2023

DIRECTORY
IRON AND STEEL PLANTS

A listing of companies and personnel operating iron- and steel-producing and finishing facilities in North America.

Also included is a listing of those companies in North America and overseas considered to be major suppliers to, or allied with, the iron- and steel-producing and processing industries.

Published by

AIST
ASSOCIATION FOR IRON & STEEL TECHNOLOGY

186 Thorn Hill Road
Warrendale, PA 15086 USA
P: +1.724.814.3000 · F: +1.724.814.3001
AIST.org

Copyright © 2023
Association for Iron & Steel Technology
186 Thorn Hill Road, Warrendale, PA 15086 USA
P: +1.724.814.3000 • F: +1.724.814.3001
AIST.org

Published annually

ISBN: 978-0-930767-10-5
ISSN: 0070-5039

Printed in the U.S.A.

Publisher — Ronald Ashburn
Editorial — Amanda Blyth, Christopher Brown, Sam Kusic,
Jennifer Vergot, Emily Williams
Graphics — Beniamina Dapra, Kyle McMullen, Carolyn Trobaugh
Sales — Cate Davidson, Vicki Dean, Doug Shymoniak,
Rebecca Smith, Stacy Varmecky

E-book is copy-protected and is intended for a single user.
It may not be shared or used by others.

As there is no charge for company or personnel listings
in this directory, the publisher assumes
no responsibility for errors that may occur.

Please direct all comments to directory@aist.org.

INTRODUCTION

The 2023 *DIRECTORY — IRON AND STEEL PLANTS* is the 20th edition published by the Association for Iron & Steel Technology. The *DIRECTORY* was first published in 1916 by Steel Publications Inc. In 1972, the Association of Iron and Steel Engineers acquired the *DIRECTORY* and published it through 2003. The *DIRECTORY* format has gradually evolved throughout its long history. Today, Sections I–III provide complete personnel and facility information for North American steel companies, including integrated, mini-mill and specialty producers, as well as service centers (I); pipe and tube manufacturers (II); and detailed facility tables (III). Section IV lists suppliers of equipment, products, and services to the worldwide iron and steel industry. Geographical indexes are included for each of the sections.

AIST would like to thank the many companies that assisted in the compilation of information for the 2023 edition. If your company is not included and you feel it should be, contact us at **directory@aist.org**, and we will consider your listing for the next edition.

Every effort has been made to keep the *DIRECTORY* useful and informative. We welcome any suggestions for improvement.

Association for Iron & Steel Technology
Warrendale, Pa., USA

Ronald E. Ashburn
Publisher and Executive Director

TABLE OF CONTENTS

I	Iron and Steel Plants Company Listings	7
II	Pipe and Tube Plants Company Listings	112
III	Iron and Steel Plants Facility Data	144
	Geographical Index Iron and Steel Plants	239
IV	Suppliers of Equipment, Products and Services	271
	Geographical Index Suppliers	577
V	Major Associations and Technical Societies With Iron and Steel Industry Interests	608
VI	Glossary of Abbreviations	615
VII	Advertisers Index	619
VIII	Alphabetical Index	621
IX	E-Book Download Instructions	640

TABLE OF CONTENTS

I   Iron and Steel Plants
Company Listings ....

II   Pipe and Tube Plants
Company Listings ....

III   Iron and Steel Plants
Facility Data ....

    Geographical Index Iron and Steel Plants ....

IV   Suppliers of Equipment,
Products and Services ....

    Geographical Index Suppliers ....

V   Major Associations and Technical Societies With Iron and Steel Industry Interests ....

VI   Glossary of Abbreviations ....

VII   Advertisers Index ....

VIII   Alphabetical Index ....

IX   E-Book Download Instructions ....

IRON and STEEL PLANTS

A

ACEROS FORJADOS ESTAMPADOS DE MONCLOVA S.A. DE C.V.
Av. Industrial No. 900
Braulio Fernandez Aguirre
Monclova, CA, 25767 Mexico
P: +52.866.636.0216
www.afemsa.mx

- Chief Exec. Officer—Alejandro Loya Galaz

PRODUCTS and/or SERVICES:
Metalwork, fabrication and forgings.

ALAMBRES Y REFUERZOS DAC S.A. DE C.V.
Playa Pie de la Cuesta 203
San Andrés Tetepílco, Iztapalapa,
Mexico City, DF, 09440 Mexico
P: +55.5539.9993; +55.5532.4709; +55.5672.1918
www.alambresyrefuerzos.com

PRODUCTS and/or SERVICES:
Wires (annealed, polished, wire rod, concertina, tec 60 shaft), steel reinforcement structures (construction ring, armor, electrowelded castle, ladder), tights (hexagonal mesh, constructive panel, expanded metal, engineering mesh, welded mesh), nails (standard and concrete).

ALGOMA STEEL INC.
105 West St.
Sault Ste. Marie, ON P6A 7B4 Canada
P: +1.705.945.2351 (Head Office and Steelworks);
+1.905.331.3400 (Burlington, ON Sales Office);
+1.403.620.2843 (Calgary, AB Sales Office)
www.algoma.com

- Chief Exec. Officer—Michael Garcia
- Chief Finance Officer—Rajat Marwah
- Vice Pres. Strategy and Chief Legal Officer—John Naccarato
- Vice Pres. Maint. and Oper. Svcs.—Loris Molino
- Vice Pres. Strategic Transformation—Mark Nogalo
- Chief H.R. Officer—Piper Lee Frech
- Vice Pres. Oprs.—Shawn Galey
- Vice Pres. Sales—Rory Brandow
- Dir. U.S. Sales and Cust. Svce.—Chris Ford
- Vice Pres. Contr. and Info. Technology—Aaron Evans
- Gen. Mgr. Steelmaking and Slabcasting—Stephen Briglio
- Gen. Mgr. Plate and Strip—Paul DeGregorio
- Gen. Mgr. DSPC and Cold Mill—Kate Kuuskman
- Gen. Mgr. Cokemaking/Ironmaking—Tom Katagis
- Gen. Mgr. EAF Oprs.—Jon Whittington
- Gen. Mgr. Engrg. Projects and Masonry—Denis Cesarin
- Gen. Mgr. Tech. Svcs.—Dan Burella
- Gen. Mgr. Ship., Transportation and Material Reprocessing—Chris McMaster

EQUIPMENT:
177 coke ovens, two BFs, two BOFs, two twin-station LMFs, one 2-strand slab casting machine, one thin-slab caster with direct rolling mill for hot coil band, three reheating furnaces, 20 annealing furnaces, a 166-in. plate finishing mill, a 106-in.-wide hot strip mill, 80-in. cold reduction and temper mills, plate Q&T line, and one pickling line.

PRODUCTS and/or SERVICES:
HRC, CRC and CTL plate (sheared, gas cut, floor, normalized, as-quenched, Q&T), coke and iron byproducts.

Annual Capacity: 2.8 million tons.

ALLEGHENY TECHNOLOGIES INC.—see ATI INC.

2023 AIST Directory — Iron and Steel Plants 7

IRON and STEEL PLANTS

ALRO STEEL
3100 E. High St.
Jackson, MI 49203 USA
P: +1.517.787.5500
F: +1.517.787.6390
steel@alro.com
www.alro.com

- Chmn. and Chief Exec. Officer—Randy Glick
- Chief Oper. Officer and Pres.—David Schmidt
- Chief Financial Officer and Exec. Vice Pres.—Steve Laten
- Vice Pres. Mktg. and Business Dev.—Brian Glick
- Vice Pres. Corporate Pur.—Dave Harrold

PRODUCTS and/or SERVICES:
Distributor of metals, industrial supplies and plastics, with more than 75 locations in 15 states. Alro offers cut-to-size metals and plastics with next-day delivery to more than 50,000 customers in North America. Alro sells a broad inventory of products under the following companies: Alro Steel, Alro Metals, Alro Metals Outlet, Alro Industrial Supply and Alro Plastics.

No. of Employees: 3,000.+

ALTASTEEL INC., a Part of Kyoei Steel Group
Mailing Address:
P.O. Box 2348
Edmonton, AB T5J 2R3 Canada

Plant Address:
9401 34th St.
Edmonton, AB T6B 2X6 Canada
P: +1.800.661.9431 (Toll-Free Sales); +1.780.468.1133
F: +1.780.468.7335
www.altasteel.com

- Sr. Vice Pres. Oprs.—Dev Kittur
- Vice Pres. Sales and Procurement—Ben Zurbrigg
- Vice Pres. H.R., Health, Safety and Environ.—Amanda Reib
- Vice Pres. Finance and Admin.—Leanne Tenbrink

EQUIPMENT:
Scrap shredder and preparation facilities, one 80-ton EAF, one LF, 3-strand continuous caster, WB billet heating furnace, 18-stand bar mill including finishing operations.

PRODUCTS and/or SERVICES:
Rebar, flat bar (round and square edge), SBQ rounds and bar, grinding media (ball stock and heat-treated grinding rod).

Annual Capacity: Semi-finished steel: 330,000 net tons.

ALTON STEEL INC.
5 Cut St.
Alton, IL 62002 USA
P: +1.618.463.4490
F: +1.618.463.4491
www.altonsteel.com

- Chief Exec. Officer—Jim Hrusovsky
- Chief Financial Officer—Jeff Dorries
- Gen. Mgr. of Oprs.—Terry Laird
- Gen. Mgr. of Sales and Qual.—Jeff Hoerr

EQUIPMENT:
One 225-net-ton EAF; one LMF; one 6-strand continuous casting machine capable of manufacturing 7 x 7-in. square billets; one 17-stand bar mill capable of manufacturing 0.750 to 3.900-in. round bar, 1.250 to 2.250-in. square bar. Two Garrett-style coilers with capability to coil 0.75 through 1.81-in.-dia. bar in coil. Two bar straighteners and one NDT eddy current machine. Two bar straighteners and one NDT eddy current machine. One bar peeler.

PRODUCTS and/or SERVICES:
Billets, slabs, and SBQ and MBQ bar and coil products.

Annual Capacity: Semi-finished: 700,000 tons. Bar product: 400,000 tons.

No. of Employees: 315.

Railroad and Shipping Facilities: Truck, rail.

IRON and STEEL PLANTS

ALTOS HORNOS DE MEXICO S.A. DE C.V. (AHMSA)
Prolongación Juárez S/N
Monclova, CA, 25770 Mexico
P: +52.86.49.33.30
www.ahmsa.com

- Chmn. Bd. of Dirs.—Alonso Ancira Elizondo
- Chief Exec. Officer—Luis Zamudio Miechielsen
- Exec. Vice Pres.—Xavier Autrey Maza
- Chief Financial Officer—Jorge Ancira Elizondo
- Gen. Counsel and Affiliated Companies—Jose Eduardo Ancira Elizondo
- Corporate Legal Affairs Dir.—Andres González Saravia Coss
- Finances Dir.—John Abbot
- Sales and Mktg. Dir.—Luis Landois
- Pur. Dir.—Gerardo García
- Steel and Technology Dir.—Armando Ferríz
- Roll., Maint. and Svcs. Dir.—Homero Perez
- H.R. (Non-Union) Dir.—Mónica Elizondo
- Labor Rels. (Union) Dir.—Enrique Rivera
- Safety and Environ. Dir.—Lorenzo González
- Pub. Affairs and Communications Dir.—Francisco Orduña
- Treasury Subdir.—Carlos Mireles
- Steelmaking Subdir.—Rogelio Ramirez
- Distr. Sales Subdir.—Luis Gutierrez
- Ind. Sales Subdir.—Daniel Riojas
- Logistic and Svce. to Cust. Subdir.—Eduardo Zamudio
- Mktg. Mgr.—Roberto Romero
- Intl. Sales Mgr.—Silverio Dávila

EQUIPMENT:
Two cokemaking plants, one sinter plant, one concentrating and pelletizing plant, two BFs, two BOF shops, three continuous slab casting machines, one hot strip line, two cold strip lines, one tinning line, one tinning/tin-free steel line, coal injection units for BFs.

PRODUCTS and/or SERVICES:
Plates, HRC, CRC, sheets, tinplate, and TFS.

Annual Capacity: 5.5 million metric tons.

Railroad and Shipping Facilities: Truck, rail.

A.M. CASTLE & CO.
1420 Kensington Road, Suite 220
Oak Brook, IL 60523 USA
P: +1.800.289.2785 (Toll-Free)
inquiries@amcastle.com
www.castlemetals.com

- Pres. and Chief Exec. Officer—Marec E. Edgar
- Exec. Vice Pres., Aerospace and Chief Supply Officer—Mark D. Zundel
- Exec. Vice Pres., Ind.—James Joyce
- Sr. Vice Pres., Strategic Accts.—Joseph Bonnema
- Sr. Vice Pres., Aerospace—Damien Mancini
- Sr. Vice Pres., Gen. Counsel and Sec.—Jeremy Steele
- Vice Pres., H.R.—Lilly Framarin
- Vice Pres., Corporate Finance and Asst. Treas.—Peter Hreska
- Vice Pres., Chief Acctg. Officer and Contr.—Edward Quinn

PRODUCTS and/or EQUIPMENT:
Provider of specialty and broad-based metals, and supply chain solutions. Distributes and processes alloy, carbon, stainless steel, nickel, aluminum, titanium, cast iron and red metals.

AMERICAN HEAVY PLATES
42722 St. Rte. 7
Clarington, OH 43915 USA
P: +1.740.331.4500
www.ahplates.com

- Co-Founder and Chief Exec. Officer—Robert Schaal
- Pres. and Chief Oper. Officer—Jack Biegalski
- Chief Financial Officer—Roxana Stoicea
- Co-Founder and Vice Pres., Admin.—Damian Brennan
- Vice Pres. Sales—Joe Curry
- Vice Pres. Oprs.—Jeff Thompson

IRON and STEEL PLANTS

EQUIPMENT:
Steel plate rolling mill (48 to 96 in. width and 3 to 22 in. thickness), plate processing services.

PRODUCTS and/or SERVICES:
ISO-certified single-source provider for heavy carbon and alloy steel plate. Focused on rapid production, processing and distribution of heavy plate and plate parts. ASTM grades include: A36, A516-60, A516-70, A572-42, A572-50, 709 GR 50, A633 GR C, A633 GR E, A830-1045, A830-1020, A829-4140, and A829-4130. Processing services include: flame cutting, stress relieving, annealing, normalizing, tempering, flattening, milling, drilling, machining, tensile testing, Charpy testing, and Brinell testing.

ARCELORMITTAL NORTH AMERICA
833 W. Lincoln Hwy., Suite 200E
Schererville, IN 46375 USA
P: +1.312.346.0300
www.northamerica.arcelormittal.com

- Chief Exec. Officer—John Brett
- Chief Admin. Officer—Neil Kohlberg
- Chief Oper. Officer—Keith Howell
- Chief Digital Officer—Antoine Dhennin
- Chief Exec. Officer, ArcelorMittal Dofasco—Ron Bedard
- Chief Exec. Officer, ArcelorMittal Mexico—Victor Manuel Martinez Cairo
- Chief Exec. Officer and Pres., AM/NS Calvert—Chuck Greene
- Vice Pres. Govt. Rels.—Marcia Miller
- Chief Exec. Officer, ArcelorMittal Long Products Canada—Stéphane Brochu
- Chief Mktg. Officer—Shelby Pixley
- Chief Mktg. Officer, Automotive—Peter Leblanc
- Chief Exec. Officer, ArcelorMittal Tubular Products North America—Ed Vore
- Dir. Communications, Corporate Responsibility—Heidi Umbhau
- Chief H.R. Officer—Maxine Stankich

AM/NS CALVERT LLC, a Joint Venture Between ArcelorMittal and Nippon Steel Corp.
1 AM/NS Way
P.O. Box 456
Calvert, AL 36513 USA
P: +1.251.289.3000
F: +1.251.289.3505
www.arcelormittal.com

- Chief Exec. Officer and Pres.—Chuck Greene
- Chief Oper. Officer—Phil Fultz
- Chief Financial Officer—Roy Mathew
- Chief Tech. Officer—Yoshiyuki Komuro
- Chief Admin. Mgr.—Chris Richards
- Chief Procurement Officer—Alex Dias

EQUIPMENT:
River terminal; slab yard; HSM (0.059 to 1 in. x 73.6 in.), design capacity: 5.84 million tons/year; PLTCM (0.012 to 0.118 in. x 73.6 in.), capacity: 2.75 million tons/year; CPL (0.059 to 0.236 in. x 73.6 in.), capacity: 1.2 million tons/year. Three HDGLs, GI/GA/AL (GI: 0.012 to 0.098 in. x 72.8 in., GA: 0.020 to 0.098 in. x 72.8 in., AL: 0.018 to 0.098 in. x 65 in.), 1,485,000 tons/year. One CAL. CRC (0.020 to 0.098 in. x 72.8 in.), capacity: 660,000 tons/year. Three inspection and slitting lines; skinpass mill; rail yard.

PRODUCTS and/or SERVICES:
Carbon flat-rolled only: HRC, HRP&O, CRC, GI, GA, AL, AHSS.

Annual Capacity: 5.3 million metric tons of finished carbon steel products.

No. of Employees: Approx. 1,600.

Railroad and Shipping Facilities: Truck, rail, barge.

ARCELORMITTAL DOFASCO G.P.
1330 Burlington St. E
P.O. Box 2460
Hamilton, ON L8N 3J5 Canada
P: +1.905.544.3761
https://dofasco.arcelormittal.com

- Pres. and Chief Exec. Officer—Ron Bedard
- Vice Pres. People and Culture—Nesha Gibson

IRON and STEEL PLANTS

- Vice Pres. Commercial—Andrew Connor
- Vice Pres. Mfg.—Dirk Francis
- Vice Pres. Finance—Rogerio Fonesca
- Vice Pres., Head of Corporate Affairs, Legal and Equality, Diversity and Inclusion—Lisa Marcuzzi
- Vice Pres. Procurement—Tony Robinson
- Vice Pres. Strategy—Vasudha Seth
- Vice Pres. Decarbonization Funding and Govt. Rels.—Tony Valeri
- Vice Pres. Technology—Herve Mouille

EQUIPMENT:
Two coke plants; pulverized coal injection facility; three BFs; one basic oxygen steelmaking facility with a 2-strand continuous slab caster; one EAF steelmaking facility with a 1-strand continuous slab caster; one hot strip mill (two reheat furnaces, 1 single-stand rougher, 7-stand finishing mill, two coilers); one stand-alone CPL; two coupled pickle line cold mills; light-gauge tower annealing line; three batch annealing facilities; two temper mills; rewind line; one electrolytic tinning line; six CGLs; one joint-venture organic coating line, two tube mills, two tube fabrication cells, tube warehouse, central shipping warehouse; utilities—five large steam boilers, two cold mill wastewater treatment plants in finishing, one acid regeneration plant, two 230-kV electrical substations, four large turbo blowers, primary wastewater treatment plant.

PRODUCTS and/or SERVICES:
Hot-rolled, cold-rolled, electrolytic tinplate, chromium-coated steel, GI, GA, AL, coke oven byproducts, pre-coated steel and tubular products.

Annual Capacity: 4.5 million tons.

No. of Employees: 5,000.

Railroad and Shipping Facilities: Rail, ship.

ARCELORMITTAL LONG PRODUCTS CANADA G.P.
4000 Route des Aciéries
Contrecoeur, QC J0L 1C0 Canada
P: +1.450.587.8600
F: +1.450.587.8777
www.long-canada.arcelormittal.com

- Chief Exec. Officer—Stéphane Brochu
- Vice Pres. and Chief Financial and Strategy Officer—Will Trower
- Vice Pres. and Chief Mktg. Officer—Philippe Boulanger
- Vice Pres. and Chief Oper. Officer—Mathieu Francoeur
- Vice Pres. and Chief Technology Officer—Louis Plante
- Vice Pres. H.R. and Communications—Hugues Fauville
- Vice Pres. and Chief Procurement Officer—Charles Fréchette
- Vice Pres. Legal Affairs, Compliance, Environ. and Security—Nadia Thibault

ArcelorMittal Contrecoeur-East
3900 Route des Aciéries
Contrecoeur, QC J0L 1C0 Canada
P: +1.450.392.3200

- Gen. Mgr.—Bertrand-Philippe Bougenot

EQUIPMENT:
DRI plant, EAFs, continuous billet and slab casting machines, wire rod and bar mill.

PRODUCTS and/or SERVICES:
Slabs, billets and wire rod.

Railroad and Shipping Facilities: Rail, ship.

ArcelorMittal Contrecoeur-West
2050 Route des Aciéries
Contrecoeur, QC J0L 1C0 Canada
P: +1.450.587.2012

EQUIPMENT:
Steel plant and bar mill.

IRON and STEEL PLANTS

ArcelorMittal Contrecoeur Recycling Center
3185 Route Marie-Victorin
Contrecoeur, QC J0L 1C0 Canada
P: +1.450.392.3200

- Mgr.—Pascal Laroche

EQUIPMENT:
Scrap processing.

ArcelorMittal Hamilton-East
690 Strathearne Ave. N
Hamilton, ON L8H 7N8 Canada
P: +1.905.528.9473

- Gen. Mgr.—Elbia Starling Pessim

EQUIPMENT:
BF, BOD, EAF, continuous caster, hot rolling mill, cold rolling mill, HDGL, annealing line.

PRODUCTS and/or SERVICES:
Wire.

ArcelorMittal Longueuil
2555 Chemin du Lac
Longueuil, QC J4N 1C1 Canada
P: +1.514.442.7700

- Mgr—Philippe Bélanger

EQUIPMENT:
Bar mill.

PRODUCTS and/or SERVICES:
Bars, SBQ, reinforcing bars.

ArcelorMittal St-Patrick
5900 Rue St-Patrick
Montreal, QC H4E 1B3 Canada
P: +1.514.762.5260

- Gen. Mgr.—Elbia Starling Pessim

EQUIPMENT:
Wire mill.

ARCELORMITTAL MEXICO
Torre Trébol Park
Av. Lázaro Cárdenas No. 2424
Col. Residencial San Agustín,
San Pedro Garza García
Monterrey, NL, 66260 Mexico
P: +01.81.1223.6700
www.mexico.arcelormittal.com

- Chief Exec. Officer—Victor Manuel Martinez Cairo
- Chief Oprs. Officer—Jose Martín Alanis Vences
- Chief Technology Officer—Jorge Nieto Morales
- Chief Financial Officer—Achal Khanna
- Dir. of Mktg. and Strategy—Santiago Rico Fernández
- Head of H.R. and Svcs.—Cynthia Arredondo Rodríguez
- Head of Legal and Compliance—Noe Galván
- Hot Strip Mill Dir.—Sergio Lima
- Chief Procurement Officer— Brenda Elizondo
- Chief Security Officer—Mauricio Domínguez Tobón

ArcelorMittal Lázaro Cárdenas
Av. Francisco J. Mujica No. 1
Lázaro Cárdenas, MC, 60950 Mexico
P: +52.753.533.1805

EQUIPMENT:
Flat Steel Segment—Four EAFs, three LFs; two VD units (RH and tank degasser); two twin-strand continuous slab casters. Long Steel Segment—One BF, two BOFs; one Oxicupula furnace; two LFs; three continuous billet casters; one wire rod rolling mill and one rebar rolling mill.

PRODUCTS and/or SERVICES:
Hot-rolled steel coils, slabs, billets, rods and wire rods.

Annual Capacity: 5.3 million metric tons crude steel.

Railroad and Shipping Facilities: Truck, rail, ship.

ArcelorMittal Celaya
Carretera Panamericana km 7.5
Tramo Celaya-Salamanca,
Rancho el Chinaco
Villagrán, GJ, 38110 Mexico

EQUIPMENT:
Two rolling mils.

PRODUCTS and/or SERVICES:
Rebar from grade 42 to 80.

IRON and STEEL PLANTS

Annual Capacity: 1.7 million tons.

Railroad and Shipping Facilities: rail.

ARCELORMITTAL MINING CANADA G.P.

Head Office
1010, de Serigny, Suite 200
Longueuil, QC J4K 5G7 Canada
P: +1.514.285.1464
F: +1.514.285.2526

Mont-Wright Mining Complex
1000, Route 389
Mont-Wright, QC G0G 1J0 Canada
P: +1.418.287.4700
F: +1.418.287.3445

Administration and Pellet Plant
24 Boul. des Îles, Suite 201
Port-Cartier, QC G5B 2H3 Canada
P: +1.418.766.2000
F: +1.418.768.2128

- Chief Exec. Officer and Pres.—Mapi Mobwano
- Vice Pres. Finance—Jean-Paul Ordioni
- Vice Pres. Procurement—Sanjay Jain
- Vice Pres. Legal Affairs and Corporate Sec.—Julie Cuddihy
- Gen. Mgr. Mining—Jonathan Hill
- Gen. Mgr. Processes—Romain Precheur
- Gen. Mgr. Maint.—Alain Brazeau
- Dir. Communications—Annie Paré

EQUIPMENT:
Two iron ore mines (Mont-Wright, QC and Fire Lake, QC), one pellet plant (Port-Cartier, QC).

PRODUCTS and/or SERVICES:
Iron ore concentrate and iron oxide pellets.

Annual Capacity: 26 million metric tons iron ore; 10 million metric tons pellets.

ARCELORMITTAL TEXAS HBI
2800 Kay Bailey Hutchison Blvd.
Portland, TX 78374 USA
P: +1.361.704.9000
office.texas@arcelormittal.com

PRODUCTS and/or SERVICES:
HBI.

Annual Capacity: 2 million metric tons.

No. of Employees: Approx. 300.

ARCELORMITTAL TUBULAR PRODUCTS—see listing page 113

ATI INC.
2021 McKinney Ave.
Suite 1100
Dallas, TX 75201 USA
P: +1.800.289.7454 (Toll-Free)
www.atimaterials.com

- Board Chair, Pres. and Chief Exec. Officer—Robert S. Wetherbee
- Sr. Vice Pres., Chief Legal and Compliance Officer—Elliot S. Davis
- Exec. Vice Pres and Chief Oper. Officer—Kimberly A. Fields
- Sr. Vice Pres., Chief Digital and Info. Officer—Timothy J. Harris
- Sr. Vice Pres., Chief Commercial and Mktg. Officer—Kevin B. Kramer
- Exec. Vice Pres., Finance and Chief Financial Officer—Don P. Newman
- Vice Pres., Internal Audit—Shelley L. Bias
- Sr. Vice Pres., Chief H.R. Officer—Elizabeth C. Powers
- Vice Pres., Environ. Affairs and Sustainability and Asst. Gen. Counsel—Lauren S. McAndrews
- Vice Pres., Treas. and Investor Rels.—Scott A. Minder
- Vice Pres., H.R.—Mary Beth Moore
- Vice Pres., Contr. and Chief Acctg. Officer—Karl D. Schwartz

ATI Specialty Rolled Products:

Brackenridge Operations
100 River Road
Brackenridge, PA 15014 USA

PRODUCTS and/or SERVICES:
Specialty stainless steel and other specialty steel sheet.

IRON and STEEL PLANTS

Natrona Heights Operations
1300 Pacific Ave.
Natrona Heights, PA 15065 USA
P: +1.724.224.1000

PRODUCTS and/or SERVICES:
Extensive range of sophisticated process and analytical equipment for pilot operations from melting to final rolling and detailed product analysis.

Latrobe Operations
242 Allvac Lane
Latrobe, PA 15650 USA

PRODUCTS and/or SERVICES:
Specialty stainless steels, high-temperature alloys, corrosion-resistant alloys, nickel-based alloys, duplex alloys and armor materials.

Louisville Operations
1500 W. Main St.
P.O. Box 3920
Louisville, OH 44641 USA

PRODUCTS and/or SERVICES:
Titanium in sheet and strip and specialty alloys.

New Bedford Operations
1357 E. Rodney French Blvd.
New Bedford, MA 02742 USA

PRODUCTS and/or SERVICES:
Titanium strip, nickel and precision-rolled strip.

Vandergrift Operations
130 Lincoln Ave.
Vandergrift, PA 15690 USA

PRODUCTS and/or SERVICES:
Specialty stainless steel in sheet and strip.

Washington Operations
500 Green St.
Washington, PA 15301 USA

PRODUCTS and/or SERVICES:
Specialty stainless, specialty alloy plate.

Monaca, PA Finishing Services
2070 Pennsylvania Ave.
Monaca, PA 15061 USA

PRODUCTS and/or SERVICES:
Surface grinding, precision grinding and polishing, abrasive saw cutting, band saw cutting—vertical and horizontal, shearing, NDT, vacuum creep flattening, FaroArm measurement scanning, water-jet cutting.

Rochester, PA Finishing Services
499 Delaware Ave.
Rochester, PA 15074 USA

PRODUCTS and/or SERVICES:
Surface grinding, abrasive saw cutting, NDT, metallic and non-metallic grit blasting.

Zelienople, PA Finishing Services
700 W. New Castle St., Rte. 228
Zelienople, PA 16063 USA

PRODUCTS and/or SERVICES:
Surface grinding, band saw cutting—vertical and horizontal.

IRON and STEEL PLANTS

B

BEAVER VALLEY ALLOY FOUNDRY CO.
4165 Brodhead Road
Monaca, PA 15061 USA
P: +1.800.900.VALU (8258) (Toll-Free);
+1.724.775.1987
F: +1.724.775.1474
cast@bvalley.com
www.bvalley.com

- Pres. and Treas.—J.B. Forster
- Vice Pres. and Sales—John B. Forster Jr.
- Sec.—Dayna Dierdorf

EQUIPMENT:
No-bake molding equipment, induction melting, vacuum spectrograph. Complete foundry facilities for patterns, castings and machining.

PRODUCTS and/or SERVICES:
Patterns, housings, rolls, rolling mill equipment, segments, covers, bearing blocks, wear plates, chutes, liners, furnace parts, guides, bars and box castings. Heat-, corrosion- and abrasion-resistant alloy steel; stainless steel; iron; ductile iron; white iron; Hadfield manganese castings and machining.

No. of Employees: 49.

BLAIR STRIP STEEL CO.
1209 Butler Ave.
New Castle, PA 16101 USA
P: +1.724.658.2611
F: +1.724.658.6548
sales@blairstripsteel.com
www.blairstripsteel.com

- Chmn. and Chief Exec. Officer—Bruce A. Kinney
- Pres. and Chief Financial Officer—Scott A. McDowell
- Vice Pres. Oprs.—Kevin R. Barren
- Vice Pres. Sales—John C. Moroco
- Gen. Mgr. — Sales and Metallurgical Svcs.—Roger Walburn
- Corporate Qual. Mgr.—Dominic R. Sikora
- Plant Mgr.—Ivan R. Clark
- Pur. Mgr.—John M. Bartko
- Gen. Foreman—Patrick Schooley
- Inside Sales Mgr.—Mary A. Schell
- Asst. Sales Mgr.—Mary Peretti
- Acctg. Mgr.—Matthew Lorello
- Regional Sales Mgrs.—Anthony R. Horn, Scott R. Kay
- Dev. Met.—Gordon A. Wilber
- Outside Processing Mgr.—Matthew Bruno

EQUIPMENT:
3-stand, 2-high cold reduction mill (Big George); 2-stand, 4-high reduction mill (Little Tom); 2-high temper mill (Old Tucker); Ebner hydrogen anneal shop; Salem HNX anneal shop; two slitters; shear line; edger/oscillating line.

PRODUCTS and/or SERVICES:
Cold-rolled strip steel in heavy thicknesses from 0.030 to 0.625 in. (0.8 mm to 16.0 mm) in low-carbon, high-carbon, alloy and custom grades. Fine blanking quality-steel (FBQ), aircraft-quality (AQ) alloys; Japanese grades (JIS); European grades (EN/DIN); BMI electromagnetic iron strip; precision thickness tolerances in narrow-width rolled precision strip steel; ribbon coils, oscillated coils and cut lengths; one-pass and gauge correction rolling; pattern-rolled finishes; spheroidized annealing; conversion. Full metallurgical laboratory for production and product development.

No. of Employees: 75.

Railroad and Shipping Facilities: Truck, rail (load containers for rail shipment).

IRON and STEEL PLANTS

BROWN STRAUSS STEEL
2495 Uravan St.
Aurora, CO 80011 USA
P: +1.800.677.2778 (Toll-Free)
info@brownstrauss.com
www.brownstrauss.com

- Pres. and Chief Oper. Officer—Kris Farris

PRODUCTS:
Distributor of wide-flange beams, structural tubing, structural channels, structural angle, structural pipe and other structural. Services include: saw cutting, cambering, track torch cutting, inventory stocking program, length/cutting optimization program and mill brokerage.

Locations:

Houston, TX
2050 FM 1405 Bldg. B
Baytown, TX 77523 USA
P: +1.877.350.5682 (Toll-Free)

Kansas City, KS
802 Kindelberger Road
Kansas City, KS 66115 USA
P: +1.800.274.0359 (Toll-Free);
+1.913.621.4000

Longview, WA
150 Panel Way
Longview, WA 98632 USA
P: +1.800.780.7607 (Toll-Free);
+1.360.501.5300

Los Angeles, CA
14970 Jurupa Ave.
Fontana, CA 92335 USA
P: +1.800.678.2778 (Toll-Free);
+1.602.233.0219

Menomonie, WI
5610 Eagle Point Road
Menomonie, WI 54751 USA
P: +1.800.274.0359 (Toll-Free)

Phoenix, AZ
3727 W. Lower Buckeye Road
Phoenix, AZ 85009 USA
P: +1.800.677.2778 (Toll-Free);
+1.602.233.0219

Salt Lake City, UT
800 S. Chestnut St.
Salt Lake City, UT 84104 USA
P: +1.800.742.4849 (Toll-Free);
+1.801.972.5328

Spokane, WA
2823 S. Craig Road
Airway Heights, WA 99224 USA
P: +1.800.780.7607 (Toll-Free);
+1.360.501.5300

Stockton, CA
4221 E. Mariposa Road
Stockton, CA 95215 USA
P: +1.800.677.2778 (Toll-Free);
+1.303.371.2200

BYER STEEL CORP.
200 W. North Bend Road
Cincinnati, OH 45216 USA
P: +1.513.821.6400
F: +1.513.821.6915
www.byersteel.com

- Chief Exec. Officer—Shayne Byer
- Pres.—Jonas Allen
- Chief Financial Officer—Mark Lefke
- Rebar Sales Mgr./Dist. and Manufactured Parts—Don Bosse
- Inside Sales — Rebar Fabrication—Renae Shell
- Sales Mgr. — Commercial Fabrication—Dan Cronin
- Acct. Mgr. — Fabrication—Debi DeBellevue
- Est. — Rebar Fabrication—Terry Kelley
- Scheduler — Rebar Fabrication—Connie Meade

EQUIPMENT:
Continuous rolling mill, 12-ft. x 68-ft. reheat furnace, four 16-in. stands, three 12-in. stands, nine 8-in. stands, 280-ft. cooling bed.

PRODUCTS and/or SERVICES:
Reinforcing bars.

Railroad and Shipping Facilities: Rail.

IRON and STEEL PLANTS

C

CALIFORNIA STEEL INDUSTRIES INC., a Nucor-JFE Co.
1 California Steel Way
P.O. Box 5080
Fontana, CA 92335 USA

Shipping and Receiving:
14000 San Bernardino Ave.
Fontana, CA 92335 USA
P: +1.909.350.6300
www.californiasteel.com

- Gen. Mgr.—Zach Moon
- Dir. of Oprs. and Qual.—Scott Starr
- Dir. of Commercial—Ricardo Bernardes
- Dir. Contr.—Francisco Peres
- Mgr. Cold Reduction and Galvanizing—Don Merchant
- Mgr. Engrg.—Hal Parker
- Mgr. Environ. Svcs.—Kathleen Brundage
- Mgr. Hot Roll. and Strip Finishings—Mehmet Ataman
- Mgr. H.R.—Luz Rodriguez-Roldan
- Mgr. Info. Svcs.—Victor Rivera
- Chief Met. and Qual. Svcs. Mgr.—Dan Goldstein
- Oprs. Mgr. Tubular Products—Russ Olgin
- Mgr. Prodn. Plan. and Logistics—Manny Lara
- Mgr. Pur.—Ed Greenwald
- Mgr. Safety and Plant Protection—Brad Bray
- Mgr. Sales Admin. and Mktg.—John Walburg
- Mgr. Maint.—Jim Lynch

EQUIPMENT:
86-in. HSM, 62-in. continuous pickle line, two HDGLs, 5-stand cold reduction, hydrogen batch annealing, 2-stand temper mill, skinpass, slitting and shear line, two ERW pipe mills and pipe coating line.

PRODUCTS and/or SERVICES:
HRP&O, galvanized, cold-rolled sheet, and ERW pipe (4.5-in.–24-in. OD).

No. of Employees: 900.

Railroad and Shipping Facilities: Truck, rail.

CARPENTER TECHNOLOGY CORP.
1735 Market St., 15th Floor
Philadelphia, PA 19103 USA
P: +1.800.654.6543 (Toll-Free Sales);
+1.610.208.2000
info@cartech.com
www.carpentertechnology.com

- Chief Exec. Officer and Pres.—Tony R. Thene
- Sr. Vice Pres. and Chief Financial Officer—Tim Lain
- Sr. Vice Pres., Gen. Counsel and Sec.—James D. Dee
- Sr. Vice Pres. and Chief Commercial Officer—Marshall Atkins
- Sr. Vice Pres. and Group Pres. — Specialty Alloys Operations Business Segment—Brian J. Malloy
- Vice Pres. and Group Pres. — Performance Engineered Products Business Segment—David Graf
- Sr. Vice Pres., Continuous Improvement—Joseph E. Haniford
- Chief Digital Officer—Shakthimani Logasundaram
- Chief Technology Officer—Suniti Moudgil
- Vice Pres. and Chief H.R. Officer—Rachelle H. Thompson

PRODUCTS and/or SERVICES:
High-performance stainless steel and specialty alloy-based materials and process solutions for critical applications in the aerospace, defense, medical, transportation energy, industrial and consumer end-use markets. Product portfolio includes stainless steels (austenitic, duplex, ferritic, martensitic, nitrogen-strengthened austenitic,

2023 AIST Directory — Iron and Steel Plants

IRON and STEEL PLANTS

precipitation-hardened); alloy and specialty steels (bearing and gear, high-strength, and valve steels); high-temperature steels and alloys; nickel-copper superalloys; titanium alloys; soft magnetic alloys; medical-grade alloys and stainless steels; controlled expansion, electrical and electronic alloys; tool and die steels; and cutting blade alloys.

Railroad and Shipping Facilities: Truck.

No. of Employees: 4,100.

Specialty Alloys Oprs.:

Carpenter Technology Corp. — Athens Oprs.
22110 Thomas L. Hammons Road
P.O. Box 219
Tanner, AL 35671 USA

EQUIPMENT:
Radial forge; finishing, inspection and metallurgical testing and laboratories.

PRODUCTS and/or SERVICES:
Aerospace materials.

Carpenter Technology Corp. — Hartsville Oprs.
205 Carpenter Technology Lane
McBee, SC 29101 USA
P: +1.843.335.7540
F: +1.843.335.5160
service@cartech.com

PRODUCTS and/or SERVICES:
Bar and wire products.

Carpenter Technology Corp. — Latrobe Oprs.
2626 Ligonier St.
Latrobe, PA 15650 USA
P: +1.800.321.6446 (Toll-Free)
service@cartech.com

EQUIPMENT:
Primary and secondary melting; finishing, inspection and metallurgical testing and laboratories.

Carpenter Technology Corp. — Latrobe Oprs., Sandy Creek
1680 Debence Dr.
Franklin, PA 16323 USA
P: +1.814.432.8575
F: +1.814.437.4765

Carpenter Technology Corp. — Latrobe Oprs., Wauseon
14614 County Road
Wauseon, OH 43567 USA
P: +1.419.335.8010
F: +1.419.330.2504

Carpenter Technology Corp. — Reading Oprs.
101 W. Bern St.
Reading, PA 19601 USA
P: +1.800.654.6543 (Toll-Free)
F: +1.610.208.2361
service@cartech.com

EQUIPMENT:
Primary melting; secondary melting; open die press; radial forge; precision HSM; finishing, inspection, and metallurgical testing and laboratories.

Carpenter Technology Corp. — Reading Oprs., Orwigsburg
116 Pinedale Industrial Road
Orwigsburg, PA 17961 USA
P: +1.888.278.1414 (Toll-Free);
 +1.570.366.1414

PRODUCTS and/or SERVICES:
Bar products.

Carpenter Technology Corp. — Shalmet, Elyria
164 Freedom Ct.
Elyria, OH 44035 USA
P: +1.440.324.3190
F: +1.440.324.6975

PRODUCTS and/or SERVICES:
Bar products.

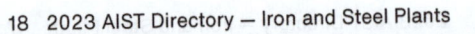

IRON and STEEL PLANTS

CASCADE STEEL ROLLING MILLS INC., a Schnitzer Co.
3200 NE Hwy. 99 W
McMinnville, OR 97128 USA
P: +1.503.472.4181
F: +1.503.434.5739

Warehouse:
3240 N. Durfee Ave.
El Monte, CA 91732 USA
P: +1.626.350.4326
www.cascadesteel.com

- Dir. Oprs.—Andre Wollmann
- Mgr. of Pur.—Andy Narkiewicz
- Mgr. Qual. Assur.—Jeff Kramer
- Supt. Steelmaking—Gary Cvitkovich
- Roll Shop Mgr.—Chuck Berrier Jr.

EQUIPMENT:
VAI 110-ton EAF, three oxy-gas burners, oxygen and coal injection lances, Danieli metallurgy station, ladle turret, 5-strand caster, dual-radius curved mold (annual capacity 800,000+ tons), two 165/45/10-ton ITI/Danieli cranes, RM-Bricmont reheat furnace, Simac: 18 mill stands, 260-ft. cooling bed, bundling equipment. Pomini rod block and rod mill. ABB electric controls.

PRODUCTS and/or SERVICES:
Rebar, rounds, coiled rebar #3 to #6, wire rod 5.5–19.5 mm.

Annual Capacity: 580,000 tons.

No. of Employees: 400.

Railroad and Shipping Facilities: Truck, rail.

CHARTER MANUFACTURING CO.
1212 W. Glen Oaks Lane
P.O. Box 217
Mequon, WI 53092 USA
P: +1.262.243.4712
F: +1.262.243.4711
www.chartermfg.com

- Chief Exec. Officer—John W. Mellowes
- Chmn. of the Board—Charles Mellowes
- Exec Vice Pres. Strategy and Corp. Dev.—Chris Wells

- Chief Financial Officer—Todd Endres
- Pres. and Gen. Mgr. Charter Steel—Tom Marry
- Vice Pres. of Supply Chain—Rebecca Fischer
- Vice Pres. Finance—Sarah Benike-Immel
- Vice Pres. Environ., Health and Safety—Erin Van Rooy
- Vice Pres. of Sales and Mktg.—Michael Skowronek,
  P: +1.262.268.2380
- Dir. Sales—Tim Spieth,
  P: +1.419.966.0917
- Dir. Mktg.—Chad Hendrickson,
  P: +1.262.268.2534
- Dir. Tech. Cust. Svce. and Qual. Assur.—Mark Henshaw,
  P: +1.262.268.2499
- Dir. Cust. Success—Brian Mekka,
  P: +1.262.268.2212
- Tech. Svcs. Mgrs.—Eric Wagner, Eric Mactavish
- Qual. Assur. Mgr.—Douglas Jones
- Vice Pres. Oprs.—Bart Reimer
- Dir. Oprs. WI—Steven Speth
- Dir. Oprs. OH—Brian Holzaepfel

PRODUCTS and/or SERVICES:
Supplier of carbon and alloy steel bar, rod and wire products with distribution and manufacturing facilities in Wisconsin and Ohio. Capabilities include steel melting, bar and rod rolling, coil processing and wire drawing. Rod and bar ranging in sizes from 7/32 in. (5.5 mm) to 1 9/16 in. (39.7 mm) dia. Straight bars 3/4 in. to 3 1/4 in., 12 ft. to 50 ft. long in bundles from 2 to 5 tons.

Annual Capacity: Approx. 1.4 million tons of SBQ.

Charter Steel – Cleveland, Ohio
4300 E. 49th St.
Cuyahoga Heights, OH 44125 USA
P: +1.216.883.3800
www.chartersteel.com

EQUIPMENT:
Meltshop: Danieli 95-ton EAF; LRF; VTD; Danieli 4-strand continuous caster—carbon and alloy. Rolling mill: Davy WB reheat furnace; 16-stand Morgan H/V breakdown and roughing

IRON and STEEL PLANTS

stands; 5-stand and 6-stand Kocks mills; Morgan 10-stand V-mill rod block; controlled Stelmor rod cooling; cooling bed; 2 abrasive saws; cold shear.

PRODUCTS and/or SERVICES:
Coiled rod and bar 7/32 in. (5.5 mm) to 1 9/16 in. (39.7 mm). Coil sizes 4,400 lbs. to 5,700 lbs.

Railroad and Shipping Facilities: Truck, rail.

Charter Steel – Fostoria, Ohio
6255 US Rte. 23
Rising Sun, OH 43457 USA
P: +1.419.457.3666
F: +1.419.457.3662
www.chartersteel.com

PRODUCTS and/or SERVICES:
Rod, bar and wire processing; hydrochloric cleaning; phos, lube, lime and polymer coatings. Sphero and lamellar annealing. Wire drawing capability. Sizes 0.140 in. (3.5 mm) to 1.469 in. (37.3 mm).

Charter Steel – Saukville, Wisconsin
1658 Cold Spring Road
Saukville, WI 53080 USA
P: +1.800.437.8789 (Toll-Free);
  +1.262.268.2400
F: +1.262.268.2340
www.chartersteel.com

EQUIPMENT:
Meltshop: Consteel 100-ton DC EAF; VAD; Concast 4-strand continuous caster—carbon and alloy. Rolling mill: Danieli WB reheat furnace; Danieli 10-stand cantilever breakdown and roughing stands; Morgan intermediates and pre-finishers. Morgan 10-stand V-mill rod block; controlled Stelmor rod cooling; Kocks 5-stand sizing mill bar outlet. Rod, bar and wire processing; hydrochloric and sulfuric cleaning; phos, lube, lime and polymer coatings; sphero and lamellar annealing; wire drawing capability.

PRODUCTS and/or SERVICES:
Coiled rod and bar: 7/32 in. (5.5 mm) to 1 3/8 in. (34.9 mm). Coil size: 4,400 lbs.

Wire sizes: 0.140 in. (3.5 mm) to 1.312 in. (33.3 mm).

Railroad and Shipping Facilities: Truck, rail.

CHICAGO HEIGHTS STEEL
211 E. Main St.
Chicago Heights, IL 60411 USA
P: +1.800.424.4487 (Toll-Free);
  +1.708.756.5648
F: +1.708.756.5628
www.chs.com

- Pres.—Bradley R. Corral
- Vice Pres. and Sales Mgr.—Steve Clark
- Treas.—Richard Gollner
- Elec. and Mech. Maint.—David Zapata
- Supt. Post Plant—Mario Cipolla
- Supt. Roll.—Jason Wagner
- Gen. Supv. Engrg.—Mark Giblin

EQUIPMENT:
Rail and billet rerolling mills.

PRODUCTS and/or SERVICES:
Angles, channels, flats, fence posts, special sections, tees, subpurlins.

Annual Capacity: 140,000 tons.

No. of Employees: 160.

Railroad and Shipping Facilities: Chicago Heights Terminal Transfer.

CHICAGO STEEL HOLDINGS LLC
700 Chase St., Suite 100
Gary, IN 46404 USA
P: +1.800.367.8110 (Toll-Free)
F: +1.219.977.4289
gbigott@upgllc.com
www.chicagosteel.net

- Vice Pres.—Chris Sekella
- Sales Dir.—Gary Bigott
- Chief Financial Officer—Mike Greco
- Acctg.—Jenny Carter
- Oprs. Mgr.—Bob Samansky
- Supv.—Brian Sowa, Jeff DeRolf
- Qual. Mgr.—Rick Gregory
- Office Mgr.—Alisa Marrero

IRON and STEEL PLANTS

PRODUCTS and/or SERVICES:
Services include: cleaning, coil jacking, inspection, oiling, CTL, precision blanking, sidetrimming, slitting, stagger winding, tension leveling and warehousing.

CLEVELAND-CLIFFS INC.
200 Public Sq., Suite 3300
Cleveland, OH 44114 USA
P: +1.216.694.5700
www.clevelandcliffs.com

- Chmn., Pres. and Chief Exec. Officer—Lourenco Goncalves
- Exec. Vice Pres. and Pres., Cleveland-Cliffs Steel—Clifford T. Smith
- Exec. Vice Pres. and Pres., Cleveland-Cliffs Services—Keith A. Koci
- Exec. Vice Pres. and Chief Financial Officer—Celso Goncalves
- Exec. Vice Pres., Environ. and Sustainability—Traci L. Forrester
- Exec. Vice Pres., Oprs.—Terry G. Fedor
- Exec. Vice Pres., Technology—Wendell Carter
- Exec. Vice Pres., Commercial—Brian Bishop
- Exec. Vice Pres., H.R., Chief Legal Officer, Chief Admin. Officer and Sec.—James D. Graham
- Exec. Vice Pres., Logistics—R. Christopher Cebula
- Vice Pres., Steelmaking—Nick Kohlhas, Dale Rupp
- Vice Pres., Tinplate and Electrical Steel—Brian James

PRODUCTS and/or SERVICES:
Cleveland-Cliffs is the largest flat-rolled steel producer in North America. Founded in 1847 as a mine operator, Cliffs also is the largest manufacturer of iron ore pellets in North America. The company is vertically integrated from mined raw materials and direct reduced iron to primary steelmaking and downstream finishing, stamping, tooling, and tubing. The company serves a diverse range of markets due to its comprehensive offering of flat-rolled carbon, stainless and electrical steel products and is the largest supplier of steel to the automotive industry in North America.

No. of Employees: 25,000 across mining, steel and downstream manufacturing operations in the U.S. and Canada.

Regional Office — Chicago
1 S. Dearborn St.
Chicago, IL 60603 USA
P: +1.312.346.0300

Regional Office — West Chester
9227 Centre Pointe Dr.
West Chester, OH 45069 USA
P: +1.513.425.5000

Research and Innovation Center
6180 Research Way
Middletown, OH 45005 USA
P: +1.844.783.3599

EQUIPMENT:
Prototype laboratories including melting, rolling, annealing and heat treating, machining and fabricating, pickling and descaling, pre-treatment and painting, and organic coatings.

PRODUCTS and/or SERVICES:
Applications engineering, advanced engineering and customer technical services. Analytic capabilities include mechanical testing, chemistry laboratory, electrical steel test labs, optical microscopy, scanning microscopy, corrosion laboratories, and exhaust materials research laboratories.

Iron Ore Facilities:

Hibbing Taconite Company (joint venture between Cleveland-Cliffs and United States Steel Corporation)
4950 County Hwy. 5 N
Hibbing, MN 55746 USA
P: +1.218.262.5950

- Plant Leadership—Dan Aagenes

EQUIPMENT:
Open-pit truck and shovel mine, concentrator utilizing single-stage crushing, AG mill and magnetic separation, pellet plant.

IRON and STEEL PLANTS

PRODUCTS and/or SERVICES:
Iron ore pellets.

Annual Capacity: 7.8 million tons.

No. of Employees: 730.

United Taconite
8470 Townline Road
Forbes, MN 55738 USA
P: +1.218.744.7800

– Plant Leadership—Nick Beukema

EQUIPMENT:
Open-pit truck and shovel mine, on-site crushing, concentrator utilizing rod mills and magnetic separation, pellet plant.

PRODUCTS and/or SERVICES:
Magnetite iron pellets.

Annual Capacity: 5.2 million tons.

No. of Employees: 540.

Northshore Mining Co.
10 Outer Dr.
Silver Bay, MN 55614 USA
P: +1.218.226.4125

– Plant Leadership—Paul Carlson

EQUIPMENT:
Open-pit truck and shovel mine, concentrator, pellet plant.

PRODUCTS and/or SERVICES:
Standard and DR-grade pellets.

Railroad and Shipping Facilities: Rail and barge.

Annual Capacity: 3.8 million tons.

No. of Employees: 590.

Minorca Mine
5950 Old Hwy. 53 N
Virginia, MN 55792 USA
P: +1.218.749.5910

– Plant Leadership—Conor McCue

EQUIPMENT:
Two open-pit iron ore mines, crushing facility, three-line concentrator, single-line straight grate pelletizing plant.

PRODUCTS and/or SERVICES:
Iron ore pellets.

Annual Capacity: 2.8 million tons.

No. of Employees: 345.

Tilden Mine
P.O. Box 2000
Ishpeming, MI 49849 USA
P: +1.906.475.3400

– Plant Leadership—Ryan Korpela

PRODUCTS and/or SERVICES:
Open-pit truck and shovel mine, single-stage primary crushing, autogenous grinding and flotation separation, pellet plant.

PRODUCTS and/or SERVICES:
Hematite concentrates.

Railroad and Shipping Facilities: Rail and barge.

Annual Capacity: 6.3 million tons.

No. of Employees: 900.

Cokemaking/Coal Mining Facilities:

Monessen Coke
345 Donner Ave.
Monessen, PA 15062 USA
P: +1.724.684.1000

– Plant Leadership—Randy E. Shelton

EQUIPMENT:
Two coke batteries, byproducts recovery process plant, boiler operations plant, biological wastewater treatment facility and barge unloading facility.

PRODUCTS and/or SERVICES:
Furnace coke and related byproducts.

No. of Employees: 185.

Princeton Coal
640 Clover Dew Dairy Road
Princeton, WV 24739 USA
P: +1.304.325.5719

– Plant Leadership—Charles Childers

IRON and STEEL PLANTS

PRODUCTS and/or SERVICES:
Coking coal and PCI.

Annual Capacity: Approx. 2.3 million tons.

Warren Coke
2234 Main Ave. SW
Warren, OH 44481 USA
P: +1.330.841.2800

– Plant Leadership—Joe Magni

EQUIPMENT:
Cokemaking facility, byproducts and powerhouse.

PRODUCTS and/or SERVICES:
Coke.

No. of Employees: 190.

HBI Facilities:

IronUnits LLC
2768 Front St.
Toledo, OH 43605 USA
P: +1.567.202.1234

– Plant Leadership—Matthew Rea

EQUIPMENT:
Direct reduction plant.

PRODUCTS and/or SERVICES:
High-quality HBI.

Railroad and Shipping Facilities: Rail, barge and heavy haul roads.

Annual Capacity: 1.9 million metric tons.

No. of Employees: 170.

Steelmaking Facilities:

Burns Harbor
250 W. U.S. Hwy. 12
Burns Harbor, IN 46304 USA
P: +1.219.787.2120

– Plant Leadership—Jean Louis Muller

EQUIPMENT:
Coke plant operations, iron producing, steel producing, hot rolling, pickling, cold rolling, annealing, galvanizing, finishing, plate rolling and heat treating.

PRODUCTS and/or SERVICES:
Hot-rolled, cold-rolled, HDG coils, as-rolled and heat-treated plate.

Annual Capacity: 5 million net tons.

No. of Employees: 3,170.

Butler Works
One Armco Dr.
Lyndora, PA 16405 USA
P: +1.724.284.2000

– Plant Leadership—Aaron Steinheiser

EQUIPMENT:
EAF, AOD unit, LMF, two double-strand continuous casters, anneal and pickle lines, one 3-stand tandem cold mill, and flat-rolled processing equipment.

PRODUCTS and/or SERVICES:
Flat-rolled electrical steels, stainless steels, stainless and carbon semi-finished slabs.

Annual Capacity: 1 million net tons.

No. of Employees: 1,130.

Cleveland Works
3060 Eggers Ave.
Cleveland, OH 44105 USA
P: +1.216.429.6000

– Plant Leadership—Chad Asgaard

EQUIPMENT:
Two BFs, two steel-producing facilities with BOFs and continuous strand casters, 84-in. HSM, pickle line, 5-stand tandem mill, hot-dip coating line (galvanize and galvanneal).

PRODUCTS and/or SERVICES:
Hot-rolled, cold-rolled, HDG sheet, semi-finished slabs.

Annual Capacity: >3 million net tons.

No. of Employees: 1,730.

Coatesville
139 Modena Road
Coatesville, PA 19320 USA
P: +1.610.383.2000

– Plant Leadership—Troy Graver

IRON and STEEL PLANTS

EQUIPMENT:
EAF, slab rolling, heat treating, annealing and blasting equipment.

PRODUCTS and/or SERVICES:
Carbon, HSLA, commercial alloy, military alloy and flame-cut steel plate. Slab rolling, heat treating, annealing and blasting. Metals conversion/processing, including stainless steel, nickel, copper and titanium alloys.

Annual Capacity: 800,000 net tons.

No. of Employees: 615.

Columbus Works
1800 Watkins Road
Columbus, OH 43207 USA
P: +1.614.492.6800

– Plant Leadership—Jason Dearth

EQUIPMENT:
72-in. HDGL, two 72-in. rewind lines.

PRODUCTS and/or SERVICES:
Galvanized sheet.

Annual Capacity: 450,000 tons.

Conshohocken
900 Conshohocken Road
Conshohocken, PA 19428 USA
P: +1.610.825.6020

– Plant Leadership—Dennis Sullivan

EQUIPMENT:
Q&T equipment, annealing, normalizing, blaster, CTL leveler.

PRODUCTS and/or SERVICES:
Coiled plate, discrete plate, military alloy, commercial alloy, heat-treated carbon.

Annual Capacity: 500,000 tons.

No. of Employees: 115.

Coshocton Works
17400 State Rte. 16
Coshocton, OH 43812 USA
P: +1.740.829.2341

– Plant Leadership—Troy Balo

EQUIPMENT:
Two Sendzimir mills, two Z-high cold reduction mills, four annealing and pickling lines, bell annealing furnaces, two bright annealing lines, two temper mills, and temper rolling, slitting and packaging equipment.

PRODUCTS and/or SERVICES:
Flat-rolled stainless steels, including austenitic (chrome-nickel), martensitic (chrome), and ferritic (chrome) grades.

No. of Employees: 390.

Dearborn Works
14661 Rotunda Dr.
Dearborn, MI 48120 USA
P: +1.313.317.8900

– Plant Leadership—LaDale Combs

EQUIPMENT:
BF, BOFs, two LMFs, VD, one dual-strand slab caster, one single-strand slab caster, PLTCM, HDGL.

PRODUCTS and/or SERVICES:
Carbon semi-finished slabs, hot-dip galvanized ZINCGRIP®, hot-dip galvannealed ZINCGRIP GA steel, AHSS.

No. of Employees: 1,290.

Indiana Harbor
3210 Watling St.
East Chicago, IN 46312 USA
P: +1.219.399.1200

– Plant Leadership—Anthony Pacilio

EQUIPMENT:
Three BFs (two operating), recycling plant, four BOFs, LMF, VD, four continuous casters, slab dimensioning facility, 80-in. HSM, pickling line, 5-stand tandem mill, batch and CAL, temper mill, two HDGLs.

PRODUCTS and/or SERVICES:
AHSS, API pipe skelp, motor laminations, automotive exposed and martensitic grades.

Annual Capacity: 5.5 million net tons.

No. of Employees: 3,715.

IRON and STEEL PLANTS

Tek and Kote
30755 Edison Road
New Carlisle, IN 46552 USA
P: +1.574.654.1000

– Plant Leadership—Allen Waitkins

EQUIPMENT:
Continuous descale cold mill, CAL.

PRODUCTS and/or SERVICES:
HDG and galvannealed sheet, electrogalvanized coil, cold-rolled sheet and annealed sheet.

Annual Capacity: 1.7 million net tons.

No. of Employees: 524.

Mansfield Works
913 Bowman St.
Mansfield, OH 44903 USA
P: +1.419.755.3011

– Plant Leadership—Thomas Hypes

EQUIPMENT:
Two EAFs, one AOD unit, LMF, thin-slab continuous caster, WB furnace, 6-stand HSM.

PRODUCTS and/or SERVICES:
Semi-finished hot bands, high-chrome ferritic and martensitic stainless steels.

Annual Capacity: >600,000 net tons.

No. of Employees: 395.

Middletown Works
1801 Crawford St.
Middletown, OH 45044 USA
P: +1.513.425.5000

– Plant Leadership—David Reinhold

EQUIPMENT:
BF, BOFs, CAS-O.B. unit, RH degasser, dual-strand slab caster, HSM, picklers, 5-stand cold mill, EGL, one HDGL, one hot-dip aluminizing line, box annealing, temper mills, open coil annealing.

PRODUCTS and/or SERVICES:
Hot-rolled, cold-rolled, AHSS, enameling steels, electrogalvanized (ZINCGRIP® ELECTROSMOOTH®) steels, HDG (ZINCGRIP), aluminized carbon and stainless steels.

Annual Capacity: 3 million net tons.

No. of Employees: 2,215.

Piedmont
2027 McLin Creek Road
Newton, NC 28658 USA
P: +1.828.464.9214

– Plant Leadership—Debbie McCurry

EQUIPMENT:
Plasma-cutting, services part leveling, warehousing and just-in-time deliveries.

PRODUCTS and/or SERVICES:
Plasma-cut steel blanks.

No. of Employees: 11.

Riverdale
13500 S. Perry Ave.
Riverdale, IL 60827 USA
P: +1.708.849.8803

– Plant Leadership—David Sena

EQUIPMENT:
Two BOFs, LMF, continuous thin-slab caster, tunnel furnace, HSM.

PRODUCTS and/or SERVICES:
Hot-rolled black bands in a full range of grades, including high-carbon and alloy.

Annual Capacity: 1 million net tons.

No. of Employees: 290.

Rockport Works
6500 N. Hwy. 231
Rockport, IN 47635 USA
P: +1.812.362.6000

– Plant Leadership—Nathaniel Johnson

EQUIPMENT:
Continuous carbon/stainless pickling line, continuous carbon/stainless cold mill, stainless CAL/pickling line, hydrogen annealing, temper mill, continuous HDG/galvannealing line.

PRODUCTS and/or SERVICES:
Cold-rolled carbon, coated and stainless steels in either the annealed

IRON and STEEL PLANTS

and pickled or temper-rolled surface condition, AHSS, 80-inch steel sheet.

No. of Employees: 480.

Steelton
215 S. Front St.
Steelton, PA 17113 USA
P: +1.717.986.2000

- Plant Leadership—George Downey

EQUIPMENT:
150-ton EAF, ladle refining, VD, three-strand continuous jumbo bloom caster, ingot teeming facility.

PRODUCTS and/or SERVICES:
Railroad blooms, specialty blooms, cast ingots and flat bars.

Annual Capacity: 1 million net tons.

No. of Employees: 450.

Weirton
100 Pennsylvania Ave.
Weirton, WV 26062 USA
P: +1.304.797.2000

- Plant Leadership—John Stubna

EQUIPMENT:
Pickler, tandem mill, batch anneal, CAL, temper mills, electro-tinplating lines, sidetrimmers.

PRODUCTS and/or SERVICES:
Cold-rolled sheet and tinplate.

No. of Employees: 870.

Zanesville Works
1724 Linden Ave.
Zanesville, OH 43701 USA
P: +1.740.450.5600

- Plant Leadership—Aaron Steinheiser

EQUIPMENT:
One anneal and pickle line, three strip anneal lines, electric box annealing furnaces, Sendzimir mill, two coating lines, one pickle/coat line, slitting line and packaging line.

PRODUCTS and/or SERVICES:
Finishing of regular grain-oriented electrical steels (GOES) and cold-rolled non-oriented electrical steels (NOES).

No. of Employees: 130.

Cleveland-Cliffs Tubular Components—see listing page 118

Tooling and Stamping Facilities: Cleveland-Cliffs Tooling & Stamping

PRODUCTS and/or SERVICES:
Advanced engineered solutions, tool design, hot- and cold-stamped steel components, and complex assemblies. Ten plants across the U.S. and Canada, and a new facility in Tennessee. Facilities feature seven large-bed, hot-stamping presses, providing 13 production lines, 81 cold-stamping presses ranging from 150 net tons to 3,000 net tons of pressing capacity, 17 large-bed, high-tonnage tryout presses, and 144 multi-axis welding assembly cells.

CLINGAN STEEL INC.
2525 Arthur Ave.
Elk Grove Village, IL 60007 USA
P: +1.847.228.6200
F: +1.847.228.6215
sales@clingansteel.com
www.clingansteel.com

- Chief Exec. Officer and Pres.—Steve Clingan
- Vice Pres. Sales and Mktg., Sales and Adv. Mgr.—Doug Clingan
- Vice Pres. Prodn./Mfg.—Tom Bulwan
- Treas.—Paulette Fischer
- Qual. Mgr.—Brian Cram
- Pur. Agt.—Ralph Herdrich

EQUIPMENT:
Five conventional slitters, one oscillate slitter, 10 edgers.

PRODUCTS and/or SERVICES:
Slit and edge carbon and stainless steel strip to order. Can provide the material as pancake coil, oscillate

IRON and STEEL PLANTS

coil, or cut lengths in both standard or precision-cut special lengths.

No. of Employees: 85.

COLUMBIANA FOUNDRY CO.
501 Lisbon Road
P.O. Box 98
Columbiana, OH 44408 USA
P: +1.330.482.3336
F: +1.330.482.9665
sales@columbianafoundry.com
www.columbianafoundry.com

- Pres.—Victor W. Nery
- Exec. Vice Pres.—Victor L. Nery

EQUIPMENT:
Two 6,000-lb. and two 2,000-lb. electric induction melting furnaces. Four solid-state programmable heat treat ovens (normalize and temper, Q&T, solution anneal).

PRODUCTS and/or SERVICES:
Iron castings from 20 lbs. to 16,000 lbs.: gray iron, ductile iron, austenitic iron, alloy iron, acicular iron. Steel, stainless steel and tool steel castings from 20 lbs to 8,000 lbs.: corrosion-resistant stainless steel, heat-resistant stainless steel, and specialty metals including cobalt- and nickel- based alloys. Columbiana Foundry Co. also has the ability to pour customized materials to meet customer-specific requirements.

COMMERCIAL METALS COMPANY
6565 N. MacArthur Blvd., Suite 800
Irving, TX 75039 USA
P: +1.214.689.4300
www.cmc.com

- Chmn., Chief Exec. Officer and Pres.—Barbara Smith
- Exec. Vice Pres.—Tracy Porter
- Sr. Vice Pres. Oprs.—Ty Garrison
- Vice Pres. — Central Div.—Steve Simpson
- Vice Pres. — Northeast Div.—Brian Halloran
- Vice Pres. — Southeast Div.—Greg Brandon
- Vice Pres. — West Div.—Steve Henderson
- Vice Pres. and Chief Supply Chain Officer—Brad Cottrell
- Vice Pres. Engrg.—Kolin Keller
- Vice Pres. and Chief H.R. Officer—Jennifer Durbin
- Dir. of Mill Oprs. — Northeast Div.—Alan Jackson
- Dir. of Mill Oprs. — Southeast Div.—Randy Marsh
- Dir. of Mill Oprs. — West Div.—Andy Sarat
- Dir. of Mill Oprs., Central Div.—Bill VanderWaal
- Dir. of Logistics, Americas Div.—Rick Jenkins
- Dir. of Energy Technology—Sam Matson
- Dir. of Environ., Americas Div.—Brad Bredesen
- Dir. of Safety, Americas Div.—Christine Lipscomb
- Environ. Mgr., Central Div.—Randy Walker
- Environ Mgr., Northeast and Southeast Div.—Alan Gillespie
- Safety Mgr., Central Div.—Jay Layton
- Safety Mgr., Northeast Div.—Brian Mayer
- Safety Mgr., Southeast Div.—Greg Hindmon
- Roll. Mill Technologies Mgr.—Greg Moore

CMC Steel Alabama
101 S. 50th St.
Birmingham, AL 35212 USA
P: +1.205.592.8981

- Dir. of Oprs.—Bryan Porter
- Meltshop Mgr.—Jonathan Ridgeway
- Roll. Mill Mgr.—Rick Wood
- Maint. Mgr.—Marty Schreiber
- Ship. and Inventory Mgr.—Glenn Marcus
- Qual. Assur. Mgr.—Marcus McCluney
- Engrg. Mgr.—Warren McWhorter
- Environ. Mgr.—Michelle Bunn
- Safety Mgr.—Santana Cazares
- Transp. Mgr.—Scott Johnson

EQUIPMENT:
DC EAF, 90-ton heat size, LMS, 4-strand continuous caster casting: 6- and 8-in. square billets and 6 x 8-in.

IRON and STEEL PLANTS

and 6 x 10-in. rectangular billets. 120-ton/hr. reheat furnace, 14-stand in-line merchant bar/structural mill.

PRODUCTS and/or SERVICES: Merchant bar and structural angles, flats, channels, and billets.

Annual Capacity: Raw steel: 750,000 net tons. Rolling mill: 600,000 net tons.

Railroad and Shipping Facilities: Truck, rail.

CMC Steel Arizona
11444 E. Germann Road
Mesa, AZ 85212 USA
P: +1.480.396.7100

AZ One

- Dir. of Mill Oprs.—Gilbert Hutton
- Meltshop Mgr.—Adrian Nieto
- Roll. Mill Mgr.—Joe Zuchowski
- Maint. Mgr.—Gareth Taylor
- Metallurgical Engrg. Technologies Mgr.—Jacob Selzer
- Environ. Mgr.—Mukonde Chama
- Safety Mgr.—Tony Hallock
- Transp. Mgr.—Patrick Cherry
- Ship. and Inventory Mgr.—David Argue

EQUIPMENT:
AC EAF 40-ton heat size, LMS, single-strand continuous caster connected to 16-stand in-line mill.

PRODUCTS and/or SERVICES: Rebar (straight and spool), studded T-post.

Annual Capacity: Rolling mill: 400,000 net tons.

AZ Two

- Dir. of Mill Oprs.—Andy Sarat
- Meltshop Mgr.—Justin Zwick
- Roll. Mill Mgr.—Adam Phillips
- Maint. Mgr.—Aaron Barredo
- Metallurgical Engrg. Technologies Mgr.—Jacob Selzer
- Environ. Mgr.—Mukonde Chama
- Safety Mgr.—Tony Hallock
- Transp. Mgr.—Patrick Cherry
- Ship. and Inventory Mgr.—David Argue

PRODUCTS and/or SERVICES: Rebar, merchant bar.

CMC Steel Arkansas
Mailing Address:
P.O. Box 1147
Magnolia, AR 71754 USA

Street Address:
100 Columbia 7B
Magnolia, AR 71753 USA
P: +1.870.234.8703

- Dir. of Mill Oprs., Central Div.—Bill VanderWaal
- Plant Mgr.—Jimmy Glass
- Roll. Mill Mgr.—Leon Whaley
- Prodn. Svcs. Mgr.—Michael Huffman
- Finishing Mgr.—Chris Otwell
- Maint. Mgr.—Randy Slaughter
- Safety Mgr.—Leonard Williams
- Environ. Mgr.—Mike Hull
- Transp. Mgr.—Abel Hernandez

EQUIPMENT:
Rail and billet steel rerolling, 40-ton/hr. reheat furnace, 14-pass merchant bar mill.

PRODUCTS and/or SERVICES: Studded T-post, flats, rounds, angles, rebar and special sections.

Railroad and Shipping Facilities: Truck, rail.

CMC Steel Florida
16770 Rebar Road
Jacksonville, FL 32234 USA
P: +1.904.266.4261

- Dir. of Oprs.—Carlos Zanoelo
- Meltshop Mgr.—Joao Feitoza
- Roll. Mill Mgr.—James Deberry
- Maint. Mgr.—Ricardo Peruchi
- Ship. and Inventory Mgr.—Rodney Thompson
- Qual. Assur. Mgr.—Alexander Renosto
- Engrg. Mgr.—Chad Foltz
- Environ. Mgr.—Anthony Cinelli
- Safety Mgr.—Jay Johnson
- Transp. Mgr.—Leslie Adams

EQUIPMENT:
AC EAF, 110-ton heat size, 4-strand continuous caster casting 5-in. billets.

IRON and STEEL PLANTS

90-ton/hr. reheat furnace, 16-stand continuous bar mill with high-speed wire rod outlet.

PRODUCTS and/or SERVICES: Billets, rebar, wire rod.

Annual Capacity: Raw steel: 760,000 net tons. Rolling mill: 550,000 net tons.

Railroad and Shipping Facilities: Truck, rail.

CMC Steel New Jersey
1 Crossman Road N
Sayreville, NJ 08871 USA
P: +1.732.721.6600

- Dir. of Oprs.—Warren Daily
- Roll. Mill Mgr.—Dick Delaney
- Maint. Mgr.—Thomas Messner
- Ship. and Inventory Mgr.—James Ruppert
- Qual. Assur. Mgr.—Biplab Sarma
- Engrg. Mgr.—Mason Compton
- Environ. Mgr.—Mark Blaire
- Safety Mgr.—Marc Miele
- Transp. Mgr.—Scott Johnson

EQUIPMENT:
AC EAF, 80-ton heat size, LMS, 5-strand continuous caster casting 4.5- and 5-in. billets. 135-ton/hr. reheat furnace, 14-stand bar mill. Epoxy coating plant.

PRODUCTS and/or SERVICES: Rebar.

Annual Capacity: Raw steel: 760,000 net tons. Rolling mill: 620,000 net tons.

Railroad and Shipping Facilities: Truck, rail.

CMC Steel Oklahoma
2353 E. Main St.
Durant, OK 74701 USA
P: +1.580.634.5200

- Dir. of Oprs.—Cole Walker
- Meltshop Mgr.—Jerry Cantu
- Roll. Mill Mgr.—Colter Prescott
- Maint./Engrg. Mgr.—Matt Skeen
- Post Shop Mgr.—Richard Davis
- Ship. and Inventory/Qual. Assur. Mgr.—Robbie Booth

- Metallurgical Engrg. Technologies Mgr.—Jacob Selzer
- Environ. Mgr.—Mike Raile
- Safety Mgr.—Coby Ragsdale
- Transp. Mgr.—Erica Reed

EQUIPMENT:
AC EAF, 45-ton heat size, LMS, single-strand continuous caster connected to 16-stand in-line mill.

PRODUCTS and/or SERVICES:
Rebar and merchant bar (straight and spool) and studded T-posts.

Annual Capacity: Rolling mill: 400,000 net tons.

Railroad and Shipping Facilities: Truck, rail.

CMC Steel South Carolina
310 New State Road
Cayce, SC 29033 USA
P: +1.803.936.3700

- Dir. of Oprs.—Brett Kunce
- Meltshop Mgr.—Ryan Peck
- Roll. Mill Mgr.—Daniel Da Rosa
- Maint. Mgr.—Mike Garcia
- Engrg. Mgr.—Tom Smith
- Ship., Inventory and Cust. Svce. Mgr.—Andrew Oseman
- Qual. Assur. Mgr.—Curtis Glenn
- Safety Mgr.—Ed Robenolt
- Environ. Mgr.—Greg Kuntz
- Transp. Mgr.—Leslie Adams

EQUIPMENT:
AC EAF, 95-ton heat size, LMS, 4-strand continuous caster casting 5- and 6.25-in. square billets and 7.625 x 5.25 in. rectangular billets. 160-ton/hr. reheat furnace, 17-stand in-line merchant bar/structural mill.

PRODUCTS and/or SERVICES:
Rebar, bar-size angles, rounds, squares, flats, channels, post, special sections and billets.

Annual Capacity: Raw steel: 840,000 net tons. Rolling mill: 800,000 net tons.

Railroad and Shipping Facilities: Truck, rail.

IRON and STEEL PLANTS

CMC Steel Tennessee
1919 Tennessee Ave.
Knoxville, TN 37921 USA
P: +1.865.867.7209

- Dir. of Oprs.—Ty Hall
- Meltshop Mgr.—Terry Tryon
- Roll. Mill Mgr.—Charles Keim
- Ship. and Inventory Mgr.—Michael Welch
- Qual. Assur. Mgr.—James Hall
- Engrg. Mgr.—Zilmar Cardoso
- Environ. Mgr.—Christopher Miles
- Safety Mgr.—James Ratledge
- Transp. Mgr.—Scott Johnson

EQUIPMENT:
AC EAF, 65-ton heat size; 3-strand continuous caster casting 5-in. billets. 90-ton/hr. reheat furnace, 17-stand continuous rolling mill.

PRODUCTS and/or SERVICES:
Rebar, plain round.

Annual Capacity: Raw steel: 600,000 net tons. Rolling mill: 600,000 net tons.

Railroad and Shipping Facilities: Truck, rail.

CMC Steel Texas
Mailing Address:
P.O. Box 911
Seguin, TX 78156 USA

Street Address:
1 Steel Mill Dr.
Seguin, TX 78155 USA
P: +1.830.372.8200

- Dir. of Mill Oprs., Central Div.—Bill VanderWaal
- Works Mgr.—Steven Hughes
- Yard and Shredder Mgr.—Joey Korzekwa
- Meltshop Mgr.—Martin Garcia
- Roll. Mill Mgr.—Chris Welfel
- Ship. and Inventory Mgr.—Alex Mims
- Qual. Assur. Mgr.—Rolando Davila
- Maint./Reliability Mgr.—Danny Avalos
- Engrg. Mgr.—Clint Watson
- Garage Mgr.—Lloyd Padalecki
- Environ. Mgr.—Wade Lindeman
- Safety Mgr.—Paul English
- Transp. Mgr.—Abel Hernandez

EQUIPMENT:
AC EAF, 120-ton heat size, LMS, 4-strand continuous caster casting 4-, 5- and 6.25-in. square billets and 7.625 x 5.25-in. rectangular billets. 175-tons/hr. reheat furnace, 17-stand in-line merchant bar/structural mill.

PRODUCTS and/or SERVICES:
Rebar, bar-size angles, rounds, squares, flats, studded T-post, channels, special sections and forging billets.

Annual Capacity: Raw steel: 1 million net tons. Rolling mills: 850,000 net tons.

Railroad and Shipping Facilities: Truck, rail.

CONTINENTAL STEEL & TUBE CO.
P.O. Box 030040
Ft. Lauderdale, FL 33303 USA
P: +1.855.954.5086 (Toll-Free);
  +1.954.332.2290
F: +1.954.332.2296
sales@continentalsteel.com
www.continentalsteel.com

- Founder/Sec.—Don Ascione, don@continentalsteel.com
- Pres.—Adam C. Ascione, adam@continentalsteel.com
- Product Mgr., Nickel/High Temp—Ben Lautredou, ben@continentalsteel.com
- Product Mgr., Stainless Steel—George Nomi, georgia@continentalsteel.com
- Product Mgr., Titanium—Andrea C. Clark, carolina@continentalsteel.com
- Product Mgr., Aluminum—Cece Basso, cece@continentalsteel.com
- Product Mgr., Carbon Steel—Michael Duffy, michael@continentalsteel.com
- West Coast Sales—Marcy Garner, marcy@continentalsteel.com
- Gen. Sales—Eddie Garcia, eddie@continentalsteel.com
- Traffic Mgr.—Vicki Pitrelli, vicki@continentalsteel.com
- Acctg. Mgr.—Megan Smith, accountant@continentalsteel.com

IRON and STEEL PLANTS

PRODUCTS and/or SERVICES:
Nickel and high-temp alloys, titanium, stainless steel, copper, brass, and bronze. Cold-rolled steel, hot-rolled steel, stainless steel, galvanized, tinplate, coils, sheet, bar, tubing, rounds, flats, strip, carbon and alloy grades in plate, pipe, rounds, shapes. Electrical steel. Coated products: GI, AL and electrogalvanized. Aluminum, titanium, alloy plate, alloy bar, alloy tubing, pipe, angles, aerospace, pre-painted steel and metals, wire, abrasion-resistant, tubing, DOM, seamless tubing, sheets, black plate, cold-drawn, cold-finished, corrosion resistant, reinforcing, rebar, shafting, spring steel, tempered steel, boiler tubes. PSQ bars.

No. of Employees: 90.

CRUCIBLE INDUSTRIES LLC
575 State Fair Blvd.
Solvay, NY 13209 USA
P: +1.800.365.1180 (Toll-Free)
F: +1.315.470.9358
sales@crucible.com
www.crucible.com

- Pres.—John Shiesley
- Vice Pres. Mfg.—Michael Sirbaugh
- Vice Pres. Oprs.—Duane Gordon

EQUIPMENT:
Arc and induction melting and vacuum arc melting furnaces, AOD, blooming mills, bar mills, rod mill, forging hammers, forging press, bar and wire cold-drawing equipment, and other cold-finishing equipment.

PRODUCTS and/or SERVICES:
Air-melted and Crucible Particle Metallurgy (CPM®) melted steel products in 300 and 400 stainless, high-speed, tool and valve grades. Available in round bar, billets, ingots, hot- and cold-rolled flats, hot-rolled squares and cold-drawn squares. Also offers conversion, laboratory testing and metallurgical services.

D

DEACERO S.A. DE C.V.
Corporate Office:
Av. Lázaro Cárdenas
No. 2333–Valle Oriente
San Pedro Garza García, NL, 66269
Mexico
P: +52.81.8368.1100
F: +01.800.851.78.11 (Toll-Free)
www.deacero.com

- Co-Chief Exec. Officers—Raul M. Gutierrez, Sergio M. Gutierrez

EQUIPMENT:
21 recycling centers (18 in Mexico and 3 in the U.S.), including 5 shredding centers. Three EAF steel works; rolling mill; 16 wire plants (14 in Mexico and 2 in the U.S.).

PRODUCTS and/or SERVICES:
Leading producer of long steel, rebar, wire and wire rod. Deacero is the largest producer of wire in Mexico with 18 production facilities and 29 distribution centers throughout North America.

Annual Capacity: Steel production: 4.5 million tons; Rolling mill: 1.4 million tons.

No. of Employees: 8,000.

IRON and STEEL PLANTS

Celaya Mill and Wire Plant
Carretera 45 Panamericana
Tramo Celaya
Salamanca km 64.8
Poblado de Chinaco, Villagrán, GJ,
38080 Mexico
P: +1.461.618.3800
F: +1.461.618.3829

EQUIPMENT:
One 100-ton EAF, one 110-ton EAF,
12-strand continuous caster and three
rolling mills.

Ramos Arizpe Mill and Wire Plant
Carretera a Monclova km 4
25000 Tramo Santa Cruz - Ojo Caliente
Ramos Arizpe, CA, 25903 Mexico

EQUIPMENT:
One 150-ton EAF.

Saltillo Mill and Wire Plant
Autopista Monterrey
Saltillo km 8.5
Ramos Arizpe, CA, 25000 Mexico
P: +1.844.432.0455;
 +1.844.432.0916
F: +1.844.432.0916

EQUIPMENT:
One 55-ton EAF, one 4-strand
continuous caster, one continuous
25-stand wire rod mill equipped with
controlled cooling.

Guadalupe Wire Plant
Av. Ruiz Cortínez No. 1421
Col. Fraccionamiento Industrial las
Américas
Guadalupe, NL, 67128 Mexico
P: +81.8131.6900
F: +81.8131.6931

EQUIPMENT:
Wire drawing mills, EGL, nail presses.

Mexicali Wire Plant
Carretera a San Luís Río Colorado
km 7.5 #2001
Gonzalez Ortega, Mexicali, BN, 21399
Mexico
P: +1.686.561.6906
F: +1.686.561.6843

EQUIPMENT:
Wire drawing mills, welding lines,
weaving lines and many finisher wire
lines.

Monterrey Wire Plant
Av. Manuel Ordoñez #770 Pte.
El Lechugal, Santa Catarina, NL, 66376
Mexico
P: +81.8389.3000
F: +81.8336.3665

EQUIPMENT:
Wire drawing mills, galvanizing lines,
welding lines, weaving lines, nail
presses and many finisher wire lines.

Puebla Wire Plant
Blvd. Mártires de Río Blanco #16
Fracc. Industrial 5 de Mayo
Puebla, PU, 72019 Mexico
P: +1.222.223.6800;
 +1.222.223.6844; 45; 46; 47
F: +1.222.223.6840

EQUIPMENT:
Wire drawing mills, galvanizing lines,
welding lines, weaving lines and many
finisher wire lines.

Tlalnepantla Wire Plant
Avenida Hidalgo Edificio 132
Fracc. Industrial
Tlalnepantla, MX, 54030 Mexico

León Industrial Wire Plant
Circuito Oleoducto No. 315
Cd. Industrial, León, GJ, 37490 Mexico
P: +1.477.740.1100
F: +1.477.740.1119

EQUIPMENT:
Wire drawing mills, galvanizing lines,
welding lines, weaving lines and many
finisher wire lines.

Morelia Industrial Wire Plant
Oriente 4 #1565
3era Etapa, Cd. Industrial
Morelia, MC, 58920 Mexico
P: +1.443.322.6500
F: +1.443.322.6508

EQUIPMENT:
Acid pickling plant, wire drawing mills,
galvanizing lines, rope and cable, and
high-carbon wires.

IRON and STEEL PLANTS

Querétaro Industrial Wire Plant
Avenida Felipe Carillo Puerto #301
Querétaro, QE, 76130 Mexico

**Mid Continent Steel and Wire Inc.—
see listing page 60**

**DOUBLE G COATINGS CO. L.P., a
Joint Venture Between Cleveland-
Cliffs Inc. and United States Steel
Corporation**
1096 Mendell Davis Dr.
Jackson, MS 39272 USA
P: +1.601.371.3460
F: +1.601.371.3466

- Pres.—Keith Mangum,
  kmangum@dgcsteel.com
- Plant Mgr.—Mark L. Chrislip,
  mchrislip@dgcsteel.com
- Contr.—Becky L. Bowers,
  becky@dgcsteel.com
- Qual. and Environ. Control Mgr.—
  Arthur L. Miller,
  amiller@dgcsteel.com
- Prodn. and Inventory Control Mgr.—
  Britt Bullock, bbullock@dgcsteel.com
- Pur. Coordinator—John Cox,
  jcox@dgcsteel.com

EQUIPMENT:
One hot-dip continuous Galvalume®/
galvanize coating line, one recoil/
inspection line, wastewater treatment
plant.

PRODUCTS and/or SERVICES:
Galvalume and galvanized sheet steel,
0.0085 in. to 0.0300 in. thick x 24 in.
to 49 in. wide; especially for pre-
painted metal building applications.

Annual Capacity: 315,000 tons.

No. of Employees: 78.

E

EATON STEEL BAR CO.
10221 Capital St.
Oak Park, MI 48237 USA
P: +1.800.527.3851 (Toll-Free);
+1.248.398.3434
sales@eatonsteel.com
www.eatonsteel.com

PRODUCTS and/or SERVICES:
SBQ distributor in North America.
Sells hot-rolled, Q&T and cold-drawn
engineered steel bar products.

Eaton Steel Corp. Taylor Plant
20601 Trolley Industrial Dr.
Taylor, MI 48180 USA
P: +1.313.291.8300
F: +1.248.837.2364

Hercules Drawn Steel Corp.
38901 Amrhein Road
Livonia, MI 48150 USA
P: +1.248.398.1950
F: +1.248.398.1938

Apollo Heat Treating
10400 Capital St.
Oak Park, MI 48237 USA
P: +1.800.527.3851 (Toll-Free);
+1.248.398.3434
sales@eatonsteel.com

**ELECTRALLOY, a G.O. Carlson
Inc. Company**
175 Main St.
Oil City, PA 16301 USA
P: +1.814.678.4100
F: +1.814.677.1342
www.electralloy.com

- Chief Oper. Officer and Pres.—Tracy
  Rudolph
- Vice Pres. Sales—Greg Chirieleison
- Vice Pres. Technology—Todd
  Tomczyk
- Sr. Vice Pres. Oprs., Plate—Gunard
  Travaglini
- Vice Pres. Sales, Plate—Craig
  Travaglini

IRON and STEEL PLANTS

- Vice Pres. and Chief Info. Officer—Peter Santucci
- Vice Pres. Production Plan.—Bart Plyler
- Mgr. Remelt Oprs.—Anthony McCoy
- Melt Supt.—Jon Haggerty
- Process Met.—Aaron Proper
- Mgr. Qual. Control—Lindsay Druschel
- Chief Chemist—Quinn Mitchell

EQUIPMENT:
One EAF, two ESR and six VAR furnaces, two AOD stations, two wire injection facilities, one continuous belt-link conveyor for casting pigs, three Midwest ingot and billet grinders, two heat treat furnaces, six stress-relief furnaces, 11 band saws, peeler and two lathes. Complete chem lab.

PRODUCTS and/or SERVICES:
Ingots, electrodes, pigs, billets, bars, block, ESR, VAR, coil rod, weld wire and cold-drawn bar. Alloys include duplex, austenitic, martensitic, ferritic and precipitation hardening stainless steels; nickel alloys; copper alloys; structural steels; tool steels; and Nitronic® 30, Nitronic 33, Nitronic 40, Nitronic 50 and Nitronic 60.

No. of Employees: Approx. 230.

Railroad and Shipping Facilities: Truck.

G.O. Carlson Plate
350 Marshallton Thorndale Road
Downingtown, PA 19335 USA-2063
P: +1.800.338.5622 (Toll-Free);
+1.610.384.2800
F: +1.610.383.3429
ctravaglini@gocarlson.com
www.electralloy.com/g-o-carlson-plate

- Vice Pres. Sales, Plate Products—Craig Travaglini
- Qual. Control Coordinator Plate—Mike Hebert

PRODUCTS and/or SERVICES:
Specialty plate and plate products. All phases of rough and finished machining, plasma-arc cutting, water-jet cutting, shearing, grinding and flattening. Stainless steel, nickel alloys, copper-nickel, and other specialty grades including austenitic, high-strength, corrosion-resistant Nitronic® 30, Nitronic 33, Nitronic 40, Nitronic 50 and Nitronic 60.

ELLWOOD GROUP INC.
P.O. Box 790
600 Commercial Ave.
Ellwood City, PA 16117 USA
P: +1.866.367.3811 (Toll-Free)
egisales@elwd.com
www.ellwoodgroup.com

- Chmn. of the Board—David E. Barensfeld
- Chief Exec. Officer and Pres.—Ben Huffman
- Chief Technology Officer—Bill Edwards

ELLWOOD CITY FORGE GROUP
800 Commercial Ave.
Ellwood City, PA 16117 USA
P: +1.800.843.0166 (Toll-Free)
ecfsales@elwd.com
www.ellwoodcityforge.com

- Pres.—Scott Boyd
- Vice Pres. of Oprs. and Gen. Mgr.—Bill Nardone
- Dir. H.R.—Danielle Book
- Vice Pres., Sales and Mktg.—Steve Ross
- Dir. Sales—Elvy Kirkham, Beau McElfresh
- Dir. Mktg.—Kathy Saunders
- Sr. Dir. Business Dev.—Mark Miller
- Dir., Engrg. and Technology—Marc Panaia

EQUIPMENT:
Open-die presses: 1,500-, 4,500- and 5,000-ton (computerized) heat treating furnaces; quench tanks; rough and semi-finish machine facilities; laboratories; and facilities for complete testing.

PRODUCTS and/or SERVICES:
Open-die air melt and remelt steel — carbon, alloy, tool, and stainless steel, nickel-alloy and aluminum forgings, including crankshafts, continuous caster rolls, spindles, couplings, table rollers, gear blanks, pinions, and work roll blanks. Fabrications and welding also available.

IRON and STEEL PLANTS

ELLWOOD City Forge Group — New Castle
712 Moravia St.
New Castle, PA 16101 USA
P: +1.724.658.9632

ELLWOOD NATIONAL FORGE
1 Front St.
Irvine, PA 16329 USA
P: +1.814.563.7522
enfsales@elwd.com
www.ellwoodnationalforge.com

- Pres.—Mike Barrett

EQUIPMENT:
2,000 ton open-die forging press, horizontal and vertical heat treatment, deep-hole boring, finish turning.

PRODUCTS and/or SERVICES:
Precision-machined steel components.

ELLWOOD National Forge — Corry
441 E. Main St.
Corry, PA 16407 USA
P: +1.814.664.9664

ELLWOOD National Forge — Warren
1045 4th Ave.
Warren, PA 16365 USA
P: +1.814.563.7522

ELLWOOD CLOSED DIE GROUP
363 N. Sam Houston Pkwy. E #630
Houston, TX 70060 USA
P: +1.800.231.6130 (Toll-Free)
sales@ellwoodcloseddiegroup.com
www.ellwoodcloseddiegroup.com

- Pres.—Richard Allener
- Vice Pres. Finance—Wayne Thompson

PRODUCTS and/or SERVICES:
Forging, heat treating, mechanical testing, machining and welding.

ELLWOOD Texas Forge — Houston
12500 Amelia Dr.
Houston, TX 77045 USA
P: +1.800.231.6130 (Toll-Free)

- Vice. and Gen. Mgr.—Mike Rollins

ELLWOOD Texas Forge — Navasota
10908 CR 419
Navasota, TX 77868 USA
P: +1.800.231.6130 (Toll-Free)

- Vice Pres. and Gen. Mgr.—Steve Ingram

ELLWOOD ENGINEERED CASTINGS
7158 Hubbard Masury Road
Hubbard, OH 44425 USA
P: +1.832.477.7101
eecsales@elwd.com
www.ellwoodengineeredcastings.com

- Pres.—Patrick F. Callihan

EQUIPMENT:
Three 55-ton coreless induction furnaces capable of melting 900 tons/day.

PRODUCTS and/or SERVICES:
Gray iron castings up to 160 tons and ductile iron castings up to 60 tons.

ELLWOOD QUALITY STEELS CO.
700 Moravia St.
New Castle, PA 16101 USA
P: +1.800.344.3396 (Toll-Free)
eqssales@elwd.com
www.ellwoodqualitysteels.com

- Pres.—Michael Morgus
- Vice Pres. Commercial—J. Kane
- Dir. Tech. Svcs.—Daniel Raiser
- Dir. Steelmaking Technology—Brendan Connolly
- Mgr. Steelmaking Oprs.—Darrin Schwartz

EQUIPMENT:
45-ton EAF with EBT; ASEA-SKF ladle furnace; ASEA ladle degasser; EMCI ladle furnace with injection; annealing furnaces; VAR furnaces; ESR furnaces.

PRODUCTS and/or SERVICES:
Carbon, low-alloy, tool and 400 series stainless steel bottom-poured ingots. Remelted ingots.

Annual Capacity: 450,000 tons.

Railroad and Shipping Facilities: Truck, rail.

ELLWOOD National Steel
1 Front St.
Irvine, PA 16329 USA
P: +1.800.344.3396 (Toll-Free)

IRON and STEEL PLANTS

PRODUCTS and/or SERVICES: Electroslag and VAR ingots in ultrahigh-quality stainless and nickel-based alloys.

NORTH AMERICAN FORGEMASTERS (Joint Venture Between ELLWOOD Group Inc. and Scot Forge)
710 Moravia St.
New Castle, PA 16101 USA
P: +1.724.656.6440
nafsales@naforgemasters.com
www.naforgemasters.com

- Pres.—Mike Kamnikar

EQUIPMENT:
4,500-ton press, 10,120-ton press with full automation capabilities, 220-ton rail bound manipulator, 110-ton mobile manipulator.

PRODUCTS and/or SERVICES: Open-die forge facility producing billet stock, solid and hollow preforms, and custom-forged shapes in sizes up to 270,00 lbs.

ESMARK STEEL GROUP, A Wholly Owned Subsidiary Of Esmark Inc.
700 Central Ave.
University Park, IL 60484 USA
P: +1.800.323.0340 (Toll-Free);
   +1.708.756.0400
F: +1.866.585.4939 (Toll-Free)
sales@steel.esmark.com
www.esmarksteelgroup.com

- Chief Exec. Officer—Roberto Alvarez
- Vice Pres. Business Dev.—David Brewer
- Vice Pres. Oprs.—John Dergentis
- Sr. Vice Pres. Pur.—Don Macintyre
- Vice Pres. Sales—Joe Darragh

PRODUCTS and/or SERVICES: Processor and distributor of value-added flat-rolled steel and producer of tinplate steel.

Railroad and Shipping Facilities: Truck.

ESG Midwest
2500 Euclid Ave.
Chicago Heights, IL 60411 USA

ESG Midwest
300 E. Joe Orr Road
Chicago Heights, IL 60411 USA

ESG Northeast
615 Liverpool Dr.
Valley City, OH 44280 USA
P: +1.800.672.5010 (Toll-Free);
   +1.330.225.7741
F: +1.330.273.6265

ESG Southeast
200 River Landing Dr. #202H
Daniel Island, SC 29482 USA
P: +1.800.323.0340 (Toll-Free)

EVRAZ NORTH AMERICA
Headquarters:
71 S. Wacker Dr., Suite 1700
Chicago, IL 60606 USA
P: +1.312.533.3555
www.evrazna.com

- Chief Exec. Officer and Pres.—Skip Herald
- Chief Commercial Officer—Jerry Reed
- Chief Financial Officer and Sr. Vice Pres.—Olesya Afanasyeva
- Chief H.R. Officer and Sr. Vice Pres.—Barbara Turk
- Chief Performance Officer and Sr. Vice Pres., Canadian Oprs.—Matthew Perkins
- Sr. Vice Pres., Recycling and Supply Chain—Steven Eldam
- Gen. Counsel and Corporate Sec.—Eileen Tierney

Facilities:

EVRAZ Portland
14400 N. Rivergate Blvd.
Portland, OR 97203 USA
P: +1.503.240.5240

- Sr. Vice Pres., Portland Business Unit—Don Hunter

PRODUCTS and/or SERVICES: Plate and coil, large-diameter line pipe, heat treating.

EVRAZ Regina
100 Armour Road
P.O. Box 1670
Regina, SK S4P 3C7 Canada
P: +1.306.924.7700

IRON and STEEL PLANTS

- Vice Pres., Regina Oprs.—Brad Forster

PRODUCTS and/or SERVICES:
Plate and coil, small- and large-diameter line pipe, OCTG.

EVRAZ Rocky Mountain Steel
1612 E. Abriendo Ave.
Pueblo, CO 81004 USA
P: +1.719.561.6000

- Sr. Vice Pres. Pueblo Business Unit—David Ferryman

PRODUCTS and/or SERVICES:
Standard and premium rail, rod and bar, seamless OCTG pipe.

EVRAZ Calgary
7201 Ogdendale Road SE
Calgary, AB T2C 2A4 Canada
P: +1.403.279.3351

- Dir., OCTG Oprs.—Jorge Garcia-Saqui

PRODUCTS and/or SERVICES:
OCTG, heat treating, threading.

EVRAZ Camrose
5302 39th St.
Camrose, AB T4V 2N8 Canada
P: +1.780.672.3116

- Oprs. Mgr.—Desmond Erickson

PRODUCTS and/or SERVICES:
Large- and small-diameter ERW line pipe.

EVRAZ Red Deer
27251 Township Road 391
P.O. Box 593
Red Deer, AB T4N 5GB Canada
P: +1.403.346.7717

- Dir., OCTG Oprs.—Jorge Garcia-Saqui

PRODUCTS and/or SERVICES:
OCTG and small-diameter line pipe, premium connections, threading.

F

FARWEST STEEL CORP.
3693 E. Game Farm Road
Springfield, OR 97477 USA
P: +1.541.686.2000
www.farweststeel.com

PRODUCTS and/or SERVICES:
Products include: plate, flat roll, tube, pipe, merchant bars, cold-finish bars, beam, grating and expanded metal, and reinforcing. Services include: CTL coil, flame cutting, HD plasma, laser cutting, structural laser cutting, forming, welding, robotic welding, shearing, saw cutting, CNC programming, rebar fabrication, rebar erection and installation. Divisions include: steel distribution, steel processing, steel advanced processing, reinforcing fabrication, reinforcing installation. Western Coating Inc. specializes in epoxy-coated rebar and alternative corrosion-resistant solutions for reinforced concrete.

Rebar — Eugene, OR
90340 Hwy. 99 N
Eugene, OR 97402 USA
P: +1.800.269.8720 (Toll-Free)
rebar.eugene.sales@farweststeel.com

Rebar — Vancouver, WA
3703 N.W. Gateway Ave.
Vancouver, WA 98660 USA
P: +1.800.793.1493 (Toll-Free)
rebar.vancouver.sales@farweststeel.com

Rose City Post-Tension — Vancouver, WA
3703 N.W. Gateway Ave.
Vancouver, WA 98660 USA
P: +1.800.250.1820 (Toll-Free)
rcpt.sales@farweststeel.com

IRON and STEEL PLANTS

Steel — Boise, ID
4421 Enterprise St.
Boise, ID 83705 USA
P: +1.800.632.5951 (Toll-Free)
steel.boise.sales@farweststeel.com

Steel — Eugene, OR
2000 Henderson Ave.
Eugene, OR 97403 USA
P: +1.800.452.5091 (Toll-Free)
steel.eugene.sales@farweststeel.com

Steel — Longview, WA
7 International Way
Longview, WA 98632 USA
P: +1.360.567.1431
dave.terry@farweststeel.com

Steel — Medford, OR
2260 Sage Road
Medford, OR 97501 USA
P: +1.800.547.9652 (Toll-Free)
steel.medford.sales@farweststeel.com

Steel — Moses Lake, WA
13583 Wheeler Road NE, Bldg. C
Moses Lake, WA 98837 USA
P: +1.509.765.1422
steel.vancouver.sales@farweststeel.com

Steel — Renton, WA
201 S.W. 34th St.
Renton, WA 98055 USA
P: +1.800.548.6623 (Toll-Free)
steel.renton.sales@farweststeel.com

Steel — Spokane Valley, WA
3808 N. Sullivan Road Bldg. 7
Spokane Valley, WA 99216 USA
P: +1.509.866.7999
steel.spokane.sales@farweststeel.com

Steel — Stockton, CA
2881 N. Navone Road
Stockton, CA 95215 USA
P: +1.866.706.5405 (Toll-Free)
steel.stockton.sales@farweststeel.com

Steel — Vancouver, WA
3703 N.W. Gateway Ave.
Vancouver, WA 98660 USA
P: +1.855.246.5052 (Toll-Free)
steel.vancouver.sales@farweststeel.com

Weld Air — Wasilla, AK
340 E. Centaur Ave.
Wasilla, AK 99654 USA
P: +1.907.373.2000

Western Coating — Auburn, WA
301 Lund Road
Auburn, WA 98001 USA
P: +1.800.835.0576 (Toll-Free)
auburn-sales@westerncoating.com

Western Coating — Ogden, UT
1250 West 2350 N
Ogden, UT 84404 USA
P: +1.800.612.5900 (Toll-Free)
sales@westerncoating.com

FERRAGON CORP.
11103 Memphis Ave.
Brooklyn, OH 44144 USA
P: +1.800.671.8655 (Toll-Free);
+1.216.671.6161
F: +1.216.671.4078
info@ferragon.com
www.ferragon.com

- Pres.—Eduardo Gonzalez
- Chief Financial Officer—David Hill
- Vice Pres. Corporate—Joe Gonzalez
- Vice Pres. Oprs.—Luis Gonzalez
- Vice Pres. Finance and Acctg.—Tony Potelicki
- Vice Pres. Commercial—Greg Kauffman
- Dir. of Qual.—Vicki Diamond
- Dir. of Info. Technology—Edwin Flores

Subsidiaries:

Autolum Processing Co.
27800 W. Jefferson Ave.
Gibraltar, MI 48173 USA
P: +1.855.772.ALUM (2586) (Toll-Free)
+1.734.727.0500
F: +1.734.722.3251
info@autolumprocessing.com
www.autolumprocessing.com

- Chief Exec. Officer—Eduardo Gonzalez
- Vice Pres. Corporate—Joe Gonzalez
- Vice Pres. Oprs.—Steve Swan
- Vice Pres. Commercial—Greg Kauffman
- Dir. of Qual.—Vicki Diamond

IRON and STEEL PLANTS

EQUIPMENT:
One 78-in. Stamco exposed slitting and inspection line with top and bottom inspection, including storage, transportation (truck) and metallurgical lab services.

PRODUCTS and/or SERVICES:
Slitting and inspection of aluminum sheet.

No. of Employees: 38.

Ferragon Specialty Steel
11103 Memphis Ave.
Cleveland OH 44144 USA
P: +1.216.600.0021
info@ferragonspecialtysteel.com
www.ferragonspecialtysteel.com

- Chief Exec. Officer—Eduardo Gonzalez
- Vice Pres. Corporate—Joe Gonzalez
- Vice Pres. Commercial—Greg Kauffman
- Sales Rep.—Bill Thoma

EQUIPMENT:
Pickling, cold reversing mill, batch and continuous anneal, cold-rolled slitting.

PRODUCTS and/or SERVICES:
Highly engineered steel strip ranging from carbon and alloy steel strip to HSLA, AHSS, and hardened and tempered grades, including storage, transportation, and metallurgical lab services.

No. of Employees: 20.

Ferrolux Metals Co.
27800 W. Jefferson Ave.
Gibraltar, MI 48173 USA
P: +1.877.566.6161 (Toll-Free);
   +1.734.727.6161
F: +1.734.722.3251
info@ferrolux.com
www.ferrolux.com

- Pres.—Eduardo Gonzalez
- Vice Pres. Corporate—Joe Gonzalez
- Gen. Mgr.—Steve Swan
- Office Mgr.—Sonia Cobos

EQUIPMENT:
Two 78-in. Stamco exposed slitting and inspection line with top and bottom inspection.

PRODUCTS and/or SERVICES:
Slitting and inspection of surface-critical flat-rolled steel, including storage, JIT transportation, and metallurgical lab services.

No. of Employees: 38.

Ferrous 85" Co.
8534 Hwy. 89, Suite No. 4
Sinton, TX 78387 USA
P: +1.361.607.6161
info@ferrous85.com
www.ferrous85.com

- Pres.—Eduardo Gonzalez
- Vice Pres. Corporate—Joe Gonzalez
- Gen. Mgr.—Mike Frausto
- Vice Pres. Commercial—Greg Kauffman
- Dir. Sales—Dennis Phelps

EQUIPMENT:
Heavy-gauge slitting line.

PRODUCTS and/or SERVICES:
Toll slitting of HR and HRP&O, including storage and transportation (truck) services.

No. of Employees: 20.

Ferrous Metal Processing
11103 Memphis Ave.
Cleveland, OH 44144 USA
P: +1.800.671.8655 (Toll-Free);
   +1.216.671.6161
F: +1.216.671.6165
info@ferrousmetalprocessing.com
www.ferrousmetalprocessing.com

- Pres.—Eduardo Gonzalez
- Vice Pres. Corporate—Joe Gonzalez
- Vice Pres. Oprs.—Chris Hinte
- Vice Pres. Sales—Dennis Phelps
- Vice Pres. Commercial—Greg Kauffman
- Cold-Rolled Mgr. and Chief Met.—Mark Slack

IRON and STEEL PLANTS

EQUIPMENT:
Push-pull pickler, heavy-gauge slitter, combination 4-high cold reversing mill, Ebner and LOI 100% hydrogen anneal furnaces, 78-in. Stamco exposed slitting and inspection line with top and bottom inspection.

PRODUCTS and/or SERVICES:
Toll processing of flat-rolled steel, CR conversion, CR slitting and inspection, warehousing, transportation (railroad and truck shipments of steel coils and sheets) and metallurgical lab services.

No. of Employees: 95.

Ferrous Metal Transfer Co. — Mississippi
38 County Road 370
Iuka, MS 38852 USA
P: +1.877.424.8655 (Toll-Free);
   +1.662.424.0115
F: +1.662.424.0311
info@ferrousmetaltransfer.com
www.ferrousmetaltransfer.com

- Chief Exec. Officer—Eduardo Gonzalez
- Vice Pres. Corporate—Joe Gonzalez
- Vice Pres. Oprs.—Lou Gonzalez
- Transp. Mgr.—Kristina Hemlinger

PRODUCTS and/or SERVICES:
Rail, truck, and barge shipments of steel coils and sheets.

No. of Employees: 19.

Ferrous Metal Transfer Co. — Ohio
11103 Memphis Ave.
Cleveland, OH 44144 USA
P: +1.216.671.8500
F: +1.216.671.3070

- Chief Exec. Officer and Pres.—Eduardo Gonzalez
- Vice Pres. Corporate—Joe Gonzalez
- Vice Pres. Oprs.—Troy Gray
- Oprs. Mgr.—Don McClain

PRODUCTS and/or SERVICES:
Rail and truck shipments of steel coils and sheets.

No. of Employees: 12.

FerrouSouth
38 County Road 370
Iuka, MS 38852 USA
P: +1.877.424.8655 (Toll-Free);
   +1.662.424.0115
F: +1.662.424.0011
info@ferrousouth.com
www.ferrousouth.com

- Pres.—Eduardo Gonzalez
- Vice Pres. Corporate—Joe Gonzalez
- Gen. Mgr.—Todd Bennett
- Vice Pres. Commercial—Greg Kauffman
- Dir. of Qual.—Vicki Diamond

EQUIPMENT:
CTL, two stretcher leveling lines—light gauge 0.053–0.165 in. x 72 in. and heavy gauge 0.135–0.565 in. x 96 in., and two slitting lines.

PRODUCTS and/or SERVICES:
Toll processing of flat-rolled product, including storage, transportation (truck, rail, barge) and metallurgical lab services.

No. of Employees: 39.

HyCAL Corp.
27800 W. Jefferson Ave.
Gibraltar, MI 48173 USA
P: +1.734.561.2000
F: +1.734.676.6048
www.hycalcorp.com

- Pres.—Eduardo Gonzalez
- Vice Pres. Corporate—Joe Gonzalez
- Gen. Mgr.—Steve Swan
- Chief Met.—Mark Blankenau
- Vice Pres. Commercial—Greg Kauffman
- Dir. of Qual.—Vicki Diamond

EQUIPMENT:
100% hydrogen continuous anneal furnace, 17 Ebner hydrogen batch furnaces, temper mill.

PRODUCTS and/or SERVICES:
Toll annealing of AHSS/UHSS, third-generation, and hardened and tempered grades.

IRON and STEEL PLANTS

FINKL STEEL
412 S. Wells St.
Chicago, IL 60607 USA
P: +1.800.DIE.BLOCK (343.25625)
  (Toll-Free);
  +1.773.975.2510
F: +1.773.348.5347
sales@finkl.com
www.finkl.com

- Chief Exec. Officer—Mark Shirley
- Chief Financial Officer—Eric Loges
- Chief Oper. Officer—David Hoffman
- Chief Info. Officer—David Laurenson
- Vice Pres. Sales and Mktg.—Steve Wasil
- Vice Pres. H.R. and Safety—Bryan Brown

Finkl Steel — Chicago
1355 E. 93rd St.
Chicago, IL 60619 USA
P: +1.773.975.2510
F: +1.773.348.5347
chicagosales@finkl.com
www.finkl.com

PRODUCTS and/or SERVICES:
Forging die steels, plastic mold steels, die casting tool steels and custom open-die forgings. Finkl open-die forgings are produced at a fully integrated production facility on Chicago's South Side and distributed domestically.

Finkl Steel — Composite
2300 W. Jefferson Ave.
Detroit, MI 48216 USA
P: +1.800.521.0420 (Toll-Free);
  +1.313.496.1226
F: +1.313.496.8599
compositesales@finkl.com

PRODUCTS and/or SERVICES:
Custom forgings and hot-work die steels.

Finkl Steel — Sorel
100 McCarthy St.
St-Joseph-de-Sorel, QC J3R 3M8
Canada
P: +1.450.746.4000
sorelsales@finkl.com
www.sorelforge.com

- Vice Pres. and Gen. Mgr.—Louis-Phillipe Lapierre-Boire

EQUIPMENT:
EAFs, VD, open-die forging presses, heat treating furnaces, machine shop, ladle metallurgy.

PRODUCTS and/or SERVICES:
Carbon, alloy steel forgings, tool and die steel, forged bars, and blocks.

Railroad and Shipping Facilities: Truck, rail.

Finkl Steel — Houston
14710 Cypress N. Houston Road
Cypress, TX 77249 USA
P: +1.281.640.2050
houstonsales@finkl.com

- Pres.—Jack Miller

FRIEDMAN INDUSTRIES INC.
1121 Judson Road, Suite 124
Longview, TX 75601 USA
P: +1.903.758.3431
www.friedmanindustries.com

- Chief Exec. Officer and Pres.—Michael J. Taylor
- Chief Financial Officer, Sec. and Treas.—Alex LaRue
- Vice Pres. Pur. and Vice Pres. Sales — Coil Div.—Jonathan Holcomb

PRODUCTS and/or SERVICES:
Steel processing, pipe manufacturing and processing, and steel and pipe distribution. The Flat Roll division operates five hot-rolled coil processing facilities with thickness/width capabilities ranging from 16 gauge through 1 in. and widths from 48 to 96 in. The Tubular division, operating under the trade name Texas Tubular Products, offers API and ASTM grade pipe, OCTG threading and semi-premium connections, and new mill reject/new secondary pipe stock.

Flat Roll Division:

East Chicago, IN Facility
4303 Kennedy Ave.
East Chicago, IN 46312 USA
P: +1.219.382.3400

IRON and STEEL PLANTS

EQUIPMENT:
Temper pass mill (36–72 in. widths, 0.054–0.625 in. gauges, 48–620 in. lengths, 80,000 lb. max coil weight), finished goods warehouse.

PRODUCTS and/or SERVICES:
Temper-passed CTL sheet and plate.

Annual Capacity: 152,000 tons.

Decatur, AL Facility
1468 Northpark Dr.
Decatur, AL 35601 USA
P: +1.903.758.3431 (Sales);
  +1.256.308.1110
F: +1.903.758.2265 (Sales)

– Vice Pres. Oprs.—Robert McCain

EQUIPMENT:
Stretcher leveler CTL line (36–96 in. widths, 0.056–0.500 in. gauges, 60–480 in. lengths, 60,000 lb. max coil weight), finished goods warehouse.

PRODUCTS and/or SERVICES:
Hot-rolled coil processing of coils up to 96 in. CTL sheet and plate up to ½-in. thick. Inventory of mill secondary and excess prime coils. Toll processing available.

Annual Capacity: 130,000 tons.

Railroad and Shipping Facilities: Truck, rail, barge.

Granite City, IL Facility
2325 North St.
Granite City, IL 62040 USA
P: +1.618.451.5426

EQUIPMENT:
Two temper pass mills (36–72 in. widths, 0.054–0.625 in. gauges, 48–999 in. lengths, 80,000 lb. max coil weight), coil storage.

PRODUCTS and/or SERVICES:
Temper-passed CTL sheet and plate.

Annual Capacity: 360,000 tons.

Hickman, AR Facility
5500 N. State Hwy. 137
Hickman, AR 72315 USA
P: +1.903.758.3431 (Sales);
  +1.870.763.8625
F: +1.903.758.2265 (Sales)

– Vice Pres. Oprs.—Steve Teeter

EQUIPMENT:
2-hi temper mill (36–72 in. widths, 0.060–0.500 in. gauges, 60–636 in. lengths, 50,000 lb. max coil weight), corrective leveling CTL line, finished goods warehouse.

PRODUCTS and/or SERVICES:
Hot-rolled coil processing. CTL sheet and plate. Inventory of mill secondary and excess prime coils. Toll processing available.

Annual Capacity: 180,000 tons.

Railroad and Shipping Facilities: Truck, rail, barge.

Sinton, TX Facility
8534 Hwy. 89, Suite 2
Sinton, TX 78387 USA
P: +1.713.454.3563

EQUIPMENT:
Stretcher leveler (36–96 in. widths, 0.0625–1.000 in. gauges, 24–720 in. lengths, 100,000 lbs. max coil weight).

PRODUCTS and/or SERVICES:
Stretcher-leveled CTL sheet and plate.

Annual Capacity: 180,000 tons.

Railroad and Shipping Facilities: Rail, truck, barge.

Tubular Division:

Texas Tubular Products Inc.—see listing page 138

IRON and STEEL PLANTS

G

GALVAPRIME S.A. DE C.V.
Privada La Puerta 2990 Interior 1
Parque Industrial La Puerta
Santa Catarina, NL, 66350 Mexico
P: +52.81.8308.7632; 7633; 7634
F: +52.81.8308.7633
info@galvaprime.com
www.galvaprime.com

- Chief Exec. Officer—Mauricio Morales
- Sales Mgr.—Luis Mercado
- Supply Chain Mgr.—Eugenio Mellando

EQUIPMENT:
Two slitters: Ga: 0.016–0.250 in. Width: 0.400–72.5 in. Coils up to 25 metric tons. Three CTL lines: Ga 0.016–0.250 in. Width: 5–72 in. Flatness: 10 Units I. Coils up to 25 metric tons. Automatic shear: Ga from 0.015–0.135 in., 120 strokes per minute. Materials: HRP&O, CR, GI, GN, AZ, PP, EG, AL and SS.

No. of Employees: 105.

GALVASID S.A. DE C.V.
Blvd. Carlos Salinas de Gortari km 10
Apodaca, NL, 66615 Mexico
P and F: +52.81.1156.0001
www.galvasid.com

PRODUCTS and/or SERVICES:
Galvasid is a subsidiary of LM Industrial Group, dedicated to adding value to hot-rolled steel bands. Galvasid offers pickling, cold-rolled, galvanizing, aluminum-zinc coating and in-line painting, as well as roll forming and other steel sheet, strip and coil products. Steel finished products are steel coils, flat sheets, and roll-formed sheets with different coatings as GI or GL in a wide variety of paints, gauges, thicknesses and lengths.

GAUTIER STEEL LTD.
80 Clinton St.
Johnstown, PA 15901 USA
P: +1.814.535.9200
F: +1.814.536.1610
sales@gautiersteel.com
www.gautiersteel.com

- Chief Exec. Officer and Pres.—Glen Buckley
- Vice Pres. Oprs.—Ken Smith
- Chief Financial Officer and Vice Pres.—Dale Gray
- Vice Pres. of Sales—Mark Groebel
- Cust. Svce.—Nathan Rock, Jeremy Dietz, Dave Shaulis
- Matls. Mgr.—Rob Gall

EQUIPMENT:
9- and 14-in. bar mills, including finishing operations.

PRODUCTS and/or SERVICES:
Carbon and alloy (MBQ, SBQ, aircraft quality grade (ACQ)) flats, sharp-corner squares, round-corner squares, special sections.

No. of Employees: 93.

Railroad and Shipping Facilities: Truck, rail.

Gautier Specialty Metals LLC
80 Clinton St.
Johnstown, PA 15901 USA
P: +1.814.535.9200
F: +1.814.536.1610
sales@gautierspecialty.com
www.gautierspecialty.com

- Pres.—Glen Buckley
- Vice Pres. Oprs.—Ken Smith
- Chief Financial Officer and Contr.—Jackie Kulback
- Gen. Mgr.—Dale Gray
- Vice Pres. of Sales—Mark Groebel
- Cust. Svce.—Jeremy Dietz, Troy Barron
- Matls. Mgr.—Rob Gall

EQUIPMENT:
51-in.-wide, 4-high plate/flat bar rolling mill.

IRON and STEEL PLANTS

PRODUCTS and/or SERVICES: AS9100D certified plate facility with capabilities including: rolling, heat treating and finishing of carbon, alloy, tool and stainless steel plates, as well as clad and canned material.

No. of Employees: 18.

Railroad and Shipping Facilities: Truck, rail.

GERDAU

GERDAU CORSA S.A.P.I. DE C.V.
Av. Ejército Nacional No. 216 Piso 2
Col. Anzures, Miguel Hidalgo,
Mexico City, DF, 11590 Mexico
P: +55.5262.7300
www.gerdaucorsa.com.mx

EQUIPMENT:
Three steel production and rolling plants, seven scrap collection and processing units.

PRODUCTS and/or SERVICES: Structural beams, rebar, bars and profiles.

Sahagún Plant
Km. 3 Ctra. Mex-Cd. Sahagún
Zona Ind. Tepeapulco
Sahagún, HD, 43990 Mexico
P: +791.913.8105

Annual Capacity: 1 million metric tons.

Tultitlán Plant
Primera Sur S/N, Independencia
Tultitlán, MX, 54915 Mexico
P: +55.5894.0044; +55.2487.2065

EQUIPMENT:
EAF.

PRODUCTS and/or SERVICES: Corrugated rod.

Annual Capacity: 200,000 metric tons.

La Presa Plant
Av. La Presa 2
Zona Industrial La Presa
Tlalnepantla, MX, 54187 Mexico
P: +55.5003.4030; +55.5062.1916

PRODUCTS and/or SERVICES: Commercial profiles. Angles, sills, squares, rounds, channels, hexagonal bars. Special lengths up to 18.3 m.

GERDAU LONG STEEL NORTH AMERICA
Executive Office:
4221 Boy Scout Blvd., Suite 600
Tampa, FL 33607 USA
P: +1.813.286.8383
F: +1.813.207.2251
www.gerdau.com

- Pres.—Chia Yuan Wang
- Vice Pres. Oprs.—Dean Peery
- Vice Pres. Sales and Mktg.—Scott Meaney
- Vice Pres. H.R.—Lorie Bryce
- Vice Pres. Sales and Operational Plan.—Carl Ash
- Chief Financial Officer—Vinicius Crescencio

Annual Capacity: Melt—7.2 million tons; rolling—5.4 million tons.

No. of Employees: 4,750.

Cambridge Mill
160 Orion Pl.
Cambridge, ON N1T 1R9 Canada
P: +1.800.265.7858 (Toll-Free);
+1.519.740.2488
F: +1.519.629.2062

- Vice Pres. and Gen. Mgr.—Tiago Beleza

EQUIPMENT:
Meltshop: 50-ton EAF, 3-strand furnace, 18-stand in-line rolling mill. Continuous caster. Rolling mill: pusher-type reheat.

PRODUCTS and/or SERVICES: Merchant rounds, squares, flats, angles, channels, special sections and rebar.

Railroad and Shipping Facilities: Truck.

IRON and STEEL PLANTS

Cartersville Mill
384 Old Grassdale Road NE
Cartersville, GA 30121 USA
P: +1.770.387.3300
F: +1.770.387.3327

- Vice Pres. and Gen. Mgr.—Rodrigo Canova

EQUIPMENT:
120-ton EAF; 4-strand continuous caster; reheat furnace; medium-section mill.

PRODUCTS and/or SERVICES:
Angles, channels, flats, wide-flange beams, standard I-beams.

Railroad and Shipping Facilities: Truck, rail.

Charlotte Mill
6601 Lakeview Road
Charlotte, NC 28269 USA
P: +1.704.596.0361
F: +1.704.597.5031

- Vice Pres. and Gen. Mgr.—Rodrigo Canova

EQUIPMENT:
75-ton EAF; 3-strand continuous caster; 15-stand continuous rolling mill.

PRODUCTS and/or SERVICES:
Billets, rebar and merchant products.

Railroad and Shipping Facilities: Truck, rail.

Jackson Mill
P.O. Box 10848
Jackson, TN 38308 USA

801 Gerdau Dr.
Jackson, TN 38305 USA
P: +1.731.424.5600
F: +1.731.422.4247

- Vice Pres. and Gen. Mgr.—Josh Wigger

EQUIPMENT:
125-ton EAF; 4-strand continuous caster; 16-stand continuous bar mill.

PRODUCTS and/or SERVICES:
Billets, merchant products, SBQ and rebar.

Railroad and Shipping Facilities: Truck, rail.

Manitoba Mill
P.O. Box 2500
27 Main St.
Selkirk, MB R1A 2B4 Canada
P: +1.800.665.0245 (Toll-Free);
+1.204.482.3241
F: +1.204.785.2193

- Vice Pres. and Gen. Mgr.—Gustavo Rodrigues

EQUIPMENT:
One 60-ton EAF; LF; continuous caster; 15-stand continuous in-line mill; automatic stackers; 3-stand heavy universal mill (UM) plate mill.

PRODUCTS and/or SERVICES:
MBQ and SBQ products, rebar, light and medium structural angles and channels, light beams and special sections.

Railroad and Shipping Facilities: Truck, rail.

Midlothian Mill
300 Ward Road
Midlothian, TX 76065 USA
P: +1.972.775.8241
F: +1.972.775.1930

- Vice Pres. and Gen. Mgr.—Daniel Rego

EQUIPMENT:
Shredder, two 150-ton EAFs. Three casting machines, total 11 strands. One bar mill, two structural and merchant mills.

PRODUCTS and/or SERVICES:
Rebar, merchant and SBQ rounds, standard beams, structural beams, piling and merchants.

Railroad and Shipping Facilities: Truck, rail.

IRON and STEEL PLANTS

Petersburg Mill
25801 Hofheimer Way
Petersburg, VA 23803 USA
P: +1.804.520.0286
F: +1.804.524.2803

- Vice Pres. and Gen. Mgr.—Jim Christina

EQUIPMENT:
Mega shredder, 150-ton EAF, near-net-shape casting X-H structural mill.

PRODUCTS and/or SERVICES:
Structural beams, piling products.

Whitby Mill
Hopkins St. S
Whitby, ON L1N 5T1 Canada
P: +1.905.668.8811
F: +1.905.668.2094

- Vice Pres. and Gen. Mgr.—Tiago Beleza

EQUIPMENT:
135-ton EAF with ladle arc furnace; 5-strand billet caster; 17-stand continuous bar mill with continuous cutting line; 15-stand structural mill with in-line straightening and bundling.

PRODUCTS and/or SERVICES:
Angles, channels, grader blades, rebar, beams, flats and billets.

Railroad and Shipping Facilities: Truck, ship.

Wilton Mill
1500-2500 W. 3rd St.
Wilton, IA 52778 USA
P: +1.563.732.3231

- Vice Pres. and Gen. Mgr.—Ricardo Rodrigues

EQUIPMENT:
One 80-ton EAF, one 3-strand continuous casting machine and rolling mill (5 ½-in. billets).

PRODUCTS and/or SERVICES:
Merchant bars, rebar, light structurals and flats, round-corner squares, SBQ flats.

GERDAU SPECIAL STEEL NORTH AMERICA
Jackson Office:
5591 Morrill Road
Jackson, MI 49201 USA
P: +1.800.876.7833 (Toll-Free);
+1.517.782.0415
www.gerdau.com/specialsteel

- Pres. Gerdau Special Steel North America—Rodrigo Belloc Soares
- Vice Pres. Sales and Technology—Luis Colembergue

Fort Smith Mill
5225 Planters Road
P.O. Box 1592
Fort Smith, AR 72916 USA
P: +1.479.646.0223

- Gen. Mgr.—John Kelleher

EQUIPMENT:
Two 55-ton EAFs, two Demag LFs/VDs, one 3-strand rotary centrifugal round caster, 12-stand 20-in. H/V rolling mill, one Kocks 500-mm PSB, three heat treat furnaces, ultrasonic testing facility, cold-finished bar facility.

PRODUCTS and/or SERVICES:
Engineered special quality carbon, alloy and bearing steel bars (hot- and cold-finished).

Annual Capacity: 550,000 tons.

Jackson Mill
3100 Brooklyn Road
Jackson, MI 49203 USA
P: +1.517.764.0311

- Vice Pres. and Gen. Mgr.—Adam Tabor

EQUIPMENT:
Two 50-ton EAFs, one Demag LF, Finkl-Mohr VAD, one 2-strand rotary centrifugal round caster, 12-stand 18-in. H/V rolling mill, one Kocks 500-mm PSB, three heat treat furnaces, ultrasonic testing facility, cold-finished bar facility, bar cutting facility.

IRON and STEEL PLANTS

PRODUCTS and/or SERVICES:
Engineered special quality carbon, alloy and bearing steel bars (hot- and cold-finished).

Annual Capacity: 300,000 tons.

Monroe Mill
3000 E. Front St.
Monroe, MI 48161 USA
P: +1.734.243.2446

- Vice Pres. and Gen. Mgr.—Daniel Mussap

EQUIPMENT:
Steelmaking: 120-ton EAF, LMF, twin tank degasser. Continuous casting: 5-strand, Danieli, 6 x 6-in. square billets. 6-stand breakdown mill. 8-stand H/V rolling mill with 8-strand Kocks RSB and three-cassette Kocks PSB, ultrasonic testing facility, cold-finished bar facility.

PRODUCTS and/or SERVICES:
Engineered special quality carbon, alloy and bearing steel bars (hot- and cold-finished).

Annual Capacity: 720,000 tons.

GLIDEWELL SPECIALTIES FOUNDRY CO. INC.
600 Foundry Road
P.O. Box 1089
Calera, AL 35040 USA
P: +1.205.668.1881
F: +1.205.668.1972
jhendrix@glidewell-foundry.com
www.glidewell-foundry.com

- Pres.—David Glidewell
- Vice Pres. Prodn./Mfg.—Brian Richey
- Vice Pres. Sales—John Hendrix
- Regional Sales Mgr.—Mark Fields

EQUIPMENT:
Two 6-ton coreless induction furnaces, foundry, fabrication and machining.

PRODUCTS and/or SERVICES:
Gray and ductile iron castings for water works, tool building, heavy construction, mining, nuclear, steel plants and coke batteries.

No. of Employees: 110.

GRANITE CITY PICKLING AND WAREHOUSE
1162 16th St.
Granite City, IL 62040 USA
P: +1.618.451.1046
F: +1.618.877.1347
info@gcpw.com
www.gcpw.com

- Chief Exec. Officer—Ford B. Cauffiel
- Pres.—Ford Tobey Cauffiel
- Plant Mgr.—Brian Watts
- Treas.—Ellen Cramer

EQUIPMENT:
72- x 0.375-in. pickle line.

PRODUCTS and/or SERVICES:
Pickling, slitting and warehousing.

GREAT LAKES METALS CORP.
8920 S. Octavia Ave.
Bridgeview, IL 60455 USA
P: +1.708.430.0500
F: +1.708.430.0505
dherpich@greatlakesmetals.com
www.greatlakesmetals.com

- Chief Exec. Officer, Pres., Treas. and Sales Mgr.—Donna Herpich
- Asst. Sales Mgr.—Karen Regan
- Pur. Agts.—Donna Herpich, Irene Mailhiot

PRODUCTS and/or SERVICES:
Full-service steel distribution warehouse specializing in stainless and structural steel. Tempered steel, tool steel, sheets and plates. Distribute aluminum, brass, extruded products, copper and bronze, hot- and cold-rolled, pickled and oiled, or galvanized steel. Metal in sheets, coil, strip, bar, flats, rounds, squares, hexagons, angles, sheet piling and H-piling. WBE/DBE/FBE certified in the State of Illinois. WBE/DBE certified in the State of Indiana. WDBE certified in the State

IRON and STEEL PLANTS

of Wisconsin. DBE certified in the State of Tennessee.

No. of Employees: 7.

GREGORY INDUSTRIES INC.
4100 13th St. SW
Canton, OH 44710 USA
P: +1.330.477.4800 (Headquarters);
 +1.866.994.4929 (Gregory Highway);
 +1.866.462.7678 (Gregory Fence);
 +1.866.997.8788 (Gregory Strut);
bporter@gregorycorp.com
www.gregorycorp.com

- Chief Exec. Officer—T. Matthew Gregory
- Vice Pres., Gregory Highway—Jeff Grover
- Vice Pres., Gregory Strut—Bob Porter
- Fence Product Mgr.—Darin Miller

PRODUCTS and/or SERVICES:
Gregory Industries specializes in galvanizing and roll-formed steel products—serving multiple industries with continuous galvanized sheet coil; highway safety guardrail and high-tension cable barrier systems; fence products; metal framing strut channel products, hangers, fasteners and accessories; welded steel tubing products; and after-fabrication "batch" HDG.

Gregory Tube—see listing page 122

GRUPO COLLADO S.A. DE C.V.
Av. Hidalgo 96
Parque Industrial Cartagena
San Antonio, Tultitlán, MX, 54900 Mexico
P: +55.5804.2200
www.collado.com.mx

- Chmn.—Guillermo Vogel Hinojosa
- Chief Exec. Officer and Dir.—Bernardo Vogel Fernandez de Castro
- Chief Financial Officer—Norberto Salas Diaz de Leon

PRODUCTS and/or SERVICES:
Semi-processed steel parts for various industries. Automatic stamping, precision machining, sheet metal and steel processing, assembly, and spot welding.

GRUPO SIMEC S.A.B. DE C.V., a Subsidiary of Industrias CH (ICH)
Av. Lázaro Cárdenas No. 601
Col. La Nogalera
Guadalajara, JA, 44440 Mexico
P: +52.55.1165.1025
ventas02@industriasch.com.mx
www.gsimec.com.mx

- Chief Exec. Officer—Rufino Vigil González
- Coordinator of Finance—Mario Moreno Cortez
- Chief Oper. Officer—Juan José Acosta Macías

EQUIPMENT:
EAF mini-mills and integrated BF production facilities in Mexico and the U.S.

PRODUCTS and/or SERVICES:
Diversified manufacturer, processor and distributor of steel wire, SBQ steels, rebar and commercial and structural long products.

Annual Capacity: Mexico and U.S.—4.9 million tons crude steel and 4.3 million tons finished.

Apizaco
Carretera Federal México-Texcoco-Veracruz km 123
Col. San Cosme Xalostoc
Apizaco-Huamantla, TL, 90460 Mexico
P: +52.241.413.1600

EQUIPMENT:
Two EBT EAFs, three ladle stations, two degassing stations, two 4-strand continuous casters, three WB reheating furnaces, three rolling mills.

PRODUCTS and/or SERVICES:
SBQ steels, rebar and merchant shapes. This plant has melting furnaces and rolling trains for bars. It manufactures hot-rolled rounds, hot-rolled hexagons, hot-rolled squares, flat bars, corrugated straight rebar,

IRON and STEEL PLANTS

commercial rounds and commercial flat bars.

Annual Capacity: Mini-mill 1: 480,000 tons billet, 444,000 tons finished. Mini-mill 2: 650,000 tons billet, 600,000 tons finished.

Cholula
Carretera Federal México-Veracruz km 123
Col. Linda Vista de Jesús
San Pedro Cholula, PU, 72760 Mexico
P: +1.800.252.7157 (Toll-Free)

EQUIPMENT:
Cold-drawn and turning equipment for bars.

PRODUCTS and/or SERVICES:
Turned, shelled and polished rounds; cold-drawn bar to bar rounds; cold-drawn roll to bar rounds; and cold-finished hexagons.

Annual Capacity: 120,000 tons.

Grupo SAN
Eje 114 No. 440, Zona Industrial
San Luis Potosí, SLP, 78395 Mexico
P: +52.444.824.5353, ext. 231
www.gruposan.com

EQUIPMENT:
Four EAFs, three continuous casters, three reheating furnaces, two rebar rolling mills, one wire rod rolling mill.

PRODUCTS and/or SERVICES:
Specializing in the production of long steels and corrugated rebar. Production and rolling plants in San Luis Potosí: two mini-mills (Aceros San Luis and Aceros DM). One processing plant in Silao, Guanajuato (CHQ Wire Mexico). Among its products are: rebar, wire rod, electrowelded wire mesh, commercial rounds, commercial squares, nails for wood and columns.

Annual Capacity: 660,000 tons billet; 610,000 tons finished.

Guadalajara
Av. Lázaro Cárdenas No. 601
Col. La Nogalera
Guadalajara, JA, 44440 Mexico

EQUIPMENT:
One EAF, one 4-strand continuous caster, five reheating furnaces, three rolling mills.

PRODUCTS and/or SERVICES:
Structural, SBQ, light structural steel and rebar. Products include I-beams, channels, angles, hot-rolled bars, fat bars, and cold-drawn bars.

Annual Capacity: 370,000 tons billet; 480,000 tons finished.

Mexicali
Carretera San Luis Rio Colorado km 11.5
Col. Gonzalez Ortega
Mexicali, BN, 21399 Mexico
P: +52.686.562.8959

EQUIPMENT:
One EAF, one 4-strand continuous caster, one WB reheating furnace, one SACK rolling mill, Linde oxygen plant, water treatment plant.

PRODUCTS and/or SERVICES:
Structural steel, light structural steel, rebar. Products include angles, rebar, channels and hot-rolled bars.

Annual Capacity: 430,000 tons billet; 250,000 tons finished product.

Railroad and Shipping Facilities: Truck, rail.

Republic Steel—see listing page 76

Tuberías Procarsa S.A. de C.V.—see listing page 138

IRON and STEEL PLANTS

H

HARRISON STEEL CASTINGS CO.
900 Mound St.
P.O. Box 60
Attica, IN 47918 USA
P: +1.765.762.2481
F: +1.765.762.2487
www.hscast.com

- Engrg.—Derek Hughes
- Prodn.—Sony Mascreen
- Pur.—Wade Harrison III
- Oprs.—Trevor Curtis
- Finance—Robert Harrison

PRODUCTS and/or SERVICES:
Carbon, low/medium-alloy and stainless steel castings, 5-axis CNC pattern router, net weight range 200–15,000 lbs., ISO 9001, PED, ABS certified, Tier 1 casting solutions with extensive machining capabilities.

HAYNES INTERNATIONAL INC.
1020 W. Park Ave.
P.O. Box 9013
Kokomo, IN 46904 USA
P: +1.800.354.0806 (Toll-Free);
+1.765.456.6012
F: +1.765.456.6905
haynessales@haynesintl.com
www.haynesintl.com

- Chief Exec. Officer, Pres. and Dir.—Michael L. Shor
- Vice Pres., Gen. Counsel and Corporate Sec.—Janice W. Gunst
- Vice Pres. Mktg. and Technology—V.R. Ishwar
- Vice Pres. Sales and Dist.—Marlin C. Losch III
- Vice Pres. Finance, Chief Financial Officer and Treas.—Daniel W. Maudlin
- Vice Pres. Corporate Affairs—Jean C. Neel
- Vice Pres. Tube and Wire Products—Scott R. Pinkham
- Vice Pres. Oprs.—David L. Strobel
- Contr. and Chief Acctg. Officer—David Van Bibber
- Vice Pres. and Chief Info. Officer—Gregory Tipton

PRODUCTS and/or SERVICES:
Manufacturer of high-performance nickel- and cobalt-based alloys used in corrosion and high-temperature applications.

Canada Sales Office
85 Beasley Crescent Apt. 15
Cambridge, ON N1T 1P5 Canada
P: +1.519.212.3471
sjohnstone@haynesintl.com

Eastern Sales and Service Center
430 Hayden Station Road
Windsor, CT 06095 USA
P: +1.800.426.1963 (Toll-Free);
+1.860.688.7771
F: +1.860.688.5550

Haynes International La Porte
3238 N. Hwy. 39
La Porte, IN 46350 USA
P: +1.800.354.0806 (Toll-Free);
+1.765.456.6012
F: +1.765.456.6905

Kokomo Manufacturing Facility
2000 W. Defenbaugh St.
Kokomo, IN 46902 USA
P: +1.800.354.0806 (Toll-Free);
+1.765.456.6012
F: +1.765.456.6905

EQUIPMENT:
Primary and secondary melting, annealing furnaces, forge press and several smaller hot mills. Four-high Steckel rolling mill and sheet product cold working equipment, including two CSMs. Located on approximately 180 acres of industrial property with more than 1.0 million square feet of building space.

PRODUCTS and/or SERVICES:
Produces sheet, plate, strip/coil, bar and billet.

La Porte Custom Metal Processing
3236 N. Hwy. 39
La Porte, IN 46350 USA
P: +1.219.326.8530

IRON and STEEL PLANTS

Southern Service Center
The Northwood Industrial Park
12241 FM 529
Houston, TX 77041 USA
P: +1.800.354.0806 (Toll-Free);
　+1.713.937.7597
F: +1.713.937.4596

Tubular Products Manufacturing Facility
3786 Second St.
Arcadia, LA 71001 USA
P: +1.800.648.8823 (Toll-Free);
　+1.318.513.7500
F: +1.318.513.7590

EQUIPMENT:
Cold pilger mills, weld mills, drawbenches, annealing furnaces and pickling facilities.

Western Sales and Service Center
14101 Rosecrans Ave., Unit A
La Mirada, CA 90638 USA
P: +1.800.531.0285 (Toll-Free);
　+1.562.407.1309
F: +1.562.407.1514

Wire Products Manufacturing Facility
158 N. Egerton Road
Mountain Home, NC 28758 USA
P: +1.800.438.7263 (Toll-Free);
　+1.828.692.5791
F: +1.828.697.9818

PRODUCTS and/or SERVICES:
Wire and welding consumables.

HEIDTMAN STEEL PRODUCTS INC.
2401 Front St.
Toledo, OH 43605 USA
P: +1.419.691.4646
F: +1.419.698.1150
www.heidtman.com

- Chief Exec. Officer and Pres.—Tim Berra

PRODUCTS and/or SERVICES:
Heidtman Steel is one of the largest privately held flat-rolled steel service center networks in North America. Processes and markets hot-rolled, cold-rolled and coated products. First operation blanks are marketed through the joint-venture National Blanking facility. Smooth clean surface (SCS) is marketed through the Butler, IN, sheet products facility. Capabilities include pickling, slitting, CTL, blanking, shearing, heavy-gauge galvanizing/galvannealing, temper/one-pass processing, edging and SCS processing, pipe and tubing. IATF and ISO certified.

Annual Capacity: 5+ million tons processing.

Butler, IN
4400 County Road 59
Butler, IN 46721 USA
P: +1.800.693.4312 (Toll-Free);
　+1.260.868.9980
F: +1.260.868.0893

Butler, IN: Sheet Products Div.
6118 County Road 42
Butler, IN 46721 USA
P: +1.800.693.4312 (Toll-Free);
　+1.260.868.9980
F: +1.260.868.1590

East Chicago, IN
4407 Railroad Ave.
East Chicago, IN 46312 USA
P: +1.219.256.7426

Erie, MI
640 Lavoy Road
Erie, MI 48133 USA
P: +1.800.521.9531 (Toll-Free);
　+1.734.848.3333
F: +1.734.848.2519

Fulton County Processing Ltd.
7800 State Route 109
P.O. Box 67
Delta, OH 43515 USA
P: +1.419.822.9266
F: +1.419.822.0408
sales@fcpltd.com
www.fcpltd.com

- Gen. Mgr.—Jeff Kunkel

EQUIPMENT:
Pickling line (0.500 x 72 in.) and four slitters (0.025–0.500 x 72 in.).

PRODUCTS and/or SERVICES:
Toll processing center.

IRON and STEEL PLANTS

Granite City, IL: Sheet Products Div. and Regional Sales
10 Northgate Industrial Dr.
Granite City, IL 62040 USA
P: +1.800.992.9310 (Toll-Free);
   +1.618.451.0052
F: +1.618.451.0240

Heidtman Tubular Products LLC—see listing page 123

National Blanking, Joint Venture
135 Fearing Blvd.
Toledo, OH 43607 USA
P: +1.419.385.0636
F: +1.419.385.2305

National Galvanizing L.P., Joint Venture
1500 Telb Road
Monroe, MI 48162 USA
P: +1.734.243.1882
F: +1.734.243.2308
www.nationalgalvanizing.com

- Gen. Mgr.—Frank Belanger
- Maint. Mgr.—Adam Barron
- Qual. Mgr.—Leon Bartley
- H.R. Mgr.—Becky Riley
- Cust. Svce. Mgr.—Tony Konczal
- Oprs. Mgr.—Michael R. Miller

PRODUCTS and/or SERVICES:
National Galvanizing offers the capability to slit off-line hot-rolled pickled, cold-rolled, galvanized or galvannealed coils.

I

INDUSTRIAS CH S.A.B. DE C.V.—see GRUPO SIMEC S.A.B. DE C.V.

IVACO ROLLING MILLS LP
1040 Hwy. 17
L'Orignal, ON K0B 1K0 Canada
P: +1.613.675.4671
F: +1.613.675.6800
www.ivacorm.com

- Pres.—Matt Walker
- Chief Financial Officer—Philippe Gauthier

Operating Plant:

Ivaco Rolling Mills LP
1040 Hwy. 17
L'Orignal, ON K0B 1K0 Canada
P: +1.613.675.4671
F: +1.613.675.6800
info@ivacorm.com

- Vice Pres. and Gen. Mgr.—Joe Olenick
- Supt. Rod Mill—Nikhil Nafade
- Dir. of Sales and Mktg.—Deron Dunbar
- Mgr. Product Qual. Assur.—Paolo Filippelli
- Dir. Finance and Contr.—Christian Levesque
- Supt. Steel Plant—Samuel Nogueira

EQUIPMENT:
75-ton EAF; LF; 3-strand casting machine; 175-mt/h Danieli reheat furnace; 4-stand Morgan housingless stand breakdown mill; 2-strand Morgan rod mill with RSMs and Stelmor/retarded cooling; two Sundco-H compactors with automatic wire tying.

PRODUCTS and/or SERVICES:
Carbon and low-alloy billets; carbon, low-alloy, and welding wire rod for drawing, cold heading, spring and special applications. Rod processing (cleaning, coating, annealing).

Annual Capacity: 625,000 tons steelmaking and casting; 900,000 tons rolling.

Railroad and Shipping Facilities: Truck, rail, ship.

IRON and STEEL PLANTS

J

JERSEY SHORE STEEL CO.
P.O. Box 5055
Jersey Shore, PA 17740 USA
P: +1.570.753.3000
F: +1.570.753.3782
Works at South Avis, PA 17721 USA
www.jssteel.com

- Pres.—David Schultz
- Dir. H.R.—Valerie Simone
- Roll. Mill Plant Supt.—Wade Potter
- Fab. Div. Plant Supt.—Matthew Bashista
- Mgr. Qual. Assur.—Chip Hoover
- Chief Financial Officer—Vern Nau

EQUIPMENT:
One continuous heating furnace, gas-fire, rail slitting mill, H&F nine stands in-line; web seven stands in-line.

PRODUCTS and/or SERVICES:
Light steel angles.

Annual Capacity: 160,000 tons.

No. of Employees: 275.

Railroad and Shipping Facilities: Truck, rail.

JSW STEEL USA
5200 E. McKinney Road
Baytown, TX 77523 USA
P: +1.281.383.5100
F: +1.281.383.1803
sales@jswsteel.us
www.jswsteel.us

- Chief Exec. Officer (interim)—Greg Manfredi
- Chief Financial Officer—Samir Kalra
- Chief Commercial Officer—Cory Raimondi
- Chief Oper. Officer Pipe—Debasish Bhowmick
- Vice Pres. Plate Oprs., Baytown—David Light
- Vice Pres. Engrg. and HSE—Matt Caprarese
- Vice Pres. Oprs.—Jonathan Shank

JSW Steel USA
500 Commercial Ave.
Mingo Junction, OH 43938 USA
P: +1.740.535.8172
sales@jswsteel.us
www.jswsteel.us

- Vice Pres. Oprs.—Mike Panzeri
- Vice Pres. Sales., Hot-Rolled Coil—Jack Morrow

PRODUCTS and/or SERVICES:
Carbon steel plate in widths from 72 in. to 155 in., thickness ranges from 0.250 in. to 6 in. and lengths up to 900 in. Grade offerings include construction, pressure vessel, rail tank car, pole tower, shipbuilding, bridge and API steel grades for pipe both onshore and offshore applications. Normalizing capability includes three heat treat furnaces for thicknesses range from 0.375 in. to 4 in. and widths from 72 in. to 144 in. Certifications include ISO-9001-2015, API 2H-0016, API 2MT1-0009, ABS, Lloyds and PED. Large-diameter line pipe for oil, gas and byproduct transmission. Grades: API-5L GR B, X42, X52, X56, X60, X65, X70, X80, A252-2, A252-3. Diameter range: 24 in., 26 in., 30 in., 36 in., 42 in. and 48 in. Wall thickness: 0.375 in. to 1 in. Length range: 40 ft. DRL to 80 ft. QRL. OD coating diameter capability range: 12 in., 14 in., 16 in., 18 in., 20 in., 22 in., 24 in., 26 in., 30 in., 36 in., 42 in. and 48 in. FBE OD thickness ranges from 12 mil min. and 26 mil max. ARO OD coating thickness ranges from 15 mil min. and 60 mil max. ID coating diameter capability range: 30 in., 36 in., 42 in. and 48 in. ID coating thickness ranges from 1.5 mil min. and 7 mil max. DJ diameter capability range: 24 in., 26 in., 30 in., 36 in., 42 in. and 48 in. Also have capabilities to meet API 2B specifications for straightness. Certifications include ISO 9001:2015, API 5L-0249 and API 2B-0041.

IRON and STEEL PLANTS

K

KLOECKNER METALS
500 Colonial Center Pkwy., Suite 500
Roswell, GA 30076 USA
P: +1.678.259.8800
F: +1.678.259.8873
kmc-marketing@kloeckner.com
www.kloecknermetals.com

- Chief Exec. Officer—John Ganem
- Chief Oper. Officer—Bart Clifford
- Chief Financial Officer—Andrea Moseley

PRODUCTS and/or SERVICES:
Carbon: coated sheets and strip, including carbon-aluminized sheet and coil; carbon cold-finished bars; cold-rolled sheets, strip and coil; enameling sheets; expanded steel; hot-dip and electrolytic galvanized sheet/strip; grating; HSS and structural pipe and tubing; hot-rolled, plain or galvanized bar; hot-rolled sheets, strip and coil; mechanical tubing; patterned steel, including embossed; perforated steel; pilings—H, pipe or sheet; plates—U.M. and sheared, floor plates and sheets; reinforcing bar (non-fabricated); structurals/welded sections, beams, channels, angles. Alloy: plate beam splitting bending/forming, beveling, burning, cambering, drill fabricating, flame cutter, ironworker, laser cutter CTL, leveler or blanking line, painting, plasma cutter, plate burning, plate sawing, press brake, sandblasting, saw, shear slitter, toll processor, trucking/transportation, welding. Stainless: PVD, pre-painted sheet and coil products, cold-rolled sheet, strip and coil; hot-rolled sheet, strip and coil. Aluminum sheet and plate, pre-painted coil products; non-heat-treated and heat-treated coil sheet plate, extrusions. Marvalum.

No. of Employees: 2,200.

KOLD ROLL DE MONTERREY S.A. DE C.V.
Francisco I. Madero 370
El Lechugal, Santa Catarina, NL, 66376 Mexico
P: +52.81.8336.1800
F: +52.81.8336.2275
info@koldroll.com
www.koldroll.com

- Pres.—Roberto Perez-Maldonado Lopez
- Oprs. Mgr.—Jose Luis Farias
- Treas. and Finance Mgr.—Raul Hernandez Ferrel

EQUIPMENT:
Round bar peeling machine, 1½-in. to 6-in. dia., straightener for 1½-in. to 6-in. dia. round bar, two round bar drawbenches, from ½-in. up to 3½ in. dia., two straighteners for ½-in. to 3½-in. dia. round bar. Three centerless grinding machines for ¾-in. to 4½-in. dia. round bar. Several saw machines for cut to specified length. Shotblaster machine for ½-in. to 3½-in. dia. round bar.

PRODUCTS and/or SERVICES:
Hot-rolled bar, any grade, size and shape. Cold-drawn (cold-rolled) round bar in SBQ grades from ½ in. to 3½ in. dia. Peeled (turned) round bar in SBQ grades from 1½-in. to 6-in. dia. Cold-drawn or peeled, then ground and polished round bar, from ¾-in. to 4½-in. dia. (pump shaft–quality). Any length up to 20 ft.

Annual Capacity: 150,000 metric tons of cold-finished products.

No. of Employees: 60.

Railroad and Shipping Facilities: Truck, rail.

IRON and STEEL PLANTS

Distribution Center
Carretera Querétaro - San Luis #22700
Bodega 13
Conjunto Industrial el Nogal
Santa Rosa Jauregui, QE, 76220 Mexico

Distribution Center 2
Agroindustrias 305 Oriente
Parque Industrial Oriente
Torreon, CA, 27272 Mexico

L

LIBERTY STEEL PRODUCTS INC.
Corporate Offices and Plant:
11650 Mahoning Ave.
North Jackson, OH 44451 USA
P: +1.800.877.3998 (Toll-Free);
+1.330.538.2236
F: +1.330.538.0833
sranelli@liberty-steel.com
www.libertysteelproducts.com

- Chief Exec. Officer and Pres.—Mark Weller
- Chief Financial Officer—Jason Mericle
- Exec. Vice Pres. Oprs.—Matt Frisby
- Exec. Vice Pres. Sales—Joe Wilson
- Vice Pres. Svce. Center Sales—Steve Ranelli
- Inside Sales Mgr.—Jennifer Good

EQUIPMENT:
Eleven processing lines.

PRODUCTS and/or SERVICES:
Liberty Steel Products Inc. sells and processes coated, cold-rolled, and hot-rolled steel sheets and coils. Products and capabilities also include embossing and pre-painted coils.

Hubbard Steel Service Center
7193 Masury Road SE
Hubbard, OH 44425 USA
P: +1.800.877.3998 (Toll-Free);
+1.330.534.7998
F: +1.330.534.8955
sranelli@liberty-steel.com

LIBERTY STEEL USA
600 Madison Ave., 19th Floor
New York, NY 10022 USA
P: +1.929.999.7407
www.libertysteelgroup.com

- Chief Exec. Officer—Gregory Jones, greg.jones@libertysteel.us
- Sr. Vice Pres. Sales and Mktg.—Tim Dillon, tim.dillon@libertysteel.us
- Chief Safety Officer—Michael C. Raabe

Liberty Bar Products
317 E. 11th St.
Chicago Heights, IL 60411 USA
P: +1.708.753.1201

- Plant. Mgr.—Bob Lopez-Acosta, bob.lopez-acosta@libertysteel.us
- Asst. Plant Mgr.—Patty Brooks, patty.brooks@libertysteel.us

PRODUCTS and/or SERVICES:
Hot-rolled bar manufacturer centrally located in the Midwest. The 13-in. bar mill provides quality, 1- to 4-in. width flat bar in thicknesses of $1/4$ in. to $3/4$ in., as well as special shape products. Can also provide annealing, shotblasting and oiling, special straightening, and saw cutting.

Liberty Engineered Wire Products
P.O. Box 313
Upper Sandusky, OH 43351 USA
P: +1.419.294.3817

Additional locations in Warren, OH, and Las Cruces, NM, USA

IRON and STEEL PLANTS

- Vice Pres./Gen. Mgr.—John Banko, john.banko@libertysteel.us
- Vice Pres. Sales and Engrg.— Jeffrey Babcock, jeff.babcock@libertysteel.us
- Plant Mgr.—Stephen Dunn

PRODUCTS and/or SERVICES: Structural mesh and pipe mesh.

Liberty Steel & Wire Peoria
7000 S.W. Adams St.
Peoria, IL 61641 USA
P: +1.800.447.6444 (Toll-Free)
F: +1.309.697.7422

- Sr. Vice Pres. Oprs.—Pieter Vanderwesthuizen
- Vice Pres. Steelworks Oprs.—Aaron Williams
- Vice Pres. Rod, Rebar and Ind. Wire Sales—Jonathan King, john.king@libertysteel.us

PRODUCTS and/or SERVICES: Construction products, industrial wire and rods.

Liberty Steel Georgetown
420 S. Hazard St.
Georgetown, SC 29440 USA
P: +1.843.485.4724
contactus@libertysteel.us

- Plant Mgr.—Dwayne Newton

EQUIPMENT:
One EAF, one LRF, one LR, 6-strand billet caster, Schloemann roughing and intermediate mill, Kocks precision sizing mill with Morgan no-twist blocks.

PRODUCTS and/or SERVICES: Wire rod in thicknesses of $7/32$ in.–$19/32$ in. and coil weight of 4,150 lbs.

Railroad and Shipping Facilities: Rail, truck, barge.

Liberty Wire Johnstown
124 Laurel Ave.
Johnstown, PA 15906 USA
P: +1.866.598.9473 (Toll-Free)
F: +1.814.532.5646
www.johnstownwire.com

- Chief Exec. Officer—Jack Miller, jack.miller@libertysteel.us
- Vice Pres. Commercial—Jack Leffler, jack.leffler@libertysteel.us

PRODUCTS and/or SERVICES: Pennsylvania-based producer of high-quality industrial wire in various grades CHQ, electrogalvanized, aluminized and spring wire. Manufacturing processes include hydrochloric acid cleaning and coating, wire drawing, electrogalvanizing, aluminizing, and continuous coil annealing.

M

MAGIC STEEL SALES
4242 Clay St.
Grand Rapids, MI 49548 USA
P: +1.616.532.4071
F: +1.616.532.0565
bkelly@magicsteelsales.com
www.magicsteelsales.com

- Vice Pres. Sales—Brendan Kelly
- Vice Pres. Oprs., Grand Rapids—Michael Welch
- Sales Mgr.—Brad Holwerda
- Prodn., Grand Rapids—Brian Williams
- Maint., Grand Rapids—Eric Tremlin
- Vice Pres. Sales, Decatur—Randall Cross
- Prodn., Decatur—David Deering

PRODUCTS and/or SERVICES: Multi-site steel service center that supplies cold-rolled, hot-rolled and coated products. Products include: hot roll, cold roll, electrogalvanize, HDG,

IRON and STEEL PLANTS

pre-paint, aluminized, galvannealed, toll processing of low-carbon, stainless and aluminum. Grade range: EDDS to 080 high strength. Slitting capacities: width: 0.5–72 in. Min. width tolerance: ±0.003 in. ID size: 20 or 24 in. Max. OD size: 72 in. Max. coil weight: 50,000 lbs. Gauge range: 0.015–0.250 in. Plants in Grand Rapids, MI, and Decatur, AL.

MAJESTIC STEEL USA
31099 Chagrin Blvd. #150
Cleveland, OH 44124 USA
P: +1.800.321.5590 (Toll-Free)
www.majesticsteel.com

- Chief Exec. Officer and Pres.—Todd M. Leebow
- Chief Financial Officer—Michele Santana
- Gen. Counsel—Chris Meyer
- Chief Mktg. Officer—Kate Mitchell
- Chief Innovation Officer—Andries De Villiers
- Chief of Staff—Kirsten Ostergard
- Chief Oper. Officer—Dave Kipe
- Chief Info. and Technology Officer—Jeff Suellentrop
- Exec. Vice Pres. Business Oprs.—Alex Fuller
- Exec. Vice Pres. Corporate Dev.—Drew McIntyre
- Exec. Vice Pres. Corporate Strategy and Business Advisor—Doug Killilea
- Exec. Vice Pres. People Strategy—Joe Cohen
- Exec. Vice Pres. Corporate Finance and Investment Plan.—Jon Gross
- Exec. Vice Pres.—Jonathan Leebow
- Sr. Vice Pres. Oprs.—Aaron Gayheart
- Sr. Vice Pres. Sales—Shannon Bibbee

PRODUCTS and/or SERVICES: Distributor and processor of flat-rolled steel, including galvanized, galvannealed, Galvalume®, aluminized, cold-rolled, phosphatized/bonderized, stainless and pre-painted.

Cleveland Service Center
5300 Majestic Pkwy.
Bedford Heights, OH 44146 USA
P: +1.440.786.2866

Fontana Service Center
11093 Beech Ave.
Fontana, CA 92337 USA
P: +1.800.445.6374 (Toll-Free)

Grand Prairie Service Center
1325 114 St.
Grand Prairie, TX 75050 USA
P: +1.972.299.5200

Houston Service Center
9302 Ley Road
Houston, TX 77078 USA
P: +1.281.243.9050

Las Vegas Service Center
5180 S. Rogers St.
Las Vegas, NV 89118 USA
P: +1.702.367.1701

Longview Service Center
850 Third Ave.
Longview, WA 98632 USA
P: +1.253.353.9494

Pittsburg Service Center
620 Clark Ave.
Pittsburg, CA 94565 USA
P: +1.800.445.6374 (Toll-Free)

Tampa Service Center
1906 Maritime Blvd.
Tampa, FL 33605 USA
P: +1.727.573.7897

MATERIAL SCIENCES CORP.
6855 Commerce Blvd.
Canton, MI 48187 USA
P: +1.734.207.4485
F: +1.877.397.6578 (Toll-Free)
info@materialsciencescorp.com
www.materialsciencescorp.com

- Chief Exec. Officer—Patrick J. Murley
- Chief Oper. Officer—Kevin McCallum
- Chief Technology Officer—Matt Murphy
- Chief Financial Officer—James L. Todd
- Dir. Pur.—Leslie Boyle-Zickuhr

IRON and STEEL PLANTS

- Dir., Info. Technology Svcs.—Dominick Wojewnik
- Vice Pres. of Business Dev., Pre-Painted Products—Allan Garrett
- Corporate Contr.—Jeff Howard
- Supply Chain Mgr.—Nancy Topp
- Dir. Product Dev.—Bryan Tullis
- Strategic Account Mgrs.—Mike Nellich, Tim O'Connor, Justin Putti, Brian Quick, Brian Robb, Tony Shillingford, Joel Turak

PRODUCTS and/or SERVICES: Coating lines, an NVH product line and electrogalvanizing services.

Canfield, OH Facility
460 W. Main St.
Canfield, OH 44406 USA
P: +1.330.533.3311
F: +1.855.864.0910

- Vice Pres. Sales, Electrogalvanized Products—Paul Pirko
- Strategic Account Mgr.—Brian Robb
- Oprs. Mgr.—John Rich
- Matls. Mgr.—Julie Minniti

PRODUCTS and/or SERVICES: Electrogalvanizing and coil coating facility, close to major highways, railroads and steel mills. Specializing in light-gauge electrogalvanized and painted products. Electrogalvanizing: gauge range 0.0078–0.0550 in.; width range 24–48 in.; max. coil weight 37,400 lbs.; max. coil OD 72 in.; starting coil ID 16, 20 or 24 in.; finished coil ID 20 in.; min. coil OD 34 in. Coil coating: gauge range 0.0078–0.0450 in.; width range 18–48 in.; max. coil weight 20,000 lbs.; max. coil OD 58 in.; starting coil ID 16–20 in.; finished coil ID 16–20 in.

Canton Research Center
6855 Commerce Blvd.
Canton, MI 48187 USA
P: +1.734.207.4485

PRODUCTS and/or SERVICES: TS16949-registered facility that provides a complete suite of NVH testing capabilities, including experimental, computer-aided engineering and materials engineering expertise. The Canton facility also contains an education center to provide training in NVH fundamentals. ITAF 16949 certified.

East Chicago, IN Facility
4407 Railroad Ave.
East Chicago, IN 46312 USA
P: +1.219.378.1930
F: +1.219.378.1933

- Oprs. Mgr.—Tim Levin
- Outside Processing Sales Mgr.—Mitch McGah

PRODUCTS and/or SERVICES: Specializes in electrogalvanized coatings that can be applied to high-strength steel coils and several other carbon steel grades. Coating line specifications: max. width incoming 72 in.; thickness 0.010–0.085 in.; min. ID 20 in.; max. ID 24 in.; max. OD incoming 80 in.; max. OD outgoing 80 in.; max. weight incoming 60,000 lbs.; max. weight outgoing 60,000 lbs.; yield strength up to 230,000 psi.

Elk Grove Village, IL Facility
2300 E. Pratt Blvd.
Elk Grove Village, IL 60007 USA
P: +1.847.439.9800

- Exec. Vice Pres., Oprs.—Mike Cocanig
- Sr. Vice Pres. Sales—Bill Stapleton
- Product Dev. Mgr.—Shawn Byrnside
- Cust. Svce. Mgr.—Jim Richert
- Tech. Dir.—Jim Blanton

PRODUCTS and/or SERVICES: Two coil coating lines (30 in. wide and 54 in. wide) along with slitting, laminating, edge trim and full inspection capabilities. 54-in. slitting line can process coated materials. ITAF 16949 certified.

Los Angeles, CA Facility
3730 Capitol Dr.
City of Industry, CA 90601 USA
P: +1.562.699.4550

PRODUCTS and/or SERVICES: Specialty coated metals along with full packaged slit and embossed products.

IRON and STEEL PLANTS

Toronto, ON Facility
1430 Martin Grove Road
Rexdale, ON M9W 4Y1 Canada
P: +1.416.743.7980
F: +1.416.743.5980

- Chief Oper. Officer—Kevin McCallum
- Dir. of Sales—Alex Davies
- Oprs. Mgr.—Jan Negrini
- Supply Chain Mgr.—Nancy Topp
- Strategic Acct. Mgrs.—Mike Nellich, Tony Shillingford

PRODUCTS and/or SERVICES:
One EGL and one coil coating line. Print pattern technology.

Walbridge, OH Facility
30610 E. Broadway St.
Walbridge, OH 43465 USA
P: +1.419.666.6130

- Oprs. Mgr.—Jeff Ramsay
- Dir. of Sales—Martin (Marty) Scott
- Inside Sales Mgr.—Andrea Taylor

PRODUCTS and/or SERVICES:
Multi-processed steel. 72-in.-wide EGL for steel and aluminum coils. 72-in.-wide multi-cut slitter and inspection line. Zinc-nickel electrogalvanized coatings. Wide-width capability for zinc plating, chemical treatments, primers, top coats, aluminum automotive pre-treatments, and/or dry lubes in one pass. MSC Walbridge is also processing automotive exposed aluminum pre-treatments for the domestic automobile industry. ITAF 16949 certified.

MATRIX METAL CASTING
1585 Dugald Road
Winnipeg, MB R2J 0H3 Canada
P: +1.204.661.6002
www.matrixmetalcasting.com

- Gen. Mgr.—Peter Hnatishin
- Office Mgr.—Heather Hnatishin

EQUIPMENT:
2,000- and 1,200-lb. induction furnace, and heat treat oven.

PRODUCTS and/or SERVICES:
Custom metal castings in steel, stainless steel, gray iron, ductile iron and aluminum.

No. of Employees: 33.

MCDONALD STEEL CORP.
100 Ohio Ave.
McDonald, OH 44437 USA
P: +1.330.530.9118
F: +1.330.530.8181
www.mcdonaldsteel.com

- Chmn.—Bill Bresnahan
- Pres.—Jim Grasso
- Chief Financial Officer and Treas.—Mark Pecchia
- Vice Pres. Sales and Mktg.—Mike Havalo
- Mgr. Oprs.—Jerry Moxley
- Dir. Qual. and Tech. Svcs.—Bill Katko
- Mgr. R&D—Glenn Kramer
- Sales and Supply Chain Mgr.—Ian Wingard

EQUIPMENT:
11-stand 14-in. cross-country hot roll special shape mill. Various warehouse straightening, de-twisting, cold shearing and saw cutting facilities.

PRODUCTS and/or SERVICES:
Symmetrical and non-symmetrical special hot-rolled shapes, rolled-in carbon and alloy steel for bridge decking and expansion joint sections, monorails, pipe spigots and couplings, truck tire rims, truck components, agricultural components, sheet piling connectors, automotive door hinge sections, industrial washers, and railroad track and car components. ISO 9001:2015 certified.

Annual Capacity: 100,000 tons.

No. of Employees: 90.

Railroad and Shipping Facilities: Truck, Direct CSXT rail sidetrack access.

IRON and STEEL PLANTS

MID-CONTINENT STEEL AND WIRE INC., a Div. of DEACERO
8411 Irvington Blvd. Suite B
Houston, TX 77022 USA
P: +1.800.867.6245 (Toll-Free)
info@mcswusa.com
www.mcswusa.com

- Chief Exec. Officer—Fernando Villanueva

PRODUCTS and/or SERVICES: Integrated manufacturer and distributor of steel wire products for the agriculture, construction and manufacturing markets. Products include: bars and beams, fasteners, fencing, industrial wires, rebar, mesh and fibers, wire strands, and wire word and billet. Brands include: Magnum fasteners, Rangemaster fencing, Stay-Tuff fencing, Designmaster fencing, DWR reinforcing and steel wire products, and DEACERO industrial steel wire and rebar.

Glendale, AZ
17505 N. 79th Ave., Suite 301
Glendale, AZ 85308 USA

Laredo, TX
6110 Bob Bullock Loop
Laredo, TX 78041 USA

New Braunfels, TX
1067 F.M. 306, Unit 102
New Braunfels, TX 78130 USA

Ontario, CA
4051 E. Santa Ana St., Suite C
Ontario, CA 91761 USA

Poplar Bluff, MO
2700 Central Ave.
Poplar Bluff, MO 63901 USA
P: +1.800.867.6245 (Toll-Free)

MILL STEEL CO.
2905 Lucerne Dr. SE
Grand Rapids, MI 49546 USA
P: +1.800.247.MILL (6455) (Toll-Free)
info@millsteel.com
www.millsteel.com

- Chief Exec. Officer—Pam Heglund
- Sr. Vice Pres. and Chief Commercial Officer—Carl Quenneville
- Sr. Vice Pres. Pur.—Joe Poot
- Vice Pres. Oprs.—Rob Vella
- Chief Financial Officer—Marc Rabitnoy

PRODUCTS and/or SERVICES: Supplier of flat-rolled carbon steel. Expertise in low- to medium-carbon steels: cold-rolled, hot-rolled, HDG, hot-dipped galvanneal, electrogalvanized, Galvalume®, aluminized, pre-paint. Processing: loop slitting, 30 slitting lines and five CTL lines. Product quality control: full-time metallurgical staff, full material certification with each shipment and A2LA-compliant labs.

Regional Processing and Distribution Centers:

Mill Steel Co.
100 Finley Ave. W
Birmingham, AL 35204 USA
P: +1.877.262.8333 (Toll-Free);
+1.205.251.8800
F: +1.205.323.8700

Mill Steel Co.
1195 Port Road
Jeffersonville, IN 47130 USA
P: +1.800.247.MILL (6455) (Toll-Free)

Mill Steel Co.
5116 36th St.
Grand Rapids, MI 49512 USA
P: +1.800.247.MILL (6455) (Toll-Free)
F: +1.616.977.9411

Mill Steel Co.
18030 Rialto St.
Melvindale, MI 48122 USA
P: +1.800.247.MILL (6455) (Toll-Free)
F: +1.313.383.6684

Mill Steel Co.
555 Gelhorn Dr.
Houston, TX 77029 USA
P: +1.800.247.MILL (6455) (Toll-Free)

IRON and STEEL PLANTS

MONARCH STEEL CO. INC.
4650 Johnston Pkwy.
Cleveland, OH 44128 USA
P: +1.800.CUT.STEL (288.7835)
  (Toll-Free);
  +1.216.587.8000
F: +1.216.587.8010
support@monarchsteel.com
www.monarchsteel.com

PRODUCTS and/or SERVICES:
Providers of hot-rolled, cold-rolled and galvanized steel products. Maintains service centers in Decatur, AL; Cadiz, KY; and Cleveland, OH. Monarch Steel produces high-quality slit-to-size steel coil, sheet, and sheared-to-size blanks and mechanical tubing.

Monarch Steel Co. Inc.
174 Roger Thomas Dr.
Cadiz, KY 42211 USA
P: +1.888.783.8823 (Toll-Free);
  +1.270.522.0491
F: +1.270.522.0496

Monarch Steel Co. Inc.
1425 Red Hat Road
Decatur, AL 35601 USA
P: +1.877.CUT.STEL (288.7835)
  (Toll-Free);
  +1.256.301.5730
F: +1.256.301.4595

N

NELSEN STEEL AND WIRE CO. INC.
9400 W. Belmont Ave.
Franklin Park, IL 60131 USA
P: +1.847.671.9700
F: +1.847.671.6833
sales@nelsensteel.com
www.nelsensteel.com

- Chief Exec. Officer—C.D. Nelsen II
- Pres.—Bill Geary
- Chief Met.—Dan Stone

EQUIPMENT:
Two batch-type stress-relieving furnaces, three drawbenches, two Schumag.

PRODUCTS and/or SERVICES:
Cold-finished steel bars.

Annual Capacity: 120,000 tons.

No. of Employees: 100.

NEW CASTLE STAINLESS PLATE LLC
549 W. State Road 38
P.O. Box 370
New Castle, IN 47362 USA
P: +1.800.349.0023 (Toll-Free);
  +1.765.529.0120
F: +1.765.529.8177
www.nestainlessplate.com

- Pres.—Michael Stateczny
- Vice Pres. Commercial—Tony Palermo
- Commercial and Plan. Mgr.—Fred Centner
- Regional Sales Mgrs.—Scott Draudt, Thomas Puetzhofen
- Inside Sales Reps.—Robin Teague, Tony Stewart

EQUIPMENT:
Hot rolling mills for plate, heat treating furnaces, pickling and finishing equipment.

PRODUCTS and/or SERVICES:
Stainless steel plate—austenitic, ferritic, martensitic, heat-resistant and duplex grades in widths up to 140 in. and

IRON and STEEL PLANTS

thicknesses ranging from 0.187 in. to 6 in.

No. of Employees: 100.

Railroad and Shipping Facilities: Truck.

NLMK (NOVOLIPETSK) USA
www.us.nlmk.com
- Chief Exec. Officer and Pres.—Robert D. Miller
- Exec. Vice Pres.—Ronald Beck
- Vice Pres. of Oprs., NLMK Pennsylvania—Bill Benson
- Vice Pres. of Oprs., NLMK Indiana—Harold B. Kincaid
- Vice Pres. of H.R. and Labor Rels.—Tom Taborek
- Chief Financial Officer—Mark Smirniw

NLMK Indiana
6500 S. Boundary Road
Portage, IN 46368 USA
P: +1.219.787.8200
www.us.nlmk.com/en/mills/indiana

EQUIPMENT:
EAF meltshop, LMF, fixed mold continuous caster, 65-in. HSM.

PRODUCTS and/or SERVICES:
Heavy-gauge hot-rolled black and pickled hot bands, HSLA, API-grade, pipe and tube grade, specialty carbon steels.

Annual Capacity: 770,000 metric tons melted, 1.2 million metric tons hot rolled.

Railroad and Shipping Facilities: Truck, rail, barge.

NLMK Pennsylvania
15 Roemer Blvd.
Farrell, PA 16121 USA
P: +1.724.983.6464
www.us.nlmk.com/en/mills/pennsylvania

EQUIPMENT:
60-in. HSM, hot-rolled temper mill, pickle line, tandem mill, hydrogen batch annealing, cold-rolled temper mills, tension leveler, Z-mill, HDG coating lines.

PRODUCTS and/or SERVICES:
Hot-rolled and cold-rolled low-carbon, high-carbon, specialty carbon, HSLA, API-grade and IF steels.

Annual Capacity: 2 million metric tons hot rolled.

Railroad and Shipping Facilities: Truck, rail, barge.

Sharon Coating
277 N. Sharpsville Ave.
Sharon, PA 16146 USA
P: +1.724.981.3545

PRODUCTS and/or SERVICES:
Galvanized and galvanneal coated sheet steel G30 through G235 and A25 through A60. Produces a variety of HDG steels, including steels for deep drawing, high-strength steels, dual-phase steels and bake-hardenable steels.

NORTH AMERICAN HÖGANÄS CO.
111 Höganäs Way
Hollsopple, PA 15935 USA
P: +1.814.479.3500
F: +1.814.479.2003
www.hoganas.com

- Pres.—Dean Howard
- Vice Pres. Finance—John Camele
- Vice Pres. Iron Powder Oprs.—David Milligan
- Vice Pres. High Alloy Oprs.—Nasser Ahmad
- Vice Pres. H.R.—David Hamaty
- Vice Pres. Supply Chain—Eric Stump
- Vice Pres. Sales—Trevor Towns

EQUIPMENT:
One 50-ton EAF, one LMF, water atomizing process, annealing furnaces and mixing stations and 5-ton induction furnace with water atomizing process. North American Höganäs High Alloys LLC: one 10,000-lb. air induction furnace, two 5,000-lb. air induction furnaces.

PRODUCTS and/or SERVICES:
Iron, alloy, electrolytic iron and stainless powders, tool steel, nickel

IRON and STEEL PLANTS

base, copper-nickel base, copper-nickel-cobalt base.

Annual Capacity: 250,000 tons.

No. of Employees: Approx. 400.

NORTH AMERICAN STAINLESS
6870 Hwy. 42 E
Ghent, KY 41045 USA
P: +1.502.347.6000
F: +1.502.347.6001;
   +1.502.347.6102
www.northamericanstainless.com

- Chmn. of the Bd.—Bernardo Velazquez
- Chief Exec. Officer and Pres.—Cris Fuentes
- Vice Pres. Mktg. and Sales—Chris Lyons
- Vice Pres. Prodn./Mfg.—Anil Yadav
- Vice Pres. of Admin. and Procurement—Todd Mitchell
- Vice Pres. of Finance and Acctg.—Pat Graph

EQUIPMENT:
Two EAFs, two AODs, one stir station, one LMF, slab continuous caster, billet continuous caster, Steckel hot rolling mill, plate annealing, cutting pickling shop, hot annealing and pickling line, six Z-mills, three cold annealing and pickling lines, bright annealing line, two grinding and polishing lines, four slitter lines, two cut-sheet lines, long products hot mill, annealing furnace and pickling for wire rod, pickling for angles, five drawing lines for bars, five grinders for bars, three bar turners, two bar furnaces, one coil blaster.

PRODUCTS and/or SERVICES:
Stainless steel coils, sheet, plate and long products.

No. of Employees: 1,500.

Railroad and Shipping Facilities: Truck, rail, barge.

NORTH STAR BLUESCOPE STEEL
6767 Country Road No. 9
Delta, OH 43515 USA
P: +1.419.822.2200
F: +1.419.822.2209
www.nsbsl.com

- Chief Exec. North America—Kristie Keast
- Pres.—Conrad Winkler
- Vice Pres. Oprs.—Jeff Joldrichsen
- Vice Pres. Sales and Mktg.—Ashley Kotowski
- Vice Pres. H.R. and H.S.E.—Kristin Malosh
- Vice Pres. Finance—Laeek Afzal

EQUIPMENT:
EAF, continuous thin-slab caster, 2-stand roughing/6-stand finishing hot strip mill.

PRODUCTS and/or SERVICES:
Hot-rolled bands for coil processors, cold-rolled strip producers, pipe and tubers, original equipment manufacturers, and steel service centers.

Annual Capacity: 3.3 million tons.

NOVA STEEL INC.
Corporate Headquarters:
6001 Irwin St.
LaSalle, QC H8N 1A1 Canada
P: +1.866.953.7751 (Toll-Free);
   +1.514.789.0511
www.novasteel.ca

PRODUCTS and/or SERVICES:
Nova Steel's product line includes a wide variety of items: Slit coils; sheets; blanks; plate and plate coils; mechanical and structural tubing; custom roll-formed shapes; structural shapes; bar products; aluminum and stainless products; front-loader buckets; pallet racking. Manufacturing, service and distribution centers in Walker, MI, USA; Baie-D'Urfé, QC; Dorval, QC; LaSalle, QC; Montreal, QC; Stoney Creek, ON; Woodstock, ON, Canada; and Ramos Arizpe, CA, Mexico.

2023 AIST Directory — Iron and Steel Plants 63

IRON and STEEL PLANTS

NUCOR CORP.
1915 Rexford Road
Charlotte, NC 28211 USA
P: +1.704.366.7000
www.nucor.com

- Chair, Chief Exec. Officer and Pres.—Leon J. Topalian
- Chief Financial Officer, Treas. and Exec. Vice Pres.—Stephen D. Laxton
- Chief Oper. Officer—David A. Sumoski
- Exec. Vice Pres., Raw Matls.—Douglas J. Jellison
- Exec. Vice Pres., Business Svcs. and Gen. Counsel—Gregory J. Murphy
- Exec. Vice Pres., Bar, Engineered Bar and Rebar Fabrication Products—John Hollatz
- Exec. Vice Pres., Sheet and Tubular Products—K. Rex Query
- Exec. Vice Pres., New Markets and Innovation D. Chad Utermark
- Exec. Vice Pres., Plate and Structural Products—Al Behr
- Exec. Vice Pres., Commercial—Daniel R. Needham

EQUIPMENT:
Fifteen bar mills: Darlington, SC; Norfolk, NE; Jewett, TX; Plymouth, UT; Auburn, NY; Birmingham, AL; Seattle, WA; Jackson, MS; Kankakee, IL; Marion, OH; Wallingford, CT; Memphis, TN; Kingman, AZ; Frostproof, FL; Sedalia, MO. Five sheet mills: Crawfordsville, IN; Blytheville, AR; Huger, SC; Decatur, AL; Ghent, KY. Three plate mills: Cofield, NC; Tuscaloosa, AL; Longview, TX. Two beam mills: Armorel, AR; Huger, SC. Three greenfield carbon steel mills under development: Brandenburg, KY (plate); Apple Grove, WV (sheet); Lexington, NC (bar). Eight tubular products facilities: Birmingham, AL; Decatur, AL; Trinity, AL; Cedar Springs, GA; Chicago, IL; Marseilles, IL; Louisville, KY; Madison, IN.

PRODUCTS and/or SERVICES:
Bar products: angles, channels, rounds, flats, rebar, squares, wire rod, hex bars, SBQ and engineered bar. Beam: manufactured housing beams, wide-flange beams, standard I-beams, channels and MC channels, angles, sheet pile sections, H pile sections, wide sheet piling. Plate: as-rolled plate, heat-treated plate. Sheet: hot-rolled, cold-rolled, floor plate, galvanized, castrip, galvannealed. Steel products: cold finish, highway and agriculture, metal building systems, rebar fabrication and distribution, joists, decking, fasteners, grating, piling, HSS pipe and tube, steel tubing, steel electrical conduit pipe, wire and mesh products, insulated panels, and racking solutions. Raw materials: scrap metal brokerage services, ferrous and non-ferrous metal recycling, logistics services, DRI.

Annual Capacity: 27,105,000 tons.

No. of Employees: 31,000+.

Bar Mill Group:

Nucor Steel Auburn Inc.
25 Quarry Road
P.O. Box 2008
Auburn, NY 13021 USA
P: +1.800.424.1494 (Toll-Free)

- Gen. Mgr.—Jason Curtis
- Contr.—Blake Turner
- Sales Mgr.—Timothy Semonich

PRODUCTS and/or SERVICES:
Reinforcing bar, merchant bar, rounds, squares, flats, angles, special shapes and SBQ.

Nucor Steel Birmingham Inc.
2301 F.L. Shuttlesworth Dr.
P.O. Box 2764
Birmingham, AL 35234 USA
P: +1.205.250.7400
F: +1.205.250.7465

- Vice Pres. and Gen. Mgr.—Kevin Barksdale
- Contr.—Matthew Greer
- Sales Mgr.—Clifford Drouet

PRODUCTS and/or SERVICES:
Reinforcing bars 10 mm/No. 3 to 57 mm/No. 18. #14J and #18J bars, hot-rolled threaded bars (SRTH) #5 through #14, 100 grade rebar by request.

IRON and STEEL PLANTS

Nucor Steel Connecticut Inc.
35 Toelles Road
P.O. Box 928
Wallingford, CT 06492 USA
P: +1.800.221.0323 (Toll-Free);
　+1.203.265.0615
F: +1.203.284.8125

- Gen. Mgr.—John Heden
- Contr.—Sandra Gutowski
- Sales Mgr.—Stephen Jurewicz

PRODUCTS and/or SERVICES:
Wire rod, rebar in coils, standard welded wire reinforcement in rolls and sheets, structural welded wire reinforcement sheets.

Nucor Steel Florida Inc.
22 Nucor Dr.
P.O. Box 8
Frostproof, FL 33843 USA
P: +1.863.546.5800 (Toll-Free)

- Vice Pres. and Gen. Mgr.—Drew Wilcox
- Contr.—Corey Allain
- Sales Mgr.—Del Benzenhafer
- Roll. Mill Mgr.—Royce Harris

PRODUCTS and/or SERVICES:
Rebar from 10 mm/#3 to 57 mm/#18 in diameter.

Nucor Steel Jackson, Inc.
3630 Fourth St.
Flowood, MS 39232 USA
P: +1.800.723.1623 (Toll-Free);
　+1.601.939.1623
F: +1.601.936.6252

- Gen. Mgr.—Trevor Saunders
- Contr.—Craig Stovall
- Sales Mgr.—Paul McKenzie

PRODUCTS and/or SERVICES:
Merchant products (rounds, flats, squares, angles and strip), SBQ, reinforcing bar and billets (MBQ and SBQ). Billet size capabilities—section: 100, 115, 130, 140 and 160 mm.

Nucor Steel Kankakee Inc.
One Nucor Way
Bourbonnais, IL 60914 USA
P: +1.800.866.3131 (Toll-Free);
　+1.815.937.3131
F: +1.815.939.5599

- Vice Pres. and Gen. Mgr.—Kevin Van De Ven
- Contr.—Kate Thompson
- Sales Mgr.—Mary Alwin

PRODUCTS and/or SERVICES:
Reinforcing bars 13 mm/No. 4 to 36 mm/No. 11, merchant rounds 1 to 1.5 in., flats 2 to 5 in., angles 1.5 to 3 in.

Nucor Steel Kingman LLC
3000 W. Old Hwy. 66
Kingman, AZ 86413 USA
P: +1.928.718.7035
F: +1.928.718.7096

- Gen. Mgr.—Matt Blitch

PRODUCTS and/or SERVICES:
Wire rod and coiled rebar.

Nucor Steel Marion Inc.
P.O. Box 1801
Marion, OH 43301 USA

912 Cheney Ave.
Marion, OH 43302 USA
P: +1.800.333.4011 (Toll-Free);
　+1.740.383.4011
F: +1.740.383.6429

- Vice Pres. and Gen. Mgr.—Eric Mitchell
- Contr.—Leslie Armstrong
- Sales Mgr.—Richard Minniti

PRODUCTS and/or SERVICES:
Reinforcing bar, rounds and signposts.

Nucor Steel Memphis Inc.
3601 Paul R. Lowry Road
Memphis, TN 38109 USA
P: +1.901.786.5900
F: +1.901.786.5901

- Vice Pres. and Gen. Mgr.—Dave Smith
- Contr.—Christina Taylor
- Sales Mgr.—Nicholas Shirilla

PRODUCTS and/or SERVICES:
Carbon and alloy steel in SBQ.

IRON and STEEL PLANTS

Nucor Steel–Nebraska
P.O. Box 309
Norfolk, NE 68702 USA

2911 E. Nucor Road
Norfolk, NE 68701 USA
P: +1.800.228.8174 (Toll-Free);
 +1.402.644.0200
F: +1.402.644.0329

- Vice Pres. and Gen. Mgr.—Johanna Threm
- Contr.—Metka Kolm
- Sales. Mgr.—Shane McGuire

PRODUCTS and/or SERVICES:
Carbon steel in SBQ and MBQ in the following shapes: angles, channels, flats, hexagons, squares and rounds.

Nucor Steel Seattle Inc.
2424 S.W. Andover St.
Seattle, WA 98106 USA
P: +1.800.677.1012 (Toll-Free);
 +1.206.933.2222
F: +1.206.933.2207

- Vice Pres. and Gen. Mgr.—Matt Lyons
- Contr.—Walter Reese
- Sales Mgr.—Ken Bowden

PRODUCTS and/or SERVICES:
Rebar No. 3/10 mm through No. 18/57 mm, rounds 0.5 through 1.5 in., angles 1.25 through 4 in., channels 3 through 6 in., flats 2 through 6 in.

Nucor Steel Sedalia LLC
500 Rebar Road
Sedalia, MO 65301 USA
P: +1.660.951.1700

- Gen. Mgr.—Ron Kessel
- Contr.—Stephanie Garrett
- Roll. Mill Mgr.—Tim Patterson
- Dist. Sales Mgr.—Andrew Stonewell

PRODUCTS and/or SERVICES:
Rebar size range from #4 to #11.

Nucor Steel–South Carolina
300 Steel Mill Road
Darlington, SC 29540 USA
P: +1.800.999.7461 (Toll-Free);
 +1.843.393.5841
F: +1.843.395.8741

- Vice Pres. and Gen. Mgr.—Tom Batterbee
- Sales Mgr.—Nick McCarthy

PRODUCTS and/or SERVICES:
Carbon and alloy steel in SBQ and rod; MBQ; and reinforcing products in the following shapes: angles, channels, flats, hexagons, reinforcing bars, rounds and wire rod.

Nucor Steel–Texas
8812 Hwy. 79 W
P.O. Box 126
Jewett, TX 75846 USA
P: +1.800.527.6445 (Toll-Free);
 +1.903.626.4461
F: +1.903.626.6290

- Vice Pres. and Gen. Mgr.—Jerald Gaines
- Contr.—Jason Bassham
- Sales Mgr.—Erik Johnson

PRODUCTS and/or SERVICES:
Carbon steel angles, channels, flats, reinforcing bars, rounds and special sections.

Nucor Steel–Utah
W. Cemetery Road
P.O. Box 100
Plymouth, UT 84330 USA
P: +1.800.453.2886 (Toll-Free);
 +1.435.458.2300
F: +1.435.458.2309

- Gen. Mgr.—Chris Locke
- Contr.—Chris Hendricksen
- Sales Mgr.—Andy Barr

PRODUCTS and/or SERVICES:
Carbon steel angles, channels, flats, reinforcing bars, rounds and squares.

Plate Mill Group:

Nucor Steel–Hertford County
P.O. Box 279
Winton, NC 27986 USA

1505 River Road
Cofield, NC 27922 USA
P: +1.252.356.3700
F: +1.252.356.3750

IRON and STEEL PLANTS

- Vice Pres. and Gen. Mgr.—Chad Beard
- Contr.—Yusef Murphy
- Sales Mgr.—Jeff Whiteman

PRODUCTS and/or SERVICES:
Carbon steel plate.

Nucor Steel Longview LLC
5400 W. Loop 281
Longview, TX 75603 USA

- Plant Mgr.—Michael Mayhall

PRODUCTS and/or SERVICES:
Carbon and alloy steel plate.

Nucor Steel Tuscaloosa Inc.
1700 Holt Road NE
Tuscaloosa, AL 35404 USA
P: +1.205.556.1310
F: +1.205.556.1482

- Gen. Mgr.—Matt Brooks
- Contr.—Mark Shearer
- Dist. Sales Mgrs.—Leslie Bonvillain, Cody Gountounas, Chase Scott

PRODUCTS and/or SERVICES:
Carbon and HSLA, HRC, and CTL plate for structural and pressure vessel applications.

Sheet Mill Group:

Nucor Steel-Arkansas
P.O. Box 30
Armorel, AR 72310 USA

7301 E. County Road 142
Blytheville, AR 72315 USA
P: +1.800.682.6727 (Toll-Free);
+1.870.762.2100
F: +1.870.762.2108

- Vice Pres. and Gen. Mgr.—Troy Brooks
- Contr.—Elmer Cherry
- Sales Mgr.—Lisa Reed

PRODUCTS and/or SERVICES:
Carbon steel sheet in hot-rolled, cold-rolled, pickled, floor plate and galvanized coils.

Nucor Steel-Berkeley
P.O. Box 2259
Mt. Pleasant, SC 29465 USA

1455 Hagan Ave.
Huger, SC 29450 USA
P: +1.843.336.6000
F: +1.843.336.6108

- Vice Pres. and Gen. Mgr.—Mike Lee
- Contr.—Nate McGaughey
- Dist. Sales Mgrs.—Todd Masters, Chris Rios, Amy Gaffney, Dave Scott, Dustin Myhand, Adam Ostoich

PRODUCTS and/or SERVICES:
Carbon steel sheet in hot-rolled, cold-rolled, pickled, galvanized and galvannealed coils.

Nucor Steel-Brandenburg
100 Ronnie Greenwell Commerce Road
Brandenburg, KY 40108 USA
P: +1.270.422.8210

- Gen. Mgr.—Johnny Jacobs
- Contr.—Brian Robinson
- Dist. Sales Mgrs.—Jake Dederich, Howie King

PRODUCTS and/or SERVICES:
Plates and heavy-gauge plates in a thickness range of 3/16 in. up to 14 in. and coils from 3/16 in. up to 1.25 in.

California Steel Industries Inc.—see listing page 17

Nucor Steel-Decatur LLC
Mailing Address:
P.O. Box 2249
Decatur, AL 35609 USA

4301 Iverson Blvd.
Trinity, AL 35673 USA
P: +1.256.301.3500
F: +1.256.301.3545

- Vice Pres. and Gen Mgr.—Brad Ford
- Contr.—Jim Brown
- Dist. Sales Mgrs.—Tim Craig, Don Fields, Todd Young, Oliverio Anaya, Jonathan Deyton, Mauricio Velasco

PRODUCTS and/or SERVICES:
Carbon steel sheet in hot-rolled, pickled, cold-rolled, galvanized and galvannealed coils.

IRON and STEEL PLANTS

Nucor Steel Gallatin LLC
4831 Hwy. 42 W
Ghent, KY 41045 USA
P: +1.800.581.3853 (Toll-Free);
    +1.859.567.3100
F: +1.859.567.3165

- Vice Pres. and Gen. Mgr.—Scott Laurenti
- Contr.—Cathy Waddell
- Dist. Sales Mgr.—Jeanne Fogarty

EQUIPMENT:
Twin-shell DC EAF (NKK-SE and MAN-GHH); 26-ft.-dia., 200-ton capacity plus heel, 140,000 max. amps, 700-volt DC; 150 MW; LMF (NKK-SE); single-strand thin-slab, 65-mm-thick, 6-stand hot rolling mill (SMS).

PRODUCTS and/or SERVICES:
HRCs, 42 to 64 in. wide, 0.055- to 0.625-in. gauge capability. Standard grades: C1006, C1008, C1010, C1015, C1017, C1019, C1020, C1021, C1022, C1025, C1026, C1030, C1035, C1050, HSLA grades, commercial and drawing quality, ASTM A-36 plate grades, ASTM and API pipe grades.

Annual Capacity: Raw steel: 1,800,000 net tons. Rolling mill: 3,000,000 net tons.

No. of Employees: 416.

Railroad and Shipping Facilities: Truck, rail, barge.

Nucor Steel–Indiana
4537 S. Nucor Road
Crawfordsville, IN 47933 USA
P: +1.800.777.0950 (Toll-Free);
    +1.765.364.1323
F: +1.765.364.1695

- Vice Pres. and Gen. Mgr.—Nathan Fraser
- Contr.—Drew Linder
- Dist. Sales Mgrs.—Kristin Donovan, Kyle Thoren, John Tomazin

PRODUCTS and/or SERVICES:
Carbon steel sheet in hot-rolled and pickled. Cold-rolled and galvanized coils.

Structural Mills:

Nucor Steel–Berkeley
P.O. Box 2259
Mt. Pleasant, SC 29465 USA

1455 Hagan Ave.
Huger, SC 29450 USA
P: +1.843.336.6000
F: +1.843.336.6108

- Vice Pres. and Gen. Mgr.—Mike Lee
- Contr.—Nate McGaughey
- Dist. Sales Mgrs.—Todd Masters, Chris Rios, Amy Gaffney, Dave Scott, Dustin Myhand, Adam Ostoich
- Sales Mgr. Beam—Andrew Fletcher

PRODUCTS and/or SERVICES:
Carbon steel beams in wide-flange, M-sections, miscellaneous and standard channels, and standard beams.

Nucor-Yamato Steel Co.
P.O. Box 1228
Blytheville, AR 72316 USA

Shipping Address:
5929 E. State Hwy. 18
Blytheville, AR 72315 USA
P: +1.800.289.6977 (Toll-Free Sales);
    +1.870.762.5500
F: +1.870.762.1130
www.nucoryamato.com

- Gen. Mgr.—Jon Witherow
- Contr.—Austin Pitzer
- Dist. Sales Mgrs.—Matthew Dyess, Carlos Esparza, Mike Greiten, Tyler McGuire, Matthew Olson

PRODUCTS and/or SERVICES:
Wide-flange structurals, special structural shapes, H-piling, sheet piling.

Nucor Tubular Products locations—see listing page 129

IRON and STEEL PLANTS

O

OHIO COATINGS CO.
2100 Tin Plate Pl.
Yorkville, OH 43971 USA
P: +1.740.859.5500
F: +1.740.859.5519
www.ohiocoatingscompany.com

- Chief Exec. Officer—David Luptak
- Exec. Vice Pres.—Jeff Yoon
- Gen. Mgr. Oprs.—Denver Green, Paul Conaway
- Vice Pres. Commercial—Lori Clark
- Gen Mgr. Raw Matl. and Cust. Svce.—Ken Kinyo
- Pur. Agt.—Melody DeFranco

EQUIPMENT:
275,000-ton Ferrostan electrolytic tinplating line with MSA electrolyte. 1,475 fpm line speed, 0.006- to 0.025-in. thickness range and 20.00- to 40.00-in. width range. In-line tension leveling, sidetrimming and induction tin reflow. GE process control and automatic stretch wrap packaging.

PRODUCTS and/or SERVICES:
Electrolytic tinplate.

Annual Capacity: 300,000 tons.

Railroad and Shipping Facilities: Rail, barge.

OLYMPIC STEEL INC.
22901 Millcreek Blvd., Suite 650
Highland Hills, OH 44122 USA
P: +1.800.321.6290 (Toll-Free);
+1.216.292.3800
F: +1.216.292.3974
info@olysteel.com
www.olysteel.com

- Chmn.—Michael D. Siegal
- Chief Exec. Officer—Richard T. Marabito
- Pres. and Chief Oper. Officer—Andrew Greiff
- Chief Financial Officer—Richard A. Manson
- Treas. and Corporate Contr.—Lisa K. Christen
- Sr. Advisor—David A. Wolfort
- Chmn., Chicago Tube & Iron—Donald R. McNeeley
- Pres., Specialty Metals—Andy Markowitz
- Pres. and Chief Oper. Officer, Chicago Tube & Iron—William Zielinski
- Regional Vice Pres. and Gen. Mgrs.—David J. Gea, James D. Post, Thomas J. Sacco
- Vice Pres., Specialty Metals—Andrew F. Wolfort
- Vice Pres., Aluminum—Brian C. Harkins
- Exec. Vice Pres., Supply Chain—Francis M. Ruane
- Vice Pres., Info. Svcs.—Christopher J. Garrett
- Vice Pres., Corporate Communications and Mktg.—Michelle Pearson-Casey
- Vice Pres., Oprs.—Terry J. Rohde
- Vice Pres., Strategic Dev.—Zachary J. Siegal
- Vice Pres., H.R.—Cassandra Powers
- Vice Pres.—Ken F. Sloan
- Managing Dir., Commercial—John J. Mooney

PRODUCTS and/or SERVICES:
Alloy: plate, heat-treated, abrasion-resistant, armor; coated: coil, sheet, blanks; cold-rolled carbon: coil, sheet, blanks; hot-rolled carbon: coil, sheet, plate; tubular and pipe products; specialty metals: stainless, aluminum, Oly Flatbrite®. Processing services include both traditional service center processes, including CTL, temper passing, stretcher leveling, slitting and shearing, as well as value-added processes and fabrication services, such as blanking, plate burning, precision machining, forming, welding, painting and kitting.

Facilities: 34 locations with more than 3.7 million sq. ft.

No. of Employees: 1,500+.

IRON and STEEL PLANTS

OPTIMUS STEEL
Old Hwy. 90
P.O. Box 3869
Beaumont, TX 77704 USA
P: +1.409.768.1211
www.optimus-steelusa.com

- Chief Exec. Officer and Pres.—Luis Barrenechea
- Vice Pres. Supply Chain—Andres Posadas
- Vice Pres. Oprs.—Ricardo Anawate
- Oprs. Mgr.—Scott Andrews

EQUIPMENT:
One EAF (120-ton capacity), one ladle refining furnace, continuous billet caster, Morgan rod mill with Stelmor cooling.

PRODUCTS and/or SERVICES:
Coiled wire rod (7/32 through 11/16 in.); rebar (size 3 to 5 bar).

Annual Capacity: 700,000 tons.

No. of Employees: 370.

Railroad and Shipping Facilities: Truck, rail, barge.

OUTOKUMPU STAINLESS USA LLC
1 Steel Dr.
P.O. Box 13000
Calvert, AL 36513 USA
P: +1.251.829.3655
www.outokumpu.com

- Chief Exec. Officer and Pres.—Tamara Weinert
- Sr. Vice Pres. Oprs.—Joachim Stolz
- Sr. Vice Pres. Sales—Carmen Pino
- Dir. Sales, Western U.S.—Ronald Archibeque
- Dir. Sales, Eastern U.S. and Canada—Bradley Small

EQUIPMENT:
Wastewater treatment plant; scrap yard; slag yard; one AC EAF (176-ton), capacity: 0.85 million tons/year; one AOD (198-ton), capacity: 1.00 million tons/year; one continuous caster (7- to 10-in. x 74-in.), capacity: 1.00 million tons/year; one slab grinding line; slab yard; one hot annealing and pickling line (0.060- to 0.400-in. x 74-in.), capacity: 0.77 million tons/year; one 20-high cold rolling stand (0.015- to 0.200-in. x 64-in.), capacity: 0.13 million tons/year; one 20-high cold rolling stand (0.020- to 0.200-in. x 74-ft.), capacity: 0.15 million tons/year; one 20-high cold rolling stand (0.008- to 0.200-in. x 54-ft.), capacity: 0.11 million tons/year; one cold annealing and pickling and skinpass line (0.014- to 0.138-in. x 74-in.), capacity: 0.50 million tons/year; one skinpass mill; one coil polishing line; one coil mill plate line (0.080- to 0.400-in. x 74-in.); two CTL lines (64-in. and 74-in.); three slitting lines (64-in. and 74-in.). 72-in.-wide coil; 200, 300 and 400 series.

PRODUCTS and/or SERVICES:
Stainless steel flat-rolled: 2D, temper, 2B, rolled-on, polish, BA finish.

Annual Capacity: Melting: 900,000 tons. Hot-rolled: 870,000 tons. Cold-rolled: 350,000 tons.

Railroad and Shipping Facilities: Truck, rail, barge.

Outokumpu Mexinox
Av. Industrias #4100
Zona Industrial Primera Sección
San Luis Potosí, SLP, 78395 Mexico
P: +52.44.48265100;
   +52.44.41371209

EQUIPMENT:
Wastewater treatment plant; bell furnaces; one hot pickling line; one mixed (hot and cold) annealing and pickling line; three cold rolling mills, one cold annealing and pickling line; one bright annealing line; four polishing lines, two skinpass mills; nine slitter lines; nine CTL lines; one continuous mill plate line (CMP); one blanking press; one laser cutting machine.

PRODUCTS and/or SERVICES:
Shape: standard sheets, standard coils, strips up to 600-mm width, blanks; BA; rolled on; tempered and #1 (for CMP); family grades: austenitics,

IRON and STEEL PLANTS

non-stabilized ferritics (430 and 434) and stabilized ferritics.

Annual Capacity: 250,000 tons.

Shipping Facilities: Truck, rail.

Outokumpu Stainless Bar Inc.
3043 Crenshaw Pkwy.
Richburg, SC 29729 USA
P: +1.803.789.5383
F: +1.803.789.3177

- Vice Pres.—Bob Beatty

PRODUCTS and/or SERVICES:
Stainless steel bar, angle, wire rod, billet, hexagon.

P

PACESETTER
1045 Big Shanty Road NW
Kennesaw, GA 30144 USA
P: +1.800.749.6505 (Toll-Free);
   +1.770.919.8000
F: +1.678.581.8800
www.teampacesetter.com

- Chief Exec. Officer—Aviva Leebow Wolmer
- Chief Financial Officer—Del Land
- Vice Pres. Oprs.—Tyler Grahovec
- Vice Pres. Sales—Kyle Daniele

PRODUCTS and/or SERVICES:
Products include: galvanized, galvannealed, Galvalume®, aluminized, cold-rolled, pre-painted and more. Services include: coil slitting, CTL, precision blanking, CNC punching, toll processing and more.

Atlanta Service Center
1100 Shallowford Road
Marietta, GA 30066 USA
P: +1.770.591.5656

Chicago Service Center
22351 Joshua Dr.
Sauk Village, IL 60411 USA
P: +1.708.757.7160

NSPS Metals (Joint Venture Between Pacesetter and Nippon Steel Americas Inc.)
10555 Wyman Gordon Dr.
Houston, TX 77095 USA
P: +1.713.999.9201

PERFILES COMERCIALES SIGOSA S.A. DE C.V.
Av. Uniones Núm. 100 Letra A
Parque Industrial del Norte
Heroica Matamoros, TM, 87316 Mexico
P: +1.868.150.1900

PRODUCTS and/or SERVICES:
This plant has hot rolling trains, and since it does not have melting furnaces, the production process begins with billets, a semi-finished steel product. Manufactures angles, channels, flat bars and beams, squares, rounds, and rebar.

Annual Capacity: 300,000 tons per year.

PRECOAT METALS, A DIV. OF SEQUA CORP.
1310 Papin St.
St. Louis, MO 63103 USA
P: +1.314.436.7010
www.precoat.com

- Pres.—Kurt Russell

PRODUCTS and/or SERVICES:
Coil coating.

IRON and STEEL PLANTS

Armorel Plant
5888 County Road E 180
Blytheville, AR 72315 USA
P: +1.870.762.6838

PRODUCTS and/or SERVICES:
24- to 64-in.-wide x 0.010- to 0.070-in.-thick aluminum, galvanized, black plate, galvannealed, cold-rolled steel, stainless steel, Galvalume®. Shape correction, interleaving, slitting, on-site rail siding, stucco embossing (non-directional).

Baltimore Plant
6754 Santa Barbara Ct.
Elkridge, MD 21075 USA
P: +1.410.796.4770

PRODUCTS and/or SERVICES:
20- to 54-in.-wide x 0.007- to 0.080-in.-thick aluminum, galvannealed, Galvalume, stainless steel, and hot-dipped and electrogalvanized. Blanking, shape correction, interleaving, slitting, stucco embossing (directional).

Birmingham Plant
3399 Davey Allison Blvd.
Hueytown, AL 35023 USA
P: +1.205.744.3200

PRODUCTS and/or SERVICES:
18- to 66.5-in.-wide x 0.010- to 0.090-in.-thick aluminum, galvanized, black plate, galvannealed, cold-rolled steel, stainless steel, Galvalume. Shape correction, slitting, Seville embossing, stucco embossing (non-directional).

Columbia Plant
650 Rosewood Dr.
Columbia, SC 29201 USA
P: +1.803.933.1300

PRODUCTS and/or SERVICES:
24- to 62-in. wide x 0.010-in. to 0.063-in.-thick aluminum, black plate, cold-rolled steel, Galvalume, galvanized, stainless steel. Blanking, interleaving, slitting, on-site rail siding, Seville embossing, stucco embossing (directional), wood grain embossing.

Greenfield Plant
1950 E. Main St.
Greenfield, IN 46140 USA
P: +1.317.462.7761

PRODUCTS and/or SERVICES:
Line 1: 24- to 49-in.-wide x 0.010- to 0.045-in.-thick galvanized, galvannealed, stainless steel, aluminum, black plate, cold-rolled steel, Galvalume. Line 2: 24- to 62-in.-wide x 0.010- to 0.060-in.-thick galvanized, galvannealed, stainless steel, aluminum, black plate, cold-rolled steel, Galvalume. Laminating, shape correction, interleaving, slitting, Seville embossing, stucco embossing (directional and non-directional).

Hawesville Plant
2604 River Road
Hawesville, KY 42348 USA
P: +1.270.689.2600

PRODUCTS and/or SERVICES:
20- to 62-in.-wide x 0.010- to 0.050-in.-thick galvanized, black plate, galvannealed, cold-rolled steel, stainless steel, Galvalume. Shape correction, interleaving, slitting, on-site rail siding, Seville embossing.

Houston Plant
16402 Jacintoport Blvd.
Houston, TX 77015 USA
P: +1.281.452.4521

PRODUCTS and/or SERVICES:
18- to 49-in.-wide x 0.008- to 0.048-in.-thick galvanized, black plate, galvannealed, cold-rolled steel, stainless steel, Galvalume. On-site rail siding.

Jackson Plant
1095 Mendell Davis Dr.
Jackson, MS 39272 USA
P: +1.601.372.0325

PRODUCTS and/or SERVICES:
24- to 62-in.-wide x 0.008- to 0.080-in.-thick aluminum, galvanized, black plate, galvannealed, cold-rolled steel, stainless steel, Galvalume. Blanking, shape correction, interleaving, slitting, off-site rail siding, prints, stucco embossing (directional).

IRON and STEEL PLANTS

Kingsbury Plant
858 E. Hupp Road
La Porte, IN 46350 USA
P: +1.219.393.3561

PRODUCTS and/or SERVICES:
24- to 72-in.-wide x 0.012- to 0.112-in.-thick aluminum, galvanized, black plate, galvannealed, cold-rolled steel, stainless steel, Galvalume. Shape correction, interleaving, slitting, on-site rail siding.

Midwest Metal Coatings Plant
#9 Konzen Ct.
Granite City, IL 62040 USA
P: +1.618.451.2971

PRODUCTS and/or SERVICES:
14- to 60-in.-wide x 0.024- to 0.160-in.-thick aluminum, galvanized, black plate, galvannealed, cold-rolled steel, stainless steel, Galvalume. Laminating, interleaving, slitting, on-site siding.

Northgate Plant
25 Northgate Industrial Dr.
Granite City, IL 62040 USA
P: +1.618.451.0909

PRODUCTS and/or SERVICES:
18- to 48.5-in.-wide x 0.008- to 0.045-in.-thick Galvalume, galvannealed, stainless steel. Shape correction.

Portage Plant
6300 U.S. Hwy. 12
Portage, IN 46368 USA
P: +1.219.763.1504

PRODUCTS and/or SERVICES:
18- to 64-in.-wide x 0.008- to 0.063-in.-thick aluminum, galvanized, black plate, galvannealed, cold-rolled steel, stainless steel, Galvalume. Shape correction, interleaving, slitting, on-site rail siding.

St. Louis Plant
4301 S. Spring Ave.
St. Louis, MO 63116 USA
P: +1.314.352.8000

PRODUCTS and/or SERVICES:
Line 1: 18- to 61-in.-wide x 0.004- to 0.040-in.-thick aluminum, galvanized, galvannealed, stainless steel, black plate, cold-rolled steel, Galvalume. Line 2: 18- to 49-in.-wide x 0.004- to 0.040-in.-thick galvanized, galvannealed, stainless steel, aluminum, black plate, cold-rolled steel, Galvalume. Laminating, shape correction, interleaving, Seville embossing.

Weirton Plant
4502 Freedom Way
Weirton, WV 26062 USA
P: +1.304.748.1557

PRODUCTS and/or SERVICES:
24- to 56-in.-wide x 0.009- to 0.057-in.-thick aluminum, galvanized, black plate, galvannealed, cold-rolled steel, stainless steel, Galvalume. Shape correction, interleaving, slitting, off-site rail siding.

PRIME METALS ACQUISITION LLC, D.B.A. PRIME METALS & ALLOYS
101 Innovation Dr.
Homer City, PA 15748 USA
P: +1.724.479.4155
F: +1.724.479.4164
mlynn@primemetals.net
www.primemetals.net

- Vice Pres. Business Dev. and Gen. Mgr.—Michael Lynn,
  P: +1.724.479.4366,
  +1.724.422.1340 (Mobile)
- Sales Mgr.—Ryan Sendro,
  P: +1.724.479.4388,
  +1.724.433.1496 (Mobile)
- Tech. Mgr.—Craig Thomas
- Vice Pres. Mfg., Safety and Environ.—Brian Knupp
- Oprs. Mgr.—Cody Affrica

EQUIPMENT:
7-ton coreless air induction furnace, 1-ton coreless air induction furnace, 20-ton AOD, band saw, billet grinder, modern laboratory.

PRODUCTS and/or SERVICES:
Bottom-poured ingots and electrodes; small ingots (pigs); toll melting services; shot; saw cutting; ingot and billet grinding; chemical laboratory services. Major grade families include

IRON and STEEL PLANTS

stainless steel, PH grades, duplex stainless, nickel-based grades, NiCo/NiCoTa/NiCoTaRe refinery grades, high-speed tool steels, cobalt-based grades, master alloys for air melt and VIM meltshops. AS 9100D, ISO 9001-2015 and PED registered.

No. of Employees: 70.

Annual Capacity: 24,000 tons.

Railroad and Shipping Facilities: Truck.

PRO-TEC COATING CO., a Joint Venture Between U. S. Steel and Kobe Steel Ltd.
5500 PRO-TEC Pkwy.
Leipsic, OH 45856 USA
P: +1.419.943.1100
F: +1.419.943.1103
www.proteccoating.com

- Pres.—Richard Veitch
- Exec. Vice Pres.—Yoichi Mukai
- Process and Equip. Mgr.—Jeff Stechschulte
- Mgr. Qual. Assur.—Jim Wurth
- Mgr. Business Plan.—Al Hueve
- Mgr. H.R.—Shannon S. Shartell

EQUIPMENT:
Two hot-dip continuous galvanize/galvannealed lines, slitter sidetrim line, inspection sidetrim line, water and solid waste reclamation unit. One CAL featuring state-of-the-art annealing furnace and water quench technology for precision cooling, temper rolling and tension leveling to produce superior flatness.

PRODUCTS and/or SERVICES:
Galvanized and galvanneal flat-rolled steel, 0.015 to 0.090 in. thick x 24 to 74 in. wide. Specializing in high-strength steels. CAL, 0.0236 to 0.090 in. thick x 32 to 65 in. wide. Specializing in advanced cold-rolled, high-strength steel.

Annual Capacity: 1.7 million tons.

Railroad and Shipping Facilities: Truck, rail.

R

RANGER STEEL
1225 N. Loop W, Suite 650
Houston, TX 77008 USA
P: +1.800.231.5014 (Toll-Free);
   +1.713.633.1306
F: +1.713.633.4827
www.rangersteel.com

PRODUCTS and/or SERVICES:
High-quality normalized steel plate, tank steel, as-rolled steel plate, HSLA steel plate for general construction, ABS grade steel and more. The complete selection of Ranger Steel plate products are ASTM and ASME certified. Services include: grade recertification, additional mechanical testing, Charpy V-notch test, ultrasonic examination and straight line burning.

Tulsa Sales Office
3104 S. Elm Pl., Suite M
Broken Arrow, OK 74012 USA
P: +1.800.231.5014 (Toll-Free);
   +1.918.246.2830
F: +1.918.246.3841

Warehouse
17628 Slover Ave.
Bloomington, CA 92316 USA
P: +1.800.231.5014 (Toll-Free);
   +1.909.419.8818

IRON and STEEL PLANTS

Warehouse
10354 Hicks Field Road
Fort Worth, TX 76179 USA
P: +1.800.231.5014 (Toll-Free);
+1.682.747.5011

Warehouse
9640 Clinton Dr.
Houston, TX 77029 USA
P: +1.800.231.5014 (Toll-Free)

Warehouse
1650 S. 81st West Ave.
Tulsa, OK 74127 USA
P: +1.800.231.5014 (Toll-Free)

RATHBONE PRECISION METALS INC.
1241 Park St.
Palmer, MA 01069 USA
P: +1.888.283.8961 (Toll-Free);
+1.413.283.8961
F: +1.413.283.9722
info@rathboneprofiles.com
www.rathboneprofiles.com

PRODUCTS and/or SERVICES:
ISO 9001:2015 certified custom manufacturer of precision cold-drawn and cold-rolled metal profiles available in 300 and 400 series stainless steel, free-cutting steel, case-hardening steel, high- and low-carbon steel, alloy steel, brass, copper, and nickel-copper. Profile configurations include unique asymmetrical profiles, gears, channel profiles, sprag profiles and linear guide profiles provided per customer blueprints. Profiles are provided in bar and coil form as well as saw-cut or sheared pieces. Markets served include medical, automotive, firearms, aircraft, agricultural equipment, power generation, telecommunication, oil exploration, industrial turbines, machine tools, electrical power tools and printing machines.

RELIANCE STEEL & ALUMINUM CO.
Corporate Headquarters:
350 South Grand Ave., Suite 5100
Los Angeles, CA 90071 USA
P: +1.213.687.7700
F: +1.213.687.8792
www.rsac.com

- Chief Exec. Officer—Karla R. Lewis
- Exec. Vice Pres. and Chief Oper. Officer—Stephen P. Koch
- Sr. Vice Pres. and Chief Financial Officer—Arthur Ajemyan
- Sr. Vice Pres. and Chief Info. Officer—Suzanne M. Bonner
- Sr. Vice Pres., Oprs.—Jeffrey W. Durham, Michael R. Hynes, Sean M. Mollins
- Sr. Vice Pres., Gen. Counsel and Corporate Sec.—William A. Smith II
- Vice Pres., Health and H.R.—Vandy C. Lupton
- Vice Pres., Corporate Initiatives—Brenda S. Miyamoto
- Vice Pres., Enterprise Risk—John A. Shatkus
- Vice Pres., Supplier Dev.—Brian M. Yamaguchi
- Vice Pres., Tax—Silva Yeghyayan

PRODUCTS and/or SERVICES:
Reliance Steel & Aluminum Co. is the largest metals service center company in North America. Reliance's family of companies encompass more than 75 brands and 315 locations with presence in 40 U.S. states and 12 countries. Reliance companies provide metals processing, inventory management services, and delivery of carbon steel, aluminum, stainless steel, brass, copper, titanium and alloy steels. Services include value-added processing such as CTL, blanking, slitting, burning, plasma burning, precision plate sawing, shearing, and more.

IRON and STEEL PLANTS

REPUBLIC STEEL
Corporate Headquarters:
2633 8th St. NE
Canton, OH 44704 USA
P: +1.330.438.5543
F: +1.330.438.5552
info@republicsteel.com
www.republicsteel.com

- Chief Exec. Officer and Pres.—Jaime Vigil
- Vice Pres. Finance and Info. Technology—Manny Viadero
- Exec. Vice Pres. Oprs.—Michael Humphrey
- Exec. Vice Pres. Commercial—James T. Thielens Jr.
- Vice Pres., Sales and Tech. Dev.—Scott Fowler
- Inside Sales Mgr.—Nick Kracker

PRODUCTS and/or SERVICES:
Carbon and alloy steel produced as bar, coil and semi-finished in the hot-rolled/cold-finished condition. Carbon and alloy bottom-poured ingots. Carbon and alloy wire.

Annual Capacity: 2,296,000 tons billet, 1,763,000 finished.

No. of Employees: 2,500.

Canton Hot Rolled Bar Plant
2633 8th St. NE
Canton, OH 44704 USA
P: +1.330.840.8521

EQUIPMENT:
Two 200-ton EAFs, one 5-strand bloom/billet caster, two LMFs, two VDs, two slag rakes. 4-strand combination bloom caster, WB furnace, 8-stand rolling mill, billet inspection line, four stationary billet grinders, saw line, QVL.

PRODUCTS and/or SERVICES:
SBQ steels, blooms and billets.

Annual Capacity: 1,247,000 tons billet.

Lackawanna Hot Rolled Bar Plant
3049 Lakeshore Road
Blasdell, NY 14219 USA
P: +1.716.827.2823

EQUIPMENT:
One three-zone WB billet reheating furnace, 17-stand mill, 5-stand sizing mill, three saw lines, QVL.

PRODUCTS and/or SERVICES:
SBQ, hot-rolled bar, rounds, squares and hexagons in cut length and coils.

Annual Capacity: 653,000 tons.

Lorain Hot Rolled Bar Plant
1807 E. 28th St.
Lorain, OH 44055 USA
P: +1.440.277.3400

EQUIPMENT:
BF, two 220-ton BOFs, one 150-ton EAF, two LMFs, VD, one 5-strand continuous bloom caster, one 6-strand billet caster, billet rolling mill, two bar rolling mills.

Annual Capacity: 1,049,000 tons billet; 900,000 tons finished.

Massillon Cold Finished Bar Plant
401 Rose Ave. SE
Massillon, OH 44646 USA
P: +1.330.837.7106

EQUIPMENT:
Cold finishing equipment (cleaning, drawing, turning, chamfering, annealing, grinding, straightening and sawing).

PRODUCTS and/or SERVICES:
SBQ and cold-finished products.

Annual Capacity: 138,000 tons.

Republic Steel Wire Processing LLC
31000 Solon Road
Solon, OH 44139 USA
P: +1.440.996.0740

EQUIPMENT:
Wire drawing and finishing equipment (cleaning and coating, drawing, annealing).

PRODUCTS and/or SERVICES:
Cold heading quality wire products.

Annual Capacity: 72,000 tons.

IRON and STEEL PLANTS

S

SAMUEL, SON & CO.
Corporate Head Office:
1900 Ironoak Way
Oakville, ON L6H 7G4 Canada
P: +1.800.267.2683 (Toll-Free)
sales@samuel.com
www.samuel.com

- Chief Exec. Officer and Pres.—Colin Osborne
- Chief Financial Officer—John Amodeo
- Pres., U.S. Service Centers—Brian Bedont
- Pres., Canadian Service Centers—Anthony Chiesa
- Gen. Counsel and Corporate Sec.—Cecile Chung
- Pres., Samuel Manufacturing—Brian Cooke
- Chief People Officer—Karen Fenton
- Chief Information Officer—Kathy McLeod
- Chief Procurement Officer—Sid Sousa
- Vice Pres., Corporate Strategy and Business Dev.—Brian Uchikata
- Vice Pres. and Gen. Mgr., Burloak Technologies—Jason Ball
- Tech. Dir.—Keyvan Hosseinkhani

PRODUCTS and/or SERVICES: Integrated network of metal manufacturing, processing and distribution divisions. Samuel provides seamless access to metals, industrial products and related value-added services. Strategically located network of metal service centers enables cost-effective distribution and just-in-time delivery. Samuel also offers metallurgical support, specialized design engineering and manufacturing services for customers who require tubular products, pressure vessels, roll forming, steel pickling services, and industrial packaging systems and supplies.

SAMUEL, SON & CO. CANADA

Alberta Locations:

Samuel, Son & Co.
1401 17th Ave. SE
Calgary, AB T2G 1J9 Canada
P: +1.800.661.4377 (Toll Free)
F: +1.403.237.0754
samuelcoilcgy@samuel.com

Samuel, Son & Co.
6125 51st St. SE
Calgary, AB T2C 3V2 Canada
P: +1.403.203.0731
F: +1.403.203.0816
calgary@samuel.com
wilkinson@samuel.com

Samuel, Son & Co.
1401 17 Ave. SE
Calgary, AB T2G 1J9 Canada
P: +1.800.661.4377 (Toll-Free)

Samuel Packaging Systems Group
7032 68th Ave. NW
Edmonton, AB T6B 3C5 Canada
P: +1.780.469.4040
F: +1.800.661.3225
packaging@samuel.com

Samuel, Son & Co.
2204 7 St.
Nisku, AB T9E 7L5 Canada
P: +1.780.434.8441

Samuel, Son & Co.
701 15th Ave.
Nisku, AB T9E 7L5 Canada
P: +1.888.972.6835 (Toll-Free)

British Columbia Locations:

Samuel, Son & Co.
1223 Derwent Way
Delta, BC V3M 5V9 Canada
P: +1.604.524.8000
F: +1.604.524.9155
customplate@samuel.com

IRON and STEEL PLANTS

Samuel, Son & Co.
300 9087C 198th St.
Langley, BC V1M 3B1 Canada
P: +1.800.356.1668 (Toll-Free)
F: +1.604.882.4968
vancouver@samuel.com

Samuel, Son & Co.
9714 Milwaukee Way
Prince George, BC V2N 5T3 Canada
P: +1.250.561.1950
F: +1.800.665.6626 (Toll-Free)
wilkinson@samuel.com

Samuel, Son & Co.
8250 130th St.
Surrey, BC V3W 8J9 Canada
P: +1.604.501.6500
F: +1.604.301.3222
vancouver@samuel.com

Samuel, Son & Co.
2278 192nd St., Unit 109
Surrey, BC V3S 3X3 Canada
P and F: +1.604.521.3700 (Toll-Free)

Samuel, Son & Co.
3141 Napier Lane
Victoria, BC V8T 5A9 Canada
P: +1.250.361.4800 (Toll-Free)
F: +1.250.361.1744
wilkinson@samuel.com

Manitoba Locations:

Samuel, Son & Co.
140 Paquin Road
Winnipeg, MB R2J 3V4 Canada
P: +1.204.661.8050
F: +1.204.663.2007
winnipeg@samuel.com

Samuel Packaging Systems Group
2073 Logan Ave., Unit 6
Winnipeg, MB R2R 0J1 Canada
P: +1.204.633.3980
F: +1.204.694.9686
manitoba_info@goval.com

New Brunswick Location:

Samuel Packaging Systems Group
115 Whiting Road
Fredericton, NB E3B 5Y5 Canada
P: +1.506.459.8898
F: +1.506.459.8916
maritimes_info@goval.com

Nova Scotia Location:

Samuel, Son & Co.
5 Burley Ct.
Dartmouth, NS B3B 2A3 Canada
P: +1.855.241.7641 (Toll-Free)
F: +1.902.481.2445
dartmouth@samuel.com

Ontario Locations:

Burloak Technologies
3280 S. Service Road W
Oakville, ON L6L 0B1 Canada
P: +1.905.592.0244

Nelson Steel
400 Glover Road
Stoney Creek, ON L8E 5X1 Canada
P: +1.905.662.1404
F: +1.905.643.4660
sales@nelsonsteel.com

Samuel, Son. & Co.
546 Elgin St.
Brantford, ON N3S 7P8 Canada
P: +1.800.465.5876 (Toll-Free)
F: +1.519.758.2782
metalblanking@samuel.com

Samuel, Son & Co.
1250 Appleby Line
Burlington, ON L7L 5G6 Canada
P: +1.905.335.9195
F: +1.905.335.3502
burlingtonprocessing@samuel.com

Samuel Packaging Systems Group
735 Oval Ct.
Burlington, ON L7L 6A9 Canada
P: +1.905.847.2770
packaging@samuel.com

IRON and STEEL PLANTS

Samuel, Son & Co.
133 Groh Ave.
P.O. Box 29059
Cambridge, ON N3C 4B1 Canada
P: +1.800.265.8719 (Toll-Free)
F: +1.519.658.5911
bothwell@samuel.com

Samuel Roll Form Group
950 Industrial Road
Cambridge, ON N3H 4W1 Canada
P: +1.519.650.2222 (Toll-Free)
F: +1.519.650.2223
sales@rollformgroup.com

Samuel Packaging Systems Group
21 Corrine Ct.
Concord, ON L4K 4W2 Canada
P: +1.905.739.1350
F: +1.905.739.1393
packaging@samuel.com

Samuel, Son & Co.
410 Nash Road N
Hamilton, ON L8H 7R9 Canada
P: +1.800.263.6504 (Toll-Free)
samuelautomotive@samuel.com
carbonflatrolled@samuel.com
nashprocessing@samuel.com
nashmetaltrading@samuel.com

Samuel, Son & Co.
1632 Burlington St. E
Hamilton, ON L8H 3L3 Canada
P: +1.905.543.8728
F: +1.905.561.2399

Samuel Packaging Systems Group
405 Exeter Road
London, ON N6E 2Z3 Canada
P: +1.519.685.0281

Samuel, Son & Co.
7455 Woodbine Ave.
Markham, ON L33R 1A7 Canada
P: +1.905.475.6464

Samuel Pressure Vessel Group
2140 Winston Park Dr., Unit 19
Oakville, ON L6J 5V5 Canada
P: +1.905.847.2770

Samuel, Son & Co.
12 Teal Ave.
P.O. Box 9930
Stoney Creek, ON L8E 3Y5 Canada
P: +1.905.561.7811
F: +1.905.662.7392
platesales@samuel.com

Quebec Locations:

Samuel, Son & Co.
21525 Clark-Graham
Baie-D'Urfé, QC H9X 3T5 Canada
P: +1.800.361.3483 (Toll-Free)
F: +1.450.669.0633
laval@samuel.com

Samuel Packaging Systems Group
3289 J.B. Deschamps
Lachine, QC H8T 3E4 Canada
P: +1.514.631.5551 (Toll-Free)
packaging@samuel.com
quebec_info@goval.com

Samuel, Son & Co.
2225 Francis Hughes
Laval, QC H7S 1N5 Canada
P: +1.800.361.0103 (Toll-Free)
F: +1.450.669.0633
laval@samuel.com

SAMUEL, SON & CO. UNITED STATES

Alabama Locations:

Samuel Packaging Systems Group
4020 Gault Ave. S
Fort Payne, AL 35967 USA
P: +1.256.845.1928
F: +1.256.845.1490
usa_info@goval.com

Samuel, Son & Co.
1400 Red Hollow Road
Birmingham, AL 35215 USA
P: +1.205.856.1300

Arizona Location:

CAID Industries
2275 E. Ganley Road
Tucson, AZ 85706 USA
P: +1.520.294.3126

IRON and STEEL PLANTS

California Locations:

Main Steel
3100 Jefferson St.
Riverside, CA 92504 USA
P: +1.951.789.3010

Burloak Technologies USA Inc.
829 Via Alondra
Camarillo, CA 93012 USA

Samuel, Son & Co.
30640 San Clemente St.
Hayward, CA 94544 USA
P: +1.800.631.9765 (Toll-Free)
F: +1.866.341.3726
california@samuel.com

Samuel, Son & Co.
12389 Lower Azusa Road
Arcadia, CA 91006 USA
P: +1.800.631.9765 (Toll-Free)
F: +1.323.722.6359
california@samuel.com

Sierra Aluminum Co.
2345 Fleetwood Dr.
Riverside, CA 92509 USA
P: +1.951.781.7800

Colorado Location:

Samuel, Son & Co.
8020 Steele St.
Denver, CO 80229 USA
P: +1.800.972.4455 (Toll-Free)
F: +1.303.422.0482
colorado@samuel.com

Florida Locations:

Samuel Roll Form Group
945 Center St.
Green Cove Springs, FL 32043 USA
P: +1.904.287.8000
F: +1.904.529.7757
sales@pilingproducts.com

Samuel, Son & Co.
8141 Eagle Palm Dr.
Riverview, FL 33578 USA
P: +1.800.227.9704 (Toll-Free)
F: +1.813.741.3333
tampa@samuel.com

Georgia Locations:

Samuel, Son & Co.
3635 Francis Cir.
Alpharetta, GA 30004 USA
P: +1.800.227.9704 (Toll-Free)
F: +1.678.527.7601
atlanta@samuel.com

Samuel Packaging Systems Group
110 Dent Dr.
Cartersville, GA 30121 USA
P: +1.770.386.8837
packaging@samuel.com

Illinois Locations:

Main Steel
2200 Pratt Blvd.
Elk Grove Village, IL 60007 USA
P: +1.847.916.1220
pete.fagan@samuel.com

Metal Spinners
802 Industrial Park Road
Rock Falls, IL 61071 USA
P: +1.815.625.0390
F: +1.260.665.7741
sales@metalspinners.com

Samuel Packaging Systems Group
1401 Davey Road
Woodridge, IL 60517 USA
P: +1.630.783.8900
F: +1.800.323.4424 (Toll-Free)
packaging@samuel.com

Indiana Location:

Metal Spinners
800 Growth Pkwy.
Angola, IN 46703 USA
P: +1.260.665.3244
F: +1.260.665.2540
sales@metalspinners.com

Louisiana Location:

Samuel, Son & Co.
1848 Beaumont Dr.
Baton Rouge, LA 70806 USA
P: +1.800.535.8468 (Toll-Free)
F: +1.225.927.0280
batonrouge@samuel.com

IRON and STEEL PLANTS

Maryland Location:

Samuel, Son & Co.
1700 Ridgley St.
Baltimore, MD 21230 USA
P: +1.800.822.3773 (Toll-Free)
F: +1.225.234.3973
baltimore@samuel.com

Michigan Location:

Samuel, Son & Co.
580 Kirts Blvd., Suite 300
Troy, MI 48084 USA
P: +1.800.521.0870 (Toll-Free)
F: +1.248.434.0422
michigan@samuel.com

Minnesota Location:

Samuel, Son & Co.
15255 Central Ave. NE
Ham Lake, MN 55304 USA
P: +1.866.361.8338 (Toll-Free)
F: +1.763.413.0075
basic-mnsales@samuel.com

Mississippi Location:

Samuel Roll Form Group
26 County Road 351
Iuka, MS 38852 USA
P: +1.662.424.1479
F: +1.662.424.1314
sales@rollformgroup.com

Missouri Location:

Missouri Metals
9970 Page Blvd.
St. Louis, MO 63132 USA
P: +1.314.222.7100
F: +1.314.222.7102
quotes@missourimetals.com

New York Locations:

Samuel, Son & Co. (Kim-Tam Logistics)
250 Lake Ave.
Blasdell, NY 14219 USA
P: +1.800.466.1073 (Toll-Free)
F: +1.716.856.3254
buffaloplatesales@samuel.com

Samuel, Son & Co.
4334 Walden Ave.
Lancaster, NY 14086 USA
P: +1.800.272.6835 (Toll-Free)
F: +1.716.681.1069
buffalo@samuel.com

Samuel, Son & Co.
21 Marway Cir.
Rochester, NY 14624 USA
P: +1.800.836.3671 (Toll-Free)
F: +1.585.426.8198
rochester@samuel.com

Ohio Locations:

Samuel, Son & Co.
1500 Coining Dr.
Toledo, OH 43612 USA
P: +1.800.537.8698 (Toll-Free)
F: +1.419.470.7040
sales@doralsteel.com

Samuel Packaging Systems Group
1455 James Pkwy.
Heath, OH 43056 USA
P: +1.740.522.2500
packaging@samuel.com

Oregon Location:

Samuel, Son & Co.
106 S.E. 223rd Ave. Bldg. B
Gresham, OR 97030 USA

Pennsylvania Locations:

Samuel, Son & Co.
10 Arch St. Bldg. #2
Carnegie, PA 15106 USA
P: +1.800.784.0242 (Toll-Free)
F: +1.412.276.2804
pittsburgh@samuel.com

Main Steel
6 Whitney Dr.
Harmony, PA 16037 USA
P: +1.724.453.3000

Samuel, Son & Co.
1760 Broadway Ave.
Hermitage, PA 16148 USA
P: +1.724.981.5042
F: +1.724.981.5857
hermitagestamping@samuel.com

IRON and STEEL PLANTS

Samuel, Son & Co.
2650 Kirila Road
Hermitage, PA 16148 USA
P: +1.610.952.0857

Samuel, Son & Co.
4990 Grand Ave.
Neville Island, PA 15225 USA
P: +1.412.865.4444
F: +1.412.865.0030
frontiersteel@samuel.com

South Carolina Location:

Samuel Packaging Systems Group
2000 K Boyer Dr.
Fort Mill, SC 29708 USA
P: +1.803.802.3203
packaging@samuel.com

Tennessee Locations:

Samuel, Son & Co.
One Eagle Way
Clinton, TN 37716 USA
P: +1.800.860.8903 (Toll-Free)
F: +1.865.457.1506
sales@doralsteel.com

Samuel, Son & Co.
1755 N. Clayton Dr.
Columbia, TN 38401 USA
P: +1.931.901.0931
tennessee@samuel.com

Texas Locations:

Samuel, Son & Co.
5022 Ashley Ct.
Houston, TX 77041 USA
P: +1.713.462.5000
F: +1.713.462.8703
houston@samuel.com

Samuel, Son & Co.
2303 Century Center Blvd.
Irving, TX 75062 USA
P: +1.800.441.0797 (Toll-Free)
F: +1.972.438.6309
dallas@samuel.com

Samuel Packaging Systems Group
623 Fisher Road
Longview, TX 75604 USA
P: +1.903.759.2761
F: +1.800.222.1800 (Toll-Free)
packaging@samuel.com

Virginia Location:

Samuel Pressure Vessel Group
58 Samuel Way
Lebanon, VA 24266 USA
P: +1.276.415.9970
F: +1.276.883.5635
spvg@samuel.com

Wisconsin Locations:

Samuel Basic Stainless
2001 S. Nikolai Ave.
Marshfield, WI 54449 USA
P: +1.866.908.9898
basic-mnsales@samuel.com

Samuel Pressure Vessel Group
2121 Cleveland Ave.
P.O. Box 767
Marinette, WI 54143 USA
P: +1.715.735.9311
F: +1.888.506.4271
spvg@samuel.com

Samuel Pressure Vessel Group
1119A Bridge St.
Tomahawk, WI 54487 USA
P: +1.715.453.5326
F: +1.715.453.6531
spvg@samuel.com

SAMUEL, SON & CO. MEXICO

Samuel, Son & Co.
Carretera Miguel Alemán km 23.5
Apodaca, NL, 66600 Mexico
P: +52.811.958.6380

Samuel, Son & Co.
Carretera 26 #1030
Hermosillo, SO, 83287 Mexico
P: +52.662.110.4020

Samuel, Son & Co.
Calle 17, #3796 Amp. Morelos
Saltillo, CH, 25013 Mexico
P: +52.844.438.6400

Samuel Associated Tube Group—see listing page **135**

IRON and STEEL PLANTS

SCHAEFFER INDUSTRIES
141 S. Western Coil Road
Lindon, UT 84042 USA
P: +1.801.785.8600
F: +1.801.785.4146
mschaeffer@sisteel.com
www.sisteel.com

- Chief Exec. Officer—George Schaeffer
- Vice Pres. Mktg., Adv. Mgr. and Pur. Agt.—Matthew Schaeffer
- Vice Pres. Sales—Ross Harrison

EQUIPMENT:
Three slitters, 6-in. pipe tube mill, one fully correctional leveler, five roll formers.

PRODUCTS and/or SERVICES:
Coil, sheet, tube, pipe, custom roll-formed profiles.

No. of Employees: 50.

Railroad and Shipping Facilities: Truck, rail.

American Tubular Products—see listing page 113

SPECIAL METALS CORP., a PCC Energy Group Co.
25201 Chagrin Blvd., Suite 250
Beachwood, OH 44122 USA
P: +1.216.755.3030
F: +1.216.755.3034
info@specialmetals.com
www.specialmetals.com

- Pres.—Tom Witheford
- Vice Pres. R&D—Shailesh J. Patel
- Intl. Sales Dir.—Paul Fielding
- Vice Pres. Global Sales—Phil MacVane

PRODUCTS and/or SERVICES:
Superalloys, nickel- and cobalt-based corrosion-resisting alloys; titanium, titanium alloys, and special stainless steels in ingot, billet, bar, powder, sheet, strip, plate, wire rod, wire and seamless tubing.

Special Metals Corp. — Huntington, WV/Burnaugh, KY/Elkhart, IN
3200 Riverside Dr.
Huntington, WV 25705 USA
P: +1.304.526.5100
F: +1.304.526.5526
info@specialmetals.com
www.specialmetals.com

- Dir. Strategic Plan.—Darrin L. Bird
- Gen. Mgr. Special Metals—David Brautigan
- Dir. of Qual. and Engrg.—Mark Holderby

EQUIPMENT:
Huntington, WV: two 35-ton EAFs, 37-ton AOD, 24-ton VIM, six VARs, 4,500-ton open-die forge press, 110-in. 2-high/4-high mill, 55-in. Steckel mill, 23-in. bar mill, 22-in. bar mill, two wire rod mills, 56-in. coil buildup line, 55-in. CAL and pickle line, 49-in. bright anneal line, 56-in. MKW cold mill, 58-in. Two tube pilger mills, various facilities for heat treating, surface preparation, cutting, straightening and testing, plate, sheet, bar, wire, seamless tubing, billet, and ingot products. Burnaugh, KY: 15-ton induction melting furnace, nine ESRs, 6,000-ton BLH extrusion press, 5.25-in.-dia. pilger mill, six ball mills, various facilities for heat treating and surface preparation of seamless tubing. Elkhart, IN: 50-in. Sendzimir cold mill, 38-in. bright anneal line, strand extensioner and slitting line, coil preparation line.

PRODUCTS and/or SERVICES:
Superalloys, nickel- and cobalt-based corrosion-resisting alloys, and special stainless steels in ingot, billet, bar, powder, sheet, strip, plate, wire rod, wire and seamless tubing.

Special Metals Corp. — New Hartford, NY/Dunkirk, NY
4317 Middle Settlement Road
New Hartford, NY 13413 USA
P: +1.315.798.2900
F: +1.315.798.2016
info@specialmetals.com
www.specialmetals.com

IRON and STEEL PLANTS

- Gen. Mgr.—Heather Simmons
- Dir., Raw Matl. Procurement—Max Bleiler

EQUIPMENT:
New Hartford, NY: one VIM, 12 VARs, four ESR furnaces, 22-in. rolling mill, 16-in. rolling mill, various facilities for heat treating, surface preparation, cutting and testing billet and bar. Dunkirk, NY: 4,500-ton open-die forge press and SX55 GFM rotary forge.

PRODUCTS and/or SERVICES:
Superalloys, nickel- and cobalt-based corrosion-resisting alloys, and special stainless steels in ingot, billet, bar, and powder, primarily for premium rotating and static aerospace applications. Product also serving sheet, strip, plate, wire rod, wire and seamless tubing.

SPECIALTY STEEL WORKS INC. (SSWI), Niagara LaSalle Corp.
1412 150th St.
Hammond, IN 46327 USA
P: +1.877.BUY.BARS (289.2277) (Toll-Free);
+1.219.853.6000
F: +1.219.853.6095

- Chief Exec. Officer—Mike Salamon
- Chief Oper. Officer—Mike Ivetich
- Chief Financial Officer—Tony Verkruyse
- Vice Pres. Commercial—Mike Flood
- Gen. Mgr.—Josh Hufford

EQUIPMENT:
Multiple drawbenches; grinders; and chamfering machines. Size range: $1/4$- through 6-in. rounds or squares; $1/4$- through 6-in. hexagons; flats from $1/4$ x $5/16$ to $3 1/2$ x 12 in. Q&T lines capable of 1–10 in. Impact shears $1/2$–$1 7/16$ in. NDT roto-bar testing capability $1/2$–5 in. Multiple bar and shape straighteners.

PRODUCTS and/or SERVICES:
Cold-finished steel bars: carbon and alloy. Drawn, turned, ground or polished bar and Custom-Cut® products. StressProof®, Fatigue-Proof®, e.t.d. 150® bars.

Corey Steel Co.
2800 S. 61st Ct.
Cicero, IL 60804 USA
P: +1.800.323.2750 (Toll-Free)
F: +1.708.735.8100

- Gen. Mgr.—Nick Beader

EQUIPMENT:
15 grinders $1/4$–6 in. up to 30 ft., three straighteners $1/4$–4 in. x 10–25 ft. and three saws. Size range: $1/8$–7 in. up to 35 ft. Six continuous drawing machines: rounds $1/4$–2 in., hexagons $5/16$–$1 1/4$ in., squares $3/8$–$7/8$ in. Two bar-to-bar drawbenches: rounds $1 3/16$–4 in., hexagons $1 1/8$–3 in., squares $7/8$–$2 1/4$ in., rectangles $3/8$ x 1 in. to $1 1/4$ x 2 in. One bar turner: rounds $1/2$–$3 1/8$ in. Two off-line chamfering machines: rounds $3/4$–$3 3/8$ in., hexagons $3/4$–$2 1/2$ in.

PRODUCTS and/or SERVICES:
Cold-drawn; TGP bars; ground and polished bars and saw cutting. Additional services: eddy current tester, bundle demagnetizing.

Michigan Seamless Tube LLC
400 McMunn St.
South Lyon, MI 48178 USA
P: +1.800.521.8416
F: +1.248.486.0296

- Gen. Mgr.—Tom Sleder

EQUIPMENT:
Rotary furnace, piercer, stretch reducing mill, Q&T, annealing, four drawbenches, cold pilger mill, and various NDT and finishing equipment. Size range: $3/4$–5 in. drawn, $3/4$–2 in. pilger, 0.083- to $7/8$-in. walls in grades 1012 to 13% chrome.

PRODUCTS and/or SERVICES:
Cold-drawn seamless tubing.

Railroad and Shipping Facilities: Truck only.

IRON and STEEL PLANTS

Niagara LaSalle Corp.
1291 S. Hwy. 67
Midlothian, TX 76065 USA
P: +1.972.723.8500
F: +1.972.775.3377

– Gen. Mgr.—Tom Sleder

EQUIPMENT:
One drawbench, size range 1–3 1/2 in.; two coil-to-bar machines, size range 3/8–1 3/16 in.; three grinders, size range 3/4–3 in.; two centerless turning machines, size range 3/4–3 in. Two close-tolerance production saws.

PRODUCTS and/or SERVICES:
Cold-finished steel bars: carbon, alloy, TGP bars.

Niagara LaSalle Corp.
16655 S. Canal St.
South Holland, IL 60473 USA
P: +1.800.323.7667 (Toll-Free)
F: +1.708.596.7262

– Gen. Mgr.—Nick Beader

EQUIPMENT:
Seven saws (3/8-in. to 18-in. dia. x 5/16-in. to 45-ft. lengths), six straighteners (9/16–7-in. dia. x 10–45 ft.), one Schumag (3/8–1 3/16 in. x 10–26 ft.) including NDT, four turn and polish lines (1/2–7 in. x 10–48 ft.), one Q&T line (3/4–2 1/8 in. x 12–45 ft.), one shotblast descaler (3/8- to 6 1/2-in. rounds and flats up to 36 in. wide x 10–45 ft.), one roto tester (1/2–3 1/2 in. x 10–45 ft.), and one chamfer machine (3/4–2 in. x 10–24 ft.).

PRODUCTS and/or SERVICES:
Cold-drawn bars, turned and polished bars, heat treating, bundle cutting and precision custom-cut pieces, descaled hot-rolled product, hot-rolled straightened bars, and NDT.

Niagara LaSalle Corp.
22700 Nagel St.
Warren, MI 48089 USA
P: +1.800.354.5660 (Toll-Free)
F: +1.586.755.9452

– Plant Mgr.—Antoine James

EQUIPMENT:
Two drawbenches, size range 1–6 in. round, 1/4–6 in. thick and 1–14.625 in. wide flats; five coil-to-bar drawing machines; two Miyazaki, three Schumag, size range 1/4–1 7/16 in.; four high-speed precision impact shears, size range 1/4–1 1/4 in., five saws (1/4 in. to 14 in., seven shotblast descalers, seven in-line and off-line straighteners (1/2 in. to 6 in. round), four shape straighteners (1/4 in. to 10 in.), four chamfer units (1/4 in. to 3 in.), in-line and off-line tester units (six mag and four roto), four stencil/bar marking units, two demag units.

PRODUCTS and/or SERVICES:
Cold-finished steel bars: carbon and alloy. Rounds, squares, hexes and special shapes.

Tulsa Centerless Bar Processing
1605 N. 168th E Ave.
Tulsa, OK 74116 USA
P: +1.918.438.0000
F: +1.918.437.2867
sales@tulsacenterless.com

– Gen. Mgr.—Evan Hudson

EQUIPMENT:
18 grinders 1/16–12 in. up to 50 ft., two roll straighteners 3/5–2 1/2 in. up to 50 ft., four press straighteners 1/2–9 in. up to 40 ft., one bar chamfering machine up to 3 in., Q&T line 3/4–2 1/2 in. up to 40 ft., off-line demagnification unit, six CNC lathes with live tooling, one CNC vertical mill with magnetic work holding, six horizontal hobs, two keyway mills 1/2–1 1/2 in. up to 40 ft., hot saw, band saw.

PRODUCTS and/or SERVICES:
Bar and parts grinding, straightening, induction heat treating, shaft and parts machining, long-length keywaying, process carbon and alloys, stainless, aluminum, titanium, composites, red metals, and other exotic materials. Bars, shafts, bushings, pins, rods and other precision components.

2023 AIST Directory — Iron and Steel Plants   85

IRON and STEEL PLANTS

SSAB AMERICAS LLC
Headquarters:
11 N. Water St., Suite 17000
Mobile, AL 36602 USA
P: +1.877.594.7726 (Toll-Free);
 +1.251.264.3800;
F: +1.251.264.3785
www.ssab.com

- Pres.—Chuck Schmitt
- Sr. Vice Pres. and Chief Commercial Officer—Jeff Moskaluk

SSAB Alabama Inc.
12400 Hwy. 43 N
Axis, AL 36505 USA
P: +1.888.592.7070 (Toll-Free);
 +1.251.662.4400
F: +1.251.662.4360

- Oprs. Mgr.—Andy Bramstedt

EQUIPMENT:
180-ton EAFs; ladle refining furnace; VTD; 120-in.-wide continuous caster; 120-in.-wide Steckel mill; 120-in.-wide plate finishing; 102-in. and 120-in.-wide Q&T lines; 120-in.-wide normalizing furnace; blast and paint line

PRODUCTS and/or SERVICES:
Discrete plate, coiled plate, coiled sheet, blast and painted product, and normalized and heat-treated plate.

Annual Capacity: 1,250,000 tons.

SSAB Central Inc.
1051 Tapscott Road
Scarborough, ON M1X 1A1 Canada
P: +1.888.576.8530 (Toll-Free);
 +1.416.321.4949
F: +1.416.321.4945

- Oprs. Mgr.—Paul Paciocco

EQUIPMENT:
19-in.-dia. work roll, 44-in.-dia. backup roll, 4-hi temper mill with outboard roll bending, 0.625–96-in. CTL line.

PRODUCTS and/or SERVICES:
Temper-leveled CTL sheet and plate, 0.188–0.625 in. thick, 48–96 in. wide, 48–720 in. long, up to 0.375 in. x 96 in. at 100,000 psi yield strength, up to 0.625-in. thickness in mild grade steels, flatness tolerances of $1/2$ ASTM for all grades and $1/4$ ASTM for a wide range of product sizes.

Annual Capacity: 300,000 tons (240,000 tons CTL, 60,000 tons plate).

SSAB Iowa Inc.
1770 Bill Sharp Blvd.
Muscatine, IA 52761 USA
P: +1.800.340.5566 (Toll-Free);
 +1.563.381.5300
F: +1.563.381.5329

- Oprs. Mgr.—Tom Cox

EQUIPMENT:
158-ton EAFs; ladle refining furnace; VTD; 120-in.-wide continuous caster; 120-in.-wide Steckel mill; 120-in.-wide plate finishing; 96-in. coil slitter.

PRODUCTS and/or SERVICES:
Discrete plate, coiled plate, coiled sheet and slit coil.

Annual Capacity: 1.25 million tons.

SSAB Minnesota Inc.
2500 W. County Road B
Roseville, MN 55113 USA
P: +1.800.383.9031 (Toll-Free);
 +1.651.631.9031
F: +1.651.631.9670

- Oprs. Mgr.—Taylor Gould

EQUIPMENT:
21-in.-dia. work roll, 45-in.-dia. backup roll, work roll bending, 0.500–96-in. CTL line.

PRODUCTS and/or SERVICES:
Temper-leveled CTL sheet and plate, 0.100–0.500 in. thick, 48–96 in. wide, 60–720 in. long, up to 0.500 in. x 96 in. at 100,000 psi yield strength, flatness tolerances of $1/2$ ASTM for all grades and $1/4$ ASTM for a wide range of product sizes.

Annual Capacity: 300,000 tons.

SSAB Texas Inc.
13609 Industrial Road, Suite 114
Houston, TX 77015 USA
P: +1.713.341.7700
F: +1.713.450.2261

- Oprs. Mgr.—Jerrel Dawkins

IRON and STEEL PLANTS

EQUIPMENT:
19-in.-dia. work roll, 44-in.-dia. backup roll, 4-hi temper mill with outboard roll bending, 0.750- to 96-in. CTL line.

PRODUCTS and/or SERVICES:
Temper-leveled CTL sheet and plate, 0.100–0.750 in. thick, 48–96 in. wide, 48–720 in. long, up to 0.500 in. x 96 in. at 100,000 psi yield strength, up to 0.750-in. thickness in mild grade steels, flatness tolerances of ½ ASTM for all grades and ¼ ASTM for a wide range of product sizes.

Annual Capacity: 300,000 tons.

SSAB Wear Solutions — Sharon, PA
251 Wheeler Place
Sharon, PA 16146 USA
P: +1.724.230.5100
sales.sharon@ssab.com
www.ssabwearsolutions.com

- Sales Mgr.—Bill Donohue
- Inside Sales Supv.—Matthew J. Wehner
- Inside Sales—Lino Rojas
- Tech. Sales Rep. (NY)—Joseph Dorma

PRODUCTS and/or SERVICES:
Offers a wide range of core steel products such as A36, Hardox and Strenx steel plate. Original manufacturers of Duroxite brand of overlay plate, pipe and pin products. Also offers complementary products of Nitronic 30 stainless steel, EN30B round bar and Bi-metal bucket protection products (chock blocks and buttons). Specializes in rebuilding equipment such as crushers and buckets. SSAB Wear Solutions manufactures truck bed liners, dozer skins, wheel loader and excavator buckets (new and rebuilt), chutes, hoppers, cyclones, hammers, screens, rebuilds, scrap grapples. Offers technical sales support through its network of technical sales representatives.

SSAB Wear Solutions — Tuscaloosa, AL
8915 Energy Lane
Northport, AL 35476 USA
P: +1.205.409.9692
sales.northport@ssab.com
www.ssabwearsolutions.com

- Managing Dir.—Ross Wylie
- Oprs. Mgr.—Allen Sullivan
- Sales Mgr.—Chris Hunter
- EHS Mgr.—Jason Hoagland
- Sr. Accountant—Kristin Bush
- Procurement Supv.—Jacob Sutton
- Ship.—Samantha Davis
- Tech. Sales Reps.— Ricky Williams (NC, SC), Chuck Harrison (North AL, GA, MS, TN), John Murphy (South AL, GA, MS), Connor Osbern (TX), Theodore David Evertz (OR)
- Inside Sales Supv.—Justin Pate
- Inside Sales—Andy Lynn, Wendy Barrett

EQUIPMENT:
Three main distribution centers complete with in-house machine and fabrication facilities.

PRODUCTS and/or SERVICES:
Offers a complete line of abrasion- and impact-resistant products, including Astralloy-V® plate; hot-rolled bar and forgings; Astralloy 8000 plate; EB-450 plate; ROC 400, 450 and 500 plate; ASTM A-514 plate; Astralloy 4800 plate; Trip-L-Tuff® plate and 11–14% manganese plate.

STANDARD STEEL LLC
500 N. Walnut St.
Burnham, PA 17009 USA
P: +1.717.248.4911
F: +1.717.248.8050
www.standardsteel.com

- Chief Exec. Officer—Yoshiro Hori
- Chief Oper. Officer and Pres.—John M. Hilton
- Sr. Vice Pres. Sales and Procurement—Tomohiro "Tony" Shinzato
- Sr. Vice Pres. and Gen. Mgr., Wheel Oprs.—Craig J. Kaniecki
- Sr. Vice Pres. Finance and Admin.—Justin Gutting

IRON and STEEL PLANTS

- Sr. Vice Pres., Engrg. and Technology—Kenichi "Ken" Shimbo
- Sr. Vice Pres. Oprs. Plan. and Gen. Mgr., Melt. and Axle Mfg.—Thomas J. Impellitteri
- Vice Pres., Safety and Security—Michael K. Petroski
- Dir. Qual.—Mark Lumadue
- Dir. H.R.—Liz Bouch
- Dir. Procurement—Trevor W. Smith

EQUIPMENT:
EAFs, closed-die press, wheel rolling mill, vertical boring mills, horizontal lathes and heat treat furnaces.

PRODUCTS and/or SERVICES:
Railway axles and wheels.

Annual Capacity: 288,000 tons.

No. of Employees: 615.

Railroad and Shipping Facilities: Truck, rail.

STEELSCAPE LLC, a Joint Venture Between Nippon Steel Corp. and BlueScope Steel Ltd.
P: +1.888.553.5521 (Toll-Free Product Inquiries and Project Assistance); +1.888.285.7717 (Toll-Free Management Support and Cust. Svce.)
www.steelscape.com

- Pres.—Sarah Deukmejian
- Vice Pres. Sales and Cust. Svce.—Scott Cooley
- Sales Mgr. East Region—Marc Fullem
- Sales Mgr. West Region—Mary Wardle
- Cust. Svce. Team Leader—Andrea Wernex-Dennis
- Tech. Mgr.—Michelle Vondran
- Architectural Specialist—Shelby Courtney

PRODUCTS and/or SERVICES:
Metal-coated and painted steels.

Annual Capacity: 446,000 metric tons metal-coated steel products; 332,000 metric tons painted steels.

Kalama, WA Facility
222 W. Kalama River Road
Kalama, WA 98625 USA
P: +1.360.673.8200

- Plant Mgr.—Norman Ross

EQUIPMENT:
One pickling line, one reversible cold rolling mill, one HDGL line, one coil coating line, one slitter, one CTL line.

Rancho Cucamonga, CA Facility
11200 Arrow Route
Rancho Cucamonga, CA 91730 USA
P: +1.909.987.4711

- Plant. Mgr.—David Gutierrez

EQUIPMENT:
One Zincalume steel line, one coil coating line, one slitter, one embosser.

STEEL DYNAMICS INC.
Corporate Office:
7575 W. Jefferson Blvd.
Fort Wayne, IN 46804 USA
P: +1.260.969.3500
F: +1.260.969.3590
www.steeldynamics.com

- Chief Exec. Officer and Pres.—Mark D. Millett
- Chief Financial Officer and Exec. Vice Pres.—Theresa Wagler
- Sr. Vice Pres. Long Products Steel Group—Chris Graham
- Sr. Vice Pres. Strategic Projects—Glenn Pushis
- Sr. Vice Pres. Flat Roll Steel Group—Barry Schneider
- Sr. Vice Pres. Metals Recycling—Miguel Alvarez
- Sr. Vice Pres. Steel Fabrication—James Anderson
- Vice Pres. and Commercial Gen. Mgr. Flat Roll Steel Group—Tommy Scruggs

No. of Employees: Approx. 81.

Butler Div.
4500 County Road 59
Butler, IN 46721 USA
P: +1.260.868.8000
F: +1.260.868.8055
www.stld.com

IRON and STEEL PLANTS

- Vice Pres. and Gen. Mgr.—Jordan Breiner
- Mgr. Casting—Aaron Larson
- Mgr. Hot Roll.—Randy Patterson
- Mgr. Melting—Conrad Fisher
- Cold Mill Fin. Mgr.—Jeff Rickman
- Mgr. Cold Roll.—Roy Perala
- Mgr. Matl. and Transp.—Dane Boykins
- Mgr. Engrg.—Dan DeWitt
- Mgr. Sales—Charles Trowbridge
- Contr.—Thomas G. Hartman

EQUIPMENT:
Twin-shell EAFs (2 pair), LFs (3), thin-slab casting machines (2), tunnel furnaces, 7-stand HSM, push-pull pickle line, continuous pickle line, 2-stand cold reversing mill, batch annealing, temper mill, galvanizing lines (2), paint line and digital paint line.

PRODUCTS and/or SERVICES:
Hot band, pickled, cold-rolled, galvanized, galvannealed and pre-painted coil.

No. of Employees: Approx. 986.

Railroad and Shipping Facilities: CSX and NS, truck.

Columbus Div.
1945 Airport Road
Columbus, MS 39701 USA
P: +1.662.245.4200
F: +1.662.848.6914
www.steeldynamics.com

- Gen. Mgr.—Dan Keown
- Mgr. Melting—Don Bryant
- Mgr. Casting—Mark Pole
- Mgr. Hot Roll.—Allen Gill
- Mgr. Fin.—Jeff McLain
- Mgr. Galvanizing and Paint—Jeff Roach
- Mgr. Ship. and Transp.—Bryant Miller
- Mgr. Engrg.—Robert Johns
- Mgr. Sales—Paul Gruseck
- Contr.—Lisa McAlexander

EQUIPMENT:
Two DC EAFs, two LMFs, two VDs, two CSP casters, two tunnel furnaces, hot strip mill, PLTCM, temper mill, batch annealing, three galvanizing lines, one push-pull pickle line, paint line.

PRODUCTS and/or SERVICES:
Hot-rolled, cold-rolled, galvanized, galvannealed, Galvalume® and painted steel coiled sheet.

Annual Capacity: 3.2 million tons.

No. of Employees: Approx. 840.

Shipping Facilities: Truck, rail and barge.

Engineered Bar Products Div.
8000 N. CR 225 E
Pittsboro, IN 46167 USA
P: +1.317.892.7000
F: +1.317.892.7010
www.sdi-pit.com

- Gen. Mgr.—Chad Bickford
- Mgr. Melting/Casting—Kale Heibult
- Mgr. Hot Roll.—Trevor Kipp
- Mgr. Fin.—Jon Plemons
- Mgr. Matl. and Transp.—Toby Powell
- Mgr. Engrg.—Greg Hoefgen
- Mgr. Sales—Jeff Cordill
- Contr.—Leon Waninger

EQUIPMENT:
EAF, LF, VTD, 3-strand continuous bloom caster, reheat furnace, bar rolling mill, precision rolling mill and bar finishing.

PRODUCTS and/or SERVICES:
SBQ and MBQ rounds and RCS 1–8 in., and rebar.

No. of Employees: Approx. 520.

Railroad and Shipping Facilities: CSX, truck.

Heartland Div.
455 W. Industrial Dr.
Terre Haute, IN 47802 USA
P: +1.812.299.4157
F: +1.812.299.3765

- Oprs. Mgr.—Roberto Bohrer
- Mgr. Sales—Melissa Brown
- Mgr. CM Roll./Finish—Bob Pershing
- Mgr. Maint./Engrg.—David Fulford
- Mgr. Logistics/Transp.—Marty Smith
- Contr.—Brad Greenwell

IRON and STEEL PLANTS

EQUIPMENT:
Continuous pickle line, 2-stand reversing cold mill, HDGL, hydrogen batch anneal, temper mill, slitter.

PRODUCTS and/or SERVICES:
Conversion of raw hot bands into galvanized and cold-rolled coils.

No. of Employees: 225.

Railroad and Shipping Facilities: Truck, rail.

Iron Dynamics Div.
4500 County Road 59
Butler, IN 46721 USA
P: +1.260.868.8402
F: +1.260.868.8953
www.steeldynamics.com

- Plant Mgr.—Paul Wierzbowski

EQUIPMENT:
Rotary hearth furnace and submerged-arc furnace.

PRODUCTS and/or SERVICES:
Liquid pig iron.

No. of Employees: Approx. 105.

Railroad and Shipping Facilities: CSX, NS, truck.

Jeffersonville
5134 Loop Road
Jeffersonville, IN 47130 USA
P: +1.812.218.1490
F: +1.812.284.9278

- Plant Mgr.—Chris Winger

EQUIPMENT:
Galvanizing and paint line.

PRODUCTS and/or SERVICES:
Light-gauge cold-rolled galvanized and Galvalume products, pre-painted coil.

No. of Employees: Approx. 101.

Railroad and Shipping Facilities: CSX and LIRC, truck.

Roanoke Bar Div.
102 Westside Blvd. NW
Roanoke, VA 24017 USA

P.O. Box 13948
Roanoke, VA 24038 USA
P: +1.540.342.1831
F: +1.540.983.7284
www.roanokesteel.com

- Gen. Mgr.—Jerry Adams
- Mgr. Melting/Casting—Derrick Walls
- Mgr. Roll. Mill—Jason Smith
- Mgr. Engrg.—Jason Johnson
- Mgr. Sales—Jordan Burkholder
- Contr.—Jason Flint
- Mgr. Matl. and Transp.—Todd Gerbers

EQUIPMENT:
EAF, 5-strand billet caster, LMF, 17-stand continuous rolling mill.

PRODUCTS and/or SERVICES:
Carbon steel billets, MBQ and SBQ products—angles, channels, rounds, flats and reinforcing bars.

No. of Employees: Approx. 437.

Railroad and Shipping Facilities: NS, truck.

Steel of West Virginia Inc., a Wholly Owned Subsidiary of Steel Dynamics Inc.
17th St. and 2nd Ave.
Huntington, WV 25703 USA

P.O. Box 2547
Huntington, WV 25726 USA
P: +1.304.696.8200
F: +1.304.529.1479
www.swvainc.com

- Vice Pres. and Gen. Mgr.—Charles Abbott
- Mgr. Roll. Mill (Mill #1)—David Bruce
- Mgr. Roll. Mill (Mill #2)—Danny Queen
- Mgr. Fabricating and Transp.—Scott Boggs
- Mgr. Melt/Cast Shop—Phillip Wolfe
- Mgr. Engrg.—David Harold
- Sales—Timothy Sizemore
- Vice Pres. Admin.—John O'Connor
- Contr.—James Johnson

IRON and STEEL PLANTS

EQUIPMENT:
EAFs (2), 3-strand continuous billet caster, continuous 24-in. mill, 22-in. cross-country special mill and fabrication equipment.

PRODUCTS and/or SERVICES:
Special steel products principally for use in construction of truck trailers, industrial lift trucks, off-highway construction equipment (such as bulldozers and graders), manufactured housing, guardrail post, merchant, solar panel farm products, rails for maglev trains and mining industry, bulb flats for shipbuilding industry.

No. of Employees: Approx. 595.

Railroad and Shipping Facilities: CSX, truck, barge.

Steel Ventures Inc., a Wholly Owned Subsidiary of Steel Dynamics Inc.
200 Harris Road
Wurtland, KY 41144 USA

P.O. Box 481
Huntington, WV 25709 USA
P: +1.606.834.8801

- Fabricating and Transp. Mgr.—Scott Boggs, sboggs@steelventuresinc.com
- Galvanizing Mgr.—Jason Rulen, jrulen@steelventuresinc.com
- Sales Mgr.—Tim Sizemore, tsizemore@steelventuresinc.com
- Sales Rep.—Jody Foster, jfoster@steelventuresinc.com

EQUIPMENT:
Galvanizing tank, miscellaneous fabricating equipment, storage facilities.

PRODUCTS and/or SERVICES:
HDG beams, channels, miscellaneous fabricated parts.

No. of Employees: Approx. 39.

Railroad and Shipping Facilities: CSX, truck.

Structural and Rail Div.
2601 County Road S 700 E
Columbia City, IN 46725 USA
P: +1.260.625.8100
F: +1.260.625.8950
www.stld-cci.com

- Gen. Mgr.—Chris Gionti
- Mgr. Roll. Mill (Mill #1)—Jeremy Cronkhite
- Mgr. Roll. Mill (Mill #2)—Todd Bashford
- Mgr. Sales—Jordan Burkholder
- Mgr. Melting—Clay Gross
- Mgr. Casting—Tom Lutes
- Mgr. Matl. and Transp.—John Horning
- Mgr. Engrg.—Jonathan Milk
- Mgr. Qual.—Valoree Varick
- Mgr. Rail Weld—Devin Crawford

EQUIPMENT:
EAFs (2), LFs (2), VTD, 4-strand continuous bloom and beam blank casting machines (2), #1 mill—breakdown mill and 3-stand universal hot rolling mill and #2 mill—21-stand continuous mill, 1 rod block, 2 spoolers.

PRODUCTS and/or SERVICES:
Parallel flange, structural merchant, rail, rebar, semi-finished, h-pile.

No. of Employees: Approx. 907.

Railroad and Shipping Facilities: NS and CF&E, truck.

The Techs, a Div. of Steel Dynamics Inc.
2400 2nd Ave.
Pittsburgh, PA 15219 USA
P: +1.412.368.4800
F: +1.412.464.3048
www.thetechs.com

- Oprs. Mgr. of The Techs—Clayton Spangler
- Mgr. Matls.—John Obel
- Mgr. Sales—Paul Navetta
- Contr.—Jim Sartori
- MetalTech Plant Mgr.—Darin Ball
- GalvTech Plant Mgr.—Fred Spannuth
- NexTech Plant Mgr.—Julie Matics

EQUIPMENT:
MetalTech—Hot/cold roll galvanizing line, GalvTech—Cold roll galvanizing

IRON and STEEL PLANTS

line, NexTech—Light-gauge cold roll galvanizing line.

PRODUCTS and/or SERVICES: HDG and galfan sheet.

No. of Employees: 224.

Railroad and Shipping Facilities: Allegheny RR, CSX, NS and truck.

Sinton Div.
8534 Hwy. 89
Sinton, TX 78387 USA
P: +1.361.424.6200
www.steeldynamics.com

- Gen. Mgr.—Dennis Black
- Mgr. Melting—Evan Wright
- Mgr. Casting—Ron Bohna
- Mgr. Hot Roll.—Bill Seres
- Mgr. Cold Roll.—Bill Glaser
- Mgr. Galvanizing and Painting—Wayne Bontempo
- Mgr. Ship. and Transp.—Rob Coward
- Mgr. Engrg.—Tom Wilcox
- Mgr. Constr.—Bryan Vogel
- Mgr. Sales—Trevor Ryals
- Contr.—Brian Prather

EQUIPMENT:
DC EAFs (2), LMFs (2), VDs (2), one intermediate thickness Nexus CSP caster, two roughing stands, two edger stands, slab cooling, two tunnel furnaces, 6-stand hot strip mill, two coilers, continuous pickle line direct coupled and also able to run in isolation to a 5-stand, 6-high tandem cold mill, temper mill, batch annealing, galvanizing line, paint line.

PRODUCTS and/or SERVICES: Hot-rolled, cold-rolled, galvanized, Galvalume® and painted steel coiled sheet.

Annual Capacity: 3.2 million tons.

No. of Employees: Approx. 500.

Shipping Facilities: Truck, rail.

STELCO INC.

Hamilton Works
386 Wilcox St.
Hamilton, ON L8L 8K5 Canada
P: +1.905.528.2511
www.stelco.com

EQUIPMENT:
Coke battery, cold reduction mill, batch annealing and temper mill, two galvanizing lines.

PRODUCTS and/or SERVICES: Coke, cold-rolled products, galvanized and galvannealed sheet steel, pre-painted sheet products.

Lake Erie Works
2330 Regional Road #3
Nanticoke, ON N0A 1L0 Canada

EQUIPMENT:
Coke battery, BF, pig iron caster, two steelmaking vessels, twin-strand slab caster, HSM, three pickling lines.

PRODUCTS and/or SERVICES: Coke, pig iron ingots, hot-rolled sheet products.

STERLING STEEL CO. LLC, a Leggett & Platt Co.
101 Ave. K
Sterling, IL 61081 USA
P: +1.815.548.7000
F: +1.815.748.7019

- Pres. and Gen. Mgr.—Kevin Mullen
- Mgr. Primary Oprs.—Jeremy May
- Mgr. Rod Mill Oprs.—Kermit L. Reins
- Contr.—Andria Keegan
- Mgr. H.R.—Cary Robbins

EQUIPMENT:
400-ton EAF, 8-strand billet caster, LMF, rod mill.

PRODUCTS and/or SERVICES: Rods.

Annual Capacity: 500,000 tons rod.

No. of Employees: 280.

Railroad and Shipping Facilities: Truck, rail.

IRON and STEEL PLANTS

SUPERIOR METALS & ALLOYS
1315 Pickering Pkwy. #300
Pickering, ON L1V 7G5 Canada
P: +1.905.427.4699
F: +1.905.686.1814
jbrunet@superiormetals.ca
www.superiormetals.ca

– Pres.—Clarence Brunet

PRODUCTS and/or SERVICES:
Steel product supply.

No. of Employees: 6.

T

TATA STEEL PLATING USA

Apollo Metals Ltd.
1001 Fourteenth Ave.
Bethlehem, PA 18018 USA
P: +1.610.867.5826
F: +1.610.419.4629
apollo.marketing@tatasteelamericas.com
www.tatasteeleurope.com/ts/about-us/sites-and-facilities/plating

– Chief Exec. Officer and Pres.—Mike Morris

PRODUCTS and/or SERVICES:
Copper- and brass-plated cold-rolled steel products in a diverse range of dimensions and surface finishes.

No. of Employees: Approx. 30.

Thomas Steel Strip Corp.
2518 W. Market St.
Warren, OH 44485 USA
P: +1.330.841.6429
tss.marketing@tatasteelamericas.com
www.tatasteeleurope.com/ts/about-us/sites-and-facilities/plating

– Chief Exec. Officer and Pres.—Mike Morris

PRODUCTS and/or SERVICES:
Electroplating of cold-rolled steel strip, nickel, nickel-cobalt and NIZN-COTE® cold-rolled steel strip.

Annual Capacity: 100,000 net tons.

No. of Employees: Approx. 220.

TERNIUM
Av. Guerrero Nte. 151
P.O. Box 66452
San Nicolás de los Garza, NL, 66452
Mexico
P: +52.81.8865.2828
www.ternium.com.mx

– Pres.—Máximo Vedoya

PRODUCTS and/or SERVICES:
Ternium produces and distributes a wide variety of high-value-added steel products in coils and sheets, including: hot-rolled steel, cold-rolled steel, galvanized steel, painted steel, long steel products (bars and wire rods), steel tubes and profiles, and metal buildings.

Plants in Mexico and USA:

Ternium Churubusco Plant
Av. Churubusco Nte. 1000
P.O. Box 64000
Monterrey, NL, 64540 Mexico
P: +52.81.8329.5000

Ternium Guerrero Plant
Av. Los Angeles Ote. 325
San Nicolás de los Garza, NL, 66452
Mexico
P: +52.81.8865.2828

Ternium Juventud Plant
Av. de la Juventud 340 Nte.
Col. Cuauhtémoc
San Nicolás de los Garza, NL, 66450
Mexico
P: +52.81.8865.2828

IRON and STEEL PLANTS

Ternium Largos Apodaca Plant
Camino al Mezquital 200
Apodaca, NL, 66440 Mexico
P: +52.81.8865.2828

Ternium Largos Puebla Plant
Autopista México Puebla km 108
San Miguel Xoxtla, PU, 72620 Mexico
P: +52.22.2372.3513

Ternium Pesquería Plant
Carretera Pesquería Los Ramones km 15
Ejido La Victoria
Pesquería, NL, 66650 Mexico
P: +52.81.8865.2828

Ternium Universidad Plant
Av. Universidad 992 Nte.
Col. Cuauhtémoc
San Nicolás de los Garza, NL, 66450 Mexico
P: +52.81.8865.2828

Ternium USA Inc.
2500 Ron Bean Road
Shreveport, LA 71115 USA
P: +1.318.698.7500

Ternium Comercial Apodaca Plant
Blvd. Carlos Salinas de Gortari km 11.5
Apodaca, NL, 66600 Mexico
P: +52.81.8135.5100

Ternium Industrial Apodaca Plant
C. G 520 Milimex
Apodaca, NL, 66637 Mexico

Ternium Ciénega de Flores Plant
Carretera a Laredo km 22.5
Ciénega de Flores, NL, 65550 Mexico
P: +52.81.8305.9113

Ternium Monclova Plant
Blvd. Harold Pape No. 1349
Colonia Elizondo
Monclova, CA, 25760 Mexico
P: +52.86.6649.7095

TIMKENSTEEL CORP.
1835 Dueber Ave. SW
Canton, OH 44706 USA
P: +1.330.471.7000
F: +1.330.458.6006
www.timkensteel.com

- Chief Exec. Officer and Pres.—Mike Williams
- Exec. Vice Pres. and Chief Commercial Officer—Kevin Raketich
- Exec. Vice Pres., Gen. Counsel and Chief H.R. Officer—Kris Syrvalin
- Exec. Vice Pres. and Chief Financial Officer—Kristopher Westbrooks
- Dir., Faircrest Steel Plant—Jim Sanders
- Dir., Harrison Steel Plant—Aman Bhatia
- Dir., Gambrinus Steel Plant—Matt Widders
- Vice Pres., Mfg.—Carolee Vanicek
- Plant Mgr., Mobile-on-Highway and Ind. Value Solutions—John Liddy

EQUIPMENT:
EAFs, VAD, jumbo bloom vertical caster, continuous strand caster, bottom-pour, forge press, bar/billet rolling mills, seamless tube mills, bar peeler, thermal treatment (quench and temper, normalize, anneal, and other), finishing, surface and internal inspection.

PRODUCTS and/or SERVICES:
SBQ bar (carbon, alloy, microalloy), seamless mechanical tubing, value-add components, blooms, billets, bottom-pour ingots.

Annual Capacity: 2 million tons.

No. of Employees: 1,850.

Faircrest Plant
4511 Faircrest St. SW
Canton, OH 44706 USA
P: +1.300.471.7000
F: +1.330.471.7416

PRODUCTS and/or SERVICES:
SBQ alloy steel.

Gambrinus Plant
2401 Gambrinus Road SW
Canton, OH 44706 USA
P: +1.330.471.7000
F: +1.330.471.5251

PRODUCTS and/or SERVICES:
Seamless mechanical tubing ranging from 1.9-in. to 13-in. dia. Alloy steel rounds up to 13-in. dia.

IRON and STEEL PLANTS

Harrison Plant
1835 Dueber Ave. SW
Canton, OH 44706 USA
P: +1.330.471.7000

PRODUCTS and/or SERVICES:
Specialty carbon and alloy steel ingots, blooms, and bars. Rounds from 1 in. through 7.5 in. and squares from 2.5 in. through 7 in.

St. Clair Plant
401 Industrial Dr.
Eaton, OH 45320 USA
P: +1.330.471.2600
F: +1.330.471.2584

PRODUCTS and/or SERVICES:
Transmission parts.

Tryon Peak Plant
205 Industrial Park Access
Columbus, NC 28722 USA
P: +1.330.471.6293
F: +1.828.894.8123

PRODUCTS and/or SERVICES:
Profile ring mill.

TimkenSteel de Mexico S. de R.L. de C.V.
Ave. Las Torres #1533
Parque Industrial La Puerta 3
Santa Catarina, NL, 66350 Mexico

TRIPLE-S STEEL HOLDINGS INC.
(Corporate Headquarters)
6000 Jensen Dr.
Houston, TX 77026 USA
P: +1.800.231.1034 (Toll-Free);
   +1.713.697.7105
F: +1.713.697.5945
gary.w.stein@sss-steel.com
www.sss-steel.com

- Chief Exec. Officer—Gary Stein

General Steel Macon, GA
4131 Broadway
Macon, GA 31206 USA
P: +1.478.746.2794
charlie.boswell@steeldeal.com

- Mgr.—Charlie Boswell

Instel Steel West, California North
450 Port Road 23
Stockton, CA 95203 USA
P: +1.209.462.4100
mark.chewning@instelsteel.com

- Mgr.—Mark Chewning

Instel Steel West, California South
8432 Almeria Ave.
Fontana, CA 92335 USA
P: +1.909.922.6300
tom.lawrence@instelsteel.com

- Mgr.—Tom Lawrence

Instel Steel Distributors, Fort Worth
3000 Braswell Dr.
Fort Worth, TX 76111 USA
P: +1.817.222.1603
justin.durst@instelsteel.com

- Mgr.—Justin Durst

Shamrock Steel Sales
238 County Road W
Odessa, TX 79763 USA
P: +1.432.337.2317
ltemple@shamrocksteelsales.com

- Mgr.—Lance Temple

Instel Steel Distributors, Houston
11310 W. Little York
Houston, TX 77041 USA
P: +1.713.937.9500
paul.pierantozzi@instelsteel.com

- Mgr.—Paul Pierantozzi

Instel Steel East
560 N. Washington Ave.
Bridgeport, CT 06604 USA
P: +1.732.770.3599
rick.perlen@instelsteel.com

- Mgr.—Rick Perlen

Instel Steel East
1641 New Market Ave.
South Plainfield, NJ 07080 USA
P: +1.908.754.8700
stewart.lichtman@instelsteel.com

- Mgr.—Stewart Lichtman

IRON and STEEL PLANTS

Instel Steel East
100 Steel Dr.
New Castle, DE 19720 USA
P: +1.908.754.8700
stewart.lichtman@instelsteel.com

– Mgr.—Stewart Lichtman

Instel Steel West, Phoenix, AZ
11001 N. 136th Ave.
Surprise, AZ 85379 USA
P: +1.909.922.6300
tom.lawrence@instelsteel.com

– Mgr.—Tom Lawrence

Instel Steel West, Salt Lake City
1887 S. 700 W
Salt Lake City, UT 84104 USA
P: +1.801.973.0911
kevin.dempsey@instelsteel.com

– Mgr.—Kevin Dempsey

Maas Hansen, California Sales Office
5555 Garden Grove Blvd., Suite 250
Westminster, CA 92683 USA
P: +1.714.236.8700
eric.allen@maashansen.com

– Mgr.—Eric Allen

Maas Hansen, Fontana, CA
13450 Napa St.
Fontana, CA 92335 USA
P: +1.909.463.3653
eric.allen@maashansen.com

– Mgr.—Eric Allen

Maas Hansen, Vernon, CA
2435 E. 37th St.
Vernon, CA 90058 USA
P: +1.323.583.6321
eric.allen@maashansen.com

– Mgr.—Eric Allen

NexCoil Steel LLC, a Triple-S Steel/NexCoil Joint Venture
300 Oceangate #430
Long Beach, CA 90802 USA
P: +1.562.432.9515
fmorrison@steelcoil.com

– Mgr.—Fred Morrison

NexCoil Steel North
1265 N. Shaw Road
Stockton, CA 95215 USA
fmorrison@steelcoil.com

– Mgr.—Fred Morrison

Instel Steel West, Denver, CO
8573 Ulster St.
Commerce City, CO 80640 USA
P: +1.303.321.9660
rod.fisher@rssteel.com

– Mgr.—Rod Fisher

Triple-S/Instel Steel Distributors, San Antonio
2042 W. Thompson Pl.
San Antonio, TX 78226 USA
P: +1.800.725.4776 (Toll-Free);
+1.210.941.1941
F: +1.210.431.0701
george.dezo@sss-steel.com

– Mgr.—George Dezo

Triple-S Steel, Salt Lake
1840 S. 700 W
Salt Lake City, UT 84104 USA
P: +1.801.433.2211
allen.mcconnell@sss-steel.com

– Mgr.—Allen McConnell

Beshert Steel Processing, a Triple-S Steel/Steel Warehouse Co. Joint Venture
15355 Jacintoport Blvd.
Houston, TX 77015 USA
P: +1.713.821.3600
christopher.long@beshertsteel.com

– Mgr.—Chris Long

Triple-S Steel Farmington, NM
1000 Malta Ave.
Farmington, NM 87401 USA
P: +1.505.327.0463
jack.hazzard@instelsteel.com

– Mgr.—Jack Hazzard

Triple-S Steel Grand Junction, CO
2189 River Road
Grand Junction, CO 81505 USA
P: +1.303.321.9660
jeff.henke@instelsteel.com

– Mgr.—Jeff Henke

IRON and STEEL PLANTS

Triple-S Steel Knoxville, TN
4800 Beverly Road
Knoxville, TN 37918 USA
P: +1.865.687.1251
stephen.briggeman@sss-steel.com

- Mgr.—Stephen Briggeman

Triple-S Steel Houston North
6000 Jensen Dr.
Houston, TX 77026 USA
P: +1.713.697.7105
adam.vieyra@sss-steel.com

- Mgr.—Adam Vieyra

Triple-S Steel Houston South
8603 Monroe Blvd.
Houston, TX 77061 USA
P: +1.713.941.1941
mike.romero@sss-steel.com

- Mgr.—Mike Romero

Tube Supply Houston
4669 Brittmoore Road
Houston, TX 77041 USA
P: +1.713.466.4130
alvaro.dominguez@tubesupply.com

- Mgr.—Alvaro Dominguez

Tube Supply Edmonton
5515 42 St. NW
Edmonton, AB T6B 3P2 Canada
P: +1.780.417.4130
cameron.sorensen@tubesupply.com

- Mgr.—Cameron Sorensen

Arbor Metals Inc. – Houston
8411 Irvington Blvd.
Houston, TX 77022 USA
P: +1.713.923.9491
bill.leavelle@metalsinc.com

- Mgr.—Bill Leavelle

Arbor Metals Inc. – Tulsa
1010 W. 37th Pl.
Tulsa, OK 74107 USA
P: +1.918.446.1671
bill.leavelle@metalsinc.com

- Mgr.—Bill Leavelle

Arbor Metals Inc. – Mobile
8639 Bellingrath Road
Theodore, AL 36582 USA
P: +1.251.653.4723
bax.kegans@arbormetals.com

- Mgr.—Bax Kegans

Arbor Metals Inc. – Dallas
811 Regal Row
Dallas, TX 75247 USA
P: +1.214.357.6161
paul.kruppa@arbormetals.com

- Mgr.—Paul Kruppa

Alamo Iron Works San Antonio
943 AT&T Center Pkwy.
San Antonio, TX 78219 USA
P: +1.210.223.6161
fdouglas@aiwnet.com

- Mgr.—Frank Douglas

Alamo Iron Works Pharr
5312 N. Cage Blvd.
Pharr, TX 78577 USA
P: +1.956.787.3800
fdouglas@aiwnet.com

- Mgr.—Frank Douglas

Alamo Iron Works Brownsville
2771 Robindale Road
Brownsville, TX 78526 USA
P: +1.956.831.4291
fdouglas@aiwnet.com

- Mgr.—Frank Douglas

BMG Metals – Richmond
950 Masonic Lane
Richmond, VA 23223 USA
P: +1.804.226.1024
stephen.briggeman@sss-steel.com

- Mgr.—Stephen Briggeman

BMG Metals – Richmond (Specialty Metals Division)
6301 Gorman Road
Richmond, VA 23231 USA
P: +1.804.226.1024
stephen.briggeman@sss-steel.com

- Mgr.—Stephen Briggeman

IRON and STEEL PLANTS

BMG Metals – Lynchburg
110 Industrial Dr.
Lynchburg, VA 24501 USA
P: +1.434.528.5000
hhoward@bmgmetals.com

- Mgr.—Hank Howard

BMG Metals – Manassas
7600 Wellingford Dr.
Manassas, VA 20109 USA
P: +1.703.330.4474
hpayton@bmgmetals.com

- Mgr.—Howard Payton

BMG Metals – Chesapeake
3325 Bus Center Dr.
Chesapeake, VA 23323 USA
P: +1.757.487.1963
stephen.briggeman@sss-steel.com

- Mgr.—Stephen Briggeman

BMG Metals – Baltimore
6945 San Tomas Road
Elkridge, MD 21075 USA
P: +1.410.355.6464
stephen.briggeman@sss-steel.com

- Mgr.—Stephen Briggeman

U

ULBRICH STAINLESS STEELS & SPECIAL METALS INC.
153 Washington Ave.
North Haven, CT 06473 USA
P: +1.800.243.1676 (Toll-Free)
info@ulbrich.com
www.ulbrich.com

PRODUCTS and/or SERVICES: Stainless steel strip, special metals strip, stainless steel and special metals foil, shaped wire, flat wire, and fine wire.

Ulbrich of California
8570 Mercury Lane
Pico Rivera, CA 90660 USA
P: +1.559.458.2340
info@ulbrich.com

Ulbrich of Illinois
12340 S. Laramie Ave.
Alsip, IL 60803 USA
P: +1.708.489.9500
F: +1.708.371.1802
info@ulbrich.com

Ulbrich of New England
153 Washington Ave.
North Haven, CT 06473 USA
P: +1.203.239.4481
info@ulbrich.com

Ulbrich Specialty Wire Products
692 Plant Road
Westminster, SC 29693 USA
P: +1.864.647.6087
F: +1.864.647.1549
info@ulbrich.com

Ulbrich Shaped Wire
55 Defco Park Road
North Haven, CT 06473 USA
P: +1.203.239.4481
F: +1.203.239.6744
info@ulbrich.com

Ulbrich Specialty Strip Mill
1 Dudley Ave.
Wallingford, CT 06492 USA
P: +1.203.239.4481
F: +1.203.239.7479
info@ulbrich.com

IRON and STEEL PLANTS

UNION DRAWN STEEL II LTD.
1350 Burlington St. E
P.O. Box 98
Hamilton, ON L8N 3A2 Canada
P: +1.800.263.9966 (Toll-Free);
 +1.905.547.4480
F: +1.905.544.3852

- Pres.—Michael P. Pitterich
- Vice Pres. and Gen. Mgr.—Jim Crompton
- Plant Mgr.—Brad Brindle

EQUIPMENT:
Bar annealing furnace, three bar drawbenches, three centerless grinders, three continuous coil drawing lines, two centerless bar turners.

PRODUCTS and/or SERVICES:
Cold-finished carbon and alloy steel bars.

No. of Employees: 63.

Railroad and Shipping Facilities: Truck.

UNION ELECTRIC STEEL CORP., a Subsidiary of Ampco-Pittsburgh Corp.
726 Bell Ave.
P.O. Box 465
Carnegie, PA 15106 USA
P: +1.412.429.7655
F: +1.412.276.1711
www.uniones.com

- Pres.—Samuel C. Lyon
- Vice Pres., U.S. Mfg.—Robert S. Grabowski
- Vice Pres., Global Supply Chain—Edward J. Siddons
- Vice Pres., Metallurgical Technology—Lew Prenni
- Vice Pres., Global Sales and Mktg.—Charles "Skip" Reinert Jr.
- Vice Pres., Finance—Katrina Mills

PRODUCTS and/or SERVICES:
Manufacturer of forged hardened steel rolls and forgings up to 80,000 lbs. finished weight.

Harmon Creek Plant
P.O. Box 151
31 Union Electric Road
Burgettstown, PA 15021 USA
P: +1.724.947.9595

- Plant Mgr.—Steve Wiard

Erie Plant
1712 Greengarden Road
Erie, PA 15106 USA
P: +1.814.452.0587

Valparaiso Plant
P.O. Box 29
Valparaiso, IN 46384 USA
P: +1.219.464.0587

- Plant Mgr.—Paul M. Ruff

UNITED STATES STEEL CORPORATION
600 Grant St.
Pittsburgh, PA 15219 USA
P: +1.412.433.1121
www.ussteel.com

- Pres. and Chief Exec. Officer—David B. Burritt
- Sr. Vice Pres., Chief Financial Officer—Christine D. Breve
- Sr. Vice Pres. of Adv. Technology Steelmaking and Chief Oper. Officer — Big River Steel Works—Daniel R. Brown
- Sr. Vice Pres. — European Solutions and Pres. — U. S. Steel Košice—James E. Bruno
- Sr. Vice Pres. and Chief Mfg. Officer — North American Flat-Rolled Segment—Scott D. Buckiso
- Sr. Vice Pres. and Chief Communications Officer—Tara Carraro
- Sr. Vice Pres. — Chief Strategy and Sustainability Officer—Richard L. Fruehauf
- Sr. Vice Pres. and Chief Financial Officer—Jessica T. Graziano
- Vice Pres., Contr. and Chief Acctg. Officer—Manpreet S. Grewal
- Sr. Vice Pres., Gen. Counsel, Chief Ethics and Compliance Officer—Duane D. Holloway

IRON and STEEL PLANTS

- Sr. Vice Pres. and Chief Commercial Officer—Kenneth Jaycox
- Sr. Vice Pres. and Chief H.R. Officer—Barry Melnkovic
- Vice Pres. Engrg. and Mfg. Support—James F. Dudek

Big River Steel
2027 State Hwy. 198
Osceola, AR 72370 USA
P: +1.870.819.3031
sales@bigriversteel.com
www.bigriversteel.com

- Chief Oper. Officer—Dan Brown
- Dir. of Product Dev.—Denis Hennessy
- Dir. of Constr.—Jim Bell

EQUIPMENT:
Two gas cleaning plants, two EAFs, two twin-station ladle treatment stations, RH degasser, two continuous casters, two tunnel furnaces, two hot mill downcoilers, covered automated coil yard, coupled pickling line and tandem cold rolling mill, batch annealing furnaces, skinpass mill, coupled universal annealing and galvanizing line.

PRODUCTS and/or SERVICES:
AHSS, electrical, hot-rolled, HRP&O, cold-rolled, cold-rolled motor lamination and galvanized steels.

Annual Capacity: 3.3 million tons raw steel

No. of Employees: 647.

Railroad and Shipping Facilities: Truck, rail and barge.

Fairfield Works
5700 Valley Road
Fairfield, AL 35064 USA
P: +1.205.783.4122

EQUIPMENT:
EAF, slab and round casters, 50-in. HGL/Galvalume line.

PRODUCTS and/or SERVICES:
Flat-rolled and tubular products.

Annual Capacity: 1.6 million tons raw steel.

Gary Works
One N. Broadway
Gary, IN 46402 USA
P: +1.219.888.2000

EQUIPMENT:
Four BFs; three top-blown BOP vessels; three bottom-blown Q-BOP vessels; VD; three LMFs; four continuous slab casters; 84-in. HSM; hot-rolled temper mill; 80-in. and 84-in. pickle lines; 52-in. 6-stand and 80-in. 5-stand cold reduction mills; electrolytic cleaning line; three batch annealing facilities; 38-in. CAL; 80-in. 1-stand, 48-in. 2-stand, and 84-in. 2-stand temper mills; 48-in. 2-stand double cold reduction mill; 37-in. and 46-in. electrolytic tinning lines.

PRODUCTS and/or SERVICES:
Hot-rolled, cold-rolled and galvanized sheet products, tin products.

Annual Capacity: 7.5 million net tons raw steel.

Granite City Works
1951 State St.
Granite City, IL 62040 USA
P: +1.618.451.3456

EQUIPMENT:
Two BFs, two top-blown BOP vessels, LMF, two continuous slab casters, 80-in. HSM, 51-in. pickle line, 56-in. 4-Stand cold reduction mill, 49-in. HDGL/Galvalume® line.

PRODUCTS and/or SERVICES:
Hot-rolled, cold-rolled and coated sheet steel products.

Annual Capacity: 2.8 million net tons raw steel.

Railroad and Shipping Facilities: Barge dock on Mississippi River.

Great Lakes Works
#1 Quality Dr.
Ecorse, MI 48229 USA
P: +1.313.749.2100

EQUIPMENT:
73-in. CGL.

IRON and STEEL PLANTS

PRODUCTS and/or SERVICES:
Galvanized sheet.

Annual Capacity: 530,000 tons.

Great Lakes Works EGL at Dearborn
3000 Miller Road
Dearborn, MI 48120 USA
P: +1.313.203.9800

EQUIPMENT:
72-in. EGL.

PRODUCTS and/or SERVICES:
Galvanized sheet.

Annual Capacity: 700,000 tons.

Midwest Plant
U.S. Hwy. 12
Portage, IN 46368 USA
P: +1.219.762.3131

EQUIPMENT:
80-in. pickle line; 52-in. and 80-in. 5-stand tandem cold reduction mills; electrolytic cleaning line; batch annealing facilities; 43-in. CAL; 54-in. and 80-in. temper mills; 54-in. double cold reduction mill; 48-in. and 72-in. HDGL; 42-in. electrolytic tinning line; 38-in. tin-free steel line.

PRODUCTS and/or SERVICES:
Tin mill products, HDG, cold-rolled and electrical lamination steels.

Minnesota Ore Operations–Keetac
1 Mine Road
Keewatin, MN 55753 USA
P: +1.218.778.8700

PRODUCTS and/or SERVICES:
Iron ore pellets.

Annual Capacity: 6 million net tons pellets.

Minnesota Ore Operations–Minntac
8819 Old Hwy. 169
P.O. Box 417
Mt. Iron, MN 55768 USA
P: +1.218.749.7589

PRODUCTS and/or SERVICES:
Iron ore pellets.

Annual Capacity: 16 million net tons pellets.

Mon Valley Works – Clairton Plant
400 State St.
Clairton, PA 15025 USA
P: +1.412.233.1800

EQUIPMENT:
Ten coke oven batteries.

PRODUCTS and/or SERVICES:
Coke.

Annual Capacity: 4.3 million tons coke.

Mon Valley Works – Edgar Thomson Plant
13th St. and Braddock Ave.
Braddock, PA 15104 USA
P: +1.412.273.7000

EQUIPMENT:
Two BFs, two top-blown BOP vessels, VD, LMF, 2-strand continuous slab caster.

PRODUCTS and/or SERVICES:
Steel slabs.

Annual Capacity: 2.9 million net tons raw steel.

Mon Valley Works – Fairless Plant
400 Middle Dr.
Fairless Hills, PA 19030 USA
P: +1.215.736.4605

EQUIPMENT:
65-in. HDGL.

PRODUCTS and/or SERVICES:
Galvanized sheet.

Mon Valley Works – Irvin Plant
Camp Hollow Road
West Mifflin, PA 15122 USA
P: +1.412.675.7459

EQUIPMENT:
80-in HSM; 64-in. and 84-in. pickle lines; 84-in. 5-stand cold reduction mill; CAL; batch and open-coil annealing facilities; 84-in. temper mill; 48-in. and 52-in. HDGL.

PRODUCTS and/or SERVICES:
Hot-rolled, cold-rolled and coated sheet; embossed sheet; Vitrenamel™ sheet; and commercial bright sheet.

IRON and STEEL PLANTS

U. S. Steel Tubular Products—see listing page 140

UPI
P.O. Box 471
Pittsburg, CA 94565 USA
P: +1.800.877.7672 (Toll-Free);
   +1.925.439.6000
F: +1.925.439.6441
www.ussupi.com

- Pres.—Michael Piekut
- Vice Pres. Oprs.—Lynnette Giacobazzi
- Vice Pres. Commercial—MD. Amin
- Gen. Counsel and Sec.—Cory Anderson
- Div. Mgr., Roll. Oprs.—Alonza Lewis
- Div. Mgr., Sheet Oprs.—Kevin Madsen
- Div. Mgr., Tin Oprs.—Markus Boro
- Div. Mgr., Reliability—Tim Kuzmicky
- Mgr., UPI Pur. Group—Tom Blasingame

EQUIPMENT:
One continuous pickle line and tandem 5-stand, 6-high cold reduction mill. One multi-purpose sheet CAL and temper rolling line. One continuous HDGL. Tinplate production—CAL, combination double cold reduction and tin temper mill, one electrolytic tinning line, one combination tin-free steel electrolytic tinning line, slitting line.

PRODUCTS and/or SERVICES:
Cold-rolled sheet, galvanized sheet, tinplate, black plate and tin-free steel HRP&O.

Annual Capacity: 1.5 million tons.

No. of Employees: 700.

Railroad and Shipping Facilities: Truck, rail.

UNIVERSAL STAINLESS & ALLOY PRODUCTS INC.
600 Mayer St.
Bridgeville, PA 15017 USA
P: +1.800.625.7610 (Toll-Free Sales);
   +1.412.257.7600
F: +1.412.257.7640
www.univstainless.com

- Chief Exec. Officer and Pres.—Dennis M. Oates
- Exec. Vice Pres. and Chief Commercial Officer—Christopher M. Zimmer
- Vice Pres. Admin., Gen. Counsel and Sec.—Paul A. McGrath
- Vice Pres. and Chief Technology Officer—Graham McIntosh
- Chief Financial Officer, Vice Pres. Finance and Treas.—Christopher T. Scanlon

EQUIPMENT:
50-ton EAF/AOD, ESR shop, VAR shop, bloom/plate mill, specialty shape mills, bar mill.

PRODUCTS and/or SERVICES:
Stainless, tool and alloy steels in ingot, bloom, billet, slab, plate, bar, and specialty shapes.

Annual Capacity: 150,000 tons.

No. of Employees: 300.

Railroad and Shipping Facilities: Truck.

Additional Facilities:

Dunkirk, NY
830 Brigham Road
Dunkirk, NY 14048 USA
P: +1.716.366.1000
F: +1.716.366.0478

- Gen. Mgr.—D. Wist
- Mgr. Maint.—K. Kuwik
- Mgr. Sales—G. Zaffalon

EQUIPMENT:
Two 14-in., one 10-in., and one continuous bar and rod mill.

PRODUCTS and/or SERVICES:
Stainless, high-temperature, and tool steel bar, wire and rod.

Annual Capacity: 50,000 tons.

No. of Employees: 230.

IRON and STEEL PLANTS

North Jackson, OH
2058 S. Bailey Road
North Jackson, OH 44451 USA
P: +1.412.257.7600 (Sales);
 +1.330.538.9621
F: +1.412.257.7640 (Sales);
 +1.330.538.9792

PRODUCTS and/or SERVICES:
Specialty steels, including nickel alloy, stainless steel, low-alloy steels. Ingots, billets, round bars (5–14 in.), forged blocks, conversion forging.

Titusville, PA
121 Caldwell St.
Titusville, PA 16354 USA
P: +1.814.827.9723
F: +1.814.827.2766

EQUIPMENT:
Five VAR furnaces.

PRODUCTS and/or SERVICES:
Specialty shapes.

V

VALBRUNA SLATER STAINLESS INC.
2400 Taylor St. W
Fort Wayne, IN 46801 USA
P: +1.260.434.2800
F: +1.260.434.2801
info@valbruna.usa
www.valbrunastainless.com

- Pres.—Massimo Amenduni Gresele
- Gen. Mgr.—Tiziano Briozzo
- Qual. Mgr.—Randy Kline
- Engrg. Mgr.—Joe Steinmetz
- Contr./Financial Officer—Tonya Brunett

EQUIPMENT:
One 10-ton electroslag refining furnace; two 10-ton VAR furnaces; 38- and 24-in. 2-high reversing mills; 2-stand, 3-high 22-in. mill; 12-stand, 12-in. continuous rolling mill with 26-in. 2-high reversing roughing mill; drawbenches; centerless grinders to 6 in.; bar peelers capacity to 8 in.; billet grinders for rounds and squares up to 20 in.; cold-drawn lines up to 1.125 in.; complete heat treating facilities with full quenching capabilities.

PRODUCTS and/or SERVICES:
Stainless steel, billets, rounds, squares, hexagons, high-temperature, corrosion- and heat-resistant alloys in billets and bars.

Annual Capacity: 75,000 tons.

No. of Employees: 130.

Railroad and Shipping Facilities: Truck.

Valbruna ASW Inc.
42 Centre St.
Welland, ON L3B 0E5 Canada
P: +1.905.735.5500
F: +1.905.735.4603
www.asw-steel.com

- Pres.—Tim Clutterbuck
- Qual. Mgr.—Mike Ackroyd
- H.R. Mgr. and Gen. Counsel—Lynn Currie
- Info. Technology Mgr.—Brian Fear
- Sales Mgr.—John Mauro
- Dir. of Tech. Sales Support—Keith Woodland
- Meltshop Mgr.—Chris Elliot

EQUIPMENT:
Two EAFs (one 100-ton and one 60-ton), LMF, VOD, AOD, VD, billet/bloom caster.

PRODUCTS and/or SERVICES:
Carbon, stainless and specialty steelmaking capabilities. Producible steel grades include 10xx series carbon

IRON and STEEL PLANTS

steel; 300 and 400 series stainless steel; 4100, 4300, 8600 and 9000 series alloy steel; and A36/44W HSLA steel. ASW Steel can produce billet (115 x 115 mm, 130 mm x 130 mm and 147 x 147 mm) and bloom (200 x 250 mm) products to 40-in. maximum length. Square tapered and cylindrical forging ingots available in 20-in. through 30-in. sections.

Annual Capacity: 150,000 tons.

Railroad and Shipping Facilities: Truck, rail and barge.

VENTURE STEEL INC.
60 Disco Road
Etobicoke, ON M9W 1LB Canada
P: +1.416.798.9396
sales@venturesteel.com
www.venturesteel.com

- Pres.—Tony Kafato
- Exec. Vice Pres.—Gary Fisher
- Vice Pres. Prodn./Mfg.—Claudio Cortina
- Vice Pres. Sales—Scott Woodland
- Pur. Agt.—Stefano Giacoboni

PRODUCTS and/or SERVICES:
Toll processing and sales of carbon steel, stainless and aluminum. Slitting, blanking, CTL, logistics and warehousing.

No. of Employees: 300.

VILLACERO
Melchor Ocampo 250
Monterrey, NL, 64000 Mexico
P: +52.81.8989.8989
ventas@villacero.com
www.villacero.com

- Chief Exec. Officer—Julio César Villarreal Guajardo

PRODUCTS and/or SERVICES:
Long and flat products—cold-rolled sheet; equal and unequal angles; flat bar; hot-rolled sheet; large-diameter pipe; rebar; round and square bars; skid sheet and plate flooring; steel plate.

Tubería Nacional S.A. de C.V.
Diego Díaz de Berlanga Sur No. 1002
San Nicolás de los Garza, NL, 66480
Mexico
P: +52.81.8989.8989

PRODUCTS and/or SERVICES:
API ERW line pipe, circular welded non-alloy steel pipe, cold-formed square tubing, channel for construction C section, dipped, galvanized, threaded and coupled conduit.

No. of Employees: 250–500.

Cintacero S.A. de C.V.
Prolongación Ruiz Cortines Ote.
No. 2500
Guadalupe, NL, 67110 Mexico

Zincacero S.A. de C.V.
Antigua Caretera a Roma km 7.5
Col. Valle del Mezquital
Apodaca, NL, 66600 Mexico
P: +52.81.8989.8989

T-H Tubería Helicoidal
Calle 5 de Mayo 3
Pesquería, NL, 66650 Mexico
P: +52.81.8989.8989

EQUIPMENT:
Pantographs; edging lines; press and shear; roll former for purlins; CTL line for hot-rolled and cold-rolled products; tension leveler; slitters for HRC and CRC; laboratory for mechanical testing of materials. Processing capacity of 840,000 tons annually.

VINTON STEEL LLC, a Part of Kyoei Steel Group
8100 Border Steel Road
Vinton, TX 79821 USA
P: +1.915.886.2000
info@vintonsteel.com
www.vintonsteel.com

- Chief Exec. Officer—Masahiro Kitada
- Deputy Gen. Mgr.—Tatsuya Fukuyama
- Vice Pres. and Procurement Dir.—Akira Andy Kosugi
- Vice Pres. Oprs. and Plant Mgr.—Juan Delgado
- Vice Pres. and Sales Dir.—David Villareal

IRON and STEEL PLANTS

- Meltshop Mgr.—Jesus Ramirez
- Ball Mill Mgr. and Asst. Plant Mgr.—Eduardo Gonzalez
- Roll. Mill Mgr.—Francisco Lucero
- Scrap Mgr.—Jim Nielsen
- Traffic Mgr.—Juan J. Rodriguez
- Scrap Pur. Mgr.—Lorena Soto
- Gen. Mgr. Reporting—Kunihiko Otomaru
- Gen. Mgr. H.R.—Victor Camacho
- Ship. and Scale Mgr.—Ernesto Sifuentes
- Qual. Assur. Supv.—Hector De Aquino
- Mech. Maint. Mgr.—Wences Samaniego
- Sr. Buyer—Manuel Gonzalez
- Inside Sales—Karla Avila, Jesus R. Nava, Fabiola Tiscareño
- Qual./Prodn. Plan. Mgr.—Guillermo Fernandez
- Prodn. Plan. Supv.—Dalia R. Martinez
- Admin. Asst.—Laura B. Clark

EQUIPMENT:
Scrap processing facilities, two EAFs, continuous casting and rolling mill.

PRODUCTS and/or SERVICES:
Reinforcing bar in sizes from #4–#18, in various lengths. ASTM standard A615 (40, 60, 75 and 80) and A706 grades. Grinding media from 0.5-in. to 4-in. dia.

Annual Capacity: 250,000 tons.

No. of Employees: 400.

VOSS INDUSTRIES

VOSS CLARK
701 Loop Road
Jeffersonville, IN 47130 USA
P: +1.812.285.7700
F: +1.812.285.7704
dovoss@vossindustries.com
www.vossindustries.com

- Chief Exec. Officer—P. Michael Voss
- Dir. of Oprs.—Douglas P. Voss
- Sales Mgr.—Ashley Hendrick
- Treas.—David Voss

EQUIPMENT:
74-in.-wide continuous pickle line with tension leveling and automated top and bottom (Parsytec) surface inspection. Three 74-in.-wide slitters. Two 1,000-ton presses.

PRODUCTS and/or SERVICES:
Pickling, slitting, stamping and blanking services.

Annual Capacity: 850,000 tons pickling. 600,000 tons slitting. 144,000 tons blanking.

No. of Employees: 125.

Railroad and Shipping Facilities: Truck, rail, barge.

Voss Taylor
7925 Beech Daly Road
Taylor, MI 48183 USA
P: +1.313.291.7500
F: +1.313.291.7504
tbilkey@vossindustries.com
www.vossindustries.com

- Chief Exec. Officer—P. Michael Voss
- Dir. of Oprs.—Steve Fischer
- Treas.—Mike Ratusznik
- Outside Sales Mgr.—Tim Bilkey
- Inside Sales Mgr.—Mary Ann Satkowiak
- Pur. Agt.—Nikki Voss-Motes

EQUIPMENT:
72-in.-wide HCl pickle line with tension leveling and automated surface inspection (Parsytec). 72-in.-wide slitting.

PRODUCTS and/or SERVICES:
Pickling, slitting, dry lube coil coating, coil pre-wash.

No. of Employees: 100.

IRON and STEEL PLANTS

W

W. SILVER INC.
9059 Doniphan Dr.
Vinton, TX 79821 USA
P: +1.877.246.3553
F: +1.915.886.5610
saleswsi@wsilverinc.com
www.wsilverinc.com

- Pres.—Luis Garcia
- Natl. Sales Mgr.—Pete Seaman
- Regional Acct. Mgrs.—Jim Cooley, Jeremy Henderson
- Mfg. Mgr.—Alfredo Cardona
- Supply Chain Mgr.—Hector Abelleyra
- Contr.—Gary Manoni
- H.R. Mgr.—Cristina Jarrell

EQUIPMENT:
Rail and billet mill.

PRODUCTS and/or SERVICES:
Reinforcing bar, light structural shapes, hot-rolled bars, fence posts, bed angles and grape stakes.

No. of Employees: 140.

WHEELING-NIPPON STEEL INC.
Penn and Main Sts.
P.O. Box 635
Follansbee, WV 26037 USA
P: +1.304.527.2800
F: +1.304.527.1063
www.wheeling-nipponsteel.com

- Pres.—Kenichi Hoshi
- Vice Pres. Commercial, Gen. Mgr. ZAM® Mktg.—William Reder
- Gen. Mgr. Commercial—Brian Petrella
- Asst. Mgr. Commercial—Daisuke Ishikawa
- Procurement Lead—Joe Kraina
- Asst. Mgr. Inside Sales—Lorrie McMahon
- Vice Pres. of Mfg.—Frank Mollica
- Gen. Mgr. Oprs.—Larry Persina
- Mgr. Oprs.—Rick Lash
- Sr. Mgr. Oprs. Svcs.—Carla Waugh
- Gen. Mgr. Qual. Assur. and Cust. Svce.—Terry Ozasa
- Mgr. Qual. Assur. and Cust. Svce.—Curtis Valero
- Sr. Tech. Svce. Rep.—Mark Guio
- Cust. Svce. Rep.—Jeff Legros
- Cust. Qual. Rep.—Derek Wayne
- Qual. Engr.—Alexa Tweedle
- Sr. Mgr. Info. Systems—Greg Lauri

EQUIPMENT:
Continuous hot-dip aluminizing and galvanizing line. Continuous HDG and Galvalume® line.

PRODUCTS and/or SERVICES:
Galvanized sheet, galvannealed sheet, aluminized sheet, Galvalume sheet and ZAM® sheet.

Annual Capacity: 700,000 tons.

No. of Employees: 175.

Railroad and Shipping Facilities: Truck, rail.

WORTHINGTON INDUSTRIES, Steel Processing Div.
200 Old Wilson Bridge Road
Columbus, OH 43085 USA
P: +1.800.844.3733 (Toll-Free)
steel@worthingtonindustries.com
www.worthingtonindustries.com
www.steel.worthingtonindustries.com

- Exec. Chmn.—John P. McConnell
- Pres. and Chief Exec. Officer—Andy Rose
- Chief Oper. Officer and Exec. Vice Pres.—Geoff G. Gilmore
- Chief Financial Officer and Exec. Vice Pres.—Joseph B. Hayek
- Sr. Vice Pres. and Chief H.R. Officer—Cathy M. Lyttle
- Vice Pres., Transformation—Bill Wertz
- Vice Pres. Corporate Communications and Brand Mgmt.—Sonya L. Higganbotham
- Vice Pres., Pur.—Cliff J. Larivey
- Chief Info. Officer—Matt Schlabig
- Contr.—Steve Witt

IRON and STEEL PLANTS

- Pres., Steel Processing—Jeff R. Klingler
- Pres., Building Products and Sustainable Energy Solutions—Eric M. Smolenski
- Treas. and Investor Rels. Officer— Marcus Rogier
- Pres. Consumer Products—Steven M. Caravati
- Vice Pres., Gen. Counsel and Sec.— Patrick Kennedy
- Pres., Consumer Products—Steve Caravati
- Vice Pres., Strategy and Innovation— Sheleemia Simmons-Taylor

PRODUCTS and/or SERVICES:
Global diversified metals manufacturing company involved in steel processing, building products, consumer products and sustainable energy solutions. Worthington's Steel Processing business segment is one of North America's largest providers of value-added carbon flat-rolled steel processing, laser welding solutions and electrical steel laminations. Products and processing capabilities include: cold-rolled steel, CTL sheets, dry film lubricant, first operation blanking, galvanized steel, hot-rolled steel, line cards, annealing, one pass rolling, oscillate slitting, pickling, slitting, and temper rolling.

Worthington – Bowling Green, KY
310 Jody Richards Dr.
Bowling Green, KY 42101 USA

Worthington – Cleveland, OH
4310 E. 49th St.
Cuyahoga Heights, OH 44125 USA

Worthington – Columbus, OH
1127 Dearborn Dr.
Columbus, OH 43085 USA

Worthington – Delta, OH
6303 County Road 10
Delta, OH 43515 USA

Worthington – Middletown, OH
1501 Made Dr.
Middletown, OH 45044 USA

Worthington – Monroe, OH
350 Lawton Ave.
Monroe, OH 45050 USA

Worthington – Porter, IN
100 Worthington Dr.
Porter, IN 46304 USA

Worthington – Rome, NY
530 Henry St.
Rome, NY 13440 USA

Worthington – Taylor, MI
11700 Worthington Dr.
Taylor, MI 48180 USA

Worthington (Tempel Steel) – Apodaca, N.L., Mexico
Andres Guajardo No. 315
Apodaca, NL, 66600 Mexico

Worthington (Tempel Steel) – Burlington, ON, Canada
5045 N. Service Road
Burlington, ON L7L 5H6 Canada

Worthington (Tempel Steel) – Chicago, IL
5500 N. Wolcott Ave.
Chicago, IL 60640 USA

Steel Processing Joint Ventures:

**SERVIACERO WORTHINGTON
(Joint Venture Between Worthington Industries and Inverzer S.A. de C.V.)**
worthington@serviacero.com
www.serviacero.com/worthington

PRODUCTS and/or SERVICES:
Steel processing services, including pickling, blanking, slitting, multi-blanking and CTL.

Serviacero Worthington – León
Blvd. Hermanos Aldama No. 4002
Col. Cd Industrial
Leon, GJ, 37490 Mexico

Serviacero Worthington – Monterrey
Arco Vial Lib. Noreste km 21.5
Ejido San Miguel
Monterrey, NL, 66050 Mexico

Serviacero Worthington – Querétaro
Ave. La Noria No. 129
Parque Ind. Qro. 2000
Santiago, QE, 76220 Mexico

IRON and STEEL PLANTS

**SPARTAN STEEL COATING CO. LLC
(Joint Venture Between Worthington
Industries and Cleveland-Cliffs Inc.)**
3300 Wolverine Dr.
Monroe, MI 48162 USA
P: +1.734.289.5400

EQUIPMENT:
HDGL.

PRODUCTS and/or SERVICES:
Toll processing for steel coils into galvanized, galvannealed and aluminized products.

Annual Capacity:

No. of Employees: 76.

**TWB CO. (Joint Venture Between
Worthington Industries and Baoshan
Iron & Steel Co. Ltd.)**
www.twbcompany.com

PRODUCTS and/or SERVICES:
Laser-welded blanks, tailor-welded aluminum blanks, laser-welded coils and other laser-welded products for the automotive industry.

TWB Co. – Antioch, TN
6050 Dana Way
Antioch, TN 37013 USA

TWB Co. – Canton, MI
7295 Haggerty Road
Canton, MI 48187 USA

TWB Co. – Glasgow, KY
119 Carroll Knicely Dr.
Glasgow, KY 42141 USA

TWB Co. – Monroe, MI
1600 Nadeau Road
Monroe, MI 48162 USA

TWB Co. – Smyrna, TN
983 Nissan Dr.
Smyrna, TN 37167 USA

TWB Co. – Valley City, OH
5569 Innovation Dr.
Valley City, OH 44280 USA

5580 Wegman Dr.
Valley City, OH 44280 USA

TWB de Mexico S.A. de C.V. – Nuevo León
Arco Vial Libramiento Noreste km 21.5, No. 7003
Monterrey, NL, 66050 Mexico

TWB de Mexico S.A. de C.V. – Puebla
km 117 Autopista Mexico Puebla S/N
Cuautlancingo, PU, 72700 Mexico

TWB de Mexico S.A. de C.V. – Silao
Blvd. Paseo de los Industriales S/N Lote IX
Silao, GJ, 36100 Mexico

TWB of Canada Inc.
100 Lingard Road
Cambridge, ON N1T 2C7 Canada

**WORTHINGTON SAMUEL COIL
PROCESSING LLC (Joint Venture
Between Worthington Industries and
Samuel Son & Co. Ltd.)**

PRODUCTS and/or SERVICES:
Steel pickling.

Worthington Samuel Coil Processing LLC – Cleveland
4600 Heidtman Pkwy.
Cleveland, OH 44105 USA

Worthington Samuel Coil Processing LLC – Twinsburg
1400 W. Enterprise Pkwy.
Twinsburg, OH 44087 USA

**WORTHINGTON SPECIALTY
PROCESSING (Joint Venture
Between Worthington Industries and
United States Steel Corporation)**
4905 S. Meridian Road
Jackson, MI 49201 USA

PRODUCTS and/or SERVICES:
Toll processing: slitting, blanking, CTL, laser blanking and warehousing.

IRON and STEEL PLANTS

COMPANIES SUPPORTING THE AIST INDIA MEMBER CHAPTER

AM/NS INDIA LTD.
27th km, Surat, Hazira Road
Hazira, GJ, 394270 India
P: +91.261.2872400

- Chief Exec. Officer—Dilip Oommen
- Dir. and Vice Pres. — Technology—Hiroyuki Nitta
- Dir. and Vice Pres. — Oprs.—Wim Van Gerven
- Dir. and Vice Pres., Sales and Mktg.—Alain Legrix de la Salle
- Dir. and Vice Pres., Finance—Takahiro Nagayoshi
- Deputy Dir., Finance—Amit Harlalka

PRODUCTS and/or SERVICES:
Integrated flat carbon steel manufacturer with a footprint across Asia, Africa, Europe, the Americas and Australia. It has fully integrated operations that span the entire value chain of steelmaking, from mining to retail. Offers more than 300 grades of steel and a product portfolio including HRC/sheet/plates, CRC/sheets, galvanized coil/sheets, pre-painted galvanized coil/sheets and plate mill plates.

Annual Capacity: 9 million metric tons.

JINDAL SAW LTD.
Jindal Centre
12 Bhikaiji Cama Pl.
New Delhi, DL, 110066 India
P: +91.11.26188345; 26188360.74
F: +91.11.26170691

- Chmn.—P.R. Jindal
- Managing Dir.—Sminu Jindal
- Group Chief Exec. Officer and Whole Time Dir.—Neeraj Kumar

PRODUCTS and/or SERVICES:
Seamless tubes and pipes, LSAW pipes (J-C-O), spiral-welded pipes, ductile iron pipes, railway wagons, etc.

JINDAL STAINLESS LTD.
Jindal Centre
12 Bhikaji Cama Pl.
New Delhi, DL, 110066 India
P: +91.011.26188345.60
F: +91.011.26170691; 26161271
info@jindalsteel.com

- Chmn.—Ratan Jindal

PRODUCTS:
Stainless steel hot-rolled strips and cold-rolled strips, modular stainless steel products.

Annual Capacity: 1.1 million metric tons melting.

JINDAL STEEL & POWER LTD. (JSPL)
Jindal Centre
12 Bhikaji Cama Pl.
New Delhi, DL, 110066 India
P: +91.11.4146.2000/6146.2000
F: +91.11.2616.1271
www.jindalsteelpower.com

- Chmn.—Naveen Jindal

PRODUCTS and/or SERVICES:
Rails—track rails: IRS 52, UIC 60 (E1 and E2), UIC 54E; crane rails: CR 80, CR 100. Parallel flange beams and columns (180–900 mm); channels (75–400 mm); angles (50–250 mm); wire rods (Grades: MS, MC and HC, EO, boron and other alloy steels) (Sizes: 5.2 mm, 5.5–20 mm); Jindal Panther TMT rebars (Grades: 500, 500D, 550, 550D, 600 and CRS) (Sizes: 6–40 mm); plates (widths: 1,500–4,900 mm, thicknesses: 5–150 mm); coils (widths: 1,500–2,500 mm, thicknesses: 5–25 mm); fabricated structures; cuts and bends; speed floor and welded wire mesh; special grade plates from Angul.

Annual Capacity: 11.6 mtpy liquid steel, 9.95 mtpy iron, 6.55 mtpy finished steel.

IRON and STEEL PLANTS

JOINT PLANT COMMITTEE (JPC)
Ispat Niketan
52/1A Ballygunge Circular Road
Kolkata, WB, 700019 India
P: +91.33.2461.4055; 4056; 4058;
 4062; 4068
F: +91.33.2461.4063
jpc-kolkata@gmail.com

- Chmn. and Sec., Ministry of Steel, Govt. of India—Smt. Rasika Chaube
- Exec. Sec.—Ranjan Bandyopadhyay

PRODUCTS and/or SERVICES: Constituted in 1964 by the Ministry of Steel, Government of India for formulating guidelines for production, allocation, pricing and distribution of iron and steel materials, JPC underwent a major transformation in 1992, when following the de-regulation of the Indian steel industry, it molded itself into a facilitator for industry, pervading knowledge on steel by forming a comprehensive and non-partisan databank—the first of its kind in the country—on the Indian iron and steel industry. Today, it is the only institution in the country officially empowered by the Ministry of Steel, Government of India to collect and report data on the Indian iron and steel industry. Accredited with ISO 9001:2015 certification, JPC is headquartered at Kolkata with regional offices in New Delhi, Kolkata, Mumbai and Chennai, and two extension centers in Bhubaneswar and Raipur that are engaged in data collection. JPC has considerably widened its variety of data, making these covetous for all policymakers in the country. JPC being a member of World Steel Association, its data is utilized to adjudge India's position in the global ranking.

JSW STEEL
Bandra Kurla Complex
Mumbai, MH, 400051 India
P: +91.22.4286.1000
F: +91.22.4286.3000
www.jsw.in

- Chmn. and Managing Dir.—Sajjan Jindal
- MVS Jt. Managing Dir. and Group Chief Financial Officer—Seshagiri Rao
- Deputy Managing Dir.—Vinod Nowal
- Joint Managing Dir. and Chief Exec. Officer—Arun Maheshwari
- Dir., Commercial and Mktg.—Jayant Acharya

PRODUCTS and/or SERVICES: Global conglomerate spread over six locations in India and with a footprint that extends to the U.S., South America and Africa. Steel plants in Karnataka, Tamil Nadu and Maharashtra have a combined installed capacity of 18 million mtpy.

KALYANI STEELS LTD.
Mundhwa, Pune, MH, 411006 India
P: +91.20.6621.5000
F: +91.20.2682.1124
kslmktg@kalyanisteels.com
www.kalyanisteels.com

Plant Locations: Pune, MH, and Hospet, KA

- Chmn.—B.N. Kalyani
- Managing Dir.—R.K. Goyal
- Dir. — Projects—P.S. Ghose
- Chief Financial Officer—B.M. Maheshwari
- Sec.—D.R. Puranik

PRODUCTS and/or SERVICES: Specialty quality carbon and alloy steels long products, hot-rolled for forging, automotive, engineering, defense and aviation applications sizes of 30–135-mm dia. rounds, 50–180-mm RCS and flats, along with as-cast sizes of 125 x 125, 160 x 160, 200 x 200, 240 x 280, and 160 dia., 200 dia. and 220 dia. Integrated steel plant comprising of: sinter plant, BF, energy optimizing furnace (EOF)-based steel meltshop with ladle refining furnace and VD, continuous caster (long products), rolling mills, auto inspection (NDT) line, power plant, railway siding, air separation unit (BOO basis). Pune plant consists of EAF-based plant with

IRON and STEEL PLANTS

RHF, VD/VOD, ESR, VAR, continuous casting facility, ingot casting facility and rolling mill

NMDC LTD.
Khanij Bhavan, Masab Tank
Hyderabad, TG, 500028 India
P: +23538713.21
F: +23538711

- Chmn. and Managing Dir.—Sunit Deb

PRODUCTS and/or SERVICES:
NMDC is India's single largest iron ore producer to the domestic steel industry. Produces more than 35 million metric tons of iron ore from three fully mechanized mines in Chhattisgarh and Karnataka. All production facilities and R&D labs are ISO 14001:2015 EMS certified. ISO 9001:2015 certified QMS. OHSAS 18001:2015 certified. In addition, the R&D lab is NABL certified. NMDC is setting up a 3.0-mtpy greenfield integrated steel plant through the BF-BOF route at Nagarnar near Jagdalpur in Bastar district of Chhattisgarh.

RASHTRIYA ISPAT NIGAM LTD. (RINL)
Administrative Bldg.
Visakhapatnam, AP, 530031 India
P: +91.891.2515854

- Chmn. and Managing Dir.—Deb Kalyan Mohanty

PRODUCTS and/or SERVICES:
Integrated shore-based steel plant located at Visakhapatnam. Produces a wide range of long steel products, including wire rods of 5.5-20 mm; thermomechanically treated rebars of sizes 8-40 mm; structurals—angles of 50 x 50 to 110 x 110 mm, channels of size 40 x 32 to 200 x 75 mm, ISMB products of 125 x 70 to 175 x 85 mm, plain rounds in size range of 16-80 mm and forged rounds of 180-240 mm size. Plant produces different grades of special steels.

Annual Capacity: 6.3 million metric tons.

TATA STEEL LTD.
Registered Office:
Bombay House
24 Homi Mody St.
Fort Mumbai, MH, 400001 India
P: +91.657.2431142
www.tatasteel.com

- Chmn.—Natarajan Chandrasekaran

PRODUCTS and/or SERVICES:
Tata Steel Group has a crude steel capacity of 34 million mtpy and a consolidated turnover of US$21.06 billion as of March 2021. Operations in 26 countries and a commercial presence in more than 50 countries.

Tata Steel BSL
B 9 to 12
Okhla Industrial Area, Phase 1
New Delhi, DL, 110020 India
P: +011.26811033
F: +91.11.46518611
www.tatasteelbsl.co.in

- Managing Dir.—Rajeev Singhal

PRODUCTS and/or SERVICES:
Tata Steel BSL, formerly known as Bhushan Steel Ltd., was established in 1989. BSL has four operating units: Angul (Odisha), Sahibabad (Uttar Pradesh), Khopoli (Maharashtra) and Hosur (Tamil Nadu). The Angul Plant is an integrated steel plant with production capacity of 5.6 million metric tons per year (mtpy) of liquid steel. The Sahibabad and Khopoli works are downstream facilities with annual capacities of 0.90 and 0.6 mtpy, respectively. In Odisha, BSL started the commercial production of steel through the DRI-EAF route in 2008-09 and increased the production capacity from 0.3 mtpy to 5.6 mtpy liquid steel through the systematic implementation of various technological units and plant facilities including two BFs, two cokemaking plants, three sinter plants, two BOF units, one twin-shell Conarc, HSM and CRM from 2003-04 until 2014. The steel plant presently has the capacity to manufacture up to 5.1 mtpy of HRC, 0.3 mtpy of billets and power generation capacity up to 442 MW for captive usage.

PIPE and TUBE PLANTS

A

AMBASSADOR PIPE & SUPPLY INC.
P.O. Box 520
Republic, MO 65738 USA
P: +1.417.744.2230
F: +1.417.744.1777
stu@ambassadorpipe.com
jeff@ambassadorpipe.com
www.ambassadorpipe.com

- Chief Exec. Officer and Treas.—
  James S. Hindman
- Pres. and Sales Mgr.—Stu Hindman
- Exec. Vice Pres., Asst. Sales
  Mgr., Pur. Agt. and Adv. Mgr.—Jeff
  Hindman
- Vice Pres. and Sec.—Vicki Hindman
- Vice Pres. Engrg. and Prodn./Mfg.
  and Chief Engr.—Lynn Walden
- Vice Pres. Sales and Mktg.—Hollie
  Hindman
- Prodn. Mgr.—David Wilson

EQUIPMENT:
Lathe cutting, lathe beveling, lathe threaders, MIG welders and spray paint equipment.

PRODUCTS and/or SERVICES:
Steel pipe and tube processing.

No. of Employees: 10.

AMERICAN CAST IRON PIPE CO. (ACIPCO)

Headquarters, AMERICAN Ductile Iron Pipe and AMERICAN Steel Pipe Divs.:
1501 31st Ave. N
Birmingham, AL 35207 USA
P: +1.205.325.7815
F: +1.205.325.8014
www.american-usa.com

PRODUCTS and/or SERVICES:
Ductile iron pipe in 4–64 in. dia. in accordance with ANSI/AWWA C151/A21/51 standard. HFW steel pipe in API grades from 12.75- to 24-in. dia. and lengths of up to 100 ft.

No. of Employees: 2,600; 1,600 at headquarters.

AMERICAN SpiralWeld Pipe Co. LLC
2061 American Italian Way
Columbia, SC 29209 USA
P: +1.800.695.2200 (Toll-Free)

EQUIPMENT:
Three plants located in Columbia, SC; Flint, MI; and Paris, TX.

PRODUCTS and/or SERVICES:
Spiral-welded carbon steel pipe per ASTM A252, A139 and A1097 standards from 24–144 in. dia. and lengths up to 50 feet. AWWA C200 standards up to 144 in.

AMERICAN PIPING PRODUCTS INC.
825 Maryville Centre Dr., Suite 310
Chesterfield, MO 63017 USA
P: +1.800.316.5737 (Toll-Free);
   +1.636.536.1775
F: +1.636.536.1363
sales@amerpipe.com
www.amerpipe.com

PRODUCTS and/or SERVICES:
Inventories a complete line of carbon, alloy and chrome-moly steel pipe, fittings, and flanges used extensively in manufacturing and construction applications and in the oil and gas and power generation industries. 50,000 tons of pipe, fittings and flanges in stock. 22-acre facility near the port of Houston and 10-acre facility outside Chicago. Services include: saw cutting, profiling, beveling, blasting and pickling, mechanical flame cutting, OD preparation, testing and threading.

Chicago Warehouse
15801 Van Drunen Road
South Holland, IL 60473 USA
P: +1.708.339.1753

PIPE and TUBE PLANTS

Houston Warehouse
11403 N. Houston Rosslyn Road
Houston, TX 77088 USA
P: +1.800.316.5737 (Toll-Free);
 +1.281.847.0693
F: +1.281.847.0953

Philadelphia Sales Office
15 Hagerty Blvd., Suite A
West Chester, PA 19382 USA
P: +1.888.277.2106 (Toll-Free)
F: +1.610.719.6005

AMERICAN STAINLESS TUBING INC.—see ASCENT TUBULAR PRODUCTS

AMERICAN TUBULAR PRODUCTS, a Div. of Schaeffer Industries
141 S. Western Coil Road
Lindon, UT 84042 USA
P: +1.801.785.8600
atpsales@sisteel.com
www.atptube.com

EQUIPMENT:
Quick-roll-change technology.

PRODUCTS and/or SERVICES:
Producer of structural steel pipe and tube in round, square and rectangle shapes.

Northern California
1265 N. Shaw Road
Stockton, CA 95215 USA
P: +1.209.465.4500

Pacific Northwest
2600 Schaeffer Way
Richland, WA 99354 USA
P: +1.801.785.8600

ARCELORMITTAL TUBULAR PRODUCTS
www.northamerica.arcelormittal.com

 – Chief Exec. Officer—Edward S. Vore
 – Chief Commercial Officer—Darren Dossi
 – Chief Technology Officer and Head of Business Strategy—Wayne Bland
 – Chief Oper. Officer North America—Fred Schuster
 – Dir. of Pur.—Brent Lesseuer

Canada Operations:

ArcelorMittal Brampton
14 Holtby Ave.
Brampton, ON L6X 2M3 Canada
P: +1.905.451.2400
F: +1.905.451.2795
brampton.tubularproducts@arcelormittal.com

 – Plant Mgr., Brampton—Mike Touhey

PRODUCTS and/or SERVICES:
Small-diameter round, square rectangle and elliptical welded tubes.

ArcelorMittal Hamilton
1330 Burlington St.
Hamilton, ON L8N 3J5 Canada
P: +1.905.544.3761
F: +1.905.549.4330
hamilton.tubularproducts@arcelormittal.com

 – Plant Mgr.—Don Stothart

PRODUCTS and/or SERVICES:
Automotive tubing.

ArcelorMittal London
2440 Scanlan St.
London, ON N5W 6H7 Canada
T: +1.519.451.7701
F: +1.519.539.6804
london.tubularproducts@arcelormittal.com

 – Plant Mgr.—Greg West

PRODUCTS and/or SERVICES:
Automotive components.

ArcelorMittal Woodstock
193 Givins St.
P.O. Box 1589
Woodstock, ON N4S 0A7 Canada
T: +1.519.537.6671
F: +1.519.539.6804
woodstock.tubularproducts@arcelormittal.com

 – Plant Mgr.—Greg West

PIPE and TUBE PLANTS

PRODUCTS and/or SERVICES:
Welded tubing, complex precision tubing.

Mexico Operations:

ArcelorMittal Monterrey
Carretera Monterrey-Saltillo km 28.2
Col. Arco Vial Libramiento Noreste
Monterrey, NL, 66050 Mexico
T: +52.81.8220.80.42
F: +52.81.8220.80.01
monterrey.tubularproducts@
arcelormittal.com

- Plant Mgr.—Marcela Garcia

PRODUCTS and/or SERVICES:
Automotive tube, non-automotive mechanical tube.

U.S. Operations:

ArcelorMittal Marion
686 W. Fairground St.
Marion, OH 43302 USA
P: +1.740.375.2299
marion.tubularproducts@
arcelormittal.com

- Plant Mgr.—Tim Hebauf

PRODUCTS and/or SERVICES:
Conveyor tube, specialty automotive tube, boiler tube.

ArcelorMittal Shelby
132 W. Main St.
Shelby, OH 44875 USA
P: +1.419.347.2424
shelby.tubularproducts@
arcelormittal.com

- Plant Mgr., Shelby—Rick Gruver

PRODUCTS and/or SERVICES:
Seamless and welded precision tubes, DOM, cold-drawn tubes.

ARCO METAL S.A. DE C.V.
Eje. 120 No. 250, Zona Industrial
San Luis Potosí, SLP, 78395 Mexico
P and F: +01.444.824.5535
ventas@arcometal.com.mx
www.arcometal.com.mx

PRODUCTS and/or SERVICES:
Square and rectangular tubes, profiles with eyebrow, purlins, doors and windows, rectangular tubular profiles, frames, rounds.

Distribution Centers:

CEDIS Mexico South
Av. Tlahuac No. 58, Fracc. Santa Isabel Industrial
Ixtapalapa, MX, 09820 Mexico
P: +01.555.581.4355
F: +01.555.581.1449

CEDIS Mexico North
Av José López Portillo 90,
San Francisco Chilpan,
Buenavista, MX, 54944 Mexico
P: +01.55.55.81.43.55
F: +01.55.55.81.14.49

CEDIS Guadalajara
Belisario Dominguez No. 2488
Col. La Federacha
Guadalajara, JA, 44300 Mexico
P: +01.33.3674.00.42

ASCENT TUBULAR PRODUCTS
1400 16th St. Suite 270
Oak Brook, IL 60523 USA
P: +1.412.462.21841
customerservice@ascenttubular.com
www.ascenttubular.com

- Chief Exec. Officer and Pres., Ascent Industries Co.—Christopher Hutter
- Exec. Vice Pres. Ascent Tubular Products—Tim Lynch

American Stainless Tubing Inc. – Troutman, NC Plant
P.O. Box 909
Troutman, NC 28166 USA
P: +1.704.878.8823
F: +1.704.878.0777
www.asti-nc.com

- Sales—Nancy Barrymore, Mike Gamage, Juanita Broussard, Jim Barrymore, Tanner Campbell

EQUIPMENT:
20 continuous pipe forming mills, slitting and welding equipment; proprietary finishing process equipment.

PIPE and TUBE PLANTS

PRODUCTS and/or SERVICES: Premium ornamental stainless steel tubing in a variety of shapes including squares, rectangles and ellipticals. ISO 9001:2015 certified.

American Stainless Tubing Inc. — Statesville, NC Plant
123 Morehead Road
Statesville, NC 28677 USA

Bristol Tubular Products - Bristol Operations
390 Bristol Metals Road
Bristol, TN 37620 USA
P: +1.423.989.4700
sales@brismet.com
www.brismet.com

- Vice Pres. of Pur., Ascent Tubular Products—Barry Newberry
- Vice Pres. Business Oprs./Logistics—Josh Ringley
- Vice Pres. Tubular Products—Rob Yepsen
- Regional Sales Dir.—David C. Terrick
- Mgr. Intl. and Special Alloy Sales—Parker Sword
- Sr. Sales Rep., Special Alloys—Jonathan W. Williams
- Outside Sales Rep.—Charles Glascock
- Mgr. Qual. Assur. and Compliance—James R. Baines III

EQUIPMENT:
20 continuous pipe forming mills (up to 3/8 to 18 in. OD); batch lines with tandem presses (from 8 to 144-in. OD with heavy wall thickness up to 1.312 in. and in 48 ft. lengths); mechanical roll forming equipment (up to 20 ft. and up to 1-in. gauge thickness); welding equipment (TIG, GTAW and PAW); cold working/planishing and secondary processing operations; in-line and off-line heat treating furnaces and localized heat treating processes; five pickling/passivation tanks; two rinse tanks; sandblasting equipment; end preparation equipment; X-ray and testing equipment.

PRODUCTS and/or SERVICES:
Welded stainless steel, high-nickel alloy, duplex, super duplex, titanium and moly pipe in sizes from 0.5 to 144 in. dia. and in lengths of up to 60 feet from continuous production line and 48 ft. from batch mill. Also supplies a wide range of round, square and rectangular ornamental tubing.

Bristol Tubular Products — Munhall Operations
1001 E. Waterfront Dr.
Munhall, PA 15120 USA
P: +1.412.462.2185

- Vice Pres. Oprs.—Dominic Baggetta

Specialty Pipe & Tube Inc. — Ohio
P.O. Box 516
3600 Union St.
Mineral Ridge, OH 44440 USA
P: +1.800.366.7473 (Toll-Free)
 +1.330.505.8262
F: +1.330.505.8260
pvass@specialtypipe.com
www.specialtypipe.com

- Sales Team—Pete Vass, Randy Bekish, Abigail Foerster-Connolly, Lisa Kaliney, Molly Klasovsky, Mark McCallister, Bryan Danks, Jason Ste. Marie

PRODUCTS and/or SERVICES:
Distributor for large-diameter, heavy wall, hot finish and seamless carbon steel pipe and mechanical tubing.

Specialty Pipe & Tube Inc. - Texas
3838 Majestic Dr.
Houston, TX 77026 USA
P: +1.800.842.5839 (Toll-Free);
 +1.713.676.2891
F: +1.713.674.9718

ATKORE INTERNATIONAL
16100 S. Lathrop Ave.
Harvey, IL 60426 USA
P: +1.800.882.5543 (Toll-Free);
 +1.708.339.1610
questions@atkore.com
www.atkore.com

- Chief Exec. Officer and Pres.—William "Bill" Waltz
- Vice Pres., Chief Financial Officer and Chief Acctg. Officer—David P. Johnson

PIPE and TUBE PLANTS

- Vice Pres., Gen. Counsel and Sec.—Daniel Kelly
- Pres., Safety and Infrastructure—Mark F. Lamps
- Pres., Elec.—John W. Pregenzer
- Vice Pres., Global H.R.—Angel Lowe
- Vice Pres., Treas. and Investor Rels.—John Deitzer
- Vice Pres. and Sr. Vice Pres., Sales—Melissa Kidd
- Vice Pres., Info. Technology—Lee Paree
- Vice Pres., Strategic Sourcing—Steve Robins
- Vice Pres., Business Dev. and Strategy—John P. Stampfel
- Vice Pres., Corporate Communications—Lisa Winter

PRODUCTS and/or SERVICES: Manufacturer of galvanized steel tubes and pipes, electrical conduit, armored wire and cable, metal framing systems, and building components; serving a wide range of construction, electrical, fire and security, mechanical, and automotive applications.

No. of Employees: 3,700 worldwide.

Allied Tube & Conduit, a Part of Atkore International
16100 Lathrop Ave.
Harvey, IL 60426 USA
P: +1.708.339.1610
www.alliedeg.us

PRODUCTS and/or SERVICES: Full line of electrical and metals products. Portfolio includes electrical metallic tubing (EMT), galvanized rigid steel conduit (GRC), intermediate metal conduit (IMC), PVC, aluminum rigid conduit, Kwik and specialty conduit, elbows, couplings and nipples, fittings, and PVC-coated conduit. Brands under Allied Tube & Conduit include True Color™, E-Z Pull®, Kwik-Fit® EMT; and Super Kwik-Couple® GRC and IMC.

ATLANTIC TUBE & STEEL INC.
1580 Meyerside Dr.
Mississauga, ON L5T 1A3 Canada
P: +1.877.665.6614 (Toll-Free);
 +1.905.670.1511
F: +1.905.670.1845
atstube@atlantictube.com

- Gen. Mgr.—Paul Cancelli
- Natl. Sales Mgr., Exhaust and Mech. Tubing—Larry Brandon
- Plant Mgr.—George Haraga
- Contr.—Marvin Bavcevic
- Matls. Mgr.—Wayne Baptiste
- Sales Reps.—Anthony Cancelli, Brad Elliott

PRODUCTS and/or SERVICES: Material types: A787 A513, A500, A500B, A500C, G40.21, 350W, GR50W. Steel grades: HRBLK, HRPO, HSLA, CRAKDQ, aluminized, galvanized, Galvalume®, ROPS. Mill length capabilities: 28 in. to 720 in. (length depends on diameter of tube). Cold saw lengths (recut) available upon request, 4 in. to 180 in.

PIPE and TUBE PLANTS

B

BERG PIPE, a Div. of EUROPIPE

Berg Pipe Panama City Corp.
5315 W. 19th St.
Panama City, FL 32401 USA
P: +1.850.769.2273
F: +1.850.763.9683
info@bergpipe.com
www.bergpipe.com

- Chmn. of the Bd.—Salko Schröter
- Chief Exec. Officer and Pres.—Ingo Riemer
- Chief Financial Officer—John Juchniewicz
- Vice Pres. Sales and Logistics—Jonathan Kirkland
- Vice Pres. Qual. Systems and Supply Chain Mgmt.—Dimitris Dimopoulos
- Dir. of Logistics—Thomas Suggs
- Dir. of Procurement—Eric Arnold
- Vice Pres. Oprs.—Andy Hicks, Paul Weber
- Mgrs. Engrg. and Maint.—Mike Hampton, Justin Beck
- Mgr. EHS—Tim Lister
- Mgr. Raw Matls.—Brink Prescott
- Dir. of H.R.—Angela Cherry
- Dir. of Info. Technology—Jay Verenakis

EQUIPMENT:
EOT cranes, pyramid roll forming facilities, plate milling machine, DSAW welding machines, sizer, end facer, hydrotester, ultrasonic tester, x-ray machine, expander.

PRODUCTS and/or SERVICES:
DSAW steel pipe 24- through 64-in. OD; wall thickness 0.25 through 1.50 in.

Annual Capacity: 400,000 tons.

No. of Employees: 300.

Railroad and Shipping Facilities: Truck, rail, barge, ship.

Berg Pipe Mobile Corp.
900 Paper Mill Road
Mobile, AL 36610 USA
P: +1.251.330.2900
F: +1.251.330.2901
info@bergpipe.com
www.bergpipe.com

Berg Pipe Houston
10375 Richmond Ave., Suite 425
Houston, TX 77042 USA
P: +1.713.465.1600
F: +1.713.827.7423
www.bergpipe.com

BRISTOL METALS LLC—–see ASCENT TUBULAR PRODUCTS

BULL MOOSE TUBE CO., a Caparo Co.
1819 Clarkson Road
Chesterfield, MO 63017 USA
P: +1.636.537.2600 (ext. 284)
www.bullmoosetube.com

- Chief Exec. Officer and Pres.—Tom Modrowski
- Exec. Vice Pres. and Chief Commercial Officer—Andy Annakin
- Vice Pres. Oprs.—Jeffrey Ostermann
- Vice Pres., Tech. Svcs. and Continuous Improvement—Jim Fink

PRODUCTS and/or SERVICES:
HSS, mechanical steel tube, sprinkler pipe.

Burlington
2170 Queensway Dr.
Burlington, ON L7R 3T1 Canada
P: +1.905.637.8261

Casa Grande
1001 N. Jefferson Ave.
Casa Grande, AZ 85122 USA
P: +1.520.836.3455

Chicago Heights
555 E. 16th St.
Chicago Heights, IL 60411 USA
P: +1.708.757.7700

PIPE and TUBE PLANTS

Elkhart
29851 County Road 20 W
Elkhart, IN 46517 USA
P: +1.574.295.8070

Gerald
406 E. Industrial Dr./Hwy. 50
Gerald, MO 63037 USA
P: +1.573.764.3315

Masury
1433 Standard Ave. SE
Masury, OH 44438 USA
P: +1.330.448.4878

Trenton
195 N. Industrial Dr.
Trenton, GA 30752 USA
P: +1.423.417.1152

C

CENTURY TUBE CORP.
22 Tannery Road
Somerville, NJ 08876 USA
P: +1.908.534.2001
F: +1.908.534.4030
centtube@aol.com
www.centurytube.net

- Vice Pres.—Nick De Angelo
- Head of Sales—Bill Vohdin

PRODUCTS and/or SERVICES:
Seven TIG welding mills. TIG welding creates a quality weld with minimal internal weld bead. All round and square polishing is completed in-house with the finishes to customer needs and specifications. TIG welding also allows Century Tube to weld to specific multiple lengths and eliminate the expense of unnecessary scrap to the customer.

CLEVELAND-CLIFFS TUBULAR COMPONENTS

Columbus
150 W. 450 S
Columbus, IN 47201 USA
P: +1.866.369.3200

- Plant Leadership—Erik R. Anderson

EQUIPMENT:
Six high-frequency ERW tube mills, four Rattunde cold saws producing CTL sizes from 25 to 102 mm dia.

PRODUCTS and/or SERVICES:
Carbon and stainless steel (aluminized or bare), HRP&O, cold-rolled, galvanized and AHSS (TRIP 700, DP 600 to 1000 grades) tubing in round, standard and complex shapes.

Annual Capacity: 100,000 tons.

No. of Employees: 205.

Walbridge
60400 E. Broadway
Walbridge, OH 43465 USA
P: +1.800.955.8031 (Toll-Free)

- Plant Leadership—Erik R. Anderson

EQUIPMENT:
Six high-frequency ERW tube mills producing sizes from 19 to 168 mm dia.

PRODUCTS and/or SERVICES:
Carbon and stainless steel (aluminized or bare), HRP&O, cold-rolled, galvanized and AHSS (TRIP 700, DP 600 to 1000 grades) tubing in round, standard and complex shapes.

Annual Capacity: 120,000 tons.

No. of Employees: 165.

CONDUIT RYMCO—see RYMCO

PIPE and TUBE PLANTS

D

DB PIPING GROUP, THE
75 Guthrie Ave.
Dorval, QC H9P 2P1 Canada
P: +1.888.893.5881 (Toll-Free);
   +1.450.435.3643
F: +1.613.342.8599
www.dbpipinggroup.com

- Pres. and Gen. Mgr.—Darko Petrovic
- Contr.—Qiguang Tian
- Dir. of Projects—Alain Laberge
- Dir. of Oprs.—Lorne Phillips
- Dir. of Sales and Mktg.—Melanie Schwery
- Project Mgr. Canada—Rick Patrick
- Projects Canada—Martin Lemieux, Alan Lavoie
- Sales and Est. U.S.—Franz Plourde
- Project Mgr. U.S.—Michael Poirier
- Drafting and Engrg. U.S.—Mark Neff
- Sales PVF — U.S./Canada—Clint Dinwiddie, Angel Rajasoorian, Carol Cross, Alain Duclos

PRODUCTS and/or SERVICES:
Stainless steel and specialty alloys for piping and fabrication.

ABE Fittings, a DB Piping Group Co.
180 Laurier Blvd., Box 86
Brockville, ON K6V 5T7 Canada
P: +1.800.668.2118 (Toll-Free)
F: +1.613.345.0160
sales@abefittings.com
www.abefittings.com

PRODUCTS and/or SERVICES:
Butt-welded stainless steel pipe and fittings in multiple alloys and specifications. NPS, ISO, OD and ID up to 30 in. light to heavy wall thickness diameters.

Douglas Barwick Inc., a DB Piping Group Co.
150 California Ave.
P.O. Box 756
Brockville, ON K6V 5W1 Canada
P: +1.613.342.8471
F: +1.613.342.4432
dbi@douglasbarwick.com

PRODUCTS and/or SERVICES:
Manufactures pipe and tubing along with a wide range of pipe fittings and accessories in stainless and other alloy steels destined mainly for the pulp and paper industry and for municipal environmental works. Principal product lines are I.D. and I.P.S. (gauge wall and Sch.5S and 10S) stainless steel pipes and fittings to ASTM A 778 and A 774 and I.P.S. stainless steel pipes and fittings to ASME SA 312/ASTM A 312 and ASME SA 403/ASTM A 403, along with a complete selection of stainless steel piping system accessories.

Douglas Brothers, a DP Piping Group Co.
423 Riverside Industrial Pkwy.
Portland, ME 04103 USA
P: +1.207.797.6771
F: +1.207.797.8385
douglas@douglasbrothers.com
www.douglasbrothers.com

PRODUCTS and/or SERVICES:
Piping and fabrication, water aeration, special builds.

Formweld Fitting Inc., a DB Piping Group Co.
8118 Progress Dr.
Milton, FL 32583 USA
P: +1.850.626.4888
F: +1.850.626.9988
sales@formweldfitting.com
www.formweldfitting.us

- Branch Mgr.—Lorne Philips
- Asst. Branch Mgr.—Brent Mason
- Sales—Clint Dinwiddie
- Prodn. Mgr.—Dennis Hudson
- Qual. and Safety Rep.—Cassidy Stowell
- Accts. Receivable, Logistics and Reception—Maura Keck

PRODUCTS and/or SERVICES:
Standard and specialized fittings. In-house specialized testing (radiography, liquid penetrant, visual,

PIPE and TUBE PLANTS

grain size verification, ferrite, hardness and positive material identification).

DETROIT TUBING MILL INC., THE
12301 Hubbell St.
Detroit, MI 48227 USA
P: +1.313.491.8823
info@detroittubingmill.com
www.detroittubingmill.com

PRODUCTS and/or SERVICES:
ISO 9001:2015 certified ERW mechanical and structural steel tubing. In-house CTL capabilities.

DURA-BOND INDUSTRIES
5790 Kennedy Ave.
Export, PA 15632 USA
P: +1.724.327.0280
F: +1.724.327.0113 (Steel Fabrication)
info@dura-bond.com
www.dura-bond.com

- Chmn.—Wayne Norris
- Pres.—Jason Norris
- Contr.—John Christy
- Vice Pres. Commercial—George Thompson
- Outside Sales—Charles Kawana
- Inside Sales Pipeline Coating/Products—Adam Norris
- Inside Sales Tubular—Jared Kamerer
- Sales Mgr. Tubular Products Western Div.—Wendy Hatz
- Accts. Payable—Anna Hall

PRODUCTS and/or SERVICES:
API LSAW, ERW pipe, coating services, heavy steel fabrication.

Dura-Bond Steel Inc. — Steel Fabrication
2658 Puckety Dr.
Export, PA 15632 USA
P: +1.724.327.0782
F: +1.724.327.0113

- Gen. Mgr.—Stan Pytlak
- Environ. Mgr.—John Hopper
- Drafting Supv.—Mark Boss
- Qual. Control/CWI On Site—Kurt Dolnack
- Shapes Coating Mgr.—Dustin Norris
- Transp. Mgr.—Marc Deal
- Est.—Raub Weimer, Shawn Luther

PRODUCTS and/or SERVICES:
Steel fabrication, custom shapes coating, ID lining, powercrete mainline coatings, pipeline products.

Dura-Bond Coating Inc.
5 N. Linden St.
Duquesne, PA 15110 USA
P: +1.412.436.2411

- Gen. Mgr. Fusion Bond Mill—Dan Swearingen
- Office/Admin. Mgr.—Barb Blum

PRODUCTS and/or SERVICES:
FBE/ARO manufactured coating applicator, coated pipe storage.

Railroad and Shipping Facilities: Barge, rail, truck.

Dura-Bond Pipe Steelton
2716 S. Front St.
Steelton, PA 17113 USA
P: +1.717.986.1100
F: +1.717.986.1104

- Exec. Vice Pres. and Gen. Mgr.—Ryan Norris
- Vice Pres. Pipe Mfg.—James Larkin
- Coating Facilities Mgmt.—Ken Leach
- Qual. Assur.—Mark Anderson
- Structural Products Mgr.—Steve Stapf
- Tubular Products Admin.—Emily Arnold
- Office Mgr.—Marianne Elliot

PRODUCTS and/or SERVICES:
Manufacturers of large OD 24–42-in. API LSAW pipe, ultrasonic weld inspection, hydrostatic expansion process. External FBE/ARO and internal linings.

Dura-Bond Pipe McKeesport
301 4th Ave.
McKeesport, PA 15132 USA
P: +1.412.267.5840

- Gen. Mgr.—Doug Nolfi
- Business Plan.—Terry Onufer
- Qual. Assur.—Sarang Muley

PRODUCTS and/or SERVICES:
HFW API line pipe from $8\,5/8$ in. through 20 in. dia. Grades up to X70 and lengths up to 80 ft.

PIPE and TUBE PLANTS

F

FAVOR STEEL & FABRICATING
4301 Coalburg Road
Birmingham, AL 35207 USA
F: +1.205.941.6800
sales@favorsteel.com
www.favorsteel.com

- Pres.—Brett L. Rayburn
- Sales Mgr.—Trae Hawkins

EQUIPMENT:
Messer plasma table Davi roll.

PRODUCTS and/or SERVICES:
Rolled and welded casing 30 in. to 180 in.

No. of Employees: 45.

FISCHER GROUP
www.fischer-group.com

PRODUCTS and/or SERVICES:
Manufactures welded mechanical stainless steel tubing in various ferritic and austenitic grades to ASTM standard A-554 and A-268 (with some exceptions). Product line consists of round tubing in 1-in. to 6-in. dia. and a variety of standard square and rectangular shapes and sizes. Can produce metric sizes as well as some specialty customized shapes and open profiles. fischer also produces tubing in D1L and Laser Plus™ welds.

fischer Canada Stainless Steel Tubing Inc.
190 Frobisher Dr.
Waterloo, ON N2V 2A2 Canada
P: +1.800.563.8823 (Toll-Free);
   +1.519.746.0088
info@fischerca.com
www.fischerca.com

- Vice Pres.—Thomas Prell
- Chief Financial Officer and H.R. Mgr.—Uta Prell
- Sales Mgr.—Joe McLinden
- Inside Sales—Lorna Hayward
- Qual. Assur. Mgr.—Glen Walter
- Matls. Mgr.—Sabrina Prell
- Ship. Coordinator—Stephen Koebel
- Environ. Coordinator—Sarah Prell

fischer USA Stainless Steel Tubing Inc.
1120 AEDC Access Road
Manchester, TN 37355 USA
P: +1.931.596.3566
F: +1.931.596.4566
sales-usa@fischer-group.com
www.fischer-usa.com

- Vice Pres.—Thomas Prell
- Plant Mgr.—Joe Franks
- Sales Mgr.—Joe McLinden
- Winglet and High Frequency Mgr.—Chris Goode
- Tube Bending Mgr.—Alex Rothweiler
- Qual. Assur. Mgr.—Bobby Simpson
- Ship. Coordinator—Christy Vogel
- Prodn. Plan.—Amanda Bryan
- Matls. Pur.—Josh Rogers

fischer Mexicana S.A. de C.V., Tubos de Acero Inoxidable
EJE 124 No. 115 Zona Industrial
San Luis Potosí, SLP, 78090 Mexico
P: +52.44.48.246966
sales-mx@fischer-group.com

- Managing Dir.—Tanja Bevc

fischer TUBETECH Inc.
190 Frobisher Dr.
Waterloo, ON N2V 2A2 Canada
P: +1.800.563.8823 (Toll-Free)
   +1.519.746.0088
info@fischerca.com
www.fischerca.com

- Vice Pres.—Thomas Prell
- Mfg. Mgr.—Wade Bauman
- Inside Sales—Kristina Prell
- Qual. Assur. Mgr.—Glen Walter
- Ship. Coordinator—Chuck Pfeiffer
- Matls. Mgr.—Lumi Duca
- Contr.—Uta Prell
- Asst. Contr.—Patti Armbuster

PRODUCTS and/or SERVICES:
Produces stainless steel tubular components and subassemblies primarily for the automotive industry:

PIPE and TUBE PLANTS

hot end inlet pipes, catalytic converter shells, collector pipes, intermediate pipes, perforated muffler pipes, tail pipes.

fischer TUBTECH S.A. de C.V.
102 Carril de San Cristóbal
Chachapa, PU, 72990 Mexico
P: +52.22.86.03.90
sales-mx@fischer-group.com

G–H

GREGORY TUBE, a Div. of Gregory Industries
715 Willo Industrial Dr.
Decatur, AL 35601 USA
P: +1.330.477.4800
www.gregorytube.com

- Vice Pres. Sales—Bob Chufar

EQUIPMENT:
Roll forming equipment, continuous and batch HDGL.

PRODUCTS and/or SERVICES:
Steel tubing, rebar spikes, tube bends, metal tube brackets, U-channel and hat channel supports, ground anchors, custom-fabricated base rails, CTL stubs.

HANNA STEEL
4527 Southlake Pkwy.
Hoover, AL 35244 USA
P: +1.800.633.8252 (Toll-Free);
 +1.205.820.5200
F: +1.205.820.5280
info@hannasteel.com
www.hannasteel.com

- Chief Exec. Officer—Marshall Akins
- Pres.—Jimmy Gustin
- Chief Oper. Officer—David Monroe
- Chief Financial Officer—Randy Raiford
- Dir. of Oprs.—Zac Davis
- Dir. of Safety—Clark Wood
- Pres., Hanna Truck Line and Gen. Mgr., Tuscaloosa—David Farmer
- Dir. of Pur.—John Simpson
- Sr. Met.—Randy Kirkland

- Outside Sales—Tony Byrd, Paul Sandlin, Patie Milton, Jeff Parks, Jeff Hager, Bruce Hager
- Inside Sales Mgr.—Tracy Sanders
- Inside Sales—Curtis Armstrong, Norman Messina, Darrell Graf, Dillon Cordes, Joey Ray

PRODUCTS and/or SERVICES:
Provides ASTM standard structural and mechanical tubing from the Southeast to the Midwest. Hanna produces tubing ranging from ½-in. square to 10-in. square in a number of square, rectangle and round sizes, with wall thicknesses through ½ in.

Fairfield Processing Div.
3812 Commerce Ave.
Fairfield, AL 35064 USA
P: +1.800.633.8252 (Toll-Free);
 +1.205.780.1111
F: +1.205.783.8366

- Gen. Mgr.—Bruce Turner
- Claims Coordinator—Tony Hayes

EQUIPMENT:
In-line HCL pickling line; continuous coating/painting line; induction curing line; two-sided high-speed reverse roll coaters.

PRODUCTS and/or SERVICES:
Coil coating up to 50,000 lbs. (24–54 in. wide, up to 72 in. OD). Processing services include: surface pre-treating, HCL pickling, continuous

PIPE and TUBE PLANTS

coat painting, dry film lubricant coating, induction-cured polymerization.

Railroad and Shipping Facilities: Rail, truck.

Pekin Processing Div.
220 Hanna Dr.
Pekin, IL 61554 USA
P: +1.309.478.3800
F: +1.309.478.3810

- Gen. Mgr.—Randy Rendfeld
- Qual. Mgr.—Roger King

EQUIPMENT:
Two tube mills.

PRODUCTS and/or SERVICES:
Tubing.

Railroad and Shipping Facilities: Rail, truck.

Tuscaloosa Tube Div.
1701 Boone Blvd.
P.O. Box 428
Northport, AL 35476 USA
P: +1.800.634.5801 (Toll-Free);
   +1.205.333.4444
F: +1.205.333.4409

- Gen. Mgr.—David Farmer
- Met.—Andrew Short

EQUIPMENT:

PRODUCTS and/or SERVICES:
Mechanical tubing, HSS.

Railroad and Shipping Facilities: Rail, truck.

HEIDTMAN TUBULAR PRODUCTS LLC
640 Lavoy Road
Erie, MI 48133 USA
P: +1.734.848.2200
www.heidtmantubular.com

- Natl. Accts. Mgr.—Jeff Terrace
- Sales Mgr.—Tanner Rippy
- Acct. Mgr.—Sherri Stone

EQUIPMENT:
ERW mill, in-line eddy current tester, in-line UV coating system.

PRODUCTS and/or SERVICES:
Serves customers in a wide variety of markets that consume mechanical and HSS tubing. Manufactures as-welded structural tubing (ASTM A500) mechanical tubing (ASTM A513), and HSLA tubing in 2 to 4 in. squares and equivalent rectangles and 1.9 to 3.5 in. rounds. Products available in hot-rolled, HRP&O and galvanized.

HOFMANN INDUSTRIES INC.
3145 Shillington Road
Sinking Spring, PA 19608 USA
P: +1.610.678.8051
F: +1.610.670.2221
sales@hofmann.com
www.hofmann.com

- Chief Exec. Officer and Pres.—Stephen P. Owens
- Vice Pres. Sales—Jeffrey Hills
- Sales Mgr.—Stephen Gallagher
- Dir. Mfg.—Mark Muchoney

PRODUCTS and/or SERVICES:
Welded steel tubing per ASTM 513A; STKM 11-A; STKM 13-A. Fabricated steel tubing, zinc-plated powder-coated steel tubing.

No. of Employees: 130.

Railroad and Shipping Facilities: Truck.

Eau Claire Div.
6405 Love Road
Eau Claire, MI 49111 USA
P: +1.269.461.3586

PIPE and TUBE PLANTS

J–L

JINDAL TUBULAR USA LLC
13092 Seaplane Road
Bay St. Louis, MS 39520 USA
P: +1.228.533.7779
F: +1.228.533.0213
sales@jindaltubular.us
www.jindaltubular.com

EQUIPMENT:
Four SAW lines, hydrostatic testing, automatic ultrasonic testing, radiography, in-house testing laboratory, external and internal coating equipment.

PRODUCTS and/or SERVICES:
Pipe manufacturing and coating facility. Manufactures, coats and internally lines large-diameter API grade pipe in diameters ranging from 24 in. to 60 in., and Water AWWA C200 grade pipe from 18 to 120 in. Wall thickness capability ranges from 0.188 in. to 1 in. in lengths up to 80 ft. State-of-the-art facility utilizes helical two-step, submerged-arc welding (HTS-SAW) in pipe manufacturing. External coating services include fusion bond epoxy, abrasion-resistant overcoat and coal tar epoxy. Internal coating services include flow efficiency epoxy liner.

Annual Capacity: 300,000 tons.

Railroad and Shipping Facilities: Rail, barge, truck.

Jindal Pipe USA Inc.
1411 565 FM Road
Baytown, TX 77523 USA
P: +1.713.457.5757
sales@jindalpipeusa.com
www.jindalpipeusa.com

EQUIPMENT:
High-frequency ERW tube mill, heat treating and threading facility.

PRODUCTS and/or SERVICES:
Line pipe, standard pipe, structural pipe and HSS between 8 5/8 to 26 in. OD. OCTG between 4 1/2 to 13 3/8 OD. HSS squares and rectangles from 7 x 7 in. to 20 x 20 in. Capable of producing pipes per API 5L, CSA, API 5CT, and ASTM specifications.

Annual Capacity: 300,000 tons ERW pipe; 150,000 tons OCTG.

Railroad and Shipping Facilities: Rail, barge, truck.

KELLY PIPE CO. LLC
11680 Bloomfield Ave.
Santa Fe Springs, CA 90670 USA
P: +1.800.305.3559 (Toll-Free)
sales@kellypipe.com
www.kellypipe.com

– Chief Exec. Officer and Pres.—Art Shelton, ashelton@kellypipe.com

PRODUCTS and/or SERVICES:
Master distributor of line and standard pipe. Kelly Pipe Co. serves all 50 states, as well as overseas, from its inventory of carbon steel pipe ranging in size from 1/8-in. to 54-in. dia. Products include welded, seamless, carbon and stainless steel pipe; pipe fittings and flanges; special alloy pipes; industrial plastic pipes; water well pipe and supplies; OCTG for green energy applications; and more. Value-added services include FBE coating, shotblasting, precision cutting, custom fabrication, cut and roll grooving, threading and beveling.

Western Region:

Western Region Headquarters, Distribution Center and Santa Fe Springs Branch
11680 Bloomfield Ave.
Santa Fe Springs, CA 90670 USA
P: +1.800.305.3559 (Toll-Free)

– Western Region Dist. Mgr.—Arne Cvek, acvek@kellypipe.com
– Branch Mgr.—Grace Fernandes, gfernandes@kellypipe.com

PIPE and TUBE PLANTS

Bakersfield Branch
19459 Flightpath Way
Bakersfield, CA 93308 USA
P: +1.661.399.4540

- Branch Mgr.—Matthew Whittaker,
mwhittaker@kellypipe.com

Phoenix Branch
1617 S. 40th Ave.
Phoenix, AZ 85009 USA
P: +1.602.256.2990

- Branch Mgr.—Dixie Buck,
dbuck@kellypipe.com

Sacramento Branch
1890 Santa Ana Ave.
Sacramento, CA 95838 USA
P: +1.800.952.5615 (Toll-Free);
+1.916.640.1859

- Branch Mgr.—Patrick Holmes,
pholmes@kellypipe.com

Salt Lake City Branch
3170 W. Directors Row
Salt Lake City, UT 84101 USA
P: +1.801.973.8200

- Branch Mgr.—Todd Smith,
tsmith@kellypipe.com

Vancouver Branch
3702 N.W. Gateway Ave.
Vancouver, WA 98660 USA
P: +1.360.737.1848

- Branch Mgr.—Barry Henning,
bhenning@kellypipe.com

Eastern Region:

Eastern Region Headquarters and Houston Branch
1624 Little York Road
Houston, TX 77093 USA
P: +1.713.692.7473

- Sr. Vice Pres.—Kevin Roberts,
kroberts@kellypipe.com
- Branch Mgr.—Tracie Callaway,
tcallaway@kellypipe.com

Broussard Branch
1027 Petroleum Pkwy.
Broussard, LA 70518 USA
P: +1.337.369.6788

- Branch Mgr.—Cole Doiron,
cdoiron@kellypipe.com

Denver Branch
8200 E. 96th Ave.
Henderson, CO 80640 USA
P: +1.800.659.7473 (Toll-Free)

- Branch Mgr.—Scott Walsh,
swalsh@kellypipe.com

Distribution Center — Savannah, GA
2535 Seaboard Coastline Dr.
Savannah, GA 31415 USA
P: +1.855.202.7473

- Oprs. Mgr.—Clint Bitzer,
cbitzer@kellypipe.com

Distribution Center — Houston, TX
10501 Sheldon Road
Houston, TX 77044 USA
P: +1.281.456.0382

- Branch Mgr.—Tracie Callaway,
tcallaway@kellypipe.com
- Oprs. Mgr.—Cesar Acevedo,
cacevedo@kellypipc.com

Distribution Center — Odessa, TX
2989 S. County Road W
Odessa, TX 79766 USA
P: +1.432.332.0273

- Branch Mgr.—Tracie Callaway,
tcallaway@kellypipe.com

Distribution Center — Wheatland, PA
100 J H Yourga Pl.
P.O. Box 337
Wheatland, PA 16161 USA
P: +1.708.331.0300

- Oprs. Mgr.—Nick Leech,
nleech@kellypipe.com

Fairless Hills Branch
95 Towpath Road
Fairless Hills, PA 19030 USA
P: +1.833.254.7473

- Branch Mgr.—Jereme Lowe,
jlowe@kellypipe.com

PIPE and TUBE PLANTS

Hammond Branch
2345 Summer St.
Hammond, IN 46320 USA
P: +1.866.431.7473 (Toll-Free);
+1.708.331.0300
F: +1.708.331.5200

- Branch Mgr.—Bill Weidner,
  bweidner@kellypipe.com

Pineville Branch
11024 Nations Ford Road
Pineville, NC 28134 USA
P: +1.855.202.7473 (Toll-Free)

- Branch Mgr.—John Bailey,
  jbailey@kellypipe.com

KVA STAINLESS INC.
191 Mangano Cir.
Encinitas, CA 92024 USA
P: +1.760.489.1500
info@kvastainless.com
www.kvastainless.com

- Pres.—Joe McCrink
- Vice Pres. Sales and Business Dev.—Douglas Gore

PRODUCTS and/or SERVICES:
Made-to-order welded tubing products including martensitic stainless steel, nickel and titanium alloys. Available in 0.5- to 2.5-in. OD, 0.016–0.110-in. wall, and 5 to 30 ft. lengths.

LONGHORN TUBE
1891 Ryan Road
Dallas, TX 75220 USA
P: +1.800.390.5029 (Toll-Free);
+1.972.556.0234
F: +1.972.556.9158
dnorris@longhorntube.com
www.longhorntube.com

- Sales—John Allen, Billy Kane, Tyler Ray, Danni Norris

PRODUCTS and/or SERVICES:
HSS; square and rectangular mechanical; custom-welded, roll-formed shapes. New expanded selection of sizes available on ASTM A787-AWG True-Galv™ galvanized tubing. Products are made from raw materials that are melted and manufactured in the USA.

M

MANNESMANN, a Business Unit of Salzgitter AG
www.mannesmann.com

Mannesmann Precision Tubes Mexico S.A. de C.V.
Calle A No. 239
Parque Industrial El Salto
El Salto, JA, 45680 Mexico
P: +52.33.3688.1107
F: +52.33.3688.1196
info.mptmx@mannesmann.com
www.mannesmann-precision-tubes.com

- Plant Mgr.—Manuel Anchondo Reynaga

PIPE and TUBE PLANTS

PRODUCTS and/or SERVICES:
Welded cold-drawn precision steel tubes, welded mechanical steel tubes. Shock absorber cylinder tubes, shock absorber container tubes, gas spring tubes. Tubes for steering cylinders, IHU hydroforming, cardan shafts, axles. ISO/TS 16949 certified.

Annual Capacity: 18,000 tons for mechanical tubes, 12,000 tons for welded cold-drawn (DOM).

No. of Employees: Approx. 350.

Salzgitter Mannesmann Stainless Tubes USA Inc.
12050 W. Little York Road
Houston, TX 77041 USA
P: +1.713.466.7278
F: +1.713.466.3769
www.mannesmann-stainless-tubes.com

- Managing Dir.—Eduardo Gomes
- Prodn. Mgr.—AJ Hemund
- Sr. Sales Mgr.—Gary Kilgore
- Sales Mgr.—Mike Rhoades
- Pur. Agt.—Richard Cervantes

EQUIPMENT:
Eight pilger mills.

PRODUCTS and/or SERVICES:
Seamless stainless steel and nickel alloy pipe and tube.

Annual Capacity: 3,000 tons.

No. of Employees: 85.

Railroad and Shipping Facilities: Truck.

MARUICHI STEEL TUBE LTD.

Maruichi American Corp.
11529 Greenstone Ave.
Santa Fe Springs, CA 90670 USA
P: +1.562.903.8600
F: +1.562.903.8601
www.macsfs.com

- Pres.—Sho Morita
- Exec. Vice Pres.—Takuhiro Ishihara
- Gen. Mgr.—Maria Anderson
- Plant Gen. Mgr.—George Gomez
- Regional Account Execs.—David Shaffer, Jaycob Camacho
- Account Execs.—Lisa Hoey, Randy Pandolini, Mariko Wood
- Qual. Assur. Engr.—Ikuyoshi Kanai
- Ship. Coordinator—Mario Parada
- Contr. and Credit Mgr.—Rico Sarreal

EQUIPMENT:
Five steel tube and pipe mills and two slitting lines.

PRODUCTS and/or SERVICES:
Square, rectangular, and round structural and mechanical tube.

Maruichi Oregon Steel Tube LLC
8735 N. Harborgate St.
Portland, OR 97203 USA
P: +1.503.737.1200
F: +1.503.737.1201
http://most.us.com

- Vice Pres.—Brian Saunders
- Plant Engrg. Mgr.—Ikuyoshi Kanai
- Account Specialist—Megan Brown
- Inside Sales Rep.—Lindsay Zaleski
- Qual. Assur. Technicians—Shawn Long, Patrick Coyle
- Ship. Mgr.—Albert Braaten
- Ship. Coordinator—Rich Gaska
- Inventory Coordinator—Rick Grigsby

PRODUCTS and/or SERVICES:
Round, square and rectangular HSS.

Annual Capacity: 150,000 tons.

Maruichi Leavitt Pipe & Tube LLC
Headquarters:
1717 W. 115th St.
Chicago, IL 60643 USA
P: +1.800.532.8488 (Toll-Free);
+1.773.239.7700
tubeman@leavitt-tube.com
www.maruichi-leavitt.com

Plant Address:
1900 W. 119th St.
Chicago, IL 60643 USA
P: +1.773.881.2639

- Chief Exec. Officer and Pres.—Shunsaku Honda
- Dir. Mktg. and Business Dev.—Joe Davy
- Regional Sales Mgr. — HSS and Mech. (Chicagoland, IN, MI)—Mike Conces

PIPE and TUBE PLANTS

- Regional Sales Mgr. — HSS and Mech. (Central and Southern IL, CO, IA, MN, MO, ND, OK, SD, NE, KS, WI, WY) — Mark Goodkind
- Regional Sales Mgr. — HSS and Mech. (AL, AR, CT, DE, GA, OH, KY, LA, MS, ME, MD, MA, NH, NJ, NY, NC, PA, RI, SC, TN, VT, VA, WA, DC, WV, Canada and Mexico) — Pat Knutson
- ASTM A53 Pipe Inside Sales — Alex Kerkstra
- Automotive Tube Inside Sales — Kyle Maloney
- HSS and Mech. Inside Sales — Bianca Ivancevich
- ASTM A53, HSS and Mech. Inside Sales — Nancy Rogers
- HSS and Mech. Inside Sales and Mktg. Specialist — Jim Erhart
- HSS and Mech. Inside Sales Support — Jan Knapp

PRODUCTS and/or SERVICES:
Electric-welded steel tubing, including ASTM A500 HSS; ASTM A513 mechanical tube, ASTM A53 standard ERW pipe, automotive tubing and specialty products.

Geneva Structural Tubes LLC
1201 R St.
Geneva, NE 68361 USA
P: +1.402.759.4401

- Plant Mgr. — Andrew Simon

EQUIPMENT:
ERW pipe mill.

PRODUCTS and/or SERVICES:
HSS from 2 x 2 to 7 x 7 in., manufactured to ASTM, CSA and A500 specifications.

Annual Capacity: 60,000 metric tons.

Maruichimex S.A. de C.V.
Circuito Japon 112
Parque Industrial San Francisco
San Francisco de los Romo, AG, 20304
Mexico
P: +52.449.910.7046
www.maruichimex.com

EQUIPMENT:
Three HFIW tube production lines: two 2-in. and one 0.5-in. Recutting machines for CTL tubes.

PRODUCTS and/or SERVICES:
Round, square and rectangular tubing in carbon and stainless steel. Automotive tubing.

Annual Capacity: 24,000 tons.

Alphametal Mexico S.A. de C.V. (Alphamex)
Municipio de Tempezala 112
Parque Industrial Del Valle De Aguascalientes
San Francisco de los Romo, AG, 20358
Mexico
P: +52.449.158.0301

PRODUCTS and/or SERVICES:
Tube processing (piercing, reducing, expanding, bending, pressing and forming).

N

NAYLOR PIPE CO.
1230 E. 92nd St.
Chicago, IL 60619 USA
P: +1.773.721.9400
F: +1.773.721.9494
sales@naylorpipe.com
www.naylorpipe.com

- Chief Exec. Officer and Pres. — John Czulno
- Chief Oper. Officer and Exec. Vice Pres. — Mike O'Rourke
- Vice Pres. Info. Technology and Sales — Mike Griffin
- Vice Pres. H.R. and Sales — Brandon Deardorff

PIPE and TUBE PLANTS

EQUIPMENT:
Six spiral butt-weld and three spiral lockseam pipe machines. 4-in. ID through 96-in. OD from 14 gauge through 1/2-in. wall capabilities.

PRODUCTS and/or SERVICES:
Carbon steel: light- to heavy-wall spiral-weld pipe and pipe pilings. Pipe systems: fittings, flanges and connections; galvanized, coated and lined. Stainless steel: spiral-weld pipe and fittings.

No. of Employees: 70+.

Railroad and Shipping Facilities: Truck, rail.

NORTHWEST PIPE CO.
201 N.E. Park Plaza Dr., Suite 100
Vancouver, WA 98684 USA
P: +1.800.989.9631 (Toll-Free);
+1.360.397.6250
www.nwpipe.com

- Chief Exec. Officer and Pres.—Scott Montross
- Chief Financial Officer—Aaron Wilkins
- Vice Pres. H.R.—Megan Kendrick
- Exec. Vice Pres.—Miles Brittain
- Sr. Vice Pres. and Gen. Mgr., Engineered Steel Pressure Pipe—Eric Stokes
- Sr. Vice Pres. and Gen. Mgr., Precast Infrastructure and Engineered Systems—Michael Wray
- Vice Pres and Gen. Mgr., Permalok—Henry Goff

PRODUCTS and/or SERVICES:
Engineered steel water pipe systems, Permalok® steel casing pipe, bar-wrapped concrete pipe, and precast and reinforced concrete products. Additional products include custom linings, coatings, joints, fittings and specialized components.

Engineered Steel Plants:

Adelanto Plant
12351 Rancho Road
Adelanto, CA 92301 USA
P: +1.760.246.3191

Parkersburg Plant
183 Northwest Dr.
Washington, WV 26181 USA
P: +1.304.863.3316

Portland Plant
12005 N. Burgard Way
Portland, OR 97203 USA
P: +1.800.824.9824 (Toll-Free);
+1.503.285.1400

Saginaw Plant
351 Longhorn Road
Saginaw, TX 76179 USA
P: +1.817.847.1402

SLRC Plant
Via Ameron No. 100
Interior B, Col. Las Adelitas
San Luis Río Colorado, SO, 83520
Mexico
P: +01152.1.6535772200

St. Louis Plant
472 Paul Ave.
St. Louis, MO 63135 USA
P: +1.314.524.1900

Tracy Plant
10100 W. Linne Road
Tracy, CA 95377 USA
P: +1.209.836.5050

NUCOR TUBULAR PRODUCTS
1915 Rexford Road
Charlotte, NC 28211 USA
www.nucortubular.com

- Chief Exec. Officer and Pres., Nucor Corp.—Leon Topalian
- Exec. Vice Pres. Sheet and Tubular Products—Rex Query
- Group Structural Sales Mgr.—Doug Rife
- Sales Mgr., Eastern Region — Structural—Jason Hollis
- Sales Mgr., Western Region — Structural—Aaron Barnett
- Sales Mgr., A53 and Sprinkler Pipe—Jeremy Cooper
- Inside Sales Supv. — Elec. Conduit—Tamatha Baker
- District Sales Mgr. — Elec. Conduit/Key Accts.—Kimberly Koontz

PIPE and TUBE PLANTS

- District Sales Mgr.— Elec. Conduit/ Southeast and OEM—Robert Sears
- District Sales Mgr. — Elec. Conduit/ Northeast—Steve Funk
- District Sales Mgr. — Elec. Conduit/ Western—Bill Desrosiers

PRODUCTS and/or SERVICES: Nucor Tubular Products (NTP) Group consists of eight tubular facilities that are strategically located in close proximity to Nucor Corp.'s sheet mills. NTP Group produces HSS steel tubing, mechanical steel tubing, piling, sprinkler pipe, galvanized tube, heat-treated tubing and electrical conduit.

Annual Capacity: 1,365,000 tons.

No. of Employees: 1,000+

Nucor Tubular Products Birmingham
3525 Richard Arrington Jr. Blvd. N
Birmingham, AL 35234 USA
P: +1.205.251.1884
F: +1.205.251.1553

- Inside Sales Supv.—Tim Nichols

Nucor Tubular Products Cedar Springs
633 Georgia Tubing Road
Cedar Springs, GA 39832 USA
P: +1.229.372.4501
F: +1.229.372.4749

- Plant Mgr.—Jim Lynch

Nucor Tubular Products Chicago
6226 W. 74th St.
Chicago, IL 60638 USA
P: +1.708.496.0380
F: +1.708.563.1950

- Gen. Mgr.—Randy Spicer
- Inside Sales Supv.—Kristen Kuzanek

Nucor Tubular Products Decatur
2000 Independence Ave. NW
Decatur, AL 35601 USA
P: +1.256.340.7420
F: +1.256.340.7415

Nucor Tubular Products Louisville
7301 Logistics Dr.
Louisville, KY 40258 USA
P: +1.502.995.5900
F: +1.502.995.5873

- Gen. Mgr.—Nickole Taylor

Nucor Tubular Products Madison LLC
4004 US-421
Madison, IN 47250 USA
P: +1.812.265.9255
F: +1.812.273.3853

- Gen. Mgr.—Josh Uhinck

Nucor Tubular Products Marseilles
1201 Broadway St.
Marseilles, IL 61341 USA
P: +1.815.795.4400
F: +1.815.795.6378

- Gen. Mgr.—Randy Spicer

Nucor Tubular Products Trinity
2000 Cooperage Way
Trinity, AL 35673 USA
P: +1.256.301.5560
F: +1.256.301.5561

PIPE and TUBE PLANTS

P

PARAGON INDUSTRIES INC.
3378 W. Hwy. 117
Sapulpa, OK 74066 USA
P: +1.918.291.4459
F: +1.918.291.0918
www.paragonindinc.com

PRODUCTS and/or SERVICES: Licensed manufacturer of API 5L line pipe and API 5CT casing products. Also manufactures proprietary-grade casings for the oilfield, as well as ASTM A53 Standard/Mechanical, A500 Structural, A252 Piling and UL Listed/FM Listed A135/A795 sprinkler pipe grades. Manufactures only rounds, in diameters ranging from 4 1/2 in. to 16 in. Wall sizes from 0.125 in. to 0.500 in. Operates a threading facility for the manufacture of API licensed threads as well as semi-premium and premium connections. Additional facilities on-site include a fusion-bonded epoxy coating facility and a heat treating facility for the manufacture of alloy casing products.

PHILLIPS TUBE GROUP
P: +1.800.841.4207 (Toll-Free)
www.phillipstube.com

– Chief Exec. Officer—Angela Phillips
– Pres.—Michael Zara

Middletown Tube Works
2201 Trine St.
Middletown, OH 45044 USA
P: +1.513.727.0080
info@middletowntube.com
www.middletowntube.com

PRODUCTS and/or SERVICES: Specializes in coated steel products. Manufactures tubes in aluminized, galvanized, galvannealed, Galvalume®, zinc-nickel, J2340 steel types and non-coated products, hot-rolled, HRP&O and cold-rolled. Also manufactures 400 series stainless steel tubing for higher corrosion-resistant products.

Phillips Tube Group of Alabama
1505 Dowzer Ave.
Pell City, AL 35125 USA
P: +1.205.338.4771
F: +1.205.338.4827

PRODUCTS and/or SERVICES: Specializes in custom tubular designs and twisted tube technology. Heat exchangers for heat pump applications.

Shelby Welded Tube
5578 State Rte. 61N
Shelby, OH 44875 USA
P: +1.800.365.1340 (Toll-Free)
F: +1.419.347.5231
info@shelbytube.com
www.shelbytube.com

PRODUCTS and/or SERVICES: Provides high-quality specialty welded tubing capable of severe fabrication in all shapes and sizes. Also specializes in small-diameter tubing from aluminized, galvanized, galvannealed, Galvalume, and zinc-nickel steels.

PHOENIX TUBE CO. INC.
1185 Win Dr.
Bethlehem, PA 18017 USA
P: +1.800.526.2124 (Toll-Free);
   +1.610.865.5337
F: +1.610.865.9832
sales@phoenixtube.com
www.phoenixtube.com

– Chief Exec. Officer—David Reale
– Pres.—Andrew Reale
– Engrg. Mgr.—Charles Kissinger
– Regional Sales—Illy Pesce, Scott Umstead, Zach Eisenreich, Ashley Marino

PRODUCTS and/or SERVICES: Stainless steel tubing, rounds, squares, rectangles, and processed flat bar for ornamental and structural applications. Distribution and service centers throughout the U.S. Full line of polishing and slitting capabilities.

PIPE and TUBE PLANTS

PLYMOUTH TUBE CO.
29W150 Warrenville Road
Warrenville, IL 60555 USA
P: +1.800.323.9506 (Toll-Free);
+1.630.393.3556
F: +1.630.393.3551
sales@plymouth.com
www.plymouth.com

- Chmn.—D.C. Van Pelt Jr.
- Chief Exec. Officer and Pres.—Drew Van Pelt
- Chief Financial Officer—Fede Barreto
- Group Vice Pres.—Chuck Banker
- Vice Pres. Strategic Initiatives—Ajay Ramaswami
- Vice Pres., Mktg.—Holly Both
- Vice Pres. H.R.—Angela Antrim
- Dir. of Finance and Acctg.—Deb Lange
- Vice Pres. Plymouth Business Systems—Mel Mendoza

PRODUCTS and/or SERVICES:
Specialty manufacturer of carbon alloy, nickel alloy and stainless precision tubing, as well as engineered shapes. All Plymouth Tube U.S. facilities are certified to ISO 9002. The carbon and alloy steel tubing facilities are further certified to QS 9000.

Railroad and Shipping Facilities: Truck, rail, barge.

Chicago, IL
4555 W. Armitage Ave.
Chicago, IL 60639 USA
P: +1.773.489.0226

PRODUCTS and/or SERVICES:
Slitting capabilities: entire coil or partial. Edging: standard AISI #1 to #6 edges or specialized custom edges. Winding options: pancake wound coils, oscillate wound coils.

East Troy, WI (Trent)
2056 Young St.
East Troy, WI 53120 USA
P: +1.262.642.7321

PRODUCTS and/or SERVICES:
Welded austenitic, ferritic, and superferritic stainless and nickel-alloy tubing, $1/8$- to 4-in. ODs, lengths up to 130 ft.

Eupora, MS
212 Industrial Park Road
Eupora, MS 39744 USA
P: +1.662.258.2420

PRODUCTS and/or SERVICES:
Welded and drawn carbon hydraulic fluid line tubing, $1/4$- to $1\ 3/4$-in. OD, and welded carbon steel tubing (DOM), $1/8$- to $1\ 3/4$-in. OD.

Hopkinsville, KY
201 Commerce Ct.
Hopkinsville, KY 42240 USA
P: +1.270.886.6631

PRODUCTS and/or SERVICES:
Extrusion facility for carbon steel, stainless steel, nickel alloy and titanium near-net extruded shapes. Must fit within a 6-in. dia.

Salisbury, MD
2000 Industrial Pkwy.
Salisbury, MD 21801 USA
P: +1.410.749.1666

PRODUCTS and/or SERVICES:
Stainless steel and nickel alloys in seamless, welded, and drawn tubing from $1/8$- to 1-in. OD with lengths to 140 ft. High-purity tubing available.

West Monroe, LA
601 Grantham Ave.
West Monroe, LA 71292 USA
P: +1.318.388.3360

PRODUCTS and/or SERVICES:
Seamless and welded stainless and nickel alloy tubing, $3/8$- to 2-in. ODs with lengths to 150 ft. U-bending available.

Winamac, IN
572 W. State Road 14
Winamac, IN 46996 USA
P: +1.574.946.3125

PRODUCTS and/or SERVICES:
Hot mill: hot-finished carbon and alloy steel tubing, 2- to 5-in. OD. Cold-drawn carbon and alloy steel tubing, $3/4$- to 5.563-in. OD. Capabilities of up to 6-in. OD.

PIPE and TUBE PLANTS

PRECITUBO
km 11.4 Carretera al Castillo
El Salto, JAL, 45685 Mexico
P: +52.33.3688.0002;
  +52.33.3688.0130;
  +52.33.3688.0042 (Sales)
www.precitubo.com.mx

- Gen. Mgr.—Miguel Angel Torres S.,
  matorress@condumex.com.mx
- Prodn. Chief—Nestor D. Camacho S.,
  ndcamachos@condumex.com.mx
- Sales Mgr.—Alfredo Hernandez R.,
  ahernan@condumex.com.mx

PRODUCTS and/or SERVICES:
Welded and seamless carbon steel tubes.

PTC ALLIANCE
Copperleaf Corporate Centre
6051 Wallace Road Ext., Suite 200
Wexford, PA 15090 USA
P: +1.412.299.7900
F: +1.412.299.2619
www.ptcalliance.com

- Chief Exec. Officer and Pres.—Cary Hart
- Chief Financial Officer—Steve Bogle
- Chief Tech. Officer—Telmo Souza

EQUIPMENT:
Eight producing plants of tube and/or pipe.

PRODUCTS and/or SERVICES:
Manufacturer and marketer of pipe and welded, seamless, and cold-drawn mechanical steel tubing and tubular shapes, fabricated parts, and chrome-plated precision bar. Major markets include steel service centers, automotive and truck, construction and agricultural equipment, machinery, and appliances. ISO 9001 and ISO/TS16949 compliant.

Facility Locations:

Alliance, OH
640 Keystone St.
Alliance, OH 44601 USA
P: +1.330.821.5700

PRODUCTS and/or SERVICES:
DOM, ERW, hot-stretched reduced solutions.

Beaver Falls, PA (2 Locations)
4400 W. Third Ave.
Beaver Falls, PA 15010 USA
P: +1.724.847.7137

PRODUCTS and/or SERVICES:
DOM, CDS solutions, value-added solutions.

Chicago Heights, IL
475 E. 16th St.
Chicago Heights, IL 60411 USA
P: +1.708.757.4747

PRODUCTS and/or SERVICES:
DOM solutions.

Darlington, PA
305 Cannelton Road
Darlington, PA 16115 USA
P: +1.800.274.8823 (Toll-Free)

PRODUCTS and/or SERVICES:
ERW, hot-stretched reduced solutions.

Fairbury, IL
23041 E. 800 North Road
Fairbury, IL 61739 USA
P: +1.815.692.4900

PRODUCTS and/or SERVICES:
DOM, ERW, value-added solutions.

Hannibal, MO — Enduro Industries
2001 Orchard Ave.
Hannibal, MO 63401 USA
P: +1.573.629.1111

PRODUCTS and/or SERVICES:
Chrome plating solutions.

Houston, TX — PTC Liberty Tubulars
13500 Industrial Road
Houston, TX 77015 USA
P: +1.713.231.2929
www.ptclibertytubulars.com

EQUIPMENT:
Danieli soaking furnace, heat treat services, hydrostatic testing, phased array ultrasonic inspection, advanced threading capabilities, integrated rail spur.

PIPE and TUBE PLANTS

PRODUCTS and/or SERVICES:
Finishing of seamless tube up to 7.625-in. OD and threading up to 13.375-in. OD.

Annual Capacity: 120,000 tons.

Liberty, TX — PTC Liberty Tubulars
1100 FM 3361
Liberty, TX 77575 USA
P: +1.713.289.5555
www.ptclibertytubulars.com

EQUIPMENT:
Two ERW mills, two threading lines with high-speed PMC machines and CNC threading, dedicated semi-premium threading line, hydrostatic testers, phased-array ultrasonic inspection system.

PRODUCTS and/or SERVICES:
ERW pipe for downhole casing and tubing applications (4.5-in. to 13.375-in. OD); processing and finishing services.

Annual Capacity: 480,000 tons.

Richmond, IN
1480 N.W. 11th St.
Richmond, IN 47374 USA
P: +1.765.259.3334

PRODUCTS and/or SERVICES:
Value-added solutions.

R

RYMCO

Conduit S.A. de C.V.
Av. Mexico Oriente No. 36
Col. Sta. Maria Tupetlac
Ecatepec de Morelos, MX, 55400
Mexico
P: +52.55.5779.8205
F: +52.55.5755.6101
www.conduit.com.mx
www.rymco.com.mx

- Dir. Gen.—Rubén Mischne

PRODUCTS and/or SERVICES:
Conduit pipe, EMT, IMC, RMC, Real Color® EMT, galvanized square pipe.

RYMCO USA
1335 Boyles St., Suite A
Houston, TX 77020 USA
P: +1.833.RYMCO.US (796.2687);
+1.832.962.7688
info@rymcousa.com
www.rymcousa.com

- Pres.—Mauricio Bielaz
- Vice Pres. Oprs.—Jesse Ghitman

PRODUCTS and/or SERVICES:
EMT pipe, IMC pipe, RMC pipe, Real Color® EMT, stainless steel RMC.

PIPE and TUBE PLANTS

S

SAMUEL ASSOCIATED TUBE GROUP

PRODUCTS and/or SERVICES: North American supplier of welded and cold-drawn stainless steel and special nickel alloy tubing. Manufacturing facilities in Canada and Mexico supply laser-, TIG-, and plasma-welded and cold-drawn stainless steel and high-nickel alloy tubular products globally. Manufactures tubing in a variety of shapes and rounds, with an extensive size range in more than 50 grades of stainless steel and high-nickel alloys.

Birmingham, AL
1400 Red Hollow Road
Birmingham, AL 35215 USA
P: +1.800.456.TUBE (8823) (Toll-Free);
 +1.205.856.1300
F: +1.205.856.1398
contactus@tubularproducts.com
www.tubularproducts.com
www.samuel.com

PRODUCTS and/or SERVICES: Straight and bent tubing, laser cut, CNC machined and fabricated components, welded subassemblies, customized, environmentally friendly packaging.

No. of Employees: 200+.

Saltillo, CA, Mexico
Calle 17, No. 3689 Amp. Morelos
Saltillo, CA, 25017 Mexico
P: +1.844.438.6400

PRODUCTS and/or SERVICES: Straight and bent tubing, laser cut, CNC machined and fabricated components, welded subassemblies, customized, environmentally friendly packaging.

No. of Employees: 200+.

Markham, ON, Canada
7455 Woodbine Ave.
Markham, ON L3R 1A7 Canada
P: +1.800.387.4217 (Toll-Free);
 +1.905.475.6464
F: +1.905.475.5202
stainlesscda@associatedtube.com
tubularsolutions@samuel.com

SEARING INDUSTRIES INC.
8901 Arrow Rte.
Rancho Cucamonga, CA 91730 USA
P: +1.909.948.3030
F: +1.909.466.0534
si@searingindustries.com
www.searingindustries.com

- Chief Exec. Officer—Lee Searing
- Pres.—Jim Searing
- Exec. Vice Pres. Finance—Margaret Cantu
- Exec. Vice Pres. Sales—Glenn Baker, Steve McDaniel
- Exec. Vice Pres. Oprs.—Richard Searing
- Plant Mgr.—Miguel Hernandez
- Lab Technician—Salvador Rodriguez

PRODUCTS and/or SERVICES: Produces ASTM A500 B/C and A1085 structural tubing, A500 Grade B/C structural pipe, A513 ornamental and mechanical tubing, and A252 pipe piling. Value-added services include transportation, laser capabilities, in-line coating, CTL, end finishing and toll processing.

Searing Industries Wyoming Inc.
5310 Clear Creek Pkwy.
Cheyenne, WY 82007 USA
P: +1.800.323.9988 (Toll-Free)

- Plant Mgr.—Victor Limon

PIPE and TUBE PLANTS

STERLING PIPE & TUBE INC.
5335 Enterprise Blvd.
Toledo, OH 43612 USA
P: +1.800.888.2013 (Toll-Free);
 +1.419.729.9756
F: +1.419.729.2757
sales@sterlingpipeandtube.com
www.sterlingpipeandtube.com

- Vice Pres. Sales and Admin.—Dennis Krout
- Regional Sales Mgr.—John Martinelli
- Dir. of Mktg.—Bill Kuhlman
- Inside Sales—Greg Denis, Kathy Ledyard
- Qual. Engr.—Cheryl Kynard
- Qual. Mgr.—Sherri Keller

EQUIPMENT:
Five tube mills.

PRODUCTS and/or SERVICES:
Supplier of electric-welded steel tubing and steel pipe. Produces round steel tubing (1–6 $5/8$-in. dia.), square steel tubing ($3/4$–3 in.) and rectangular steel tubing (1 $1/2$ x $3/4$–4 x 2 in.), as well as mechanical tubing.

Railroad and Shipping Facilities: Truck.

T

T&B TUBE CO.
4000 E. 7th Ave.
Gary, IN 46403 USA
P: +1.219.979.8100
F: +1.219.979.8101
www.tbtube.com

- Pres.—Jack Jones
- Oprs. Mgr.—Kevin Barker
- Inside Sales—Jay Vasquez, Ed Ciechomski
- Acct. Mgr.—Christine Schwartz
- Acct. Rep.—Melissa Fernandez

EQUIPMENT:
Five tube mills, five high-speed recut machines.

PRODUCTS and/or SERVICES:
Specializing in manufacturing CTL steel tube for a variety of applications and customers that include: point-of-purchase displays, outdoor products, tube fabricators and various other OEMs. ISO 9001:2000 certified.

TENARIS
www.tenaris.com

- Chmn. and Chief Exec. Officer—Paolo Rocca
- Chief Financial Officer—Alicia Móndolo
- Chief Ind. Officer—Antonio Caprera
- Chief Supply Chain Officer—Gabriel Casanova
- Chief Digital and Info. Officer—Alejandro Lammertyn
- Chief H.R. Officer—Luis Scartascini
- Chief Technology Officer—Marcelo Ramos
- Pres., USA—Luca Zanotti
- Pres., Canada—Ricardo Prosperi
- Pres., Mexico—Sergio de la Maza
- Commercial Dir., USA—Laura Urrutia

PRODUCTS and/or SERVICES:
OCTG, onshore and offshore line pipe, seamless and ERW tubes, premium connections, coiled tubing, sucker rods, OCTG accessories.

Tenaris AlgomaTubes
547 Wallace Terrace
Sault Ste. Marie, ON P6C 1L9 Canada
P: +1.705.941.6717
lcarlucci@tenaris.com

PRODUCTS and/or SERVICES:
Seamless and welded pipe, premium connections.

PIPE and TUBE PLANTS

TenarisAmbridge
23rd St. and Duss Ave.
Ambridge, PA 15003 USA
P: +1.724.251.2515

- Plant Mgr.—Frank Corona

EQUIPMENT:
Seamless tube mill.

PRODUCTS and/or SERVICES:
Seamless tubing and pipe.

Annual Capacity: 450,000 tons.

No. of Employees: 256.

TenarisBayCity
7960 State Hwy. 35
Bay City, TX 77414 USA
P: +1.979.323.5200
rcheyne@tenaris.com

EQUIPMENT:
Barrel-type piercing mill, 6-stand mandrel mill, 4-stand extracting mill, induction furnace, 24-stand stretch-reduction mill, roll pass measurement system.

PRODUCTS and/or SERVICES:
Seamless tubes.

Annual Capacity: 600,000 tons.

Tenaris Baytown
2600 E. Grand Pkwy. S
Baytown, TX 77523 USA
P: +1.281.841.7709
rpatron@tenaris.com

- Dir. of Oprs.—Rafael Patron

EQUIPMENT:
Pipe and tube finishing mill.

PRODUCTS and/or SERVICES:
Heat treating, threading and premium connections.

TenarisCamanche
2011 7th Ave.
Camanche, IA 52730 USA
P: +1.563.242.0000
F: +1.563.242.9408

- Plant Mgr.—Steve Lawrence

EQUIPMENT:
ERW pipe mill and threading equipment.

PRODUCTS and/or SERVICES:
Produces pipe from 4 1/2 to 8 5/8 in. and related HSS. Pipe manufactured to API, ASTM and A500 specifications.

Annual Capacity: 250,000 tons.

TenarisConroe
669 FM 3083
Conroe, TX 77301 USA
P: +1.936.539.2136

PRODUCTS and/or SERVICES:
Heat treatment and finishing of pipe.

TenarisHickman
5000 N. County Road 967
Blytheville, AR 72315 USA
P: +1.870.766.5000

EQUIPMENT:
High-speed ERW pipe mill. Slitter. Heat treating, threading.

PRODUCTS and/or SERVICES:
Produces pipe from 1 1/2 to 4 1/2 in. and manufactured to API, CSA, ASTM and A500 specifications.

Annual Capacity: 250,000 tons.

TenarisKoppel
6403 Sixth Ave.
Koppel, PA 16136 USA
P: +1.724.843.7100

EQUIPMENT:
EAF.

PRODUCTS and/or SERVICES:
Continuous cast round billets. Heat treating.

Annual Capacity: 600,000 tons.

No. of Employees: 259.

TenarisWilder
100 Steel Plant Road
Wilder, KY 41071 USA
P: +1.859.292.6060

- Plant Mgr.—James Montgomery

EQUIPMENT:
Two ERW pipe mills. 4 1/2 to 16 in. OD.

PIPE and TUBE PLANTS

PRODUCTS and/or SERVICES:
Welded pipe, pipe threading.

Annual Capacity: 600,000 tons.

Tenaris Coiled Tubes LLC (Downhole Center)
8615 E. Sam Houston Pkwy.
Houston, TX 77044 USA
F: +1.281.458.2883

- Vice Pres.—Martin Urcola
- Oprs. Dir.—Luis Reyes

PRODUCTS and/or SERVICES:
HFW carbon steel tube and pipe.

Annual Capacity: 40,000 metric tons.

Tenaris Coiled Tubes LLC (Subsea Center)
8762 Clay Road
Houston, TX 77080 USA
F: +1.713.460.1500

- Vice Pres.—Martin Urcola
- Oprs. Dir.—Luis Reyes

PRODUCTS and/or SERVICES:
Laser-welded stainless steel tube and pipe.

Annual Capacity: 3,200 metric tons.

TenarisTamsa
km 433.7 Carr. Mexico - Veracruz
Via Xalapa
Veracruz, VE, 91697 Mexico
P: +52.229.989.1100.1322
omartinez@tamsa.com.mx

PRODUCTS and/or SERVICES:
Seamless tubes, sucker rods, components.

Annual Capacity: 1,230,000 metric tons.

TEXAS TUBULAR PRODUCTS INC.
3681 FM 250
Lone Star, TX 75668 USA
P: +1.800.270.4856 (Toll-Free)
F: +1.903.639.3239
www.texastubular.com

- Vice Pres. Oprs.—Howard Henderson
- Vice Pres. and Gen. Mgr.—Michael Thompson

EQUIPMENT:
Two ERW pipe mills, finished goods warehouse.

PRODUCTS and/or SERVICES:
Distributor of new mill secondary/reject pipe. Producer of ERW annealed carbon steel pipe in API line pipe grades and ASTM grades A500B and A53B from 2 $^3/_8$ in. to 8 $^5/_8$ in. OD. 36–72 in. widths, 0.054–0.625 in. gauges, 48–999 in. lengths, 80,000 lb. max coil weight.

Annual Capacity: 60,000 tons.

Railroad and Shipping Facilities: Rail, truck.

TUBAC S.A. DE C.V.
Av. Lázaro Cárdenas No. 329
Ote. Int. 3E, Col. Valle Oriente
San Pedro Garza García, NL, 66269
Mexico
P: +51.81.8299.4242
hernando@tubac.com.mx
www.tubac.com.mx

PRODUCTS and/or SERVICES:
Manufacturing of steel pipe with spiral-welded seam, various diameters, thicknesses and lengths. Supply and installation of steel pipe and special pieces. In-plant inner and outer coating of steel pipe and structures, hydrostatic testing. Docking and interconnections.

TUBERÍAS PROCARSA S.A. DE C.V., a Subsidiary of Industíias CH (ICH)
Prolongación Francisco I. Madero s/n
Zona Industrial, Cd. Frontera
Monclova, CA, 25680 Mexico
P: +1.866.636.2266 (Toll-Free);
   +1.866.636.0970 (Toll-Free Sales)
contacto@procarsa.mx
www.procarsa.mx

PRODUCTS and/or SERVICES:
Pipelines for hydrocarbon transportation, drilling pipes, pile pipes, water pipes, round- and square-section pipes for structural uses and pipes for marine platforms, among many

PIPE and TUBE PLANTS

others. ERW, DSAW, HSAW, and epoxy coatings for pipes.

Annual Capacity: 750,000 metric tons.

TUBESA S.A. DE C.V.
Culiacán No. 123, Int. 1307
Colonia Hipódromo, Del. Cuauhtémoc
Mexico City, DF, 06100 Mexico
P: +52.55.5271.9311
F: +52.55.5271.9357
sales@tubesa.com
www.tubesa.com

PRODUCTS and/or SERVICES:
Spiral-welded carbon steel pipe in lengths up to 88 feet (26.82 m), 20 to 120 in. dia., and sprinklers ¼ to 1 in.

TUBULAR STEEL INC.
Headquarters and St. Louis Sales Office:
1031 Executive Parkway Dr.
St. Louis, MO 63141 USA
P: +1.314.851.9200
F: +1.314.851.9336
info@tubularsteel.com
www.tubularsteel.com

– Pres.—Todd Roberts

PRODUCTS and/or SERVICES:
Products include: square and rectangular structural tubing; stainless steel bar, pipe and tube; welded pipe; seamless carbon mechanical tubing; as-welded mechanical tubing; alloy mechanical tubing; seamless pipe; DOM, honed and hydraulic tubing. Services include: sales, delivery, cutting, finishing and quality assurance.

Cleveland Sales Office and Service Center
7440 Deer Trail Lane
Lorain, OH 44053 USA
P: +1.440.960.6100
F: +1.440.960.6105

Houston Sales Office and Service Center
27700 Highway Blvd.
Katy, TX 77493 USA
P: +1.281.371.5200
F: +1.281.371.5204

Los Angeles Sales Office and Service Center
2750 N. Locust Ave.
Rialto, CA 92376 USA
P: +1.909.429.6900
F: +1.909.429.6939

St. Louis Service Center
7220 Polson Lane
Hazelwood, MO 63042 USA

Savannah Sales Office
P: +1.800.388.7563 (Toll-Free)
F: +1.912.748.2409

Metalcraft Enterprises – Fabrication Operations
202 Industrial Dr.
New Haven, MO 63068 USA
P: +1.573.237.3016
F: +1.573.237.2330

TWIN BROTHERS MARINE LLC
Port of West St. Mary
322 Twin Brothers Road
Franklin, LA 70538 USA
P: +1.337.923.4981
F: +1.337.923.4349
frontdesk@tbmc.com
www.tbmc.com

– Pres.—Darrell J. Webster
– Vice Pres. Finance—Wayne P. Theriot
– Dir. of Business Dev.—Ranis Avet

EQUIPMENT:
Three tubular rolling mills.

PRODUCTS and/or SERVICES:
Heavy industrial steel fabricator of offshore oil and gas platforms and steel modules, and manufacturer of large-diameter, heavy-wall tubular products, pressure vessels, cargo tanks, cement kilns, debarkers, suction piles, bridge piles, etc. In-house special pipe manufacturing capability. ISO 9001:2015 certified.

Railroad and Shipping Facilities: Truck, highway, rail, ship, water.

PIPE and TUBE PLANTS

U–V

U. S. STEEL TUBULAR PRODUCTS
460 Wildwood Forest Dr., Suite 300S
Spring, TX 77380 USA
P: +1.877.893.9461
F: +1.281.671.3879
www.usstubular.com

- Head of Tubular Solutions—Scott M. Dorn

PRODUCTS and/or SERVICES:
North America's largest fully integrated tubular products manufacturer. OCTG offerings include casing and tubing, connections, and accessories. Standard and line pipe offerings include seamless, HFEW, API 5L, A106 seamless carbon, A252 piling, A54 seamless and welded, and A523 cable circuit. U. S. Steel Tubular Products also provides casing, tubular and rig site services.

Annual Capacity: 1.9 million net tons.

Fairfield Tubular Operations
5700 Valley Road
Fairfield, AL 35064 USA
P: +1.205.783.4150

PRODUCTS and/or SERVICES:
Seamless steel casing from 4 1/2 to 9 7/8 in. OD; standard pipe from 4 1/2 to 8 5/8 in. OD.

Annual Capacity: 750,000 tons.

Lone Star Tubular Operations
6866 Hwy. 259 S
Lone Star, TX 75668 USA
P: +1.903.656.6521

EQUIPMENT:
Two tube mills.

PRODUCTS and/or SERVICES:
Full body normalized ERW tubular products.

Lorain Tubular Operations
2199 E. 28th St.
Lorain, OH 45055 USA
P: +1.440.240.2500

PRODUCTS and/or SERVICES:
OCTG, casing, standard and line pipe, couplings.

U. S. Steel Oilwell Services and Offshore Operations
9518 E. Mt. Houston Road
Houston, TX 77050 USA
P: +1.281.458.9944

PRODUCTS and/or SERVICES:
Full-length threading of pipe from 3 1/2 to 20 in. OD, premium finishing and processing services, proprietary tubing and casing accessories. Inspection services including full-body ultrasonic, weld line, electromagnetic, visual, dry or wet special-end-area and dye penetration. Pipe storage.

Wheeling Machine Products
5411 Industrial Dr. S
Pine Bluff, AR 71602 USA
P: +1.870.247.5945

EQUIPMENT:
Two facilities in Pine Bluff, AR, and Hughes Spring, TX.

PRODUCTS and/or SERVICES:
Couplings and specialized couplings from 2.375 in. to 20 in.

UNITED TUBE CORP.
960 Lake Road
Medina, OH 44256 USA
P: +1.800.321.TUBE (8823) (Toll-Free);
  +1.330.725.4196
F: +1.330.723.2092
sales@unitedtube.com
www.unitedtube.com

- Vice Pres. Sales—Jack Bretz
- Inside Sales—Tim Gaertner, Mark Segedi, Justin Traft

PRODUCTS and/or SERVICES:
Manufacturer of quality mechanical welded steel tubing, using materials such as: HRP&O, cold-rolled commercial quality, United high-yield

PIPE and TUBE PLANTS

structural steel tubing; galvanized; HSLA pickled and oiled. Variety of sizes and gauges available, including round, square and rectangle.

US PREMIER TUBE MILLS
2855 Michigan Road
Madison, IN 47250 USA
P: +1.812.265.7001
F: +1.812.274.0345
contact@usptmills.com
www.usptmills.com

PRODUCTS and/or SERVICES: High-quality fully galvanized steel fence pipe and tubing for the high security, industrial/commercial, and residential markets. Available in a variety of gauges, diameters and lengths of more than 40 ft. Offers polyester and polyolefin powder coating meeting ASTM F1043 and ASTM F934 standards.

No. of Employees: 111.

VALLOUREC CANADA
407 2nd St. SW, Suite 1830
Calgary, AB T2P 2Y3 Canada
P: +1.403.233.0119
sales.vca-can@vallourec.com
www.vallourec.com

PRODUCTS and/or SERVICES: Seamless hot-rolled steel tubes for all applications. Carbon steels, alloyed and special steels. Various sizes available.

Vallourec Canada St. John's
10 St. Anne's Crescent
Paradise, NL A1L 1K1 Canada
P: +1.709.687.3035
sales.vca-can@vallourec.com
www.vallourec.com

PRODUCTS and/or SERVICES: Seamless hot-rolled steel tubes for all applications. Premium connections field services.

VALLOUREC STAR LP
2669 Martin Luther King Jr. Blvd.
Youngstown, OH 44510 USA
P: +1.330.742.6300
F: +1.330.742.6315
info@vallourec.com

- Pres.—Eric Shuster
- Dir., Safety and Qual.—Sean Smith
- Gen. Mgr. Oprs., North—John Kettler
- Gen. Mgr. Oprs., South—Karl Crouch
- Mgr., H.R.—Ryan Hutchison
- Mgr. Meltshop, MPM Oprs. and Ship.—Mark Rambo
- Mgr. FQM Oprs.—Jake Buzzard
- Plant Mgr., Muskogee—James Lester

EQUIPMENT:
One 90-metric-ton (100-short-ton) EAF; one 3-strand bloom caster; one ladle refining station, two seamless pipe mills, 2 3/8- to 10 3/4-in. dia., heat treat, threading, inspection.

PRODUCTS and/or SERVICES: Seamless pipe.

Annual Capacity: 550,000 tons.

No. of Employees: 500+.

VEST INC.
6023 Alcoa Ave.
Vernon, CA 90058 USA
P: +1.800.521.6370 (Toll-Free)
 +1.323.581.8823
sales@vestinc.com
www.vestinc.com

- Pres.—Yoshiki Murakami
- Gen. Mgr.—Kaz Sawai

EQUIPMENT:
Six tube mills.

PRODUCTS and/or SERVICES: Electric welded carbon steel tubing. Ornamental tubing (1/2-in.–3 in. squares and rectangles, .035 in. to .120 in. thickness), A513 mechanical tubing (5/8-in. to 4 in. OD), and A500 HSS (1 1/2 in. to 10 in. squares and rectangles, up to 5/8-in. thick).

No. of Employees: 85.

Railroad and Shipping Facilities: Truck, rail.

PIPE and TUBE PLANTS

W–Z

WELSPUN TUBULAR LLC
9301 Frazier Pike
Little Rock, AR 72206 USA
P: +1.501.301.8800
F: +1.501.490.1759
www.welspun.com

- Vice Pres. Exec. Mgmt.—Snehal Patel
- Vice Pres. Mktg.—Todd Phillips
- Asst. Vice Pres. QAOC—P.N. Mahida
- Dir. Supply Chain Mgmt.—Mihir Desai

PRODUCTS and/or SERVICES:
Up to 80-ft. large-diameter spiral pipe, HFIW small-diameter pipe and coating plant.

ZEKELMAN INDUSTRIES INC.
227 W. Monroe St., Suite 2600
Chicago, IL 60606 USA
P: +1.312.275.1600
info@zekelman.com
www.zekelman.com

- Exec. Chmn. and Chief Exec. Officer—Barry Zekelman
- Chief Financial Officer—Michael J. Graham
- Pres. Z Modular and Exec. Vice Pres. Zekelman Industries—Michael McNamara
- Exec. Vice Pres. and Chief Oper. Officer, Tubular Products Div.—Tom Muth
- Exec. Vice Pres. and Chief Commercial Officer Atlas Tube—Randy Boswell
- Pres. HSS and Piling—Jeff Cole
- Pres. Elec.—Jim Hays
- Pres. Standard Pipe—Kevin Kelly
- Pres. Fence and Mech.—Nick Shubat
- Pres. Sharon Tube—Dan Reilly
- Exec. Vice Pres. of Strategic Procurement—Michael E. Mechley

PRODUCTS and/or SERVICES:
HSS, electrical conduit, electrical fittings, standard pipe, mechanical tube, pipe piling, fence, DOM, sprinkler, OCTG products, line pipe, modular construction services.

Annual Capacity: 2.7 million tons.

No. of Employees: 2,700+.

Atlas Tube Headquarters
1855 E. 122nd St.
Chicago, IL 60633 USA
P: +1.800.733.5683 (Toll-Free)
+1.773.646.4500
info@atlastube.com
www.atlastube.com

Atlas Tube
171 Cleage Dr.
Birmingham, AL 35217 USA
P: +1.800.956.5440 (Toll-Free)
+1.205.520.0238
F: +1.205.520.9813

Atlas Tube
6651 E. St. Hwy. 137
Blytheville, AR 72315 USA
P: +1.870.838.2000
F: +1.870.838.6630

Atlas Tube
13101 Eckles Road
Plymouth, MI 48170 USA
P: +1.734.738.5600
F: +1.734.738.5604

Atlas Tube Canada
200 Clark St.
P.O. Box 970
Harrow, ON N0R 1G0 Canada
P: +1.519.738.5000

Atlas Tube Canada
#5 Agri Park Road
Oak Bluff, MB R4G 0A5 Canada
P: +1.800.665.7602 (Toll-Free);
+1.204.953.3107

Hayes Modular Group
8108 FM N. 973
Austin, TX 78724 USA
P: +1.512.276.1011
www.hayesmodular.com

PIPE and TUBE PLANTS

Picoma Headquarters
9208 Jeffrey Dr.
Cambridge, OH 43725 USA
P: +1.800.PICOMA1 (742.6621)
www.picoma.com

Sharon Tube Headquarters
100 Martin Luther King Jr. Blvd.
Farrell, PA 16121 USA
P: +1.800.245.8115 (Toll-Free)
info@sharontube.com
www.sharontube.com

Sharon Tube
1800 Hunter Ave.
Niles, OH 44446 USA
info@sharontube.com
www.sharontube.com

Wheatland Tube Headquarters
One Council Ave.
Wheatland, PA 16161 USA
P: +1.800.257.8182 (Toll-Free)
info@wheatland.com
www.wheatland.com

Wheatland Tube
4435 S. Western Blvd.
Chicago, IL 60609 USA
info@wheatland.com
www.wheatland.com

Wheatland Tube
901 Dietz Road
Warren, OH 44483 USA
info@wheatland.com
www.wheatland.com

Z Modular Headquarters
227 W. Monroe St., Suite 2600
Chicago, IL 60606 USA
P: +1.800.733.5606
www.z-modular.com

Z Modular
3944 Valley E. Industrial Dr.
Birmingham, AL 35217 USA

Z Modular
710 Swanner Loop
Killeen, TX 76543 USA

Z Modular
50 Goodrich Dr.
Kitchener, ON N2C 2L3 Canada

Z Modular
6205 S. Arizona Ave.
Chandler, AZ 85248 USA

Z Modular — Design
200 Clark St.
P.O. Box 970
Harrow, ON N0R 1G0 Canada

Z Modular — Engineering
100 W. Big Beaver Road, Suite 390
Troy, MI 48084 USA

IRON and STEEL PLANT FACILITIES

NORTH AMERICAN FACILITIES

Coke Oven Batteries..145
Blast Furnaces..147
DRI and HBI Plants 149
Basic Oxygen Furnaces......................................150
Electric Arc Furnaces...152
Specialty Alloy and Foundry Facilities 163
Continuous Casters 175
Hot Strip Mills 191
Plate Mills..197
Cold Mills 199
Galvanizing Lines 204
Canadian and U.S. Long Products Mills...........210
Pipe and Tube Mills...220

Note: Data in all tables are in metric units unless otherwise noted.

IRON and STEEL PLANT FACILITIES

NORTH AMERICAN COKE OVEN BATTERIES

Company	Battery no.	Oven type(s)	Start-up year	Ovens per battery	Capacity (m³)	Fuel gas
CANADA						
Algoma Sault Ste. Marie, ON	7	Wilputte	1959	60	21	BFG COG
	8	Wilputte	1968	60	31	BFG COG
	9	Wilputte	1979	57	31	BFG COG
ArcelorMittal North America Dofasco G.P. No. 2 CP Hamilton, ON	4, 5	Koppers-Becker	1967	53	19	BFG COG
Dofasco G.P. No. 3 CP Hamilton, ON	6	Didier	1978	53	35	BFG COG
Stelco Inc. Hamilton Works Hamilton, ON	7	McKee/Otto	1972	83	32	COG
Lake Erie Works Nanticoke, ON	LEW #1	Otto	1981	45	45	COG
UNITED STATES						
Bluestone Resources Inc. Birmingham, AL	3	Koppers	1952	30	16	COG
	4	Koppers	1956	30	16	COG
	5	Koppers	1958	60	16	COG
Cleveland-Cliffs Inc. Burns Harbor, IN	1	Otto	1983	82	39	BFG COG
	2	Still/Otto	1994	82	39	COG
Middletown Works Middletown, OH	1	Wilputte	1953	76	21	COG
Monessen Coke Monessen, PA	1B	Koppers-Becker	1981	37	23	COG
	2	Koppers-Becker	1980	19	23	COG
Warren Coke Warren, OH	4	Koppers	1979	85	20	COG

IRON and STEEL PLANT FACILITIES

NORTH AMERICAN COKE OVEN BATTERIES

Company	Battery no.	Oven type(s)	Start-up year	Ovens per battery	Capacity (m^3)	Fuel gas
Drummond Co. Inc. ABC Coke Birmingham, AL	1A	Wilputte	1968	78	31	COG
	5	Koppers	1947	25	20	COG
	6	Koppers	1953	29	20	COG
DTE Energy Services EES Coke River Rouge, MI	5	Krupp Wilputte	1992	85	40	COG
SunCoke Energy Gateway Energy and Coke Co. Granite City, IL	A, B, C	SunCoke	2009	40	54	–
Haverhill North Coke Co. I Franklin Furnace, OH	A, B, C	SunCoke	2005	2x40; 1x20	52	–
Haverhill North Coke Co. II Franklin Furnace, OH	D, E, F	SunCoke	2008	2x40; 1x20	52	–
Indiana Harbor Coke Co. East Chicago, IN	A, B, C, D	SunCoke	1998	67	49	–
Jewell Coke Co. Vansant, VA	2D, 2E, 3B, 3C, 3F, 3G	SunCoke	1963	17–36	49	–
Middletown Coke Co. Middletown, OH	A, B, C	SunCoke	2011	2x40; 1x20	54	–
United States Steel Corporation Mon Valley Works Clairton Plant Clairton, PA	1, 2, 3	Wilputte	1955	64	18	COG
	13, 14, 15	Carl Still	No. 13 and 14 – 1989; No. 15 – 1979	61	18	COG
	19, 20	Koppers-Becker	No. 19 – 1976; No. 20 – 1977	87	24	COG
	B	Carl Still	1982	75	42	COG
	C	UHDE	2012	84	42	COG

IRON and STEEL PLANT FACILITIES

NORTH AMERICAN BLAST FURNACES

Company	Blast furnace ID	Stated capacity* '000 mt/year	mt/day	Hearth dia. (m)	Working vol. (m^3)	Charging method
CANADA						
Algoma Sault Ste. Marie, ON	7	2,540	7,620	10.67	2,478	Skip
ArcelorMittal North America Dofasco G.P. Hamilton, ON	2	1,000	2,903	7.33	1,062	Belt
	3 (idle)	790	2,268	6.61	925	Skip
	4	1,450	4,264	8.53	1,609	Skip
Stelco Inc. Lake Erie Works Nanticoke, ON	1	2,120	6,169	10.29	2,418	Belt
MEXICO						
Altos Hornos de México Monclova, CA	5	1,910	5,443	11.20	2,210	Belt
	6 (idle)	1,270	3,719	8.41	1,392	Belt
ArcelorMittal North America ArcelorMittal Mexico Lázaro Cárdenas, MC	1	–	–	8.99	1,712	Belt
UNITED STATES						
Cleveland-Cliffs Inc. Burns Harbor, IN	C	2,480	6,786	10.73	2,645	Belt
	D	2,480	6,786	10.82	2,600	Belt
Cleveland Works Cleveland, OH	5	1,440	3,946	8.99	1,546	Skip
	6	1,370	3,765	8.99	1,598	Skip
Dearborn Works Dearborn, MI	C	1,990	5,443	9.22	1,797	Belt
Indiana Harbor East East Chicago, IN	IH - 7	–	–	13.72	4,134	Belt
Indiana Harbor West East Chicago, IN	IH - 3 (idle)	–	–	8.99	1,586	Skip
	IH - 4	–	–	9.98	2,044	Skip
Middletown Works Middletown, OH	3	2,090	5,897	9.17	1,493	Skip

IRON and STEEL PLANT FACILITIES

NORTH AMERICAN BLAST FURNACES

Company	Blast furnace ID	Stated capacity* '000 mt/year	Stated capacity* mt/day	Hearth dia. (m)	Working vol. (m^3)	Charging method
United States Steel Corporation	4	1,360	3,810	8.79	1,496	Skip
Gary Works	6	1,230	3,447	8.53	1,506	Skip
Gary, IN	8	1,070	2,994	7.80	1,299	Skip
	14	2,540	7,439	11.73	3,244	Skip
Granite City Works	A (idle)	1,200	3,600	8.31	1,435	Skip
Granite City, IL	B	1,200	3,600	8.31	1,402	Skip
Mon Valley Works	1	1,090	3,175	8.79	1,541	Skip
Edgar Thomson Plant Braddock, PA	3	1,000	2,903	7.70	1,380	Skip

*Based on 2021 data.

IRON and STEEL PLANT FACILITIES

NORTH AMERICAN DRI AND HBI PLANTS

Company	Module	Start-up year	Stated capacity (million mt/year)	Technology	Product type
CANADA					
ArcelorMittal North America Long Products Canada G.P. Contrecoeur, QC	I	1973	0.40	Midrex	CDRI
	II	1977	0.60	Midrex	CDRI
MEXICO					
ArcelorMittal North America ArcelorMittal Mexico Lázaro Cárdenas, MC	I	1997	1.20	Midrex	CDRI
	II A	1988	0.50	HYL III	CDRI
	II B	1988	0.50	HYL III	CDRI
	III A	1991	0.50	HYL III	CDRI
	III B	1991	0.50	HYL III	CDRI
Ternium Puebla, PU	2P5	1995	0.93	HYL III	CDRI
Monterrey, NL	3M5	1983	0.78	HYL/ Energiron ZR	CDRI
	4M	1998	0.95	HYL/ Energiron ZR	HDRI
UNITED STATES					
ArcelorMittal North America ArcelorMittal Texas HBI Portland, TX	1	2016	2.00	Midrex	HBI
Cleveland-Cliffs Inc. IronUnits LLC Toledo, OH	1	2020	1.90	Midrex	HBI
Nucor Corp. Nucor Steel Louisiana LLC Convent, LA	1	2013	2.50	HYL/ Energiron ZR	CDRI

IRON and STEEL PLANT FACILITIES

NORTH AMERICAN BASIC OXYGEN FURNACES

Company	Type/ product	Year of start-up/ revamp	Furnace type	Stated capacity (million mt/ year)	No. converters	Working vol. (m³)	Heat size (mt)
CANADA							
Algoma Sault Ste. Marie, ON	Carbon/ flat	1970/ 1995	LD	3.2	2	232	238
ArcelorMittal North America Dofasco G.P. Hamilton, ON	Carbon/ flat	1978	KOBM	2.7	1	187	320
Rio Tinto Iron and Titanium Sorel-Tracy, QC	Carbon/ long, round	1986/ 2014	KOBM	0.6	1	80	115
Stelco Inc. Lake Erie Works Nanticoke, ON	Carbon/ flat	1980/ 1997	LD	2.5	2	291	245
MEXICO							
Altos Hornos de México Plant 1 Monclova, CA	Carbon/ flat	1971	LD	1.0	3	58	75
Plant 2 Monclova, CA	Carbon/ flat	1976/ 1994	LD	3.4	2	125	150
ArcelorMittal North America ArcelorMittal Mexico Lázaro Cárdenas, MC	Carbon/ round	1976	LD	2.6	2	#1: 95; #2: 91	115
UNITED STATES							
Cleveland-Cliffs Inc. Burns Harbor, IN	Carbon, IF/flat	1969	LD	4.6	3	255	278
Cleveland Works – East Cleveland, OH	Carbon, IF, AHSS	1961	LD	2.3	2	217	248
Cleveland Works – West Cleveland, OH	Carbon, AHSS	1956	LD	1.8	2	130	198
Dearborn Works Dearborn, MI	Carbon, IF/flat	1963	LD	2.6	2	185	232
Indiana Harbor No. 3 S.P. East Chicago, IN	Carbon, IF/flat	1970	LD	3.6	2	250	250

IRON and STEEL PLANT FACILITIES

NORTH AMERICAN BASIC OXYGEN FURNACES

Company	Type/ product	Year of start-up/ revamp	Furnace type	Stated capacity (million mt/ year)	No. convert-ers	Working vol. (m^3)	Heat size (mt)
Indiana Harbor No. 4 S.P. East Chicago, IN	Carbon, IF/flat, CRML	1966	LD	3.2	2	185	230
Middletown Works Middletown, OH	Carbon, IF	1969/ 2017/ 2021	LD	2.5	2	169	203
Riverdale, IL	Carbon/ flat	1959/ 2006/ 2012	LD	1.0	2	57	82
United States Steel Corporation Gary Works, No. 1 BOP Shop Gary, IN	Carbon	1965	LD	3.9	3	143	202
Gary Works, No. 2 QBOP Shop Gary, IN	Carbon, IF	1973	QBOP	3.9	3	154	202
Granite City Works Granite City, IL	Carbon	1967	LD	2.7	2	204	208
Mon Valley Works Edgar Thomson Plant Braddock, PA	Carbon, IF	1972	LD	2.7	2	183	225

IRON and STEEL PLANT FACILITIES

NORTH AMERICAN ELECTRIC ARC FURNACES

Company	No. of furnaces	Original furnace manufacturer	Heat size (mt)	Shell dia. (m)	Transformer max. operating cap. (MVA)	Stated cap. ('000 mt/year)
CANADA						
AltaSteel Inc., Part of Kyoei Steel Edmonton, AB	1	IHI	68	5.5	60	360
ArcelorMittal North America Dofasco G.P. Hamilton, ON	1	Fuchs	167	8.2	120	1,350
Long Products Canada G.P. Contrecoeur-East Contrecoeur, QC	1 (#3)	Siemens VAI	141	6.7	130	900
	1 (#4)	Siemens VAI	141	6.7	130	900
Long Products Canada G.P. Contrecoeur-West Contrecoeur, QC	1	SMS Siemag	98	6.4	110	600
EVRAZ North America EVRAZ Regina Regina, SK	1	Siemens VAI	133	6.1	62	520
	1	EMPCO	133	6.1	67	680
Finkl Steel Finkl Steel — Sorel St-Joseph-de-Sorel, QC	1	Tenova	37	4.6	13	80
Gerdau Long Steel North America Cambridge, ON	1, not melting	EMPCO	38	4.6	33	360
Manitoba Mill Selkirk, MB	1	SMS Siemag	54	4.8	54	394
Whitby Mill Whitby, ON	1	Superior	122	6.6	120	949
Ivaco Rolling Mills LP L'Orignal, ON	1	Lectromelt, Rev. Tenova	69	4.8	45	650
Valbruna ASW Steel Inc. Welland, ON	1	EMPCO	64	5.8	50	200
	1	Whiting	64	5.2	30	120
Weir ESCO Port Hope, ON	1	Tenova	5	2.4	3	3.8

IRON and STEEL PLANT FACILITIES

NORTH AMERICAN ELECTRIC ARC FURNACES

Company	No. of furnaces	Original furnace manufacturer	Heat size (mt)	Shell dia. (m)	Transformer max. operating cap. (MVA)	Stated cap. ('000 mt/year)
MEXICO						
Altos Hornos de México Monclova, CA	1	Siemens VAI	190	7.4	140	1,200
ArcelorMittal North America ArcelorMittal Mexico Lázaro Cárdenas, MC	4	NKK	222	7.9	190	950
Atlax S.A. Xalostoc, TL	1	Danieli	70	5.5	70	500
Deacero S.A. de C.V. Celaya, GJ	1	Danieli	102	5.5	85	2,000
	1	Danieli	120	–	–	
Ramos Arizpe, CA	1	Danieli	150	–	–	1,500
Saltillo, CA	1	Danieli	54	4.5	55	480
Gerdau Gerdau Corsa S.A.P.I. de C.V. Tultitlán, DF	1	Danieli	55	5.4	56	385
Grupo Simec Grupo SAN Aceros DM San Luis Potosí, SLP	1	Danieli, Rev. Primetals Technologies	54	4.6	60	400
Grupo SAN Aceros San Luis San Luis Potosí, SLP	1	Heroult	20	3.4	13	121
	1	Whiting	20	3.4	15	145
	1	Whiting	33	3.4	15	150
Talleres y Aceros S.A. de C.V. Ixtaczoquitlán, VZ	1	Primetals Technologies	100	–	80	1,200
	1	Danieli	50	4.3	48	310
Tenaris TenarisTamsa Veracruz, VZ	1	Tenova	164	7.6	132	1,200
Ternium Bar/Rod Div. Apodaca, NL	1	Danieli	106	5.8	70	600
Bar/Rod Div. Puebla, PU	1	Fuchs	140	7.1	140	1,330

IRON and STEEL PLANT FACILITIES

NORTH AMERICAN ELECTRIC ARC FURNACES

Company	No. of furnaces	Original furnace manufacturer	Heat size (mt)	Shell dia. (m)	Transformer max. operating cap. (MVA)	Stated cap. ('000 mt/year)
Ternium (cont'd)	1	Danieli	145	7.3	208	825
Flat Products Div. Monterrey, NL	1	Fuchs	145	7.3	156	825
UNITED STATES						
American Cast Iron Pipe Co. Birmingham, AL	2	Lectromelt	2	1.7	1	–
	1	Whiting	5	2.1	3	–
	1	American Bridge	14	3.3	8	–
	1	Demag	64	9.3	70	–
Arkansas Steel Associates LLC Newport, AK	1	Whiting	45	4.6	33	273
ATI Inc. ATI Specialty Rolled Products Brackenridge, PA	1	Danieli	100	6.1	55	360
ATI Specialty Rolled Products Latrobe, PA	1	Primetals Technologies	23	3.8	18	100
Bradken Bradken Engineered Products Atchison, KS	1	Whiting	59	3.8	8	24
	1	Lectromelt		2.7	3	
	1	Lectromelt		3.4	4	
	1	Whiting		3.4	6	
Carpenter Technology Corp. Latrobe, PA	1, not melting	American Bridge	23	3.7	13	14
	1	J.T. Cullen/ Swindell	32	4.1	15	37
Reading, PA	4	Swindell-Dressler	15	3.4	4	136
	1	Swindell-Dressler	15	3.7	6	136
	1	Lectromelt	38	4.1	17	136

IRON and STEEL PLANT FACILITIES

NORTH AMERICAN ELECTRIC ARC FURNACES

Company	No. of furnaces	Original furnace manufacturer	Heat size (mt)	Shell dia. (m)	Transformer max. operating cap. (MVA)	Stated cap. ('000 mt/year)
Cascade Steel Rolling Mills Inc. McMinnville, OR	1	Fuchs	100	6.4	84	900
Charter Manufacturing Co. Charter Steel – Cleveland Cuyahoga Heights, OH	1	Danieli	81	5.2	75	616
Charter Steel – Saukville Saukville, WI	1	Fuchs	90	5.1	65	570
Cleveland-Cliffs Inc. Butler Works Butler, PA	3, not melting	Swindell-Dressler	159	6.7	56	275
	1	SMS Siemag	161	–	170	908
Coatesville, PA	1	American Bridge, Rev. Primetals Technologies	150	6.7	67	798
Indiana Harbor East Chicago, IN	1, not melting	Lectromelt, Rev. Fuchs	105	6.7	60	454
Mansfield Works Mansfield, OH	1 (#8)	American Bridge	122	6.1	28	545
	1 (#9)	voestalpine	122	6.7	49	
Steelton, PA	1	NKK-United	127	7.0	120	998
Commercial Metals Company CMC Steel Alabama Birmingham, AL	1	NKK-SE, Rev. Superior Machine	77	5.9	79	653
CMC Steel Arizona Mesa, AZ	1	Danieli	35	4.7	30	354
CMC Steel Florida Jacksonville, FL	1	Danieli	90	6.7	95	617
CMC Steel New Jersey Sayreville, NJ	1	Demag	77	6.4	80	653
CMC Steel Oklahoma Durant, OK	1	Danieli	41	4.7	33	360
CMC Steel South Carolina Cayce, SC	1	BSE	100	5.5	80	776

IRON and STEEL PLANT FACILITIES

NORTH AMERICAN ELECTRIC ARC FURNACES

Company	No. of furnaces	Original furnace manufacturer	Heat size (mt)	Shell dia. (m)	Transformer max. operating cap. (MVA)	Stated cap. ('000 mt/year)
Commercial Metals Company (cont'd) CMC Steel Tennessee Knoxville, TN	1	Techint	65	5.9	69	544
CMC Steel Texas Seguin, TX	1	Superior Machine	109	6.7	80	943
Crucible Industries LLC Solvay, NY	1	Lectromelt	36	4.6	20	45
Electralloy Oil City, PA	1	Lectromelt	23	4.0	13	82
Ellwood Group Inc. Ellwood National Steel Irvine, PA	1	American Bridge	41	4.6	18	53
Ellwood Quality Steels Co. New Castle, PA	1	Concast	41	4.3	42	410
EVRAZ North America EVRAZ Rocky Mountain Steel Pueblo, CO	1	Siemens VAI	127	6.7	67	1,100
Finkl Steel Finkl Steel — Chicago Chicago, IL	1	SMS Siemag	75	5.8	75	573
Gerdau Long Steel North America Cartersville, GA	1	Demag, Rev. Superior Machine	104	6.7	85	925
Charlotte, NC	1	Fuchs, Rev. Superior Machine	37	5.0	40	468
Midlothian, TX	1	EMPCO, Rev. Siemens VAI	136	5.8	115	650
	1	EMPCO, Rev. Superior Machine	136	6.7	140	850
Petersburg, VA	1	Fuchs	136	6.7	120	965
St. Paul, MN	1, not melting	voestalpine	86	6.0	–	502

IRON and STEEL PLANT FACILITIES

NORTH AMERICAN ELECTRIC ARC FURNACES

Company	No. of furnaces	Original furnace manufacturer	Heat size (mt)	Shell dia. (m)	Transformer max. operating cap. (MVA)	Stated cap. ('000 mt/year)
Wilton, IA	1	Whiting	73	5.1	31	322
Gerdau Special Steel North America Fort Smith, AR	2	Lectromelt	54	4.6	40	550
Jackson, MI	2, not melting	Lectromelt	41	4.3	27	300
Monroe, MI	1	Whiting, Rev. Primetals Technologies	113	6.1	75	600
GKN Hoeganaes Corp. Gallatin, TN	1	Demag, Rev. Superior Machine	54	4.6	45	300
Harrison Steel Castings Co. Attica, IN	1	Heroult	7	2.7	8	15
	1	Lectromelt	18	3.4	10	36
	1	Lectromelt	18	3.4	13	36
Haynes International Inc. Kokomo, IN	1	Lectromelt	5	2.7	3	–
	1	Swindell-Dressler	14	3.4	7	18
Hensley Industries Dallas, TX	1	Lectromelt	4.5	2.1	4	15
	1	Universal	4.5	2.1	4	15
JSW Steel USA Mingo Junction, OH	1	Tenova	250	8.8	157	1,500
Keokuk Steel Castings Keokuk, IA	1	Whiting	9	2.7	5	34
Kobelco Metal Powder Seymour, IN	1, not melting	Whiting	15	3.7	18	57
Leggett & Platt Sterling Steel Co. LLC Sterling, IL	1, not melting	Lectromelt	336	9.8	175	608
	1 (#8)	Fuchs	331	9.8	188	1,090
Liberty Steel USA Liberty Steel & Wire Peoria Peoria, IL	1	Amerifab, Siemens VAI	163	6.7	115	744

IRON and STEEL PLANT FACILITIES

NORTH AMERICAN ELECTRIC ARC FURNACES

Company	No. of furnaces	Original furnace manufacturer	Heat size (mt)	Shell dia. (m)	Transformer max. operating cap. (MVA)	Stated cap. ('000 mt/year)
Liberty Steel USA (cont'd) Liberty Steel Georgetown Georgetown, SC	1	Demag, Rev. Superior Machine	77	5.8	65	454
	1	Demag, Rev. Superior Machine	77	5.8	62	454
Maynard Steel Casting Co. Milwaukee, WI	1 (#4)	Lectromelt	5	2.4	2	6
	1 (#5)	Whiting	5	2.4	4	6
	1 (#6)	Lectromelt	7	2.7	4	8
	1 (#7)	Lectromelt	18	3.4	10	16
Metaltek International Sandusky International Div. Sandusky, OH	1	Lectromelt	9	2.7	3	4
	1	Lectromelt	9	2.7	3	4
NLMK NLMK Indiana Portage, IN	1	Danieli	118	7.0	120	680
North American Höganäs Co. Hollsopple, PA	1	Lectromelt, Rev. Fuchs, NKK-SE	45	3.8	30	160
North American Stainless Ghent, KY	1	SMS Demag	140	–	155	800
	1	Siemens VAI	–	–	–	800
North Star BlueScope Steel Delta, OH	1	Fuchs, Rev. Superior Machine	171	7.6	140	1,905
Nucor Corp. Nucor Steel–Arkansas Blytheville, AR	2	MAN GHH	148	7.3	2 x 81	2,450
Nucor Steel Auburn Inc. Auburn, NY	1	SMS Demag	64	5.3	45	499
Nucor Steel–Berkeley Huger, SC	2	MAN GHH	154	7.6	180	2,956
Nucor Steel Birmingham Inc. Birmingham, AL	1	Sarralle	52.5	5.2	54	500

IRON and STEEL PLANT FACILITIES

NORTH AMERICAN ELECTRIC ARC FURNACES

Company	No. of furnaces	Original furnace manufacturer	Heat size (mt)	Shell dia. (m)	Transformer max. operating cap. (MVA)	Stated cap. ('000 mt/year)
Nucor Steel–Decatur LLC Trinity, AL	2	NKK-SE (DC), Rev. SMS Demag, Superior Machine	165	7.3	2 x 123	3,100
Nucor Steel Florida Inc. Frostproof, FL	1	Danieli	39	4.7	33	450
Nucor Steel Gallatin LLC Ghent, KY	1	NKK-SE, Rev. SMS Siemag	172	7.9	2 x 75	1,452
Nucor Steel–Hertford County Cofield, NC	1	MAN GHH	150	7.3	88	1,542
Nucor Steel–Indiana Crawfordsville, IN	2	Brown-Boveri	118	6.7	2 x 90	2,304
Nucor Steel Jackson Inc. Flowood, MS	1	Tenova	53	5.1	48	454
Nucor Steel Kankakee Inc. Bourbonnais, IL	1	Danieli	73	5.8	73	794
Nucor Steel Kingman LLC Kingman, AZ	1, not melting	Fuchs	91	7.3	80	454
Nucor Steel Longview LLC Longview, TX	1 (D)	Lectromelt	23	4.0	10	110
	1 (E)	Lectromelt	23	4.0	6	
Nucor Steel Marion Inc. Marion, OH	1	EMCI	48	4.7	45	345
Nucor Steel Memphis Inc. Memphis, TN	1	Danieli	94	6.7	120	891
Nucor Steel–Nebraska Norfolk, NE	1	MAN GHH	95	6.3	90	1,134
Nucor Steel Seattle Inc. Seattle, WA	1	Fuchs	100	6.6	92	855
Nucor Steel Sedalia LLC Sedalia, MO	1	Danieli	39	4.7	33	450

IRON and STEEL PLANT FACILITIES

NORTH AMERICAN ELECTRIC ARC FURNACES

Company	No. of furnaces	Original furnace manufacturer	Heat size (mt)	Shell dia. (m)	Transformer max. operating cap. (MVA)	Stated cap. ('000 mt/year)
Nucor Corp. (cont'd) Nucor Steel–South Carolina Darlington, SC	1	MAN GHH	109	7.3	2 x 34	907
Nucor Steel–Texas Jewett, TX	1	SMS Concast	91	6.7	110	907
Nucor Steel Tuscaloosa Inc. Tuscaloosa, AL	1	MAN GHH	122	7.1	96	1,200
Nucor Steel–Utah Plymouth, UT	2	American Bridge, Rev. Fuchs	51	4.6	35	908
Nucor-Yamato Steel Co. Blytheville, AR	1	Demag, Rev. Superior Machine	109	6.7	110	2,632
Optimus Steel LLC Beaumont, TX	1	Krupp, Rev. Superior Machine	113	6.7	120	750
Outokumpu Stainless USA LLC Calvert, AL	1	Siemens VAI	165	8	155	1,000
Republic Steel Canton Hot Rolled Bar Plant Canton, OH	1	Swindell-Dressler, Tenova, Danieli	200	7.9	110	820
	1, not melting	American Bridge	91	6.1	20	272
Lorain Hot Rolled Bar Plant Lorain, OH	1, not melting	SMS Concast	136	–	–	907
SSAB Americas SSAB Alabama Inc. Axis, AL	1	Fuchs	159	7.6	140	1,270
SSAB Iowa Inc. Muscatine, IA	1	Demag	141	7.3	140	1,134

IRON and STEEL PLANT FACILITIES

NORTH AMERICAN ELECTRIC ARC FURNACES

Company	No. of furnaces	Original furnace manufacturer	Heat size (mt)	Shell dia. (m)	Transformer max. operating cap. (MVA)	Stated cap. ('000 mt/year)
Standard Steel LLC Burnham, PA	1, not melting	Lectromelt	35	4.3	10	54
	1, not melting	American Bridge	35	4.4	15	39
	1	Tenova	65	5.2	30	116
Steel Dynamics Inc. Engineered Bar Products Div. Pittsboro, IN	1	Demag	91	6.1	80	725
Flat Roll Group Butler Div. Butler, IN	2	Fuchs, Rev. Superior Machine	150	7.3	120	2,900
Flat Roll Group Columbus Div. Columbus, MS	2	SMS Demag	158	7.6	160	3,100
Flat Roll Group Southwest-Sinton Div. Sinton, TX	2	SMS group	185	8.5	176	3,100
Roanoke Bar Div. Roanoke, VA	1	Danieli	90	5.5	56	590
Steel of West Virginia Inc. Huntington, WV	2	Lectromelt	59	4.6	28	265
Steel Ventures Inc. Wurtland, KY	2, not melting	Lectromelt	47	4.6	25	272
Structural and Rail Div. Columbia City, IN	2	Demag	109	6.7	120	2,000
Tenaris TenarisKoppel Koppel, PA	1	Krupp, Rev. Demag	77	5.8	67	450
TimkenSteel Corp. Faircrest Plant Canton, OH	1	Krupp	171	7.3	120	805
Harrison Plant Canton, OH	1, not melting	Swindell-Dressler	122	6.7	54	1,111
	1, not melting	Swindell-Dressler	122	6.7	40	

2023 AIST Directory — Iron and Steel Plants

IRON and STEEL PLANT FACILITIES

NORTH AMERICAN ELECTRIC ARC FURNACES

Company	No. of furnaces	Original furnace manufacturer	Heat size (mt)	Shell dia. (m)	Transformer max. operating cap. (MVA)	Stated cap. ('000 mt/year)
Union Electric Steel Corp. Carnegie, PA	1	Lectromelt	54	4.4	13	–
United States Steel Corporation Big River Steel Osceola, AR	2	SMS	150	7.0	2 x 123	2,900
Fairfield Works Fairfield, AL	1	SMS	155	7.6	156	1,600
Universal Stainless & Alloy Products Inc. Bridgeville, PA	1	American Bridge, Rev. APT Technologies, SMS Siemag	45	4.6	30	95
Valbruna Slater Stainless Inc. Fort Wayne, IN	1	Lectromelt	15	3.4	5	18
	1	Lectromelt	18	3.7	18	68
Vallourec Star LP Youngstown, OH	1	Fuchs, Rev. Superior Machine	92	6.1	70	725
Vinton Steel LLC, Part of Kyoei Steel Vinton, TX	1	Fuchs	32	3.7	20	272
	1	Lectromelt	32	3.7	20	
Weir ESCO Newton, MS	1	Lectromelt	7	2.9	5	9
	1	Swindell-Dressler	7	2.9	5	9
Whemco Lehigh Specialty Melting Latrobe, PA	1	Lectromelt	34	4.0	20	54

IRON and STEEL PLANT FACILITIES

NORTH AMERICAN SPECIALTY ALLOY AND FOUNDRY FACILITIES

Company	Annual cap. (metric tons)	Melting type	No. of furnaces	Avg. heat size (metric tons)	Casting method
CANADA					
Alloy Casting Industries Ltd. New Hamburg, ON	136	Air melt	3	0.68	Air-set/no-bake
Bradken Bradken Engineered Products London, ON	4,000	Air melt	5	7.71	Air-set/no-bake
Bradken Mineral Processing Mont-Joli, QC	35,000	Air melt	1	8.16	
Canada Alloy Castings Co. Kitchener, ON	295	Air melt	5	12.70	Air-set/no-bake
Castech Metallurgy Thetford-Mines, QC	680	—	1	9.07	Air-set/no-bake, green sand — vert. parted
Finkl Steel Finkl Steel — Sorel St-Joseph-de-Sorel, QC	80,000	EAF	1	37.00	Ingot
Foothills Steel Foundry Ltd. Calgary, AB	187	Air melt	—	—	Air-set/no-bake, gas-hardened/coldbox, shell mold, green sand — horiz. parted, green sand — vert. parted
Highland Foundry Ltd. Surrey, BC	4,354	Air melt	7	4.54	Air-set/no-bake, gas-hardened/coldbox, green sand — horiz. parted, squeeze/semi-solid, lost foam
Kubota Metal Corp. Fahramet Division Orillia, ON	—	EAF/Air melt	2/6	2.72/ 3.63	Air-set/no-bake, green sand — horiz. parted, centrifugal
M A Steel Foundry Ltd. Calgary, AB	68	Air melt	1	1.36	Air-set/no-bake
Molten Metallurgy Inc. Paris, ON	—	Air melt	5	2.27	Air-set/no-bake

IRON and STEEL PLANT FACILITIES

NORTH AMERICAN SPECIALTY ALLOY AND FOUNDRY FACILITIES

Company	Annual cap. (metric tons)	Melting type	No. of furnaces	Avg. heat size (metric tons)	Casting method
Peninsula Alloy Inc. Stevensville, ON	181	Air melt	4	8.85	Air-set/no-bake, plaster mold
Valbruna ASW Inc. Welland, ON	200,000	EAF	1	64.00	Ingot/continuous
	120,000	EAF	1	64.00	
Weir ESCO Port Hope, ON	3,800	EAF	1	5.44	Air-set/no-bake, gas-hardened/coldbox
MEXICO					
Acerlan S.A. de C.V. San Juan del Rio, QA	—	EAF/Air melt	2/4	7.26/ 12.70	Air-set/no-bake, gas-hardened/coldbox, shell mold
Corporacion Pok S.A. de C.V. Tlajomulco de Zuniga, JA	—	Air melt	8	7.71	—
Fimex S.A. de C.V. Guadalajara, JA	181	Air melt	3	0.91	Air-set/no-bake, green sand — horiz. parted
Frisa Steel Monterrey, NL	350,000	EAF	1	50.00	Ingot
Fundidora Morelia S.A. de C.V. Morelia, MC	73	Air melt	6	10.89	Air-set/no-bake
Magotteaux Magotteaux S.A. de C.V. Monterrey, NL	272	Air melt	2	3.63	Air-set/no-bake
Mayran Castings San Pedro, CA	—	Air melt	4	22.68	Air-set/no-bake
Ramsa S.A. de C.V. San Luis Potosí, SLP	—	Air melt	6	5.44	Air-set/no-bake, shell mold, investment, centrifugal
UNITED STATES					
Advanced Centrifugal Cambridge, WI	—	Air melt	6	2.72	Air-set/no-bake, shell mold, green sand — horiz. parted, centrifugal

IRON and STEEL PLANT FACILITIES

NORTH AMERICAN SPECIALTY ALLOY AND FOUNDRY FACILITIES

Company	Annual cap. (metric tons)	Melting type	No. of furnaces	Avg. heat size (metric tons)	Casting method
American Foundry Group Inc. Muskogee, OK	—	Air melt	4	5.44	Air-set/no-bake, shell mold, investment
Plant 1 Bixby, OK	—	Air melt	3	3.18	Air-set/no-bake, investment, green sand — horiz. parted, squeeze/semisolid
American Spincast Inc. Belton, TX	165	Air melt	6	0.82	Centrifugal
Ashland Foundry & Machine Works Ashland, PA	—	Air melt	7	12.25	Air-set/no-bake
Astech Inc. Vassar, MI	127	Air melt	3	1.36	Air-set/no-bake, investment, green sand — horiz. parted, green sand — vert. parted
ATI Inc. ATI Specialty Rolled Products Brackenridge, PA	360,000	EAF	1	100	Ingot/continuous
		EAF	1	23.00	
Badger Alloys Inc. Milwaukee, WI	—	Air melt	9	16.33	Air-set/no-bake
Bahr Bros. Mfg. Marion, IN	—	Air melt	4	3.40	Air-set/no-bake, lost foam
Bay Cast Inc. Bay City, MI	907	EAF/Air melt	1/6	21.78/124	Air-set/no-bake
Beaver Valley Alloy Foundry Co. Monaca, PA	227	Air melt	4	4.99	Air-set/no-bake
Berkley Machine Works & Foundry Co. Norfolk, VA	18,144	—	—	—	—
Blue Creek Foundry El Campo, TX	136	Air melt	2	—	Air-set/no-bake, shell mold, centrifugal
Bradken Bradken Engineered Products Atchison, KS	24,000	EAF	4	58.97	Air-set/no-bake

2023 AIST Directory — Iron and Steel Plants 165

IRON and STEEL PLANT FACILITIES

NORTH AMERICAN SPECIALTY ALLOY AND FOUNDRY FACILITIES

Company	Annual cap. (metric tons)	Melting type	No. of furnaces	Avg. heat size (metric tons)	Casting method
Bradken (cont'd) Bradken Engineered Products Tacoma, WA	6,500	EAF	2	20.87	Air-set/no-bake, green sand — horiz. parted, green sand — vert. parted
Carpenter Technology Corp. Latrobe, PA	14,000	EAF	1 (idle)	23.00	Ingot
	37,000	EAF	1	32.00	
Reading, PA	136,000	EAF	4	15.00	Ingot/continuous
	136,000	EAF	1	15.00	
	136,000	EAF	1	38.00	
Cast Tools Inc. Racine, WI	—	Air melt	—	—	Gas-hardened/coldbox, investment
Castalloy Corp. Waukesha, WI	363	Air melt	4	3.63	Air-set/no-bake, shell mold
Central Machine & Tool Enid, OK	—	Air melt	1	1.36	Air-set/no-bake, permanent mold-gravity/tilt pour, green sand — horiz. parted
Centrifugal Castings Inc. Temple, TX	—	Air melt	7	5.24	Centrifugal
Cleveland-Cliffs Inc. Butler Works Butler, PA	908,000	EAF	1	161	Continuous
Coatesville, PA	798,000	EAF	1	150	Ingot/continuous
Mansfield Works Mansfield, OH	545,000	EAF	1 (#8)	122	Continuous
	545,000	EAF	1 (#9)	122	Continuous
Steelton, PA	454,000	EAF	1	127	Ingot/continuous
Columbia Steel Portland, OR	—	EAF/Air melt	4/4	2.72	Air-set/no-bake, green sand — horiz. parted
Columbiana Foundry Co. Columbiana, OH	454	Air melt	7	—	Air-set/no-bake, gas-hardened/coldbox, lost foam
Commercial Casting Co. Fontana, CA	363	Air melt	4	8.16	Air-set/no-bake

IRON and STEEL PLANT FACILITIES

NORTH AMERICAN SPECIALTY ALLOY AND FOUNDRY FACILITIES

Company	Annual cap. (metric tons)	Melting type	No. of furnaces	Avg. heat size (metric tons)	Casting method
Coronado Steel Co. Youngstown, OH	—	Air melt	3	0.23	Air-set/no-bake, shell mold, investment
Crucible Industries LLC Solvay, NY	45,000	EAF	1	36.00	Ingot
Davis Alloys Sharpsville, PA	—	—	—	—	Pig
Delta Centrifugal Corp. Temple, TX	—	Air melt	8	7.26	Centrifugal
Duraloy Technologies Scottdale, PA	236	Air melt	13	10.89	Air-set/no-bake, centrifugal
Durametal Corp. Muncy, PA	—	Air melt	6	13.61	Air-set/no-bake, green sand
DW Clark Inc. East Bridgewater, MA	91	Air melt	5	21.77	Air-set/no-bake, centrifugal
Eagle Alloy Inc. Muskegon, MI	—	Air melt	11	23.13	Shell mold, investment, permanent mold-gravity/tilt pour
Eagle Foundry Co. Eagle Creek, OR	—	Air melt	2	4.99	Air-set/no-bake
Effort Foundry Inc. Bath, PA	54	Air melt	4	1.63	Air-set/no-bake
Electralloy Oil City, PA	82,000	EAF	1	23.00	Ingot/pig
Ellwood Group Inc. Ellwood National Steel Irvine, PA	53,000	EAF	1	41.00	Ingot
Ellwood Quality Steels Co. New Castle, PA	410,000	EAF	1	41.00	Ingot
Finkl Steel Finkl Steel — Chicago Chicago, IL	573,000	EAF	1	75.00	Ingot
Fisher Cast Steel Products Inc. West Jefferson, OH	91	Air melt	5	5.44	Air-set/no-bake, investment
GKN Hoeganaes Corp. Gallatin, TN	300,000	EAF	1	54.00	Powder

IRON and STEEL PLANT FACILITIES

NORTH AMERICAN SPECIALTY ALLOY AND FOUNDRY FACILITIES

Company	Annual cap. (metric tons)	Melting type	No. of furnaces	Avg. heat size (metric tons)	Casting method
Grass Valley Steelcast Grass Valley, CA	23	—	1	0.91	Green sand — horiz. parted
Harbor Castings Canton, OH	—	Air melt	2	0.91	Investment
Harrison Steel Castings Co. Attica, IN	15,000	EAF	1	7.00	Air-set/no-bake
	36,000	EAF	1	18.00	
	36,000	EAF	1	18.00	
Haynes International Inc. Kokomo, IN	18,000	EAF	1	5.00	Ingot/pig
		EAF	1	14.00	
Henderson Manufacturing Co. Inc. Pittsburg, TX	200	Air melt	1	0.91	Air-set/no-bake
Hensley Industries Dallas, TX	13,608	EAF	1	4.50	Air-set/no-bake, shell mold, green sand — horiz. parted
Howell Foundries LLC St. Francisville, LA	—	Air melt	3	1.36	Air-set/no-bake
Huron Casting Inc. Pigeon, MI	2,994	Air melt	9	45.36	Air-set/no-bake, shell mold
International Casting Corp. New Baltimore, MI	4,536	Air melt	3	3.63	Air-set/no-bake, green sand — horiz. parted
J & L Fiber Services Inc. Waukesha, WI	544	Air melt	—	—	—
Kennametal Inc. Latrobe, PA	—	Air melt	10	3.45	Air-set/no-bake, gas-hardened/coldbox, green sand — horiz. parted
Kenosha Steel Castings Kenosha, WI	181	EAF	1	4.54	Air-set/no-bake
Keokuk Steel Castings Keokuk, IA	34,000	EAF	1	9.00	Air-set/no-bake
Kobelco Metal Powder Seymour, IN	57,000	EAF	1 (idle)	15.00	Powder

IRON and STEEL PLANT FACILITIES

NORTH AMERICAN SPECIALTY ALLOY AND FOUNDRY FACILITIES

Company	Annual cap. (metric tons)	Melting type	No. of furnaces	Avg. heat size (metric tons)	Casting method
KPF Steel Foundry Kahoka, MO	1,814	Air melt	4	0.54/ 1.09	Air-set/no-bake, gas-hardened/coldbox
The Lawton Standard Family of Companies Damascus Steel Casting Co. Novi, MI	181	Air melt	2	0.91	Air-set/no-bake, investment, green sand – horiz. parted, green sand – vert. parted
QESC LLC Houston, TX	10,886	EAF/Air melt	2/2	19.96/ 6.35	Air-set/no-bake
Temperform Corp. Novi, MI	181	Air melt	5	4.54	Air-set/no-bake
M E Global Inc. Duluth, MN	—	EAF	3	32.66	Air-set/no-bake, gas-hardened/coldbox, lost foam
Tempe, AZ	—	EAF	3	17.69	Air-set/no-bake
Maca Supply Co. Springville, UT	45	Air melt	15	24.49	Air-set/no-bake, gas-hardened/coldbox
Magotteaux Magotteaux Inc. Pulaski, TN	—	EAF/Air melt	3/2	13.61/ 9.08	Air-set/no-bake, green sand — vert. parted
Maynard Steel Casting Co. Milwaukee, WI	6,000	EAF	1 (#4)	5.00	Air-set/no-bake, gas-hardened/coldbox, green sand — horiz. parted
	6,000		1 (#5)	5.00	
	8,000		1 (#6)	7.00	
	16,000		1 (#7)	18.00	
MCC International McDonald, PA	181	Air melt	7	18.14	Centrifugal
McConway & Torley LLC Pittsburgh, PA	54,431	EAF	3	18.14	Green sand — vert. parted
Meltec Seattle, WA	—	Air melt	4	4.08	Air-set/no-bake, gas-hardened/coldbox, green sand — horiz. parted
MetalTek International Pevely, MO	—	—	8	21.95	Air-set/no-bake, green sand — horiz. parted

IRON and STEEL PLANT FACILITIES

NORTH AMERICAN SPECIALTY ALLOY AND FOUNDRY FACILITIES

Company	Annual cap. (metric tons)	Melting type	No. of furnaces	Avg. heat size (metric tons)	Casting method
MetalTek International (cont'd) Sandusky International Div. Sandusky, OH	4,000 / 4,000	EAF / EAF	1 / 1	9.00 / 9.00	Centrifugal
Midwest Metal Products Inc. Winona, MN	127	Air melt	1	1.36	Air-set/no-bake
Minncast Inc. Fridley, MN	—	Air melt	3	4.08	Air-set/no-bake
Monett Metals Inc. Monett, MO	145	Air melt	4	2.72	Air-set/no-bake, investment
National Foundry & Manufacturing Co. Inc. Crane, TX	—	Air melt	1	0.45	Green sand — horiz. parted
North American Höganäs Co. Hollsopple, PA	160,000	EAF	1	45.00	Ingot/powder
North American Stainless Ghent, KY	800,000 / 800,000	EAF / EAF	1 / 1	140 / —	Continuous
North Star Casteel Products Inc. Seattle, WA	181	Air melt	2	1.81	Shell mold, green sand — horiz. parted
Northern Stainless Corp. Pewaukee, WI	109	Air melt	4	2.27	Air-set/no-bake
Northfield Manufacturing Inc. Westland, MI	136	Air melt	3	—	Air-set/no-bake, gas-hardened/coldbox
Nucor Corp. Nucor Steel Longview LLC Longview, TX	110,000	EAF / EAF	1 (D) / 1 (E)	23.00 / 23.00	Ingot
Omaha Steel Castings Co. Wahoo, NE	544	Air melt	2	5.44	Air-set/no-bake, green sand — horiz. parted
Omega Castings Inc. Battle Creek, MI	38	Air melt	2	0.91	Air-set/no-bake, shell mold

IRON and STEEL PLANT FACILITIES

NORTH AMERICAN SPECIALTY ALLOY AND FOUNDRY FACILITIES

Company	Annual cap. (metric tons)	Melting type	No. of furnaces	Avg. heat size (metric tons)	Casting method
Outokumpu Stainless USA LLC Calvert, AL	900,000	EAF	1	160	Continuous
Pacific Alloy Castings South Gate, CA	2,177	Air melt	3	9.53	Air-set/no-bake, green sand — horiz. parted
Pearce Foundry & Machine Works Prairieville, LA	187	Air melt	3	10.89	Air-set/no-bake
Penatek Industries Inc. Odessa, TX	—	Air melt	5	6.80	Permanent mold — gravity/tilt pour, centrifugal
Philadelphia Naval Shipyard Foundry Philadelphia, PA	—	—	12	10.89/36.29	Air-set/no-bake
Quaker City Castings Inc. Salem, OR	—	Air melt	7	31.75	Air-set/no-bake, centrifugal
Regal Cast Inc. Lebanon, PA	36	Air melt	3	4.99	Air-set/no-bake
Remelt Services Darlington, SC	–	Air melt	2	4.50	Ingot/pig
Republic Steel Canton Hot Rolled Bar Plant Canton, OH	820,000 272,000	EAF EAF	1 (idle) 1 (idle)	200 91	Ingot/continuous
Rock Island Arsenal Rock Island, IL	—	EAF/Air melt	2/6	2.72/3.63	Air-set/no-bake, centrifugal
Roemer Electric Steel Foundry Longview, WA	181	Air melt	3	3.63	Air-set/no-bake, green sand — horiz. parted
Sawbrook Steel Casting Co. Lockland, OH	544	EAF	1	3.63	Air-set/no-bake, squeeze/semisolid, green sand — vert. parted
Seabee Foundry Hampton, IA	127	Air melt	6	0.91	Air-set/no-bake
Shenango Industries Inc. Terre Haute, IN	374	Air melt	—	—	Centrifugal

IRON and STEEL PLANT FACILITIES

NORTH AMERICAN SPECIALTY ALLOY AND FOUNDRY FACILITIES

Company	Annual cap. (metric tons)	Melting type	No. of furnaces	Avg. heat size (metric tons)	Casting method
Sivyer Steel Corp. Bettendorf, IO	18,144	EAF	3	27.22	Air-set/no-bake, gas-hardened/coldbox
Smith Castings Inc. Kingsford, MI	45	Air melt	2	1.36	Air-set/no-bake, green sand — horiz. parted
Southern Alloy Corp. Sylacauga, AL	109	Air melt	8	5.44	Air-set/no-bake
Southern Cast Products Inc. Meridian, MS	—	Air melt	4	6.35	Air-set/no-bake
Southwest Steel Casting Co. Longview, TX	907	EAF/Air melt	2/2	7.26/3.63	Air-set/no-bake, gas-hardened/coldbox
Spanish Fork Foundry Spanish Fork, UT	112	Air melt	6	6.35	Air-set/no-bake, green sand — horiz. parted, lost foam
Spokane Industries Inc. Spokane Valley, WA	454	EAF/Air melt	2/2	4.54/0.18	Air-set/no-bake, investment, green sand — horiz. parted
Spuncast Inc. Watertown, WI	—	Air melt	—	—	Centrifugal
	—	Air melt	6	10.89	
St. Louis Precision Casting Co. St. Louis, MO	82	Air melt	—	—	Air-set/no-bake
Stainless Foundry & Engineering Inc. Milwaukee, WI	—	Air melt	8	5.99	Air-set/no-bake, investment, green sand — horiz. parted, green sand — vert. parted
Standard Alloys & Mfg. Port Arthur, TX	—	Air melt	12	17.69	Air-set/no-bake, gas-hardened/coldbox, investment
Standard Steel LLC Burnham, PA	54,000	EAF	1 (idle)	35.00	Ingot
	39,000	EAF	1 (idle)	35.00	
	116,000	EAF	1	65.00	
Star Foundry and Machine Salt Lake City, UT	—	Air melt	3	5.44	Air-set/no-bake, green sand — horiz. parted

IRON and STEEL PLANT FACILITIES

NORTH AMERICAN SPECIALTY ALLOY AND FOUNDRY FACILITIES

Company	Annual cap. (metric tons)	Melting type	No. of furnaces	Avg. heat size (metric tons)	Casting method
Steeltech Ltd. Grand Rapids, MI	56	Air melt	5	2.72	Air-set/no-bake, shell mold, investment, centrifugal
Strategic Materials Corp. South Gate, CA	22	Air melt	—	—	—
Sturm Inc. Barboursville, WV	—	Air melt	3	0.91	Air-set/no-bake, shell mold, investment, centrifugal
Talladega Castings & Machine Co. Talladega, AL	—	Air melt	3	—	Air-set/no-bake
The Taylor & Fenn Co. Windsor, CT	—	Air melt	7	16.10	Air-set/no-bake
Techni-Cast Corp. South Gate, CA	—	—	8	6.35	Centrifugal
Tidewater Castings Inc. Portsmouth, VA	—	Air melt	2	0.45	—
TimkenSteel Corp. Faircrest Plant Canton, OH	805,000	EAF	1	171	Ingot/continuous
Harrison Plant Canton, OH	1,111,000	EAF	1	122	Ingot/continuous
		EAF	1	122	
Trident Alloys Inc. Springfield, MA	—	Air melt	2	1.36	Air-set/no-bake
Trumbull Metal Specialties Niles, OH	1,200	Air melt	6	2.79	Air-set/no-bake
Union Electric Steel Corp. Burgettstown, PA	—	EAF	1	54.00	Ingot
Universal Stainless & Alloy Products Inc. Bridgeville, PA	95,000	EAF	1	45.00	Ingot
North Jackson, OH	—	Vacuum melt	1	16.00	Ingot
Valbruna Slater Stainless Inc. Fort Wayne, IN	18,000	EAF	1	15.00	Ingot/pig
	68,000	EAF	1	18.00	

IRON and STEEL PLANT FACILITIES

NORTH AMERICAN SPECIALTY ALLOY AND FOUNDRY FACILITIES

Company	Annual cap. (metric tons)	Melting type	No. of furnaces	Avg. heat size (metric tons)	Casting method
Victoria Precision Alloys Victoria, TX	—	Air melt	3	2.09	Air-set/no-bake, green sand — horiz. parted, green sand — vert. parted
Waukesha Foundry Co. Inc. Waukesha, WI	—	Air melt	11	19.96	Air-set/no-bake, lost foam, plaster mold
Wear-Tek Spokane, WA	181	Air melt	6	3.17	Air-set/no-bake, green sand — horiz. parted
Weir ESCO Newton, MS	9,000	Air melt	—	—	Air-set/no-bake, green sand — horiz. parted
	9,000	EAF	2	7.26	—
Portland, OR	2,359	EAF/Air melt	3/1	27.22/ 3.27	Air-set/no-bake, gas-hardened/coldbox, shell mold, investment, green sand — horiz. parted, green sand — vert. parted
West Coast Foundry Vernon, CA	—	—	—	—	Sand
Wheelabrator Cast Products Group Walterboro, SC	131	Air melt	4	4.99	—
Whemco Lehigh Specialty Melting Latrobe, PA	54,000	EAF	1	34.00	Ingot
Whemco Steel Castings Midland, PA	—	EAF	1	—	Air-set/no-bake
Winsert Inc. Marinette, WI	136	Air melt	3	2.00	Shell mold
Wirco Foundry Champaign, IL	—	EAF/Air melt	2/6	2.27/ 0.27	Air-set/no-bake, green sand, centrifugal
Wollaston Alloys Inc. Braintree, MA	227	Air melt	8	8.50	Air-set/no-bake, shell mold

IRON and STEEL PLANT FACILITIES

NORTH AMERICAN CONTINUOUS CASTERS

Company	No. of units	Mill builder, start-up/ revamp	Mold type	No. of strands	Ladle cap. (mt)	Cast product	Stated cap. ('000 mt/ year)	Product dimensions (mm)
CANADA								
Algoma Sault Ste. Marie, ON	1	Mannesmann Demag 1979	Curved	2	227	Slab	1,906	203 x 1,016–2,159
	1	Danieli 1997	Straight, funnel	2	227	Slab	2,178	89 x 787–1,600
AltaSteel Inc., Part of Kyoei Steel Edmonton, AB	1	Koppers 1974	Straight	3	68	Billet	331	150–200 sq.
ArcelorMittal North America Dofasco G.P. Hamilton, ON	1	Mannesmann Demag/ Hitachi Zosen 1987	Straight	2	317	Slab	2,450	218 x 740–1,600
	1	VAI 1996	Straight	1	167	Slab	1,400	218 x 740–1,600
Long Products Canada G.P. Contrecoeur-East Contrecoeur, QC	1	Concast/VAI 1972/ 1972/2006	Curved	6	141	Billet	862	120–160 sq.
	1	VAI 1978	Straight	1	141	Slab	907	203 x 762–1,550
Long Products Canada G.P. Contrecoeur-West Contrecoeur, QC	1	Concast 1974	Curved	4	104	Billet	454	120–150 sq.
EVRAZ North America EVRAZ Regina Regina, SK	1	Pecor/ Mesta/ Primetals Technologies 1987/2016	Curved	1	135	Slab	1,300	254/203 x 1,016–2,210

2023 AIST Directory — Iron and Steel Plants 175

IRON and STEEL PLANT FACILITIES

NORTH AMERICAN CONTINUOUS CASTERS

Company	No. of units	Mill builder, start-up/ revamp	Mold type	No. of strands	Ladle cap. (mt)	Cast product	Stated cap. ('000 mt/ year)	Product dimensions (mm)
Gerdau Long Steel North America Manitoba Mill Selkirk, MB	1	Danieli 1997	Curved	3	54	Billet, bloom	390	170–254 sq.; 178 x 406
Whitby, ON	1	Concast 1981/2006	Curved	5	123	Billet	907	130 sq.; 140 x 187; 152 x 254
Ivaco Rolling Mills LP L'Orignal, ON	1	Concast 1975/1982	Curved	4	68	Billet	363	140 sq.
	1	Concast 2015	Curved	3	68	Billet	635	160 sq.
Rio Tinto Iron & Titanium Sorel-Tracy, QC	1	Rokop 1986	Curved	4	110	Billet, round	517	130–160 sq.; 215 dia.
Stelco Inc. Lake Erie Works Nanticoke, ON	1	Mannesmann Demag 1980/1997	Curved	2	250	Slab	2,650	240 x 1,050–2,030
Valbruna ASW Steel Inc. Welland, ON	1	Danieli 1987	Curved	3	64	Billet, bloom	363	115–146 sq.; 203 x 254
MEXICO								
Aceros del Noreste-Acenor Chihuahua, CI	1	Rokop 1977	Vertical	2	30	Billet	109	100–150 sq.
	1	Continua International 1959	Vertical	2	14	Billet	54	50–75 sq.
Aceros Nacionales Tlalnepantla, MX	1	Mannesmann Demag 1977	Curved	4	50	Billet	159	83–107 sq.
	1	Mannesmann Demag 1973	Curved	4	50	Billet	159	83–107 sq.

IRON and STEEL PLANT FACILITIES

NORTH AMERICAN CONTINUOUS CASTERS

Company	No. of units	Mill builder, start-up/ revamp	Mold type	No. of strands	Ladle cap. (mt)	Cast product	Stated cap. ('000 mt/ year)	Product dimensions (mm)
Altos Hornos de México (AHMSA) Monclova, CA	1	Siemens VAI 2014	Straight	1	150	Slab	1,200	152–203; 1,524–2,464
	1	Mannesmann Demag/ Hitachi/ Corus 1995/2010	Curved	2	150	Slab	1,500	200–300 x 990–1,990
	1	Mannesmann Demag/ Hitachi 1983	Curved	2	150	Slab	1,100	200 x 838–1,575
	1	Mannesmann Demag 1976	Curved	2	150	Slab	750	200 x 838–1,066
ArcelorMittal North America ArcelorMittal Mexico Lázaro Cárdenas, MC	1	Hitachi-Zosen/SMS Siemag 1988/2010	Curved	2	220	Slab	2,000	200–250 x 965–1,930
	1	Hitachi-Zosen 1988	Curved	2	220	Slab	2,000	200–250 x 965–1,930
	1	Siemens VAI 1976/1998	Curved	6	109	Billet	750	100–150 sq.
	1	Siemens VAI 1976/1996	Curved	6	109	Billet	750	127 sq.
	1	Siemens VAI 1976/1996	Curved	6	109	Billet	750	127 sq.
Deacero S.A. de C.V. Celaya, GJ	2	Danieli 2006	Curved	6	91	Billet	1,000	160–170 sq.
Saltillo, CA	1	Danieli 1999	Curved	4	57	Billet	700	160–215 dia.
Fonderia San Luis Potosí, SL	1	Danieli 1975/2005	Curved	4	68	Billet	400	120–130 sq.

IRON and STEEL PLANT FACILITIES

NORTH AMERICAN CONTINUOUS CASTERS

Company	No. of units	Mill builder, start-up/ revamp	Mold type	No. of strands	Ladle cap. (mt)	Cast product	Stated cap. ('000 mt/ year)	Product dimensions (mm)
Gerdau Gerdau Corsa S.A.P.I. de C.V. Tultitlán, MX	1	Danieli 1985	Curved	3	60	Billet	500	130–150 sq.
Grupo Simec Apizaco-Huamantla, TL	1	Danieli 2010	Curved	4	78	Billet	562	115–160 sq.
	1	Danieli 2017	Curved	3	90	Round	600	300–500 dia.
Guadalajara, JA	1	Mannesmann-Demag 1977	Curved	4	64	Billet	350	115–160 sq.
Mexicali, BS	1	Mannesmann-Demag 1993	Curved	4	73	Billet	430	115–160 sq.
Talleres y Aceros S.A. de C.V. Veracruz, VZ	1	Danieli 1992	Curved	4	54	Billet	450	100–140 sq.
	1	Castrip 2017	Twin roll	1	100	Strip	655	0.9–1.8 x 1,345–1,680
TenarisTamsa Veracruz, VZ	1	Mannesmann-Demag 1986	Curved	5	132	Billet, round	800	215–368 dia.
Ternium Apodaca, NL	1	Danieli 1993	Curved	5	82	Billet	660	130 sq.
Monterrey, NL	2	SMS Concast 1994	Funnel	1	181	Slab	2,200	50 x 787–1,346
Puebla, PU	1	Concast 1996/1997/1998	Curved	5	118	Billet	600	130–160 sq.; 215 rd.
UNITED STATES								
Alton Steel Inc. Alton, IL	1	Mannesmann Demag 1986/2006	Straight	6	191	Billet, bloom	726	102 x 235–394; 178 sq.

IRON and STEEL PLANT FACILITIES

NORTH AMERICAN CONTINUOUS CASTERS

Company	No. of units	Mill builder, start-up/ revamp	Mold type	No. of strands	Ladle cap. (mt)	Cast product	Stated cap. ('000 mt/ year)	Product dimensions (mm)
Arkansas Steel Associates LLC Newport, AR	1	Mitsubishi/ Rokop 1994	Curved	2	34	Billet, bloom	318	100–175 sq.; 178 x 432
ATI Inc. ATI Specialty Rolled Products Brackenridge, PA	1	Concast 1978	Curved	1	113	Slab	454	203 x 660–1,320
Carpenter Technology Corp. Reading, PA	1	Concast 1978	Curved	2	45	Billet, bloom	100	127 x 203–254
Cascade Steel Rolling Mills Inc. McMinnville, OR	1	Danieli 1991	Curved	5	100	Billet	635	137–160 sq.
Charter Manufacturing Co. Charter Steel –Cleveland Cuyahoga Heights, OH	1	Danieli 2006	Curved	4	77	Billet	590	140–178 sq.
Charter Steel – Saukville Saukville, WI	1	Concast 1991	Curved	4	91	Billet	499	140 sq.
Cleveland-Cliffs Inc. Burns Harbor, IN	1	Mannesmann Demag/ VAI/SMS 1975/2004/ 2010	Curved	2	277	Slab	1,815	254 x 965–1,930
	1	VAI/ SteelPlantech 1986/2015	Straight	2	277	Slab	2,904	254 x 965–2,159

IRON and STEEL PLANT FACILITIES

NORTH AMERICAN CONTINUOUS CASTERS

Company	No. of units	Mill builder, start-up/ revamp	Mold type	No. of strands	Ladle cap. (mt)	Cast product	Stated cap. ('000 mt/ year)	Product dimensions (mm)
Cleveland-Cliffs Inc. (cont'd) Butler Works Butler, PA	1	Mannesmann Demag 1970	Curved	2	159	Slab	454	203 x 660–1,600
	1	Mannesmann Demag 1981	Curved	2	159	Slab	454	203 x 660–1,320
Cleveland Works East Cleveland, OH	1	Mannesmann Demag/ Hitachi-Zosen 1983	Curved	2	250	Slab	2,632	229 x 864–1,854
Cleveland Works West Cleveland, OH	1	Mannesmann Demag 1993	Curved	2	200	Slab	1,815	229 x 610–1,626
Coatesville, PA	1	Concast 1969/ 1988/2013	Curved	1	150	Slab	681	305 x 2,159
Dearborn Works Dearborn, MI	1	Mannesmann Demag/ Hitachi-Zosen/SMS Siemag 1986/2006	Straight	2	230	Slab	2,359	203 x 965–1,880
	1	Concast 1996	Curved	1	230	Slab	1,180	203 x 762–1,524

180   2023 AIST Directory — Iron and Steel Plants

IRON and STEEL PLANT FACILITIES

NORTH AMERICAN CONTINUOUS CASTERS

Company	No. of units	Mill builder, start-up/ revamp	Mold type	No. of strands	Ladle cap. (mt)	Cast product	Stated cap. ('000 mt/ year)	Product dimensions (mm)
Indiana Harbor East No. 2 S.P. (idle) East Chicago, IN	1	Mannesmann Demag/ Hitachi-Zosen 1985	Curved	1	200	Slab	1,089	235 x 889–1,930
	1	Mannesmann Demag/ Hitachi-Zosen 1986/1989	Curved	2	200	Slab	1,452	235 x 610–1,524
Indiana Harbor East No. 3 S.P. (idle) East Chicago, IN	2	Sumitomo/ Primetals Technologies 1983/2016	Curved/ straight	1	259	Slab	1,724	254 x 1,067–2,032
Indiana Harbor East No. 4 S.P. East Chicago, IN	1	Mannesmann Demag/ Hitachi-Zosen 1972/2000	Straight	2	236	Slab	2,722	235 x 864–1,676
Indiana Harbor Long Carbon (idle) East Chicago, IN	1	Paul Wurth 1990	Curved	4	227	Billet	544	178 sq.
Mansfield Works Mansfield, OH	1	Siemens VAI 1995	Straight	1	127	Slab	681	133 x 635–1,270
Middletown Works Middletown, OH	1	Mannesmann Demag/VAI 1972/1995	Curved	2	204	Slab	2,722	229 x 1,016–1,320
Riverdale, IL	1	SMS 1996	Funnel	1	82	Slab	907	56 x 940–1,600
Steelton, PA	1	Mannesmann Demag 1983	Curved	3	136	Bloom	1,089	370 x 600

IRON and STEEL PLANT FACILITIES

NORTH AMERICAN CONTINUOUS CASTERS

Company	No. of units	Mill builder, start-up/ revamp	Mold type	No. of strands	Ladle cap. (mt)	Cast product	Stated cap. ('000 mt/ year)	Product dimensions (mm)
Commercial Metals Company CMC Steel Alabama Birmingham, AL	1	Rokop/ VAI-Pomini 1992	Curved	4	79	Billet, bloom	653	120–203 sq.; 152 x 203–254
CMC Steel Arizona Mesa, AZ	1	Danieli 2009	Curved	1	32	Billet	368	130 sq.
CMC Steel Florida Jacksonville, FL	1	Rokop 1976	Curved	4	91	Billet	726	130 sq.
CMC Steel New Jersey Sayreville, NJ	1	Danieli 1996	Curved	6	77	Billet	681	115–130 sq.
CMC Steel Oklahoma Durant, OK	1	Danieli 2018	Curved	1	44	Billet	326	130 sq.
CMC Steel South Carolina Cayce, SC	1	Mannesmann Demag 1991	Curved	4	89	Billet, bloom	692	127–133 sq.; 159 x 194
CMC Steel Tennessee Knoxville, TN	1	Rokop 2000	Curved	3	54	Billet	363	127 sq.
CMC Steel Texas Seguin, TX	1	Concast 2006	Curved	4	111	Billet, bloom	1,008	102–159 sq.; 184 x 137
EVRAZ North America EVRAZ Rocky Mountain Steel Pueblo, CO	1	Mannesmann Demag 1994/2005	Curved	6	136	Rounds	998	195–311 dia.

IRON and STEEL PLANT FACILITIES

NORTH AMERICAN CONTINUOUS CASTERS

Company	No. of units	Mill builder, start-up/ revamp	Mold type	No. of strands	Ladle cap. (mt)	Cast product	Stated cap. ('000 mt/ year)	Product dimensions (mm)
Gerdau Long Steel North America Cartersville, GA	1	VAI/ Primetals Technologies 1999/2018	Curved	4	107	Billet, bloom, beam blank	726	130–160 sq.; 160 x 230–320; 285 x 175 x 77
Charlotte, NC	1	Concast/ Rokop 1979	Curved	3	41	Billet	381	114–127 sq.
Jackson, TN	1	Rokop/VAI 1981/2003	Curved	4	127	Billet	590	133–159 sq.; 117–152 x 168–178
Midlothian, TX	1	Concast 1975	Curved	4	136	Billet	726	165 sq.
	1	Concast 1981	Curved	5	136	Billet, bloom, beam blank	885	127–152 x 178–254; 305 x 152–210 x 75–100
	1	Concast 1991	Curved	2	136	Beam blank	544	431–711 x 220–305 x 51
Petersburg, VA	2	SMS Concast 1999	Curved	2	136	Beam blank	1,089	406–1,041 x 229–368 x 51
St. Paul, MN (idle)	1	Various/ Danieli 1994/2014	Curved	4	82	Billet, bloom	544	152–165 sq.
Wilton, IA	1	Koppers/ various 1976	Curved	3	73	Billet	299	140 sq.

IRON and STEEL PLANT FACILITIES

NORTH AMERICAN CONTINUOUS CASTERS

Company	No. of units	Mill builder, start-up/ revamp	Mold type	No. of strands	Ladle cap. (mt)	Cast product	Stated cap. ('000 mt/year)	Product dimensions (mm)
Gerdau Special Steel North America Fort Smith, AR	1	Vallourec 1984	Straight, centrifugal	3	50	Rounds	426	140–228 dia.
Jackson, MI	1	Vallourec 1974	Straight, centrifugal	2	50	Rounds	272	170–179 dia.
Monroe, MI	1	Danieli 2012	Curved	4	116	Billet	817	152–240 sq.
JSW Steel USA Mingo Junction, OH	1	Mannesmann Demag 1983	Curved	2	285	Slab	2,359	288 x 990 x 2032
Leggett & Platt Sterling Steel Co. LLC Sterling, IL	1	Concast 1980	Curved	8	350	Billet	1,430	130 sq.
Liberty Steel USA Liberty Steel & Wire Peoria Peoria, IL	1	Concast 1998	Curved	6	159	Billet	744	127 sq.
Liberty Steel Georgetown Georgetown, SC	1	Danieli 1989	Curved	6	73	Billet	907	120 sq.
Mid American Steel and Wire Madill, OK	1	Rokop 1976	Curved	3	32	Billet	272	158 sq.
NLMK NLMK Indiana Portage, IN	1	Danieli 1997	Curved	1	118	Slab	635	206 x 990–1,524
North American Stainless Ghent, KY	1	SMS Demag 2000	Straight	1	136	Slab	1,216	200 x 600–1,600
	1	Danieli 2007	Curved	4	136	Billet	200	200 sq.

IRON and STEEL PLANT FACILITIES

NORTH AMERICAN CONTINUOUS CASTERS

Company	No. of units	Mill builder, start-up/ revamp	Mold type	No. of strands	Ladle cap. (mt)	Cast product	Stated cap. ('000 mt/ year)	Product dimensions (mm)
North Star BlueScope Steel Delta, OH	1	Sumitomo/ Siemens VAI 1996/2006	Straight	1	172	Slab	1,906	100 x 990– 1,575
Nucor Corp. Nucor Steel– Arkansas Blytheville, AR	2	SMS 1992/1994	Straight, funnel	1	150	Slab	2,450	50–70 x 914– 1,625
Nucor Steel Auburn Inc. Auburn, NY	1	Concast/ various 1975/1990/ 2005/2007	Curved	3	67	Billet	500	127– 159 sq.
Nucor Steel–Berkeley Huger, SC	1	SMS 1996/2013	Straight, funnel	1	159	Slab	1,450	50–65 x 900– 1,920
	1	SMS 2000/2019	Straight, funnel	1	159	Slab	1,450	50–65 x 900– 1,920
	1	SMS Concast 1998	Curved	4	159	Bloom, billet, beam blank	910	160 sq.; 160 x 230; 77 x 220 x 330
Nucor Steel Birmingham Inc. Birmingham, AL	1	Rokop 1993	Curved	3	54	Billet	454	140 sq.
Nucor Steel– Decatur LLC Trinity, AL	2	Sumitomo 1997	Straight	2	180	Slab	2,381	90 x 915– 1,625
Nucor Steel Florida Inc. Frostproof, FL	1	Danieli 2020	Curved	1	45	Billets	380	130 sq.
Nucor Steel Gallatin LLC Ghent, KY	1	SMS 1995	Funnel	1	181	Slab	1,600	65 x 1,067– 1,650
	1	Danieli 2021	Vertical curved	1	181	Slab	3,100	110 x 900– 1,870

IRON and STEEL PLANT FACILITIES

NORTH AMERICAN CONTINUOUS CASTERS

Company	No. of units	Mill builder, start-up/ revamp	Mold type	No. of strands	Ladle cap. (mt)	Cast product	Stated cap. ('000 mt/ year)	Product dimensions (mm)
Nucor Corp. (cont'd) Nucor Steel–Hertford County Cofield, NC	1	Danieli 2000	Straight, funnel	1	154	Slab	2,269	135–160 x 1,830–3,125
Nucor Steel–Indiana Crawfordsville, IN	2	SMS 1989/1994	Straight, funnel	1	118	Slab	907	50 x 915–1,397
	1 (idle)	Castrip 2002	Twin roll	1	100	Strip	490	0.9–1.8 x 1,345–1,410
Nucor Steel Jackson Inc. Flowood, MS	1	Concast 2009	Curved	3	50	Billet	550	100–160 sq.
Nucor Steel Kankakee Inc. Bourbonnais, IL	1	Rokop 1986	Curved	4	77	Billet	794	115–160 sq.
Nucor Steel Marion Inc. Marion, OH	1	Gladwin/ Rokop 1984	Straight	4	47	Billet	345	115–140 sq.
Nucor Steel Memphis Inc. Memphis, TN	1	Danieli 2008	Curved	3	91	Rounds	771	267–511 dia.
Nucor Steel–Nebraska Norfolk, NE	1	Concast 1997/2014	Curved	5	100	Billet, rounds	907	168 sq., 157–225 dia.
Nucor Steel Seattle Inc. Seattle, WA	1	Concast 1985/2005	Curved	4	107	Billet	998	130–160 sq.
Nucor Steel Sedalia LLC Sedalia, MO	1	Danieli 2020	Curved	1	45	Billet	380	130 sq.
Nucor Steel–South Carolina Darlington, SC	1	Rokop 1993	Curved	4	109	Billet	907	133–178 sq.

IRON and STEEL PLANT FACILITIES

NORTH AMERICAN CONTINUOUS CASTERS

Company	No. of units	Mill builder, start-up/ revamp	Mold type	No. of strands	Ladle cap. (mt)	Cast product	Stated cap. ('000 mt/ year)	Product dimensions (mm)
Nucor Steel–Texas Jewett, TX	1	Concast 2005	Curved	5	82	Billet, bloom	907	160 sq.; 152 x 228
Nucor Steel Tuscaloosa Inc. Tuscaloosa, AL	1	Concast 1996	Curved	1	136	Slab	1,200	135 x 1,016– 2,565
Nucor Steel–Utah Plymouth, UT	1	Rokop 1981	Curved	4	54	Billet, bloom	907	165 sq.; 127–140 x 215–292
Nucor-Yamato Steel Co. Blytheville, AR	1	Concast/ Sumitomo 1988	Curved	4	113	Bloom, beam blank, slab	1,361	200 x 280– 470; 370–400 x 460–510 x 120; 155 x 330–935
	1	Concast/ Sumitomo 1993	Curved	2	113	Beam blank, slab	1,270	410–513 x 600– 1,150 x 120–165; 155 x 1,045
	1	Castrip 2012	Twin roll	1	109	Strip	613	0.7–2.0 x 1,345– 1,680
Optimus Steel Beaumont, TX	2	Concast/ various, 1976/2004	Curved	4	113	Billet	590	130– 152 sq.
Outokumpu Stainless USA LLC Calvert, AL	1	VAI 2012	Straight	1	160	Slab	1,000	180–240 x 800– 1,900

IRON and STEEL PLANT FACILITIES

NORTH AMERICAN CONTINUOUS CASTERS

Company	No. of units	Mill builder, start-up/ revamp	Mold type	No. of strands	Ladle cap. (mt)	Cast product	Stated cap. ('000 mt/ year)	Product dimensions (mm)
Republic Steel Canton Hot Rolled Bar Plant Canton, OH	1	Danieli 1995	Curved	4	195	Bloom	780	254 x 330
	1	Danieli 2005	Curved	5	195	Billet, bloom	613	170–254 sq.; 178–254 x 305–406
Lorain Hot Rolled Bar Plant Lorain, OH (idle)	1	Mannesmann Demag 1983	Curved	6	200	Billet, bloom, round	907	150–267 sq.; 152–311 dia.
	1	Mannesmann Demag 1995	Curved	5	200	Billet, bloom, round	1,089	267 sq.; 310 x 370; 267–342 dia.
SSAB Americas SSAB Alabama Inc. Axis, AL	1	VAI 2001	Straight	1	168	Slab	1,134	152 x 3,048
SSAB Iowa Inc. Muscatine, IA	1	Mannesmann Demag 1997	Straight	1	144	Slab	1,134	153 x 3,048
Steel Dynamics Inc. Engineered Bar Products Div. Pittsboro, IN	1	Demag/SMS 1996/2004	Curved	3	91	Billet, bloom	653	178 sq.; 262 x 358
Flat Roll Group Butler Div. Butler, IN	2	SMS 1996, 1998	Funnel	1	150	Thin slab	3,000	65 x 915–1,625
Flat Roll Group Columbus Div. Columbus, MS	2	SMS Siemag 2008, 2011	Straight, funnel	1	150	Thin slab	3,086	55–80 x 914–1,930
Flat Roll Group Southwest- Sinton Div. Sinton, TX	1	SMS 2021	Funnel	1	210	Thin slab	2,700	110–140 x 1035–2134

IRON and STEEL PLANT FACILITIES

NORTH AMERICAN CONTINUOUS CASTERS

Company	No. of units	Mill builder, start-up/ revamp	Mold type	No. of strands	Ladle cap. (mt)	Cast product	Stated cap. ('000 mt/ year)	Product dimensions (mm)
Roanoke Bar Div. Roanoke, VA	1	Danieli 1982	Curved	5	77	Billet	544	100–152 sq.
Steel of West Virginia Inc. Huntington, WV	1	Concast 1975	Curved	3	59	Billet, beam blank	254	100 sq.; 248 x 152
Structural and Rail Div. Columbia City, IN	1	SMS 2002	Curved	4	109	Bloom, beam blank	1,160	430–1,005 x 260–420 x 78–90; 152–254 x 254–305
	1	Siemens VAI 2010	Curved	4–5	109	Billet, bloom	1,160	178–203 sq; 203–254 x 254–356
Tenaris TenarisKoppel Koppel, PA	1	Arbed/ Danieli 1984/2021	Curved	4	83	Round	544	165–270 dia.
TimkenSteel Corp. Faircrest Plant Canton, OH	1	SMS Concast 2014	Straight	3	175	Bloom	900	280–460 x 430–610
Harrison Plant Canton, OH (idle)	1	Sumitomo/ Concast 1992	Curved	4	118	Bloom	590	280 x 375
United States Steel Corporation Big River Steel Osceola, AR	2	SMS 2016, 2019	Funnel	1	150	Slab	3,300	55–85 x 900–1,930

IRON and STEEL PLANT FACILITIES

NORTH AMERICAN CONTINUOUS CASTERS

Company	No. of units	Mill builder, start-up/ revamp	Mold type	No. of strands	Ladle cap. (mt)	Cast product	Stated cap. ('000 mt/ year)	Product dimensions (mm)
United States Steel Corporation (cont'd) Fairfield Works Fairfield, AL (idle)	1	SMS Demag/ SMS Concast 1984/2020	Curved	4	154	Round	850	267–343 dia.
	1	Fives-Cail Babcock 1988	Straight	1/2	154	Slab	1,750	254 x 762–2,540
Gary Works No. 1 BOP Gary, IN	1	USS/SMS 1967/ 1982/2016	Straight	1	200	Slab	1,742	230 x 914–2,006
	2	Concast/ SMI 1986	Straight	2	204	Slab	3,339	230 x 1,168–2,388
	1	VAI 1991	Straight	Single/ twin	204	Slab	1,906	230 x 813–2,642
Granite City Works Granite City, IL	1	VAI 1986/2015	Straight	Single/ twin	209	Slab	1,814	220 x 889–2,210
	1	Concast 1990	Curved	1	209	Slab	1,307	220 x 890–2,032
Great Lakes Works Ecorse, MI	1	Concast 1977	Curved	Single/ twin	231	Slab	1,996	244 x 762–2,515
	1	Concast/ Sumitomo 1987	Straight	2	231	Slab	2,541	244 x 610–1,930
Mon Valley Works Edgar Thomson Plant Braddock, PA	1	Davy Distington 1992	Straight	2	227	Slab	2,541	203 x 710–1,675
Vallourec Star LP Youngstown, OH	1	Concast/ Wean United 1986/2009	Curved	3	90	Round	730	222–286 dia.

IRON and STEEL PLANT FACILITIES

NORTH AMERICAN HOT STRIP MILLS

Company	Mill builder Start-up/ modernization	Reheat furnaces (No.) and type (manufacturer)	Roughing mill (No.) and type of stands/edgers	Finishing mill (No. of stands)/looper type	Finished sizes Thickness x width, mm	Stated cap. '000 mt/year
CANADA						
Algoma 106-Inch Strip Mill Sault Ste. Marie, ON	Dominion Engineering Works 1982	(3) WB	(1) 2-hi reversing with edger, (1) 4-hi plate reversing mill with edger; HAGC	(6) Pneumatic	1.50–12.70 x 762–2,540	680 strip + 410 plate
Direct Strip Production Complex Sault Ste. Marie, ON	Danieli, United/Siemens 1997	(2) Tunnel (ANDRITZ METALS Bricmont)	(1) Non-reversing with hydraulic edger	(6) 4-hi, pos. and neg. roll bending and shifting	1.00–15.88 x 800–1,600	2,000
ArcelorMittal North America Dofasco G.P. Hamilton, ON	Dominion Engineering Works/Hitachi, GE/Toshiba, Primetals Technologies 1983/1987, 2001, 2020	(2) 12-zone WB (Italimpianti)	(1) 2-hi reversing with attached entry edger	(7) Electric	1.52–12.70 x 762–1,600	4,700
Stelco Inc. Lake Erie Works Nanticoke, ON	Wean United, Dominion Engineering Works/CGE, GE 1983/1988–2000	(2) Pusher (Tenova Salem), (1) WB (Stein-Huertey)	(1) 4-hi reversing with coupled entry edger	(6): (3) Pneumatic, (2) low-inertia electric	2.03–15.88 x 889–1,880	3,300
MEXICO						
Altos Hornos de México Monclova, CA	Hitachi, United Engineering/GE, Siemens 1967/1992, 1995, 2010	(2) 10-zone WB (Davy)	(1) 2-hi reversing with (2) edgers	F0 stand + (6)	1.22–12.70 x 584–1,626	2,800

2023 AIST Directory — Iron and Steel Plants

IRON and STEEL PLANT FACILITIES

NORTH AMERICAN HOT STRIP MILLS

Company	Mill builder Start-up/ modernization	Reheat furnaces (No.) and type (manufacturer)	Roughing mill (No.) and type of stands/ edgers	Finishing mill (No. of stands)/ looper type	Finished sizes Thickness x width, mm	Stated cap. '000 mt/ year
Ternium MC1 Guerrero, NL	Lewis 1923/1964/ 2007: automation, roughing mill and furnace	(1) 9-zone WB (Tenova Techint)	(1) 2-hi reversing with coupled edger, (1) 4-hi reversing	(6)	1.40 x 711– 1,117	1,000
MC2 Guerrero, NL	SMS Demag/ Siemens 1994/2nd caster 1998/2nd downcoiler 2000	(2) Tunnel	N/A	(6)	0.91– 12.70 x 914– 1,372	1,500
MC3 Churubusco, NL	Blaw-Knox/ United GE 1994/mod. 1996/ 2001–2002	(1) 9-zone pusher (Tenova Salem), (1) 9-zone WB (Tenova Techint)	(1) 4-hi reversing with attached edger	(6) Hydraulic	1.90– 15.60 x 760– 1,524	2,400
UNITED STATES						
ArcelorMittal North America AM/NS Calvert LLC Calvert, AL	SMS Siemag 2010	(3) WB (Tenova LOI Italimpianti)	(1) 2-hi, (1) 4-hi	(7)	1.50– 25.40 x 800– 1,860	5,400
ATI Inc. ATI Specialty Rolled Products Brackenridge, PA	Siemens VAI 2014	(2) WB, car-bottom, induction	(1) 4-hi reversing with coupled edger	(7) Hydraulic	1.78– 21.00 x 711– 2,083	–
California Steel Industries Inc. a Nucor-JFE Co. Fontana, CA	Kaiser Engineering/ GE 1958/1969, 1974, 1976, 1989–1992, 1997	(2) Hydraulic WB (Chugai-Ro and Tenova Core)	(1) 2-hi RSB; (5) 4-hi with edgers on last (4) stands	(6)	1.37– 15.88 x 711– 1,880	2,700

IRON and STEEL PLANT FACILITIES

NORTH AMERICAN HOT STRIP MILLS

Company	Mill builder Start-up/ modernization	Reheat furnaces (No.) and type (manufacturer)	Roughing mill (No.) and type of stands/ edgers	Finishing mill (No. of stands)/ looper type	Finished sizes Thickness x width, mm	Stated cap. '000 mt/year
Cleveland-Cliffs Inc. Burns Harbor, IN	United Engineering 1966/mod. 1986/1998, 2003	(3) 5-zone pusher (Rust)	(2) 2-hi, (3) 4-hi with edgers on last 4 stands	(7)	1.45–12.70 x 660–1,930	4,100
Butler Works Butler, PA	Bliss, Continental/ Westinghouse 1957	(4) Pushers, 3 zones	(1) 4-hi reversing with (2) edgers	(5) Electric	1.70–6.40 x 635–1,270	600
Cleveland Works Cleveland, OH	MESTA/GE 1971/1988–1998, 2003–2005	(3) 5-zone pusher (Lotus)	(3) 2-hi, (2) 4-hi, with VSB and (4) edgers	(7) Electric on stands 1–3, Hydraulic on stands 4–7	1.42–19.05 x 711–1,905	3,000
Dearborn Works Dearborn, OH (idle)	Blaw-Knox 1974/1990, 2002, 2007	(3) 8-zone WB (Swindell)	(2) 2-high and (2) 4-high; (1) VSB and (3) close-coupled edgers	(7) Electric	1.47–13.34 x 683–1,585	3,600
Indiana Harbor East East Chicago, IN	United Engineering/ GE 1965/1990/ 1992/2001/ 2018–2020	(3) WB (Italimpianti and Voest-Alpine)	(3) 2-hi, (3) 4-hi, with VSB and (5) edgers	(6) Electric on stands 1–3, Hydraulic on stands 4–6	1.93–9.50 x 660–1,859	4,900
Mansfield Works Mansfield, OH	United, Bliss/ Siemens VAI 1952/1995	(1) WB, 5 zones	(1) 2-hi reversing	(6) Hydraulic	2.00–12.70 x 635–1,270	500

IRON and STEEL PLANT FACILITIES

NORTH AMERICAN HOT STRIP MILLS

Company	Mill builder Start-up/ modernization	Reheat furnaces (No.) and type (manufacturer)	Roughing mill (No.) and type of stands/ edgers	Finishing mill (No. of stands)/ looper type	Finished sizes Thickness x width, mm	Stated cap. '000 mt/ year
Cleveland-Cliffs Inc. (cont'd) Middletown Works Middletown, OH	United/ Westinghouse, Siemens 1966/1999	(1) Pusher, 5 zones, and (3) WBs, 8 zones	(3) 2-hi, (3) 4-hi; VSB and (5) attached edgers	(7) Pneumatic + Electric	1.80– 9.50 x 635– 2,032	5,400
Riverdale, IL	SMS/ Siemens 1996	(1) Tunnel	N/A	(7)	1.07– 17.00 x 914– 1,585	900
JSW Steel USA Mingo Junction, OH	Blaw-Knox, United Engineering/ GE 1965/2001	(3) Pusher	(1) 2-hi, (4) 4-hi, VSB and (4) edgers	(6)	1.50– 9.50 x 800– 1,930	2,800
NLMK NLMK Indiana Portage, IN	Sack/ MESTA/ Danieli/ Converteam 1992/2006/ 2020	(1) Pusher (OFU) with Tenova Adapt Skids	(1) 2-hi reversing	(5) Electric	1.78– 19.00 x 813– 1,549	1,000
NLMK Pennsylvania Farrell, PA	United Engineering 1966/1999	(3) 3-zone pusher, ((2) Rust, (1) Tenova Salem)	(1) 4-hi reversing with edger	(6) Hydraulic	1.50– 16.46 x 838– 1,359	1,800
North Star BlueScope Steel Delta, OH	Danieli 1997	(1) Tunnel, (1) heated transfer	(2) 4-hi, (1) edger	(6)	1.30– 12.70	2,700
Nucor Corp. Nucor Steel–Arkansas Blytheville, AR	SMS/ Siemens 1992	(2) Roller hearth tunnel with (2) shuttles	–	(6) Hydraulic	1.40– 15.88 x 914– 1,635	2,300
Nucor Steel–Berkeley Huger, SC	SMS/ Siemens 1996/2015	(2) Roller hearth tunnel with (2) shuttles	–	(7) Hydraulic	1.40– 15.88 x 914– 1,905	2,300

IRON and STEEL PLANT FACILITIES

NORTH AMERICAN HOT STRIP MILLS

Company	Mill builder Start-up/ modernization	Reheat furnaces (No.) and type (manufacturer)	Roughing mill (No.) and type of stands/ edgers	Finishing mill (No. of stands)/ looper type	Finished sizes Thickness x width, mm	Stated cap. '000 mt/year
Nucor Steel–Decatur LLC Trinity, AL	MHI/INNSE/ Siemens 1996	(2) Roller hearth tunnel with (2) shuttles	(1) 2-hi, (1) 4-hi, (1) edger	(5) Electric	1.40–19.05 x 914–1,651	2,300
Nucor Steel Gallatin LLC Ghent, KY	SMS/Siemens/ Danieli 1995/1996 (F6); 2020 (roughing stands)	(1) Tunnel with 9 zones and swivel ferry system	(2) 4-hi	(6)	1.40–17.40 x 1,029–1,626	1,500
Nucor Steel–Indiana Crawfordsville, IN	SMS/Westinghouse/ Siemens 1989; 1992 (F5), 1995 (F6)	(2) Roller hearth tunnel with (2) shuttles	–	(6) Hydraulic	1.47–15.88 x 914–1,397	1,900
Steel Dynamics Inc. Flat Roll Group Butler Div. Butler, IN	SMS/ Siemens 1996	(2) Tunnel (ANDRITZ METALS Bricmont)	–	(7) Hydraulic	1.09–12.70 x 991–1,588	2,700
Flat Roll Group Columbus Div. Columbus, MS	SMS/TMEIC 2007/2011 (tunnel furnace)	(2) Roller hearth tunnel with (2) shuttles	–	(6) Hydraulic	1.50–19.20 x 927–1,930	3,100
Flat Roll Group Southwest-Sinton Division Sinton, TX	SMS/TMEIC 2021	(1) 116-m tunnel	(2) 4-high, (2) edgers	(6) Hydraulic	1.20–25.40 x 1,016–2,134	2,700
United States Steel Corporation Big River Steel Osceola, AR	SMS 2016	(1) Tunnel, SMS	N/A	(6) Hydraulic	1.47–25.40 x 900–1,980	2,830

IRON and STEEL PLANT FACILITIES

NORTH AMERICAN HOT STRIP MILLS

Company	Mill builder Start-up/ modernization	Reheat furnaces (No.) and type (manufacturer)	Roughing mill (No.) and type of stands/ edgers	Finishing mill (No. of stands)/ looper type	Finished sizes Thickness x width, mm	Stated cap. '000 mt/ year
United States Steel Corporation (cont'd) Gary Works Gary, IN	Blaw-Knox/ GE 1967/1993– 1994	(4) Pusher (Rust)	VSB and (3) 2-hi, (3) 4-hi with last (5) edgers	(7) Electric	1.80– 25.40 x 711– 1,981	5,700
Granite City Works Granite City, IL	MESTA/GE 1966/1978, 1992/1996/ 2004/2009	(4) Electro-mechanical WB (Tenova Salem)	(2) 2-hi (2) 4-hi with (4) edgers	(7)	1.45– 18.08 x 602– 1,991	3,300
Mon Valley Works Irvin Plant West Mifflin, PA	MESTA 1938/1995, 1998	(5) 3-zone pushers (Rust)	(1) 2-hi, (4) 4-hi, last (3) with edgers	(6)	1.52– 10.16 x 635– 1,676	2,500

IRON and STEEL PLANT FACILITIES

NORTH AMERICAN PLATE MILLS

Company	Mill configuration	Slab sizes (thick x width x length, mm)	Finished sizes (thick x width, mm)	Discrete or coil	Stated cap. ('000 mt/year)
CANADA					
Algoma Sault Ste. Marie, ON	(1) 2-hi rougher with edger, (1) 4-hi plate mill with rougher/finisher	206 x 1,168–2,184 x 3,607–9,804	6.35–76 x 1,270–3,810	Discrete and coil	910
EVRAZ North America EVRAZ Regina Regina, SK	Finishing mill	152–203 x 1,016–1,981 x 8,890–9,373	9.53–76 x 1,016–1,981	Discrete and coil	1,000
MEXICO					
Altos Hornos de México (AHMSA) Monclova, CA	(1) 4-hi reversing rougher, (1) 4-hi reversing finisher	152–250 x 914–2,438 x 2,032–8,763	7.92–51 x 1,422–3,048	Discrete	630
	(1) 4-hi reversing Steckel	155–250 x 914–2,438 x 1,524–8,765	4.5–50 x 1,600–3,200	Discrete	1,000
UNITED STATES					
Cleveland-Cliffs Inc. Burns Harbor – 110-Inch Burns Harbor, IN	(1) 2-hi reversing rougher, (1) 4-hi reversing finisher	102–305 x 914–1,930 x 1,372–3,759	4.75–25 x 1,219–2,540	Discrete	330
Burns Harbor – 160-Inch Burns Harbor, IN	(1) 2-hi reversing rougher, (1) 4-hi reversing finisher	102–305 x 914–1,930 x 1,778–6,655	4.75–102 x 1,219–3,861	Discrete	710
Coatesville – 140-Inch Coatesville, PA	(1) 4-hi reversing	102–406 x 965–2,540 x 1,067–4,369	4.75–711 x 1,524–3,353	Discrete	500
Coatesville – 206-Inch Coatesville, PA	(1) 4-hi reversing	229–406 x 1,270–2,540 x 2,159–4,369	15.88–711 x 3,556–4,953	Discrete	50
Conshohocken, PA	(2) 4-hi reversing Steckel	102–305 x 1,016–2,692 x 1,727–7,315	3.56–76 x 1,219–2,642	Discrete and coil	410

IRON and STEEL PLANT FACILITIES

NORTH AMERICAN PLATE MILLS

Company	Mill configuration	Slab sizes (thick x width x length, mm)	Finished sizes (thick x width, mm)	Discrete or coil	Stated cap. ('000 mt/year)
Cleveland-Cliffs Inc. (cont'd) Gary Plate Gary, IN	Finishing mill	102–305 x 1,143–2,032 x 1,727–7,417	4.75–38 x 1,219–3,861	Discrete	580
EVRAZ North America EVRAZ Portland Portland, OR	(2) 4-hi reversing Steckel	102–381 x 1,219–3,099 x 2,540–10,262	4.75–203 x 1,219–3,505	Discrete and coil	1,090
JSW Steel (USA) Inc. Baytown, TX	(1) 2-hi reversing rougher, (1) 4-hi reversing finisher	203–305 x 914–1,829 x 1,092–3,861	7.94–152 x 1,829–3,861	Discrete	710
Nucor Corp. Nucor Steel–Hertford County Cofield, NC	(1) 4-hi	127–152 x 1,829–3,175 x 4,064–15,240	7.94–76 x 1,829–3,175	Discrete	1,000
Nucor Steel Longview LLC Longview, TX	(1) 4-hi reversing	Ingot casting: 813 x 1,524 x 3,302	19.05–311 x 3,048	Discrete	160
Nucor Steel Tuscaloosa Inc. Tuscaloosa, AL	(1) 4-hi reversing Steckel	134 x 1,067–2,565 x 8,128–19,507	19.05–64 x 1,067–2,540	Discrete and coil	1,090
SSAB Americas SSAB Alabama Inc. Axis, AL	(1) 4-hi reversing Steckel	152 x 1,524–3,150 x 6,096–19,202	4.57–76 x 1,524–3,099	Discrete and coil	1,130
SSAB Iowa Inc. Muscatine, IA	(1) 4-hi reversing Steckel	152 x 1,524–3,124 x 5,588–22,352	4.57–76 x 1,524–3,099	Discrete and coil	1,130

IRON and STEEL PLANT FACILITIES

NORTH AMERICAN COLD MILLS

Company	Mill ID	Configuration (No./type of stands)	Nominal width (max/avg., mm)	Finished sizes thick x width (mm)	Stated cap. ('000 mt/year)
CANADA					
Algoma Sault Ste. Marie, ON	80-in. RCM	(1) 4-hi RV	1,880/1,200	0.38–3.40 x 1,880	363
	80-in. Temper Mill	(1) 4-hi	1,880/1,200	0.38–4.32 x 1,880	635
ArcelorMittal North America Dofasco G.P. Hamilton, ON	No. 1 CPCM	(5) 4-hi tandem	1,626/1,181	1.90–5.08 (HB) 0.18–2.16 (CR) x 660–1,626	1,179
	No. 1 56-in. TCM	(5) 4-hi tandem	1,226/940	1.78–7.37 x 685–1,225	416
	No. 2 72-in. TCM	(5) 4-hi tandem	1,143	0.32–3.43 x 685–1,626	1,300
Long Products Canada G.P. Contrecoeur, QC	No. 1	(1) RV	1,308/1,092	0.38–3.23 x 610–1,308	227
	No. 2	(1) RV	1,308/1,092	0.38–3.23 x 610–1,308	227
Stelco Inc. Hamilton Works Hamilton, ON	No. 2 Temper Mill	(1) 4-hi	1,295	0.30–3.40 x 457–1,295	299
	No. 3 Temper Mill	(1) 4-hi	1,854	0.51–5.08 (HB) 0.51–3.45 (CR)x 610–1,854	544
	Cold Mill	(4) 4-hi tandem	1,854	0.33–4.17 x 610–1,854	1,451
	Cold Mill	(5) 4-hi tandem	1,143	0.18–0.61 x 457–1,143	453

IRON and STEEL PLANT FACILITIES

NORTH AMERICAN COLD MILLS

Company	Mill ID	Configuration (No./type of stands)	Nominal width (max/avg., mm)	Finished sizes thick x width (mm)	Stated cap. ('000 mt/year)
MEXICO					
Altos Hornos de México (AHMSA) Monclova, CA	60-in. RCM	(1) 4-hi RV	1,525/1,142	0.30–1.12 x 1,118–1,524	90
	TCM	(4) 4-hi tandem	1,320/1,083	0.46–2.67 x 1,320	840
	TCM	(5) 4-hi tandem	965/892	0.18–0.91 x 965	375
	No. 1 Temper Mill	(2) 4-hi tandem	965/887	0.15–0.36 x 965	200
	No. 2 Temper Mill	(1) 4-hi no RV	1,320/1,071	0.46–2.64 x 965	625
APM Monterrey, NL	21.5 and 56 x 56 TCM	(4) 4-hi tandem	1,270	0.36–3.43 x 610–1,270	720
Ternium Monterrey, NL	Cold Mill No. 1	(1)	1,067/902	0.36–3.05 x 585–1,092	91
	Cold Mill No. 2	(1)	1,016/864	0.20–1.52 x 610–1,000	120
	Cold Mill No. 3	(1)	1,257/1,041	0.23–2.16 x 838–1,257	209
	Cold Mill No. 4	(1)	1,320/1,118	0.42–3.05 x 610–1,320	218
UNITED STATES					
ArcelorMittal North America AM/NS Calvert LLC Calvert, AL	PLTCM	(5) 4-hi tandem	1,870/1,448	0.30–3.00 x 800–1,870	2,500
California Steel Industries Inc., a Nucor-JFE Co. Fontana, CA	TCM	(5) 4-hi	1,200	0.20–3.50 x 610–1,524	907
	Temper Mill	(2) 4-hi tandem	1,200	0.23–3.43 x 610–1,524	327
Cleveland-Cliffs Inc. Burns Harbor, IN	80-in. TCM	(5) 4-hi tandem	1,880	0.36–3.18 x 610–1,880	1,814

IRON and STEEL PLANT FACILITIES

NORTH AMERICAN COLD MILLS

Company	Mill ID	Configuration (No./type of stands)	Nominal width (max/avg., mm)	Finished sizes thick x width (mm)	Stated cap. ('000 mt/year)
Butler Works Butler, PA	No. 2 TCM	(4) 4-hi tandem	1,270	0.33–6.35 x 610–1,270	299
	No. 3 TCM	(3) 4-hi tandem	1,283	0.15–2.54 x 610–1,283	544
Cleveland Works Cleveland, OH	84-in. TCM	(5) 4-hi tandem	1,854/ 1,372	0.48–3.18 x 890 x 1,930	1,197
Coshocton Works Coshocton, OH	36 Z-Mill (ZR-22BB-40)	(1) 20-hi Z-mill	980	0.25–4.45 x 660–980	55
	52 Z-Mill (ZR-22-52)	(1) 20-hi Z-mill	1,295	0.38–5.59 x 838–1,295	79
	No. 1 Z-hi CRM	(1) 18-hi Z-mill	959	0.46–4.57 x 508–960	52
	No. 2 Z-hi CRM	(1) 18-hi Z-mill	711	0.20–3.18 x 457–711	27
	30 Temper Mill	(1) 2-hi temper	749	0.25–1.90 x 305–750	15
	48 Temper Mill	(1) 2-hi temper	1,283	0.25–3.81 x 533–1,283	54
Dearborn Works Dearborn, MI	PLTCM	(5) 6-hi tandem	1,829/ 1,270	0.37–2.67 x 737–1,829	1,905
Middletown Works Middletown, OH	No. 3 CSM	(5) 4-hi tandem	1,930/ 1,320	0.38–3.30 x 610–1,930	2,722
	No. 5 Temper Mill	(1) 4-hi	1,854/ 1,397	0.35–3.20 x 610–1,930	726
	No. 6 Temper Mill	(1) 4-hi	1,930/ 1,320	0.40–2.92 x 610–1,930	1,542
Rockport Works Rockport, IN	Continuous Cold Mill	(5) tandem: (3) 4-hi + (2) 6-hi	2,032	0.30–4.04 x 508–2,032	2,086
	No. 1 Temper Mill	(1), 4-hi	2,057	0.30–4.04 x 508–2,057	1,542
Tek and Kote New Carlisle, IN	CDCM	(4) 6-hi tandem	1,680/ 1,250	0.40–2.40 x 850–1,680	1,500
Zanesville Works Zanesville, OH	No. 1 Z-Mill	(1) 20-hi Z-mill	1,118	0.38–3.81 x 559–1,118	113

IRON and STEEL PLANT FACILITIES

NORTH AMERICAN COLD MILLS

Company	Mill ID	Configuration (No./type of stands)	Nominal width (max/avg., mm)	Finished sizes thick x width (mm)	Stated cap. ('000 mt/year)
NLMK NLMK Pennsylvania Farrell, PA	No. 4 TCM	(5) 4-hi tandem	1,270/1,090	0.25–3.10	910
	No. 26 Sendzimir Mill	(1) 20-hi Z-mill	1,270/1,090	0.38–3.20	90
	No. 27 Temper Mill	(1) 4-hi	1,270/1,090	0.38–3.20	90
	No. 28 Temper Mill	(1) 4-hi	1,270/1,090	0.25–3.10	410
Nucor Corp. Nucor Steel-Arkansas Blytheville, AR	CM1 RV/Temper Mill	(1) 4-hi	1,590/1,295	0.30–2.79 x 915–1,590	205 (temper); 650 (RV)
	CM2 RV/Temper Mill	(1)	1,651	0.25 x 915–1,650	327 (temper); 200 (RV)
	CM2 S6H RV Mill	(1) 6-hi	1,651	0.25 x 915–1,650	345
Nucor Steel-Berkeley Huger, SC	RV Mill 1	(1)	1,651	0.28 x 915–1,650	453
	RV Mill 2	(1)	1,829	0.33 x 915–1,830	680
	Temper Mill	(1)	1,829	0.28 x 915–1,830	680
Nucor Steel-Decatur LLC Trinity, AL	Tandem Mill	(4) 4-hi	1,830/1,245	0.30–4.06 x 915–1,650	1,179
	Temper Mill	(1)	1,651	0.30 x 915–1,650	1,089
Nucor Steel-Indiana Crawfordsville, IN	RV Mill	(1) 4-hi	1,525/1,200	0.36–2.54 x 865–1,385	635
	RV/Temper Mill	(1) 4-hi	1,525/1,200	0.36–1.93 x 865–1,385	454 (temper); 109 (RV)
Steel Dynamics Inc. Flat Roll Group Butler Div. Butler, IN	RV Mill	(2) 4-hi RV	1,575/1,234	0.23–4.19 x 915–1,575	907

IRON and STEEL PLANT FACILITIES

NORTH AMERICAN COLD MILLS

Company	Mill ID	Configuration (No./type of stands)	Nominal width (max/avg., mm)	Finished sizes thick x width (mm)	Stated cap. ('000 mt/year)
Heartland Div. Terre Haute, IN	Cold Mill	(2)	1,524/ 1,200	0.25–1.27 x 1,040–1,525	726
United States Steel Corporation Big River Steel Osceola, AR	PLTCM	(5) 4-hi tandem	1,850/ 1,300	0.25–3.00 x 915–1,850	1,179
	SPM1	(1) 4-hi	1,800/ 1,245	0.32–1.50 x 915–1,800	
Fairfield Works Fairfield, AL	52	(6) 4-hi	1,257	0.30–2.79 x 1,257	1,361
Gary Works Gary, IN	80	(5) 4-hi	1,880/ 1,364	0.36–3.40 x 710–1,880	2,631
	52	(6) 4-hi	1,168	0.18–0.69 x 1,168	748
Granite City Works Granite City, IL	56	(4) 4-hi	1,270/ 1,050	0.48–2.08 x 610–1,270	708
Midwest Plant Portage, IN	84	(5) 4-hi	1,930/ 1,041	0.30–4.19 x 1,930	1,996
	80	(5) 4-hi	1,829	0.30–3.05 x 610–1,830	1,252
Mon Valley Works Irvin Plant West Mifflin, PA	52	(5) 4-hi	1,219	0.18–2.03 x 510–1,200	590
UPI Pittsburg, CA	60 PLTCM	(5) 6-hi tandem	1,422/ 1,184 (sheet); 870 (tin)	0.20–2.54 x 610–1,372	1,497

IRON and STEEL PLANT FACILITIES

NORTH AMERICAN GALVANIZING LINES

Company	Line no., name	Coating types	Thickness (mm) Min	Thickness (mm) Max	Max width (mm)	Stated cap. ('000 mt/year)
CANADA						
ArcelorMittal North America Dofasco G.P. Hamilton, ON	No. 3	GI, GA	0.20	1.1	1,321	220
	No. 4	GI, AZ	0.25	2.3	1,537	236
	No. 5	GI, GA	0.51	2.1	1,829	490
	No. 6	GI, GA, AL, Al-Si	1.00	4.3	1,651	650
Dofasco G.P. Côteau-du-Lac Montreal, QC	No. 1	GI, GA	0.23	3.4	1,372	230
Dofasco G.P. Windsor Windsor, ON	No. 1	GI, GA	0.40	2.1	1,829	440
Material Sciences Corp. Toronto, ON	No. 1 EG	–	0.20	2.4	1,524	41
Stelco Inc. Hamilton Works Hamilton, ON	3CGL	GI	0.30	1.2	1,320	181
	Z-Line	GI, GA	0.58	2.1	1,830	470
MEXICO						
Galvasid S.A. de C.V. (Grupo Industrial LM) Apodaca, NL	No. 1	GI, AZ	0.34	2.8	1,525	340
Nucor Corp. Nucor-JFE Steel Mexico Silao, GT	No. 1	GI, GA	0.40	2.6	1,850	400
POSCO Mexico Altamira, TM	CGL 1	GI, GA	0.40	2.0	1,900	400
	CGL 2	GI, GA	0.40	2.3	1,860	500
Ternium Centro Industrial Ternium Pesquería, NL	No. 1	GI, GA	0.31	1.5	>1,650	356
Monclova, CA	IMSA	GI, AZ	0.20	1.9	1,270	250
San Nicolás de los Garza, NL	H-G No. 1	GI	0.20	1.9	1,295	130
	H-G No. 2	GI, GA	0.25	2.7	1,295	136
	H-G No. 3	GI, AZ	0.20	1.2	1,270	150

IRON and STEEL PLANT FACILITIES

NORTH AMERICAN GALVANIZING LINES

Company	Line no., name	Coating types	Thickness (mm) Min	Thickness (mm) Max	Max width (mm)	Stated cap. ('000 mt/year)
Tenigal SRL de C.V. Monterrey, NL	Tenigal 1	GI, GA	0.40	2.6	1,850	400
Universidad Plant Monterrey, NL	No. 2	GI, GA	0.25	2.0	1,270	145
	No. 3	GI, AZ	0.21	3.4	1,219	226
	No. 4	GI	0.28	0.9	1,270	272
Villacero Cintacero Guadalupe, NL	EG	–	0.30	3.2	711	48
Zincacero Apodaca, NL	HDGL	GI	0.26	1.5	1,244	91
UNITED STATES						
ArcelorMittal North America AM/NS Calvert LLC Calvert, AL	HDGL1	GI, GA	0.50	2.3	1,870	500
	HDGL3	GI, GA	0.50	2.5	1,670	500
	HDGL4	GI, AL, AL-SI	0.30	2.5	1,670	520
California Steel Industries Inc., a Nucor-JFE Co. Fontana, CA	No. 1	GI, GA	0.38	4.3	1,524	430
	No. 2	GI, GA	0.25	1.5	1,321	300
Cleveland-Cliffs Inc. Burns Harbor, IN	HDGL	GI, GA	0.51	2.0	1,829	550
Cleveland Works Cleveland, OH	HDGL	GI, GA	0.55	2.5	1,830	650
Columbus, OH	HDGL	GI, GA	0.50	1.7	1,829	400
Dearborn Works Dearborn, MI	HDGL	GI, GA	0.57	2.7	1,829	454
Indiana Harbor East East Chicago, IN	5 CGL (idle)	GI, GA	0.51	2.5	1,830	–
Indiana Harbor West East Chicago, IN	No. 2	GI, GA	0.38	4.8	1,830	557
Middletown Works Middletown, OH	No. 2 EG	–	0.48	1.9	1,900	454
	No. 3	GI	0.53	3.5	1,880	508
	No. 4	AL	0.38	3.5	1,575	426

IRON and STEEL PLANT FACILITIES

NORTH AMERICAN GALVANIZING LINES

Company	Line no., name	Coating types	Thickness (mm) Min	Thickness (mm) Max	Max width (mm)	Stated cap. ('000 mt/year)
Cleveland-Cliffs Inc. (cont'd) Rockport Works Rockport, IN	CGL	GI, GA	0.46	2.0	2,032	907
Tek and Kote New Carlisle, IN	KCGL	GI, GA	0.38	2.3	1,829	454
	EG	–	0.43	2.0	1,829	454
Double G Coatings Co. L.P. Jackson, MS	DGC	GI, AZ	0.23	0.8	1,245	286
Gregory Industries Inc. Canton, OH	No. 1	GI, GA	0.76	4.6	495	132
Material Sciences Corp. Canfield Metal Coating Canfield, OH	EG	–	0.20	2.0	1,219	60
Electric Coating Technologies East Chicago, IN	EG	–	0.25	2.2	1,829	181
MSC Walbridge Coatings Inc. Walbridge, OH	No. 1 EG	–	0.46	2.5	1,829	363
National Galvanizing L.P. Monroe, MI	No. 1	GI, GA	1.52	6.4	1,219	204
NLMK NLMK Pennsylvania Sharon, PA	No. 2	GI	0.30	1.8	1,524	250
	No. 3	GI, GA	0.51	2.5	1,829	454
North Star BlueScope Steel Steelscape LLC Kalama, WA	No. 2	GI	0.26	1.2	1,295	191
Steelscape LLC Rancho Cucamonga, CA	No. 1	AZ	0.30	0.9	1,270	200
Nucor Corp. Nucor Steel–Arkansas Blytheville, AR	No. 1	GI	0.30	2.7	1,575	544
	No. 2 CAGL	GI, GA; GF, ZM, CAL capable	0.23	2.7	1,900	454
Nucor Steel–Berkeley Huger, SC	No. 1	GI, GA	0.25	2.7	1,676	635

IRON and STEEL PLANT FACILITIES

NORTH AMERICAN GALVANIZING LINES

Company	Line no., name	Coating types	Thickness (mm) Min	Thickness (mm) Max	Max width (mm)	Stated cap. ('000 mt/year)
Nucor Steel–Decatur LLC Trinity, AL	No. 1	GI, GA	0.51	6.3	1,829	544
Nucor Steel Gallatin LLC Ghent, KY	No. 1 PAGL	GI, GA, pickled	–	6.4	1,854	454
Nucor Steel–Indiana Crawfordsville, IN	No. 1	GI	0.38	3.3	1,346	318
Precoat Metals Elkridge, MD	EG	–	0.18	1.5	1,372	64
PRO-TEC Coating Co. Leipsic, OH	CGL 1	GI, GA	0.58	2.6	1,880	544
	CGL 2	GI, GA	0.38	1.7	1,702	454
	CGL 3	GI, GA	0.60	2.7	1,670	454
Spartan Steel Coating LLC Monroe, MI	No. 1	GI, GA	0.46	1.9	1,575	544
Steel Dynamics Inc. Flat Roll Group Butler Div. Butler, IN	No. 1	GI, GA	1.02	4.2	1,575	544
	No. 2	GI, GA	0.25	1.9	1,575	327
Flat Roll Group Columbus Div. Columbus, MS	CGL 1	GI, GA	0.25	1.5	1,829	408
	CGL 2	GI, AZ	0.46	3.3	1,829	349
	CGL 3	GI, AL, AL-SI	0.33	4.1	1,829	363
Flat Roll Group Heartland Div. Terre Haute, IN	No. 1	GI	0.25	1.5	1,854	318
Flat Roll Group Jeffersonville Plant Jeffersonville, IN	–	GI, AZ	0.30	1.1	1,524	272
Flat Roll Group Southwest-Sinton Div. Sinton, TX	No. 1	GI, GA, AZ	0.25	4.0	1,930	499
	No. 2	AZ	0.25	1.5	1,829	272
GalvTech Pittsburgh, PA	No. 1	GI, GF	0.38	1.2	1,550	431
MetalTech Pittsburgh, PA	No. 1	GI, GF	1.02	4.1	1,320	340

IRON and STEEL PLANT FACILITIES

NORTH AMERICAN GALVANIZING LINES

Company	Line no., name	Coating types	Thickness (mm) Min	Thickness (mm) Max	Max width (mm)	Stated cap. ('000 mt/year)
Steel Dynamics Inc. (cont'd) NexTech Turtle Creek, PA	No. 1	GI, GF	0.18	0.5	1,092	154
Tata Steel Plating Apollo Metals Bethlehem, PA	EGL	–	0.10	1.8	830	50
Thomas Steel Strip Corp. Warren, OH	EGL	–	0.10	1.7	724	80
Ternium Ternium USA Inc. Shreveport, LA	No. 1	GI, AZ	0.33	3.2	1,372	236
United States Steel Corporation Big River Steel Osceola, AR	HDGL 1	GI, CAL capable	0.36	3.0	1,850	490
Fairfield Works Fairfield, AL	No. 5 DualLine	GI, AZ	0.30	1.0	1,257	272
Granite City Works Granite City, IL	Triple G	GI, AZ	0.23	0.9	1,245	254
Great Lakes Works Ecorse, MI	No. 1 CGL	GI, GA	0.58	2.0	1,854	472
	No. 1 EGL (idle)	–	0.41	1.8	1,880	–
Great Lakes Works EGL at Dearborn Dearborn, MI	DESCCo (idle)	–	0.56	1.7	1,854	–
Midwest Plant Portage, IN	72-in. GACT	GI, GA	0.56	3.2	1,829	454
	No. 3 CL	GI	0.23	0.9	1,245	245
Mon Valley Works Fairless Plant Fairless Hills, PA	GAL3	GI, GA	0.37	2.0	1,626	299
Mon Valley Works Irvin Plant West Mifflin, PA	GAL1	GI	0.91	4.3	1,321	200
	GAL2	GI	0.36	1.6	1,219	160
UPI Pittsburg, CA	No. 2 CC	GI, GA	0.38	3.2	1,410	363

IRON and STEEL PLANT FACILITIES

NORTH AMERICAN GALVANIZING LINES

Company	Line no., name	Coating types	Thickness (mm) Min	Thickness (mm) Max	Max width (mm)	Stated cap. ('000 mt/year)
Wheeling-Nippon Steel Inc. Follansbee, WV	No. 1 AGL	GI, GA, GF, ZAM, AL	0.36	2.7	1,549	363
	No. 2 CGL	GI, AZ	0.20	1.2	1,270	272
Worthington Industries Delta, OH	No. 1	GI, GA	0.64	6.4	1,575	363

IRON and STEEL PLANT FACILITIES

CANADIAN AND U.S. LONG PRODUCTS MILLS

Company	Equipment manufacturer	Reheat furnace type, supplier	Mill stand layout, qty. of stands	Product size (mm) and shape range or type of mill	Stated cap. ('000 mt/ year)
CANADA					
AltaSteel Inc., Part of Kyoei Steel Edmonton, AB	Danieli	WB, Danieli	IN, 16	50–152 x 6–51 flats, 25.4–102 rounds and sq.	350
ArcelorMittal North America Long Products Canada G.P. Contrecoeur-East Contrecoeur, QC	Brightside/ Morgan	Pusher, Salem	IN, 25	5.5–19 wire rod, 12.7–22.2 coiled rounds	415
Long Products Canada G.P. Contrecoeur-West Contrecoeur, QC	SIMAC	Pusher, Salem	IN, 16	10M–35M rebar, flats	450
Long Products Canada G.P. Longueuil Longueuil, QC	Birdsboro/ Danieli	WB, Bendotti	IN, 16	178 x 19–25.4 x 51 flats, 14.3–102 rounds, 12.7–16 sq., 152 wide-grade blade	315
Gerdau Long Steel North America Cambridge, ON	Danieli	Pusher, Bricmont	IN, 18	19–51 angles, #3–#8 rebar, small special sections	330
Manitoba No. 4 Mill Selkirk, MB	SMS Schloemann	WB, Salem	RV IN, 15	19 x 4.8–102 x 25.4 channels, 9.5–38.4 sq., 12.7–32 rounds, #3–#11 rebar	300
Manitoba No. 5 Mill Selkirk, MB	Quad/Danieli	–	RV, 2	Special sections, structural, beams	100
Whitby Bar Mill Whitby, ON	Ferrco/Danieli	Pusher, Ferrco	IN, 18	25–102 flats, 38–90 angles, 76 channels, #4–#11 rebar	500

IRON and STEEL PLANT FACILITIES

CANADIAN AND U.S. LONG PRODUCTS MILLS

Company	Equipment manufacturer	Reheat furnace type, supplier	Mill stand layout, qty. of stands	Product size (mm) and shape range or type of mill	Stated cap. ('000 mt/year)
Whitby Structural Mill Whitby, ON	Quad	Pusher, Bricmont	IN, 15	125–305 flats, 100–150 angles, 100–250 channels	600
Ivaco Rolling Mills L'Orignal, ON	Morgan	WB, Danieli	IN, 32	4.8–25.4 wire rod, #3–#5, 10M–15M coiled rebar	810
Max Aicher North America Hamilton, ON	1–2: Morgardshammar, 3–16: Birdsboro	WB, Italimpianti	IN, 18	15–65 rounds, #5–#20, 15–55 mm rebar	300
UNITED STATES					
Alton Steel Inc. Alton, IL	Birdsboro/ Moeller-Neumann	WB, Bloom	IN CC, 17	19–100 rounds, 19–36 hexagons, 35–51 sq., 19–46 coils	250
ATI Inc. ATI Specialty Materials Richburg, SC	Danieli	Induction, Ajax	IN, 18	Bar/wire rod	–
Byer Steel Corp. Cincinnati, OH	AB Steel	WB, AB Steel	IN, 16	#3–#11, 10M–35M rebar	50
Carpenter Technology Corp. Latrobe, PA	Morgardshammar/ Kocks	Roller hearth and induction	IN, 3	Wire, rod, SBQ	–
Reading, PA	SMS	2 WB, 5 batch, induction, Surface Combustion	RV IN, 17		32
Talley Metals Hartsville, SC	Morgardshammar	Induction, conveyor	IN, 27		32
Cascade Steel Rolling Mills Inc. McMinnville, OR	SIMAC/Pomini/ Danieli	Pusher, Bricmont	IN, 26	5.5–19 wire rod, 12–76 rounds, #3–#18 rebar, #3–#6 coiled rebar	400

IRON and STEEL PLANT FACILITIES

CANADIAN AND U.S. LONG PRODUCTS MILLS

Company	Equipment manufacturer	Reheat furnace type, supplier	Mill stand layout, qty. of stands	Product size (mm) and shape range or type of mill	Stated cap. ('000 mt/year)
Charter Manufacturing Co. Charter Steel –Cleveland Cuyahoga Heights, OH	Morgan/Kocks	WB, Davy	IN, 43	19–40 coils, 5.5–19 wire rod, 19–83 precision round bar	675
Charter Steel –Saukville Saukville, WI	Morgan/Kocks/Danieli	WB, Danieli	IN, 33	19–35 coils, 5.5–19 wire rod	620
Cleveland-Cliffs Inc. Steelton 20" Mill Steelton, PA	United/Birdsboro	Pusher, Rust	CC, 6	Railroad rails, specialty blooms, flat bars, ingots	54
Steelton 28" Mill Steelton, PA	United/Birdsboro	WB, Danieli	RV CC, 5		396
Commercial Metals Company CMC Steel Alabama Birmingham, AL	Pomini/Danieli	Pusher, Bricmont	IN, 14	Medium-section rebar	495
CMC Steel Arizona Mesa, AZ	Danieli	Induction, Elind	IN, 16	#4–#11 rebar, fence post, #3–#8 spooled rebar	300
CMC Steel Arkansas Magnolia, AR	Sakai	WB, Bricmont	IN, 12	Angles, fence post	167
CMC Steel Florida Jacksonville, FL	Laguna-Artea/Danieli	Pusher, Bricmont	IN, 26	5.5–17.5 rod, #3–#5 coiled rebar, #3–#11 rebar	500
CMC Steel New Jersey Sayreville, NJ	Danieli	WB, Core	IN, 18	#3–#11 rebar, handrail	610
CMC Steel Oklahoma Durant, OK	Danieli	Induction, Bricmont	IN, 16	#4–#11 rebar, fence post, #3–#8 spooled rebar	300

IRON and STEEL PLANT FACILITIES

CANADIAN AND U.S. LONG PRODUCTS MILLS

Company	Equipment manufacturer	Reheat furnace type, supplier	Mill stand layout, qty. of stands	Product size (mm) and shape range or type of mill	Stated cap. ('000 mt/year)
CMC Steel South Carolina Cayce, SC	Danieli	WB, AC Ledbetter	IN, 17	12.7–64 sq., 12.7–90 rounds, #3–#8 rebar	720
CMC Steel Tennessee Knoxville, TN	Pomini	Pusher, Olsen Industries	IN, 17	#4–#11 rebar	550
CMC Steel Texas Seguin, TX	Danieli	WB, Surface Combustion	IN, 17	38–152 flats, 25.4–102 angles, 75–152 channels, #3–#18 rebar	720
Crucible Industries LLC 14" Hand Mill Solvay, NY	–	Batch	CC, 6	4.8–19 x 76–203 flats, 19–152 sq., 47.6–559 round bars	10
26" Mill Solvay, NY	Birdsboro	–	RV, 1		–
EVRAZ North America EVRAZ Rocky Mountain Steel Pueblo, CO	Danieli	WB, Danieli	Tandem, 16	Rail	600
	Morgan/Various	WB, ITAM	IN, 28	5–19 wire rod, #3–#6, 10M, 15M coiled rebar	415
Franklin Industries Franklin, PA	Various	WB	CC, 15	0.95–1.33# fence post, 1–4# sign post	50
Gerdau Long Steel North America Cartersville, GA	SMS Meer/ Danieli	WB, Bricmont	RV IN, 13	Medium section	650
Charlotte, NC	Morgardshammar	Pusher, Bricmont	IN, 15	25.4–63.5 flats, 25.4–50.8 angles, 12.7–34.9 rounds, #4–#11 rebar	330
Jackson, TN	Morgards- hammar/ Danieli	Pusher, Bricmont	IN, 16	50.8–152.4 flats, 25.4–101.6 angles, 50.8 x 25.4–127 x 89 unequal angles, 76.2–127 channels, 16–50 sq., #4–#18 rebar	500

2023 AIST Directory — Iron and Steel Plants   213

IRON and STEEL PLANT FACILITIES

CANADIAN AND U.S. LONG PRODUCTS MILLS

Company	Equipment manufacturer	Reheat furnace type, supplier	Mill stand layout, qty. of stands	Product size (mm) and shape range or type of mill	Stated cap. ('000 mt/year)
Gerdau Long Steel North America (cont'd) Midlothian Bar Mill Midlothian, TX	Ferrco/SMS	WB, Danieli	IN, 19	44.5–76.2 flats, 15.9–101.2 rounds, #3–#11 rebar	450
Midlothian Large Section Mill Midlothian, TX	Quad	WB, Bricmont	RV IN, 11	W12–W24, flat piling	545
Midlothian Medium Section Mill Midlothian, TX	SMS Meer	WB, ITAM	IN, 14	S3–W14 beams, 100–250 channels	800
Petersburg, VA	SMS Meer	WB, Fives Stein	RV IN, 8	Heavy section	1,000
St. Paul, MN (idle)	Ferrco/Kocks/Danieli	Pusher, North American	IN, 18	Bar	450
Wilton, IA	Ferrco/Danieli/SIMAC	Pusher, Bricmont	IN, 16	Angles, flats, rounds, squares	320
Gerdau Special Steel North America Fort Smith, AR	Ferrco/Kocks/Danieli	WB, Danieli	IN, 18	Bar	500
Jackson, MI	Danieli/Morgardshammar	Pusher, Bricmont	IN, 16	Bar	270
Monroe, MI	Ferrco/Kocks/Danieli	WB, Danieli	IN, 18	Bar	500
Jersey Shore Steel Co. Jersey Shore, PA	Danieli/Various	WB, Bricmont	IN, 17	Light section, bed angles	120
Liberty Steel USA Liberty Bar Products Chicago Heights, IL	Des-Eng-Con	Pusher, Flinn & Dreffein	CC, 10	25–100 flats	60
Liberty Steel & Wire Peoria Peoria, IL	BlawKnox	Pusher, Siemens	IN, 25	Wire rod	680

IRON and STEEL PLANT FACILITIES

CANADIAN AND U.S. LONG PRODUCTS MILLS

Company	Equipment manufacturer	Reheat furnace type, supplier	Mill stand layout, qty. of stands	Product size (mm) and shape range or type of mill	Stated cap. ('000 mt/ year)
Liberty Steel Georgetown Georgetown, SC	SMS Scholemann/ Kocks	Pusher, AFC Holcroft	IN, 25	Wire rod	540
Leggett & Platt Sterling Steel Co. LLC Sterling, IL	Morgan/ Birdsboro	Pusher, Bricmont	RV CC, 21	25.4–229 rounds, 63.5–203.round corner sq., #4–#18 rebar	454
Nucor Corp. Nucor Steel Auburn Inc. Auburn, NY	SIMAC/NKK/ Danieli	WB, Bendotti	IN, 18	Light-section angles, channels, rounds, flats, rebar	450
Nucor Steel–Berkeley Huger, SC	Danieli	WB, Bricmont	IN, 15	W101–W406 beams, C127–C381 channels, 152 angle	720
Nucor Steel Birmingham Inc. Birmingham, AL	Danieli	Pusher	IN, 16	#4–#18 rebar, rounds	600
Nucor Steel Connecticut Inc. Wallingford, CT	Morgan	Pusher	IN, 25	5.5–16 wire rod	270
Nucor Steel Florida Inc. Frostproof, FL	Danieli	Induction, Danieli	IN, 16	#4–#11 rebar, #3–#8 coiled rebar	380
Nucor Steel Jackson Inc. Flowood, MS	Danieli/SIMAC	Pusher, Bricmont	IN, 18	25.4–127 x 4.4–305 flats, 25.4–51 angles, 12.7–25.4 sq., 12.7–45 rounds, #3–#11 rebar	360

IRON and STEEL PLANT FACILITIES

CANADIAN AND U.S. LONG PRODUCTS MILLS

Company	Equipment manufacturer	Reheat furnace type, supplier	Mill stand layout, qty. of stands	Product size (mm) and shape range or type of mill	Stated cap. ('000 mt/year)
Nucor Corp. (cont'd) Nucor Steel Kankakee Inc. Bourbonnais, IL	Danieli	Pusher, Bricmont	IN, 14	50–127 x 12.7 flats, 38 x 38 angles, 12.7–25.4 sq., 25.4–38 rounds, #3–#11 rebar	675
	SMS	WB, Bendotti	IN, 16	101.6–304.8 flats, 76.2–152.4 angles, 76.2–254 channels, 41.3–92 rounds, #14–#18 rebar	500
Nucor Steel Kingman LLC Kingman, AZ	Danieli	WB, Danieli	IN, 28	Wire rod, rebar	360
Nucor Steel Marion Inc. Marion, OH	SMS/Danieli	Pusher, SMS	IN, 16	16–32 rounds, #3–#11 rebar, 1.75#–5# sign post	360
Nucor Steel Memphis Inc. Memphis, TN	Danieli	WB	RV IN, 9	SBQ rounds	550
Nucor Steel–Nebraska Norfolk, NE	Danieli/ Morgardshammar/ Kocks	WB, Nucor	IN, 31	5.6–19 wire rod, 19–79 rounds, 19–35 coiled rounds, 17.5–33.3 hexagons	540
	Danieli	WB, Bricmont	IN, 18	76–102 x 50–76 angles, 12.7–52 sq., 12.7–52 rounds, 17.5–52 hexagons	405
Nucor Steel Seattle Inc. Seattle, WA	Danieli	Pusher, Bricmont	IN, 18	25–152 flats, 32–102 angles, 76–152 channels, 12.7–38 rounds, #3–#18 rebar	730
Nucor Steel Sedalia LLC Sedalia, MO	Danieli	Induction, Danieli	IN, 16	#4–#11 rebar, #3–#8 spooled rebar	380

IRON and STEEL PLANT FACILITIES

CANADIAN AND U.S. LONG PRODUCTS MILLS

Company	Equipment manufacturer	Reheat furnace type, supplier	Mill stand layout, qty. of stands	Product size (mm) and shape range or type of mill	Stated cap. ('000 mt/year)
Nucor Steel–South Carolina Darlington, SC	Morgardshammar/Pomini/ SMS Meer/ Danieli	WB, Bricmont	IN, 18	6.4–26 x 38–76 flats, 25.4–51 x 25.4–51 angles, 51 channels, 14.3–56 rounds, #4–#11 rebar, 6–19 wire rod	495
	Danieli	Pusher, SMS	IN, 32	6.4–25.4 x 101.6–203 flats, 44.5–152.4 x 28.6–101.6 angles, 63.5–152.4 channels, 14.3–55.6 rounds, #8–#11 rebar	500
Nucor Steel–Texas Jewett, TX	Danieli	Pusher	IN, 18	Flats, angles, unequal leg angles, channels, squares, rounds, rebar, special sections	700
	Danieli	WB	IN, 18		600
Nucor Steel–Utah Plymouth, UT	Danieli	Pusher, Nucor/Core	IN, 11	Flats, 75–152 angles, unequal leg angles, 75–254 channels, squares, rounds, #5–#18 rebar	540
	Danieli	WB, Bricmont/ Danieli	IN, 18	Flats, 25.4–50.8 angles, unequal leg angles, 25.4–50.4 channels, squares, rounds, #3–#8 rebar, fence post, special sections, #3–#8 spooled rebar	450

IRON and STEEL PLANT FACILITIES

CANADIAN AND U.S. LONG PRODUCTS MILLS

Company	Equipment manufacturer	Reheat furnace type, supplier	Mill stand layout, qty. of stands	Product size (mm) and shape range or type of mill	Stated cap. ('000 mt/year)
Nucor-Yamato Steel Co. Large Section Mill Blytheville, AR	Kawasaki	WB, ITAM	RV, 4	Wide-flange beam, H-piling, sheet piling, standard I-beams, channels, structural shapes	1,170
Medium Section Mill Blytheville, AR	SMS/Kawasaki/ Danieli	Pusher, Davy McKee	RV, 5		900
Optimus Steel LLC Beaumont, TX	Morgan/Danieli	Pusher, Ofenbau-Union	IN, 25	5.5–17.5 wire rod, #3–#11 rebar	750
Republic Steel Canton Hot Rolled Bar Plant Canton, OH	Danieli	WB	IN, 8	Billets, squares	–
Lackawanna Hot Rolled Bar Plant Blasdell, NY	–	WB	IN, 25	25–165 rounds, 98.4–216 round corner sq., 22.2–64 hexagons, 19–30 coiled rod, 22.2–42.9 coiled hexagons	653
Lorain Hot Rolled Bar Plant Lorain, OH (idle)	BlawKnox/ Morgan	WB	IN, 30	7.5–21 wire rod, 19.8–31 coiled rounds	381
Steel Dynamics Inc. Engineered Bar Products Div. Pittsboro, IN	SMS/Danieli/ Morgardshammar	WB, Core	RV CC, 21	25.4–229 rounds, 63.5–203 round corner sq., #4–#18 rebar	300
	Pomini/Danieli	WB, ITAM	IN, 19	19.1–89 precision rounds, 25.4–63.5 round corner sq., #4–#18 rebar	650
Kentucky Electric Steel Div. Ashland, KY	Birdsboro/ Morgan-Pomini/ Siemens	Pusher, Amsier-Morton	CC IN, 11	6.4–75.0 x 38.1–305 flats	305

IRON and STEEL PLANT FACILITIES

CANADIAN AND U.S. LONG PRODUCTS MILLS

Company	Equipment manufacturer	Reheat furnace type, supplier	Mill stand layout, qty. of stands	Product size (mm) and shape range or type of mill	Stated cap. ('000 mt/ year)
Roanoke Bar Div. Roanoke, VA	Danieli	Pusher, Bricmont	IN, 17	25.4–152 x 4.8 flats, 25.4–102 angles, 76.2–102 channels, 12.7–16 sq., 16–38 rounds, #4–#11 rebar	450
Steel of West Virginia Inc. No. 1 Mill Huntington, WV	MEECO/Danieli	Pusher, Bricmont	CC, 6	Structural beams, channels, special shape sections	95
No. 2 Mill Huntington, WV	Quad/Danieli	Pusher, Bricmont	IN, 11		225
Structural and Rail Div. Columbia City, IN	SMS Meer	WB, SMS Meer	IN, 15	Beams, channels, pilings, rails	450
	Danieli	WB, SMS Meer	IN, 12	#3–#8 coiled rebar, coiled rounds	450
TimkenSteel Corp. Faircrest Plant Canton, OH	Birdsboro/Telis/ Bricmont/ Mitsubishi	Pusher, Centro/ Danieli	IN, 19	100–406 round bars	1,000
Harrison Plant Canton, OH	Danieli/SMS	WB	RV IN, 14	25–250 round bars	850
Vinton Steel LLC, Part of Kyoei Steel Vinton, TX	Various	Pusher, Salem	CC IN, 13	Rebar, rounds	360
W. Silver Inc. Vinton, TX	BlawKnox/ Various	WB, Fives Stein	IN, 12	Fence posts, angles, sign posts	120

IRON and STEEL PLANT FACILITIES

NORTH AMERICAN PIPE AND TUBE MILLS

Company	Product	Manufacturing process	Product size dia. range, mm (min-max)	API licensed	Heat treatment capabilities	Stated cap., ('000 mt/year)
CANADA						
ArcelorMittal Tubular Products Brampton, ON	Mech. tubing welded cold-sized	ERW	12.0–76.2	No	No	58
Hamilton, ON	Precision-welded automotive tubing	ERW	12.0–165.0	No	No	168
	Welded cold-sized tubing		50.8–165.0			
	Mech. tubing		31.8–317.5			
Woodstock, ON	Line pipe	ERW	60.3–178.0	Yes	Yes	107
	HSS		50.8 sq.; 101.6 x 203.0			
	Cold-drawn welded tubing		12.8–141.2			
	Mech. tubing welded cold-sized		19.1–190.5			
Atlantic Tube & Steel Inc. Mississauga, ON	Mech. and struct. tubing	ERW	19.1–158.8	No	No	–
Bull Moose Tube Co., A Caparo Co. Burlington, ON	Mech. tubing	ERW	15.9–101.6	No	No	73
Canadian Phoenix Steel Products Ltd. Toronto, ON	Spiral-welded pipe	HSAW	254–2,438	No	No	
The DB Piping Group Douglas Barwick Inc. Brockville, ON	Light wall pipe	PAW	19.1–2,438	No	Anneal	–
DFI Corp. Edmonton, AB	Struct. piling	ERW	114.3–406.4	No	No	–

IRON and STEEL PLANT FACILITIES

NORTH AMERICAN PIPE AND TUBE MILLS

Company	Product	Manufacturing process	Product size dia. range, mm (min–max)	API licensed	Heat treatment capabilities	Stated cap., ('000 mt/year)
EVRAZ North America EVRAZ Calgary Calgary, AB	OCTG casing, OCTG tubing	ERW	60.3–244.5	Yes	Yes	225
EVRAZ Camrose Camrose, AB	Line pipe	ERW	219.0–406.4	Yes	No	180
	Large-dia. pipe	DSAW	609.6–1,067			135
EVRAZ Red Deer Red Deer, AB	OCTG casing, line pipe	ERW	114.3–339.7	Yes	Yes	170
EVRAZ Regina Regina, SK	Large-dia. pipe	HSAW	660.4–1,524	Yes	No	500
	Line pipe	ERW	406.4–609.6			175
	OCTG tubing	ERW	60.3–88.9			62
J.M. Lahman Mfg. Inc. Linwood, ON	Mech. tubing	ERW	19.1–127.0	No	No	–
Nova Steel Inc. Nova Steel Inc. Baie-D'Urfé, QC	HSS mech. tubing	ERW	12.7–50.8	No	No	–
Nova Steel Inc. Woodstock, ON	Automotive tubing	ERW	25.4–101.6	No	No	100
Nova Tube (Delta) LaSalle, QC	HSS	ERW	38.1–152.4	No	No	–
Nova Tube Inc. Montreal, QC	Welded pipe	ERW	21.3–168.3	No	No	–
Quali-T-Group Inc. Quali-T-Tube Bromont, QC	HSS struct. tubing, mech. tubing	ERW	19.1–88.9	No	No	–
Samuel Associated Tube Group Associated Tube Canada Markham, ON	Welded, welded and drawn tubing	GTAW, PAW, CD	4.8–168.3	No	Bright anneal, special tempers	–

2023 AIST Directory — Iron and Steel Plants 221

IRON and STEEL PLANT FACILITIES

NORTH AMERICAN PIPE AND TUBE MILLS

Company	Product	Manufacturing process	Product size dia. range, mm (min–max)	API licensed	Heat treatment capabilities	Stated cap., ('000 mt/year)
Spiralco St. Felix-de-Kingsey, QC	Spiral pipe and tubing	HSAW	406.4–4,064	No	No	–
Tenaris AlgomaTubes Sault Ste. Marie, ON	Welded tubing	ERW	60.3–323.9	Yes	Yes	363
Precision Tube Canada ULC Red Deer, AB	Coiled tubing	HFW, LW	25.4–127.0	Yes	No	–
Welded Tube of Canada Corp. Concord, ON	OCTG casing and line pipe, mech. tubing, HSS, struct. tubing, pilings, line pipe, tubing, ROPS	ERW	19.1–273.1	Yes	Q&T	318
Zekelman Industries Inc. Atlas Tube Canada Harrow, ON	HSS tubing, OCTG casing and line pipe, pipe piles	ERW	114.3–406.4	Yes	Yes	–
Atlas Tube Canada Oak Bluff, MB	HSS struct. tubing	ERW	–	No	No	–
MEXICO						
Aermotor Monterrey, NL	Mech. tubing	ERW	–	No	No	–
ArcelorMittal Tubular Products Monterrey Escobedo, NL	Mech. tubing welded cold-sized tubes	ERW	12.7–168.3	Yes	No	140
Arco Metal S.A. de C.V. San Luis Potosí, SL	Mech. tubing, HSS tubing	ERW	12.7–76.2	No	No	–
Forza Steel Salinas Victoria, NL	HSS tubing	ERW	–	Yes	Yes	–
	Helicoidal pipe	HSAW	508.0–3,048			
	Line pipe	ERW	101.6–508.0			

IRON and STEEL PLANT FACILITIES

NORTH AMERICAN PIPE AND TUBE MILLS

Company	Product	Manufacturing process	Product size dia. range, mm (min–max)	API licensed	Heat treatment capabilities	Stated cap., ('000 mt/year)
LM Perfiles y Herrajes S.A. de C.V. Apodaca, NL	HSS tubing, mech. tubing	ERW	12.7–152.4	No	Yes	–
Nippon Steel Pipe Mexico Silao, GJ	Automotive tubing	ERW	22.2–80.0	No	No	22
Nova Steel Inc. Nova Steel Mexico Saltillo, CA	Automotive tubing	ERW	152.4	No	No	73
Precitubo El Salto, JA	Seamless tubing	CD	9.5–101.6	–	–	9
	Welded tubing	ERW	19.1–79.4			11
Productos Laminados de Monterrey (Prolamsa) A4C-Sankin Precision Tube S.A. de P.I. Escobedo, NL	Automotive pipe	ERW	–	No	No	–
Prolamsa S.A. de C.V. Escobedo, NL	HSS tubing, mech. tubing	ERW	–	No	No	–
Pytco S.A. de C.V. Frontera, CA	Mech. tubing, HSS, OCTG casing and tubing, OCTG line pipe	ERW, HFW	12.7–273.0	Yes	Yes	18
Salzgitter Group Mannesmann Precision Tubes Mexico S.A. de C.V. El Salto, JA	Cold-drawn precision tubing	CD	12.7–17.8	No	No	18
	Welded size-rolled precision tubing	ERW	20.0–76.2			20
Samuel Associated Tube Group Tubos Samuel de México Saltillo, CA	Welded tubing	GTAW, PAW, LW	6.4–63.5	–	Bright anneal	–

IRON and STEEL PLANT FACILITIES

NORTH AMERICAN PIPE AND TUBE MILLS

Company	Product	Manufacturing process	Product size dia. range, mm (min–max)	API licensed	Heat treatment capabilities	Stated cap., ('000 mt/year)
Swecomex S.A. de C.V. (Grupo Carso) Panuco, VE	DSAW line pipe	LSAW	–	Yes	No	–
TenarisTamsa Veracruz, VE	OCTG casing and line pipe, seamless mech. tubing	PPR	60.3–406.4	Yes	Yes	1,116
		CD	–			
Ternium San Nicolás de los Garza, NL	OCTG casing and line pipe, mech. tubing	ERW	–	Yes	Yes	–
Tubac S.A. de C.V. San Pedro Garza García, NL	Pipe casing	DSAW	508.0–3,658	No	No	–
Tubacero Monterrey, NL	OCTG casing, line pipe	ERW, LSAW, HSAW	168.3–3,810	Yes	Yes	726
Spiral Plant Salinas Victoria, NL	OCTG large-dia. spiral-welded line pipe	HSAW	–	Yes	Yes	–
Tuberia Laguna Gomez Palacio, DU	Line pipe	ERW	60.3–609.6	Yes	Yes	250
Tuberías Procarsa S.A. de C.V., a Subsidiary of Industrías CH (ICH) Monclova, CA	Line pipe, spiral line pipe	ERW	50.8–609.6	Yes	Yes	750
		HSAW	508.0–2,235			
		DSAW	457.2–1,219			
Tubesa S.A. de C.V. Mexico City, DF	Spiral-welded pipe	HSAW	–	–	–	–
Villacero T-H Tubería Helicoidal Pesqueria, NL	OCTG large-dia. spiral-welded line pipe	HSAW	508.0–3,048	Yes	No	–

IRON and STEEL PLANT FACILITIES

NORTH AMERICAN PIPE AND TUBE MILLS

Company	Product	Manufacturing process	Product size dia. range, mm (min–max)	API licensed	Heat treatment capabilities	Stated cap., ('000 mt/year)
Tubería Nacional S.A. de C.V. San Nicolás de los Garza, NL	Conduction pipe	ERW	21.3–168.3	Yes	Yes	–
	OCTG casing and line pipe		12.7–152.4			
UNITED STATES						
American Cast Iron Pipe Co. American Spiralweld Pipe Co. Columbia, SC	Spiral-welded line pipe	ERW, HSAW	3,658	No	No	–
American Spiralweld Pipe Co. Flint, MI	Pipe	ERW, HSAW	1,524–1,676	No	No	–
American Steel Pipe Birmingham, AL	OCTG casing and line pipe	ERW	273.0–609.6	Yes	Anneal	–
American Consolidated Industries Inc. Parthenon Tube Inc. LaVergne, TN	Tubing	Welded	10.0–101.6	No	–	–
American Tubular Products (Div. of Schaeffer) Lindon, UT	HSS, pipe	ERW	60.3–168.3	–	–	–
ArcelorMittal Tubular Products Marion, OH	AW mech. tubing	ERW	25.4–152.4	–	–	59
Shelby, OH	Welded precision tubing	ERW	31.7–317.5	–	Q&T	198
	Hot-finish seamless tubing	GTAW	55.6–171.4			
	Cold-drawn welded tubing	DOM	19.0–304.8			
	Cold-drawn seamless precision tubing	CD	34.9–196.8			

IRON and STEEL PLANT FACILITIES

NORTH AMERICAN PIPE AND TUBE MILLS

Company	Product	Manu-facturing process	Product size dia. range, mm (min–max)	API licensed	Heat treatment capabilities	Stated cap., ('000 mt/year)
Atkore International Allied Tube & Conduit Corp. De Pere, WI	Electrical conduit	ERW	–	–	–	–
Allied Tube & Conduit Corp. Harvey, IL	Electrical conduit	ERW	12.7–152.4	–	–	–
Allied Tube & Conduit Corp. Phoenix, AZ	Mech. tubing, HSS	ERW	–	–	–	–
Ascent Tubular Products American Stainless Tubing Inc. Troutman, NC	Stainless tubing	–	11–127	–	–	–
Bristol Tubular Products Bristol, TN	Mech. tubing	GTAW, ERW	12.7–3,658	No	Anneal	–
Bristol Tubular Products Munhall, PA	Pipe and tubing	GTAW, ERW, SAW, PAW	11.4–324	–	Anneal	54
Avis Industrial Corp. James Steel & Tube Co. Madison Heights, MI	HSS	ERW	33.4–168.3	No	–	–
AZZ Tubular Products Crowley, TX	OCTG casing and line pipe	Pilger mill, ERW	25.4–114.3	Yes	Normalize, Q&T	–
Berg Pipe, a Div. of EUROPIPE Berg Pipe Mobile Corp. Mobile, AL	Large-dia. spiral-welded line pipe	HSAW	609.6–1,422	Yes	Yes	163
Berg Pipe Panama City Corp. Panama City, FL	DSAW straight-seam line pipe	LSAW	609.6–1,524	Yes	Yes	218

IRON and STEEL PLANT FACILITIES

NORTH AMERICAN PIPE AND TUBE MILLS

Company	Product	Manufacturing process	Product size dia. range, mm (min–max)	API licensed	Heat treatment capabilities	Stated cap., ('000 mt/ year)
Borusan Mannesmann Baytown, TX	OCTG casing and line pipe	HFW	114.3–273.1	Yes	Yes	250
Bull Moose Tube Co., a Caparo Co. Casa Grande, AZ	Mech. tubing	ERW	–	No	No	–
Chicago Heights, IL	Mech. tubing	ERW	19.1–76.2	No	No	54
Elkhart, IN	HSS tubing	ERW	50.8–305.0	No	No	227
Gerald, MO	Mech. tubing	ERW	12.7–114.3	No	No	91
Masury, OH	Sprinkler pipe; A135/A795	ERW	25.3–114.3	No	No	73
Trenton, GA	HSS tubing	ERW	12.7–203.2	No	No	136
California Steel Industries Inc. a Nucor-JFE Co. Fontana, CA	OCTG casing, line pipe, pilings	ERW, HFW	168.3–406.4	Yes	Weld seam normalize	227
	Pilings, line pipe	ERW, HFW	219.0–609.6	Yes		363
Century Tube Corp. Somerville, NJ	Struct. tubing	GTAW	19.0–114.3	No	–	–
Chen International Wildwood, FL	Precision-welded pipe	GTAW	12.7–2,032	No	Anneal	–
Cleveland-Cliffs Tubular Components Columbus, IN	Automotive tubing	ERW	38.1–88.9	No	No	–
Walbridge, OH	Mech. tubing, HSS tubing	ERW	19.1–168.3	No	No	–
The DB Piping Group Douglas Bros. Portland, ME	Tubing, fabrication	GTAW	26.6–1,219	No	Yes	–
Dundee Products Dundee, MI	HSS	ERW, CD	16.0–79.4	–	–	–

IRON and STEEL PLANT FACILITIES

NORTH AMERICAN PIPE AND TUBE MILLS

Company	Product	Manu-facturing process	Product size dia. range, mm (min–max)	API licensed	Heat treatment capabilities	Stated cap., ('000 mt/year)
Dura-Bond Industries Dura-Bond Coating Duquesne Duquesne, PA	Coated pipe	FBE, dual-layer ARO	114.3–914.4	N/A	No	6.264 mil. linear ft.
Dura-Bond Pipe McKeesport McKeesport, PA	Line pipe	HFW	219.0–508.0	Yes	Weld seam normalize	220
Dura-Bond Pipe Steelton Steelton, PA	Line pipe	LSAW, UOE	609.6–1,067	Yes	–	400
EVRAZ North America EVRAZ Portland Portland, OR	Large-dia. pipe	HSAW	660.4–1,524	Yes	No	225
EVRAZ Rocky Mountain Steel Pueblo, CO	Seamless OCTG casing	Seamless	177.8–244.5	Yes	Yes	135
EXLTUBE Kansas City, MO	Struct. and mech. tubing, OCTG line pipe	ERW	33.4–111.0	Yes	Yes	–
			63.5–194.0			
Felker Bros. Corp. Felker Piping Products Marshfield, WI	Pipe and tubing	ERW	355.6–2,438	No	–	–
Hanna Steel Corp. Pekin, IL	Mech. tubing, HSS	ERW	21.3–273.0	No	No	–
Tuscaloosa, AL	Mech. tubing, HSS	ERW	12.7–127.0	No	No	–
Jackson Tube Service Inc. Piqua, OH	Tubing, sections	ERW	10.0–76.2	No	Anneal	–
Jindal Tubular USA LLC Bay St. Louis, MS	Large-dia. spiral-welded pipe	HSAW	609.6–1,524	Yes	No	300

IRON and STEEL PLANT FACILITIES

NORTH AMERICAN PIPE AND TUBE MILLS

Company	Product	Manufacturing process	Product size dia. range, mm (min–max)	API licensed	Heat treatment capabilities	Stated cap., ('000 mt/year)
JSW Steel (USA) Inc. Baytown, TX	OCTG casing and tubing, line pipe	ERW, DSAW	609.6–1,219	Yes	No	227
Kirk Eastern Inc. Gardner, MA	Mech. tubing	Welded	9.3–63.5	No	–	–
Kloeckner Metals California Steel and Tube City of Industry, CA	Mech. tubing	ERW	12.7–88.9	–	–	–
Leggett & Platt Aerospace Valley Metals Poway, CA	Precision-welded and redrawn tubing	Welded	15.2–2,286	No	–	–
Western Pneumatic Tube Co. Kirkland, WA	Welded and cold-drawn tubing	Welded	19.0–304.8	No	–	–
Lock Joint Tube Chattanooga, TN	Pipe and tubing sections	ERW, rolling	16.0–101.6	No	No	–
South Bend, IN	Pipe and tubing sections	ERW, rolling	16.0–168.3	Yes	Yes	–
Temple, TX	Pipe and tubing sections	ERW, rolling	16.0–79.4	No	No	–
Longhorn Tube LP Dallas, TX	HSS	ERW, rolling	12.7–203.2	–	–	–
Louisiana Steel Inc. Louisiana, MO	Custom steel tubing	CD	33.3–406.4	No	Stress relieve	–
Mach Industrial Group Houston, TX	Steel tubing	GTAW, ERW, SAW, PAW	508.0–3,658	–	Q&T	–
Major Metals Co. Mansfield, OH	Steel tubing	ERW	15.9–79.4	No	No	–

IRON and STEEL PLANT FACILITIES

NORTH AMERICAN PIPE AND TUBE MILLS

Company	Product	Manufacturing process	Product size dia. range, mm (min-max)	API licensed	Heat treatment capabilities	Stated cap., ('000 mt/year)
Maruichi Steel Tube Ltd. Geneva Structural Tubes LLC Geneva, NE	Welded pipe	ERW	205.6–711.2	No	No	100
Maruichi American Corp. Santa Fe Springs, CA	Mech. tubing, HSS	ERW	21.3–324.0	No	No	–
Maruichi Leavitt Pipe & Tube LLC Chicago, IL	Mech. tubing, struct. pipe	ERW, rolling	12.7–304.8	Yes	Yes	–
Maruichi Oregon Steel LLC Portland, OR	HSS	Welded, seamless	63.5–254	No	–	150
Metal-Matic Inc. Bedford Park, IL	DOM seamless tubing, precision tubing	PPR, ERW, CD	–	No	Anneal	–
Middletown, OH	DOM seamless tubing, precision tubing	PPR, ERW, CD	31.8–114.3	No	Anneal	–
Minneapolis, MN	DOM seamless tubing, precision tubing	PPR, ERW, CD	9.5–89.0	No	Anneal, normalize, non-decarburize, stress relieve	–
National Oilwell Varco Grant Prideco Navasota, TX	OCTG drill pipe	Friction weld	60.5–194.0	Yes	Q&T	3
Naylor Pipe Co. Chicago, IL	Spiral pipe	DSAW	101.6–2,438	No	–	–
Nippon Steel Pipe America Inc. Seymour, IN	Automotive tubing	ERW	15.9–89.1	No	Anneal	–

IRON and STEEL PLANT FACILITIES

NORTH AMERICAN PIPE AND TUBE MILLS

Company	Product	Manufacturing process	Product size dia. range, mm (min–max)	API licensed	Heat treatment capabilities	Stated cap., ('000 mt/year)
Northwest Pipe Co. Adelanto, CA	Cylinder pipe	ERW	304.8–1,524	–	–	–
Parkersburg, WV	Spiral-welded pipe	ERW	304.8–3,962	–	–	–
Portland, OR	Spiral pipe and tubing	ERW	101.6–406.4	–	–	–
Saginaw, TX	Spiral-welded pipe	GTAW	3,200	–	–	–
St. Louis, MO	Casing pipe	ERW	762.0–3,810	–	–	–
Nucor Tubular Products Birmingham, AL	Pipe, round tubing, specialty tubing	ERW	12.7–324.0	No	No	–
Cedar Springs, GA	Round hollow struct. tubing	ERW	12.5–50.8	No	No	–
Chicago, IL	Round hollow struct. tubing, HSS	ERW	60.9–168.3	No	No	–
Decatur, AL	Round hollow struct. tubing, HSS	ERW	127.0–406.4	No	No	–
Louisville, KY	Round hollow struct. tubing	ERW	12.5–101.6	No	No	–
Madison, IN	Mech. tubing	ERW	12.7–82.5	No	In-line quench	–
Marseilles, IL	Round hollow struct. tubing, HSS	ERW	42.2–324.0	No	No	–
Trinity, AL	Round hollow struct. tubing, HSS	ERW	60.3–219.0	No	Yes	–
Warehouse Systems Los Angeles, CA	Mech. and struct. tubing	ERW	12.7–127.0	—	—	—

IRON and STEEL PLANT FACILITIES

NORTH AMERICAN PIPE AND TUBE MILLS

Company	Product	Manufacturing process	Product size dia. range, mm (min-max)	API licensed	Heat treatment capabilities	Stated cap., ('000 mt/year)
Okaya Shinnichi Corp. of America Charlotte, NC	Precision-welded tubing	GTAW	60.0–180.0	No	–	6
Paragon Industries Inc. Sapulpa, OK	OCTG 5CT casing, 5L line pipe, mech. pipe, struct. tubing, piling pipe, sprinkler pipe	HFW	114.3–406.4	Yes	Seam normalize, Q&T	–
Stephenville, TX	OCTG 5CT casing, 5L line pipe, mech. pipe, struct. tubing, sprinkler pipe	HFW	25.0–114.3	Yes	Seam normalize, Q&T	–
PCC Energy Group Greenville Tube Clarksville, AR	Seamless tubing, welded and drawn tubing	DOM	3.18–38.1	No	–	–
RathGibson Janesville, WI	Pipe and tube, seamless tubing	GTAW, PPR	12.7–152.4	No	Anneal	–
RathGibson North Branch, NJ	Welded tubing	PAW, LBW, TIG	2.0–203.2	No	Anneal	–
Special Metals Corp. Burnaugh, KY	Seamless tubing	Pilger mill	133.4	No	Yes	–
Special Metals Corp. Huntington, WV	Seamless tubing	Pilger mill	12.7–241.3	No	Anneal	–
Phillips Tube Group Middletown Tube Works Middletown, OH	Tubing	ERW	10.0–127.0	No	–	–
Phillips Tube Group of Alabama Pell City, AL	Welded tubing	ERW	10.0–127.0	No	–	–

IRON and STEEL PLANT FACILITIES

NORTH AMERICAN PIPE AND TUBE MILLS

Company	Product	Manu-facturing process	Product size dia. range, mm (min–max)	API licensed	Heat treatment capabilities	Stated cap., ('000 mt/year)
Shelby Welded Tube Shelby, OH	Welded tubing	LSAW	16.0–76.2	No	–	–
Phoenix Tube Co. Inc. Bethlehem, PA	Tubing	GTAW	12.7–304.8	–	–	–
Plymouth Tube Co. East Troy, WI	Tubing	Welded	16.0–50.8	No	–	–
			6.4–101.6		Anneal	
Eupora, MS	DOM welded mech. tubing	GTAW, ERW, CD	6.4–44.5	No	–	–
Salisbury, MD	Seamless and welded tubing	ERW, CD	3.2–25.4	No	–	–
West Monroe, LA	Seamless and welded tubing	GTAW, ERW, CD	12.7–38.0	No	–	–
Winamac, IN	Hot-finished steel tubing	–	31.8–152.4	No	Q&T	–
	Steel tubing	CD	22.2–127.0			
Prolamsa Axis Pipe and Tube Bryan, TX	HSS tubing, OCTG casing and tubing, OCTG line pipe	ERW	60.3–406.4	Yes	Yes	272
Prolamsa Inc. Laredo, TX	HSS profile pipes/tubing, mech. tubing	ERW	–	No	No	–
PTC Alliance Alliance, OH	Tubing	DOM, ERW, HSR	19.1–273.1	No	–	–
Beaver Falls, PA	Tubing	DOM, CD	76.2–304.8	No	Anneal, harden	–
Chicago Heights, IL	Conduit steel tubing	ERW, DOM	16.0–267.0	No	–	–
Darlington, PA	Tubing, seamless line pipe	ERW, HSR	19.0–273.0	No	–	68
Fairbury, IL	Steel tubing	DOM, ERW	–	No	–	–

IRON and STEEL PLANT FACILITIES

NORTH AMERICAN PIPE AND TUBE MILLS

Company	Product	Manu-facturing process	Product size dia. range, mm (min–max)	API licensed	Heat treatment capabilities	Stated cap., ('000 mt/year)
PTC Alliance (cont'd) Hannibal, MO	Tubing and hollow rods	–	12.7–254.0	No	Induction harden	–
Roscoe Moss Co. Los Angeles, CA	Spiral casing pipe	HSAW	143.0–1,524	No	No	–
Salzgitter Group Salzgitter Mannesmann Stainless Tubes USA Inc. Houston, TX	Seamless pipe and tubing	Pilger mill	6.4–101.6	–	–	3
Searing Industries Inc. Rancho Cucamonga, CA	Struct. pipe and tubing, mech. tubing, ornamental sections	ERW	33.4–168.3	No	No	–
Specialty Steel Works Inc. Michigan Seamless Tube LLC South Lyon, MI	Seamless pipe and tubing	CD	19.0–127.0	Yes	Anneal, Q&T	–
Sterling Pipe & Tube Inc. Toledo, OH	Mech. tubing, pipe	ERW	26.7–168.3	No	–	–
Stupp Corp. Baton Rouge, LA	Spiral-welded line pipe	HSAW	609.6–1,524	Yes	No	225
	Line pipe	ERW	273.0–609.6	Yes	Anneal	450
Swepco Tube Clifton, NJ	Pipe and tubing, heavy-wall pipe, struct. tubing	GTAW, ERW	50.8–2,438	–	Q&T	–
T&B Tube Co. Gary, IN	Tubing	–	9.5–76.2	No	–	–
Tejas Tubular Products Inc. Stephenville, TX	Tubing	ERW	66.7–90.0	Yes	–	–

IRON and STEEL PLANT FACILITIES

NORTH AMERICAN PIPE AND TUBE MILLS

Company	Product	Manu-facturing process	Product size dia. range, mm (min–max)	API licensed	Heat treatment capabilities	Stated cap., ('000 mt/year)
Tenaris TenarisAmbridge Ambridge, PA	Seamless pipe	MPM	60.3–153.7	Yes	Q&T	450
TenarisBayCity Bay City, TX	Seamless pipe	PPR	114.3–219.0	–	Yes	544
TenarisCamanche Camanche, IA	Welded pipe	ERW	114.3–219.1	Yes	No	250
TenarisConroe Conroe, TX	OCTG casting and line pipe	ERW	114.3–219.1	Yes	Yes	–
TenarisHickman Blytheville, AR	Welded pipe	ERW	60.3–114.3	Yes	Q&T	250
	OCTG casing and line pipe	ERW	60.3–406.4	Yes	Yes	–
TenarisWilder Wilder, KY (idle)	Welded pipe	ERW	114.3–406.4	Yes	No	400
Tenaris Coiled Tubes LLC Houston, TX	OCTG line pipe	ERW	19.0–127.0	Yes	Yes	–
	OCTG line pipe, coiled tubing		9.5–127.0			
TimkenSteel Corp. Gambrinus Plant Canton, OH	Seamless mech. tubing	Assel mill	48.3–330.0	No	Q&T, anneal, normalize, stress relieve	–
Tubacex Group Salem Tube Greenville, PA	Tubing, seamless tubing, cold-drawn tubing	GTAW, CD	3.2–50.8	No	–	–
Tubular Industries Spring House, PA	Pipe, tubing, struct. sections, HSS	ERW, SAW	19.0–168.3	–	–	–
Twin Brothers Marine LLC Franklin, LA	Heavy-wall pipe	DSAW	711.0–5,639	No	Post-weld heat treat	36

2023 AIST Directory — Iron and Steel Plants 235

IRON and STEEL PLANT FACILITIES

NORTH AMERICAN PIPE AND TUBE MILLS

Company	Product	Manu-facturing process	Product size dia. range, mm (min–max)	API licensed	Heat treatment capabilities	Stated cap., ('000 mt/ year)
U. S. Steel Tubular Products Fairfield Tubular Operations Fairfield, AL	Seamless OCTG casing and drill pipe, standard and line pipe	PPR, HSR	114.3–250.8	Yes	Q&T, HSR	653
Lone Star Tubular Operations Lone Star, TX (idle)	OCTG casing	ERW, HFW	114.3–178.0	Yes	Q&T, HSR, normalize, anneal	286
Lorain Tubular Operations Lorain, OH (idle)	Seamless OCTG casing and drill pipe, standard and line pipe	PPR	257.0–609.6	Yes	Q&T	272
US Premier Tube Mills Madison, IN	Tubing	ERW	35.0–101.6	No	–	–
Vallourec Star LP Houston, TX	Seamless casing, tubing and line pipe	PPR, ERW	–	Yes	Yes	–
Muskogee, OK	Seamless tubing	PPR	–	Yes	Yes	–
Youngstown, OH	Seamless casing, tubing and line pipe	PPR, MPM	127.0–273.0	Yes	No	499
			50.8–178.0		Yes	
Vest Inc. Vernon, CA	Struct., mech., orna-mental tubing	ERW	15.9–152.4	No	No	–
Villacero Tex-Tube Houston, TX	Mech. tubing, OCTG casing and line pipe	ERW	60.3–219.0	Yes	Yes	127
Webco Industries Inc. Kellyville Specialty Tube Kellyville, OK	Coiled tubing	Seam-welded	6.4–44.5	No	–	–
Mannford Specialty Tube Mannford, OK	Straight and coiled tubing	LW	–	No	–	–

IRON and STEEL PLANT FACILITIES

NORTH AMERICAN PIPE AND TUBE MILLS

Company	Product	Manufacturing process	Product size dia. range, mm (min–max)	API licensed	Heat treatment capabilities	Stated cap., ('000 mt/year)
Oil City Tube Oil City, PA	Welded and cold-drawn mech. tubing	ERW, CD	–	No	–	–
Southwest Tube Sand Springs, OK	Tubing, cold-drawn welded tubing, cold-drawn seamless tubing	ERW, CD	–	No	–	–
Star Center Tube Sand Springs, OK	Large-dia. tubing	–	–	No	–	–
Welded Tube of Canada Corp. Lackawanna, NY	OCTG casing	ERW	114.3–244.5	Yes	Q&T	318
Welspun Tubular LLC Little Rock, AR	Large-dia. spiral pipe, HFIW small-dia. pipe	HFW, ERW	168.3–508.0	Yes	Yes	210
		HSAW	610.0–1,625			350
Youngstown Tube Co. Youngstown, OH	Water well casing pipe, sprinkler pipe	ERW	0.8–6.6	No	–	–
Zekelman Industries Inc. Atlas Tube Birmingham, AL	Struct. and mech. pipe and tubing	GTAW	25.4–168.2	No	No	–
Atlas Tube Blytheville, AR	HSS tubing, pipe piling	ERW	73.0–711.2	No	No	–
Atlas Tube Chicago, IL	Piling, mech. tubing	ERW	33.4–508.0	No	No	–
Atlas Tube Plymouth, MI	HSS tubing	ERW	–	Yes	No	–
Sharon Tube Farrell, PA	Mech. tubing	ERW	16–168.3	Yes	Q&T, SRA, full anneal, normalize	–
		DOM	12.7–228.6			
Sharon Tube Niles, OH	Mech. tubing	ERW	–	No	Yes	–

IRON and STEEL PLANT FACILITIES

NORTH AMERICAN PIPE AND TUBE MILLS

Company	Product	Manufacturing process	Product size dia. range, mm (min–max)	API licensed	Heat treatment capabilities	Stated cap., ('000 mt/year)
Zekelman Industries (cont'd) Wheatland Tube Chicago, IL	Conduit, mech. tubing	ERW	–	No	–	–
Wheatland Tube Sharon, PA	Mech. tubing	ERW, CD	–	No	Yes	–
Wheatland Tube Warren, OH	Mech. tubing	ERW	–	Yes	Yes	–
Wheatland Tube Wheatland, PA	Mech. tubing	CD	–	Yes	Anneal	–

GEOGRAPHICAL INDEX IRON and STEEL PLANTS

UNITED STATES

ALABAMA

AXIS
  SSAB
    ALABAMA INC.... 86, 160, 188, 198

BIRMINGHAM
  ABC COKE 146
  AMERICAN CAST IRON
    PIPE CO..................112, 154
    (AMERICAN DUCTILE
    IRON PIPE)....................112
    (AMERICAN STEEL PIPE).. 112, 225
  BLUESTONE
    RESOURCES INC. 145
  CMC STEEL
    ALABAMA 27, 155, 182, 212
  FAVOR STEEL & FABRICATING....121
  MILL STEEL CO................... 60
  NUCOR CORP.
    (NUCOR STEEL
    BIRMINGHAM INC.)........64, 158,
                              185, 215
    (NUCOR
    TUBULAR PRODUCTS
    BIRMINGHAM) 130, 231
  SAMUEL, SON & CO. 79
    (SAMUEL ASSOCIATED
    TUBE GROUP)................. 135
  ZEKELMAN INDUSTRIES INC.
    (ATLAS TUBE)............ 142, 237
    (Z MODULAR) 143

CALERA
  GLIDEWELL SPECIALTIES
    FOUNDRY CO. INC. 47

CALVERT
  AM/NS
    CALVERT LLC.... 10, 192, 200, 205
  OUTOKUMPU
    STAINLESS USA LLC....... 70, 160,
                              171, 187

DECATUR
  FRIEDMAN INDUSTRIES INC. 42
  GREGORY TUBE..................122
  MAGIC STEEL SALES 57
  MONARCH STEEL CO. INC. 61

  NUCOR TUBULAR
    PRODUCTS DECATUR 130, 231
  WORTHINGTON INDUSTRIES 107

FAIRFIELD
  HANNA STEEL FAIRFIELD
    PROCESSING DIV..............122
  UNITED STATES STEEL
    CORPORATION
    (FAIRFIELD TUBULAR
    OPERATIONS)............140, 236
    (FAIRFIELD WORKS) 100, 162,
                            190, 203, 208

FORT PAYNE
  SAMUEL PACKAGING
    SYSTEMS GROUP 79

HOOVER
  HANNA STEEL...................122

HUEYTOWN
  PRECOAT METALS............... 72

MOBILE
  ARBOR METALS INC...............97
  BERG PIPE
    MOBILE CORP............117, 226
  SSAB AMERICAS LLC 86

NORTHPORT
  HANNA STEEL
    TUSCALOOSA TUBE DIV....... 123
  SSAB WEAR SOLUTIONS......... 87

PELL CITY
  PHILLIPS TUBE GROUP
    OF ALABAMA 131, 232

SYLACAUGA
  SOUTHERN ALLOY CORP. 172

TALLADEGA
  TALLADEGA CASTINGS &
    MACHINE CO..................173

TANNER
  CARPENTER
    TECHNOLOGY CORP............18

2023 AIST Directory — Iron and Steel Plants

GEOGRAPHICAL INDEX IRON and STEEL PLANTS

TRINITY
NUCOR CORP.
(NUCOR STEEL-
DECATUR LLC) 67, 159, 185,
195, 202, 207
(NUCOR TUBULAR
PRODUCTS TRINITY) 130, 231

TUSCALOOSA
HANNA STEEL CORP. 228
NUCOR STEEL
TUSCALOOSA INC. 67, 160,
187, 198

ALASKA

WASILLA
FARWEST STEEL CORP. –
WELD AIR. 38

ARIZONA

CASA GRANDE
BULL MOOSE TUBE CO. 117, 227

CHANDLER
ZEKELMAN INDUSTRIES INC.
(Z MODULAR) 143

GLENDALE
MID CONTINENT STEEL
AND WIRE 60

KINGMAN
NUCOR STEEL
KINGMAN LLC 65, 159, 216

MESA
CMC STEEL ARIZONA 28, 155,
182, 212

PHOENIX
ALLIED TUBE &
CONDUIT CORP. 226
BROWN STRAUSS STEEL. 16
KELLY PIPE CO. LLC 125

SURPRISE
INSTEL STEEL WEST. 96

TEMPE
M E GLOBAL INC. 169

TUCSON
CAID INDUSTRIES 79

ARKANSAS

BLYTHEVILLE
NUCOR CORP.
(NUCOR STEEL-
ARKANSAS). 67, 158, 185,
194, 202, 206
(NUCOR-YAMATO
STEEL CO.) 68, 160, 187, 218
PRECOAT METALS. 72
TENARISHICKMAN. 137, 235
ZEKELMAN INDUSTRIES INC.
(ATLAS TUBE). 142, 237

CLARKSVILLE
PCC ENERGY GROUP
(GREENVILLE TUBE). 232

FORT SMITH
GERDAU SPECIAL STEEL
NORTH AMERICA
FORT SMITH MILL 46, 157,
184, 214

HICKMAN
FRIEDMAN INDUSTRIES INC. 42

LITTLE ROCK
WELSPUN TUBULAR LLC. . . . 142, 237

MAGNOLIA
CMC STEEL ARKANSAS 28, 212

NEWPORT
ARKANSAS STEEL
ASSOCIATES LLC. 154, 179

OSCEOLA
UNITED STATES STEEL
CORPORATION
(BIG RIVER STEEL) 100, 162,
189, 195, 203, 208

GEOGRAPHICAL INDEX IRON and STEEL PLANTS

PINE BLUFF
   U. S. STEEL TUBULAR PRODUCTS
   (WHEELING MACHINE
   PRODUCTS).................. 140

CALIFORNIA

ADELANTO
   NORTHWEST PIPE CO....... 129, 231

ARCADIA
   SAMUEL, SON & CO.............. 80

BAKERSFIELD
   KELLY PIPE CO. LLC 125

BLOOMINGTON
   RANGER STEEL
   (WAREHOUSE)..................74

CAMARILLO
   BURLOAK TECHNOLOGIES
   USA INC. 80

CITY OF INDUSTRY
   CALIFORNIA STEEL AND TUBE... 229
   MATERIAL SCIENCES CORP....... 58

EL MONTE
   CASCADE STEEL
   ROLLING MILLS INC.
   (WAREHOUSE) 19

ENCINITAS
   KVA STAINLESS INC...............126

FONTANA
   BROWN STRAUSS STEEL..........16
   CALIFORNIA STEEL
   INDUSTRIES INC...........17, 192,
                    200, 205, 227
   COMMERCIAL CASTING CO...... 166
   INSTEL STEEL WEST
   (CALIFORNIA SOUTH).......... 95
   MAAS HANSEN.................. 96
   MAJESTIC STEEL USA 57

GRASS VALLEY
   GRASS VALLEY STEELCAST..... 168

HAYWARD
   SAMUEL, SON & CO.............. 80

LA MIRADA
   HAYNES INTERNATIONAL INC......51

LONG BEACH
   NEXCOIL STEEL LLC............. 96

LOS ANGELES
   NUCOR TUBULAR PRODUCTS
   (NUCOR WAREHOUSE
   SYSTEMS) 231
   RELIANCE STEEL &
   ALUMINUM CO. 75
   ROSCOE MOSS CO.............. 234
   VEST INC.......................141

ONTARIO
   MID CONTINENT STEEL
   AND WIRE.................... 60

PICO RIVERA
   ULBRICH OF CALIFORNIA 98

PITTSBURG
   MAJESTIC STEEL USA 57
   UNITED STATES STEEL
   CORPORATION
   (UPI)................ 102, 203, 208

POWAY
   VALLEY METALS................. 229

RANCHO CUCAMONGA
   SEARING
   INDUSTRIES INC..........135, 234
   STEELSCAPE LLC 88, 206

RIALTO
   TUBULAR STEEL INC. 139

RIVERSIDE
   MAIN STEEL..................... 80
   SIERRA ALUMINUM CO........... 80

SACRAMENTO
   KELLY PIPE CO. LLC 125

SANTA FE SPRINGS
   KELLY PIPE CO. LLC 124
   MARUICHI
   AMERICAN CORP. 127, 230

GEOGRAPHICAL INDEX IRON and STEEL PLANTS

SOUTH GATE
   PACIFIC ALLOY CASTINGS 171
   STRATEGIC
      MATERIALS CORP. 173
   TECHNI-CAST CORP. 173

STOCKTON
   AMERICAN TUBULAR
      PRODUCTS NORTHERN
      CALIFORNIA 113
   BROWN STRAUSS STEEL. 16
   FARWEST STEEL CORP. 38
   INSTEL STEEL WEST
      (CALIFORNIA NORTH). 95
   NEXCOIL STEEL NORTH. 96

TRACY
   NORTHWEST PIPE CO. 129

VERNON
   MAAS HANSEN 96
   VEST INC. 236
   WEST COAST FOUNDRY 174

WESTMINSTER
   MAAS HANSEN, CALIFORNIA 96

COLORADO

AURORA
   BROWN STRAUSS STEEL. 16

COMMERCE CITY
   INSTEL STEEL WEST. 96

DENVER
   SAMUEL, SON & CO. 80

GRAND JUNCTION
   TRIPLE-S STEEL 96

HENDERSON
   KELLY PIPE CO. LLC 125

PUEBLO
   EVRAZ ROCKY
      MOUNTAIN STEEL 37, 156,
                           182, 213, 228

CONNECTICUT

BRIDGEPORT
   INSTEL STEEL EAST 95

NORTH HAVEN
   ULBRICH STAINLESS STEELS &
      SPECIAL METALS INC. 98
   (ULBRICH OF
      NEW ENGLAND). 98
   (ULBRICH SHAPED WIRE) 98

WALLINGFORD
   NUCOR STEEL
      CONNECTICUT INC. 65, 215
   ULBRICH SPECIALTY
      STRIP MILL 98

WINDSOR
   HAYNES INTERNATIONAL INC. 50
   THE TAYLOR & FENN CO. 173

DELAWARE

NEW CASTLE
   INSTEL STEEL EAST 96

FLORIDA

FORT LAUDERDALE
   CONTINENTAL STEEL
      & TUBE CO. 30

FROSTPROOF
   NUCOR STEEL
      FLORIDA INC. 65, 159, 185, 215

GREEN COVE SPRINGS
   SAMUEL ROLL FORM
      GROUP. 80

JACKSONVILLE
   CMC STEEL
      FLORIDA 28, 155, 182, 212

MILTON
   FORMWELD FITTING INC. 119

GEOGRAPHICAL INDEX IRON and STEEL PLANTS

PANAMA CITY
BERG PIPE
PANAMA CITY CORP. 117, 226

RIVERVIEW
SAMUEL, SON & CO. 80

TAMPA
GERDAU LONG STEEL
NORTH AMERICA 44
MAJESTIC STEEL USA 57

WILDWOOD
CHEN INTERNATIONAL. 227

GEORGIA

ALPHARETTA
SAMUEL, SON & CO. 80

CARTERSVILLE
GERDAU LONG STEEL
NORTH AMERICA
CARTERSVILLE MILL 45, 156, 183, 213
SAMUEL PACKAGING
SYSTEMS GROUP 80

CEDAR SPRINGS
NUCOR TUBULAR PRODUCTS
CEDAR SPRINGS 130, 231

KENNESAW
PACESETTER 71

MACON
GENERAL STEEL 95

MARIETTA
PACESETTER 71

ROSWELL
KLOECKNER METALS. 54

SAVANNAH
KELLY PIPE CO. LLC 125
TUBULAR STEEL INC. 139

TRENTON
BULL MOOSE TUBE CO. 118, 227

IDAHO

BOISE
FARWEST STEEL CORP. 38

ILLINOIS

ALSIP
ULBRICH OF ILLINOIS. 98

ALTON
ALTON STEEL INC. 8, 178, 211

BEDFORD PARK
METAL-MATIC INC.. 230

BOURBONNAIS
NUCOR STEEL
KANKAKEE INC.. . . . . 65, 159, 186, 216

BRIDGEVIEW
GREAT LAKES METALS CORP. 47

CHAMPAIGN
WIRCO FOUNDRY. 174

CHICAGO
CLEVELAND-CLIFFS INC.
(REGIONAL OFFICE) 21
FINKL STEEL —
CHICAGO. 41, 156, 167
MARUICHI LEAVITT
PIPE & TUBE LLC. 127, 230
NAYLOR PIPE CO.. . . . . .128, 230
NUCOR TUBULAR
PRODUCTS CHICAGO. 130, 231
PLYMOUTH TUBE CO. 132
WORTHINGTON
(TEMPEL STEEL) 107
ZEKELMAN INDUSTRIES INC. 142
(ATLAS TUBE). 142, 237
(WHEATLAND TUBE). 143, 238
(Z MODULAR) 143

CHICAGO HEIGHTS
BULL MOOSE TUBE CO.. . . . . . .117, 227
CHICAGO HEIGHTS STEEL 20
ESMARK STEEL GROUP
(ESG MIDWEST) 36
LIBERTY BAR PRODUCTS 55, 214
PTC ALLIANCE 133, 233

GEOGRAPHICAL INDEX IRON and STEEL PLANTS

CICERO
COREY STEEL CO.................84

ELK GROVE VILLAGE
CLINGAN STEEL INC. 26
MAIN STEEL......................80
MATERIAL SCIENCES CORP.......58

FAIRBURY
PTC ALLIANCE 133, 233

FRANKLIN PARK
NELSEN STEEL AND WIRE
CO. INC........................61

GRANITE CITY
FRIEDMAN INDUSTRIES INC. 42
GRANITE CITY PICKLING AND
WAREHOUSE 47
HEIDTMAN STEEL
PRODUCTS INC.
(SHEET PRODUCTS DIV.).......52
PRECOAT METALS CO.
(MIDWEST METAL
COATINGS PLANT) 73
(NORTHGATE PLANT)...........73
SUNCOKE ENERGY
(GATEWAY ENERGY
AND COKE CO.) 146
U. S. STEEL –
GRANITE CITY
WORKS.............100, 148, 151,
196, 203, 208

HARVEY
ALLIED TUBE &
CONDUIT CORP..........116, 226
ATKORE INTERNATIONAL 115

MARSEILLES
NUCOR
TUBULAR PRODUCTS
MARSEILLES 130, 231

OAK BROOK
A.M. CASTLE & CO. 9

PEKIN
HANNA STEEL
(PEKIN
PROCESSING DIV.) 123, 228

PEORIA
LIBERTY STEEL &
WIRE PEORIA 56, 157, 184, 214

RIVERDALE
CLEVELAND-CLIFFS
RIVERDALE....... 25, 151, 181, 194

ROCK FALLS
METAL SPINNERS 80

ROCK ISLAND
ROCK ISLAND ARSENAL 171

SAUK VILLAGE
PACESETTER
(CHICAGO SERVICE CENTER) ...71

SOUTH HOLLAND
AMERICAN PIPING
PRODUCTS INC................112
NIAGARA LASALLE CORP.........85

STERLING
STERLING STEEL
CO. LLC 92, 157, 184, 215

UNIVERSITY PARK
ESMARK STEEL GROUP..........36

WARRENVILLE
PLYMOUTH TUBE CO.............132

WOODRIDGE
SAMUEL PACKAGING
SYSTEMS GROUP 80

INDIANA

ANGOLA
METAL SPINNERS 80

ATTICA
HARRISON STEEL
CASTINGS CO......... 50, 157, 168

BURNS HARBOR
CLEVELAND-CLIFFS
BURNS HARBOR 23, 145, 147,
150, 179, 193,
197, 200, 205

GEOGRAPHICAL INDEX IRON and STEEL PLANTS

BUTLER
HEIDTMAN STEEL
  PRODUCTS INC.................51
  (SHEET PRODUCTS DIV.).......51
STEEL DYNAMICS INC.
  (FLAT ROLL GROUP
  BUTLER DIV.).........88, 161, 188,
                    195, 202, 207
  (IRON DYNAMICS DIV.)......... 90

COLUMBIA CITY
STEEL DYNAMICS INC. –
  STRUCTURAL
  AND RAIL DIV...... 91, 161, 189, 219

COLUMBUS
CLEVELAND-CLIFFS
  TUBULAR COMPONENTS
  (COLUMBUS)............. 118, 227

CRAWFORDSVILLE
NUCOR STEEL-
  INDIANA..... 68, 159, 186, 202, 207

EAST CHICAGO
CLEVELAND-CLIFFS
  INDIANA HARBOR......... 24, 150,
                        151, 155,
                    181, 193, 205
  (EAST)......................147
  (LONG CARBON) 181
  (WEST) 147
FRIEDMAN INDUSTRIES INC. 41
HEIDTMAN STEEL
  PRODUCTS INC..................51
MATERIAL
  SCIENCES CORP...........58, 206
SUNCOKE ENERGY
  (INDIANA HARBOR
  COKE CO.).................. 146

ELKHART
BULL MOOSE TUBE CO...... 118, 227
SPECIAL METALS CORP. 83

FORT WAYNE
STEEL DYNAMICS INC............. 88
VALBRUNA SLATER
  STAINLESS INC....... 103, 162, 173

GARY
CHICAGO STEEL
  HOLDINGS LLC................. 20

CLEVELAND-CLIFFS
  GARY PLATE................ 198
T&B TUBE CO...............136, 234
U. S. STEEL –
  GARY WORKS........ 100, 148, 151,
                   190, 196, 203

GREENFIELD
PRECOAT METALS............... 72

HAMMOND
KELLY PIPE CO. LLC 126
SPECIALTY STEEL WORKS INC.
  (NIAGARA LASALLE CORP.) 84

JEFFERSONVILLE
MILL STEEL CO. 60
STEEL DYNAMICS INC. –
  FLAT ROLL GROUP
  JEFFERSONVILLE
  PLANT 90, 207
VOSS CLARK....................105

KOKOMO
HAYNES
  INTERNATIONAL INC........... 50,
                        157, 168

LA PORTE
HAYNES INTERNATIONAL 50
  (CUSTOM METAL
  PROCESSING) 50
PRECOAT METALS
  (KINGSBURY PLANT) 73

MADISON
NUCOR TUBULAR PRODUCTS
  MADISON LLC............ 130, 231
US PREMIER TUBE MILLS ... 141, 236

MARION
BAHR BROS .MFG................165

NEW CARLISLE
CLEVELAND-CLIFFS INC.
  (TEK AND KOTE).......25, 201, 206

NEW CASTLE
NEW CASTLE STAINLESS
  PLATE LLC....................61

2023 AIST Directory – Iron and Steel Plants 245

GEOGRAPHICAL INDEX IRON and STEEL PLANTS

PITTSBORO
STEEL DYNAMICS INC. –
ENGINEERED BAR
PRODUCTS DIV........... 89, 161, 188, 218

PORTAGE
NLMK INDIANA 62, 158, 184, 194
PRECOAT METALS............... 73
UNITED STATES STEEL
CORPORATION
(MIDWEST PLANT)....101, 203, 208

PORTER
WORTHINGTON INDUSTRIES 107

RICHMOND
PTC ALLIANCE 134

ROCKPORT
CLEVELAND-CLIFFS
ROCKPORT WORKS 25, 201, 206

SCHERERVILLE
ARCELORMITTAL
NORTH AMERICA 10

SEYMOUR
KOBELCO METAL
POWDER 157, 168
NIPPON STEEL PIPE
AMERICA INC.................. 230

SOUTH BEND
LOCK JOINT TUBE
IRELAND ROAD 229

TERRE HAUTE
SHENANGO INDUSTRIES INC. 171
STEEL DYNAMICS INC. –
FLAT ROLL GROUP
HEARTLAND DIV...... 89, 203, 207

VALPARAISO
UNION ELECTRIC STEEL CORP.... 99

WINAMAC
PLYMOUTH TUBE CO........132, 233

IOWA

BETTENDORF
SIVYER STEEL CORP.............172

CAMANCHE
TENARISCAMANCHE........ 137, 235

HAMPTON
SEABEE FOUNDRY 171

KEOKUK
KEOKUK STEEL
CASTINGS................ 157, 168

MUSCATINE
SSAB IOWA INC..... 86, 160, 188, 198

WILTON
GERDAU LONG STEEL
NORTH AMERICA
WILTON MILL 46, 157, 183, 214

KANSAS

ATCHISON
BRADKEN ENGINEERED
PRODUCTS 154, 165

KANSAS CITY
BROWN STRAUSS STEEL..........16

KENTUCKY

ASHLAND
STEEL DYNAMICS INC. –
KENTUCKY ELECTRIC
STEEL DIV.................... 218

BOWLING GREEN
WORTHINGTON INDUSTRIES 107

BRANDENBURG
NUCOR STEEL-
BRANDENBURG............... 67

BURNAUGH
SPECIAL METALS CORP......83, 232

GEOGRAPHICAL INDEX IRON and STEEL PLANTS

CADIZ
  MONARCH STEEL CO. INC. 61

GHENT
  NORTH AMERICAN
    STAINLESS 63, 158, 170, 184
  NUCOR STEEL
    GALLATIN LLC 68, 159,
        185, 195, 207

GLASGOW
  TWB CO. 108

HAWESVILLE
  PRECOAT METALS. 72

HOPKINSVILLE
  PLYMOUTH TUBE CO. 132

LOUISVILLE
  NUCOR TUBULAR PRODUCTS
    LOUISVILLE. 130, 231

WILDER
  TENARISWILDER 137, 235

WURTLAND
  STEEL DYNAMICS INC. –
    STEEL VENTURES INC. 91, 161

LOUISIANA

ARCADIA
  HAYNES INTERNATIONAL INC.
    (TUBULAR PRODUCTS
    MANUFACTURING FACILITY) 51

BATON ROUGE
  SAMUEL, SON & CO. 80
  STUPP CORP. 234

BROUSSARD
  KELLY PIPE CO. LLC 125

CONVENT
  NUCOR STEEL
    LOUISIANA LLC 149

FRANKLIN
  TWIN BROTHERS
    MARINE LLC 139, 235

PRAIRIEVILLE
  PEARCE FOUNDRY &
    MACHINE WORKS 171

SHREVEPORT
  TERNIUM USA INC.. . . . . 94, 208

ST. FRANCISVILLE
  HOWELL FOUNDRIES LLC 168

WEST MONROE
  PLYMOUTH TUBE CO. 132, 233

MAINE

PORTLAND
  DOUGLAS BROTHERS 119, 227

MARYLAND

BALTIMORE
  SAMUEL, SON & CO. 81

ELKRIDGE
  BMG METALS 98
  PRECOAT METALS. 72, 207

SALISBURY
  PLYMOUTH TUBE CO. 132, 233

MASSACHUSETTS

BRAINTREE
  WOLLASTON ALLOYS INC. 174

EAST BRIDGEWATER
  DW CLARK INC. 167

GARDNER
  KIRK EASTERN INC. 229

NEW BEDFORD
  ATI SPECIALTY ROLLED
    PRODUCTS 14

PALMER
  RATHBONE PRECISION
    METALS INC.. 75

2023 AIST Directory — Iron and Steel Plants   247

GEOGRAPHICAL INDEX IRON and STEEL PLANTS

SPRINGFIELD
    TRIDENT ALLOYS INC............173

MICHIGAN

BATTLE CREEK
    OMEGA CASTINGS INC...........170

BAY CITY
    BAY CAST INC..................165

CANTON
    MATERIAL SCIENCES CORP....... 57
      (CANTON RESEARCH
      CENTER) 58
    TWB CO....................... 108

DEARBORN
    CLEVELAND-CLIFFS
      DEARBORN WORKS ... 24, 147, 150,
                        180, 193, 201, 205
    U. S. STEEL -
      GREAT LAKES WORKS
      EGL AT DEARBORN 101, 208

DETROIT
    DETROIT TUBING MILL
      INC., THE 120
    FINKL STEEL — COMPOSITE.......41

DUNDEE
    DUNDEE PRODUCTS............ 227

EAU CLAIRE
    HOFMANN INDUSTRIES INC...... 123

ECORSE
    U. S. STEEL -
      GREAT LAKES WORKS........ 100,
                        190, 208

ERIE
    HEIDTMAN STEEL
      PRODUCTS INC.................51
      (HEIDTMAN TUBULAR
      PRODUCTS LLC) 123

FLINT
    AMERICAN SPIRALWELD
      PIPE CO................... 112, 225

GIBRALTAR
    AUTOLUM PROCESSING CO....... 38
    FERROLUX METALS CO........... 39
    HYCAL CORP.................... 40

GRAND RAPIDS
    MAGIC STEEL SALES 56
    MILL STEEL CO.................. 60
    STEELTECH LTD. 173

ISHPEMING
    CLEVELAND-CLIFFS INC.
      (TILDEN MINE) 22

JACKSON
    ALRO STEEL 8
    GERDAU SPECIAL STEEL
      NORTH AMERICA 46
      (JACKSON MILL).......... 46, 157,
                         184, 214
    WORTHINGTON SPECIALTY
      PROCESSING 108

KINGSFORD
    SMITH CASTINGS INC............172

LIVONIA
    HERCULES DRAWN
      STEEL CORP. 33

MADISON HEIGHTS
    JAMES STEEL & TUBE CORP..... 226

MELVINDALE
    MILL STEEL CO.................. 60

MONROE
    GERDAU SPECIAL STEEL
      NORTH AMERICA
      MONROE MILL 47, 157, 184, 214
    NATIONAL
      GALVANIZING L.P..........52, 206
    SPARTAN STEEL
      COATING CO. LLC 108, 207
    TWB CO....................... 108

MUSKEGON
    EAGLE ALLOY INC. 167

NEW BALTIMORE
    INTERNATIONAL
      CASTING CORP................ 168

GEOGRAPHICAL INDEX IRON and STEEL PLANTS

NOVI
   DAMASCUS STEEL
      CASTING CO.................. 169
   TEMPERFORM CORP. 169

OAK PARK
   APOLLO HEAT TREATING......... 33
   EATON STEEL BAR CO............ 33

PIGEON
   HURON CASTING INC............ 168

PLYMOUTH
   ZEKELMAN INDUSTRIES INC.
      (ATLAS TUBE)............ 142, 237

RIVER ROUGE
   DTE ENERGY SERVICES
      (EES COKE).................. 146

SOUTH LYON
   MICHIGAN SEAMLESS
      TUBE LLC................84, 234

TAYLOR
   EATON STEEL CORP.............. 33
   VOSS TAYLOR....................105
   WORTHINGTON INDUSTRIES 107

TROY
   SAMUEL, SON & CO. 81
   ZEKELMAN INDUSTRIES INC.
      (Z MODULAR —
      ENGINEERING)............... 143

VASSAR
   ASTECH INC.....................165

WALKER
   NOVAL STEEL INC................ 63

WARREN
   NIAGARA LASALLE CORP......... 85

WESTLAND
   NORTHFIELD
      MANUFACTURING INC. 170

MINNESOTA

DULUTH
   M E GLOBAL INC................ 169

FORBES
   CLEVELAND-CLIFFS
      (UNITED TACONITE) 22

FRIDLEY
   MINNCAST INC. 170

HAM LAKE
   SAMUEL, SON & CO................81

HIBBING
   CLEVELAND-CLIFFS
      (HIBBING TACONITE CO.) 21

KEEWATIN
   UNITED STATES STEEL
      CORPORATION
      (MINNESOTA ORE
      OPERATIONS–KEETAC)........101

MINNEAPOLIS
   METAL-MATIC INC................ 230

MT. IRON
   UNITED STATES STEEL
      CORPORATION
      (MINNESOTA ORE
      OPERATIONS–MINNTAC).......101

ROSEVILLE
   SSAB MINNESOTA INC............ 86

SILVER BAY
   CLEVELAND-CLIFFS
      (NORTHSHORE MINING CO.) ... 22

ST. PAUL
   GERDAU LONG STEEL
      NORTH AMERICA
      ST. PAUL MILL........ 156, 183, 214

VIRGINIA
   CLEVELAND-CLIFFS
      (MINORCA MINE) 22

WINONA
   MIDWEST METAL
      PRODUCTS INC................170

GEOGRAPHICAL INDEX IRON and STEEL PLANTS

MISSISSIPPI

BAY ST. LOUIS
  JINDAL TUBULAR
    USA LLC.................124, 228

COLUMBUS
  STEEL DYNAMICS INC. —
  FLAT ROLL GROUP
    COLUMBUS DIV...........89, 161,
                      188, 195, 207

EUPORA
  PLYMOUTH TUBE CO........132, 233

FLOWOOD
  NUCOR STEEL
    JACKSON INC.....65, 159, 186, 215

IUKA
  FERROUS METAL TRANSFER CO.
    - MISSISSIPPI.................40
  FERROUSOUTH.................40
  SAMUEL ROLL FORM GROUP......81

JACKSON
  DOUBLE G COATINGS
    CO. L.P..................33, 206
  PRECOAT METALS...............72

MERIDIAN
  SOUTHERN CAST
    PRODUCTS INC................172

NEWTON
  WEIR ESCO 162, 174

MISSOURI

CHESTERFIELD
  AMERICAN PIPING
    PRODUCTS INC................112
  BULL MOOSE TUBE CO..........117

GERALD
  BULL MOOSE TUBE CO......118, 227

HANNIBAL
  PTC ALLIANCE 133, 234

HAZELWOOD
  TUBULAR STEEL INC............139

KAHOKA
  KPF STEEL FOUNDRY...........169

KANSAS CITY
  EXLTUBE 228

LOUISIANA
  LOUISIANA STEEL INC..........229

MONETT
  MONETT METALS INC...........170

NEW HAVEN
  METALCRAFT ENTERPRISES —
    FABRICATION OPERATIONS... 139

PEVELY
  METALTEK INTERNATIONAL.....169

POPLAR BLUFF
  MID CONTINENT STEEL
    AND WIRE 60

REPUBLIC
  AMBASSADOR PIPE &
    SUPPLY INC..................112

SEDALIA
  NUCOR STEEL
    SEDALIA LLC 66, 159, 186, 216

ST. LOUIS
  MISSOURI METALS 81
  NORTHWEST PIPE CO.......129, 231
  PRECOAT METALS...........71, 73
  ST. LOUIS PRECISION
    CASTING CO. 172
  TUBULAR STEEL INC............139

NEBRASKA

GENEVA
  GENEVA STRUCTURAL
    TUBES LLC 128, 230

NORFOLK
  NUCOR STEEL-
    NEBRASKA.......66, 159, 186, 216

WAHOO
  OMAHA STEEL CASTINGS CO.....170

GEOGRAPHICAL INDEX IRON and STEEL PLANTS

NEVADA

LAS VEGAS
   MAJESTIC STEEL USA 57

NEW JERSEY

CLIFTON
   SWEPCO TUBE 234

NORTH BRANCH
   RATHGIBSON 232

SAYREVILLE
   CMC STEEL
     NEW JERSEY 29, 155, 182, 212

SOMERVILLE
   CENTURY TUBE CORP....... 118, 227

SOUTH PLAINFIELD
   INSTEL STEEL EAST 95

NEW MEXICO

FARMINGTON
   TRIPLE-S STEEL 96

LAS CRUCES
   LIBERTY ENGINEERED
     WIRE PRODUCTS.............. 55

NEW YORK

AUBURN
   NUCOR STEEL
     AUBURN INC. 64, 158, 185, 215

BLASDELL
   REPUBLIC STEEL
    (LACKAWANNA HOT
    ROLLED BAR PLANT) 76, 218
   SAMUEL, SON & CO...............81

DUNKIRK
   SPECIAL METALS CORP. 83
   UNIVERSAL STAINLESS
     & ALLOY PRODUCTS INC. 102

LACKAWANNA
   WELDED TUBE OF CANADA...... 237

LANCASTER
   SAMUEL, SON & CO...............81

NEW HARTFORD
   SPECIAL METALS CORP. 83

NEW YORK
   LIBERTY STEEL USA............. 55

ROCHESTER
   SAMUEL, SON & CO...............81

ROME
   WORTHINGTON INDUSTRIES 107

SOLVAY
   CRUCIBLE
     INDUSTRIES LLC 31, 156,
                              167, 213

NORTH CAROLINA

CHARLOTTE
   GERDAU LONG STEEL
     NORTH AMERICA
     CHARLOTTE MILL 45, 156,
                              183, 213
   NUCOR CORP................... 64
   OKAYA SHINNICHI CORP.
     OF AMERICA................. 232

COFIELD
   NUCOR STEEL-
     HERTFORD COUNTY 66, 159,
                              186, 198

COLUMBUS
   TIMKENSTEEL CORP.
     TRYON PEAK PLANT........... 95

MOUNTAIN HOME
   HAYNES INTERNATIONAL
    (WIRE PRODUCTS
    MANUFACTURING FACILITY) 51

NEWTON
   CLEVELAND-CLIFFS
     PIEDMONT..................... 25

GEOGRAPHICAL INDEX IRON and STEEL PLANTS

PINEVILLE
KELLY PIPE CO. LLC 126

STATESVILLE
AMERICAN STAINLESS
TUBING INC. 115

TROUTMAN
AMERICAN STAINLESS
TUBING INC. 114, 226

OHIO

ALLIANCE
PTC ALLIANCE 133, 233

BEACHWOOD
SPECIAL METALS CORP. 83

BEDFORD HEIGHTS
MAJESTIC STEEL USA 57

BROOKLYN
FERRAGON CORP................. 38

CAMBRIDGE
ZEKELMAN INDUSTRIES INC. 143

CANFIELD
MATERIAL
SCIENCES CORP...........58, 206

CANTON
GREGORY
INDUSTRIES INC...........48, 206
HARBOR CASTINGS 168
REPUBLIC STEEL................. 76
(CANTON HOT
ROLLED BAR PLANT)....... 76, 160, 171, 188, 218
TIMKENSTEEL CORP. 94, 173
(FAIRCREST PLANT) 94, 161, 189, 219
(GAMBRINUS PLANT) 94, 235
(HARRISON PLANT).... 95, 161, 189

CINCINNATI
BYER STEEL CORP.............16, 211

CLARINGTON
AMERICAN HEAVY PLATES 9

CLEVELAND
CLEVELAND-CLIFFS INC...........21
(CLEVELAND
WORKS LLC).......... 23, 147, 150, 180, 193, 201, 205
FERRAGON CORP.
(FERRAGON
SPECIALTY STEEL)............ 39
(FERROUS METAL
PROCESSING) 39
(FERROUS METAL
TRANSFER CO. – OHIO)........ 40
MAJESTIC STEEL USA 57
MONARCH STEEL CO. INC. 61
WORTHINGTON INDUSTRIES 107
(WORTHINGTON SAMUEL
COIL PROCESSING LLC) 108

COLUMBIANA
COLUMBIANA
FOUNDRY CO. 27, 166

COLUMBUS
CLEVELAND-CLIFFS
COLUMBUS WORKS 24, 205
WORTHINGTON
INDUSTRIES 106, 107

COSHOCTON
CLEVELAND-CLIFFS
COSHOCTON WORKS...... 24, 201

CUYAHOGA HEIGHTS
CHARTER STEEL –
CLEVELAND 19, 155, 179, 212

DELTA
FULTON COUNTY
PROCESSING LTD. 51
NORTH STAR
BLUESCOPE STEEL 63, 158, 185, 194
WORTHINGTON
INDUSTRIES 107, 209

EATON
TIMKENSTEEL CORP.
ST. CLAIR PLANT............... 95

ELYRIA
CARPENTER
TECHNOLOGY CORP............18

GEOGRAPHICAL INDEX IRON and STEEL PLANTS

FRANKLIN FURNACE
SUNCOKE ENERGY
(HAVERHILL
NORTH COKE CO. I) 146
(HAVERHILL
NORTH COKE II)............... 146

HEATH
SAMUEL PACKAGING
SYSTEMS GROUP 81

HIGHLAND HILLS
OLYMPIC STEEL INC................ 69

HUBBARD
ELLWOOD ENGINEERED
CASTINGS..................... 35
LIBERTY STEEL
PRODUCTS INC................ 55

LEIPSIC
PRO-TEC COATING CO. 74, 207

LOCKLAND
SAWBROOK STEEL
CASTING CO. 171

LORAIN
REPUBLIC STEEL
(LORAIN HOT
ROLLED BAR PLANT)....... 76, 160, 188, 218
TUBULAR STEEL INC............. 139
U. S. STEEL
TUBULAR PRODUCTS
(LORAIN TUBULAR
OPERATIONS)........... 140, 236

LOUISVILLE
ATI SPECIALTY
ROLLED PRODUCTS.............14

MANSFIELD
CLEVELAND-CLIFFS
MANSFIELD WORKS........ 25, 155, 166, 181, 193
MAJOR METALS CO.............. 229

MARION
ARCELORMITTAL
TUBULAR PRODUCTS
(MARION)................. 114, 225
NUCOR STEEL
MARION INC.. ......65, 159, 186, 216

MASSILLON
REPUBLIC STEEL
(MASSILLON
COLD FINISHED BAR PLANT) ... 76

MASURY
BULL MOOSE TUBE CO...... 118, 227

MCDONALD
MCDONALD STEEL CORP......... 59

MEDINA
UNITED TUBE CORP............. 140

MIDDLETOWN
CLEVELAND-CLIFFS INC.
(MIDDLETOWN WORKS).... 25, 145, 147, 151, 181, 194, 201, 205
(RESEARCH AND
INNOVATION CENTER).........21
METAL-MATIC INC............... 230
MIDDLETOWN
TUBE WORKS 131, 232
SUNCOKE ENERGY
(MIDDLETOWN COKE CO.)..... 146
WORTHINGTON INDUSTRIES 107

MINERAL RIDGE
SPECIALTY PIPE & TUBE INC...... 115

MINGO JUNCTION
JSW STEEL USA 53, 157, 184, 194

MONROE
WORTHINGTON INDUSTRIES 107

NILES
TRUMBULL METAL
SPECIALTIES 173
ZEKELMAN INDUSTRIES INC.
(SHARON TUBE).......... 143, 237

NORTH JACKSON
LIBERTY STEEL
PRODUCTS INC................ 55
UNIVERSAL STAINLESS
& ALLOY PRODUCTS...... 103, 173

PIQUA
JACKSON TUBE SERVICE INC. ... 228

GEOGRAPHICAL INDEX IRON and STEEL PLANTS

RISING SUN
   CHARTER STEEL —
      FOSTORIA, OHIO 20

SANDUSKY
   METALTEK SANDUSKY
      INTERNATIONAL DIV. 158, 170

SHELBY
   ARCELORMITTAL
      TUBULAR PRODUCTS
      (SHELBY) 114, 225
   SHELBY WELDED TUBE 131, 233

SOLON
   REPUBLIC STEEL WIRE
      PROCESSING LLC 76

TOLEDO
   CLEVELAND-CLIFFS
      IRONUNITS LLC 23, 149
   HEIDTMAN STEEL
      PRODUCTS INC. 51
   NATIONAL BLANKING 52
   SAMUEL, SON & CO. 81
   STERLING PIPE &
      TUBE INC. 136, 234

TWINSBURG
   WORTHINGTON SAMUEL
      COIL PROCESSING LLC 108

UPPER SANDUSKY
   LIBERTY ENGINEERED
      WIRE PRODUCTS 55

VALLEY CITY
   ESG NORTHEAST 36
   TWB CO. 108

WALBRIDGE
   CLEVELAND-CLIFFS
      TUBULAR COMPONENTS
      (WALBRIDGE) 118, 227
   MATERIAL
      SCIENCES CORP. 59, 206

WARREN
   CLEVELAND-CLIFFS
      WARREN COKE 23, 145
   LIBERTY ENGINEERED
      WIRE PRODUCTS 55

THOMAS STEEL
      STRIP CORP. 93, 208
ZEKELMAN INDUSTRIES INC.
   (WHEATLAND TUBE). 143, 238

WAUSEON
   CARPENTER
      TECHNOLOGY CORP. 18

WEST CHESTER
   CLEVELAND-CLIFFS INC.
      (REGIONAL OFFICE) 21

WEST JEFFERSON
   FISHER CAST STEEL
      PRODUCTS INC. 167

YORKVILLE
   OHIO COATINGS CO. 69

YOUNGSTOWN
   CORONADO STEEL CO. 167
   VALLOUREC STAR LP 141, 162,
                             190, 236
   YOUNGSTOWN TUBE CO. 237

ZANESVILLE
   CLEVELAND-CLIFFS
      ZANESVILLE WORKS 26, 201

OKLAHOMA

BIXBY
   AMERICAN FOUNDRY
      GROUP INC. 165

BROKEN ARROW
   RANGER STEEL 74

DURANT
   CMC STEEL
      OKLAHOMA 29, 155, 182, 212

ENID
   CENTRAL MACHINE & TOOL 166

KELLYVILLE
   KELLYVILLE SPECIALTY TUBE ... 236

MADRILL
   MID AMERICAN STEEL
      AND WIRE 184

GEOGRAPHICAL INDEX IRON and STEEL PLANTS

MANNFORD
   MANNFORD SPECIALTY TUBE ... 236

MUSKOGEE
   AMERICAN FOUNDRY
      GROUP INC. 165
   VALLOUREC STAR LP 236

SAND SPRINGS
   WEBCO INDUSTRIES
      (SOUTHWEST TUBE).......... 237
      (STAR CENTER TUBE)......... 237

SAPULPA
   PARAGON
      INDUSTRIES INC.......... 131, 232

TULSA
   ARBOR METALS INC............... 97
   RANGER STEEL 75
   TULSA CENTERLESS BAR
      PROCESSING 85

OREGON

EAGLE CREEK
   EAGLE FOUNDRY CO............. 167

EUGENE
   EUGENE STEEL 38
   FARWEST REBAR................ 37

GRESHAM
   SAMUEL, SON & CO............... 81

MCMINNVILLE
   CASCADE STEEL
      ROLLING MILLS INC........ 19, 155, 179, 211

MEDFORD
   FARWEST STEEL CORP........... 38

PORTLAND
   COLUMBIA STEEL 166
   EVRAZ PORTLAND 36, 198, 228
   MARUICHI OREGON
      STEEL TUBE LLC.......... 127, 230
   NORTHWEST PIPE CO. 129, 231
   WEIR ESCO 174

SALEM
   QUAKER CITY CASTINGS INC. 171

SPRINGFIELD
   FARWEST STEEL CORP........... 37

PENNSYLVANIA

AMBRIDGE
   TENARISAMBRIDGE 137, 235

ASHLAND
   ASHLAND FOUNDRY &
      MACHINE WORKS 165

BATH
   EFFORT FOUNDRY INC........... 167

BEAVER FALLS
   PTC ALLIANCE 133, 233

BETHLEHEM
   APOLLO METALS LTD......... 93, 208
   PHOENIX TUBE CO. INC. 131, 233

BRACKENRIDGE
   ATI SPECIALTY
      ROLLED PRODUCTS....... 13, 154, 165, 179, 192

BRADDOCK
   U. S. STEEL
      MON VALLEY WORKS —
      EDGAR THOMSON
      PLANT 101, 148, 151, 190

BRIDGEVILLE
   UNIVERSAL STAINLESS &
      ALLOY PRODUCTS INC........ 102, 162, 173

BURGETTSTOWN
   UNION ELECTRIC
      STEEL CORP.
      HARMON CREEK PLANT ... 99, 173

BURNHAM
   STANDARD STEEL LLC.... 87, 161, 172

GEOGRAPHICAL INDEX IRON and STEEL PLANTS

BUTLER
CLEVELAND-CLIFFS
BUTLER WORKS 155, 166, 180, 193, 201

CARNEGIE
SAMUEL, SON & CO. 81
UNION ELECTRIC
STEEL CORP. 99, 162

CLAIRTON
U. S. STEEL
MON VALLEY WORKS —
CLAIRTON PLANT 101, 146

COATESVILLE
CLEVELAND-CLIFFS
COATESVILLE............. 23, 155, 166, 180, 197

CONSHOHOCKEN
CLEVELAND-CLIFFS
CONSHOHOCKEN......... 24, 197

CORRY
ELLWOOD NATIONAL FORGE —
CORRY...................... 35

DARLINGTON
PTC ALLIANCE 133, 233

DOWNINGTOWN
G.O. CARLSON PLATE............. 34

DUQUESNE
DURA-BOND
COATING INC............120, 228

ELLWOOD CITY
ELLWOOD CITY GROUP 34

ERIE
UNION ELECTRIC STEEL
CORP. ERIE PLANT 99

EXPORT
DURA-BOND INDUSTRIES 120
(DURA-BOND
STEEL INC. - STEEL
FABRICATION................ 120

FAIRLESS HILLS
KELLY PIPE CO. LLC 125
U. S. STEEL
MON VALLEY WORKS —
FAIRLESS PLANT......... 101, 208

FARRELL
NLMK
PENNSYLVANIA 62, 194, 202
ZEKELMAN INDUSTRIES INC.
(SHARON TUBE).......... 143, 237

FRANKLIN
CARPENTER
TECHNOLOGY CORP.............18
FRANKLIN INDUSTRIES 213

GREENVILLE
SALEM TUBE.................... 235

HARMONY
MAIN STEEL......................81

HERMITAGE
SAMUEL, SON & CO. 81, 82

HOLLSOPPLE
NORTH AMERICAN
HÖGANÄS CO......... 62, 158, 170

HOMER CITY
PRIME METALS
ACQUISITION LLC 73

IRVINE
ELLWOOD GROUP INC.
(ELLWOOD
NATIONAL FORGE) 35
(ELLWOOD
NATIONAL STEEL)..... 35, 156, 167

JERSEY SHORE
JERSEY SHORE STEEL CO.... 53, 214

JOHNSTOWN
GAUTIER STEEL LTD. 43
(SPECIALTY METALS LLC)...... 43
LIBERTY WIRE JOHNSTOWN 56

KOPPEL
TENARISKOPPEL 137, 161, 189

GEOGRAPHICAL INDEX IRON and STEEL PLANTS

LATROBE
ATI SPECIALTY
 ROLLED PRODUCTS 14, 154
CARPENTER
 TECHNOLOGY CORP. 18, 154,
  166, 211
 KENNAMETAL INC. 168
 LEHIGH SPECIALTY MELTING..... 162
 WHEMCO 174

LEBANON
REGAL CAST INC. 171

LYNDORA
CLEVELAND-CLIFFS
 BUTLER WORKS 23

MCDONALD
MCC INTERNATIONAL........... 169

MCKEESPORT
DURA-BOND PIPE
 MCKEESPORT 120, 228

MIDLAND
WHEMCO STEEL CASTINGS 174

MONACA
ATI SPECIALTY ROLLED
 PRODUCTS 14
BEAVER VALLEY
 ALLOY FOUNDRY CO. 15, 165

MONESSEN
CLEVELAND-CLIFFS
 MONESSEN COKE......... 22, 145

MUNCY
DURAMETAL CORP............... 167

MUNHALL
BRISTOL TUBULAR
 PRODUCTS 115, 226

NATRONA HEIGHTS
ATI SPECIALTY ROLLED
 PRODUCTS 14

NEVILLE ISLAND
SAMUEL, SON & CO. 82

NEW CASTLE
BLAIR STRIP STEEL CO........... 15
ELLWOOD GROUP INC.
 (ELLWOOD CITY
 FORGE GROUP) 35
 (ELLWOOD QUALITY
 STEELS CO.) 35, 156, 167
 (NORTH AMERICAN
 FORGEMASTERS) 36

OIL CITY
ELECTRALLOY 33
WEBCO INDUSTRIES
 OIL CITY TUBE 237

ORWIGSBURG
CARPENTER
 TECHNOLOGY CORP............ 18

PHILADELPHIA
CARPENTER
 TECHNOLOGY CORP............ 17
PHILADELPHIA NAVAL
 SHIPYARD FOUNDRY 171

PITTSBURGH
MCCONWAY & TORLEY LLC 169
SAMUEL, SON & CO.............. 81
STEEL DYNAMICS INC.
 (GALVTECH) 207
 (METALTECH) 207
 (THE TECHS).................. 91
UNITED STATES STEEL
 CORPORATION 99

READING
CARPENTER
 TECHNOLOGY CORP. 18, 154,
  166, 179, 211

ROCHESTER
ATI SPECIALTY
 ROLLED PRODUCTS............ 14

SCOTTDALE
DURALOY TECHNOLOGIES....... 167

SHARON
NLMK USA
 (SHARON COATING) 62
SSAB WEAR SOLUTIONS......... 87
ZEKELMAN INDUSTRIES INC.
 (WHEATLAND TUBE)......... 238

GEOGRAPHICAL INDEX IRON and STEEL PLANTS

SHARPSVILLE
DAVIS ALLOYS 167

SINKING SPRING
HOFMANN INDUSTRIES INC...... 123

SOUTH AVIS
JERSEY SHORE STEEL CO........ 53

SPRING HOUSE
TUBULAR INDUSTRIES 235

STEELTON
CLEVELAND-CLIFFS
STEELTON................ 26, 155,
166, 181, 212
DURA-BOND PIPE
STEELTON............... 120, 228

TITUSVILLE
UNIVERSAL STAINLESS 103

TURTLE CREEK
STEEL DYNAMICS INC. -
NEXTECH 208

VANDERGRIFT
ATI SPECIALTY ROLLED
PRODUCTS 14

WASHINGTON
ATI SPECIALTY ROLLED
PRODUCTS 14

WEST CHESTER
AMERICAN PIPING
PRODUCTS INC.................113

WEST MIFFLIN
U. S. STEEL
MON VALLEY WORKS –
IRVIN PLANT............. 101, 196,
203, 208

WEXFORD
PTC ALLIANCE 133

WHEATLAND
KELLY PIPE CO. LLC 125
ZEKELMAN INDUSTRIES INC.
(WHEATLAND TUBE)......143, 238

ZELIENOPLE
ATI SPECIALTY ROLLED
PRODUCTS 14

SOUTH CAROLINA

CAYCE
CMC STEEL
SOUTH CAROLINA......... 29, 155,
182, 213

COLUMBIA
AMERICAN SPIRALWELD
PIPE CO. LLC. 112, 225
PRECOAT METALS
COLUMBIA PLANT............. 72

DANIEL ISLAND
ESG SOUTHEAST................. 36

DARLINGTON
NUCOR STEEL-
SOUTH CAROLINA......... 66, 160,
186, 217
REMELT SERVICES 171

FORT MILL
SAMUEL PACKAGING
SYSTEMS GROUP 82

GEORGETOWN
LIBERTY STEEL
GEORGETOWN............ 56, 158,
184, 215

HARTSVILLE
TALLEY METALS..................211

HUGER
NUCOR STEEL-
BERKELEY 67, 68, 158, 185,
194, 202, 206, 215

MCBEE
CARPENTER
TECHNOLOGY CORP............18

RICHBURG
ATI SPECIALTY MATERIALS.......211
OUTOKUMPU STAINLESS
BAR INC. 71

258 2023 AIST Directory — Iron and Steel Plants

GEOGRAPHICAL INDEX IRON and STEEL PLANTS

WALTERBORO
  WHEELABRATOR CAST
    PRODUCTS GROUP............174

WESTMINSTER
  ULBRICH SPECIALTY WIRE
    PRODUCTS................... 98

TENNESSEE

ANTIOCH
  TWB CO....................... 108

BRISTOL
  BRISTOL TUBULAR
    PRODUCTS.............. 115, 226

CHATTANOOGA
  LOCK JOINT TUBE.............. 229

CLINTON
  SAMUEL, SON & CO.............. 82

COLUMBIA
  SAMUEL, SON & CO.............. 82

GALLATIN
  GKN HOEGANAES CORP......157, 167

JACKSON
  GERDAU LONG STEEL
    NORTH AMERICA
    JACKSON MILL........45, 183, 213

KNOXVILLE
  CMC STEEL
    TENNESSEE......30, 156, 182, 213
  TRIPLE-S STEEL 97

LAVERGNE
  PARTHENON TUBE INC.......... 225

MANCHESTER
  FISCHER USA STAINLESS
    STEEL TUBING INC. 121

MEMPHIS
  NUCOR STEEL
    MEMPHIS INC.....65, 159, 186, 216

PULASKI
  MAGOTTEAUX INC.............. 169

SMYRNA
  TWB CO....................... 108

TEXAS

AUSTIN
  HAYES MODULAR GROUP........142

BAY CITY
  TENARISBAYCITY........... 137, 235

BAYTOWN
  BORUSAN MANNESMANN....... 227
  JINDAL PIPE USA INC..............124
  JSW STEEL (USA) INC.... 53, 198, 229
  TENARISBAYTOWN 137

BEAUMONT
  OPTIMUS STEEL LLC..... 70, 160, 187

BELTON
  AMERICAN SPINCAST INC. 165

BROWNSVILLE
  ALAMO IRON WORKS 97

BRYAN
  PROLAMSA AXIS PIPE
    AND TUBE 233

CONROE
  TENARISCONROE 137, 235

CRANE
  NATIONAL FOUNDRY &
    MANUFACTURING CO. INC. 170

CROWLEY
  AZZ TUBULAR PRODUCTS 226

CYPRESS
  FINKL STEEL – HOUSTON.........41

DALLAS
  ARBOR METALS INC...............97
  ATI INC..........................13
  HENSLEY INDUSTRIES...... 157, 168
  LONGHORN TUBE LP 126, 229

GEOGRAPHICAL INDEX IRON and STEEL PLANTS

EL CAMPO
   BLUE CREEK FOUNDRY 165

FORT WORTH
   INSTEL STEEL DISTRIBUTORS 95
   RANGER STEEL 75

GRAND PRAIRIE
   MAJESTIC STEEL USA 57

HOUSTON
   AMERICAN PIPING
      PRODUCTS INC 113
   ARBOR METALS INC 97
   BERG PIPE HOUSTON 117
   BESHERT STEEL PROCESSING ... 96
   BROWN STRAUSS STEEL 16
   ELLWOOD CLOSED DIE GROUP ... 35
      (ELLWOOD TEXAS FORGE) 35
   HAYNES INTERNATIONAL 51
   INSTEL STEEL DISTRIBUTORS 95
   KELLY PIPE CO. LLC 125
      (DISTRIBUTION CENTER) 125
   MACH INDUSTRIAL GROUP 229
   MAJESTIC STEEL USA 57
   MID-CONTINENT STEEL AND
      WIRE INC. 60
   MILL STEEL CO. 60
   NSPS METALS 71
   PRECOAT METALS 72
   PTC LIBERTY TUBULARS 133
   QESC LLC 169
   RANGER STEEL 74
      (WAREHOUSE) 75
   RYMCO USA 134
   SALZGITTER MANNESMANN
      STAINLESS TUBES
      USA INC. 127, 234
   SAMUEL, SON & CO. 82
   SPECIALTY PIPE & TUBE INC 115
   SSAB TEXAS INC 86
   TENARIS COILED TUBES LLC 235
      (DOWNHOLE CENTER) 138
      (SUBSEA CENTER) 138
   TEX-TUBE 236
   TRIPLE-S STEEL
      HOLDINGS INC. 95
      (HOUSTON NORTH) 97
      (HOUSTON SOUTH) 97
   TUBE SUPPLY HOUSTON 97
   U. S. STEEL
      TUBULAR PRODUCTS
      (OILWELL SERVICES AND
      OFFSHORE OPERATIONS) 140
   VALLOUREC STAR LP 236

HUGHES SPRINGS
   U. S. STEEL
      TUBULAR PRODUCTS
      (WHEELING MACHINE
      PRODUCTS) 140

IRVING
   COMMERCIAL METALS
      COMPANY 27
   SAMUEL, SON & CO. 82

JEWETT
   NUCOR STEEL-
      TEXAS 66, 160, 187, 217

KATY
   TUBULAR STEEL INC. 139

KILLEEN
   ZEKELMAN INDUSTRIES
      (Z MODULAR) 143

LAREDO
   MID CONTINENT STEEL
      AND WIRE 60
   PROLAMSA INC 233

LIBERTY
   PTC LIBERTY TUBULARS 134

LONE STAR
   TEXAS TUBULAR
      PRODUCTS INC 138
   U. S. STEEL
      TUBULAR PRODUCTS
      (LONE STAR TUBULAR
      OPERATIONS) 140, 236

LONGVIEW
   FRIEDMAN INDUSTRIES INC. 41
   NUCOR STEEL
      LONGVIEW LLC 67, 159,
                        170, 198
   SAMUEL PACKAGING
      SYSTEMS GROUP 82
   SOUTHWEST STEEL
      CASTING CO. 172

MIDLOTHIAN
   GERDAU LONG STEEL
      NORTH AMERICA
      MIDLOTHIAN MILL 45, 156, 214
   NIAGARA LASALLE CORP 85

GEOGRAPHICAL INDEX IRON and STEEL PLANTS

NAVASOTA
ELLWOOD TEXAS FORGE 35
NATIONAL OILWELL
  VARCO (GRANT PRIDECO)..... 230

NEW BRAUNFELS
MID CONTINENT STEEL
  AND WIRE 60

ODESSA
KELLY PIPE CO. LLC 125
PENATEK INDUSTRIES INC........171
SHAMROCK STEEL SALES 95

PARIS
AMERICAN SPIRALWELD
  PIPE CO......................112

PHARR
ALAMO IRON WORKS 97

PITTSBURG
HENDERSON
  MANUFACTURING CO. INC. ... 168

PORT ARTHUR
STANDARD ALLOYS & MFG. 172

PORTLAND
ARCELORMITTAL
  TEXAS HBI................ 13, 149

SAGINAW
NORTHWEST PIPE CO. 129, 231

SAN ANTONIO
ALAMO IRON WORKS 97
TRIPLE-S/INSTEL STEEL
  DISTRIBUTORS 96

SEGUIN
CMC STEEL
  TEXAS...........30, 156, 182, 213

SINTON
FERROUS 85" CO. 39
FRIEDMAN INDUSTRIES INC. 42
STEEL DYNAMICS INC. -
  FLAT ROLL GROUP
  SOUTHWEST-
    SINTON DIV. 92, 161,
                188, 195, 207

SPRING
U. S. STEEL
  TUBULAR PRODUCTS......... 140

STEPHENVILLE
PARAGON INDUSTRIES INC...... 232
TEJAS TUBULAR
  PRODUCTS INC............... 234

TEMPLE
CENTRIFUGAL
  CASTINGS INC................ 166
DELTA CENTRIFUGAL CORP. 167
LOCK JOINT TUBE.............. 229

VICTORIA
VICTORIA PRECISION ALLOYS 174

VINTON
VINTON STEEL LLC 104, 162, 219
W. SILVER INC. 106, 219

UTAH

LINDON
AMERICAN TUBULAR
  PRODUCTS 113, 225
SCHAEFFER INDUSTRIES 83

ODGEN
FARWEST STEEL CORP. —
  WESTERN COATING 38

PLYMOUTH
NUCOR STEEL-
  UTAH............ 66, 160, 187, 217

SALT LAKE CITY
BROWN STRAUSS STEEL..........16
INSTEL STEEL WEST............. 96
KELLY PIPE CO. LLC 125
STAR FOUNDRY AND
  MACHINE....................172
TRIPLE-S STEEL 96

SPANISH FORK
SPANISH FORK FOUNDRY 172

SPRINGVILLE
MACA SUPPLY CO............... 169

GEOGRAPHICAL INDEX IRON and STEEL PLANTS

VIRGINIA

CHESAPEAKE
  BMG METALS 98

LEBANON
  SAMUEL PRESSURE
    VESSEL GROUP 82

LYNCHBURG
  BMG METALS 98

MANASSAS
  BMG METALS 98

NORFOLK
  BERKLEY MACHINE
    WORKS & FOUNDRY CO 165

PETERSBURG
  GERDAU LONG STEEL
    NORTH AMERICA
    PETERSBURG MILL 46, 156, 183, 214

PORTSMOUTH
  TIDEWATER CASTINGS INC. 173

RICHMOND
  BMG METALS 97
    (SPECIALTY METALS DIV.) 97

ROANOKE
  STEEL DYNAMICS INC. -
    ROANOKE BAR DIV. 90, 161, 189, 219

VANSANT
  SUNCOKE ENERGY
    (JEWELL COKE CO.) 146

WASHINGTON

AIRWAY HEIGHTS
  BROWN STRAUSS STEEL 16

AUBURN
  WESTERN COATING 38

KALAMA
  STEELSCAPE LLC 88, 206

KIRKLAND
  WESTERN PNEUMATIC
    TUBE CO 229

LONGVIEW
  BROWN STRAUSS STEEL 16
  FARWEST STEEL CORP. 38
  MAJESTIC STEEL USA 57
  ROEMER ELECTRIC STEEL
    FOUNDRY 171

MOSES LAKE
  FARWEST STEEL CORP. 38

RENTON
  FARWEST STEEL CORP. 38

RICHLAND
  AMERICAN
    TUBULAR PRODUCTS
    PACIFIC NORTHWEST 113

SEATTLE
  NORTH STAR CASTEEL
    PRODUCTS INC 170
  NUCOR STEEL
    SEATTLE INC 66, 159, 186, 216

SPOKANE
  WEAR-TEK 174

SPOKANE VALLEY
  FARWEST STEEL CORP. 38
  SPOKANE INDUSTRIES INC. 172

TACOMA
  BRADKEN ENGINEERED
    PRODUCTS 166

VANCOUVER
  FARWEST REBAR 37
    (FARWEST STEEL CORP.) 38
    (FARWEST STEEL CORP. –
    ROSE CITY POST-TENSION) 37
  KELLY PIPE CO. LLC 125
  NORTHWEST PIPE CO 129

WEST VIRGINIA

BARBOURSVILLE
  STURM INC 173

GEOGRAPHICAL INDEX IRON and STEEL PLANTS

FOLLANSBEE
WHEELING-NIPPON
STEEL INC. 106, 209

HUNTINGTON
PCC ENERGY GROUP
(SPECIAL
METALS CORP.) 83, 232
STEEL DYNAMICS INC. –
STEEL OF WEST
VIRGINIA INC. 90, 161, 189, 219

PARKERSBURG
NORTHWEST PIPE CO. 231

PRINCETON
CLEVELAND-CLIFFS
PRINCETON COAL. 22

WASHINGTON
NORTHWEST PIPE CO. 129

WEIRTON
CLEVELAND-CLIFFS
WEIRTON. 26
PRECOAT METALS. 73

WISCONSIN

CAMBRIDGE
ADVANCED CENTRIFUGAL 164

DE PERE
ALLIED TUBE &
CONDUIT CORP.. 226

EAST TROY
PLYMOUTH TUBE CO. 132, 233

JANESVILLE
RATHGIBSON 232

KENOSHA
KENOSHA STEEL CASTINGS. 168

MARINETTE
SAMUEL PRESSURE
VESSEL GROUP. 82
WINSERT INC.. 174

MARSHFIELD
FELKER PIPING PRODUCTS 228
SAMUEL BASIC STAINLESS. 82

MENOMONIE
BROWN STRAUSS STEEL. 16

MEQUON
CHARTER
MANUFACTURING CO. 19

MILWAUKEE
BADGER ALLOYS INC.. 165
MAYNARD STEEL
CASTING CO. 158, 169
SAMUEL PRESSURE
VESSEL GROUP 82
STAINLESS FOUNDRY &
ENGINEERING INC. 172

RACINE
CAST TOOLS INC.. 166

SAUKVILLE
CHARTER STEEL –
SAUKVILLE 20, 155, 179, 212

TOMAHAWK
SAMUEL PRESSURE
VESSEL GROUP. 82

WATERTOWN
SPUNCAST INC. 172

WAUKESHA
CASTALLOY CORP. 166
J & L FIBER SERVICES INC. 168
WAUKESHA FOUNDRY CO. INC. . . .174

WYOMING

CHEYENNE
SEARING INDUSTRIES
WYOMING INC.. 135

2023 AIST Directory — Iron and Steel Plants 263

GEOGRAPHICAL INDEX IRON and STEEL PLANTS

CANADA

ALBERTA

CALGARY
EVRAZ CALGARY............ 37, 221
FOOTHILLS STEEL
  FOUNDRY LTD................ 163
M A STEEL FOUNDRY LTD........ 163
SAMUEL, SON & CO............... 77
VALLOUREC CANADA............ 141

CAMROSE
EVRAZ CAMROSE 37, 221

EDMONTON
ALTASTEEL INC........ 8, 152, 175, 210
DFI CORP....................... 220
SAMUEL PACKAGING
  SYSTEMS GROUP 77
TUBE SUPPLY EDMONTON 97

NISKU
SAMUEL, SON & CO............... 77

RED DEER
EVRAZ RED DEER 37, 221
PRECISION TUBE
  CANADA ULC 222

BRITISH COLUMBIA

DELTA
SAMUEL, SON & CO............... 77

LANGLEY
SAMUEL, SON & CO............... 78

PRINCE GEORGE
SAMUEL, SON & CO............... 78

SURREY
HIGHLAND FOUNDRY LTD. 163
SAMUEL, SON & CO............... 78

VICTORIA
SAMUEL, SON & CO............... 78

MANITOBA

OAK BLUFF
ZEKELMAN INDUSTRIES
  (ATLAS TUBE CANADA)... 142, 222

SELKIRK
GERDAU LONG STEEL
  NORTH AMERICA
  MANITOBA MILL 45, 152, 176, 210

WINNIPEG
MATRIX METAL CASTING......... 59
SAMUEL, SON & CO............... 78
  (SAMUEL PACKAGING
  SYSTEMS GROUP)............. 78

NEW BRUNSWICK

FREDERICTON
SAMUEL PACKAGING
  SYSTEMS GROUP 78

NEWFOUNDLAND AND LABRADOR

PARADISE
VALLOUREC CANADA
  ST. JOHN'S 141

NOVA SCOTIA

DARTMOUTH
SAMUEL, SON & CO............... 78

ONTARIO

BRAMPTON
ARCELORMITTAL
  TUBULAR PRODUCTS
  (BRAMPTON)............ 113, 220

BRANTFORD
SAMUEL, SON. & CO. 78

GEOGRAPHICAL INDEX IRON and STEEL PLANTS

BROCKVILLE
ABE FITTINGS................119
DOUGLAS BARWICK INC..... 119, 220

BURLINGTON
BULL MOOSE TUBE CO.......117, 220
SAMUEL, SON & CO................ 78
 (SAMUEL PACKAGING
  SYSTEMS GROUP).............. 78
WORTHINGTON INDUSTRIES
 (TEMPEL STEEL) 107

CAMBRIDGE
GERDAU LONG STEEL
 NORTH AMERICA
 CAMBRIDGE MILL.....44, 152, 210
HAYNES INTERNATIONAL INC..... 50
SAMUEL, SON & CO.............. 79
 (SAMUEL ROLL
  FORM GROUP)................ 79
TWB OF CANADA INC............ 108

CONCORD
SAMUEL PACKAGING SYSTEMS
 GROUP....................... 79
WELDED TUBE OF
 CANADA CORP................ 222

ETOBICOKE
VENTURE STEEL INC............ 104

HAMILTON
ARCELORMITTAL
 NORTH AMERICA
 (DOFASCO G.P.)....... 10, 145, 147,
                      150, 152, 175,
                      191, 199, 204
 (LONG PRODUCTS
  CANADA G.P.)..............12, 113
 (TUBULAR PRODUCTS) 220
MAX AICHER
 NORTH AMERICA 211
SAMUEL, SON & CO............. 79
STELCO INC.
 HAMILTON WORKS..........92, 145,
                          199, 204
UNION DRAWN STEEL II LTD....... 99

HARROW
ZEKELMAN INDUSTRIES INC.
 (ATLAS TUBE CANADA)...142, 222
 (Z MODULAR – DESIGN) 143

KITCHENER
CANADA ALLOY
 CASTINGS CO................ 163
ZEKELMAN INDUSTRIES INC.
 (Z MODULAR)................ 143

LINWOOD
J.M. LAHMAN MFG. INC.......... 221

LONDON
ARCELORMITTAL
 TUBULAR PRODUCTS
 (LONDON) 113
BRADKEN...................... 163
SAMUEL PACKAGING
 SYSTEMS GROUP 79

L'ORIGNAL
IVACO ROLLING
 MILLS LP 52, 152, 176, 211

MARKHAM
SAMUEL, SON & CO.............. 79
 (SAMUEL ASSOCIATED
  TUBE GROUP CANADA) ... 135, 221

MISSISSAUGA
ATLANTIC TUBE &
 STEEL INC............... 116, 220

NANTICOKE
STELCO INC.
 LAKE ERIE WORKS 92, 147,
                         150, 176, 191

NEW HAMBURG
ALLOY CASTING
 INDUSTRIES LTD.............. 163

OAKVILLE
BURLOAK TECHNOLOGIES....... 78
SAMUEL, SON & CO.............. 77
 (SAMUEL PRESSURE
  VESSEL GROUP) 79

ORILLIA
KUBOTA METAL CORP........... 163

PARIS
MOLTEN METALLURGY INC...... 163

PICKERING
SUPERIOR METALS & ALLOYS 93

2023 AIST Directory — Iron and Steel Plants 265

GEOGRAPHICAL INDEX IRON and STEEL PLANTS

PORT HOPE
    WEIR ESCO 152, 164

REXDALE
    MATERIAL SCIENCES CORP.
    (TORONTO, ON FACILITY) 59

SAULT STE. MARIE
    ALGOMA
        STEEL INC. 7, 145, 147, 150,
        175, 191, 197, 199
    TENARIS
        ALGOMATUBES 136, 222

SCARBOROUGH
    SSAB CENTRAL INC.............. 86

STEVENSVILLE
    PENINSULA ALLOY INC.......... 164

STONEY CREEK
    NOVA STEEL INC................. 63
    SAMUEL, SON & CO.............. 79
    (NELSON STEEL) 78

TORONTO
    CANADIAN PHOENIX STEEL
        PRODUCTS LTD............... 220
    MATERIAL SCIENCES CORP...... 204

WATERLOO
    FISCHER GROUP
        (FISCHER CANADA
        STAINLESS STEEL
        TUBING INC.)...................121
        (FISCHER TUBETECH) 121

WELLAND
    VALBRUNA ASW INC. 103, 152,
        164, 176

WHITBY
    GERDAU LONG STEEL
        NORTH AMERICA
        WHITBY MILL 46, 152, 176
        (BAR MILL)................... 210
        (STRUCTURAL MILL)...........211

WINDSOR
    ARCELORMITTAL
        DOFASCO G.P.
        (WINDSOR) 204

WOODSTOCK
    ARCELORMITTAL
        TUBULAR PRODUCTS
        (WOODSTOCK).......... 113, 220
    NOVA STEEL INC.............. 63, 221

QUEBEC

BAIE-D'URFÉ
    NOVA STEEL INC.............. 63, 221
    SAMUEL, SON & CO.............. 79

BROMONT
    QUALI-T-TUBE.................. 221

CONTRECOEUR
    ARCELORMITTAL
        LONG PRODUCTS
        CANADA G.P. 11, 149, 199
        (CONTRECOEUR-EAST).....11, 152,
        175, 210
        (CONTRECOEUR
        RECYCLING CENTER)...........12
        (CONTRECOEUR-WEST).....11, 152,
        175, 210

DORVAL
    DB PIPING GROUP, THE 119
    NOVA STEEL INC................. 63

LACHINE
    SAMUEL PACKAGING
        SYSTEMS GROUP 79

LASALLE
    NOVA STEEL INC.
        (NOVA TUBE (DELTA)) 63, 221

LAVAL
    SAMUEL, SON & CO.............. 79

LONGUEUIL
    ARCELORMITTAL
        NORTH AMERICA
        (LONG PRODUCTS
        CANADA G.P.
        LONGUEUIL).............. 12, 210
        (MINING CANADA G.P.).........13

MONT-JOLI
    BRADKEN...................... 163

GEOGRAPHICAL INDEX IRON and STEEL PLANTS

MONT-WRIGHT
   ARCELORMITTAL MINING
      CANADA G.P. 13

MONTREAL
   ARCELORMITTAL NORTH AMERICA
     (DOFASCO G.P.
     CÔTEAU-DU-LAC) 204
     (LONG PRODUCTS
     CANADA G.P. ST-PATRICK) 12
   NOVA STEEL INC.
     (NOVA TUBE INC.) 63, 221

PORT-CARTIER
   ARCELORMITTAL MINING
      CANADA G.P. 13

SOREL-TRACY
   RIO TINTO IRON AND
      TITANIUM................ 150, 176

ST. FELIX-DE-KINGSEY
   SPIRALCO 222

ST-JOSEPH-DE-SOREL
   FINKL STEEL —
     SOREL 41, 152, 163

THETFORD-MINES
   CASTECH METALLURGY 163

SASKATCHEWAN

REGINA
   EVRAZ REGINA............. 36, 152,
                        175, 197, 221

MEXICO

AGUASCALIENTES

SAN FRANCISCO DE LOS ROMO
   ALPHAMETAL MEXICO
     S.A. DE C.V................... 128
   MARUICHIMEX S.A. DE C.V....... 128

BAJA CALIFORNIA

MEXICALI
   DEACERO S.A. DE C.V.
     (MEXICALI WIRE PLANT) 32
   GRUPO SIMEC............... 49, 178

CHIHUAHUA

CHIHUAHUA
   ACEROS DEL
     NORESTE-ACENOR............176

COAHUILA

FRONTERA
   PYTCO S.A. DE C.V.............. 223

MONCLOVA
   ACEROS FORJADOS
     ESTAMPADOS DE
     MONCLOVA S.A. DE C.V. 7
   ALTOS HORNOS
     DE MEXICO
     S.A. DE C.V. (AHMSA)....... 9, 147,
                           150, 153, 177,
                           191, 197, 200
   TERNIUM 94, 204
   TUBERÍAS PROCARSA
     S.A. DE C.V............... 138, 224

RAMOS ARIZPE
   DEACERO S.A. DE C.V.
     (RAMOS ARIZPE MILL
     AND WIRE PLANT) 32, 153
     (SALTILLO MILL AND
     WIRE PLANT) 32
   NOVA STEEL INC................. 63

SALTILLO
   DEACERO S.A. DE C.V. 153, 177
   NOVA STEEL MEXICO........... 223
   SAMUEL, SON & CO............... 82
     (SAMUEL ASSOCIATED
     TUBE GROUP
     (TUBOS SAMUEL
     DE MÉXICO))............. 135, 223

SAN PEDRO
   MAYRAN CASTINGS 164

TORREON
KOLD ROLL DE
MONTERREY S.A. DE C.V. 55

DISTRITO FEDERAL

MEXICO CITY
ALAMBRES Y REFUERZOS
DAC S.A. DE C.V. 7
TUBESA S.A. DE C.V. 139, 224

DURANGO

GOMEZ PALACIO
TUBERIA LAGUNA 224

GUANAJUATO

CELAYA
DEACERO S.A. DE C.V. 153, 177

LEON
DEACERO S.A. DE C.V.
(LEON INDUSTRIAL
WIRE PLANT) 32
SERVIACERO WORTHINGTON 107

SILAO
GRUPO SAN
(CHQ WIRE MEXICO)........... 49
NIPPON STEEL PIPE MEXICO 223
NUCOR-JFE STEEL MEXICO 204
TWB DE MEXICO S.A. DE C.V. 108

VILLAGRÁN
ARCELORMITTAL MEXICO
(ARCELORMITTAL CELAYA) 12
DEACERO S.A. DE C.V.
(CELAYA MILL
AND WIRE PLANT)............. 32

HILDALGO

SAHAGÚN
GERDAU
CORSA S.A.P.I. DE C.V.......... 44

JALISCO

EL SALTO
MANNESMANN
PRECISION TUBES
MEXICO S.A. DE C.V. 126, 223
PRECITUBO................133, 223

GUADALAJARA
ARCO METAL S.A. DE C.V. 114
FIMEX S.A. DE C.V............... 164
GRUPO SIMEC
S.A.B. DE C.V...........48, 49, 178

TLAJOMULCO DE ZUNIGA
CORPORACION
POK S.A. DE C.V. 164

MEXICO

BUENAVISTA
ARCO METAL S.A. DE C.V. 114

ECATEPEC DE MORELOS
RYMCO
(CONDUIT S.A. DE C.V.) 134

IXTAPALAPA
ARCO METAL S.A. DE C.V. 114

TLALNEPANTLA
ACEROS NACIONALES 176
DEACERO S.A. DE C.V.
(TLALNEPANTLA
WIRE PLANT) 32
GERDAU CORSA S.A.P.I DE C.V.... 44

TULTITLÁN
GERDAU CORSA
S.A.P.I. DE C.V. 44, 153, 178
GRUPO COLLADO S.A. DE C.V..... 48

MICHOACÁN

LÁZARO CÁRDENAS
ARCELORMITTAL MEXICO
(ARCELORMITTAL
LÁZARO CÁRDENAS).......12, 147,
149, 150, 153, 177

GEOGRAPHICAL INDEX IRON and STEEL PLANTS

MORELIA
  DEACERO S.A. DE C.V.
    (MORELIA INDUSTRIAL
    WIRE PLANT) 32
  FUNDIDORA
    MORELIA S.A. DE C.V.......... 164

NUEVO LEÓN

APODACA
  GALVASID S.A. DE C.V. 43, 204
  LM PERFILES Y
    HERRAJES S.A. DE C.V........ 223
  SAMUEL, SON & CO.............. 82
  TERNIUM 153, 178
    (COMERCIAL
    APODACA PLANT) 94
    (INDUSTRIAL
    APODACA PLANT) 94
    (LARGOS APODACA PLANT).... 94
  VILLACERO
    (ZINCACERO
    S.A. DE C.V.) 104, 205
  WORTHINGTON
    (TEMPEL STEEL) 107

CHURUBUSCO
  TERNIUM 192

CIÉNEGA DE FLORES
  TERNIUM 94

ESCOBEDO
  ARCELORMITTAL
    TUBULAR PRODUCTS
    (MONTERREY) 222
  PROLAMSA
    (PROLAMSA A4C
    SANKIN PRECISION
    TUBE S.A. DE P.I.)............. 223
    (PROLAMSA S.A. DE C.V.)...... 223

GUADALUPE
  DEACERO S.A. DE C.V.
    (GUADALUPE WIRE PLANT)..... 32
  VILLACERO
    (CINTACERO
    S.A. DE C.V.) 104, 205

GUERRERO
  TERNIUM 192

MONTERREY
  AERMOTOR 222
  APM 200
  ARCELORMITTAL MEXICO
    (MONTERREY) 12, 114
  FRISA STEEL 164
  MAGOTTEAUX S.A. DE C.V....... 164
  SERVIACERO WORTHINGTON 107
  TENIGAL SRL DE C.V............. 205
  TERNIUM 149, 154, 178, 200, 205
    (CHURUBUSCO PLANT) 93
  TUBACERO..................... 224
  TWB DE MEXICO S.A. DE C.V. 108
  VILLACERO 104
    (TUBERIA NACIONAL)......... 225

PESQUERÍA
  T-H TUBERÍA HELICOIDAL ... 104, 224
  TERNIUM
    (CENTRO INDUSTRIAL
    TERNIUM).................... 204
    (PESQUERÍA PLANT)........... 94

SALINAS VICTORIA
  FORZA STEEL.................. 222
  TUBACERO SPIRAL PLANT 224

SAN NICOLÁS DE LOS GARZA
  TERNIUM 93, 224
    (GUERRERO PLANT)........... 93
    (JUVENTUD PLANT)............ 93
    (UNIVERSIDAD PLANT)......... 94
  VILLACERO
    (TUBERÍA NACIONAL
    S.A. DE C.V.) 104

SAN PEDRO GARZA GARCÍA
  DEACERO S.A. DE C.V. 31
  TUBAC S.A. DE C.V. 138, 224

SANTA CATARINA
  DEACERO S.A. DE C.V.
    (MONTERREY WIRE PLANT).... 32
  GALVAPRIME S.A. DE C.V. 43
  KOLD ROLL DE
    MONTERREY S.A. DE C.V....... 54
  TIMKENSTEEL DE
    MEXICO S. DE R.L. DE C.V. 95

GEOGRAPHICAL INDEX IRON and STEEL PLANTS

PUEBLA

CHACHAPA
  FISCHER
    TUBTECH S.A. DE C.V. 122

CHOLULA
  GRUPO SIMEC................... 49

CUAUTLANCINGO
  TWB DE MEXICO S.A. DE C.V. 108

PUEBLA
  DEACERO S.A. DE C.V.
    (PUEBLA WIRE PLANT)......... 32
  TERNIUM 149, 153, 178

SAN MIGUEL XOXTLA
  TERNIUM
    LARGOS PUEBLA PLANT 94

QUERÉTARO

QUERÉTARO
  DEACERO S.A. DE C.V.
    (QUERÉTARO INDUSTRIAL
      WIRE PLANT) 33

SAN JUAN DEL RIO
  ACERLAN S.A. DE C.V............ 164

SANTA ROSA JAUREGUI
  KOLD ROLL DE
    MONTERREY S.A. DE C.V....... 55

SANTIAGO
  SERVIACERO WORTHINGTON 107

SAN LUIS POTOSÍ

SAN LUIS POTOSÍ
  ARCO METAL S.A. DE C.V. ... 114, 222
  FISCHER
    MEXICANA S.A. DE C.V.........121
  FONDERIA 177
  GRUPO SAN..................... 49
    (ACEROS DM)............. 49, 153
    (ACEROS SAN LUIS) 49, 153
  OUTOKUMPU MEXINOX 70
  RAMSA S.A. DE C.V............. 164

SONORA

HERMOSILLO
  SAMUEL, SON & CO.............. 82

SAN LUIS RÍO COLORADO
  NORTHWEST PIPE CO........... 129

TAMAULIPAS

ALTAMIRA
  POSCO 204

HEROICA MATAMOROS
  PERFILES COMERCIALES
    SIGOSA S.A. DE C.V............71

TLAXCALA

APIZACO-HUAMANTLA
  GRUPO SIMEC.............. 48, 178

XALOSTOC
  ATLAX S.A...................... 153

VERACRUZ

PANUCO
  SWECOMEX S.A. DE C.V.
    (GRUPO CARSO) 224

VERACRUZ
  TALLERES Y
    ACEROS S.A. DE C.V. 178
  TENARISTAMSA ... 138, 153, 178, 224

SUPPLIERS OF EQUIPMENT, PRODUCTS and SERVICES

A

A. LINDEMANN INC.
1005 8th Ave.
Glenshaw, PA 15116 USA
P: +1.412.487.7282
F: +1.412.487.7298
sales@alindemann-usa.com
www.alindemann.us

- Exec. Vice Pres.—Steve King

PRODUCTS and/or SERVICES:
HSS circular, TCT circular, thin kerf circular, orbital circular and bandsaw blades.

No of Employees: 25.

A. Lindemann Inc.
2115 Shore St.
High Point, NC 27263 USA
P: +1.336.886.2744

No. of Employees: 3.

AAVISHKAR MACHINERY PVT. LTD.—see GREENFIELD TECH PROJECTS

ABB INC.
305 Gregson Dr.
Cary, NC 27511 USA
P: +1.800.435.7365
www.abb.com

High Power Rectifiers Div.

- Sales Mgr., High Power Rectifiers—Joe Frisch, P: +1.262.785.3272, joe.frisch@us.abb.com

PRODUCTS and/or SERVICES:
DC EAF rectifier systems, AC EAF arc regulation systems (ARCARE). Offers a range of rectification technology and system sizes for converting alternating current to direct current for various industrial production requirements in primary metal and chemical applications, and for specialty power supplies. ABB High Power Rectifiers can service any make or model of rectifier and offer spare parts, training, calibration services, preventive maintenance, system studies, upgrades and revamps.

LV and MV Drives

- Metals Segment Mgr.—Douglas Ferrante, P: +1.678.316.7794, douglas.ferrante@us.abb.com

PRODUCTS and/or SERVICES:
Variable speed drives, drive systems, spare parts, and services for greenfield and brownfield projects.

Measurement Products:

Force Measurement PG
24 Commerce Dr.
Danbury, CT 06810 USA
P: +1.203.790.8588

- Sales Metals—Ryan Sweda, P: +1.716.673.6856, ryan.sweda@us.abb.com; David Patterson, P: +1.717.329.5451, david.w.patterson@us.abb.com

PRODUCTS and/or SERVICES:
Strip flatness measurement and control (Stressometer), strip tension measurement, roll force measurement, strip position and width measurement, and load cell weighing systems.

ABB Inc. Metals Systems
Office:
1425 Discovery Pkwy.
Wauwatosa, WI 53226 USA

Mail/Shipping:
16250 W. Glendale Dr.
New Berlin, WI 53151 USA
www.abb.com/metals

- Industry Lead and Industry Group Mgr. — Metals Systems, USA and Canada—Siraj Boudighar, P: +1.262.395.1745; +1.262.227.0638 (Mobile) siraj.boudighar@us.abb.com

2023 AIST Directory — Iron and Steel Plants 271

SUPPLIERS of EQUIPMENT, PRODUCTS and SERVICES

PRODUCTS and/or SERVICES: Electrical power and automation solutions for the iron and steel industry. Digital solutions, AC and DC motors, variable speed drives, PLCs and DCSs, level 1, level 2 control systems, mathematical models and MES solutions for melting, casting, hot rolling, cold rolling and process lines. Full-scope supplier, service, support, consultancy and parts.

Hitachi ABB Power Grids
901 Main Campus Dr.
Raleigh, NC 27606 USA
P: +1.800.290.5290 (Toll-Free)
power-grids@hitachi-powergrids.com
www.hitachiabb-powergrids.com

- Contact—Pradeep Chaudhary, P: +1.434.489.2368, pradeep.chaudhary@hitachi-powergrids.com
- Contact — Mktg. and Promotions, Transformers North America—Mike Levesque, P: +1.919.760.0459, mike.levesque@hitachi-powergrids.com

PRODUCTS and/or SERVICES: EAF transformers, power substation transformers, series reactors, rectifier transformers, auto-regulating transformers, rebuilding services, and field diagnostic and monitoring.

ABBOTT MACHINE CO.
700 W. Broadway
Alton, IL 62002 USA
P: +1.618.465.1898
mike@abbottmachineco.com
www.abbottmachineco.com

- Pres.—Mike St. Peters
- Roll Shop Foreman—Jerry King

PRODUCTS and/or SERVICES: Rebuilds, retrofits, new and used machinery sales, cylindrical grinding services, plant service repairs.

No. of Employees: 30.

ABP INDUCTION LLC
1460 Livingston Ave.
North Brunswick, NJ 08902 USA
P: +1.732.932.6400
F: +1.732.828.7274
www.abpinduction.com

PRODUCTS and/or SERVICES: Leading supplier of induction furnaces and heating systems for the metals and metalworking industries. ABP's heating division focuses on billet and bar heating, slab and strip heating, and pipe and rail heating applications. The heating systems are built using a modular design to be as flexible as possible for each customer's applications. By employing the principles of sustainable technology, ABP provides foundries and steel plants the opportunity for economic growth while balancing social and ecological concerns.

ACE INDUSTRIES
6295 McDonough Dr.
Norcross, GA 30093 USA
P: +1.800.733.2231 (Toll-Free)
F: +1.800.628.3648 (Toll-Free)
ccappel@aceindustries.com
www.aceindustries.com

- Chief Exec. Officer and Pres.—Josh Arwood
- Chief Financial Officer—Cheryl Rossborough
- Chief Oprs. Officer—Daniel Arwood
- Sales Mgr.—Dan Carmichael

PRODUCTS and/or SERVICES: Overhead crane manufacturer. Hoist and repair parts in stock. Wire rope hoists, chain hoists, repair parts, electrification, crane sales, parts, rigging, service and warranty, modification.

No. of Employees: 200+.

ACE WORLD COMPANIES INC.
10200 Jacksboro Hwy.
Fort Worth, TX 76135 USA
P: +1.817.237.7700
F: +1.817.237.2777
www.aceworldcompanies.com

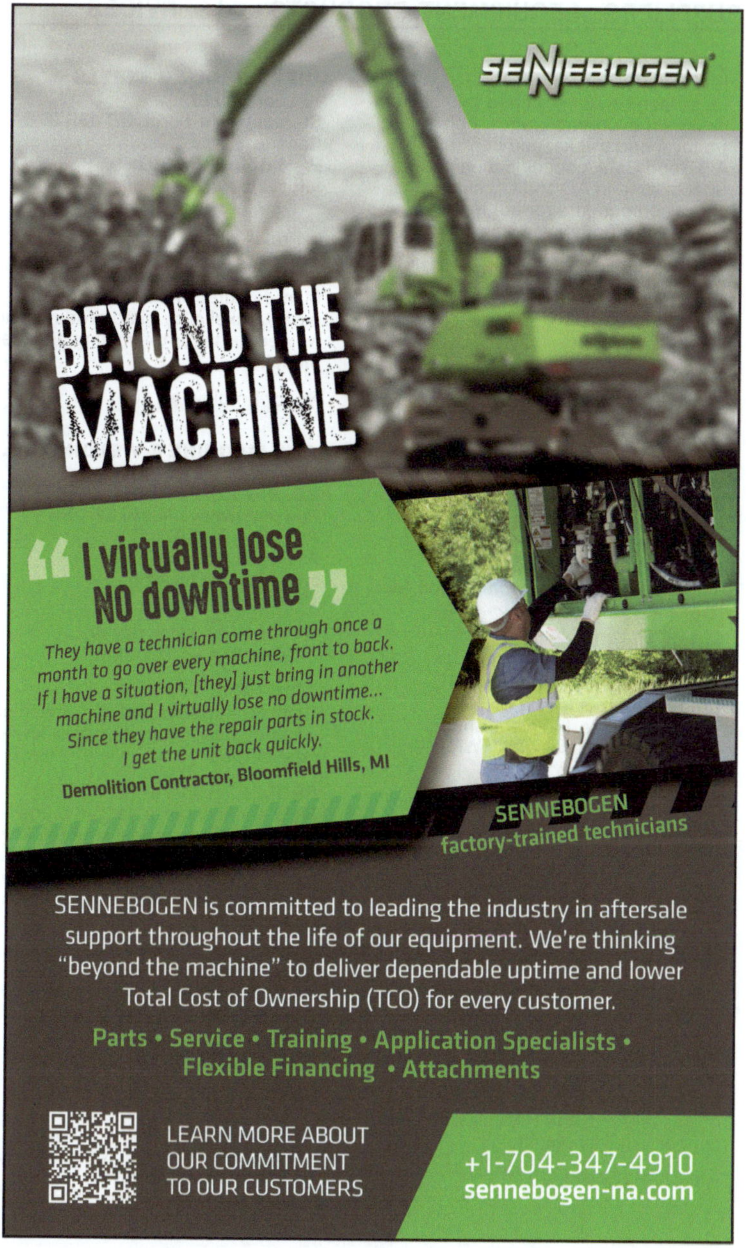

See listing page 509

SUPPLIERS of EQUIPMENT, PRODUCTS and SERVICES

PRODUCTS and/or SERVICES: Manufacturers of standard and custom-designed overhead cranes, hoists, trolleys, end trucks, and controls for AIST and CMAA specification cranes. Specializing in AC and DC mill-duty crane components for hot metal and other production applications. Complete source for replacement parts and refurbishing.

No. of Employees: 120, including 8 engineers.

ACI, A HOWDEN CO.—see HOWDEN GROUP

ACI HOLDING LLC, dba American Combustion International
3500 Lenox Road NE, Suite 1500
Atlanta, GA 30326 USA
P: +1.678.354.8230
F: +1.678.669.2841
jodi.wheeler@americancombustion.com
www.americancombustion.com

- Gen. Mgr.—Vivek Gautam
- Vice Pres. Sales and Mktg.—Al Bentz
- Dir. of Engrg.—Richard Masi
- Control Expert—Igor Diagilev
- Process Expert—Valera Shifrin
- Spare Parts Sales—Jodi Wheeler

EQUIPMENT:
EAF combustion technologies that include multi-function burners, supersonic oxygen injection, post-combustion, offgas analysis, valve train design and construction, control systems, carbon injection, copper sidewall panels, EAF process optimization, and ladle heating and drying systems.

PRODUCTS and/or SERVICES:
PyreJet™ multi-function burners, PyreTron™ burners, PyrOx™ burners, ALARC™-Jet supersonic oxygen injectors, ALARC-PC, ALARC-TDL offgas analysis and BASILISK™ series copper sidewall panels.

No. of Employees: 10.

ACIERS RÉGIFAB STEELS
16 Léon-XIII St.
St-Joseph-de-Sorel, QC J3R 3T8
Canada
P: +1.855.955.0397
info@aciersregifab.com
www.aciersregifab.com

- Pres.—Yanick Mathieu

PRODUCTS and/or SERVICES:
Manufacturer of abrasion-resistant parts, nickel alloy plate products, and welded parts for the mining and steel industries.

No. of Employees: 100.

ACME MACHINE & WELDING CO.
46 Anchor Inn Road
P.O. Box 1099
Punxsutawney, PA 15767 USA
P: +1.814.938.6702
F: +1.814.938.5945
acme@acmemw.com
www.acmemw.com

- Pres.—R.J. McSorley Jr.
- Sales Mgr.—Mike Meko

EQUIPMENT:
Complete manual and CNC machining, welding, fabricating, stress relieving, gear cutting.

PRODUCTS and/or SERVICES:
Field service: portable ID-OD line boring, milling, journal squirrel, key cutting, rigging, optics and Faro laser tracker technology, press rebuilding, gearbox/gear reducer repair, crusher repair/rebuild.

ADL INSULFLEX INC.
94 Willmott St.
Cobourg, ON K9A 0E9 Canada
P: +1.905.377.1488
F: +1.905.377.1484
custserv@adlinsulflex.com
www.adlinsulflex.com

- Pres.—Nichola Walt
- Vice Pres. and Gen. Mgr.—Steve Allan
- Contr.—Henry Climaco
- Sales Mgr.—J. MacDonald
- EU Sales Mgr.—Werner Pattberg

SUPPLIERS of EQUIPMENT, PRODUCTS and SERVICES

- EU Tech. Sales—Igor Golyzhbin
- Growth Admin.—Kelly Silk
- Cust. Svce.—Erica Miller
- Sales Admin.—Amanda Ingram

PRODUCTS and/or SERVICES:
Insulflex® high-temperature protection products are available worldwide through a network of 700 distributors in 60 countries. Insulflex products include EAF cable cover, Pyreflect, Pyrojacket®, Pyrotape, Pyrosleeve® Pyroblanket, Pyrosealant, Pyro-rope, Thermo-sleeve, Firesleeve, Kevtex and Silicaflex. Insulflex products are used to protect hoses, cables, wiring and other equipment from molten splash and intense radiant heat to 3,000°F (1,650°C).

ADL Insulflex Inc. (USA)
Watertown, NY 13601 USA
P: +1.800.461.9323 (Toll-Free)
F: +1.800.461.9328 (Toll-Free)

ADL Insulflex Inc. (Germany)
Finkenhof 12
Essen, 45134 Germany
P: +49.0201.43.063.223
F: +49.0201.43.063.224

ADS MACHINERY CORP.
1201 Vine Ave. NE
P.O. Box 1027
Warren, OH 44482 USA
P: +1.330.399.3601
F: +1.330.399.1190
ads@adsmachinery.com
www.adsmachinery.com
www.coatingline.com

- Pres.—Dale C. Minton
- Vice Pres. Sales—K. Ramalingam
- Shop Supt.—Ted Miller
- Design Supt.—Joe Gladysz
- Pur. Agt.—Laura Flaviano

EQUIPMENT:
Boring mills, lathes, milling machines, drill presses, grinders, welders, planer-shaper, testing equipment. Complete heavy machine shop and assembly equipment.

PRODUCTS and/or SERVICES:
Engineering, design and manufacture of strip processing lines and equipment for ferrous and non-ferrous material in coil form (e.g., cleaning lines, tension level lines, anneal lines, coating lines, pickle lines and galvanizing lines).

No. of Employees: 50.

ADVANCED ENERGY
1595 Wynkoop St., Suite 800
Denver, CO 80202 USA
P: +1.800.446.9167 (Toll-Free)
info@aei.com
www.advancedenergy.com

- Chief Exec. Officer and Pres.—Steve Kelley
- Exec. Vice Pres. and Chief Financial Officer—Paul Oldham
- Exec. Vice Pres. and Chief Oprs. Officer—Eduardo Bernal
- Exec. Vice Pres., Gen. Counsel and Corporate Sec.—Elizabeth K. Vonne
- Exec. Vice Pres. and Global Head of Sales—John Donaghey
- Sr. Vice Pres. and Chief People Officer—Rory O'Byrne
- Sr. Vice Pres. and Chief Technology Officer—Randy Heckman
- Sr. Vice Pres., Plasma Power Products—Jürgen Braun
- Vice Pres., Medical Power Products—Shrinidhi Chandrasekharan
- Sr. Vice Pres., Ind. Power Products—Maria Cortez
- Sr. Vice Pres., Corporate Dev.—Kevin Fairbairn
- Sr. Vice Pres. of Strategic and Corporate Mktg.—Peter Gillespie
- Sr. Vice Pres., High Volume Products—Emdrem Tan

PRODUCTS and/or SERVICES:
Designs and manufactures highly engineered, precision power conversion, measurement and control solutions for mission-critical applications and processes. AE's power solutions enable customer innovation in complex applications for a wide range of industries including semiconductor equipment, industrial, manufacturing, telecommunications,

SUPPLIERS OF EQUIPMENT, PRODUCTS and SERVICES

data center computing and healthcare. With engineering know-how and responsive service and support around the globe, the company builds collaborative partnerships to meet technology advances, propel growth for its customers and innovate the future of power.

ADVANCED GAUGING TECHNOLOGIES, L.L.C.
8430 Estates Ct.
Plain City, OH 43064 USA
P: +1.614.873.6691
F: +1.614.873.6770
sales@advgauging.com
www.advgauging.com

- Pres.—Scott Cook
- Sales and Mktg.—Nick Hunkar
- Sales—Michael DeBanto
- Oprs. and Technology Mgr.—Todd Allen
- Office Asst.—Melisa Williams

PRODUCTS and/or SERVICES: Manufacturer of non-contact isotope and laser on-line thickness gauges, multi-width gauges, sheet-width gauges and flatness gauges. Service for all brands of isotope thickness gauges worldwide.

No. of Employees: 16.

ADVANCED MACHINE & ENGINEERING
2500 Latham St.
Rockford, IL 61103 USA
P: +1.815.962.6076
F: +1.815.962.6483
info@ame.com
www.ame.com

- Chmn. of the Bd.—Willy Goellner
- Chief Exec. Officer and Pres.—Dietmar Goellner
- Sales Mgr.—Steve Schubert

PRODUCTS and/or SERVICES: High-production saws from AMSAW: carbide circular saws for bars or billets up to 760 mm, rails (with optional drill units), profile, plates, pipes, or tubes either single or in layers. Complete sawing systems including material handling, measuring weighing and other peripheral operations. Speed-cut resharpenable carbide saw blades.

No. of Employees: 135.

ADVANCED SYSTEMS INDUSTRIAL PRODUCTS
1020 W. 14 Mile Road
Clawson, MI 48017 USA
P: +1.877.436.0302 (Toll-Free);
 +1.248.658.1900
F: +1.866.285.5139
dmcdonald@advancedsystems-inc.com
www.asip-usa.com

- Pres.—Rob Rich
- Exec. Vice Pres. and Cust. Svce. Mgr.—Dan McDonald
- Contr.—Ronda Bussa
- Acctg.—Linda Gerard

PRODUCTS and/or SERVICES: MAXDOOR vertical lift fabric doors, rubber doors, other industrial doors.

AEROMET INDUSTRIES INC.
739 S. Arbogast St.
Griffith, IN 46319 USA
P: +1.800.899.7442 (Toll-Free);
 +1.219.924.7442
F: +1.219.924.6732
chris.benton@aerometindustries.com
www.aerometindustries.com

- Pres.—Fred Wahlberg
- Vice Pres. and Sales Mgr.—Gus Sitaras
- Vice Pres. Engrg. and Chief Engr.—Drew Wahlberg
- Asst. Sales Mgr.—Doug Couch
- Adv. Mgr.—Chris Benton

EQUIPMENT:
Union floor bar, large-capacity lathe.

PRODUCTS and/or SERVICES: Mandrel repair, custom and stock coil-wrapping products, emergency breakdown work, large-capacity-job shop, machine shop.

No. of Employees: 54.

SUPPLIERS of EQUIPMENT, PRODUCTS and SERVICES

AFC-HOLCROFT
49630 Pontiac Trail
Wixom, MI 48393 USA
P: +1.248.624.8191
F: +1.248.624.3710
sales@afc-holcroft.com
www.afc-holcroft.com

- Chief Exec. Officer and Pres.—William Disler
- Vice Pres. of Sales—Tracy Dougherty

PRODUCTS and/or SERVICES:
Supplier of industrial heat treating furnaces and equipment.

No. of Employees: 120+.

AGM WELDING
1062 O'Block Road
Pittsburgh, PA 15239 USA
P: +1.724.601.8855
F: +1.724.519.7353
agmwelding@yahoo.com

- Owner—Gus P. Mathews Jr.

PRODUCTS and/or SERVICES:
Supplier of high-alloy welding electrodes for the maintenance and hardfacing industry. Welding cable available in all sizes.

AIC NORTH AMERICA CORP.
885 Third Ave., 17th Floor
New York, NY 10020 USA
P: +39.0365.826333
F: +39.0365.826336
aic@aicnet.it
www.aicnet.it

- Chief Exec.—Marco Capitanio
- Pres.—Dino Capitanio
- Regional Sales Mgr. and Tech. Dir.—Antonio Ambra
- Adv. Mgr.—Andrei Molchan
- Chief Engr.—Stefano Arondi

PRODUCTS and/or SERVICES:
AIC is a system integrator providing advanced and tailored automation solutions for the steel industry, with the aim to continuously improve efficiency, competitiveness and safety of production processes in long product rolling mills and continuous casting machines. AIC provides experience and technical know-how for engineering, AC and DC drives, PLC, and SCADA for complete level 0, 1 and 2 automation and process control. Rolling Mill Automation Control System (RACS) integrated platform is specially developed for all mill applications and requirements. AIC is also present in Europe, South America and India. The latest developments are in the field of robotics and mechatronics, including billet, coils and bundles automatic tagging and bundles automatic tying machines.

No. of Employees: 62.

AIM MARKET RESEARCH
102 Harmony Pl.
Harmony, PA 16037 USA
P: +1.412.889.0516
mliebman@aimmarketresearch.com
www.aimmarketresearch.com

- Pres.—Marc Liebman

PRODUCTS and/or SERVICES:
Publishes steel plant location maps, including: Steel Plants of North America (shows all BOF and EAF shops, new edition May 2021), Continuous Casters of North America, Steel and Ferroalloy Plants of North America, Hot Strip and Plate Mills of North America (new edition June 2020), Hot Strip Steel Pickling Plants of North America (new edition May 2020), Metallic (Galvanized) Coating Plants of North America (new edition August 2020), Metallic (Galvanized) Coating Plants of Europe, Steel Plants of Latin America, Steel Plants of Europe—East and West, and three foundry maps of North America: Steel, Aluminum and Ductile Iron. Also publishes map of Coil Coaters of North America (new edition May 2020), Aluminum Extruders of North America (new edition January 2021) and Extruder Coaters of North America (January 2021). AIM also has available data covering major process areas such as EAF meltshops, continuous casters, hot strip and plate mills, cold mills, pickling lines, galvanizing lines, annealing facilities, etc.

AIST
ASSOCIATION FOR IRON & STEEL TECHNOLOGY
Register Now
at AISTech.org
Steel's #1 Conference and Exposition
AISTech®
» 8-11 May 2023 » Huntington Place » Detroit, Mich., USA
GLOBAL EVENT SPONSORS
SUPER BOOTH
THE SYSTEMS GROUP
AISTech.org

SUPPLIERS of EQUIPMENT, PRODUCTS and SERVICES

AIR CLEANING BLOWERS LLC
1521 U.S. Hwy. 9W, Bldg. 4C-4D
Selkirk, NY 12158 USA
P: +1.518.635.4169
marketing@aircleaningblowers.com
www.aircleaningblowers.com

- Mktg. Coordinator—Joseph Seitz

PRODUCTS and/or SERVICES:
Air cleaning blowers.

No. of Employees: 7.

AIR PRODUCTS
1940 Air Products Blvd.
Allentown, PA 18106 USA
P: +1.800.654.4567 (Toll-Free)
F: +1.800.272.2724 (Toll-Free)
info@airproducts.com
www.airproducts.com/ironsteel

PRODUCTS and/or SERVICES:
Leading global industrial gas supplier (oxygen, nitrogen, argon, hydrogen, carbon dioxide) with a comprehensive range of industrial gases, gas supply options and cost-efficient technologies. Air Products' industrial gas plant network has a 99.95% reliability record of providing on-time deliveries. On-site gas production solutions provide cost-effective, reliable and dedicated supply, tailored to operating needs. From the meltshop to the rolling mill, Air Products helps companies realize operating cost savings through proprietary technologies in combustion, gas injection, atmosphere control and remote monitoring, as well as a broad portfolio of decarbonization solutions to help companies lower their carbon footprint.

AIR-THERM INC.
310 Victoria Ave.
Montreal, QC H3Z 2M9 Canada
P: +1.514.482.2067
F: +1.514.482.6806
info@air-therm.com
www.air-therm.com

- Pres.—Sig Baltuch
- Vice Pres. Engrg.—Ted Baltuch

PRODUCTS and/or SERVICES:
Gravity ventilation, inlet louvers, CFD modeling, low-profile ventilators.

No. of Employees: 143.

AIR TRAC CORP.
P.O. Box 2238
Sarasota, FL 34230 USA
P: +1.866.580.5814 (Toll-Free)
info@airtraccorp.com
www.airtraccorp.com

- Chief Exec. Officer—Ron Kalka
- Vice Pres. Mktg.—Linda Casagrande
- Chief Engr.—Ken Higginson

PRODUCTS and/or SERVICES:
Provides fresh/filtered/cooled/heated air for overhead crane cabs, electrical rooms, motors. Traveling exhaust, traveling air, industrial ventilation, pneumatic conveying, design, supply, dust collection.

AIRCENTRIC CORP.
12250 Inkster Road
Redford, MI 48239 USA
P: +1.313.937.2131
F: +1.313.937.2346
cdwyer@aircentric.com
www.aircentric.com

- Pres.—Cynthia Dwyer

PRODUCTS AND/OR SERVICES:
Heat exchangers, blowers, and air compressors sales and service. Certified WBE company.

No. of Employees: 10.

AIS GAUGING
5350 N. 13th St.
Terre Haute, IN 47805 USA
P: +1.877.843.9247 (Toll-Free);
   +1.812.466.5478
F: +1.812.460.1295
sales@aisgauging.com
service@aisgauging.com
www.aisgauging.com

- Pres.—John Young
- Vice Pres. Svce. and Engrg.—Glenn Wrightsman

SUPPLIERS of EQUIPMENT, PRODUCTS and SERVICES

PRODUCTS and/or SERVICES: Coating weight and thickness measurement, control, and data management services.

No. of Employees: 25.

AJAX TOCCO MAGNETHERMIC CORP.
1745 Overland Ave. NE
Warren, OH 44483 USA
P: +1.800.547.1527 (Toll-Free);
  +1.330.372.8511
F: +1.330.372.8608
www.ajaxtocco.com

- Pres.—Thomas Illencik
- Vice Pres. of Global Sales—John Caruso
- Vice Pres. of Tech. Sales—Jeff Deeter
- Vice Pres. Channel Dev.—William Vennette
- Installation and Contract Product Mgr.—Tom Vogan
- Gen. Mgr. Svce. Oprs.—Scott Tewell
- Dir. Global Svcs.—Gary Andrews
- Sales Mgr.—Nick Katradis

PRODUCTS and/or SERVICES: Induction heating and melting equipment.

Michigan Mfg. Center
30100 Stephenson Hwy.
Madison Heights, MI 48071 USA
P: +1.248.399.8601
F: +1.248.399.8603

- Gen. Mgr.—Keith Anderson

Cleveland Mfg. Center
3800 Harvard Ave.
Cleveland, OH 44105 USA
P: +1.440.943.3300
F: +1.440.833.0391

- Gen. Mgr.—John Manocchio

MIS Service Center
1745 Overland Ave. NE
Warren, OH 44483 USA
P: +1.800.547.1527 (Toll-Free);
  +1.330.372.8511
F: +1.330.372.8659

- Sales—Mark Mihalick

Southwest Service Center
5807 W. Marshall Ave.
Longview, TX 75604 USA
P: +1.800.252.9839 (Toll-Free);
  +1.903.297.2526
F: +1.903.297.1547

- Gen. Mgr.—Tracy Dula

Southeast Service Center
6325 Highway 431
Albertville, AL 35950 USA
P: +1.265.279.1200
F: +1.256.279.1201

- Mgr.—Tim Stracener

PRODUCTS and/or SERVICES: Designs, builds to print, and repairs induction heating coils and transformers for the iron, steel and heat treating industries. Pickup and delivery services available. Emergency and general repair or rebuilding of channel and coreless melting coils and equipment, including repair/replacement of water-cooled cables and spare parts.

Ajax Tocco/Lectrotherm
8984 Meridian Cir. NW
North Canton, OH 44720 USA
P: +1.330.443.6600
F: +1.330.443.6610

- Gen. Mgr. Aftermarket Sales—Joe Hawkins

ALFA & ASSOCIATES
2006 Broad Hill Farms
Coraopolis, PA 15108 USA
P: +1.412.559.6185
F: +1.724.457.6125
info@alfainc.com

- Pres.—Larry Rich
- Exec. Vice Pres.—Frances Banks
- Mgr. Engrg.—Alison Rich
- Mgr. Tech. Svcs.—Daniel Ference
- Mgr. Business Dev.—Amy Rich
- Mgr. Applications and Training—Paul DiNubila
- Mgr. Field Svcs.—Thomas Garcia

PRODUCTS and/or SERVICES: Advanced engineering services that incorporate finite element

SUPPLIERS OF EQUIPMENT, PRODUCTS and SERVICES

mathematical heat transfer and CFD modeling; furnace design and engineering; furnace inspections; plantwide energy assessments; combustion engineering; instrumentation; automation and control; calibration and tuning; burner performance and design; feasibility studies; due diligence; expert witnessing; diagnostics; analysis and studies; operator and maintenance training; cooling bed analysis; reheating/heat treating process optimization.

ALKEGEN
Williams Square – Central Tower
5215 N. O'Connor Blvd.
Irving, TX 75039 USA
P: +1.716.768.6500
info@alkegen.com
www.alkegen.com

– Chief Exec. Officer and Pres.—John C. Dandolph

PRODUCTS and/or SERVICES:
High-temperature insulation products for thermal management applications.

No. of Employees: 9,000+ worldwide.

Alkegen — Manchester, CT
One Colonial Road
Manchester, CT 06042 USA
P: +1.860.646.1233
F: +1.860.646.4917

ALLEGHENY ALLOY INC.
400 Cyrus St.
Jeannette, PA 15644 USA
P: +1.724.527.3730
F: +1.724.527.3422
alleghenyalloy@gmail.com

– Pres.—John F. DeBlasio

EQUIPMENT:
Shear; press brakes; plate roll; expanded metal machine; plasma cutting torch; seam welder (filler metal); seam welder (fusion); bar draw and straightener; welders for MIG, TIG and sub-arc.

PRODUCTS and/or SERVICES:
Cast and fabricated alloy products for heat resistance, as used in furnaces. Products include centrifugal cast and fabricated radiant tube assemblies, recuperator tubes, burner tubes, pickling hooks, furnace muffles and furnace roll assemblies, inner covers, generator retort tubes, cast skids, tray assemblies, fittings, skid buttons, furnace curtains, retorts, heating elements (rod, ribbon and coil), belt wrappers, recuperator tubes (Hazen), fan/shaft assemblies, roller rails, rollers. Generator catalyst, galvanizing line: pot roll bushings, sleeves; pot roll ends, arms; sink roll washers, arms; snout castings, chute castings, stabilizing roll ends, half bushings, inserts, spider castings, roll drivers, spreader castings. Continuous galvanizing line: zinc rolls, guide rolls, roll supports, pinch rolls, stabilizing rolls, bimetallic rolls, radiant and burner tubes.

No. of Employees: 35.

ALLIED MINERAL PRODUCTS
2700 Scioto Pkwy.
Columbus, OH 43221 USA
P: +1.614.876.0244
info@alliedmin.com
www.alliedmineral.com

PRODUCTS and/or SERVICES:
Monolithic refractories, IFB, fire clay brick, high-alumina brick. Calcium silicate boards, vermiculite boards and ceramic fiber products. BF taphole clay, casthouse refractories and shapes, cement-free castables, gunning mixes, reheat furnace refractories, plastics, ramming mixes, EAF spouts, delta sections, tundish shapes and castables, spinel well blocks, impact pads, coke oven specialties, engineering and installation capability.

SUPPLIERS of EQUIPMENT, PRODUCTS and SERVICES

ALLIED SYSTEMS CO.
21433 S.W. Oregon St.
Sherwood, OR 97140 USA
P: +1.503.625.2560
F: +1.503.625.7269
wagner@alliedsystems.com
www.alliedsystems.com

- Pres.—Jeff Rink
- Sales—Ron Vandlac
- Vice Pres. Prodn./Mfg.—Aaron Bruce
- Treas.—Wolfgang Mann
- Pur. Agt.—Gary Barendrick
- Chief Engr.—Gerry Keagbine

EQUIPMENT:
Complete engineering and manufacturing facilities.

PRODUCTS and/or SERVICES:
Off-road heavy-lift mobile equipment: lift up to 50-ton slabs; 80 tons of coils; elevating transporters to 280-ton capacity.

No. of Employees: 250.

ALLOR MANUFACTURING INC.
12534 Emerson Dr.
P.O. Box 1540
Brighton, MI 48116 USA
P: +1.248.486.4500
F: +1.248.486.4040
www.allorplesh.com

- Chief Exec. Officer and Pres.—Tony Allor
- Plant Mgr.—Anthony Rossi
- Engr. Mgr.—Jim Kitson
- Pur. Mgr.—Gary Anderson
- Chief Est. Mgr.—Jon Hatton

EQUIPMENT:
More than 85 pieces of manufacturing equipment, including: turning, milling, grinding, welding and fabricating equipment, as well as 21 CNC machining centers and more than 35 tons of overhead crane capacity. Offers in-house engineering, precision machining, fabricating, grinding and welding.

PRODUCTS and/or SERVICES:
Custom-designed levelers, complete tension leveler systems, leveler work rolls, and backup or thrust bearings. Allor also rebuilds and refurbishes OEM leveler equipment. Material handling line includes heavy-duty steel conveyors to move large steel or aluminum coils, sheet, billets, bar, beam, plate, slabs or metal scraps. Allor's cooling bed systems are made to move large hot plates or bars of steel/aluminum. Can rebuild and make new dummy bars for casters. Also makes all types of custom bearings, wheels, rollers and cam followers.

No. of Employees: 70.

ALLOY ENGINEERING CO., THE
844 Thacker St.
Berea, OH 44017 USA
P: +1.440.243.6800
F: +1.440.243.6489
sales@alloyengineering.com
www.alloyengineering.com

- Chief Exec. Officer—Lee Watson
- Vice Pres., Sales and Mktg.—Maryann Remner
- Pur. Agt.—Joe Pipik

EQUIPMENT:
TIG, MIG and plasma arc welders; bending and forming machines; vertical and horizontal machining centers; HD plasma burning tables.

PRODUCTS and/or SERVICES:
High-nickel alloy and stainless steel fabrications for high-temperature and corrosive environments.

No. of Employees: 85.

ALLSTRAP STEEL & POLY STRAPPING SYSTEMS
1719 Kenny Road
Columbus, OH 43212 USA
P: +1.614.486.7722
sales@allstrap.com
www.allstrap.com

PRODUCTS and/or SERVICES:
Battery-powered strapping tool and semi-automatic lines. Fast strapping tool repair.

No. of Employees: 14.

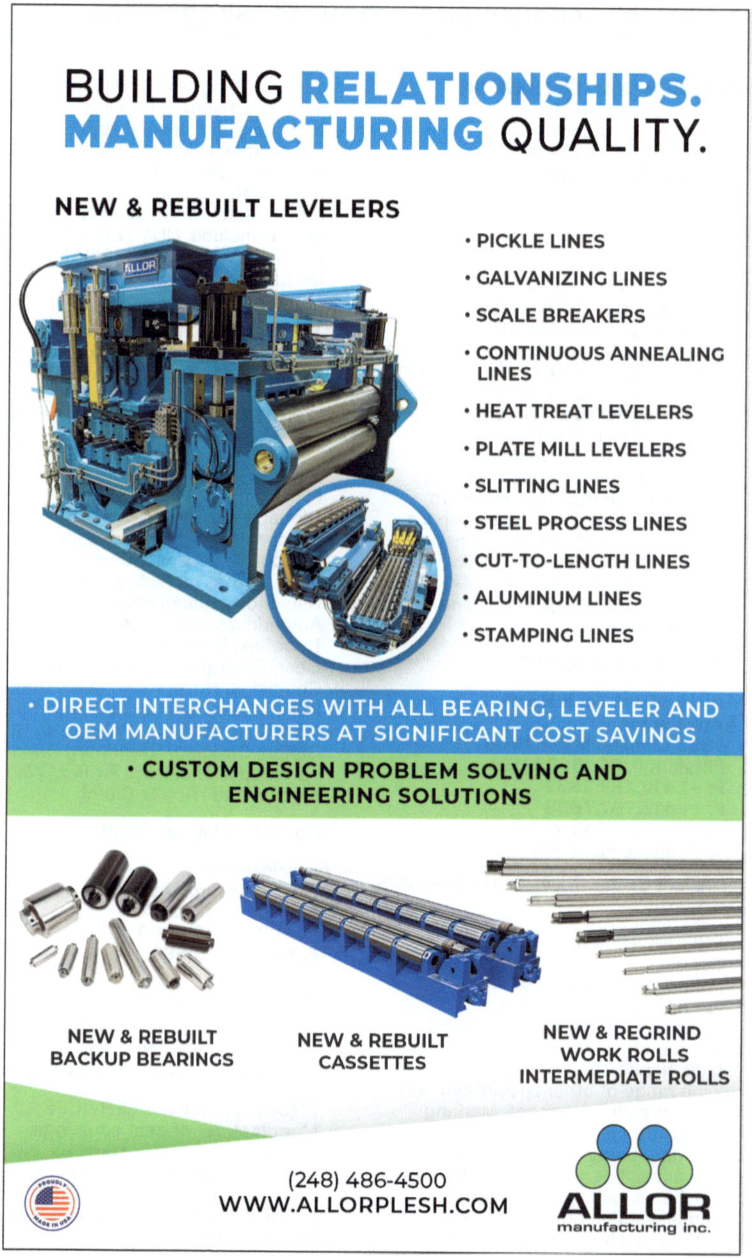

See listing page 284

SUPPLIERS of EQUIPMENT, PRODUCTS and SERVICES

ALPINE METAL TECH GMBH
Buchbergstrasse 11
4844 Regau, Austria
P: +43.7672.78134.0
F: +43.7672.25429
office@alpinemetaltech.com
www.alpinemetaltech.com

- Exec. Officer—Christian Preslmayr

PRODUCTS and /or SERVICES: Develops, designs, produces, and services special plants and machines for rolling, processing, and handling of long products, product identification and product inspection, as well as complete packages for continuous casting machines and special applications for the testing, production, and handling of aluminum wheels as well as fire training simulators for different fields of the aerospace industry. Alpine Metal Tech operates globally under the brands NUMTEC, GEGA, KNORR, MAKRA, AMAKON, MAGNEMAG, SIMULATION and INTERMATO.

No. of Employees: 500.

Alpine Metal Tech North America Inc.
4853 Campbells Run Road
Pittsburgh, PA 15205 USA
P: +1.412.787.2832
F: +1.412.787.7638
na@alpinemetaltech.com
www.alpinemetaltech.com

- Chief Exec. Officer and Pres.—Justin Willott

PRODUCTS and/or SERVICES: Supplier of machinery to the steel industry in the areas of: marking, reading, tracking, torch cutting, deburring, scarfing, ladle shroud manipulators, powder feeders, tundish/ladle heating and drying, and a wide range of other specialized and custom-built equipment. Marking systems include: hot metal spray marking, hot and cold stamping machines, hot and cold paint marking machines, and specialty identification and inspection equipment. Torch cutting machines include: caster cutoff, slitting, subdividing and special shapes. Deburring for billets, blooms and slabs, and special applications. Scarfing machine solutions include: 4-sided, 2-sided, strip, band, robotic, manipulator and portable systems. Alpine Metal Tech's steel industry brands include: NUMTEC, GEGA, KNORR, MAGNEMAG, AMAKON and INTERMATO.

ALTRA INDUSTRIAL MOTION
300 Granite St., Suite 201
Braintree, MA 02184 USA
P: +1.781.917.0600
F: +1.781.843.0709
info@altramotion.com
www.altramotion.com

PRODUCTS and/or SERVICES: Global designer and manufacturer of clutches and brakes, couplings, gearing and power transmission component product lines marketed under 24 well-known manufacturing brands: Ameridrives, Bauer Gear Motor, Bibby Turboflex, Boston Gear, Delroyd Worm Gear, Formsprag Clutch, Guardian Couplings, Huco, Kilian Manufacturing, Kollmorgan, Lamiflex, Marland Clutch, Matrix, Nuttall Gear, Portescap, Stieber Clutch, Stromag, Svendborg Brakes, TB Wood's, Thomson, Twiflex, Warner Electric and Wichita Clutch.

No. of Employees: 9,100.

Ameridrives
1802 Pittsburgh Ave.
Erie, PA 16502 USA
P: +1.814.480.5000
F: +1.814.453.5891
info@ameridrives.com
www.ameridrives.com

- Product Mgr. Universal Joints and Gear Spindles—Nick Jenkins
- Global Sales Mgr.—Tim Nageli

PRODUCTS and/or SERVICES: Manufacturer of gear couplings, universal joints, gear spindles, disc, and diaphragm couplings servicing the metals, power generation, petrochemical, rubber and general heavy industries.

SUPPLIERS OF EQUIPMENT, PRODUCTS and SERVICES

Ameridrives — Gear Couplings
2000 Clovis Barker Road
San Marcos, TX 78666 USA
P: +1.814.480.5000
info@ameridrives.com
www.ameridrives.com

- Product Mgr. Gear Couplings—Chris Jackson
- Global Sales Mgr.—Tim Nageli

PRODUCTS and/or SERVICES:
Manufacturer of gear couplings, gear spindles, disc, and diaphragm couplings servicing the metals, power generation, petrochemical, rubber and general heavy industries.

AM HEALTH AND SAFETY INC.
5177 Campbells Run Road
Pittsburgh, PA 15205 USA
P: +1.412.429.0560
F: +1.412.429.5122
bmomyer@amhealthandsafety.com
www.amhealthandsafety.com

- Pres./Owner—Barry J. Momyer
- Regional Sales Mgrs., Pittsburgh Area—Tyrone Snyder, Barb Cummings, Steve Rihel
- Regional Sales Mgr., Cleveland Area—Mary Zitek
- Regional Sales Mgrs., Chicago Area—Mary Bernhard, Kim Duha
- Pur. Agt.—Theresa Subsara
- Mktg. Coordinator—Barbara E. Momyer

PRODUCTS and/or SERVICES:
Professional industrial hygiene, safety, radiation safety and environmental consulting services. In addition, safety data sheets (SDS) authoring, employee safety and health training, third-party health, safety and environmental audits/inspections, OSHA consultative services, toxicology reviews, indoor air quality studies, noise exposure and control consulting, ergonomics, construction safety, staff augmentation, occupational medicine.

No. of Employees: 22.

AMENDOLA ENGINEERING INC.
15711 Detroit Ave.
Lakewood, OH 44107 USA
P: +1.216.521.5900
F: +1.216.521.5905
g.amendola@amendola-eng.com
www.amendola-eng.com

- Pres.—Gary A. Amendola

PRODUCTS and/or SERVICES:
Water quality engineering: conceptual engineering for new and upgraded wastewater treatment systems. Water quality programs: NPDES and pre-treatment permitting; mixing zone demonstrations, near-field dilution modeling, outfall diffuser design; wasteload allocations; Section 301(g), fundamentally different factors, mercury and water quality variances; Section 316(a) thermal demonstrations; Section 316(b) CWIS; point source and ambient water quality studies; toxicity investigations (TREs/TIEs). Environmental auditing (EPCRA, CAA, NESHAPs, RCRA, CWA, TSCA). Contingency planning: RCRA, SPCC, SWPPP. Other specialties: CERCLA PRP services; natural resource damage assessments; dioxins (source investigations, inventories); expert services for environmental litigation.

AMEPA AMERICA INC.
31250 Solon Road, Unit 17
Solon, OH 44139 USA
P: +1.440.337.0005
F: +1.440.318.1027
info@amepa.com

- Chief Engr.—Pete Krause
- Engr.—Brian Hanz
- System Technician—Jeff Reitz

PRODUCTS and/or SERVICES:
Specializes in process control to the North American steel industry. Other technologies include the coal flow measurement (CFM), used to measure pulverized coal injection (PCI) into the BF; the thermographic slag detection (TSD) system for the BOF/EAF/AOD, used to measure and control the transfer of slag; the residual steel detection (RSD) system, used to

SUPPLIERS of EQUIPMENT, PRODUCTS and SERVICES

maximize caster yield by automating the tundish draining practice; the surface roughness measurement (SRM), using non-contact methods to measure sheet/strip surface roughness conditions, in real time, directly in the line of the rolling mill; and oil film measurement (OFM), using non-contact methods to measure oil/lubricants thickness of sheet/strip, in real time, directly in the line of the rolling mill.

AMERICAN AIR FILTER CO. INC.
9920 Corporate Campus Dr.
Suite 2200
Louisville, KY 40223 USA
P: +1.800.830.3461 (Toll-Free)
fieldservice@aafintl.com
www.aafintl.com

PRODUCTS and/or SERVICES:
Designs, engineers, services, and manufactures air pollution control products and systems for sinter plants, coke oven plants, coal mills, BFs, iron desulfurization, BOFs, hot metal transfer, EAFs, AOD refining, scarfing, ferroalloy furnaces, material handling systems. Provides manufacturing and services for such products as: fabric filters, electrostatic precipitators, scrubbers, evaporative coolers, forced-air coolers, radiant coolers, energy recovery systems, nuisance filters, multi-cartridge filters, multi-cyclones, cyclones, industrial fans, stacks, silencers, hoods and ventilation systems.

AMERICAN CHEMICAL TECHNOLOGIES INC.
1892 Hydraulic Dr.
Howell, MI 48855 USA
P: +1.866.945.1041 (Toll-Free)
sales@americanchemical.com
www.americanchemtech.com

- Pres.—Kevin Kovanda
- Exec. Vice Pres.—Ross Kovanda

PRODUCTS and/or SERVICES:
As a result of the sale of American Chemical Technologies' (ACT's) asset to Shell at the end of 2019, ACT has transitioned into a belting division and steel processing fluids supplier. ACT purchased an existing conveyor belt distributor in Gary, IN, and created a Conveyor Belt Division under ACT. Capabilities include all standard and specialty heavy-duty industrial conveyor belt and components, including sidewall pocket EAF raw material belts, DRI pipe belts, and high-temperature-resistant belts. For steel processing, ACT has aligned with formulating chemists, application engineers and technical sales representatives who will provide solutions and value to all aspects of steel finishing operations: pickle oils, rolling oils, temper fluids, cleaners and more.

No. of Employees: 45.

AMERICAN GFM CORP.
1200 Cavalier Blvd.
Chesapeake, VA 23323 USA
P: +1.757.487.2442
F: +1.757.487.4712
sales@agfm.com
www.gfm-global.com

- Pres.—Michael Kralowetz
- Vice Pres.—Brad Fair
- Dir. of Sales, Small Arms Radial Forging Machines and Spare Parts, Svce.—Dieter Lubinger

PRODUCTS and/or SERVICES:
Radial and precision forging machines.

No. of Employees: 140.

AMERICAN GREEN VENTURES (SPILLFIX)
180 Towerview Ct.
Cary, NC 27513 USA
P: +1.919.535.8278
kate.dean@am-green.com
www.spillfix.com

Standard Conveyor Belt IN STOCK
High Temperature Belt, MSHA Belt, Oil Resistant,
Coal Handling, DRI, Coke and Ore Pellet Belt

Side-wall Pocket Belts for EAF Raw Material Delivery

CALL or EMAIL for RFQ Price and Availability

Gary Hanson / 269-830-6870   gary@belt.doctor
Ross Kovanda / 248-521-3351   ross@belt.doctor

" Pride in Personal Service Continues "

CONVEYOR BELT DIVISION

AMERICAN CHEMICAL TECHNOLOGIES, INC.

SUPER BOOTH
AISTech 2023
Global Event Sponsor

Corporate Office:
American Chemical Technologies, Inc
1892 Hydraulic Drive
Howell, MI 48855 USA

Advanced Rubber Technologies
Division of American Chemical Technologies
201 Mississippi St. Door V-129
Gary, IN 46402 USA

SUPPLIERS of EQUIPMENT, PRODUCTS and SERVICES

- Exec. Vice Pres. Sales and Mktg.—
  Kate Dean

PRODUCTS and/or SERVICES:
SpillFix industrial absorbent and spill remediation products.

No. of Employees: 10.

AMERICAN ROLLER BEARING CO.
1331 4th St. Dr. NW
Hickory, NC 28601 USA
P: +1.828.624.1460
F: +1.828.624.1462
orders@amroll.com
www.amroll.com

- Chief Exec. Officer and Pres.—
  Benjamin S. Succop

PRODUCTS and/or SERVICES:
Designs, manufactures, services and repairs tapered roller, cylindrical roller, spherical roller, spherical plain, and ball bearings for heavy-duty steel mill applications. With sizes up to 84 in., American's line of bearings cover industry standard radial and thrust bearings, as well as engineered specials to meet unique application demands. Mill applications including bearings for gearboxes, work rolls, backup rolls, screwdown mechanisms, vertical rolls, converters and more. Patented Blended Bevel® inner races are standard for American's line of four-row cylindrical roller roll neck bearings and available from stock on many popular roll neck sizes. American also offers an in-house bearing reconditioning program.

AMERIFAB INC.
3501 E. 9th St.
Indianapolis, IN 46201 USA
P: +1.317.231.0100
F: +1.317.231.0144
sales@amerifabinc.com
www.amerifabinc.com

- Chief Exec. Officer—Rick Manasek
- Pres.—Andrew Akers
- Sales—Todd Soja, Debbie Sullivan, Sean Collins

PRODUCTS and/or SERVICES:
AmeriBronze®, AmeriSpline®, AmeriAntiSlag®, AmeriPanelization® patented technologies, and AmeriSlagSlot™ patent-pending technologies, including the full complement of proprietary technologies for EAF, LMF, BOF/BOP and AOD furnace and caster equipment, including water-cooled sidewall and roof systems, water-cooled duct systems, upper shells, bottom shells, current-conducting electrode arms, EAF, LMF and RHF revamps, plus BOF/BOP and AOD hoods. Engineering capabilities include 3D modeling, offgas system heat/mass/flow modeling balance and FEA.

AMETEK

AMETEK Inc.
1100 Cassatt Road
Berwyn, PA 19312 USA
P: +1.610.647.2121
www.ametek.com

- Chmn. and Chief Exec. Officer—
  David A. Zapico
- Chief Financial Officer and Exec. Vice Pres.—William J. Burke
- Chief Commercial Officer—Emanuela Speranza
- Chief Info. Officer and Vice Pres.—
  Stewart Douglas
- Pres. Electronic Instruments—Tony J. Ciampitti, John W. Hardin, Thomas C. Marecic
- Pres. Electromechanical Group—
  Dave Hermance
- Chief Admin. Officer—Ronald J. Oscher
- Vice Pres., Investor Rels. and Treas.—
  Kevin Coleman

PRODUCTS and/or SERVICES:
Manufacturer of electronic instruments and electromechanical devices.

AMETEK Factory Automation
1080 N. Crooks Road
Clawson, MI 48017 USA
P: +1.248.435.0700
F: +1.248.435.8120
apt.sales@ametek.com
www.ametekfactoryautomation.com

RADIAL FORGING TECHNOLOGY

- New RX Design
- Highly Energy Efficient – Large energy savings
- Stepless stroke rate
- Less Hydraulics
- Unmatched Flexibility
- Closer Tolerances
- Easy to Program
- Highest Quality
- Robust and Stable
- Low maintenance

GFM
Ennser Strasse 14
A-4403 Steyr Austria
Tel: 0 72 52/898 0
Email: info@gfm.at
www.gfm-global.com

American GFM Corp.
1200 Cavalier Blvd
Chesapeake, VA 23323
Tel: 757-487-2442
Email: sales@agfm.com
www.gfm-global.com

SUPPLIERS of EQUIPMENT, PRODUCTS and SERVICES

- Dir. Engrg.—Jack Pattee
- Contr.—Ron Jayroe
- Product/Sales Dir.—Blake Cawley

PRODUCTS and/or SERVICES:
Continuous process position feedback solutions for extreme applications. Expertise in system automation in the following industries: iron, steel, and non-ferrous metal processing, die casting and fabrication, plastic processing, packaging, wood products, press automation, and specialty machinery. Processes utilizing continuous linear or rotary feedback for roll positioning, secondary metals processing, lateral/sideguides, WB furnaces, slitters and cutters, extrusion equipment, heavy movable structures, and more. Manufacturing technology: GEMCO brand non-contact (magnetostrictive) linear displacement transducers (LDTs), mill-duty housings, high-speed programmable limit switches (PLSs), PLC resolvers, cable reel sensors, programmable limit switches, LDT and resolver interface cards, rotary limit switches, and SEMELEX safety meters for process stop time calculation for safe distances. B/W Controls brand intrinsically safe liquid level sensors and leak detection solutions, CATRAC heavy-duty hose/cable management systems and heavy-duty industrial brakes.

No. of Employees: 110.

AMETEK Land
Wreakes Lane
Dronfield, Derbyshire, S18 1DJ U.K.
P: +44.0.1246.417691
land.enquiry@ametek.com
www.ametek-land.com

PRODUCTS and SERVICES:
Monitors and analyzers.

No. of Employees: 144.

AMETEK Process Instruments
150 Freeport Road
Pittsburgh, PA 15238 USA
P: +1.412.828.9040
F: +1.412.826.0399
www.ametekpi.com

PRODUCTS and/or SERVICES:
Process analyzers and instrumentation.

AMETEK Surface Vision
1288 San Luis Obispo Ave.
Hayward, CA 94544 USA
P: +1.877.926.4639 (Toll-Free);
   +1.510.431.6767
F: +1.510.431.6730
surfacevision.info@ametek.com
www.ameteksurfacevision.com

- Div. Vice Pres. and Business Unit Mgr.—Justin Smith
- Div. Vice Pres. and Global Business Mgr.—Mike Hevey
- Div. Vice Pres. Sales, Projects and Svcs.—Jason Zyglis
- Div. Vice Pres. — Oprs.—Alan Terry
- Dir. Business Unit Contr.—Lincoln Drake
- Dir. H.R.—Nancy Bradbury
- Global Legal Dir.—Sevican Celik

PRODUCTS and/or SERVICES:
SmartView, SmartAdvisor for complete surface inspection, process monitoring and root-cause defect analysis.

No. of Employees: 140.

AMI INTERNATIONAL S. DE R.L. DE C.V.
Blvd. LIC Gustavo Diaz Ordaz #402
Col. Rincon de Sta. Maria
Monterrey, NL, 64650 Mexico
P: +011.52.81.1001.4050
info@amiautomation.com
www.amiautomation.com

- Chief Exec. Officer—Octavio Rodriguez
- Vice Pres.—Fernando Martinez
- Dir. Ind. Systems—Bernardo Sainz
- Dir. Meltshops Solutions—Carlos Adrian de los Santos

PRODUCTS and/or SERVICES:
AMI Automation is an international automation and control solutions company with a focus on designing, manufacturing, and implementing innovative technology solutions to provide process improvements that help make companies more efficient. Industries served include steel, mining,

SUPPLIERS OF EQUIPMENT, PRODUCTS and SERVICES

cement, pulp and paper, and oil and gas. AMI Automation combines 30+ years of experience with automation and controls including artificial intelligence to assist customers with the challenges of implementing and upgrading to new technology solutions. In addition to new equipment, AMI can add updates to older existing equipment for cost-effective process improvements. AMI can provide repairs and spares as well as preventive maintenance programs. AMI's team of experienced, specialized engineers is available for consulting, custom design, training and technical support. AMI Automation consists of two groups: The Industrial Systems Group focus is on drive solutions while the Meltshops Solutions group is focused on EAF optimization.

No. of Employees: 250+.

AMIAD WATER SYSTEMS
120-J Talbert Road
Mooresville, NC 28117 USA
P: +1.800.243.4583 (Toll-Free);
 +1.704.662.3133
F: +1.704.662.3155
infousa@amiad.com
www.amiadusa.com

- Pres.—Michael Poth
- Business Dev. Mgr.—Omry Levin
- Dir. Ind./Municipal Sales and Mktg.— Piero Suman

PRODUCTS and/or SERVICES:
Manufacture and supply automatic, self-cleaning filters. Products include stainless and carbon steel automatic, self-cleaning filters with 10 to 3,500 micron, and the AMF series of thread filters for both potable and wastewater filtration down to 2 micron. Amiad technology can be found among the following applications: pre-treatment for UV and membranes, tertiary wastewater treatment, surface and well water supply treatment, water reuse, and cooling water.

AMRESIST INC., a Bray Co.
2045 Silber Road
Houston, TX 77055 USA
P: +1.713.682.0000
F: +1.713.682.0080
sales@amresist.com
www.amresist.com

- Vice Pres. Engrg.—Richard DeBuck
- Vice Pres. Sales and Regional Sales Mgr. — West and Southeast—Keith McElroy
- Regional Sales Mgr. — Northeast— Jim Clark

EQUIPMENT:
Valves and actuators: Acris, Isoria, Mammouth Valves; C-series actuators.

PRODUCTS and/or SERVICES:
Tight-shutoff PFA and rubber-lined butterfly/ball valves for pickling acid, galvanizing solution, and general water applications. Sizes from ½-in. to 160-in. dia. Full in-house valve automation capabilities.

No. of Employees: 1,200.

AMTEC HYDRACLAMP INC., a Div. of Higginson Equipment Inc.
1175 Corporate Dr., Unit 1
P.O. Box 5011
Burlington, ON L7R 3Z4 Canada
P: +1.905.335.8233
F: +1.905.335.6074
inquiries@amtechydraclamp.com
www.amtechydraclamp.com

- Pres.—Caryes Allan
- Vice Pres. Sales and Mktg.—Josh Cosford

PRODUCTS and/or SERVICES:
Standard and custom-engineered hydraulic clamping devices, including nuts, rings, pads, and cylinders for rolling mills, casters, presses, metal processing lines and machine tools. Custom-designed integrated pressure control systems for oil or grease, quick-disconnect fittings, manual and electric pumps to 10,000 psi or higher.

No. of Employees: 24.

SUPPLIERS of EQUIPMENT, PRODUCTS and SERVICES

ANDREW S. MCCREATH & SON INC.
1649 Bobali Dr.
Harrisburg, PA 17104 USA
P: +1.717.364.1440
F: +1.717.364.1640
service@mccreathlabs.com
www.mccreathlabs.com

- Pres.—Robert Kozicki
- Vice Pres.—Michael Carmon

PRODUCTS and/or SERVICES: Inspection, sampling and testing of raw materials used by steel mills or foundries. Weight verification via barge survey, pile survey and scale weight verification.

No. of Employees: 40.

ANDRITZ AG
Stattegger Strasse 18
Graz, 8045 Austria
P: +43.316.6902.0
welcome@andritz.com
www.andritz.com

- Chief Exec. Officer and Pres.—Joachim Schönbeck
- Managing Bd.—Joachim Schönbeck, Domenico Iacovelli, Norbert Nettesheim, Humbert Köfler, Wolfgang Semper
- Business Area Mgr. for ANDRITZ Metals—Guido Burgel

PRODUCTS and/or SERVICES: Global supplier of complete lines for the production and processing of cold-rolled strip made of carbon steel, stainless steel, aluminum and other non-ferrous metals. The lines comprise equipment for pickling, cold rolling, annealing and heat treatment, surface finishing, strip coating and finishing, punching and deep drawing, and regeneration of pickling acids. The business area also supplies turnkey furnace systems for the steel, copper, and aluminum industries; burners and refractory products; as well as a comprehensive service for welding systems for the metalworking industry. The Schuler Group, in which ANDRITZ has a stake of more than 95%, offers presses, automation solutions, dies, process know-how and services for the entire metal forming industry. Its customers include car manufacturers and their suppliers, as well as companies in the forging, household appliance, packaging, energy and electrical industries. Offers coin minting technology and system solutions for the aerospace industry, rail transport, and manufacture of large pipes.

No. of Employees: 29,616 worldwide.

ANDRITZ Metals Germany GmbH
Stephanopeler Str. 22
Hemer, D-58675 Germany

P.O. Box 1655
Hemer, D-58656 Germany
P: +49.2372.540
F: +49.2372.54200
welcome.metalsgermany@andritz.com
www.andritz.com/metals

- Chmn. and Managing Dir.—Guido Burgel

PRODUCTS and/or SERVICES: Turnkey systems for the processing of stainless steel, coated metals, non-ferrous metals and special materials. Cold rolling mills for reducing, skinpassing and finish-rolling in 20-high, S6-high (18-high), 12-high, 6-high, 4-high, and 2-high designs, and in combinations of 2-high/4-high or 4-high/S6-high design, available as one-way, reversing or tandem mill, in-line and off-line. Shape control systems for cold rolling mills and strip processing lines. Roll grinders. Strip processing lines for annealing, pickling, shotblasting, metal coating, hot-dip galvanizing, plastic coating, painting, surface conditioning, tension leveling, coil preparation, coil buildup, grinding, polishing, etc. Finishing lines for cutting-to-length, slitting, sidetrimming, rewinding and inspection. Automation—Complete electrical equipment, including drive systems, process automation, and level 2 systems for cold rolling mills, strip processing lines and finishing lines. Technological control systems

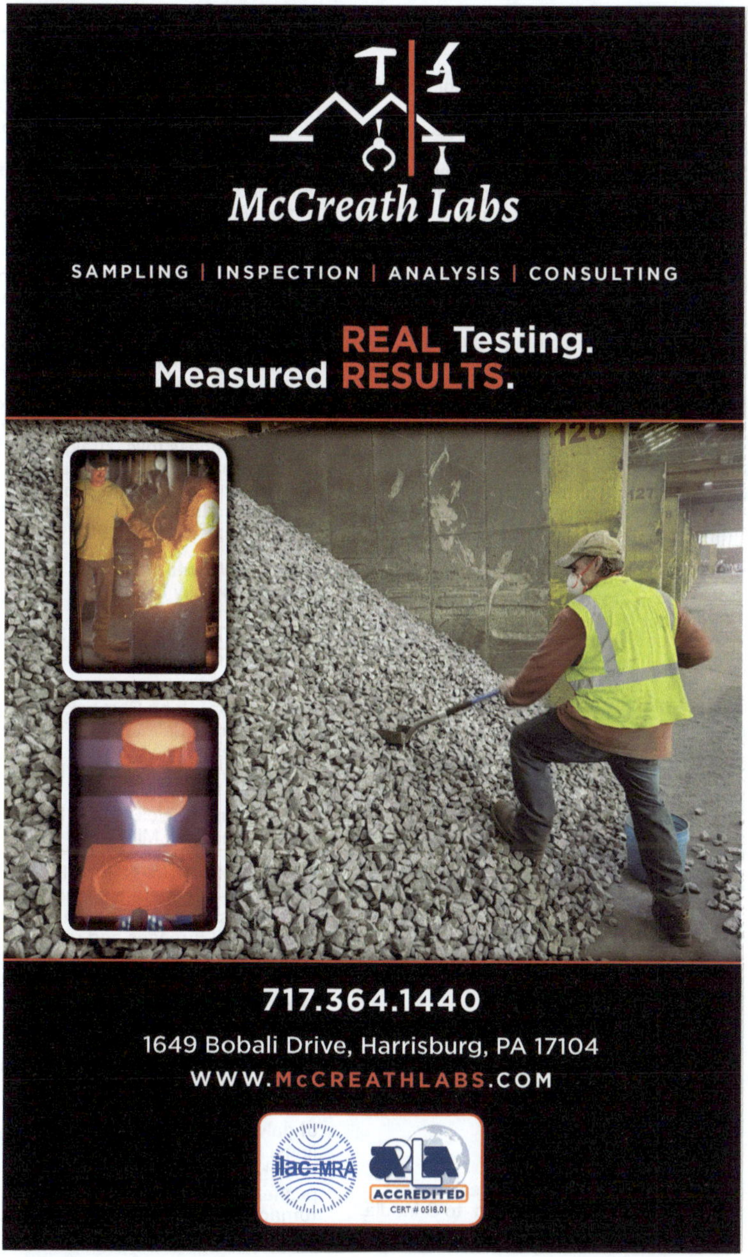

See listing page 294

SUPPLIERS of EQUIPMENT, PRODUCTS and SERVICES

for cold rolling mills, such as thickness control systems (AGC), automatic flatness control systems (AFC) as well as fully automatic roll change systems for rolling mills. Revamps and modernization of existing production equipment dedicated team of engineers, commissioning specialists and experienced field personnel with knowledge in design, engineering and process optimization. After-sales services and spare part business. Provides service solutions such as maintenance, training, technical expert operations, technology support and equipment evaluations. Spare part storage for some critical items to ensure the shortest possible lead times on special parts. Furnaces—planning, engineering, supply, installation, and start-up of furnace systems for thermal processes and accessory installations to the steel industry. Burners and refractory—industrial burners, complete heating systems, and combustion equipment for a wide range of thermal industrial applications, particularly in the steel and aluminum industry, the forging industry, and in many other high-temperature processes.

No. of Employees: 300.

ANDRITZ Metals USA Inc.
130 Main St.
P.O. Box AB
Callery, PA 16024 USA
P: +1.724.538.3180
F: +1.724.538.3056
metals.usa@andritz.com
www.andritz.com/metals
www.linkedin.com/company/andritz
www.youtube.com/c/andritzgroup

- Pres.—Josh Gossner
- Vice Pres. Oprs. and Mill Svcs.— James Jeschke Jr.
- Vice Pres. Sales, Capital—Michael Finan
- Vice Pres. Sales, Aftermarket— Michael Mason

EQUIPMENT:
Manufacture of strip processing machinery. Rolls from 3/4-in. to 8-in. dia. induction hardened.

PRODUCTS and/or SERVICES:
Headquarters of ANDRITZ Metals USA Inc. and home of Herr-Voss Stamco and ASKO technologies. Designer, manufacturer, and installer of precision roller and tension levelers, CTL lines, slitting lines, inspection lines for both ferrous and non-ferrous metals in coil form. Manufacturing of new capital processing equipment and rebuilding of levelers and processing equipment. Field service, mechanical engineering, electrical engineering. In-house engineering and feasibility studies. Rebuild and repair miscellaneous mill equipment for hot mills and cold mills and processing lines. Centerless grinding process rolls, straightener/ journal repair and chrome plating service for processing equipment. Standard rolls, high-abrasion rolls and rolls for more than 100,000 yield.

ANDRITZ Metals USA Inc.
500 Technology Dr.
Canonsburg, PA 15317 USA
P: +1.724.746.2300
F: +1.724.746.9420

- Vice Pres. Innovation and Project Execution—John Chrobak
- Aftermarket Sales Dir. — Furnaces— John Trenkelbach
- Aftermarket Sales Mgr. — Furnaces— Timothy Dixon
- Aftermarket Sales Mgr. — Processing Lines and Roll. Mills—Ron Piotrowski

PRODUCTS and/or SERVICES:
Furnaces—Complete engineering for the design and construction of industrial furnaces and related equipment. Project engineering and detailed design of furnaces and mechanical handling equipment. Project management, cost control, detailed schedule control, procurement/purchasing, expediting/ inspection and construction management. Turnkey installation of galvanizing/annealing processing lines, thin-cast strip facilities, walking hearth and WB furnaces, continuous pusher furnaces, coil annealing furnaces, rotary hearth furnaces, roller hearth, and batch-type furnaces for

ANDRITZ METALS

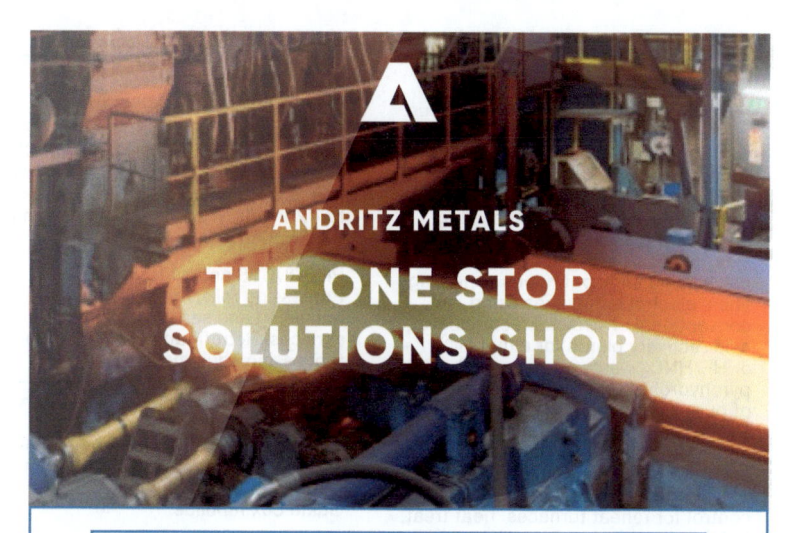

THE ONE STOP SOLUTIONS SHOP

ASKO KNIVES	HERR-VOSS STAMCO	BRICMONT
MAERZ	SUNDWIG	SOUTEC
SELAS	FBB BURNERS	SCHULER

EQUIPMENT
ANDRITZ METALS designs and builds equipment for the processing of carbon steel, stainless steel, and non-ferrous metal including pickling lines, coating lines, levelers, cut to length lines, slitting lines as well as continuous or batch furnaces for reheating slabs, blooms, billets, and structural shapes.

REBUILD AND RETROFIT
ANDRITZ METALS offers mechanical, electrical, automation and safety rebuilds, and retrofits to make your old equipment better and safer than new. We have extensive experience working on equipment at mills, service centers, processors and fabricators.

PARTS AND SERVICE
ANDRITZ METALS specializes in supplying parts and services for rolling mills and strip processors to meet any and all needs. Our knowledge of a wide variety of metals equipment allows us to supply, inspect and recondition all types of rolls, knives, bearings and other parts. We also provide a wide range of mechanical and electrical components for ANDRITZ equipment as well as for many other brands in the industry.

ENGINEERED SUCCESS

ANDRITZ METALS USA Inc. / 130 Main Street / Callery, PA 16024 / USA
+1 (724) 538 0207 / andritz.com/metals / metals.usa@andritz.com

ANDRITZ

SUPPLIERS of EQUIPMENT, PRODUCTS and SERVICES

reheating and heat treating of ferrous, aluminum, and other non-ferrous metals. Strip Processing—Design and furnish complete continuous, push-pull pickling lines for both carbon steel and stainless steel strip, annealing and pickling lines for stainless steel, electrolytic cleaning lines, hot-dip galvanizing and continuous annealing lines, electroplating lines using conventional or Gravitel technologies, acid recovery plants for either HCl or HF/HNO_3 waste streams, and pyrohydrolysis for the production of pure oxides. Cold rolling mills. Flatness shape rolls. Controls—Design, engineering, and installation of computerized monitoring and control of mill processes. Totally automated control for reheat furnaces, heat treat, batch anneal furnaces, soaking pits, continuous casters and EAFs. Custom-designed systems for galvanize line coating control, continuous caster and furnace simulation, product tracking, material handling, and energy management. Extensive experience in process modeling for heat transfer applications. Engineering Services—Analysis and consulting services: applied FEA, including heat transfer and thermal stress, thermodynamic analysis, failure analysis, structural analysis, high-temperature materials technology and heating process development. Engineering: feasibility/planning studies, furnace optimization studies, layout/conceptual design studies, field engineering, start-up assistance, cost estimating, furnace inspection/evaluation, energy and safety audits. Training: maintenance and operations training for BF and stoves, EAFs, continuous casters, soaking pits, reheat furnaces, boilers, rolling mills and strip processing.

ANDRITZ Metals USA Inc.
2970 Duss Ave.
Ambridge, PA 15003 USA
P: +1.724.251.8745
P: +1.724.251.8747

– Plant Mgr.—Al Leo

EQUIPMENT:
Grinding: 2-in. dia. to 60-in. dia. x 30-ft. 5-in. horizontal boring mill, 48-in. CNC lathe, 60-in. CNC VTL. Machine shop and assembly floor. Grinding: 3-in. dia. to 42-in. dia. x 24 ft. CNC lathes and CNC boring mills.

PRODUCTS and/or SERVICES:
Processing rolls, mill rolls, dynamic balancing and seamless pipe mill services. Retrofit and service center processing equipment. Installation of equipment. Retrofit engineering—mechanical, electrical and civil. Service for process and mill equipment. Chrome and EDT textured rolls. HGC and AGC cylinder rebuilds and testing. Chock repairs and bearing repairs. Guide box rebuilds.

ANDRITZ Metals USA Inc.
1079 Lot #1 Industry Dr.
Chesterton, IN 46304 USA
P: +1.219.764.8586
F: +1.219.764.8597

– Plant Mgrs.—Bill Donaldson, Silverio Napules

EQUIPMENT:
Roll grinders from 2-in. dia. to 60 in. x 28 ft.; roll lathes 5-in. dia. to 60-in. dia.; milling. Centerless grinding $5/16$-in. dia. to 4-in. dia. Backup bearing grinding $1 1/4$-in. dia. to $3 1/2$-in. dia.

PRODUCTS and/or SERVICES:
Roll reconditioning service. Roll turners, grinding, EDT texturing, shotblast, polishing, hard chrome plating up to 32-in. dia. x 18 ft. Grinding process rolls, straightener/journal repair and optic alignment. Field service, tension level module rebuilds, journals and backup support repair.

ANDRITZ Metals USA Inc.
15600 Vincennes Ave.
South Holland, IL 60473 USA

– Plant Mgr.—Bill Donovan

PRODUCTS and/or SERVICES:
Rotary and shear knife regrinding services.

SUPPLIERS OF EQUIPMENT, PRODUCTS and SERVICES

ANDRITZ Metals USA Inc.
600 Huey Road
Rock Hill, SC 28730 USA

- Plant Mgr.—Dick Heatherington

PRODUCTS and/or SERVICES:
Manufacturing and regrind services for knives, blades, liners, wear plates and accessories for the metal producing, processing and recycling industries.

ANDRITZ Metals Netherlands B.V.
Willem Fenegastraat 10
1096 BN Amsterdam, The Netherlands

- Plant Mgr.—Branislav Petrov

PRODUCTS and/or SERVICES:
Manufacturing and regrind services for knives, blades, liners, wear plates and accessories for the metal producing, processing and recycling industries.

ANDRONACO INDUSTRIES
4855 Broadmoor Ave.
Kentwood, MI 49512 USA
P: +1.616.554.4600
F: +1.616.554.9304
creeves@andronaco.com
www.andronaco.com

- Chief Exec. Officer and Pres.—Ralph Mallozzi
- Vice Pres. Sales—Colleen Reeves
- Chief Engr.—Joe Beaumont

EQUIPMENT:
Advanced structural corrosion-resistant fluid processing piping systems for steel pickling lines.

PRODUCTS and/or SERVICES:
Engineered structural composite piping systems, lined steel piping systems, fiberglass piping systems, fiberglass and dual laminate chemical storage tanks, composite ball, butterfly, and check valves, expansion joints, lined hoses, and related fluid processing mechanical components.

No. of Employees: 350.

ANGSTROM INC.
12890 Haggerty Road
Belleville, MI 48111 USA
P: +1.734.697.8058
F: +1.734.697.3544
www.angstrom-inc.com

- Pres.—John R. Schneider
- Vice Pres. Sales and Mktg.—Randy S. Moffat

PRODUCTS and/or SERVICES:
OES for steel analysis. Computerized readout and source updates for aging spectrometers. Sample preparation equipment for slag analysis, including ring and puck mills and briquette presses.

No. of Employees: 25.

ANGUIL ENVIRONMENTAL SYSTEMS INC.
8855 N. 55th St.
Milwaukee, WI 53223 USA
P: +1.414.365.6400
F: +1.414.365.6410
sales@anguil.com
www.anguil.com

- Chief Exec. Officer—Gene Anguil
- Chief Oper. Officer—Deb Anguil
- Pres.—Chris Anguil
- Vice Pres. Engrg.—Mike Disabato
- Dir. Mktg.—Kevin Summ
- Sales Mgr.—Scott Bayon
- Chief Engr.—Jeff Weiss

PRODUCTS and/or SERVICES:
Supplies air pollution control systems (thermal and catalytic oxidizers), water treatment technologies, and energy recovery equipment for manufacturing facilities and industrial applications. Turnkey solutions and services for environmental compliance.

SUPPLIERS of EQUIPMENT, PRODUCTS and SERVICES

ANT AUTOMATION
651 Holiday Dr., Suite 400
Pittsburgh, PA 15220 USA
P: +1.412.736.9170
info@ant-automation.com
www.ant-automation.com

- Chief Exec. Officer and Pres.—Aldo Javier Barreiro
- Exec. Vice Pres.—Marcelo Michalek
- Chief Engr.—Fabian Alberto Barreiro

PRODUCTS and/or SERVICES:
Industry 4.0, industry digitalization, cloud-based platforms, ladle/torpedo/LMF/EAF/CCM hot spot detection, 3D SCADA, VR plant simulation, virtual commissioning, synthetic environments, digital twin development, plant optimization, operation training, infrared image processing, process models, optimization models, automation, engineering, commissioning, applying new technologies.

No. of Employees: 20.

APEX CONTROL SYSTEMS INC.
751 N. 21st St.
Sebring, OH 44672 USA
P: +1.330.938.2588
F: +1.330.938.6865
tom@apexcontrol.com

- Chief Exec. Officer and Pres.—Thomas Drakulich

PRODUCTS and/or SERVICES:
Motor control systems and equipment, magnet controls, magnet rectifiers, brake rectifiers, crane controls, DC motor drives and controls, cabs and control houses, AC crane controls, DC crane controls, resistors, operator stations, pendants, consoles, festoon systems, VF controls, and motors.

No. of Employees: 60.

AQ TRANSFORMER SOLUTIONS INC.
823 Fairview Road
Wytheville, VA 24382 USA
P: +1.540.970.7016
F: +1.540.206.2995
sachin.gupta@aqgroup.com
https://www.aqgroup.com/en/aqtransformersolutionsinc/aq-transformer-solutions-inc

- Pres.—Matt Gregg
- Vice Pres. Mktg.—Dan Day
- Treas.—Judy Cox
- Sales and Adv. Mgr.—Sachin Gupta

PRODUCTS and/or SERVICES:
Transformers, rectifiers and filters.

No. of Employees: 100.

ARKO BY PMP
Carretera Miguel Alemán km 26, #1040
Apodaca, NL, 66633 Mexico
P: +52.81.8367.8030
F: +52.81.8367.9230
ventas@arko.mx
www.pmpgrupo.mx

- Chief Exec. Officer—Porfirio Gonzalez
- Chief Financial Officer—Diego Garza
- Sales Mgr.—Gregorio Salas

PRODUCTS and/or SERVICES:
Water-cooled equipment: ducts (parallel flow, spiral), panel flip and turn, roof panels (iron, copper), sidewall panels (iron, copper), combi panels (iron, copper), electric delta, water-cooled delta, roof ladle furnace, BOF chimney. Maintenance and installation services: LF installation, EAF installation, panel removal, panel repair, engineering services, process analysis. Mechanical components: ladle, scrap ladles, transfer cars, turrets, lower shell, upper shell, roof ladles, carbon injectors, conductive electrode arms, post-combustion camera. Spare parts and commercial products.

No. of Employees: 136.

SUPPLIERS OF EQUIPMENT, PRODUCTS and SERVICES

ARMOR PROTECTIVE PACKAGING
P.O. Box 828
Howell, MI 48844 USA
P: +1.800.365.1117 (Toll-Free);
 +1.517.546.1117
F: +1.248.573.0241
www.armorvci.com

- Vice Pres. Sales and Mktg.—David Yancho

PRODUCTS and/or SERVICES:
Rust prevention and rust removal products. ARMOR offers a full of line of rust prevention packaging materials designed to protect ferrous and nonferrous metals thanks to ARMOR's proprietary VCI Nanotechnology™ for vapor corrosion inhibitors. Products include ARMOR WRAP® paper, ARMOR POLY® film, the ARMOR SHIELD® line of desiccants, emitters, foam pads, and Metal Rescue® Rust Remover Bath and Dry Coat™ rust preventive.

ARVA AG TECHNOLOGICAL CONSULTING
Loostrasse 3
CH 8803 Rueschlikon, Switzerland
P: +66.89.124.33.45;
 +66.89.991.21.17 (Mobile)
arva@hispeed.ch
arva_ag@protonmail.ch

- Chief Exec. Officer—Arthur Vaterlaus

PRODUCTS and/or SERVICES:
Continuous casting engineering and technical assistance. Technological consulting: precision mold level control (PCV), tundish vortex prevention, mold stirring by whirl-SEN, 3D-parabolic mold taper, extended machine and alignment life by month-long sequence casting anti-stress technology, the world's first and original continuous straightening method, secondary cooling for high casting speed and even strand surface temperature.

No. of Employees: 3.

ARVOS SCHMIDTSCHE SCHACK LLC
6500 Brooktree Road, Suite 300
Wexford, PA 15090 USA
P: +1.724.759.2802
F: +1.724.935.6580
robert.boucher@arvos-group.com
www.shg-schack.com

- Managing Dir.—Robert Boucher
- Sr. Sales Mgr.—James Geisler

PRODUCTS and/or SERVICES:
Recuperators for all types of steel mill furnaces, BF gas-fired boilers, DRI heat recovery systems, waste heat boilers.

AS METALS TECHNOLOGIES
Via S. Balestra 7
Lugano, Cantone Ticino, 6900
Switzerland
P: +41.79.921.37.58
 +41.79.194.94.05
F: +41.91.921.37.58
info@asmetalstechnologies.com
c.giorgi@asmetalstechnologies.com
www.asmetalstechnologies.com

- Chief Exec. Officer and Pres.—Carlo Giorgi

EQUIPMENT:
Dedusting systems, water treatment plants.

PRODUCTS and/or SERVICES:
Centrifugal fans, special anti-wear fans, pulse-jet baghouse, ESP, water-cooled parts, spare parts. Engineering for dedusting systems, water treatment plants, etc.

No. of Employees: 25–30.

ASSA ABLOY/MEGADOOR USA
350 Dividend Dr.
Peachtree City, GA 30269 USA
P: +1.419.343.3002
F: +1.770.631.9086
www.assaabloyentrance.com

- Sales—Robert Moulton
- Pur.—Kimberly Vargas
- Svce.—Mark Hagl
- Parts—Sonny Holloway

SUPPLIERS of EQUIPMENT, PRODUCTS and SERVICES

PRODUCTS and/or SERVICES:
Door systems, heavy industrial rubber doors and vertical lift fabric doors for mining, heavy industry and transportation.

ATLANTIC TRACK & TURNOUT CO.
400 Broadacres Dr., Suite 415
Bloomfield, NJ 07003 USA
P: +1.800.631.1274 (Toll-Free)
F: +1.973.748.4520
info@atlantictrack.com
www.atlantictrack.com

- Pres.—P.A. Hughes
- Vice Pres., Crane Runway Div.—F.J. Jroski
- Vice Pres., Railroad Div.—J.P. McDonald
- Vice Pres., Transit Div.—P.J. Schuler
- Natl. Sales Mgr., Crane Runway Div.—N.J. Jroski
- Eastern Sales Mgr., Railroad Div.—J.A. Boosel
- Western Sales Mgr., Railroad Div.—R.W. Beard
- Export Sales—D.A. Olortegui
- Corporate Pur.—M. Martinez
- ATRS Installation Oprs. Mgr.—R. Swope
- Flash-Weld Oprs. Mgr.—J. Horvath

PRODUCTS and/or SERVICES:
Crane rail, railroad rail, track accessories, overhead crane runways, rubber nose clips and pads, tieback linkage systems, special and standard trackwork, crane runway surveys, rail changeouts, and flash butt welding. Cutting, drilling and fabrication of rail products.

AUSTRALTEK LLC
800 Old Pond Road, Suite 706K
Bridgeville, PA 15017 USA
P: +1.412.257.2377
F: +1.412.257.2388
info@australtek.com
www.australtek.com
www.steeltracking.com
www.iot4i.com
www.mes.australtek.com
www.oeeasy.com

- Chief Exec. Officer—Federico Ahualli
- Pres.—Cesar Agostino
- Vice Pres. Oprs.—Santiago Picco
- Vice Pres. Sales—Juan Sagasti
- Vice Pres. Mktg.—Cris Miller

EQUIPMENT:
RFID sensors and readers for extreme temperature and long distance. Physical tracking of hot ladles, tundish, torpedo cars and caster sections. Automatic detection of ladle arrival and departure up to 60 ft. away and 750°F. Automatic hot ladle numbering with high-temperature RFID. Radar-based ladle freeboard and tundish level detection. Radar-based width measurement, product shape and camber detection for hot and cold strips, slabs, and plates. IIOT hardware for digital and analog sensors conversion. IIOT routers. PLC to cloud gateways. Wireless devices for rapid deployment.

PRODUCTS and/or SERVICES:
MES system for meltshop, caster, hot and cold mills. Finishing lines automation. Electrical engineering, PLC, HMI, AC/DC and servodrives. Instrumentation. Field networks. Site management and supervision. Level 2, MES-ERP integration, machine learning, machine vision, special developments. Process OEE calculation and reporting. Cloud data analysis tools. Digital transformation. Maintenance, performance and asset aging tracking. Breakdown reduction. Statistical process control. Energy efficiency metering tools, on-line monitoring of consumptions. Analysis of productivity and efficiency of machines. On-time/downtime calculation. Process dashboards. Automatic delay and loss tracking for industrial equipment. Remote monitoring and smartphone apps. Web-based, fully scalable platform. Supports multiple sites information comparison with centralized configuration. 100% integration compatibility with floor plant PLC, SCADA and MES systems.

No. of Employees: 26.

SUPPLIERS OF EQUIPMENT, PRODUCTS and SERVICES

AUTOMATION PRODUCTS INC. – DYNATROL® DIV.
3030 Maxroy St.
Houston, TX 77008 USA
P: +1.800.231.2062 (Toll-Free);
   +1.713.869.0361
F: +1.713.869.7332
sales@dynatrolusa.com
www.dynatrolusa.com

- Contact—Jeff Rommel

PRODUCTS and/or SERVICES: Dynatrol® quality measurement and control equipment for continuous in-line measurement of density, specific gravity, percent solids or percent concentration of quenchants, such as brine, caustic soda solutions, oil, water or oil-water emulsions, as well as lubricants and slurries at most process conditions in steel plants. Level detectors are used for high-, intermediate- or low-level detection of bulk solids in baghouse applications, dust collection systems, and bulk solids storage application in hoppers, silos and bins. Additional Dynatrol products include viscometers, liquid level detectors, sensors, gauges and measuring devices, level control, etc.

B

B&H MACHINE INC.
15001 Lincoln St. SE
P.O. Box 96
Minerva, OH 44657 USA
P: +1.330.868.6425
F: +1.330.868.4699
sales@bhcylinders.com
www.bhcylinders.com

- Pres. of Sales and Engrg.—Brady Koble
- Pres. of Oprs.—Nathan Bush
- Pur. Agt.—Chad Leach
- Chief Engr.—Ron Wilhelm

PRODUCTS and/or SERVICES: Manufacturers of heavy-duty hydraulic and pneumatic cylinders, special design cylinders, Pathon cylinders. Also cylinder repair service.

No. of Employees: 23.

B.E. SPERANZA INC.
201 S. Colfax Ave.
Griffith, IN 46319 USA
P: +1.219.922.4170
F: +1.219.922.4167
besperanza@besperanza.com

- Pres.—Michael B. Speranza

PRODUCTS and/or SERVICES: Saar Metall oxygen lance tips, lance maintenance, copper products and repairs for metallurgical furnaces, Piccardi electrode jointer, torque station, electrode handling tools, Alpine Metal Tech (Magnemag, Numtec, Gega brands) marking, reading, vision systems, caster equipment, Ravarini electrostatic oilers.

B.S.A. S.R.L.
33 Via Tirso
San Giuliano Milanese (MI), 20098 Italy
P: +39.029.8284024
F: +39.029.8289887
bsa@termostahl.it
www.bsarolls.it

- Pres.—Marco Galeotti

PRODUCTS and/or SERVICES: Rolls, backup bearings and other components for levelers.

No. of Employees: 45.

SUPPLIERS of EQUIPMENT, PRODUCTS and SERVICES

BALTIMORE AIRCOIL CO. (BAC)
7600 Dorsey Run Road
Jessup, MD 20794 USA
P: +1.410.799.6200
info@baltimoreaircoil.com
www.baltimoreaircoil.com

- Pres.—Don Fetzer
- Vice Pres. — Business Dev.—Adam Bee
- Vice Pres. — Global Mktg.—Preston Blay
- Vices Pres. — Business Transformation—Tim Buzby
- Vice Pres. — External Affairs—Brad Considine
- Vice Pres. — Global Finance—Katie Feltz
- Vice Pres. and Managing Dir. — EMEIA—David Jacobs
- Vice Pres. and Managing Dir. — Americas—Greg Lowman
- Vice Pres. — Global Products and Technology Innovation—Luke Rubino
- Vice Pres. — Global H.R.—Dasie Thames

EQUIPMENT:
Baltimore Aircoil Co. (BAC) is a supplier of environmentally friendly cooling towers and condensers, providing high-capacity modular evaporative cooling equipment for open- and closed-loop systems.

PRODUCTS and/or SERVICES:
Evaporative cooling towers, closed-loop cooling towers, evaporative condensers and hybrid products. Advanced coil options, including cleanable coils, cleanable headers, split circuits, extended surface coils, ASME "U" stamp coils and low-pressure drop designs. Evaporative cooling for caster mold water, EAFs, BOFs, BFs, annealing furnaces, induction furnaces, hot strip mills, motor cooling, effluent cooling, contact and non-contact water. Factory authorized parts and service.

BAR STOCK SPECIALTIES
11710 Charles Road
Houston, TX 77041 USA
P: +1.713.849.0055
F: +1.713.466.3583
info@gobarstock.com
www.gobarstock.com

- Sales Mgr.—Mike Uriarte
- Pur. Agt.—Doug Karis

EQUIPMENT:
Grinding capabilities up to 3 in.; four cold-drawing machines with a max finished dia. of 1¼ in. and lengths up to 40 ft.; two bar peeling machines from 0.394–2 in.; four straighteners with 2-in. max capacity.

PRODUCTS and/or SERVICES:
Drawing, peeling, grinding, straightening, cutting, toll processing.

No. of Employees: 40.

BAR1 TRANSPORTATION
1016 Shantz Pl.
Crossfield, AB T0M 0S0 Canada
P: +1.403.941.5008;
 +1.403.605.4924 (Mobile)
bar1transportation@outlook.com
www.bar1transportation.com

- Contact—Frank J. Barone

PRODUCTS and/or SERVICES:
Transportation and logistics services.

No. of Employees: 5.

BEARING MANUFACTURING INDIA
206 A, Flying Colors, 2nd Floor Above Croma, P.D.U. Marg, Mulund – West, Mumbai, MH, 400080 India
P: +91.22.25640000
shrenik@bmibearings.com
www.bmibearings.com

- Vice Pres. Mktg.—Shrenik Sheth
- Pur. Agt.—Mr. Soni

PRODUCTS and/or SERVICES:
Roller and ball bearings.

SUPPLIERS OF EQUIPMENT, PRODUCTS and SERVICES

BEARING SERVICE CO.
630 Alpha Dr.
RIDC Industrial Park
Pittsburgh, PA 15238 USA
P: +1.412.963.7710
F: +1.412.963.8005
www.bearing-service.com

- Pres.—William J. Banks
- Mfg. Mgr.—Robert Lutz
- Sales Mgr.—William Moser
- Area Vice Pres.—John Schoessel

PRODUCTS and/or SERVICES:
Distributor and manufacturer of standard and special ball and roller bearings, tension leveler, and Z-mill bearings with engineering and application services. Reclamation and remanufacturing of bearings, all types, including spherical roller and split pedestal for continuous caster applications. Distributor for major manufacturers of work roll bearings; backup roll bearings; and all types of industrial bearings, power transmission and fluid sealing products for the primary metals industry.

No. of Employees: 110.

BEDA OXYGENTECHNIC USA INC.
49910 Calcutta Smith Ferry Road
Calcutta, OH 43920 USA
P: +1.330.382.9811
F: +1.330.382.9812
bedausa@beda.com
www.beda.com

- Pres.—Volker Hornung
- Gen. Mgr.—Don Featherstone
- Project Mgr.—Mark Beckner II

PRODUCTS and/or SERVICES:
Oxygen lancing safety equipment; EAF burner safety devices; argon ladle coupling (automatic and manual); oxygen system inspections.

No. of Employees: 3.

BENETECH INC.
2245 Sequoia Dr., Suite 300
Aurora, IL 60506 USA
P: +1.630.844.1300 (Toll-Free)
F: +1.630.844.0064
info@benetechusa.com
www.benetechglobal.com

- Pres.—Ron Pircon
- Vice Pres. Sales West—John Pircon
- Vice Pres. Sales East—Michael Shahed

PRODUCTS and/or SERVICES:
Dust suppression; conveyor belt systems, components and engineering; engineered transfer systems; wash-down systems; wet dust extraction; dust collection; load zone containment; belt cleaners; modular skirt board systems; belt support; and plant assessments. Brands include MaxZone, MaxZone Plus, Dustinator and J-Glide.

No. of Employees: 500.

BERRY METAL CO.
2408 Evans City Road
Harmony, PA 16037 USA
P: +1.724.452.8040
F: +1.724.452.4115
info@berrymetal.com
www.berrymetal.com

- Chief Exec. Officer and Pres.—George A. Boy
- Chief Oper. Officer—Michael Diana
- Dir. of EAF Technology and Applications—Christopher S. Farmer

PRODUCTS and/or SERVICES:
Provides engineering, technical services and a full line of custom solutions (new equipment, engineered improvements and repair services) for BOF, BF and EAF steelmakers to maximize steelmaking furnace operations. Full-service organization with precision manufacturing capabilities and industry expertise delivering project management, operational assistance, field service and "boots on the ground" technical support. ISO 9001-2015 certified. Featured BF/BOF equipment/engineered solutions: UltraLife® copper

SUPPLIERS of EQUIPMENT, PRODUCTS and SERVICES

and cast-iron stave lining technology; lining wear monitoring systems; BF and hot blast stove valves; taphole drill and mud gun equipment; probes; tuyere stocks; water-cooled oxygen lances; split-flow and double-flow post-combustion lances; deskulling and slag splashing lances; camera lances for BOFs and degassers; solids/oxygen injection lances for BOF, Q-BOP and degassers. EAF optimization solutions include: chemical energy packages, lime injection, copper panels and boxes; oxy-gas burners, oxygen lances; carbon and lime injection burners; water-cooled panels; boxes and housings; Sentinel™ water leak detection; valve controls; and specialty repairs for the EAF market.

BETA LASERMIKE PRODUCTS (An NDC Technologies Brand)
8001 Technology Blvd.
Dayton, OH 45424 USA
P: +1.937.233.9935
F: +1.937.233.7284
info@ndc.com
www.ndc.com/betalasermike

- Pres.—Marti Nyman
- Vice Pres. Sales—Stefano Cicetti
- Mktg. and Communications Mgr.—Jay Luis

EQUIPMENT:
Non-contact length and speed measurement gauges.

PRODUCTS and/or SERVICES:
LaserSpeed® Pro.

BIJUR DELIMON INTERNATIONAL FARVAL/BIJUR/LUBESITE
2685 Airport Road
Kinston, NC 28504 USA
P: +1.800.526.5211 (Toll-Free);
 +1.252.527.6001
F: +1.252.522.2913
sales@bijurdelimon.com

- Sales Mgr.—Jim Hamilton
- Gen. Mgr.—Mark Gerlach
- Lead Application Engr.—Tom Byrd

EQUIPMENT:
Large turning centers, CNC machining centers, CNC lathes, honing and grinding machines, hydraulic testing equipment.

PRODUCTS and/or SERVICES:
Designers and manufacturers of Farval and Delimon heavy-duty centralized lubricating equipment to dispense oil and grease lubricants. Manual and automatic lubricators, air-operated and electric motor-driven. Metered dispensing equipment includes LubeSite single-point lubricators, Dualine blocks, injectors and progressive dividers. System timers/controllers and monitoring devices available.

BIRMINGHAM RAIL & LOCOMOTIVE
5205 5th Ave. N
Birmingham, AL 35020 USA
P: +1.205.424.7245
F: +1.205.424.7436
www.bhamrail.com

- Pres.—Jo Ann Cary
- Vice Pres. Oprs.—Barry Hillgartner
- Vice Pres. Sales—Ryan Jenkins
- Locomotive — Dir. of Oprs.—Jimmy May

EQUIPMENT:
Fabrication equipment: saws, punches, shears, drills, vertical rail forming.

PRODUCTS and/or SERVICES:
Carbon steel rails, light T rail, heavy T rails, crane rails, joint bars, rail clips, crane rail technical services, turnouts and related other track material (OTM) railroad accessories, complete locomotive rebuilds, parts, and on-site preventive maintenance and troubleshooting.

No. of Employees: 76.

SUPPLIERS OF EQUIPMENT, PRODUCTS and SERVICES

BK-SERVICES – Germany, Represented by Hawk Industrial Products
100 Fairway Park Blvd. Unit 312
Ponte Vedra Beach, FL 32082 USA
P: +1.412.576.1699
hipcorp@outlook.com

- Rep. and Owner, Hawk Industrial Products—Chris Hawk

PRODUCTS and/or SERVICES:
Experienced supplier of steel plant technology. Designs, manufactures and commissions turnkey EAFs, LMFs, and foundry furnace projects. Non-stick ladle roof, covers and splash guard for all VTD operations. Scope includes all levels of visualization, current-conducting electrode arms, ladles, scrap buckets and transport cars, burner and lance technology, refractory cooling blocks, burner boxes, as well as complete hydraulic systems and hydro cylinders.

No. of Employees: 100.

BLACKHAWK "COMBUSTIONEERING" LTD.
589 Cannon St. E
Hamilton, ON L8L 2G6 Canada
P: +1.905.547.5757
F: +1.905.549.1848
jim@blackhawkcombustion.com
www.blackhawkcombustion.com

- Gen. Mgr.—Jim Walton
- Mgr. — Instrumentation—Doug Whitelaw
- Sec./Contr.—Margaret Ronald
- Strategic Business Mgr., Steel Industry—David Hartwell
- Sr. Combustion Engr.—George Faulkner

PRODUCTS and/or SERVICES:
Industrial combustion, instrumentation, burners, technical support, specialized steel mill services, oxy-fuel systems, ladle pre-heaters, tundish pre-heaters.

No. of Employees: 15.

BLASCHAK ANTHRACITE
Rte. 54
P.O. Box 12
Mahanoy City, PA 17948 USA
P: +1.570.773.2113
F: +1.570.773.0569
www.blaschakanthracite.com

- Chief Exec. Officer and Pres—Boyd Kreglow
- Chief Financial Officer—Roger Allsop
- Vice Pres Sales, Mktg. and Business Dev.—Andrew Meyers
- Supt. Prodn. and Logistics—Francis Curran
- Chief Engr.—Shawn Frye

EQUIPMENT:
Heavy-media WEMCO system with Dyna Whirlpool separator. Two Marion 7450 draglines; three 185S DEMAGs; CAT 777 trucks.

PRODUCTS and/or SERVICES:
Producing supplier of anthracite used for charge carbon and injection carbon. Anthracite coal mining, preparation and distribution company. Multiple surface mines, multiple prep plants and bagging plant. Producers of high-carbon, low-ash and low-volatile anthracite coal. Product delivered by bulk, pneumatic tanker, rail, barge or ocean vessel. Bagged anthracite also available.

No. of Employees: 150.

BLASTECH MOBILE
12400 Hwy. 43 N
Axis, AL 36505 USA
P: +1.346.224.5161
patti.fretwell@tfwarren.com
www.tfwarren.com

- Pres.—Terry Warren
- Gen. Mgr.—Andy Walter
- Sales—Patti Fretwell

EQUIPMENT:
Automated blast cleaning and coating application.

PRODUCTS and/or SERVICES:
Blast and prime steel plate on an automated line. Services include burning, beveling and rolling.

SUPPLIERS of EQUIPMENT, PRODUCTS and SERVICES

BLOOM ENGINEERING CO. INC.
100 Vista Dr.
Charleroi, PA 15022 USA
P: +1.412.653.3500
F: +1.412.653.2253
info@bloomeng.com
www.bloomeng.com

- Chief Exec. Officer and Pres.—David Boyce
- Vice Pres. Sales and Applications—Frank Beichner
- Vice Pres. Tech. Svcs.—David Schalles
- Vice Pres. Project Mgmt.—Michael Binni
- Vice Pres. Engrg.—Jerry Ennis
- Dir. — Sales and Business Dev. — Steel Industry—Scott Brown
- Dir. Global Key Accts. — Aluminum—Clive Lucas
- Mgr. Process Heating Applications—Bruce Cain
- Spare Parts—Lyndsey Kramer
- Svce.—Kerry Henderson

EQUIPMENT:
Refractory casting/dryout, welding, painting, product assembly, R&D test furnaces.

PRODUCTS and/or SERVICES:
Combustion system design, burners, valves, fuel skids, on-site combustion service, combustion controls, combustion training, CFD modeling.

BM GROUP POLYTEC S.P.A.
Via Roma, 151
38083 Borgo Chiese (TN), Italy
P: +39.0465.621794
F: +39.0465.621202
sales@bmgroup.com
www.polytec.bmgroup.com

- Chief Exec. Officer—Dario Abbà
- Chief Oper. Officer—Massimo Zanotti
- Chief Sales Officer—Andrea Tonini
- Chief Technology Officer—Mirko Bottini
- Events, Corporate Communication and Mkt. Dev.—Anna Zoppirolli

PRODUCTS and/or SERVICES:
Robotic cells for steel industry: meltshop, rolling mills, pipe mills.

POLYTEC USA Corp.
1800 W. Loop S, Suite 1740
Houston, TX 77027 USA

- Chief Exec. Officer—Nicola Bertoni
- Chief Technology Officer—Gianluca Maccani

BMD COMPANY LLC
5368 N. Beacon Dr.
Youngstown, OH 44515 USA
P: +1.330.727.4501
F: +1.330.799.9636
manoj@bmdcompanyllc.com

- Pres.—Manoj K. Sharma

PRODUCTS and/or SERVICES:
Offers technical solutions and resources. Manufacturers supply rolls for hot and cold sheet, bar, wire, and tube mills, plus slitter tooling, custom fabrication and machining, stamping and blanking, castings, and more.

No. of Employees: 1.

BOC WATER HYDRAULICS INC.
12024 Salem-Warren Road
Salem, OH 44460 USA
P: +1.330.332.4444
F: +1.330.332.1650
www.bocwaterhydraulics.com

- Chief Exec. Officer—Donald R. Olson
- Pres.—Todd D. Olson
- Vice Pres. Mktg.—John D. Fisher
- Pur. Agt.—Abbey Aegerter
- Chief Engr.—Jeff DeCort

PRODUCTS and/or SERVICES:
Manufacture high-pressure water hydraulic valves and systems. Descale, directional control and press controls. Flow and pressure unlimited. Remanufacture facility.

No. of Employees: 40.

SUPPLIERS OF EQUIPMENT, PRODUCTS and SERVICES

BOGNAR AND CO. INC.
5th Floor, 731-733 Washington Road
Pittsburgh, PA 15228 USA
P: +1.412.344.9900
F: +1.412.344.9909
admin@ejbognar.com
www.ejbognar.com

- Chief Oper. Officer—C.A. Bognar
- Exec. Vice Pres.—Debra Ray
- Vice Pres. Tech. Sales and Svcs.—E.J. Gross

PRODUCTS and/or SERVICES: Industrial carbons, metallurgical and petroleum-based carbon products, and anthracite coal. Custom processing/crushing, blending, packaging, drying and screening. Bognar and Co. Inc. operates four manufacturing plants in the U.S. together with its associated companies, E.J. Bognar Inc. and Carb-Rite Co., to provide carbon product to most major steel mills in the U.S. and Canada.

BOLDROCCHI SRL
Viale Trento e Trieste 93
Biassono (MI), 20853 Italy
P: +39.039.2202.1
F: +39.039.2754.200
boldrocchi@boldrocchi.eu
www.boldrocchigroup.com

- Pres.—M. Boldrocchi
- Chief Exec. Officer—M. Bailo
- Gen. Mgr.—F. Chiesa
- Intl. Oprs. Exec. Dir.—Giuliamaria Meriggi
- Fan Div. Mgr.—Sergio Di Vincenzo
- Air Pollution Control Div. Mgr.—Luca Maiocchi
- Air Cooler Div. Mgr. Transformers—Roberto Ruffolo
- Air Cooler Div. Mgr. Generators—Stefano Vertemati
- North American Sales Office—Giuliamaria Meriggi, P: +1.678.741.7000, meriggi@boldrocchi.us
- India Sales Office—Nokesh Aggarwal, P: +91.124.426.0391, F: +91.124.426.0396, nokesh@boldrocchi.in
- France Sales Office—Emmanuel Eglaine, P: +33.474190032, F: +33.474190306, emmanuel.eglaine@boldrocchi.fr
- Germany Sales Office—Markus Szirmay, P: + 49.5594.6534859, szirmay@boldrocchi.eu
- Spain Sales Office, Madrid—David Martin, P: +34.810520716, martin@boldrocchi.eu
- Mexico Sales Office, Mexico City—info@boldrocchi.com.mx
- China Sales Office, Shanghai—Jian Lu, P: +86.136.7165.8139, jian.lu@boldrocchi.eu

PRODUCTS and/or SERVICES: International engineering and manufacturing firm. Wide-ranging portfolio of solutions, including fans, blowers and compressors; environmental solutions; heat exchangers and coolers for large transformers and motors; noise protection; heavy-duty dampers and diverters and gas turbine ancillaries air intake; bypass stack; diverter dampers and hot gas silencers. Also offers an array of on-site services, providing turnkey projects.

No. of Employees: 500.

BOLLFILTER CORP.
22635 Venture Dr.
Novi, MI 48375 USA
P: +1.248.773.8200
F: +1.248.773.8201
boll@bollfilter.com
www.bollfilterusa.com

- Pres.—Michele LaTorre

PRODUCTS and/or SERVICES: Automatic self-cleaning filters for hydraulic oils; lube oils; automatic self-cleaning strainers for process water and roll cooling emulsions; manual simplex/duplex basket strainers; spare parts.

SUPPLIERS of EQUIPMENT, PRODUCTS and SERVICES

BOSSTEK
1607 W. Chanute Road
Peoria, IL 61615 USA
P: +1.309.693.8600
F: +1.309.693.8605
info@bosstek.com
www.bosstek.com

- Chief Exec. Officer—Edwin Peterson

PRODUCTS and/or SERVICES:
Dust suppression, odor control, area cooling.

No. of Employees: 12.

BOWEN TECHNICAL PRODUCTS & SERVICES
6000 Blackstone Ct.
Johnston, IA 50131 USA
P: +1.515.278.5966
dbowen0769@mchsi.com

- Pres.—Douglas E. Bowen

EQUIPMENT:
Industrial sewing machines, testing equipment, raw materials.

PRODUCTS and/or SERVICES:
Custom-made high-temperature and molten metal protective curtains, sleeves, jackets, and blankets.

No. of Employees: 12.

BPI INC.
612 S. Trenton Ave.
Pittsburgh, PA 15221 USA
P: +1.412.371.8554
F: +1.412.371.9984
www.bpiminerals.com

- Chief Exec. Officer—Joe Quigley

PRODUCTS and/or SERVICES:
Synthetic slags, calcium aluminates, calcium silicates, magnesium oxide, silicon carbide, silicon, aluminum silicate, aluminum oxide, ferroalloys, dolomite, spent steel mill refractories, refractory fillers. ISO 9001 certified.

No. of Employees: 100.

BRADBURY CO. INC., THE
1200 E. Cole
Moundridge, KS 67107 USA
P: +1.620.345.6394
F: +1.620.345.6381
bradbury@bradburygroup.com
www.bradburygroup.com

- Chief Exec. Officer—David Cox
- Pres.—Ryan Durst
- Industry Sales Leader, Processing Lines—Jim Sugars

PRODUCTS and/or SERVICES:
Manufacturer of coil processing equipment, including advanced hydraulic levelers and CTL lines.

No. of Employees: 340.

BRADLEY LIFTING CORP., an Xtek Co.
1030 Elm St.
York, PA 17403 USA
P: +1.717.848.3121
F: +1.717.843.7102
sales@bradleylifting.com
www.bradleylifting.com

- Gen. Mgr.—Scott R. Salisbury

PRODUCTS and/or SERVICES:
Design and manufacture of mill-duty, below-the-hook lifting equipment. On-staff licensed professional engineers ensure compliance with ASME B30.20 and BTH-1 standards. Services include repair and reconditioning of all brands of lifting equipment. Experienced with manufacturing and repairing motorized coil grabs, laminated ladle hooks, slab and sheet lifters, tongs, rotating crane hooks, roll and chock handling equipment, vacuum lifters, ingot handling equipment, plus much more. Registered: ISO 9001 and ISO 14001.

BRANDENBURG
501 W. Lake St., Suite 204
Elmhurst, IL 60126 USA
P: +1.800.932.2869 (Toll-Free)
email@brandenburg.com
www.brandenburg.com

SUPPLIERS OF EQUIPMENT, PRODUCTS and SERVICES

- Pres.—Tom Little
- Vice Pres.—Jack Jasinowski

PRODUCTS and/or SERVICES:
Demolition, asbestos abatement, dismantling, environmental remediation, scrap processing, utility disconnection and relocation, piling, and excavating services specializing in the steel industry.

No. of Employees: 800.

BRANDT ENGINEERED PRODUCTS
Box 1876, 302 Mill St.
Regina, SK S4P 3E1 Canada
P: +1.306.791.7557
jrizk@brandt.ca
tbest@brandt.ca
aharapiak@brandt.ca
www.brandt.ca

- Territory Mgrs.—Joseph Rizk, Terry Best

EQUIPMENT:
CNC vertical and horizontal boring mills, automated laser cutting, five-axis water jet, plasma table, plate-bending roll/brake, CNC lathes, annealing furnace, powder coat and liquid painting, and other large-scale industrial equipment.

PRODUCTS and/or SERVICES:
Contract manufacturing, including: material handling, beveling, hydrotesting, swaging, threading, coupling screw-on, inspection, destructive testing, weigh-measure-stencil, coating, and packaging/bundling equipment, in addition to large-scale and production machining, engineering and field services, industrial repair, and 24/7 customer service.

No. of Employees: 4,500.

BRAUN MASCHINENFABRIK GMBH
Gmundner Strasse 76
Voecklabruck, A-4840 Austria
P: +43.7672.72463
F: +43.7672.75652
office@braun.at
www.braun-tech.com

- Chief Exec. Officer and Pres.— Lennart M. Braun
- Engrg. Mgr.—Stefan Purrer
- Prodn./Mfg. Mgr.—Manuel Teufl
- Treas.—Renate Kroiss
- Sec.—Andrea Iglseder
- Sales Mgrs.—Norbert Asamer, Alexander Zeischka, Alfred Schmuckermayer
- Sales Engrs.—Michel van Gasselt, Joachim Schendl
- Pur. Mgr.—Thomas Berndl

BRAUN Machine Technologies LLC
6545 Market Ave. N, Suite 100
North Canton, OH 44720 USA
P: +1.330.777.5433
office@braun.at
www.braun-tech.com

- Chief Exec. Officer and Pres.— Lennart M. Braun
- Sr. Area Sales Mgr. U.S. and Canada—Norbert Asamer, n.asamer@braun.at
- Treas.—Renate Kroiss

PRODUCTS and/or SERVICES:
High-performance abrasive saws, combined abrasive/cold circular saws and combined abrasive/friction saws for cutting of all steel grades and shapes; high-pressure surface grinding machines for defect removal and for bright grinding (conditioning of ingots, blooms, billets and slabs); deburring grinding machines; associated material handling, environmental and automation systems. Technical expertise; consulting and planning engineering, manufacturing and site services; preventive maintenance, revamping and upgrading; spare part supply.

No. of Employees: 100.

BRICKING SOLUTIONS
1144 Village Way
Monroe, WA 98272 USA
P: +1.360.794.1277
info@brickingsolutions.com
www.brickingsolutions.com

SUPPLIERS of EQUIPMENT, PRODUCTS and SERVICES

- Managing Dir.—Heather Harding
- Vice Pres. and Global Sales Mgr.—Paul Herrick
- Tech. Sales Mgr.—Jeff Mirisola

EQUIPMENT:
Custom bricking machines and custom refractory maintenance equipment.

PRODUCTS and/or SERVICES:
Bricking machines, torpedo ladle bricking machines, safety cages, custom kiln access ramps, conveyors.

No. of Employees: 13.

BRILEX INDUSTRIES INC.
1201 Crescent St.
Youngstown, OH 44501 USA
P: +1.330.744.1114
F: +1.330.744.1125
sales@brilex.com
www.brilex.com

- Chief Exec. Officer—Doyle Hopper
- Pres.—Steve Davinsizer
- Plant 1 Mgr.—Ryan Engelhardt
- Plant 2 Mgr.—Mike Horne
- Estg. Mgr.—Thomas Benyo
- Brilex Technical Solutions Gen. Mgr.—Josh Vitale
- Engrg. Sales Mgr.—Eric Curry

EQUIPMENT:
Complete heavy steel plate and structural facility equipped with 12 horizontal boring mills (CNC and manual), nine vertical machining centers (planner and gantry), two vertical turning centers including a double ram with live spindle on each and a single ram with live spindle, eight horizontal lathes (CNC and manual), vertical turret lathes (CNC), thermal stress-relieving furnaces, shotblast facilities, paint rooms, welding positioners up to 70,000 lb., turning rolls, sub-arc welding equipment, robotic welder, full machining, fabrication and assembly capabilities. 350,000-sq.-ft. heavy manufacturing facilities, with up to 35 ft. under hook.

PRODUCTS and/or SERVICES:
Complete manufacturing, engineering, detailing, fabrication, machining, rolling and assembly of heavy equipment and machinery for the steel industry. Examples: furnace shells, tundishes, tundish cars, ladles, ladle cars, scrap buckets, coil handling equipment, terminal equipment and almost any other steel or foundry equipment.

No. of Employees: 150.

BROKK INC.
17321 Tye St. SE, Suite B
Monroe, WA 98272 USA
P: +1.360.794.1277
F: +1.360.805.2521
info@brokkinc.com
www.brokk.com

- Chief Exec. Officer—Martin Krupicka
- Pres.—Lars Lindgren
- Vice Pres. Oprs.—Mike Martin

PRODUCTS and/or SERVICES:
Remote-controlled demolition equipment for cleaning ladles, runners, tapholes, cupolas and tearing out refractory.

No. of Employees: 200.

BROWN TRANSPORT INC.
6387 SR 122
P.O. Box 6
West Alexandria, OH 45381 USA
P: +1.800.226.1391 (Toll-Free)
F: +1.937.787.4345
mbrown@browntransportinc.com
www.browntransportinc.net

- Pres.—Mickey Brown

PRODUCTS and/or SERVICES:
Bulk commodity carrier, transporting various dry bulk commodities, including lime and scrap iron throughout the Midwest.

No. of Employees: 33.

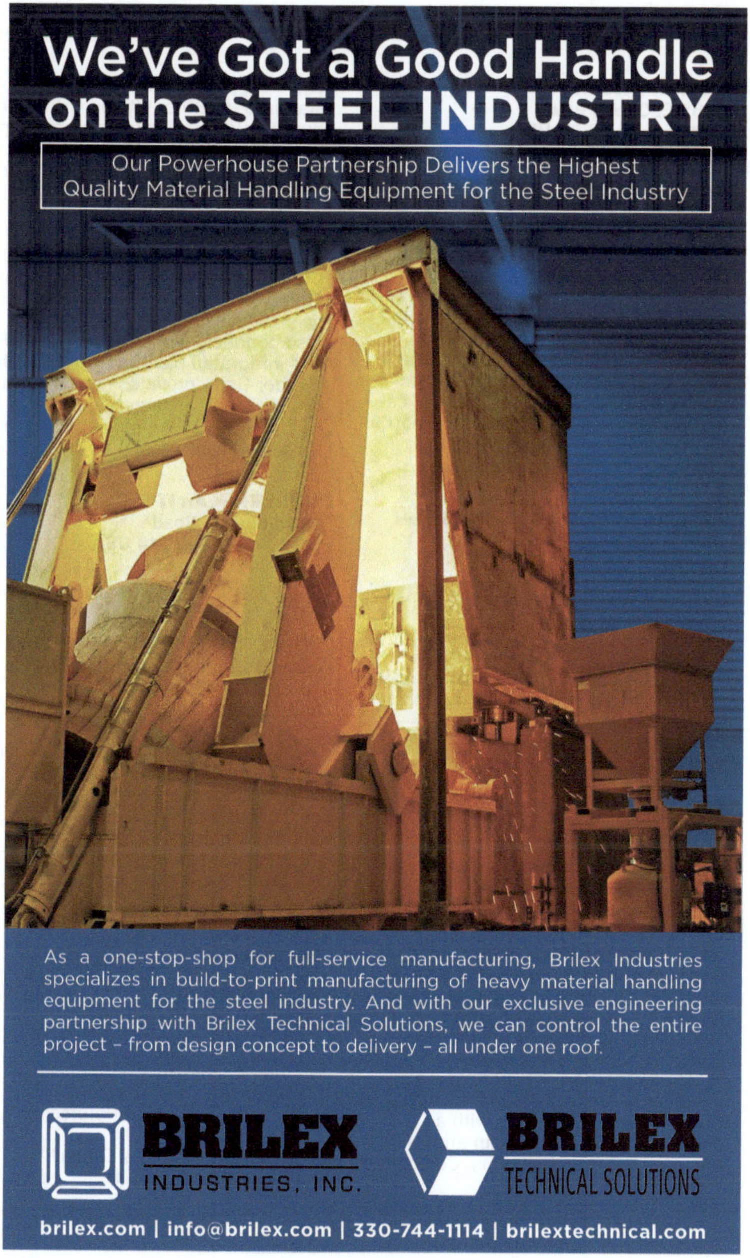

See listing page 312

SUPPLIERS of EQUIPMENT, PRODUCTS and SERVICES

BRUKER AXS INC.
5465 E. Cheryl Pkwy.
Madison, WI 53711 USA
P: +1.800.234.9729 (Toll-Free)
F: +1.608.276.3006
info.baxs@bruker.com
www.bruker.com/axs

PRODUCTS and/or SERVICES: Laboratory and mobile OES spark spectrometers, CS/ONH gas analyzers, metal cleanliness inspection, inclusion analysis, laboratory and handheld XRF spectrometers, PMI, XRDs, phase analysis, process automation systems, 24/7/365 customer service, technical and professional applications support, and customer training courses.

BSE AMERICA, Subsidiary of Badische Stahl Engineering GmbH
1811 Sardis Road N, Suite 210
Charlotte, NC 28270 USA
P: +1.704.553.1582
F: +1.704.553.2317
patrick.hansert@bse-kehl.de
www.bse-kehl.de/en

- Chief Exec. Officer—Markus Menges
- Vice Pres. Americas—Patrick Hansert
- Vice Pres. Sales North America—Henning Karbstein
- Treas.—Marc Sester
- Office Mgr.—Martha Mace

PRODUCTS and/or SERVICES: Badische offers hardware solutions, consulting services and training with a focus on safety at the EAF and LF, such as the EBT taphole manipulator (THM) for clearing, cleaning and taphole channel installation. MultiROB for temperature/sample-taking with automatic cartridge change available for the EAF as well as LF. EAF inspection via the door or sidewall panel. Various lance manipulators for O_2 and carbon injection, as well as temperature/sample manipulators. Current-conducting arms with a detachable head: aluminum arms and patented copper-steel arms. Complete chemical energy packages with a standard (fixed) or tiltable virtual lance burners (VLBs). Customized revamps for EAFs and LFs; finite network method (FNM) for an optimized current density analysis. Smart leakage detection (SLD) of leaks above 6 gpm, total mast control (TMC) for maintenance-free mast positioning. Consulting and training services for meltshops and rolling mills with focus on productivity and cost reduction. Also conducts logistics studies for EAF and integrated plants. Together with Bender Corp. provides environmental concepts and engineering services for all type of mills. Webinars and online trainings available.

BUEHLER — An ITW Co.
41 Waukegan Road
Lake Bluff, IL 60044 USA
P: +1.847.295.6500
info@buehler.com
www.buehler.com

PRODUCTS and/or SERVICES: Manufacturer and innovator of Wilson hardness testers, DiaMet software and a complete line of metallographic equipment and consumables. Metallographic equipment: sectioning, mounting press, grinders/polishers, microscopes, hardness testers and consumables. Services include process improvement, laboratory assistance, education, training, preventive maintenance and service worldwide.

BUELTMANN GMBH
Hoennestr. 31
Neuenrade, 58809 Germany
P: +49.2394.18.0
info@bueltmann.com
www.bueltmann.com

- Chief Exec. Officer—Andreas Bueltmann
- Svce. Mgr.—Ansgar Peterschulte, P: +49.2394.18.113
- Sales Dir.—Andreas Zimball, P: +49.2394.18.253

SUPPLIERS OF EQUIPMENT, PRODUCTS and SERVICES

Bueltmann US LP
4175 Warren Sharon Road
Vienna, OH 44473 USA
P: +1.330.437.4446
gb@bueltmann.com
www.bueltmann.com

- Sales Mgr. U.S. and Canada—George Burnet, P: +1.330.437.4446; +1.724.900.3861 (Mobile)

PRODUCTS and/or SERVICES: Machinery and complete processing solutions for makers of ferrous and non-ferrous long products and tubular products, including: peeling (turning) machines, straightening machines, stretching and detwisting machines, drawing machines (drawbenches, spinner blocks, bull blocks, roll drawing), separating systems, pointing machines, swaging machines, internal gripper systems for tube drawing without pointing, cutting machines, chamfering lines, handling systems, finishing lines, production lines, bundling and packaging lines, extrusion press billet heaters, non-contact dimension and surface assessment systems, continuous annealing lines, technology consulting, and investment project consulting.

No. of Employees: 150.

BUFFALO TRANSFORMER SERVICES
10 Simonds St.
Lockport, NY 14094 USA
P: +1.716.698.4635
chadcurtis@buffalotransformerservices.com
www.buffalotransformerservices.com

- Pres. and Engr.—Chad W. Curtis

PRODUCTS and/or SERVICES: Expert transformer service provider for furnace, rectifier, power and all other specialty types of transformers. Providing in-shop repair, rewind, and reconditioning, including on-site electrical testing, load tap changer inspection and overhaul, internal and external inspections, regasketing, LV buss repair and resealing, oil processing, and control panel upgrades.

No. of Employees: 10.

BULK EQUIPMENT CORP.
720 W. US Hwy. 20
Michigan City, IN 46360 USA
P: +1.844.688.BULK (2855)
info@bulkequip.com
www.bulkequip.com

PRODUCTS and/or SERVICES: Wheel loaders, fork trucks, reach stackers, magnets, articulated dump trucks, rigid frame haul trucks, excavators, dozers, graders, scrapers, skid steers, carry deck and rough terrain cranes, scissor and boom lifts, on- and off-road semi tractors, trailers, custom-built steel hauling equipment, transporters, pickup trucks, vans, flatbeds, tow tractors, and other equipment needs.

BURNS INDUSTRIAL EQUIPMENT INC.
210 Thorn Hill Road
Warrendale, PA 15086 USA
P: +1.412.856.9253
F: +1.412.372.2941
www.burnslift.com

- Pres.—Christopher J. Burns
- Vice Pres.—Michael Burns

PRODUCTS and/or SERVICES: Yale lift trucks, Hyster heavy-capacity pneumatic and solid-tired forklifts and ram tractors, Combilift four-directional forklifts, mobile robots and Taylor Dunn personnel carriers. Sales, service, parts and rentals.

BUSCH VACUUM SOLUTIONS
516 Viking Dr.
Virginia Beach, VA 23452 USA
P: +1.757.463.7800
F: +1.757.453.7407
info@buschusa.com
www.buschvacuum.com

SUPPLIERS of EQUIPMENT, PRODUCTS and SERVICES

PRODUCTS and/or SERVICES:
Oil-lubricated rotary vane vacuum pumps, dry claw vacuum pumps and compressors, dry-screw vacuum pumps, vacuum boosters, dry running rotary vane vacuum pumps, rotary lobe blowers, liquid ring vacuum pumps, side channel blowers, scroll vacuum pumps, and customized systems including 3 and 4 stage dry-running mechanical vacuum pumping systems for steel degassing. Eight service centers and a fleet of field service technicians nationwide.

No. of Employees: 500+.

BUSHMAN EQUIPMENT INC.
W133N4960 Campbell Dr.
Menomonee Falls, WI 53051 USA
P: +1.800.338.7810 (Toll-Free);
 +1.262.790.4200
F: +1.262.790.4202
custinfo@bushman.com
www.bushman.com

– Gen. Mgr.—Pete Kerrick

PRODUCTS and/or SERVICES:
Designs and manufactures custom-engineered material handling equipment for use in a variety of high-capacity/high-duty-cycle industrial and mill applications. The company is a single-source supplier for below-the-hook and floor-based material handling solutions.

BUTECH BLISS
550 S. Ellsworth Ave.
Salem, OH 44460 USA
P: +1.330.337.0000
F: +1.330.337.0800
sales@butech.com
www.butechbliss.com

– Pres.—John R. Buta
– Exec. Vice Pres.—Jock Buta
– Engrg. Mgr.—Matt Huston
– Vice Pres. Sales and Mktg.—
 Zeb Edgerly
– Mgr. of Roll. Mill Sales—Randy Smrek

PRODUCTS and/or SERVICES:
Design and build metal processing equipment to individual customers' specifications. Products include 2- and 4-high reversing cold mills, temper mills and skinpass mills for ferrous and non-ferrous metals. Downcoilers, roll changers, new HGC cylinders, and HGC cylinder rebuild and repair services. The 400,000-plus-sq.-ft. technology center offers mechanical and electrical engineering, full-service subcontract manufacturing, both large and small machining, including 5-axis machining capability, welding, large-capacity in-house stress relieving and shotblasting, and complete assembly. Facility for the manufacture or rebuild of large rolling mill equipment featuring 200-ton crane capacity, large machining centers and railcar access. Edge trim scrap choppers, hydraulic roller levelers, plate levelers, edge trimmers, crop shears, flying shears, heavy-gauge CTL lines, push-pull pickle line equipment and heavy-gauge slitting lines, extrusion equipment; forging presses; repair and reconditioning for crucibles; and molds and hearths for ESR, VAR, electron beam melting (EBM), or plasma arc melting (PAM) applications.

No. of Employees: 290.

SUPPLIERS OF EQUIPMENT, PRODUCTS and SERVICES

C

C&E PLASTICS INC.
2500 State Rte. 168
Georgetown, PA 15043 USA
P: +1.724.947.4949
F: +1.724.947.5150
scott.barwell@ceplastics.com
www.ceplastics.com

- Pres.—Clifford D. Crighton
- Strip Product Mgr.—Tony Furka
- Plant Mgr.—Ron Castelli

EQUIPMENT:
Thermoplastic fabricating equipment for cutting, fusion butt welding, extrusion welding, hand welding, machining, forming and hot testing plastic products; 30,000-sq.-ft. manufacturing space under cranes; 24/7 field service.

PRODUCTS and/or SERVICES:
Design, engineer, fabricate, install, commission, and service custom plastic process equipment for pickling, cleaning, plating, anodizing and other surface treatments; continuous and push-pull tanks, covers, piping, fume abatement, containment.

No. of Employees: 30+.

CALDERYS, a Member of Imerys
43 Quai de Grenelle
75015 Paris, France
P: +33.1.49.55.63.00
info@calderys.com
www.calderys.com

- Sr. Vice Pres.—Michel Cornelissen

PRODUCTS and/or SERVICES:
Global provider of refractory products, engineering solutions, and installation services for ironmaking, steelmaking, foundry, aluminum, cement and lime, oil and chemical, and boilers and incinerators. Calderys, a fully owned subsidiary of Imerys, has a global network of 19 plants in 16 countries with a combined production capacity of 600,000 metric tons.

No. of Employees: 2,300+.

Calderys USA Inc.
917 Francis St. W
Jacksonville, AL 36265 USA
P: +1.256.435.9342
usa@calderys.com

- Dir. of Sales Americas, Iron and Steel—Daniel Silva

CALDWELL GROUP INC., THE
4080 Logistics Pkwy.
Rockford, IL 61109 USA
P: +1.800.628.4263 (Toll-Free);
   +1.815.229.5667
F: +1.815.229.5686
www.caldwellinc.com

- Chief Exec. Officer and Pres.—Doug Stitt

PRODUCTS and/or SERVICES:
Designers and manufacturers of a complete line of below-the-hook lifting equipment. Coil handling equipment includes telescopic grabs, C-hooks, rim grabs, ID lifters and upenders. Sheet handling equipment includes telescopic grabs, vacuum lifters and magnet beams. Other products include ingot grabs and slab tongs, rotating crane blocks, Posi-Turner® load rotation systems, pallet lifters, custom-designed tongs, a wide range of lifting and spreader beams, and a complete jib and gantry crane line. All products conform to ASME B30.20 and BTH-1.

No. of Employees: 135.

CAMCORP INC.
9732 Pflumm Road
Lenexa, KS 66215 USA
P: +1.877.226.2677
info@camcorpinc.com
www.camcorpinc.com

SUPPLIERS of EQUIPMENT, PRODUCTS and SERVICES

- Pres.—John Rothermel
- Chief Oper. Officer—Dan Bruyn
- Vice Pres. Sales—Jim Weber

EQUIPMENT:
Pulse-jet dust collectors, cartridge dust collectors, CAM-AIRO vertical cartridge dust collectors, reverse-air baghouses, cyclones, bin vents, pneumatic conveying, bulk bag unloaders, bag dump stations, rotary air locks, scale hoppers, silos and surge hoppers.

PRODUCTS and/or SERVICES:
Equipment designed to application, in-house manufacturing, aftermarket parts and components.

No. of Employees: 75.

CARB-RITE CO.—see BOGNAR AND CO. INC.

CARBIDE INDUSTRIES LLC
4400 Bells Lane
Louisville, KY 40211 USA
P: +1.502.775.4100
F: +1.502.775.4200
sales@carbidellc.com
www.carbidellc.com

- Pres.—Ara Hacet
- Exec. Vice Pres.—Brent McWhorter
- Sales Mgrs.—Kathy Darby, David King
- Tech. Mgrs.—Stewart Robinson, Greg Brasel

EQUIPMENT:
Submerged-arc electric furnace.

PRODUCTS and/or SERVICES:
Calcium carbide, slag conditioning, EAF injection, desulfurization reagents, acetylene, Steelmaking 101 classes, calcium carbide safety sessions.

No. of Employees: 150.

CARBINITE METAL COATINGS
463 Brownsdale Road
Renfrew, PA 16053 USA
P: +1.724.586.5659
F: +1.724.586.1144
sue@carbinite.com
www.carbinite.com

- Chief Exec. Officer—M. Sue Freyvogel
- Chief Tech. Officer—Drew Meier
- Sales—John Hamblin

PRODUCTS and/or SERVICES:
Provides grip solutions for the unique challenges in the steel industry. Carbinite's textured tungsten-carbide coating increases the coefficient of friction in applications where improvements in grip would benefit production, including coiling and expanding mandrels, bridle and drive rolls, gripper wedges, and payoff reels. A textured coating allows for better control of strip tension, eliminating slip and telescoping. Pulling tension earlier on mandrels and reels reduces processing time and improves mill output. Carbinite also provides non-slip safety coatings for metal flooring, metal stair edges and forklift forks. Carbinite is metallurgically bonded to the base metal and is guaranteed to not crack, chip or peel. Coating can be reapplied without additional buildup. On-site service is available to minimize downtime.

No. of Employees: 13.

CARL ZEISS MICROSCOPY LLC
One N. Broadway
White Plains, NY 10601 USA
P: +1.800.233.2343 (Toll-Free Customer Service);
+1.914.681.7627
www.zeiss.com/metals

PRODUCTS and/or SERVICES:
Manufacturer of multi-modal microscope systems. For the metals industry, Zeiss offers a vast array of multi-modal microscopy solutions focused on five key areas: chemistry, crystallography, dimensional measurement, tomography, and determining processing parameters. Through its portfolio of light, X-ray and electron microscopes, Zeiss helps customers in the metals industry solve both routine characterization and advanced R&D problems through integrated and connected solutions such as digital imaging, spectroscopy,

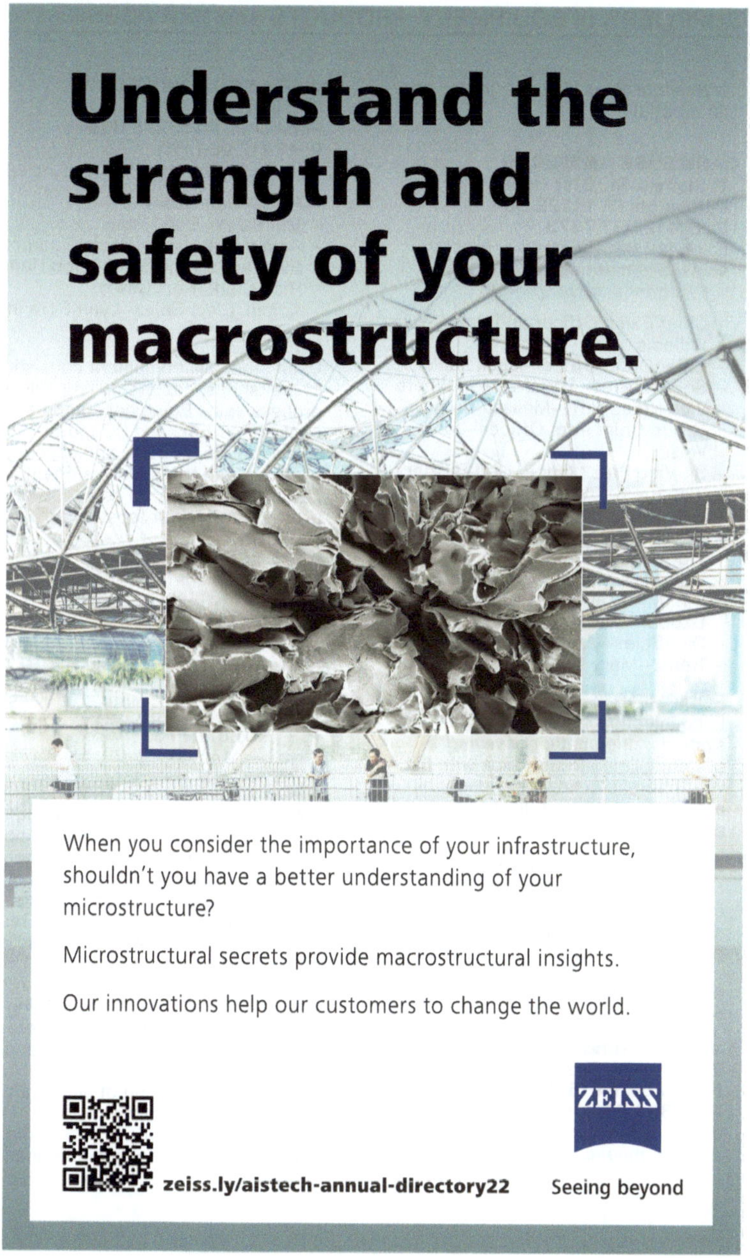

SUPPLIERS of EQUIPMENT, PRODUCTS and SERVICES

crystallography, 3D tomography and data handling.

CARMEUSE AMERICAS
11 Stanwix St., 21st Floor
Pittsburgh, PA 15222 USA
P: +1.412.527.7873
F: +1.412.995.5570
salesinfo@carmeuse.com
www.carmeuse.com/na-en

- Chief Exec. Officer and Pres.—Yves Willems
- Chief Oper. Officer—Jack Fahler
- Sr. Vice Pres., Legal—Kevin Whyte
- Vice Pres., H.R.—Melissa Croll
- Group Chief Info. Officer—Jose Voisin
- Sr. Vice Pres., Oprs.—Jeff Bittner
- Vice Pres., Finance—Jonathan Bright
- Vice Pres., Engrg.—Alain Baert
- Vice Pres., Sales and Mktg.—Phil Piggott
- Vice Pres., Supply Chain—Eric Segal
- Dir., Mktg. and Innovation—Eric Dzuba
- Dir., Sales—Andrew Fluder
- Treas.—Mary Colin

EQUIPMENT:
Lime injection systems; lime slaking systems; pneumatic conveying systems; lime storage silos with bin vent filters; silo flow promotion: bin actuators, aeration buttons, air pads and/or compactors.

PRODUCTS and/or SERVICES:
Lime handling solutions and optimization; lime storage; lime slaking solutions and optimization; lime products; and limestone products.

No. of Employees: 2,000 in North America/4,000 globally.

Carmeuse Innovation Center
3600 Neville Road
Pittsburgh, PA 15225 USA
P: +1.866.780.0974
innovation@carmeuse.com
www.carmeuse.com/na-en/innovation

CASEY EQUIPMENT CORP.
275 Kappa Dr.
Pittsburgh, PA 15238 USA
P: +1.412.963.1111
www.caseyusa.com

- Pres.—Don Casey
- Mill Sales—Bob Huber
- Admin. Mill Sales—Paula Guenther
- Elec. and Crane Sales—Bob Hamilton, Rich Clark, Kurt Casey
- Admin. Elec. Sales—Lynn Soranno

EQUIPMENT:
Used steel mill equipment consisting of meltshops, casters, rolling mills and process lines. Electrical equipment consisting of AC and DC motors, crane motors, control, brakes, circuit breakers and transformers. Plant: 700,000 sq. ft. on 58 acres, 38 cranes up to 60 tons, four repair shops and inventory storage.

PRODUCTS and/or SERVICES:
Selling used steel mill equipment both domestically and internationally.

CASTER MAINTENANCE CO.
215 Mississippi St.
Gary, IN 46402 USA
P: +1.901.871.7737
www.castermaint.com

PRODUCTS and/or SERVICES:
Caster segment repairs; incoming testing and inspections; disassembly and metal overspill removal; inspection of frames, rolls, bearings and all other components; bearing, housing and rotary joint reclamation; off-line testing of cooling jackets, sprays, hydraulic systems and lubrication systems; roll reconditioning (includes overlaying to customer specifications); piping rehabilitations (including complete replacement fabrication); reassembly and alignment to specifications; complete final testing of all systems and functions; engineering and technical support; data interfacing with predictive/preventive maintenance programs.

SUPPLIERS of EQUIPMENT, PRODUCTS and SERVICES

CASTING CONSULTANTS INC.
526 Meadow Dr.
Utica, NY 13502 USA
P: +1.585.766.3536 (Mobile)
casting@omeansea.net

- Pres.—Edward S. Szekeres

PRODUCTS and/or SERVICES: Educational and training programs for continuous casting technology. Metallurgical and engineering consulting on design, specification and operation of strand casting facilities. Analysis of as-cast quality, strand breakouts and solidification-related problems.

CATTRON NORTH AMERICA INC.
655 N. River Road NW, Suite A
Warren, OH 44483 USA
P: +1.234.806.0018
sales.us@cattron.com
www.cattron.com

PRODUCTS and/or SERVICES: Hardware-to-machine controls via wireless connectivity that protect people and resources, maximize productivity and accelerate ROI. Remote-control solutions include both standard configurations and engineered-to-order systems tailored to meet customer-specific applications across a variety of markets such as industrial, transportation, safety systems, underground mining and more.

CBMM NORTH AMERICA INC.
1000 Omega Dr., Suite 1110
Pittsburgh, PA 15205 USA
P: +1.412.221.7008
northamerica@cbmm.com
www.cbmm.com

- Gen. Mgr.—Jim Boyle
- Commercial Mgr. Special Products—Rodolfo Morgado
- Sales Mgr.—Chris Hoffman
- Tech. Mkt. Dev. Mgr. — Auto—C. Matt Enloe
- Tech. Mkt. Dev. Mgr. — Pipeline—Aaron Litschewski
- Logistics Mgr.—Tracey Miller

PRODUCTS and/or SERVICES: Ferroniobium/ferrocolumbium—standard grade; ferroniobium—vacuum grade; nickel niobium—vacuum grade; niobium metal—reactor grade, commercial grade; niobium oxide—high purity, optical grade; niobium compounds (by special request in batch form).

CENTRO-METALCUT
7550 Quantum Ct.
Caledonia, IL 61011 USA
P: +1.815.885.1300
F: +1.815.885.1370
cmsales@quantumdi.com
www.centrometalcut.com

- Chief Exec. Officer and Pres.—Danny Pearse
- Exec. Vice Pres.—David J. Culvey
- Sales Mgr.—Derek Wheeler
- Adv. Mgr.—Angie Ostler

PRODUCTS and/or SERVICES: Abrasive saws, gantry abrasive saws, pivot abrasive saws, wet cutting abrasive saws, abrasive lab saws, conditioning stationary grinders, conditioning track grinders, overhead grinding machines, handling equipment, system automation, spare parts and more.

No. of Employees: 105.

CERCO INC.
27301 Fort St.
Trenton, MI 48183 USA
P: +1.734.675.6090;
 +1.734.558.5286 (Mobile)
F: +1.734.675.7861

- Pres.—Carl E. Rigg
- Vice Pres. and Chief Engr.—Randal Rigg
- Sec. and Treas.—Barbara Rigg

PRODUCTS and/or SERVICES: Manufacturer of quality refractory shapes and in-plant refractory installation services.

No. of Employees: 14.

Caster Maintenance Co.
ISO 9001: 2008 Certified

GARY, IN • BIRMINGHAM, AL • GRANITE CITY, IL

American Craftsmanship

No Matter What You Call Them, We Can Help.

WHETHER YOUR MILL CALLS THEM SPRAY BARS, HEADERS, BARS, ZONES OR ANYTHING ELSE we understand what you're talking about.

For new and reconditioned sprays, skilled modifications and supply of hard to procure items like machined components and spray nozzle weld adapters, Caster Maintenance Co has the know-how to help your Strip, Funnel, CSP, Slab, Bloom or Billet Caster perform at its best.

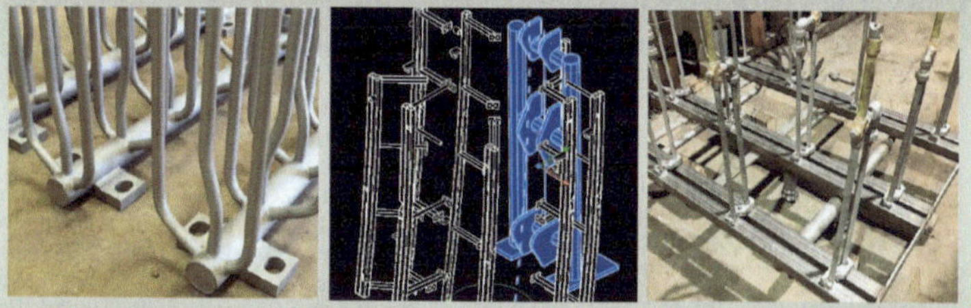

CALL US! *at* (901) 871-7737 *to get started on your next solution*
MESSAGE US! *www.facebook.com/CasterMaintCo*
TWEET US! *www.twitter.com/CasterMaintCo*

Quality. Price. Delivery.

SUPER BOOTH

See listing page 320

SUPPLIERS of EQUIPMENT, PRODUCTS and SERVICES

CERVIS INC.
170 Thorn Hill Road
Warrendale, PA 15086 USA
P: +1.724.741.9000
F: +1.724.741.9001
sales@cervis.net
www.cervisinc.com

- Pres. and Dir. Sales, Mktg. and Svce.—Kevin Hadley
- Vice Pres. Sales—Randy Butter
- Exec. Sales Mgrs.—Keith Stauffer, Rafael Lozada
- Mgr., Canada—Robert Grimshaw

PRODUCTS and/or SERVICES: Industrial wireless remote controls, overhead crane controls, HMI interface design and electronic machine controls.

CG THERMAL LLC
8950 Dutton Dr.
Twinsburg, OH 44087 USA
P: +1.330.405.0844, ext. 309
www.cgthermal.com

- Pres.—Richard Chandler
- Sr. Vice Pres.—Greg Becherer
- Vice Pres., Sales and Mktg.—Joan Bova

PRODUCTS and/or SERVICES: Pickling tank heat exchangers for steel, stainless steel and nickel alloy operations. Fluoropolymer lined pipe and vessels.

CHIZ BROS. INC.
2117 Lincoln Blvd.
Elizabeth, PA 15037 USA
P: +1.412.384.5220
F: +1.412.384.2358
mrhoa@chizbros.com
www.chizbros.com

- Pres.—Mark A. Rhoa

PRODUCTS and/or SERVICES: Suppliers of all types of refractory materials, castables and IFB. Unifrax distributor for ceramic fiber blankets, papers, textiles and modules. Also carries non-refractory-ceramic-fiber (RCF) bio-soluble fiber products. Inventory contains a complete line of both Fiberfrax ceramic fiber and refractory products. Custom gasket die cutting, vacuum-cast ceramic fiber products, burner blocks, refractory pre-cast shapes and engineered fabricated assemblies.

No. of Employees: 15.

CID ASSOCIATES INC.
730 Ekastown Road, Rte. 228
Sarver, PA 16055 USA
P: +1.724.353.0300
F: +1.724.353.0308
sales@cidbuildings.com
www.cidbuildings.com

- Pres.—Scott S. Docherty
- Vice Pres.—Casey S. Docherty
- Vice Pres. Engrg.—Gary Murray
- Chief Financial Officer—Jackie Bott
- Sec.—Erica Leonberg
- Oprs. Mgr.—Matt Hensel
- Regional Sales Mgrs.—Ray Simon, Jason Goehring, Brendan Docherty

PRODUCTS and/or SERVICES: Liftable buildings mainly for the steel industry, control pulpits, computer centers, crane cabs, electrical enclosures, motor control centers, guard shelters, scale houses and gas analyzer buildings. Manufacturer of electrical and pneumatic control systems, panels, consoles, desks and motor control centers. CID's control panel shop is cUL 508A listed. Pre-engineered buildings and high-tech construction such as computer centers, clean rooms, in-plant offices; turnkey interior-retrofit packages.

No. of Employees: 70.

CIM-TECH INC.
1951 Morthland Dr.
Valparaiso, IN 46385 USA
P: +1.219.476.0302
rudy.tolkamp@cim-techsvc.com
www.cim-techsvc.com

- Pres.—Rudy Tolkamp
- Treas.—Brian Greubel

PRODUCTS and/or SERVICES: Provides full-service engineering, as well as supply of thermocouples,

CiD STEEL BUILDINGS inc.

POWER DISTRIBUTION CENTERS

Complete Customizing to Meet All Your Needs

CID DOES EVERYTHING

- Engineering & Design
- Building
- Engineer Stamped Drawings
- State Approval
- Equipment Installation
- Electrical Ratings
- 1 & 2 Hour Fire Ratings
- Blast Resistant
- Interconnection of Equipment
- UL Listed Control Panels
- Grounding of Equipment
- Custom Logo and Paint Job
- Fire Suppression
- Control Consoles
- MCC, PLC
- Testing Before Shipment
- Freight

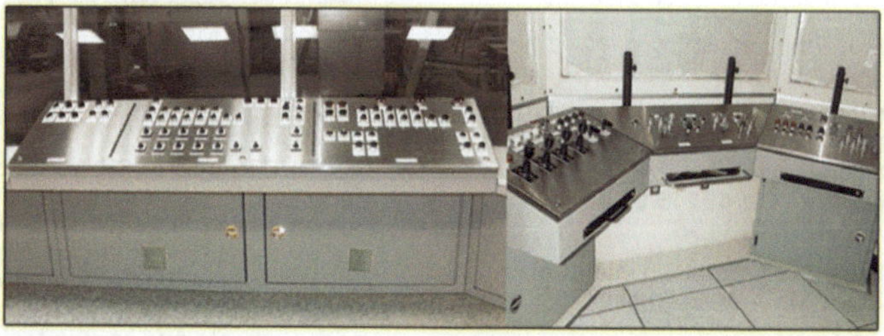

CiD LIFTABLE

PPS Third Party Inspectors

State Registered

c UL

Steel

CiD STEEL BUILDINGS, inc
Phone: (724) 353-0300 • Fax: (724) 353-0308
730 Ekastown Rd., Rt.228 • Sarver, PA 16055
sales@cidbuildings.com • www.cidbuildings.com

See listing page 324

SUPPLIERS of EQUIPMENT, PRODUCTS and SERVICES

control cabinets, custom equipment, graphite and pre-cast shapes. Complete program management from start to finish, including scope, evaluation, budgeting, engineering and project management. Expertise in design, engineering, and supply of equipment for BFs, stoves and casthouses. Specialties include EAFs, caster alignments, steelmaking upgrades, BF relines, taphole replacement, hearth repair, natural gas injection, cooling system design and optimization, refractory, mechanical, piping, instrumentation, and controls. Additional services include construction engineering, solid modeling, FEA, thermal modeling, CFD, AutoCAD, 3D plant layout, raster editing and automated raster-to-vector conversion. Design and supply of custom equipment, prototype development, on-site consultation, inspection, troubleshooting and investigation. Custom training for BF personnel in stove operation, control room operation and casthouse practice. Capabilities include process engineering, fluid flow (compressible and non-compressible), machine design, hydraulics, heat transfer, high-temperature design, process design, electrical design and instrumentation, arc flash studies, casting design, refractory design, process modeling and animation/motion analysis.

No. of Employees: 34.

CINCINNATI GASKET & INDUSTRIAL GLASS
40 Illinois Ave.
Cincinnati, OH 45215 USA
P: +1.513.761.3458

- Pres.—Lawrence J. Uhlenbrock
- Sales Mgr.—Matt Uecker

EQUIPMENT:
Metal fabrication, welding (including light-gauge TIG), glass cutting and polishing, die cutting, stamping, water jet, light machining, and assembly.

PRODUCTS and/or SERVICES:
Gaskets for gearboxes, piping, strainers, gas lines, roll chock gaskets, etc., from a wide variety of materials for any application. Industrial glass: heat shield windows, windows for crane cabs, pulpits and mobile/slag handling equipment, and furnace viewports using combinations of heat-resistant glass (borosilicate, quartz, etc.), heat-reflecting glass, and/or impact-resistant laminated glass to protect operators from heat, splatter, impact and explosions. Quick-change industrial-style windows for any application.

CINCINNATI THERMAL SPRAY—see CTS INC.

CIVIL & ENVIRONMENTAL CONSULTANTS INC.
700 Cherrington Pkwy.
Moon Twp., PA 15108 USA
P: +1.800.365.2324 (Toll-Free)
F: +1.412.429.2114
hdravecky@cecinc.com
www.cecinc.com

- Chief Exec. Officer and Pres.—Ken Miller
- Chief Oper. Officer—Daniel Szwed
- Chief Financial Officer—Rick Richardson
- Chief Tech. Officer—Paul Tomiczek III
- Chief Strategic Officer—Mary Guinee
- Corporate Mfg. Lead—Harry Dravecky
- Pittsburgh Mfg. Lead—David Larson
- Sr. Mktg. Mgr.—Emily Chiodo

PRODUCTS and/or SERVICES:
Complete scope of services ranging from selecting or acquiring a new site for development, to maintaining compliance in today's heavily regulated environment. Air quality services: measurements and source testing; permitting; compliance; emission inventory development/dispersion modeling. Environmental services: mergers and acquisitions support; RCRA/CERCLA; soil/groundwater investigation and remediation; waste

SUPPLIERS OF EQUIPMENT, PRODUCTS and SERVICES

characterization; management and reporting; facility decommissioning; demolition planning; permitting. Civil engineering services: site infrastructure and utility design; geotechnical engineering; transportation engineering. Manufacturing infrastructure services: pre-project planning (PPP); detailed design; construction support. Water-related services: treatability testing; industrial process water design; industrial wastewater treatment and reuse. Compliance services: auditing and environmental compliance plans; industrial hygiene assessments and programs; EH&S compliance and management systems; process safety and risk management programs. GIS and data management services: spatial and image analyses; geoprocessing; cartography and visualization; custom application development; web GIS and internet mapping; field and survey data integration; mobile- and tablet-based data collection tools. Survey/geospatial services: land surveying; bathymetric/hydrographic surveys; unmanned aerial systems (UAS); 3D LiDAR scanning and imagery.

No. of Employees: 1,100.

CLARKE ROLLER AND RUBBER LTD.
485 Southgate Dr.
Guelph, ON N1G 3W6 Canada
P: +1.519.763.7655
F: +1.519.763.7699
general@clarkeroller.com
www.clarkeroller.com

- Pres.—Rob Wolstenholme
- Tech. Sales Mgr.—Jeff Garrard

EQUIPMENT:
90,000-sq.-ft. rubber and polyurethane plant; 54,000-sq.-ft. polyurethane div.; 20,000-sq.-ft. polymer compounding div.; 23,000-sq.-ft. facility in Montreal, QC, Canada.

PRODUCTS and/or SERVICES:
Rubber and polyurethane roller coverings. Complete roll fabrications, repairs and balancing. CNC grinding and grooving. Custom compounding available for all types of steel mill applications.

No. of Employees: 75.

CLAUDIUS PETERS PROJECTS GMBH
Schanzenstrasse 40
Buxtehude, 21614 Germany
P: +49.4161.706.0
F: +49.4161.706.270
projects@claudiuspeters.com
www.claudiuspeters.com

- Managing Dir.—Frank Christian Siefert
- Managing Dir. Global Sales—Kurt Herrmann
- Treas.—Manfred Fitschen

EQUIPMENT:
Engineering office and workshop for production of core equipment for bulk handling.

PRODUCTS and/or SERVICES:
Engineering and manufacturing of coal grinding, drying and injection systems for BFs, high-pressure injection systems for other metallurgical applications, pneumatic transport systems.

No. of Employees: 400.

CLAYTON ENGINEERING CO.
685 Millers Run Road
Bridgeville, PA 15017 USA
sales@clayeng.net
www.claytonengineering.com
www.shop.claytonengineering.com

- Pres.—Mark G. Murman
- Vice Pres.—Jordan Murman
- Vice Pres. Sales—Don Bohn

PRODUCTS and/or SERVICES:
AC/DC motors and drives; tachometers; hot metal detectors; laser, proximity and photoelectric sensors; PLCs, HMI, SCADA and industrial computers; communications and networking; panel meters and instruments; mechanical power transmission; electrical power distribution and protection; enclosures;

SUPPLIERS of EQUIPMENT, PRODUCTS and SERVICES

motor control and MCCs; brakes; AC and DC crane controls.

No. of Employees: 35.

CLEVELAND GEAR CO. INC.
3249 E. 80th St.
Cleveland, OH 44104 USA
P: +1.800.423.3169 (Toll-Free)
F: +1.216.641.0616
emcternan@clevelandgear.com
www.clevelandgear.com

- Pres.—Dana Lynch
- Mgr. Engrg.—John Zamiska
- Vice Pres. Mfg.—Mike Grace
- Vice Pres. Sales and Mktg.—Ed McTernan
- Regional Sales Mgrs.—Jim Murphy, Dan Kaspar
- Inside Tech. Support—Fleming Shy, Brian Cichra
- Vice Pres. Finance—Robert Wightman

EQUIPMENT:
Gleason/Pfauter gear hobbers up to 2.4-m dia. Worm thread grinders up to 14-in.-dia. worm threads.

PRODUCTS and/or SERVICES:
Manufactures open gearing, including worms, helical, double helical and spur gears. Also provides a wide variety of enclosed gear drives: Standard worm gear reducers (1.33-in. to 36-in. C.D.), helical shaft-mount and screw conveyor drives, standard parallel shaft and custom-designed reducers. Cleveland Gear also repairs reducers of all types and will reverse-engineer dimensional "drop-in" replacements for obsolete gear drives. Field service and on-site borescope inspection of enclosed drives and gearing is provided.

No. of Employees: 110.

CMI HEAVY INDUSTRIES
2677 Winger Road
P.O. Box 20
Stevensville, ON L0S 1S0 Canada
P: +1.905.382.7000
sales@cmihi.com
www.cmihi.com

- Pres.—David Rapone
- Vice Pres.—Brian Rapone
- Contr.—Shawn Rapone
- Prodn.—Richard Rapone

PRODUCTS and/or SERVICES:
Mill products and solutions for all areas of steelmaking. CMI's area of expertise lies in the manufacturing and refurbishment of large mill components and assemblies for hot strip mills, casters, coke ovens, cold finishing mills and blast furnaces. Key processes include: proprietary twin-head submerged-arc overlaying, and robotic hardfacing to buildup of surfaces. Fully equipped 130,000 sq. ft. facility features 100 ton lifting capacity with 30 ft. under the hooks, two sandblast and two paint booths, late-model CNC machinery and highly skilled staff.

CNC DESIGN PTY. LTD.
Unit 2, 137–145 Rooks Road
Nunawading, VIC, 3131 Australia
P: +61.3.9417.2820
michael_sutherland@cncdesign.com.au
www.cncdesign.com

- Pres.—Bruce Rowley
- Sales Mgr.—Michael Sutherland
- Asst. Sales Mgr.—Sorin Purdea

PRODUCTS and/or SERVICES:
Motion control and drive-based solutions and CNC retrofitting. CNC Design is the exclusive Siemens representative for machine tool products in Australia, New Zealand and Southeast Asia, providing support sales, engineering and service. More than 150 people located in offices in Australia, Indonesia, New Zealand, Thailand, Malaysia and Singapore. Complete mechatronic solution provider to machine builders and end customers, and complete electrical and mechanical upgrading/retrofitting of roll grinders for the steel industry worldwide.

No. of Employees: 160.

SUPPLIERS OF EQUIPMENT, PRODUCTS and SERVICES

COLT AUTOMATION
6175 Kestrel Road
Mississauga, ON L5T 1Z2 Canada
P: +1.905.625.6600
info@coltauto.com
www.coltauto.com

- Sales Mgr.—Stuart Cordrey
- Adv. Mgr.—David Sait

PRODUCTS and/or SERVICES:
Complete feed lines, cradle feed lines, uncoilers, straighteners, peelers/threaders, threading tables, electronic servo feeders, micro feeders, zig zag feeders and more.

No. of Employees: 50.

COLT INTERNATIONAL BV
Korte Oyen 4
Katwijk Noord-Brabant, 5433
The Netherlands
P: +31.485399922;
   +31.622947832
niek.menting@nl.coltgroup.com
www.colt-ventilation.com

- Chief Exec. Officer—Mark Oliver
- Sales Mgr.—Niek Menting
- Adv. Mgr.—Sarah Al Mouden

PRODUCTS and/or SERVICES:
Design, manufacturing and supply of natural building ventilation systems for the steel industry. The product folio contains industrial heavy-duty roof ventilators and louvers.

No. of Employees: 200.

COLUMBIA MACHINE WORKS INC.
1940 Oakland Pkwy.
Columbia, TN 38401 USA
P: +1.931.388.6202
F: +1.931.381.8128
john@columbiamachineworks.com
www.columbiamachineworks.com
www.electrodehandling.com

- Chief Exec. Officer and Pres.—John K. Langsdon III
- Gen. Mgr./Pur.—Steve Thomason
- Chief Financial Officer—Rolanda Thurman
- Electrode Handling—Mike Yarbrough
- Engrg.—Jack Sowell

PRODUCTS and/or SERVICES:
Electrode handling products, large-capacity machining, large-capacity fabrication, assembly and industrial maintenance.

No. of Employees: 70.

COMBUSTION DYNAMICS LLC
Mailing Address:
P.O. Box 1339
Covington, GA 30015 USA

Main Office and Plant Address:
4250 Davis Academy Road
Rutledge, GA 30663 USA
P: +1.706.557.7552
F: +1.706.557.7690
terrypulliam@gmail.com

- Pres.—Terry Pulliam

EQUIPMENT:
Fully staffed on-site CNC machine shop, fabrication, repair and testing facilities.

PRODUCTS and/or SERVICES:
EAF equipment consisting of new/modified oxy-fuel burner designs, existing burner/lance repairs; combustion replacement parts; carbon and lime injection systems as well as replacement of consumable parts; valve train upgrades, repairs and preventive maintenance service; design, upgrades and supply of ladle and tundish pre-heaters and drying systems; combustion system troubleshooting analysis; operating crew training; operators panel upgrades.

No. of Employees: 15.

SUPPLIERS of EQUIPMENT, PRODUCTS and SERVICES

CONDUCTIX-WAMPFLER
10102 F St.
Omaha, NE 68127 USA
P: +1.800.521.4888 (Toll-Free);
+1.402.339.9300
F: +1.402.339.9627
www.conductix.us

- Pres.—Lon Miller
- Chief Financial Officer—Stuart Zastrow
- Dirs. of Sales—Don Jones, Kyle Creasy, Brian Roberts (U.S.)
- Dir. of Mktg.—Andrew Dierks

PRODUCTS and/or SERVICES: Heavy-duty conductor bar systems, spring- and motor-driven cable reels, cable festoon systems, slip ring assemblies, pushbutton pendants, radio remote controls, and data transmission systems.

No. of Employees: 265.

CONSERO INC.
9607 Gayton Road, Suite 110
Henrico, VA 23238 USA
P: +1.804.359.8448
F: +1.804.359.9199
info@conseroinc.com
www.conseroinc.com

- Chief Exec. Officer, Pres. and Sales Mgr.—Daniel J. Cunningham

PRODUCTS and/or SERVICES: Hot metal detectors and sensors. Thermal cameras.

No. of Employees: 3.

CONTRACTORS & INDUSTRIAL SUPPLY INC.—see MAZZELLA COMPANIES

CONTROL CHIEF CORP.
200 Williams St.
Bradford, PA 16701 USA
P: +1.814.362.6811
F: +1.814.368.4133
sales@controlchief.com
www.controlchief.com

- Managing Partner and Chief Financial Officer—Tim Bean
- Managing Partner and Chief Mktg. Officer—Brian Landries
- Managing Partner and Chief Technology Officer—Jake Bryner

PRODUCTS and/or SERVICES: Manufacturer of industrial wireless remote control solutions. Products include: Advantage Series receivers, L Series transmitters, Raymote®, MU&Go®, MU&Go®plus+™, TrainChief® plus+™, Lightweight OCUs, Summit Series, TeleChief® Series and Access 1000™. Services include: engineering, sales, marketing, customer service, installation and repair service, and manufacturing.

CONTROLES Y SISTEMAS (C&S) SRL
Garibaldi 611
San Nicolas, BA, B2900DOM Argentina
P: +54.33.644.26734
cpuccini@controlesysistemas.com.ar

- Chief Exec. Officer—Carlos Puccini
- Pres.—Adriana Serafini
- Vice Pres. Eng.—Fernando Albertario
- Treas.—Antonela Rodriguez Nuciari
- Sec.—Agustín Benitez
- Chief Engr.—Pablo Pochettino

PRODUCTS and/or SERVICES: Magnaposi electronic sensor for catenary measurement in deep bath pickling lines. Positioning systems for coke ovens and industrial electronics. Overload protection for DC motors. Industrial electronics.

No. of Employees: 10.

CORE METALS GROUP LLC
133 Franklin St.
Aurora, IN 47001 USA
P: +1.812.926.3399
jbarrett@ferroglobe.com
www.ferroglobe.com

- Vice Pres.—Chris Bowes
- Product Mgr.—Jeff Barrett

330   2023 AIST Directory — Iron and Steel Plants

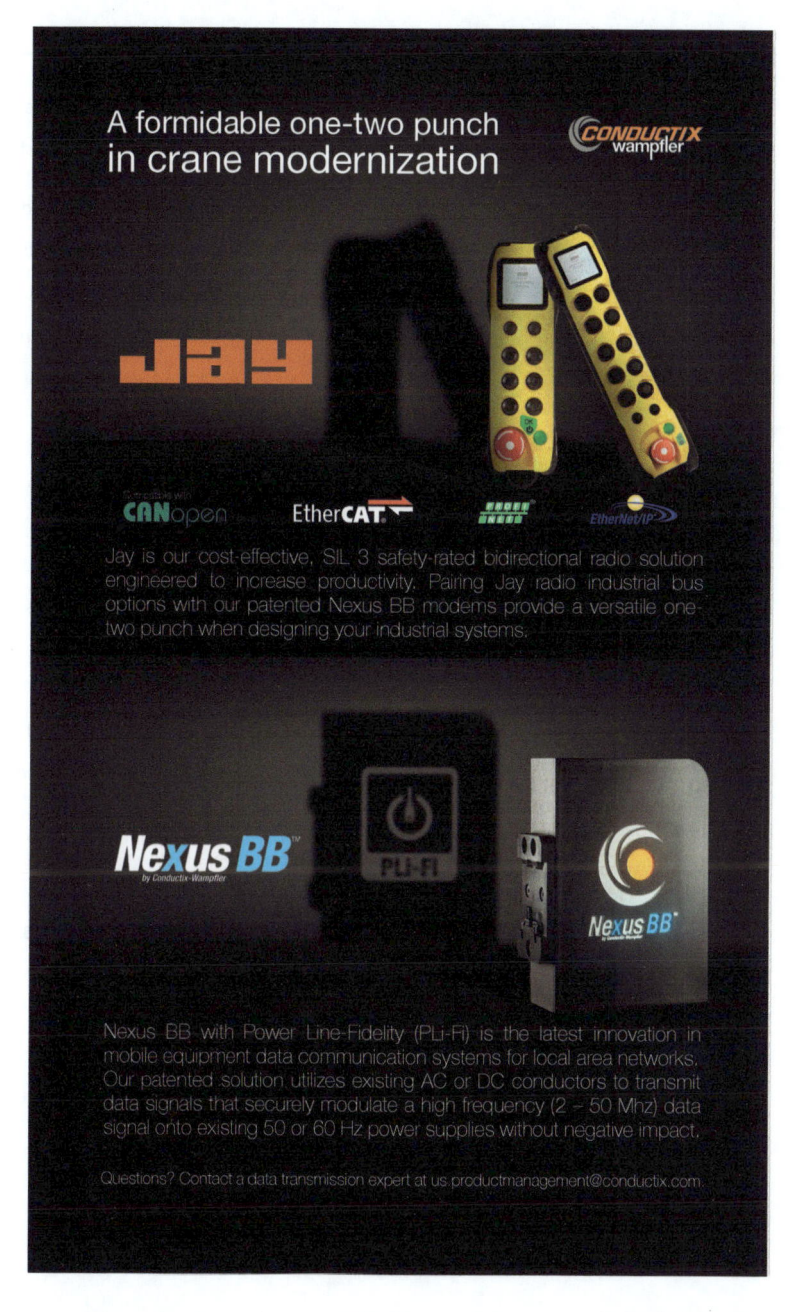

SUPPLIERS of EQUIPMENT, PRODUCTS and SERVICES

PRODUCTS and/or SERVICES:
Fluorspar, calcium aluminates and full-service custom blending of desulfurizers, slag conditioners, manufacturer of FeSi.

No. of Employees: 94.

COREWIRE LTD.
Station Road W
Ash Vale, Aldershot
Hampshire, GU12 5LZ U.K.
P: +44.1252.517766
info@corewire.com
www.corewire.com

- Managing Dir.—Alasdair Boag
- Treas.—Ian Welch
- Commercial Dir.—Ray Anstee
- Sales Mgr.—Sascha Plewka
- Adv. Mgr.—Adrian Leek
- Tech. Dir.—Ioannis Grammenos

PRODUCTS and/or SERVICES:
Manufacturers of Weldclad hardsurfacing consumables for reclaiming and cladding of steel mill rolls. Manufacturers of Cortech hardfaced steel mill rolls.

No. of Employees: 100.

CORPORATESEARCH LLC
Columbus, OH 43147 USA
P: +1.614.352.1453
msmythe@corporatesearchusa.com
www.corporatesearchusa.com

- Principal—Michele Smythe

PRODUCTS and/or SERVICES:
U.S. and global customized recruiting and search services in manufacturing industries, including all metals.

CRANE 1 SERVICES
Field Support Center
1027 Byers Road
Miamisburg, OH 45342 USA
P: +1.937.704.9900
F: +1.937.704.9921
www.crane1.com

- Chief Exec. Officer and Pres.—Thomas Boscher
- Chief Financial Officer—Joe Schivone
- Vice Pres. Sales and Mktg.—Chris Lauletta
- Chief Oper. Officer—Justin Roberts

PRODUCTS and/or EQUIPMENT:
Super-regional provider of overhead crane service, inspection, repair, maintenance, below-the-hook solutions and new crane systems including crane components (brakes, power limits, gearboxes, hook blocks and upper sheave nests) fabrication, rebuild and repair.

No. of Employees: 380.

Crane 1 (Formerly D&S Hoist and Crane)
3100 Casteel Dr.
Coraopolis, PA 15108 USA
P: +1.412.490.3215
F: +1.412.788.4435
craneinfo@dshoistandcrane.com
www.dshoistandcrane.com

- Vice Pres.—Steven Celaschi

EQUIPMENT:
Overhead cranes.

PRODUCTS and/or SERVICES:
Crane and lift equipment, overhead cranes, inspections, maintenance, overhead crane safety, parts, rebuilds, new crane manufacturing, below-the-hook lifting devices, OSHA crane inspections, ASME crane inspections, crane runways, hoists.

No. of Employees: 30.

Magnetic Lifting Technologies US, a Crane 1 Business
3877 Wilmington Road
New Castle, PA 16105 USA
P: +1.724.202.7987
F: +1.724.202.7966
info@mltus.com
www.mltus.com

- Gen. Mgr.—Mike Gordon
- Engrg.—Kirk Bowser
- Natl. Sales—Rick Frischolz
- Sales Mgr.—Kim Kasler

EQUIPMENT:
Industrial electromagnets.

SUPPLIERS OF EQUIPMENT, PRODUCTS and SERVICES

PRODUCTS and/or SERVICES: Industrial lifting magnets, lead protection, electromagnets, remanufactured magnets, magnetic road sweepers, scrap handling magnets, coil handling magnets, underwater magnets, hot work magnets, magnet safety inspections, electromagnet training, electromagnet parts, magnet rectifiers.

No. of Employees: 36.

CROWN TECHNOLOGY INC.
7513 E. 96th St.
P.O. Box 50426
Indianapolis, IN 46250 USA
P: +1.317.845.0045
F: +1.317.845.9086
info@crowntech.com
www.crowntech.com

- Chief Exec. Officer—Joseph C. Peterson
- Pres.—Carrie Benko
- Vice Pres. Finance—Jeff Buckner
- Vice Pres. Sales—Scott Peterson
- Tech. Dir.—Tucker Maurer
- Regional Vice Pres. Sales—Chuck Amori
- Regional Sales Mgr.—Dave Jaap
- Regional Sales Mgr. Mexico—Fernando Flores Ramon
- Cust. Svce.—Karen Ghesquiere

PRODUCTS and/or SERVICES: HCl and sulfuric acid inhibitors, extenders, accelerators, rinse aids and galvanizing cleaners for steel pickling. Oils and metalworking lubricants. Dust control and freeze conditioning agents for mineral handling. Also corrosion inhibitors for oil and gas drilling, pickling chemicals for stainles;s steel, lime coating additives, industrial floor cleaners, strip stain-preventing chemicals, pre-treatment chemicals, electroless copper inhibitors/accelerators, aqueous chemical toll-blending, sulfuric acid recovery systems and pickling line consulting. ISO 9001:2008 certified.

No. of Employees: 33.

CSD ENGINEERS
500 Mosites Way, Suite 200
Pittsburgh, PA 15205 USA
P: +1.412.489.9050
F: +1.412.489.6598
info@csdengineers.com
www.csdengineers.com

- Chief Exec. Officer—Vance H. Williams
- Exec. Vice Pres. and Gen. Mgr.—Joseph R. Perri

PRODUCTS and/or SERVICES: Project management, process engineering, mechanical engineering, civil engineering, structural engineering, piping design, electrical engineering, automation, field services.

No. of Employees: 85.

CTS INC. (CINCINNATI THERMAL SPRAY)
5901 Creek Road
Cincinnati, OH 45242 USA
P: +1.513.793.0670
F: +1.513.793.4254
www.cts-inc.net

PRODUCTS and/or SERVICES: Provides customized coatings to solve problems related to aggressive impact wear, galling, high-temperature oxidation, atmospheric corrosion, acidic resistance and electrical resistance. Thermal spray processes: wire combustion, powder combustion, electric arc, HVOF and plasma.

CV ENGINEERING
3400 McKnight E. Dr.
Pittsburgh, PA 15237 USA
P: +1.412.364.2180
F: +1.412.364.8922
info@cvengineering.com
www.cvengineering.com

- Pres.—Kalyan Sennerikuppam
- Exec. Vice Pres. Oprs.—Sharat Gottumukkala

PRODUCTS and/or SERVICES: Provides multi-disciplinary engineering services to the metals industries. Services include: feasibility studies,

SUPPLIERS of EQUIPMENT, PRODUCTS and SERVICES

budget estimations, project management, facility engineering covering civil, structural, foundations, architectural, HVAC, piping, electrical substations, power distribution, equipment electrics (including raceway, cable and termination schedules), lighting and grounding (including lightning protection), and electrical studies, which includes: arc flash study, relay coordination, short circuit and power quality study and grounding study. Steel experience includes: materials handling, EAFs, LMFs, VTDs, RH degassers, continuous casters, thin-slab casters, reheat furnaces, long and flat product hot rolling mills, compact strip mills, cold rolling mills, process lines, and galvanizing lines. Provides service for greenfield installations and upgrades to existing brownfield installations.

No. of Employees: 37.

D

D&S HOIST AND CRANE—see CRANE 1 SERVICES

DALFORSÅN AB
Industrivägen 11
Vikmanshyttan, 776 70 Sweden
P: +46.225.595460
info@dalforsan.se
www.dalforsan.se

- Chief Exec. Officer—Dan Norman
- Vice Pres. Engrg. and Sales Mgr.—Henrik Stigers
- Treas.—Mats Olhans

EQUIPMENT:
Mainly rollers and roller jackets for continuous casters. All types, with and without internal cooling.

PRODUCTS and/or SERVICES:
Manufacture of rolls and roll sets for casting machines. Refurbishment of casting machine and rolling mill rolls. Contract machining of heavy-duty rolls and mechanical components. Specialize in weld cladding, weld surfacing.

No. of Employees: 47.

DALTON INDUSTRIES LLC
2800 Alliance Dr.
Waterford, MI 48328 USA
P: +1.248.673.0755
F: +1.248.673.7863
info@daltonind.com
www.daltonind.com

- Chief Exec. Officer and Pres.—T. Steven Tolliver
- Engrg. Mgr.—Paul McArthur
- Contr.—Tom Fairbrother
- Gen. Mgr.—Jerry Thomas
- Office Mgr.—Cindy Diehm
- Est.—Tim Thomas
- Qual.—Craig Johnson
- Pur.—Don Shellnut
- Sales—Dennis Buda, Kelly Moore, Bob Nesbitt

EQUIPMENT:
Large fabricating and machining, 100,000-sq.-ft., 100-ton lifting capacity, 1,000-ton press brake, large floor mills/vertical mills, in-house stress-relief furnaces, blast and paint room, roll welding equipment, lathes, and balancing equipment.

PRODUCTS and/or SERVICES:
Full service. Build new or repair hot mills, caster, BF, coke plant.

No. of Employees: 70.

SUPPLIERS OF EQUIPMENT, PRODUCTS and SERVICES

DANIELI & C. OFFICINE MECCANICHE SPA
41 Via Nazionale
Buttrio (UD), I-33042 Italy
P: +39.0432.195.8111
F: +39.0432.195.8289
info@danieli.com
www.danieli.com

- Chmn.—G.P. Benedetti
- Chief Exec. Officers—G. Mareschi Danieli, R. Paolone
- Div. Mgrs. Electric Steelmaking, Continuous Casting—R. Paolone, R. Sellan, A. Tellatin
- Div. Mgrs. Long Products—R. Paolone, F. Mulinaris, C. Fabbro
- Div. Mgr. Forging, Extrusion, Seamless Pipes, Heating, Heat Treatment—M. Totis
- Div. Mgr. Heat Treatment—F. Pere
- Div. Mgrs. Flat Products—L. Coianiz, M. Bulfone, F. Bortolussi, M. Turchetto, M. Girardi, T. Settimo
- Div. Mgr. Plant Engrg.—G. Mareschi Danieli
- Div. Mgrs. Engrg. Products—A. Di Giacomo, S. Giacomelli
- Div. Mgrs. Advisory Svcs. for Plant Start-Up and Commissioning—I. Grgic
- Div. Mgr. Danieli Construction and Site Mgmt. Svcs.—F. Casarsa, P. Saccuman
- Div. Mgrs. Automation and Process Control Systems—A. Mordeglia, A. Ardesi
- Div. Mgrs. Recycling—R. Calligaro, E. Betts, M. Padovan
- Div. Mgrs. Danieli Cust. Svcs.—G. Carnelutti, A. Vallan
- Key Acct. Mgmt.—A. Mordeglia, L. Morsut, P. Losso, A. Diasparro, L. Mottes, A. Colussi, C. Chang, M. Knights, N. Patrizi, G. van Hattum
- Procurement, Logistics, Mfg.—M. Di Giacomo, M. Rinaldis
- Admin. and Controlling Auditing—A. Brussi, M. Marinutti, A. Deana
- H.R. Mgrs.—S. Stafisso, P. Perabo

EQUIPMENT:
Fully equipped R&D, design, engineering, manufacturing and testing facilities.

PRODUCTS and/or SERVICES:
Turnkey plants and systems (Danieli Plant Engineering); beneficiation, pelletizing and direct reduction plants (Danieli Centro Metallics); ironmaking and steelmaking plants (Danieli Corus, Danieli Centro Met); slab casters (Danieli Davy Distington); flat products casting, rolling and processing (Danieli Wean United, Danieli Fata Hunter, Innoval Technology); speciality mills and strip finishing lines (Danieli Fröhling); long products rolling mills (Danieli Morgårdshammar); process control systems (Danieli Automation); conditioning, drawing and finishing lines (Danieli Centro Maskin); EMS and induction heating systems (Danieli Rotelec); extrusion and forging plants (Danieli Breda); heating systems (Danieli Centro Combustion, Danieli Olivotto Ferré); seamless tube mills (Danieli Centro Tube); longitudinal and spiral-welded pipe plants (Danieli W + K); ecological systems (Danieli Environment); recycling systems (Danieli Centro Recycling); cranes for the metals industry (Danieli Centro Cranes); plant construction and erection (Danieli Construction, Fata EPC); technical service and spare parts (Danieli Service).

No. of Employees: 9,100.

Danieli Automation
Via B. Stringher 4
Buttrio (UD), 33042 Italy
P: +39.432.518111
F: +39.432.673177
info@dca.it
www.dca.it

- Pres.—A. Mordeglia
- Chief Exec. Officer—A. Ardesi
- Sales Dir.—E. Plazzogna

PRODUCTS and/or SERVICES:
Production management systems (MES), data analytics and business intelligence, and automation and process control systems for the metals and steel industry. Robotics for metals applications, instrumentation and equipment for production quality control, power distribution, drives and

SUPPLIERS of EQUIPMENT, PRODUCTS and SERVICES

induction heating systems design and manufacturing, electrical and automation control equipment, HW integrator, SW development, electric/electronic engineering, consulting, installation/start-up service, training, after-sales assistance, and plant and personnel safety systems.

No. of Employees: 434.

Danieli Corp.
600 Cranberry Woods Dr., Suite 200
Cranberry Twp., PA 16066 USA
P: +1.724.778.5400
F: +1.724.778.5401
www.danieli.com

- Pres.—P. Losso
- Chief Exec. Officer—M. Sattolo
- Chief Financial Officer—P. Pizzolato
- Dir. Oprs.—P. Deano
- After Sales Svce. Dir.—P. Saccavini
- Service Hubs Oprs. Dir.—K. Shillam

PRODUCTS and/or SERVICES:
Marketing and sales for all Danieli product lines, project management, after-sales customer support, spare parts, field service, electrical and automation services, equipment reconditioning on- and off-site, long-term maintenance, and service agreements.

Danieli Corus BV
Rooswijkweg 291, 1951 ME
Velsen-Noord, The Netherlands
P: +31.251.500.500
F: +31.251.500.501
www.danieli-corus.com

- Managing Dir.—N. Bleijendaal

PRODUCTS and/or SERVICES:
Engineering, equipment, automation and control, and consulting services within the following areas: ironmaking, steelmaking and gas cleaning facilities for the primary aluminum industry.

Danieli FATA Hunter
Strada Statale 24, km 12
Pianezza (TO), 10044 Italy
P: +39.11.96681
F: +39.11.9668355
www.danielifatahunter.com

- Chief Exec. Officer—A. Lombardi
- Div. Mgrs. Aluminium Casting, Rolling, and Coil Coating Lines—M. Girardi, M. Milocco
- Dir. Sales and Proposals—F. Chiappa
- Dir. Oprs.—M. Mazza

PRODUCTS and/or SERVICES:
Design and supply of process equipment for the production of aluminum, steel and stainless steel flat-rolled products. The FATA Hunter product lines for the aluminum sector include: continuous casters, cold rolling mills, foil rolling mills, finishing equipment (stretcher and tension leveling lines, foil separators and slitters, caster and mill automation system packages). Supplier of continuous coil coating lines for aluminum and steel.

Danieli Rotelec
Tours Mercuriales F-93176
Bagnolet Cedex, Paris, France
P: +33.1.49.72.22.63
info@danieli-rotelec.fr

- Chief Exec. Officer—P. Declercq
- Pres.—Antonello Mordeglia
- Bd. Members—P. Declercq, Alessandro Brussi

EQUIPMENT:
Manufacturing plant in St. Quentin Fallavier near Lyon, France.

PRODUCTS and/or SERVICES:
Complete range of EMSs for continuous casting machines, for high-end, automotive, specialty and stainless steels: mold-, strand- and final-EMS with rotative magnetic fields for billet and bloom casters; Multi-Mode® EMS, in-roll and box-type strand EMS with linear traveling magnetic fields for slab casters; Multi-Mode electromagnetic brake (EMBr) with static magnetic fields for thin-slab casters. Induction bar edge heaters for hot strip mills. Induction full-bar heaters in transversal and longitudinal magnetic flux technology for flat product. Metallurgical, mechanical, and electrical hands-on training, start-up services and after-sales process assistance

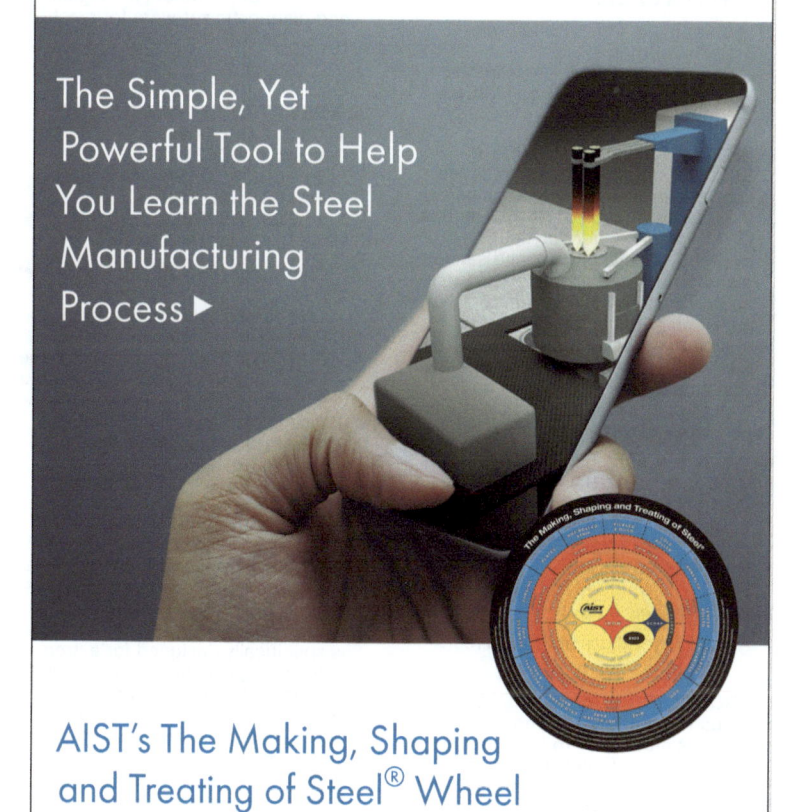

The Simple, Yet Powerful Tool to Help You Learn the Steel Manufacturing Process ▶

AIST's The Making, Shaping and Treating of Steel® Wheel

A FREE, one-of-a-kind interactive tool that illustrates the steelmaking process from start to finish. Try it yourself at AIST.org/Resources.

*Created in collaboration with Purdue University Northwest's Center for Innovation Through Visualization and Simulation and assistance from the Colorado School of Mines.

SUPPLIERS of EQUIPMENT, PRODUCTS and SERVICES

Danieli Taranis LLC
54 Chesser Crane Road
Chelsea, AL 35043 USA
P: +1.205.678.7451

- Chief Exec. Officer and Pres.—Colin Feather
- Chief Oper. Officer—A. Nardone
- Spares and Cust. Svce.—Jeffrey Rozycki

PRODUCTS and/or SERVICES:
Electrics, automation, and process controls for plants and equipment for the metals industry in North America. LV/MV drives, induction heating systems, special gauges and sensors, manufacturing of advanced process control systems. HW integrator, SW development, electric/electronic engineering, consulting, installation/start-up services, training, after-sales assistance, spares, erection and construction services, and plant and personnel safety systems.

DATA-LINC GROUP
1125 12th Ave. NW, Suite B-2
Issaquah, WA 98027 USA
P: +1.425.882.2206
F: +1.425.867.0865
info@data-linc.com
www.data-linc.com

- Gen. Mgr./Mktg. and Sales Mgr.—K.M. Perlbachs

PRODUCTS and/or SERVICES:
Industrial-grade wired and non-licensed wireless modems. Products include: SRM8 family of intelligent spectrum, FHSS, high-speed, long-range license-free, simultaneous, dual protocol modems that support edge computing; CIX family of long-range protocol to I/O and I/O to I/O extender radio modems; HSM family of high-speed, long-range OFDM/DSSS modems in both 2.43 GHz and 5 GHz bands; PLR family of medium-range Ethernet, serial and I/O radio modems; SRM6 family of long-range FHSS Ethernet and serial radio modems; dial-up/leased line family of wire modems; and antennas, cables and lightning arrestors. Data-Linc'c no-cost services include WiDE (wireless network design) software; RF path studies/site surveys; pre- through post-sale technical support; RF network configuration, management and diagnostic software for most of Data-Linc's SRM8 and SRM6 families of FHSS modems.

DAUBERT CHEMICAL CO. INC.
4700 S. Central Ave.
Chicago, IL 60638 USA
P: +1.800.688.0459 (Toll-Free);
+1.708.496.7350
F: +1.708.796.7367
www.daubertchemical.com

- Chief Exec. Officer and Pres.—Matt Puz
- Chief Financial Officer and Vice Pres.—Tim Henderson
- Exec. Vice Pres. Oprs.—Mark Pawelski
- Exec. Vice Pres. Technology—Mike Duncan
- Vice Pres. Sales—Frank Vella
- Vice Pres. Commercial Dev.—Matthew McGinnis

EQUIPMENT:
Leading provider of specialty coatings and adhesives for the steel, automotive transportation and general manufacturing industries. Daubert's TecPlex® line of high-performance calcium sulfonate steel mill greases is specifically designed for extreme industrial applications and provides long-lasting protection to critical components without relying on polymers or solid additives that can clog lines and filters, or chemical additives that will deplete at high temperatures leading to eventual bearing wear after sustained use. Daubert also manufactures legacy brand names such as Tectyl®, Nox-Rust®, Daubond® and V-Damp®.

DAUBERT CROMWELL
12701 S. Ridgeway Ave.
Alsip, IL 60803 USA
P: +1.800.535.3535 (Toll-Free);
+1.708.293.7750
F: +1.708.293.7765
info@daubertcromwell.com
www.daubertcromwell.com

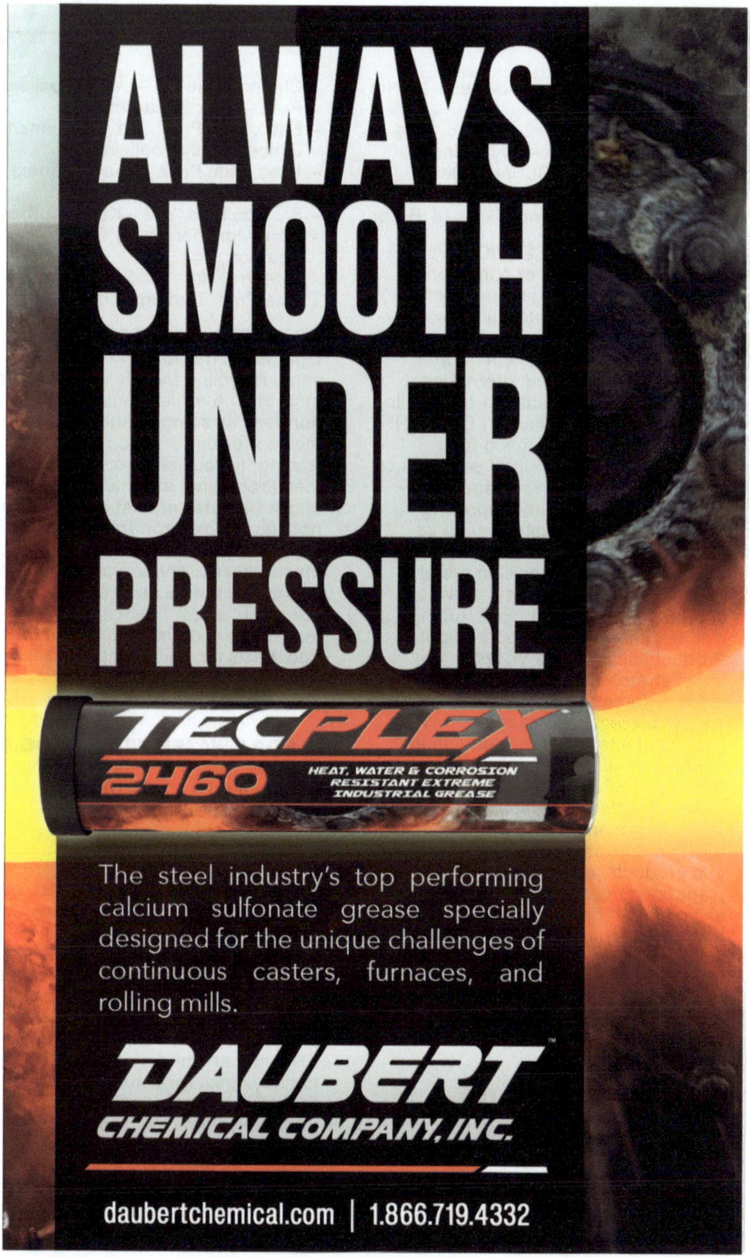

See listing page 338

SUPPLIERS of EQUIPMENT, PRODUCTS and SERVICES

- Chief Exec. Officer and Pres.—Martin J. Simpson
- Chief Oper. Officer and Exec. Vice Pres. Global Oprs.—Roy Galman
- Vice Pres. Global Business Dev.—Scott Kotvis
- Vice Pres., Sales and Mktg.—J. Bitter

PRODUCTS and/or SERVICES:
Global manufacturer of corrosion inhibitor (VCI) packaging products, including rust-preventive liquids, to protect metal parts, equipment, machinery and components during storage, domestic and international shipping, and parts subject to handling during processing. Daubert Cromwell VCI products are also used for preservation and lay-up of seasonal or long-term equipment storage. OEM-approved manufacturer supplying VCI products to industries such as automotive, electronics, aerospace, heavy equipment, precision metal machining, steel and steel service centers, underground pipes/tubing, military, energy, and export shipping. Product line includes VCI poly film, bags, stretch film, shrink film, sheeting, plus reinforced scrim and paper for use as rust-protective packaging, pallet liners and interleaving. Products are nitrite-free, amine-free, recyclable, RoHS and REACH compliant. Daubert Cromwell offers technical analysis and application assistance, lab testing, audits of corrosion inhibitor processes and products, and on-site training for plant personnel concerned with quality, shipping and handling. Company headquarters are in the U.S., with sales and manufacturing operations in Europe, Mexico, China and Brazil. Distributors are located throughout the U.S. and in more than 40 countries. ISO 9001:2015 certified.

DAVID J. JOSEPH CO., THE
300 Pike St.
Cincinnati, OH 45202 USA
P: +1.513.419.6200
F: +1.513.419.6227
www.djj.com

- Chmn. of the Bd.—Leon Topalian
- Pres.—Mark Schaefer
- Exec. Vice Pres. and Chief Financial Officer—Kelly Poellein
- Exec. Vice Pres.—Noah Hanners, David J. Steigerwald
- Sr. Vice Pres. H.R.—Karen Luther
- Gen. Mgr., Ferroalloy Group—Lucas Reinhart
- Vice Pres. Intl. Trading—Ryan Eckert
- Vice Pres. Trading—Chris Stout

PRODUCTS and/or SERVICES:
Operates a network of over 60 U.S. scrap recycling facilities that process more than 5 million tons of ferrous and non-ferrous scrap annually. Services include ferrous and non-ferrous scrap trading; ferrous and non-ferrous metal recycling; international scrap and substitutes marketing; ferroalloy, nodular and pig iron trading; global supply chain expertise; industrial scrap management services; independently owned fleet of railcars; railcar leasing, purchase, sales, financing, engineering, inspection and dismantling; self-serve auto parts recycling; and mill services.

No. of Employees: 1,900.

DE NORA WATER TECHNOLOGIES
2000 McClaren Woods Dr.
Coraopolis, PA 15108 USA
P: +1.412.788.8300
info.dnwt@denora.com
www.denora.com

PRODUCTS and/or SERVICES:
Water and wastewater solutions focused on filtration, biological and adsorption technologies, all disinfection processes, instrumentation, and contract operating services. Products include: capital controls analyzers; TETRA biological reactors; EST eductors and ejectors; TETRA filter systems (gravity and pressure); Fe and Mn removal plus other in-organics removal; ClorTec on-site hypochlorite generators; chlorine dioxide generators; vacuum regulators; UAT reverse osmosis systems.

SUPPLIERS OF EQUIPMENT, PRODUCTS and SERVICES

DEC INDUSTRIES LTD.
2240 43rd Ave.
Lachine, QC H8T 2J8 Canada
P: +1.514.636.5740
F: +1.514.636.5743
sales@decindustries.com
www.decindustries.com

- Pres.—Dave Chaudry
- Vice Pres. Prodn./Mfg.—Suresh Patel
- Sec.—Chynna St. Amour
- Chief Engr.—Claude Tessier

PRODUCTS and/or SERVICES:
Complete fabrication, machining, customizing and assembly, including hydraulic lubrication, piping, and electrical wiring and testing of hot and cold mill, process line, continuous line and furnace equipment: uncoilers, looper towers, bridles, tension levelers, shears, rotary shears, recoilers, beltwrappers, inspection stations, peeler flatteners, mill stands, roller aprons, tundish cars, mold housings, withdrawal straighteners, starter bars, dummy bar assemblies, eccentric mill stands, sidetrimmers, slitters, stacker assemblies, conveyors, AGC cylinders, rolls, chocks, mandrels, segments, sideguides and exclusive manufacturer of Dominion Gearflex couplings.

DEEP SOUTH CRANE & RIGGING
15324 Airline Hwy.
Baton Rouge, LA 70817 USA
P: +1.877.490.4371 (Toll-Free)
jbowen@deepsouthcrane.com
www.deepsouthcrane.com

- Chief Exec. Officer—Camile Landry
- Pres.—Mitch Landry
- Exec. Vice Pres.—Thad Lentz
- Vice Pres.—Jeremy Landry
- Sales Mgr.—John Bowen
- Chief Engr.—Derek Elliott

EQUIPMENT:
Cranes up to 3,000 tons, proprietary VersaCrane fleet, self-propelled modular transporters (SPMTs), rigging equipment, capabilities to engineer and fabricate rigging steel matting, steel bridges, etc.

PRODUCTS and/or SERVICES:
Crane lifts, heavy hauling and transport engineering for specialized rigging and lift plans. From feasibility studies to final execution, Deep South provides custom solutions and expertise for turnaround, maintenance, and capital projects in North and South America.

No. of Employees: 800.

DELLNER BUBENZER
20026 Hickory Twig Way
Spring, TX 77388 USA
P: +1.832.482.4830
info@dellnerbubenzer.com
www.dellnerbubenzer.com

- Pres.—Joel Cox
- Exec. Sales Mgr.—Mike Astemborski
- Vice Pres.—Lauren Lasin-Tum

PRODUCTS and/or SERVICES:
Industrial brakes, brake systems and brake monitoring.

No. of Employees: 14 in the U.S., 200+ worldwide.

DELTA STEEL TECHNOLOGIES
2204 Century Center Blvd.
Irving, TX 75062 USA
P: +1.972.438.7150
F: +1.972.579.0100
main@deltasteeltech.com
www.deltasteeltech.com

- Pres.—Joseph Savariego

PRODUCTS and/or SERVICES:
Designs, manufactures, re-manufactures and rebuilds steel mill equipment and OEM components. Products include: temper mills, rotary shears, stretch levelers, equalizers (tension leveling system), CTL lines, slitting lines, robotic applications, pickling lines, cold rolling mills, galvanizing lines, paint lines, and material handling equipment. Industrial services include: engineering/reverse engineering; heavy fabrication; heavy machining; hydraulic cylinder rebuilds; gearbox repairs/rebuilds; custom and complex fabrications; and custom manufacturing of all types of machinery.

SUPPLIERS of EQUIPMENT, PRODUCTS and SERVICES

DELTA USA INC.
600 N. Bell Ave. Bldg. 2, Suite 180
Carnegie, PA 15106 USA
P: +1.412.429.3574
F: +1.412.429.3348
www.delta-usa.com

- Sales Mgr.—Jay Kane

PRODUCTS and/or SERVICES:
Sales, service and application engineering for Delta mill-duty sensors, including hot metal detectors, loop scanners, laser barriers, retro-reflective lasers with high-temperature reflectors, heavy-duty pulse generators. FT time-of-flight and TL triangulation measurement sensors and systems for dimensional and position measurement. XD 4000 stereoscopic width gauge for hot and cold strip measurement. Velas Laser speed gauges for speed and length measurement.

DESHAZO LLC
200 Kilsby Cir.
Bessemer, AL 35022 USA
P: +1.800.926.2006 (Toll-Free)
F: +1.205.664.3668
kcalma@deshazo.com
www.deshazo.com

- Chief Exec. Officer—Guy K. Mitchell III
- Exec. Vice. Pres.—Tray Ivey
- Crane Pres.—Cliff Denson
- Automation Pres.—Chris McCulley
- Vice Pres. Mfg.—Chuck Tucker

PRODUCTS and/or SERVICES:
Original equipment manufacturer of overhead cranes, hoists, automated material handling equipment, as well as provider of replacement parts, on-site service, inspections, repairs, upgrades, and rebuilds of all crane and hoist makes and models.

No. of Employees: 445.

DIALIGHT
1501 Rte. 34 S
Farmingdale, NJ 07727 USA
P: +1.732.751.5891
info@dialight.com
www.dialight.com

PRODUCTS and/or SERVICES:
LED lighting for industrial applications and hazardous locations.

DIBENEDETTO APPRAISAL SERVICES (DAS), Member of the TDI Group LLC
700 Blaw Ave., Suite 101B
P.O. Box 38591
Pittsburgh, PA 15238 USA
P: +1.412.826.4950
F: +1.412.826.4959
drd@tdigrp.com
www.tdigrp.com

- Pres.—David R. DiBenedetto Sr.
- Vice Pres.—David R. DiBenedetto Jr.

PRODUCTS and/or SERVICES:
Certified machinery and equipment appraisals. Valuation services of complete integrated steel producing, mini-mill and scrap processing facilities. Accurate, confidential reporting compliant with the Uniform Standards of Professional Appraisal Practice (USPAP); appraisal solutions meeting stringent industry requirements—mergers and acquisitions, litigation, insurance reviews, corporate restructuring, capital improvement, ESOP valuation, bankruptcy and turnaround services. Accredited member: The Equipment Appraisers of North America (EANA), Association of Machinery & Equipment Appraisers (AMEA), and American Society of Appraisers (ASA). Senior appraiser on staff.

No. of Employees: 6.

DILLON INDUSTRIAL FAN CO.
31 Bedding Pl.
Johnson City, TN 37604 USA
P: +1.423.948.0141
difco97@gmail.com

- Pres.—David E. Tolson
- Vice Pres.—Gerri Tolson

PRODUCTS and/or SERVICES:
Industrial man-cooler fans, wall vent fans, product cooling, under-table cooling fans, "super quiet" industrial fans.

Get Involved With AIST's
29 Technology Committees

Technology Committee membership offers:

- An enhanced network of peers

- A forum to collectively solve problems

- Opportunities to advance individual technical know-how

Make the most of your membership.
Find a committee at AIST.org.

Join today!

2023 AIST Directory — Iron and Steel Plants   343

SUPPLIERS of EQUIPMENT, PRODUCTS and SERVICES

DITH REFRACTORIES
100 Matawan Road
Matawan, NJ 07747 USA
P: +1.217.778.0886
F: +1.732.242.1068
kyle.kingsbury@dith.com
www.dithrefractories.com

- Vice Pres. Refractory Technology—Kyle Kingsbury
- Dir. of Sales—Jerry King
- Admin. and Logistics—Rita Arya

PRODUCTS and/or SERVICES:
Flow control products for casting, including slidegate and isostatic refractories. Shaped products such as bricks (mag carbon, AMC, mag/chrome)—ferrovanadium in a variety of packaging styles.

No. of Employees: 35.

DIXON VALVE & COUPLING CO.
1 Dixon Sq.
Chestertown, MD 21620 USA
P: +1.877.963.4966 (Toll-Free)
sales@dixonvalve.com
www.dixonvalve.com

PRODUCTS and/or SERVICES:
Manufacturer and supplier of hose couplings, valves, dry-disconnects, swivels, and other fluid transfer and control products. The company's global reach includes a wide range of products for numerous industries including petroleum exploration, refining, transportation, chemical processing, food and beverage, steel, fire protection, construction, mining, and manufacturing. Brands include: GSM Hose; Swivel Joints; King Safety Cable; King Safety Whip Sock; Boss-lock, EZ Boss-Lock, Vent-Lock Safety Cam & Groove; Holedall; FloMAX Fuel System; Eagle Bellows Seal Valves; and Dix-Lock Couplings.

DLZ INDUSTRIAL LLC
316 Tech Dr.
Burns Harbor, IN 46304 USA
P: +1.219.764.4700
F: +1.219.764.4156
www.dlz.com

- Pres.—Kurt S. Schmiegel
- Vice Pres.—Craig Nagdeman
- Div. Mgrs.—Andrew Kincaid, Tony Toscani, Don Williams Jr., Charles Anderson, Ray Radjenovich
- Project Mgrs.—Richard McDonald, Keith Nay, John Sprouse, William Wick, Don Bonnema, Sam Elomar, Nathan Sederstrom, Aziz Omara

PRODUCTS and/or SERVICES:
A vertical integrated design service provider: design and industrial surveying including 3D scanning; through engineering (geotechnical, structural, mechanical and electrical) with architectural design; precision machinery and laser tracker; specialty services (drone and hydrographic surveying), field engineering, materials testing and construction administration; and drilling.

No. of Employees: 115.

DOVER HYDRAULICS INC.
2996 Progress St.
Dover, OH 44622 USA
P: +1.800.394.1617 (Toll-Free);
   +1.330.364.1617
F: +1.330.343.4994
www.doverhydraulics.com

- Chief Exec. Officer and Pres.—Bob Sensel
- Exec. Vice Pres.—Dayne Thomas
- Vice Pres. Engrg.—Eric Kinsey
- Vice Pres. Sales and Mktg.—Gretchen Boring
- Dir. Sales and Mktg.—J.C. Raies
- Sales Mgr.—Jim Karl
- Sales Engr.—Rob Sensel

PRODUCTS and/or SERVICES:
Repairs hydraulic and pneumatic cylinders (including AGC and oscillation), pumps, motors and valves. Full engineering, field service and fabrication departments. Dover also serves North American steelmakers with strategic partners in Europe, including ALBA torch cutting equipment, Kamat high-pressure triplex piston pumps for descaling, and Sibre industrial brake systems.

PROBLEM SOLVED
SINCE 1916

SERVICING THE STEEL INDUSTRY FOR OVER 60 YEARS

Your trusted source for dependable **INDUSTRIAL AND PRECISION SURVEYING** now pleased to offer **INDUSTRIAL ENGINEERING**. A comprehensive capital and maintenance project support team.

Extensive experience in:
- Safety, engineering, and environmental
- Cokemaking
- Ironmaking
- Steelmaking
- Refining and casting
- Rolling and processing – hot strip mills
- Rolling and processing – cold strip mills
- Rolling and processing – plate mills
- Energy and utilities
- Material movement and overhead cranes

SUPER BOOTH

OFFICE 1.877.425.5359 | ONLINE WWW.DLZ.COM

SUPPLIERS of EQUIPMENT, PRODUCTS and SERVICES

DRAFTO CORP.
P.O. Box 158
100 Pressler Ave.
Cochranton, PA 16314 USA
P: +1.814.425.7445
F: +1.814.425.8048
sales@drafto.com
www.drafto.com

- Chief Exec. Officer and Pres.—Bruce Wesley
- Vice Pres. Sales and Engrg.—Dave Kiser

PRODUCTS and/or SERVICES: Overhead material handling equipment for the steel industry. Drafto weigh systems have an NTEP Certification of Conformance and can be certified as legal for trade. Coil lifters available with rotation and weighing to handle both hot or cold coils (with coil edge damage prevention and electronic sensing), narrow aisle coil lifters, patented Coil Guard edge protector modules. Crane scale weighing systems with RF or direct-readout interfacing to customer computer systems, hot metal weighing in upper sheave nest (overhead crane). Rotahook® motorized rotating hook blocks; Rotahook crane scale systems; sheet lifters; slab tongs; patented Autolatch® remote-controlled gravity latch; replacement hook blocks; sheaves; hoist rope drums and laminated hot-riveted ladle hooks.

DRESSEL TECHNOLOGIES LLC
1674 Hawthorn Dr.
Pawleys Island, SC 29585 USA
P and F: +1.843.237.8337
gregdressel@dresseltech.com
www.dresseltech.com

- Principal Consultant—Gregory L. Dressel

PRODUCTS and/or SERVICES: Commissioning, final acceptance test and line management services provided in steel meltshop operations and quality control; equipment and technology experience, including scrap yards, EAF, BOF, LF, degassers, ladles, and slab and billet casters (CCM). Expert witness work for legal cases. Expertise in molten steel and slag process engineering for the economical manufacture of low-carbon aluminum-killed sheet steels, all grades of wire rod, and tool steels made using scrap, DRI, HBI, pig iron and hot metal. On-site services provided for elimination of surface pinholes; internal inclusions; slab and billet surface slag and bleeders; shape and rhomboidity; and other quality issues. Marketing and sales services provided for steelmaking equipment and consumables.

DREVER INTERNATIONAL—see SMS GROUP

DROPSA USA INC.
15809 Claire Ct.
Macomb, MI 48042 USA
P: +1.586.566.1540
F: +1.586.566.1541
sales@dropsausa.com
www.dropsa.com

- Pres.—Ron Newsome
- Vice Pres.—Jason Craft
- Vice Pres. Mktg.—Ryan Mikolasik
- Sec.—Luba Mazuro
- Sales Mgr.—Kevin Howes
- Regional Sales Mgrs.—Wayne Gaskill, Tim Fawcett, Brad Gray, Mike Vandewiele, Adam Keen
- Pur. Agt.—Matt Stoyanoff
- Chief Engr.—Mark Butler
- Inside Sales—Kelli Zaranek, Nicole German
- Qual. Mgr.—Mike Monicatti

PRODUCTS and/or SERVICES: Develops lubrication systems and applications which are currently employed by many producers working in different industry segments. Centralized lubrication systems, sales, design, engineering and service for North America.

No. of Employees: 20.

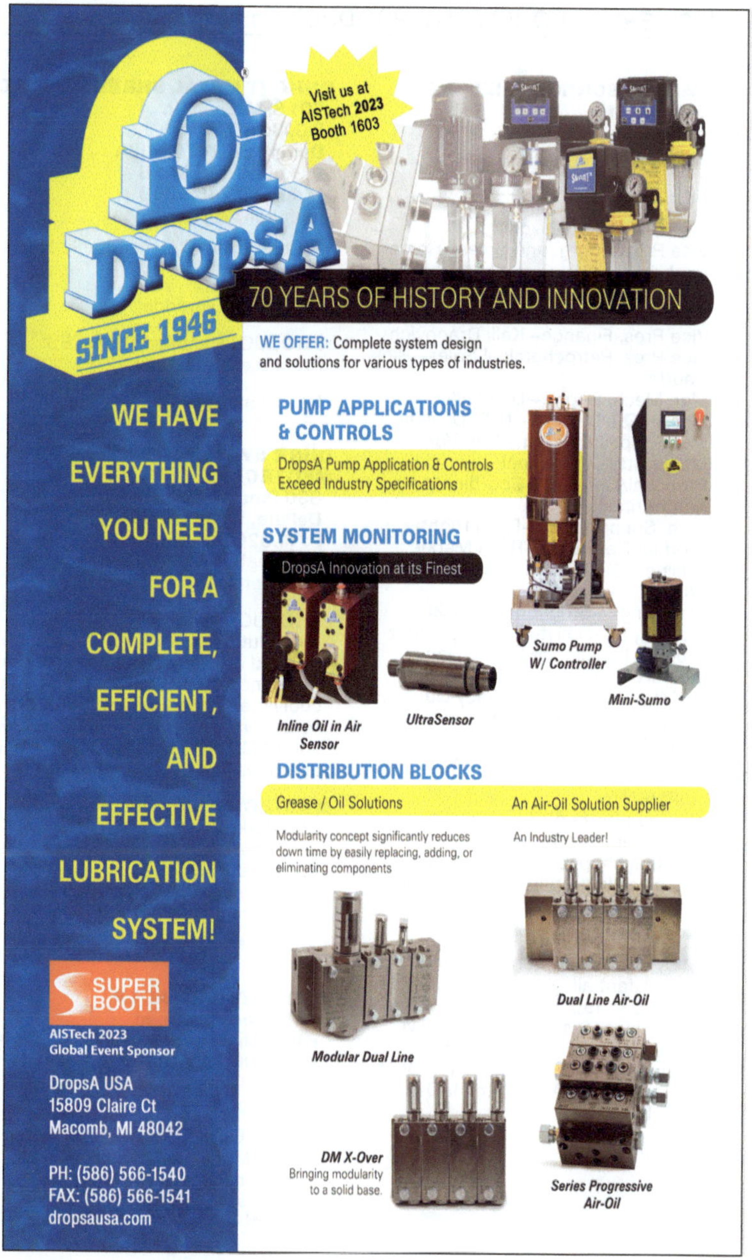

See listing page 346

SUPPLIERS of EQUIPMENT, PRODUCTS and SERVICES

DURALOY TECHNOLOGIES INC.
120 Bridge St.
Scottdale, PA 15683 USA
P: +1.724.887.5100
sales@duraloy.com
www.duraloy.com

- Pres.—Vince Schiavoni
- Vice Pres. Engrg. and Sales—Roman Pankiw
- Vice Pres. and Gen. Mgr.—Dale Smodic
- Vice Pres. Finance—Kelli Dragovich
- Vice Pres. Petrochemical Sales—Rick Kauffman
- Mgr. Mech. Engrg.—Dan Miller
- Mgr. of Qual. Assur.—M.E. Dove III
- Mgr. Proposal Engrg.—Don Voke
- Maint. Supv.—Tom Lock
- Proposal/Contracts Coordinator—Anna Krinock
- Tech. Support Mgr.—Ryan Richter
- Product Dev. Engr.—Ryan Markle
- Business Dev./Tech. Support—Tim Wilson
- Plant Engr.—Stephen Ozoroski
- Welding Specialist—Josh Melendez
- Product Excellence Engr.—Daniel Limpert
- Sr. Mfg. Design Engr.—Lacy Dunmyre
- Design Engr.—Alexis Palo
- Project Engr.—Evan Brown
- Lab Technician—Earl Kinneer

EQUIPMENT:
Static foundry, centrifugal foundry, machine shop, pattern shop, fabrication shop, all NDT equipment including radiography, metallurgical testing laboratory.

PRODUCTS and/or SERVICES:
Duraloy corrosion-, abrasion- and heat-resistant alloy castings. Tubes, furnace rolls, radiant tube assemblies, skids, fittings, assemblies. Exclusive manufacturers of nickel aluminide plate furnace rolls, Super 22H®, 22H®, Supertherm®, TMA® and the MO-RE® family of alloys.

No. of Employees: 200.

DURANT METAL SHREDDING LLC
701 S. McLean Dr.
P.O. Box 1732
Durant, OK 74702 USA
P: +1.580.745.9558
F: +1.580.745.9358
joefulton57@gmail.com

- Chief Exec. Officer—Joe L. Fulton

EQUIPMENT:
Automobile shredder.

PRODUCTS and/or SERVICES:
Processed scrap metal.

No. of Employees: 25.

DÜRR SYSTEMS INC. (DÜRR MEGTEC)
830 Prosper St.
DePere, WI 54115 USA
P: +1.920.336.5715
durrmegtecinquiries@durrusa.com
www.durr-megtec.com

PRODUCTS and/or SERVICES:
Air pollution control (APC) equipment: wet and dry electrostatic precipitators (new and rebuilds), evaporative gas cooling and conditioning, venturi scrubbers, acid gas scrubbers, SCR and SNCR NOx control solutions, and upgrades to existing equipment.

MEGTEC TurboSonic Inc.
550 Parkside Dr., Suite A-14
Waterloo, ON N2L 5V4 Canada
P: +1.519.885.5513
durrmegtecinquiries@durrusa.com
www.durr-megtec.com

- Sales Mgr.—Margarita Murach

DYNAINDUSTRIAL LP
277 Sherwood Road
RM of Sherwood, SK S4K 0A8 Canada
P: +1.306.359.7088
sales@dynaindustrial.com
www.dynaindustrial.com

- Chief Exec. Officer—Darrin Craig
- Gen. Mgr.—Marland Ottenbreit
- Product Dev.—Mike Suchan
- Business Dev.—Troy Tait, Jason Schoff
- Dir. of Sales—Victoria Rhodes

SUPPLIERS OF EQUIPMENT, PRODUCTS and SERVICES

EQUIPMENT:
CNC lathe turning capacity of 47-in. dia. x 240 in. length. CNC vertical milling to 30 in. x 35 in. x 70 in. length. Boring mill capacity up to 33 ft. of travel. Full contouring 6-axis and 5-axis boring mills. 60-ton overhead crane. Sub-arc welders.

PRODUCTS and/or SERVICES:
Customer design, build and engineering; large CNC boring mill work; steel fabrication and welding; turnkey assemblies; hydraulic cylinder rebuild and manufacture; industrial hard chrome plating; heavy industrial equipment repair. Products include: double joining lines, pipe collapse testers, pipe handling equipment, plasma cutoffs, ID clamps, ID welders, top guides, sideguides, etc.

No. of Employees: 110.

DYNAMIC MILL SERVICES CORP.
P.O. Box 49609
Charlotte, NC 28277 USA
P: +1.704.542.4494
inbound@dynamicms.com
www.dynamicms.com

– Sales Mgr.—Ernesto "Ernie" Bosch

PRODUCTS and/or SERVICES:
Bearings, bearing inner races, bearing components, etc.; extreme lubricants; couplings, spindles, universal joints, clutches, etc.; gears, gear reducers, gearboxes; electric motors; labyrinth rings; machined parts; fabrications; castings (normally no pattern cost); forgings; chains, chain products, sprockets; guards; laser product gauges; rolls and roll rings (iron, steel, forged and carbide); guides; guide rollers; induction heaters; rolling mill personnel training; pass and roll design; slit rolling expertise; bearing reconditioning and modifying; chain reconditioning; gear and gearbox repair, rebuilding and improving; maintenance and millwright services; electric motor repair; custom design of parts, assemblies, guides, etc. (normally at no cost); alignment, installation, measurement, scanning, surveying, tracking and dynamic analysis services (all multi-dimensional, highly precise, very rapid and laser-based).

E

EAFAB CORP.
4 Industrial Park Dr.
Oakdale, PA 15071 USA
P: +1.724.693.8800
F: +1.724.693.8450
sales@eafabcorp.com
www.eafabcorp.com

– Chief Exec. Officer and Pres.— Claudia Leal
– Vice Pres. Engrg.—Pedro Quiroga
– Vice Pres. Sales and Mktg.—Mark G. Kropf

EQUIPMENT:
More than 130,000 sq. ft. of fabrication space in North America. Crane lift capacities up to 100 tons.

PRODUCTS and/or SERVICES:
Manufacturer of water-cooled equipment and heavy steel fabrications, including: roof and sidewall panels, roof structures, upper and lower shell structures, gantry assemblies, tilt platforms, mast columns, current conducting arms, tap gates, scrap buckets, ladles, ladle turrets, tundishes, LF roofs with pipe or smooth plate

SUPPLIERS of EQUIPMENT, PRODUCTS and SERVICES

technology, as well as fixed-position options, Consteel pans and hoods, and complete offgas systems, caster spray bars, and runout rolls. In-house machining and stress-relieving for optimum quality control. Can provide design engineering, project management and equipment design solutions. All designs are generated under a 3D base to verify all aspects of the design and simulate working conditions. EAFab will verify that all designs meet not only fabrication standards, but also the objectives of customers. Have the capabilities to perform detailed FEA utilizing Inventor, motion analysis, interference analysis and state-of-the-art fluid simulations. EAFab also provides a panel assurance program to manage, inspect and repair sidewall, roof, and sump panels, providing a cost control for water-cooled equipment.

No. of Employees: 200.

EBNER FURNACES INC.
224 Quadral Dr.
Wadsworth, OH 44281 USA
P: +1.330.335.1600
F: +1.330.335.1605
sales@ebnerfurnaces.com
www.ebnerfurnaces.com

- Managing Dir.—Herbert Gabriel
- Vice Pres. Sales, U.S. and Canada—B.J. Austin

PRODUCTS and/or SERVICES: Full-solution provider of thermal processing solutions. EBNER manufactures continuous and batch-type thermal processing facilities for steel, copper and aluminum semi-finished products industries worldwide. EBNER HICON® and HICON/H2® solutions provide minimal processing time, temperature uniformity for consistent properties, rapid cooling for automotive AHSS and hardened steels, and clean end products. EBNER equipment processes semi-finished products including coils, strip, rod/wire, plate and shapes.

EDDISONS CJM
Dunlop Way
Scunthorpe, DN16 3RN U.K.
P: +44.0.1724.334411
F: +44.0.1724.334422
charles.moses@eddisons.com
www.eddisons.com

- Dir.—Charles W. Moses

PRODUCTS and/or SERVICES: Qualified valuers of metals processing equipment; specializing in the worldwide sale of used steel mills and process plants.

No. of Employees: 20.

EDWARDS VACUUM, Part of the Atlas Copco Group
6416 Inducon Corporate Dr.
Sanborn, NY 14132 USA
P: +1.800.848.9800 (Toll-Free)
info@edwardsvacuum.com
www.edwardsvacuum.com

PRODUCTS and/or SERVICES: Mechanical dry vacuum pumps for secondary metallurgy/steel degassing. Edwards' vacuum solutions offer reasonable redundancies for each ladle size and process ensuring highest uptime. Largest installed base of dry pumps in the global steel industry with a global footprint of manufacturing, sales and service.

EES COKE BATTERY LLC
P.O. Box 18309
River Rouge, MI 48218 USA

- Vice Pres.—David Smith
- Plant Mgr.—Mike Krchmar

PRODUCTS and/or SERVICES: Cokemaking.

ELCON TECHNOLOGIES, Div. of Gagne Technical Services
1901 Mayview Road Unit 10
Bridgeville, PA 15017 USA
P: +1.412.822.8250
F: +1.412.822.8254
mikegagne@elcontech.com
www.elcontech.com

SUPPLIERS OF EQUIPMENT, PRODUCTS and SERVICES

- Pres.—Michael Andrew Gagne
- Finance—Andrew Gagne
- Oprs.—Evan Gagne

EQUIPMENT:
SCADA, machinery control, custom electrical, electrical machines, process control panels, cellular controls and cybersecurity software.

PRODUCTS and/or SERVICES:
Engineering design for process, field service and electromechanical repair.

No. of Employees: 25.

EM MOULDS SPA
Via della Repubblica 257
Fornaci di Barga (LU), 55051 Italy
P: +39.0583.70071
F: +39.0583.700791
info@coppermoulds.com
www.coppermoulds.com

PRODUCTS and/or SERVICES:
Copper mold tubes, copper plate molds, stainless steel water jackets and miscellaneous related hardware for continuous casting.

EMG-USA INC.
8555 Sweet Valley Dr.
Cleveland, OH 44125 USA
P: +1.330.372.4418
F: +1.330.372.4431
patric.jobst@emg-automation.com
www.emg-automation.com

- Vice Pres. Sales and Oprs.—Patric Jobst
- Sales—Mike Gilbert, Mark Szabados
- Svce.—Dennis Carr

PRODUCTS and/or SERVICES:
Strip guiding and steering equipment, sensors, hydraulic power units, servovalves. Electromagnetic strip stabilizing systems. QA systems, on-line oil layer determination, on-line surface roughness measurement, on-line material property measurement.

EMPCO
910 Hopkins St.
Whitby, ON L1N 6A9 Canada
P: +1.905.666.1744
info@empco.com
www.empco.com

- Dir.—Robert Wunsche
- Mech. Design Mgr.—Arthur Craigwell
- Special Projects Designer—Marek Michalski
- Plant Mgr.—Steve Bumbacco

PRODUCTS and/or SERVICES:
Supplier of EAFs and ancillary electrometallurgical equipment to steelmakers. Products include: SIOS™ simplified iron ore to steel process used directly in EAF with pellet technology; AUTO-REACT™ electrode arms with automatic impedance control; UNIGATE™ slag door sealing; SCORPIO™ temperature and sampling device through wall panel; SSR™ self-supporting roof; UNILANCE™ 40-MW burner/lance; CuRe™ (Copper)/FeRe™ (carbon steel) panels; OMNIVALVE™ automatic panel temperature control; and INCONEL ducts.

ENCORE MATERIALS INC.
P.O. Box 58184
Pittsburgh, PA 15209 USA
P: +1.412.848.1916
encore.david13@gmail.com
davidj1142@gmail.com

- Pres.—David J. Jacobs
- Vice Pres. Oprs.—Faith Goetz
- Research—Jeddi Tomich

PRODUCTS and/or SERVICES:
Recycles spent materials including mag carbon ladle bricks, pre-cast alumina ladle bottoms, ladle slidegates and nozzles, 65% and above alumina ladle bricks, EAF/BOF bricks from relines, and alumina grinding wheels.

ENERTIME
1 rue du Moulin des Bruyères
Courbevoie, 92400 France
P: +33.0.1.75.43.15.40
gilles.david@enertime.com
www.enertime.com

SUPPLIERS of EQUIPMENT, PRODUCTS and SERVICES

- Pres.—Gilles David
- Sales Mgr.—Siavash Barkhordar

PRODUCTS and or SERVICES:
Organic rankine cycle units that can produce electricity from industrial waste heat. Range: 100 kWel to 6,000 kWel. High-temperature, high-power heat pump to produce heat from industrial waste heat. Range 2.5 MWth to 7 MWth. Natural gas turbo-expander from 300 kW to 3 MW.

No. of Employees: 28.

ENPROTECH INDUSTRIAL TECHNOLOGIES LLC
4259 E. 49th St.
Cleveland, OH 44125 USA
P: +1.216.206.0800

3234 N. St. Road 39
La Porte, IN 46350 USA
P: +1.219.326.6900
dsnyder@enprotech.com
www.enpromech.com

- Pres.—Bob Owen
- Div. Sales Mgr.—Dave Snyder

PRODUCTS and/or SERVICES:
Enprotech specializes in servicing, repairing, and optimizing heavy manufacturing equipment to increase productivity. With more than 100 years of OEM heavy industrial manufacturing know-how, from remanufactured components to roll, caster and mandrel systems, Enprotech delivers optimized solutions both on- and off-site to drive productivity optimization. Operating 24/7 to meet all customer needs, especially emergency repairs. Solutions include: component manufacturing and repair, machining, welding, part replacement services through direct shipment to customer locations or on-site installation of manufactured replacement parts. Design services, engineering solutions and more.

ENVEA INC.
2623 Kaneville Ct.
Geneva, IL 60134 USA
P: +1.630.262.4400
F: +1.630.262.6220
sales.usa@envea.global
www.envea.global

- Pres.—Malek Hattar
- Vice Pres. Engrg.—Frank Alvarez
- Adv. Mgr.—Kathleen Klimek
- Acctg.—Lauri Prohaska

PRODUCTS and/or SERVICES:
Multi-gas and dust analyzers for emissions, process monitors for solids and bulk powder, particulate and broken bag leak detectors and filter leak monitors, mercury analyzers, and ambient air analyzers and fenceline ambient monitors.

No. of Employees: 12.

E.P.R. S.R.L.
Via Don Angelo Questa 41
Vobarno (BS), 25079 Italy
P: +39.0365.61181
F: +39.0365.599191
info@epr.it
www.epr.it

- Chief Exec. Officer and Sales Mgr.—Nicola Saletti
- Pres.—Eugenio Saletti
- Sec.—Barbara Saletti
- Chief Engr.—Matteo Tessadori

PRODUCTS and/or SERVICES:
Lathe machines, milling machines, welding machines and cardan shafts from size 180 to 890.

ERIE COPPER WORKS
230 N. State Road
Medina, OH 44256 USA
P: +1.330.725.5590
F: +1.330.723.0267
www.eriecopperworks.com

- Chief Exec. Officer—David A. Surgeon
- Pres.—David G. Berg,
  dave.berg@eriecopperworks.us
- Vice Pres.—Jesse Barrowcliff,
  jesse.barrowcliff@eriecopperworks.us

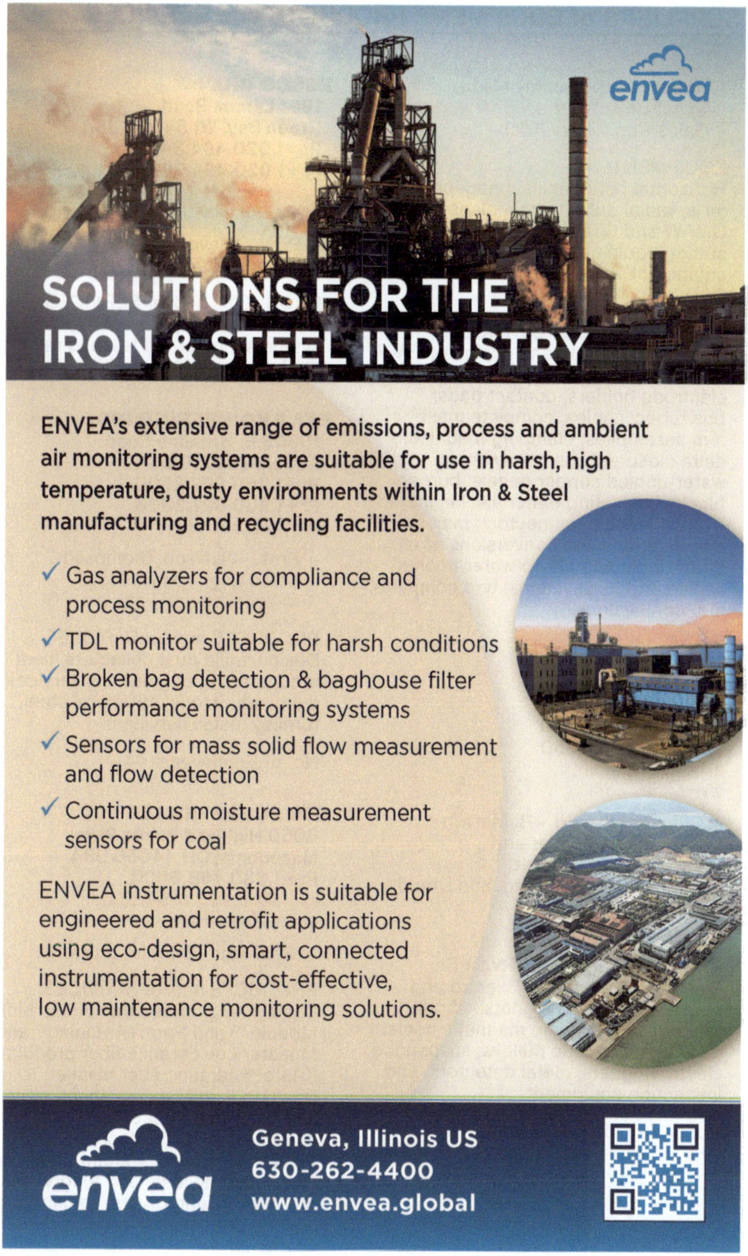

SUPPLIERS of EQUIPMENT, PRODUCTS and SERVICES

- Admin. Asst.—Tammy Mikut,
  tammy.mikut@eriecopperworks.us
- Sales Rep.—Terry Koch

EQUIPMENT:
Horizontal boring mills, bridgeport mills, radial drills, lathes, planers, GMAW and GTAW equipment, plasma-cutting equipment, pipe bender, NDT equipment, overhead crane system, CAD.

PRODUCTS and/or SERVICES:
Repair, fabrication and design of EAF/LMF components for AC/DC furnaces; electrode holders; contact pads; bus tubes; cables; complete mast arm assemblies; clamping modules; delta closures; bus bar systems; water-cooled copper panels; burner blocks; insulating materials; laminated shunts; flexible connectors; major modifications and conversions of all types, including air- to water-cooled cables and bus systems, and complete arm conversions.

ERIEZ
2200 Asbury Road
Erie, PA 16506 USA
P: +1.814.835.6000
F: +1.814.838.4960
eriez@eriez.com
www.eriez.com

- Chmn. of the Bd.—R. Merwin
- Chief Exec. Officer and Pres.—L. Guenthardt
- Global Sr. Dir. of Mktg. and Brand Mgmt.—J. Blicha
- Pur. Mgr.—T. Popoff

PRODUCTS and/or SERVICES:
Magnetic skelp drums, electro and permanent lifting magnets, vibratory feeders, high-volume magnetic coolant cleaners, magnetic pulleys, suspended electromagnets, metal detectors, and inspection equipment.

No. of Employees: 860.

ESSCO INC.
1991 Larsen Road
Green Bay, WI 54303 USA
P: +1.920.494.3480
F: +1.920.494.3483
sales@esscoincorporated.com
www.esscoincorporated.com

- Pres.—Steve Whitman
- Sales Mgr.—John Ryf

PRODUCTS and/or SERVICES:
Roll cleaning equipment. Doctor systems, doctor blades, and related engineering and consulting work.

ETA ENGINEERING INC.
10605 E. Baseline Road
Avilla, IN 46710 USA
P: +1.260.897.2800
F: +1.260.897.2338
www.etaapc.com

- Pres.—Jamison Thompson
- Sales Engr.—Kevin Floyd,
  kfloyd@etaapc.com

PRODUCTS and/or SERVICES:
Design/build dust collectors, heat recuperators, engineering services, ductwork, hoods, structural steel, turnkey install services.

No. of Employees: 44.

ETS SCHAEFER LLC
8050 Highland Pointe Pkwy.
Macedonia, OH 44056 USA
P: +1.330.468.6600
sales@etsschaefer.com
www.etsschaefer.com

- Gen. Mgr.—Dennis Guilmette

PRODUCTS and/or SERVICES:
Custom-engineered monolithic Monster Module™ and Perm+A+Lining® and Monster Loc ceramic fiber products. K-Lite™ ceramic fiber blanket; traditional and custom shape stud-weld and anchored fiber block. Furnace shells, roofs, walls, doors (with PosiSeal® closure system), flues, ducts and dampers; ladle and tundish covers, pre-heaters and dryers; soaking pit covers; protective thermal screens and

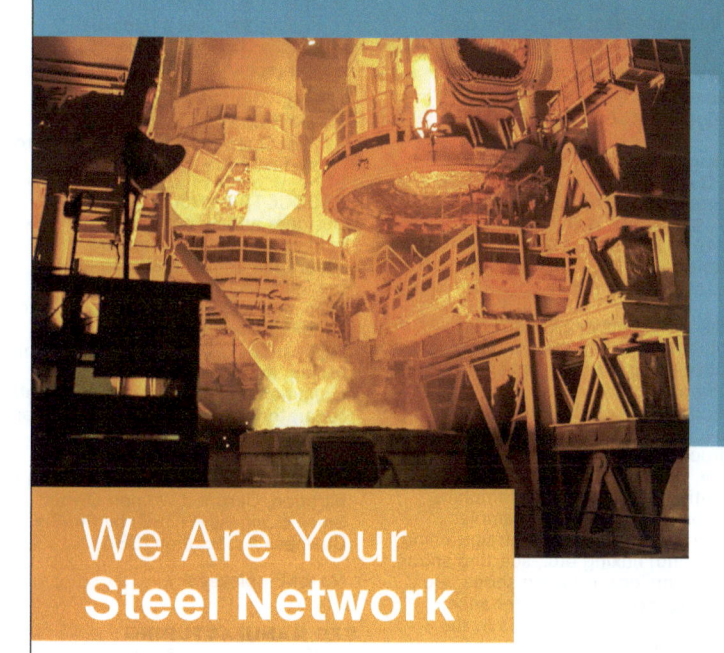

SUPPLIERS of EQUIPMENT, PRODUCTS and SERVICES

covers. Relining and refurbishment of existing equipment. Field installation and repair services.

No. of Employees: 50+

EVERTZ KG, EGON/ETS
Birkenweiher 60–80
Solingen, D-42651 Germany

Mailing Address:
P.O. Box 101008
Solingen, D-42610 Germany
P: +49.212.223.11.0
F: +49.212.223.11.149
info@evertz-group.com
www.evertz-group.com

PRODUCTS and/or SERVICES: Continuous casting technology, electroplating, mechanical engineering, grinding technology, welding technology, steel construction, slab logistics, electromagnets, hydroengineering, plant engineering. Scope of work includes setup and operation of individual or complete business segments, for example: finishing shops including straightening, ultrasound, fluxing etc., scarfing shops, cutting services, grinding shops, etc., including repair and maintenance. Also processes titanium within the production process as well.

ETS Evertz Technology Service U.S.A. Inc.
Midd Cities Industrial Complex
2601 S. Verity Pkwy., Bldg. 21A
Middletown, OH 45044 USA
P: +1.513.422.8400
F: +1.513.422.9400
smiller@etsusainc.com
www.evertzusa.com

– Div. Mgr.—Steve Miller

PRODUCTS and/or SERVICES: Grinding of slabs, blooms, billets, steel slugs, rounds, ingots, etc., including torch cutting in in-house facility. Range of duty covers the entire responsibility for production and quality according to ISO 9001-2015.

EXACTRATION
194 Harshfield Lane
Shepherdsville, KY 40165 USA
P: +1.502.531.9018 (Office);
   +1.502.376.6442 (Mobile)
sales@exactration.com
www.exactration.com

– Pres.—Debbie Terrell,
  P:+1.502.377.0009
– Chief Oper. Officer—Brent D. Terrell,
  P: +1.502.376.6442

PRODUCTS and/or SERVICES: Designer and manufacturer of industrial liquid filtration and separation equipment/systems for the following industries: steel and aluminum mills; industrial wastewater; grinding, honing and polishing applications; parts washers; machining, milling, and turning. Products and equipment include: bar-type magnetic separators (patented technology); oil separators (patented technology); bag filtration; custom-engineered skids; vacuum, pressure and/or drum filtration. Certified Woman Owned Small Business (WOSB) by the Small Business Association (SBA).

No. of Employees: 7.

EZG MANUFACTURING
1833 N. Riverview Road
Malta, OH 43758 USA
P: +1.800.417.9272 (Toll-Free)
sales@ezgmfg.com
www.ezgmfg.com

PRODUCTS and/or SERVICES: Mobile refractory mixers ranging in size from 300 to 3,000+ lbs. All mixers are fully customizable but come standard with hydraulic drive, hydraulic dump as well as bolt-in abrasion-resistant drum liners and variable speed control for the paddles. EZG Manufacturing also offers a refractory mixer/pump combination with a unique cleanout on the pump for minimal downtime changing wear plates. All products are built in the U.S. at EZG's Malta, OH, facility. With expertise in custom fabrication, any and all models can be

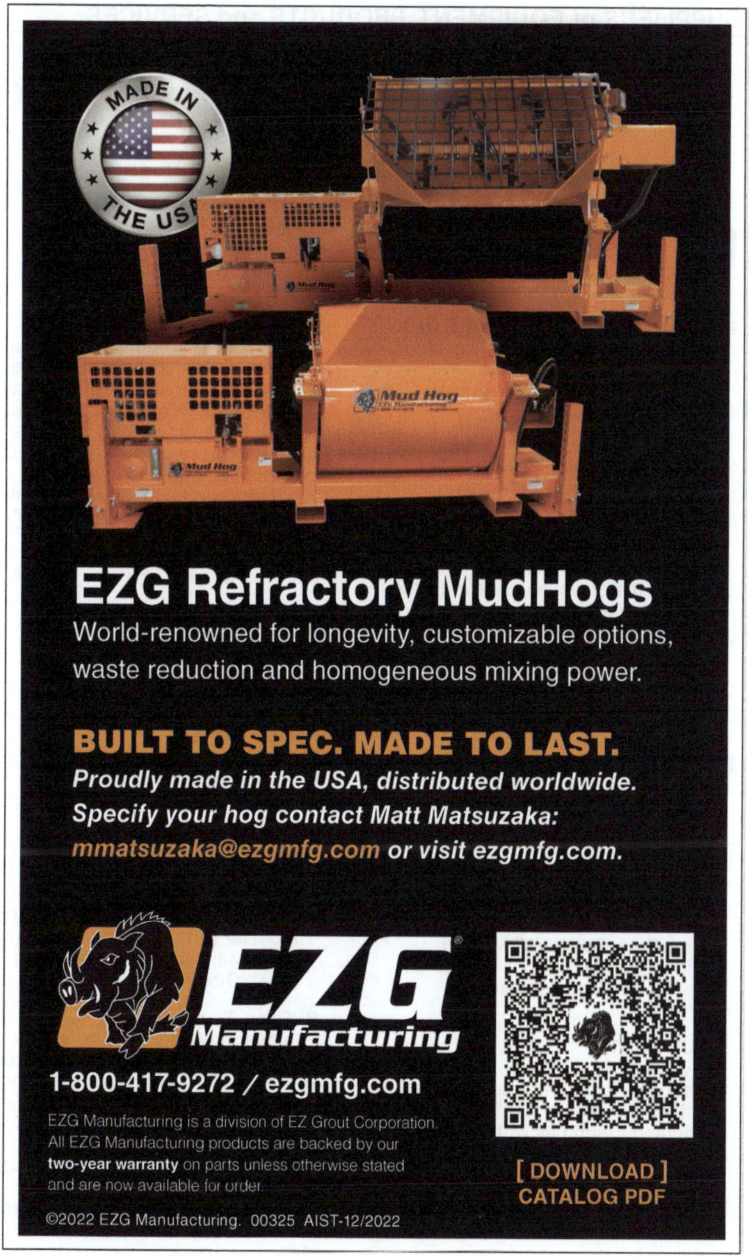

See listing page 356

SUPPLIERS of EQUIPMENT, PRODUCTS and SERVICES

built for specific customer needs. All equipment comes with a 30-day money back guarantee as well as a two-year warranty.

F

FABREEKA INTERNATIONAL INC.
1023 Turnpike St.
Stoughton, MA 02072 USA
P: +1.800.322.7352 (Toll-Free)
info@fabreeka.com
www.fabreeka.com

- Gen. Mgr.—David Meyer
- Corporate Contr.—Joseph Micciche

PRODUCTS and/or SERVICES:
Structural thermal break in buildings, impact shock, vibration and noise isolation materials, engineering design service available for use on cranes, mill tables, foundations, scales and stops, and any equipment requiring protection from shock and vibration.

No. of Employees: 33.

FABRIS INC.
1216 S. Service Road
Stoney Creek, ON L8E 5C4 Canada
P: +1.905.643.4111
F: +1.905.643.3355
insidesales@fabris.com
www.fabris.com

- Pres.—Carole P. Fabris
- Vice Pres. Oprs.—Bill Mackie
- Vice Pres. Sales—Tom R. Statham
- Team Lead Eng.—Jonathan Thompson

EQUIPMENT:
Fully equipped CNC machining operations, including 5-axis multi-task machining, EDM, DMLS 3D printing technology, high bay with 24-ft. clearance, 40-ton lifting capacity, certified ISO 9001:2015 and API Q1 (9th edition) Quality Management System, fully integrated ERP system.

PRODUCTS and/or SERVICES:
Fabris guiding systems for rod, bar and shape mills, including 2-, 3- and 4-roller entry guides; FABCAM® mill alignment camera; Fabris SCS® spiral cooling system; rest bars; twisters; slitters; delivery guides; and various mill spare components. In-house engineering, design, and consulting to all major rod, bar and shape mill designs.

No. of Employees: 85.

FALK PLI
Corporate Office:
6370 Ameriplex Dr., Suite 100
Portage, IN 46368 USA

Remote Offices:
Mobile, AL and Pittsburgh, PA
P: +1.888.965.1143 (Toll-Free)
www.falk-pli.com

- Chief Exec. Officer and Pres.—Michael Falk
- Chief Oper. Officer and Dir. of H.R.—Dorothy Falk
- Project Mgrs.—Jeff Nix (IN), Nate Plooster (IN), Mark Wellensiek (IN), Scott Meltzer (IN), Jerrod Bolz (PA), Jason Gibson (AL)

PRODUCTS and/or SERVICES:
Engineering and surveying services including: precision 3D laser metrology and alignment; advanced laser tracking measurement and alignment; advanced laser scanning and 3D modeling for as-built condition and design; structural verification; structural deformation, interference, and clash detection reporting; land surveying; construction administration; BIM ready, live 3D

FABRIS®
a solutions provider.

With over 50 years in the Steel Industry, we have a wide variety of solutions to keep your mill rolling.

Traversing Restbars
allow for quick and accurate pass changes

- Honors existing mill attachment points and guide base, no machining on your stands required
- Made from stainless steel and specifically tailored to your mill ensuring perfect fit, operation and longevity

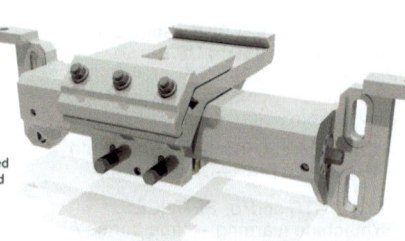

Our **roller entry guides** keep your product on the pass

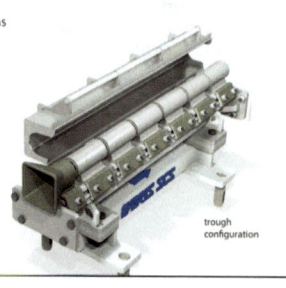

- Single point, centralized adjustment during operation
- 2, 3 and 4 roller configurations
- Rigid, stainless steel construction
- Broad size range

SCS
SPIRAL COOLING SYSTEM

Maximize your mill speed while meeting your quenching requirements on all bar sizes. Not just controlled cooling, but *correct cooling*

- Fewer surface defects and better scale control
- Available in Box, Trough and Restbar-mounted configurations

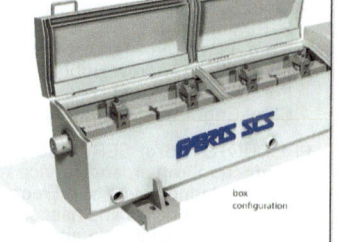

box configuration

Contact Us

www.fabris.com   ✉ info@fabris.com
☎ 905.643.4111

trough configuration

See listing page 358

SUPPLIERS of EQUIPMENT, PRODUCTS and SERVICES

crane and crane rail measurement during operations.

No. of Employees: 45.

FALKONRY INC.
10020 N. De Anza Blvd., Suite 200
Cupertino, CA 95014 USA
P: +1.408.461.9286
info@falkonry.com
www.falkonry.com

- Chief Exec. Officer—Nikunj Mehta
- Exec. Vice Pres.—Crick Waters

PRODUCTS and/or SERVICES: AI/machine learning — time-series AI product suite, predictive maintenance, condition monitoring.

No. of Employees: 50.

FARRAND CONTROLS, a Div. of Ruhle Co. Inc.
99 Wall St.
Valhalla, NY 10595 USA
P: +1.914.761.2600
F: +1.914.287.4038
sales@ruhle.com
www.ruhle.com

- Chief Exec. Officer and Pres.—Frank S. Ruhle
- Exec. Vice Pres.—Robert E. Ruhle
- Sales Mgr.—Andrew Hubbard
- Pur. Agt.—Frank Lantz
- Chief Engr.—James Brentano

PRODUCTS and/or SERVICES: Manufacture, repair, and service rotary and linear Inductosyn® and Electrosyn® position transducers and associated electronics. Specialize in application of linear Inductosyn cassette transducers for hydraulic cylinder positioning in AGC systems for rolling mills.

No. of Employees: 68.

FASTWAY INC.
9794 Leavitt Road
State Rte. 58
Elyria, OH 44035 USA
P: +1.440.707.4016
F: +1.440.707.4020
tearls@fastwayinc.com
www.fastwayinc.com
www.fastwaysafety.com

- Gen. Mgr.—Tom Earls

PRODUCTS and/or SERVICES: Industrial baghouse service; inspections, maintenance and repairs; NESHAP and Title V inspections; baghouse parts, safety equipment and supplies sales.

No. of Employees: 6.

FEDERAL-MOGUL DEVA GMBH
Schulstr. 20, Postfach 1160
Stadtallendorf, D-35260 Germany
P: +49.6428.7010
F: +49.6428.701108
info@deva.de
www.deva-bearings.com

- Gen. Mgr.—Stefan Rittmann
- Mfg. Mgr.—Hendryk Pfeuffer
- Financial Mgr.—Wilhelm Rönninger
- Application Mgr.—Hubert Kraeuter
- Regional Sales Mgr.—Willian Baretto

PRODUCTS and/or SERVICES: Design, manufacturing and distribution of maintenance-free, self-lubricating sliding bearings.

No. of Employees: 200.

FERROSER LTD.
Ebubekir Caddesi No. 30/1 Sancaktepe
Istanbul, 34887 Turkey
P: +90.216.466.5980
F: +90.216.466.5984
info@ferroser.com.tr
www.ferroser.com.tr

- Chief Exec. Officer—Serdar Ozdogan
- Sec.—Sukran Bakir
- Vice Pres. Sales—Ismail Ozalp

PRODUCTS and/or SERVICES: Tundish metering nozzles, flying and stationary nozzles for nozzle

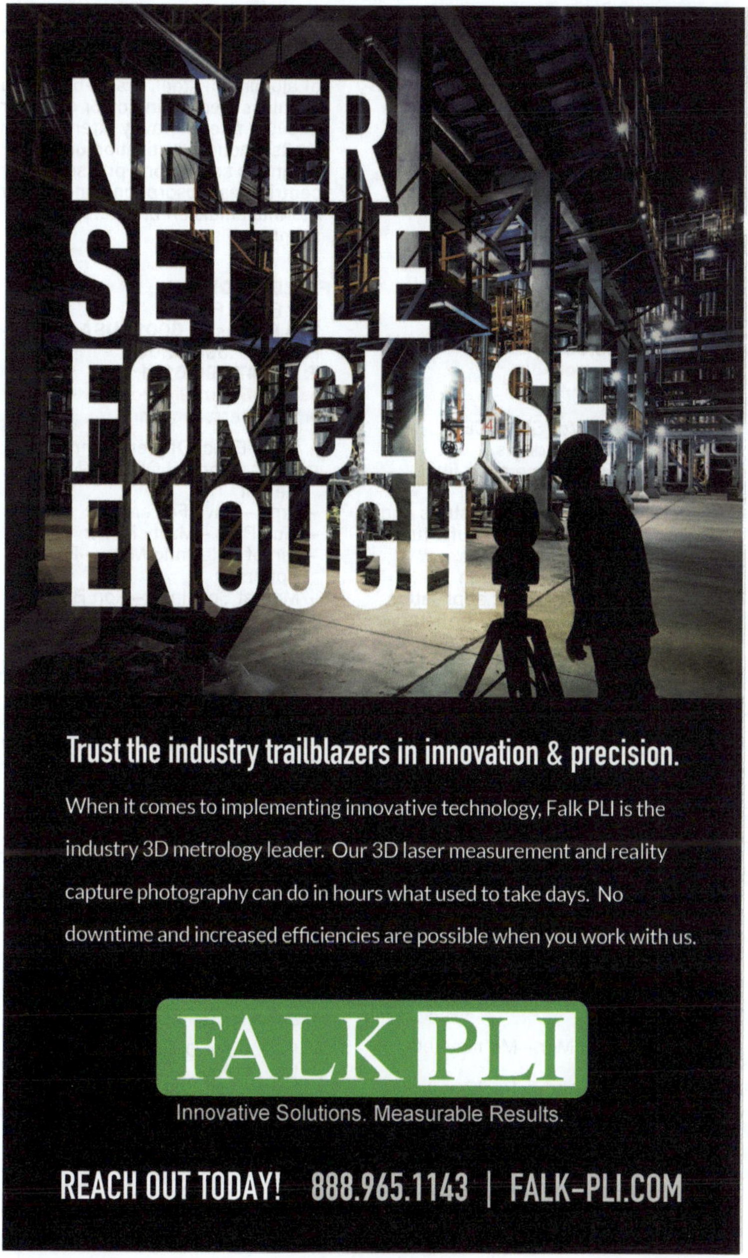

See listing page 358

SUPPLIERS of EQUIPMENT, PRODUCTS and SERVICES

changing systems in tundishes, nozzle changing mechanisms, ladle slidegate mechanisms, hardfaced wear plates for cement, mining and steel industry, distribution of tubular Cu molds, graphite electrodes, refractories.

No. of Employees: 30.

FIBRECAST
3264 Mainway
Burlington, ON L7M 1A7 Canada
P: +1.866.323.0084
info@fibrecast.com
www.fibrecast.com

PRODUCTS and/or SERVICES: Vacuum-formed products, polycrystalline fiber, ceramic fiber, modules, textiles, ropes, high-temperature die-cut gasket/strips and precast refractory. As a manufacturer and distributor of refractories, FibreCast can custom-design solutions to meet specific application requirements. Fibrecast's proprietary tooling and mold design allows for a 1- to 2-week turnaround on new vacuum-formed shapes from drawing board to prototype.

FILTERTECH INC.
113 Fairgrounds Dr.
P.O. Box 527
Manlius, NY 13104 USA
P: +1.315.682.8815;
F: +1.315.682.8825;
info@filtertech.com
www.filtertech.com

- Principal and Dir.—Joseph El-Hindi
- Dir./Qual. Control Mgr.—Lawrence El-Hindi
- Domestic Sales Mgr. and Mktg. Mgr.—Jamal El-Hindi
- Foreign Sales Mgr.—Mohammed Al-Bedour
- Prodn. Mgr.—Andriy Pechenyy
- Engrg. Mgr.—Mehdi Meghezzi
- Field Svce. Mgr.—Richard Riddell
- Pur. Mgr.—Jill Laskowski

PRODUCTS and/or SERVICES: Designs and builds complete rolling mill coolant filtration systems for rolling of aluminum, steel, brass, bronze, and stainless steel, using oil or emulsion. Vacuum filters, gravity filters, retention tanks, vacuum distillation units, magnetic separators, pressure filters, centrifuges, absorption candle filters, thermal emulsion breakers and oil skimmers.

FINZER ROLLER
129 Rawls Road
Des Plaines, IL 60018 USA
P: +1.847.390.6200
F: +1.847.390.6201
sales@finzerroller.com
www.finzerroller.com

- Chief Exec. Officer—John Finzer
- Chief Financial Officer—Michael Hefner
- Pres.—Dave Finzer
- Vice Pres.—Marty Finzer
- Dir. of Sales and Mktg.—Randy Apperson
- Market Specialist—Ron Bradley

PRODUCTS and/or SERVICES: New and refurbished rubber and polyurethane rollers, in-house machine shop for new cores and repairs, specialty roller products and coatings, multiple manufacturing plants providing national coverage.

No. of Employees: 300.

FIVES GROUP

Fives Bronx Inc.
8817 Pleasantwood Ave. NW
North Canton, OH 44720 USA
P: +1.330.244.1960
F: +1.330.244.1961
fivesbronx-sales@fivesgroup.com
www.fivesgroup.com

- Pres.—Jon Dunn
- Dir. of Oprs.—Gary Lisitsa
- Dir. of Sales and Mktg.—Ricardo Sierra
- Mgr. of Aftermarket, Sales—Carter Dulaney
- Mgr. of Aftermarket, Engrg.—Matthew Owens

SUPPLIERS OF EQUIPMENT, PRODUCTS and SERVICES

PRODUCTS and/or SERVICES:
A complete range of tube finishing equipment: hydrostatic pipe testers, end finishing machines, and packaging solutions for seamless and welded tubular products, as well as tube mills.

Fives Bronx Ltd.
Ham Lane, Kingswinford
West Midlands, DY6 7JU U.K.
P: +44.0.1384.286829
fivesbronxuk-sales@fivesgroup.com
www.fivesgroup.com

- Managing Dir.—Jon Dunn
- Spares Mgr.—Stewart Lane

PRODUCTS and/or SERVICES:
Manufacturer of tube, pipe, bar and section straighteners.

Fives North American Combustion Inc.
4455 E. 71st St.
Cleveland, OH 44105 USA
P: +1.800.626.3477 (Toll-Free)
F: +1.216.373.4237
fna.sales@fivesgroup.com
www.fivesgroup.com

- Chief Exec. Officer—Stephan Paech
- Vice Pres., Sales and Mktg.—Charles Schroer
- Vice Pres., Engrg. and Technology—Tom Robertson

PRODUCTS and/or SERVICES:
Provides an integrated array of products and services, complementing combustion burner products which focus on lowest emissions, highest efficiency and decarbonization strategies, process tuning, fuel trains, safety PLC-based control panels, furnace automation solutions, IIoT smart manufacturing and more.

North American Construction Services Ltd.
5000 Commerce Ave.
Birmingham, AL 35210 USA
P: +1.800.786.0849 (Toll-Free)
nacs.sales@fivesgroup.com
www.fivesgroup.com

- Chief Exec. Officer—Stephan Paech

- Vice Pres., Sales and Mktg.—Charles Schroer
- Gen. Mgr.—Matt Owen

PRODUCTS and/or SERVICES:
Provides steel and aluminum processing furnace solutions and complete furnace life cycle services: small repairs to rebuilds, refractory services and outages, maintenance, relines, and more.

Fives Steel Business Line
c/o Fives Stein SA
108-112 Ave. de la Liberté
Maisons-Alfort, 94701 France
P: +33.1.45.18.65.35;
  +33.3.20.49.35.00;
  +1.419.522.1080 (in the U.S.)
steel@fivesgroup.com
www.fivesgroup.com

- Exec. Vice Pres.—Philippe Cruiziat
- Vice Pres., Sales—Kevin Bertermann, Kristiaan Van Teutem, Stéphane Mehrain
- Dir., Innovation and Technology—Jean-Paul Nauzin

PRODUCTS and/or SERVICES:
Provides process expertise, innovative technologies and digital tools for steelmakers: strategic consulting and process optimization services; reheating furnaces; induction heaters; cold rolling mills and strip processing lines for carbon, stainless and silicon steels.

Fives ST. Corp.
1 Park Centre Dr., Suite 210
Wadsworth, OH 44281 USA
P: +1.234.217.9070
F: +1.234.217.8629
steel@fivesgroup.com
www.fivesgroup.com

- Pres.—Daniel Balcer
- Vice Pres. Sales—Kevin Bertermann
- Exec. Asst.—Laurie Sutherland

PRODUCTS and/or SERVICES:
Process expertise, consulting, design, engineering services. Furnaces, cold rolling mills, skinpass mills, strip processing lines.

SUPPLIERS of EQUIPMENT, PRODUCTS and SERVICES

FLAME TECHNOLOGIES INC.
703 Cypress Creek Road
Cedar Park, TX 78613 USA
P: +1.800.749.3682 (Toll-Free)
www.flametechnologies.com

PRODUCTS and/or SERVICES:
Caster torches, emergency cutoff torches, cutting nozzles, scrap-cutting torches and nozzles, billet slab-cutting torches, gas manifold cabinets, exothermic cutting equipment, carbon arc gouging equipment, safety equipment, and safety training. Provider of HydroMist flash evaporative cooling fans.

FLANDERS
8101 Baumgart Road
Evansville, IN 47725 USA
P: +1.855.875.5888 (Toll-Free);
+1.812.567.7421
F: +1.812.867.2687
info@flandersinc.com
www.flandersinc.com

- Chief Exec. Officer—John Oliver

PRODUCTS and/or SERVICES:
Manufactures and repairs large electric motors, power systems and aftermarket products, and engineers systems integration and automation solutions for metals, mining, power utilities, alternative energy and other heavy industries.

FLETCHER ENGINEERED SOLUTIONS
402 High St.
Huntington, WV 25705 USA
P: +1.304.525.7811
sales@jhfletcher.com
www.jhfletcher.com

- Chief Exec. Officer—Greg Hinshaw
- Pres.—Rod Duncan
- Sales Mgr. of New Business Dev.—Jeff Kemper
- Sales Engr.—Cass O'Connell

EQUIPMENT:
Demolition machines, door closers, ladle access devices, material handling equipment, furnace/de-bricking equipment.

PRODUCTS and/or SERVICES:
Engineered equipment, engineering surveys, specialized equipment design, safety audits.

No. of Employees: 200.

FLEXOSPAN
P.O. Box 515 Railroad St.
Sandy Lake, PA 16145 USA
P: +1.800.245.0396 (Toll-Free)
F: +1.724.376.3864
www.flexospan.com

- Pres.—Lauri Frederick
- Vice Pres.—Laurel McLallen
- Sec./Treas.—Lou Ann Miller
- Vice Pres. Sales—Jessica Hoovler
- Chief Engr.—Scot Nottingham
- Business Dev.—Tom Hubert

PRODUCTS and/or SERVICES:
Metal building panels and accessories.

No. of Employees: 49.

FLOLO CORP., THE
1400 Harvester Road
West Chicago, IL 60185 USA
P: +1.630.595.1010
F: +1.630.595.1327
www.flolo.com

- Gen. Mgr.—George Flolo
- Svcs. Mgr.—Gregg Flolo
- Chief Engr.—Michael McBlaine
- Sales Rep.—Ray Ossowski

PRODUCTS and/or SERVICES:
Electric motors, electric motor controls, VFDs, engineered control systems, motion control equipment, electric motor repair, vibration analysis, mechanical repair, electronic repair.

No. of Employees: 47.

Get Top-Notch Steel Industry Education & Endless Networking Opportunities at

AIST's Spring 2023 Technology Training Conferences

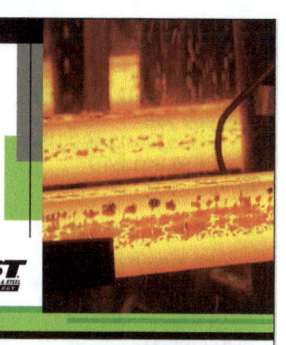

Core Steelmaking Processes

Modern Electric Steelmaking —
A Practical Training Seminar
- 20–24 February 2023
- San Antonio, Texas, USA
- CMC Steel Texas

Cold Rolling Fundamentals —
A Practical Training Seminar
- 20–23 February 2023
- San Antonio, Texas, USA
- Steel Dynamics Inc. – Flat Roll Group Southwest-Sinton Division

Advanced Cold Rolling: 201
- 23–24 February 2023
- San Antonio, Texas, USA

Long Products Rolling —
A Practical Training Seminar
- 28 February–2 March 2023
- Orlando, Fla., USA
- Nucor Steel Florida Inc.

The Making, Shaping and Treating of Steel: 101
- 21–22 March 2023
- Indianapolis, Ind., USA
- Nucor Steel–Indiana

Essential Support Systems

Steel Mill Combustion Thermal Systems
- 21–23 March 2023
- Cleveland, Ohio, USA
- Fives North American Combustion Inc.

29th Crane Symposium
- 12–14 June 2023
- Pittsburgh, Pa., USA

Product & Technology Development

Scrap Supplements & Alternate Ironmaking 9
- 6–8 March 2023
- Orlando, Fla., USA

Digital Transformation Forum for the Steel Industry
- 7–8 March 2023
- Pittsburgh, Pa., USA

International Symposium on New Developments in Advanced High-Strength Sheet Steels
- 19–22 June 2023
- Vail, Colo., USA

AIST is committed to presenting superior conferences, expositions and technical training to better serve those involved in the iron and steel community, including steel manufacturers, suppliers, consumers and academics.

To register and get updated conference information, visit AIST.org

SUPPLIERS of EQUIPMENT, PRODUCTS and SERVICES

FLUIDTECHNIK USA INC.
P.O. Box 715
Uwchland, PA 19480 USA
P: +1.610.321.2407
F: +1.610.321.2409
jpalmer@fluidtechnikusa.com
www.fluidtechnikusa.com

- Pres.—John Palmer
- Pur. Agt. and Inside Sales—Carol Palmer

EQUIPMENT:
Fluid power systems and controls.

PRODUCTS and/or SERVICES:
Inoxihp water hydraulic plunger pumps, valves and controls; EPE and Fluidtechnik bladder, diaphragm, and piston-type accumulators; FOX pressure switches and diaphragm accumulators; Delta Delage high-pressure ball valves; Dusterloh radial piston motors, air motors and air starters; Rollstar planetary gear reducers and hydraulic motors; complete water (descaling) and oil hydraulic systems.

No. of Employees: 12.

FLUOR METALS
100 Fluor Daniel Dr.
Greenville, SC 29607 USA
P: +1.864.281.4400
bradley.godbey@fluor.com
www.fluor.com

- Vice Pres. and Gen. Mgr.—Harish Jammula
- Sr. Dir. — Oprs.—Vince Rosales
- Dir. of Sales—Bradley Godbey
- Sr. Advisor—Joe Turner

PRODUCTS and/or SERVICES:
Global engineering, procurement and construction (EPC) services for the metals industry.

FOERSTER INSTRUMENTS INC.
140 Industry Dr.
Pittsburgh, PA 15275 USA
P: +1.412.788.8976
sales.us@foerstergroup.com
www.foerstergroup.com

- Pres.—Jason Wilburn

PRODUCTS and/or SERVICES:
NDT equipment, training and service.

No. of Employees: 61.

FORCE CONTROL INDUSTRIES INC.
3660 Dixie Hwy.
Fairfield, OH 45014 USA
P: +1.513.868.0900
F: +1.513.868.2105
info@forcecontrol.com
www.forcecontrol.com

PRODUCTS and/or SERVICES:
Industrial clutches and brakes featuring oil shear technology, including MagnaShear motor brakes and crane brakes, Positorq tension brakes, Posistop pneumatic brakes, and Posidyne clutch brakes.

No. of Employees: 40.

FOREMOST ENVIRONMENTAL CONSULTING INC.
P.O. Box 2086
Cranberry Twp., PA 16066 USA
P: +1.724.776.5369
jskubak@zbzoom.net

- Pres.—James Skubak

PRODUCTS and/or SERVICES:
Environmental consulting services for the primary metals industries, including: air emissions inventories, reporting and permitting; NPDES permitting; hazardous waste management, spill prevention and DOT/HazMat training; environmental contingency plans, including SPCC, FRP, ICP, HWCP and RMP; stormwater pollution prevention plans; Tier 2 and TRI reporting.

FOSBEL INC.
20600 Sheldon Road
Cleveland, OH 44142 USA
P: +1.800.553.7887 (Toll-Free); +1.216.362.3900
fosbel.inc@fosbel.com
www.fosbel.com

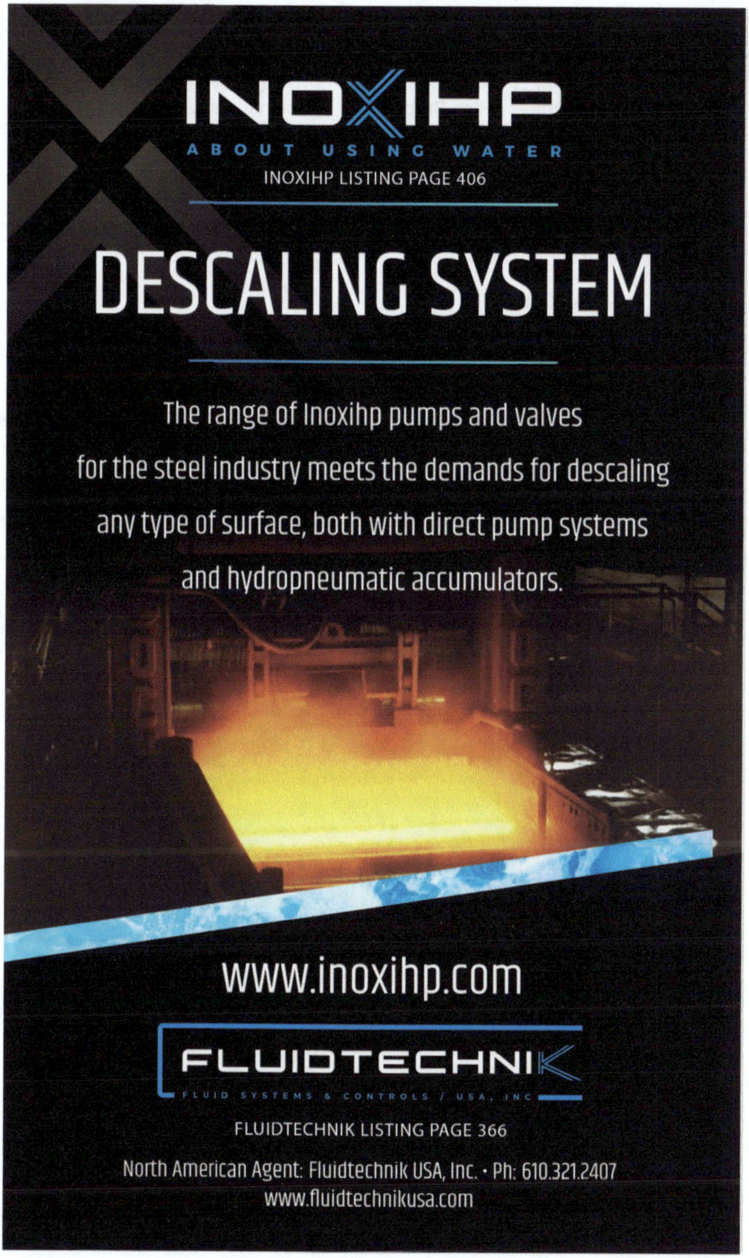
INOXIHP
ABOUT USING WATER
INOXIHP LISTING PAGE 406
DESCALING SYSTEM
The range of Inoxihp pumps and valves
for the steel industry meets the demands for descaling
any type of surface, both with direct pump systems
and hydropneumatic accumulators.
www.inoxihp.com
FLUIDTECHNIK
FLUID SYSTEMS & CONTROLS / USA, INC
FLUIDTECHNIK LISTING PAGE 366
North American Agent: Fluidtechnik USA, Inc. • Ph: 610.321.2407
www.fluidtechnikusa.com

SUPPLIERS of EQUIPMENT, PRODUCTS and SERVICES

- Chief Exec. Officer—Eric Yaszemski
- Chief Financial Officer—Rich Barberic
- Global Dir. H.R.—Robin Carlin
- Global Safety Dir.—Jason Barnes
- Managing Dir. — Americas and Business Unit Dir. — Glass—Bob Chambers
- Managing Dir. — Asia-Pacific and Business Unit Dir. — Coke—Tom McKinley
- Tech. Dir.—Sean Gilbride
- Mktg. Dir./Financial Analyst—Bob Forsythe
- Vice Pres. Business Dev.—Ernie Goffi

PRODUCTS and/or SERVICES:
Complete coke battery maintenance program, including proprietary COMIT™ condition monitoring system, ceramic welding, gunning, and unique brickwork technologies such as MICOWALL™ and MONOWALL™ patented coke oven wall and corbel rebuild systems.

No. of Employees: 500 worldwide.

Wahl Refractory Solutions LLC, a Fosbel Co.
767 State Rte. 19 S
Fremont, OH 43420 USA
P: +1.800.837.WAHL (9245) (Toll-Free);
 +1.419.334.2658
info@wahlref.com
www.wahlref.com

PRODUCTS and/or SERVICES:
Designs, manufactures and formulates custom-made monolithic and pre-cast refractory solutions.

FUCHS LUBRICANTS CO.
17050 Lathrop Ave.
Harvey, IL 60426 USA
P: +1.708.333.8900
www.fuchs.com/us

- Sales—Nathan Lechene
- Mktg.—Jen Martin,
 marketing.us@fuchs.com

EQUIPMENT:
Oil and lubricant blending, chemical reactors, grease manufacturing, graphite processing.

PRODUCTS and/or SERVICES:
High-temperature, high-performance, water-resistant greases, hot and cold rolling oils, gear oils, hydraulic oils, casting fluids, morgoils, forging lubricants, rust preventives, wire rope lubricants, automotive approved pre-lubes. Seven manufacturing plants in North America.

No. of Employees: 5,000.

G

GALLETTA ENGINEERING CORP.
501 Holiday Dr., Suite 105
Pittsburgh, PA 15220 USA
P: +1.412.261.3357
F: +1.412.281.8489
mail@galletta.com
www.galletta.com

- Managing Partner, Pres.—Bernard Bombara
- Managing Partner, Vice Pres.—Dan Smith

PRODUCTS and/or SERVICES:
Providing full-service, multi-discipline consulting engineering services to the metals and mining industries. Capabilities include: program management, project management, construction management, and construction engineering design services in the civil, structural, mechanical, HVAC, process/utility piping, electrical, controls/instrumentation and environmental

OIL SHEAR CLUTCHES AND BRAKES FOR STEEL MILLS

You Can't Buy a Longer Lasting Brake for Steel Mill Applications!

The benefits of Oil Shear Technology
- Years of Maintenance Free Life*
- No Adjustment—Ever!
- No Regular Disc Change
- Totally Enclosed Sealed Design
- Not Affected by Chips, Scale, Oil, Water, Grease, Heat or Cold
- Reduced Down Time
- Operational Cost Savings

*Annual fluid change recommended for maximum performance and life.

Call 800-829-3244

Force Control Industries, Inc.
Fairfield, OHIO USA
Ph: 513-868-0900
Email: info@forcecontrol.com
www.forcecontrol.com

FORCE CONTROL EST. 1969

SUPPLIERS of EQUIPMENT, PRODUCTS and SERVICES

disciplines. Specialties include: conceptual and feasibility studies, cost estimating, FEA and analytical modeling, machine design, forensic engineering, control architecture design and software development, piping systems analysis, field engineering, and inspection services. Steel industry expertise extends to most aspects of specialty steel, stainless steel and carbon steel production and includes (among others): mining, raw material handling, coke and byproducts, iron production, desulfurization, scrap handling, BOP/BOF steelmaking, EAF/DC steelmaking, ladle metallurgy, reheat and trimming, slab/billet/bloom casting, reheat/heat treating furnaces, hot strip/plate/bar rolling, pipe/tube mills, cooling beds, pickling, cold rolling and finishing of strip and long products, strip annealing and coating, strip sidetrimming and slitting, CTL/leveling/flattening lines, storage/packaging and shipping of finished products, fume and dust collection systems, wastewater treatment systems, utility systems, power distribution and substation design, sitework/stormwater drainage, traffic/scales, railroads, radiation detection, maintenance/repair shops, roll shops, mill buildings, crane runways, landfills, and lagoons.

GAMMA-TECH LLC
200 Benham St.
Dayton, KY 41074 USA
P: +1.859.581.6300
dpflaum@gammatech.us
www.gammatech.us

- Pres.—Dan Pflaum
- Vice Pres. Oprs. and Cust. Svce.—Clark Scott

PRODUCTS and/or SERVICES:
Distributor and service provider of CrossBelt recycled metal analyzer. Analytical equipment for composite analysis of bulk recycled metals run through units on conveyor belts. Specializing in ferrous, stainless and aluminum scrap.

No. of Employees: 7.

GANTREX INC.
6000 Town Center Blvd., Suite 240
Canonsburg, PA 15317 USA
P: +1.800.242.6873 (Toll-Free)
F: +1.412.655.3814
sales@gantrex.com
www.gantrex.com

- Chief Oper. Officer.—Maarten Impens
- Pres. and Gen. Mgr.—Mark Veydt
- Sales Mgr., Canada—Joby George
- Sales Mgr., USA—Mark Tinney
- Mgr. of Inside Sales—Tom Berringer
- Mgr. of Engrg./Oprs.—Srini Punukollu
- Plant Coordinator—Roger Wall
- Qual. Mgr.—Dan Thajer
- Pur. Agt.—Jason Kumar
- Installation Mgr.—Jerry Sarver
- Contr.—Bethann DePretis
- Regional Sales Mgrs.—Chuck Thompson, Dan Sandu, Sean Ryan, Joshua Hernandez, Mike Larkin

PRODUCTS and/or SERVICES:
Crane rail and fastening systems, raid pad, crane girder tiebacks, hydraulic bumpers, cable protection systems, crane rail installations, welding and runway surveys.

No. of NAM Employees: 60.

GARLOCK FAMILY OF COMPANIES
1666 Division St.
Palmyra, NY 14522 USA
P: +1.800.448.6688 (Toll-Free)
F: +1.315.597.3173
info@garlock.com
www.garlock.com

- Vice Pres., Commercial—Bill Ruhl
- Sr. Applications Engr.—Matt Tones
- Sales, U.S.—Stephen Huether

PRODUCTS and/or SERVICES:
Industrial fluid sealing products: Garlock Klozure: KLOZURE® oil seals (radial lip seals), bearing isolators (non-contact labyrinth seals) and mechanical seals. Garlock Sealing Technologies:

AIST
ASSOCIATION FOR IRON & STEEL TECHNOLOGY
HOT OFF THE LINE
AND DIRECT TO YOU
SteelNews.com is your gateway to everything that's happening in the steel industry!
STEELNEWS.com TOP STORIES
Get the latest news at SteelNews.com

SUPPLIERS of EQUIPMENT, PRODUCTS and SERVICES

Metallic, compressed and GYLON® gasketing, valve and pump packing, hydraulic seals, molded rubber products, and expansion joints.

No. of Employees: 1,887 globally.

GENERAL KINEMATICS
5050 Rickert Road
Crystal Lake, IL 60014 USA
P: +1.815.455.3222
info@generalkinematics.com
www.generalkinematics.com

- Pres.—Thomas Musschoot
- Mkt. Dir. Mining—Derek Kerkera
- Vice Pres. North America Sales—Jim Egan
- Regional Sales—Will Lichtenberger, Mark Magill, Brian Story, Rob Wasilewski, Bob Huffer, Kevin Oyster, Ed Paterchak, Tom Doepker

PRODUCTS and/or SERVICES: Vibratory feeders, conveyors and screens for processing difficult to severe material under harsh process conditions, including large induction furnace feeders, reduced iron pellet screens, dry and wet quenching conveyors, and coal and coke feeders.

GEORG NORTH AMERICA INC.
307 Eastpark Dr.
Roanoke, VA 24019 USA
P: +1.540.977.0404, ext. 111
F: +1.540.977.2781
www.georg.com

PRODUCTS and/or SERVICES: Roll grinders, roll shop equipment, lathes for roll, turbine and general applications, turning and milling machining centers, milling machines in portal and single-column design, multi-spindle drilling machines, and machines for special applications.

GERLINGER CARRIER CO.
665 Murlark Ave. NW
Salem, OR 97304 USA
P: +1.503.585.4191
F: +1.503.364.2213
rodc@gerlingercarrier.com
www.gerlingercarrier.com

PRODUCTS and/or SERVICES: Straddle carrier design and manufacture, with a wide range of machines specifically designed for heavy lifts and long loads. Lift capacities ranging from 30,000 lbs. to 90,000 lbs. and available in a wide range of package sizes.

GESCO INC. (GRINDING ENGINEERING SERVICES CO.)
711 4th St.
Beaver Falls, PA 15010 USA
P: +1.800.376.6911 (Toll-Free)
F: +1.724.846.8600
sales@gescoinc.net
www.gescoinc.net

- Pres. and Treas.—John T. Jasko
- Vice Pres. and Sec.—James E. Rimmel
- Mgr. Prodn./Mfg.—Thomas Firm
- Sales. Mgr.—Michael Chinchilla
- Contr./Qual. Mgr.—Jennifer Chinchilla

EQUIPMENT:
Surface grinders (horizontal spindle) up to 42 in. wide x 200 in. long x 42 in. high. Rotary surface grinder (blanchard) 48-in. swing x 18 in. high. Cylindrical grinders up to 30-in. swing x 168 in. Cl. Rotary surface grinders (vertical spindle) 30 in. x 12 in. high.

PRODUCTS and/or SERVICES: Reconditioning and remanufacturing of shear and slitter knives, tool steel and carbide, including bar mill knives and rotary crop knives. Repair of butt welder dies and forging dies. Roll grinding including crowning. Manufacturers and distributors of shear knives, slitter knives and associated products, liners, wear plates, and rocker plates. Inventory services: perform knife inventory at mill level, including shear knives, bar mill knives

PRECISION TOOL ENGINEERING

ISO 9001 Registered by BSI Certificate No. FM 586120

Re-Conditioning & Re-Manufacturing:
Shear & Slitter Knives, Slab Knives, Forging Dies, Rotary Crop Knives, Welder Die Repair & Bar Mill Knives

Manufacturers & Distributors of:
Shear, Bar Mill & Slitter, Rotary Crop Knives, Hot Mill & Flying Shear Knives, Spacers & Stripper Rings

On-site and Database Inventory Control

Slitter & Shear Knife Problem Solving

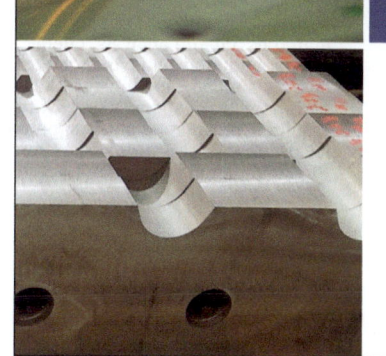

GRINDING
ENGINEERING
SERVICES
Gesco

Service Is Our Middle Name
Beaver Falls, PA 15010
724-846-8700 • GescoInc.net

SUPPLIERS of EQUIPMENT, PRODUCTS and SERVICES

and curve crop knives. Anticipate new knife orders and delivery time using estimated number of grinds remaining and current reconditioning practices. Maintain database of usage, history and current inventory. ISO 9001:2015 Certificate No. FM5861220 BSI Group America Inc.

GFG PEABODY INC., a Subsidiary of Primetals Technologies
N53 W24900 S. Corporate Cir.
Sussex, WI 53089 USA
P: +1.262.372.4515
gfg.sales@gfg-peabody.com
www.gfg-peabody.com

- Pres.—Kevin Buchanan

EQUIPMENT:
Mechanical and electrical assembly and testing, finish painting.

PRODUCTS and/or SERVICES:
Engineering design and manufacture of coil coating solutions, roll coaters, electrostatic oilers and laminators.

GLASSPORT CYLINDER WORKS
1250 McKean Ave.
Charleroi, PA 15022 USA
sales@tristatehyd.com
www.tristatehyd.com

- Pres.—James D. Palmer II
- Prod. Mgr.—James Pierrard
- Shop Foreman—Ronald Dugger

EQUIPMENT:
Complete machine and fabrication shop, lathes to 36 ft., milling machines, horizontal and vertical boring mills to 52 in., CNC machining, welding, bore welder and bronze overlay, hydraulic test stands, crane capacity to 27 tons.

PRODUCTS and/or SERVICES:
Manufacturer and rebuilder of mill-type cylinders, OEM and mill user, standard and custom design, in-house engineering and drafting, rebuilds, including failure analysis and design improvements.

No. of Employees: 60.

GLOBAL GAUGE CORP.
3200 Kettering Blvd.
Moraine, OH 45439 USA
P: +1.937.254.3500
sales@globalgauge.com
www.globalgauge.com

- Pres.—Tim McCormick
- Dir. of Oprs.—Tom Fairchild
- Sales, Mktg. and Business Dev.—Bill McCormick

PRODUCTS and/or SERVICES:
Measurement and control solutions for materials producers/processors. Crop optimization, slab measurement, centerline and cross-width strip thickness measurement, coating measurement, bar imaging/thermal profile, width measurement, and crop shear control solutions. Also produces lab-based gauges for confirming thickness, profile, density and coating weight values.

GLOBAL STRATEGIC SOLUTIONS INC.
16317 Woolwine Road
Charlotte, NC 28278 USA
P: +1.704.488.7969
F: +1.704.583.2361
drhornby62@gmail.com

- Pres.—Sara A. Hornby

PRODUCTS and/or SERVICES:
Consulting services for the international steel, foundry and related industries: Lean Six Sigma analysis and black belt assistance; process surveys; EAF process optimization (raw materials, charge analysis, chemical energy and tools, industrial gas use, energy use); new technology evaluation and recommendations; expert witness testimony; marketing studies; patent illustrations to U.S. and international PPO standards.

SUPPLIERS OF EQUIPMENT, PRODUCTS and SERVICES

GLUNT INDUSTRIES INC.
319 N. River Road NW
Warren, OH 44483
P: +1.330.399.7585
F: +1.330.393.0387
sales@glunt.com
www.glunt.com

EQUIPMENT:
Horizontal floor and table mills to 8-in. spindle, 12-ft. vertical x 55-ft. horizontal travels, CNC mills, lathes and machining centers. Planer mills, vertical boring mills to 18-ft. dia., welding facilities for large or small fabrications, automatic, CNC, semi-automatic and sub-arc welding, 60-ton crane capability.

PRODUCTS and/or SERVICES:
Heavy machining, replacement, repair and redesign parts for the ferrous and non-ferrous industries, including: melting facilities, casters, rolling mills, finish equipment and power plants. Specializing in mandrels, spindles, chocks and rolls (new and repaired).

GMB HEAVY INDUSTRIES
5165 Timberlea Blvd.
Mississauga, ON L4W 2S3 Canada
P: +1.905.282.9395, ext. 225
F: +1.905.282.9440
iainb@gmbindustries.com
www.gmbindustries.com

- Pres.—Gordon Muir
- Vice Pres. Procurement/Mfg.—Wayne Baxter
- Sales Dir.—Iain Barnie
- Pur. Agts.—Jim Ward, Paul Apostolou
- Chief Engr.—Fil Cadete

EQUIPMENT:
Full machining, fabricating and assembly facilities.

PRODUCTS and/or SERVICES:
Design, development, engineering, manufacturing and installations of complete turnkey systems for rolling mill equipment, including finishing ends, cooling beds and spare parts.

No. of Employees: 65.

GO2 PARTNERS INC.
6285 Schumacher Park Dr.
West Chester, OH 45069-4806
P: +1.888.273.1617 (Toll-Free)
F: +1.888.524.1347 (Toll-Free)
tim.doyle@go2partners.com
www.go2partners.com/operations/material-id

- Sales Mgr.—Tim Doyle
- Partners—Dan Schroer, Dave Carlin

PRODUCTS and/or SERVICES:
Label and tag solutions, RFID, scanners, printers, electronic hardware (most makes and models), material identification solutions, protective packaging, e-commerce technology, and marketing logistics.

No. of Employees: 145.

GOAD CO.
144 S. Kentucky Ave.
Independence, MO 64053 USA
P: +1.800.733.4623 (Toll-Free)
F: +1.816.836.2113
www.goadco.com

- Chmn. of the Bd. and Pres.—Curtis Goad
- Oprs. Mgr.—Tyler Good
- Business Dev.—Jon Barrows
- Sr. Project Mgr.—Owen Gordon
- Est. and Field Svcs.—David Phelps

EQUIPMENT:
Equipment for metal fabrication, thermoplastic and fiberglass (FRP) plastic fabrication, coatings application, and corrosion-resistant linings application for stainless steel, rubber, PVC, PTFE, PE, PP, PVDF, CPCV and other lining systems.

PRODUCTS and/or SERVICES:
Metal and plastic tanks and corrosion-resistant linings for pickling, metal treating, plating, and cleaning and waste containment. Corrosion-resistant linings, including stainless steel, rubber, PVC, PTFE, PE, PP, PVDF, CPCV and other lining systems. Corrosion-resistant fume handling systems and ductwork. TANKeye® leak and pre-leak

SUPPLIERS of EQUIPMENT, PRODUCTS and SERVICES

detection system. Field inspection and relining/repair services.

No. of Employees: 20.

GONTERMANN-PEIPERS GMBH
Hauptstrasse 20
Siegen, NRW, 57074 Germany
P: +49.271.60.0
F: +49.271.60.200
khabitzki@gontermann-peipers.de
www.gontermann-peipers.de

- Regional Sales Mgr.—Klaus Habitzki
- Local Agent for U.S. (QUALICAST)—Chris Law

EQUIPMENT:
Casting (DPS and spincasting) and machining for rolls up to 265 metric tons finished weight.

PRODUCTS and/or SERVICES:
Double-poured or DP-forged backup rolls for plate, hot and cold rolling mills. Work rolls for plate and hot rolling mills. Rolls for long product mills. Rolls for aluminum and steel mills.

No. of Employees: 560.

Gontermann-Peipers America Inc.
3208 Brookline Dr. W
Mobile, AL 36693 USA
P: +1.251.635.9595
rsteinhagen@gontermann-peipers.de
www.gontermann-peipers.de

- Regional Sales Mgr.—Klaus Habitzki
- Chief Engr.—Raphael Steinhagen

PRODUCTS and/or SERVICES:
Technical service for rolling mill rolls.

No. of Employees: 2.

GORMAN-RUPP CO.
600 S. Airport Road
Mansfield, OH 44903 USA
P: +1.419.755.1011
F: +1.419.755.1251
grsales@gormanrupp.com
www.grpumps.com

- Chief Exec. Officer and Pres.—Scott King
- Vice Pres. Engrg.—Craig Redmond
- Vice Pres. Mktg. and Sales—Tony Chirico
- Gen. Mgr.—D.J. Daniels
- Sales Mgr.—Travis Eighinger
- Ind. Sales Mgr.—Jeff Hannan
- Adv. Mgr.—Cyndi Hoffner
- Pur. Agt.—Ken Westfield

PRODUCTS and/or SERVICES:
Pumps and pumping equipment.

No of Employees: 450.

GPM INC.
4432 Venture Ave.
Duluth, MN 55811 USA
P: +1.218.722.9904
bkolquist@gpmco.com
www.gpmco.com

- Chief Exec. Officer—Peter Haines
- Vice Pres. Mktg.—Blake Kolquist
- Sales Mgr.—Jeremy Jackson
- Chief Engr.—Jim Bittinger
- Sales Rep.—Adam Christensen

PRODUCTS and/or SERVICES:
Submersible slurry pumps, turnkey pumping packages.

No. of Employees: 70.

GRAFTECH INTERNATIONAL LTD.
982 Keynote Cir.
Brooklyn Heights, OH 44131 USA
P: +1.216.676.2000
www.graftech.com

- Chief Exec. Officer and Pres.—Marcel Kessler
- Chief Oper. Officer and Exec. Vice Pres.—Jeremy Halford
- Vice Pres. Sales — Americas—Mark Chrisman
- Dir. Cust. Tech. Svce. — Americas—Rodrigo Corbari

PRODUCTS and/or SERVICES:
Graphite electrodes, needle coke.

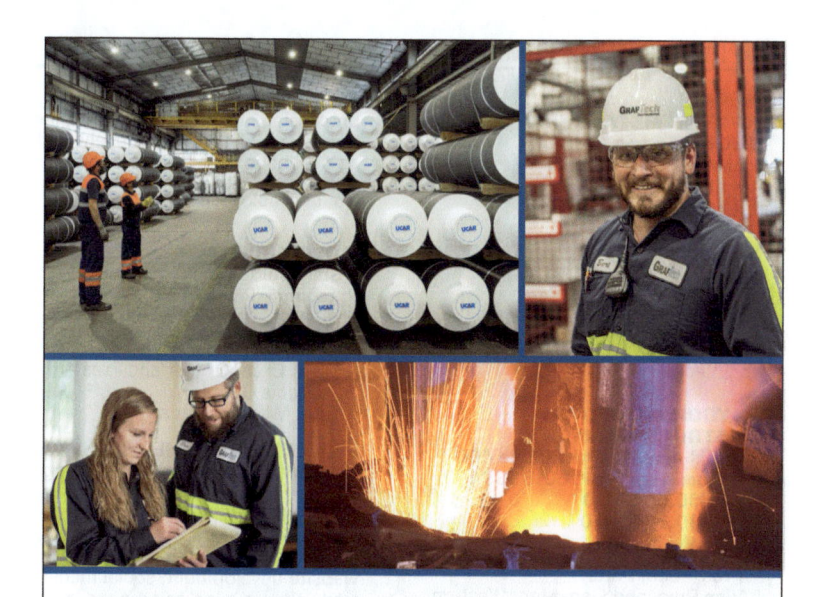

MAXIMIZING STEEL PRODUCTIVITY
THROUGH TECHNOLOGY AND SERVICE LEADERSHIP

- Leading manufacturer of high-quality graphite electrode products with over 135 years of experience researching and developing graphite- and carbon-based solutions

- Highly engineered, industry-leading technical services and solutions, including ArchiTech® Furnace Productivity System

- Over 135 patents and published patent applications

- Substantially vertically integrated into petroleum needle coke production

Enabling the Sustainability of Steel

GrafTech International

www.graftech.com

982 Keynote Circle
Brooklyn Heights, Ohio 44131

SUPPLIERS of EQUIPMENT, PRODUCTS and SERVICES

GRAPHITE METALLIZING CORP.
1050 Nepperhan Ave.
Yonkers, NY 10703 USA
P: +1.914.968.8400
F: +1.914.968.8468
eric.ford@graphalloy.com
www.graphalloy.com

- Vice Pres.—Eric Ford

PRODUCTS and/or SERVICES:
GRAPHALLOY® high-temperature bearings.

GRAYCOR INDUSTRIAL CONSTRUCTORS INC.
Two Mid America Plaza, Suite 400
Oakbrook Terrace, IL 60181 USA
P: +1.630.684.7110
F: +1.630.684.7120
www.graycor.com

- Pres.—Sam Potter
- Vice Pres. and Gen. Mgr., Western U.S. Oprs.—Shawn Anderton
- Gen. Mgr., Metals—Pat Kouns

PRODUCTS and/or SERVICES:
Heavy industrial construction and rebuilding in the steel industry focusing on coke batteries, BFs, steelmaking facilities, casters, hot and cold mills, metallurgical furnaces, environmental facilities, and coating lines. Construction services include, but are not limited to: demolition, salamander removal, BF delining, excavation, concrete work, structural steel erection, heavy rigging, equipment installation, refractory installation, boilermaker work, piping and general trades.

GREENFIELD TECH PROJECTS
21/1 Alaknanda Society
Nr. Dental College Road
Manipur, Bopal-Ghuma Road
Ahmedabad, GJ, 38005 USA8 India
P: +91.972.770.1693
krishpy.aavishkar@gmail.com
https://greenfieldtechprojects.com

PRODUCTS and/or SERVICES:
Manufactures minerals, refractory, cement, food, castables, agriculture, building and construction, and fertilizer processing equipment. Also supplies turnkey projects and is actively working on utilization of industrial wastes.

No. of Employees: 15.

GROWTHHIVE
4 Smithfield St.
Pittsburgh, PA 15222 USA
P: +1.412.201.1900
www.growthhive-strategy.com

- Chief Exec. Officer and Pres.— Francois Gau
- Gen. Mgr.—Amanda Uhme

PRODUCTS and/or SERVICES:
Full-service marketing firm offering B2B inbound and outbound solutions for industry and tech companies grounded in strategy. Offers strategic marketing services, data analytics, website development, social media, PR, trade show design and management, and creation and production of sales and brand literature.

GUILD INTERNATIONAL
7273 Division Dr.
Bedford, OH 44146 USA
P: +1.440.232.5887
F: +1.440.232.5878
sales@guildint.com
www.guildint.com

- Vice Pres. Sales—Mark Wagner

PRODUCTS and/or SERVICES:
Coil joining and end welding machines for steel processing, tube producing and stamping applications. Guild International's line of patented equipment includes laser welders, arc welders and resistance welders. Guild International also produces a full line of tube mill entry equipment including uncoilers, speed funnels, flatteners and accumulators.

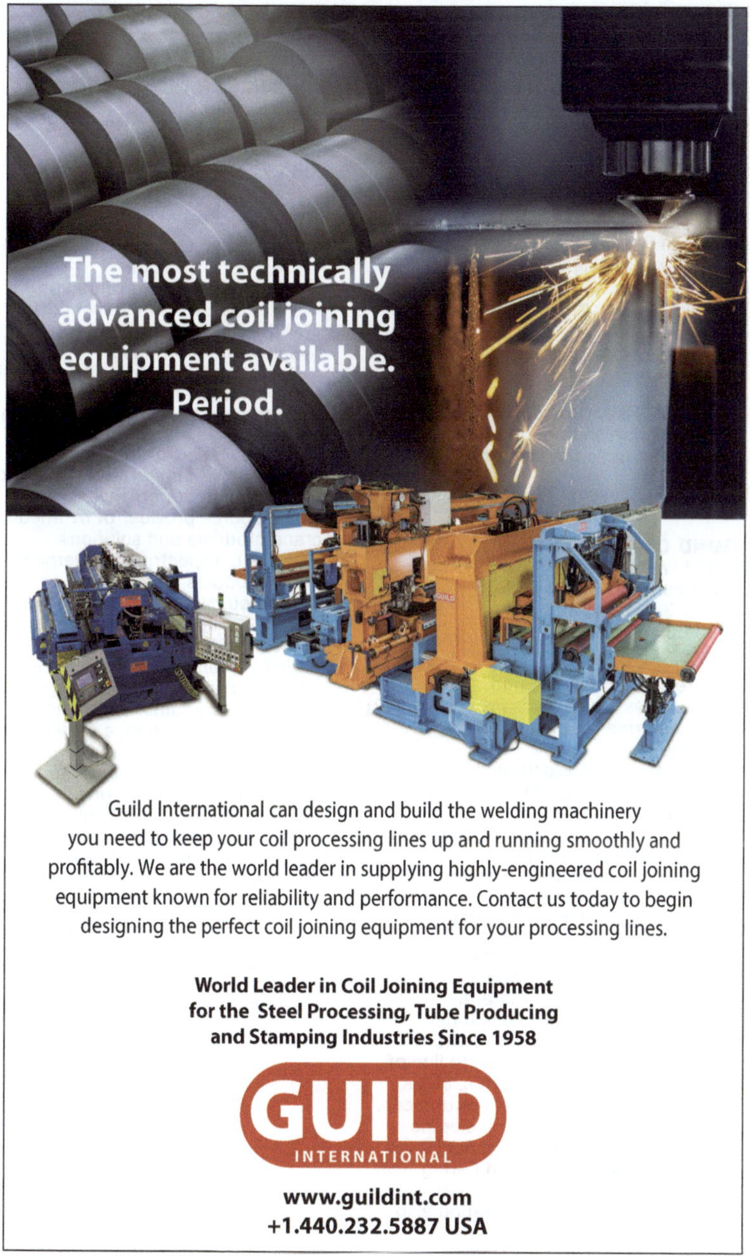

See listing page 378

SUPPLIERS of EQUIPMENT, PRODUCTS and SERVICES

GULF STATES ENGINEERING INC.
600 Azalea Road
Mobile, AL 36609 USA
P: +1.251.460.4646
F: +1.251.460.4649
tim.morris@gseeng.com
www.GSEeng.com

- Chief Exec. Officer and Pres.— Timothy Morris
- Vice Pres.—Tom Wade, Karen Brown
- Vice Pres. — Project Mgmt.—Lane Sesi
- Vice Pres. — Oprs. Mgr.—Matthew Roberts

PRODUCTS and/or SERVICES:
Construction engineering, procurement and construction management.

No. of Employees: 100.

GUND CO. INC., THE
2121 Walton Road
St. Louis, MO 63114 USA
P: +1.314.423.5200
F: +1.314.423.9009
www.thegundcompany.com

- Pres.—Stephen P. Gund
- Business Mgr. Metals Processing and Transformer Applications—Freddy Lugo
- Business Mgr. Electronics/Switchgear Applications—Diego Legorreta
- Business Mgr. Rotating Equipment Applications—Steve Ulm
- Product Specialist — Elastomeric Matls.—Greg Watson
- Cust. Svce. Mgr.—Tim Marien

PRODUCTS and/or SERVICES:
Manufacturer of engineered thermoset composite materials and custom-fabricated electrical insulating components for power systems equipment. Complete line of insulation materials for EAFs, LMFs, smelting furnaces, induction furnaces, transformers, switchgears, electric motors and generators. Product lines include gaskets, seals and O-ring products. Kitting, assembly and component design consultation also available.

G.W. BECKER INC.
2600 Kirila Blvd.
Hermitage, PA 16148 USA USA
P: +1.724.983.1000
F: +1.724.983.1818
sales@gwbcrane.com
www.gwbcrane.com

- Chief Exec. Officer—George Becker
- Pres.—Chris Becker
- Engrg. Mgr.—David Umbaugh
- Svce. Mgr.—Justin Wellendorf
- Mktg. Dir.—Elyssa Wiesen
- Sales Mgr.—Ron Piso
- Regional Sales Mgrs.—Art Goforth, Dave Yetso, Fred Pokrywka, Don Cioffi, Jim Walkama, Mike Lucatorto

PRODUCTS and/or SERVICES:
A CMAA "OEM Integrated Overhead Crane Manufacturer." Full-service, single-source provider of overhead crane products and solutions. Offers a full spectrum of overhead crane products and services throughout North America, including: manufacturing of custom overhead cranes to CMAA specifications or *AIST Technical Report No. 6*, packaged crane equipment, freestanding runway systems, workstations, jibs, hoists, OSHA and maintenance inspections with PM, field service and repair, component rebuilds, operator and maintenance training, runway surveys and inspections, engineering analysis, design engineering, modernizations, automation control and integration, and turnkey installation, as well as parts distribution. Provides specialized expertise and long-term planning solutions for maintaining overhead crane equipment.

No. of Employees: 50+.

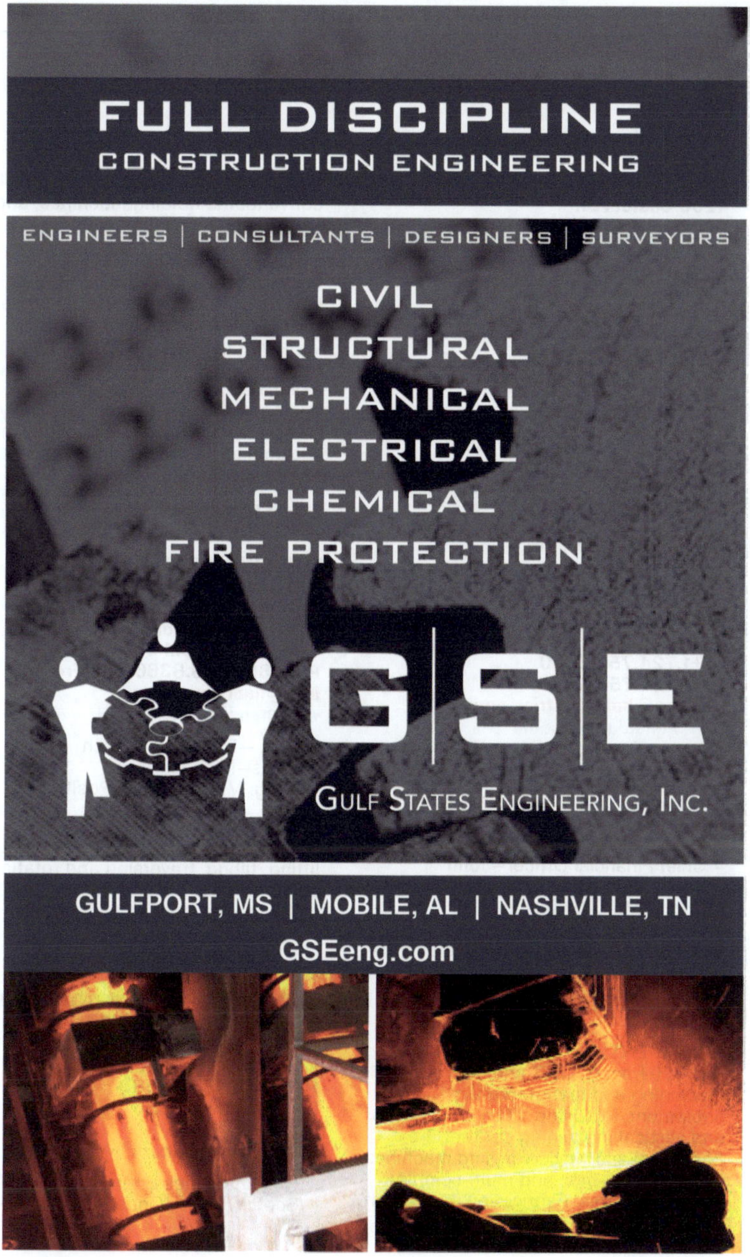

See listing page 380

SUPPLIERS of EQUIPMENT, PRODUCTS and SERVICES

H

H&K EQUIPMENT
4200 Casteel Dr.
Coraopolis, PA 15108 USA
P: +1.800.272.9953 (Toll-Free);
   +1.412.490.5300
F: +1.412.494.0975
info@hkequipment.com
www.hkequipment.com

- Pres.—George Koch
- Exec. Vice Pres. and Sales Mgr.—Peter Cicero

PRODUCTS and/or SERVICES:
Lift trucks, railcar movers, personnel carriers, sweepers, scrubbers, sales, rentals, parts, service.

No. of Employees: 119.

HALL INDUSTRIES INC.
514 Mecklem Lane
Ellwood City, PA 16117 USA
P: +1.724.752.2000
F: +1.724.758.1558
sserene@hallindustries.com
www.hallindustries.com

- Chief Exec. Officer and Pres.—Jonathan Hall
- Vice Pres. Mktg. and Sales—Mark Hall
- Vice Pres. Prodn./Mfg.—Frank Schlafhauser
- Chief Financial Officer—John Schlafhauser
- Engrg. Mgr., Wheels and Components—Mark McGinley
- Sales Mgr., Wheels and Components—Scott Serene
- Sales Mgr., Coke Oven Products—Ed Hall

EQUIPMENT:
100,000+ sq. ft. CNC and conventional machining and manufacturing equipment, including VTLs, horizontal and vertical machining centers, horizontal and vertical milling machines, and various lathes and multi-spindle screw machines. Fabrication equipment including plasma and oxyfuel burning tables, full CNC robotic welding cell, conventional welding machines, and various support equipment.

PRODUCTS and/or SERVICES:
Forged steel crane wheels, industrial wheels, wire rope sheaves and rollers heat treated up to 62Rc in a wide variety of carbon, alloy steel, and stainless-steel grades. Also produces axles, bearing housings, spacers, end caps and other wheel assembly components. Provides complete wheel assemblies and fabricated housings to suit application.

No. of Employees: 300.

HANDLING SPECIALTY MANUFACTURING LTD., a Whiting Co.
219 S. Service Road W
Grimsby, ON L3M 4G1 Canada
P: +1.800.559.8366 (Toll-Free)
info@handling.com
www.handling.com

- Pres.—Thomas E. Beach
- Sales—Michael Roper
- Mktg. Mgr.—Michael Poeltl

PRODUCTS and/or SERVICES:
Design and manufacture of custom lifting, tilting, traversing and rotating equipment for the steel/metals industry, including the ladle relining lift.

No. of Employees: 120.

HANNECARD ROLLER COATINGS INC. – ASB INDUSTRIES
1031 Lambert St.
Barberton, OH 44203 USA
P: +1.330.753.8458
F: +1.330.753.7550
info@asbindustries.com
www.hannecard.com

- Regional Sales Engrs.—Charles Kay, Scott Whitten, Chris Slabbert

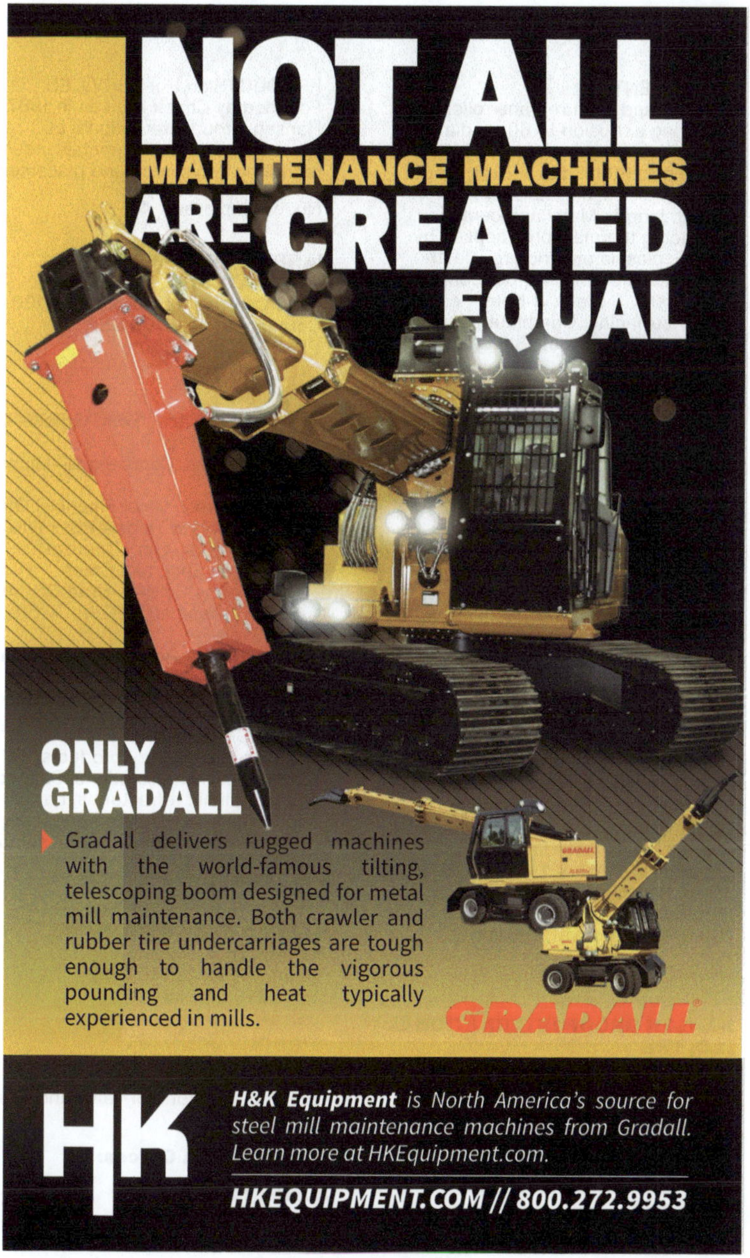

See listing page 382

SUPPLIERS of EQUIPMENT, PRODUCTS and SERVICES

EQUIPMENT:
Rubber and polyurethane roller covering extrusion to 60-in. dia. x 26-ft. length; urethane: rotational casting to 60-in. dia. x 26-ft. length. MONKAL® casting to 20-in. dia. x 9.5-ft. length. Metal and ceramic surfacing thermal spray applied by HVOF, plasma electric arc, electric arc, and wire-powder (rod) combustion processes. S-Met®, S-Kote®, cold spray surfacing. Complete grinding and machining facility, including horizontal mills, CNC vertical mills to 110 in., roll and OD grinder to 60 x 288 in. with CNC controls and crowning capabilities, lathe capacity to 56 x 252 in., CNC machining, belt grinding, diamond polishing, chatter-free polishing, tapers and crowning.

PRODUCTS and/or SERVICES:
Roller maintenance, repair and grinding; dynamic roll balancing; rubber and polyurethane roller coverings for the metal industry, MONKAL polyurethane roller coating. Thermal spray coatings for wear and grip, including bridle rolls, mandrel segments, furnace hearth rolls, pot rolls, bar and rod table rolls, wire blocks, hydraulic pistons, chocks, and pumps. On-site processing. Submerged-arc roll welding and plasma transferred arc (PTA). Disassembly and assembly. Specialized coating systems designated as Cascoat® caster mold plates. Licensee of Nippon Steel Hardfacing for hot-dip coating components. ISNet certified, Thermal Spray Operator certification.

No. of Employees: 26.

HANSEN GROUP INTERNATIONAL LLC, THE
3840 Williamsburg Park Blvd., Unit 1
Jacksonville, FL 32257 USA
P: +1.904.448.5200
hheinold@hansengroupinc.com
www.hansengroupinc.com

- Chief Exec. Officer and Pres.—Hank Heinold

PRODUCTS and/or SERVICES:
Founded by Chuck Hansen in 1987, Hansen Group International LLC specializes in retained metals industry recruiting, job search and placement.

No. of Employees: 4.

HARBISONWALKER INTERNATIONAL
1305 Cherrington Pkwy., Suite 100
Coraopolis, PA 15108 USA
P: +1.412.375.6600
customer-service@thinkhwi.com
www.thinkhwi.com

- Chmn. and Chief Exec. Officer—Carol Jackson
- Sr. Vice Pres. Commercial—Michael Werner
- Sr. Vice Pres., Chief Financial Officer and Corporate Treas.—Ross Wilkin
- Sr. Vice Pres., Gen. Counsel, Corporate Sec., and Chief Compliance Officer—Brad Cramer
- Sr. Dir., Commercial Oprs. — Steel— Jim Skelly
- Sr. Dir. Value-Added Svcs.—William Wagstaff
- Sr. Mgr. Mktg.—Crawford Murton

PRODUCTS and/or SERVICES:
Supplier of refractory products and refractories lining solutions. Shaped and monolithic refractories, basic and alumino-silicate, comprehensive refractories management and solutions.

No. of Employees: 2,000.

HAROLD BECK & SONS INC.
11 Terry Dr.
Newtown, PA 18940 USA
P: +1.215.968.4600
sales@haroldbeck.com
www.haroldbeck.com

PRODUCTS and/or SERVICES:
Electric actuators for valve and damper control.

Regional Sales Offices:

Austin, TX
P: +1.512.639.2982
jpmangan@haroldbeck.com

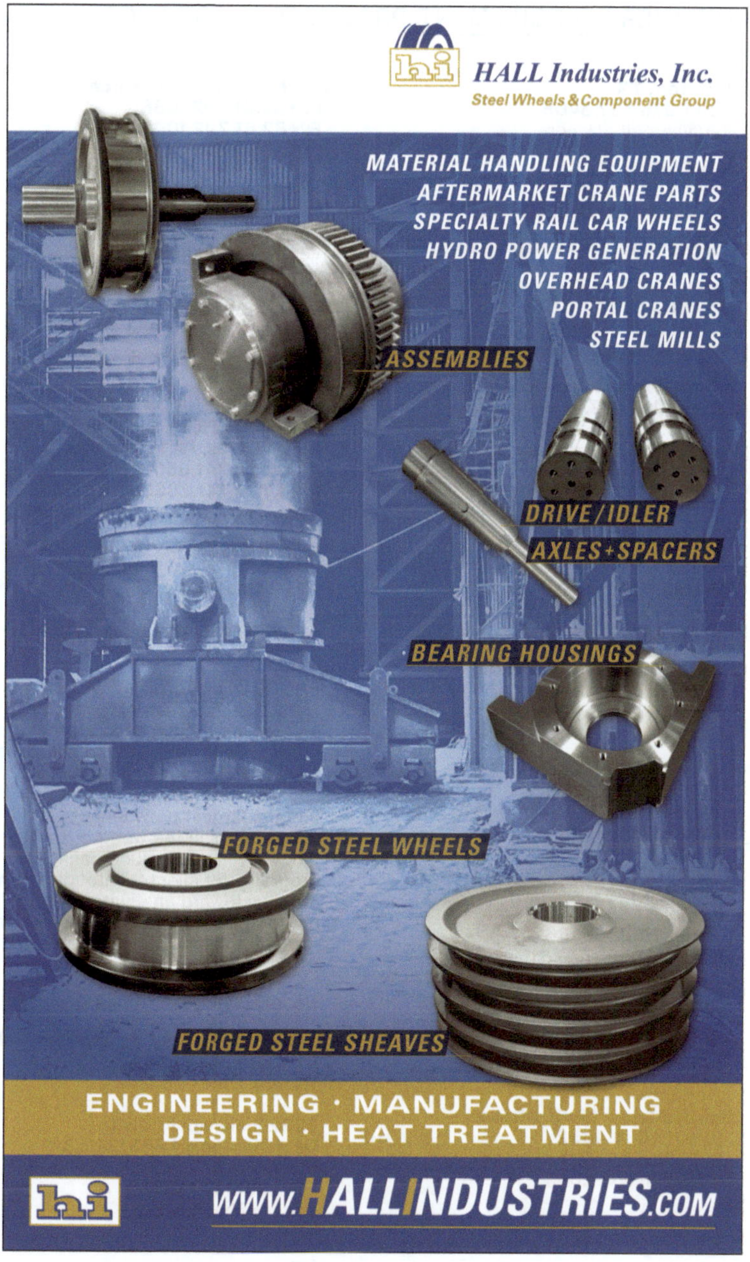

See listing page 382

SUPPLIERS of EQUIPMENT, PRODUCTS and SERVICES

Houston, TX
P: +1.936.597.8408
tat@haroldbeck.com

San Francisco, CA
P: +1.707.782.8101
tffadloun@haroldbeck.com

International Sales Representatives:

Australia/New Zealand: Acrodyne
P: +61.3.8727.7800
F: +61.3.9729.8699
info@acrodyne.com.au

Brazil: Top Componentes
P: +55.11.3637.1669
F: +55.11.2099.1430
aurelio@topcomponentes.com.br

Canada (Eastern): Provan
P: +1.514.332.3230
F: +1.514.332.3552
pkurylowicz@provan.ca

Canada (Western)
P: +1.215.378.7297
wmf@haroldbeck.com

Colombia: Laps Ingenieria
P: +57.1.7223321
F: +57.1.3182870782
ventas@lapsingenieria.com

India
P: +91.98.1830.3045;
+91.98.7339.7773
ark@haroldbeck.in

Mexico/Central America: Master Control S.A.
P: +52.81.8324.7737;
+52.81.8367.1862
F: +52.81.8337.4781
esteban.arjona@mastercontrolsa.com

P.R. China
P: +86.21.6212.1211
F: +86.21.6225.2697
beckgd@126.com

South Africa: Limit Africa
P: +017.634.4852
F: +086.773.8211
sales@limitsa.co.za

South Korea: Turbo-Tech
P: +82.61.792.1088
F: +82.61.792.1092
turbo@turbotech.co.kr

Turkey: Arfen Teknoloji
P: +90.212.876.79.54
F: +90.212.876.79.55
info@arfenteknoloji.com

United Kingdom: IPT Engineering
P: +44.1623.862.990
F: +44.1623.869.304
david@iptengineering.com

HARSCO ENVIRONMENTAL
300 Seven Fields Blvd., Suite 300
Seven Fields, PA 16046 USA
P: +1.724.741.6600
F: +1.724.741.2033
www.harsco-environmental.com

- Regional Pres., North America—Ed Ramsey
- Regional Engrg. Dir., North America—Justin Vendemia
- Commercial Dir., North America—Joe Burkey

PRODUCTS and/or SERVICES: Harsco Environmental recovers and recycles metal and repurposes products into value-added solutions. At over 145 sites in more than 30 countries, Harsco Environmental is one the largest providers of steel mill services in the world. Provides innovative and product management programs for clients. Through its shift in focus toward an environmental platform, Harsco views customer needs through the lens of sustainability and meeting environmental goals.

No. of Employees: 10,000+.

Performix/Harsco Environmental
101 Tidewater Road NE
Warren, OH 44483 USA

5222 Indianapolis Blvd.
East Chicago, IN 46312 USA
P: +1.330.372.1781
F: +1.330.372.1314
kstone@harsco.com

SUPPLIERS OF EQUIPMENT, PRODUCTS and SERVICES

- Gen. Mgr.—Jennifer Lucas
- Mgr. Business Dev.—Brian F. Conlon
- Cust. Svce.—Kimberly Stone

EQUIPMENT:
Crushing, drying, screening, mixing, briquetting and bagging equipment, and chemical and physical lab analysis devices.

PRODUCTS and/or SERVICES:
Calcium aluminate, synthetic slag, ladle slag deoxidizers, desulfurizers, hot top compounds and toll briquetting.

No. of Employees: 35.

HASTEC GROUP

HASTEC Engineering Inc. and HASTEC REBS Inc.
8-45 Hannover Dr.
St. Catharines, ON L2W 1A3 Canada
P: +1.905.687.9194
F: +1.905.687.9988
sales@hastec.com
www.hastec.com

- Pres.—Hardy Siegmund

PRODUCTS and/or SERVICES:
HASTEC Engineering—Specialists in descaling, offering a complete line of descaling equipment for CSP casters, rolling mills and forging presses. Distribution partner in North and South America for HYDROWATT descale pumps. HASTEC REBS—Specialists in air-oil lubrication technology. Manufactures Turbolube air-oil systems for casters, hot mills, cold mills, rod and bar mills, table rolls, roll grinders, cranes, and combustion fan bearings. Exclusive distributor for REBS lubrication products for Canada, USA, Mexico and South America.

No. of Employees: 15.

HATCH LTD.
2800 Speakman Dr.
Mississauga, ON L5K 2R7 Canada
P: +1.905.855.7600
F: +1.905.855.8270
www.hatch.com

- Global Managing Dir., Energy—Robert Francki
- Global Managing Dir., Infrastructure—Michael Schatz
- Managing Dir., Bulk Metals—Joe Petrolito
- Managing Dir., Base Metals—Tina Armstrong
- Managing Dir., Minerals—Andrea De Mori Bajolin
- Managing Dir., Digital—Alim Somani
- Global Dir., Iron and Steel—Paul Towsey
- Global Dir., Technology, Commercial Dev.—Melanie Price
- Global Dir., Iron and Steel Decarbonization—David Mysko
- Dir., Iron and Steelmaking Technologies—David Rudge

PRODUCTS and/or SERVICES:
Consulting engineers specializing in process control and automation, direct reduction, EAF melting, oxygen steelmaking, billet, bloom, round and slab casters, rolling mills. Providing information systems and comprehensive engineering services, including problem-solving, optimization, retrofits, planning, feasibility studies, environmental services, site selection, market studies, project and construction management, and start-up assistance with detailed design for the iron/steel and non-ferrous industries.

No. of Employees: 9,000.

Hatch Associates Consultants Inc.
Gateway View Plaza
1600 W. Carson St., Suite 1
Pittsburgh, PA 15219 USA
P: +1.412.497.2000
F: +1.412.497.2212

- Regional Managing Dir.—Ted Lyon
- Dirs., Engrg. and Project Delivery—Dan Haslett, John Visnesky
- Dir., Downstream—David Irvine
- Dir., Downstream Technologies—Nigel Blackmore

Additional Offices:

Abu Dhabi, United Arab Emirates
P: +971.2.201.8700

SUPPLIERS of EQUIPMENT, PRODUCTS and SERVICES

- Dir.—Roy Dabbous

Beijing, China
P: +86.10.8500.2288

- Commercial Dir.—Tracy Wang

Belo Horizonte, MG, Brazil
P:+55.31.3308.7200

- Dir. — Metals—Kezer Almeida

Brisbane, QLD, Australia
P: +61.7.3166.7777

- Regional Mgr. Dir.—Jan Kwak
- Dir. — Metals—Claude D'Cruz

Gurugram, India
P: +91.124.460.9200

- Dir.—Ruby Rajvanshi

Johannesburg, South Africa
P: +27.11.239.5300

- Regional Managing Dir.—Pierre Olivier
- Dir. — Metals—Arne Weissenberger

London, U.K.
P: +44.020.7906.5100

- Dir.—Julian Clark

Montréal, QC, Canada
P: +1.514.861.0583

- Regional Mgr. Dir.—Stephane Raymond

Santiago, Chile
P: +56.22.430.2600

- Regional Managing Dir. South America—Nabil Habib
- Dir. — Metals—Vicente Alfaro

Hatch IAS
7000 Industrial Blvd.
Aliquippa, PA 15001 USA
P: +1.724.375.5500
F: +1.724.375.7700
terry.gerber@hatch.com
www.hatch.com

- Regional Dir.—Terry Gerber

HAUHINCO
1325 Evans City Road
Evans City, PA 16033 USA
P: +1.724.789.7050
F: +1.724.789.7056
khuffman@hauhinco.com
www.hauhinco.com

- Pres.—Ron Osselborn
- Sales Mgr.—Keith Huffman

PRODUCTS and/or SERVICES:
Water hydraulic system components, including high-pressure pumps, valves, hydraulic valve blocks, control technology and modular systems.

HAVER & BOECKER NIAGARA
225 Ontario St.
St. Catharines, ON L2R 7B6 Canada
P: +1.800.325.5993 (Toll-Free)
info@haverniagara.ca
www.haverniagara.com

- Pres., North American and Australian Oprs.—Karen Thompson
- Vice Pres., North American and Australian Oprs.—Peter Kilmurray

PRODUCTS and/or SERVICES:
Modular screen media, tensioned screen media, specialty screen media, inclined vibrating screens, linear vibrating screens, scarabaeus pelletizing disc, pulse condition monitoring, pulse vibration analysis, pulse impact testing.

No. of Employees: 200+.

HEG LTD.
Bhilwara Towers, A-12, Sector 1
Noida, NCR Delhi, 201301 India
P: +91.120.439.0300
F: +91.120.427.7841
manish.gulati@lnjbhilwara.com
www.hegltd.com

- Chmn. and Chief Exec. Officer—Ravi Jhunjhunwala
- Exec. Dir.—Manish Gulati, P: +91.981.060.2295 (Mobile)
- Sr. Mgr. — Intl.—Madhur Sharma, P: +91.966.736.2227 (Mobile)
- Regional Sales Mgr., USA—Hemant Sanghvi, P: +1.412.523.3641 (Mobile)

SUPPLIERS OF EQUIPMENT, PRODUCTS and SERVICES

PRODUCTS and/or SERVICES:
Graphite electrodes (UHP, SHP and HP), graphite specialties and graphite fines. Annual capacity: 80,000 MT. Electrode size range extends up to 30-in. dia. ISO 9001:2008 and ISO 14001:2004 certified company.

HEICO FASTENING SYSTEMS
2377 8th Ave. NW
Hickory, NC 28601 USA
P: +1.828.261.0184
info@heico-group.us
www.heico-lock.us

- Sales Mgr., North America—Luke Reed
- Sales Engr., Northeast U.S. and Eastern Canada—Michael Palmer
- Sales Engr., South Central U.S.—Bruce Bourgeois
- Sales Engr., Western U.S. and Western Canada—John Murphy
- Sales Engr.—Upper Midwest U.S. and Central Canada—Mike Taylor
- Sales Engr., Southeast U.S. and North American Applications Engr.—Scott Dekoker
- Cust. Svce. Mgr.—Elisha Fox
- Cust. Svce.—Melanie Walker

PRODUCTS and/or SERVICES:
Highly engineered fastening products for securing critical bolted joints found throughout the iron and steel industry. HEICO-LOCK wedge locking washers and HEICO-TEC tensioning systems ensure safety, accuracy and lifespan of vital bolted connections. IATF 16949 and ISO 9001 certified.

No. of Employees: 32 (U.S.); 500+ (Global).

HEIDENHAIN CORP.
333 E. State Pkwy.
Schaumburg, IL 60173 USA
P: +1.847.490.1191
F: +1.847.490.3931
info@heidenhain.com
www.heidenhain.us

- Chief Exec. Officer—David Doyle
- Chief Financial Officer—David Armstrong
- Dir. of Mktg. Communications—Tom Wyatt

PRODUCTS and/or SERVICES:
CNC controls, linear encoders, rotary encoders, length gauges, digital readouts.

No. of Employees: 200.

HELMKE – MOTORS AND DRIVES, Represented by Hawk Industrial Products
100 Fairway Park Blvd., Unit 312
Ponte Vedra Beach, FL 32082 USA
P: +1.412.576.1699
hipcorp@outlook.com

- Rep. and Owner, Hawk Industrial Products—Chris Hawk

PRODUCTS and/or SERVICES:
German motor manufacturer of LV, MV and HV three-phase IEC motors and drive systems, DC motors and transformers for all industrial needs. Specializes in the field of individual and custom-built motors and drive solutions. Maintains a warehouse with more than 200 HELMKE medium- and high-voltage motors and 50,000 low-voltage HELMKE motors and other brands (Siemens and ABB Motors).

No. of HELMKE Employees: 230.

HELWIG CARBON PRODUCTS
8900 W. Tower Ave.
Milwaukee, WI 53224 USA
P: +1.414.354.2411
F: +1.800.365.3113 (Toll-Free)
carboncrew@helwigcarbon.com
www.helwigcarbon.com

- Pres.—Mark Umhoefer
- Vice Pres. Engrg.—Nitin Kulkarni
- Treas.—Tom Lauer
- Sales Mgr.—Kevin Koenitzer

PRODUCTS and/or SERVICES:
Carbon graphite brushes, brush holders, and constant force springs for electric motors and generators. Shaft

SUPPLIERS of EQUIPMENT, PRODUCTS and SERVICES

grounding/bearing protection kits for motors with VFDs.

No. of Employees: 250.

HENKEL (LOCTITE)
One Henkel Way
Rocky Hill, CT 06067 USA
P: +1.860.571.2601
F: +1.860.571.5430
www.henkel-adhesives.com/us/en/industries

PRODUCTS and/or SERVICES: Maintenance and repair products, training, adhesives, sealants, and lubricants.

Henkel
32100 Stephenson Hwy.
Madison Heights, MI 48071 USA
P: +1.248.583.9300
F: +1.248.583.2976
www.henkel-adhesives.com/us/en/industries/metal-processing

- Dir. Mktg.—Emily Mullins
- Dir. Business—Andrea Coggins
- Adv. Mgr.—Matina Kakar

PRODUCTS and/or SERVICES: Provides specialty chemicals and services for the processing of flat-rolled steel.

No. of Employees: 1,200 in North America.

HERAEUS ELECTRO-NITE CO. LLC
541 S. Industrial Dr.
Hartland, WI 53029 USA
P: +1.800.558.9008 (Toll-Free)
F: +1.267.685.4170
info.electro-nite.us@heraeus.com
www.heraeus-electro-nite.com

- Dir. Sales and Mktg.—Thomas Coleman
- Mktg. Mgr.—Christopher Carr

PRODUCTS and/or SERVICES: Produces a full range of molten metal immersion sensors used to measure and control requirements such as: temperature, oxygen activity, carbon, hydrogen, nitrogen, metal and slag chemistries, etc. These measurements are direct-contact immersion solutions in molten metal through HEN-developed technologies such as: Celox®, HYDRIS®, Positherm®, Multilance®, CasTemp®, QuiK-Slag®, QuiK-Spec® Samplers, ArMOR®, QUBE™, CoreTemp and other innovative on-line/in-situ solutions for control of the molten metal process.

HERKULES NORTH AMERICA
101 River St.
Ford City, PA 16226 USA
P: +1.724.763.9050
F: +1.724.763.3890
sales@herkulesusa.com
www.herkulesusa.com

- Pres.—Thorsten Mehlhorn
- Sr. Vice Pres. Sales—Robert Curler Jr.
- Vice Pres. Sales—Howard Adams, Michael Chociej Jr., Robert Klingensmith, Justin Snedeker, Eric Klenner, Claire Float

EQUIPMENT: Heavy machining, fabrication and assembly shops. 100,000 sq. ft. with crane capacities up to 80 tons.

PRODUCTS and/or SERVICES: Manufacturers of roll shop equipment, including roll grinders, roll lathes, special roll machining system, roll handling equipment, turnkey roll shops and roll shop management systems. Also rebuilds/retrofits all listed equipment.

HERMETIK HYDRAULIK AB
Skärviksvägen 4
Djursholm, Danderyd, 18261 Sweden
P: +46.70.323.1060
info@hermetik.com
www.hermetik.com

- Chief Exec. Officer, Pres. and Head of Design—Jürgen Gaydoul
- Vice Pres. Mktg.—Aaron Weller
- After Sales—Claudia Recke
- Chief Svce. Officer—Steffen Kulling

PRODUCTS and/or SERVICES: Provides full-service engineering; complete program management from start to finish; design and supply of

SUPPLIERS of EQUIPMENT, PRODUCTS and SERVICES

customer equipment; high-pressure water plunger pump <250 MPa (36,250 psi), 2,500 l/min. (660 gpm, power <2,500 kW (3,399 hp); rotary and stationary nozzles; rotary nozzles for water milling—multi-passes/descaling; high-pressure water valves; mobile descaling systems; descalers for all mill types; power control electrical systems for descalers; turnkey equipment and services; water filters; training; spare parts; refurbishment; and global services.

No. of Employees: 10.

HICKMAN, WILLIAMS & CO.
Pittsburgh Office:
2009 Mackenzie Way, Suite 120
Cranberry Twp., PA 16066 USA
P: +1.724.772.3090
F: +1.724.772.3066
www.hicwilco.com

- Chief Exec. Officer and Pres.—Robert Davis
- Tech. Mgr.—Jim Csonka

PRODUCTS and/or SERVICES: Services metals producers and related industries with an array of products, including foundry coke, ferroalloys, briquetted alloys, specialty metals and alloys, carbon additives, abrasives, pig iron, fused silica, metal filters, anthracite coal, met coke products, and lime.

Birmingham Office
22 Inverness Center Pkwy., Suite 160
Birmingham, AL 35242 USA
P: +1.205.322.2344

- Vice Pres. and Regional Mgr.—Ben Rankin

California Office
8838 Calabash Ave.
Fontana, CA 92335 USA
P: +1.909.822.5591
F: +1.909.822.7595

- Regional Sales Mgr.—Glenn Schneider

Chattanooga Office
6918 Shallowford Road, Suite 311
Chattanooga, TN 37421 USA
P: +1.423.867.6457
F: +1.423.867.6428

- Sales Engr.—Jeremy McLimans

Cincinnati Office
Columbia Plaza
250 E. Fifth St., Suite 300
Cincinnati, OH 45202 USA
P: +1.513.621.1946
F: +1.513.621.0024

- Chief Financial Officer and Vice Pres.—Stuart Shroyer

Texas Office
2505 Texas Dr., Suite 107
Irving, TX 75062 USA
P: +1.214.441.9040
F: +1.214.441.9258

- Sales Engr.—Kyle L. Watt

La Porte Manufacturing Div.
2321 W. Progress Dr.
La Porte, IN 46350 USA
P: +1.219.379.5199
F: +1.219.324.0208

- Regional Foundry Mgr.—Gene Holloway
- Regional Steel Mgr.—Dean Daenens

Melting Materials Div.
3420 Messer Airport Hwy.
Birmingham, AL 35222 USA
P: +1.205.322.2347
F: +1.205.328.3649

- Plant Mgr.—Wes Pearson

Subsidiary:

Hickman, Williams Canada Inc.
140 McGovern Dr., Unit 13
Cambridge, ON N3H 4R7 Canada
P: +1.519.650.1910
F: +1.519.650.0714

- Regional Sales Mgr.—Bill Van Beers

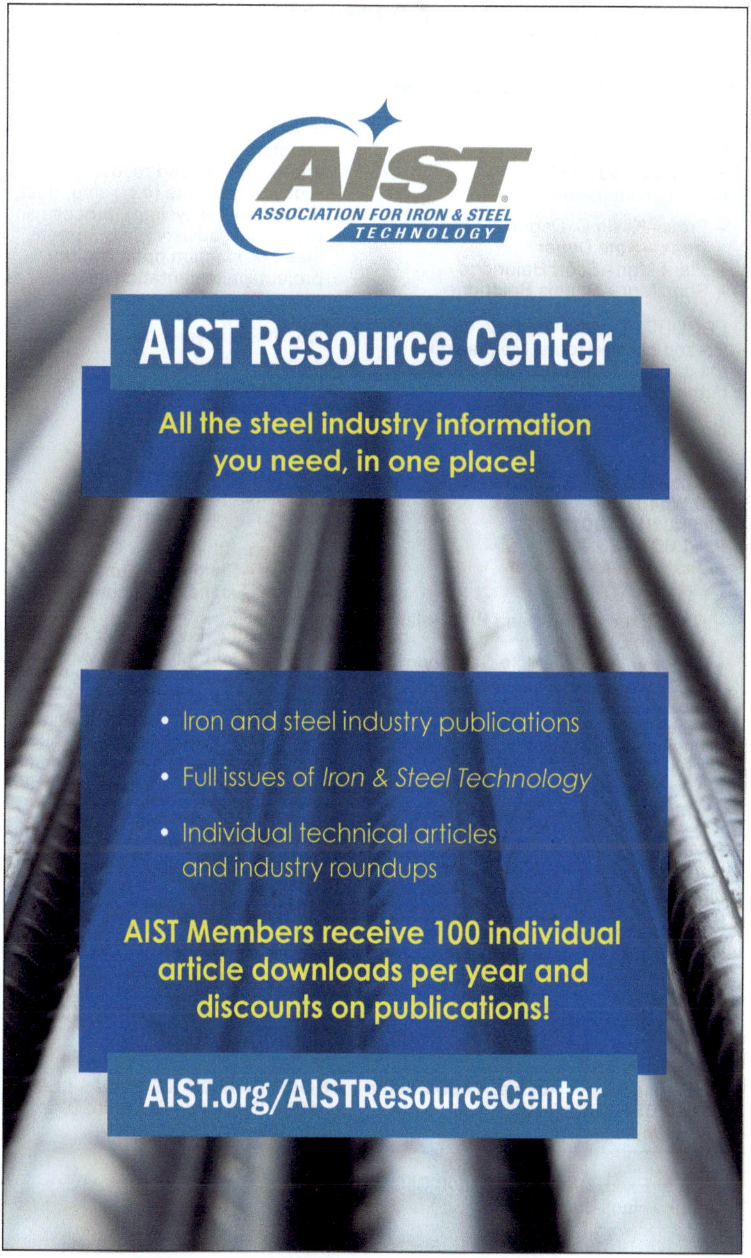
AIST
ASSOCIATION FOR IRON & STEEL
TECHNOLOGY
AIST Resource Center
All the steel industry information
you need, in one place!
• Iron and steel industry publications
• Full issues of Iron & Steel Technology
• Individual technical articles
and industry roundups
AIST Members receive 100 individual
article downloads per year and
discounts on publications!
AIST.org/AISTResourceCenter

SUPPLIERS of EQUIPMENT, PRODUCTS and SERVICES

HIGHLAND CARBIDE TOOL CO. INC.
741 Northeast Dr.
Irwin, PA 15642 USA
P: +1.724.863.7151
F: +1.724.863.7152
www.highlandcarbide.com

- Pres.—Kevin C. Deger
- Treas.—Kate Deger
- Plant Mgr.—Scott Baldridge
- Ship. Mgr.—Dennis Baldridge

PRODUCTS and/or SERVICES:
Brazed carbide tools. Mechanical tools. Carbide inserts. High-speed steel cutting blades (Steelcraft).

No. of Employees: 10.

HILLIARD BRAKE SYSTEMS
100 W. 4th St.
Elmira, NY 14901 USA
P: +1.607.733.7121
rdoud@hilliardcorp.com
www.hilliardcorp.com

- Chief Exec. Officer and Pres.—Jan van den Blink
- Exec. Vice Pres.—Mike Cantando
- Vice Pres. Sales—Mike Long
- Vice Pres. Engrg.—Matthew Cowan
- Vice Pres. Mktg.—Mike Long
- Vice Pres. Prodn./Mfg.—Steve Chesboro
- Adv. Mgr.—Rob Doud
- Chief Engr.—Brent Barron

PRODUCTS and/or SERVICES:
Caliper disc brakes, modular brakes, electric brakes, brake control systems, overrunning clutches, backstops, portable filtration.

No. of Employees: 475.

HJK CONSULTING ENGINEERS GMBH
Am Ipfbach 55
St. Florian, Upper Austria, 4490 Austria
P: +43.664.8872.7465
office@hjkcon.com
www.hjkcon.com

- Chief Exec. Officer, Pres. and Sales Mgr.—Hans-Joerg Klapf

PRODUCTS and/or SERVICES:
Consulting services, feasibility studies in iron- and steelmaking, production, maintenance and quality optimization, energy-saving and recovery, residual recovery services (e.g., slag, dust, refractories recycling), process and production advisory (e.g., green steel, production optimization), project implementation services, and secondhand facility advisory.

No. of Employees: 10–50.

HOH ENGINEERS INC.
623 Cooper Ct.
Schaumburg, IL 60173 USA
P: +1.312.346.8131
F: +1.312.424.3699
info@hohgroup.com
www.hohgroup.com

- Chmn., Chief Exec. Officer and Pres.—Santiago Garcia
- Chief Financial Officer—David M. Torelli
- Mgr. Elec. Engr.—Peter B. Leonard
- Mgr. Civil Engr.—Brent A. Profilio
- Dir. of Project Mgmt.—Nick M. Raskovich
- Mgr. Mech. and Process Engrg.—Nolan S. Kaplan
- Mgr. Structural Engrg.—David N. Bilow
- Mgr. Architecture—Johnny Bueno-Abdala

PRODUCTS and/or SERVICES:
Project management and engineering for the development of effective plant design, installations and operations. Complete mini-mills and fully integrated facilities. Robotics and automation integration. Fire protection and security systems. Control of hazardous wastes and emissions to comply with present-day federal regulations.

HOISTCAM BY NETARUS LLC
4855 Brookside Ct., Suite B
Norfolk, VA 23502 USA
P: +1.757.819.4600
F: +1.757.585.3534
sales@hoistcam.com
www.netarus.com

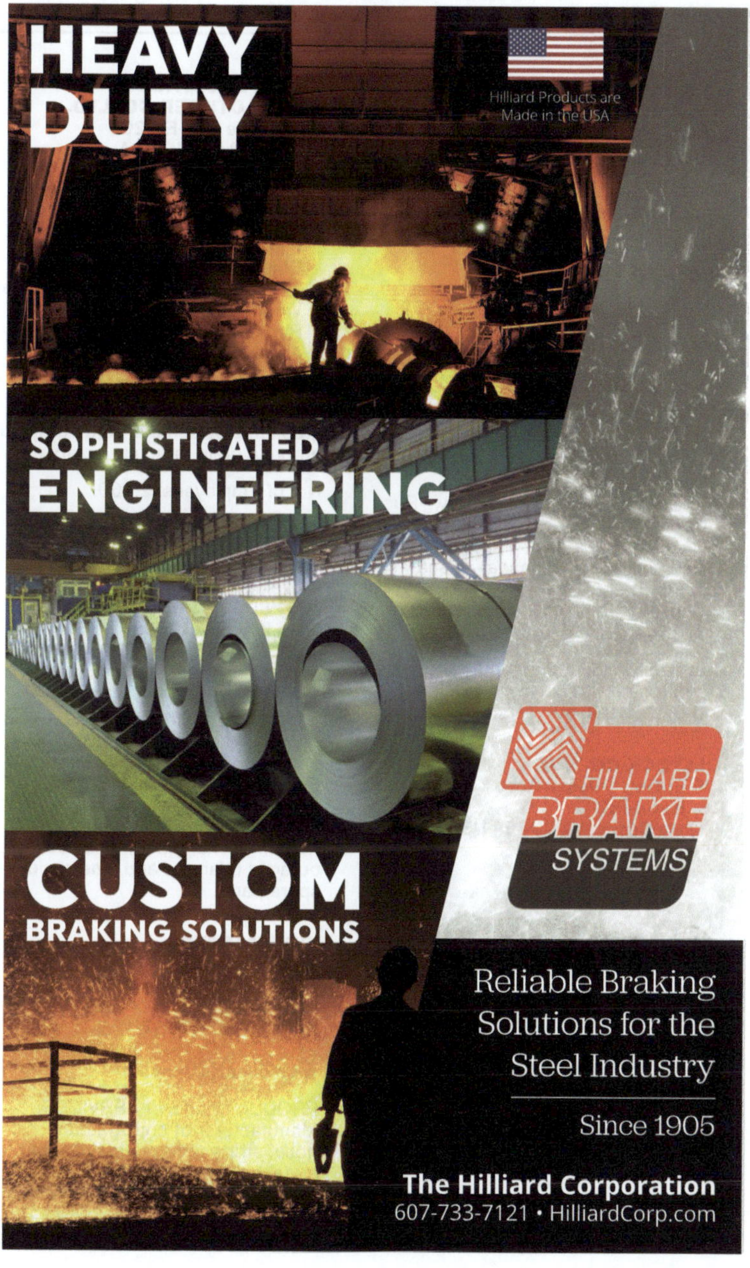

See listing page 394

SUPPLIERS of EQUIPMENT, PRODUCTS and SERVICES

- Chief Exec. Officer—Christopher Machut
- Pres.—Mark B. Shaw

PRODUCTS and/or SERVICES:
Safety and productivity solutions for cranes, material handling equipment, logistics and operations teams.

No. of Employees: 12.

HOLLAND
1000 Holland Dr.
Crete, IL 60417 USA
P: +1.708.672.2300
F: +1.708.672.0119
sales@hollandco.com
www.hollandco.com

- Pres.—Jordan Wolf
- Exec Vice Pres. Business Dev.—Russ Gehl
- Natl. Dir. Sales, U.S.—Maggie Vuono
- Natl. Sales Mgr., Canada—Taisha Poulin
- Gen. Mgr. Rail Svcs.—Rob Rosencrans

PRODUCTS and/or SERVICES:
Crane rail welding: flash-butt and thermite; in-track flash-butt welding and track inspection services.

HOLLTECK CO. INC.
105 S. First Colonial Road
P.O. Box 4453
Virginia Beach, VA 23454 USA
P: +1.757.425.7282
F: +1.757.425.5530
www.hollteck.co.uk/hollteck-worldwide.htm

- Pres.—Paul Holland
- Vice Pres.—Stephen Holland
- Sec./Treas.—Michael Holland

PRODUCTS and/or SERVICES:
Rolling mill guide equipment for rod, bar, SBQ and merchant products, including light and medium sections. Roller and friction-type guides as standard or custom-made.

No. of Employees: 30.

HONGJI ELECTRODE MANUFACTURER CO. LTD.
333 Maple Ave. E #200
Vienna, VA 22180 USA
P: +1.888.861.6158 (Toll-Free)
F: +1.206.338.2402
contact@sagegroupcorp.com
www.hongji.sagegroupcorp.com

- Chief Exec. Officer—Huitao Ge
- Pres. and Vice Pres. Sales—Yinhai Liu
- Vice Pres. Mktg.—Wei Li
- Regional Sales Mgr.—Ben Lee
- Adv. Mgr.—Kent Paonili

PRODUCTS and/or SERVICES:
Graphite electrode, carbon blocks, graphite blocks, high-purity graphite, graphite grain, graphite scrap, etc.

No. of Employees: 2,500.

HORSBURGH & SCOTT
5114 Hamilton Ave.
Cleveland, OH 44114 USA
P: +1.800.424.6514 (Toll-Free);
   +1.216.431.3900;
   +1.216.432.5888 (24-Hr. Svce. Line)
inquiry@horsburgh-scott.com
www.horsburgh-scott.com

- Chief Exec. Officer and Pres.—Randy Burdick

PRODUCTS and/or SERVICES:
Industrial gears, gearboxes, pinions, shafts, reverse engineering, power transmissions, repair, field service/outages (planned and emergency), spare parts.

HOSE MASTER
1233 E. 222nd St.
Cleveland, OH 44117 USA
P: +1.800.221.2319 (Toll-Free)
F: +1.216.481.7557
info@hosemaster.com
www.hosemaster.com

PRODUCTS and/or SERVICES:
Manufacturer of corrugated metal hose, stripwound metal hose and metal bellows expansion joints for steel manufacturing applications. Applications include: coke oven and coke byproducts, lime injection, oxygen

SUPPLIERS OF EQUIPMENT, PRODUCTS and SERVICES

lance hoses, steam lines, gas lines, lubrication lines, vacuum degassers, caster cut-off torches, furnace door cooling water, tap hole drills, and spray chamber cooling lines.

HOTWORK-USA
223 Gold Rush Road
Lexington, KY 40503 USA
P: +1.859.276.1570
F: +1.859.276.1583
hotwork@hotwork.com
www.hotwork.com

- Chief Exec. Officer—Tom Graham Jr.
- Vice Pres.—Justin Jones
- Cust. Svce.—Stephenie Haden

PRODUCTS and/or SERVICES:
Refractory dryout and heat-up services for coke ovens, BFs, hot blast stoves, DRI vessels, reheat furnaces, galvanize pots, and other refractory-lined facilities.

HOWDEN GROUP
Old Govan Road
Renfrew, Lanarkshire, PA4 8XJ
Scotland, U.K.
www.howden.com

- Chief Exec. Officer—Ross B. Shuster
- Chief Financial Officer—Alastair Irvine
- Chief Oper. Officer—Massimo Bizzi
- Chief H.R. Officer—Stuart Dalgleish
- Gen. Counsel—Jen Robertson
- Pres. Asia Pacific—Camille Levy
- Pres. China—Harold Lang
- Pres. Americas—Mark Sanders
- Pres. EMENA—Fred Hearle
- Pres. Africa—Eric Vemer
- Vice Pres. Global Aftermarket—Feilim Coyle
- Vice Pres. Strategy and Business Dev.—Amit Bhargava

PRODUCTS and/or SERVICES:
Air and gas handling products, services and support for the metal industry. Howden builds fans, heaters, and blowers engineered to improve efficiency, emission levels and reliability. The Howden family includes more than 90 brands, including American Standard, Buffalo Forge, Canadian Blower, Covent Fans, Green Fans, Novenco, Roots Blowers, Sturtevant Fans, TLT-Babcock, Westinghouse Fans, and more. Global network with locations in more than 30 countries.

No. of Employees: 6,000 worldwide.

HUBBELL
4301 Cheyenne Dr.
Archdale, NC 27263 USA
P: +1.336.434.2800
F: +1.336.434.2801
www.hubbell.com

PRODUCTS and/or SERVICES:
International manufacturer of quality electric and electronic products for a broad range of industrial, construction and utility applications. Brands include: Cableform, EC&M, Gleason Reel, Hubbell Industrial Controls, Metron, and Powerohm Resistors.

HUNT VALVE CO.
1913 E. State St.
Salem, OH 44460 USA
P: +1.800.321.2757 (Toll-Free)
F: +1.330.337.3754
www.huntvalve.com

- Chief Exec. Office and Pres.—Charles Ferrer
- Vice Pres., Chief Financial and Admin. Officer—Peter Bellin
- Vice Pres. Oprs. and Supply Chain—Michael Johnston
- Vice Pres. Engrg.—Andrew Pfister

PRODUCTS and/or SERVICES:
Descale spray valves, water hydraulic directional control valves, specialty hydraulic cylinders, rotary distributors.

No. of Employees: 75.

HY-DAC RUBBER MFG.
301 S. Main St.
Smithton, IL 62285 USA
P: +1.618.233.2129
F: +1.618.233.2361
dstellhorn@hy-dac.com

- Gen. Mgr./Owner—David Stellhorn
- Regional Sales Mgr.—Randy Polk

SUPPLIERS of EQUIPMENT, PRODUCTS and SERVICES

EQUIPMENT:
Rubber roll extruders, machine lathes, boilers, overhead cranes, welder.

PRODUCTS and/or SERVICES:
Rubber-covered rolls for the steel and brass industries. In-house machine shop.

No. of Employees: 20.

HY-PRO FILTRATION
6810 Layton Road
Anderson, IN 46011 USA
P: +1.317.849.3535
info@hyprofiltration.com
www.hyprofiltration.com

PRODUCTS and/or SERVICES:
Manufactures filtration products for lubrication and hydraulic systems, including filter assemblies, filter elements, mobile and off-line filtration systems, breathers, vacuum dehydration units, turbine oil and diesel fuel coalesce skids, ion charge bonding acid scavenging elements, soluble varnish removal, and fluid analysis equipment.

No. of Employees: 100.

HYDRO INC.
834 W. Madison St.
Chicago, IL 60607 USA
P: +1.312.738.3000
info@hydroinc.com
www.hydroinc.com

- Founder and Chief Exec. Officer—George Harris

PRODUCTS and/or SERVICES:
Independent aftermarket pump services. Engineered pump rebuilding, engineered upgrades, engineering services, engineered replacement parts, 24/7 emergency services, pump performance testing up to 5,000 hp, wireless condition monitoring, comprehensive field services, reliability services, on-site pump training and worldwide service centers.

HydroAire Inc.
834 W. Madison St.
Chicago, IL 60607 USA
P: +1.312.738.3000
F: +1.312.738.3226
www.hydroinc.com

- Chief Exec. Officer and Pres.—George Harris
- Vice Pres. Ind. Sales and Svce.—Ken Babusiak

PRODUCTS and/or SERVICES:
Specializing in the rebuilding and upgrading of engineered pumps such as those used in descaling, central hydraulics, BF recycle and other steel mill applications. In addition, HydroAire provides engineering, wireless condition monitoring, field service and pump performance testing, as well as offering new pumps and replacement parts.

No. of Employees: Chicagoland—175; Worldwide—454.

HYDROTHRIFT CORP.
1301 Sanders Ave. SW
Massillon, OH 44648 USA
P: +1.330.837.5141
F: +1.330.837.0558
sales@hydrothrift.com
www.hydrothrift.com

- Pres.—Paul Heston

PRODUCTS and/or SERVICES:
Closed-loop cooling systems, heat exchanger sales and repair.

No. of Employees: 30.

HYSTER CO.
1400 Sullivan Dr.
Greenville, NC 27834 USA
P: +1.800.HYSTER1 (497.8371)
  (Toll-Free)
information@hyster.com
www.hyster.com

PRODUCTS and/or SERVICES:
Materials handling equipment, lift trucks, fleet management services, telemetry, parts and service. Lifting capacities of up to 105,000 lbs.

SUPPLIERS OF EQUIPMENT, PRODUCTS and SERVICES

I

I²R POWER
4300 Chamber Ave. SW
Canton, OH 44706 USA
P: +1.330.588.3000
F: +1.330.588.3007
www.i2rpower.com

- Pres.—Michael G. Pinney, mike.pinney@i2rpower.com
- Dir.—Karl J. Schwenk, karl.schwenk@i2rpower.com
- Sales Engr.—Dane Schwartz, dane.schwartz@i2rpower.com

PRODUCTS and/or SERVICES: Designer/manufacturer of air- and water-cooled cables for a wide array of thermal processing applications: EAF, VIM, VAR, ESR, hot isostatic press, submerged arc, induction heating, crystal growing. Comprehensive service/remanufacture of EMS equipment, including caster and ladle stirrers alike. Provide products/services to the end user, as well as OEMs.

IBA AMERICA LLC
370 Winkler Dr., Suite C
Alpharetta, GA 30004 USA
P: +1.770.886.2318
F: +1.770.886.9258
sales@iba-america.com
www.iba-america.com

- Chief Exec. Officer—Horst Anhaus
- Pres. and Chief Engr.—Scott Bouchillon
- Contr.—Carol Denovchek
- Oprs. Mgr.—Eric Snyder

PRODUCTS and/or SERVICES: Measurement systems for process insight in industrial production, power generation and energy distribution plants. The iba system consists of hardware and software components for acquiring, recording, analyzing and processing measurement data. Due to the modular design, the iba system can be adapted comfortably to various tasks and is scalable at any time. iba's team of application and consulting engineers also provides best practices with regard to data collection, PC control, automated test systems, on-line diagnostics and condition monitoring, automated maintenance and quality reporting systems, edge analytics, business intelligence tools, and customized application-specific solutions.

No. of Employees: 10–15.

ICL-IP AMERICA INC.
622 Emerson Road, Suite 500
St. Louis, MO 63141 USA
P: +1.800.666.1200 (Toll-Free)
ipacustomer.service@icl-group.com
www.fyrquel.com

PRODUCTS and/or SERVICES: Fyrquel®, Fyrlube®, fire-resistant hydraulic fluids, phosphate ester hydraulic fluids.

No. of Employees: 500+.

IDOM INC.
330 S. Second Ave., Suite 600
Minneapolis, MN 55401 USA
P: +1.612.331.8905
miles@idom.com
info@idom.com
www.idom.com

- Pres. U.S. Oprs.—Thomas Lorentz
- Vice Pres. U.S. Oprs.—Javier Alvarez
- Vice Pres. Business Dev.—Miles Shephard
- Dir., Metals and Minerals—Andoni Borjabez

PRODUCTS and/or SERVICES: Basic/detailed engineering services and construction management.

No. of Employees: 3,800.

SUPPLIERS of EQUIPMENT, PRODUCTS and SERVICES

IKEUCHI USA INC.
4722 Ritter Ave.
Blue Ash, OH 45242 USA
P: +1.513.942.3060
F: +1.513.942.3064
info@ikeuchi.us
www.ikeuchi.us

- Pres.—Seiro Matsui
- Sales Mgr.—Yasunori Washizuka

PRODUCTS and/or SERVICES:
Precision-made spray nozzles for descaling. Nozzle headers with internal brushes for manual cleaning in areas where nozzle clogging is a concern for minimal downtime. Cooling mist nozzles for casting lines. A variety of nozzles designed to lower costs and make maintenance easier, combined with a team of professionals to support and advise. Nozzles not only for the iron and steel industry itself, but also to help with dust suppression, employee cooling and other fringe needs.

No. of Employees: 9.

ILLINOIS ELECTRIC WORKS
2161 Adams St.
Granite City, IL 62040 USA
P: +1.618.451.6900
F: +1.618.451.6940
chad@illinoiselectric.com
www.illinoiselectric.com

- Pres.—Dale Hamil
- Exec. Vice Pres.—Trent Hamil
- Sales Mgr.—Chad Travnicek

PRODUCTS and/or SERVICES:
Motor repairs to 50,000 hp, pumps, blowers, cranes, motor controls service and new products, and generator testing and repair.

No. of Employees: 70.

IMS SYSTEMS INC.
519 Myoma Road
Mars, PA 16046 USA
P: +1.724.772.9772
F: +1.724.772.9786
sales@imssystems.com
www.imssystems.com

- Chief Exec. Officer—Chris Lackinger

PRODUCTS and/or SERVICES:
Non-contact, on-line, real-time measurement of thickness, profile, wedge, crown, width, edge drop, contour, flatness, coating weight, passline, tube, diameter, tube OD/ovality, and tube wall thickness of ferrous and non-ferrous metals, in hot and cold applications.

IN-PLACE MACHINING CO.
3811 N. Holton St.
Milwaukee, WI 53212 USA
P: +1.414.562.2000
F: +1.414.562.2932
help@inplace.com
www.inplace.com

- Pres.—Dean Flint
- Vice Pres. Tech. Svcs.—Miron Mironczuk
- Sr. Vice Pres. Sales and Mktg.—Dina Maihi

EQUIPMENT:
Portable welding, drilling, milling, boring, facing and turning machine tools. A wide range of both manual and CNC machine shop equipment. Optical alignment tooling and an entire fleet of 3D precision measurement and machine alignment tooling including laser trackers, portable 3D scanners and long-range scanners, portable measuring arms, and CT scanning machines.

PRODUCTS and/or SERVICES:
Extensive on-site and in-shop machining, R-stamp certified welding and Metalstitch® cold cast iron repair services. Large-scale diamond wire cutting and core drilling services. Upgrades and/or corrective machining of hot and cold rolling mill housings, gearboxes, pinion stands, drive motors, handling/processing equipment, cranes, BOF, EAF, casters, and BFs. As divisions of IPM, OASIS Alignment Services and Exact Metrology make up the Measurement and Alignment Services Group. Services include machine alignment inspections and

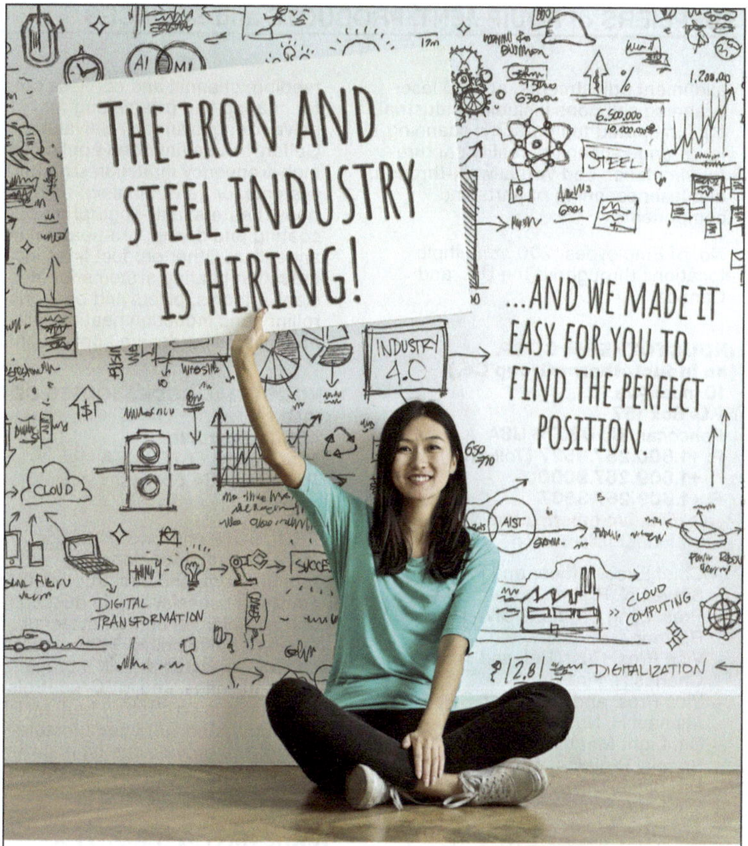

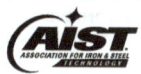

SUPPLIERS of EQUIPMENT, PRODUCTS and SERVICES

alignment adjustments, and 3D laser scanning solutions including industrial CT (computed tomography) scanning, long-range scanning, reality capture for simulation and virtual walk-through, and laser scanning of parts and components.

No. of Employees: 200 at multiple locations throughout the U.S. and Canada.

INDUCTOTHERM CORP.
(an Inductotherm Group Co.)
10 Indel Ave.
P.O. Box 157
Rancocas, NJ 08073 USA
P: +1.800.257.9527 (Toll-Free);
  +1.609.267.9000
F: +1.609.267.3537
sales@inductotherm.com
www.inductotherm.com

- Chief Exec. Officer and Pres.—Satyen N. Prabhu
- Pres. Long Products Div.—Bernard M. Raffner
- Vice Pres. Cust. Rel. and Training—Charles H. Fink Jr.
- Vice Pres. and Gen. Mgr. Sales—Michael H. Nutt
- Dir. Light Metal Applications and Special Projects—Charles W. Vivian
- Dir. Sales, USA—Robert C. Keshecki
- Dir. Long Products Div.—Bert Armstrong
- Capital Sales, Long Products Div.—David Cernava
- Mgr., Intl. Sales—Gregory Bossong
- Managing Dir. Inductotherm Group Canada—Paul Webber
- Sales Mgr. Inductotherm Group México—Oscar De León

PRODUCTS and/or SERVICES: Manufactures a complete line of induction melting, holding, pouring, heating, and coating equipment for thermal applications in air or controlled atmospheres for the metals industry. Coreless and channel furnaces with capabilities up to 500 tons; power supplies up to 42,000 kW; automated pouring systems; computer controls; charge handling systems; pre-heating, drying and feeding; channel and coreless pots for coating and pre-melting for galvanize, galvanneal, Galvalume®, Galfan® and aluminized applications; high-frequency induction strip heating systems for galvannealing; tin reflow; boost heaters; anti-fingerprint; paint coating and drying; pre-heating; weld annealing. Other product lines include induction heating systems for ingots, slabs, blooms, billets and bars prior to rolling; and induction heating for rail and mill roll hardening applications.

INDUSTRIAL ACCESSORIES CO. (IAC)
4800 Lamar Ave.
Mission, KS 66202 USA
P: +1.913.384.5511
www.iac-intl.com

PRODUCTS and/or SERVICES: Fully integrated engineering, procurement, and construction (EPC) contractor specializing in dust control and air pollution control systems, dry material handling, pneumatic conveying systems, bulk storage and transloads, and MCC/controls. IAC's unique position as both an EPC contractor and OEM manufacturer allows it to provide customers with everything from full plant builds to replacement components.

INDUSTRIAL MAINTENANCE WELDING & MACHINING CO. INC.
1431 W. Pershing Road
Chicago, IL 60609 USA
P: +1.773.376.6526
F: +1.773.376.0631
www.imwnet.com

PRODUCTS and/or SERVICES: Quality job shop servicing all areas of heavy manufacturing with a focus on all steelmaking and finishing operations. With more than 300,000 sq. ft. of manufacturing space and over 100,000 lbs. lifting capacity, IMW is able to service large work as well as small. In-house trucking provides around-the-clock services to help with any daily or emergency requirements.

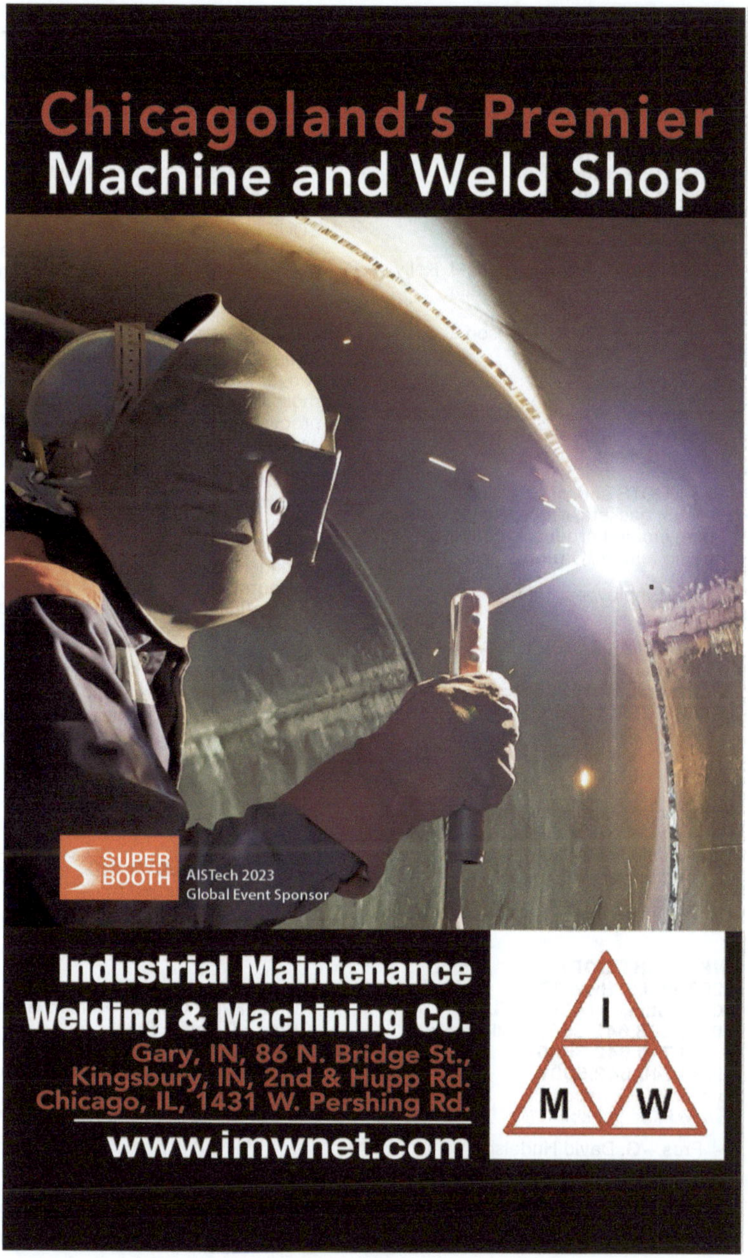

See listing page 402

SUPPLIERS of EQUIPMENT, PRODUCTS and SERVICES

INDUSTRIAL RUBBER PRODUCTS CO.
726 Trumbull Dr.
Pittsburgh, PA 15205 USA
P: +1.412.276.6400
F: +1.412.276.4900
irp@irpgroup.com
www.irpgroup.com

- Chief Exec. Officer—Frank J. Kelly Jr.
- Acctg. Coordinator—Angelia Impellicceiri
- Sales Mgr.—David Murison
- Pur. Agt.—Mike Daley

EQUIPMENT:
Vulcanizers, extruders, lathes, grinders, presses, overhead cranes, tow motors, tractor trailers.

PRODUCTS and/or SERVICES:
V-belts, gaskets, rubber hose, metal hose, molded products, conveyor belting and MRO rubber products.

No. of Employees: 15.

INDUSTRIAL SCIENTIFIC CORP.
1 Life Way
Pittsburgh, PA 15205 USA
P: +1.412.788.4353
F: +1.412.788.8353
info@indsci.com
www.indsci.com

PRODUCTS and/or SERVICES:
Provider of gas detection products and services that keep workers safe in hazardous environments.

No. of Employees: 1,200.

INFOSIGHT CORP.
20700 U.S. Hwy. 23
Chillicothe, OH 45601 USA
P: +1.888.642.3600 (Toll-Free);
   +1.740.642.3600
F: +1.740.642.5001
info@infosight.com
www.infosight.com

- Pres.—G. David Hudelson
- Chief Financial Officer—Rob Underhill
- Sec.—Barbara Robertson
- Dir. of Automation—Jeff Good
- Dir. of Laser Printers and Tag Products—Joseph B. Morelli
- Gen Mgr., Laser Product Dev. and Oprs.—Edward O'Neal
- Prodn. Mgr.—John Redfearn
- Pur. Mgr.—Becky Dolan

EQUIPMENT:
30,000 sq. ft. of manufacturing space; full panel shop; grinder; paint booth; three welders; two 10-ton cranes; three full CNC machining centers with automatic tool changers with three additional mills; various saws; two lathes; one shear; one brake; one radial arm drill press; tag coating and processing lines; standard product assembly and testing facility.

PRODUCTS and/or SERVICES:
Automatic dot-peen marking equipment, automatic ink spray systems, automatic direct laser marking systems, robot integration into automatic systems, manual and automatic laser printers for metal tags, custom equipment, laser-markable metal tags, 24/7 technical service, installation and start-up services, vision reading systems, standard and custom design capabilities including mechanical and engineering software; R&D department for new product development.

No. of Employees: 65.

INJECTION ALLOYS INC.
1700 Made Industrial Dr.
Middletown, OH 45044 USA
P and F: +1.513.422.8819
info.iausa@injectionalloys.com
www.injectionalloys.com

- Chief Exec. Officer—Ramiro Becerra
- Pres.—Dominic Stekly
- Exec. Vice Pres.—Manuel Franco
- Vice Pres. Prodn./Mfg.—Luis Acosta
- Treas.—Nubia Clem
- Sales Mgrs.—Adalid Ramirez, Mike Farley

PRODUCTS and/or SERVICES:
Supplier of cored injection wires. Hi-Core® product line is a calcium-based group of ultrahigh metallurgical

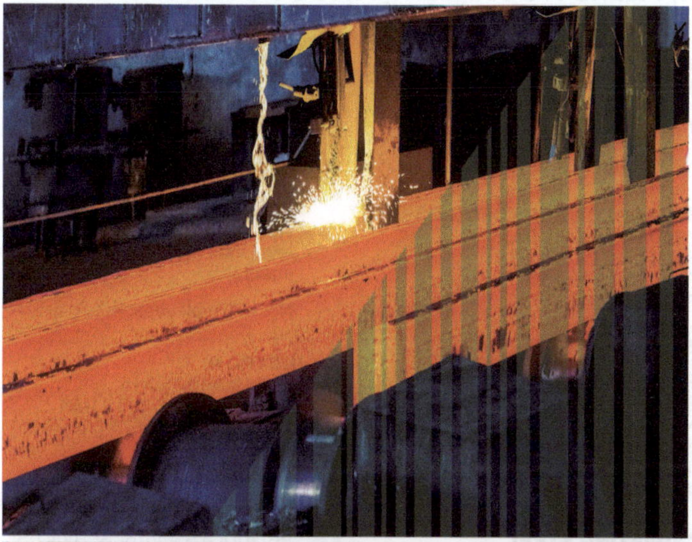

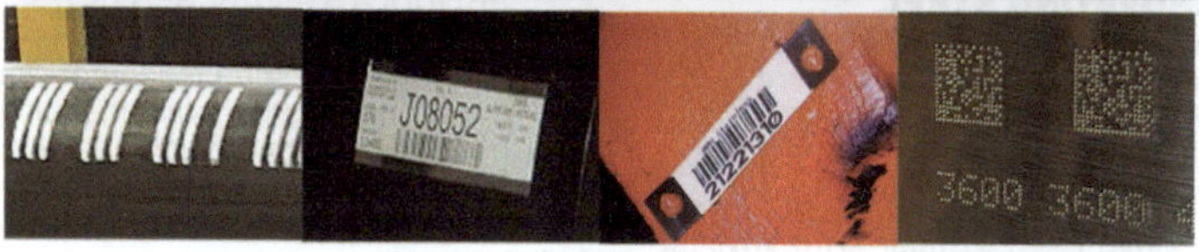

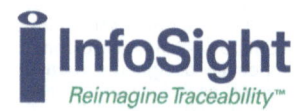

SUPPLIERS of EQUIPMENT, PRODUCTS and SERVICES

performance wires. Also supply a complete line of conventional cored wire products and wire feeder machines.

No. of Employees: 100.

INNERSPEC TECHNOLOGIES INC.
2940 Perrowville Road
Forest, VA 24551 USA
P: +1.434.948.1301
F: +1.434.948.1313
sales@innerspec.com
www.innerspec.com

PRODUCTS and/or SERVICES: Specializes in high-performance NDT solutions with a focus on electromagnetic acoustic transducer ultrasonic testing (UT), dry-coupled UT, and eddy current solutions.

INNOVATING STEEL
Malecon Cisneros 124
Miraflores, Lima, 00018 Peru
P: +51.9.96488727
tito.voysest@innovatingsteel.com
www.innovatingsteel.com

– Chief Exec. Officer—Tito Voysest

PRODUCTS and/or SERVICES: Flow control products, refractory bricks, water-cooled panels, steel mill machinery, balers, shears, MgO-based raw materials, graphite electrodes. Exclusively serving South America.

No. of Employees: 7.

INOXIHP S.R.L.
Via Garibaldi 89
Nova Milanese (MB), 20834 Italy
P: +39.0362.19.01.11
F: +39.0362.19.01.008
a.dovico@inoxihp.com
www.inoxihp.com

– Business Dev. Mgr.—Alessandro Dovico

PRODUCTS and/or SERVICES: Engineering and manufacturing of components and systems for high-pressure water. Descaling and rolling mill applications, press applications and hydraulic testing. Reciprocating plunger pumps, air- and oil-actuated valves 2/3 way, on/off water-actuated valves 2/3 way, stop-balanced valves, flow proportional valves air- and oil-actuated, air-actuated pressure-regulating valves, check valves, accumulator shutoff valves, level indicators, pre-filling valves, and manifolds.

No. of Employees: 40.

INSTRON
825 University Ave.
Norwood, MA 02062 USA
P: +1.800.877.6674 (Toll-Free)
web@instron.com
www.instron.com

– Metals Mkt. Mgr.—Dean Lovewell

PRODUCTS and/or SERVICES: Universal testing machines, dynamic and fatigue testing machines, impact drop tower testing machines, impact pendulum testing machines, automated testing systems, materials testing accessories, and materials testing software.

No. of Employees: 1,000+.

INTECO PTI
4950 S. Royal Atlanta Dr., Suite A
Tucker, GA 30084 USA
P: +1.770.934.9502
sales@intecopti.com
www.intecopti.com

PRODUCTS and/or SERVICES: Designs and builds plants for the production of carbon steels including specialty steels and super alloys. Inteco's product portfolio comprises melting (EAF, SAF, IF), refining (LF, VD/VOD, AOD, RH-VCP), casting (bottom pouring, vacuum ingot casting), continuous billet and bloom casting (specially designed vertical continuous caster) as well as special melting and remelting (VIM, VIMP, ESR, Pressure ESR, ESRR®, VAR) technology.

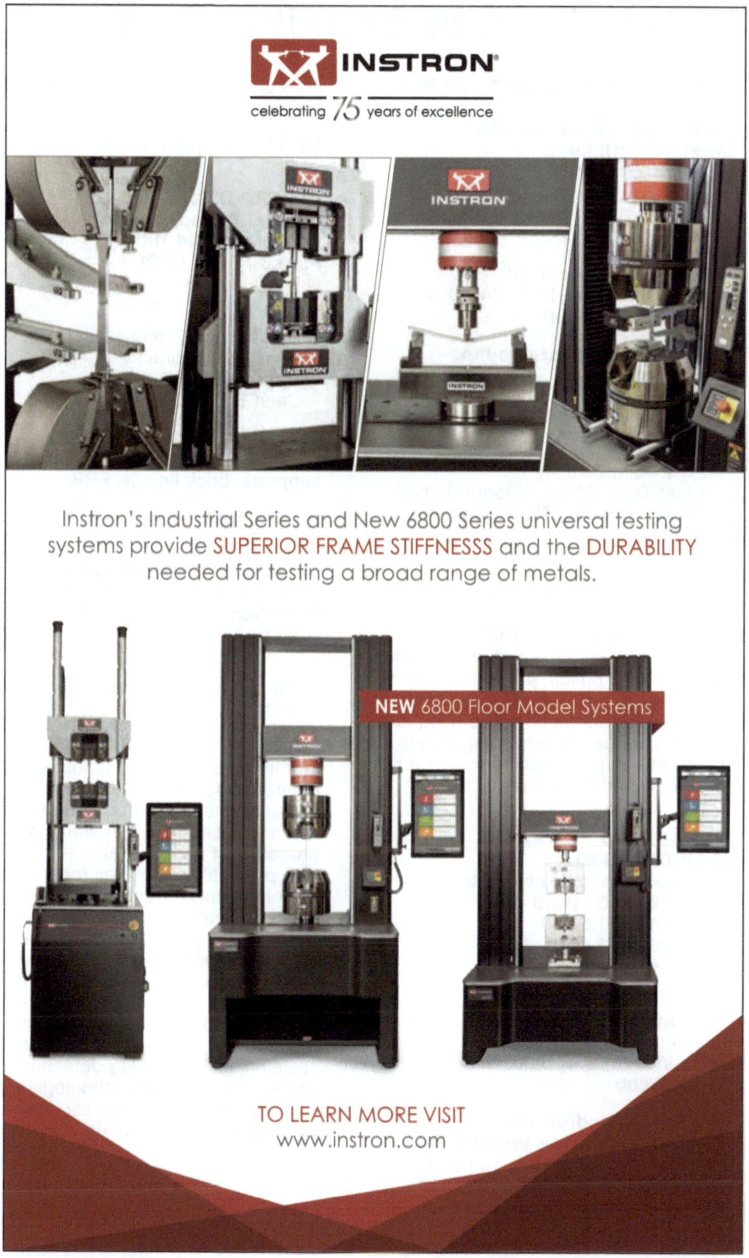

See listing page 406

SUPPLIERS of EQUIPMENT, PRODUCTS and SERVICES

INTEGRATED MILL SYSTEMS INC.
1702 Joseph Lloyd Pkwy.
Willoughby, OH 44094 USA
P: +1.440.918.9900
F: +1.440.918.9901
www.integratedmillsystems.com

Integrated Mill Systems Inc. – Pittsburgh Office
8800 Barnes Lake Road
North Huntingdon, PA 15642 USA
P: +1.724.861.3500

Integrated Mill Systems Inc. – Midwest Office
1110 Arrowhead Ct.
Crown Point, IN 46307 USA
P: +1.219.765.9757

- Pres.—Jim Zelazny
- Chief Tech. Officer—Robert Urban
- Chief Financial Officer—Marius Juodisius
- Sales Dir.—Jeff Daugherty
- Gen. Mgr.—Jason Strobel
- Business Mgr.—Dennis Golias

PRODUCTS and/or SERVICES: Process automation solutions provider. IMS designs, builds, programs, and implements level 1 control systems, primarily for the metals producing and processing market, providing a wide range of equipment and services for both new and retrofit projects.

INTEGRATED POWER SERVICES (IPS)
3 Independence Pointe, Suite 100
Greenville, SC 29615 USA
P: +1.864.451.5600
F: +1.864.451.5601
services@ips.us
www.ips.us

- Chief Exec. Officer and Pres.—John Zuleger
- Sr. Vice Pres. of Sales and Mktg.—Jon Webb

PRODUCTS and/or SERVICES: Electric motor repair services, field services and distribution, as well as remanufacturing, in-house coil manufacturing of B-Stage fully cured coils and VPI engineered insulation systems.

No. of Employees: 1,000.

INTEREP INC.
400 Old Y Road
Golden, CO 80401 USA
P: +1.303.277.0401
sales@interepinc.com
www.interepinc.com

- Chief Exec. Officer—C.J. Horecky
- Pres.—Carl Horecky
- Treas.—Grace Burge
- Chief Engr.—Daniel Corral

PRODUCTS and/or SERVICES: Dampers, expansion joints, fans, pipe supports, brick linings, FRP.

No. of Employees: 8.

INTERFLOW TECHSERV INC.
3449 Technology Dr., Unit 202
North Venice, FL 34275 USA
P: +1.941.480.1111
jim.dorricott@interflowtechserv.com

- Managing Dir.—James D. Dorricott
- Tech. Dir.—Lawrence J. Heaslip

PRODUCTS and/or SERVICES: Mathematical process simulation laboratory for computational models of heat transfer, fluid flow and solidification in metallurgical processes. Fluid flow laboratory with physical capabilities for tracer dispersion measurement, velocimetry and liquid metal flow visualization. Steelmaking process analysis and software development. Design and process optimization services for liquid steel transfer operations, including furnaces, ladles, tundishes and molds. Development of control and sensing systems, including slag detection and level measuring technologies. Educational and training services in steelmaking and continuous casting.

SUPPLIERS OF EQUIPMENT, PRODUCTS and SERVICES

INTERNATIONAL KNIFE & SAW INC.
1435 N. Cashua Road
Florence, SC 29501 USA
P: +1.800.354.9872 (Toll-Free);
  +1.843.292.1459
F: +1.843.664.1103
jcarr@iksinc.com

- Vice Pres. Sales—Jeff Carr
- Chief Engr.—Joshua Gibson

PRODUCTS and/or SERVICES:
Shear blades, slitter knives, sidetrimmers, slitter spacers, sheet slitter blades, separator tooling, disc and spacers, stripper rings, arbor shims, tooling software, slitter training services, tube cutoff knives, machine ways, and scrap chopper knives.

No. of Employees: 70+.

INTERNATIONAL TECHNICAL CERAMICS LLC (ITC)
13001 Old Denton Road
Fort Worth, TX 76177 USA
P: +1.817.337.9889
F: +1.817.337.3883
office@itccoatings.com
www.itccoatings.com

PRODUCTS and/or SERVICES:
High-temperature, energy-efficient ceramic coatings.

INTERPOWER INDUCTION USA
3578 Van Dyke Road
Almont, MI 48003 USA
P: +1.810.798.9201
F: +1.810.798.9301
mrugg@interpowerinduction.com

- Chief Exec. Officer and Pres.—Gary Gariglio
- Dir. of Sales—Mike Rugg
- Adv. Mgr.—Kristin Grifka
- Chief Engr.—Mark Beygelman

EQUIPMENT:
Induction heating equipment.

PRODUCTS and/or SERVICES:
Material handling, water cooling systems, induction coils and turnkey systems.

No. of Employees: 75.

IOMES GROUP LTD.
28 Queen's Road Central
Hong Kong, Hong Kong, P.R. China
P: +85.281.932.369
info@myindustrialoperations.com
www.myindustrialoperations.com

- Pres.—Corrado Licata

PRODUCTS and/or SERVICES:
Heavy industry expert services and IIoT solutions for process quality control.

No. of Employees: 12.

IRWIN CAR AND EQUIPMENT
9953 Broadway, Rte. 993
P.O. Box 409
Irwin, PA 15642 USA
P: +1.724.864.8900
F: +1.724.864.8909
dfitzpatrick@irwincar.com
www.irwincar.com

- Chief Exec. Officer and Pres.— William Baker
- Sr. Vice Pres.—David J. Fitzpatrick
- Vice Pres. Engrg. and Qual. Control— Terry R. Steiner
- Mgr. of Engrg. and AGV Sales—Joe Parker
- Product Line Mgr., Atlas Car and Railroad Products—Bill Springer
- Product Line Mgr., Phillips Products— Dave Felt
- Vice Pres. Supply Chain—Perry Sumner

EQUIPMENT:
130,000+-sq.-ft. manufacturing facilities with 30-ton-capacity overhead cranes, fully equipped CNC machine shops with six CNC VTLs with turning capacity to 40 in., four CNC lathes, CNC milling machines; a fully equipped heavy fabrication facility with dedicated manufacturing cells for new industrial car and equipment manufacture, truck assembly and repair, full-service traction motor repair and rebuild shop in-house with full wheel truing capabilities; light- to heavy-duty general fabrication, prototypes and mechanical assembly. State-of-the-art quality control inspection lab. Additional production

SUPPLIERS of EQUIPMENT, PRODUCTS and SERVICES

and warehousing facilities in Blairsville, PA; Waynesburg, PA; Beckley, WV; Logan, WV; Big Rock, VA; and West Frankfort, IL.

PRODUCTS and/or SERVICES: Custom-engineered and -manufactured industrial cars and heavy-duty material handling equipment for heavy industry, including self-propelled and non-propelled transfer cars, furnace cars, ladle cars, scrap cars, coil cars, ingot cars, locomotives, AGVs, transporters, steerable trailers; also heavy-duty truck and bogie assemblies, crane wheels, sheave wheels, custom steel wheels and wheel assemblies, turntables, scrap and charging buckets, bulk material handling equipment, mine and tunneling cars, and spare parts.

No. of Employees: 180.

ISB STEEL TECH [Principal Companies are Atomat SpA and Bendotti (Forni Industriali Bendotti SpA)]
615 Crystal Dr.
Spartanburg, SC 29302 USA
P: +1.803.238.4400
keith@isbsteel.com

- Pres.—Keith Bacon

PRODUCTS and/or SERVICES: CNC machinery for notching/marking, turning, grinding and combination machines; related tooling for all machines; TC wire mesh and TiC guide rollers. Pre-fabricated reheat furnaces: walking beam, pusher and walking hearth; level 1 and 2 controls; specialized high-aluminum refractory for pusher furnaces.

ISRA VISION PARSYTEC AG
Pascalstrasse 16
Aachen, 52076 Germany
P: +49.0.2408.92700.0
F: +49.0.2408.92700.500
info@isravision.com
www.isravision.com

- Exec. Bd.—Hans Jürgen Christ, Martin Heinrich, Jens Magenheimer

PRODUCTS and/or SERVICES: Supplies surface inspection systems and full quality monitoring throughout metal production and processing. The EXPERT5i software solutions allow the customer to prepare customized surface quality and yield management applications while integrating surface quality data with process data.
The ISRA VISION Group, with its headquarter offices in Darmstadt and Aachen, does business on a global level through locations in 25 other branch offices around the world.

ISRA Vision Parsytec Inc.
4470 Peachtree Lakes Dr.
Berkeley Lake, GA 30096 USA
P: +1.770.449.7776
F: +1.770.449.0399
info@isravision.com
www.isravision.com

- Pres.—Brian Heil
- Mktg. Mgr.—Tim Boldt

PRODUCTS and/or SERVICES: Automated metal surface inspection systems for all applications and process stages in metal strip production. Surface quality yield management software. Quality management systems.

No. of Employees: 800+.

ITIPACK SYSTEMS
919 Zelco Dr.
Burlington, ON L7L 4Y2 Canada
P: +1.905.220.0551
info@itipacksystems.com
www.itipacksystems.com

- Pres.—Arnold Hulzebosch
- Gen. Mgr.—Chris Hulzebosch
- NA-BD/Sales Dir.—Kyle Jager

PRODUCTS and/or SERVICES: Leading provider of integrated strapping solutions. Manufactures fully automatic and semi-automatic (standard and customizable) strapping machines for hot coils, cold coils, slit coils, plates, long products, billets and ingots; seal-less and weld-seal strapping heads available. Additional

itipack

ADVANCED EFFICIENCY

Itipack Systems is a world leader in integrated strapping solutions.

Each one of our systems shares in our firm commitment towards high value, optimum performance, and long-lasting results. We provide top-of-the-line machinery for strapping steel and aluminum products.

Services

- Custom Engineering & Manufacturing
- Strapping head and machine repairs
- Preventative maintenance plans
- Strapping head rebuild program
- Strapping head training

Need something a little different?

We relish the opportunity to innovate custom solutions that fits our customer's unique needs.

Industry Equipment

- ID/Radial
- OD/Circumferential
- Long Products
- Slit Coils

Schedule a visit today
info@itipacksystems.com or call
+1.905.220.0551

itipacksystems.com   919 Zelco Dr, Burlington, ON L7L 4Y2, Canada

SUPPLIERS of EQUIPMENT, PRODUCTS and SERVICES

design/engineering and manufacturing solutions for specialty applications, including specialty machines for strapping high-strength steels/X-Grade materials, OD strapping on mandrels, OD/ID combo strapping machines, and various dual-head strapping machine solutions. North America parts and service departments, complete with comprehensive head rebuild/repair and service/training programs. Itipack also supplies robotic coil debanding and marking/labelling/tagging/laser etching systems to many steel mills.

ITR
902 4th Ave.
Bethlehem, PA 18018 USA
P: +1.610.867.0101
F: +1.610.867.2341
info@itr.com
www.itr.com

- Chief Exec. Officer—Jonathan Davis
- Chief Tech. Officer—Andrew Lauden
- Vice Pres. Sales—Brad Kintner

PRODUCTS and/or SERVICES: Provides PdM services, continuous monitoring and analysis solutions and reliability consulting. PdM services include vibration analysis, oil analysis, IR thermography, ultrasonic testing, motor amplification, motor testing and applications engineering. Exclusive vibration analysis hardware and software specifically designed for accurate data acquisition and analysis of the complex variable load, variable speed equipment found throughout the steel industry. ITR provides Industry 4.0 solutions, remote, wireless, on-site and/or on-line data acquisition and analysis options and works closely with customers to design PdM partnerships based on their objectives. Service plans and hardware options to accommodate any plant size, location or budget.

No. of Employees: 40+.

IVC TECHNOLOGIES
210 S. West St.
Lebanon, OH 45036 USA
P: +1.800.525.1269 (Toll-Free);
   +1.513.932.4678
F: +1.513.932.4980
ivc-info@ivctechnologies.com
www.ivctechnologies.com

- Pres.—Pete Epperson
- Vice Pres. Business Dev.—Jim Smith
- Vice Pres. CBM Oprs.—Fred Gallardo
- Vice Pres. Adv. Testing—Bob Miller
- Mktg. Coordinator—Christie Schmidt
- Contr.—Pam Murphy

PRODUCTS and/or SERVICES: Condition-based monitoring services—vibration analysis, infrared thermography, visual inspection, CBM program assessments. Advanced testing services—CBM training and certification, Modal/ODS, torque, Motion Amplification™, remote monitoring, crane and turret testing, rolling mill testing.

J

JACOBSON & ASSOCIATES
14571 Regatta Lane
Naples, FL 34114 USA
P: +1.847.735.7250
jej@jacobsonsteel.com

- Pres.—John E. Jacobson

PRODUCTS and/or SERVICES: Customer satisfaction measurement, management consulting, market analysis.

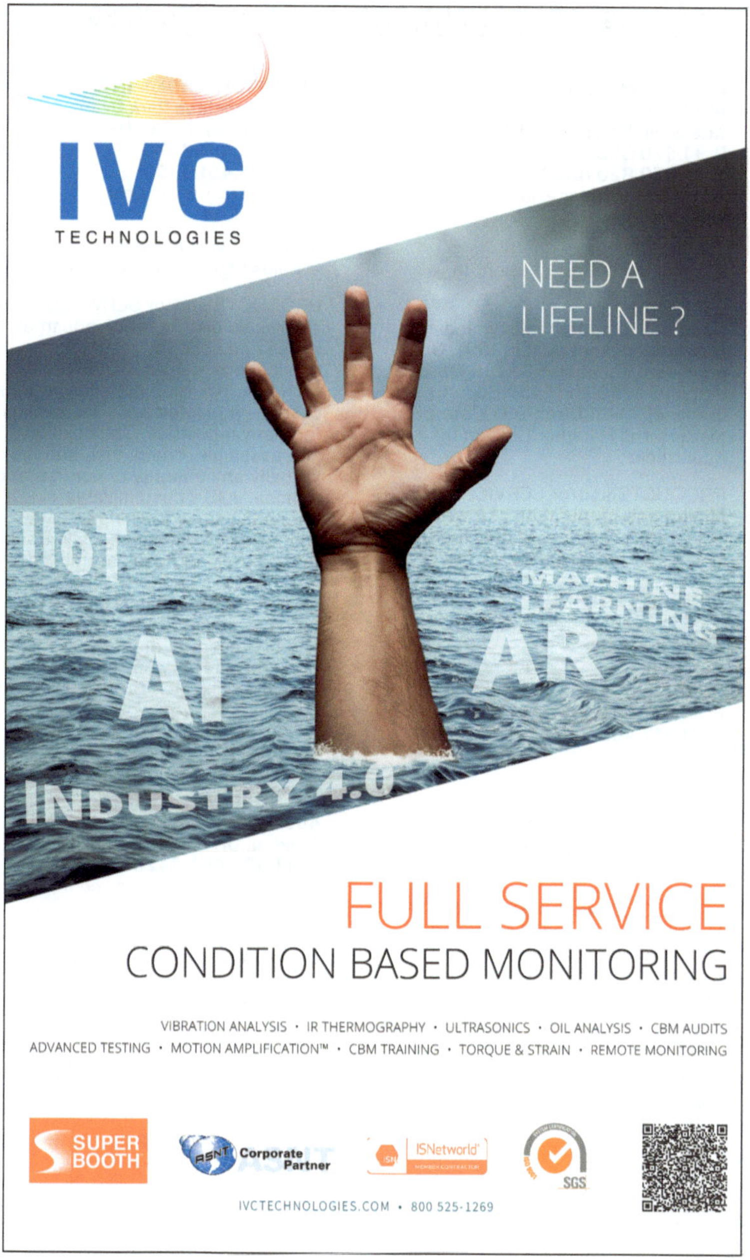

See listing page 412

SUPPLIERS of EQUIPMENT, PRODUCTS and SERVICES

JEDDO COAL CO.
144 Brown St.
Yatesville, PA 18640 USA
P: +1.570.825.0138
F: +1.570.820.8369
rpagnotti@peirealty.net
www.jeddocoal.com

- Pres.—James Pagnotti
- Sales Mgr.—Robert Pagnotti

EQUIPMENT:
Computer-operated heavy media preparation plant built in 1997. Open-pit mining equipment—8700 Marion dragline, 1250 and 1450 Bucyrus Erie draglines, D-11 dozer, 992 Caterpillar loaders and Haulpak 120-ton off-road haul trucks.

PRODUCTS and/or SERVICES:
Mining and preparation of low-ash/high-carbon anthracite coal, permitted coal ash disposal space.

No. of Employees: 76.

JENDCO CORP.
368 Butler St.
Pittsburgh, PA 15223 USA
P: +1.412.782.1957
F: +1.412.408.3531
ahaberman@jendco.com
www.jendco.com

- Pres.—John R. Matschner Jr.
- Svce. Mgr.—Andy Haberman
- Pur. Mgr.—Mary McGuire
- Expeditor—Rhonda Hamilton

PRODUCTS and/or SERVICES:
Manufacturer of radiation-based equipment for mold level control for continuous casting machines throughout the world. Services include engineering, technical support, start-up assistance, field maintenance service, and scintillation detector repairs and sales. Also provide leak testing and analysis.

JGB ENTERPRISES INC.
115 Metropolitan Park Dr.
Liverpool, NY 13088 USA
P: +1.315.451.2770
F: +1.315.451.8503
webassist@jgbhose.com
www.jgbhose.com

- Pres.—Kevin Kilkelly
- Sales Mgr.—Renee Capria

PRODUCTS and/or SERVICES:
Wholesale distributor of industrial hoses and hose fittings for all applications. JGB's custom hose fabrication division provides in-house custom-fabricated hose assemblies for many industries. Can quickly cut, assemble, crimp, test, and label virtually any quantity or configuration of hose. JGB's customizable, interactive hose tracking website supports customers' needs in tracking the life cycle of hose assemblies. JGB also provides audit services for the refinery/petrochemical industry for process, steam, water, air, nitrogen and hydrocarbon drain hoses. JGB has branches in Houston, TX; Charlotte, NC; St. Louis, MO; Buffalo, NY; and Liverpool, NY.

No. of Employees: 500.

JMP SOLUTIONS INC.
4026 Meadowbrook Dr., Unit 143
London, ON N6L 1C9 Canada
P: +1.905.464.2428
kpottruff@jmpsolutions.com
www.jmpsolutions.com

- Pres.—Scott Shawyer
- Vice Pres. Engrg.—Laurens VanPagee
- Vice Pres. Sales—Darryl King

PRODUCTS and/or SERVICES:
Control systems engineering and automation services for integrated steel mills.

No. of Employees: 275.

SUPPLIERS OF EQUIPMENT, PRODUCTS and SERVICES

JNE GROUP OF COMPANIES

JNE Automation
176 Shaw St.
Hamilton, ON L8L 3P7 Canada
P: +1.905.529.5122
F: +1.905.529.1974
automation@jnegroup.com
www.jnegroup.com/automation

- Business Dev. Mgr.—Nathan Terbrack

PRODUCTS and/or SERVICES:
JNE Automation works with steel industry clients to modernize legacy control systems and integrate new automation technologies. Specializing in continuous process automation applications such as process control, safety, material handling, plant utility and visualization systems. Typical design-build-program projects include DCS/PLC control panels, HMI screens, motor control centers, operator control stations and desks, and pre-fabricated control rooms. JNE Automation's proven approach to legacy migrations is phased to ensure that normal operations are maintained throughout the migration process. JNE Automation offers professional on-site support and management services such as feasibility studies, site validation, commissioning, start-up and acceptance testing.

JNE Consulting Ltd.
176 Shaw St.
Hamilton, ON L8L 3P7 Canada
P: +1.905.529.5122
F: +1.905.529.1974
info@jnegroup.com
www.jnegroup.com/consulting

- Pres.—John Ng
- Vice Pres. Sales—Keith Taylor
- Business Dir., Steel—Steve Bohm

JNE Consulting U.S.A.
103 Gamma Dr., Suite 160
Pittsburgh, PA 15238 USA
P: +1.412.963.1950
F: +1.412.963.1618

- Gen. Mgr.—David Anderson

PRODUCTS and/or SERVICES:
Provides a wide range of multi-disciplinary engineering services for metals clients around the world; accommodating both large and small projects as well as supporting sustaining operations. Engineering services include feasibility and front-end studies with conceptual engineering, detail and construction engineering for all disciplines, full project estimating, planning/scheduling for the entire project, with emphasis on shutdowns, commissioning and start-up, training, safety analysis (period safety review), and safety program development.

No. of Employees: 300.

JOHANNES HUEBNER CORP.
271 17th St. NW, Suite #1750
Atlanta, GA 30363 USA
P: +1.843.642.5452
F: +1.866.869.5611 (Toll-Free)
celine.limbacher@huebner-giessen.com
www.huebner-giessen.com

- Chief Exec. Officer—Frank Tscherney
- Treas.—Oliver Ruespeler
- Sales Mgr., U.S./Canada—Marvin Limbacher
- Sales Support/Office Mgr.—Lisa Hill
- Inside Sales Rep.—Celine Limbacher

PRODUCTS and/or SERVICES:
Heavy-duty encoders (incremental and absolute), magnetic encoders, electronic overspeed switches, electronic position switches, DC tach, mechanical and electrical accessories, modernization service, motors and generators.

No. of Employees: 100.

SUPPLIERS of EQUIPMENT, PRODUCTS and SERVICES

JOHN COCKERILL INDUSTRY
435 W. Wilson St.
Salem, OH 44460 USA
P: +1.330.332.4661
F: +1.330.332.1853
www.johncockerill.com

- Co. Mgr.—Larry Garcia
- Dir. of Projects—Bruce Parker
- Head of Sales—Marc Carter,
  P: +1.330.941.9170

PRODUCTS and/or SERVICES: Markets all of the products and services of John Cockerill Industry on the NAFTA market (design, modernization and maintenance of cold rolling mills, steel galvanizing lines, thermal, including heat treatment furnaces and chemical treatment equipment for steel, specialized equipment, solutions for recovering heat lost in high-energy-consuming industries and turnkey factories). These products are marketed under brands such as EFCO™ and UVK™.

No. of Employees: 60.

JOHNSON POWER LTD.
2530 Braga Dr.
Broadview, IL 60155 USA
P: +1.708.345.4300
F: +1.708.345.4315
tmillirons@johnsonpower.com
www.johnsonpower.com

- Chmn. of the Bd. and Pres.—Lisa C. Johnson
- Vice Pres.—Robert Honig
- Vice Pres. Engrg. and Chief Engr.—Jay Lavieri
- Vice Pres. Sales, Mktg.—Tim Millirons
- Vice Pres. Prodn./Mfg.—Peter Bobula
- Treas.—Arlene Johnson
- Sec.—Robert Honig
- Cust. Svce.—Ron Gagner, Rich Nendza, Bryon Stites, Karl Milosheff, Ernie Sarley
- Regional Sales Mgr.—Brad Pollock

PRODUCTS and/or SERVICES: High-performance industrial universal joints. Featuring GWB, Voith, Maina, Spicer and Con-Vel universal joints. Custom design assistance and engineering readily available.

No. of Employees: 45.

J.R. MERRITT CONTROLS INC.
55 Sperry Ave.
Stratford, CT 06615 USA
P: +1.203.381.0100
F: +1.203.381.0400
info@jrmerritt.com
www.jrmerritt.com

PRODUCTS and/or SERVICES: Designs and manufactures precision-engineered joysticks and operator chair systems tailored specifically for the steel industry. Comprehensive line of control solutions that can be custom configured to a range of steel mill machinery to improve operator productivity, comfort and safety.

No. of Employees: 45.

JTEKT NORTH AMERICA CORP.
7 Research Dr.
Greenville, SC 29607 USA
P: +1.800.331.5696 (Toll-Free)
inquiries@jtekt.com
www.jtekt-na.com

- Chief Exec. Officer and Pres.—Kenji Okamatsu
- Exec. Vice Pres. and Chief Oper. Officer—Gary Bourque
- Vice Pres., Business Dev.—Craig Woodford
- Exec. Vice Pres., Mfg.—Tsutomu Kimura
- Vice Pres., Mfg.—James Gregory
- Exec. Advisor—Mary Hirabayashi
- Chief Financial Officer—Brian Williamson
- Exec. Dir., Sales—Marc Dickison
- Exec. Dir., Pur.—Paul Dygert

PRODUCTS and/or SERVICES: Automotive systems and components, bearings; needle, roller and ball bearings; and machine tools and mechatronics.

No. of Employees: 5,000 in North America.

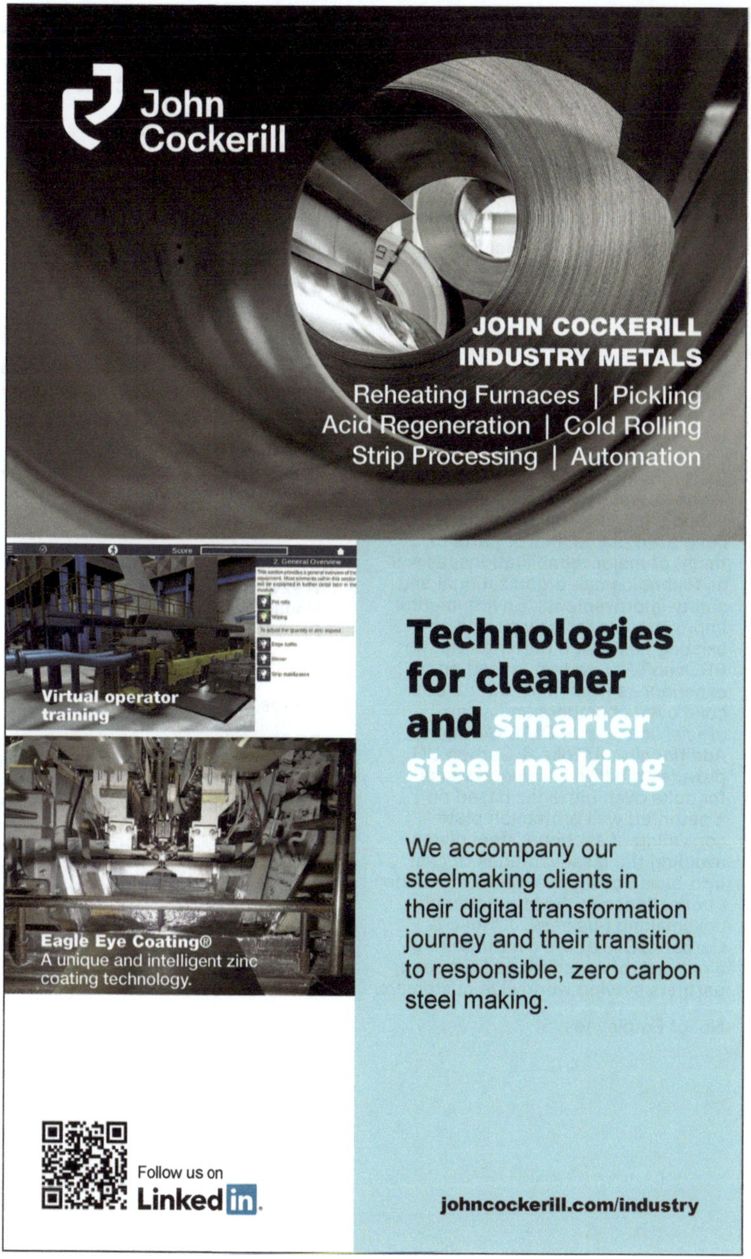

See listing page 416

SUPPLIERS of EQUIPMENT, PRODUCTS and SERVICES

JUKOKE & CARBON UG
Zur Gummershardt 5b
Gummersbach, NRW, 51647 Germany
P: +01149.2261.288.040
F: +01149.2261.288.625
ulrich.kochanski@jukokecarbon.eu
www.jukokecarbon.eu

- Managing Dir. and Chief Exec. Officer—Ulrich Kochanski
- Managing Dir. and Chief Financial Officer—Jana Kochanski

PRODUCTS and/or SERVICES:
Engineering, consulting, safety, inspections, supervision, improvements, studies, and design for cokemaking technologies related to process, operation, maintenance, optimization, (hot) repairs and environmental issues. Technological and organizational support for all installations of new coke oven plants and/or parts of them, of major rehabilitations, as well as technological, organizational and safety improvements. Environmental improvements for new as well as existing coke oven batteries via the PROven® NG system (based on experiences from more than 2,400 coke oven chambers and as an official licensee of DMT, Germany). Additionally, JUKoke & Carbon UG provides modern bracing systems for coke oven batteries based on a patented wall protection plate consisting of sectional steel plates avoiding the disadvantages of cast iron-based designs. With four decades of experience in the international cokemaking business, JUKoke & Carbon UG is at the center point of a network of experienced European partners serving worldwide customers.

No. of Employees: 5.

JVCKENWOOD USA CORP.
1440 Corporate Dr.
Irving, TX 74038 USA
P: +1.972.819.0700
F: +1.678.474.4730
ecomm@us.jvckenwood.com
www.kenwood.com/usa/com

- Exec. Vice Pres. and Gen. Mgr.—Mark Jasin
- Sales Mgr., LMR Div.—Dave Brandkamp

EQUIPMENT:
Digital and analog two-way radios and systems for plantwide and wide-area communications.

PRODUCTS and/or SERVICES:
NEXEDGE® digital portable and mobile radios, analog radios, custom radio systems, IP-based radio systems.

JVI VIBRATORY EQUIPMENT
11929 Brittmoore Park Dr.
Houston, TX 77041 USA
P: +1.832.467.3720
sales@jvivibratoryequipment.com
www.jvivibratoryequipment.com

- Pres.—Rob Bishop

PRODUCTS and/or SERVICES:
Manufactures a broad line of vibratory equipment including electromechanical and electromagnetic vibratory feeders, conveyors, grizzlies, screens, and spiral elevators — all designed to feed, dose, spread, batch, sift, screen, recycle, reclaim, separate, or elevate dry bulk solid materials. JVI custom designs every machine to meet the exact application and work envelope requirements of customers.

SUPPLIERS OF EQUIPMENT, PRODUCTS and SERVICES

K

KALENBORN ABRESIST CORP.
5541 N. State Road 13
Urbana, IN 46990 USA
P: +1.800.348.0717 (Toll-Free)
F: +1.260.774.3832
info@abresist.com
www.kalenborn.us

- Pres.—Craig Frendewey
- Dir. of Prodn.—Scott Dietrich
- Dir. of Finance—Troy Ray
- Supply Chain Mgr.—Kathy Stroh
- National Sales Mgr.—Russ Bauer
- Midwest Regional Sales Mgr.—James Dunchuck

PRODUCTS and/or SERVICES:
Flume design, installation and repair and a complete array of engineered wear protection materials for the iron and steel industry. Brands include ABRESIST fused cast basalt; KALOCER alumina ceramic including the KALBOND adhering system; KALCRET hard compound (cast, troweled or sprayed); and KALMETALL iron-alloy castings and overlay weldings.

KARK GMBH
Cuxhavener Strasse 60b
Hamburg, 21149 Germany
P: +49.40.797.004.40
F: +49.40.797.004.50
sales@kark.de
www.kark.de

- Sales Mgrs.—Kerstin Loeffler, Arwed Braeunig

EQUIPMENT:
Fabricating and machining capabilities: CNC lathes, CNC machining centers, CNC coordinate measuring machines, modern welding equipment, CAD-CAM technology, etc.

PRODUCTS and/or SERVICES:
Kafix composite rolls and axial clamping systems, hybrid cast carbide (HCC) rolls and rings, Kafix CBN inserts, Kafix COOL roll cooling, Kafix TC and Kafix PM roll rings, Kark EAF current-conducting aluminum electrode arms, Kark ECS electrode aerosol spray cooling system, engineering and consulting, all kinds of spare and wear parts.

No. of Employees: 100.

KASTALON INC.
4100 W. 124th Pl.
Alsip, IL 60803 USA
P: +1.708.389.2210
F: +1.708.389.0432
www.kastalon.com

- Pres.—Bob DeMent
- Chief Engr.—Paul Werstler
- Sales Admin.—Kim Mioni

EQUIPMENT:
CNC roll grinders, CNC lathes, CNC polyurethane processing equipment, CNC roll covering equipment. Polyurethane blending systems.

PRODUCTS and/or SERVICES:
Custom polyurethane solutions for iron and steel production and processing, including engineered polyurethane expanding mandrel sleeves and filler plates, slitter stripper tires, threading aprons, crane bumpers, coil storage pads, steady rest polyurethane gib blocks, Kastalon polyurethane thrust collars, roll drivers, C-hook pads, coil peeler knife edges, coil car pads, Fork-Kushion® lift truck bumpers, over-arm separator spacers, and custom-cast polyurethane products to the customer's specification. Rollers and wheels covered in engineered Kastalon Polyurethane® have a high load-bearing capacity and are able to withstand wear, abrasions and tearing, and resist water, oil, grease and chemicals.

No. of Employees: 75.

SUPPLIERS of EQUIPMENT, PRODUCTS and SERVICES

KENNAMETAL INC.
525 William Penn Pl., Suite 3300
Pittsburgh, PA 15219 USA
www.kennametal.com

- Chief Exec. Officer and Pres.—Christopher Rossi
- Chief Financial Officer and Vice Pres.—Patrick Watson
- Chief Technology Officer and Vice Pres.—Carlonda Reilly
- Vice President and Chief Admin. Officer—Judith L. Bacchus
- Vice Pres. Kennametal, Pres., Metal Cutting Segment—Sanjay Chowbey
- Vice Pres. Kennametal, Pres. Infrastructure Segment—Franklin Cardenas
- Vice Pres., Sec. and Gen. Counsel—Michelle R. Keating
- Vice Pres. and Corporate Contr.—John Witt

PRODUCTS and/or SERVICES:
Manufacturer of cutting tools, wear components and high-temperature wear materials utilized in iron and steel mills.

No. of Employees: Approx. 8,700.

KENNEDY INDUSTRIES
4925 Holtz Dr.
Wixom, MI 48393 USA
P: +1.248.684.1200
F: +1.248.486.0955
sharkness@kennedyind.com

PRODUCTS and/or SERVICES:
Centrifugal pumps, valves, valve automation, heat tracing, heat transfer products, pump repair and field service, hosted SCADA system.

KETTENWULF INC.
322 Thornton Road, Suite 101
Lithia Springs, GA 30122 USA
P: +1.678.433.0210
F: +1.678.433.0215
usa@kettenwulf.com
www.kettenwulfusa.com

- Dir. of Sales—Brian Ludvigsen
- Sales Mgrs.—Chris Pfahl, Simon Tabke, Luis Jimenez, Steve Fleckenstein, John Cabrera

PRODUCTS and/or SERVICES:
Made-to-order engineered conveyor chains, sprockets and shafts. On-site chain inspection services and installation support.

KIEWIT
8900 Renner Blvd.
Lenexa, KS 66219 USA
P: +1.913.928.7000
www.kiewit.com

PRODUCTS and/or SERVICES:
Kiewit is one of North America's largest engineering and construction organizations. Employee-owned with a network of subsidiaries in the U.S., Canada and Mexico, Kiewit offers full engineering, procurement and construction services in a variety of markets such as industrial, including metals and heavy industrial; transportation; oil, gas and chemical; power; building; water/wastewater; and mineral processing/mining.

No. of Employees: 28,800.

KIMZEY SOFTWARE SOLUTIONS
230 N. 1680 E, Bldg. S1
St. George, UT 84790 USA
P: +1.435.900.6777
kelly@kssco.com
www.kssco.com

- Chief Exec. Officer—Kerry Kimzey
- Pres.—Kyle Kimzey
- Sales Mgr.—Tyson Oldroyd
- Asst. Sales Mgr.—Hunter Kimzey
- Adv. Mgr.—Kelly Howell

PRODUCTS and/or SERVICES:
Kimzey Software Solutions (KSS) offers MetalTrax, a fully integrated Windows application designed to handle all of the needs of metal service centers. MetalTrax includes general ledger, accounts receivable, accounts payable, inventory control, sales order/quoting, purchasing, production and prospect manager modules. Users can quickly navigate menus, which include features such as the following: remnant tracking, bar coding, lot tracking, quick quotes, back orders and more. Reports can be accessed via the menus

SUPPLIERS OF EQUIPMENT, PRODUCTS and SERVICES

or designed by the user with any ODBC-compliant reporting tool such as Crystal Reports, Excel or Access. KSS also offers Trax-it, a graphical document imaging system designed to scan, store, index, and retrieve mill test reports, customer drawings, shipping documents, vendor invoices and other critical paperwork. In addition, Trax-it includes batch scanning and annotation capabilities and allows users to fax or email multiple MTRs directly to the customer.

No. of Employees: 15.

KINETIC CO., THE
P.O. Box 200
Greendale, WI 53129 USA
P: +1.414.425.8221
F: +1.414.425.7927
www.knifemaker.com

- Pres.—Cash Masters

PRODUCTS and/or SERVICES:
Shear knives, rotary knives, slitters and slitter tooling, hot crop shear blades, scrap choppers, sidetrimmers, tube cutoff knives, liners, guide rolls, and Sendzimir mill rolls. Regrinding of knives.

KINTNER INC.
100 Hafner Ave.
Pittsburgh, PA 15223 USA
P: +1.412.781.3000
F: +1.412.781.3301
chrissy@kintner.com
sales@kintner.com
www.kintner.com

- Chief Exec. Officer, Pres. and Sales Mgr.—Samuel Kintner,
  sam@kintner.com
- Vice Pres.—John Kintner
- Treas.—Ted Kintner, ted@kintner.com
- Office Mgr.—Chrissy Kintner,
  chrissy@kintner.com

PRODUCTS and/or SERVICES:
Furnace rolls, radiant tubes, charge/discharge rolls, piers/work supports, WBs, furnace trays, door castings, hot riders, electric heating elements, serpentine grids, skid rails, galvanizing snouts, recuperator castings, furnace muffles, sink roll arms and retorts.

No. of Employees: 7.

KLUBER LUBRICATION
Av. La Montaña #109
Querétaro, QE, 76220 Mexico
P: +01.442.229.5700
jcruz@kluber.com.mx
www.kluber.com.mx

PRODUCTS and/or SERVICES:
Lubricants, greases and oils.

No. of Employees: 70–90.

KOCKS PITTSBURGH CO., Affiliate of Friedrich Kocks GmbH & Co.
504 McKnight Park Dr.
Pittsburgh, PA 15237 USA
P: +1.412.367.4174
F: +1.412.367.3648
sales@kockspittsburgh.com
spares@kockspittsburgh.com
fieldsvc@kockspittsburgh.com

- Chmn. of the Bd.—Ali Bindernagel
- Pres.—Patrick E. Connell
- Gen. Mgr. Sales—Glyn D. Ellis
- Finance Mgr.—Gregory P. DeCesare
- Svce. Engr.—Thomas Niederwoehrmann
- Spare Parts Sales—Anne Glinsky

PRODUCTS and/or SERVICES:
Design, manufacture, and service of rolling mills for rod, bar and tubular products, including 3-roll reducing and sizing blocks (RSB) for precision rolling of rod and bar, stretch-reducing blocks (SRB), precision sizing mills, planetary elongators (KRM), and rotating hot saws for seamless and welded tube and pipe. Modern technology packages, including size control systems (SCS) enabled by advanced in-line gauge (4D Eagle) for high quality and production.

SUPPLIERS of EQUIPMENT, PRODUCTS and SERVICES

KOCSIS USA
11755 S. Austin Ave.
Alsip, IL 60803 USA
P: +1.513.256.4881
F: +1.937.522.0807
www.kocsisusa.com

PRODUCTS and/or SERVICES:
Maintenance support for hot strips, continuous casters and pickle lines. Offers engineered roll welding solutions, which include roll performance tracking, custom welding processes, inventory management and technical support. Also offers a wide range of machining, inspection and assembly capabilities, and reconditioning and manufacturing of the following types of equipment: pinch rolls, wrapper rolls, caster rolls, deflector rolls, entry guides, table roll assemblies and flash trimmers.

KONECRANES PLC
Group Headquarters:
P.O. Box 661 (Koneenkatu 8)
Hyvinkaa, FI-05801 Finland
T: +358.20.427.11
F: +358.20.4272099
sales.uk@konecranes.com
www.konecranes.co.uk

EQUIPMENT:
Port cranes, lift trucks, overhead cranes, hoists, machine tools, lifting equipment. Manufacturing facilities in Springfield, OH, USA; Houston, TX, USA; Watertown, WI, USA; Edmonton, AB, Canada; and Sorocaba, SP, Brazil.

PRODUCTS and/or SERVICES:
Crane servicing, hoist servicing, spare parts, machine tool servicing, modernizations, repairs, service contracts.

No. of Employees: Approx. 19,000.

Konecranes Inc.
4401 Gateway Blvd.
Springfield, OH 45502 USA
P: +1.800.934.6976 (Toll-Free)
www.konecranesusa.com

PRODUCTS and/or SERVICES:
Manufacture and service of standardized and specialized cranes and hoists for the steel and metals, pulp and paper, petrochemical, automotive, nuclear, power, ports and shipyards, general manufacturing, mining, intermodal and rail, and energy-from-waste industries. Crane service centers located across North and South America providing 24/7 emergency, as well as inspections and preventive maintenance. Replacement and spare parts for all crane brands. Crane engineering and redesign to upgrade or provide solutions to the changing applications of the EOT cranes and/or individual components on the cranes. Formal training for crane operators and maintenance personnel at the Konecranes Training Institute.

KONRAD CORP.
1421 Hanley Road
Hudson, WI 54016 USA
P: +1.800.359.4200 (Toll-Free Sales);
 +1.715.386.4200
F: +1.715.386.4219
www.konradcorp.com

- Chief Exec. Officer and Pres.—
 Ken Konrad
- Vice. Pres.—Jenny Konrad, Dan
 Konrad

EQUIPMENT:
Complete machining and fabricating capabilities; CNC mills and lathes, gear manufacturing equipment, grinding capabilities, and extensive CAD/CAM system.

PRODUCTS and/or SERVICES:
Design and manufacture steel rolling mill equipment, industrial equipment, and replacement parts, including custom single components, drive spindle assemblies and complete mill stands. Konrad also specializes in repairing and refurbishing customers' used equipment.

No. of Employees: 40.

SUPPLIERS OF EQUIPMENT, PRODUCTS and SERVICES

KOYO BEARINGS NORTH AMERICA—
see JTEKT NORTH AMERICA CORP.

KRESS CORP.
227 W. Ilinois St.
Brimfield, IL 61517 USA
P: +1.309.446.3395
F: +1.309.446.9625
sales@kresscarrier.com
www.kresscarrier.com

- Pres.—Rita Kress
- Dir. of Engrg.—Dan Boettcher
- Dir. of Product Support Mktg.—David Denman
- Dir. of Prodn.—Rich Hendrick
- Dir. of Finance—Clarence Carr
- Mktg. Mgr.—Nathan Kress
- Product Support Mgr.—Clint Summers

PRODUCTS and/or SERVICES:
Custom-made material handling equipment, including slag pot carriers, slab carriers, straddle carriers, pallet carriers, tundish dumpers, coil carriers, container handlers, personnel carriers, ladle carriers and scrap bucket carriers. Complete design, engineering, manufacturing, spare parts and support.

No. of Employees: 200.

KRK ASSOCIATES INC.
Columbiana, OH 44408 USA
P: +1.330.533.1099
info@krkassoc.com
www.krkassoc.com

- Chmn.—Kenneth R. Kunz
- Pres.—Keith M. Kunz
- Sec.—T.L. Kunz

PRODUCTS and/or SERVICES:
Sales agents for BPI Inc.: raw materials (i.e., calcium aluminates, MgO, aluminas, sulfur, pyrites, dololime, DeOx Sil, Koverall insulators, topping powders). MinMet Minerals: tundish insulators. Sales agents for Unifrax Engineered Thermal Components Inc. (fiber shapes for hot top applications).

No. of Employees: 4.

KSB SUPREMESERV NORTH AMERICA
5000 Wrightsboro Road
Grovetown, GA 30813 USA
P: +1.800.241.2702
info@pumps911.com
www.pumps911.com

- Vice Pres.—Jan Avramov

PRODUCTS and/or SERVICES:
Service, repair, and spare parts for all makes and models of pumps, and related rotating equipment. Complete engineering and machining of parts with the ability to custom-manufacture and re-engineer replacement parts and pumps. 24-hour emergency service, pump installation, removal, commissioning and start-up services. Field testing and troubleshooting, with system analysis. New centrifugal pumps for descaling, water treatment, cooling and other steel manufacturing processes.

KSB SupremeServ By KSB Dubric
3737 Laramie Dr. NE
Comstock Park, MI 49321 USA
P: +1.616.784.6355
jeff.koeper@ksb.com

- Pres.—Jeff Koeper

KSB SupremeServ By GIW Industries
Georgia:
968 Ferrous Road
Thomson, GA 30824 USA
P: +1.706.595.5950

Florida:
1351 FL-60
Mulberry, FL 33860 USA
P: +1.863.425.4961

Fort McMurray:
220 Maclennan Crescent
Fort McMurray, AB T9H 4E8 Canada
P: +1.780.713.3457
john.mitchell@ksb.com

- Svce. Dir.—John Mitchell

SUPPLIERS of EQUIPMENT, PRODUCTS and SERVICES

KSB SupremeServ/KSB Inc.
Virginia:
4415 Sarellen Road
Henrico, VA 23231 USA
P: +1.804.222.1818

California:
19234 Flightpath Way
Bakersfield, CA 93308 USA
P: +1.800.641.7540 (Toll-Free)
matt.erickson@ksb.com

- Svce. Dir.—Matt Erickson

KSB SupremeServ Canada/KSB Pumps Inc.
Ontario:
5205 Tomken Road
Mississauga, ON L4W 3N8 Canada
P: +1.905.568.9200

Edmonton:
7127 68 Ave. NW
Edmonton, AB T6B 3T6 Canada
P: +1.780.485.2420
chris.madia@ksb.com

- Vice Pres.—Chris Madia

KSB SupremeServ Mexico
Av. Peñuelas No. 19
San Pedrito Peñuelas
Querétaro, QE, 76148 Mexico
P: +52.442.427.5500
alfonso.donan@ksb.com

- Svce. Dir.—Alfonso Donan

KSB SupremeServ By Standard Alloys
1145 Kerry Thomas Dr.
Port Arthur, TX 77640 USA
P: +1.800.231.8240 (Toll-Free);
+1.409.983.3201
richard.martinez@ksb.com

Port Arthur, TX (Foundry)
201 W. Lakeshore Dr.
Port Arthur, TX 77640 USA

Deer Park, TX (Repair Center)
1101 Howard Dr.
Deer Park, TX 77536 USA
P: +1.281.476.5500

Louisiana (Repair Center)
1927 Commercial Dr.
Port Allen, LA 70767 USA
P: +1.225.379.6097

- Pres.—Richard Martinez

KT-GRANT
3073 Rte. 66
Export, PA 15632 USA
P: +1.724.468.4700
F: +1.724.468.8188
sales@kt-grant.com
www.kt-grant.com

- Chief Exec. Officer—Michael Riska
- Dir. Sales and Mktg.—Chris Beiter
- Sr. Dir., Acct. Mgmt.—William Stevenson
- Sr. Dir., Engrg. and Mfg.—Timothy Aretz
- Southern Regional Mgr.—Kevin Cartwright
- Dir., Tech. Svcs.—Richard Thomas

PRODUCTS and/or SERVICES:
Design and manufacturing of specialty remote-controlled mechanical refractory and scale removal equipment. Services include all furnace types, ladle, tundish, casthouse troughs and runners, EAF, BOF, BOP maintenance. Taphole drilling and insert equipment for EBT and BOF vessels. Slag skimmers, slag door pushers, special demolition equipment, custom meltshop projects, safe scale and buildup removal from all industrial vessel types.

KTSDI LLC
801 E. Middletown Road
North Lima/Youngstown, OH 44452 USA
P: +1.330.783.2000
F: +1.330.965.9921
sales@ktsdi.com
www.ktsdi.com

- Mgr.—Ken Timmings

EQUIPMENT:
Complete fabrication, machining and production for mobile equipment.

SUPPLIERS OF EQUIPMENT, PRODUCTS and SERVICES

PRODUCTS and/or SERVICES:
Slag pot carriers, pallet transporters, scrap trailers, CASK VCT transporters, forklifts, AGVs. Authorized dealer for Kessler axles and transfer cases. ISO 9001:2015 certified.

KUBOTA MATERIALS CANADA CORP.
25 Commerce Road
Orillia, ON L3V 6L6 Canada
P: +1.800.461.0260 (Toll-Free)
F: +1.705.325.5887
kmc_g.sales@kubota.com
www.kubotamaterials.com

EQUIPMENT:
Green sand, no-bake and centrifugal casting. Full machine and fabrication shop facilities, including TIG, pulsed and hot wired TIG, MIG, plasma arc and orbital welding. Pattern shop facilities.

PRODUCTS and/or SERVICES:
Full line of heat-, corrosion- and wear-resistant alloys to 5,000 lbs. Wide range of specialty alloys and innovative products for the steel industry, including skid buttons and riders for WB and pusher furnace applications. Radiant tubes and furnace rolls for CGL/CAL/EGL and heat treat applications. Sink and stab rolls for zinc pots. Dry rolls for thin-slab (tunnel and reheat furnace) processes. Coiler drums for Steckel mill applications. All manufactured under ISO 9001:2015 standards. In-house testing includes chemical, physical, metallurgical and non-destructive disciplines. Extensive in-house R&D program.

No. of Employees: 340.

KUTTNER NORTH AMERICA
211 N. Franklin St.
Port Washington, WI 53074 USA
P: +1.262.284.4483
AISTDirect@KuttnerNA.com
www.KuttnerNA.com

- Pres.—Robert Fechner
- Vice Pres. Oprs.—Adel Rahman
- Vice Pres. Engrg.—James Ruka
- Cust. Svce. and Parts—Karen Wilkens

PRODUCTS and/or SERVICES:
Planning, design, delivery, construction and commissioning of steel mill equipment systems such as: dense phase pulverized coal injection systems; oxygen/coal injection lances; coking plants; rolling mill technology; casthouse high-efficiency fume collection, including fabric filter; sintering plants and emission controls; waste heat recovery and power generation; hot stove combustion air pre-heaters; and mill waste iron recovery systems using the Oxycup®.

No. of Employees: 20+.

KYTOLA INSTRUMENTS
900 Old Roswell Lakes Pkwy., Suite 120
Roswell, GA 30076 USA
P: +1.678.701.3569
F: +1.514.448.5151
flow@kytola.com
www.kytola.com

- Chief Exec. Officer—Sakari Häyrynen
- Pres.—Hans Kos
- Sales Mgr.—Jari Auvinen
- Regional Sales Mgrs.—Martin Valois, Lisa Doud
- Adv. Mgr.—Sanna Lattunen
- Pur. Agt.—Bert Hogendoorn
- Chief Engr.—Kai Mikkola

PRODUCTS and/or SERVICES:
Flowmeters and instrumentation, oil lubrication systems, oil analyzers.

No. of Employees: 150.

SUPPLIERS of EQUIPMENT, PRODUCTS and SERVICES

L

L&L SPECIAL FURNACE CO. INC.
20 Kent Road
Aston, PA 19014 USA
P: +1.610.459.9216
F: +1.610.459.3689
sales@llfurnace.com
www.llfurnace.com

PRODUCTS and/or SERVICES: Designers and builders of high-temperature furnaces, ovens and quench tanks. Specializing in batch production furnaces and ovens, particularly applications requiring high uniformity and controlled atmosphere.

LAKOS FILTRATION SOLUTIONS
1365 N. Clovis Ave.
Fresno, CA 93727 USA
P: +1.559.255.1601
F: +1.559.255.8093
info@lakos.com
www.lakos.com

PRODUCTS and/or SERVICES: Filtration solutions to improve process reliability and water use by easily removing scale from cooling towers and sumps as well as extending spray nozzle and pump life. High-efficiency continuous filtration solutions featuring no moving parts, low/steady pressure drop and automated purge options.

LAMIFLEX INC.
1610 Woodstead Ct., Suite 440
The Woodlands, TX 77380 USA
P: +1.832.251.0200
F: +1.832.251.0201
lamiflexus@lamiflex.com
www.lamiflex.com

- Chief Exec. Officer—Adrian Robert
- Gen Mgr.—Jan Persson

PRODUCTS and/or SERVICES: Supplier of transport packaging solutions mainly in the steel, aluminum and cable industries. Products include materials, machines, services, and process improvements with methods and tools to develop and implement the optimal packaging solution and processes for packing. Also provides services for recycling or reuse of products or product systems.

No. of Employees: 65.

LAP OF AMERICA LASER APPLICATIONS LLC
161 Commerce Road, Suite 6
Boynton Beach, FL 33426 USA
P: +1.561.416.9263
F: +1.561.416.9263
info@lap-laser.com
www.lap-laser.com

PRODUCTS and/or SERVICES: Supplies laser projection and measurement solutions. For the steel industry, LAP provides laser-based systems that measure dimensions such as width, thickness, length, diameter and straightness in rolling processes.

LAVISA
Mazarik 25
Mexico City, DF, 11560 Mexico
P: +52.55.000.3600
dcoutino@lavisa.net
www.lavisa.net

- Chief Exec. Officer—Alfredo Garcia
- Sales Mgr.—Diego Coutiño
- Pur. Agt.—Laura Bautista

PRODUCTS and/or SERVICES: Distributor of pipes, valves and fittings.

No. of Employees: 60.

LECHLER INC.
445 Kautz Road
St. Charles, IL 60174 USA
P: +1.630.377.6611
F: +1.630.377.6657
info@lechlerusa.com
www.lechlerusa.com

LET'S GET SOCIAL

Follow AIST on our social media channels to **get the inside scoop!**

SUPPLIERS of EQUIPMENT, PRODUCTS and SERVICES

- Chief Exec. Officer and Pres.—Adolf Pfeiffer
- Dir., Metallurgical Div.—Tito Torres
- Vice Pres. Sales and Mktg.—Ned Mansour
- Engrg. Mgr.—Budi Francisco
- Mgr. Oprs. and Continual Improvement—Dinesh Patel

PRODUCTS and/or SERVICES:
Spray nozzle technology. Provides engineering solutions and products for descaling, roll cooling, continuous casting, pickling lines, air and pollution control, gas cooling, and dust suppression.

LECO CORP.
**3000 Lakeview Ave.
St. Joseph, MI 49085 USA
P: +1.800.292.6141 (Toll-Free);
   +1.269.985.5496
F: +1.269.982.8987**
info@leco.com
www.leco.com

- Pres. Sales—Chris Warren
- Pres. Oprs.—Carl Warren
- Vice Pres. USA and Canada Sales—Dave Valensi
- Pur. Dir.—Tom Blank

PRODUCTS and/or SERVICES:
Manufactures analytical instruments for rapid elemental determination in inorganic and metals applications using combustion/fusion/OES techniques. Metallographic equipment (sectioning machines, grinders/polishers, macro- and micro-indentation hardness testers and numerous microscopes/optical accessories) is also offered for materials testing and structural examination.

No. of Employees: 800.

LEHIGH ANTHRACITE COAL
**1233 E. Broad St.
Tamaqua, PA 18252 USA
P: +1.570.668.9060**
derek.altenbaugh@resfuel.com
www.lehighanthracite.com

- Chief Exec. Officer and Pres.—Jeff Specht
- Chief Oper. Officer—John Hadesty
- Sales Mgr. U.S. Industrial/Export—Derek Altenbaugh
- Sales Mgr. Southeast U.S.—Chuck Jones
- Sales Mgr. Bagged—Matt Stahler
- Pur. Agt.—Bill Strauch
- Oprs. Mgr.—Cody Bartkoski

EQUIPMENT:
300 tons/hour processing plant, rail siding, approx. 8,000 acre continuous mine site.

PRODUCTS and/or SERVICES:
High-carbon, low-sulfur, low volatile anthracite injection and charge carbon.

Annual Capacity: 375,000 tons.

No. of Employees: 112.

Railroad and Shipping Facilities: Truck, rail and barge.

LENOX INSTRUMENT CO. INC.
**265 Andrews Road
Trevose, PA 19053 USA
P: +1.800.356.1104 (Toll-Free);
   +1.215.322.9990, ext. 106
F: +1.215.322.6126**
sales@lenoxinst.com
www.lenoxinst.com

- Pres.—John W. Lang
- Vice Pres. Sales and Mktg.—William J. Lang
- Mktg. Mgr.—Richard Parello

PRODUCTS and/or SERVICES:
Durable furnace cameras for use in reheat furnaces, VDs, ladle metallurgy, EAFs, tunnel furnaces, annealing furnaces, continuous galvanizing and galvannealing lines, continuous casters, BFs, sintering and pellet operations, and other high-temperature processes.

No. of Employees: 30.

Seamless Transitions,
From Start to Finish
It's so much more satisfying when everything just flows. When every step of the process blends from one instrument to the next, it's not just your samples that are smoother. LECO's complete analysis solutions streamline the process with durable and intuitive equipment for repeatable results from start to finish.
Whether you're a high-throughput, busy laboratory or working on specialized, unique analyses, the LECO solution will work for you.
Sample Preparation
Hardness Testing
Microscopic Examination
Elemental Analysis
Glow Discharge Spectrometry
Phone: 1-800-292-6141 | info@leco.com
www.leco.com | © 2022 LECO Corporation
LECO
EMPOWERING RESULTS

SUPPLIERS of EQUIPMENT, PRODUCTS and SERVICES

EDW. C. LEVY CO.
9300 Dix Ave.
Dearborn, MI 48120 USA
P: +1.313.429.2200
www.edwclevy.com

- Exec. Chmn.—Ed Levy Jr.
- Chief Exec. Officer and Pres.—S. Evan Weiner
- Vice Pres. and Chief Financial Officer—Brad Critchfield
- Vice Pres. Steel Mill Svcs. USA—Russ Burke
- Vice Pres. Intl. Oprs., Flame Svcs. and Technology—Clyde Kirkwood

EQUIPMENT:
20 slag processing plants with a capacity of 14 million tons/year, 2.5 million tons/year recovered metallics; eight scrap management facilities; steel slab scarfing facilities; burrless cutting and slitting machines.

PRODUCTS and/or SERVICES:
Slag handling, processing and commercialization with metal recovery. Slag marketing. Shredded scrap upgrading through copper removal. Mobile equipment specialist. Waste stream optimization. Mill scale handling and marketing. Scrap yard management. Scrap marketing. Material handling and processing for the steel and foundry industries. Ladle and furnace refractory separating and recycling. Analytical laboratory services. Mobile equipment rental. Slab scarfing and burrless cutting/slitting services. Donze steel cutting torches and supplies. BF slag granulator operating and maintenance management. Fe beneficiation. Phosphorus remediation. Plant Tuff silicon fertilizer. Levy specialty products include: CemStar, LevyLite, VitraSpar, Durabase and Duraberm.

No. of Employees: 2,500.

LEVY MARKETERS FOR INDUSTRY + TECH—see GROWTHHIVE

LEXICON INC.
8900 Fourche Dam Pike
Little Rock, AR 72206 USA
P: +1.501.490.4200
F: +1.501.490.4411
lexiconinfo@lexicon-inc.com
www.lexicon-inc.com

- Chief Exec. Officer and Pres.—Patrick Schueck
- Exec. Vice Pres.—Michael Hupp

PRODUCTS and/or SERVICES:
Structural steel, platework and pressure vessel fabrication; civil; steel erection; piping; mechanical equipment installation; and plant maintenance services (including shutdown/turnaround).

LEYBOLD VACUUM
6005 Enterprise Dr.
Export, PA 15632 USA
P: +1.800.764.5369 (Toll-Free)
F: +1.724.325.3577
info.ex@leybold.com
www.leybold.com

- Gen. Mgr.—Henrique Triboni
- Business Line Mgr. High Vacuum—Brad Cramer
- Business Line Mgr. Ind. Vacuum—Steven Shrawder
- Business Line Mgr. Svce.—Greg Greinke
- Contr.—Renée Nauyokas
- Sr. Mgr. H.R.—Valerie Mooney
- Head of Mktg.—Corrie Freudenstein

PRODUCTS and/or SERVICES:
Vacuum pumping systems; high vacuum leak detectors; vacuum sensors; vacuum pump repair services.

No. of Employees: 105.

LHOIST NORTH AMERICA
5600 Clearfork Main St., Suite 300
Forth Worth, TX 76109 USA
P: +1.682.774.2037
ian.saratovsky@lhoist.com
www.lhoist.com

DURABLE FURNACE CAMERA SYSTEMS

Monitor:
- Flame Characteristics
- Process Flow
- Product Orientation
- Refractory Conditions
- Other problems before damage occurs

Made and Serviced in USA

Why Use Lenox Furnace Camera Systems?
- Designed to be rugged & durable for the brutal atmosphere of the steel industry
- Proven reliable dual cooling system, highest camera resolution with superior optics
- Minimal maintenance and operating costs once correctly installed
- Backed by an industry leading two year warranty
- Flexibility in choice of penetration lengths, viewing angles, water or low consumption air-cooling and a selection of portable water-cooled or air-cooled models
- Lenox know-how, expertise and installation / field service.

Lenox Instrument Company
265 Andrews Road, Trevose, PA 19053

USA 800-356-1104 / FAX 215-322-6126
Worldwide 215-322-9990
sales@lenoxinst.com
http://www.lenoxinst.com

SUPPLIERS of EQUIPMENT, PRODUCTS and SERVICES

- Vice Pres. Prodn./Mfg.—Mark Milner

PRODUCTS and/or SERVICES: Lime, hydrated lime, enhanced hydrated lime, sorbents, air pollution control.

No. of Employees: 1,200.

LIFE CYCLE ENGINEERING
4360 Corporate Road
Charleston, SC 29405 USA
P: +1.843.744.7110
F: +1.843.725.1603
rheisler@lce.com
www.lce.com

PRODUCTS and/or SERVICES: Reliability Consulting Group (RCG) specializes in asset management, reliability, and maintenance solutions for industrial and government markets allowing public and private enterprises to gain increased profitability through greater capacity, increased uptime and improved quality.

No. of Employees: 500.

LIMAB NORTH AMERICA INC.
3122 Fincher Farm Road, Suite 722
Matthews, NC 28105 USA
P: +1.704.321.0760
sales@limab.com
www.limab.com

- Chief Exec. Officer and Pres.—Lars Granlund
- Sales Mgr. North America—Michael Spurgin
- Treas.—Ann Wiig
- Chief Engr.—Anthony Godair

PRODUCTS and/or SERVICES: Laser-based measurement sensors and systems for dimensional measurements on hot and cold metals on long and flat products. The LIMAB profiler series of products includes the BarProfiler 3D for bars and billets, TubeProfiler for dimensions and straightness on tubes, WireProfiler 3D for wire rod and SlabProfiler 3D for measurement of slabs, among other systems. Limab also sells many different laser sensors for various applications. Measurement of width, length, thickness, camber and flatness on flat products.

No. of Employees: 4 and local representatives.

LINCOLN ELECTRIC CO., THE
22801 St. Clair Ave.
Cleveland, OH 44117 USA
P: +1.216.481.8100
F: +1.216.486.1751
www.lincolnelectric.com

- Chmn., Chief Exec. Officer and Pres.—Christopher L. Mapes
- Exec. Vice Pres., Chief Financial Officer and Treas.—Gabriel Bruno
- Exec. Vice Pres., Chief Oper. Officer—Steven B. Hedlund
- Exec. Vice Pres., General Counsel and Sec.—Jennifer I. Ansberry
- Exec. Vice Pres., Chief H.R. Officer—Michele R. Kuhrt
- Exec. Vice Pres., Chief Info. Officer—Lisa A. Dietrich
- Sr. Vice Pres., Strategy and Business Dev.—Geoffrey P. Allman
- Sr. Vice Pres. and Pres., International—Peter Pletcher
- Sr. Vice Pres. and Pres., Harris Products Group—Gregory D. Doria
- Sr. Vice Pres. and Pres., International Welding—Thomas A. Flohn
- Sr. Vice Pres and Pres., North America, Americas Welding—Doug S. Lance
- Sr. Vice Pres. Sales—Michael S. Mintun
- Sr. Vice Pres. and Pres., Global Automation, Cutting and Additive Business—Michael J. Whitehead

PRODUCTS and/or SERVICES: Engineers, designs and manufactures arc welding solutions, automated joining, assembly and cutting systems, plasma and oxy-fuel cutting equipment and has a leading global position in the brazing and soldering alloys market. Lincoln Electric Co. operates 56 manufacturing locations in 19 countries.

EDW C LEVY CO
Mill Services
SOLUTIONS FOR YOUR ENVIRONMENT®

At Levy, our forward-thinking, client-first approach to providing services and solutions that are specially designed to meet the unique needs of our steel mill customers has set us apart from our competition. Our innovative technologies deliver the results you need today, while building a more sustainable, greener tomorrow.

- **Vertically Integrated Solutions Provider**
- **Technical Specialist in Granulation, Material Analysis, Engineered Aggregates & Co-Product Management**
- **Comprehensive Scrap Management & Logistics**
- **Expert in slag processing and metal recovery**
- **World-Class Enterprise Asset Management**
- **Patented Flame Technologies for Slab Sizing and Conditioning**

SINCE 1918
LEVY
SOLUTIONS FOR YOUR ENVIRONMENT®

edwclevy.com

See listing page 430   2023 AIST Directory — Iron and Steel Plants   433

SUPPLIERS of EQUIPMENT, PRODUCTS and SERVICES

LINDE
10 Riverview Dr.
Danbury, CT 06810 USA
P: +1.844.44LINDE (445.4633)
(Toll-Free)
www.linde.com

- Chief Exec. Officer—Sanjiv Lamba

PRODUCTS and/or SERVICES:
Global industrial gases and engineering company. Provides high-quality gases, application technologies and services to a variety of end markets including manufacturing and primary metals, chemicals, food and beverage, electronics, energy, healthcare, and aerospace. Linde's industrial gases are used in countless applications, from life-saving oxygen for hospitals to high-purity and specialty gases for electronics manufacturing, hydrogen for clean fuels, and much more.

No. of Employees: 80,000.

Linde
10 Riverview Dr.
Danbury, CT 06810 USA
P: +1.844.44LINDE (445.4633)
(Toll-Free)
F: +1.800.772.9985 (Toll-Free)
contactus@linde.com
www.lindeus.com

- Exec. Dir. — Metals, Combustion and Energy—Pravin Mathur

PRODUCTS and/or SERVICES:
Linde produces, sells and distributes industrial gases to steel and non-ferrous mills worldwide. Linde's industrial gases are used extensively in metal production to lower costs, improve energy efficiency, deliver environmental benefits and improve productivity. Iron- and steelmaking application technologies include gas injection systems, oxygen enrichment, ladle pre-heating, and more. Gases supplied include oxygen, nitrogen, argon, carbon dioxide, helium, hydrogen, and specialty gases. Gases can be supplied and delivered depending on volume needs, from cylinders to on-site gas production.

Praxair Surface Technologies
1500 Polco St.
Indianapolis, IN 46222 USA
P: +1.317.240.2500
F: +1.317.240.2426
www.praxairsurfacetechnologies.com

- Pres.—Todd Skare
- Vice Pres. Technology and Innovation—Derek Hileman
- Business Dev. Dir.—Michael Brennan
- Business Mgr., Laser, New Castle, PA—Roland Gassmann
- R&D Associate Dir.—Michael Helminiak

PRODUCTS and/or SERVICES:
Offers wear and corrosion protection services on process rolls via thermal spray coatings and laser weld overlays. Common applications are in use on pickle, cold rolling, annealing, hot-dip and plating.

LINTORFER EISENGIESSEREI GMBH
Rehhecke 83–87
Ratingen, 40885 Germany
P: +49.2102.3806.45
F: +49.2102.3806.39
le@lintorfereg.de
www.lintorfereg.de

- Chief Exec. Officers—Gunnar Jentsch, Wolfgang Schulz
- Sales Mgr.—Wolfgang Schulz
- Chief Engr.—Gunnar Jentsch

PRODUCTS and/or SERVICES:
Manufacturer of ingot molds and accessories of nodular cast iron and cast iron with lamellar graphite. Weight per piece of up to 20 tons.

No. of Employees: 80.

LISMAR INC., a Burke Porter Group Co.
730 Plymouth Ave. NE
Grand Rapids, MI 49505 USA
P: +1.603.879.9497
info@lismar.com
www.lismar.com

- Vice Pres., North American Sales—Sean McHugh

Linde is here to help you look ahead

Maximizing efficiency and flexibility in steel production

Steelmakers face intense market conditions and must search for ways to remain competitive. Linde's gas applications optimize your process and help you keep moving forward. Linde's industrial gases and technologies are used extensively in metal production to lower cost, improve energy efficiency, deliver environmental benefits, and improve productivity. The iron and steelmaking application technologies include gas injection systems, oxy-fuel combustion, ladle pre-heating, hydrogen steelmaking, and more.

If you want to keep pace with tomorrow's competition, you need a partner by your side for whom top quality, process optimization, and enhanced productivity are part of daily business.

Visit www.lindeus.com or call 1.844.44LINDE to find out more about our gases for steelmaking applications.

The Linde logo and the Linde wordmark are trademarks or registered trademarks of Linde plc or its affiliates.

Copyright © 2022, Linde plc. 10/2022

SUPPLIERS of EQUIPMENT, PRODUCTS and SERVICES

PRODUCTS and/or SERVICES:
Design, development, installation and service of roll surface and subsurface inspection instrumentation. LISMAR's automatic inspection systems detect surface defects through eddy current and surface wave technology. For subsurface defects, ultrasonic technology is applied. LISMAR also revamps and modernizes existing grinders, from mechanical reworks on-site to complete rebuilds, revamps reinstallations and integrations.

LITTELL STEEL CO.
220 Brady St.
New Brighton, PA 15066 USA
P: +1.724.843.5212
F: +1.724.843.5211
www.littellsteel.com

- Pres.—Robert M. Thaw
- Vice Pres.—Scott Durbin
- Est./Sales—Troy Hall
- Project Mgrs.—Nate Bedford, B.J. Patterson
- Pur. Agt.—Dan Kohlman
- Prodn. Coordinator—Gene McLaughlin

EQUIPMENT:
180,000-sq.-ft. building with 15 cranes (10- to 20-ton). Various types of carbon steel fabrication and welding, shears, press brakes, 85-ft. CNC burning and drill table, plasma cutting hydraulic girder fixture, three track-mounted drills, sandblast and sophisticated paint application system, saws.

PRODUCTS and/or SERVICES:
Girders (crane and bridge), trusses, weldments, building steel, bins, hoppers, miscellaneous metals. Structural steel fabrication and construction.

No. of Employees: 55.

LJB INC.
2500 Newmark Dr.
Miamisburg, OH 45342 USA
P: +1.937.259.5166
info@ljbinc.com
www.ljbinc.com

- Chief Exec. Officer—Rod Summer

PRODUCTS and/or SERVICES:
National engineering company licensed in all 50 U.S. states. Turnkey design/construction, fall protection systems, fall protection training, walking working surface engineering/safety, digital safety systems, and mobile applications hazard risk assessments.

No. of Employees: 160.

LOGIKA TECHNOLOGIES INC.
10-30 Mural St.
Richmond Hill, ON L4B 1B5 Canada
P: +1.905.597.7272
F: +1.905.597.7278
info@logikatech.com
www.logikatech.com

- Pres.—Russell Cote
- Applications Engrg. Mgr.—Rashik Laxman
- Regional Sales Mgrs.—Stephen Rogozynski, Aravin Shan, John Reading
- India Sales Mgr.—Ravi Sabhlok

PRODUCTS and/or SERVICES:
Ruggedized optical sensors and camera systems intended for use in extremely harsh industrial environments. The sensors and camera systems contain state-of-the-art electronics, optics and firmware. They are "armor plated" so they survive and thrive in harsh industrial environments, while still being easy to maintain. Logika also provides comprehensive applications engineering support for all products. Products include high-dynamic-range furnace camera systems, hot metal detectors, loop scanners, laser distance meters, optical barriers, pyrometers and machine vision–based image processing solutions.

LOGISTICS ETC.
2840 Dupont Commerce
Fort Wayne, IN 46825 USA
P: +1.260.246.9293
greg@logisticsetc.com
www.logisticsetc.com

SUPPLIERS OF EQUIPMENT, PRODUCTS and SERVICES

- Chief Exec. Officer—Greg McClain
- Vice Pres.—James Patrick

PRODUCTS and/or SERVICES:
Logistics/transportation.

No. of Employees: 250.

LUDECA INC.
1425 N.W. 88th Ave.
Doral, FL 33172 USA
P: +1.305.591.8935
F: +1.305.591.1537
info@ludeca.com
www.ludeca.com

- Pres.—Frank Seidenthal
- Vice Pres.—Alan Luedeking
- Asst. Sales Mgr.—Ron Lambert
- Adv. Mgrs.—Ana Maria Delgado, Dieter J. Seidenthal
- Chief Engr.—Pedro Casanova

PRODUCTS and/or SERVICES:
Laser alignment tools for rotating machinery. V-belt pulley alignment tools. Vibration, balancing, ultrasound and condition monitoring tools. Bearing heaters. Pre-cut SS shims. Consultation services, equipment rentals and training courses.

No. of Employees: 50+.

LUMAR METALURGICA LTDA.
Rodovia MG 232 km 09 No. 70
Santana do Paraiso, MG,
35179-000 Brazil
P: +55.31.38.281.000
www.lumarmetals.com.br

- Ind. Dir.—Willian Dos Reis Lima
- Tech. Dir.—Breno Totti Maia

EQUIPMENT:
Lance tip, oxygen lance, oxygen injectors, burners, contact plate, carbon lance, water cooler panel, duct, tuyeres, slagless technology, protect block technology, flexox, power carbon.

PRODUCTS and/or SERVICES:
Engineering and repair of meltshop equipment.

LUTHER HOLTON ASSOCIATES INC.
206-175 Longwood Road S
Hamilton, ON L8P 0A1 Canada
P: +1.905.521.9121
info@lutherholtonassoc.com
www.lutherholtonassoc.com

- Pres.—Luther J. Holton
- Engrg.—John A. Forsythe

PRODUCTS and/or SERVICES:
Rolling mill automation systems and services. On-line and off-line mill models.

M

M. BRASHEM INC./MBI ROLLS LLC
14023 N.E. 8th St.
Bellevue, WA 98007 USA
P: +1.425.641.1566
F: +1.425.641.1583
info@mbigraphite.com
www.mbigraphite.com

- Pres.—Marvin Brashem
- Vice Pres.—Mark Brashem

- Regional Sales Mgrs.—Phil Buchanan, Mike Bower, Brad Ratkiewicz, Nathan Engstrom

PRODUCTS and/or SERVICES:
Graphite electrodes; carbon electrodes; carbon and graphite blocks — extruded, vibro-molded and iso-molded; and mill rolls.

SUPPLIERS of EQUIPMENT, PRODUCTS and SERVICES

MACHINE CONCEPTS INC.
2167 State Rte. 66
P.O. Box 127
Minster, OH 45865 USA
P: +1.419.628.3498
www.machineconcepts.com

- Pres.—John Eiting
- Vice Pres. and Gen. Mgr.—Dale Broering
- Mgr. Process Line Equip.—Kirk Dicke

PRODUCTS and/or SERVICES:
Engineers and providers of: coil processing line equipment and lines (coil prep, tension leveling, inspection, sampling, re-banding, shear); multi-roll levelers with optional auto cassette exchange; tension levelers; flatteners; auto flat shape measuring systems; sidetrimmers and scrap choppers; slitters; back tension devices; payoff reels; tension reels; bridles; belt wrappers; shears (helical drum, flying, traversing and guillotine); accumulators; steering rolls; cleaning sections; coil cars; cut sheet conveyors and stackers; roll de-chocking systems; custom-designed equipment solutions; engineering studies; repair of other OEM equipment and upgrading services.

MACK MANUFACTURING INC.
7205 Bellingrath Road
Theodore, AL 36590 USA
P: +1.251.653.9999
F: +1.251.653.1365
sales@mackmfg.com
www.mackmfg.com

- Chief Exec. Officer and Pres.—Nevin E. McElderry
- Vice Pres. Mktg. and Adv. Mgr.—Matthew Davidson

PRODUCTS and/or SERVICES:
Buckets and grapples for handling scrap, iron ore, mill scale, etc.

MACPHERSON & COMPANY
2809 Mahoning Ave. NW
Warren, OH 44483 USA
P: +1.440.243.6565
F: +1.440.243.2211
sales@macphersonglass.com
www.macphersonglass.com

- Chief Exec. Officer—Jane MacPherson
- Vice Pres. Prodn./Mfg.—David Carlisle

PRODUCTS and/or SERVICES:
Manufacturer of custom-engineered industrial safety window systems for protection from molten metal reactions, blast, explosion, heavy impact, extreme heat and from radiant light transmission for eye safety. Designs special glass and windows for applications such as furnace pulpits, crane cabs, mobile equipment, caster stations, billet cranes, tapping stations, soaking pits, and any other dangerous areas where operators need protection. Safety window systems feature the EASY-RELEASE Retainer thumb-push lock system for tool-free quick changes for heavy splatter areas. Manufacturer of HOOGOVENS, SAFE-SHIELD, and MULTI-GLASS impact-resistant glasses; BPS heat shield and 101 Glass extreme radiant heat-resistant glass; custom pull-down shades and rolling glare shields to reduce the blinding light during steelmaking. Also supplies tempered IRR soda lime glass made in the U.S.A., plus many different types of special sight glass including for tuyeres, cameras boxes and lasers. MacPherson & Company also provides on-site technical consultations to determine the best-suited products for each application's environment to provide maximum safety solutions. Over 50 years of experience as a worldwide supplier of safety windows for mill workers' protection. Family-owned business and WBENC certified. HUBZone manufacturing facility.

No. of Employees: <25.

SUPPLIERS OF EQUIPMENT, PRODUCTS and SERVICES

MAGALDI TECHNOLOGIES LLC
30000 Mill Creek Ave.
Alpharetta, GA 30022 USA
P: +1.800.620.6921 (Toll-Free);
+1.678.705.9219
salesna@magaldi.com
www.magaldi.com

PRODUCTS and/or SERVICES:
Engineers, designs and manufactures steel belt conveyors to handle bulk materials for severe applications such as those found in coal-fired power plants, foundries, steel mills, mineral processing plants, cement plants, waste-to-energy plants and solid-fuel power plants.

MAGNECO/METREL INC.
740 Waukegan Road, Suite 212
Deerfield, IL 60015 USA
P: +1.630.543.6660
marketing@magneco-metrel.com
www.magneco-metrel.com

PRODUCTS and/or SERVICES:
Manufacturer of Metpump brand colloidal silica (sol-gel) bonded monolithic, pumpable refractories. Metpump products are ideal for endless lining repair programs and rebuilds of blast furnaces, reheat furnaces and torpedo ladles. In addition to repairs, MMI manufactures large shapes for casthouses, EAF delta sections, ladle safety linings and other special shapes.

MAGNETECH INDUSTRIAL SERVICES INC.
800 Nave Road SE
Massillon, OH 44646 USA
P: +1.800.837.1614 (Toll-Free)
F: +1.330.830.3520
www.magnetech.com

PRODUCTS and/or SERVICES:
Specializes in repair, rewind and refurbishment of industrial equipment from the transformer to the driven component: AC/DC motors and generators; motor control centers; fans/blowers; transformers; switchgear and circuit breakers; overhead cranes; and lifting magnets. Magnetech also provides preventative and predictive maintenance; comprehensive field services including planned outage services; and 24/7 emergency services.

Service Center Locations:

Boardman, OH
821 Bev Road
Boardman, OH 44512 USA
P: +1.330.758.0941

Hammond, IN
1825 Summer St.
Hammond, IN 46320 USA
P: +1.219.937.1000

Huntington, WV
501 8th Ave. W
Huntington, WV 25701 USA
P: +1.304.529.3264

Saraland, AL
701 Bill Myles Dr. W
Saraland, AL 36571 USA
P: +1.251.675.0855

Columbus, GA (Southern Rewinding)
5277 Chumar Dr.
Columbus, GA 31904 USA
F: +1.706.317.5545

MAGNETEK
N49 W13650 Campbell Dr.
Menomonee Falls, WI 53051 USA
P: +1.800.288.8178 (Toll-Free);
+1.262.783.3500
F: +1.262.783.3510
sales@magnetek.com
www.columbusmckinnon.com/magnetek

Divs.: Electromotive Systems, Telemotive and Enrange Radio Remote Controls, and Mondel Brakes

- Chief Exec. Officer and Pres.—David Wilson
- Vice Pres. Mktg.—Lynn Bostrom
- Dir. Sales and Mktg.—Dan Beilfuss
- Pur. Agt.—Jim Schultz

EQUIPMENT:
Complete manufacturing facility for controls, brakes, power delivery systems and radio remote controls.

SUPPLIERS of EQUIPMENT, PRODUCTS and SERVICES

PRODUCTS and/or SERVICES:
AC adjustable frequency controls, DC digital and magnet controls, standard-duty through mill-duty applications. Industrial brakes, mill-duty brakes and heavy-duty disc brakes. Overhead traveling crane conductor bar systems, festoon cable systems and radio remote controls. Automation and engineering capabilities and services. Magnetek is a Columbus McKinnon brand.

No. of Employees: 340.

MAGNETIC LIFTING TECHNOLOGIES US—see CRANE 1 SERVICES

MAINA ORGANI DI TRASMISSIONE S.P.A.
Corso Alessandria, 160
Asti (AT), 14100 Italy
P: +39.0141.492811
F: +39.0141.492873
sales@maina.it
info@maina.it
www.maina.it

- Pres.—Francesca Parroni Maina
- Chief Exec. Officer—Fiorenzo Orlandinotti

EQUIPMENT:
Fully equipped machine and assembly shop for production of power transmission units. Complete gear cutting, boring, turning and grinding facilities.

PRODUCT and/or SERVICES:
Manufacturer of gear spindles, universal shafts, gear couplings, safety elements with all production facilities located in Italy (270,000 sq. ft.). Provides engineering services including FEA, field service, reverse engineering, gear spindle and universal shaft reconditioning. Operating in 90 countries. ISO 9001 and OHSAS 18001 certified.

No. of Employees: 130.

MAINTOCARE
3 Pooja Business Centre, DA-8
Shakarpur, New Delhi, DL, 110092 India
P: +91.98.10707648
F: +91.11.22450607
acadim@gmail.com
www.maintocare.com

- Chief Exec. Officer—Sushil K. Varshney
- Vice Pres.—M. Dayal
- Sec.—V. Shilpaa
- Sales Mgr.—Pramod Saini

PRODUCTS and/or SERVICES:
Technical training and troubleshooting consultancy services for steel plants. Highly experienced steel industry engineers who can analyze problems relating to process, operation, maintenance, or projects and suggest cost-effective practical solutions for improvement.

No. of Employees: 10.

MAJOR
225 N. Montcalm Blvd.
Candiac, QC J5R 3L6 Canada
P: +1.450.659.7681
F: +1.450.659.5570
info@majorflexmat.com
www.majorflexmat.com

- Pres.—Bernard Betts
- Sr. Dir. Global Sales—Ian Edwards
- Dir. Product Technology—Lars Braünling

EQUIPMENT:
Screening equipment.

PRODUCTS and/or SERVICES:
FLEX-MAT tensioned screens, FLEX-MAT modular panels, FLEX-MAT sensors, woven screens.

No. of Employees: 200+.

MAINA
ORGANI DI TRASMISSIONE
Since 1886

Maina Organi di Trasmissione is a worldwide leader in engineering and manufacturing power transmission equipment for industrial plants.

Maina's Maintenance Facilities in the USA

- Chicago, IL
- Green Bay, WI
- Portland, OR
- Greenville, SC
- Savannah, GA
- West Monroe, LA
- Youngstown, OH
- Miami, FL

DNV
ISO 9001 · ISO 45001

www.Maina.it
Corso Alessandria, 160
14100 Asti (Italy)
Phone: +39 0141 492811
info@maina.it

SUPPLIERS of EQUIPMENT, PRODUCTS and SERVICES

MALMEDIE INC.
1275 Glenlivet Dr., Suite 100
Allentown, PA 18106 USA
P: +1.484.224.2949
F: +1.484.224.2999
us@malmedie.com
www.malmedie.com

PRODUCTS and/or SERVICES:
Mechanical couplings for various industrial applications worldwide. Malmedie develops, designs, manufactures and distributes gear, drum, flange, and safety couplings (torque limiters).

MANAGEMENT SCIENCE ASSOCIATES INC., Metals and Advanced Manufacturing Div.
6565 Penn Ave.
Pittsburgh, PA 15206 USA
P: +1.412.362.2000
F: +1.412.661.6442
infomamfg@msa.com
www.msa.com/home/our-businesses/metals

- Chief Exec. Officer—Alfred Kuehn
- Pres.—Joe Reddy
- Sr. Vice Pres.—Patrick J. Gallagher
- Client Oprs. Dir.—Todd Zahniser

EQUIPMENT:
Multiple-certification disaster recovery—business continuity centers, turnkey server, client, networking equipment. MSA-hosted applications and software as a service offering.

PRODUCTS and/or SERVICES:
Design, development and installation of process control and information management systems. Products and services include Blending Optimization Software Suite (BOSS™), Raw Material Data Aggregation Service (RMDAS™), scrap yard management systems, thermal and metallurgical models (EAF/BOF), refining models (AOD, VOD, LMF), level 2 meltshop systems, legacy systems remediation, custom software development and forecasting, and other analytical consulting engagements.

MAPOMEGA INC.
5605 N. MacArthur Blvd.
10th Floor
Irving, TX 75038 USA
stephane@mapomega.com
www.mapomega.com

- Chief Exec. Officer—Stephane Duchemin

PRODUCTS and/or SERVICES:
MapOmega helps businesses of all sizes to reduce accidents and optimize resources with cloud-based devices and standardization. MapOmega's core product is a fully automated Safety Cross, which samples safety data remotely at workstations and distributes consolidated information in real time at all levels of decisions across an organization and beyond. Safety Cross automates critical tasks, locally or remotely, to deliver data quickly and accurately to identify and to address spot issues or recurrent safety problems in the field. Customers can schedule a demo online and request a complimentary automated Safety Cross by visiting MapOmega's website or following them on social media.

No. of Employees: 5.

MARMACOR INC.
Sahrayicedit Ataturk Cad. Mesa Koz Plaza, No. 69/222
Kadikoy, 34734 Istanbul, Turkey
P: +90.216.373.1744
F: +90.216.373.1773
marmacor@marmacor.com
www.marmacor.com

- Dir.—Niyazi Ozdemir

PRODUCTS and/or SERVICES:
Rolls for steel rolling mills, seamless tube mills, straightening rollers, static and spun cast rings and sleeves. Mill spares.

No. of Employees: 110.

SUPPLIERS OF EQUIPMENT, PRODUCTS and SERVICES

MATRIX TECHNOLOGIES INC.
1760 Indian Wood Cir.
Maumee, OH 43537 USA
P: +1.419.897.7200
www.matrixti.com

- Chief Exec. Officer and Pres.—David Blaida
- Vice Pres., Project Svcs. Div.—Ronald M. England
- Chief Financial Officer—Dan Pruss
- Sr. Dir. Strategic Technology—Tim Lemoine
- Dir. Oprs.—Jason Perry
- Dir. Ind. Systems Div.—Terry Du Moulin
- Dir. Project Mgmt.—Deborah Zimmerman
- Dir. Info. Technology—Craig Varner
- Dir. H.R.—Lisa Behrendt

PRODUCTS and/or SERVICES:
Control and information system integration, manufacturing execution and intelligence systems, and engineering, procurement and construction services.

No. of Employees: 300+.

MATTHEWS MARKING SYSTEMS
3159 Unionville Road, Suite 500
Cranberry Twp., PA 16066 USA
P: +1.800.775.7775 (Toll-Free)
info@matw.com
www.matthewsmarking.com

PRODUCTS and/or SERVICES:
Matthews Marking Systems offers a wide range of marking and coding technologies for metal product manufacturers, including inkjet and laser. Solutions available include permanent and removable ink, 2D and bar code marking, machine-readable symbol marking, and custom-designed solutions to meet customer application requirements.

MAXCESS
1211 W. 22nd St., Suite 804
Oak Brook, IL 60523 USA
P: +1.844.MAXCESS (629.2377)
sales@maxcessintl.com
www.maxcessintl.com

PRODUCTS and/or SERVICES:
Customized end-to-end web handling solutions. Maxcess' global service network includes the product brands of RotoMetrics (rotary dies and accessories), Fife (guiding systems), Tidland (slitting systems and winding components), MAGPOWR (tension control systems), Webex (precision rolls), Valley Roller (rubber-covered rolls), and Componex (dead shaft idler technology).

MAZZELLA COMPANIES
21000 Aerospace Pkwy.
Cleveland, OH 44142 USA
P: +1.440.239.7000
F: +1.440.239.7010
marketing@mazzellacompanies.com
www.mazzellacompanies.com

- Chief Exec. Officer—Tony Mazzella
- Dir. of Mktg.—Mike Minissale
- Exec. Vice Pres. Sales, Lifting Businesses—Glen Powers
- Mktg. Mgr.—Mike Close
- Dir. of Pur.—Jim Takacs

EQUIPMENT:
Number of proof test beds: 23; largest capacity test bed: 660,000 lbs.; number of sewing machines: 34; number of swagers: 29; largest capacity swager: 2,500 tons.

PRODUCTS and/or SERVICES:
Provides lifting solutions, offering all styles of slings, overhead cranes, hoists and engineered lifting devices. Also provides training, in-field inspection and repair services.

No. of Employees: 700.

SUPPLIERS of EQUIPMENT, PRODUCTS and SERVICES

Mazzella CIS
1241 Foster Ave.
Nashville, TN 37210 USA
P: +1.615.256.8658
dschock@cisrigging.com
www.electrode-handling.com

- Chief Exec. Officer and Pres.—Tom Schiller
- Dir. of Business Dev.—Scott Tant
- Tech. and Safety Support—David Schock
- Field Svce. Technicians—Rick Spurlock, Cody Mathis

PRODUCTS and/or SERVICES: Electrode addition tools (torque devices and wrenches, chain wrenches, manual clamp collars, wishbone spacers, aluminum spinner wrenches, vertical automatic addition tongs (VAAT) and tilt tables); lift plugs (graphite and metal) and lift plug storage boxes; cushioned lift devices and shock absorbers, including slidegate lift systems and cushioned lift baskets; electrode recovery equipment (rings, tongs and tools); carbon electrode lifting tongs and on-furnace smelter jointing; elebia© automatic safety hooks. Patented No-Touch™ electrode handing system with upending table, vertical auto-edition tong, and spinning hydraulic torque device. Lifting and rigging products offered for the steel industry include custom-fabricated wire rope; shackles, hoists; alloy chain sling assemblies; fall protection devices; trolleys; beam clamps; and crane and rigging systems, all professionally engineered to meet the highest OSHA-compliant safety certifications and ANSI/ASME standards. Also offers services including site surveys to determine exact product needs, on-site and remote equipment safety inspections and repair; load, proof and destructive testing; on-site and classroom rigging safety and training; and consulting.

No. of Employees: 20.

MCCLUSKEY & ASSOCIATES INC.
1106 Ohio River Blvd., Suite 605
Sewickley, PA 15143 USA
P: +1.412.741.1612
F: +1.412.741.5336
sales@mccluskeyandassociates.com

- Pres.—John P. McCluskey
- Vice Pres.—John P. McCluskey Jr.
- Pur. Agt.—Sue Glasgow

PRODUCTS and/or SERVICES: Industrial building heating, ventilation and air conditioning systems; control room and motor room ventilation, pressurization equipment, and severe-duty air conditioning units; fiberglass pickle line fume exhaust systems; industrial fans, dampers, louvers, air rotation and unit heaters.

MCKEES ROCKS FORGINGS, Subsidiary of Trinity Industries Inc.
75 Nichol Ave.
McKees Rocks, PA 15136 USA
P: +1.800.223.2818 (Toll-Free)
www.mckeesrocksforgings.com

- Inside Sales Supv.—Janet Kastan
- Inside Sales—Donnie Hickie
- Engrg. Mgr.—Zachary Herbert

PRODUCTS and/or SERVICES: Produces a wide range of forged circular products for use in the industrial market, including crane wheels, industrial wheels, sheave wheels, gear blanks, rollers, and other circular forgings. McKees Rocks Forgings can produce forgings from 10 to 52 in. dia. and in weights up to 6,000 lbs. in almost any steel grade, and can produce almost any closed-die circular forging and crane wheel to customer specifications.

MCKEOWN INTERNATIONAL INC.
1111 Ace Road
Princeton, IL 61356 USA
P: +1.815.261.0072
F: +1.815.879.8209
mckeown@mckeowninternational.com
www.mckeowninternational.com

- Pres.—Patrick McKeown
- Chief Oper. Officer—Julie Liu

SUPPLIERS OF EQUIPMENT, PRODUCTS and SERVICES

- Gen. Mgr.—David Ison
- Treas.—Kerry Tang
- Adv. Mgr.—Nicole Noethan

PRODUCTS and/or SERVICES:
Mag-carbon brick for BOF, EAF and ladle applications; mag-dolomite, mag chrome brick for AOD, VOD linings and copper smelters; AMC brick for steel ladles; high-alumina brick for steel mills and foundries; EAF and LMF electrodes; silica brick/fireclay for the glass industry and coke oven batteries; insulating brick and ceramic fiber for most every metal and furnace application, and functional refractories (ladle shroud, stopper rod, slidegate). Services: turnkey services including engineering, manufacturing/fabrication; installation and maintenance for all caster components such as water jackets, mold tubes, mold assemblies, segments, including refurbishing, containment rolls, spray zones, dummy bars and torch/shear systems. Turnkey services for coke oven batteries including battery inspection, refractory and structural repair; ceramic welding for maintenance and operations management; and other metallurgical products such as cored wire, stainless steel flex hoses, ladle and tundish cover heaters, graphite electrodes.

MIG Refractories USA
1111 Ace Road
Princeton, IL 61356 USA
P: +1.815.261.0072
F: +1.815.879.8209
mckeown@mckeowninternational.com
www.mckeowninternational.com

- Pres.—Patrick McKeown
- Sales Mgr. and Pur. Agt.—David Ison
- Adv. Mgr.—Nicole Noethan

PRODUCTS and/or SERVICES:
Mag carbon bricks, pre-cast shapes and monolithics.

No. of Employees: 50.

MCNEIL INDUSTRIES – MAXAM BEARINGS
835 Richmond Road
Painesville, OH 44077 USA
P: +1.440.721.0400
F: +1.440.721.0401
sales@mcneilindustries.com
www.mcneilindustries.com

PRODUCTS and/or SERVICES:
MAXAM bearings in plain, spherical, cylindrical and full-complement designs, whose proprietary design enables them to tolerate high temperatures, harsh environments, contamination, and heavy or shock loads providing service life that is 4 to 10 times longer than typical standard bearings. McNeil Guide Systems pin, bushing and ball retainer sets for stamping and molding tooling bearing guidance.

MECON LTD.
Vivekananda Path, P.O. Doranda
Ranchi, JH, 834002 India
F: +0651.2482189.2214
P: +0651.2483000
ranchi@meconlimited.co.in
www.meconlimited.co.in

- Chmn. and Managing Dir.—Atul Bhatt
- Dir. (Projects)—Salil Kumar
- Dir. (Finance)—RH Juneja
- Dir. (Commercial)—Sanjay Kumar Verma
- Dir. (Tech.)—Arun Kumar Agarwal

PRODUCTS and/or SERVICES:
MECON Ltd., formerly known as Metallurgical & Engineering Consultants (India) Ltd., is a public sector undertaking under the Indian Ministry of Steel. Provides frontline engineering, consultancy and contracting, and a full range of services required for setting up of a project from concept to commissioning including turnkey execution. Competency in EPC execution of various projects in the areas of coke oven batteries and byproduct plants, BFs, rolling mills, ports and material handling, and special projects demanding core engineering and technological skills.

SUPPLIERS of EQUIPMENT, PRODUCTS and SERVICES

Also provides design, engineering and consultancy services for the international market.

MELTER S.A. DE C.V.
Calle C No. 511
Parque Industrial Almacentro
Apodaca, NL, 66600 Mexico
P: +52.81.8000.9600
sales@melter.com.mx
www.melter.com.mx

- Chief Exec. Officer—Carlos Uribe
- Gen. Dir.—Carlos Gutierrez
- Sales Mgr., Southern USA and Canada—Roy Aleman
- Sales Mgr., Northern USA—Jorge Guajardo

PRODUCTS and/or SERVICES:
Complete engineering, project design, fabrication, and testing of EAFs, including water-cooled elements and systems such as lower and upper shells, roofs, LMFs, individual panels (steel and copper), slag doors, tunnels, dropout chambers, pre-heater connecting car pan (consteel), water-cooled ductwork, etc. Mechanical components include electrode arms, superstructures, masts, gantry beams, ladles, scrap buckets, and the fabrication of tube and shell heat exchangers and pressure vessels (ASME stamp). Engineering and fabrication of heat recuperators, air coolers, and economizers.

MERIT PUMP & EQUIPMENT CO. INC.
975 Lincoln Way W
P.O. Box 960
Wooster, OH 44691 USA
P: +1.800.700.8265 (Toll-Free);
  +1.330.262.7867
F: +1.330.262.6200
sales@meritpump.com
www.meritpump.com

- Chief Exec. Officer and Pres.—John E. Dunbar
- Gen. Mgr.—Mike Dunbar
- Sales Mgr.—David Edwards
- Shop Mgr. and Field Svce.—Colin Saffel
- Jobs Coordinator—John W. Dunbar

PRODUCTS and/or SERVICES:
Kobe triplex pumps for Morgoil bearing applications, high-pressure lubrication, hydraulic and descaling systems. Kobe Master Distributor North Americas repair/sales/distribution. Full repair, field service, troubleshooting for Kobe and various pumps, including: Kobe, Weatherford, Myers/Aplex, Stancor, All-Flo, HydraCell, Fairbanks Morse, Aurora and Pacer. Pump repair, sales, system fabrication, design and troubleshooting.

No. of Employees: 6.

META-FIND, INC
16 Fox Ridge
Roslyn, NY 11576 USA
P: +1.212.867.8100
mikeh@meta-findny.com
www.meta-findny.com

- Pres.—Michael R. Heineman

PRODUCTS and/or SERVICES:
Executive search consultants for metallurgical and material engineers.

METAL PRODUCTS AND ENGINEERING – U.S. LLC
447 S. Sullivan St.
Hobart, IN 46342 USA
P: +1.219.942.2050
F: +1.219.942.6408
info@mpe-us.com
www.mpe-us.com

- Pres.—Robert T. McGuire

PRODUCTS and/or SERVICES:
Distributors of the AGELLIS electromagnetic level measurement and slag detection system for mold level measurement, tundish level measurement, EAF level measurement, and slag detection in ladles and EAFs. Also offers the WADECO line of microwave measurement instruments and level switches.

SUPPLIERS OF EQUIPMENT, PRODUCTS and SERVICES

METALHEAP.COM
3490 US 1, Bldg. 11C
Princeton, NJ 08540 USA
P: +1.609.278.1041
info@metalheap.com
www.metalheap.com

- Pres.—Gitanjali Aggarwal

PRODUCTS and/or SERVICES:
Software services to manage/sell surplus/excess/seconds including pipe, plate, structural and coil. Provides private listing sites as well as a common marketplace to allow best possible realization.

No. of Employees: 1.

METALLON
432, 9 de Julio St.
San Nicolás, BA, B2900HGJ Argentina
P: + 011.54.9.336.421.1990
jorge.madias@metallon.com.ar
graciela.palmerio@metallon.com.ar
www.metallon.com.ar

- Pres.—Jorge Madias
- Sec.—Graciela Palmerio

PRODUCTS and/or SERVICES:
Consulting, training, met lab, and library services for ironmaking, steelmaking, rolling, finishing, product development and foundries.

No. of Employees: 4.

METALTEK INTERNATIONAL
905 E. St. Paul Ave.
Waukesha, WI 53188 USA
P: +1.262.544.7777
F: +1.262.544.7843
www.metaltek.com

- Chief Exec. Officer—EJ Kubick
- Vice Pres. Sales and Mktg.—Rod Anderson

EQUIPMENT:
AOD vessels, induction melting, heat treating, centrifugal casting, sand molding and casting, investment molding and casting, NDT, chem labs, x-ray, mechanical testing.

PRODUCTS and/or SERVICES:
Wear-, heat- and corrosion-resistant centrifugal, sand, and investment castings in a full range of bronze, stainless, nickel, cobalt, and specialty alloys.

Divs.:

Carondelet Corp.
P: +1.636.475.2143

- Business Dev.—Tim Falleri

Wisconsin Centrifugal
P: +1.262.544.7760

- Business Dev.—Andy Griffin

Wisconsin Investcast
P: +1.920.206.8336

- Business Dev.—Mike McCleary

Sandusky International
P: +1.419.609.4025

- Business Dev.—Joe Fratoe

Sandusky Ltd.
P: +44.1592.773030

- Business Dev.—Graeme Duncan

MI-JACK PRODUCTS INC.
3111 W. 167th St.
Hazel Crest, IL 60429 USA
P: +1.708.596.5200
info@mi-jack.com
www.mi-jack.com

- Pres.—Michael Lanigan

PRODUCTS and/or SERVICES:
Travelift® rubber-tired gantry (RTG) cranes. Travelift RTG cranes handle steel material including, but not limited to, slabs, coils, ingots, plates, rebar, billets and more. All Mi-Jack gantry cranes are manufactured to ISO 9001:2015 certified standards.

SUPPLIERS of EQUIPMENT, PRODUCTS and SERVICES

MICHELS CONSTRUCTION INC.
817 Main St.
Brownsville, WI 53006 USA
P: +1.920.583.3132
kschwart@michels.com
www.michels.us

EQUIPMENT:
Drill rigs, jet trucks, one-pass trenchers, drills, mixers, pumps and support equipment.

PRODUCTS and/or SERVICES:
Deep foundations, dewatering, earth retention systems, federal infrastructure, ground improvement, industrial construction and marine construction.

No. of Employees: 8,000.

MICRO-EPSILON AMERICA
8120 Brownleigh Dr.
Raleigh, NC 27617 USA
P: +1.919.787.9707
F: +1.919.787.9706
me-usa@micro-epsilon.com
www.micro-epsilon.com

– Managing Dir.—Martin Dumberger

PRODUCTS and/or SERVICES:
Sensor systems for displacement, distance, position and thickness. 2D/3D measurement technology, laser scanners, micrometers, fiber optic sensors. Sensors for color recognition and color measurement. Infrared temperature sensors and thermal imaging cameras. Measurement and inspection systems for metal, rubber and tire, plastics, and painting.

No. of Employees: 1,200 worldwide.

MICROCRANES INC.
10000 N.E. 7th Ave., Suite 330-A
Vancouver, WA 98685 USA
P: +1.360.768.5104
info@microcranes.com
www.smartrigcranes.com

– Chief Exec. Officer—Josh Clark

PRODUCTS and/or SERVICES:
Portable multi-purpose floor cranes and compact industrial hoists. Manual, electric and battery-powered options. For use indoors, outdoors or on rooftops for a variety of above-the-hook rigging applications; from steel erection, glazing, aircraft and construction to facility maintenance and aircraft repairs. Offerings: 2,000-lb.-capacity M1 Model (battery-powered with hydraulic boom) and 1,200-lb.-capacity T1 Model (electric or hand-crank winch/hand-pump jack). No operator license required for most North American agencies (under 1-ton rule).

No. of Employees: 3.

MICROPOLY/PHYMET INC.
75 N. Pioneer Blvd.
Springboro, OH 45066 USA
P: +1.937.743.8061
F: +1.937.568.6743
www.micropoly.com

– Pres. and Treas.—Amy Minck Lachman
– Chief Engr.—Brandon Collins

PRODUCTS and/or SERVICES:
MicroPoly® solid lubricants.

No. of Employees: 20.

MID-CONTINENT COAL AND COKE CO.
20600 Chagrin Blvd., Suite 850
Cleveland, OH 44122 USA
P: +1.216.283.5700
F: +1.216.283.0328
sales@midcontinentcoke.com
www.midcontinentcoke.com

PRODUCTS and/or SERVICES:
All sizes of metallurgical and petroleum coke products, including coke breeze, buckwheat, nut and furnace coke. Anthracite coal. Dry coke products include charge and injection carbon. Also provides contract screening and material handling services in various mills.

SUPPLIERS OF EQUIPMENT, PRODUCTS and SERVICES

MID RIVER MINERALS INC.
4675 Weitz Road
Morris, IL 60450 USA
P: +1.815.941.SLAG (7524)
F: +1.815.941.0426
www.midriverminerals.com

- Pres.—Anthony P. Augius
- Vice Pres.—Paul A. Augius

PRODUCTS and/or SERVICES:
Full-service custom blending and bagging of high-calcium lime, dolomitic lime, calcium aluminate, spar, sand, and a full line of synthetic and artificial slags. Custom packaging from 25# to 4000#. Transloading of rail and warehousing services.

MIDDOUGH INC.
1901 E. 13th St., Suite 400
Cleveland, OH 44114 USA
P: +1.216.367.6000
F: +1.216.367.6020
www.middough.com

Offices located in Ashland, KY; Buffalo, NY; Chicago, IL; Cleveland, OH; Merrillville, IN; Madison, WI; Pittsburgh, PA; and Maumee, OH.

- Chief Exec. Officer and Chmn.—Ron Ledin
- Chief Oper. Officer and Pres.—Carl Wendell
- Chief Financial Officer—Dan O'Connor
- Vice Pres. and Gen. Mgrs.—Bob Necciai, Rich Hayes, Dan Lowry
- Sr. Project Mgrs.—Kevin Moore, Tony Nuzzo, Clay Piper, David Schmidt, Jim Weinheimer
- Sr. Technology Mgrs.—Nitin Mahajan, Tony Sansone, Pete Sortisio, Bryan Turney

PRODUCTS and/or SERVICES:
Major project solutions engineers, project managers and construction managers—comprehensive services for studies, planning, preliminary, and detail engineering, as well as structural inspections, welding engineering, construction management, personnel facilities, industrial engineering, and plant modeling and design-build—including CAD, FEA, CFD, BIM, 3D CADD, estimating, scheduling, procurement, specifications, testing, inspection and start-up—serving integrated mills, mini-mills, and non-ferrous metals, process, foundry and utilities industries. Specialists for casters, hot and cold rolling mills for both flat rolling and bar rolling projects, BOP shop, including vessel and ladle design and maintenance, coke plants, BFs, EAFs, chemical process, power plants, arc furnaces, water systems, energy management and conservation, industrial furnaces, machine design, dust and fume collection, material handling, air and water pollution control, processing lines, electrical distribution, including high-voltage and computer automation systems.

No. of Employees: 500.

MIDREX TECHNOLOGIES INC.
3735 Glen Lake Dr., Suite 400
Charlotte, NC 28208 USA
P: +1.704.373.1600
F: +1.704.373.1611
info@midrex.com
www.midrex.com

- Pres. and Chief Oper. Officer—Stephen Montague
- Chief Oper. Officer—K.C. Woody
- Vice Pres. — Oprs.—Chris Hayes
- Vice Pres. — Commercial—Will Dempsey
- Dir. — Engrg.—John Teeters
- Mgr. Mktg. and Communications—Lauren Lorraine

PRODUCTS and/or SERVICES:
DRI technologies for production of cold DRI, hot DRI and HBI; ferrous mineral processing, technology testing and development. Midrex Direct Reduction Process.

No. of Employees: 175.

SUPPLIERS of EQUIPMENT, PRODUCTS and SERVICES

MIDWEST INDUSTRIAL SUPPLY INC.
1101 3rd St. SE
Canton, OH 44707 USA
P: +1.800.321.0699 (Toll-Free)
F: +1.888.890.4429 (Toll-Free)
custserv@midwestind.com
lynn.cielec@midwestind.com

- Pres.—Steven Vitale
- Vice Pres. of Ind. Sales—Lynn Cielec
- Adv. Mgr.—Liz Campbell
- Pur. Agt.—Jason Tomci
- Chief Chemist—Cheryl Detloff

PRODUCTS and/or SERVICES:
Dust control of particulate matter from entering the air and water, including fugitive dust from stockpiles, steel mills and industrial facilities. Environmentally safe, reliable and effective dust control products. Managed Service Program provides a comprehensive, site-specific solution to excess dust caused by the frequent use of unpaved roads by major industrial operations.

No. of Employees: 100.

M.N. DASTUR & CO. (P) LTD.
P-17 Mission Row Extension
Kolkata, WB, 700013 India
P: +91.33.2225.5420; 0500
F: +91.33.2225.1422; 7101
kolkata@dastur.com
www.dastur.com

- Chmn. and Managing Dir.—R.M. Dastur

PRODUCTS and/or SERVICES:
Independent consulting engineering firm with expertise in the areas of process design and innovation, operations improvement, energy and carbon management, engineering, and techno-economics of iron- and steelmaking operations. Has successfully engineered mega-scale projects for steelmakers, governments, banks, and other investors from the conceptualization stage to the implementation stage. Headquartered in Kolkata, India, with offices in Düsseldorf, Germany; New Jersey, USA; Toronto, ON, Canada; Tokyo, Japan; Abu Dhabi, UAE; and Manama, Bahrain. Indian operations include offices in Chennai, Mumbai, Bengaluru, New Delhi, Bhubaneswar and Hyderabad.

Dastur International Inc.
650 From Road, Suite 158
Paramus, NJ 07652 USA
P: +1.201.261.2300
F: +1.201.261.2334
paramus@dastur.com

MODULOC CONTROL SYSTEMS LTD., a Rotalec Group Co.
22B London Road, Woolmer Green
Knebworth, Hertfordshire SG3 6JP U.K.
P: +44.0.1438.817792
sales@moduloc-intl.com
www.moduloc-intl.com

PRODUCTS and/or SERVICES:
Laser distance meters, hot metal detectors, thickness gauges, induction loop sensors, molten metal level measurement, crane positioning radar, laser doppler velocimeters, pyrometers.

MOFFITT CORP.
1351 13th Ave. S, Suite 130
Jacksonville Beach, FL 32250 USA
P: +1.904.241.9944
F: +1.904.246.8333
ilachut@moffittcorp.com
www.moffittcorp.com

- Chief Exec. Officer and Pres.—John Moffitt
- Exec. Vice Pres.—Blake Edgeworth
- Chief Financial Officer—Phil Spano
- Vice Pres. Sales—Mark Hannah
- Vice Pres. Engrg.—Mike Berry
- Dir. of Project Engrg.—Richard Pereira
- Natl. Sales Mgr.—Seth Nickol

PRODUCTS and/or SERVICES:
Industrial ventilation system design, natural ventilation systems, industrial ventilation contracting and installation, MoffittVent natural ventilators, MatrixVent natural ventilators, DeltaStream adiabatic natural cooling units, EcoStream wall louvers, fan sales and service.

SUPPLIERS OF EQUIPMENT, PRODUCTS and SERVICES

Moffitt Mechanical
1351 13th Ave. S, Suite 130
Jacksonville Beach, FL 32250 USA
P: +1.904.241.9944
F: +1.904.246.8333
ilachut@moffittcorp.com

- Chief Exec. Officer and Pres.—John Moffitt
- Exec. Vice Pres.—Blake Edgeworth

PRODUCTS and/or SERVICES:
Industrial ventilation contracting and installation.

MOLYNEUX INDUSTRIES INC.
621 Cliff Mine Road
Coraopolis, PA 15108 USA
P: +1.724.695.3406
F: +1.724.695.3407
sales@molyneuxindustries.com
www.molyneuxindustries.com

PRODUCTS and/or SERVICES:
Designs and manufactures adjustable crane rail clips, rail pads, girder tiebacks, sole plates, and customized engineering solutions for crane runways.

MOOG FLO-TORK
1701 N. Main St.
Orrville, OH 44667 USA
P: +1.330.682.0010
F: +1.330.683.6857
sales@ft.moog.com
www.flotork.com

- Ind. Sales Mgr.—Allen Ruef
- Pur. Agt.—Bob Starling
- Sr. Sales Coordinator—Tim Kimball
- Sales Coordinator—Patrick Gordon

PRODUCTS and/or SERVICES:
Manufacturer of hydraulic and pneumatic rack-and-pinion rotary actuators. Torque ranges to 50,000,000 in.-lbs.

No. of Employees: 120.

MOON FABRICATING CORP.
700 W. Morgan St.
Kokomo, IN 46901 USA
P: +1.765.459.4194
F: +1.765.452.6090
gveach@moontanks.com
www.moontanks.com

- Pres.—Greg Veach
- Vice Pres.—Shawn Pannell
- Treas. and Pur. Agt.—Todd Veach
- Est./Engr.—Greg Talkington

EQUIPMENT:
Complete fabrication and tank lining facility. 12-ft. x 40-ft. vulcanizer. Crane capacity: 60,000 lbs.

PRODUCTS and/or SERVICES:
Custom plate metal fabrication, tanks, stacks, ducts. Applications of corrosion-resistant linings. Rubber, Koroseal, fiberglass, products for pickling, plating and acid regeneration.

No. of Employees: 50.

MORE S.R.L.
Via S. Lucia 7
Gemona del Friuli (UD), 33013 Italy
P: +39.0432.973511
F: +39.0432.970676
info@more-oxy.com
www.more-oxy.com

- Pres. and Chief Engr.—Simone Marcuzzi
- Managing Dir.—Massimo Iacuzzi
- Sales Mgr.—Ivo Filipovic
- Asst. Sales Mgr.—Giovanni Londero
- Regional Sales Mgr.—Robby McGill III
- Svce. Mgr.—Christian Spiz
- Regional Svce. Mgr.—Dylan McGill

PRODUCTS and/or SERVICES:
Complete engineering, fabrication and testing facilities. Offgas analysis system; dynamic post-combustion management; EAF sidewall fix injection system; oxy-fuel burner systems; temperature and sampling manipulators; carbon and lime pneumatic injection systems;

SUPPLIERS of EQUIPMENT, PRODUCTS and SERVICES

consumable lance manipulators; water-cooled lance manipulators.

No. of Employees: 80.

MORGAN ADVANCED MATERIALS — THERMAL CERAMICS
2102 Old Savannah Road
Augusta, GA 30903 USA
P: +1.706.796.4200
marketing.tc@morganplc.com
www.morganthermalceramics.com

- Chief Exec. Officer—Pete Raby

PRODUCTS and/or SERVICES: High-temperature insulation fibers, refractory and microporous products supplied to the iron and steel market.

No. of Employees: 9,000.

MORGAN ENGINEERING
1049 S. Mahoning Ave.
Alliance, OH 44601 USA
P: +1.330.823.6130
F: +1.330.823.9249
www.morganengineering.com

- Chief Exec. Officer and Pres.—Mark L. Fedor
- Chief Financial Officer—Scott Thomas
- Vice Pres. Engrg.—Ken Maurer
- Regional Sales Mgrs.—David Heppner, Greg Novickoff, David Hackworth
- Morgan Heppenstall/Blawknox Product Mgr.—John Lizak
- Morgan Argentina—Lauro Picasso
- Vice Pres. Mfg.—Jim Caserta
- Chief Engr.—Nelson E. Baker
- Pur. Mgr.—Mike Lyons

PRODUCTS and/or SERVICES: Parent company of Morgan Automation, Morgan Engineering, Morgan Heppenstall/Blawknox and Morgan Kinetic Structures. As a group the Morgan companies provide consultation, design development, detailed engineering, manufacturing, installation and commissioning of the following products: human-operated and autonomous overhead bridge cranes for unique, demanding and severe requirements; automation of moving machines, structures and process lines; engineering consultation services; special lifting devices for below-the-crane-hook applications, bulk material handling and custom attachments to new and existing machinery; development and supply of mechanization and automation for movable stadium roofs and other large movable structures; spare parts and repair services for all of the above.

MOTION
1605 Alton Road
Birmingham, AL 35210 USA
P: +1.800.526.9328 (Toll-Free)
F: +1.205.957.5290
www.motion.com

- Chief Exec. Officer and Pres.—Randy Breaux
- Exec. Vice Pres. Supply Chain, Oprs. Support, Mktg. and Enterprise Excellence—Joe Limbaugh
- Vice Pres. Group Exec.—Jay Carwan
- Vice Pres. Dist., Logistics and Oprs.—John Watwood
- Exec. Vice Pres., Branch Oprs.—Kevin Storer
- Vice Pres. — Canada—Brent Pope
- Vice Pres. — Southeast Group—Jon Tart
- Vice Pres. Automation—Aurelio Banda
- Vice Pres. Fluid Power—David Mayer
- Mgr. Graphic Design—Robert Hernandez

PRODUCTS and/or SERVICES: Industrial parts distributor of bearings, mechanical power transmission, electrical and industrial automation, hydraulic and industrial hose, hydraulic and pneumatic components, industrial products, safety products, and material handling. Services include technical expertise, comprehensive and innovative training programs for customers and employees, satellite-based computerized national inventory management, integrated services and documented cost reduction. 700+ locations in North America, including 20 distribution centers.

No. of Employees: 7,000+.

SUPPLIERS OF EQUIPMENT, PRODUCTS and SERVICES

MOTOROLA SOLUTIONS
500 W. Monroe St.
Chicago, IL 60661 USA
P: +1.888.325.9336
info-na@motorolasolutions.com
www.motorolasolutions.com

PRODUCTS and/or SERVICES:
Two-way radio systems and devices, LTE broadband, GPS location tracking, alarm and event management, dispatch and incident management software, PTT applications, video security and analytics, access control, man down alerts, lone worker applications.

No. of Employees: 14,000.

MOVARESA
Ave. Burocratas #352 L-4
Col. Cumbres 2 Sector
Monterrey, NL, 64610 Mexico
P: +52.81.8311.5900
info@movaresa.com
www.movaresa.com

- Chief Oper. Officers and Pres.—Roberto Martin, Jose Figueroa

PRODUCTS and/or SERVICES:
International engineering sales representative company (manufacturers' representative) established in Mexico. For more than 45 years, MOVARESA has been involved in selling equipment, tools, services, repairs, spare parts, capital goods, consumable products, automation, technology, and robots to the following industries in Mexico: steel, aluminum, crane manufacturing, forging, foundry, mining, metal mechanic, metal stamping, scrap metal recycling, cement and power generation. High level of expertise in technical sales of components, spare parts, repair services, and equipment for heavy industries, with primary focus on the steel, metalworking and mining industries.

MRSI — MAINTENANCE - RELIABILITY SOLUTIONS INC.
425 Caro Lane
Chapin, SC 29036 USA
P: +1.803.231.8227
F: +1.803.298.5986
ship@m-rsi.com
www.m-rsi.com

- Pres.—Jeff Blankenship

PRODUCTS and/or SERVICES:
Titan Bearings, Kingsbury Bearings, Kingsbury/Messinger Bearings, IVC, power transmission product and slewing ring bearing consulting, Liebherr North America representative. Specialty bearing and rotating solution specialist.

No. of Employees: 1.

MTS SENSORS—see TEMPOSONICS LLC

MTUS TECHNOLOGY INC.
3057 Nationwide Pkwy.
Brunswick, OH 44212 USA
P: +1.330.220.0833
F: +1.330.220.0933
info@mtus-technology.com
www.mtus-technology.com

- Sales Contacts—Dragos Preda, Rick Liptak

PRODUCTS and/or SERVICES:
Consulting, engineering and supply of plants for: VD, vacuum carbon deoxidation (VCD), VOD, vacuum oxygen heating (VOH), vacuum metal distillation (MD), vacuum ingot teeming (VIT), Rheinmetall Heraeus (RH). Automatic connections for stirring gas (automatic ladle gas coupling systems, LF, EAF, tundish, VD and VOD, and stirring stations), automatic manipulators for sampling and measurements at EAF, LF, VD/VOD and caster; wire feeding machines, process gas analyzers, bath level control (mold, filling height of ladles when teeming EAF, slag pot level height and further filling heights of different metallurgical vessels); material handling/alloying systems.

SUPPLIERS of EQUIPMENT, PRODUCTS and SERVICES

MUNROE INC.
1820 N. Franklin St.
Pittsburgh, PA 15233 USA
P: +1.412.231.0600
F: +1.412.231.0647
munroe@munroeinc.com
www.munroeinc.com

- Pres.—Robert T. Woodings
- Vice Pres. Finance—Richard Bralich
- Vice Pres. Oprs./Pur.—Robert Vinson
- Vice Pres. Sales—Anthony Manuel
- Contr.—Scott Shankel
- Gen. Mgr. Constr.—Joseph Rodichok
- Plant Mgr., Youngstown, OH—Tim Thompson
- Plant Mgr., Ringgold, GA—Michael Anchondo
- Pur. Mgr.—Rich Tommarello
- Chief Engr.—Kevin Craig
- Qual. Control Mgr.—Marty O'Connell

EQUIPMENT:
Youngstown, OH, plant: computerized, automated weld overlay equipment, tube and pipe bending equipment, shears, forming equipment, welding equipment, automatic panel welding line, submerged-arc welding, vessel manipulators, fin welding line, and heavy overhead cranes. Ringgold, GA, plant: swaging, tube bending and fin welding equipment, automatic submerged-arc panel welding line.

PRODUCTS and/or SERVICES:
Design and manufacture of BOF water-cooled hoods, ASME code pressure vessels, heat exchangers, fractionating columns, jacketed pipe and tubular boiler components, waterwall panels, overlaid panels, superheater and reheater elements, economizer elements, tube bending, boiler headers, studded tubing, complete boiler house installation, field construction services including boiler and BOF hood repair, heat exchanger retubing, code welding and pressure vessel alterations, and EAF roofs.

No. of Employees: 200.

N

NALCO WATER, AN ECOLAB CO.
1601 W. Diehl Road
Naperville, IL 60564 USA
P: +1.337.305.2430
boesteves@ecolab.com
www.ecolab.com/nalco-water

- Chief Exec. Officer—Christophe Beck
- Pres.—Darrell Brown
- Sr. Mktg. Mgr., Global PMI—Bárbara Tufano

PRODUCTS and/or SERVICES:
Leading provider of water treatment, water management and process improvements to the industrial sector. Nalco Water's solutions comprise proprietary chemistry, engineering expertise along with automation and digital solutions to ensure steel producers meet their key goals in a safe and sustainable manner.

No. of Employees: 48,000+.

NANJING REFMIN CO. LTD.
Suite 1230, New Century Plaza
1 Taiping South Road
Nanjing, Jiangsu, 210000 P.R. China
P: +025.5703.3909
F: +025.5703.3900
info@refmin.com.cn
www.refmin.com.cn

- Pres.—Jun Wang
- Sales Mgr.—Ivan Wong

PRODUCTS and/or SERVICES:
Refractories.

No. of Employees: 10.

454   2023 AIST Directory — Iron and Steel Plants

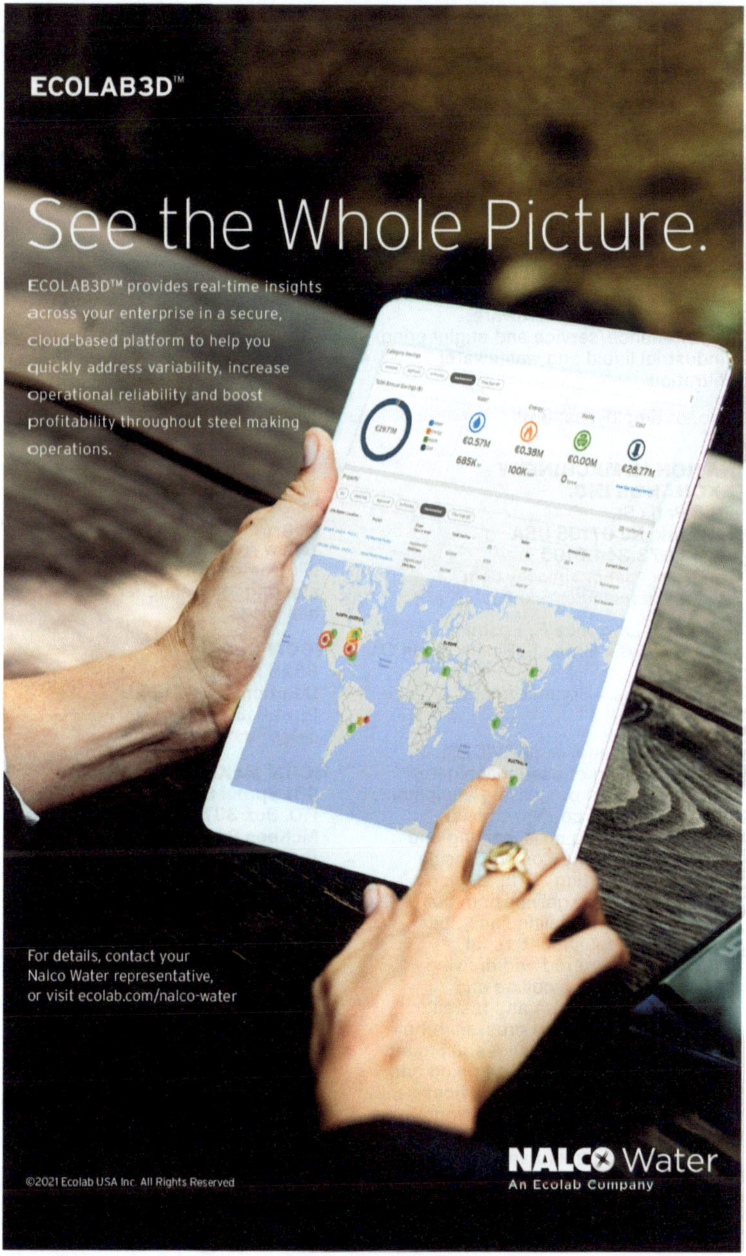

See listing page 454

SUPPLIERS of EQUIPMENT, PRODUCTS and SERVICES

NATIONAL FILTER MEDIA
309 N. Braddock St.
Winchester, VA 22601 USA
P: +1.800.336.7300 (Toll-Free);
+1.540.773.4780
F: +1.540.773.4781
midwescofilter@nfm-filter.com
www.nfm-filter.com

PRODUCTS and/or SERVICES:
Baghouse filter bags, cartridges, pleated elements, hardware, maintenance/service and engineering, industrial liquid and wastewater filtration.

No. of Employees: 350.

NATIONAL MACHINERY EXCHANGE INC.
158 Paris St.
Newark, NJ 07105 USA
P: +1.973.344.6100
andreia@nationalmachy.com
www.nationalmachy.com

- Pres.—Lawrence R. Epstein
- Vice Pres.—Bruce L. Pinelli, Brian O. Epstein
- Sales Dirs.—Bryan Byrne, Ray Alvarez

PRODUCTS and/or SERVICES:
Buying/selling of used machinery, including: steel processing equipment, rolling mills (all configurations), Sendzimir rolling mills, casting and rolling equipment, coil processing equipment (slitting, CTL, tension leveling, edging, galvanizing, coil coating, and annealing lines), bar processing equipment, rebar equipment, wire rod and drawing equipment, spring coiling and wire forming, forging and fastener equipment, extrusion presses, tube mills and tube processing equipment, fabrication equipment, stamping and specialty presses. Other services include auctions and liquidations; industrial real estate; and logistics, project management and appraisals.

No. of Employees: 25.

NCCM CO.

North America:

NCCM River Falls (Headquarters)
2555 Prairie Dr.
River Falls, WI 54022 USA
P: +1.715.425.5885
sales@nccmco.com
www.nccmco.com

- Chief Exec. Officer—Brent Niccum
- Pres.—Jewels Niccum
- Chief Oprs. Officer—Cole Niccum
- Dir. Global Sales and Mktg.—Kai Vöhl
- Gen. Mgr. of Oprs. (Spain)—Joan Compte
- Oprs. Mgr. McKees Rocks—Dave Shearer
- Natl. Chinese Sales Mgr.—Nathan Xu

PRODUCTS and/or SERVICES:
Non-woven mill roll products—Premier Yellow rolls, wringer rolls, bridle rolls, oiler/de-oiler rolls, deflector rolls, steering rolls, snubber rolls, wiper bars, mill wipes.

NCCM Dearborn
8526 Brandt St.
Dearborn, MI 48126 USA
P: +1.313.584.9696
sales@nccmco.com

NCCM McKees Rocks
401 Sproul St.
P.O. Box 337
McKees Rocks, PA 15136 USA
P: +1.800.252.3358 (Toll-Free);
+1.412.771.2200
F: +1.412.771.5777
sales@nccmco.com

Europe:

NCCM Barcelona
Vial Nord, 9 Nave 1
08170 Montornés del Valle
Barcelona, Spain
P: +34.935.181.856
sales@nccmco.com

NCCM International Sales Office
Im Diebesgarten 1
Frankenberg/Eder, 35066 Germany
P: +49.151.2540.4346
sales@nccmco.com

AIST
ASSOCIATION FOR IRON & STEEL TECHNOLOGY
2023
media kit
Your connection to the GLOBAL STEEL INDUSTRY.
Partner with AIST and expand your reach!
Print Advertising
Digital Advertising
Sponsorships
AIST Sales Team
+1.724.814.3000, ext. 2
sales@aist.org
AIST.org

SUPPLIERS of EQUIPMENT, PRODUCTS and SERVICES

Asia:

NCCM Shanghai
Room 1940, No. 755
Huaihai Zhong Road
E. Bldg. of New Hualian Mansion
Shanghai, 200020 P.R. China
P: +86.021.54503002
sales@nccmco.com

NDC TECHNOLOGIES
8001 Technology Blvd.
Dayton, OH 45424 USA
P: +1.937.233.9935
F: +1.937.233.7284
info@ndc.com
www.ndc.com/metals-processing

- Pres.—Marti Nyman
- Vice Pres. Engrg.—Mike Ramsey
- Vice Pres. Sales and Cust. Svce.—Stefano Cicetti
- Mktg. and Communications Mgr.—Jay Luis

EQUIPMENT:
Measurement systems for hot and cold rolling mill, continuous caster, plate mill, strip process line, coating line, pipe and tube mill applications.

PRODUCTS and/or SERVICES:
Non-contacting length and speed measurement gauges; infrared coating weight and coating thickness gauges.

NEW YORK BLOWER CO.
7660 S. Quincy St.
Willowbrook, IL 60527 USA
P: +1.800.208.7918 (Toll-Free)
nyb@nyb.com
www.nyb.com

- Chief Exec. Officer and Pres.—Tim O'Hare
- Vice Pres. Engrg.—David Maletich
- Vice Pres. Prodn./Mfg.—Scott Hamilton
- Vice Pres. Sales—Greg Whittington
- Sales Mgr.—Rory King
- Asst. Sales Mgr.—Ben Zastrow
- Adv. Mgr.—Margaret Wood

PRODUCTS and/or SERVICES:
Centrifugal fans, axial fans, industrial blowers, aftermarket service, field service, remote monitoring equipment. AMCA accredited laboratory.

No. of Employees: 500.

NEWARK BRUSH CO. LLC
1 Silver Ct.
Springfield, NJ 07081 USA
P: +1.973.376.1000
F: +1.973.376.9888
boleary@newarkbrush.com
www.newarkbrush.com

- Pres.—Brian O'Leary
- Contr. and Pur. Agt.—Ramon Matti

EQUIPMENT:
Manufacturing, balancing, trimming, repairing and refurbishing various brush rolls, including high-temperature furnace brush rolls.

PRODUCTS and/or SERVICES:
Manufacturing, engineering and reconditioning brush rolls used for primary metals production. High-temperature brush rolls, tower brush rolls, scrubber brush rolls, steering brush rolls, custom brush rolls. Manufactures coil-wound brushes, sectional brushes, internally welded brush packages and strip brushes. Many fill materials available, including polymers, abrasives and wires. Refurbishing and refilling of brush rolls.

No. of Employees: 25.

United Engineered Products
8150 Business Way
Plain City, OH 43064 USA
P: +1.937.644.3515
sales@unitedengineeredproducts.com
www.unitedengineeredproducts.com

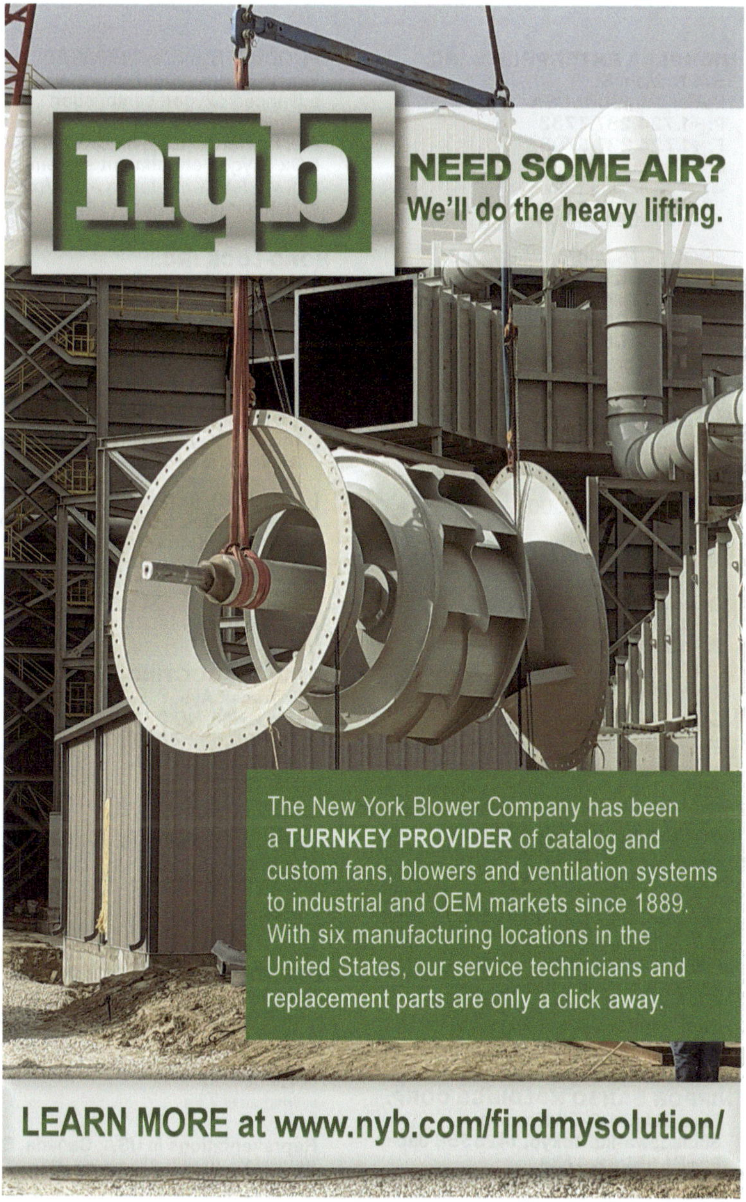

See listing page 458

SUPPLIERS of EQUIPMENT, PRODUCTS and SERVICES

NICHOLAS ENTERPRISES INC.
514 N. Main St.
Butler, PA 16001 USA
P: +1.724.287.7733
F: +1.724.287.5708
dmarlin@nicholasinc.com
www.nicholasinc.com

- Sales—Dean Marlin

PRODUCTS and/or SERVICES:
Services two river terminals on the Ohio and Allegheny Rivers, rail reload in Dubois, PA. Transfer, from barge and rail, warehouse, and distribution of industrial products, steel, oil, lumber, chemicals, coal, salt and fertilizer. Value-added services including steel burning and welding. Norfolk Southern railroad steel unit trains direct barge to rail, and lifts up to 120 tons.

No. of Employees: 60.

NIDEC INDUSTRIAL SOLUTIONS
243 Tuxedo Ave.
Cleveland, OH 44131 USA
P: +1.216.642.1230
F: +1.216.642.6037
metals@nidec-industrial.com
www.nidec-industrial.com

PRODUCTS and/or SERVICES:
Electrical and automation solutions for ironmaking, steelmaking, continuous casters, hot rolling, cold rolling and finishing. Low- and medium-voltage motors and drives and mill-duty encoders. Also supplies power conditioning solutions to ensure energy stability throughout the plant. Designs turnkey control solutions that integrate with existing systems. Solutions include: retrofitting DC and AC drives; design and engineering, installation, start-up, and project management; level 0 to level 3 control systems; and service and support.

NIPPON SANSO HOLDINGS CORP.
Toyo Bldg., 1-3-26 Koyama
Shinagawa-ku, Tokyo, 1428558 Japan
P: +81.551.42.4734
hagiharay.qxr@tn-sanso.co.jp
www.tn-sanso.co.jp/en

PRODUCTS and/or SERVICES:
Industrial gas manufacturer with advanced oxygen combustion technologies offering SCOPE-Jet, Oxy-fuel burner for EAF, Innova-Jet low-NOx oxygen enrichment system and Innova-Jet Swing for oxy-fuel/oxygen-enriched combustion.

NORD-LOCK INC.
1200 Clifford Ball Dr.
Clinton, PA 15026 USA
P: +1.412.279.1149
F: +1.412.279.1185
bolting@nord-lock.com
www.nord-lock.com

- Distr. Dir.—Julie Pereyra
- Inside Sales Support—Denise Barton, Melissa Howcroft

PRODUCTS and/or SERVICES:
Nord-Lock Bolt Securing System for safe locking for bolted joints, even when exposed to severe vibration and dynamic loads.

No. of Employees: 25.

NORDFAB DUCTING
150 Transit Ave.
Thomasville, NC 27360 USA
P: +1.800.532.0830 (Toll-Free)
F: +1.336.889.7873
info@nordfab.com
www.nordfab.com

PRODUCTS and/or SERVICES:
Modular system of ducting for dust collection and industrial ventilation.

No. of Employees: 150.

NORTEK S.A.
Polígono Los Leones
s/n, Pinseque, Zaragoza, 50298 Spain
P: +34.976.656999
F: +34.976.656784
nortek@nortek.es
www.nortek.es

Representations in USA, Canada, Spain, Italy, U.K., Brazil, Argentina, Peru, Chile, Mexico, South Korea, China and India.

SUPPLIERS OF EQUIPMENT, PRODUCTS and SERVICES

- Chief Exec. Officer—Frederic Llamerd
- Pres.—Alejandro Segrelles
- Chief Exec. Officer North America—Rafael Lazo
- Eng. Vice Pres.—Anselmo Garcia

U.S. Groups:

U.S. Nortek Inc.
4 Farnum St.
Worcester, MA 01602 USA
P: +1.774.314.4006
nortek@nortek.es

EQUIPMENT:
Modern workshop for the production of all types of lubrication and emulsion systems, components, and equipment. Large fabrications, including complete lubrication and emulsion systems, vacuum dehydrators, air/oil systems, grease systems, magnetic separators, pressure vessels, filtration, specialized cooling nozzles, and API 610, API 614 and CE certified lube systems.

PRODUCTS and/or SERVICES:
Design and supply of lubrication systems, including centralized oil circulating systems, centralized grease and air/oil systems, progressive distributors, oil emulsion systems, descaler systems, water systems, cooling systems, pumps, filters, and specialized valves and components. Engineering, installation and commissioning services for lubrication, water, hydraulics, pneumatics and descaler systems.

No. of Employees: 70.

NORTH AMERICAN CRANE BUREAU INC. (NACB)
224 W. Central Blvd.
Altamonte Springs, FL 32714 USA
P: +1.800.654.5640 (Toll-Free)
F: +1.407.869.8778
nacbgroup@cranesafe.com
www.cranesafe.com

PRODUCTS and/or SERVICES:
Crane operator training, crane operator certification, inspector training, rigging training, signal person training, crane simulators, training aids.

NOVASPECT INC., an Emerson Automation Solutions Local Business Partner
1124 Tower Road
Schaumburg, IL 60173 USA
P: +1.847.956.8020
F: +1.847.885.8200
bpaz@novaspect.com
www.novaspect.com

- Chief Exec. Officer and Pres.—Joe Simchak
- Account Mgr.—Brian Paz

PRODUCTS and/or SERVICES:
Fisher control valves and regulators, Emerson Delta V DCS, Emerson AMS device manager asset management software, Anderson-Greenwood Crosby safety relief valves, Emerson valve automation and isolation products (Vanessa, KTM, Yarway, Keystone, Clarkson); gate, globe, check, safety and control valve repair services. Machinery reliability: Emerson CSI6500 Machinery Health Monitor prediction and protection systems, Emerson CSI 2140 Machinery Health Analyzer, Emerson wired and wireless vibration monitoring transmitters; alignment/balancing services on rotating equipment. Chesterton mechanical pump seals, packing, gaskets and repair services. Asset reliability consulting services.

No. of Employees: 330.

SUPPLIERS of EQUIPMENT, PRODUCTS and SERVICES

NSK AMERICAS
4200 Goss Road
Ann Arbor, MI 48105 USA
P: +1.800.675.9930 (Toll-Free)
F: +1.734.913.7510
www.nskamericas.com

- Chief Exec. Officer and Pres. NSK Americas—Brian Parsons
- Exec. Vice Pres.—Hiromasa Orito
- Chief Financial Officer and Treas.—Brent Parkinson
- Sr. Vice Pres. of ABU/IBU—Mike Stofferahn
- Vice Pres. of Supply Chain—Ed Jabri
- Sr. Engrg. Mgr.—Bimal Nathwani

PRODUCTS and/or SERVICES:
Global manufacturer of ball and rolling bearings, linear motion technology, automotive components and steering systems, with domestic and international manufacturing capabilities. NSK also offers a full range of services, including reconditioning, ball screw repair, product integration, application engineering, and preventive maintenance and reliability services.

No. of Employees: 3,000.

NTN BEARING CORP. OF AMERICA
1600 E. Bishop Ct.
Mt. Prospect, IL 60056 USA
P: +1.800.468.6528 (Toll-Free)
F: +1.847.294.1230
www.ntnamericas.com

- Pres.—Pete Eich
- Vice Pres., Ind. Aftermarket Sales—Scott Eiss
- Vice Pres., Ind. OE Sales—Tom Mohrdieck
- Dir. Mktg.—Georgianne Dickey
- Dir. of Mktg. and Tech. Svcs.—Jim Misch
- Mgr. — Field Svce. Engrg. — Metals—Majkol Spirovski
- Regional Sales Mgr., Eastern Region—Oscar Joyner
- Regional Sales Mgr., Central Region—Paul Bancherau
- Regional Sales Mgr., Midwest Region—Ross Freeman
- Regional Sales Mgr., South Eastern Region—Arthur Smith
- Regional Sales Mgr., South Western Region—Matt Boganowski
- Regional Sales Mgr., Western Region—JD Martin

PRODUCTS and/or SERVICES:
Full-line manufacturer of precision anti-friction ball and roller bearings for the iron and steel mill industry.

NU-TECH RESOURCES
112 Woodshire Dr.
Pittsburgh, PA 15215 USA
P: +1.412.782.4833
www.nu-techresources.com

- Contacts—Carol Huff, P: +1.412.848.8095, carol@nu-techresources.com; David Huff, P: +1.412.848.4893, david@nu-techresources.com

PRODUCTS and/or SERVICES:
Silica and fireclay brick; fused silica; carbon, graphite and silicon carbide refractory shapes; high-temperature insulation for BFs, stoves and coke ovens.

No. of Employees: 2.

NUFLUX
2395 State Rte. 5
Cortland, OH 44410 USA
P: +1.330.399.1122
F: +1.330.399.1135
info@nuflux.com
www.nuflux.com

- Pres.—Rob White
- Vice Pres. Engrg.—Frank Kemeny
- Vice Pres. Prodn./Mfg.—Steve Sanfrey

EQUIPMENT:
Blending and packaging equipment.

PRODUCTS and/or SERVICES:
Calcium carbide–based slag modifiers; patented EAF calcium carbide injection technology; silicon carbide–based slag modifiers; synthetic slag fluidizers; aluminum deoxidizers; desulfurizers;

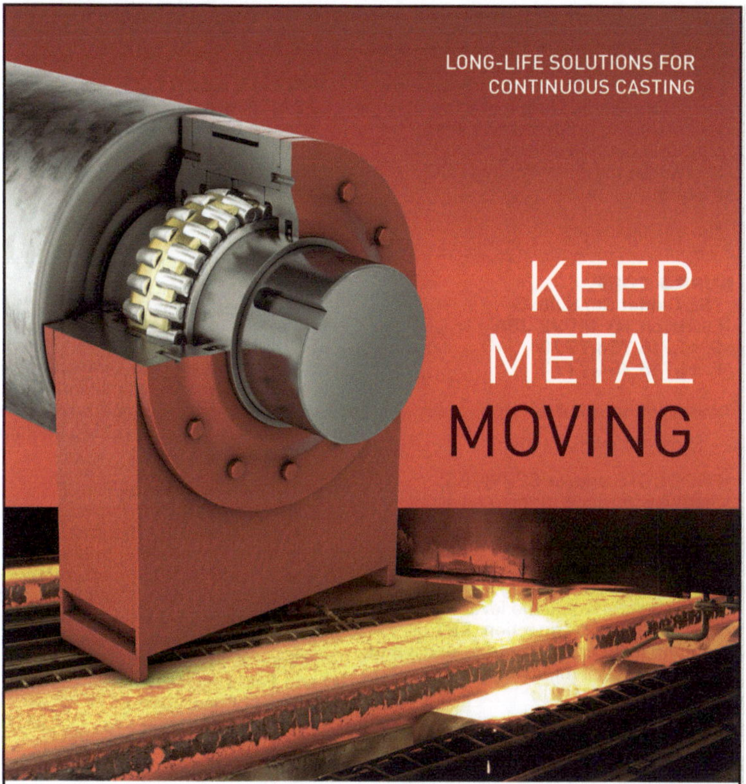

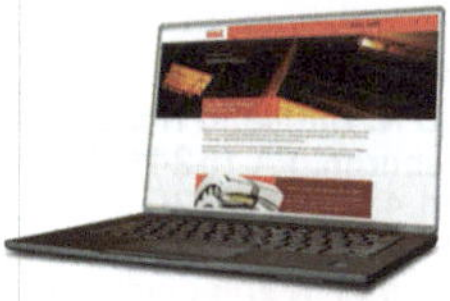

See listing page 462

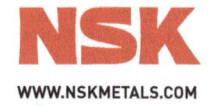

SUPPLIERS of EQUIPMENT, PRODUCTS and SERVICES

calcium aluminate; tundish fluxes and insulators; cored wire; metallurgical and meltshop process consulting; carbon reduction strategies and alternative materials to lower CO_2 footprint.

No. of Employees: 13.

NUPRO CORP.
755 Center St., Suite 3
Lewiston, NY 14092 USA
P: +1.716.754.7770
F: +1.716.754.7773
fkemeny@nuprocorp.com
www.nuprocorp.com

- Pres.—Frank Kemeny

PRODUCTS and/or SERVICES: SlagView furnace tapping advisory system, AutoTap automated furnace tapping, SlagTracker ladle-to-tundish slag detection, TruStir ladle stirring control, thermal imaging systems, ladle skimming control, ladle level detection, furnace interior inspection, EBT sanding inspection, vision systems and image analysis, metallurgical process consulting.

No. of Employees: 8.

NUTTALL GEAR LLC
2221 Niagara Falls Blvd.
Niagara Falls, NY 14304 USA
P: +1.716.298.4100
F: +1.716.298.4101
info@nuttallgear.com
www.nuttallgear.com

- Gen. Mgr.—Don Wierbinski
- Product Mgr.—Michael Suszek
- Natl. Sales Mgr., Nuttall Gear Products—John Proven

EQUIPMENT:
State-of-the-art gear production facility. Extensive helical and worm gear machining and gearbox service facility. On-site load testing equipment for gearboxes.

PRODUCTS and/or SERVICES: Enclosed gearboxes for recoilers/uncoilers, levelers, flatteners, pinion stands, accumulators, bridle drives and slitters. Custom gearboxes for the metals industry. Complete line of Delroyd brand worm gear reducers and Moduline brand concentric shaft reducers. Reverse engineering, rebuild and field service capabilities for all brands of gearboxes.

No. of Employees: 100.

O

OCMET INC.
1700 N. Highland Road, Suite 400
Pittsburgh, PA 15241 USA
P: +1.412.831.5620
F: +1.412.831.5626
sales.engineer@ocmet.com
www.ocmet.com

- Chief Exec. Officer—D.F. Bricmont
- Pres. and Chief Oper. Officer—W.A. McSorley
- Sales Engrs.—P. Jordan, O. Phillips, D. Kelly, J. Manchak
- Design Engr.—A. McSorley
- Project Mgr.—K. Picard
- Admin.—L. Albrecht, K. Secen

PRODUCTS and/or SERVICES: Design, engineering, and supply of components and spare parts for steel processing equipment. Typical applications include components for all types of reheat furnaces, continuous and batch anneal furnaces, and galvanizing lines. Products include furnace doors (charge, discharge,

SUPPLIERS OF EQUIPMENT, PRODUCTS and SERVICES

inspection and access) and operating hardware, skid pipes, riders, furnace rolls, radiant tubes, heat-resistant castings (alloy, steel and iron), water-cooled fabrication, mechanical equipment (pushers, peel bars, tables and conveyors), diffusers, sink/stabilizing rolls and arms, sink/stabilizing roll sleeves and bushings. Regional offices in Indiana, South Carolina and Texas.

ODDA DIGITAL SYSTEM AS
Holmavegen 29
Odda, Hordaland, 5750 Norway
P: +47.481.22.587
post@oddadigitalsystem.no
www.oddadigitalsystem.no

- Chief Exec. Officer—Rune Torblå
- Pres.—Ingvald Torblå
- Vice Pres. Global Sales—Michael Iversen

PRODUCTS and/or SERVICES:
Custom-developed business products, software integration, and digitalization planning for visual tracking and registration. Odda offers software solutions that can integrate different data sources, automate daily work, offer full production traceability, provide real-time financial and production reporting, and generate report packages like MRB and SMDR. Other solutions include full business systems for handling shift data and standardizing the way the clients input and store data, and stop management system to monitor machines and log all events related to stops and reduced production.

No. of Employees: 20.

OHIO MAGNETICS INC.
5400 Dunham Road
Maple Heights, OH 44137 USA
P: +1.800.486.6446 (Toll-Free);
  +1.216.662.8484
F: +1.216.662.2911
sales@ohiomagnetics.com
www.ohiomagnetics.com

- Sales Mgr.—Tim Schuh
- Territory Sales Mgr.—Walter Civovic
- Inside Sales—Devin Collins
- Chief Engr.—Robert Wright

EQUIPMENT:
Electrolifting magnets, permanent and electromagnetic separators, pulleys, drums, magnet controllers, and magnet power supplies.

PRODUCTS and/or SERVICES:
Lifting magnet systems and magnetic separation equipment for the steel, scrap processing, waste recycling, mining and rail industries. Ohio brand of products includes standard and specialized circular, bipolar, and rectangular lifting magnets as well as power supplies, including rectifiers, power take-off and hydraulic-driven generators, and magnet controls. Stearns brand includes magnetic separation equipment, including standard and alternating pole magnetic drums for auto shredders, electric or permanent over-the-belt magnets, magnetic pulleys, and specialized wet or dry magnetic separators. A full-service repair facility that is able to remanufacture all manufacturers' brands of magnets to original specifications. ISO 9001 certified.

OIL SKIMMERS INC.
12800 York Road
Cleveland, OH 44133 USA
P: +1.440.237.4600
info@oilskim.com
www.oilskim.com

PRODUCTS and/or SERVICES:
Oil skimmers, oil removal systems, and oil water separators for recovering all types of floating waste oils, greases and fats from water. Turnkey and custom-engineered solutions available.

SUPPLIERS of EQUIPMENT, PRODUCTS and SERVICES

**OILCO LIQUID HANDLING SYSTEMS,
A Div. of Valeur Corp.**
596 Ridge Road
P.O. Box 226
Monmouth Junction, NJ 08852 USA
P: +1.732.329.4666
F: +1.732.329.9422
sales@oilco-usa.com
www.oilco-usa.com

EQUIPMENT:
CNC multi-axis machines, milling lathes, automatic welders, full machine and fabrication shop, testing facility, paint booth, miscellaneous equipment.

PRODUCTS and/or SERVICES:
Extensive line of swivel joints in 2 in. through 24 in., water treatment–compatible units, top- and bottom-loading assemblies, floating suction, vapor return systems, steam-jacketed assemblies, and transfer and roof drain assembly components.

ONPOINT, Part of Koch Engineered Solutions
4111 E. 37th St. N
Wichita, KS 67220 USA
P: +1.212.290.2300
onpointsales@kes.global
www.onpointsolutions.com

PRODUCTS and/or SERVICES:
Portfolio of digital solutions that enable more efficient, optimized performance. Brands include CORTEX advanced analytics platform, Ember digital combustion assistant, and ZoloSCAN laser-based combustion monitoring and diagnostic systems.

OPTA GROUP LLC
407 Parkside Dr.
Waterdown, ON L0R 2H0 Canada
P: +1.905.689.7361
F: +1.905.689.3915
www.optagroupllc.com

- Chief Exec. Officer—John Dietrich
- Chief Commercial Officer—Mike Ball
- Chief Oper. Officer—William Kodatsky
- Vice Pres. Sales and Mktg.—Chad Carl
- Vice Pres. Product Technology and Supply Chain—Jose Lujan
- Pur.—Gary Spolarich

EQUIPMENT:
Desulfurization injection equipment, mixers, grinders, sieving units, powder injection, dryers, transportation, railroad and shipping facilities.

PRODUCTS and/or SERVICES:
Metal and alloy products; granules—custom sizing and formulation for use in iron desulfurization. Reagents and conditioners: injection blends—variety of Mg sizes and alloys for use in iron desulfurization; carriers—series of XR products for higher yield iron application and traditional lime/spar product line; slag conditioners—series of steel ladle additives for desulfurization; fluxes and insulators—reactive fluxes and insulators for tundish and ladle applications for inclusion removal and control.

Opta Group LLC
2111 Industrial Dr.
Regina, SK S4P 3Y3 Canada
P: +1.306.585.1911
F: +1.306.585.2012
www.optagroupllc.com

Opta Group LLC
205 Plymouth LaPorte Trail
State Hwy. 104
Walkerton, IN 46574 USA
P: +1.574.586.9559
F: +1.574.586.9625
www.optagroupllc.com

Opta Group LLC
300 Corporate Pkwy. 118N
Amherst, NY 14226 USA
P: +1.716.446.8914
F: +1.716.446.8911
www.optagroupllc.com

Affival Inc.
Schreiber Industrial Park, Bldg. 210
14th St. and 3rd Ave.
New Kensington, PA 15068 USA
P: +1.412.826.9430
F: +1.412.826.1070
www.optagroupllc.com/affival

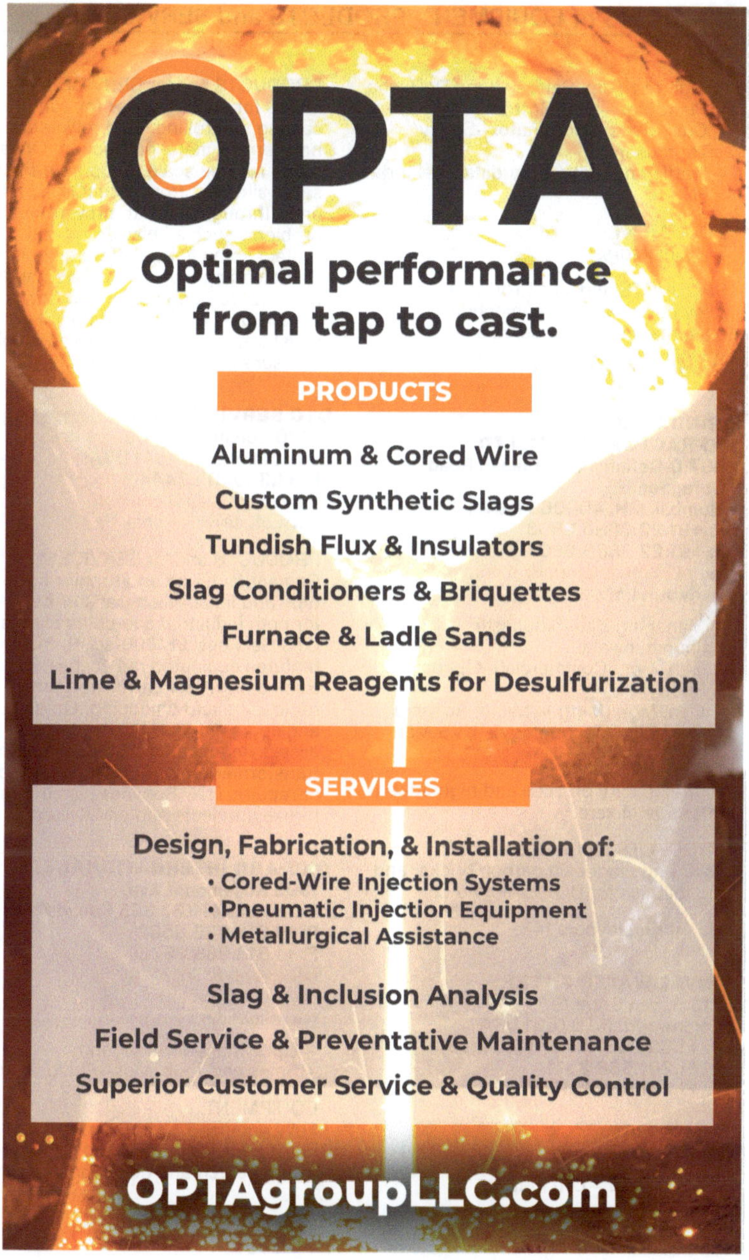

See listing page 466

SUPPLIERS of EQUIPMENT, PRODUCTS and SERVICES

- Mgr. of Equip. Sales—Glenn DeRusha
- Plant Mgr.—Curt Britton
- Cust. Svce. Coordinator—Shelly Thompson
- Traffic and Matls. Coordinator—Linda Hill

EQUIPMENT:
Wire injectors.

PRODUCTS and/or SERVICES:
Alloy cored wire, wire injection equipment and field service.

No. of Employees: 76.

ORIND SPECIAL REFRACTORIES PVT. LTD.
607 D-Definity, Jayprakash Road Goregaon (E),
Mumbai, MH, 400063 India
P: +91.22.2686.6803
F: +91.22.2686.6804
mumbai.office@orindref.com
www.orindref.com

- Managing Dir.—Siddharth Jhunjhunwala
- Gen. Mgr. (Commercial)—Sundar Shetty
- Gen. Mgr. (Mktg.)—Manoj Acharya
- Gen. Mgr. (Technology)—KVS Mani

EQUIPMENT:
High-capacity presses and high-speed intensive mixers.

PRODUCTS and/or SERVICES:
AMC and magnesia carbon bricks, and monolithics for BOF, EAF and LF.

No. of Employees: 143.

ORIVAL WATER FILTERS
213 S. Van Brunt St.
Englewood, NJ 07631 USA
P: +1.800.567.9767 (Toll-Free);
   +1.201.568.3311
F: +1.201.568.1916
filters@orival.com
www.orival.com

- Pres.—Reuven Schwartz
- Chief Engr.—Lou Mattos

PRODUCTS and/or SERVICES:
Filters for cooling water for continuous casting, hot rolling, cold rolling and non-ferrous metal production. Orival filters remove scale, airborne particles, sand, silt, etc., from recirculated and once-through water to prevent quality problems such as black digs and protect spray nozzles from clogging. Self-cleaning individual filters handle up to 12,000 gpm; unlimited flowrate capabilities. ASME U-stamp, oil-resistant, high-temperature and high-pressure units are available.

OTC SERVICES INC.
1776 Constitution Ave.
Louisville, OH 44641 USA
P: +1.330.871.2444
bwoost@otcservices.com
www.otcservices.com

PRODUCTS and/or SERVICES:
Remanufacturing and repair of dry-type and liquid-filled transformers for both industrial and utility clients. OTC Services' 98,000-sq.-ft. facility features dedicated rail access, large-truck delivery and a 100-ton crane for loading and unloading. On-site engineers are available to properly assess, manage, and execute customer transformer remanufacturing projects or repairs. OTC Services also offers turnkey projects and on-site repair.

OXY-ARC INTERNATIONAL LP
1395 Rosemount Ave.
Cornwall, ON K6J 3E5 Canada
P: +1.613.938.6502
F: +1.613.938.2673
info@oxy-arc.com
www.oxy-arc.com
www.linkedin.com/company/oxy-arc

- Oprs. Mgr.—Tim Magoon
- Sales and Tech. Mgr.—Fabio Santolo

EQUIPMENT:
Fully equipped 10,000-sq.-ft. production, assembly, and repair facility with research and development center.

SUPPLIERS OF EQUIPMENT, PRODUCTS and SERVICES

PRODUCTS and/or SERVICES: Manufacturer of the CanCut™ line of flame cutting equipment specializing in caster cutoff and slab dimensioning machine torches, ultrahigh-capacity ingot, tundish, and scrap-cutting machine torches, heavy-duty emergency cutoff hand torches, scrap-cutting hand torches, and hand-scarfing torches, along with associated cutting tips and nozzles. Iron powder delivery systems for automatic and hand torches for alloy cutting. Designer of gas-saving manifold systems and drop stations for cutting processes. Supplier of application-specific thermal-protected rubber hoses and stainless steel braided hoses. Oxygen lance holders and safety valve assemblies. Complete line of flashback arrestors and custom aluminized and fire-resistant protective clothing for operator safety. On-site equipment setup, calibration and personnel training. Repairs, modifications and custom design services for all products and competitors' offerings. North American agent for STS Selected Technological Supplies S.r.l. of Udine, Italy, which designs, manufactures, and supplies equipment, plants and services for the global steelmaking industry. Their range of products covers EAFs, LFs, continuous casting machines, torch cutting machines, cooling beds and lifting systems, rolling mills and meltshop auxiliary systems, as well as complete in-house development of automation.

No. of Employees: 10.

OXYLANCE INC.
2501 27th St. N
Birmingham, AL 35234 USA
P: +1.205.322.9906
dcowart@oxylance.com
www.oxylance.com

PRODUCTS and/or SERVICES: Exothermic cutting systems, burning bars, lance pipe, underwater cutting and welding rods, safety equipment, and related accessories for the primary metals and demolition industries.

P

PALING TRANSPORTER LTD.
1632 Burlington St. E
Hamilton, ON L8H 3L3 Canada
P: +1.905.561.3444
info@palingtransporter.com
www.palingtransporter.com

- Chief Exec. Officer and Pres.—Bob Charczuk
- Gen. Mgr.—Cameron Evans
- Dir. of Business Affairs—Karolina Charczuk

PRODUCTS and/or SERVICES: Design and manufacture of self-propelled, self-elevating, heavy-load transporters, slag handling transporters, coil lift trucks, forklifts and related equipment for the steel industry.

No. of Employees: 40.

PALMER WAHL INSTRUMENTS INC.
234 Old Weaverville Road
Asheville, NC 28804 USA
P: +1.828.658.3131
F: +1.828.658.0728
info@palmerwahl.com
www.palmerwahl.com

- Pres.—Stephen J. Santangelo
- Vice Pres. Sensors—Michael Blount
- Vice Pres. Oprs.—Mark Morse
- Product Dev. Mgr.—Jim Eldridge

SUPPLIERS of EQUIPMENT, PRODUCTS and SERVICES

PRODUCTS and/or SERVICES: Manufacturer of custom-engineered resistance temperature detectors (RTDs) and thermocouple sensors for temperature-critical applications; multi-point assemblies, tube skin thermocouples, mineral-insulated thermocouples and RTDs; thermowells; precision industrial digital, bimetal and filled system thermometers; pressure and temperature chart recorders and accessories; temperature recording labels; handheld infrared thermometers, RTD and thermocouple meters and probes. ISO 9001:2015 certified.

PANNIER CORP.
207 Sandusky St.
Pittsburgh, PA 15212 USA
P: +1.412.323.4900
F: +1.412.323.4962
sales@pannier.com
www.pannier.com

Plant:
1130 Old Butler Plank Road
Glenshaw, PA 15116 USA
P: +1.412.492.1400

- Pres.—John E. Visconti, Scott D. Heddaeus
- Dir. of Sales—Michael E. Leard
- Intl. Sales Mgr.—Michael W. Roy
- Product Mgr., Metal and Plastics Tags—Jeremy Rocco
- Product Specialist, Ink Jet—John Burke
- Product Specialist, Contact Printing—John Gorman
- Product Specialist, Indenting—Domenic Liberto
- Product Specialist, Dot Peen and Laser—Dan Wertz

PRODUCTS and/or SERVICES: Metal tag printing and attaching systems for bar code identification of slabs, billets, blooms, ingots, wire and bar during casting, pickling, and annealing. Embossed metal tags for marking joists and structural steel. Contact and inkjet printers for marking shapes, sheet, strip, tinplate, bar and tubes in a variety of applications. All types of indenting equipment, including stamps, stamping hammers, and programmable stampers for marking hot or cold semi-finished and finished products. Laser marking systems for various applications.

No. of Employees: 100.

PARTS SUPER CENTER
7555 Woodland Dr., Suite A
Indianapolis, IN 46278 USA
P: +1.888.997.4763 (Toll-Free)
sales@pscparts.com
www.partssupercenter.com

PRODUCTS and/or SERVICES: Licensed provider of OEM General Electric (GE) renewal parts and life-extension solutions for transformers, drives and controls, circuit breakers and switchgear, and motors. Part identification services available.

PAUL WURTH SA—see SMS GROUP

PCE INSTRUMENTS UK LTD.
Unit 11 South Point Business Park
Ensign Way, Southampton
Hampshire, SO31 4RF U.K.
P: +44.0.2380.98703.0
F: +44.0.2380.98703.9
info@pce-instruments.co.uk
www.pce-instruments.com

- Contact—John Mulligan

PRODUCTS and/or SERVICES: Measuring instruments, thickness meters, durometers, torque meters, calipers, thermometers, scales, balances, vibration meters, borescopes, thermal imaging cameras, force meters.

No. of Employees: 50.

SUPPLIERS OF EQUIPMENT, PRODUCTS and SERVICES

PENN RADIANT
8105 Perry Hwy.
Pittsburgh, PA 15237 USA

LTL Freight and Warehouse:
CXL 10 Plum St.
Verona, PA 15147 USA
P: +1.800.438.2503 (Toll-Free);
 +1.412.635.2503
F: +1.412.635.8016
info@pennradiant.com
mlieb@pennradiant.com
patty@pennradiant.com
www.pennradiant.com

PRODUCTS and/or SERVICES: Industrial HVAC equipment. Specializing in railcar thaw shed applications and heating equipment for thawing to extract coal and steel scrap as well as pre-heating coke frozen in railcars. U.S.-made gas-fired industrial infrared tube heaters by Space Ray, RSTP models, as well as straight and U-tube available in negative pressure/vacuum and positive pressure tube heaters. High-intensity RSCA and DK model radiant ceramic heaters by Space Ray. Radiant portable gas heaters (top pot, salamander, red rocket, construction) that require no electricity for spot heating in freeze protection applications for industrial spaces. Space Ray model RFPA10, RFPA21, and RFPA25 (high-pressure model). U.S.-made gas-fired portable construction-type space heaters from 400,000 Btu to 8,000,000 Btu capacities. Gas indirect-fired industrial heaters as well as portable makeup air heaters by SureFlame and Heat Wagon. Also portable torches by SureFlame (Sure Flame). Electric infrared heaters, both portable and fixed, by Aitken and Fostoria/TPI. Replacement electric metal sheath infrared/radiant heating elements; 2 kW and 4.5 kW metal sheath elements for 4 kW, 6 kW, and 13.5 kW heaters; as well as Quartz Halogen element tubes, for Aitken, Fostoria and TPI (models FHK, CHK elements, Marley and Chromalox infrared radiant electric heaters (2,000 W and 4,500 W individual replacement heater elements). Industrial fixed and portable drum fans by Penn Fan/PennFan in sizes 24- to 60-in. dia. also available in custom sizes and explosion-proof specifications. Americ portable ventilators/exhaust fans. DC-powered crane cab heaters as well as crane cab fans. Portable AC units by Kwikool, WayCool Evaporative cooling units by Schaefer and WayCool and ProKool replacement pads. Also carries replacement parts for Space Ray, SunStar, Gas Fired Products, Heat Wagon, Sure Flame, Fostoria, Aitken, Penn Fan, Schaefer Ventilation, KING Electric products and more.

PENNA FLAME INDUSTRIES
1856 State Rte. 588
Zelienople, PA 16063 USA
P: +1.724.452.8750
F: +1.724.452.0484
andrewo@pennaflame.com
www.pennaflame.com

– Vice Pres.—Andrew Orr

EQUIPMENT:
Robotic precision surface-hardening cells, induction-hardening robotic cell, CNC lathes, grinders, mills, polisher, roll-hardening machines, spin flame hardening, progressive flame hardening, tempering ovens, cryogenic treating, stress-relieving furnaces, 290-ton hydraulic press, non-contact IR pyrometers, thermal imaging camera.

PRODUCTS and/or SERVICES:
Custom selective hardening of wheels, rollers, sheaves, plate and rolls/shafts. Flame hardening, induction hardening, stress relieving, tempering, shrink fitting and cryogenic treatment. Robotic cells, thermal imaging camera, complete process control and traceability. Flame hardening services and induction hardening services.

No. of Employees: 28.

SUPPLIERS of EQUIPMENT, PRODUCTS and SERVICES

PENNSYLVANIA EQUIPMENT INC.
P.O. Box 61
180 Lincoln Ave.
Grove City, PA 16127 USA
P: +1.724.458.6162
paequip@zoominternet.net
www.paequip.com
www.bridgecranes.com

- Chmn. of the Bd. and Pres.—Thomas R. Noone

EQUIPMENT:
500,000-sq.-ft. warehousing and manufacturing facility, 155-ton crane capacity.

PRODUCTS and/or SERVICES:
Provider of steel mill cranes, rebuilds, engineering and installation. Crane parts: motors, brakes and controls. Used steel mill machinery and machine tools. Certified machinery and equipment appraisals. Turnkey rigging and shipping services, dismantling, match marking of complete plants or one machine. Purchase, sell and marketing services for surplus assets.

No. of Employees: 25.

PENSCO LLC
P.O. Box 451
Connoquenessing, PA 16027 USA

Street Address:
431 Upper Harmony Road
Evans City, PA 16033 USA
P: +1.724.789.7286
F: +1.724.789.7891
pgweakland1@aol.com
www.penscohvac.com

- Chief Exec. Officer and Pres.— Patrick Weakland

PRODUCTS and/or SERVICES:
Industrial plant heating and makeup air equipment, service and consulting. Manufacturer's representative for Hasting HVAC industrial and heavy commercial heating equipment. Direct- and indirect-fired makeup air units. Air rotation heaters and floor furnaces. Air handling units using gas, steam, hot water and electric. Split system and chilled water heating and cooling units. Evaporative coolers. Dravo Inc.: specializing in parts, replacement units, bill of materials, wiring diagrams, etc., including upgrades to or conversion from obsolete controls for the older Dravo units. Experienced service work for old Dravo units.

No. of Employees: 1.

PERFORMANCE IMPROVEMENT INC.
59 Enmore Ave.
Hamilton, ON L9G 2H4 Canada
P: +1.905.317.5838
david.marshall@pionline.ca
www.pionline.ca

- Process Equip. and Power Generation—D. Marshall
- Refractories—S. Hutchings

PRODUCTS and/or SERVICES:
Integrated steel mill (primary end) process equipment and refractory specialists with a unique focus on plant reliability improvement in difficult applications for air, gas and water: maintenance reliability support, BF relines and outages, coke oven byproducts, energy, utilities and wastewater treatment plants. Process technologies include: NSE (copper staves) TD Co. GMBH (BF and stove process valves), Peel Jones copper products (tuyeres, coolers and plates), AVK Donkin (coke oven gas valves), Dango & Dienenthal (water filters), Evolution (control, ball and triple eccentric valves), Shelley Machine (complicated fabrication and machining, plus repairs) and Great Lakes Equipment Repair Group. Refractory lining systems include: pre-cast shapes and linings. Process gas recovery and decarbonization systems include: Clayton Walker (gas holders) and Combined Power Generation Co. (multi-fuel power generation systems).

No. of Employees: 18.

SUPPLIERS OF EQUIPMENT, PRODUCTS and SERVICES

PEWAG CHAIN INC.
600 W. Crossroads Pkwy.
Bolingbrook, IL 60440 USA
P: +1.800.526.3924 (Toll-Free);
 +1.630.226.6020
F: +1.630.759.0788
ala@pewagchain.com
www.pewagchain.com

- Pres.—Michael Uhrenbacher
- Product Mgr., Tire Protection Chain Div.—Al Atkinson

PRODUCTS and/or SERVICES:
Tire protection chains, conveyor chains, lifting chains, chain slings, lifting clamps, lifting magnets, lifting points.

PFEIFFER VACUUM
24 Trafalgar Sq.
Nashua, NH 03063 USA
P: +1.603.578.6524
contact@pfeiffer-vacuum.com
www.pfeiffer-vacuum.com

PRODUCTS and/or SERVICES:
Turnkey design and manufacturing of pumping systems for steel and other metal degassing and vacuum furnaces. Experience in RH, VD and VOD applications. Pfeiffer Vacuum manufactures all of the equipment needed to provide a complete pumping system or individual components and leak detection equipment for qualifying the system for processing. Gas-cooled Okta G Series pumps are suited for degassing applications where the pumps must operate at elevated pressure and quickly evacuate large volumes. Okta G Series pumps decrease system complexity and improve reliability of the degassing vacuum system.

PHILIP DOYLE MANUFACTURING INC.
95 Covington St.
Hamilton, ON L8E 2Y4 Canada
P: +1.905.561.0545
F: +1.905.561.5858
info@philipdoyle.com
www.philipdoyle.com

PRODUCTS and/or SERVICES:
Custom-designed portable pulpits, control rooms, electrical rooms, noise control enclosures, in-plant offices, operator crane cabins, manipulator cabs, storage rooms, personnel booths, air locks, acoustical doors and windows. Complete line of industrial severe- and mill-duty air conditioners engineered for overhead cranes, mill pulpits, electrical rooms and coke oven vehicles, designed to operate continuously in corrosive environments with high temperatures, humidity, radiant heat, fine dust particles, dirt, acid fumes, gases and vibration. Custom-designed AC units. Specialized mobile air conditioners and casting floor personnel coolers. Pressurization fan filter units. All units use environmentally friendly refrigerants. Qualified HVAC refrigeration service technicians available. Patented dual-pane sealed windows for hot, dirty environments with excessive radiant heat. Stainless steel operator consoles.

PHILIPPI-HAGENBUCH INC.
7424 W. Plank Road
Peoria, IL 61604 USA
P: +1.309.697.9200
F: +1.309.697.2400
sales@philsystems.com
www.philsystems.com

- Pres.—Danette Swank
- Chief Engr.—LeRoy Hagenbuch
- Vice Pres. Sales and Mktg.—Josh Swank

PRODUCTS and/or SERVICES:
Rear-eject scrap steel bodies, end dump scrap steel bodies, hot slag bodies, J-Hook systems and other off-highway truck enhancements, and mobile water tanks for off-highway trucks.

No. of Employees: 5.

SUPPLIERS of EQUIPMENT, PRODUCTS and SERVICES

PHOENIX SERVICES LLC
4 Radnor Corporate Center
100 Matsonford Road, Suite 520
Radnor, PA 19087 USA
P: +1.610.347.0444
F: +1.610.347.0443
info@phoenix-services.com
www.phoenix-services.com

- Chief Exec. Officer and Pres.—Mark Porto
- Chief Financial Officer—Bob Richard
- Exec. Vice Pres. Oprs. North America—Steve Hall
- Exec. Vice Pres. Special Oprs. and Projects—Dave Chapman
- Exec. Vice Pres. Intl.—Venky Srambikal
- Sr. Vice Pres. Sales and Mktg.—Jeff Mellen
- Sr. Vice Pres. Procurement and Assets—Clint McGinty
- Dir. of Cust. Oprs.—Carl Erickson

PRODUCTS and/or SERVICES:
Core services include slag handling, utilizing slag pot carriers or the traditional slag digging with front-end loaders; recovery and sizing of metal to customer's specifications; and processing of slag for use by steel mill customers or marketing processed slag material for aggregate use. Also offers customized scrap handling and processing; charge box loading and transport; scrap upgrading; ladle and furnace refractory tearout and taphole drilling; road sweeping and watering service for dust control; vacuum truck service; locomotive transport service; mobile equipment rental; ladle transport service and a number of other services.

PICO CHEMICAL CORP.
400 E. 16th St.
Chicago Heights, IL 60411 USA
P: +1.708.757.4910
F: +1.708.757.4940
info@picochemical.com
www.picochemical.com

- Chief Exec. Officer—Richard Pisarski Jr.
- Pres.—Richard Pisarski Sr.
- Vice Pres. Sales—Ted Meehan
- Sales Mgr.—Mike DeLisa

PRODUCTS and/or SERVICES:
ISO 9001:2015 certified. Manufacturer of environmentally friendly industrial chemicals and lubricants to clean, condition, lubricate, and protect steel and steel-related processes. Products include: roll grinding and machining lubricants; continuous casting lubricants; fire-resistant hydraulic fluids; and maintenance/machine lubricants; rust and corrosion inhibitors; rust removers; heat transfer fluids; freeze control agents; de-icing fluids; railroad switch/switch plate lubricants, water jet/plasma cutting table coolants and conditioners, slab/billet scale inhibitors, fuel and coke oven gas cleaning additives; dust control compounds and maintenance cleaners. Specialized equipment for chemical and lubricant applications.

No. of Employees: 15.

PIEDMONT HOIST AND CRANE INC.
3350 Temple School Road
Winston-Salem, NC 27107 USA
P: +1.888.845.5646 (Toll-Free)
rvanderbeck@piedmonthoist.com
www.piedmonthoist.com

PRODUCTS and/or SERVICES:
CMAA and AIST spec. designed overhead and gantry cranes, special hoists, transfer cars and heavy AGVs, bi-rails and monorails, runways, turnkey installations, semi- and full automation, anti-skewing controls, load testing, inspections, and repair.

PITTEK DIV. OF SWINDELL DRESSLER INTERNATIONAL CO.
5100 Casteel Dr.
Coraopolis, PA 15108 USA
P: +1.412.788.7100
F: +1.412.788.7110
tschultz@swindelldressler.com
www.pittek.com

- Tech. Sales—Ronald J. Orth, Tim Schultz

NOTES FROM A LEADER

Becky E. Hites, President, Steel-Insights LLC

I began my steel career in 1988 working as an associate equity analyst following company equities in the steel, aluminum, mining and manufacturing industries. I was fortunate to work in South Carolina with an engineer who was an Iron & Steel Society member. When I left in 1996, I wasn't willing to give up my access to the monthly magazine, so I became a member.

I moved to New York City and joined an investment bank involved in privatizing the steel industry in Eastern Europe. I maintained my membership even though I didn't have time to fully utilize the resources of the association. My first boss had instilled in me an appreciation for the value that the association provides. It offers so much more today through its research platform and committees.

In 2003, I joined Peter F. Marcus at the steel industry brain trust he had built, World Steel Dynamics. It wasn't until I started my own consulting group that I was able to become more involved in AIST. I missed my steel mill clients and arranged to attend the Southeast Member Chapter annual meeting to reconnect. I was invited to give a presentation, which laid the groundwork for my relationship with the chapter, including serving as the chapter chair in 2019 and this year as secretary and representative to the AIST Board of Directors.

The mentoring among members is one of my favorite things about the association. Creation of a safe space of empowerment for our younger members to grow has been a priority of the Southeast Member Chapter.

AIST membership is affordable, provides growth opportunities, pushes the expansion of one's comfort zone, gives opportunities for one to present before peers, and is supported by senior executives in every significant steel-producing organization. And if you haven't been to AISTech, I encourage you to attend, as it's the largest steel industry gathering in the U.S. I highly recommend the investment of time and energy in AIST to every industry participant. The steel industry is a family of sorts, and AISTech is the event that connects us all. ✦

AIST MEMBER CHAPTERS

Get involved with your local Member Chapter! Visit **AIST.org** or contact **Jill Liberto** at **+1.724.814.3046** or **jliberto@aist.org**.

SUPPLIERS of EQUIPMENT, PRODUCTS and SERVICES

PRODUCTS and/or SERVICES:
Hot and cold rolling mill fume exhaust systems, industrial ventilation systems, motor room ventilation systems, process and system improvements.

PITTSBURGH AIR SYSTEMS – AIR INDUSTRIAL INC.
208 Bilmar Dr.
Pittsburgh, PA 15205 USA
P: +1.412.539.1234
F: +1.412.539.1245
sales@pittsburghairsystems.com
www.pittsburghairsystems.com

PRODUCTS and/or SERVICES:
Specialized ventilation equipment, custom manufactured equipment and HVAC. Products include heavy/severe-duty industrial HVAC units, commercial HVAC units, pressurization/filtration units, fans, dampers, heaters, makeup air units, air filters, and energy recovery systems. Capabilities also include turnkey projects involving layout, supply of equipment, installation and start-up.

PKG EQUIPMENT INC.
367 Paul Road
Rochester, NY 14624 USA
P: +1.877.615.6460 (Toll-Free);
   +1.585.436.4650
F: +1.585.436.3751
carla@pkgequip.com
info@pkgequipment.com
www.pkgequipment.com

- Chief Exec. Officer—Stephen Pontarelli
- Chief Financial Officer—Maria Pontarelli
- Chief Oper. Officer—Carla Pontarelli
- Engrg. Mgr.—Terry Stadtmiller

EQUIPMENT:
Box and pan brake; two crane bays: 50 ft. x 144 ft., 15-ton capacity and 35 ft. x 195 ft., 10-ton capacity; five 1-ton jib cranes; 30-ton iron worker; lower plate bending rolls: $3/8$ in. x 8 ft.; plate burning table; press brakes: 440-ton (10 ft.); shearing: $1/4$ in. x 10 ft. mild steel and $3/16$ in. x 10 ft. stainless steel; two plastic butt welders: 2 in. x 10 ft.; two plastic formers: 1 in. x 10 ft.; grit blast room: 30 ft. x 20 ft. x 14 ft. 6 in. high; paint booth: 30 ft. x 24 ft. x 20 ft. high; curing oven: 6 ft. x 7 ft. x 7 ft. high; heat stripping oven: 9 ft. 6 in. x 8 ft. x 10 ft. high, CNC router, orbital welding system, SAW system. Computer-controlled flat butt fusion and corner fusion plastic welding machine: $2\ 3/8$ in. x 13 ft. 6 in.

PRODUCTS and/or SERVICES:
Designs, engineers, manufactures, and installs carbon steel, stainless steel and thermoplastic tanks for annealing, galvanizing, pickling, cleaning, rinsing, and plating, including push-pull tanks, continuous strip process tanks and recirculation tanks. Other equipment includes hoods, covers, ducting and scrubbers. Turnkey galvanizing, pickling, cleaning, plating and ventilation systems are also available including instrumentation, automation, recirculation and filtration equipment. Performs field service work including repairs and modifications. Replacements parts, such as granite keepers, spray headers and steam injectors, are also available.

POLYONICS
28 Industrial Park Dr.
Westmoreland, NH 03467 USA
P: +1.603.352.1415
F: +1.603.352.1936
info@polyonics.com
www.polyonics.com

PRODUCTS and/or SERVICES:
Manufactures highly engineered coated label and tag materials for tracking and identifying steel throughout the milling process. Polyonics HIGHdegree label and tag materials are rated up to 1,112°F (600°C) and offer high durability and abrasion resistance for long-term retention of critical bar code information.

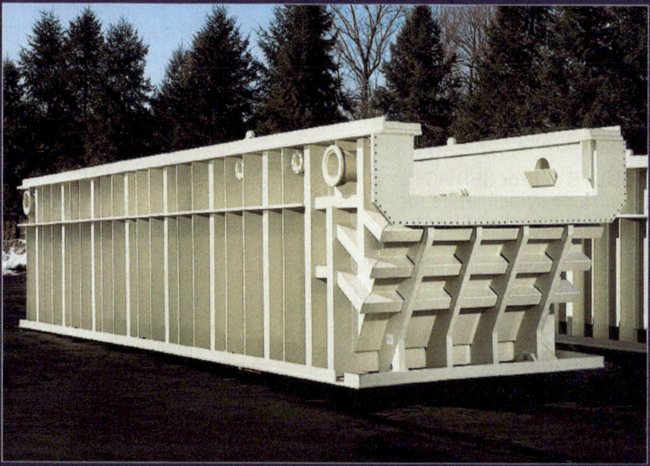

See listing page 476

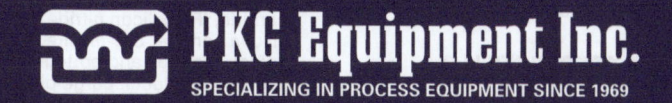

SUPPLIERS of EQUIPMENT, PRODUCTS and SERVICES

POLYTEC INC.
16400 Bake Pkwy.
Irvine, CA 92618 USA
P: +1.949.943.3033
info@polytec.com
www.polytec.com

PRODUCTS and/or SERVICES:
Laser surface velocimeters for non-contact speed and length measurements in steel processing applications, including casting, hot rolling, cold rolling, plate, tube/pipe and more.

POWER ELECTRONICS® INTERNATIONAL INC.
561-8 Plate Dr.
East Dundee, IL 60118 USA
P: +1.847.428.9494
F: +1.847.428.7744
sales@peinfo.com
www.peinfo.com

PRODUCTS and/or SERVICES:
Steel mill high-temperature AC electronic motor and crane controls. Crane/hoist robust VFDs and soft starts designed for heavy-duty applications. All products are designed, engineered and manufactured in the U.S.A. Smooth-Move® brand soft starts; Micro-Speed® Smart-Move®, CX®, and Ultra® Series (MV-Ultra™ and MX-Ultra™); MX® and MMV® Multi-Vector® (for hoist without mechanical load brakes). Complete control panels designed to your specifications and PE® Ready-Built™ Bridge Panel series. Advanced crane options for Ultra Series™ drives include anti-sway crane control (PE SAM™ Swing Amplitude Manager™), anti-twist system (PE360™), PE Smart-Set™ and PE Remote Keypad.

POWER RESOURCES LLC
8511 Atascocita Lake Way
Humble, TX 77346 USA
P: +1.304.639.5088
jim@powerresourcesllc.com
www.powerresourcesllc.com

- Pres.—James R. Molnar

PRODUCTS and/or SERVICES:
Executive recruiting in metals, tubing and energy industries.

No. of Employees: 1.

PRCO AMERICA INC.
P.O. Box 30
Glenshaw, PA 15116 USA
P: +1.412.837.2798
F: +1.270.277.1952
info@prco-america.com
www.prco-america.com

- Pres.—Changsheng Qi
- Mgr. Finance—Joan Taylor
- Gen. Mgr. — USA and Canada—Bill Porter
- Plant Mgr. Mayfield, KY—Barry Heath
- Regional Mgr. North USA—Aaron Ingalls
- Regional Mgr. West USA—Jim Mack
- Regional Mgr. South—Dave Westphal
- Regional Mgr. Midwest—Steve Zakutansky
- Sales Mgr. MI, OH, KY—Jim McMillan

PRODUCTS and/or SERVICES:
Full-line manufacturer and supplier of refractories for heavy industry. PRCO America Inc. is a wholly owned subsidiary of Puyang Refractories Group Co. Ltd. Supplies refractories for BF, BOF, EAF, AOD, tundishes, steel ladles, iron transfer ladles, torpedo ladles, reheat and industrial furnaces. Seventeen manufacturing facilities with more than 5,000 employees, the PRCO Group supplies refractories to the ferrous, non-ferrous, glass and cement industries. PRCO products include: Brick: mag chrome, mag carbon, alumina mag carbon/mag alumina carbon (AMC/MAC), high-alumina, magnesia, dolomite, alumina silicon carbide, IFB, silicon nitride-bonded silicon carbide, SIC-mullite, alumina-spinel, fire/clay and bottom-pour tiles. Pre-cast products: purge plugs, seating blocks, well blocks, nozzles, deltas, ladle bottoms, skimmer blocks, impact pads, dams and weirs. Functional parts: slide plates, ladle shrouds, stopper rods, upper/lower nozzles, SENs and metering nozzles. Monolithics:

Are You Hiring?

Filling open positions with the right candidate can be difficult...

But it doesn't have to be.

AIST members can post iron and steel industry-related job openings for FREE on AIST's Employment Board.

Not a member? Contact Beniamina Dapra at bdapra@aist.org or +1.724.814.3058 for more information.

AIST.ORG/EMPLOYMENTBOARD

SUPPLIERS of EQUIPMENT, PRODUCTS and SERVICES

ramming mixes, gunning mixes, tundish spray mixes, dry vibe mixes, self-flow castables and shotcrete. Others: environmentally friendly taphole clay.

PRECISIONED COMPONENTS LLC
25 Barton Chapel Road
Apple Grove, WV 25502 USA
P: +1.304.576.2622
F: +1.304.576.2013
precisionedcomponentsllc@eafrepair.com
www.eafrepair.com

PRODUCTS and/or SERVICES:
Specialty welding and fabrication shop with emphasis on meltshop services. Welding services range from basic carbon steel to more exotic nickel, stainless steel and copper alloys.

PRECISION MACHINE INC.—see XTEK INC.

PRECISION SURFACE TECHNOLOGIES INC.
649 S. Service Road
Grimsby, ON L3M 4E8 Canada
P: +1.905.643.4244
F: +1.905.643.4246
sales@precisionrolls.com
www.precisionrolls.com

- Pres.—Greg Schneider, P. Eng.
- Sales Mgr.—Andrew Schneider
- Vice Pres. Admin.—A. Mazzotti
- Office Admin.—Carissa Goldstein
- Cust. Svce.—Mark Gish

PRODUCTS and/or SERVICES:
Roll manufacturing, roll repair, chrome plating, thermal spray, heat treating, cylindrical grinding.

PRIMETALS TECHNOLOGIES LTD.
Global Headquarters:
566 Chiswick High Road
Bldg. 11, Chiswick Park
W4 5YA London, U.K.
contact@primetals.com
www.primetals.com

- Chief Exec. Officer—Satoru Iijima

PRODUCTS and/or SERVICES:
Leading provider of engineering, plant building and life cycle services for the metals industry. Offers a complete technology, product, and services portfolio that includes integrated electrics and automation, digitalization, and environmental/green steel solutions. This covers every step of the iron and steel production chain—from the raw materials to the finished product—and includes the latest rolling solutions for the non-ferrous metals sector. Primetals Technologies is a joint venture of Mitsubishi Heavy Industries and partners, with around 7,000 employees worldwide.

PRIMETALS TECHNOLOGIES USA LLC
USA Headquarters:
5895 Windward Pkwy.
Alpharetta, GA 30005 USA
P: +1.770.740.3800

- Chief Exec. Officer—Ralf Hanneken

USA — Alabama
701 Market St. NW
Decatur, AL 35603 USA

USA — Arkansas
101 Terra Road
Blytheville, AR 72315 USA
P: +1.870.762.1905

USA — Kentucky
199 Montgomery Road
Ghent, KY 41045 USA
P: +1.501.350.1997

USA — Massachusetts
93 Gilmore Dr.
Sutton, MA 01590 USA
P: +1.508.755.6111

USA - Michigan
470 Paw Paw Ave.
Benton Harbor, MI 49022 USA
P: +1.269.927.3591

USA - Mississippi
1961 Airport Road, MS Door #9
Columbus, MS 39701 USA
P: +1.662.245.4598

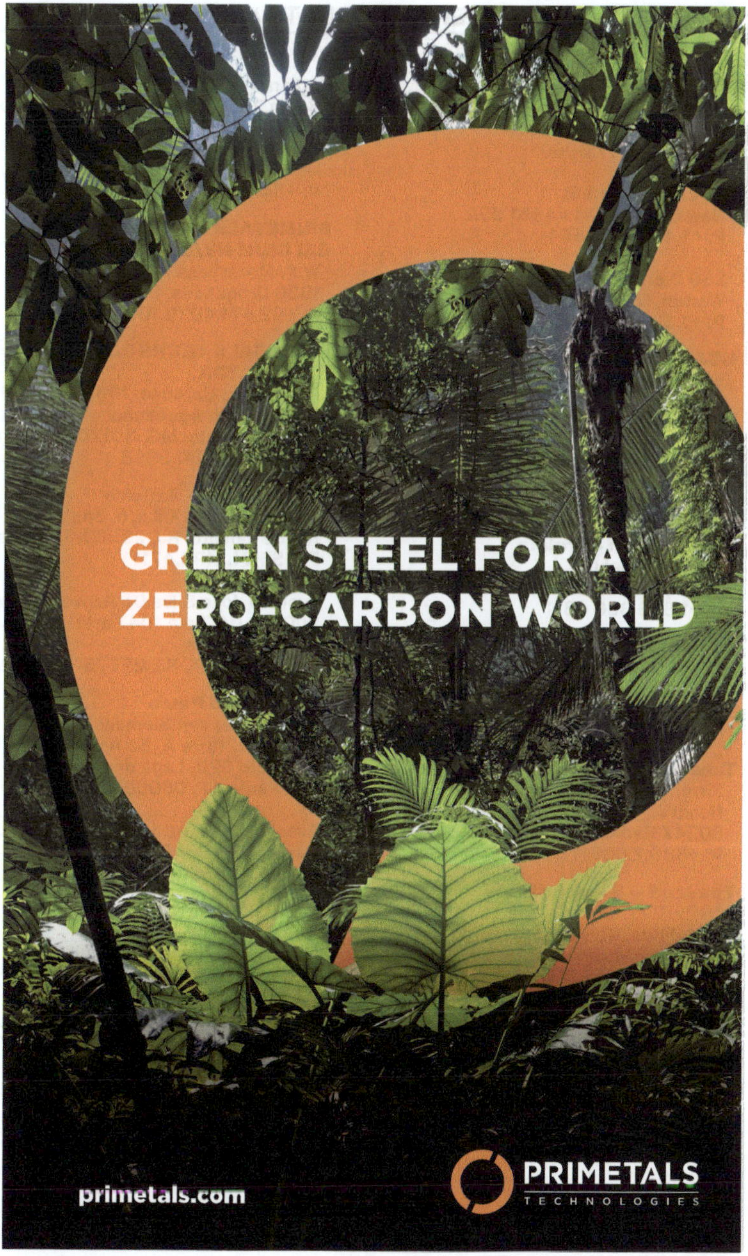

See listing page 480

SUPPLIERS of EQUIPMENT, PRODUCTS and SERVICES

USA — Ohio
3605 Warren Meadville Road
Cortland, OH 44410 USA
P: +1.330.637.6060

81 E. Washburn St.
New London, OH 44851 USA
P: +1.419.929.1554

250 Dietz Road NE
Warren, OH 44483 USA
P: +1.330.637.6060

USA — Pennsylvania
501 Technology Dr.
Canonsburg, PA 15317 USA
P: +1.724.514.8500

220 Commerce Dr., Suite 105
Fort Washington, PA 19034 USA
P: +.215.947.7333

USA — South Carolina
1287 S. Steel Cir.
Huger, SC 29450 USA
P: +1 843 336 4811

PRIMETALS TECHNOLOGIES AUSTRIA GMBH
Turmstrasse 44
4031 Linz, Austria
P: +43.732.6592.0

Taiwan — Representative Office
Siwei 4th Road, Lingya District
Room A, 4F, Si Wei Bldg., No. 7
80247 Kaohsiung, Taiwan
P: +886.7.5361750

Thailand — Branch Office
2922/277 Charn Issara Tower II
24th Floor, New Petchburi Road
Bangkapi, Huaykwang
Bangkok 10310, Thailand
P: +66.830383434

United Arab Emirates — Representative Office
Office 3709, JLT Cluster I,
Platinum Tower, Jumeirah Lake Towers
Dubai, United Arab Emirates
P: +971.44.560383

Vietnam — Representative Office
Room 2006, 20th Floor, Sun Wah Tower
115 Nguyen Hue St.
Ben Nghe Ward, District 1
Ho Chi Minh City, Vietnam
P: +84.28.3914.3003

PRIMETALS TECHNOLOGIES BELGIUM NV/SA
W.A. Mozartlaan 4, Bldg. Amadeus
1620 Drogenbos, Belgium
P: +32.471.40.10.10

PRIMETALS TECHNOLOGIES BRAZIL LTDA.
Rua Matias Cardoso, 169 — Sala 601
Bairro Santo Agostinho
Belo Horizonte, MG, 30170-050, Brazil
P: +55.31.3330.3856

Brazil — Rio de Janeiro
Avenida João XXIII s/n, Santa Cruz
Rio de Janeiro, RJ, 23560-352, Brazil
P: +55.21.3198.4711

Avenida Jose Silva De Azevedo Neto,
200, BL 04, Sala 104 Parte
Barra da Tijuca
Rio de Janeiro, RJ, 22775-056, Brazil

Brazil — São Paulo
Rua Werner von Siemens, 111
Prédio 11, Torre A, 3o Andar,
Conjunto 32B, Lapa de Baixo
São Paulo, SP, 05069-010, Brazil

Avenida Tamboré 1400, Bairro Tamboré
Barueri, SP, 06460-000, Brazil
P: +55.31.3330.3856

Brazil — Serra
Rua 6 B; Setor II;
Quadra 14A, Lote 14; Civit II
Serra, ES, 29168-085, Brazil

Brazil — Volta Redonda
Rua Nossa Senhora da Conceição, 20
Conforto, Volta Redonda, RJ,
27260-390, Brazil
P: +55.21.3344.6468

Rudovia Lucia Meira, BR 393, km 5.001
s/n Volta Redonda,
RJ, 27260-390, Brazil

SUPPLIERS OF EQUIPMENT, PRODUCTS and SERVICES

PRIMETALS TECHNOLOGIES CHINA LTD.
No. 7 S. Zhong Huan Nan Road
Bldg. C, ChaoYang District
100102 Beijing, P.R. China

China — Changxing
2518 Fazhan Dadao
ChangXing High-Tech Zone
313100 Huzhou, P.R. China
P: +86.572.6601027

China — Shanghai
8F, Bldg. MT 1
No. 229 Haowen Road, MixC Park
Minhang District
201103 Shanghai, P.R. China
P: +86.21.53206000

China — Tangshan
1698 N. Weiguo Road, High-Tech Zone
063000 Tangshan, P.R. China

PRIMETALS TECHNOLOGIES SERVICES LTD.
Gangchang Road S
Lubei District
063000 Tangshan, P.R. China

PRIMETALS TECHNOLOGIES CZECH REPUBLIC S.R.O.
28 Října 2663/150
702 00 Ostrava, Czech Republic
P: +420.597.400.660

PRIMETALS TECHNOLOGIES GERMANY GMBH
Bunsenstraße 43
91058 Erlangen, Germany
P: +49.9131.9886.0

Germany — Fürth
Breslauer Straße 10
90766 Fürth, Germany
P: +49.9131.9886.0

Germany — Saarbrücken
Werner-von-Siemens-Allee 4
66115 Saarbrücken, Germany
P: +49.9131.9886.0

Germany — Willstätt-Legelshurst
Reithallenstraße 1
77731 Willstätt-Legelshurst, Germany
P: +49.9131.9886.0

PRIMETALS TECHNOLOGIES INDIA PVT. LTD.
5th Floor, Tower - C, DLF IT Park-I,
08 Major Arterial Road, New Town
(Rajarhat),
Kolkata 700156, India
P: +91.33.66291000

India — Mumbai
Plot No. D-41/1, TTC, MIDC, Turbhe
4000705 Navi Mumbai, MH, India
P: +91.22.6761.5100

India — Mumbai — Concast India Ltd. (Group Co.)
47-48, Jolly Maker Chambers II,
Nariman Point
400021 Mumbai, MH, India
P: +91.22.2202.0414

PRIMETALS TECHNOLOGIES JAPAN LTD.
6-22, Kannon Shinmachi
4-Chome, Nishi-ku
733-8553 Hiroshima, Japan
P: +81.82.291.2181

Japan — Tokyo
34-6, Shiba 5-Chome
12F Shin-Tamachi Building, Minato-ku
108-0014 Tokyo, Japan
P: +81.3.5765.5275

PRIMETALS TECHNOLOGIES KOREA LTD.
Jaehwa Square 16th Floor, 311
Dongmak-ro Mapo-gu
04156 Seoul, South Korea
P: +82.2.3149.8003

PRIMETALS TECHNOLOGIES MEXICO S. DE R.L. DE C.V.
Miguel Aleman km 26,
Parque Industrial Milimex
Apodaca, NL, 66637 Mexico
P: +52.81.81.96.0909

PRIMETALS TECHNOLOGIES POLAND SP. Z O.O.
ul. Stefana Korbońskiego 14
30-443 Kraków, Poland
P: +48.12.211.43.00

Poland — Rzeszów
ul. Majora Wacława Kopisto 8B
35-315 Rzeszów, Poland
P: +48.883.313.793

SUPPLIERS of EQUIPMENT, PRODUCTS and SERVICES

PRIMETALS TECHNOLOGIES RUSSIA LLC
Karla Libknekhta Str., 4
620075 Ekaterinburg, Russia
P: +7.343.37.92.395

Russia — Moscow
Gilyarovskogo Str., 10
Bldg. 1, Floor 4
129090 Moscow, Russia
P: +7.495.114.5518

PRIMETALS TECHNOLOGIES SAUDI ARABIA GMBH
P.O. Box 1656, Mergab Tower, 1st Floor
Al Madinah Al Munawarah St.
31951 Al-Jubail, Saudi Arabia
P: +966.13.361.4559

PRIMETALS TECHNOLOGIES SLOVAKIA S.R.O.
Němcovej 30
040 01 Košice, Slovakia
P: +421.55.7979820

PRIMETALS TEKNOLOJI SANAYI VE TICARET A.Ş.
Yakacik Cad. No. 111
34870 Istanbul, Turkey
P: +90.216.459.3160

PRIMETALS TECHNOLOGIES UKRAINE LLC
Dmytra Yavornitskogo Ave. 1A
Office 401, Slaviya Business Center
49005 Dnipro, Ukraine
P: +38.056.731.97.90

Ukraine — Kiev
4-B Mykoly Hrinchenka Str.
3038 Kiev, Ukraine
P: +38.044.233.7200

PRIMETALS TECHNOLOGIES LTD.

United Kingdom — Christchurch
9 Enterprise Way, Aviation Park W
Bournemouth International Airport
BH23 6EW Christchurch, Dorset, U.K.
P: +44.1202.33.1407

United Kingdom — Scunthorpe
Warren Road
DN15 6XH Scunthorpe
North Lincolnshire, U.K.
P: +44.1724.280360

United Kingdom — Sheffield
Unit S, Europa Link
S9 1XU Sheffield, South Yorkshire, U.K.
P: +44.1709.726500

United Kingdom — Stockton-on-Tees
7 Fudan Way
TS17 6ER Stockton-on-Tees
Durham, U.K.
P: +44.1642.662276

PRO-CHEM-CO INC.
Ripley and Schneider Sts.
Lake Station, IN 46405 USA
P: +1.219.962.8554
F: +1.219.962.7459
jjtaglia@pro-chem-co.com
www.pro-chem-co.com

– Co-Pres.—James J. Taglia, V. Thomas Taglia

EQUIPMENT:
ISO 9001-certified toll blending, chemical processing facility, 375,000-gallon enclosed bulk storage capacity. Production batch sizes range from 50 to 20,000 gallons.

PRODUCTS and/or SERVICES:
Manufactures and markets a full line of hot mill rolling oils, pickling oils for sheet and tin, sheet mill rolling oils, tin mill rolling oils, double cold reduction mill rolling oils, reversing mill rolling oils, final stand mill detergents, temper mill fluids for cold-rolled and galvanized, rust preventives, slushing oils, edge sealants, rinse additives for pickle lines, roll grinding coolants, hydraulic oils, waterproof bearing greases, specialty solvents, heavy-duty maintenance cleaners, acetyl tributyl citrate (ATBC), and butyl stearate oil (BSO). In addition, Pro-Chem-Co. Inc. supplies a full line of process cleaners to both tin and sheet mill processes including, but not limited to, galvanizing lines, annealing lines, coating lines and stand-alone cleaning lines. Also manufactures a full line of metalworking fluids, including machining and grinding fluids, metalforming lubricants, wire drawing lubricants, cleaners, and corrosion

SUPPLIERS OF EQUIPMENT, PRODUCTS and SERVICES

preventives. Toll manufacturing and private labeling services available.

No. of Employees: <50.

PROCESSBARRON
2770 Welborn St.
P.O. Box 1607
Pelham, AL 35124 USA
P: +1.205.663.5330
F: +1.205.663.6037
www.processbarron.com

- Pres.—Ken Nolen
- Vice Pres. Sales South—Ashley Doyal
- Vice Pres. Sales North—Chad Snyder
- Chief Revenue Officer—Ken Buttery
- Mktg.—Marcy Miller, Jennifer Smith
- Dir. Bulk Matls. Handling—David Cantu
- Dir. of Air Handling—Allen Ray
- Chief Financial Officer—Andrew Carter
- Sales Dirs.—Joe Waite, John Toitch, J.B. Calhoun, Russell Powell

EQUIPMENT:
Heat exchangers, bulk materials handling systems, ash handling systems, air handling systems, multi-clone dust collectors, baghouse and scrubber ID fans, dampers, high-temperature and fabric expansion joints, BF goggle valves, LMF dust systems, silos, stacks, industrial efficiency program.

PRODUCTS and/or SERVICES:
Design, manufacture and installation of fans, technical field services, and fan rebuilds.

PROCO PRODUCTS INC.
P.O. Box 590
Stockton, CA 95201 USA
P: +1.209.943.6088
F: +1.209.943.0242
sales@procoproducts.com
www.procoproducts.com

PRODUCTS and/or SERVICES:
Rubber expansion joints, PTFE convoluted expansion joints, PTFE-lined rubber expansion joints, ducting joints and rubber duckbill check valves. US$2.5 million expansion joint inventory.

PROMECON
Steinfeldstr. 5
Barleben, 39179 Germany
P: +49.39206.512.0
F: +49.39203.512.202
info@promecon.com
www.promecon.com

PRODUCTS and/or SERVICES:
Manufactures and installs high-technology measurement systems for the monitoring and optimization of thermal processes such as coal-fired boilers, cement kilns, smelter processes and others.

PROMECON USA Inc.
2125 Center Ave., Suite 507
Fort Lee, NJ 07024 USA
P: +1.330.465.0738
usa@promecon.com

PROTON PRODUCTS INC.
1590 S. Coast Hwy., Suite 13
Laguna Beach, CA 92651 USA
P: +1.949.981.1909
www.protonproducts.com
www.linkedin.com/company/proton-products

- Pres.—Grant Latimer
- Sales Mgr.—Greg Goss

PRODUCTS and/or SERVICES:
Non-contact speed and length measurement and non-contact diameter measurement.

No. of Employees: Approx. 100.

PROXITRON INC.
9607 Gayton Road, Suite 110
Henrico, VA 23238 USA
P: +1.804.359.8448
F: +1.804.359.9199
info@proxitroninc.com
www.proxitroninc.com

- Pres.—Dan Cunningham

PRODUCTS and/or SERVICES:
Hot metal detectors; inductive sensors; pyrometers; airflow sensors.

No. of Employees: 3.

SUPPLIERS of EQUIPMENT, PRODUCTS and SERVICES

PRUFTECHNIK INC., Part of Fluke Reliability
7821 Bartram Ave.
Philadelphia, PA 19153 USA
P: +1.844.242.6296
usa@pruftechnik.com
www.pruftechnik.com

PRODUCTS and/or SERVICES:
Laser alignment systems, including OPTALIGN® and ROTALIGN® for shaft alignment systems across sectors; condition monitoring systems including VIBXPERT® and VIBGUARD® for vibration analyses across a range of applications.

PSI METALS NORTH AMERICA INC.
Park West Two
2000 Cliff Mine Road, Suite 600
Pittsburgh, PA 15275 USA
P: +1.412.747.0900
F: +1.412.747.0901
swilson@psimetals.com
www.psimetals.com

PRODUCTS and/or SERVICES:
Develops intelligent software for the production of steel, aluminum and other metals. The PSI metals software solution optimizes processes to increase throughput, increase profit and yield, manage inventory, improve quality and due date adherence. PSI Metals offers a variety of intelligent solutions for planning, manufacturing execution, logistics, quality, scheduling, energy, automation and plant optimization.

PSNERGY
152 W. 12th St.
Erie, PA 16501 USA
P: +1.814.504.2326
sales@psnergy.com
www.psnergy.com

- Pres.—Carl Nicolia
- Vice Pres. Engrg.—Chris Wyant
- Vice Pres. Sales—Roy Hardy

PRODUCTS and/or SERVICES:
Total combustion solutions: combustion monitoring systems, waste heat recovery, combustion tuning services, combustion training.

PT TECH LLC®
1441 Wolf Creek Trail
Wadsworth, OH 44281 USA
P: +1.330.239.4933
F: +1.330.239.4465
pttinfo@pttech.com
www.pttech.com

- Pres.—Jason Rebucci
- Vice Pres. Sales—Doug Herr

PRODUCTS and/or SERVICES:
Hoist brakes, bridge brakes for cranes and torque limiters for metal strip leveling and other mill applications (AC and DC caliper disc brakes and hydraulic disc brakes and torque limiters for the steel industry).

No. of Employees: 50+.

PYROTEK INC.
705 W. 1st Ave.
Spokane, WA 99201 USA
P: +1.509.926.6212
www.pyrotek.com

PRODUCTS and/or SERVICES:
High-strength ISOMAG® structural insulation boards for refractory systems used in iron- and steelmaking.

SUPPLIERS OF EQUIPMENT, PRODUCTS and SERVICES

Q

QUAD ENGINEERING INC.
90 Sheppard Ave. E, Suite 700
Toronto, ON M2N 3A1 Canada
P: +1.416.391.3755
F: +1.416.391.3645
www.quadeng.com

– Pres.—Michael Levick

PRODUCTS and/or SERVICES:
Equipment for rolling steel, titanium, aluminum, copper and special metals. Equipment design, supply, custom retrofits and upgrades of rolling mill machinery, including: reversing blooming mills, 2-high and universal mill stands for long products; peel bars, pinch rolls, shears, cooling beds, stacking and packing lines: 4-high temper mills, cold mills, and hot mills for flat products, including all terminal equipment and AGC systems. Custom equipment design and supply for both long and flat-rolled products. Steel mill process engineering, including long-term capital planning, production improvement planning, and process simulations of rolling mills for both long and flat products. Operation services, including operation assessments, pass design, physical pass design modeling, operations consulting and customized operator training rolling courses. Stress analysis, thermal analysis and failure analysis using complex 3D finite element techniques. Meltshop engineering services, including: offgas systems, and baghouse and specialized equipment design and supply. Installation, engineering and construction services, including: civil, utilities, mechanical and project management.

No. of Employees: 40.

Affiliated Companies:

Quad Infotech Inc.
90 Sheppard Ave. E, Unit 603
Toronto, ON M2N 6X3 Canada
P: +1.416.391.3755
F: +1.416.391.3645
info@QUADINFOTECH.com
www.quadinfotech.com

PRODUCTS and/or SERVICES:
Quad Mill Operation System (QMOS) specifically designed and developed for the long steel products industry. QMOS enables users to plan and schedule the production of the meltshop and the rolling mill while optimizing the process and yield. QMOS is able to monitor the quality of the produced steel and provide quality execution of the product. QMOS consists of all functions of a meltshop, from loading of the scrap to the melting, refining, and production of billet and bloom. It also deals with ladle and mold management. The rolling mill modules track the assignment of the billet to the order, up to loading of the billet to the reheat furnace, rolling, bundling and all sorts of after-production operations. It also provides a comprehensive roll shop management system for the rolls, guides, bearings and chocks, and stand building.

Quad Training
90 Sheppard Ave. E, Suite 700
North York, ON M2N 3A1 Canada
P: +1.416.391.3755, ext. 226
j.kennedy@quadeng.com
www.quadeng.com

– Pres.—Joseph Kennedy

PRODUCTS and/or SERVICES:
Complete on-site operation and training services including on-site operator training customized to a rolling mill's product and shape range. Training includes classroom pass design and rolling theory with

SUPPLIERS of EQUIPMENT, PRODUCTS and SERVICES

customized work sessions designed from actual setup sheets and pass designs. Hands-on rolling classes using Quad's containerized lab training mill, which is shipped to the customer's mill site for training their mill crews. Quad R-factor system and training designed to show operators how they are operating the mill compared to the setup sheet plan. Operational troubleshooting, pass design and commissioning services designed to help operators get the most out of their mill equipment.

QUAKER HOUGHTON
901 E. Hector St.
Conshohocken, PA 19428 USA
P: +1.610.832.4000
www.quakerhoughton.com

- Chief Exec. Officer—Andy Tometich
- Chmn. of the Board—Michael Barry
- Sr. Vice Pres, Chief Financial Officer and Treas.—Shane Hostetter
- Sr. Vice Pres., Gen. Counsel and Corporate Sec.—Robert T. Traub
- Sr. Vice Pres., Global H.R. and Chief H.R. Officer—Kym Johnson
- Sr. Vice Pres., Global Oprs., EHS and Procurement—Wilbert Platzer
- Exec. Vice Pres., Global Specialty Business and Chief Strategy Officer—Joseph A. Berquist
- Sr. Vice Pres., Chief Technology Officer—Dave Slinkman
- Sr. Vice Pres. and Managing Dir., APAC—Dieter Laininger
- Sr. Vice Pres. and Managing Dir., EMEA—Adrian Steeples
- Sr. Vice Pres. and Managing Dir., Americas—Jeewat Bijlani
- Sr. Dir. of Metals, U.S. and Canada—Matt Knapik
- Vice Pres., Global Metals—Dirk Wouters

PRODUCTS and/or SERVICES:
Developer, producer and marketer of custom-formulated chemical specialty products for various heavy industrial and manufacturing applications. Offers and markets chemical management services, equipment solutions, technical solutions and engineering solutions. Products for the steel industry include rolling lubricants, corrosion preventives, metal finishing compounds, hydraulic fluids, specialty greases and industrial lubricants.

No. of Employees: 4,000 worldwide in consolidated subsidiaries.

QUAL-FAB INC.
34250 Mills Road
Avon, OH 44011 USA
P: +1.440.327.5000
F: +1.440.327.5599
sales@qual-fab.net
www.qual-fab.net

PRODUCTS and/or SERVICES:
Manufacturer of stainless and high-nickel-alloy products for the steel industry. Main products include inner covers of all style, radiant heater tubes (both cast and wrought), fans, furnace rolls, recuperator tubes, pickle hooks, cooling tubes, dampers, zinc arms "pot roll-arms", forced cooler assemblies, and many styles of convector plates, charge plates, diffusers, and plenum chambers.

QUALICAST CORP.
P.O. Box 538
Chester Heights, PA 19017 USA
P: +1.610.358.9398
F: +1.610.358.9391
www.qualicastcorp.com

- Vice Pres. Sales—Christopher Law

EQUIPMENT:
Sand and centrifugal castings, and full machining services.

PRODUCTS and/or SERVICES:
Work rolls, backup rolls, coiler drums, garrett drums, zinc pot rollers, screwdown nuts, worm gears, galvanizing furnace rolls, mill drives couplings and reducers. Various iron, high-alloy steel and bronze castings for steel mills.

No. of Employees: 250.

SUPPLIERS OF EQUIPMENT, PRODUCTS and SERVICES

R

R&G LABORATORIES INC.
217 Hobbs St., Suite 105
Tampa, FL 33619 USA
P: +1.813.643.3513
F: +1.813.793.4429
cheryl@randglabs.com
www.randglabs.com

- Pres.—Charles Boswell
- Sales and Adv. Mgr.—Cheryl Huff

PRODUCTS and/or SERVICES:
Complete lubricant solutions provider. State-of-the-art laboratory that can handle anything from basic engine oil analysis to varnish detection testing from turbine systems. Offers a complete line of products, which include: Oil Safe, Des-Case, CheckFluid, Grease Safe/Label Safe Products.

No. of Employees: 10.

RABCO ENERGY SOLUTIONS INC.
14786 Greenleaf Valley Dr.
Chesterfield, MO 63017 USA
P: +1.636.536.0386
tcohen@rabcosolutions.com
www.rabcosolutions.com

- Chief Exec. Officer and Pres.—Tab Cohen

EQUIPMENT:
Waste heat recovery.

PRODUCTS and/or SERVICES:
Free energy solutions.

No. of Employees: 5.

RACO INTERNATIONAL L.P.
3350 Industrial Blvd.
Bethel Park, PA 15102 USA
P: +1.888.289.7226 (Toll-Free);
    +1.412.835.5744
F: +1.412.835.0338
www.racointernational.com

- Pres.—Reinhard Wilke
- Gen. Mgr.—Michael A. Bock

PRODUCTS and/or SERVICES:
Manufacturer of electric cylinders and actuators with precision ball or Acme screws to position or move any object or load. Thrusts to 200,000 lbs., speeds to 30 in./sec. and strokes to 20 ft. Cylinders are built for heavy-duty industrial applications.

RAD-CON INC.
13001 Athens Ave., Suite 300
Cleveland, OH 44107 USA
P: +1.440.871.5720
F: +1.216.221.1135
sales@rad-con.com
www.rad-con.com

- Pres.—Christopher J. Messina
- Vice Pres. Oprs.—Michael W. McDonald

EQUIPMENT:
Bell-type batch annealing equipment (BAF), Entec CAPS™ level 2 batch annealing models.

PRODUCTS and/or SERVICES:
Hydrogen convection bell-type batch annealing furnaces and level 2 optimization of batch annealing facilities (both HNx and hydrogen). Process consulting for batch annealing improvement, including reducing running costs, improving cleanliness and avoiding stickers. Equipment used for recrystallize annealing of cold-rolled steel sheet/strip, for spheroidize annealing of medium/high-carbon alloy steels, and for other heat treating processes of ferrous and non-ferrous metals.

No. of Employees: 25.

SUPPLIERS of EQUIPMENT, PRODUCTS and SERVICES

RADCOMM SYSTEMS CORP.
2931 Portland Dr.
Oakville, ON L6H 5S4 Canada
P: +1.905.829.9290
F: +1.905.829.1406
inquiries@radcommsystems.com
www.radcommsystems.com

- Chief Exec. Officer—Steve Steranka
- Pres.—Andrew Haber
- Vice Pres. Prodn./Mfg.—Barry Rudnicki
- Treas.—Siew-Hon Ang
- Sales Mgr.—Scott Aikin
- Regional Sales Mgr.—Josh Hunter

PRODUCTS and/or SERVICES:
Radiation detection systems; vehicle and rail portal monitors; grapple and magnet radiation detection systems; conveyor and offgas radiation detection systems; charge bucket radiation detection systems; handheld and portable units; laboratory and quality assurance equipment; supervisory software; customized solutions.

No. of Employees: 30.

RADIAN ROBOTICS
70 Lancing Dr.
Hamilton, ON L8W 3A1 Canada
P: +1.905.639.7370
www.radianrobotics.com

- Pres.—Jim Kay
- Sales Mgr.—Bill Smith

PRODUCTS and/or SERVICES:
Robotic solutions for the metals industry. Fully automatic robotic systems designed for destrapping and product identification, including hot slab marking and labeling, hot billet marking and labeling, hot coil marking and labeling, cold coil marking and labeling, strapping solutions, laser etching, long product marking and tagging, piece count verification, and custom robotic applications.

No. of Employees: 32.

RADIOMETRIC SERVICES AND INSTRUMENTS LLC (RSI)
4507 Metropolitan Court, Unit J
Frederick, MD 21704 USA
P: +1.301.874.3494
F: +1.301.874.3499
info@rsi-xray.com
www.rsi-xray.com

- Pres. and Vice Pres. Engrg.—Dino Jardina
- Gen. Mgr.—Mike Cook
- Global Sales Mgr.—Clyde Hunt
- Mktg. Mgr.—Angela Retzos
- S/W Mgr.—Tom Ryan
- Test and Svce. Mgr.—Chris Gockley
- West Virginia Svce. Mgr.—Todd Bolinger

PRODUCTS and/or SERVICES:
X-ray thickness gauge systems for hot mills, cold mills and process lines; new coating gauge systems; upgrade packages for existing thickness and coating gauge systems; x-ray sensor repair (DMC x-ray sources, detectors, standard magazines); spare parts for thickness gauges and coating gauges; service and support for x-ray and isotope thickness and coating gauges. Service centers in Maryland, West Virginia and Ohio, USA; and Beijing, China.

RAMM METALS
1555 Indian River Blvd. B113
Vero Beach, FL 32960 USA
P: +1.772.713.1970
F: +1.772.299.4426
bg@rammglobal.com
www.rammglobal.com
www.rammsand.com

- Managing Partner—Brian George
- Partner—Pat George
- Consultant—Michael Pierce
- Comptr.—Mark Sinicrope
- Business Dev. Mgr.—Daniel Kurtz
- Qual. Engrg.—Horacio Lima

EQUIPMENT:
Supplier of engineering castings, ladle sands and scrap for recycling.

RADIAN ROBOTICS

100% NORTH AMERICAN

Radian Robotics is a worldwide leader in turnkey robotic solutions for the metals industry.

Our North American office provides convenient access to innovative robotic products and services throughout North and South America, as well as Australia and New Zealand.

Need something a little different?
We relish the opportunity to innovate custom solutions that fits our customer's unique needs.

Call: +1-905-639-7370

Learn more at radianrobotics.com

Services:

- Hot & cold coil marking, tagging, and de-banding
- Slabs & billet marking and tagging
- Long product tagging
- Product identification and verification
- Inner diameter welding for coils
- Custom applications

Methods:

- Single nozzle & dot matrix marking
- Laser-etching
- Hot/cold product labeling
- Stud nailing/welding
- Coil de-strapping/de-banding

SUPPLIERS of EQUIPMENT, PRODUCTS and SERVICES

PRODUCTS and/or SERVICES:
Ingot molds, stools and accessories. Iron and steel slag pots, coke oven doors and frames in CG iron. Also, goosenecks and charging hole frames and covers for coke ovens. Refractory plugs for coke oven doors. Scrap metals such as coolant scrap, steel turnings and manganese scrap. Also low-alloy scrap and tool steel scrap. Pig molds. Grate bars for sintering plants. Engineering design services for complete ingot-making manufacturer lines. Dried and screened mill scale in bulk or bags. Ladle sands in bags.

No. of Employees: 4.

RAPID GEAR
1596 Strasburg Road
Kitchener, ON N2R 1E9 Canada
P: +1.519.748.4828
F: +1.519.748.5528
renato.foti@rapidgear.com
www.rapidgear.com

- Pres.—Tania Sabados
- Vice Pres.—Renato Foti
- Engrg.—Clay Williams
- Prodn.—Jamie Bradie

EQUIPMENT:
Gear cutting up to 200 in.

PRODUCTS and/or SERVICES:
Gearing, gearbox repair, custom precision machining, engineering, field service.

No. of Employees: 60.

RAW MATERIAL SERVICES LLC
500 Nolf Road
Nazareth, PA 18064 USA
P: +1.610.746.3920;
    +1.610.216.8583 (Mobile)
wjmcguire@verizon.net
www.rawmaterialservices.com

- Pres.—William J. McGuire

PRODUCTS and/or SERVICES:
Raw material supply consultation for the steel industry, specializing in coal, metallurgical coke and iron ore (lump, pellets and fines).

RDSTOLZ ENGINEERING LLC
676A Enterprise Dr.
Lewis Center, OH 43035 USA
P: +1.614.890.5704
F: +1.614.259.3201
j.boggs@tepgroup.com

PRODUCTS and/or SERVICES:
Contract engineering/bulk material handling specialists.

No. of Employees: 12.

R.E. WARNER & ASSOCIATES INC.
25777 Detroit Road, Suite 200
Westlake, OH 44145 USA
P: +1.440.835.9400
F: +1.440.835.9474
contactus@rewarner.com
www.rewarner.com

- Pres.—Ted Beltavski
- Vice Pres. Metals Mkt. and Chief Oper. Officer—Frank Johnson
- Project Dir., Engrg.—Ed Dziubek
- Project Mgrs.—Matt Benovic, Jeff Spangler, Jim Lender, Dave Brunner, Jen Kalin

PRODUCTS and/or SERVICES:
Full-service, multi-discipline consulting engineering firm offering professional services in civil, structural, mechanical, piping, electrical engineering, architecture, and surveying to the metal production and processing industry. Engineering services include preliminary, conceptual, and detailed engineering, cost estimates, construction administration and start-up assistance on projects involving material handling, steelmaking, continuous casting, rolling mills and finishing mills. Also offers complete industrial surveying services, precise alignment and elevation of new or existing equipment for a variety of mills, construction surveying, plant and utility locating, geographic information systems (GIS), plant mapping, aerial drone mapping, 3D laser scanning, 3D CAD modeling and point cloud recognition, and 3D laser tracking. Capabilities extend to ferrous, non-ferrous and non-metallic materials. Steel industry experience includes

SUPPLIERS of EQUIPMENT, PRODUCTS and SERVICES

BFs, steelmaking, rolling/hot strip mills, finishing mills, water treatment, facilities, energy management and infrastructure inspection programs.

READING ANTHRACITE CO.
200 Mahantongo St.
Pottsville, PA 17901 USA
P: +1.570.622.5150
F: +1.570.622.2612
www.readinganthracite.com

- Chmn. of the Bd.—John W. Rich Jr.
- Pres.—Brian R. Rich
- Exec. Vice Pres.—Michael Rich
- Vice Pres.—Mark Pishock
- Dir. of Oprs.—Jeffrey A. Gliem
- Gen. Mgr.—Frank Derrick
- Sec.—Robert M. Ryan
- Steel Div. Mgr.—Melissa Jones

EQUIPMENT:
Two dryers on-site, five rail sidings, five processing plants, eight active mine sites.

PRODUCTS and/or SERVICES:
Anthracite injection and charge carbon (high carbon, low sulfur, low volatiles) shipped via truck pneumatic tankers, rail and barge.

No. of Employees: 200.

RED BUD INDUSTRIES
200 B&E Industrial Dr.
Red Bud, IL 62278 USA
P: +1.618.282.3801
rbi@redbudindustries.com
www.redbudindustries.com

- Pres.—Kalin Liefer
- Vice Pres. Mktg. and Sales—Dean Linders

PRODUCTS and/or SERVICES:
Coil processing equipment; CTL and multi-blanking lines; light-, medium- and heavy-gauge slitters; stretcher levelers.

No. of Employees: 200.

REDECAM USA LLC
5970 Fairview Road, Suite 440
Charlotte, NC 28210 USA
P: +1.704.969.8811
redecam.usa@redecam.com
www.redecam.com

- Pres.—Salvatore Gallo
- Dir. of Business Dev.—Niccolò Griffini

PRODUCTS and/or SERVICES:
Baghouse filters, deNOx systems, extreme high-temperature bag filters, wagon tippler bag filter, nuisance filters, multi-input integrated systems ESPS (electrostatic precipitators), deSOx systems, DSI (dry sorbent injection), cyclones, coal mill explosion-proof bag filters, cyclones for DRI material handling, DRI explosion-proof bag filters, coke oven battery bag filters, coke dry quenching cyclone secondary dedusting, ESP secondary dedusting, baghouse waste heat recovery.

No. of Employees: 120.

REDHAWK INDUSTRIES
42-215 Washington St., A #1
Palm Desert, CA 92211 USA
P: +1.800.987.5031 (Toll-Free)
F: +1.800.987.8127 (Toll-Free)
redhawk@redhawkindustriesllc.com
www.redhawkindustriesllc.com

- Principal—Scott Hess

PRODUCTS and/or SERVICES:
Specializes in metal protection for the steel industry. Providing high-quality industrial packaging products used by mills, metal coaters, metal service centers and manufacturers. Redhawk's comprehensive line of products protect material from moisture, corrosion and physical damage during shipping, handling and storage: Plastic ID protection rings, edge protection, poly-weave w/VCI, corrugated plastic donuts, VCI film, desiccant and poly-sheeting.

No. of Employees: 1–10.

FAMOUS READING ANTHRACITE

LEADING THE INDUSTRY SINCE 1871

CHARGE & INJECTION CARBON
(PROUDLY MINED IN THE U.S.A.)

High Carbon
Low Sulfur
Low Volatiles

Request information or a quote:

Melissa Jones, Steel Division Manager
Email: melissaj@racoal.com
C: 570-401-0592

Jeff Gliem, Director of Operations
Email: jeffg@racoal.com
C: 570-640-9940

See listing page 494

SUPPLIERS of EQUIPMENT, PRODUCTS and SERVICES

REDSTONE MACHINERY LLC
44 Skyline Dr.
Plainville, CT 06062 USA
P: +1.860.747.2211
F: +1.860.747.2215
home@redstonemachinery.com
www.redstonemachinery.com

– Pres.—Jay Nyczak

PRODUCTS and/or SERVICES:
Buys and sells secondhand and new steel mill equipment and complete plants internationally. Main groups of equipment include: melting (including remelting), casting, long and flat product rolling, forging, seamless and welded tube manufacturing, cold bar and wire processing, coil processing. Asset liquidation services. Exclusive agent for Nuova Carpenteria Odolese Spa (NCO) for USA and Canada. NCO is a supplier of complete bar mills, rod mills, and related machinery and equipment. Equipment includes reheating furnaces, rolling mills, shears, high-speed bar delivery systems, in-line thermal processing, cooling beds and conveyors, straighteners, coiling and compacting machinery, handling and packaging, roll shop equipment, power and automation, laboratory equipment, auxiliary services (water treatment, hydraulic and lubrication, overhead cranes, etc.). NCO provides installation, start-up, training, maintenance, upgrades and other services.

REGAL REXNORD MOTION CONTROL SOLUTIONS
111 W. Michigan St.
Milwaukee, WI 53045 USA
P: +1.866.739.6673 (Toll-Free Customer Care);
 +1.414.643.3000
www.regalrexnord.com

– Pres. Regal Rexnord MCS—Kevin Zaba
– Vice Pres. Global Sales and Mktg.— Chad Hartley

PRODUCTS and/or SERVICES:
Manufacturer of power transmission gear drives, bearings, couplings, industrial chain, brakes, powertrain drive components, and conveying solutions, including repair and diagnostics. Includes the following brands: Centa, Kop-Flex, Jaure, Rexnord, Falk and Perceptiv.

No. of Employees: 25,000+ worldwide.

REICHARD INDUSTRIES LLC
338 S. Main St.
Columbiana, OH 44408 USA
P: +1.330.482.5511
F: +1.330.482.3743
kreichard@reichardind.com
www.reichardind.com

– Pres.—Keith A. Reichard

EQUIPMENT:
170,000-sq.-ft. manufacturing, heavy fabricating equipment, CNC plate burning machines, plate rolling and forming, 100-ton max. crane, 25-ft. stress-relieving furnace, vertical boring mills up to 25-ft. dia., horizontal boring mills, welding positioner up to 75,000-lb. capacity, 40 ft. x 40 ft. layout floor.

PRODUCTS and/or SERVICES:
Design/build hot metal handling equipment, teeming and transfer ladles (10–350 T), hot metal cars (150–500 T), clamshell scrap buckets, tundishes, ladle transfer cars, bells and hoppers, bosh and tuyere jackets, gas seals, rotating distributors, AOD and BOF vessels/cones, bails, hooks, BOF ductwork, EAF shells, reverse engineering, on-site inspections, FEA, emergency field crew service, contract machinery and fabricating.

No. of Employees: 90.

REINHAUSEN MANUFACTURING INC.
2549 N. 9th Ave.
Humboldt, TN 38343 USA
P: +1.731.784.7681
www.reinhausen.com

– Pres.—Bernhard Kurth

SUPPLIERS OF EQUIPMENT, PRODUCTS and SERVICES

PRODUCTS and/or SERVICES:
Load tap changers and transformer accessories. REINHAUSEN's MR tap-changers are designed for the high output and large number of tap-change operations on the EAF. The VACUTAP® VR I HD vacuum tap-changer, for example, delivers 600,000 tap change operations without maintenance and only requires a new diverter switch insert after 1.2 million tap-change operations. REINHAUSEN also supplies transformer accessories that withstand the tough conditions experienced in the steel works and monitor the safe and long-term operation of the furnace transformer.

REMIOR INDUSTRIES INC.
9165 N.W. 96th St.
Medley, FL 33178 USA
P: +1.305.883.8722
F: +1.305.883.9534
remior@bellsouth.net
www.remiorindustries.com

- Pres.—Lazaro R. Remior
- Exec. Vice Pres. and Treas.—Emilio Remior
- Vice Pres. and Sec.—Marta L. Remior
- Vice Pres. Prodn./Mfg.—Felix J. Robles
- Sales Mgr.—Roly Remior
- Asst. Sales Mgr. and Pur. Agt.—Jennifer Remior
- Pur. Agt.—Julia Vizcardo

PRODUCTS and/or SERVICES:
Manufacture and install miscellaneous metals products: steel stairs, railings, columns, fences, gates and others.

No. of Employees: 20.

RENOLD INC.
100 Bourne St.
Westfield, NY 14787 USA
P: +1.716.326.3121
F: +1.716.326.8229
www.renoldajax.com

- Chief Exec. Officer—Robert Purcell
- Pres.—Mike Conley
- Vice Pres. Prodn./Mfg.—Don Ellison
- Treas.—Kevin McCann
- Sales Mgr.—Kelly Boser

- Regional Sales Mgrs.—Tom Burleton, David Werther
- Pur. Agt.—Angelyn Achilles
- Chief Engr.—David Zebrak

PRODUCTS and/or SERVICES:
Spindles, couplings, universal joints, special gearing and gearboxes, elastomeric couplings, clutches.

No. of Employees: 50.

REXA INC.
4 Manley St.
West Bridgewater, MA 02379 USA
P: +1.508.584.1199
sales@rexa.com
www.rexa.com

PRODUCTS and/or SERVICES:
Designs and manufactures self-contained, closed-loop electrohydraulic valve actuators and damper drives for critical applications throughout the metals processing industry.

RFTS LLC
P.O. Box 161
Lempster, NH 03605 USA
P: +1.203.927.6545
rftsii@aol.com
www.linkedin.com/in/louisnizet

- Pres.—Louis Nizet

PRODUCTS and/or SERVICES:
Capital investment equipment for metallurgical industries, including metal rolling mills and related processing equipment, peripheral and related spares parts, including rolling mill (2-hi, 4-hi, 6-hi and 20-hi cluster, Z-hi mills, bonding mills and wire mills), process lines (zero-burr slitter, CTL, blanking, TLL, galv), thickness gauges (on-line and profile), flatness control shapemeters, mill rolls (hot and cold) and process rolls, chocks and bearings, knives and shear blades, strip degreasing, cleaning and wiping systems, industrial bearings, 20-hi (Z mill) cluster mills backing assemblies and related spares. Also provides aluminum casthouse equipment and automation.

SUPPLIERS of EQUIPMENT, PRODUCTS and SERVICES

RGS MILL PRODUCTS CORP.
4622 N. 52 W
P.O. Box 1597
La Porte, IN 46350 USA
P: +1.219.326.5000
F: +1.219.326.5001
rgsmill@frontier.com

- Pres.—James N. Donnelly
- Treas.—Susan Mlekush
- Chief Engr.—Rob Conn

PRODUCTS and/or SERVICES: Designer and manufacturer of descaling hoods for hot strip, plate, bar, and structural mills. Furnace charge door assemblies (Flexi panels) for pusher and WB reheat furnaces. Services include: parts support, field engineering, engineering studies, installation supervision and CADD.

No. of Employees: 8.

RHI MAGNESITA
Kranichberggasse 6
Vienna, 1120 Austria
P: +43.50213.0
F: +43.5021236213
www.rhimagnesita.com

PRODUCTS and/or SERVICES: Global supplier of high-grade refractory products, systems and services for industrial high-temperature processes exceeding 1,200°C in a wide range of industries, including steel, cement, non-ferrous metals and glass, among others. Vertically integrated value chain, from raw materials to refractory products and full performance-based solutions. The company has more than 12,000 employees in 28 main production sites and more than 70 sales offices.

RITTERTECH, A Div. of Motion & Control Enterprises
100 Williams Dr.
Zelienople, PA 16063 USA
P: +1.724.452.6000
F: +1.724.452.0766
www.mceautomation.com

Service Centers: Zelienople, PA; Erie, PA; Pewaukee, WI; Mokena, IL; Warren, MI; Clinton Twp., MI; Hammond, IN; Munster, IN.

- Chief Exec. Officer—Charley Hale
- Chief Sales and Mktg. Officer—Ben Hensler
- Eastern Regional Sales Mgr.—Tony Ramey
- Western/Central Regional Sales Mgr.—Tim Hake
- Connector Sales Dir.—Joe Jelinek
- Tech. Sales Dir.—Steve Taylor
- Chief Financial Officer—Michelle Burnettee

PRODUCTS and/or SERVICES: Hydraulic, pneumatic, filtration and lubrication components featuring Parker Hannifin products. Complete design, consultation, assembly and installation services for fluid power systems. Evaluation and repairs of hydraulic and lubrication components. Industrial lubrication equipment featuring Graco (Trabon) grease, oil and air/oil. Hydraulic industrial tool and workholding products through Enerpac.

No. of Employees: 150.

RMI — RAW MATERIALS AND IRONMAKING GLOBAL CONSULTING
1992 Easthill Dr.
Bethlehem, PA 18017 USA
P: +1.610.442.3527 (Mobile)
joe.poveromo@rawmaterialsiron.com
joe.poveromo@gmail.com

- Pres.—Joseph J. Poveromo

PRODUCTS and/or SERVICES: Consulting on impact of raw materials (ferrous, coke, flux) on ironmaking operations; ironmaking process economics; technical marketing of ironmaking raw materials and services on a global basis; technical and economic evaluation including market studies of iron ore mining properties, iron ore-based metallics (pig iron, HBI, DRI), agglomeration facilities;

SUPPLIERS OF EQUIPMENT, PRODUCTS and SERVICES

alternative ironmaking (including direct reduction) evaluations.

No. of Employees: 1.

RNP INDUSTRIES INC.
112 Prevost Blvd.
Boisbriand, QC J7G 2S2 Canada
P: +1.888.697.5355
F: +1.450.537.2651
frank.pieters@rnpind.com
www.rnpind.com

- Pres.—Frank Pieters
- Vice Pres.—Michelle Boudreau
- Chief Engr.—Danny Morisette

PRODUCTS and/or SERVICES:
Semi-robotic arm for chipping out slag and foundry brick.

No. of Employees: 10.

ROSER TECHNOLOGIES INC.
347 E. Industrial Dr.
Titusville, PA 16354 USA
P: +1.814.827.7717
F: +1.814.827.7742
tkelly@rosertech.com

- Chief Exec. Officer and Pres.—Jack A. Roser
- Chief Oper. Officer—Thomas R. Kelly
- Chief Financial Officer—Samuel R. Swartzfager
- Vice Pres. Oprs.—Chad M. Nicewonger
- Vice Pres. Engrg.—Timothy G. Kritikos
- Tech. Acct. Mgrs.—Thomas A. Beres, Scott M. Watkins
- Qual. Mgr.—Zack Hutchinson

EQUIPMENT:
Large machining capacity, nickel and copper electroplating, HVOF spray coating of continuous caster liner plates.

PRODUCTS and/or SERVICES:
Continuous caster mold and segment manufacture and repair. Large-component fabrication and machining. Roll overlay and machining.

No. of Employees: 100.

Vertical Seal Co.
162 Chapman Road
Pleasantville, PA 16341 USA
P: +1.814.589.7031
F: +1.814.589.7628

- Chief Exec. Officer and Pres.—Jack A. Roser
- Chief Oper. Officer—Thomas R. Kelly
- Chief Financial Officer—Samuel R. Swartzfager
- Vice Pres. Oprs.—Chad M. Nicewonger
- Bearing Dept. Plant Mgr./Sales—Jack Kennedy
- Bearing Dept. Mgr.—Chris Lindquist
- Tech. Acct. Mgrs.—Benjamin Remaley, Ryan Smith

EQUIPMENT:
Centrifugal cast babbitting machines; custom dual-head CNC vertical grinder for roll sleeves; bushing expander; vertical and horizontal lathes and grinders; milling machines.

PRODUCTS and/or SERVICES:
New and reconditioned oil film bearing sleeves and bushings (Mesta, Iverson, Morgoil, etc.). Babbitting of bushings, pinion stands, turbine and generator bearings, wear parts. Repair and manufacture of roll bearing chocks. Replacement parts for oil film bearings.

No. of Employees: 65.

ROSS CONTROLS
950 Woodward Heights
Ferndale, MI 48220 USA
P: +1.248.764.1800
bob.winsand@rosscontrols.com
www.rosscontrols.com

- Chief Exec. Officer and Pres.—Jeff Hand
- Global Product Mgr., Poppet Tech—Bob Winsand
- New Projects, Panels and Systems—Kirk Bolton
- Vice Pres. Global Safety Dev.—Chris Brogli
- Mgr. Safety Dev. (Americas)—Eric Cummings
- Vice Pres. Global Engrg.—Jay Dalal

SUPPLIERS of EQUIPMENT, PRODUCTS and SERVICES

- Vice Pres. Sales (Americas)—Don Swanson
- Tech. Svce.—Mike Kramer, Jon Jolly

PRODUCTS and/or SERVICES:
Global leader in fluid power safety. Designs and manufactures pneumatic and hydraulic solutions for the iron and steel industry. Based in the USA, ROSS also has full-service design and manufacturing locations in Germany, Japan, China, France, India, Brazil and the U.K. ROSS' mill-duty product range includes: turnkey control panels, control reliable safety valves, proportional technology, EnergySaver® systems, LOTO valves, directional control POPPET valves, heavy-duty flow controls, manual lever valves, baghouse and dust collection systems, and air preparation equipment.

ROTATOR PRODUCTS LTD.
101 Innovation Dr., Unit 8
Woodbridge, ON L4H 0S3 Canada
P: +1.905.856.2653
F: +1.905.856.3407
sales@rotatorproducts.com
www.rotatorproducts.com

- Pres.—Ajay Bajaj
- Contr.—Fanny Ko
- Pur. Agt.—Susan Russell
- Tech. Support—Satish Nathan

PRODUCTS and/or SERVICES:
Lenze, Delta and Siemens drives, oil skimmers, Enidine and Jarret shock absorbers, Magnetek crane controls, Dellner Bubenzer and Mondel brakes, Galvi polyurethane bumpers, GMT rubber bumpers, Ringfeder locking devices, Falk/Rexnord couplings and gearboxes, Ringfeder clutches and couplings, Hycomp carbon fiber self-lubricating bushings, Brother gearboxes and Geared motors, Conductix-Wampfler conductor bars, cable festoon, and cable reels. Duff Norton actuators, Reuland AC motors, Eaton Cutler Hammer contactors. Filnor: disconnect switches, power resistors, fuse blocks. Gear couplings, disc couplings, torsionally soft couplings, load limiters for cranes. EPC and Huebner encoders.

ROVISYS
1455 Danner Dr.
Aurora, OH 44202 USA
P: +1.330.995.8169
www.rovisys.com

PRODUCTS and/or SERVICES:
Global systems integration and software development company. Automation partner for new installations, upgrades and legacy migrations. Experience with level 1, 2 and 3 systems as well as the latest historians and MES. Provides turnkey, single-source solutions for metals production, from the process through management reports.

R.T. PATTERSON CO. INC.
230 Third Ave.
Pittsburgh, PA 15222 USA
P: +1.412.227.6600
F: +1.412.227.6614
pgh-info@rtpatterson.com
www.rtpatterson.com

- Pres.—W. Johnson
- Gen. Mgr. Engrg.—L. Friedline

PRODUCTS and/or SERVICES:
Multi-disciplined engineering and consulting services. Preparation of: feasibility and development studies; cost analysis, design concepts, facilities planning, field and structural inspections; project management; design and construction engineering; equipment and construction specifications; construction and cost control services; CPM Primavera scheduling; CADD services; PLC/control system services and simulation software.

Crown Point Office
2080 N. Main St., Suite 1
Crown Point, IN 46307 USA
P: +1.219.838.2500
F: +1.219.838.2555
cpi-info@rtpatterson.com

SUPPLIERS OF EQUIPMENT, PRODUCTS and SERVICES

Evansville Office
6500 Interchange Road S
Evansville, IN 47715 USA
P: +1.812.473.8654
F: +1.812.473.8658
evv-info@rtpatterson.com

East Moline, IL Office
1033 7th St., Suite 4
East Moline, IL 61244 USA
P: +1.309.203.1928
mli-info@rtpatterson.com

RUBICON REFRACTORIES INC.
5028 Columbia Ave.
Hammond, IN 46327 USA
P: +1.219.932.4152
F: +1.219.932.6533
www.rubiconrefractories.com

- Pres.—Thomas J. Schwer
- Vice Pres. and Sec.—Lisa M. Schwer

EQUIPMENT:
Buildings: one 85,000 sq. ft., one 3,000 sq. ft. Mixers: one 7,500-lb. mixer; two 1,500-lb. mixers. Overhead cranes: one 15-ton, on 10-ton, one 5-ton, one 2-ton. Trucks: one tractor trailer, one 32,000-lb.-capacity straight. Two convection ovens capable of treating shapes over 20 tons, measuring 20 ft. x 30 ft. x 12 ft.; steel fabrication complete with CNC plasma burning and rolling equipment.

PRODUCTS and/or SERVICES:
Steel: EAF deltas/donuts, stir and injection lances, ladle bottoms, ladle lip rings, ladle covers, tundish covers, tundish linings, castable materials, various roofs, fume hoods, pre-heat walls and covers, EAF runners, breast blocks, BF runners/spouts, BF covers and other various pre-cast shapes. Foundry: ladle inserts and various shapes. Coke oven: doors, lintels and other various shapes.

No. of Employees: 30.

RUHLIN CO., THE
6931 Ridge Road
Sharon Center, OH 44274 USA
P: +1.330.239.2800
F: +1.330.239.1828
gseanor@ruhlin.com
www.ruhlin.com

- Chief Exec. Officer and Pres.—Jim Ruhlin
- Treas.—Sean Demlow
- Business Dev. Mgr. and Sales Mgr.—Don Rife
- Gen. Mgr., Ind. Div.—George Seanor

PRODUCTS and/or SERVICES:
Heavy industrial construction in the steel industry. Self-performed construction services include, but are not limited to: design-build services, demolition, excavation, bearing and sheet piling, concrete work, foundations, structural steel erection, structural steel rehabilitation, precision equipment installation, vessel repair, coupling, alignment, equipment repair, rigging, and machinery moving.

No. of Employees: 350.

RUSSULA CORP.
559 Main St., Unit 202
Fiskdale, MA 01518 USA
P: +1.774.452.4411
sales@russulacorp.com
www.russula.com

- Chief Exec. Officer—Keith Fiorucci
- Mktg. Mgr.—Mary House
- Regional Dir. of Sales—Fermin de la Maza

EQUIPMENT:
AC and DC drives, DC drive rebuilds, mechanical and electrical/automation equipment for rod, bar and section mills, reheat furnaces, water treatment facilities.

PRODUCTS and/or SERVICES:
Engineering equipment and services for steel industry, industrial water treatment plants and process improvement/consulting.

No. of Employees: 220 worldwide, 12 in U.S.

SUPPLIERS of EQUIPMENT, PRODUCTS and SERVICES

S

SAFETY LAMP OF HOUSTON INC.
1816 Rotary Dr.
Humble, TX 77338 USA
P: +1.281.964.1019
F: +1.281.964.1040
www.safetylampofhouston.com

- Gen. Mgr.—J.C. Reeves
- Pres.—Deborah A. Reeves

PRODUCTS and/or SERVICES:
Wolf low-voltage pneumatic lamps for hazardous areas, wet areas, caster spray chambers, rolling mills and coke ovens.

SAINT-GOBAIN PERFORMANCE CERAMICS & REFRACTORIES
Plant 6, 1 New Bond St.
Worcester, MA 01606 USA
P: +1.508.795.5264
ceramics.refractories@saint-gobain.com
www.ceramicsrefractories.saint-gobain.com

PRODUCTS and/or SERVICES:
Design, development and production of engineered ceramics and refractory products for extreme operating conditions and high-temperature industrial applications. Provides full design and supply of refractories for the BF and operations downstream of the BF, including taphole mixes, concretes for trough and runners, and alumina silicon carbide carbon bricks for torpedo ladles. Engineered ceramic burner solutions for industrial heating applications, including custom-built products designed to meet customers' needs.

SALEM-REPUBLIC RUBBER CO.
475 W. California Ave.
Sebring, OH 44672 USA
P: +1.800.686.4199 (Toll-Free);
   +1.330.938.9801
F: +1.330.938.9809
sholt@salem-republic.com
www.salem-republic.com

- Pres.—Drew Ney
- Dir. of Sales and Mktg.—Sarah Holt

PRODUCTS and/or SERVICES:
High-temperature fiberglass-covered rubber hose for water cooling of the EAF roof, EAF shell and EAF electrode arm. Manufactures furnace door hose, power cable assembly cover hoses, gunite hose, carbon powder injection hose, oxygen charging hose, spool pieces and expansion joints, and all types of hose with flanged ends.

SANGRAF INTERNATIONAL INC.
Global Headquarters:
3171 Independence Dr.
Livermore, CA 94551 USA
P: +1.216.800.9999
livermore@sangrafintl.com
johannesburg@sangrafintl.com
sao-paulo@sangrafintl.com
geneva@sangrafintl.com
www.sangrafintl.com

PRODUCTS and/or SERVICES:
Fully integrated global manufacturer of premium graphite electrodes for the steel, ferrous and non-ferrous metal industries. SANGRAF is exclusively dedicated to graphite electrodes. With offices and manufacturing in major steel-producing areas of the world (Livermore, CA, USA; Geneva, Switzerland; Johannesburg, South Africa; São Paulo, Brazil; Beijing, P.R. China; and Wan Chai, Hong Kong), SANGRAF provides lean supply chain solutions, local support and dedicated service teams.

SANYO SEIKI CO. LTD.
Hamasaki 1-2-8-7F
Asaka, Saitama, 3510033 Japan
P: +81.48.486.1100
F: +81.48.486.1101
h-watanabe@sanyoseiki.co.jp
www.sanyoseiki.co.jp/en

From Narni, Italy, to the North American Market

SANGRAF
INTERNATIONAL

BRINGING YOU QUALITY ELECTRODES AND UNMATCHED TECHNICAL SERVICE

OPERATIONAL HEADQUARTERS
LIVERMORE, CALIFORNIA

INTERNATIONAL SALES OFFICES
JOHANNESBURG, SOUTH AFRICA | SÃO PAULO, BRAZIL | GENEVA, SWITZERLAND
HONG KONG | BEIJING, CHINA

UHP GRAPHITE ELECTRODES UP-TO 30"

SANGRAF International is a fully integrated global manufacturer of UHP graphite electrodes for the steel, ferrous and non-ferrous metal industries.

SANGRAF International provides:

» Global Technical Team with *Real* Industry Expertise «
» Global Footprint with Manufacturing in *both Asia and Europe* «

3171 Independence Dr. | Livermore, CA 94551
USA +1 216 800 9999 | sangrafintl.com

See listing page 502

SUPPLIERS of EQUIPMENT, PRODUCTS and SERVICES

- Engrg. Dir.—Kenichi Harano
- Mfg. Dir.—Hisashi Mori
- Sales Dir.—Takeshi Takiguchi
- Sales Mgr.—Tomoyuki Katoh
- Overseas Sales Mgr.—Hiro Watanabe

EQUIPMENT:
40 CNC machines, three vacuum furnaces.

PRODUCTS and/or SERVICES:
Forming rolls for welded tube/pipe mills. All raw materials used for products are forged in Japan.

No. of Employees: 190.

SST Forming Roll Inc.
1318 Busch Pkwy.
Buffalo Grove, IL 60089 USA
P: +1.847.215.6812
info@sstformingroll.com
www.sanyoseiki.co.jp/english

- Pres.—T. Takiguchi
- Gen. Mgr. of Oprs.—Stan Green
- Gen. Mgr. of Engrg.—Rick Yamashita

PRODUCTS and/or SERVICES:
Forming roll, straightener roll, feed roll, FEA analysis. Sanyo Seiki and SST have a design team consisting of more than 20 engineers and offer FEA with six units located in the U.S. and Japan.

No. of Employees: 10.

SARCLAD NORTH AMERICA LP
317 E. Carson St., Suite 241
Pittsburgh, PA 15219 USA
P: +1.412.466.2000
sales@sarclad.com
www.sarclad.com

PRODUCTS and/or SERVICES:
Rollscan—eddy current and ultrasonic surface and subsurface inspection equipment for flat product mill rolls. Rolltex—EDT (electrodischarge texturing) Multi Servo Array machines for strip mill rolls. Strand condition monitors—fully automated in-chain systems and off-line continuous caster measuring sleds for gap, alignment, spray, bend, roll condition.

SARCO (SOUTH AFRICAN ROLL CO. PTY. LTD.)
8 Mc Colm Blvd.
Vanderbijlpark, Gauten
1900 South Africa
P: +27.16.910.7000
F: +27.16.986.0660
marketing@sarco.co.za
www.sarco.co.za

- Chief Exec. Officer—Harold Pretorius
- Sales Mgr.—Stephanus van der Walt

EQUIPMENT:
Six main-frequency induction furnaces, with a total melting capacity of 86 metric tons. Horizontal spin-cast machine. Sand reclamation plant with four continuous sand mixers. Six large capper (top hat) furnaces and two bogie hearth furnaces. Roll machine shop with roughing lathes, CNC lathes and double-head milling machines.

PRODUCTS and/or SERVICES:
Cast rolls and sleeves for steel mills. Spin-cast rolls (600–840 mm dia.): ICDP, HSS and HiCr rolls. Static-cast rolls (280–1,600 mm dia., max. weight of 86 metric tons): alloy cast steel, graphitic steel, nodular cast iron (pearlitic, bainitic and acicular). Ferrous casting ranging from 5–60 metric tons for the general engineering market.

No. of Employees: 120.

SARGENT ELECTRIC CO.
2740 Smallman St.
Pittsburgh, PA 15222 USA
P: +1.412.391.0588
www.sargentelectric.com

- Pres.—Rob Smith
- Chief Oper. Officer—Denis St. Pierre
- Chief Financial Officer—Beth Lawrence
- Div. Mgr. Pittsburgh—Ben Patton
- Safety—Matthew J. Babilon
- Util. Div. Mgr. Columbus, OH—Joe Ebersbach, P: +1.949.413.8518

PRODUCTS and/or SERVICES:
Serves all segments of the iron and steel industry, and offers a full range of electrical project management, design/build and construction management

Sargent Electric Company

Proudly Serving the Iron & Steel Industry since 1907.

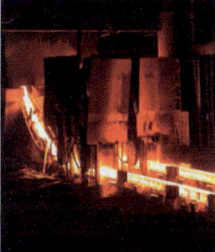

Pittsburgh, PA
412.391.0588

Northwest, IN
219.397.0133

De Pere, WI
920.413.5353

Columbus, OH
380.400.3200

Lewiston, ME
207.815.5252

Sargent Electric Company provides a full range of Electrical, Instrumentation, Wireless, and TeleData services for:

- Grassroots Projects
- Major Capital Projects
- In-Plant Projects
- Blanket Maintenance Agreements
- Outages / Turnarounds
- 24/7 Emergency Call-Outs

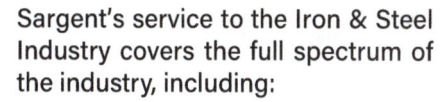

Sargent's service to the Iron & Steel Industry covers the full spectrum of the industry, including:

- Blast Furnaces
- Casters
- Rolling Mills
- Furnace Re-Lines
- Finishing Lines
- Power & Utilities
- Pipe Mills
- Rebuilds
- Iron Ore Processing

@SargentElectric

www.sargentelectric.com

See listing page 504

SUPPLIERS of EQUIPMENT, PRODUCTS and SERVICES

services. Provides electrical, instrumentation, wireless, fiber optic and teledata services for industries including oil and gas (upstream, midstream and downstream), power generation (nuclear, coal, gas, renewables and hydroelectric), power transmission and distribution, chemical/petrochemical, industrial, communications, commercial, heavy highway and rail, water, as well as operations and maintenance services (24/7 call-out and in-plant) for all sectors. Sargent serves strategic customers nationwide from offices in Pittsburgh, PA; East Chicago, IN; Green Bay, WI; Columbus, OH; and Lewiston, ME.

Northwest Indiana (NWI) Office
601 E. Chicago Ave.
East Chicago, IN 46312 USA
P: +1.219.397.0133

- Div. Mgr.—Tim Baker

SARRALLE EQUIPOS SIDERURGICOS
S.L. Barrio Landeta, apdo. 1
Azpeitia, 20730 Spain
P: +34.943.157088
F: +34.943.157290
sarralle@sarralle.com
www.sarralle.com

- Area Sales Mgr.—Eduardo Bilbao
- Proposal Engrg. Mgr.—Aitor Odriozola

PRODUCTS and/or SERVICES: Proprietary engineering and equipment supplier with several fabricating workshops focused on the steel industry. Sarralle offers equipment, metallurgical, field and construction technical services, including: EAFs, LFs, VDs and VODs, continuous casters (billet/bloom/slabs), rolling mills, finishing and processing lines, as well as auxiliary plants including fume dedusting, ferroalloy handling systems, and water treatment plants.

No. of Employees: 400.

North American Office:
Sarralle USA
210 Sixth Ave.
Pittsburgh, PA 15222 USA
P: +1.412.418.4129
akurzinski@sarralleusa.com
www.sarralle.com

- Dir. of Sales North America—Alan D. Kurzinski

SCANTECH INTERNATIONAL PTY. LTD.
143 Mooringe Ave.
Camden Park, South Australia, 5038 Australia
P: +61.88.350.0200
F: +61.88.350.0188
sales@scantech.com.au
www.scantech.com.au

- Chief Exec. Officer—David Lindeberg
- Chief Tech. Officer—Luke Balzan
- Chief Mktg. Officer—Henry Kurth
- Chief Financial Officer—Valerie Steer
- Vice Pres. Engrg.—Adrian Bridgland
- Vice Pres. Prodn./Mfg.—Mark Triggs
- Sales Mgr.—Andrew Brodie
- North American Svce. Engr.—Alex Bartle-Smith

PRODUCTS and/or SERVICES: GEOSCAN and COALSCAN elemental analyzer range, TBM and CM 100 moisture analyzer range, SizeScan PSD/volume analyzer, manufacturing and service support of analyzers for cokemaking, ironmaking and steelmaking.

No. of Employees: 40.

SCHENCK PROCESS LLC
7901 NW 107th Terrace
Kansas City, MO 64153 USA
P: +1.816.891.9300
cmm-sales@schenckprocess.com
www.schenckprocess.com

- Pres.—Jay Brown
- Sr. Vice Pres.—Dan Gilman
- Sales Dir.—Brad Suter
- Mktg. Mgr.—Laura Hanley

SUPPLIERS OF EQUIPMENT, PRODUCTS and SERVICES

EQUIPMENT:
Weighing, feeding, pneumatic injection, dense phase pneumatic conveying and filtration.

PRODUCTS and/or SERVICES:
Weighfeeders, crane scales, ladle weighing scales, load cells, valves, rail weighing systems, pressure vessels, parts and services.

No. of Employees: 550.

SCHENK VISION
1830 Wooddale Dr., Suite 500
Woodbury, MN 55125 USA
P: +1.651.730.4090
F: +1.651.730.1955
schenkmarcon@yahoo.com
www.schenkvision.com

- Chief Exec. Officer—Jochen Koenig
- Vice Pres. Sales—Chris Toepfert
- Sales Mgr.—Mark Cornell

PRODUCTS and/or SERVICES:
EasyInspect automatic optical surface inspection system for metal inspection Together with EasyMeasure, EasyInspect for metal inspection continuously optimizes the complete metal production process.

No. of Employees: 25.

SCHNEIDER ELECTRIC
35 rue Joseph Monier
Rueil-Malmaison, Ile-de-France, 92500 France
P: +1.877.342.5173
mo.ahmed@se.com
www.schneider-electric.com/en/work/solutions/for-business/metals

- Chief Exec. Officer—Jean-Pascal Tricoire

PRODUCTS and/or SERVICES:
Global manufacturer and supplier of energy and automation hardware, software and services. Brands: Modicon PACs, Wonderware SCADA, Foxboro safety PLCs, Altivar variable speed drives, Premset MV switchgear, Aveva industrial software, Square D, Telemecanique and more. Products: MV switchgear, LV/MV drives, transformers, LV power distribution products, intelligent MCC, energy management/energy efficiency systems, asset performance management, PLCs, SCADA, autonomous crane automation, integrated plant automation systems, process optimization, digitalization, AR/VR applications for workforce efficiency (training and maintenance), data centers, UPS, harmonic filters, and more. Services: Cybersecurity risk analysis and mitigation, energy efficiency audits, control systems modernization and migration, asset performance management, remote condition monitoring, electrical distribution risk assessment, power management, power systems engineering, energy purchasing programs, renewable energy projects, and more.

No. of Employees: 140,000.

SCHONSHECK INC.
50555 Pontiac Trail
Wixom, MI 48393 USA
P: +1.248.669.8800
www.schonsheck.com

- Pres.—Kent Burzynski
- Vice Pres.—Ron Kuznicki

PRODUCTS and/or SERVICES:
Design-build, general contracting, and supply-erect services for heavy industrial/crane buildings and operation/office facilities.

No. of Employees: 13.

SCHUST
4483 County Road 19
Auburn, IN 46706 USA
P: +1.260.925.6550
info@schust.com
www.schust.com

- Pres.—John Rothermel
- Vice Pres. Tech. Resources—Keith Blair
- Vice Pres. Engrg.—Ty Knox

SUPPLIERS of EQUIPMENT, PRODUCTS and SERVICES

PRODUCTS and/or SERVICES:
Turnkey dust collection/ventilation systems; specialty hooding systems; engineering studies and environmental audits; baghouse upgrades, maintenance and sheet metal fabrication/installation.

No. of Employees: 90.

Pittsburgh Office
1639 Pine Hollow Road, Suite A
McKees Rocks, PA 15136 USA
P: +1.412.771.8850
info@schust.com

Schust Mexico
Lázaro Cárdenas No. 2321 Pte (Piso 3)
Col. Residencial San Agustin
San Pedro Garza García, NL,
66260 Mexico
P: +011.52.811.001.6983
juan@schustmexico.com

SEAUD SRL
Strada dei Pioppi 29
Remanzacco (UD), I-33047 Italy
P: +39.0432.667194
F: +39.0432.668266
sea@seaud.it

- Pres.—Augusto Casarin
- Vice Pres. and Sales Mgr.—Giovanni Casarin
- Pur. Agt.—F.E.T. Casarin

EQUIPMENT:
Modern CNC workshop for machining and assembly of machines. Warehouse for secondhand equipment.

PRODUCTS and/or SERVICES:
Dealer of secondhand machines for the steel industry: peeling, straightening, grinding machines, combined drawing machines, etc.

No. of Employees: 15.

SEIRIS
Chemin de la Julienne
Le Coudray-Montceaux, 91830 France
P: +33.1.69.01.33.33
F: +33.1.69.01.33.33
contact@seiris-sa.com
www.seiris-sa.com

- Sales Mgr.—Baptiste Boucharel

PRODUCTS and/or SERVICES:
Fabric expansion joints, metallic expansion joints, rubber expansion joints, PTFE expansion joints, flexible hoses.

No. of Employees: 50.

SELAS HEAT TECHNOLOGY CO. LLC
11012 Aurora-Hudson Road
Streetsboro, OH 44241 USA
P: +1.800.523.6500 (Toll-Free);
   +1.216.662.8800
F: +1.216.663.8954
sales@selas.com
www.selas.com

PRODUCTS and/or SERVICES:
Combustion control equipment, pre-mix/nozzle mix burners, regulators, flow control, package burners, radiant tubes, recuperative burners. Combustion control systems, pre-mix/nozzle mix burners, regulators, flow control systems, combustion safety devices, infrared burners, ribbon burners, boiler burners, fuel-saving devices.

SEMAC LLC
2345 167th St.
Hammond, IN 46323 USA
P: +1.219.934.0559
info@semacmachinery.com
www.semacmachinery.com

- Gen. Mgr.—John Hall
- Sales Mgr.—William Rashin

PRODUCTS and/or SERVICES:
Design, manufacture and implementation of custom industrial machinery. Provides new equipment, existing equipment upgrades, feasibility/engineering studies, and build-to-print/spare parts. Provides innovative solutions for improved safety, reliability, efficiency, productivity and increased overall profitability to the end user.

No. of Employees: 12.

SUPPLIERS OF EQUIPMENT, PRODUCTS and SERVICES

SEMPER EXETER PAPER CO.
2617 Legends Way
Crestview Hills, KY 41017 USA
P: +1.210.373.3397
vquinones@semperexeter.com
www.semperexeter.com

- Sales Mgr.—Rob Webster Jr.
- Regional Sales Mgr.—Vic Quinones

PRODUCTS and/or SERVICES:
Supplier of industrial protective packaging solutions for the steel and metals industry. Products include steel wrap, VCI stretch film, edge protectors (paper/plastic), interleaving paper, surface protection films, desiccants and more.

No. of Employees: 100.

SENNEBOGEN LLC
1957 Sennebogen Trail
Stanley, NC 28164 USA
P: +1.704.347.4910
F: +1.704.347.8894
sales@sennebogen-na.com
www.sennebogen-na.com

- Pres.—Constantino Lannes
- Regional Business Mgrs.—Billy Miller, David LaFleur, Gerry Beaulieu, Greg Roberts, Jacob Storedahl, James Gonzalez, Kyle Barton, Max Tratar, Michael Carpenter, Mike Furda, Nate House, Ryan Zenor, Scott Robertson, Stephen Davidson
- Sales Mgr.—Colleen Miller
- Svce. Mgr.—Paul Quistorff
- Parts and Traffic Mgr.—Jason Ellenberger
- Mktg. Mgr.—Ryan Kolb

PRODUCTS and/or SERVICES:
SENNEBOGEN purpose-built material handling equipment. Operating wt.: 818 M "E"—48,060 lbs.; 818 R-HD "E"—55,115 lbs.; 818 Stationary "E"—66,000 lbs.; 821 M "E"—52,800 lbs.; 821 R-HD "E"—57,982 lbs.; 821 Stationary "E"—66,000 lbs.; 825 M "E"—57,600 lbs.; 825 R-HD "E"—66,000 lbs.; 825 Stationary—66,000 lbs.; 830 M "E"—84,900 lbs.; 830 M-HD "E"—88,185 lbs.; 830 M-HD-S "E"—90,390 lbs.; 830 M-T "E"—91,300 lbs.; 830 R-HD "E"—96,780 lbs.; 830 R-HDD "E"—96,780 lbs.; 830 Stationary "E"—118,000 lbs.; 835 M "E"—100,000 lbs.; 835 R-HD "E"—120,151 lbs.; 835 Stationary "E"—162,800 lbs.; 840 M "E"—100,000 lbs.; 840 R-HD "E"—130,072 lbs.; 850 M "E"—142,600 lbs.; 850 R-HD "E"—151,016 lbs.; 850 Stationary "E"—193,600 lbs.; Green Hybrid 855 M "E"—169,756 lbs.; Green Hybrid 855 R-HD "E"—182,984 lbs.; Green Hybrid 860 M "E"—169,756 lbs.; Green Hybrid 860 R-HD "E"—192,905,000 lbs.; Green Hybrid 860 Stationary "E"—227,000 lbs.; 870 M "E"—203,900 lbs.; 870 R-HD "E"—205,690 lbs.; 870 Stationary "E"—246,400 lbs.; 875 M "E"—308,644 lbs.; 875 R-HD "E"—308,644 lbs.; 895 Hybrid M "E"—780,000 lbs.; 895 Hybrid R-HD "E"—780,000 lbs.; 895 Hybrid Rail "E"—780,000 lbs.; 6100HD DB—221,000 lbs.; 6180HD DB—398,000 lbs.; 8100 EQ Crawler "E"—284,396 lbs.; 8100 EQ Stationary "E"—283,800–310,200 lbs.; 8130 EQ Crawler "E"—310,852 lbs.; 8130 EQ Stationary "E"—283,800–310,200 lbs.; 8160 EQ Crawler "E"—363,763 lbs.; 8160 EQ Stationary "E"—363,000 lbs.; 8320 EQ Crawler "E"—573,202 lbs.; 8320 EQ Stationary "E"—573,202 lbs.; 8400 EQ Crawler "E"—705,479 lbs.; 8400 EQ Stationary "E"—705,479 lbs.

SENTEK CORP.
1300 Memory Lane N
Columbus, OH 43209 USA
P: +1.614.586.1123
F: +1.614.586.1192
info@sentekcorp.com
www.sentekcorp.com

- Pres.—Niklas Almstedt
- Exec. Vice Pres.—Ann Almstedt

PRODUCTS and/or SERVICES:
Gauging and shape systems, thickness and coat weight gauges, x-ray and isotope sensors and sources, inductive work roll heating at strip edges, gauge mechanical refits, rolling mill troubleshooting, gauge alignment

SUPPLIERS of EQUIPMENT, PRODUCTS and SERVICES

and calibration, sealed-source leak testing, electronics upgrades, obsolete component solutions, NIST-traceable sample certification.

SES LLC (STEEL EQUIPMENT SPECIALISTS)
1507 Beeson St.
Alliance, OH 44601 USA
P: +1.330.821.3322
F: +1.330.821.6350
ses@seseng.com
www.seseng.com

- Pres.—James R. Boughton
- Chief Exec. Officer—Rich C. Retort
- Chief Oper. Officer—Tim Hostetler
- Chief Financial Officer—Scott E. Stedman
- Chief Business Officer—Steve Sirota
- Vice Pres. Engineered Equip. Sales—Jason Erb
- Vice Pres. Outside Sales—Dan Cullen
- Vice Pres. Technology—Tim Rohde
- Vice Pres. Redesign and Rebuild—David Woy

PRODUCTS and/or SERVICES: Designers and builders of specialty mill equipment, specialty rolling mills and process lines for the metals, metals-forming and related industries. Equipment capabilities include complete process lines, process line revamps and retrofits, pickle lines, tension level lines, CTL lines, slitting lines, sidetrimming lines, inspection lines, transfer cars, transporters and all associated meltshop equipment; slab handling equipment; long product handling and processing equipment, including bar, tube and pipe handling systems; strip processing equipment; coil handling equipment; custom-designed and -built equipment; automation and level 1 and 2 system design; complete system integration, PLC, drives and HMI integration; power and control system design; and facilities engineering.

No. of Employees: 160.

SES Salico Finishing and Processing
1507 Beeson St.
Alliance, OH 44601 USA
P: +1.330.821.3322
F: +1.330.821.6350

Italy:
Viale Lombardia 10
Molteno, Lecco (LC), 23847 Italy

- Dir. U.S. Oprs.—Rich C. Retort
- Dir. Intl. Oprs.—Jose M. Gerbolés de Gáldiz
- Mgr. — Business Dev.—John Wallace
- Mgr. — Tech. Oprs.—César Martín

Achenbach SES
1507 Beeson St.
Alliance, OH 44601 USA
P: +1.330.821.3322
F: +1.330.821.6350
www.achenbach-ses.com

Germany:
Siegener Straße 152
Kreuztal, 57223 Germany

- Dir. U.S. Oprs.—Rich C. Retort
- Dir. Intl. Oprs.—Andre Barten
- Mgr. Business Dev.—John Wallace
- Mgr. Tech. Oprs.—Jörg Schneider

SGM MAGNETICS CORP.
6441 19th St. E, Bldg. E
Sarasota, FL 34243 USA
P: +1.866.693.4815
www.sgmmagneticsusa.com

- Pres.—Robert Melenick
- Sales—David Baker

PRODUCTS and/or SERVICES: Magnetic solutions for material handling systems and separation technology specializing in ferrous and non-ferrous metals, offering turnkey solutions within the steel and recycling industry. SGM Magnetics manufactures electro and electro-permanent lifting magnets, spreader beams, eddy current separators, drum magnets, magnetic pulleys, overbelt magnets, x-ray, color, and sensor sorter separators along with control panels, auxiliary devices and structures. SGM's service department offers technical

CUSTOMER DRIVEN SOLUTIONS

For your material handling equipment and automation service needs.

SES and SES Automation take improving your company's processes and performance to a whole new level. Our equipment and services are tailored to meet and exceed your specific manufacturing needs.

- Complete Design and Manufacture of Specialty Equipment
- Transfer Cars & Melt Shop Equipment
- Long Product Handling Equipment
- Coil Handling and Strip Processing Equipment
- Slab Handling Equipment
- Redesign and Rebuild Existing Equipment
- Automation and Level I/II System Design
- Complete System Integration
- Power & Control System Design
- Facilities Engineering

SES
People-Driven Solutions

1507 Beeson St.
Alliance, OH 44601
330.821.3322
www.seseng.com

See listing page 510 — 2023 AIST Directory — Iron and Steel Plants 511

SUPPLIERS of EQUIPMENT, PRODUCTS and SERVICES

assistance, troubleshooting, repairs on- and off-site, design-build services along with preventive maintenance programs, and a wide range inventory of spare parts.

No. of Employees: 150.

SHIMADZU SCIENTIFIC INSTRUMENTS INC.
7102 Riverwood Dr.
Columbia, MD 21046 USA
P: +1.800.477.1227 (Toll-Free)
F: +1.410.381.1222
www.ssi.shimadzu.com

- Pres.—Yoshiaki Maeda
- Vice Pres. Sales—Patrick Fromal
- Treas.—Naohiro Nakada
- Regional Sales Mgrs.—Sarah Braseth, Greg Vandiver, Iain Green, Jordan Frost, Bruce Thompson, Ken Umbarger, Matthew Chaidez, Faith Hays
- Adv. Mgr.—Kevin McLaughlin

PRODUCTS and/or SERVICES:
Sales of analytical instrumentation: atomic absorption spectrophotometers, ICP spectrometers, tensile testers, hardness testers, XRF spectrometers.

SHINAGAWA ADVANCED MATERIALS AMERICAS
3555 Gilchrist Road
Mogadore, OH 44260 USA
P: +1.330.628.1118
F: +1.330.628.1334
info@shinagawa-usa.com
www.shinagawa-usa.com

- Chief Exec. Officer—Heiki Miki
- Pres.—Jay Theiss
- Vice Pres. Sales and Tech. Svce.—Steve Campbell
- Treas.—Rob Owsiany
- Tech. Mgr.—Jim Gilmore

PRODUCTS and/or SERVICES:
Develops, manufactures, and markets high-performance ceramics, refractory products, mold powders, and flow control systems for the iron and steel, foundry, glass, and industrial markets.

No. of Employees: 45.

SHOWA DENKO CARBON INC.
478 Ridge Road
P.O. Box 2947201
Ridgeville, SC 29472 USA
P: +1.843.875.3200
info@showadenkocarbon.com
www.showadenkocarbon.com

PRODUCTS and/or SERVICES:
UHP graphite electrodes, specialty carbon and graphite granular materials, fine carbon.

SHUB MACHINERY
4608 Oakside Point
Marietta, GA 30067 USA
P: +1.770.490.0299
barry@shubmachinery.com
www.shubmachinery.com

- Chief Exec. Officer—Barry Shub
- Pres.—Stanley Shub

PRODUCTS and/or SERVICES:
Machinery and equipment dealer.

No. of Employees: 5.

SHUTTLELIFT
49 E. Yew St.
Sturgeon Bay, WI 54235 USA
P: +1.920.743.8650
sales@shuttlelift.com
www.shuttlelift.com

- Pres.—Erich Pfeifer
- Dir. of Sales and Mktg.—Brock R. Rubens

PRODUCTS and/or SERVICES:
Manufacturer of material handling RTG cranes with capacities ranging from 30 to 1,000+ tons.

No. of Employees: 250.

SICON AMERICA LP
11390 Old Roswell Road, Suite 126
Alpharetta, GA 30009 USA
P: +1.678.527.1432
F: +1.678.527.1410
info@sicon-america.com
www.sicon-america.com

- Chief Exec. Officers—Heiner Guschall, Sebastian Schuelke

SUPPLIERS OF EQUIPMENT, PRODUCTS and SERVICES

EQUIPMENT:
Plants for processing and cleaning scrap as well as the recycling of residue generated by scrap processing and cleaning. Processing solutions for up to 400 tph.

PRODUCTS and/or SERVICES:
Scrap shredders (EcoShred), non-ferrous metal separation and sorting plants, HMS cleaning, ScrapTuning®, EcoScan.

No. of Employees: >25.

SIDOCK GROUP INC.
45650 Grand River Ave.
Novi, MI 48374 USA
P: +1.248.349.4500
F: +1.248.349.1429
wsidock@sidockgroup.com
www.sidockgroup.com

- Pres.—Bill Sidock

PRODUCTS and/or SERVICES:
Consulting, architectural, civil, structural, mechanical, electrical, and process engineering for integrated mills, foundries and processing facilities.

SIGNAL METAL INDUSTRIES INC.
850 E. Pioneer Dr.
Irving, TX 75061 USA
P: +1.800.527.8989 (Toll-Free);
   +1.972.438.1022
F: +1.972.445.0418
sales@signalmetal.com
www.signalmetal.com

PRODUCTS and/or SERVICES:
Specializes in the design of ladles, charge buckets, and ladle j-hooks. Signal Metal Industries can also provide turnkey manufacturing, including fabrication, machining, thermal stress relief, and assembly of heavy equipment and machinery for the steelmaking industry using customer-supplied drawings. Signal Metal Industries has 200,000 sq. ft. of heavy manufacturing area under roof, situated on a total of 22 acres, equipped with large-capacity overhead cranes exceeding 150 tons of lifting capacity. On-site ASME-certified stress-relief oven and state-of-the-art paint facility.

SIL-BASE CO. INC.
4 Juniper St.
McKeesport, PA 15132 USA
P: +1.412.751.2314
F: +1.412.751.2100
office@silbase.com
www.silbase.com

- Pres.—Carole Suey Nguyen
- Vice Pres. and Gen. Mgr.—Ngoc (Nick) Nguyen
- Sales Mgr.—Brigitte Nguyen
- Pur. Mgr.—Christina Nguyen

PRODUCTS and/or SERVICES:
Z-bar coke oven door liners, Flex-Sil, Sil-Bord, solid coke oven door liners, skid tile, reheat furnace doors, jamb brick, burner blocks.

No. of Employees: 15.

SIMMERS CRANE DESIGN & SERVICES CO.
1134 Salem Pkwy.
Salem, OH 44460 USA
P: +1.330.332.3300
F: +1.330.332.3322
sales@simmerscrane.com
www.simmerscrane.com

- Pres. — Midwest Region—Ross Muhleman
- Pres. — Northeast Region—Paul Kit
- Pres. — Southwest Region—Mark Kastner
- Oprs. Mgr.—Pat DeChellis
- Pur. Mgr.—Suzanne Schisler

PRODUCTS and/or SERVICES:
Overhead crane engineering and field services, crane modernizations, inspections, routine and comprehensive maintenance/repair, capacity and end-of-life analysis, redesign/enhancement of obsolete OEM parts, crane runway analysis/inspections, manufacturer of EOT Cranes CMAA Class A-D, fall protection systems.

No. of Employees: 260.

SUPPLIERS of EQUIPMENT, PRODUCTS and SERVICES

SIMPSON TECHNICAL SALES INC.
212 University Dr.
Aliquippa, PA 15001 USA
P: +1.724.375.7713
david@simpson-tech.com
david.b.simpson@comcast.net
www.simpson-tech.com

- Pres.—David B. Simpson

PRODUCTS and/or SERVICES:
Castings, forgings, machining, fabrications and gears.

No. of Employees: 2.

SINTERMET LLC
222 N. Park Dr.
West Hills Industrial Park
Kittanning, PA 16201 USA
P: +1.800.922.1229 (Toll-Free);
+1.724.548.7631
F: +1.724.545.1824
www.sintermet.com

PRODUCTS and/or SERVICES:
Tungsten-carbide rod mill rolls, ShurLock and ShurClad composite rolls, titanium carbide guide rolls, wire flattening and forming rolls, rotary knives for slitting and sidetrimming.

S.I.T. AMERICA INC.
205 S. Atlantic Ave.
Pittsburgh, PA 15224 USA
P: +1.412.371.8114
F: +1.412.371.8115
sitamerica@gmail.com

- Pres.—Jason Carfagna

PRODUCTS and/or SERVICES:
North American agent for STEIN Injection Technology GmbH, providing pneumatic conveying and injection systems and solutions for all applications using dry bulk material, mainly in the steel and foundry industry. Also supply wear-resistant pipeline accessories that include ceramic-lined elbows and ceramic-lined flexible hose.

No. of Employees: 1.

SLIPNOT®
2545 Beaufait St.
Detroit, MI 48207 USA
P: +1.800.754.7668 (Toll-Free)
F: +1.313.923.4555
info@slipnot.com
www.slipnot.com

PRODUCTS and/or SERVICES:
Specialized safety flooring products and surface technologies for walkways, entryways, stairs, ladders and more. Products include floor plates, grating, perforated plate, flattened expanded metal, stair treads, ladder rungs/covers and handrails, which are used for new construction or retrofitting over existing slippery areas. SLIPNOT products can be utilized for coolant, lubricant and recycling trenches, crossovers, catwalks, mezzanines, walkways, operator platforms, lift tables, and various other applications. SLIPNOT safety products retain traction in the most demanding environments, even when submerged in oil and other substances.

SMS GROUP

SMS group GmbH
Eduard-Schloemann-Straße 4
Düsseldorf, 40237 Germany
P: +49.211.881.0
communications@sms-group.com
www.sms-group.com

SMS group Inc.
100 Sandusky St.
Pittsburgh, PA 15212 USA
P: +1.412.231.1200
info@sms-group.com
www.sms-group.us

- Chief Exec. Officer and Pres.—Doug Dunworth
- Chief Oper. Officer—Thomas Fest
- Chief Sales Officer—Jens Oliver Haupt
- Chief Financial Officer—Peter Fernie
- Vice Pres. of Sales—Chad Donovan
- Vice Pres. of Metallurgy—Andy Gribben
- Vice Pres. of Roll. Mills—Keith Watson
- Vice Pres. of EA—Matt Korzi

SMS group

At SMS group, we have made it our mission to create a carbon-neutral and sustainable metals industry. We supply the technology to produce and recycle all major metals which gives us a key role in the transformation towards a green metals industry.

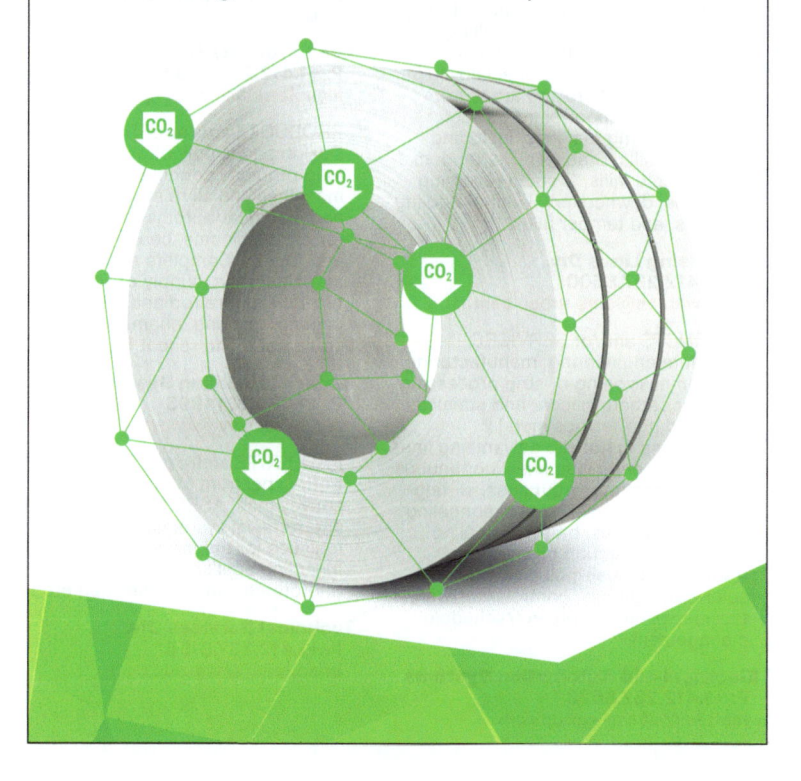

SUPPLIERS of EQUIPMENT, PRODUCTS and SERVICES

Metallurgy, Steelmaking and Continuous Casting Div.
P: +1.412.237.8578
andy.gribben@sms-group.com

PRODUCTS and/or SERVICES: Complete engineering, manufacturing, and commissioning of steelmaking and continuous casting equipment for metallurgical plants. Specializing in EAFs, oxygen converters, LFs, VD systems, metallurgical refining facilities, continuous slab casters, CSP plants, gas cleaning plants, energy recovery facilities and submerged-arc furnaces.

Flat Rolling Mill Div.
P: +1.412.237.8500
keith.watson@sms-group.com

PRODUCTS and/or SERVICES: Complete engineering, manufacturing, and supply of hot and cold rolling mill equipment for the ferrous and non-ferrous industries. Specializing in both hot and cold rolling areas from the furnace dropout point through cold processing facilities, including reversing mills, Steckel mills, tandem hot and cold mills, 2-stand reversing cold mills, downcoilers, laminar cooling systems, and temper mills.

Processing Lines Div.
P: +1.412.237.8500
keith.watson@sms-group.com

PRODUCTS and/or SERVICES: Complete engineering, manufacturing, and commissioning of strip processing lines for carbon, silicon, and stainless steel and non-ferrous metals. Specializing in hot-dip galvanizing lines, continuous annealing lines, continuous pickling lines, cross-cut lines, slitting lines, tension leveling lines, annealing and pickling lines, bright annealing lines, coil inspection preparation/rewind lines, push-pull pickling lines, color-coating lines, controls/software, facilities planning, project/schedule management.

Electrical and Automation Systems
P: +1.412.237.8523
matt.korzi@sms-group.com

PRODUCTS and/or SERVICES: Design, supply, and service of automation and electrical equipment for steelmaking, continuous casting rolling mill and process lines equipment for ferrous and non-ferrous plants. Specializing in complete automation systems comprising technological controls, sequence controls, automating data-related connections and level 2 computer models.

Tube and Pipe Div.
P: +1.412.237.8289
steve.marzina@sms-group.com

PRODUCTS and/or SERVICES: Complete engineering, manufacturing, and supply of tube and welded pipe mill equipment, seamless tube mills, tube finishing, pilger mills, and copper tubing.

Long Products Div.
P: +1.412.237.8955
nicholas.klipa@sms-group.com

PRODUCTS and/or SERVICES: Design and supply of complete long products continuous casting machines and all related mechanical and electrical/automation equipment for billets, blooms, beam blanks and rounds. Complete engineering, manufacturing, supply of section and billet mills, wire rod and bar mills, peeling, grinding, chamfering, handling equipment, and reheat furnaces.

Material Handling Systems/AMOVA
P: +1.330.881.1996
carl.brockway@amova.eu

PRODUCTS and/or SERVICES: Entire spectrum of automated conveyance, ASRS (automatic storage and retrieval systems) and packaging logistics for the metals industry, including applications for flat-rolled, roll-formed and semi-finished products.

Technical Services Div.
P: +1.412.237.8155
brian.rea@smsgroup.com

SUPPLIERS OF EQUIPMENT, PRODUCTS and SERVICES

PRODUCTS and/or SERVICES:
Provide comprehensive maintenance, field service, and spare parts services for steel works/continuous casting (flat and long products), tubes and welded pipe, extrusion press, closed- and open-die forging, ring rolling, non-ferrous technology, and heat treating from one single source. Modernization and refurbishment services for all major OEM equipment.

SMS digital Div.
P: +1.412.237.8232
markus.schulte@sms-group.com

PRODUCTS and/or SERVICES:
Merging process know-how, engineering model and automation expertise with advanced data analytics and IT competence generating added value in the metals industry. Digital solutions of The Learning [Steel] Plant are in the areas of asset health, product quality, production planning, and energy management and are made possible by the infrastructure of the SMS Data Factory.

SMS GROUP S.P.A.
Via Udine 103
Tarcento (UD), 33017 Italy
P: +39.0432.799111
sales.spa@sms-group.com
www.sms-group.com

- Chief Exec. Officer and Pres.—
  Marco Asquini
- Chief Sales Officer—Alberto Bregante
- Sales and Mktg. Dir. (Metallurgy)—
  Andrea Lanari
- Sales and Mktg. Dir. (Reheating Technology)—Pietro Della Putta
- Sales and Mktg. Dir. (Long Products)—Nicola Redolfi

PRODUCTS and/or SERVICES:
Design, manufacturing, and supply of meltshops and related auxiliary areas, reheating furnaces and heat treatment lines, hot rolling mills, mini-mill plants, and turnkey jobs. Feasibility studies, technical assistance, technological/practical training.

SMS INDIA PVT. LTD.
Plot No. 286, Udyog Vihar, Phase II
Gurugram, HR, 122016 India
P: +91.124.435.1500
www.sms-group.com

- Chief Exec. Officer and Managing Dir.—Ulrich Greiner-Pachter
- Chief Financial Officer and Dir.—
  Sumendra Jain
- Chief Sales Officer—Pino Tese

PRODUCTS and/or SERVICES:
Design, engineering, manufacturing and supply of ironmaking, cokemaking, steelmaking, hot rolling (flat and long), mini-mill plants, reheating furnaces, processing lines, non-ferrous, waste recycling and related auxiliaries including turnkey jobs. Engineering and supply also includes complete electrics/automation including implementation of digitalization. Supply is followed by installation and commissioning including supervision support. Diversification includes turnkey projects in the field of electrical substations, railway workshops, oil and gas sector, etc. Feasibility studies, technical assistance, technological/practical training, after-sales service, spares management, etc., are also covered during project life cycle and onward.

DREVER INTERNATIONAL S.A.
Parc Scientifique du Sart Tilman
Alée des Noisetiers 15
B-4031 Angleur, Liège, Belgium
P: +32.0.43666262
F: +32.0.43666323
www.drever.be

- Chief Exec. Officer—Jean Pierre Crutzen
- Vice Pres. Sales and Mktg.—
  Serge Vanderheyden

PRODUCTS and/or SERVICES:
Continuous annealing furnaces and galvanizing plants for carbon steel strip and annealing of stainless steel strip.

2023 AIST Directory — Iron and Steel Plants 517

SUPPLIERS of EQUIPMENT, PRODUCTS and SERVICES

Drever International USA
100 Sandusky St.
Pittsburgh, PA 15212 USA
P: +1.412.237.8525
sales@drever.us

- Sales Mgr.—Paul Debski

PAUL WURTH SA
P.O. Box 2233
32 rue d'Alsace
Luxembourg, L-1022 Luxembourg
P: +352.4970.1
paulwurth@paulwurth.com
www.paulwurth.com

- Chmn. of the Bd.—Torsten Heising
- Chief Exec. Officer—Georges Rassel
- Chief Tech. Officer and Chief Oprs. Officer—Thomas Hansmann
- Chief Admin. and Financial Officer—Frank Wagener

SOFIS CO. INC.
554 Bocktown Cork Road
Clinton, PA 15026 USA
P: +1.724.378.2670
F: +1.724.378.3719
tsofis@sofiscompany.com
www.sofiscompany.com

- Pres—William J. Sofis Jr.
- Sec. and Treas.—Ted W. Sofis

EQUIPMENT:
Underbridge inspection cranes, gunite equipment, lift vans.

PRODUCTS and/or SERVICES:
Gunite and refractory installation, refractory materials, concrete repair, epoxy injection, chemical grouting, fireproofing, bridge repair, rigging and inspection services.

SOFTWEB SOLUTIONS INC. — an Avnet Co.
7950 Legacy Dr., Suite 250
Plano, TX 75024 USA
P: +1.866.345.7638
mehul.nayak@softwebsolutions.com
www.softwebsolutions.com

PRODUCTS and/or SERVICES:
Industrial automation, IoT solutions, AI services, augmented reality use in manufacturing, data science services.

No. of Employees: 500.

SONGER SERVICES
2755A Park Ave.
Washington, PA 15301 USA
P: +1.724.884.0184
F: +1.724.884.0185
www.songerservices.com

- Chmn.—Joseph C. Meneskie
- Chief Exec. Officer and Pres.—Gregg S. Preterot
- Exec Vice Pres. and Chief Oper. Officer.—Mike Armold
- Chief Financial Officer—Sean Ream
- Vice Pres. Cost, Contracts and Proposals—William C. Yockel
- Vice Pres. Oprs.—David Toennies
- Vice Pres. Engrg.—Lauren Culbertson
- Gen. Mgr. Engrg.—Terry J. Jackson
- Gen. Mgr.—Glenn Reed
- Gen. Mgr. Midwest—Thomas Jarka
- Dir. EHS—Jason W. Savasta
- Gen. Mgr. Canada Oprs.—Mike Hubbs
- Labor Rels. and H.R. Principal—Robert C. Hoover
- Sr. Consultant—Richard J. Kline

PRODUCTS and/or SERVICES:
General contractor — heavy industrial markets, maintenance, project management and field engineering.

SOUTHERN ALLOY CORP.
36280 U.S. Hwy. 280
P.O. Box 1168
Sylacauga, AL 35150 USA
P: +1.256.245.5237
F: +1.256.245.4992
www.southernalloy.com

- Chmn. of the Bd. and Pres.—Billy T. Bobbitt
- Exec. Vice Pres. Oprs.—Jim Snowden
- Vice Pres. Mktg.—Lee Bobbitt
- Treas.—Henry Nunnelley
- Regional Sales Mgrs.—Andy Housch, Jason Green
- Pur. Agt.—Anita Tharp

SUPPLIERS OF EQUIPMENT, PRODUCTS and SERVICES

EQUIPMENT:
Induction melting furnaces, heat treating furnaces, pattern shop, machine shop, chemical analysis control with Siemens x-ray unit.

PRODUCTS and/or SERVICES:
Entry and delivery guides, rest bars, coupling boxes and spindles, sideguards and roller boxes, straightener rolls, skids and doors for reheat furnaces, castings for meltshop and rolling mill.

No. of Employees: 80, including four metallurgical engineers.

S.P. KINNEY ENGINEERS INC.
143 1st Ave.
P.O. Box 445
Carnegie, PA 15106 USA
P: +1.800.356.1118 (Toll-Free)
F: +1.412.276.6890
info@spkinney.com
www.spkinney.com

PRODUCTS and/or SERVICES:
New and refurbished automatic backwashing strainers, automatic stove reversal systems, hot blast stoves, hot blast stove burners, gas and air valves (shutoff, regulating and safety), chimney valves, blowoff valves, hot blast valves (gate and mushroom), hot blast valve seats, snort valves, check and relief valves, cold blast valves, mixer valves, open hearth stack cap valves, goggle valves (vertical gate, swing and hydraulic ram types), butterfly valves, quick-opening valves, backdrafting valves, tower, orifice and venturi gas scrubbers, spray nozzles, moisture eliminators, main mixers, electric gas stack igniters, cinder notch stoppers, expanded slag process (Kinney-Osborne), motor actuators.

SPRAYING SYSTEMS CO.
200 W. North Ave.
Glendale Heights, IL 60139 USA
P: +1.630.665.5000
www.spray.com/industries/steel-and-metal-manufacturing

PRODUCTS and/or SERVICES:
Provides spray nozzles and accessories, complete integrated systems, support services (performance validation testing, wear life testing), and expertise to the steel industry. Offers a complete line of products designed specifically for use in steel mills, including cooling in continuous casting, hot mill and finishing mill operations, descale, coating, rinsing and cooling for pickling lines, gas conditioning, pollution control, quenching and cooling in cokemaking operations, and many other applications.

SPRINGER CO.
P.O. Box 26
Zelienople, PA 16063 USA
P: +1.412.980.5475
dj@springercompanyinc.com
www.springercompanyinc.com

– Pres.—D.J. Springer

PRODUCTS and/or SERVICES:
Manufacturer's representative for 14 sales partners around the U.S., offering equipment repair, on-site work, engineering services, design services, upgrades and retrofits to the steel and non-ferrous industries.

SPUNCAST INC.
W6499 Rhine Road
Watertown, WI 53098 USA
P: +1.920.261.7853
F: +1.920.261.7977
sales@spuncast.com
www.spuncast.com

PRODUCTS and/or SERVICES:
Steel centrifugal foundry selling specialty alloy tubing to OEM and aftermarket manufacturers. Offers over 180 alloys, tight tolerance machining, extensive product warranties and five degreed metallurgists on staff. Industries served include mining, oil and gas, water treatment, food processing, aerospace, steel production, defense, power generation, shipbuilding and more.

SUPPLIERS of EQUIPMENT, PRODUCTS and SERVICES

SSS CLUTCH CO. INC.
610 W. Basin Road
New Castle, DE 19720 USA
P: +1.302.322.8080
F: +1.302.322.8548
engineering@sssclutch.com
www.sssclutch.com

- Pres.—Morgan L. Hendry
- Mgr. Application Engrg.—Randall Attix
- Sr. Project Engr.—David Haldeman
- Project Engr.—Garrett McKay
- Engrg. and Business Dev. Mgr.—Eileen Mulvena
- Dir. Latin America Sales—Frank Dougherty
- Inside Sales and Office Mgr.—Suzie Wham

PRODUCTS and/or SERVICES:
North and South American affiliate of SSS Gears Ltd. supplying automatic-engaging, gear-type, overrunning clutches used in a wide range of applications. SSS Clutches are in service in: gas turbine–driven naval ship main propulsion of 50+ navies worldwide, 1,300+ gas turbine–driven, peak-load generators for synchronous condensing (spinning reserve, VARs and voltage support); more than 475 steam turbines with powers up to 400 MW in baseload, combined-cycle plants; nearly 100 clutches for steam turbine powers up to 200 MW in a combined heat and power cogeneration; hundreds of dual-driven boiler feed pumps; more than 2,000 diesel engine–driven, rotating UPS generators; hundreds of dual-driven pumps; dual-driven compressors, many for steel mill BOF main blowers; and dual-driven gas recirculation and boiler ID and FD fans for petrochemical, process and refinery energy recovery applications; thousands of turning gear and gas turbine starter drives.

No. of Employees: 11 in USA, 60 in U.K.

STANDARD ELECTRIC SUPPLY CO.
222 N. Emmber Lane
Milwaukee, WI 53233 USA
P: +1.800.776.8222 (Toll-Free);
+1.414.272.8100
F: +1.414.272.8111
tchristopher@standardelectricsupply.com
www.standardelectricsupply.com

- Pres.—Larry Stern
- Vice Pres. Finance—Tom Poehlman
- Vice Pres. Mktg. and Sales—Mike Harvey
- Dir. of Sales—Tammy Christopher
- Dir. of Engrg.—Bill Hirschinger
- Pur. Agt./Sales Support—Debbie Haley
- Engr. Mgrs.—Kyle Brooks, Mike Wojda
- Acct. Mgrs.—Tony Abbott, Nick Guzick, Josh Cox

PRODUCTS and/or SERVICES:
Full-line electrical distributor emphasizing industrial automation and control products with a focus on the OEM and MRO marketplace.

No. of Employees: 150–200.

Regional Headquarters
9900 Westpoint Dr., Suite 142
Indianapolis, IN 46256 USA
P: +1.877.219.7782

STANDARD MACHINE, a Brand of The Timken Co.
868 60th St. E
Saskatoon, SK S7K 8G8 Canada
P: +1.306.931.3343
canadasales@standardmachine.ca
www.standardmachine.ca

- Gen. Mgr.—Jason Young

PRODUCTS and/or SERVICES:
Gears, gear reducers, Hamilton Gear products, Philadelphia Gear products, custom gear drives, machining/fabricating, repairs/refurbishment, engineering services, field services.

No. of Employees: 105.

SUPPLIERS OF EQUIPMENT, PRODUCTS and SERVICES

STEEL EQUIPMENT CORP.
40 Elmhurst Road
Pittsburgh, PA 15220 USA
P: +1.412.721.6945
dlemster@steelequip.com
www.steelequip.com

- Pres.—Dev Earle Lemster

PRODUCTS and/or SERVICES:
Buy, sell, appraise and liquidate used steel mill equipment, including primary steelmaking, rolling mills, overhead cranes, product finishing, miscellaneous material handling and electrical equipment. Consulting services for long products rolling mill projects.

No. of Employees: 2.

STEELTAGS.COM
9209 Emerson Ave.
Miami, FL 33154 USA
P: +1.305.393.8669
harri@steeltags.com
www.steeltags.com

- Pres.—Harri Fenzl

PRODUCTS and/or SERVICES:
Tags and labels, ribbons, printers, attachment solutions, clips, welding guns.

No. of Employees: 65.

STEVENS ENGINEERS & CONSTRUCTORS
7850 Freeway Cir., Suite 100
Middleburg Heights, OH 44130 USA
P: +1.440.234.7888
F: +1.440.234.1967
info@stevensec.com
www.stevensec.com

- Chief Exec. Officer—Vicki Anderson
- Pres.—Scott Snyder
- Chief Financial Officer—Tony DeLuca
- Business Dev. Mgrs.—Paul Dellemonache, Bill Bucina, Craig Barras, Ken Miles

PRODUCTS and/or SERVICES:
Full-service industrial engineering and contracting firm with individual business units in Middleburg Heights, OH; Canonsburg, PA; and Hobart, IN; providing a wide range of engineering and construction services. On capital projects, STEVENS provides complete design-build capabilities. STEVENS' engineering arm, CDMG, is a full-scale, multi-discipline engineering firm offering feasibility studies, project management and construction management, as well as being a Nucor distributor offering pre-engineered buildings. Construction and maintenance services—demolition, excavation, equipment and process system installations, machinery moving, equipment setting and precision alignment, heavy welding, ductwork/furnace maintenance, heavy rigging, structural steel erection, building and pre-engineered building erection, civil work including building and equipment foundations, slab on grade and pre-cast concrete, repair to high-pressure process equipment and systems.

No. of Employees: 450.

STIMPLE & WARD CO.
3400 Babcock Blvd.
Pittsburgh, PA 15237 USA
P: +1.800.792.6457 (Toll-Free);
+1.412.364.5200
F: +1.412.364.5299
www.swcoils.com

- Chmn. of the Bd. and Pres.—Raymond M. Love
- Prodn./Mfg.—George Dietz
- Treas.—Thomas J. Love
- Sales Mgr.—Mark Van Cura

EQUIPMENT:
Spreaders, curing ovens, edge winding machines and coil taping equipment.

PRODUCTS and/or SERVICES:
Electric motor coils for repair of mill-duty motors. Brake, blowout, contactor and solenoid coils. Magnet wire distribution.

No. of Employees: 30.

SUPPLIERS of EQUIPMENT, PRODUCTS and SERVICES

STUCCHI USA
1105 Windham Pkwy.
Romeoville, IL 60446 USA
P: +1.847.956.9720
F: +1.847.956.9723
sales@stucchiusa.com
www.stucchiusa.com

PRODUCTS and/or SERVICES:
ISO 9001/Vision 2000 certified manufacturer of hydraulic quick disconnects for a variety of industries including construction, agriculture, automation, chemical, off-shore and land-based oil and gas, pulp and paper, plastics, public utilities, and many others. Stucchi designs and manufactures quick coupling products in a variety of sizes and port configurations ranging from 1/8 inch to 2 1/2 inch sizes to accommodate a wide field of application requirements. Pressure capabilities extending to 10,000 psi working pressure, imperial and metric standard port configurations, materials from brass to 316 stainless steel, and an assortment of seal options are available.

STEULER-KCH GMBH
Berggarten 1
56427 Siershahn, Germany
P: +49.2623.600.409
kai.schwickert@steuler-kch.de
https://linings.steuler.de/en/business-areas/refractory-linings.html

- Exec. Vice Pres.—Ulf Frohneberg
- Vice Pres. Sales—Kai Schwickert

PRODUCTS and/or SERVICES:
Globally recognized technology partner in the field of refractory systems, with special emphasis on direct reduction processes and H_2 atmospheres. The Steuler team conducts research and development and works closely with plant design engineers and operators to provide project-specific advice and refractory solutions to contribute to the production of clean steel.

No. of Employees: 2,800 worldwide.

SUEZ WATER TECHNOLOGIES & SOLUTIONS—see **VEOLIA WATER TECHNOLOGIES & SOLUTIONS**

SUMITOMO DRIVE TECHNOLOGIES
4200 Holland Blvd.
Chesapeake, VA 23323 USA
P: +1.757.485.3355
mike.clark@shi-g.com
www.sumitomodrive.com

- Chief Exec. Officer—Jim Solomon
- Vice Pres. Mktg.—Sara Zimmerman
- Vice Pres. Prodn./Mfg.—Tony Barlett
- Treas.—Nate Flora
- Vice Pres. Sales—Jon Murphy
- Adv. Mgr.—Phil Zarate

PRODUCTS and/or SERVICES:
Gearmotors, gearboxes, speed reducers, Paramax, Cyclo, Hyponic, BBB, HBB, Hansen, CycloSmart, DriveSmart, Invertek, Luftex.

No. of Employees: 350.

SUNCOKE ENERGY
1011 Warrenville Road, 6th Floor
Lisle, IL 60532 USA
P: +1.630.824.1000
F: +1.630.824.1001
suncokeinfo@suncoke.com
www.suncoke.com

PRODUCTS and/or SERVICES:
Supplies high-quality coke to the integrated steel industry under long-term, take-or-pay contracts that pass through commodity and certain operating costs to customers. . Cokemaking facilities located in Illinois, Indiana, Ohio and Virginia, USA; and Brazil. Additionally, provides export and domestic coal handling services to the coke, coal, steel and power industries. Material handling terminals with the collective capacity to blend and transload more than 25 million tons each year, strategically located to reach Gulf Coast, East Coast, Great Lakes and international ports.

SUPPLIERS of EQUIPMENT, PRODUCTS and SERVICES

SUPERIOR ENGINEERING LLC
2345 167th St.
Hammond, IN 46323 USA
P: +1.219.844.7030;
 +1.630.378.8080 (Bolingbrook, IL);
 +1.440.234.9972 (Middleburg
 Heights, OH)
info@supereng.com
www.superiorengineering.com

- Gen. Mgr., IL, IN, and OH Offices—Bill Heuer
- Branch Mgr. — IL—Steve Vernengo
- Branch Mgr. — OH—Jim Fennessy
- Mech. Dept. Mgr.—Kent Troxel
- Elec., Instrumentation and Controls Dept. Mgr.—Scott Dewes
- Struct./Civil Dept. Mgr.—Todd Moore
- Process Dept. Mgr.—Rich Skarvan
- Projects Dept. Mgr.—Corey Clevenger
- Dir. of Business Dev.—Paul Wojcik

PRODUCTS and/or SERVICES:
Complete program management: scoping, evaluation, budgeting, engineering, and project management for the iron and steel, foundry, and allied industries. Services cover consultation, project/construction management, fast-track and turnkey projects, computerized analyses, 3D CAD, specifications and bid analyses, as well as complete construction design documentation. Specialties include mechanical, piping, pressure vessels, instrumentation, programmable controllers, program development, BF relines, pickle lines, EGLs, hot metal desulfurization, power generation, material handling, air and water pollution control, mill buildings, foundations, electrical power distribution and control, plant layout, and construction scheduling and management.

SUPERIOR MACHINE CO. OF S.C. INC.
692 N. Cashua Dr.
Florence, SC 29502 USA
P: +1.843.468.9200
F: +1.843.468.9173
sales@smco.net
www.smco.net

- Pres.—John Ham
- Vice Pres. Engrg.—Mike Honeygosky
- Vice Pres. Sales—Cary Andrews
- Vice Pres. Field Svce.—Dennis Freeman
- Vice Pres. Finance—Robert G. Vassy
- H.R.—Cathey Allen
- Matls. Mgr.—Bill Barnett

EQUIPMENT:
Vertical boring mills to 20-ft. dia.; horizontal boring mills: 40-ft. horizontal travel, 15-ft. vertical travel; lathes: up to 14-ft. swing and up to 58 ft. between centers; surface grinding: 84-in. dia., 24-in. thickness; rolls: 1 1/2-in. capacity, 10 ft. wide; press brake: 1,000 tons x 14 ft.; hydraulic press: 1,800-ton capacity; stress-relieving: 14 x 14 x 14 ft.—gas-fired, thermostatically controlled, CNC flame and plasma cutting. Complete fleet of field service trucks, including installation and testing equipment.

PRODUCTS and/or SERVICES:
Complete design engineering, project management, feasibility studies, and installation services for turnkey retrofitting and upgrading EAFs, continuous casting machines, and secondary refining. Supplier of fabricated replacement components for EAFs, including: shells, roofs, electrode arms, gantries, tilt platforms, water-cooled panels and offgas ductwork. Upgrading and replacement components for continuous casters, including: tundishes, cars, molds, oscillators, segments, starter bars, runout/cross-transfer systems. Design and implement PLC systems for EAFs and continuous casters, including water and hydraulic controls. Steel mill-related equipment, including: charging buckets, ladles, crane bales and other heavy fabrications. Field service capability for installation of new mill equipment, scheduled outages and emergency repair work.

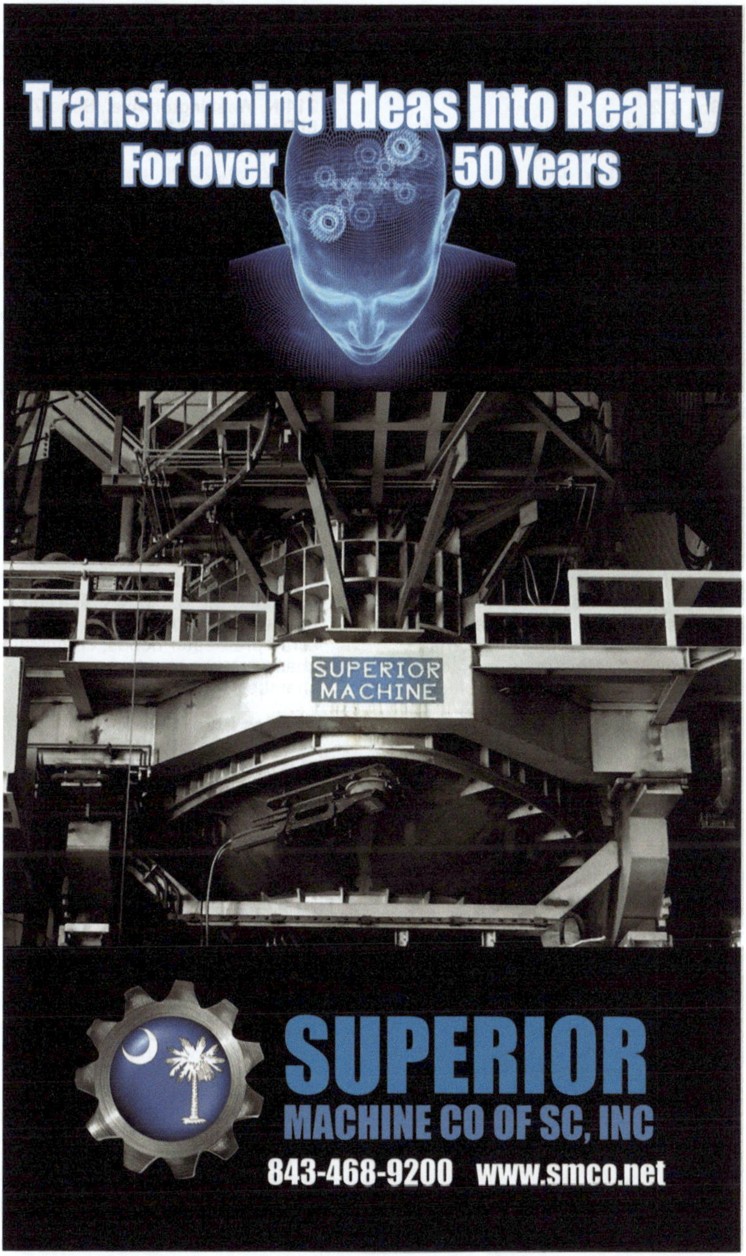

See listing page 524

SUPPLIERS of EQUIPMENT, PRODUCTS and SERVICES

SWERIM AB
Box 812
971 25 Luleå, Sweden
P: +46.10.489.09.70
www.swerim.se/en

- Chief Exec. Officer—Pontus Sjöberg
- Business Area Mgr. Metallurgy—Mikael Larsson
- Business Area Mgr. Prodn. Technology—Tania Irebo Schwartz
- Business Area Mgr. Matl. Dev.—Magnus Andersson
- Business Area Mgr. Pilot and Demo.—Daniel Palo
- Chief Financial Officer—Per Södergren
- H.R. Mgr.—Britta Bolin
- Business Dev.—Maria Lundberg, Marianne Magnelöv

PRODUCTS and/or SERVICES: Conducts needs-based industrial R&D concerning metals and their route from raw material to finished product. Applied research in pilot plants in the field of process metallurgy, metalworking, heating and furnace technology, refractories, surface conditioning, process control, and measurement technology. Consulting, computer modeling and simulation of metallurgical processes.

THE SYSTEMS GROUP
214 N. Washington Ave., Suite 700
El Dorado, AR 71730 USA
P: +1.870.862.1315
www.tsg.bz

- Chief Exec. Officer—Charles A. Hays Jr.
- Chief Financial Officer—Vicki Peace
- Pres.—Lee Morgan
- Vice Pres. and Gen. Mgr., Systems Plant Services—Tony Lollar
- Vice Pres. and Gen. Mgr., Systems Spray-Cooled—Scott Ferguson
- Vice Pres. and Gen. Mgr., Systems Fab & Machine—Elizabeth Nations

No. of Employees: 800.

Systems Contracting
214 N. Washington Ave., Suite 700
El Dorado, AR 71731 USA
P: +1.870.862.1315
http://contracting.tsg.bz

PRODUCTS and/or SERVICES: Process piping, structural concrete, structural steel erection, equipment setting and alignment, plant maintenance services, boiler and pressure vessel installation, service and repair, machining, and fabrication services.

Systems Spray-Cooled Equipment
877 Seven Oaks Blvd., Suite 500
Smyrna, TN 37167 USA
P: +1.615.366.7772
http://spraycooled.tsg.bz

PRODUCTS and/or SERVICES: Designing, manufacturing and installing Systems' patented spray-cooled equipment, including: EAF upper shells, roofs and D.E.S. elbows; AOD and BOF hoods; LMF hoods; offgas ducting; scrap pre-heater hoods; combustion chambers; dropout boxes; spray chambers.

Systems Plant Services
214 N. Washington Ave., Suite 700
El Dorado, AR 71730 USA
P: +1.870.862.1315
http://plantservices.tsg.bz

PRODUCTS and/or SERVICES: Regular facility maintenance, equipment changeouts, new equipment fabrication and installation, on-site/off-site support.

Systems Fab & Machine
151 Pickering Dr.
El Dorado, AR 71730 USA
P: +1.870.862.1393
http://fabmachine.tsg.bz

PRODUCTS and/or SERVICES: Steel fabrication services, structural steel, buildings, process structures, furnaces, specialized fabrication, vessels, material handling and storage, duct fabrication.

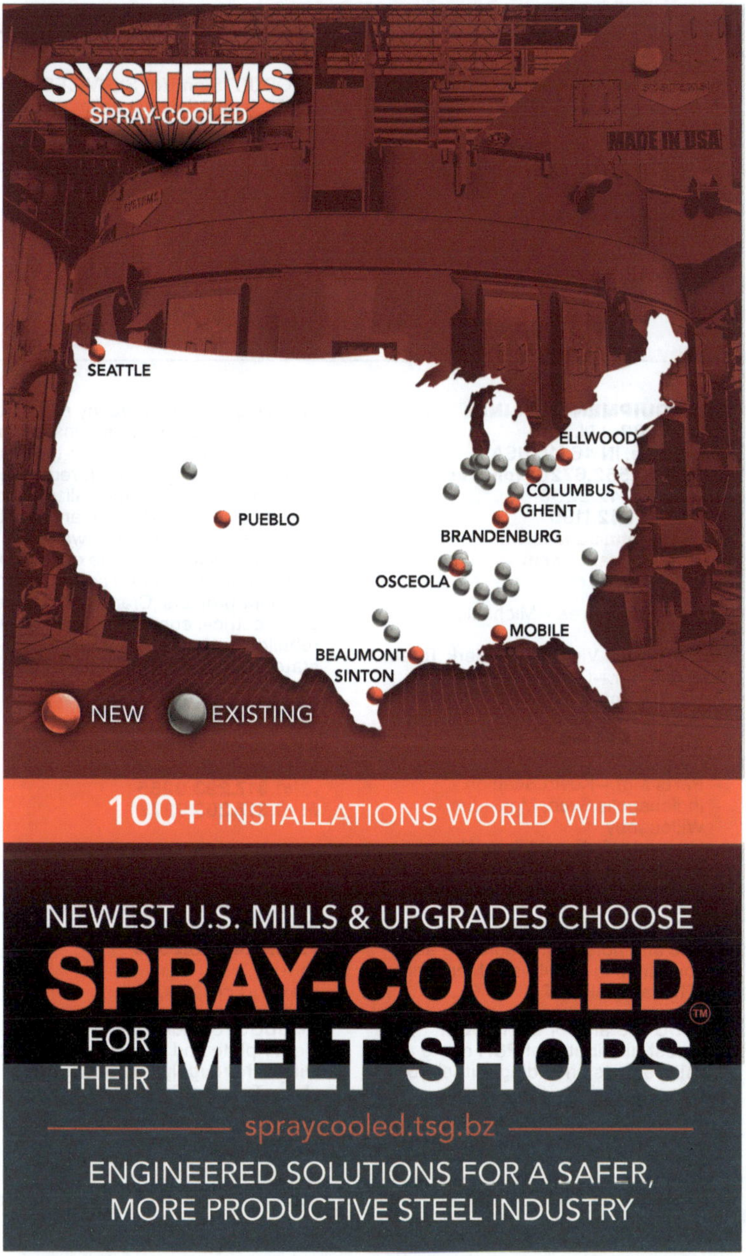

See listing page 526

SUPPLIERS of EQUIPMENT, PRODUCTS and SERVICES

Systems SMAC — Self-Maintaining Air Cleaner
2414 E. Matthews Ave. E
Jonesboro, AR 72401 USA
P: +1.870.819.9000
https://smac.tsg.bz

PRODUCTS and/or SERVICES:
SMAC industrial dust collection unit designed for the harsh environment of steel mills. Room pressurization, dust applications, transformer vaults, DRI, MCC rooms.

T

T&M EQUIPMENT CO. INC.
2880 E. 83rd Pl.
Merrillville, IN 46410 USA
P: +1.800.552.6720 (Toll-Free);
 +1.219.942.2299
F: +1.219.942.1180
mikemal@tmcranes.com
mford@tmcranes.com
www.tmcranes.com

- Owner and Pres.—Michael Malatestinic
- Owner and Vice Pres.—Mark Turek
- Svce. Mgr.—Chris Koller
- North Central IN and MI Sales—Glen Tiller
- Southern IN Sales—Mike Decker
- Steel Sales Engr.—Michael Ford
- Parts Mgr.—Kevin Scanlon
- Indianapolis Svce. Mgr.—Jim Willoughby
- Kentucky Sales—Melody Nees
- Indianapolis Sales—Jim Broadbent
- Inside Sales—Elaine Kalantzis

EQUIPMENT:
Crane and hoist manufacturing and reconditioning facilities in Merrillville and Indianapolis, IN.

PRODUCTS and/or SERVICES:
Midwest distributor of P&H crane and hoist products, including authentic replacement parts. Supplying customers in MI, IL, IN, OH and KY, USA. Engineering designer and manufacturer of overhead cranes and hoists for the steel, automotive, paper, aluminum, chemical, cement and other industries. Two crane service centers, providing 24/7 emergency repairs and service, as well as routine inspection and repair functions. Below-the-hook lifting device engineering, redesign and manufacturing. Specialized and specifically tailored crane and hoist inspection programs. Runway rail installations and mainline conductor installations and crane construction are frequent projects. Crane mechanical and electrical component assembly rebuilds, including lifting devices. Solid-state AC and DC electrical controls.

Indianapolis Office
6501 N. Guion Road
Indianapolis, IN 46268 USA
P: +1.888.237.2499 (Toll-Free);
 +1.317.293.9255
F: +1.317.293.9277

T. BRUCE SALES INC.
9 Carbaugh St.
West Middlesex, PA 16159 USA
P: +1.724.528.9961
F: +1.724.528.2050
tbruce@tbrucesales.com
www.tbrucesales.com

PRODUCTS and/or SERVICES:
Heavy plate and structural fabricator with a thoroughly equipped machine shop. T. Bruce Sales Inc. specializes in material handling equipment and custom machine building. Services include cutting, sawing, rolling and welding, CNC machining, stress relieving, blast cleaning, painting and testing.

SUPPLIERS OF EQUIPMENT, PRODUCTS and SERVICES

T-T ELECTRIC USA
P.O. Box 180074
Delafield, WI 53018 USA
P: +1.262.244.0581
sales@ttelectricusa.com
www.ttelectricusa.com

PRODUCTS and/or SERVICES: Supplier of high-quality AC motors, DC motors and DC drives. Offering flexible product designs allowing for easy adaptation to fit customer requirements. DC motors feature high output-torque-to-frame-size ratios, flexibility, adaptability for replacement motors, and designs made specifically for easy maintenance. AC motors feature a wide speed range, high overload capacity, cast-iron end shields for vibration damping, and modular designs for a high degree of flexibility. Suitable for rotary shears, flying shears, uncoiler/recoilers, flatteners, and stamping presses.

No. of Employees: 5.

TALLMAN TECHNOLOGIES INC.
2220 Industrial St.
Burlington, ON L7P 1A1 Canada
P: +1.905.335.3491
F: +1.905.335.5896
sales@tallmantechnologies.ca
www.tallmantechnologies.ca

- Chief Exec. Officer and Pres.—Michael J. Strelbisky
- Sr. Application Engr.—Majid Zamani
- Product Mgr. Cast Products—Aaron Strelbisky

PRODUCTS and/or SERVICES: Supplier of BOF and EAF technologies to reduce CO_2 emissions, improve productivity and reduce costs as well as technical consulting services on equipment commissioning/optimization, carbon and flux injection modeling/optimization, and development of BOF blowing and other refining practices. Patented steelmaking technologies include: Tallman Supersonic Carbon Injectors (TSCi) to reduce carbon and energy consumption; EAF sidewall camera; cold shroud (focused post-combustion) to reduce CO_2 emissions, slopping and increase BOF scrap ratio and productivity; Focused Swirl Cool—high-intensity cooled centrifugal BOF converter lance tips; and Internal Lance Support System (ILSS) to eliminate bending of post-combustion distributor lances. BOF steelmaking products/services include: lances and lance tips, parabolic lance tips, twisted lance tips, post-combustion (PCD) lances, tapered lances, and complete repair and maintenance program for BOF lances. EAF steelmaking products/services include: EAF cameras, burners, injectors, lance tips, and cast copper water-cooled panels. Ironmaking products and services include: auxiliary stave cooler for remediation of damaged staves, BF tuyeres (dual-chamber, high-velocity, spiral, dual and flooded chamber), BF coolers and BF cigar coolers complete with calorizing and hardfacing on critical high-wear areas, and high-temperature BF tuyere inserts/reducers. Other products and services include: centrifugal and sand cast copper and bronze components, including slippers, wear plates, gear blankets and liners. Repair/repair services of all cast water-cooled components. Specialty welding of dissimilar metals including copper, carbon and stainless steels.

TAMINI TRASFORMATORI S.R.L.
Viale Cadorna, 56/A
Legnano (MI), 20025 Italy
P: +39.02.98205.1
F: +39.02.98230322
info@tamini.it
www.tamini.it

- Chief Exec. Officer—Sergio Agosta
- Chief Oper. Officer—Riccardo Reboldi
- Commercial Dir.—Danilo Dosi

SUPPLIERS of EQUIPMENT, PRODUCTS and SERVICES

Tamini Transformers USA LLC — Pittsburgh, PA Office
518 Broad St., Suite 001
Sewickley, PA 15143 USA
P: +1.412.534.4263
F: +1.412.356.5974
g.urso@tamini.com
www.tamini.it

- Managing Dir.—Gary M. Urso

PRODUCTS and/or SERVICES: Energy transformers, including design, manufacturing, testing, commissioning, maintenance, repair, redesign and revamping. Products for diverse industrial sectors (i.e., steel, aluminum, mining, oil and gas, chemical, and transportation) and the electrical power provider sectors (production, distribution and transmission). Industrial units include: furnace transformers, reactors, power and rectifier transformers. Power units include: transformers for electricity generation, transmission and distribution, phase shifting transformers, and shunt reactors for both conventional and renewable sources. "Green Transformers" having environmental, safety and technical benefits for industrial and power applications that utilize both natural and synthetic ester fluids. Services include technical assistance in each phase of the transformer life cycle, experienced specialists, and complete service portfolio.

TARRANT HYDRAULIC SERVICE— see MOTION

TASACO INC.
300 Century Park S, Suite 212
Birmingham, AL 35226 USA
P: +1.205.823.2105
F: +1.205.823.2185

- Vice Pres. and Treas.—Mike Taylor
- Vice Pres.—Russ Elkan
- Office Mgr.—Erin Mardis

PRODUCTS and/or SERVICES: Refractory, pre-cast shapes, carbons, lances, lance pipe, quick-change nozzles, mold powder, magnesia fluxes, safety clothing, Spar, Spar Lime, ladle shrouds and funnel shrouds.

TAYLOR DEVICES INC.
90 Taylor Dr.
North Tonawanda, NY 14120 USA
P: +1.716.694.0800
F: +1.716.695.6015
www.taylordevices.com

- Chmn. of the Bd.—John Burgess
- Chief Exec. Officer—Tim Sopko
- Chief Financial Officer—Mark McDonough
- Pres.—Alan Klembczyk
- Vice Pres. Oprs.—Todd Avery
- Vice Pres. Engrg.—Paul Crvelin
- Chief Engr.—Don Horne
- Sales Dirs.—Robert Schneider, Craig Winters
- Pur. Mgr.—Robert Conrad
- Sec.—Eric Armenat

PRODUCTS and/or SERVICES: Hydraulic shock absorbers for mill and heavy industrial service. Applications include overhead cranes, transfer cars, ladle cars, continuous caster runouts, grinding machines, coke plant machinery and more. Custom hydraulic components for aerospace and commercial use.

No. of Employees: 115.

TAYLOR MACHINE WORKS INC.
3690 N. Church Ave.
Louisville, MS 39339 USA
P: +1.662.773.3421
contact_sales@taylorbigred.com
www.taylorbigred.com

- Dir. of Sales—Hal Nowell
- Gen. Sales Mgr.—Barry Black

PRODUCTS and/or SERVICES: Forklifts, cushion tire trucks, material handling equipment and safety equipment.

No. of Employees: 1,000.

TAYLOR
WE ARE TAYLOR
Your COMPLETE Heavy-Lift Supplier
for the Iron and Steel Industry
FOLLOW US ON SOCIAL MEDIA
You Can DEPEND On Big Red
TAYLOR
www.taylorbigred.com
AISTech
BOOTH
2208

SUPPLIERS of EQUIPMENT, PRODUCTS and SERVICES

TAYLOR-WINFIELD TECHNOLOGIES INC.
3200 Innovation Pl.
Youngstown, OH 44509 USA
P: +1.800.523.4899 (Toll-Free);
   +1.330.259.8500
F: +1.330.259.8538
sales@taylor-winfield.com
www.taylor-winfield.com

- Chief Exec. Officer—Doyle Hopper
- Pres.—Donnie Wells
- Vice Pres. Sales—Rick Kitchokoff
- Vice Pres. Business Dev.—Blake Rhein
- Vice Pres. Oprs. and Engrg.—Rory McDonnell
- Product Mgr.—Robert Kornack
- Product Specialist—Matt Keller
- Engrg. Mgr.—Nick Maillis
- Plant Mgr.—Rick Severs

EQUIPMENT:
150,000-sq.-ft. assembly and manufacturing with an on-site laser coil joining R&D laboratory.

PRODUCTS and/or SERVICES:
Fully integrated OEM manufacturer of various coil-joining welders, including the new Eclipse X1 solid-state fiber laser welder and accessories, induction post-weld heat treatment (PWHT) systems, and existing welder rebuilds/upgrades. Other services include: OEM machine spare parts, copper products and worldwide on-site field service.

TDI GROUP LLC
P.O. Box 38657
Pittsburgh, PA 15238 USA
P: +1.412.826.4950
F: +1.412.826.4959
sales@tdigrp.com
www.tdigrp.com

- Pres.—David R. DiBenedetto Sr.
- Vice Pres. Ind. Sales—David R. DiBenedetto Jr.

PRODUCTS and/or SERVICES:
Supplier of used and remanufactured mechanical and electrical equipment to the metals industry, providing brokerage and consignment services, removal, rigging, and demolition services. Project support, export packaging and logistics services upon request.

No. of Employees: 5.

TECHNICAL WEIGHING SERVICES INC.
1004 Reder Road
Griffith, IN 46319 USA
P: +1.219.924.3366
F: +1.219.924.4566
mailroom@techweigh.com
www.techweigh.com

PRODUCTS and/or SERVICES:
Engineers, manufactures and installs weighing systems, in-motion crane weigh systems, roll force measurement systems and strip tensions systems for the steel industry throughout the U.S. and worldwide. Provides solutions ranging from repairs and replacements for all brands of load cells, to complete integrated control and material handling solutions and weighing systems.

TECHNOS INC.
7016 FM 3009
Schertz, TX 78154 USA
P: +1.210.651.9393
F: +1.210.651.1258
info@technosfans.com
www.technosfans.com

- Pres.—Derrick Dowden
- Vice Pres.—Mike Hatfield
- Chief Financial Officer—Robin Dawson
- Field Svce. Mgr.—Stephen Adams

EQUIPMENT:
Cincinnati 600-ton press brake; 50-in. x 31-ft. lathe; Ryazan 44-in. CNC lathe with Fanuc controls; King 84-in. VBM, 1-in. x 10-ft. plate roll; key seat machines; 12-ft. x 24-ft. auto plasma cutter; and Hoffman balancing machine capable up to 100,000 lbs.

PRODUCTS and/or SERVICES:
Designs, fabricates, repairs and installs industrial fans, including wheels, housings, dampers, expansion

WELDING INNOVATION IS IN OUR CORPORATE DNA

Henry Ford and Thomas Edison observing Taylor-Winfield's technician welding in 1927

Taylor-Winfield's Eclipse X1® Laser Welder

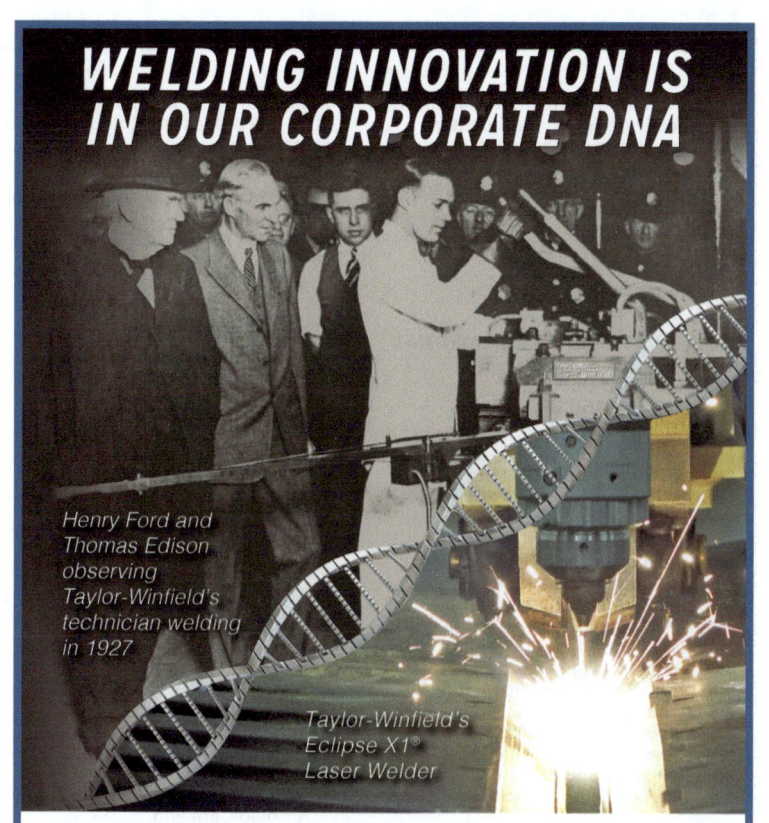

140-YEAR LEGACY OF PROVIDING THE MOST ADVANCED WELDERS TO THE METALS PROCESSING INDUSTRY

Since 1882, we have been developing innovative welding techniques for some of America's more historic manufacturers and greatest inventors. Today, Taylor-Winfield Technologies is continuing to develop the world's most advanced welding technologies for continuous steel process lines around the globe.

Contact us today for more information on our innovative line of coil joining welders.

Taylor Winfield TECHNOLOGIES, INC.

www.taylor-winfield.com
+1.330.259.8500

SUPPLIERS of EQUIPMENT, PRODUCTS and SERVICES

joints, wear-resistant liners and shafts specifically designed for the steel industry. Offers performance upgrades, PM and rebuild/retrofits of existing induced-draft baghouse equipment. Technos' field crews are certified and trained full-time employees in all phases of fan repairs.

No. of Employees: 75.

TECHNOVATIONS INTERNATIONAL INC. (TII)
198 Duck Pond Dr.
Groton, MA 01450 USA
P: +1.978.842.4587;
   +1.978.798.0320
technovationsintl@gmail.com
www.technovations.ws

- Pres.—Ram K. Iyengar

PRODUCTS and/or SERVICES:
TII associates provide technical services for the manufacture of high-performance thick steel plates including controlled reheating of ingots, shape factor rolling, heat treatment and product quality improvement for a steel company in Ohio. TII develops and implements best practices for process and resource efficiency, improving product performance, and training in end-use applications.

No. of Associates: 3.

TEMCO INDUSTRIES INC.
670 Steubenville Pike
Burgettstown, PA 15021 USA
P: +1.724.947.7700
F: +1.724.947.5700
sales@temcoind.com
www.temcoind.com

- Gen. Mgr.—Andrew Mitch
- Oprs.—C. Henderson

EQUIPMENT:
Burn tables, press brakes, MIG/TIG welding, lathes, rollers, iron works, saws, heavy-lift bridge cranes.

PRODUCTS and/or SERVICES:
Custom plate, pipe and structural fabrications. Capability to produce a wide variety of components for steel mill processing equipment and machinery.

TEMPOSONICS LLC, an Amphenol Co.
3001 Sheldon Dr.
Cary, NC 27513 USA
P: +1.919.677.0100
F: +1.919.677.0200
info.us@temposonics.com
www.temposonics.com

- Chief Exec. Officer and Pres.—Jeffrey A. Graves
- Exec. Vice Pres.—Brian T. Ross

PRODUCTS and/or SERVICES:
Linear position sensors.

No. of Employees: 443.

TENOVA S.p.A.
Via Gerenzano 58
Castellanza (VA), 21053 Italy
P: +39.331.444111
F: +39.331.444390
tenova@tenova.com
www.tenova.com

- Chief Exec. Officer—Roberto Pancaldi
- Exec. (Upstream Business Unit)—Paolo Argenta
- Exec. (Downstream Business Unit)—Antonio Catalano
- Exec. (Pomini Business Unit)—Paolo Gaboardi
- Exec. (Material Handling Business Unit)—Silvio Leoni
- Chief Communications Officer—Sara Secomandi
- Mktg. Mgr.—Marina Carrea

PRODUCTS and/or SERVICES:
Worldwide partner for sustainable, innovative and reliable solutions in the metals industry, and, through the well-known TAKRAF and DELKOR brands, in the mining industries. From hydrometallurgy to port facilities, DRI to EAF, reheating furnaces to heat treatment furnaces, cold rolling mills to processing lines and roll grinding and texturing, Tenova provides technology to minimize the environmental impact

SUPPLIERS OF EQUIPMENT, PRODUCTS and SERVICES

of clients and improve the quality of their products.

No. of Employees: 2,200.

Americas:

Tenova Inc.
100 Corporate Center Dr.
Cherrington Corporate Center
Coraopolis, PA 15108 USA
P: +1.412.262.2240
F: +1.412.262.2055
tenova.usa@tenova.com
- Chief Exec. Officer and Pres.—Francesco Memoli
- Chief Financial Officer—Hernan Mompo
- Vice Pres. Metal Making—Kyle Shoop
- Vice Pres. Reheat and Specialty Furnaces—Thomas Walsh
- Dir. Heat Treat and Strip Processing—Mike Allan
- Vice Pres. Furnace Process Technology—Bill Barraclough
- Vice Pres. Pomini Roll Grinders—Alfredo Brambilla
- Vice Pres. Cold Rolling—Frank Byus

Tenova HYL
HYL Technologies S.A. de C.V.
Av. Múnich 101, Col. Cuauhtémoc
San Nicolás de los Garza, NL, 66450
México
P: +52.81.8865.2801
F: +52.81.8865.2810
hyl@tenova.com
- Chief Exec. Officer and Pres.—Stefano Maggiolino
- Commercial Dir.—Jorge E. Martinez

Tenova Goodfellow Inc.
10 Kingsbridge Garden Cir., Suite 601
Mississauga, ON L5R 3K6 Canada
P: +1.905.507.3330
- Chief Exec. Officer—Marcello Pozzi

Germany:

Tenova LOI Thermprocess
LOI Thermprocess GmbH
Schifferstrasse 80
Duisburg, 47059 Germany
P: +49.203.8039.8900
loi@tenova.com

- Managing Dir.—Christian Schrade

P.R. China:

Tenova Technologies (Tianjin) Co. Ltd.
Room 802-806, T5 Bldg.,
No. 2, Han's Plaza
Yard Ronghua S. Road
Beijing Economic & Technologic Development Zone
Beijing, 100176 P.R. China
P: +86.10.8447.5656
F: +86.10.8447.5858
titb.cn@tenova.com

- Managing Dir.—Guido Molteni

India:

Tenova Technologies Pvt. Ltd.
I Think Techno Campus,
A Wing, 5th Floor
Pokhran Road No. 2
Behind TCS, Thane (West)
Mumbai, MH, 400607 India
P: +91.22.61045700
F: +91.22.61045701
tenova.in@tenova.com

- Managing Dir.—Shirvaikar Shirish

Russia:

Tenova East Europe LLC
Lane Elektricheskiy, House 3/10, Bldg. 4
Moscow, 123557 Russia
P: +7.495.995.95.07
F: +7.495.995.95.07
temos@tenova.com

- Managing Dir.—Lucio Puracchio

South Africa:

Tenova Pyromet
Tenova South Africa (PTY) Ltd.
Midrand Business Park Bldg. #4
563 Old Pretoria Main Road
Halfway House, Midrand 1685
Johannesburg, South Africa
P: +27.11.480.2000
F: +27.86.743.0389
pyromet@tenova.com

- Sr. Vice Pres.—Chris Oertel

SUPPLIERS of EQUIPMENT, PRODUCTS and SERVICES

Vietnam:

Tenova Representative Office Vietnam
6th Floor, Empire Tower
26-28 Ham Nghi St.
Dist. 1, Ho Chi Minh City, Vietnam
P:+84.28.39111.388
F: +84.28.39111.399
tenova.vn@tenova.com

- Chief Rep. Officer—Giuseppe Zanzi

Tenova TAKRAF:

TAKRAF GmbH
Torgauer Strasse 336
Leipzig, 04347 Germany
P: +49.341.2423.500
F: +49.341.2423.510
info@takraf.com

- Sales Dir., TAKRAF—Frank Enderstein

TAKRAF USA Inc.
Regency Plaza
4643 S. Ulster St., Suite 900
Denver, CO 80237 USA
P: +1.303.714.8050
F: +1.303.770.6307

TENUTE SRL
5 Via Leonardo da Vinci
Cambiago (MI), 20040 Italy
P: +39.02.9506523
F: +39.02.9506603
commerciale@tenutesrl.it
www.tenutesrl.com

- Chief Exec. Officer—Raffaello Ravanelli

PRODUCTS and/or SERVICES:
Seals and sealing systems.

No. of Employees: 52.

THERMA-FAB INC.
42421 Gilbert Dr.
Titusville, PA 16354 USA
P: +1.814.827.9455
F: +1.814.827.0047
office@thermafab.com
www.thermafab.com

- Chief Exec. Officer, Pres. and Sales Engr.—Butch Prichard
- Qual. Control and Plant Mgr.—Mark Corbett
- Gen. Mgr., Internal Sales and Office Mgr.—Peggi Corbett
- Applications Engr.—Maryann Hartman

EQUIPMENT:
60,000-sq.-ft. plant. Welders, saws, grinders, presses, positioner, compressor, fork trucks, cranes, oven, scales, heat treat furnace.

PRODUCTS and/or SERVICES:
Castings (all alloys) small to large. All processes (sand, invest, die, shell). Forgings, machining, industrial patterns, centrifugal cast tubes, fabrication (small to medium) for the steel industry and cast-iron observation door assemblies and the petrochemical industry.

No. of Employees: 13.

THERMAL-FLEX SYSTEMS INC.
1831 Middletown Ave.
Northford, CT 06472 USA
P: +1.203.484.2776
info@tflexsys.com
www.tflexsys.com

- Pres.—Daniel Santagata
- Sales Mgr.—Jerry Santagata

PRODUCTS and/or SERVICES:
Crane rail heating systems and controls.

No. of Employees: 10.

THERMO FISHER SCIENTIFIC
22 Alpha Road
Chelmsford, MA 01824 USA
P: +1.978.663.2300
F: +1.978.667.4146
sales.gauging@thermofisher.com
www.thermofisher.com/metals

- Sales Mgrs. (North America)—Mike Kadar, Polly Whitehouse
- Tech. Product Mgr.—Chris Burnett

536   2023 AIST Directory — Iron and Steel Plants

SUPPLIERS OF EQUIPMENT, PRODUCTS and SERVICES

EQUIPMENT:
On-line non-contact thickness and coating weight gauges for hot and cold rolling mills, providing flat sheet dimensional measurements.

PRODUCTS and/or SERVICES:
Single-point and instantaneous profile thickness gauges, hot zinc coating weight gauges, other metal and non-metallic coating measurement and control systems.

No. of Employees: 80,000.

Thermo Fisher Scientific (Electron Microscopy Products)
5350 N.E. Dawson Creek Dr.
Hillsboro, OR 97124 USA
www.thermofisher.com/EM

EQUIPMENT:
Imaging and analytical applications for R&D, non-metallic inclusion analysis for process improvements, and quality control.

PRODUCTS and/or SERVICES:
SEM, TEM, EDS, and focused ion beam (FIB) systems and in-house expertise provide market-leading products such as Apreo SEM, Helios PFIB and Explorer MQA.

THERMO FISHER SCIENTIFIC (ECUBLENS) SARL
En Vallaire Ouest C, Ch. de Verney 2
Ecublens, VD, 1024 Switzerland
P: +41.21.694.71.11
info.spectrometry@thermofisher.com
www.thermofisher.com/elemental

- Sales Mgr. (North America)—Matt Cerutti, matt.cerutti@thermofisher.com

PRODUCTS and/or SERVICES:
Optical emission and x-ray instruments for elemental and phase analysis of solids and liquids. ARL iSpark, ARL easySpark metals analyzers; ARL 9900, ARL QUANT'X EDXRF, ARL OPTIM'X WDXRF, ARL PERFORM'X WDXRF spectrometers, ARL EQUINOX Series XRD instruments, ARL SMS 2300/3300/3500 automation systems for metals analysis.

No. of Employees: 130,000.

THOMPSON INDUSTRIAL SERVICES LLC
104 N. Main St.
Sumter, SC 29150 USA
P: +1.803.773.8005
F: +1.803.773.1955
cwise@thompsonind.com
www.thompsonindustrialservices.com

- Chief Exec. Officer and Pres.—William "Billy" Ford
- Vice Pres. Sales—Larry Rocco
- Sales Mgr.—Jeremy Knight

PRODUCTS and/or SERVICES:
Safe, quality life cycle industrial cleaning service solutions from critical path pre-commissioning and on-site operations support to major, comprehensive outages. Oil flushing and ultra-filtration to 1 micron, chemical cleaning, dry/wet/sludge vacuuming, automated hydroblasting, high-volume and ultrahigh-pressure hydroblasting and cutting, combustible dust removal, cryogenic (dry ice) cleaning, pneumatic/hydro-vacuum excavation, and custom specialty solutions.

No. of Employees: 1,000.

TIMKEN CO., THE
4500 Mount Pleasant NW
North Canton, OH 44720 USA
P: +1.234.262.3000
www.timken.com

- Chmn. of the Bd.—John M. Timken Jr.
- Chief Exec. Officer and Pres.—Richard G. Kyle
- Exec. Vice Pres. and Group Pres.—Andreas Roellgen
- Exec. Vice Pres. and Pres. Ind. Motion—Christopher Coughlin
- Exec. Vice Pres. and Chief Financial Officer—Philip D. Fracassa
- Exec. Vice Pres., H.R.—Natasha Pollock

SUPPLIERS of EQUIPMENT, PRODUCTS and SERVICES

PRODUCTS and/or SERVICES:
Friction management and industrial motion products and services.

No. of Employees: 18,000.

TITAN BEARINGS
425 Caro Lane
Chapin, SC 29036 USA
P: +1.803.298.5986;
+1.803.231.8227 (Mobile)
ship@m-rsi.com
www.m-rsi.com
www.titanbearing.com

- Pres.—Jeff Blankenship
- Vice Pres.—Jeff Kusnier,
  jeff@m-rsi.com

PRODUCTS and/or SERVICES:
Specialty bearing and rotating solutions for heavy industry.

No. of Employees: 2.

TMEIC CORP. AMERICAS
1325 Electric Road
Roanoke, VA 24018 USA

Mailing/Receiving Address:
2060 Cook Dr.
Salem, VA 24153 USA
P: +1.540.283.2000
F: +1.540.283.2001
www.tmeic.com

- Chief Exec. Officer—Manmeet Bhatia
- Exec. Vice Pres.—Masashi Yamamoto
- Chief Financial Officer—Hubert Mensah
- Ind. Systems Vice Pres.—Declan Daly
- Technology Vice Pres.—Paul Bixel
- Commercial Dir.—Darren Honaker
- Industry Segment Leader—Kevin Bort
- Sales Mgrs.—Bryan Beard, Thomas Daum, Greg Podlecki, Ernesto Rivera, Tony Adams, Rob Brunelli

EQUIPMENT:
Automation solutions for hot strip mills, cold mills, long products, and process lines including a full range of AC and DC drives and motors, industrial controllers, software, and plant services.

PRODUCTS and/or SERVICES:
AC and DC variable speed drives and motors ranging from 10 to 50,000 kW. Comprehensive metals automation solutions from simple drive upgrades to full process systems with process modeling. Drive system installations for applications such as hot mills, cold mills, bar mills and process lines.

No. of Employees: 2,200.

TML TECHNIK GMBH
Daimlerstrasse 14-16
Monheim am Rhein
NRW, 40789 Germany
P: +49.2173.9575.100
info@tml.de
www.tml.de

- Pres.—Christof Mikat
- Vice Pres. Sales—Michael Hobden

EQUIPMENT:
Production facilities for welding, laser cutting, machining, fabricating, and assembly of all manufactured products and equipment, including a workshop to produce hydraulic hoses and pipes.

PRODUCTS and/or SERVICES:
Mobile and stationary steel mill equipment. Debricking machines for ladles and furnaces. Slag raking machines. Charging machines for EAFs. Taphole repair machines. EBT-drilling units. Converter service machines. All machines are available diesel-hydraulic or electric-hydraulic driven. Operation from the cabin and/or radio remote controlled.

No. of Employees: 102.

SUPPLIERS of EQUIPMENT, PRODUCTS and SERVICES

TMS INTERNATIONAL LLC
Southside Works, Bldg. 1, Third Floor
2835 E. Carson St.
Pittsburgh, PA 15203 USA
P: +1.412.678.6141
F: +1.412.675.8291

1155 Business Center Dr.
Horsham, PA 19044 USA
P: +1.215.956.5500
F: +1.215.956.5589

2901 Carlson Dr., Suite 100
Hammond, IN 46323 USA
P: +1.219.864.0044
F: +1.219.864.0045
www.tmsinternational.com

- Chief Exec. Officer and Pres.—Raymond S. Kalouche
- Chief Oper. Officer, Raw Matl. and Optimization Group and Pres.—J. David Aronson
- Pres., Environ. and Ind. Svcs. Group—Richard L. Santello Jr.
- Exec. Vice Pres., Oprs. North America—Mark Whalen
- Exec. Vice Pres., Oprs. Intl.—Michael Costa
- Sr. Vice Pres., Chief Financial Officer—Kirk D. Peters
- Sr. Vice Pres. and Gen. Counsel—Caitlin Gifford
- Sr. Vice Pres., North American Trading and Business Dev., Raw Matl. and Optimization Group—Hank Wilson

EQUIPMENT:
Shredders, shears, balers, cranes, railcars, specialized mobile equipment and eddy current separators.

PRODUCTS and/or SERVICES:
Domestic and international provider of a full range of outsource steel mill and environmental services. Services include raw materials purchasing and sales worldwide; scrap management; scrap optimization; extruded product services; installation and operation of complete slag processing and metal recovery systems; slag pot carriers; raw material and finished product handling; lancing and shearing; environmental services; mobile equipment rental; maintenance and slag sales; scarfing (surface conditioning) and ancillary services. The company also provides Scrap OptiMiser® and Gen Blend+® optimization software, proprietary purchasing and melt-chemistry optimization programs that determine the optimal scrap mix for every heat melt order and ensure the lowest-cost liquid steel; and the Alloy Blending System (ABS), a comprehensive software package that allows customers to create value within their melting operations. TMS is also a leading provider of transportation and recycling, hydroexcavation, vacuum and container management services, serving a wide variety of industrial customers, including customers in the chemical and petrochemical industries.

TOKAI CARBON GE LLC
6210 Ardrey Kell Road, Suite 270
Charlotte, NC 28277 USA
P: +1.800.828.6601 (Toll-Free)
www.tokaicarbonusa.com

- Vice Pres. of Sales, Mktg. and Tech. Svce.—Jay McCloy,
  jay.mccloy@tokaicarbon.com

EQUIPMENT:
Four graphite electrode manufacturing facilities in Ozark, AR, USA; Hofu, Japan; Shiga, Japan; and Grevenbroich, Germany.

PRODUCTS and/or SERVICES:
14-in. to 32-in.-dia. graphite electrodes.

No. of Employees: 2,300 (consolidated).

TORCUP OF WESTERN PENNSYLVANIA AND NORTHERN OHIO
3530 Tuscarawas Road
Beaver, PA 15009 USA
P: +1.724.494.2306
F: +1.610.250.2700
torcupwpa@verizon.net
www.torcup.com

- Sales Rep.—Jeffrey Young

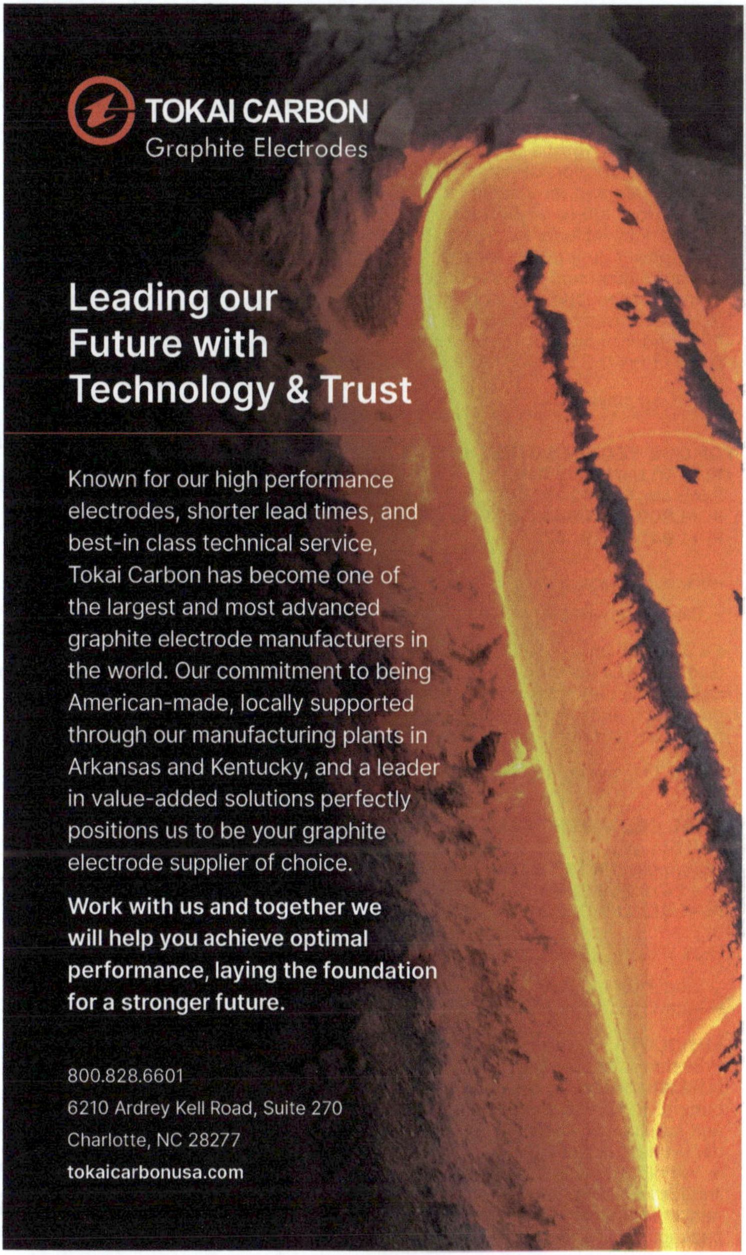

See listing page 540

SUPPLIERS of EQUIPMENT, PRODUCTS and SERVICES

PRODUCTS and/or SERVICES: Manufactures, sells, services, and rents hydraulic, battery-powered, pneumatic and electronic torque wrenches to heavy industry. TorcUP tools can provide safe and repeatable torque values from 100 to 58,000 ft-lbs. Applications include: heavy equipment, wind, power generation, oil and gas production and exploration, rail transportation, and many others. Sales representatives across the U.S. and throughout the world. TorcUP tools are made in the U.S.

No. of Employees: 1.

TORQUE TECHNOLOGIES INC.
1623 W. University Ave.
Sarasota, FL 34243 USA
P: +1.800.813.0844 (Toll-Free)
F: +1.941.358.9647
brad@torq-tech.com
www.goizperusa.com

- Sales Mgr.—Bradley Binks

PRODUCTS and/or RESOURCES—Guibe gearboxes for hot and cold rolling mills and finishing lines. Goizper pneumatic and hydraulic clutch-brakes for shears and other applications.

No. of Employees: 10.

TOTAL EQUIPMENT CO.
400 5th Ave.
Coraopolis, PA 15108 USA
P: +1.412.269.0999
F: +1.412.269.0262
info@totalequipment.com
www.totalequipment.com

- Vice Pres. of Oprs.—Kurt Duckworth
- Vice Pres. of Sales—Eric Solverson

PRODUCTS and/or SERVICES: Provides sales, service, parts, installation, accessories, and rentals for pumps, compressors, blowers, mixers and mechanical seals. 45-man service department is available in-house or in-field with 24-hour emergency service available. Total Equipment Co. has an in-house machine shop and a packaging area. Other services offered include: vertical turbine rebowls, air-end rebuilds, vibration analysis, field balancing, oil sampling, leak detection and laser alignment.

No. of Employees: 105.

TR ELECTRONIC
955 Green Valley Road
London, ON N6N 1E4 Canada
P: +1.800.709.3300 (Toll-Free U.S.);
 +1.800.265.9483 (Toll-Free Canada)
F: +1.519.452.1177
customercare@trelectronic.com
www.trelectronic.com

- Pres.—Tod Warner
- Regional Sales Mgrs.—Paul Evans, John Hice, Keith Croxdale, Craig Moore, Jon Jacobs, Shawn Zumbrum, Todd Renier
- Pur. Agt.—Jeff Whitney
- Chief Engr.—Kevin Condorato

PRODUCTS and/or SERVICES: Rotary absolute encoders, linear transducers, cable retractors, string pots, laser distance measurement, sensors, switches, machine lighting, die protection.

No. of Employees: 24.

USA Head Office
200 E. Big Beaver
Troy, MI 48083 USA
P: +1.800.709.3300
F: +1.248.244.2283
customercare@trelectronic.com
www.trelectronic.com

TRAMCO PUMP CO.
1428 Sherman Road
Romeoville, IL 60446 USA
P: +1.312.243.5800
sales@tramcopump.com
www.tramcopump.com

- Pres.—John P. Obermaier

PRODUCTS and/or SERVICES: Manufacture/distribute pumps for various applications; sump, sewage, slurries, sludge, scale, condensate, booster and high-viscosity liquids. Has the following types of pumps available:

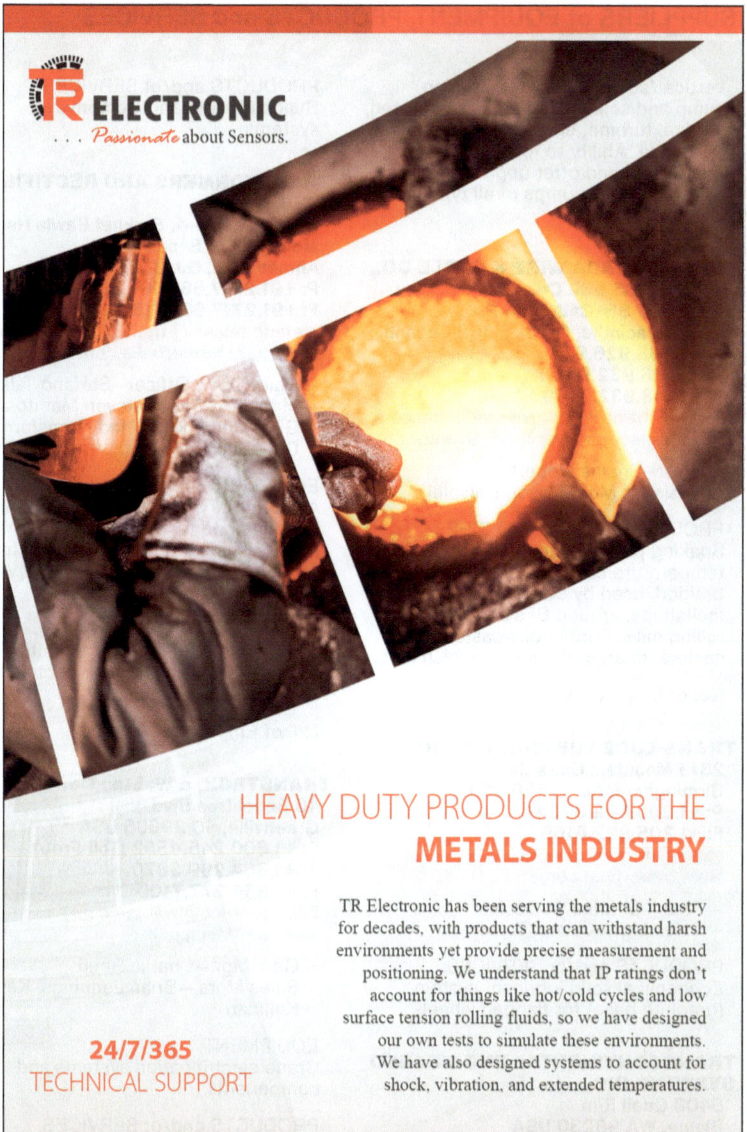

See listing page 542

SUPPLIERS of EQUIPMENT, PRODUCTS and SERVICES

vertical/submersible/self-priming sump and solids handling, air-operated, vertical turbine, engine driven, ANSI, split case. Ability to retrofit existing installation and offer upgrades. Repair capabilities for pumps of all types and sizes.

TRANS CANADA WIRE & CABLE CO., a Div. of NCS Intl. Co.
201-1005 Ste-Catherine Ave.
Saint-Hyacinthe, QC J2S 8C6 Canada
P: +1.888.926.9473 (Toll-Free);
   +1.613.932.9450
F: +1.613.932.7450
tcwc7@transcanadawireandcable.com
www.transcanadawireandcable.com

- Pres.—Shaine Nobert
- Business Mgr.—Jason Betsalel

PRODUCTS and/or SERVICES:
Soaking pit cable and FG2000 high-temperature cables, stainless steel braided, used by steel mills in their meltshops, around BFs and EAFs, hot rolling mills, continuous casters, slab casters, charging cranes, tundish cars.

No. of Employees: 6.

TRANS-LUBE LUBRICANTS INC.
2315 Mountain Oaks Cir.
Birmingham, AL 35226 USA
P: +1.205.822.3934
F: +1.205.822.6169
sales@trans-lube.com
www.trans-lube.com

- Pres.—Charles W. Davis
- Sales Mgr.—Jaime Reyes

PRODUCTS and/or SERVICES:
Economical solid lubricant system (graphite base) for flanged wheels.

TRANSCONTINENTAL ENGINEERED SYSTEMS INC.
5408 Quail Run
Blaine, WA 98230 USA
P: +1.360.371.7212
F: +1.360.371.0575
dc.penfold@tepgroup.com

PRODUCTS and/or SERVICES:
Bulk material handling conveyor systems.

TRANSFORMERS AND RECTIFIERS (INDIA) LTD.
S.N.4217 P/3-4, Sarkhef Bawla Hwy.
Moraiya, TA: Sanad Dist.
Ahmedabad, GJ, 382212 India
P: +91.2717.661.661
F: +91.2717.661.716
stefano.talassi@transformerindia.com
www.transformerindia.com

- Chief Oper. Officer—Stefano Talassi
- Managing Dir.—Sateyen Mamtora
- Gen. Mgr. Mktg. — Ind. Transformer Div.—Bijoyen Das

EQUIPMENT:
All necessary manufacturing, material handling and testing equipment required for transformer manufacturing up to 1,200 kv class and 1,000 MVA. KEMA approved product.

PRODUCTS and/or SERVICES:
Transformers for EAF, LF, induction furnace, substation power, rectifiers and special applications.

No. of Employees: 1,600.

TRANSTECH, a Wabtec Co.
46 Beechtree Blvd.
Greenville, SC 29605 USA
P: +1.800.245.4552 (Toll-Free);
   +1.864.299.3870
F: +1.864.277.7100
infotranstech@wabtec.com
www.transtech.com

- Gen. Mgr.—Charlie Reed
- Sales Mgrs.—Brian Jennings, Kevin Keilman

EQUIPMENT:
Crane electrification systems and components.

PRODUCTS and/or SERVICES:
Crane collector systems and components, insulators, collectors, cable reels, and festoon systems.

SUPPLIERS OF EQUIPMENT, PRODUCTS and SERVICES

TRE SERVICES INC.
21 Leonberg Road
Cranberry Twp., PA 16066 USA
P: +1.724.538.5444
F: +1.724.538.5441
taleb@treservices.com
www.treservices.com

- Chief Engr.—Taleb Talaat

PRODUCTS and/or SERVICES:
Refractory engineering, including product specifications and applications, supply, and field installation/inspection.

No. of Employees: 10.

TREBNICK SYSTEMS INC.
215 S. Pioneer Blvd.
Springboro, OH 45066 USA
P: +1.937.743.1550
F: +1.937.743.1558
gregg@trebnick.com

- Pres.—Linda Trebnick
- Exec. Vice Pres.—Aaron Trebnick
- Sales Solutions Mgr.—Gregg Trebnick

PRODUCTS and/or SERVICES:
Label and tag manufacturer, RFID, printers, and service.

No. of Employees: 25.

TRI-STATE HYDRAULICS
1250 McKean Ave.
Charleroi, PA 15022 USA
P: +1.724.483.1790
F: +1.724.489.0911
sales@tristatehyd.com
www.tristatehyd.com

- Pres.—James D. Palmer II
- Sec. and Treas.—Scott D. Palmer

PRODUCTS and/or SERVICES:
Full-line fluid power products distributor and service company. Products include hydraulic pumps, valves, motors and cylinders, cylinder repairs, servo valves and controllers, position sensors, filtration, accumulators, lubrication equipment, hydraulic and air tools, custom seals, hydraulic bumpers and shock absorbers, hose assemblies, hydraulic power units. Locations and offices: Charleroi, PA; Johnstown, PA; Cleveland, OH; Carrollton, KY; Decatur, AL; Morgantown, WV; and Charleston, SC.

No. of Employees: 60.

TRIBCO INC.
18901 Cranwood Pkwy.
Cleveland, OH 44128 USA
P: +1.216.486.2000
F: +1.216.486.2099
info@tribco.com
www.tribco.com

- Mktg. Mgr.—Nick Bade

PRODUCTS and/or SERVICES:
100% Kevlar composite brake pads, discs and shoes.

No. of Employees: <50.

TRICON WEAR SOLUTIONS
P.O. Box 101447
Birmingham, AL 35219 USA
P: +1.205.956.2567
F: +1.205.956.9703
www.triconwearsolutions.com

- Chief Exec. Officer—Todd Plate
- Chief Financial Officer—Michael Symasek
- Prod. Mgr.—David Terakedis
- Sales Dir.—B.J. Osborne
- Mktg. Dir.—Vance Moody

EQUIPMENT:
Torch cutting, forming and welding.

PRODUCTS and/or SERVICES:
Abrasion-resistant materials and fabrications.

No. of Employees: 170.

TUBE-MAC® PIPING TECHNOLOGIES LTD.
853 Arvin Ave.
Stoney Creek, ON L8E 5N3 Canada
P: +1.905.643.8823
F: +1.905.643.0643
info@tube-mac.com
www.tube-mac.com

SUPPLIERS of EQUIPMENT, PRODUCTS and SERVICES

PRODUCTS and/or SERVICES: Complete piping systems, layout, manufacturing, project management and/or turnkey installation, oil flushing and testing of non-welded piping/tubing systems of various steel mill equipment. Product line includes: Tube-Mac® 37° Flare Flanges, TMI Retain Ring Flanges, PYPLOK® mechanically attached fittings, precision pipe and tubes both in carbon steel or stainless steel, high-pressure ball valves, hoses and pipe supports.

TULLOCH ENGINEERING
71 Black Road, Unit 8
Sault Ste. Marie, ON P6B 0A3 Canada
P: +1.705.949.1457
F: +1.705.949.9606
mark.coleman@tulloch.ca
www.tulloch.ca

- Pres.—Mark Tulloch
- Chief Financial Officer—Dave Tulloch
- Mech. Chief Engr.—Nathan Lambert

PRODUCTS and/or SERVICES: General engineering mechanical, structural, civil (BFs, BOPs, mill buildings, tube mills, coke ovens and byproducts). Piping, machine design, pressure piping, 3D modeling, laser scanning, bridges, roads, sewers, drainage, surveying, mill buildings, crane runways, office buildings, roof systems, building envelopes.

No. of Employees: 350.

TYK AMERICA INC.
301 Brickyard Road
Clairton, PA 15025 USA
P: +1.412.384.4259
F: +1.412.384.4242
jimk@tykamerica.com
www.tykamerica.com

- Chief Exec. Officer—Nobutaka Ushigome
- Pres.—Andrew Elksnitis
- Exec. Vice Pres. and Gen. Sales Mgr.—James Karamanos

PRODUCTS and/or SERVICES: Global manufacturer and supplier of innovative refractory materials for BFs, iron transfer vessels, BOFs, RH degasser vessels and snorkels, steel ladles, EAFs, and continuous casting applications. TYK's product line includes a full range of brick shapes and materials for furnaces and ladles, pre-cast shapes, lances, purging plugs, flow control nozzles and plates for many slidegate systems, as well as its own TN-60, 80 and 100 series ladle gates. TYK is also a leading supplier of Isostatically pressed SENs, ladle shrouds and stoppers for continuous casters. TYK's advanced ceramics include diesel particulate filters (DPF), saggars (for lithium ion powder production), metal matrix shot sleeves (for die casting), as well as many other advanced materials.

No. of Employees: 800.

U

UESCO CRANES
5908 W. 118th St.
Alsip, IL 60803 USA
P: +1.800.325.8372 (Toll-Free);
 +1.708.385.7700
F: +1.708.385.6889
cranes@uesco.us
www.uescocranes.com

- Chief Exec. Officer—Ryan D. Marks
- Regional Sales Mgrs.—Brad Cole, Brian Jones, Tad Boyle

PRODUCTS and/or SERVICES: Manufacturer of engineered overhead cranes, motorized gantry cranes, trolleys and runway systems. Uesco

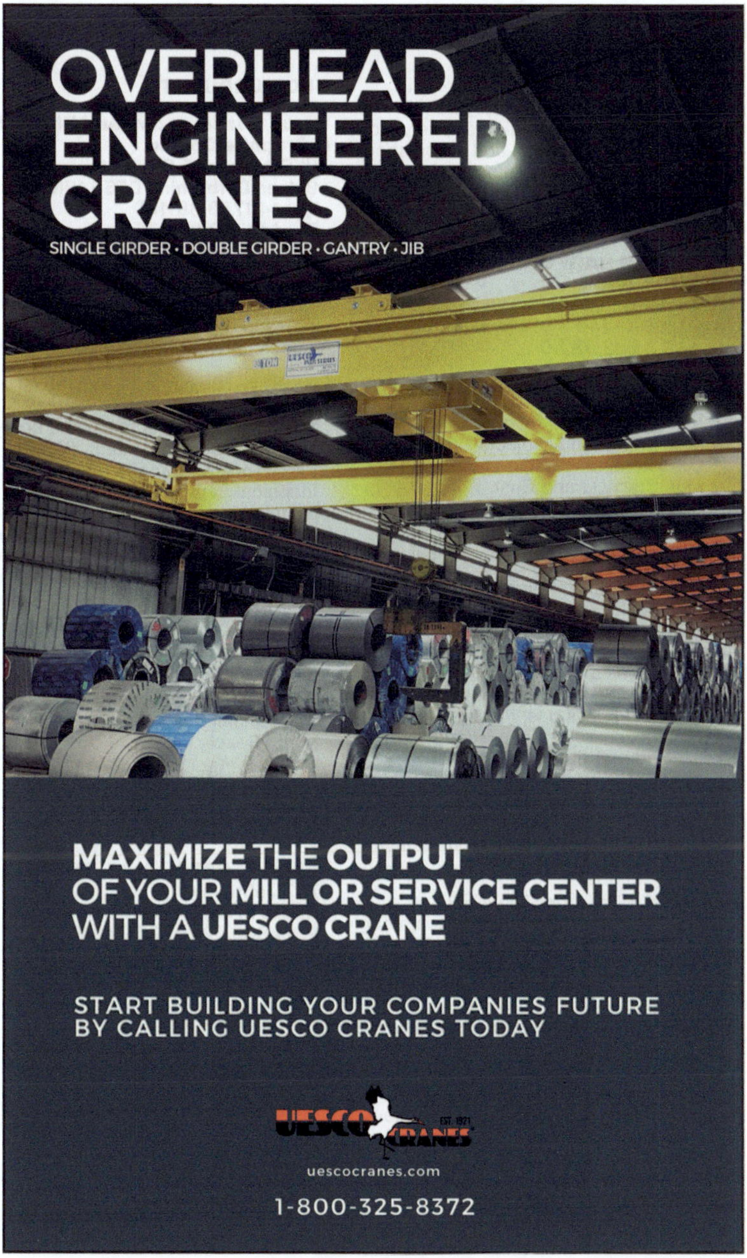

See listing page 546

SUPPLIERS of EQUIPMENT, PRODUCTS and SERVICES

Cranes builds both single girder and double girder cranes in top-running and under-running configurations. Also provides modernization and automation services for existing equipment.

No. of Employees: 50.

UHT—UVÅN HAGFORS TEKNOLOGI AB
Kistagången 2
Kista, SE-16440 Sweden
P: +46.8.622.08.80
info@uht.se
www.uht.se

- Managing Dir.—Christoffer Lundström
- Mgr. Engrg. and Projects—Joakim Lundstöm
- Mgr. Start-Up and Cust. Support—Carl-Johan Rick

EQUIPMENT:
AOD and Creusot-Loire-Uddeholm (CLU) converter refining equipment for the stainless steel and ferroalloy industry. Complete AOD and CLU deliveries or as key components supply. This includes a gas mixing station with the possibility of using superheated steam as process gas; tuyeres; hydraulic converter drive (HCD); level 1 PLC and real-time level 2 UTCAS process control; and GRANSHOT metal granulation units to the iron, steel and ferroalloy industry, with up to 360 metric tons/hour capacity from runner, torpedo or ladle.

PRODUCTS and/or SERVICES:
Consulting/feasibility studies, customer pilot GRANSHOT tests, basic and detailed engineering, in-house production, assembly and factory acceptance testing, supervision, commissioning and start-up, training and on-site support, process guarantees, process support, and process optimization. Service, spare parts and upgrades: converter solution for AOD and CLU, process control (UTCAS) for EAF, AOD/BOF, LF, VD/VOD, gas mixing station, metal granulation unit—GRANSHOT to produce granulated pig iron (GPI).

UKCG GROUP LTD.

Group Headquarters and UK Carbon & Graphite Co. Ltd.
UKCG House, 5 Strutt St.
Belper, Derbyshire, DE56 1UN U.K.
P: +44.1773.881130
F: +44.1773.881138
enquiries@uk-cg.com
www.uk-cg.com

- Managing Dir.—Greg Pitts
- Group Mfg. Dir.—Richard Moore
- Tech. Svce. Dir.—Alfonso Martinez

PRODUCTS and/or SERVICES:
Specializes in a range of carbon and graphite products backed up by an expert technical team. UKCG's UK Carbon & Graphite and UKCG Technical Services divisions offer complete technical solutions and EAF optimization. Product range includes electrodes for EAF/LMF applications up to 28-in. dia. Also provides technical services at no additional cost, including full technical regulation analysis, recommendations and adjustments to improve furnace operation.

UKCG Technical Services
350 Lincoln Road, Floor 2
Miami Beach, FL 33139 USA
technicalservice@uk-cg.com
www.uk-cg.com

- Tech. Sales Dir.—John McAuliffe

ULTRA ELECTRONICS, ENERGY
707 Jeffrey Way
Round Rock, TX 78680 USA
P: +1.800.321.0796 (Toll-Free)
sean.coakley@ultra-nspi.com
www.ultra.energy

- Gen. Mgr.—Sean Coakley

PRODUCTS and/or SERVICES:
Specialty industrial thermocouples, including metal sheathed, base metal and noble metal thermocouple assemblies. Product line includes MgO and platinum assemblies, vacuum-sealed assemblies, platinum wire, and base metal assemblies and wire. Also offers protection tubes, thermowells, plastic thermocouples, resistance

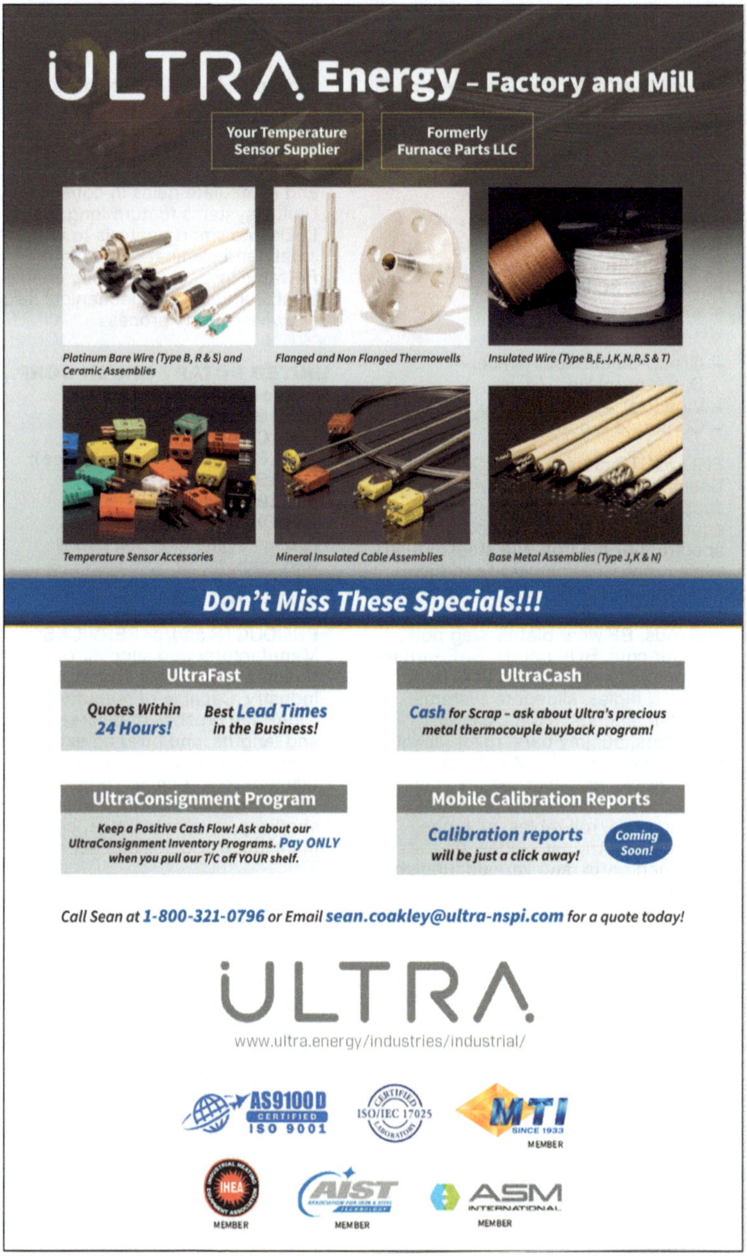
ULTRA Energy - Factory and Mill
Your Temperature Sensor Supplier
Formerly Furnace Parts LLC
Platinum Bare Wire (Type B, R & S) and Ceramic Assemblies
Flanged and Non Flanged Thermowells
Insulated Wire (Type B,E,J,K,N,R,S & T)
Temperature Sensor Accessories
Mineral Insulated Cable Assemblies
Base Metal Assemblies (Type J,K & N)
Don't Miss These Specials!!!
UltraFast
Quotes Within 24 Hours!
Best Lead Times in the Business!
UltraCash
Cash for Scrap - ask about Ultra's precious metal thermocouple buyback program!
UltraConsignment Program
Keep a Positive Cash Flow! Ask about our UltraConsignment Inventory Programs. Pay ONLY when you pull our T/C off YOUR shelf.
Mobile Calibration Reports
Calibration reports will be just a click away!
Coming Soon!
Call Sean at 1-800-321-0796 or Email sean.coakley@ultra-nspi.com for a quote today!
ULTRA
www.ultra.energy/industries/industrial/
AS9100D CERTIFIED ISO 9001
CERTIFIED ISO/IEC 17025 LABORATORY
MTI SINCE 1933 MEMBER
IHEA MEMBER
AIST MEMBER
ASM INTERNATIONAL MEMBER

SUPPLIERS of EQUIPMENT, PRODUCTS and SERVICES

temperature detectors, hardware and connectors in a wide variety of styles and sizes. Fully accredited calibration and repair services.

UMECC
9468 Meridan Way
West Chester, OH 45069 USA
P: +1.888.966.6322 (Toll-Free)
F: +1.513.336.6185
mail@umecc.com
www.umecc.com

- Group Chief Exec. Officer—
  D. (George) He
- Vice Pres.—Anderson Hu
- Corporate Product Mgr.—Brown R. Yin

PRODUCTS and/or SERVICES: Design, engineering, manufacturing, supply and commissioning of heavy equipment, covering the entire spectrum of the iron and steel industry. Wide range of engineered products and equipment, including coke oven castings, BF valves, staves, BF drill bits and rods, BF wear plates, slag pots, transfer cars, BOF hoods, EAF furnace equipment, water-cooled panels, scrap buckets, ladles, slidegate systems, slidegate springs, molds, caster segments, dummy bars, roller jackets, bearing housings, HSM rolls, cold mill rolls, chocks and accessories, spindles, screwdowns, reheat furnace skids, cooling beds, roll tables, all types of castings, stripper blades, tie rods, machined parts, and various tundish and ladle refractories.

UNIFRAX LLC—see ALKEGEN

UNILUX INC.
59 N. 5th St.
Saddle Brook, NJ 07663 USA
P: +1.201.712.1266
F: +1.201.712.1366
unilux@unilux.com
www.unilux.com

PRODUCTS and/or SERVICES: Provides inspection solutions that give operators the ability to confirm quality at full production speed. Edge Tech provides a real-time view of the trimmed edge, eliminating waste and re-trim due to improper knife settings or nicked blade edges. Edge Trim is an ideal retrofit to make existing lines more efficient with fast ROI and immediate gains in consistency. Unilux systems feature long-life LEDs and smart controls to improve safety and eliminate downtime. Portable inspection strobes enable troubleshooting of mechanical issues, anywhere in the process.

UNITED ROTARY BRUSH CORP., Engineered Products Div.
8150 Business Way
Plain City, OH 43064 USA
P: +1.800.896.0003 (Toll-Free);
  +1.937.644.3515
F: +1.937.642.3552
jeffp@united-rotary.com
epdsales@united-rotary.com
www.united-rotary.com

- Sales Rep.—Jeff Purcell

PRODUCTS and/or SERVICES: Manufacturer and supplier of industrial brushes to the steel and aluminum industry. Capable of manufacturing wide-face brushes of diverse diameters and lengths, and offer an extensive selection of abrasive and non-abrasive filament to suit unique applications. Other services include complete shaft repair, maintenance, bearing installation and delivery service.

UNITED STATES CONTROLS
8511 Foxwood Ct.
Poland, OH 44514 USA
P: +1.330.758.1147
F: +1.330.758.7976
www.unitedstatescontrols.com

- Chief Exec. Officer and Pres.—
  Desmond J. McDonald
- Commercial Mgr.—Lisa L. Quinn
- Oprs. Mgr.—Rod Christensen
- Sales Dir.—Ken Flowers

PRODUCTS and/or SERVICES: Specializes in manufacturing precision spray systems used by the metals rolling processing industries to apply coolant and lubricants to

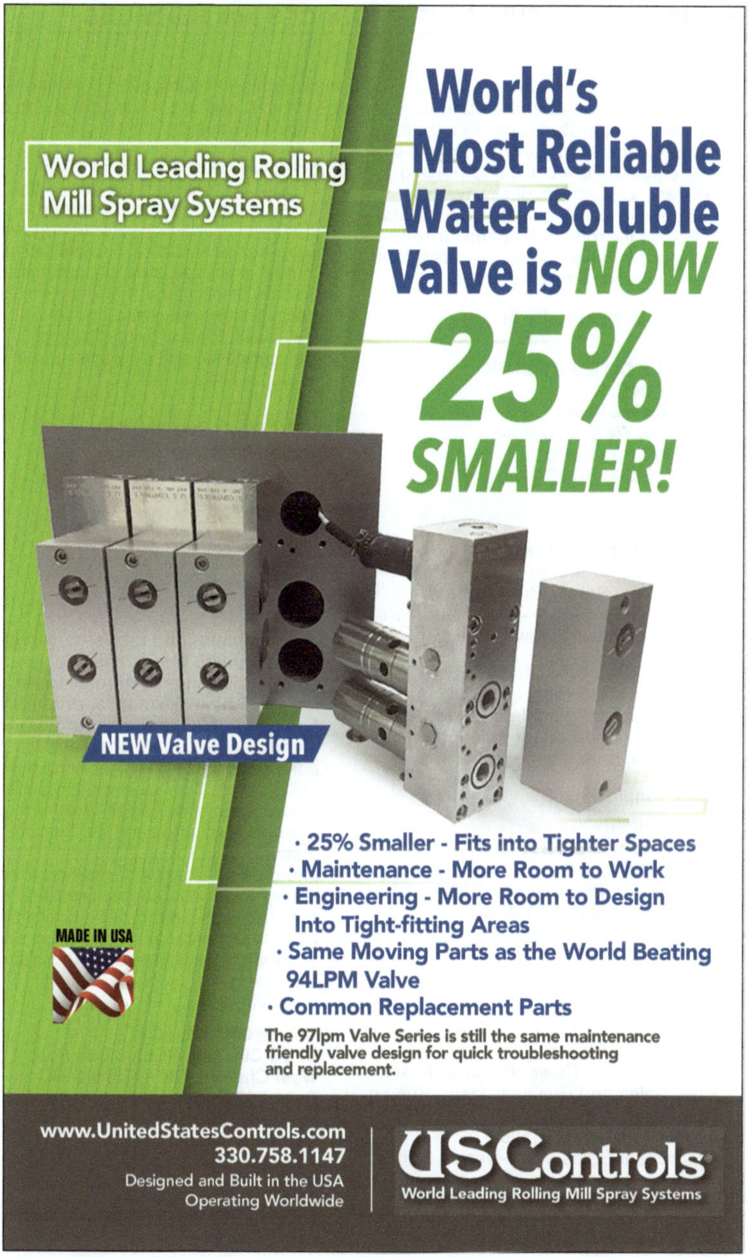

See listing page 550

SUPPLIERS of EQUIPMENT, PRODUCTS and SERVICES

rolls and strip. USC spray systems are actuated by automatic flatness sensors, temperature control inputs, manually operated control stations or USC electrical controls, and pulsing software. USC offers spray systems for applying water-soluble and mineral oil liquids for roll cooling and/or roll heating. All systems are CAD designed to suit customer requirements.

No. of Employees: 25–50.

UNITED STATES ROLLER WORKS INC.
1901 Elm Hill Pike
Nashville, TN 37210 USA
P: +1.615.391.3300
F: +1.615.391.5003
usrw@usrwinc.com
www.unitedstatesrollerworks.com

- Pres.—James R. Robers
- Vice Pres.—Richard D. Howell
- Vice Pres. Sales—Brad Robers
- Acct. Mgmt./Sales—Ellen Randolph
- New Business—Drew Robers

PRODUCTS and/or SERVICES:
Rubber-covered rolls; core design and fabrication; complete roll repair; thermal spray hardcoat rolls; chrome rolls; metal rolls; copper rolls.

No. of Employees: 30.

UNIVERSAL INDUSTRIAL GASES LLC
3001 Emrick Blvd., Suite 320
Bethlehem, PA 18020 USA
P: +1.610.559.7967
F: +1.610.515.0945
info@uigi.com
www.uigi.com

- Chief Exec. Officer and Pres.—Samuel D. Piazza
- Chief Oper. Officer—Kevin A. Baker
- Dir. Sales and Business Dev.—Steven G. Ruoff
- Sales Mgr.—Eric Blance
- Merchant Sales Mgr.—Nazilla Nahid

EQUIPMENT:
New and used air separation plants, tanks, and related equipment for producing and supplying oxygen, nitrogen and argon for use in iron and steel facilities.

PRODUCTS and/or SERVICES:
Supply of oxygen, nitrogen, and argon from UIG-owned and -operated or customer-owned on-site air separation/liquefaction facilities. Project execution of new and used air separation plants on sale-of-equipment and sale-of-gas basis. Engineering and consultant services, along with operations, maintenance, and upgrade support to air separation plants.

UNIVERSAL URETHANE PRODUCTS INC.
410 First St.
Toledo, OH 43605 USA
P: +1.419.693.7400
F: +1.419.693.2363
sales@universalurethane.com
www.universalurethane.com

PRODUCTS and/or SERVICES:
Polyurethane- and rubber-covered rolls including bridle rolls, blocker rolls, coater rolls, squeegee rolls, tower rolls, cell rolls, hold-down rolls, print rolls and pinch rolls, urethane and rubber mandrel sleeves and segments such as unwind and rewind sleeves, temper mill sleeves, filler sleeves, expander sleeves and slitter rings, urethane coil storage pads and saddles, custom molding of parts of all sizes, shapes and custom-designed, replacement snow plow blade edges, urethane stock flat sheet, round rod and square bar, jobsite technical assistance. Complete steel and aluminum core building and balancing.

UPA TECHNOLOGY
8963 Cincinnati-Columbus Road
West Chester, OH 45069 USA
P: +1.513.755.1380
F: +1.513.755.1381
mjustice@upa.com
www.upa.com

- Pres.—Mike Justice
- Exec. Vice Pres.—Susan Justice

SUPPLIERS OF EQUIPMENT, PRODUCTS and SERVICES

PRODUCTS and/or SERVICES: Coatings measurement instrumentation and lubricant measuring equipment.

No. of Employees: 6–10.

U.S. BORAX | RIO TINTO
200 E. Randolph, Suite 7100
Chicago, IL 60601 USA
P: +1.773.270.6500
www.borax.com

- Mgr. Tech. Mktg. and Strategic Mktg.— Frank Wawrzos, frank.wawrzos@riotinto.com
- Sr. Dev. Specialist, Americas—Fred Ascherl, fred.ascherl@riotinto.com
- Specialist Tech. Market Dev.— Emmanuel Laval, emmanuel.laval@riotinto.com; Maryam Moravej, maryam.moravej@riotinto.com
- Regional Tech. Svce. Mgr., APAC— Kee Lung, kee.lung@riotinto.com
- Dev. Specialist, APAC—Allen Zheng, allen.zheng@riotinto.com
- Mgr. Tech. Mktg., APAC—Songlin Shi, songlin.shi@riotinto.com

PRODUCTS and/or SERVICES: Dehybor®: Anhydrous borate to stabilize stainless steel slag. Neobor®: Pentahydrate borax used in metalworking fluids. Optibor®: Boric oxide used to strengthen metal alloys and steel. Potassium pentaborate and potassium tetraborate: For fluxes for stainless steel.

No. of Employees: 1,000+ globally.

U.S. TSUBAKI POWER TRANSMISSION LLC
301 E. Marquardt Dr.
Wheeling, IL 60090 USA
P: +1.847.459.9500
F: +1.847.459.9520
sales@ustsubaki.com
www.ustsubaki.com

PRODUCTS and/or SERVICES: Roller chain, engineering class chain, sprockets, power transmission components, KabelSchlepp cable and hose carriers.

USA BORESCOPES
3061 Bearden Road
Clarksville, TN 37043 USA
P: +1.931.362.3304
sales@usaborescopes.com
www.usaborescopes.com

- Pres.—Jennifer French
- Vice Pres. Sales—Shayne Gallo
- Asst. Sales Mgr.—Mike Costello

PRODUCTS and/or SERVICES: Borescopes, videoscopes, pipe inspection services.

No. of Employees: 8.

V

VAHLE INC.
407 Cane Island Pkwy.
Katy, TX 77494 USA
P: +1.713.465.9796
F: +1.713.465.1851
sales@vahleinc.com
www.vahleinc.com

- Pres.—Diego Sanchez

PRODUCTS and/or SERVICES: Conductor rails and busbar systems for cranes, hoists, transport. Battery charging systems, communications systems, positioning systems, control systems, custom design, installation, service and maintenance.

No. of Employees: 100.

SUPPLIERS of EQUIPMENT, PRODUCTS and SERVICES

VAIL RUBBER WORKS INC.
521 Langley Ave.
P.O. Box 64
St. Joseph, MI 49085 USA
P: +1.269.983.1595
www.vailrubber.com

Plant Location:
124 Salco Road E
Axis, AL 36505 USA
P: +1.251.675.5544

- Pres.—Vail Harding
- Vice Pres. Sales and Technology—Matthew J. Hanley
- Qual. Mgr.—Leasha Sherer

EQUIPMENT:
Rubber- and polyurethane-covered rolls/rollers; Masroll vacuum rolls; steel roll cores, new and repaired; wringer roll and bridle roll covers: Z Series, X Series, CK-Series, polyurethane, PolyCast, Polyfire and PolyTek. High-velocity thermal spray. Ceramic furnace rolls. Non-woven mill rolls. Millwright services. NDT and dynamic balance work performed in-house. Flatbed truck fleet. ISO 9001 certified.

No. of Employees: 125.

VALVES INC.
1291 Airport Road
P.O. Box 1186
Aliquippa, PA 15001 USA
P: +1.724.378.0600
F: +1.724.378.8057
www.valvesinc.com

- Pres. and Pur. Agt.—George Wilson
- Regional Sales Mgr.—Bobbie Boustead
- Chief Engr.—Werner Reppermund

PRODUCTS and/or SERVICES:
Valve reconditioning and valve sales. Reconditioning of standard water, oil, fuel, gas, steam and strainer valves. Reconditioning and redesign/modification of BF and coke plant valves. Mechanical, thermal expansion and hydraulic expansion goggle valves.

No. of Employees: 19.

VELCO GMBH
Haberstrasse 40
Velbert, 42551 Germany
P: +49.2051.20870
F: +49.2051.208720
info@velco.de
www.velco.de/en

- Gen. Mgr.—Christian Wolf

EQUIPMENT:
Refractory gunning machines, gunning robots for EAF, ladle, RH degasser, EAF foaming slag production by injection of carbon or lime, ladle metallurgy by injection of lime, carbon, etc. Reinjection of filter dusts into EAF. Injection of Ti fines into BF.

PRODUCTS and/or SERVICES:
GUNMIX moistening system, gunning machines for refractory repairs, gunning robots, injection equipment.

No. of Employees: 50.

VENETA USA LLC
One Broadway, 14th Floor
Cambridge, MA 02142 USA
P: +1.617.401.2180
F: +1.617.401.3716
alberto.maccatrozzo@venetausa.us
www.venetausa.us

- Sales Mgr.—Alberto Maccatrozzo

PRODUCTS and/or SERVICES:
Industrial minerals. Premium iron pyrite of natural origin (iron disulfide, FeS_2) for high-sulfur, free machining steel grades. Main product: Sulfex 1050 in lump size.

VENTILATION SYSTEMS LLC
P.O. Box 99386
Pittsburgh, PA 15233 USA
P: +1.412.761.0826
tglass@ventsystemspgh.com
www.ventsystemspgh.com

- Pres.—Thomas A. Glassbrenner

PRODUCTS and/or SERVICES:
Natural gravity ventilation equipment for steel mill buildings. Air-Therm Gravitec Vent. Roof ventilators for

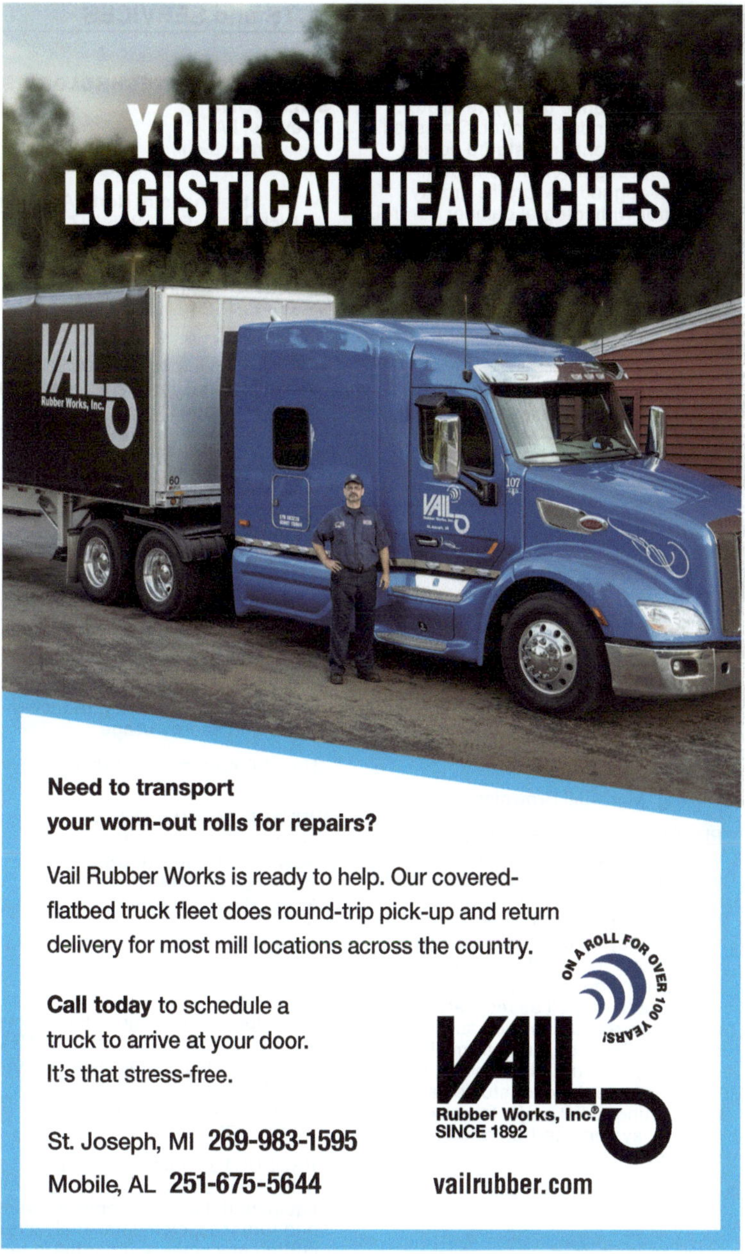

See listing page 554

SUPPLIERS of EQUIPMENT, PRODUCTS and SERVICES

industrial buildings. VG Ventilator—high-performance gravity ventilator. Tulip-shaped ridge monitor. Clamshell monitors. L Vent—registered design, low-profile, lightweight ventilator. M Vent—rugged low-profile gravity ventilator with integral damper control. Louvers—high free area industrial grade. Fixed blade or adjustable, intake or exhaust. Bladed ventilation fans—axial power driven, supply or exhaust.

VENTILATORENFABRIK OELDE GMBH
Robert-Schuman-Ring 21
Oelde, 59302 Germany
P: +49.25.22.75.0
F: +49.25.22.75.2.50
info@venti-oelde.de
www.venti-oelde.com

- Sales Mgr.—Sergej Woltschenko

EQUIPMENT:
Fans, filters and scrubbers.

No. of Employees: 247.

VEOLIA WATER TECHNOLOGIES
945 S. Brown School Road
Vandalia, OH 45377 USA
P: +1.800.337.0777 (Toll-Free)
www.veoliawatertech.com

- Mktg. Mgr.—Jill Browning

PRODUCTS and/or SERVICES:
Water and wastewater treatment solutions, specialized technologies and resource management expertise to the steel industry. Provides integrated treatment systems for supply water, contact and non-contact cooling circulation loops, coal yard runoff and wastewater, as well as recovery of in-process resources such as alkaline cleaners. Services range from chemical supply, system troubleshooting, mobile water treatment, water studies and pilot testing to EP projects, operator training, system start-up and operation contracts.

VEOLIA WATER TECHNOLOGIES & SOLUTIONS
Trevose, PA
www.watertechnologies.com/industries/primary-metals

- Dir. Steel Industry North America—Rick Toste, P: +1.905.517.5961, rick.toste@veolia.com
- Primary Metals Industry Team Leader—Ryan Goodman, P: +1.217.246.1360, ryan.goodman@veolia.com

PRODUCTS and/or SERVICES:
Veolia provides innovative solutions in water treatment and recycle/reuse, process fouling and corrosion control, and digital monitoring and control solutions. Veolia offers a comprehensive set of chemical, equipment, and digital-enabled services and products to help customers optimize water resources and overcome process challenges. With operations in more than 130 countries, Veolia works with customers across all industries including steel and primary metals processors to improve their processing assets' reliability and optimize their efficiency, reducing water and energy usage.

No. of Employees: 10,000+.

VERDER SCIENTIFIC INC.
11 Penns Trail, Suite 300
Newtown, PA 18940 USA
P: +1.267.757.0351
F: +1.267.757.0358
info-us@verder-scientific.com
www.verder-scientific.com

- Pres.—Georg Schick
- Vice Pres.—Kyle James
- Regional Sales Mgrs.—Kyle James (Retsch), Cesar Ballester (ELTRA), Michael Hager (Carbolite Gero), Matthias Ziegenhagen (QATM), Edward Lim (Microtrac MRB)
- Adv. Mgr.—Erin Lorensini

PRODUCTS and/or SERVICES:
Mills, sieve shakers, sampling equipment, high-temperature ovens and furnaces, elemental analyzers, cutting machines and hardness testers,

SUPPLIERS OF EQUIPMENT, PRODUCTS and SERVICES

particle size and shape analyzers, and gas adsorption measurement systems.

No. of Employees: 45.

VERICHEK TECHNICAL SERVICES INC.
3000 Industrial Blvd.
Bethel Park, PA 15102 USA
P: +1.412.854.1800
sales@verichek.net
www.verichek.net

- Pres. Sales—Tim Moury
- Vice Pres. Oprs.—Evan Sivetz
- Vice Pres. Financials—Jeff Froetschel

PRODUCTS and/or SERVICES: OES, XRD, XRF, RA, coating thickness, hardness, ISO accredited calibration, PMI, inspection and training.

No. of Employees: 18.

VESUVIUS USA
5510 77 Center Dr.
Charlotte, NC 28217 USA
P: +1.980.296.6400
www.vesuvius.com

- Vice Pres., Advanced Refractories NAFTA—Cedric Woindrich
- Vice Pres., Flow Control NAFTA—Patrick Rienks
- Finance Dir., Flow Control NAFTA—Ashley Phagan
- Finance Dir., Advanced Refractories NAFTA—Aasta Hughes
- Commercial Dir., Advanced Refractories USA—John Olsav
- Commercial Dir., Advanced Refractories Canada—Pablo Serafin
- Commercial Dir., Flow Control USA/Canada—Paul Batt

PRODUCTS and/or SERVICES: Vesuvius provides a full range of engineering services and solutions to customers worldwide, principally serving the steel and foundry industries. Vesuvius' Flow Control business unit supplies consumable refractories and fluxes products, systems, robotics, digital services and technical services. Vesuvius' Advanced Refractories business unit supplies specialist refractory materials for lining vessels such as BFs, ladles and tundishes. Along with these materials, Vesuvius provides advanced installation technologies (including robots), CFD capabilities and laser systems for measuring refractory wear. The Digital Services group within Vesuvius provides products that include temperature sensors, oxygen, hydrogen and sublance probes, iron oxide, and metal sampling.

Cust. Svce. and Flow Control Div.
1404 Newton Dr.
Champaign, IL 61821 USA
P: +1.217.351.5000
F: +1.217.351.5031

- Flow Control Systems NAFTA—Jon Guido

Foundry Divs.:

Foseco
20200 Sheldon Road
Cleveland, OH 44142 USA
P: +1.440.826.4548
F: +1.440.243.7658

- Vice Pres., Foundry NAFTA—Manuel Delfino
- Finance Dir., Foundry NAFTA—Lisa Miao
- Commercial Dir., Foundry—Mario Seixas

Vesuvius Canada
333 Prince Charles Dr.
Welland, ON L3B 5P4 Canada
P: +1.905.732.4441
F: +1.950.735.8245

- Oprs. and Tech. Mgr.—Tom Serravalle

Vesuvius Mexico
Carretera a San Miguel km 1
Col. Jardines de San Rafael
Guadalupe, NL, 67110 Mexico
P: +52.81.83.194500
F: +52.81.83.194599

- Commercial Dir. Steel (Flow Control/Advanced Refractories) Mexico—Marisol Ocampo

SUPPLIERS of EQUIPMENT, PRODUCTS and SERVICES

VH ENTERPRISES INC.
1564 Village Dr.
Pittsburgh, PA 15237 USA
F: +1.412.367.0146
vheinc@verizon.net

- Pres.—Virginia Hixenbaugh
- Dir. Technology—Dennis Hixenbaugh

PRODUCTS and/or SERVICES:
Industrial application baghouses, system evaluation and troubleshooting, reporting and interfacing, combustion process analysis, miscellaneous dust control, greenhouse gas inventories, reporting, and reductions.

No. of Employees: 2.

VIPER IMAGING
2406 Valleydale Road
Birmingham, AL 35244 USA
P: +1.205.677.3700
F: +1.205.278.5830
contact@viperimaging.com
www.viperimaging.com

PRODUCT and/or SERVICES:
With a specialty in steel mill refractory monitoring solutions, Viper Imaging is a FLIR Platinum Partner and a leading supplier of thermal imaging systems and industrial process monitoring equipment. Viper's systems and software have been installed in a variety of commercial applications for metals, oil and gas, energy production and distribution, industrial automation, and elevated body temperature (EBT) detection.

No. of Employees: 17.

VIRGINIA CRANE (FOLEY MATERIAL HANDLING)
11327 Virginia Crane Dr.
Ashland, VA 23005 USA
P: +1.804.798.1343
F: +1.804.798.7843
www.virginiacrane.com

- Chief Exec. Officer—Dale Foley
- Pres.—Richard Foley

PRODUCTS and/or SERVICES:
Manufacturers of custom-engineered automated overhead and gantry cranes as well as components compliant with CMAA and *AIST Technical Report No. 6* specifications. Also crane modernization, inspection and repair services.

VISHAY PRECISION GROUP CANADA ULC (KELK)
48 Lesmill Road
Toronto, ON M3B 2T5 Canada
P: +1.416.445.5850
F: +1.416.445.5972
kelk@vpgsensors.com
www.kelk.com

- Sales and Mktg.—Hiro Kitagawa
- Regional Sales Mgrs.—Hiro Kitagawa, Al Boluarte, John Shen, Kejun Eric Liang, Musab Al-Lami, Aydin Saurcan, Peter Morrell, Howard He
- Mktg.—Binne Youn, ext. 1151

EQUIPMENT:
Machine shop, sheet metal shop, electronics, mechanics and optics lab. Force calibrating presses to 5,000 tons. Test and measuring equipment for digital and analog electronics, mechanics, and optics.

PRODUCTS and/or SERVICES:
Roll force load cells of all shapes and sizes. Strip tension measurement systems, Monobloc tensiometer systems for process lines, Accuband strip width gauge and crop optimization system, Accuscan light curtain—hot metal detector, Accuplan plate outline gauges, Accuspeed laser velocimeters. Weighing systems for continuous casters, cranes and other applications. Absolute displacement transducers and fluid pressure transmitters.

No. of Employees: 100.

VIRGINIA CRANE®

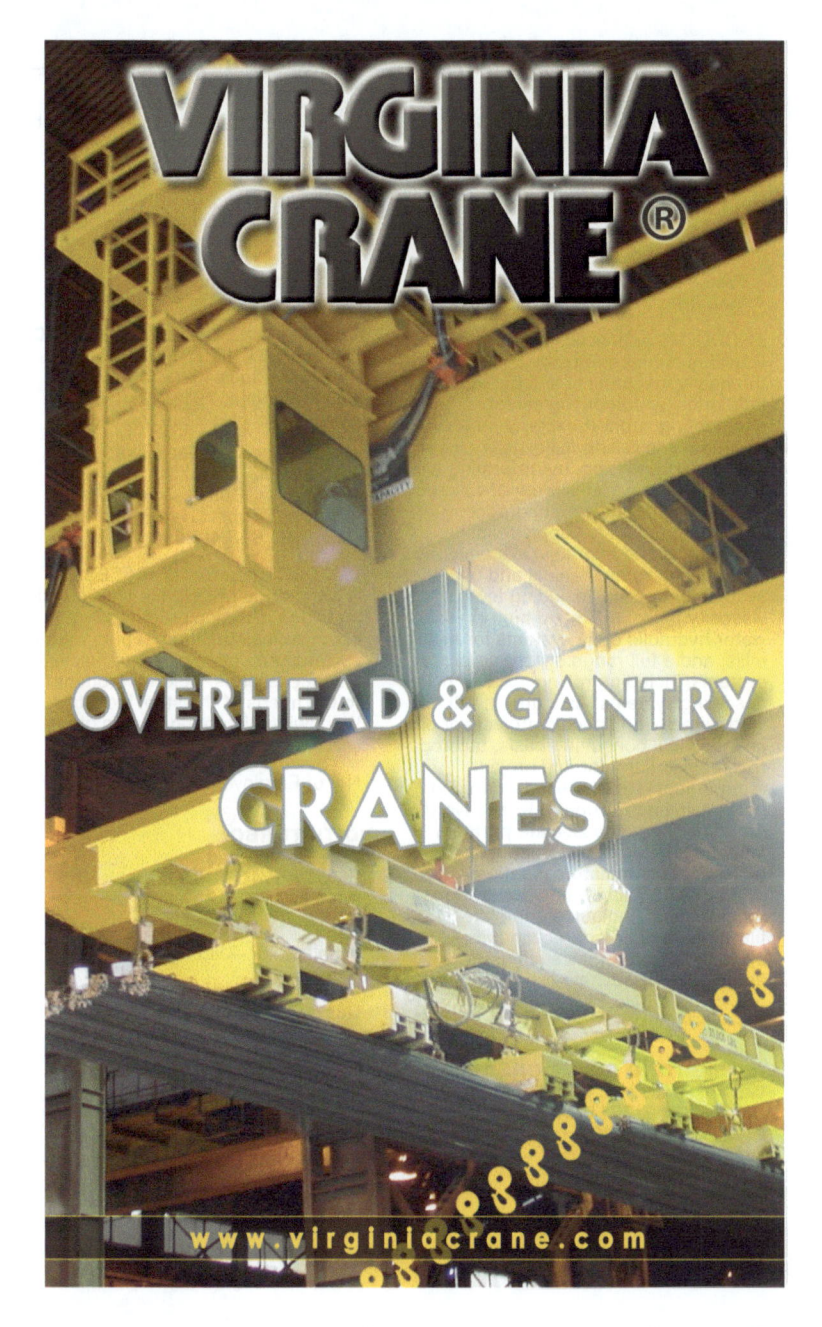

OVERHEAD & GANTRY CRANES

www.virginiacrane.com

SUPPLIERS of EQUIPMENT, PRODUCTS and SERVICES

VISTA SYSTEM AND PRODUCT ENGINEERS (VISTA SPE LLC)
7211 Linwood Road
Racine, WI 53402 USA
P: +1.262.639.3117
chazj@ticon.net
www.vistaspe.com

- Pres.—Chuck/Charles Johnson
- Vice Pres.—Gordon H. Enderle

PRODUCTS and/or SERVICES:
Provides engineering services in the heavy mechanical and hydraulic industries by combining senior engineering support experience with experience in rolling mills, heavy metals industries, extrusion, hydroforming and forging press systems. Provides project engineering for design, upgrades, and new projects to supply reliable mechanical and hydraulic systems. Expertise is in mechanical and oil system hydraulics, including low-viscosity fluids; 97/3 and high-pressure water hydraulic drive systems for heavy mills; and a full range of forging press systems, including rolling mill and billet descaling systems. As a group, will work directly on specific projects or on an individual consulting basis, tailored to specific customer and project requirements, from offices located in Italy, mainland Europe, U.K. and North America. Product associate partners including: bladder, piston and gas ballasted accumulators meeting ASME, CE, CSA, ABS and other worldwide requirements, including complete filtration and coolant reclamation systems for industries such as automotive powertrain machining.

No. of Employees: 4+.

VM5 LIGHTING SOLUTIONS LLC
1951 S. Parco Ave. Unit A
Ontario, CA 91761 USA
P: +1.909.635.2301
info@vm5lighting.com
www.vm5lighting.com

- Pres.—Douglas Su
- Vice Pres. Engrg.—Jing Mo
- Vice Pres. Sales and Mktg.—Ralph Mosheo
- Sales Mgr.—Dennis Spaulding

PRODUCTS and/or SERVICES:
Extremely high-temperature LED fixtures.

No. of Employees: 15.

VOESTALPINE BÖHLER WELDING UTP MAINTENANCE GMBH
Elsässer Straße 10
Bad Krozingen, 79189 Germany
www.voestalpine.com/welding

- Managing Dir.—Jan Hilkes,
  P: +49.2381.271751
- Vice Pres. Business Dev. M&R—Siegbert Hafenscherer,
  P: +49.7633.409214

PRODUCTS and/or SERVICES:
A wide range of long-life welding filler metals to increase productivity and optimize maintenance, repair, wear and surface protection, welding machines and accessories. Tailored products to the needs of the steel industry. Worldwide distribution and a global service network.

No. of Employees: 2,300.

VOITH TURBO
25 Winship Road
York, PA 17406 USA
P: +1.717.767.3200
www.usa.voithturbo.com

- Sales Mgr.—Jim Fraser

PRODUCTS and/or SERVICES:
Designs, manufactures and services advanced mechanical power transmission equipment used in rotating machinery for industrial applications. Products include universal joint shafts (up to 1,300-mm swing), torque-limiting safety couplings, FlexPad Roll End Hubs and torque diagnostic/condition-monitoring equipment.

VM5™ LIGHTING SOLUTIONS

Finally, an energy saving LED light that will take the heat
Reduce Carbon Footprint

- Operating Temperature up to 239°F
- Fixtures Replace 1000, 400, and 250 Watt Metal Halide
- Constant Light Output Over Temperature
- Patented Solid State LED Driving Technology
- No Active Cooling Necessary
- Long Lasting, Reduce Maintenance Cost
- Lowest Total Cost of Ownership

info@vm5lighting.com www.vm5lighting.com Tel: (909) 635-2301

SUPPLIERS of EQUIPMENT, PRODUCTS and SERVICES

VOLLMER AMERICA INC.
5 Lime Kiln Road
Canaan, CT 06018 USA
P: +1.860.824.5157
info@vollmeramerica.com
www.vollmeramerica.com

- Pres.—Karim Alshurafa

PRODUCTS and/or SERVICES:
Produces a complete line of measurement and control equipment for the metals industry, including contact and non-contact continuous thickness gauges, contact and optical flatness measurement and control equipment, hydraulic rolling mill upgrades, and inspection equipment for specialty applications.

VR MASTER CO. LTD.
19/41, 19/43 Chuanchuen Modus Centro Village M. 2, Klongkluea Pakkred, Nonthaburi, 11120 Thailand
P: +66.25752616
F: +66.25752615
ekkasit@vr-master.com
www.vr-master.com

- Chief Exec. Officer and Pres.—
  Ekkasit Smanchat

PRODUCTS and/or SERVICES:
Automation and drives system, AC/DC motors, sensors for steel industry, MCC, switchgear, solar PV inverter, energy storage, medium-voltage motors/drives.

No. of Employees: 15.

W

W. L. GORE & ASSOCIATES INC.
101 Lewisville Road
P.O. Box 1200
Elkton, MD 21921 USA
P: +1.800.437.5427 (Toll-Free U.S.);
   +1.410.506.3560
F: +1.410.506.0107
filterbags@wlgore.com
www.gore.com/filterbags

- Sales—Kim Burnham
- Mktg.—Uta Holzmann

PRODUCTS and/or SERVICES:
Inventor and supplier of ePTFE membrane filtration products and air filtration solutions for compliance in standard or aggressive EAF baghouse environments. New technical developments in regulatory technologies for metallurgical industries, including GORE® LOW DRAG Filter Bags, GORE Low Emission Filter Bags ($PM_{2.5}$) as well as products for the removal of mercury, NOx, SOx and dioxins.

WALBRIDGE
777 Woodward Ave., Suite 300
Detroit, MI 48226 USA
P: +1.412.723.1050
F: +1.313.234.0841
mmiskevics@walbridge.com
www.walbridge.com

- Contact—Michael Miskevics

PRODUCTS and/or SERVICES:
General contractor and foundation and equipment installation contractor.

No. of Employees: 1,000.

WALCO
303 Allens Ave.
Providence, RI 02905 USA
P: +1.401.467.6500
F: +1.401.941.4451
ellisw@walcokip.com
www.walcokip.com

- Chief Exec. Officer and Pres.—Ellis S. Waldman

THE BEST FOR THE BEST

TERRA & URANOS welding machines.

Your challenge is to JOIN materials made of metal. You know how to weld constructions for bridges, machines and power plants. In your job you do not need "a" solution, YOU DESERVE the best. Our offering includes a unique portfolio of welding application services, high end welding consumables, accessories and welding machines – we are your Full Welding Solution Provider.

Scan for more infos

voestalpine Böhler Welding
www.voestalpine.com/welding

voestalpine
ONE STEP AHEAD.

SUPPLIERS of EQUIPMENT, PRODUCTS and SERVICES

PRODUCTS and/or SERVICES:
Automation and controls for all metal processing equipment, AGC, electronic and rolling mill service.

No. of Employees: 85.

WALKER MAGNETICS, a Div. of Industrial Magnetics Inc.
1385 S. M 75
Boyne City, MI 49712 USA
P: +1.800.962.4638 (WMAGNET) (Toll-Free)
sales@magnetics.com
www.magnetics.com

- Chief Business Dev. Officer—Dennis O'Leary
- Natl. Sales Mgr.—Kristian Knights

PRODUCTS and/or SERVICES:
Magnetic material handling solutions for moving scrap, billets, slabs, plate, coils, bundles, pipe, structurals or high-temperature materials. Walker also rebuilds all makes and models of magnets.

WEBER SENSORS LLC
4462 Bretton Ct., Bldg. 1, Suite 7
Acworth, GA 30101 USA
P: +1.888.520.6691 (Toll-Free);
   +1.770.592.6630
F: +1.770.592.6640
sales@captor.com
www.captor.com
www.weber-sensors.de

- Chief Exec. Officer—John Pitcher

PRODUCTS and/or SERVICES:
Sales, service, manufacturing of sensors, and application engineering for hot and cold steel processes. Products include: foto-captor hot metal detectors; flow-captor solid-state flow switches and monitors for water, oil, and most liquids with up to 80% semisolids; vent-captor solid-state airflow switches and monitors for air cooling systems; and proxi-captor induction-based industrial proximity detection.

WELLS ENGINEERING PSC
6900 Houston Road, Suite 38
Florence, KY 41042 USA
P: +1.859.282.7538
jcook@wellsengineering.com
www.wellsengineering.com

- Chief Exec. Officer and Pres.— Patrick Wells
- Chief Oper. Officer—Jim Cook
- Vice Pres. Sales—Kraig Storbeck
- Key Account Sales Engr. — Metals— Brad Denham

PRODUCTS and/or SERVICES:
Power system consulting engineering: EPC and EPCM projects, HV/MV/LV substations and power distribution, protection relay system design, substation automation, system studies (short circuit, coordination, load analysis, power quality, mitigation, capacitors/reactors/SVCs, arc flash studies and mitigation, grounding), DC power design and upgrades, power system maintenance, and testing services.

No. of Employees: 18.

WHEMCO INC. (CSS)
#5 Hot Metal St., Suite 300
Pittsburgh, PA 15203 USA
P: +1.412.390.2700
F: +1.412.390.2737
www.whemco.com

- Chief Exec. Officer and Pres.— Charles (Curly) Novelli
- Vice Pres. Engrg., Capital Projects and Maint.—Ben Heck
- Vice Pres. Product Technology—Chris Hrizo
- Vice Pres. Sales and Mktg.—Frank Pearson IV
- Vice Pres. Sales and Tech. Svce.— Tom Kane

PRODUCTS and/or SERVICES:
Worldwide supplier of heavy industrial components for the metals, mining, power generation, shipbuilding, nuclear, commercial, heavy equipment manufacturing and national defense industries. Technical excellence in

SUPPLIERS OF EQUIPMENT, PRODUCTS and SERVICES

core competencies of melting, casting, forging, heat treating and machining.

WHEMCO Steel Castings Inc. (SCH), an Affiliate of WHEMCO Inc.
601 W. 7th Ave.
Homestead, PA 15120 USA
P: +1.412.464.4400
F: +1.412.464.1950

- Gen. Mgr.—Howard Zeigler

EQUIPMENT:
Complete roll shop, CNC lathes, CNC roll grinders to 72-in. cast-iron and steel rolls. Vertical boring mills to 20 ft., horizontal boring mills, duplex mills, planer mills to 17 ft. x 40 ft. Heat treating: two hood furnaces, 12 car-bottom furnaces, water and polymer quench facilities.

PRODUCTS and/or SERVICES:
Complete roll/machine shop and heat treat facility that produces finished cast steel backup rolls for various rolling mill applications, finished machined mill housings, large chocks, die blocks, and a variety of components for mining, material handling, power generation, primary metal manufacturers, metal processing and heavy equipment manufacturers. Carbon and alloy castings from 5,000 to 150,000 lbs. ship weight. Domestic and international sales. Cranes up to 250-ton lifting capacity; maximum clearance below hook: 100 ft.

WHEMCO Steel Castings Inc. (SCM), an Affiliate of WHEMCO Inc.
One 12th St.
Midland, PA 15069 USA
P: +1.724.643.7001
F: +1.724.643.5569

- Gen. Mgr.—Frank Moldovan

EQUIPMENT:
60-ton EAF, two 9-ton induction furnaces, 18 gas-fired annealers, pattern shop, six large casting pits. Three tracer lathes with 55- to 65-in. capacity. Two CNC lathes: one with 42-in. capacity and one with 73-in. capacity.

PRODUCTS and/or SERVICES:
Steel foundry that static casts steel backup rolls for various rolling mill applications, mill housings, large chocks, die blocks, components for mining, material handling, power generation, primary metal manufacturers, metal processing and heavy equipment manufacturers. Major casting products include slag pots for ferrous and non-ferrous applications, coiler drums for Steckel mill applications, and numerous commercial castings. Pour weight: 240,000 lbs. Domestic and international sales.

WHEMCO Ohio Foundry Inc. (WOF), an Affiliate of WHEMCO Inc.
1600 McClain Road
Lima, OH 45804 USA
P: +1.419.222.2111
F: +1.419.222.2318

- Pres.—John Hribar
- Plant Mgr.—Jerry Malone

EQUIPMENT:
Two 30-ton coreless induction melting furnaces, three 25-ton coreless induction melting furnaces, state-of-the-art computerized vertical centrifugal casting machine to 500 tons, numerous heat treating furnaces, a complete roll shop including vertical boring mills, 10- to 300-hp engine lathes, duplex mills, 14- to 72-in. roll grinders, NC lathes, CNC lathes.

PRODUCTS and/or SERVICES:
Cast iron foundry. Products include vertically spun-cast and static-cast iron and chrome iron rolls for hot, cold, and plate mill rolling applications. Domestic and international sales.

Lehigh Heavy Forge Corp. (LHF), an Affiliate of WHEMCO Inc.
275 Emery St.
Bethlehem, PA 18015 USA
P: +1.610.332.8100
F: +1.610.332.8102

- Pres.—James J. Romeo

SUPPLIERS of EQUIPMENT, PRODUCTS and SERVICES

EQUIPMENT:
Size: 850,000-sq.-ft. facility. 300-ton crane capacity; 4,500- and 10,000-ton presses; 12- to 25-ft. VBMs—CNC and tracer; lathes to 138 in. x 75 ft. long; 7- and 8-in. spindle—CNC HBMs; CNC roll grinders; boring and honing to 75 ft. x 30-in. dia.; heat treating, quenching and cryogenic treatment to –200°F; on-site mechanical test lab; ultrasonic and magnetic particle inspection (MPI) testing.

PRODUCTS and/or SERVICES:
Open-die forging and forged components to the power generation, pressure vessel, oil and gas, defense, and metals industries. Core competencies include custom forging, heat treating and machining. 10,000-ton open-die hydraulic press produces the largest forgings in the Western Hemisphere with ship weights exceeding 166 tons. Operates a 4,500-ton open-die hydraulic press for work roll forgings, billets and smaller forgings of various configurations with ship weights starting at 10 tons. Products include forged work rolls for steel and aluminum mills; hot or cold rolling applications; nuclear reactor components; pressure vessels; large discs; cylinders; shells and heads for generators; press cylinders; and other large, custom open-die forgings. Core competencies include forging, custom heat treating and custom machining. Shipped weights to 450,000 lbs.

Erie Forge & Steel Inc. (EFS), an Affiliate of WHEMCO Inc.
1341 W. 16th St.
Erie, PA 16502 USA
P: +1.814.452.2300
F: +1.814.459.9170

- Pres.—Dave Harned
- Plant Mgr.—Steve Woods

EQUIPMENT:
Machine shop: 300,000 sq. ft. Heat treat: 113,000 sq. ft. Under-roof available storage: 50,400 sq. ft. Lifting capabilities: main bay 160,000 lbs., auxiliary bay north 200,000 lbs., auxiliary bay south 119,000 lbs., heat treat south 100,000 lbs., heat treat north 200,000 lbs. Roughing/finishing lathes (14 available): up to 85-in. dia. x 53 ft. overall length (OAL), up to 60-in. dia. x 82 ft. OAL. Boring lathes (two available): solid bore/trepan 3- to 30-in. dia., hognose 6.75- to 60-in. dia., honing 1.5- to 19-in. dia. vertical boring machines (two available): 132-in. table dia. x 10 ft. high, 209-in. max. swing. Horizontal boring mills (four available): 10-in. max. dia. Planer mills (manual, two available): up to 6 ft. wide x 6 ft. high x 36 ft. long. Planer mill (CNC): up to 78 in. wide x 6 ft. high x 36 ft. long. Cylindrical grinding: up to 48-in. dia. x 64 ft. long. Heat treatment capabilities: horizontal product limit 7 x 7 x 70 ft. long x 150,000 lbs. Welding capabilities: shielding metal arc welding, gas tungsten arc, gas metal arc, submerged arc and electroslag.

PRODUCTS and/or SERVICES:
Supplier of new and refurbished marine propulsion components for the U.S. Navy's fleet of aircraft carriers, destroyers, submarines and support ships. Forges, heat treats, machines, clads and assembles marine shafts. Manufactures items to military or ABS requirements. Ability to manufacture shafts in sizes up to 70 ft. in overall length.

Lehigh Specialty Melting Inc. (LSM), an Affiliate of WHEMCO Inc.
107 Gertrude St.
Latrobe, PA 15650 USA
P: +1.724.537.7731
F: +1.724.539.0645

- Pres.—Chad Ireland
- Vice Pres. Sales—Mark Wolford
- Plant Mgr.—Greg Gigliotti

EQUIPMENT:
40-ton EAF, VD, casting pits, gas-fired annealers, flame cutting, billet grinding.

PRODUCTS and/or SERVICES:
Produces bottom-poured steel ingots for the domestic forging industry. Specializes in the melting of vacuum stream degassed, argon shrouded carbon and alloy steel ingots for a

SUPPLIERS OF EQUIPMENT, PRODUCTS and SERVICES

variety of applications from 12.75 to 55 in. dia. Products include smooth and corrugated ingot sizes of 13-in. dia. to 63-in. dia. and weights from 5,700 lbs. to 79,500 lbs. each.

United Rolls Inc. (URI), an Affiliate of WHEMCO Inc.
1400 Grace Ave. NE
Canton, OH 44705 USA
P: +1.330.456.2761
F: +1.330.456.2085

- Pres.—John Hribar
- Gen. Mgr.—Joe Shipley

EQUIPMENT:
Foundry: five induction furnaces (two 35-ton, one 30-ton and two 15-ton), two 45-ton horizontal centrifugal casting machines, 60-ton crane capacity. Machine shop: three HBMs, one VBM, 10 heat treating furnaces, four roll grinders, 14 lathes, three duplex milling machines, grinding capacity 62 x 436 in. roughing, turning capacity 75 x 360 in. and 42 x 588 in., 60-ton crane capacity.

PRODUCTS and/or SERVICES:
Rolling mill supplier offering horizontally centrifugal cast-iron rolls; hot isostatic pressed rolls and high-speed steel rolls for hot strip, cold strip, plate, and roughing mill applications; cored and drilled rolls for the rubber and plastic industries; and rolls for long products.

Johnstown Specialty Castings Inc. (JSC), an Affiliate of WHEMCO Inc.
545 Central Ave.
Johnstown, PA 15902 USA
P: +1.814.535.9164
F: +1.814.536.0868

- Oprs. Mgr.—Mark Stahl,
  P: +1.814.330.7034 (Mobile)
- Sales Mgr.—Ed Serafin

EQUIPMENT:
500-ton plate press, two tempering furnaces 900–1,400°F, two hardening furnaces 1,550–2,000°F, oil or water quenching options, multi-spindle drilling system, double-headed plate planer, large and small industrial metalworking saws, and large and small drilling operations.

PRODUCTS and/or SERVICES:
Lorain® hot-rolled alloy steel liners for rod and ball mills for the coal, cement and minerals industries.

Whemco International GmbH, Germany Office, an Affiliate of WHEMCO Inc.
Am Kirschgarten 30
Schulzendorf, 15732 Germany
P: +49.337.624.0038

- Dir.—Volker Schaffer,
  vschaffer@whemco.com

PRODUCTS and/or SERVICES:
Commercial and technical assistance for customers outside the Western Hemisphere. Network of agents around the world, a strongly established distributor in Eastern Asia, and a technical service team and manufacturing facilities in the U.S.

WHITING CORP.
26000 S. Whiting Way
Monee, IL 60449 USA
P: +1.800.WHITING (944.8464)
   (Toll-Free)
F: +1.708.587.2001
info@whitingcorp.com
www.whitingcorp.com

- Pres.—Jeff Kahn
- Crane Sales Mgr., Northern U.S. and Western Canada—Ben Thomas
- Crane Sales Mgr., Southwestern U.S. and Mexico—Frank Bailey
- Crane Sales Mgr., Eastern U.S. and Eastern Canada—Robert Smilak

PRODUCTS and/or SERVICES:
Manufactures specialized and standard overhead cranes for the metal producing and processing market. Also produces robust overhead cranes for automotive stamping and assembly facilities, paper mills, nuclear and non-nuclear power generating facilities, refuse and waste facilities, and other material handling applications. Modernizations and component upgrades for rerating

SUPPLIERS of EQUIPMENT, PRODUCTS and SERVICES

and dynamic application changes. Replacement OEM parts for Whiting and Conco overhead cranes. Whiting also produces railcar maintenance equipment such as portable electric jacks, transfer tables, turntables, and single- or double-axle drop tables.

WHITING EQUIPMENT CANADA INC.
350 Alexander St.
P.O. Box 217
Welland, ON L3B 5P4 Canada
P: +1.905.732.7585
F: +1.905.732.2366
jbartok@whiting.ca
www.whiting.ca

- Chief Exec. Officer and Pres.—H.R. Kroeker
- Engrg. Mgr.—W. Duncan
- Chief Financial Officer—N. Sestili
- Dir., Metallurgical and Crane Product Group—J. Bartok
- Dir. Procurement—P. Dano

EQUIPMENT:
Fabrication shop, machining shop, CSA 47.1, 47.2; ANSI; ASME Section 8, Div. 1; ASME Section I and ASME B31.3; NB-R; AISE Spec. 9; ISO 9001:2015; Certified PEO Certificate of Authorization.

PRODUCTS and/or SERVICES:
Heavy industrial equipment: EAFs, AOD converter systems, ladles, charge buckets, transfer cars, turn tables, cranes, process monitoring computer control and regulators for EAFs, upgrades to EAF equipment, resistance rod holding furnaces, cupolas.

No. of Employees: 45.

WIKA MOBILE CONTROL LP
1540 Orchard Dr.
Chambersburg, PA 17201 USA
P: +1.717.217.2200
F: +1.717.263.7845
sales.us.wmc@wika.com
www.wika-mc.com

- Gen. Mgr. and Dir. of Sales and Mktg.—Gary Peck
- Engrg. Mgr.—Jason Miller

PRODUCTS and/or SERVICES:
Manufactures overload protection, weighing, and control systems for crane and lifting applications. Offers a full line of force sensors including compression load cells, load pins, force transducers and tensiometers. These systems and sensors meet OEM and retrofit requirements in lifting applications.

No. of Employees: 50.

WINKLE INDUSTRIES
2080 W. Main St.
Alliance, OH 44601 USA
P: +1.330.823.9730
F: +1.330.823.9788
www.winkleindustries.com

- Dir. of Sales—Mark Volansky

EQUIPMENT:
Design, manufacture, and remanufacturing of lifting devices, crane products and mill equipment, such as lifting magnets, mechanical lifting devices, spreader beams, hook blocks, electric brake assemblies/parts, brake shoe relining, brake wheels, limit stops, cable reels, drum assemblies and electromagnetic devices.

PRODUCTS and/or SERVICES:
Full-service engineering, manufacturing and remanufacturing of lifting devices, crane products, and mill equipment. Specializations include magnetic and mechanical lifting devices for the steel industry. Auxiliary magnet equipment such as magnet controllers, generators, rectifiers, battery backup systems and meter packages. Precision CNC/conventional machining and fabrication. Distributor of Cutler-Hammer electrical components, inventory management and consolidation programs. Aftermarket and engineering services.

No. of Employees: 75+.

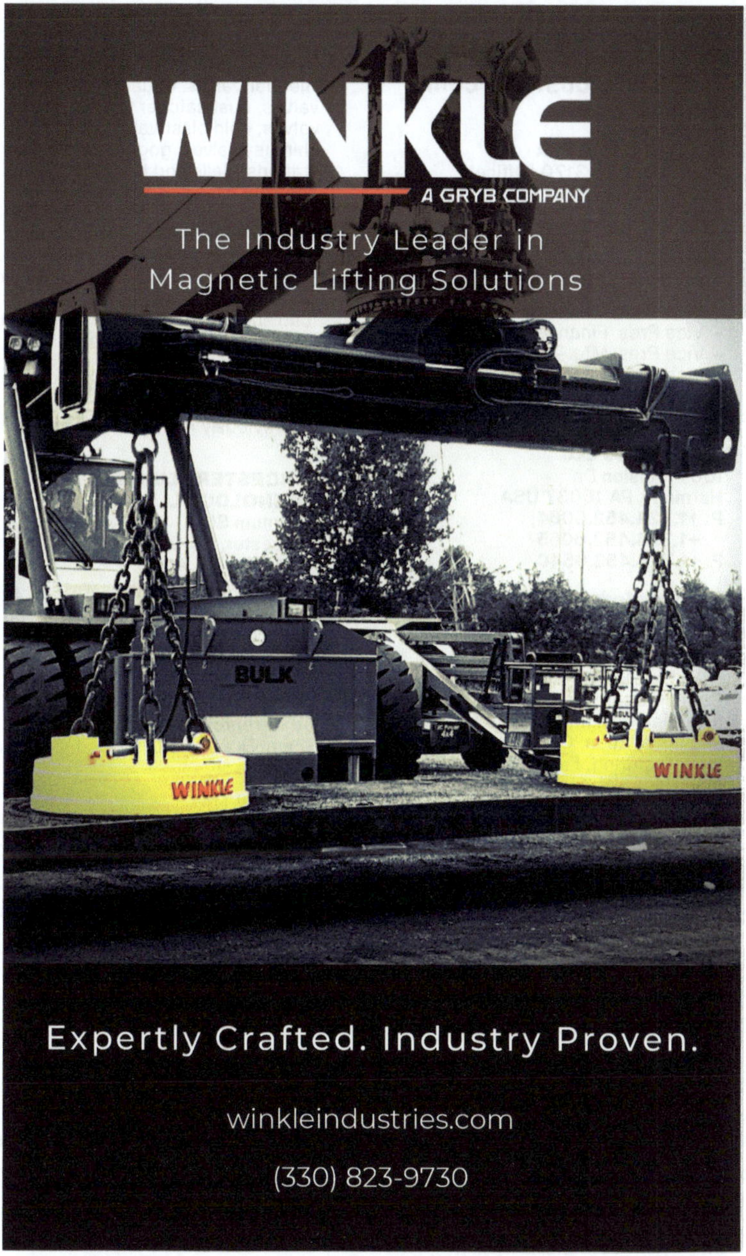

See listing page 568

SUPPLIERS of EQUIPMENT, PRODUCTS and SERVICES

WOODINGS INDUSTRIAL CORP.
Clay Ave.
P.O. Box 851
Mars, PA 16046 USA
P: +1.724.625.3170 (Office);
  +1.724.625.3131 (Plant)
F: +1.724.625.3176
rwoodings@woodings.com
www.woodings.com

- Pres.—Robert T. Woodings
- Vice Pres. Sales—Tony Cook
- Vice Pres. Finance—Rick Bralich
- Vice Pres. Mfg.—Bob Vinson
- Vice Pres. Engrg.—Joe Saxinger
- Cust. Rels. Mgr.—Anna Marie Nellis

Progressive Power Technologies LLC
100 Precision Dr.
Harmony, PA 16037 USA
P: +1.724.452.6064;
  +1.724.452.6065
F: +1.724.452.6540

Woodings Industrial Corp.
330 N. Leona Ave.
Garden City, MI 48135 USA

EQUIPMENT:
Complete turnkey capabilities including design, engineering, supply and installation. Complete in-house manufacturing. Fully integrated manufacturing facilities, consisting of forging, fabricating, machining and engineering.

PRODUCTS and/or SERVICES:
Design and engineering of equipment. Casthouse floor design, furnace tapping equipment, hot metal tapping equipment for the ferrous and non-ferrous industry. Taphole drills (conventional and soaking bar). Hydraulic drills. Tilting runners systems. Hydraulic clay guns. Rebuilding of clay guns. Tuyere stocks, tuyere stock removal machines. Heavy-duty mill-type cylinders, rebuilding services, specialty mill equipment. Stopper rods, argon lance handling devices, EAF mast raising columns, roller boxes. Soaking bar hammers. Ladle cleaning stations. Ladle cars. Bleeder valves, equalizer and relief valves, dust catcher valves. Hot blast valves, cold blast valves, burner valves, chimney valves, goggle valves. Sensor stations. Bells and hoppers, chutes and seal valves. Bell-less tops. BOF measuring probes. BOF taphole drills. Charging machines. In-burden and above-burden probes, burnout tables, disappearing steps, torch-cut tables, cross-transfer tables, tundish cars and tundishes. Continuous caster repair. Continuous caster segments. Coke oven equipment. Design, engineering, studies and project management. Repair and reconditioning services for all previously mentioned products.

WORCESTER FLUIDS TECHNOLOGY LLC
4 Farnum St.
Worcester, MA 01602 USA
P: +1.774.314.4006
lazor@fluids-tech.com
www.worcesterfluidstechnology.com
www.fluids-tech.com

- Chief Exec. Officer—Rafael Lazo
- Field Engrg.—John Gasparik

Other representations: P.R. China, Spain, Brazil, Peru, Mexico, Sweden and India.

EQUIPMENT:
Fluids systems and equipment supply, engineering and consultant services. Includes lubrication, hydraulic, water, cooling, descaler, air/oil, grease, and pneumatic systems and components, including filtration systems. Specialized engineering and simulation software for these systems. Tribology studies. Fluids systems for rolling mills (ferrous and non-ferrous).

PRODUCTS and/or SERVICES:
Design and supply of complete lubrication, water, hydraulics, pneumatics, grease, air/oil and descaler systems. Specialized fluids design and simulation software for steel mill applications. Tribology studies and analysis. Complete mill

SUPPLIERS OF EQUIPMENT, PRODUCTS and SERVICES

audits, commissioning services, site services, spare parts and complex fluid systems analysis.

No. of Employees: 15.

WORLD WIDE METRIC INC.
37 Readington Road
Branchburg, NJ 08876 USA
P: +1.732.247.2300
F: +1.732.247.7258
sales@worldwidemetric.com
www.worldwidemetric.com

- Chief Exec. Officer—George Contos
- Treas.—Theo Contos
- Sec.—Anthee Contos
- Mktg.—Brooke Pawlowski

PRODUCTS and/or SERVICES:
Valves, actuation, flanges and gaskets; hydraulic fittings, tubing and clamps; pipe couplings and repair clamps; expansion joints, protective tapes, press fitting and drain systems.

No. of Employees: 45.

WORLDBRIDGE PARTNERS OF TOLEDO INC.
33 N. Huron St.
Toledo, OH 43604 USA
P: +1.419.537.1100
F: +1.419.537.8730
gfruchtman@worldbridgepartners.com
www.worldbridgepartners.com

- Pres.—Gary Fruchtman

PRODUCTS and/or SERVICES:
Executive search firm specializing in recruiting top talent for the primary steel and steel value-added industries (specifically the pipe and tube industries).

No. of Employees: 12.

WORLDWIDE MATERIAL HANDLING
32 Forestwood Dr.
Romeoville, IL 60446 USA
P: +1.888.650.9473
sales@wwmh.net
www.wwmh.net

PRODUCTS and/or SERVICES:
Wire mesh decking, pallet rack protection, pallet rack repair.

No. of Employees: 40.

WKW INDUSTRIAL SERVICES
202 W. Bridge Dr.
Morgan, PA 15064 USA
P: +1.724.338.4601
sales@wkwindustrialservices.com
www.wkwsales.com

- Chief Exec. Officer—Ken Walden
- Sales Mgr.—Phil Ponikvar

PRODUCTS and/or SERVICES:
Solutions provider for fabrication and machining needs representing various types of machine shops in the steel industry.

No. of Employees: 2.

WPT POWER CORP.
1600 Fisher Road
Wichita Falls, TX 76307 USA
P: +1.940.761.1971
info@wptpower.com
www.wptpower.com

- Pres.—Lane Brock
- Vice Pres. and Sales Mgr.—Byron Baber
- Mktg. Mgr.—Steve St. John
- Chief Engr.—Bryan Schaffner
- Pur. Mgr.—Tyler Kisner

PRODUCTS and/or SERVICES:
Industrial clutches and brakes, power take-off products (PTOs), hydraulic pump drives.

No. of Employees: 30.

SUPPLIERS of EQUIPMENT, PRODUCTS and SERVICES

W.S. HAMPSHIRE INC.
365 Keyes Ave.
Hampshire, IL 60140 USA
P: +1.800.541.0251 (Toll-Free);
+1.847.683.4400
F: +1.847.683.4407
info@wshampshire.com
www.wshampshire.com

- Chief Exec. Officer and Pres.—Jeff Pope
- Chief Oper. Officer—Brian Loftus
- Sales Rep.—Kevin Pope

PRODUCTS and/or SERVICES: Provides custom fabrication of composite bearings, bushings and other wear parts featuring Ryertex® composites and technical plastics. Ryertex composite laminates, such as C/CG/G3/G7/G11/G10/FR4, BR60 and BR70, for applications including strippers, wipers, fiber bearings, wear plates, thrust collars, block bearings with collar and bearing shells. Technical plastics, such as nylon (filled or unfilled), UHMW and PTFE (including bronze filled), for applications including chock liners, spindle slipper pads, coupling box inserts, thrust collars for roll stands, table and gate rolls for pickle lines, filler plates or mandrel segments for payoff or rewind mandrel, and slinger rings. Will partner with operations, maintenance and engineering teams to replace traditional materials such as steel, brass, bronze and Micarta with non-metallic materials. Main drivers address problems with high-stress applications and operating conditions, including high-load, high-temperature, corrosive or difficult to lubricate.

WS THERMAL PROCESS TECHNOLOGY INC.
8301 W. Erie Ave.
Lorain, OH 44053 USA
P: +1.440.385.6829
F: +1.440.960.5454
wsinc@flox.com
www.flox.com

- Pres.—Joachim G. Wuenning

PRODUCTS and/or SERVICES: New generation of direct- and indirect-fired gas burners with integrated heat exchangers providing maximum efficiency with minimal NOx emissions. The Rekumat® self-recuperative burner is available in both direct- and indirect-fired versions, each of which is available in alloy or ceramic composition.

X

XTEK INC.
11451 Reading Road
Cincinnati, OH 45241 USA
P: +1.888.332.XTEK (9835) (Toll-Free);
+1.513.733.7800
F: +1.513.733.7939
sales@xtek.com
www.xtek.com

- Chief Exec. Officer and Pres.—Roger Miller
- Chief Financial Officer and Pres.—Kristin Farrell
- Vice Pres., Cincinnati and XE Oprs.—Tom Thole
- Vice Pres., Maint. Svcs. Group and Pres., Xtek Precision Machine—John Mayhan
- Vice Pres., Admin.—Jennifer King

EQUIPMENT: Complete machining, heat treating, carburizing and assembly facilities for all products listed. Service/recondition facility for maintenance of coupling,

EDITORS: Vladimir B. Ginzburg and Naum M. Kaplan

HIGHLIGHTING THE REVOLUTIONARY RECENT TECHNOLOGICAL ADVANCEMENTS IN FLAT STEEL ROLLING

Advanced Steel Plants for Production of Hot-Rolled Flat Products
PB-520 US$150

Advanced Equipment for Production of Hot-Rolled Flat Products
PB-521 US$150

Find solutions to modernize existing plants and design new facilities at AIST.org

SUPPLIERS of EQUIPMENT, PRODUCTS and SERVICES

gear, wheel and other mill-related products.

PRODUCTS and/or SERVICES:
Gearing (spur, helical, herringbone and bevels). Forged and hardened rolls. Wheels (track/crane, brake, sheave, rollers and assemblies). Geared couplings (mill, motor type), coupling grease. Universal joints. Specialty rolls (coiler pinch rolls, leveler, blocker). Mill screw and nut assemblies. Below-the-hook lifting equipment.

Xtek Canada — Avon Engineering
1680 Brampton St.
Hamilton, ON L8H 351 Canada
P: +1.800.844.8117 (Toll-Free);
    +1.905.689.7994
F: +1.855.720.1220
tech@avonengineering.com
sales@avonengineering.com
www.avonengineering.com

- Gen. Mgr.—Tom Mulhern

EQUIPMENT:
Machining, assembly and reconditioning facility for all products listed.

PRODUCTS and/or SERVICES:
Below-the-hook lifting devices. Upenders, inverters and lift tables. Coil packaging equipment. Service/reconditioning facility for maintenance of this equipment, plus crane wheel assemblies and gearboxes.

Xtek Europe s.r.o.
Domazlicka 180a
Plzen, 318 00 Czech Republic
P: +420.377.331.377
F: +420.377.320.585
sales@xtek.com
www.xtek.com

- Dir.—Roman Stichenwirth

EQUIPMENT:
Machining, heat treating and assembly facility for wheel products. Service/reconditioning facility for maintenance of crane wheel assemblies, geared couplings and universal joints.

PRODUCTS and/or SERVICES:
Manufacture of crane wheels, tires, guide rollers, sheave wheels and related wheel assemblies.

Bradley Lifting Co., an Xtek Co.—see listing page 310.

Xtek Precision Maintenance
1231 S. Third St.
Paducah, KY 42001 USA
P: +1.270.443.8444
www.xtekprecisionmaintenance.com

- Svce. Mgr.—Kevin Harper
- Prodn. Mgr.—Alan Sexton
- Machine Shop Foreman—Clayton Parker
- Field Maint. Mgr.—Ray Fennel
- Mechanic Shop Foreman—Jason Garner
- Weld Shop Supv.—Jon Thweatt
- Oprs. Support Mgr.—Cameron Castle
- Admin.Svcs. Mgr.—Amy Glover

EQUIPMENT:
Milling, drilling, turning, welding and fabrication, service/recondition facility for mill-related products.

PRODUCTS and/or SERVICES:
Machining and repair of mill-related products, including gearboxes, drivetrain spindles and specialty equipment. Field service maintenance and machining.

No. of Employees: 80+.

SUPPLIERS OF EQUIPMENT, PRODUCTS and SERVICES

Y

YATES INDUSTRIES INC.
23050 E. Industrial Dr.
St. Clair Shores, MI 48080 USA
P: +1.586.778.7680
F: +1.586.778.6565
www.yatesind.com

- Pres.—William H. Yates III
- Vice Pres.—Mark T. Cook
- Prodn./Mfg. Mgr.—Jim Warneke
- Treas.—Sallie Walsh
- Sales Mgr.—Steve Cavera
- Pur. Agt.—Scott Malik
- Chief Engr.—Donald Baaso

EQUIPMENT:
Turning equipment capable of 65-in. dia. x 320-in. B.C., lathes, boring mills, honing equipment, 10,000 psi test stands.

PRODUCTS and/or SERVICES:
Manufacturer of hydraulic and pneumatic cylinders, cylinder repairs for all departments of the steel mills (shop size 145,000 sq. ft.—St. Clair Shores, MI; 85,000 sq. ft.—Yates Alabama, 55 Refreshment Pl., Decatur, AL; and 75,000 sq. ft.—Yates Georgia, 7750 The Bluffs, Austell, GA., Yates Cylinders Ohio, 550 Bellbrook Ave., Xenia, OH).

No. of Employees: 212.

YS TECH CO. LTD.
40-11 Minamiseiwarncho
Suita, Osaka, 5640038 Japan
P: +81.6.4860.7770
https://ys-tech.jp

PRODUCTS and/or SERVICES:
Heat-proof label and tag products for identification and bar coding of hot steel, including slabs, coils, billets, bars and wire coils. Heat resistance to 1,800°F. Print labels in standard thermal transfer printers. Resistant to pickling, acid baths and powder coating processes. Automated and manual labeling devices to improve product identification for hot steel, including: slab, coil and billet.

YS Tech Co. Ltd.
509-30 Duke St. W
Kitchener, ON N2H 3W5 Canada
P: +1.519.489.4950
F: +1.519.489.4953
www.heatprooflabel.com

- Pres.—Koji Age
- Vice Pres.—Kenji Takehisa
- Sales Mgr.—Paul Porter

YS Tech Co. Ltd.
12747 Olive Blvd., Suite 300
St. Louis, MO 63304 USA
P: +1.314.872.2129
d.olson@ystech-gn.com
www.heatprooflabel.com

- Sales Mgr.—Dereck Olson

SUPPLIERS of EQUIPMENT, PRODUCTS and SERVICES

Z

ZANASI USA
9490 Hemlock Lane N
Maple Grove, MN 55369 USA
P: +1.763.593.1907
F: +1.763.593.1941
jason.spangler@zanasiusa.com
www.zanasiusa.com

- Pres.—Gary O'Hearn
- Vice Pres. Oprs.—Jason Spangler
- Vice Pres. Sales—Todd Fox

PRODUCTS and/or SERVICES:
Industrial inkjet equipment and solutions.

No. of Employees: 9.

ZAPTECH
15 Piedmont Center
3575 Piedmont Road NE, Suite 710
Atlanta, GA 30305 USA
P: +1.770.925.8125
F: +1.770.921.5635
ekaterina_galperina@yahoo.com
www.zaptechcorporation.com

- Pres.—Grigori Galperine
- Chief Financial Officer and Mktg.—Ekaterina Galperina

PRODUCTS and/or SERVICES:
Steelmaking technology.

ZERO GRAVITY FILTERS
12300 Emerson Dr.
Brighton, MI 48116 USA
P: +1.248.486.3500
F: +1.248.486.3501
jwiest@zgfilters.com
www.zgfilters.com

- Chief Exec. Officer—J. Todd Bruhn

PRODUCTS and/or SERVICES:
Automatic magnetic separators, automatic backwashing permanent media filters, centrifugal separators and oil/water separators for cleaning sections, cold mills, roll grinding, scale pits, cooling towers, tube mills, continuous annealing lines and paint/finishing lines.

No. of Employees: 10.

ZOLO TECHNOLOGIES—see ONPOINT

GEOGRAPHICAL INDEX SUPPLIERS

UNITED STATES

ALABAMA

ALBERTVILLE
  AJAX TOCCO
    MAGNETHERMIC CORP. 282

AXIS
  BLASTECH MOBILE. 307
  VAIL RUBBER WORKS INC. 554

BESSEMER
  DESHAZO LLC. 342

BIRMINGHAM
  BIRMINGHAM RAIL &
    LOCOMOTIVE. 306
  HICKMAN, WILLIAMS & CO. 392
    (MELTING MATERIALS DIV.). . . . 392
  MOTION 452
  NORTH AMERICAN
    CONSTRUCTION
    SERVICES LTD. 363
  OXYLANCE INC. 469
  TASACO INC. 530
  TRANS-LUBE
    LUBRICANTS INC. 544
  TRICON WEAR SOLUTIONS. 545
  VIPER IMAGING 558

CHELSEA
  DANIELI TARANIS LLC. 338

DECATUR
  PRIMETALS TECHNOLOGIES
    USA LLC. 480
  TRI-STATE HYDRAULICS 545
  YATES ALABAMA 575

JACKSONVILLE
  CALDERYS USA INC. 317

MOBILE
  FALK PLI. 358
  GONTERMANN-PEIPERS
    AMERICA INC. 376
  GULF STATES
    ENGINEERING INC. 380

PELHAM
  PROCESSBARRON 485

SARALAND
  MAGNETECH INDUSTRIAL
    SERVICES INC. 439

SYLACAUGA
  SOUTHERN ALLOY CORP. 518

THEODORE
  MACK MANUFACTURING INC. 438

ARKANSAS

BLYTHEVILLE
  PRIMETALS TECHNOLOGIES
    USA LLC. 480

EL DORADO
  THE SYSTEMS GROUP 526
    (SYSTEMS
    CONTRACTING). 526
    (SYSTEMS
    FAB & MACHINE) 526
    (SYSTEMS
    PLANT SERVICES). 526

JONESBORO
  SYSTEMS SMAC. 528

LITTLE ROCK
  LEXICON INC. 430

CALIFORNIA

BAKERSFIELD
  KSB SUPREMESERV/
    KSB INC. 424

CUPERTINO
  FALKONRY INC. 360

FONTANA
  HICKMAN, WILLIAMS & CO. 392

FRESNO
  LAKOS FILTRATION
    SOLUTIONS. 426

GEOGRAPHICAL INDEX SUPPLIERS

HAYWARD
AMETEK SURFACE VISION. 292

IRVINE
POLYTEC INC. 478

LAGUNA BEACH
PROTON PRODUCTS INC. 485

LIVERMORE
SANGRAF INTERNATIONAL INC. 502

ONTARIO
VM5 LIGHTING SOLUTIONS LLC 560

PALM DESERT
REDHAWK INDUSTRIES 494

SAN FRANCISCO
HAROLD BECK & SONS 386

STOCKTON
PROCO PRODUCTS INC. 485

COLORADO

DENVER
ADVANCED ENERGY 276
TAKRAF USA INC. 536

GOLDEN
INTEREP INC. 408

CONNECTICUT

CANAAN
VOLLMER AMERICA INC. 562

DANBURY
ABB INC. - FORCE MEASUREMENT PG 271
LINDE 434

MANCHESTER
ALKEGEN. 283

NORTHFORD
THERMAL-FLEX SYSTEMS INC. 536

PLAINVILLE
REDSTONE MACHINERY LLC 496

ROCKY HILL
HENKEL (LOCTITE). 390

STRATFORD
J.R. MERRITT CONTROLS INC. 416

DELAWARE

WILMINGTON
SSS CLUTCH CO. INC. 520

FLORIDA

ALTAMONTE SPRINGS
NORTH AMERICAN CRANE BUREAU INC. (NACB) 461

BOYNTON BEACH
LAP OF AMERICA LASER APPLICATIONS LLC. 426

DORAL
LUDECA INC. 437

JACKSONVILLE
HANSEN GROUP INTERNATIONAL LLC 384

JACKSONVILLE BEACH
MOFFITT CORP. 450
(MOFFITT MECHANICAL) 451

MEDLEY
REMIOR INDUSTRIES INC. 497

MIAMI
STEELTAGS.COM 521

MIAMI BEACH
UKCG TECHNICAL SERVICES. . . . 548

578   2023 AIST Directory — Iron and Steel Plants

GEOGRAPHICAL INDEX SUPPLIERS

MULBERRY
   KSB SUPREMESERV
      BY GIW INDUSTRIES INC. 423

NAPLES
   JACOBSON & ASSOCIATES 412

NORTH VENICE
   INTERFLOW TECHSERV INC. 408

PONTE VEDRA BEACH
   HELMKE —
      MOTORS AND DRIVES 389

SARASOTA
   AIR TRAC CORP. 280
   SGM MAGNETICS CORP. 510
   TORQUE TECHNOLOGIES INC. ... 542

TAMPA
   R&G LABORATORIES INC. 489

VERO BEACH
   RAMM METALS 490

GEORGIA

ACWORTH
   WEBER SENSORS LLC 564

ALPHARETTA
   IBA AMERICA LLC 399
   MAGALDI
      TECHNOLOGIES LLC. 439
   PRIMETALS TECHNOLOGIES
      USA LLC. 480
   SICON AMERICA LP 512

ATLANTA
   ACI HOLDING LLC. 274
   JOHANNES HUEBNER CORP. 415
   ZAPTECH 576

AUGUSTA
   MORGAN
      ADVANCED MATERIALS —
      THERMAL CERAMICS 452

AUSTELL
   YATES GEORGIA. 575

BERKELEY LAKE
   ISRA VISION PARSYTEC INC. 410

COLUMBUS
   SOUTHERN REWINDING. 439

GROVETOWN
   KSB SUPREMESERV
      NORTH AMERICA 423

LITHIA SPRINGS
   KETTENWULF INC. 420

MARIETTA
   BALD EAGLE AIR KINETICS. 304
   SHUB MACHINERY. 512

NORCROSS
   ACE INDUSTRIES 272

PEACHTREE CITY
   ASSA ABLOY/
      MEGADOOR USA. 301

ROSWELL
   KYTOLA INSTRUMENTS. 425

RUTLEDGE
   COMBUSTION DYNAMICS LLC ... 329

SUWANEE
   JVCKENWOOD USA CORP. 418

THOMSON
   KSB SUPREMESERV
      BY GIW INDUSTRIES. 423

TUCKER
   INTECO PTI 406

ILLINOIS

ALSIP
   DAUBERT CROMWELL 338
   KASTALON INC. 419
   KOCSIS USA 422
   UESCO CRANES. 546

ALTON
   ABBOTT MACHINE CO. 272

GEOGRAPHICAL INDEX SUPPLIERS

AURORA
    BENETECH INC. 305

BOLINGBROOK
    PEWAG CHAIN INC. 473
    SUPERIOR
        ENGINEERING LLC 524

BRIMFIELD
    KRESS CORP. 423

BROADVIEW
    JOHNSON POWER LTD. 416

BUFFALO GROVE
    SST FORMING ROLL INC. 504

CALEDONIA
    CENTRO-METALCUT. 322

CHAMPAIGN
    VESUVIUS USA 557

CHICAGO
    DAUBERT CHEMICAL CO. INC. ... 338
    HYDRO INC. 398
        (HYDROAIRE INC.) 398
    INDUSTRIAL MAINTENANCE
        WELDING & MACHINING
        CO. INC. 402
    MIDDOUGH INC. 449
    MOTOROLA SOLUTIONS 453
    U.S. BORAX | RIO TINTO. 553

CHICAGO HEIGHTS
    PICO CHEMICAL CORP. 474

CRETE
    HOLLAND LP 396

CRYSTAL LAKE
    GENERAL KINEMATICS 372

DEERFIELD
    MAGNECO/METREL INC. 439

DES PLAINES
    FINZER ROLLER 362

EAST DUNDEE
    POWER ELECTRONICS®
        INTERNATIONAL INC. 478

ELMHURST
    BRANDENBURG 310

GENEVA
    ENVEA INC. 352

GLENDALE HEIGHTS
    SPRAYING SYSTEMS CO. 519

GRANITE CITY
    ILLINOIS ELECTRIC WORKS 400

HAMPSHIRE
    W.S. HAMPSHIRE INC. 572

HARVEY
    FUCHS LUBRICANTS CO. 368

HAZEL CREST
    MI-JACK PRODUCTS INC.. 447

LAKE BLUFF
    BUEHLER 314

LISLE
    SUNCOKE ENERGY 522

MOKENA
    RITTERTECH 498

MONEE
    WHITING CORP. 567

MORRIS
    MID RIVER MINERALS INC. 449

MT. PROSPECT
    NTN BEARING CORP.
        OF AMERICA. 462

NAPERVILLE
    NALCO WATER,
        AN ECOLAB CO. 454

OAK BROOK
    MAXCESS. 443
    TAMINI TRANSFORMERS
        USA LLC. 530

OAKBROOK TERRACE
    GRAYCOR INDUSTRIAL
        CONSTRUCTORS INC. 378

GEOGRAPHICAL INDEX SUPPLIERS

PEORIA
   BOSSTEK 310
   PHILIPPI-HAGENBUCH INC. 473

PRINCETON
   MCKEOWN
      INTERNATIONAL INC. 444
   MIG REFRACTORIES USA 445

RED BUD
   RED BUD INDUSTRIES 494

ROCKFORD
   ADVANCED MACHINE &
      ENGINEERING 277
   CALDWELL GROUP INC., THE 317

ROMEOVILLE
   STUCCHI USA 522
   TRAMCO PUMP CO. 542
   WORLDWIDE MATERIAL
      HANDLING 571

SCHAUMBURG
   HEIDENHAIN CORP. 389
   HOH ENGINEERS INC. 394
   NOVASPECT INC. 461

SMITHTON
   HY-DAC RUBBER MFG. 397

SOUTH HOLLAND
   ANDRITZ METALS USA INC. 298

ST. CHARLES
   LECHLER INC. 426

WEST CHICAGO
   FLOLO CORP. 364

WEST FRANKFORT
   IRWIN CAR AND EQUIPMENT 410

WHEELING
   U.S. TSUBAKI POWER
      TRANSMISSION LLC 553

WILLOWBROOK
   NEW YORK BLOWER CO. 458

INDIANA

ANDERSON
   HY-PRO FILTRATION 398

AUBURN
   SCHUST 507

AURORA
   CORE METALS GROUP LLC 330

AVILLA
   ETA ENGINEERING INC. 354

BURNS HARBOR
   DLZ INDUSTRIAL LLC 344

CHESTERTON
   ANDRITZ METALS USA INC. 298

CROWN POINT
   INTEGRATED MILL
      SYSTEMS INC. –
      MIDWEST OFFICE 408
   R.T. PATTERSON CO. INC. 500

EAST CHICAGO
   PERFORMIX/HARSCO
      ENVIRONMENTAL 386
   SARGENT ELECTRIC CO. 506

EAST MOLINE
   R.T. PATTERSON CO. INC. 501

EVANSVILLE
   FLANDERS 364
   R.T. PATTERSON CO. INC. 501

FORT WAYNE
   LOGISTICS ETC. 436

GARY
   CASTER MAINTENANCE CO. 320

GRIFFITH
   AEROMET INDUSTRIES INC. 277
   B.E. SPERANZA INC. 303
   TECHNICAL WEIGHING
      SERVICES INC. 532

GEOGRAPHICAL INDEX SUPPLIERS

HAMMOND
MAGNETECH INDUSTRIAL
  SERVICES INC. 439
RITTERTECH 498
RUBICON
  REFRACTORIES INC. 501
SEMAC LLC 508
SUPERIOR ENGINEERING LLC ... 524
TMS INTERNATIONAL LLC 540

HOBART
METAL PRODUCTS AND
  ENGINEERING – U.S. LLC 446
STEVENS ENGINEERS &
  CONSTRUCTORS. 521

INDIANAPOLIS
AMERIFAB INC. 290
CROWN TECHNOLOGY INC. 333
PARTS SUPER CENTER 470
PRAXAIR SURFACE
  TECHNOLOGIES. 434
STANDARD ELECTRIC SUPPLY ... 520
T&M EQUIPMENT CO. INC. 528
  (INDIANAPOLIS OFFICE). 528

KOKOMO
MOON FABRICATING CORP. 451

LA PORTE
ENPROTECH INDUSTRIAL
  TECHNOLOGIES LLC. 352
HICKMAN, WILLIAMS & CO.
  (LA PORTE
  MANUFACTURING DIV.) 392
RGS MILL
  PRODUCTS CORP. 498

LAKE STATION
PRO-CHEM-CO INC. 484

MERRILLVILLE
MIDDOUGH INC. 449
T&M EQUIPMENT CO. INC. 528

MICHIGAN CITY
BULK EQUIPMENT CORP. 315

MUNSTER
RITTERTECH 498

PORTAGE
FALK PLI 358

TERRE HAUTE
AIS GAUGING 280

URBANA
KALENBORN
  ABRESIST CORP. 419

VALPARAISO
CIM-TECH INC. 324

WALKERTON
OPTA GROUP LLC 466

IOWA

JOHNSTON
BOWEN TECHNICAL
  PRODUCTS & SERVICES 310

KANSAS

LENEXA
CAMCORP INC. 317
KIEWIT 420

MISSION
INDUSTRIAL ACCESSORIES
  CO. (IAC). 402

MOUDRIDGE
BRADBURY CO. INC., THE 310

WICHITA
ONPOINT 466

KENTUCKY

ASHLAND
MIDDOUGH INC. 449

CARROLLTON
TRI-STATE HYDRAULICS 545

CRESTVIEW HILLS
SEMPER EXETER PAPER CO. 509

DAYTON
GAMMA-TECH LLC. 370

GEOGRAPHICAL INDEX SUPPLIERS

FLORENCE
  WELLS ENGINEERING PSC 564

GHENT
  PRIMETALS TECHNOLOGIES
    USA LLC. 480

LEXINGTON
  HOTWORK-USA 397

LOUISVILLE
  AMERICAN AIR FILTER
    CO. INC. 288
  CARBIDE INDUSTRIES LLC 318

PADUCAH
  XTEK PRECISION
    MAINTENANCE 574

SHEPHERDSVILLE
  EXACTRATION 356

LOUISIANA

BATON ROUGE
  DEEP SOUTH CRANE
    & RIGGING. 341

PORT ALLEN
  KSB SUPREMESERV
    BY STANDARD ALLOYS 424

MAINE

LEWISTON
  SARGENT ELECTRIC CO. 506

MARYLAND

CHESTERTOWN
  DIXON VALVE &
    COUPLING CO. 344

COLUMBIA
  SHIMADZU SCIENTIFIC
    INSTRUMENTS INC. 512

ELKTON
  W. L. GORE &
    ASSOCIATES INC. 562

FREDERICK
  RADIOMETRIC SERVICES AND
    INSTRUMENTS LLC (RSI) 490

JESSUP
  BALTIMORE AIRCOIL CO. 304

MASSACHUSETTS

BRAINTREE
  ALTRA INDUSTRIAL MOTION..... 286

CAMBRIDGE
  VENETA USA LLC 554

CHELMSFORD
  THERMO FISHER SCIENTIFIC 536

FISKDALE
  RUSSULA CORP. 501

GROTON
  TECHNOVATIONS
    INTERNATIONAL INC. (TII)..... 534

NORWOOD
  INSTRON 406

STOUGHTON
  FABREEKA
    INTERNATIONAL INC.......... 358

SUTTON
  PRIMETALS TECHNOLOGIES
    USA LLC. 480

WEST BRIDGEWATER
  REXA INC. 497

WORCESTER
  SAINT-GOBAIN
    PERFORMANCE CERAMICS &
    REFRACTORIES. 502
  U.S. NORTEK INC. 461
  WORCESTER FLUIDS
    TECHNOLOGY LLC 570

2023 AIST Directory — Iron and Steel Plants   583

GEOGRAPHICAL INDEX SUPPLIERS

MICHIGAN

ALMONT
  INTERPOWER INDUCTION USA............ 409

ANN ARBOR
  NSK AMERICAS 462

BELLEVILLE
  ANGSTROM INC.................. 299

BENTON HARBOR
  PRIMETALS TECHNOLOGIES USA LLC..................... 480

BOYNE CITY
  WALKER MAGNETICS........... 564

BRIGHTON
  ALLOR MANUFACTURING INC.... 284
  ZERO GRAVITY FILTERS......... 576

CLAWSON
  ADVANCED SYSTEMS INDUSTRIAL PRODUCTS...... 277
  AMETEK FACTORY AUTOMATION................ 290

CLINTON TWP.
  RITTERTECH.................... 498

COMSTOCK PARK
  KSB SUPREMESERV BY KSB DUBRIC................. 423

DEARBORN
  EDW. C. LEVY CO. 430
  NCCM DEARBORN.............. 456

DETROIT
  SLIPNOT®........................514
  WALBRIDGE 562

FERNDALE
  ROSS CONTROLS 499

GARDEN CITY
  WOODINGS INDUSTRIAL CORP............ 570

HOWELL
  AMERICAN CHEMICAL TECHNOLOGIES INC.......... 288
  ARMOR PROTECTIVE PACKAGING 301

KENTWOOD
  ANDRONACO INDUSTRIES 299

MACOMB
  DROPSA USA INC............... 346

MADISON HEIGHTS
  AJAX TOCCO MAGNETHERMIC CORP....... 282

NOVI
  BOLLFILTER CORP.............. 309
  SIDOCK GROUP INC............. 513

REDFORD
  AIRCENTRIC CORP.............. 280

RIVER ROUGE
  EES COKE BATTERY LLC........ 350

ST. CLAIR SHORES
  YATES INDUSTRIES INC.......... 575

ST. JOSEPH
  LECO CORP. 428
  VAIL RUBBER WORKS INC. 554

TRENTON
  CERCO INC..................... 322

TROY
  TR ELECTRONIC................ 542

WARREN
  RITTERTECH.................... 498

WATERFORD
  DALTON INDUSTRIES LLC 334

WIXOM
  AFC-HOLCROFT................ 278
  KENNEDY INDUSTRIES.......... 420
  SCHONSHECK INC.............. 507

GEOGRAPHICAL INDEX SUPPLIERS

MINNESOTA

DULUTH
GPM INC. 376

MAPLE GROVE
ZANASI USA. 576

MINNEAPOLIS
IDOM INC. 399

WOODBURY
SCHENK VISION 507

MISSISSIPPI

COLUMBUS
PRIMETALS TECHNOLOGIES
USA LLC. 480

LOUISVILLE
TAYLOR MACHINE
WORKS INC. 530

MISSOURI

CHESTERFIELD
RABCO ENERGY
SOLUTIONS INC. 489

INDEPENDENCE
GOAD CO.. 375

KANSAS CITY
SCHENCK PROCESS LLC. 506

ST. LOUIS
GUND CO. INC., THE 380
ICL-IP AMERICA INC. 399
JGB ENTERPRISES INC. 414
YS TECH CO. LTD. 575

NEBRASKA

OMAHA
CONDUCTIX-WAMPFLER 330

NEW HAMPSHIRE

AMHERST
OPTA GROUP LLC 466

LEMPSTER
RFTS LLC 497

NASHUA
PFEIFFER VACUUM 473

WESTMORELAND
POLYONICS 476

NEW JERSEY

BLOOMFIELD
ATLANTIC TRACK &
TURNOUT CO.. 302

BRANCHBURG
WORLD WIDE METRIC INC. ...... .571

ENGLEWOOD
ORIVAL WATER FILTERS. 468

FARMINGDALE
DIALIGHT 342

FORT LEE
PROMECON USA INC. 485

MATAWAN
DITH REFRACTORIES 344

MONMOUTH JUNCTION
OILCO LIQUID HANDLING
SYSTEMS. 466

NEWARK
NATIONAL MACHINERY
EXCHANGE INC. 456

NORTH BRUNSWICK
ABP INDUCTION LLC 272

PARAMUS
DASTUR INTERNATIONAL INC. ... 450

PRINCETON
METALHEAP.COM 447

2023 AIST Directory — Iron and Steel Plants 585

GEOGRAPHICAL INDEX SUPPLIERS

RANCOCAS
INDUCTOTHERM CORP. 402

SADDLE BROOK
UNILUX INC. 550

SPRINGFIELD
NEWARK BRUSH CO. LLC 458

NEW YORK

BUFFALO
JGB ENTERPRISES INC. 414
MIDDOUGH INC. 449

ELMIRA
HILLIARD BRAKE SYSTEMS 394

LEWISTON
NUPRO CORP. 464

LIVERPOOL
JGB ENTERPRISES INC. 414

LOCKPORT
BUFFALO TRANSFORMER
SERVICES 315

MANLIUS
FILTERTECH INC. 362

NEW YORK CITY
AIC NORTH AMERICA CORP. 278

NIAGARA FALLS
NUTTALL GEAR LLC 464

PALMYRA
GARLOCK FAMILY OF
COMPANIES 370

ROCHESTER
PKG EQUIPMENT INC. 476

ROSLYN
META-FIND, INC 446

SANBORN
EDWARDS VACUUM. 350

SELKIRK
AIR CLEANING BLOWERS LLC . . . 280

TONAWANDA
TAYLOR DEVICES INC. 530

UTICA
CASTING CONSULTANTS INC. . . . 322

VALHALLA
FARRAND CONTROLS. 360

WATERTOWN
ADL INSULFLEX INC. 276

WESTFIELD
RENOLD INC. 497

WHITE PLAINS
CARL ZEISS
MICROSCOPY LLC 318

YONKERS
GRAPHITE
METALLIZING CORP. 378

NORTH CAROLINA

ARCHDALE
HUBBELL 397

ASHEVILLE
PALMER WAHL
INSTRUMENTS INC. 469

CARY
ABB INC. 271
AMERICAN GREEN VENTURES
(SPILLFIX) 288
TEMPOSONICS LLC 534

CHARLOTTE
BSE AMERICA. 314
DYNAMIC MILL
SERVICES CORP. 349
GLOBAL STRATEGIC
SOLUTIONS INC. 374
JGB ENTERPRISES INC. 414
MIDREX TECHNOLOGIES INC. . . . 449
REDECAM USA LLC 494
TOKAI CARBON GE LLC 540
VESUVIUS USA 557

GREENVILLE
HYSTER CO. 398

586 2023 AIST Directory — Iron and Steel Plants

GEOGRAPHICAL INDEX SUPPLIERS

HICKORY
 AMERICAN ROLLER
  BEARING CO. 290
 HEICO FASTENING SYSTEMS 389

HIGH POINT
 A. LINDEMANN INC. 271

KINSTON
 BIJUR DELIMON
  INTERNATIONAL
  FARVAL/BIJUR/LUBESITE 306

MATTHEWS
 LIMAB NORTH AMERICA INC. 432

MOORESVILLE
 AMIAD WATER SYSTEMS 293

RALEIGH
 HITACHI ABB POWER GRIDS 272
 MICRO-EPSILON AMERICA 448

SALISBURY
 BK-SERVICES 307

STANLEY
 SENNEBOGEN LLC 509

THOMASVILLE
 NORDFAB DUCTING 460

WINSTON-SALEM
 PIEDMONT HOIST AND
  CRANE INC. 474

OHIO

ALEXANDRIA
 BROWN TRANSPORT INC. 312

ALLIANCE
 ACHENBACH SES. 510
 MORGAN ENGINEERING 452
 SES LLC
  (STEEL EQUIPMENT
  SPECIALISTS) 510
 SES SALICO FINISHING AND
  PROCESSING 510
 WINKLE INDUSTRIES 568

AURORA
 ROVISYS. 500

AVON
 QUAL-FAB INC. 488

BARBERTON
 HANNECARD
  ROLLER COATINGS INC. –
  ASB INDUSTRIES 382

BEDFORD
 GUILD INTERNATIONAL 378

BEREA
 ALLOY ENGINEERING
  CO., THE 284

BOARDMAN
 MAGNETECH INDUSTRIAL
  SERVICES INC. 439

BROOKLYN HEIGHTS
 GRAFTECH
  INTERNATIONAL LTD.. 376

BRUNSWICK
 MTUS TECHNOLOGY INC. 453

CALCUTTA
 BEDA OXYGENTECHNIC
  USA INC. 305

CANTON
 I²R POWER. 399
 MIDWEST INDUSTRIAL
  SUPPLY INC. 450
 UNITED ROLLS INC. 567

CHILLICOTHE
 INFOSIGHT CORP. 404

CINCINNATI
 CINCINNATI GASKET &
  INDUSTRIAL GLASS 326
 CTS INC. 333
 DAVID J. JOSEPH CO., THE 340
 HICKMAN, WILLIAMS & CO. 392
 XTEK INC. 572

2023 AIST Directory — Iron and Steel Plants   587

GEOGRAPHICAL INDEX SUPPLIERS

CLEVELAND
  AJAX TOCCO
    MAGNETHERMIC CORP. 282
  CLEVELAND GEAR CO. INC. 328
  EMG-USA INC. 351
  ENPROTECH INDUSTRIAL
    TECHNOLOGIES LLC. 352
  FIVES NORTH AMERICAN
    COMBUSTION INC. 363
  FOSBEL INC. 366
  FOSECO 557
  HORSBURGH & SCOTT. 396
  HOSE MASTER 396
  LINCOLN ELECTRIC CO., THE. . . . 432
  MAZZELLA COMPANIES. 443
  MID-CONTINENT COAL AND
    COKE CO. 448
  MIDDOUGH INC. 449
  NIDEC INDUSTRIAL
    SOLUTIONS. 460
  OIL SKIMMERS INC. 465
  RAD-CON INC. 489
  TRI-STATE HYDRAULICS 545
  TRIBCO INC.. 545

COLUMBIANA
  KRK ASSOCIATES INC. 423
  REICHARD INDUSTRIES LLC. 496

COLUMBUS
  ALLIED MINERAL PRODUCTS 283
  ALLSTRAP STEEL & POLY
    STRAPPING SYSTEMS 284
  CORPORATESEARCH LLC. 332
  SARGENT ELECTRIC CO. 506
  SENTEK CORP. 509

CORTLAND
  NUFLUX 462
  PRIMETALS TECHNOLOGIES
    USA LLC. 482

DAYTON
  BETA LASERMIKE PRODUCTS . . . 306
  NDC TECHNOLOGIES 458

DOVER
  DOVER HYDRAULICS INC. 344

ELYRIA
  FASTWAY INC.. 360

FAIRFIELD
  FORCE CONTROL
    INDUSTRIES INC.. 366

FRANKLIN
  CRANE 1 SERVICES 332

FREMONT
  WAHL REFRACTORY
    SOLUTIONS LLC 368

LAKEWOOD
  AMENDOLA
    ENGINEERING INC. 287

LEBANON
  IVC TECHNOLOGIES 412

LEWIS CENTER
  RDSTOLZ ENGINEERING LLC. . . . 492

LIMA
  WHEMCO OHIO
    FOUNDRY INC. 565

LORAIN
  WS THERMAL PROCESS
    TECHNOLOGY INC. 572

LOUISVILLE
  OTC SERVICES INC.. 468

MACEDONIA
  ETS SCHAEFER LLC 354

MALTA
  EZG MANUFACTURING. 356

MANSFIELD
  GORMAN-RUPP CO. 376

MAPLE HEIGHTS
  OHIO MAGNETICS INC.. 465

MASSILLON
  HYDROTHRIFT CORP.. 398
  MAGNETECH INDUSTRIAL
    SERVICES INC.. 439

MAUMEE
  MATRIX TECHNOLOGIES INC.. . . . 443
  MIDDOUGH INC.. 449

588   2023 AIST Directory — Iron and Steel Plants

GEOGRAPHICAL INDEX SUPPLIERS

MEDINA
    ERIE COPPER WORKS............ 352

MIAMISBURG
    LJB INC......................... 436

MIDDLEBURG
    STEVENS ENGINEERS &
        CONSTRUCTORS..............521

MIDDLEBURG HEIGHTS
    SUPERIOR ENGINEERING LLC ... 524

MIDDLETOWN
    ETS EVERTZ TECHNOLOGY
        SERVICE U.S.A. INC........... 356
    INJECTION ALLOYS INC. 404

MINERVA
    B&H MACHINE INC.............. 303

MINSTER
    MACHINE CONCEPTS INC........ 438

MOGADORE
    SHINAGAWA ADVANCED
        MATERIALS AMERICAS 512

MORAINE
    GLOBAL GAUGE CORP. 374

NEW LONDON
    PRIMETALS TECHNOLOGIES
        USA LLC..................... 482

NORTH CANTON
    AJAX TOCCO/
        LECTROTHERM 282
    BRAUN MACHINE
        TECHNOLOGIES LLC...........311
    FIVES BRONX INC............... 362
    TIMKEN CO., THE 537

NORTH LIMA/YOUNGSTOWN
    KTSDI LLC 424

ORRVILLE
    MOOG FLO-TORK................451

PAINESVILLE
    MCNEIL INDUSTRIES –
        MAXAM BEARINGS........... 445

PLAIN CITY
    ADVANCED GAUGING
        TECHNOLOGIES, L.L.C. 277
    UNITED ENGINEERED
        PRODUCTS 458
    UNITED ROTARY
        BRUSH CORP................. 550

POLAND
    UNITED STATES CONTROLS..... 550

SALEM
    BOC WATER
        HYDRAULICS INC.............. 308
    BUTECH BLISS 316
    HUNT VALVE CO. 397
    JOHN COCKERILL INDUSTRY 416
    SIMMERS CRANE DESIGN &
        SERVICES CO. 513

SEBRING
    APEX CONTROL
        SYSTEMS INC. 300
    SALEM-REPUBLIC
        RUBBER CO.................. 502

SHARON CENTER
    RUHLIN CO., THE 501

SOLON
    AMEPA AMERICA INC............ 287

SPRINGBORO
    MICROPOLY/PHYMET INC. 448
    TREBNICK SYSTEMS INC. 545

SPRINGFIELD
    KONECRANES INC. 422

STREETSBORO
    SELAS HEAT TECHNOLOGY
        CO. LLC 508

TOLEDO
    UNIVERSAL URETHANE
        PRODUCTS INC................ 552
    WORLDBRIDGE PARTNERS OF
        TOLEDO INC...................571

TWINSBURG
    CG THERMAL LLC 324

GEOGRAPHICAL INDEX SUPPLIERS

VANDALIA
   VEOLIA WATER
      TECHNOLOGIES.............. 556

VIENNA
   BUELTMANN US LP 315

WADSWORTH
   EBNER FURNACES INC.......... 350
   FIVES ST. CORP................. 363
   PT TECH LLC®.................. 486

WARREN
   ADS MACHINERY CORP.......... 276
   AJAX TOCCO
      MAGNETHERMIC CORP....... 282
      (MIS SERVICE CENTER) 282
   CATTRON NORTH
      AMERICA INC.................. 322
   GLUNT INDUSTRIES INC.......... 375
   MACPHERSON & COMPANY 438
   PERFORMIX/HARSCO
      ENVIRONMENTAL 386
   PRIMETALS TECHNOLOGIES
      USA LLC..................... 482

WEST CHESTER
   GO2 PARTNERS INC.............. 375
   IKEUCHI USA INC. 400
   UMECC 550
   UPA TECHNOLOGY 552

WESTLAKE
   R.E. WARNER &
      ASSOCIATES INC.............. 492

WILLOUGHBY
   INTEGRATED MILL
      SYSTEMS INC. 408

WOOSTER
   MERIT PUMP & EQUIPMENT
      CO. INC...................... 446

XENIA
   YATES CYLINDERS OHIO 575

YOUNGSTOWN
   BMD COMPANY LLC 308
   BRILEX INDUSTRIES INC..........312
   TAYLOR-WINFIELD
      TECHNOLOGIES INC. 532

OKLAHOMA

DURANT
   DURANT METAL
      SHREDDING LLC 348

OREGON

HILLSBORO
   THERMO FISHER SCIENTIFIC 537

SALEM
   GERLINGER CARRIER CO.
      (GCC INC.).................... 372

SHERWOOD
   ALLIED SYSTEMS CO............ 284

PENNSYLVANIA

ALIQUIPPA
   HATCH IAS..................... 388
   SIMPSON TECHNICAL
      SALES INC. 514
   VALVES INC. 554

ALLENTOWN
   AIR PRODUCTS................. 280
   MALMEDIE INC. 442

AMBRIDGE
   ANDRITZ METALS USA INC....... 298

ASTON
   L&L SPECIAL FURNACE
      CO. INC...................... 426

BEAVER
   TORCUP OF WESTERN
      PENNSYLVANIA AND
      NORTHERN OHIO 540

BEAVER FALLS
   GESCO INC.
      (GRINDING ENGINEERING
      SERVICES CO.)................ 372

BERWYN
   AMETEK INC.................... 290

GEOGRAPHICAL INDEX SUPPLIERS

BETHEL PARK
   RACO INTERNATIONAL L.P........ 489
   VERICHEK TECHNICAL
      SERVICES INC................ 557

BETHLEHEM
   ITR............................412
   LEHIGH HEAVY FORGE CORP.... 565
   RMI—RAW MATERIALS AND
      IRONMAKING GLOBAL
      CONSULTING 498
   UNIVERSAL INDUSTRIAL
      GASES LLC 552

BLAIRSVILLE
   IRWIN CAR AND EQUIPMENT 410

BRADFORD
   CONTROL CHIEF CORP.......... 330

BRIDGEVILLE
   AUSTRALTEK LLC 302
   CLAYTON ENGINEERING CO..... 327
   ELCON TECHNOLOGIES......... 350

BURGETTSTOWN
   TEMCO INDUSTRIES INC......... 534

BUTLER
   NICHOLAS ENTERPRISES INC.... 460

CALLERY
   ANDRITZ METALS USA INC....... 296

CANONSBURG
   ANDRITZ METALS USA INC....... 296
   GANTREX INC. 370
   PRIMETALS TECHNOLOGIES
      USA LLC..................... 482
   STEVENS ENGINEERS &
      CONSTRUCTORS..............521

CARNEGIE
   DELTA USA INC. 342
   S.P. KINNEY ENGINEERS INC......519

CHAMBERSBURG
   WIKA MOBILE CONTROL LP 568

CHARLEROI
   BLOOM ENGINEERING
      CO. INC..................... 308
   GLASSPORT CYLINDER
      WORKS...................... 374
   TRI-STATE HYDRAULICS 545

CHESTER HEIGHTS
   QUALICAST CORP............... 488

CLAIRTON
   TYK AMERICA INC............... 546

CLINTON
   NORD-LOCK INC................. 460
   SOFIS CO. INC. 518

COCHRANTON
   DRAFTO CORP................... 346

CONSHOHOCKEN
   QUAKER HOUGHTON 488

CORAOPOLIS
   ALFA & ASSOCIATES............. 282
   CRANE 1....................... 332
   DE NORA WATER
      TECHNOLOGIES............... 340
   H&K EQUIPMENT 382
   HARBISONWALKER
      INTERNATIONAL 384
   MOLYNEUX INDUSTRIES INC......451
   PITTEK DIV. OF
      SWINDELL DRESSLER
      INTERNATIONAL CO. 474
   TENOVA INC.................... 535
   TOTAL EQUIPMENT CO. 542

CRANBERRY TWP.
   DANIELI CORP.................. 336
   FOREMOST ENVIRONMENTAL
      CONSULTING INC............. 366
   HICKMAN, WILLIAMS & CO...... 392
   MATTHEWS MARKING
      SYSTEMS..................... 443
   TRE SERVICES INC.............. 545

ELIZABETH
   CHIZ BROS. INC................. 324

ELLWOOD CITY
   HALL INDUSTRIES INC........... 382

GEOGRAPHICAL INDEX SUPPLIERS

ERIE
AMERIDRIVES 286
ERIE FORGE & STEEL INC. 566
ERIEZ 354
PSNERGY. 486
RITTERTECH 498

EVANS CITY
HAUHINCO 388
PENSCO LLC 472

EXPORT
KT-GRANT 424
LEYBOLD VACUUM 430

FORD CITY
HERKULES NORTH AMERICA 390

FORT WASHINGTON
PRIMETALS TECHNOLOGIES
  USA LLC 482

GEORGETOWN
C&E PLASTICS INC 317

GLENSHAW
A. LINDEMANN INC. 271
PANNIER CORP. 470
PRCO AMERICA INC 478

GROVE CITY
PENNSYLVANIA
  EQUIPMENT INC. 472

HARMONY
AIM MARKET RESEARCH 278
BERRY METAL CO 305
PROGRESSIVE POWER
  TECHNOLOGIES LLC. 570

HARRISBURG
ANDREW S. McCREATH &
  SON INC. 294

HERMITAGE
G.W. BECKER INC. 380

HOMESTEAD
WHEMCO STEEL
  CASTINGS INC.. 565

HORSHAM
TMS INTERNATIONAL LLC 540

IRWIN
HIGHLAND CARBIDE TOOL
  CO. INC. 394
IRWIN CAR AND EQUIPMENT 409

JEANNETTE
ALLEGHENY ALLOY INC. 283

JOHNSTOWN
JOHNSTOWN SPECIALTY
  CASTINGS INC.. 567
TRI-STATE HYDRAULICS 545

KITTANNING
SINTERMET LLC 514

LATROBE
LEHIGH SPECIALTY
  MELTING INC. 566

MAHANOY
BLASCHAK ANTHRACITE 307

MARS
IMS SYSTEMS INC. 400
WOODINGS
  INDUSTRIAL CORP. 570

MCKEESPORT
SIL-BASE CO. INC. 513

MCKEES ROCKS
MCKEES ROCKS FORGINGS 444
NCCM MCKEES ROCKS 456
SCHUST 508

MIDLAND
WHEMCO STEEL
  CASTINGS INC.. 565

MOON TWP.
CIVIL & ENVIRONMENTAL
  CONSULTANTS INC. 326

MORGAN
WKW INDUSTRIAL SERVICES 571

NAZARETH
RAW MATERIAL
  SERVICES LLC 492

NEW BRIGHTON
LITTELL STEEL CO. 436

GEOGRAPHICAL INDEX SUPPLIERS

NEW CASTLE
MAGNETIC LIFTING
  TECHNOLOGIES US 332

NEW KENSINGTON
AFFIVAL INC. 466

NEWTOWN
HAROLD BECK & SONS INC. 384
VERDER SCIENTIFIC INC. 556

NORTH HUNTINGDON
INTEGRATED MILL
  SYSTEMS INC. 408

OAKDALE
EAFAB CORP. 349

PHILADELPHIA
PRUFTECHNIK INC. 486

PITTSBURGH
AGM WELDING 278
ALPINE METAL TECH NORTH
  AMERICA INC. 286
AM HEALTH AND SAFETY INC. 287
AMETEK PROCESS
  INSTRUMENTS. 292
ANT AUTOMATION. 300
BEARING SERVICE CO. 305
BOGNAR AND CO. INC. 309
BPI INC. 310
CARMEUSE AMERICAS. 320
  (CARMEUSE INNOVATION
  CENTER) 320
CASEY EQUIPMENT CORP. 320
CBMM NORTH AMERICA INC. 322
CSD ENGINEERS 333
CV ENGINEERING 333
DIBENEDETTO APPRAISAL
  SERVICES 342
DREVER INTERNATIONAL USA. ... 518
ENCORE MATERIALS INC. 351
FALK PLI. 358
FOERSTER
  INSTRUMENTS INC. 366
GALLETTA
  ENGINEERING CORP. 368
GROWTHHIVE. 378
HATCH ASSOCIATES
  CONSULTANTS INC. 387
INDUSTRIAL RUBBER
  PRODUCTS CO. 404
INDUSTRIAL SCIENTIFIC CORP. ... 404

JENDCO CORP. 414
JNE CONSULTING U.S.A. 415
KENNAMETAL INC. 420
KINTNER INC. 421
KOCKS PITTSBURGH CO. 421
MANAGEMENT SCIENCE
  ASSOCIATES INC. 442
MIDDOUGH INC. 449
MUNROE INC. 454
NU-TECH RESOURCES 462
OCMET INC. 464
PANNIER CORP. 470
PENN RADIANT. 471
PITTSBURGH AIR SYSTEMS –
  AIR INDUSTRIAL INC. 476
PSI METALS NORTH
  AMERICA INC. 486
R.T. PATTERSON CO. INC. 500
SARCLAD NORTH
  AMERICA LP 504
SARGENT ELECTRIC CO. 504
SARRALLE USA 506
S.I.T. AMERICA INC. 514
SMS GROUP INC. 514
STEEL EQUIPMENT CORP. 521
STIMPLE & WARD CO. 521
TDI GROUP LLC. 532
TMS INTERNATIONAL LLC 540
VENTILATION SYSTEMS LLC. 554
VH ENTERPRISES INC. 558
WHEMCO INC. (CSS) 564

PLEASANTVILLE
VERTICAL SEAL CO. 499

POTTSVILLE
READING ANTHRACITE CO. 494

PUNXSUTAWNEY
ACME MACHINE &
  WELDING CO. 274

RADNOR
PHOENIX SERVICES LLC 474

RENFREW
CARBINITE METAL COATINGS ... 318

SANDY LAKE
FLEXOSPAN. 364

SARVER
CID ASSOCIATES INC. 324

2023 AIST Directory — Iron and Steel Plants   593

GEOGRAPHICAL INDEX SUPPLIERS

SCOTTDALE
DURALOY
TECHNOLOGIES INC. 348

SEVEN FIELDS
HARSCO ENVIRONMENTAL. 386

SEWICKLEY
MCCLUSKEY &
ASSOCIATES INC. 444

TAMAQUA
LEHIGH ANTHRACITE COAL 428

TITUSVILLE
ROSER TECHNOLOGIES INC. 499
THERMA-FAB INC. 536

TREVOSE
LENOX INSTRUMENT CO. INC. . . . 428
VEOLIA WATER
TECHNOLOGIES &
SOLUTIONS. 556

UWCHLAND
FLUIDTECHNIK USA INC. 366

WARRENDALE
BURNS INDUSTRIAL
EQUIPMENT INC. 315
CERVIS INC. 324

WASHINGTON
SONGER SERVICES. 518

WAYNESBURG
IRWIN CAR AND EQUIPMENT 410

WEST MIDDLESEX
T. BRUCE SALES INC. 528

WEXFORD
ARVOS SCHMIDTSCHE
SCHACK LLC. 301

YATESVILLE
JEDDO COAL CO. 414

YORK
BRADLEY LIFTING CORP. 310
VOITH TURBO 560

ZELIENOPLE
PENNA FLAME INDUSTRIES 471
RITTERTECH. 498
SPRINGER CO. 519

RHODE ISLAND

PROVIDENCE
WALCO 562

SOUTH CAROLINA

CHAPIN
MRSI –
MAINTENANCE - RELIABILITY
SOLUTIONS INC. 453
TITAN BEARINGS 538

CHARLESTON
LIFE CYCLE ENGINEERING 432
TRI-STATE HYDRAULICS 545

FLORENCE
INTERNATIONAL KNIFE &
SAW INC. 409
SUPERIOR MACHINE CO. OF
S.C. INC. 524

GREENVILLE
FLUOR METALS 366
INTEGRATED POWER
SERVICES (IPS). 408
JTEKT NORTH
AMERICA CORP. 416
TRANSTECH—A WABTEC CO. . . . 544

HUGER
PRIMETALS TECHNOLOGIES
USA LLC. 482

PAWLEYS ISLAND
DRESSEL
TECHNOLOGIES LLC. 346

RIDGEVILLE
SHOWA DENKO CARBON INC. . . . 512

ROCK HILL
ANDRITZ METALS USA INC. 299

GEOGRAPHICAL INDEX SUPPLIERS

SPARTANBURG
ISB STEEL TECH.................410

SUMTER
THOMPSON INDUSTRIAL
SERVICES LLC 537

TENNESSEE

CHATTANOOGA
HICKMAN, WILLIAMS & CO....... 392

CLARKSVILLE
USA BORESCOPES 553

COLUMBIA
COLUMBIA MACHINE
WORKS INC. 329

HUMBOLDT
REINHAUSEN
MANUFACTURING INC. 496

JOHNSON CITY
DILLON INDUSTRIAL FAN CO..... 342

NASHVILLE
MAZZELLA CIS................. 444
UNITED STATES ROLLER
WORKS INC. 552

SMYRNA
SYSTEMS SPRAY-COOLED
EQUIPMENT 526

TEXAS

AUSTIN
HAROLD BECK & SONS 384

CEDAR PARK
FLAME TECHNOLOGIES INC..... 364

DEER PARK
KSB SUPREMESERV
BY STANDARD ALLOYS 424

FORT WORTH
ACE WORLD COMPANIES INC.... 272

INTERNATIONAL TECHNICAL
CERAMICS LLC (ITC).......... 409
LHOIST NORTH AMERICA 430

HOUSTON
AMRESIST INC.................. 293
AUTOMATION PRODUCTS INC. –
DYNATROL® DIV. 303
BAR STOCK SPECIALTIES 304
HAROLD BECK & SONS 386
JGB ENTERPRISES INC..........414
JVI VIBRATORY EQUIPMENT......418
KONECRANES INC. 422
POLYTEC USA CORP. 308

HUMBLE
POWER RESOURCES LLC 478
SAFETY LAMP OF
HOUSTON INC................. 502

IRVING
ALKEGEN 283
DELTA STEEL TECHNOLOGIES....341
HICKMAN, WILLIAMS & CO....... 392
MAPOMEGA INC. 442
SIGNAL METAL
INDUSTRIES INC.............. 513

KATY
VAHLE INC. 553

LONGVIEW
AJAX TOCCO
MAGNETHERMIC CORP. 282

PLANO
SOFTWEB SOLUTIONS INC. 518

PORT ARTHUR
KSB SUPREMESERV
BY STANDARD ALLOYS 424

ROUND ROCK
ULTRA ELECTRONICS,
ENERGY..................... 548

SAN MARCOS
AMERIDRIVES –
GEAR COUPLINGS 287

SCHERTZ
TECHNOS INC................... 532

GEOGRAPHICAL INDEX SUPPLIERS

SPRING
DELLNER BUBENZER 341

THE WOODLANDS
LAMIFLEX INC. 426

WICHITA FALLS
WPT POWER CORP. 571

UTAH

ST. GEORGE
KIMZEY SOFTWARE
  SOLUTIONS. 420

VIRGINIA

ASHLAND
VIRGINIA CRANE
  (FOLEY MATERIAL
  HANDLING) 558

BIG ROCK
IRWIN CAR AND EQUIPMENT 410

CHESAPEAKE
AMERICAN GFM CORP. 288
SUMITOMO DRIVE
  TECHNOLOGIES. 522

FOREST
INNERSPEC
  TECHNOLOGIES INC. 406

HENRICO
CONSERO INC. 330
KSB SUPREMESERV/
  KSB INC. 424
PROXITRON INC. 485

NORFOLK
HOISTCAM BY NETARUS LLC 394

ROANOKE
GEORG NORTH AMERICA INC. ... 372
TMEIC CORP. AMERICAS 538

VIENNA
HONGJI ELECTRODE
  MANUFACTURER CO. LTD. 396

VIRGINIA BEACH
BUSCH VACUUM SOLUTIONS 315
HOLLTECK CO. INC. 396

WINCHESTER
NATIONAL FILTER MEDIA. 456

WYTHEVILLE
AQ TRANSFORMER
  SOLUTIONS INC. 300

WASHINGTON

BELLEVUE
M. BRASHEM INC./
  MBI ROLLS LLC 437

BLAINE
TRANSCONTINENTAL
  ENGINEERED
  SYSTEMS INC. 544

ISSAQUAH
DATA-LINC GROUP 338

MONROE
BRICKING SOLUTIONS 311
BROKK INC. 312

SPOKANE
PYROTEK INC. 486

VANCOUVER
MICROCRANES INC. 448

WEST VIRGINIA

APPLE GROVE
PRECISIONED
  COMPONENTS LLC 480

BECKLEY
IRWIN CAR AND EQUIPMENT 410

HUNTINGTON
FLETCHER ENGINEERED
  SOLUTIONS. 364
MAGNETECH INDUSTRIAL
  SERVICES INC. 439

GEOGRAPHICAL INDEX SUPPLIERS

LOGAN
    IRWIN CAR AND EQUIPMENT 410

MORGANTOWN
    TRI-STATE HYDRAULICS 545

WISCONSIN

BROWNSVILLE
    MICHELS CONSTRUCTION INC.......... 448

DELAFIELD
    T-T ELECTRIC USA 529

DEPERE
    DÜRR SYSTEMS INC............. 348

GREEN BAY
    ESSCO INC..................... 354
    SARGENT ELECTRIC CO......... 506

GREENDALE
    KINETIC CO., THE. 421

HARTLAND
    HERAEUS ELECTRO-NITE CO. LLC 390

HUDSON
    KONRAD CORP. 422

MADISON
    BRUKER AXS INC. 314
    MIDDOUGH INC.................. 449

MADISON HEIGHTS
    HENKEL 390

MENOMONEE FALLS
    BUSHMAN EQUIPMENT INC...... 316
    MAGNETEK 439

MILWAUKEE
    ANGUIL ENVIRONMENTAL SYSTEMS INC. 299
    HELWIG CARBON PRODUCTS.... 389
    IN-PLACE MACHINING CO. 400
    REGAL REXNORD MOTION CONTROL SOLUTIONS......... 496
    STANDARD ELECTRIC SUPPLY CO.................. 520

PEWAUKEE
    RITTERTECH.................... 498

PORT WASHINGTON
    KUTTNER NORTH AMERICA 425

RACINE
    VISTA SYSTEM AND PRODUCT ENGINEERS (VISTA SPE LLC).............. 560

RIVER FALLS
    NCCM RIVER FALLS (HEADQUARTERS)............ 456

STURGEON BAY
    SHUTTLELIFT 512

SUSSEX
    GFG PEABODY INC.............. 374

WATERTOWN
    KONECRANES INC. 422
    SPUNCAST INC. 519

WAUKESHA
    METALTEK INTERNATIONAL..... 447

WAUWATOSA
    ABB INC. METALS SYSTEMS 271

ARGENTINA

BUENOS AIRES

SAN NICOLÁS
    CONTROLES Y SISTEMAS (C&S) SRL 330
    METALLON..................... 447

AUSTRALIA

QUEENSLAND

BRISBANE
    HATCH ASSOCIATES CONSULTANTS INC............ 388

GEOGRAPHICAL INDEX SUPPLIERS

SOUTH AUSTRALIA

CAMDEN PARK
SCANTECH INTERNATIONAL
PTY. LTD. 506

VICTORIA

NUNAWADING
CNC DESIGN PTY. LTD. 328

AUSTRIA

GRAZ
ANDRITZ AG 294

LINZ
PRIMETALS TECHNOLOGIES
AUSTRIA GMBH 482

REGAU
ALPINE METAL TECH GMBH 286

ST. FLORIAN
HJK CONSULTING
ENGINEERS GMBH 394

VIENNA
RHI MAGNESITA 498

VOECKLABRUCK
BRAUN
MASCHINENFABRIK GMBH. 311

BELGIUM

DROGENBOS
PRIMETALS TECHNOLOGIES
BELGIUM NV/SA 482

LIEGE
DREVER INTERNATIONAL S.A. 517

BRAZIL

ESPÍRITO SANTOS

SERRA
PRIMETALS TECHNOLOGIES
BRAZIL LTDA. 482

MINAS GERAIS

BELO HORIZONTE
HATCH ASSOCIATES
CONSULTANTS INC. 388
PRIMETALS TECHNOLOGIES
BRAZIL LTDA. 482

SANTANA DO PARAISO
LUMAR METALURGICA LTDA. 437

RIO DE JANEIRO

RIO DE JANEIRO
PRIMETALS TECHNOLOGIES
BRAZIL LTDA. 482

VOLTA REDONDA
PRIMETALS TECHNOLOGIES
BRAZIL LTDA. 482

SÃO PAULO

SÃO PAULO
PRIMETALS TECHNOLOGIES
BRAZIL LTDA. 482
SANGRAF INTERNATIONAL. 502

SOROCABA
KONECRANES INC. 422

GEOGRAPHICAL INDEX SUPPLIERS

CANADA

ALBERTA

CROSSFIELD
BAR1 TRANSPORTATION 304

EDMONTON
KONECRANES INC. 422
KSB SUPREMESERV
CANADA/KSB PUMPS INC. 424

FORT MCMURRAY
KSB SUPREMESERV BY
GIW INDUSTRIES INC. 423

ONTARIO

BURLINGTON
AMTEC HYDRACLAMP INC. 293
FIBRECAST 362
ITIPACK SYSTEMS 410
TALLMAN
TECHNOLOGIES INC. 529

CAMBRIDGE
HICKMAN, WILLIAMS
CANADA INC. 392

COBOURG
ADL INSULFLEX INC. 274

CORNWALL
OXY-ARC INTERNATIONAL LP ... 468

GRIMSBY
PRECISION SURFACE
TECHNOLOGIES INC. 480

GUELPH
CLARKE ROLLER AND
RUBBER LTD. 327

HAMILTON
BLACKHAWK
"COMBUSTIONEERING" LTD. ... 307
JNE GROUP OF COMPANIES
(JNE AUTOMATION) 415
(JNE CONSULTING LTD.) 415
LUTHER HOLTON
ASSOCIATES INC. 437
PALING TRANSPORTER LTD. 469
PERFORMANCE
IMPROVEMENT INC. 472
PHILIP DOYLE
MANUFACTURING INC. 473
RADIAN ROBOTICS 490
XTEK CANADA–
AVON ENGINEERING 574

KITCHENER
RAPID GEAR 492
YS TECH CO. LTD. 575

LONDON
JMP SOLUTIONS INC. 414
TR ELECTRONIC 542

MISSISSAUGA
COLT AUTOMATION. 329
GMB HEAVY INDUSTRIES 375
HATCH LTD. 387
KSB SUPREMESERV
CANADA/KSB PUMPS INC. 424
TENOVA GOODFELLOW INC. 535

NORTH YORK
QUAD TRAINING 487

OAKVILLE
RADCOMM SYSTEMS CORP. 490

ORILLIA
KUBOTA MATERIALS
CANADA CORP. 425

RICHMOND HILL
LOGIKA TECHNOLOGIES INC. ... 436

SAULT STE. MARIE
TULLOCH ENGINEERING 546

ST. CATHERINES
HASTEC GROUP
(HASTEC
ENGINEERING INC.) 387
(HASTEC REBS INC.) 387
HAVER & BOECKER NIAGARA ... 388

STEVENSVILLE
CMI HEAVY INDUSTRIES 328

GEOGRAPHICAL INDEX SUPPLIERS

STONEY CREEK
    FABRIS INC. 358
    TUBE-MAC® PIPING
        TECHNOLOGIES LTD. 545

TORONTO
    QUAD ENGINEERING INC. 487
        (QUAD INFOTECH INC.) 487
    VISHAY PRECISION GROUP
        CANADA ULC (KELK) 558

WATERDOWN
    OPTA GROUP LLC 466

WATERLOO
    MEGTEC TURBOSONIC INC. 348

WELLAND
    WHITING EQUIPMENT
        CANADA INC. 568

WELLINGTON
    VESUVIUS CANADA 557

WEST GRIMSBY
    HANDLING SPECIALTY
        MANUFACTURING LTD. 382

WHITBY
    EMPCO 351

WOODBRIDGE
    ROTATOR PRODUCTS LTD. 500

QUEBEC

BOISBRIAND
    RNP INDUSTRIES INC. 499

CANDIAC
    MAJOR 440

LACHINE
    DEC INDUSTRIES LTD. 341

MONTREAL
    AIR-THERM INC. 280
    HATCH ASSOCIATES
        CONSULTANTS INC. 388

SAINT-HYACINTHE
    TRANS CANADA WIRE &
        CABLE CO. 544

ST-JOSEPH-DE-SOREL
    ACIERS RÉGIFAB STEELS 274

SASKATCHEWAN

REGINA
    BRANDT ENGINEERED
        PRODUCTS 311
    OPTA GROUP LLC 466

RM OF SHERWOOD
    DYNAINDUSTRIAL LP 348

SASKATOON
    STANDARD MACHINE 520

CHILE

SANTIAGO
    HATCH ASSOCIATES
        CONSULTANTS INC. 388

CZECH REPUBLIC

OSTRAVA
    PRIMETALS TECHNOLOGIES
        CZECH REPUBLIC S.R.O 483

PLZEN
    XTEK EUROPE S.R.O. 574

FINLAND

HYVINKAA
    KONECRANES PLC 422

GEOGRAPHICAL INDEX SUPPLIERS

FRANCE

COURBEVOIE
ENERTIME .... .351

LE COUDRAY-MONTCEAUX
SEIRIS 508

MAISONS-ALFORT
FIVES STEEL BUSINESS LINE 363

PARIS
CALDERYS .... .317
DANIELI ROTELEC 336

RUEIL-MALMASION
SCHNEIDER ELECTRIC 507

GERMANY

AACHEN
ISRA VISION PARSYTEC AG ...... .410

BAD KROZINGEN
VOESTALPINE BÖHLER
WELDING UTP
MAINTENANCE GMBH 560

BARLEBEN
PROMECON 485

BUXTEHUDE
CLAUDIUS PETERS
PROJECTS GMBH 327

DUISBURG
LOI THERMPROCESS GMBH 535

DÜSSELDORF
SMS GROUP GMBH .... .514

ERLANGEN
PRIMETALS TECHNOLOGIES
GERMANY GMBH 483

ESSEN
ADL INSULFLEX INC 276

FRANKENBERG/EDER
NCCM INTERNATIONAL
SALES OFFICE 456

FÜRTH
PRIMETALS TECHNOLOGIES
GERMANY GMBH 483

GUMMERSBACH
JUKOKE & CARBON UG .... .418

HAMBURG
KARK GMBH .... .419

HEMER
ANDRITZ METALS
GERMANY GMBH 294

KREUZTAL
ACHENBACH SES 510

LEIPZIG
TAKRAF GMBH 536

MONHEIM AM RHEIN
TML TECHNIK GMBH 538

NEUENRADE
BUELTMANN GMBH .... .314

OELDE
VENTILATORENFABRIK
OELDE GMBH 556

RATINGEN
LINTORFER
EISENGIESSEREI GMBH 434

SAARBRÜCKEN
PRIMETALS TECHNOLOGIES
GERMANY GMBH 483

SCHULZENDORF
WHEMCO
INTERNATIONAL GMBH 567

SIEGEN
GONTERMANN-
PEIPERS GMBH 376

SIERSHAHN
STEULER-KCH GMBH 522

2023 AIST Directory — Iron and Steel Plants 601

GEOGRAPHICAL INDEX SUPPLIERS

SOLINGEN
EVERTZ KG, EGON/ETS......... 356

STADTALLENDORF
FEDERAL-MOGUL
  DEVA GMBH................. 360

VELBERT
VELCO GMBH.................. 554

WILLSTÄTT-LEGELSHURST
PRIMETALS TECHNOLOGIES
  GERMANY GMBH............. 483

HONG KONG

HONG KONG
IOMES GROUP LTD.............. 409
SANGRAF INTERNATIONAL...... 502

INDIA

DELHI

NEW DELHI
MAINTOCARE................... 440

NOIDA
HEG LTD...................... 388

GUJARAT

AHMEDABAD
GREENFIELD TECH
  PROJECTS 378
TRANSFORMERS AND
  RECTIFIERS (INDIA) LTD....... 544

HARYANA

GURUGRAM
HATCH ASSOCIATES
  CONSULTANTS INC........... 388
SMS INDIA PVT. LTD.............517

JHARKHAND

RANCHI
MECON LTD.................... 445

MAHARASHTRA

MUMBAI
BEARING MANUFACTURING
  INDIA....................... 304
ORIND SPECIAL
  REFRACTORIES PVT. LTD...... 468
PRIMETALS TECHNOLOGIES
  INDIA PVT. LTD.
  (CONCAST INDIA LTD.)........ 483
TENOVA TECHNOLOGIES
  PVT. LTD.................... 535

NAVI MUMBAI
PRIMETALS TECHNOLOGIES
  INDIA PVT. LTD. 483

WEST BENGAL

KOLKATA
M.N. DASTUR & CO. (P) LTD........ 450
PRIMETALS TECHNOLOGIES
  INDIA PVT. LTD. 483

ITALY

ASTI

ASTI
MAINA ORGANI DI
  TRASMISSIONE S.P.A. 440

BRESCIA

VOBARNO
E.P.R. S.R.L..................... 352

GEOGRAPHICAL INDEX SUPPLIERS

LECCO

MOLTENO
SES SALICO FINISHING AND
PROCESSING 510

LUCCA

FORNACI DI BARGA
EM MOULDS SPA 351

MILAN

BIASSONO
BOLDROCCHI SRL 309

CAMBIAGO
TENUTE SRL 536

MELEGNANO
TAMINI
TRASFORMATORI S.R.L. 529

SAN GIULIANO MILANESE
B.S.A. S.R.L. 303

MONZA AND BRIANZA

NOVA MILANESE
INOXIHP S.R.L. 406

TORINO

PIANEZZA
DANIELI FATA HUNTER 336

TRENTO

BORGO CHIESE
BM GROUP
POLYTEC S.P.A. 308

UDINE

BUTTRIO
DANIELI & C. OFFICINE
MECCANICHE SPA 335
DANIELI AUTOMATION 335

GEMONA DEL FRIULI
MORE S.R.L. 451

REMANZACCO
SEAUD SRL 508

TARCENTO
SMS GROUP S.P.A. 517

VARESE

CASTELLANZA
TENOVA S.P.A. 534

JAPAN

ASAKA
SANYO SEIKI CO. LTD. 502

HIROSHIMA
PRIMETALS TECHNOLOGIES
JAPAN LTD. 483

SUITA
YS TECH CO. LTD. 575

TOKYO
NIPPON SANSO
HOLDINGS CORP. 460
PRIMETALS TECHNOLOGIES
JAPAN LTD. 483

LUXEMBOURG

LUXEMBOURG
PAUL WURTH SA 518

2023 AIST Directory — Iron and Steel Plants 603

GEOGRAPHICAL INDEX SUPPLIERS

MEXICO

DISTRITO FEDERAL

MEXICO CITY
  LAVISA 426

NUEVO LEÓN

APODACA
  ARKO BY PMP 300
  MELTER S.A. DE C.V. 446
  PRIMETALS TECHNOLOGIES
    MEXICO S. DE R.L. DE C.V. 483

GUADALUPE
  VESUVIUS MEXICO 557

MONTERREY
  AMI INTERNATIONAL
    S. DE R.L. DE C.V. 292
  MOVARESA 453

SAN NICOLÁS DE LOS GARZA
  HYL TECHNOLOGIES
    S.A. DE C.V. 535

SAN PEDRO GARZA GARCÍA
  SCHUST MEXICO 508

QUERÉTARO

QUERÉTARO
  KLUBER LUBRICATION 421
  KSB SUPREMESERV MEXICO 424

NETHERLANDS

AMSTERDAM
  ANDRITZ METALS
    NETHERLANDS B.V. 299

VELSEN-NOORD
  DANIELI CORUS BV 336

NORWAY

ODDA
  ODDA DIGITAL SYSTEM AS 465

PERU

MILAFLORES
  INNOVATING STEEL. 406

POLAND

KRAKOW
  PRIMETALS TECHNOLOGIES
    POLAND SP. Z O.O. 483

RZESZÓW
  PRIMETALS TECHNOLOGIES
    POLAND SP. Z O.O. 483

P.R. CHINA

BEIJING
  HATCH ASSOCIATES
    CONSULTANTS INC. 388
  PRIMETALS TECHNOLOGIES
    CHINA LTD. 483
  SANGRAF INTERNATIONAL. 502
  TENOVA TECHNOLOGIES
    (TIANJIN) CO. LTD. 535

HUZHOU
  PRIMETALS TECHNOLOGIES
    CHINA LTD. 483

NANJING
  NANJING REFMIN CO. LTD. 454

SHANGHAI
  NCCM SHANGHAI 458
  PRIMETALS TECHNOLOGIES
    CHINA LTD. 483

TANGSHAN
  PRIMETALS TECHNOLOGIES
    (CHINA LTD.) 483
    (SERVICES LTD.) 483

GEOGRAPHICAL INDEX SUPPLIERS

RUSSIA

EKATERINBURG
PRIMETALS TECHNOLOGIES
RUSSIA LLC 484

MOSCOW
PRIMETALS TECHNOLOGIES
RUSSIA LLC 484
TENOVA EAST EUROPE LLC 535

SAUDI ARABIA

AL-JUBAIL
PRIMETALS TECHNOLOGIES
SAUDI ARABIA GMBH......... 484

SLOVAKIA

KOŠICE
PRIMETALS TECHNOLOGIES
SLOVAKIA S.R.O............. 484

SOUTH AFRICA

JOHANNESBURG
HATCH ASSOCIATES
CONSULTANTS INC........... 388
SANGRAF INTERNATIONAL...... 502
TENOVA PYROMET 535

VANDERBIJLPARK
SARCO (SOUTH AFRICAN
ROLL CO. PTY. LTD.).......... 504

SOUTH KOREA

SEOUL
PRIMETALS TECHNOLOGIES
KOREA LTD. 483

SPAIN

AZPEITIA
SARRALLE EQUIPOS
SIDERURGICOS.............. 506

BARCELONA
NCCM BARCELONA............. 456

PINSEQUE
NORTEK S.A.................... 460

SWEDEN

DJUSHOLM
HERMETIK HYDRAULIK AB 390

KISTA
UHT—UVÅN HAGFORS
TEKNOLOGI AB 548

LULEÅ
SWERIM AB 526

VIKMANSHYTTAN
DALFORSÅN AB 334

SWITZERLAND

CANTONE TICINO
AS METALS TECHNOLOGIES..... 301

EXCUBLENS
THERMO FISHER SCIENTIFIC
(ECUBLENS) SARL............ 537

GENEVA
SANGRAF INTERNATIONAL...... 502

RUESCHLIKON
ARVA AG TECHNOLOGICAL
CONSULTING 301

GEOGRAPHICAL INDEX SUPPLIERS

TAIWAN

KAOHSIUNG
PRIMETALS TECHNOLOGIES AUSTRIA GMBH (TAIWAN — BRANCH OFFICE) 482

THAILAND

BANGKOK
PRIMETALS TECHNOLOGIES AUSTRIA GMBH (THAILAND — BRANCH OFFICE) 482

PAKKRED
VR MASTER CO. LTD. 562

TURKEY

ISTANBUL
FERROSER LTD. 360
MARMACOR INC. 442
PRIMETALS TEKNOLOJI SANAYI VE TICARET A.Ş. 484

UKRAINE

DNIPRO
PRIMETALS TECHNOLOGIES UKRAINE LLC 484

KIEV
PRIMETALS TECHNOLOGIES UKRAINE LLC 484

UNITED ARAB EMIRATES

ABU DHABI
HATCH ASSOCIATES CONSULTANTS INC. 387

DUBAI
PRIMETALS TECHNOLOGIES AUSTRIA GMBH (UNITED ARAB EMIRATES — BRANCH OFFICE) 482

UNITED KINGDOM

ALDERSHOT
COREWIRE LTD. 332

BELPER
UK CARBON & GRAPHITE CO. LTD. 548
UKCG GROUP LTD. 548

CHRISTCHURCH
PRIMETALS TECHNOLOGIES LTD. 484

DRONFIELD
AMETEK LAND 292

KINGSWINFORD
FIVES BRONX LTD. 363

KNEBWORTH
MODULOC CONTROL SYSTEMS LTD. 450

LANARKSHIRE/RENFREW
HOWDEN GROUP 397

LONDON
HATCH ASSOCIATES CONSULTANTS INC. 388
PRIMETALS TECHNOLOGIES LTD. 480

SCUNTHORPE
EDDISONS CJM 350
PRIMETALS TECHNOLOGIES LTD. 484

SHEFFIELD
PRIMETALS TECHNOLOGIES LTD. 484

GEOGRAPHICAL INDEX SUPPLIERS

SOUTHAMPTON
   PCE INSTRUMENTS UK LTD...... 470

STOCKTON-ON-TEES
   PRIMETALS
      TECHNOLOGIES LTD.......... 484

VIETNAM

HO CHI MINH CITY
   PRIMETALS TECHNOLOGIES
      AUSTRIA GMBH
      (VIETNAM —
      BRANCH OFFICE) 482
   TENOVA
      (REPRESENTATIVE
      OFFICE VIETNAM)............ 536

MAJOR ASSOCIATIONS and TECHNICAL SOCIETIES with IRON AND STEEL INDUSTRY INTERESTS

AIR & WASTE MANAGEMENT ASSOCIATION
Koppers Bldg.
436 Seventh Ave., Suite 2100
Pittsburgh, PA 15219 USA
P: +1.800.270.3444 (Toll-Free);
+1.412.232.3444
F: +1.412.232.3450
info@awma.org
www.awma.org

–Exec. Dir.—Stephanie Glyptis

ALLIANCE DES MINERAIS, MINÉRAUX ET MÉTAUX (A3M)
17 Rue de l'Amiral Hamelin
Paris, 75116 France
P: +33.0.1.40.76.44.50
www.a3ms.fr

–Pres.—Stéphane Delpeyroux

ALLIANCE FOR AMERICAN MANUFACTURING
711 D St. NW, 3rd Floor
Washington, DC 20004 USA
P: +1.202.393.3430
info@aamfg.org
www.americanmanufacturing.org

–Pres.—Scott Paul

ALUMINUM ASSOCIATION, THE
1400 Crystal Dr., Suite 430
Arlington, VA 22202 USA
P: +1.703.358.2960
info@aluminum.org
www.aluminum.org

–Chief Exec. Officer and Pres.—
Charles Johnson

AMERICAN CERAMIC SOCIETY, THE (ACERS)
550 Polaris Pkwy., Suite 510
Westerville, OH 43082 USA
P: +1.866.721.3322 (Toll-Free);
+1.614.890.4700
F: +1.614.899.6109
www.ceramics.org

–Exec. Dir.—Mark Mecklenborg

AMERICAN COKE AND COAL CHEMICALS INSTITUTE
25 Massachusetts Ave. NW, Suite 800
Washington, DC 20001 USA
P: +1.724.772.1167
information@accci.org
www.accci.org

–Pres.—David C. Ailor

AMERICAN FOUNDRY SOCIETY INC.
1695 N. Penny Lane
Schaumburg, IL 60173 USA
P: +1.800.537.4237 (Toll-Free);
+1.847.824.0181
F: +1.847.824.7848
www.afsinc.org

–Chief Exec. Officer—Doug Kurkul

AMERICAN GALVANIZERS ASSOCIATION INC.
6881 S. Holly Cir., Suite 108
Centennial, CO 80112 USA
P: +1.720.554.0900
F: +1.720.554.0909
aga@galvanizeit.org
www.galvanizeit.org

–Exec. Dir.—Melissa Lindsley

AMERICAN GEAR MANUFACTURERS ASSOCIATION
1001 N. Fairfax St., Suite 500
Alexandria, VA 22314 USA
P: +1.703.684.0211
F: +1.703.684.0242
tech@agma.org (Technical Issue)
www.agma.org

–Pres.—Matthew E. Croson

AMERICAN INSTITUTE OF MINING, METALLURGICAL AND PETROLEUM ENGINEERS (AIME)
12999 E. Adam Aircraft Cir.
Englewood, CO 80112 USA
P: +1.303.948.4255
F: +1.888.702.0049 (Toll-Free)
aime@aimehq.org
www.aimehq.org

–Exec. Dir.—L. Michele Lawrie-Munro

MAJOR ASSOCIATIONS and TECHNICAL SOCIETIES with IRON AND STEEL INDUSTRY INTERESTS

AMERICAN INSTITUTE OF STEEL CONSTRUCTION
130 E. Randolph St., Suite 2000
Chicago, IL 60601 USA
P: +1.312.670.2400
www.aisc.org

- Pres.—Charles J. Carter

AMERICAN IRON AND STEEL INSTITUTE (AISI)
25 Massachusetts Ave. NW, Suite 800
Washington, DC 20001 USA
P: +1.202.452.7100
www.steel.org

- Chief Exec. Officer and Pres.—Kevin Dempsey

AMERICAN METALS SUPPLY CHAIN INSTITUTE
1101 King St., Suite 360
Alexandria, VA 22314 USA
info@amsci.us
www.amsci.us

- Pres. and Intl. Trade Counsel—Richard Chriss

AMERICAN WELDING SOCIETY (AWS)
8669 N.W. 36 St., #130
Miami, FL 33166 USA
P: +1.800.443.9353 (Toll-Free)
www.aws.org

- Chief Exec. Officer—Gary Konarska II

AMERICAN WIRE PRODUCERS ASSOCIATION
908 King St., Suite 320
Alexandria, VA 22314 USA
P: +1.703.299.4434
info@awpa.org
www.awpa.org

- Exec. Dir.—Emily Bardach

ASM INTERNATIONAL
9639 Kinsman Road
Materials Park, OH 44073 USA
P: +1.440.338.5151
F: +1.440.338.4634
memberservicecenter@asminternational.org
www.asminternational.org

- Exec. Dir.—Sandy Robert

ASME INTERNATIONAL (American Society of Mechanical Engineers)
Two Park Ave.
New York, NY 10016 USA
P: +1.800.843.2763 (Toll-Free)
customercare@asme.org
www.asme.org

- Exec. Dir.—Thomas Costabile

ASSOCIAÇÃO BRASILEIRA DE METALURGIA, MATERIAIS E MINERAÇÃO (ABM)
Rua Antonio Comparato 218
São Paulo, SP, 04605-030 Brazil
P: +55.11.5534.4333
www.abmbrasil.com.br

- Exec. Pres.—Horacidio Leal Barbosa Filho

ASSOCIATION FOR IRON & STEEL TECHNOLOGY (AIST)
186 Thorn Hill Road
Warrendale, PA 15086 USA
P: +1.724.814.3000
F: +1.724.814.3001
memberservices@aist.org
www.aist.org

- Exec. Dir.—Ronald E. Ashburn

ASSOCIATION OF WOMEN IN THE METAL INDUSTRIES (AWMI)
19 Mantua Road
Mt. Royal, NJ 08061 USA
P: +1.856.423.3201
F: +1.856.423.3420
awmi@talley.com
www.awmi.org

- Exec. Dir.—Haley Brust

MAJOR ASSOCIATIONS and TECHNICAL SOCIETIES with IRON AND STEEL INDUSTRY INTERESTS

ASSOCIAZIONE ITALIANA DI METALLURGICA (AIM)
Via Filippo Turati 8
20121 Milan, Italy
P: +39.02.76021132;
   +39.02.76397770
F: +39.02.76020551
aim@aimnet.it
www.metallurgia-italiana.net

– Sec. Gen.—Federica Bassani

ASTM INTERNATIONAL
100 Barr Harbor Dr.
P.O. Box C700
West Conshohocken, PA 19428 USA
P: +1.610.832.9500
F: +1.610.834.3636
service@astm.org
www.astm.org

– Pres.—Katharine E. Morgan

BRAZIL STEEL INSTITUTE
11 Rua do Mercado, 18th Floor
Rio de Janeiro, RJ, 20010-120, Brazil
P: +55.21.3445.6300
F: +55.21.2262.2234
acobrasil@acobrasil.org.br
www.acobrasil.org.br

– Exec. Pres.—Marco Polo de Mello Lopes

CÁMARA NACIONAL DE LA INDUSTRIA DEL HIERRO Y DEL ACERO (CANACERO)
Amores 338 Col. Del Valle
Mexico City, DF, 03100 Mexico
P: +52.55.5448.8160
info@canacero.org.mx
www.canacero.org.mx

– Dir. Gen.—Salvador Quesada Salinas

CANADIAN INSTITUTE OF STEEL CONSTRUCTION
445 Apple Creek Blvd., Suite 102
Markham, ON L3R 9X7 Canada
P: +1.905.604.3231
info@cisc-icca.ca
www.cisc-icca.ca

– Chief Exec. Officer and Pres.—Edward Whalen

CANADIAN STEEL PRODUCERS ASSOCIATION (CSPA)
270 Albert St., Suite 402
Ottawa, ON K1P 5G8 Canada
P: +1.613.238.6049
www.canadiansteel.ca

– Chief Exec. Officer and Pres.—Catherine Cobden

CASTING INDUSTRY SUPPLIERS ASSOCIATION (CISA)
7431 E. State St. #234
Rockford, IL 61108 USA
P: +1.815.226.1527
mark@cisa.org
www.cisa.org

– Exec. Dir.—Mark Ziegler

CHINESE SOCIETY FOR METALS, THE
No. 76 Xueyuan Nanlu, Haidian District
Beijing, 100081 P.R. China
P: +86.10.6521.1205/1206
F: +86.10.6512.4122
csmoffice@csm.org.cn
www.csm.org.cn

CONCRETE REINFORCING STEEL INSTITUTE (CRSI)
933 N. Plum Grove Road
Schaumburg, IL 60173 USA
P: +1.847.517.1200
F: +1.847.517.1206
www.crsi.org

– Chief Exec. Officer and Pres.—Danielle Kleinhans

ENGINEERS' SOCIETY OF WESTERN PENNSYLVANIA
337 4th Ave.
Pittsburgh, PA 15222 USA
P: +1.412.261.0710
eswp@eswp.com
www.eswp.com

– Gen. Mgr.—David Teorsky

MAJOR ASSOCIATIONS and TECHNICAL SOCIETIES with IRON AND STEEL INDUSTRY INTERESTS

EUROPEAN STEEL ASSOCIATION, THE (EUROFER)
172 Ave. de Cortenbergh
1000 Brussels, Belgium
P: +32.02.738.79.20
mail@eurofer.be
www.eurofer.eu

– Dir. Gen. — Axel Eggert

FABRICATORS & MANUFACTURERS ASSOCIATION INTERNATIONAL (FMA)
2135 Point Blvd.
Elgin, IL 60123 USA
P: +1.888.394.4362 (Toll-Free)
 +1.815.399.8700
info@fmanet.org
www.fmamfg.org

– Chief Exec. Officer and Pres. — Ed Youdell

FORGING INDUSTRY ASSOCIATION
6363 Oak Tree Blvd.
Independence, OH 44131 USA
P: +1.216.781.6260
F: +1.216.781.0102
info@forging.org
www.forging.org

– Exec. Dir. — James Warren

Forging Industry Educational and Research Foundation
foundation@forging.org
www.fierf.org

– Exec. Dir. — Angela Gibian

GALVANIZERS ASSOCIATION
6347 King Road
Marine City, MI 48039 USA
P: +1.810.765.4747
F: +1.810.765.4646
info@galvanizersassociation.com
http://galvanizersassociation.com

– Exec. Dir. — Christopher Nevison

GERMAN STEEL FEDERATION (Wirtschaftsvereinigung Stahl)
Französische Str. 8
10117 Berlin, Germany

Sohnstraße 65
40237 Düsseldorf, Germany
P: +49.211.6707.0;
 +49.0.30.23.25.546-0
F: +49.211.6707.310
info@wvstahl.de
www.stahl-online.de

– Chief Exec Officer and Pres. — Hans Jürgen Kerkhoff

INDUSTRIAL HEATING EQUIPMENT ASSOCIATION
P.O. Box 110578
Lakewood Ranch, FL 34211 USA
P: +1.859.356.1575
F: +1.859.356.0908
www.ihea.org

– Exec. Vice Pres. — Anne Goyer

INSTITUTE FOR BRIQUETTING AND AGGLOMERATION
1301 Service Road
West Barnstable, MA 02668 USA
P: +1.219.865.2378
iba@agglomeration.org
www.agglomeration.org

– Exec. Dir. — James Torok

INSTITUTE OF ELECTRICAL AND ELECTRONICS ENGINEERS INC. (IEEE)
3 Park Ave., 17th Floor
New York, NY 10016 USA
P: +1.212.419.7900
contactcenter@ieee.org
www.ieee.org

– Exec. Dir. and Chief Oper. Officer — Stephen Welby

MAJOR ASSOCIATIONS and TECHNICAL SOCIETIES with IRON AND STEEL INDUSTRY INTERESTS

INSTITUTE OF SCRAP RECYCLING INDUSTRIES INC. (ISRI)
1250 H St. NW, Suite 400
Washington, DC 20005 USA
P: +1.202.662.8500
isri@isri.org
www.isri.org

–Pres.—Robin K. Wiener

INSTITUTO ARGENTINO DE SIDERURGIA (IAS)
Av. Central y Calle 19 Oeste
San Nicolás de los Arroyos, BA, 2900 Argentina
P: +54.336.4461805
F: +54.336.4462989
siderurgia@siderurgia.org.ar
www.siderurgia.org.ar

–Gen. Dir.—Alejandro Hermida

INTERNATIONAL IRON METALLICS ASSOCIATION LTD. (IIMA)
One Bell Lane
Lewes, East Sussex,
England, BN7 1JU, U.K.
P: +44.7952.191.950
www.metallics.org

–Sec. Gen.—John Atherton

INTERNATIONAL STAINLESS STEEL FORUM
Avenue de Tervueren 270
1150 Brussels, Belgium
P: +32.2.702.8900
issf@issf.org
www.worldstainless.org

–Sec. Gen.—Tim Collins

IRON AND STEEL INSTITUTE OF JAPAN, THE
3-2-10 Tekko Kaikan, 5th Floor
Nihonbashi-Kayabacho
Chuou-ku, Tokyo, 103-0025 Japan
P: +81.3.3669.5931
F: +81.3.3669.5934
www.isij.or.jp

–Pres.—Sumio Kozawa

JAPAN IRON AND STEEL FEDERATION, THE
3-2-10, Nihonbashi Kayabacho
Chuo-ku, Tokyo, 103-0025 Japan
P: +81.3.3669.4811
F: +81.3.3664.1457
www.jisf.or.jp

–Managing Dir.—Hiroyoshi Suzuki

JERNKONTORET
Box 1721
Kungsträdgårdsgatan 10
SE-111 87 Stockholm, Sweden
P: +46.8.679.17.00
office@jernkontoret.se
www.jernkontoret.se

–Managing Dir. and Chief Exec. Officer—Annika Roos

LATIN AMERICAN STEEL ASSOCIATION (ALACERO)
Rua Capitão Antonio Rosa, 409
São Paulo, SP, 01443-010, Brazil
P: +55.11.94055.3138
alacero@alacero.org
www.alacero.org

–Exec. Dir.—Alejandro Wagner

METAL POWDER INDUSTRIES FEDERATION
105 College Road E
Princeton, NJ 08540 USA
P: +1.609.452.7700
info@mpif.org
www.mpif.org

–Chief Exec. Officer and Exec. Dir.—James P. Adams

METAL TREATING INSTITUTE (MTI)
123 Maple Row Blvd. #530
Hendersonville, TN 37075 USA
P: +1.904.249.0448
F: +1.904.249.0459
info@heattreat.net
www.heattreat.net

–Chief Exec. Officer—Tom Morrison

MAJOR ASSOCIATIONS and TECHNICAL SOCIETIES with IRON AND STEEL INDUSTRY INTERESTS

METALS SERVICE CENTER INSTITUTE
4201 Euclid Ave.
Rolling Meadows, IL 60008 USA
P: +1.847.485.3000
F: +1.847.485.3001
info@msci.org
www.msci.org

– Chief Exec. Officer and Pres. — M. Robert Weidner III

MHI
8720 Red Oak Blvd., Suite 201
Charlotte, NC 28217 USA
P: +1.704.676.1190
F: +1.704.676.1199
www.mhi.org

– Chief Exec. Officer — John Paxton

THE MINERALS, METALS & MATERIALS SOCIETY (TMS)
5700 Corporate Dr., Suite 750
Pittsburgh, PA 15237 USA
P: +1.800.759.4867 (U.S. and Canada); +1.724.776.9000
F: +1.724.776.3770
tmsgeneral@tms.org
www.tms.org

– Exec. Dir. — James J. Robinson

NATIONAL ASSOCIATION OF STEEL PIPE DISTRIBUTORS
1501 E. Mockingbird Lane, Suite 212
Victoria, TX 77904 USA
P: +1.361.574.7878
info@naspd.com
www.naspd.com

– Exec. Dir. — Susannah Porr

NATIONAL CORRUGATED STEEL PIPE ASSOCIATION (NCSPA)
14070 Proton Road, Suite 100 LB 9
Dallas, TX 75244 USA
P: +1.972.850.1907
F: +1.972.490.4219
info@ncspa.org
www.ncspa.org

– Exec. Dir. — Michael McGough

NATIONAL MINING ASSOCIATION
101 Constitution Ave. NW, Suite 500 E
Washington, DC 20001 USA
P: +1.202.463.2600
F: +1.202.463.2666
cbernstein@nma.org
www.nma.org

– Chief Exec. Officer and Pres. — Rich Nolan

NATIONAL SLAG ASSOCIATION
112 Airport Road, Suite 304
Coatesville, PA 19320 USA
P: +1.610.857.5356
administration@nationalslag.org
www.nationalslag.org

– Pres. — Charles Ochola

NATIONAL SOCIETY OF PROFESSIONAL ENGINEERS
1420 King St.
Alexandria, VA 22314 USA
P: +1.888.285.NSPE (6773)
F: +1.703.684.2821
memserv@nspe.org
www.nspe.org

– Exec. Dir. and Chief Exec. Officer — Monika Schulz

REFRACTORIES INSTITUTE, THE
1300 Sumner Ave.
Cleveland, OH 44115 USA
P: +1.216.241.7333
F: +1.216.241.0105
info@refractoriesinstitute.org
www.refractoriesinstitute.org

SAE INTERNATIONAL
400 Commonwealth Dr.
Warrendale, PA 15096 USA
P: +1.724.776.4841
F: +1.724.776.0790
customerservice@sae.org
www.sae.org

– Chief Exec. Officer — David L. Schutt

MAJOR ASSOCIATIONS and TECHNICAL SOCIETIES with IRON AND STEEL INDUSTRY INTERESTS

SME
1000 Town Center, Suite 1910
Southfield, MI 48075 USA
P: +1.313.425.300
communications@sme.org
www.sme.org

- Exec. Dir. and Chief Exec. Officer— Robert Willig

SOCIETY OF TRIBOLOGISTS AND LUBRICATION ENGINEERS (STLE)
840 Busse Hwy.
Park Ridge, IL 60068 USA
P: +1.847.825.5536
F: +1.847.825.1456
information@stle.org
www.stle.org

- Exec. Dir.—Edward P. Salek

SOCIETY OF WOMEN ENGINEERS (SWE)
130 E. Randolph St., Suite 3500
Chicago, IL 60601 USA
P: +1.312.596.5223
hq@swe.org
www.swe.org

- Chief Exec. Officer and Exec. Dir.— Karen Horting

SPECIALTY STEEL INDUSTRY OF NORTH AMERICA
3050 K St. NW
Washington, DC 20007 USA
P: +1.800.982.0355 (Toll-Free); +1.202.342.8630
F: +1.202.342.8451
info@ssina.com
www.ssina.com

STAHLINSTITUT VDEH—see GERMAN STEEL FEDERATION

STEEL FOUNDERS' SOCIETY OF AMERICA
780 McArdle Dr., Unit G
Crystal Lake, IL 60014 USA
P: +1.815.455.8240
www.sfsa.org

- Exec. Vice Pres.—Raymond W. Monroe

STEEL MANUFACTURERS ASSOCIATION (SMA)
1150 Connecticut Ave. NW, Suite 1125
Washington, DC 20036 USA
P: +1.202.296.1515
F: +1.202.296.2506
info@steelnet.org
www.steelnet.org

- Pres.—Philip K. Bell

STEEL TUBE INSTITUTE
2516 Waukegan Road, Suite 172
Glenview, IL 60025 USA
P: +1.847.461.1701
F: +1.209.224.8645
dcrawford@steeltubeinstitute.org
www.steeltubeinstitute.org

- Exec. Dir.—Dale L. Crawford

WIRE ASSOCIATION INTERNATIONAL INC., THE
71 Bradley Road, Suite 9
Madison, CT 06433 USA
P: +1.203.453.2777
sfetteroll@wirenet.org
www.wirenet.org

- Exec. Dir.—Steven J. Fetteroll

WORLD STEEL ASSOCIATION (worldsteel)
Ave. de Tervuren 270
1150 Brussels, Belgium
P: +32.2.702.8900
F: +32.2.702.8899
steel@worldsteel.org
www.worldsteel.org

- Dir. Gen.—Edwin Basson

GLOSSARY of ABBREVIATIONS

A

AGC . . . . automatic gauge control
AGV . . . . automated guided vehicle
AHSS . . advanced high-strength steel
AI. . . . . artificial intelligence
AL . . . . Galvalume®
ANSI . . . American National Standards Institute
AOD . . . argon oxygen decarbonization
API . . . . . American Petroleum Institute
ARO . . abrasion-resistant overcoating
ASME . . . . American Society of Mechanical Engineers
ASTM . . . . American Standard of Testing and Materials
AWS . . . . . . American Welding Society
AZS. . . . . alumina/zirconia/silica

B

BF . . . . blast furnace
BFG. . . . . blast furnace gas
BIM . . . . . building information modeling
BOF. . . . . basic oxygen furnace
BOP . . . . basic oxygen process

C

CAD/CADD . . computer-aided design/ and drafting
CAL. . . . . continuous annealing line
CAS-OB . . . composition adjustment by sealed argon bubbling – oxygen blowing
CC . . . . cross-country
CD . . . . cold drawn
CDRI . . . . cold direct reduced iron
CFD . . . . computational fluid dynamics
CGL . . . . . continuous galvanizing line
CMMS . . . . . computerized maintenance management software
CNC . . . . . computer numerical control
COG . . . . coke oven gas
CPL . . . . continuous pickle line
CRC . . . . cold-rolled coil
CRM . . . . cold rolling mill

CSONH . . . . carbon, sulfur, oxygen, nitrogen and hydrogen
CSP . . . . compact strip production
CTL . . . . cut to length
CVC . . . . . . continuously variable crown

D

DCS . . . . . . distributed control systems
DOM . . . . drawn over mandrel
DRI . . . . direct reduced iron
DRL . . . . double random length
DSAW . . . . double submerged-arc weld

E

EAF . . . . electric arc furnace
EBM . . . . electron beam melting
EBT . . . . eccentric bottom tap
EDDS . . . . . . extra deep-drawing steel
EDM . . electrical discharge machining
EDS . . . . energy dispersive x-ray spectroscopy
EDT . . . . . . electric discharge texturing
EGL . . . . electrogalvanizing line
EHS . . . environment, health and safety
EMS . . . . electromagnetic stirring
EMT . . . . electrical metallic tubing
EOT . . . . electric overhead traveling
EPC/EPCM engineering, procurement and construction/ construction management
ERMC . . . . . electrical rigid metal conduit
ERP . . . . . enterprise resource planning
ERW . . . . electric resistance weld
ESR . . . . electroslag remelting

F

FBE . . . . fusion-bonded epoxy
FEA . . . . finite element analysis

GLOSSARY of ABBREVIATIONS

G

GA .... galvannealed
GI .... galvanized
GIS .. geographic information systems
GL .... aluminum zinc
GMAW .... gas metal arc weld
GTAW .... gas tungsten arc weld

H

H.R. .... human resources
H/V .... horizontal and vertical
HAGC ..... hydraulic automatic gauge cylinder
HBI .... hot briquetted iron
HBM ...... horizontal boring machine
HCI/HCL .... hydrochloric acid
HD .... high definition
HDG .... hot-dip galvanized
HDGL .... hot-dip galvanizing line
HFEW ... high-frequency electric weld
HFIW .... high-frequency induction welding
HFW .... high-frequency welding
HGC .... hydraulic gap control
HIP .... hot isostatic press
HMI .... human machine interface
HRC .... hot-rolled coil
HRP&O .... hot-rolled picked and oiled
HSAW .... helical submerged-arc weld
HSLA .... high-strength low-alloy
HSM .... hot strip mill
HSS .... hollow structural sections
HVAC .... heating, ventilation and air conditioning
HVOF ...... high-velocity oxygen fuel

I

ICP ...... inductively coupled plasma
ID .... inside diameter
IF .... interstitial free
IFB .... insulating firebrick
IMC .... intermediate metal conduit
IN .... in-line
IoT/IIoT ... Internet of Things/Industrial Internet of Things
IR .... infrared
ISO .... International Organization for Standardization

K

KOBM ...... Klöckner Oxygen Bottom Maxhüte

L

LBW .... laser beam welding
LD .... Linz-Donawitz
LF .... ladle furnace
LMF .... ladle metallurgy furnace
LOTO .... lockout/tagout
LRF .... ladle refining furnace
LSAW .... longitudinal submerged-arc weld
LTL .... less than load
LW .... laser welding

M

MBQ .... merchant bar quality
MCC .... motor control center
MES . manufacturing execution system
MIG .... metal inert gas welding
MPM .... mandrel pipe mill
mt .... metric tons
mtpy .... metric tons per year

N

N/A .... not applicable
NDT .... non-destructive testing
NPS .... nominal pipe size
NVH .. noise, vibration and harshness

O

OCTG ...... oil country tubular goods
OD .... outside diameter

GLOSSARY of ABBREVIATIONS

OEE . . overall equipment effectiveness
OEM . original equipment manufacturer
OES . . . . optical emission spectroscopy
OSHA . . . . Occupational Safety and Heath Administration
PAM . . . . plasma arc melting
PAW . . . . plasma arc welding

P

PCB . . . . polychlorinated biphenyl
PCI . . . . pulverized coal injection
PdM . . . . predictive maintenance
PLC . . . . programmable logic controller
PLM . . . . project life cycle management
PLS . . . . . programmable limit switches
PLTCM . . picking line and tandem cold rolling mill
PM . . . . preventive maintenance
PPR . . . . plug piercing and rolling
PSQ . . . . pump shaft–quality
PTA . . . . plasma transferred arc
PTFE . . . . polytetrafluoroethylene
PVD . . . . physical vapor deposition

Q

Q-BOP . . . . quick-quiet basic oxygen process
Q&T . . . . quench and temper
QA . . . . quality assurance
QRL . . . . quadruple random length
QVL . . . . quality verification line

R

R&D . . . . . . research and development
RCS . . . . round corner squares
RFID . . . radio frequency identification
RH . . . . Ruhrstahl-Heraeus
RHF . . . . rotary hearth furnace
RMC . . . . rigid metallic conduit
ROB . . . . railroad over bridge
ROPS . . roll-over protective structures
RSB . . . . reducing sizing block
RTD . . resistance temperature detector
RTG . . . . rubber-tired gantry
RUB . . . . railroad under bridge
RV . . . . reversing

S

SBQ . . . . special bar quality
SCADA . . supervisory control and data acquisition
SCNR . . . . selective non-catalytic reduction
SCR . . . . . selective catalytic reduction
SEM . . . scanning electron microscopy
SEN . . . . submerged-entry nozzle
SRA . . . . stress relief annealed

T

TCM . . . . tandem cold mill
TEM transmission electron microscopy
TFS . . . . tin-free steel
TGP . . . . . turned, ground and polished
TIG . . . . tungsten inert gas

U

UHP . . . . ultrahigh-power
UHSS . . . . ultrahigh-strength steel
UOE . . . . . U-ing, O-ing and expanding
UPS . . . . . uninterruptible power supply
UST . . . . underground storage tank

V

VAD . . . . vacuum arc degassing
VAR . . . . vacuum arc remelting
VBM . . . . vertical boring machine
VD . . . . vacuum degasser
VFD . . . . variable frequency drive
VIM . . . . vacuum induction melting
VOD . vacuum oxygen decarburization
VSB . . . . vertical scalebreaker
VTD . . . . vacuum tank degasser
VTL . . . . vertical turning lathes

GLOSSARY of ABBREVIATIONS

W

WB . . . . walking beam
WBENC . . . . Women's Business Enterprise National Council
WR . . . . work roll

X

XRD. . . . . x-ray diffractometer
XRF. . . . . x-ray fluorescent

Z

ZAM . . zinc, aluminum and magnesium

ADVERTISERS INDEX

A

ABP INDUCTION LLC 275
AIR PRODUCTS .... .281
ALLOR MANUFACTURING INC. ... 285
AMERICAN CHEMICAL
   TECHNOLOGIES INC. 289
AMERICAN GFM CORP. .... .291
ANDREW S. MCCREATH &
   SON INC. 295
ANDRITZ METALS USA INC. 297

B

BRILEX INDUSTRIES INC. .... .313

C

CARL ZEISS
   MICROSCOPY LLC. .... .319
CARMEUSE AMERICAS. .... .321
CASTER MAINTENANCE CO. 323
CID ASSOCIATES INC. 325
CONDUCTIX-WAMPFLER .... .331

D

DAUBERT CHEMICAL CO. INC. ... 339
DLZ INDUSTRIAL LLC 345
DROPSA USA INC. 347

E

ENVEA INC. 353
EZG MANUFACTURING 357

F

FABRIS INC. 359
FALK PLI .... .361
FLUIDTEKNIK USA INC./
   INOXIHP S.R.L. 367
FORCE CONTROL
   INDUSTRIES INC. 369

G

GESCO INC. (GRINDING
   ENGINEERING
   SERVICES CO.) 373
GRAFTECH
   INTERNATIONAL LTD. 377
GUILD INTERNATIONAL 379
GULF STATES
   ENGINEERING INC. 381

H

H&K EQUIPMENT 383
HALL INDUSTRIES INC. 385
HERAEUS ELECTRO-NITE
   CO. LLC .... .391
HILLIARD BRAKE SYSTEMS. 395

I

INDUSTRIAL MAINTENANCE
   WELDING & MACHINING
   CO. INC. 403
INFOSIGHT CORP. 405
INSTRON. 407
ITIPACK SYSTEMS 411
IVC TECHNOLOGIES .... .413

J

JOHN COCKERILL INDUSTRY .... .417

L

LECO CORP. 429
LENOX INSTRUMENT CO. INC. ... .431
EDW. C. LEVY CO. 433
LINDE 435

M

MAINA ORGANI DI
   TRASMISSIONE S.P.A. .... .441

2023 AIST Directory — Iron and Steel Plants

ADVERTISERS INDEX

N

NALCO WATER,
    AN ECOLAB CO............... 455
NEW YORK BLOWER CO......... 459
NSK AMERICAS................. 463

O

OPTA GROUP LLC 467

P

PKG EQUIPMENT INC............ 477
PRIMETALS
    TECHNOLOGIES LTD.......... 481

R

RADIAN ROBOTICS 491
READING ANTHRACITE CO. 495

S

SANGRAF
    INTERNATIONAL INC.......... 503
SARGENT ELECTRIC CO......... 505
SENNEBOGEN LLC 273
SES LLC (STEEL EQUIPMENT
    SPECIALISTS)................511
SMS GROUP....................515
SUPERBOOTH.................. 523
SUPERIOR MACHINE CO.
    OF S.C. INC................... 525
THE SYSTEMS GROUP 527

T

TAYLOR MACHINE
    WORKS INC. 531
TAYLOR-WINFIELD
    TECHNOLOGIES INC.......... 533
TITAN BEARINGS 539
TOKAI CARBON GE LLC 541
TR ELECTRONIC................ 543

U

UESCO CRANES................ 547
ULTRA ELECTRONICS,
    ENERGY 549
UNITED STATES CONTROLS 551

V

VAIL RUBBER WORKS INC. 555
VIRGINIA CRANE
    (FOLEY MATERIAL
    HANDLING) 559
VM5 LIGHTING
    SOLUTIONS LLC...............561
VOESTALPINE BÖHLER
    WELDING UTP
    MAINTENANCE GMBH 563

W

WINKLE INDUSTRIES............ 569

INDEX

A

A. LINDEMANN INC. 271
AAVISHKAR MACHINERY
    PVT. LTD. . . . . see GREENFIELD
        TECH PROJECTS
ABB INC. 271
ABBOTT MACHINE CO. 272
ABP INDUCTION LLC 272
ACE INDUSTRIES 272
ACERLAN S.A. DE C.V. 164
ACEROS DEL
    NORESTE-ACENOR. 176
ACEROS FORJADOS ESTAMPADOS
    DE MONCLOVA S.A. DE C.V. 7
ACEROS NACIONALES 176
ACE WORLD COMPANIES INC. . . . 272
ACI, A HOWDEN CO. . . . . see HOWDEN
        GROUP
ACI HOLDING LLC. 274
ACIERS RÉGIFAB STEELS 274
ACME MACHINE &
    WELDING CO. 274
ADL INSULFLEX INC. 274
ADS MACHINERY CORP. 276
ADVANCED CENTRIFUGAL 164
ADVANCED ENERGY 276
ADVANCED GAUGING
    TECHNOLOGIES, L.L.C. 277
ADVANCED MACHINE &
    ENGINEERING 277
ADVANCED SYSTEMS
    INDUSTRIAL PRODUCTS 277
AERMOTOR 222
AEROMET INDUSTRIES INC. 277
AFC-HOLCROFT 278
AGM WELDING 278
AIC NORTH AMERICA CORP. 278
AIM MARKET RESEARCH 278
AIR & WASTE MANAGEMENT
    ASSOCIATION. 608
AIR CLEANING BLOWERS LLC . . . 280
AIR PRODUCTS 280
AIR-THERM INC. 280
AIR TRAC CORP. 280
AIRCENTRIC CORP. 280
AIS GAUGING 280
AJAX TOCCO
    MAGNETHERMIC CORP. 282
ALAMBRES Y REFUERZOS
    DAC S.A. DE C.V. 7
ALFA & ASSOCIATES. 282
ALGOMA. 7, 145, 147, 150,
        175, 191, 197, 199

ALKEGEN 283
ALLEGHENY ALLOY INC. 283
ALLEGHENY
    TECHNOLOGIES INC. . . . see ATI INC.
ALLIANCE DES MINERAIS,
    MINÉRAUX ET MÉTAUX 608
ALLIANCE FOR AMERICAN
    MANUFACTURING. 608
ALLIED MINERAL PRODUCTS 283
ALLIED SYSTEMS CO. 284
ALLOR MANUFACTURING INC. . . . 284
ALLOY CASTING
    INDUSTRIES LTD. 163
ALLOY ENGINEERING
    CO., THE 284
ALLSTRAP STEEL & POLY
    STRAPPING SYSTEMS 284
ALPINE METAL TECH GMBH 286
ALRO STEEL 8
ALTASTEEL INC. 8, 152, 175, 210
ALTON STEEL INC. 8, 178, 211
ALTOS HORNOS DE MEXICO
    S.A. DE C.V. (AHMSA) 9, 147,
        150, 153, 177,
        191, 197, 200
ALTRA INDUSTRIAL MOTION. 286
ALUMINUM ASSOCIATION 608
A.M. CASTLE & CO. 9
AM HEALTH AND SAFETY INC. . . . 287
AM/NS INDIA LTD. 109
AMBASSADOR PIPE &
    SUPPLY INC. 112
AMENDOLA ENGINEERING INC. . . 287
AMEPA AMERICA INC. 287
AMERICAN AIR FILTER
    CO. INC. 288
AMERICAN CAST IRON
    PIPE CO. 112, 154, 225
AMERICAN CERAMIC
    SOCIETY 608
AMERICAN CHEMICAL
    TECHNOLOGIES INC. 288
AMERICAN COKE AND COAL
    CHEMICALS INSTITUTE 608
AMERICAN CONSOLIDATED
    INDUSTRIES INC. 225
AMERICAN FOUNDRY
    GROUP INC. 165
AMERICAN FOUNDRY
    SOCIETY INC. 608
AMERICAN GALVANIZERS
    ASSOCIATION INC. 608
AMERICAN GEAR
    MANUFACTURERS
    ASSOCIATION. 608

2023 AIST Directory — Iron and Steel Plants   621

INDEX

AMERICAN GFM CORP. 288
AMERICAN GREEN VENTURES
  (SPILLFIX) 288
AMERICAN HEAVY PLATES 9
AMERICAN INSTITUTE OF MINING,
  METALLURGICAL
  AND PETROLEUM
  ENGINEERS (AIME) 608
AMERICAN INSTITUTE OF STEEL
  CONSTRUCTION 609
AMERICAN IRON AND STEEL
  INSTITUTE (AISI) 609
AMERICAN METALS SUPPLY
  CHAIN INSTITUTE 609
AMERICAN PIPING
  PRODUCTS INC. 112
AMERICAN ROLLER
  BEARING CO. 290
AMERICAN SPINCAST INC. 165
AMERICAN STAINLESS
  TUBING INC. . . . . see ASCENT
                TUBULAR PRODUCTS
AMERICAN TUBULAR
  PRODUCTS 113, 225
AMERICAN WELDING
  SOCIETY (AWS) 609
AMERICAN WIRE PRODUCERS
  ASSOCIATION 609
AMERIFAB INC. 290
AMETEK 290
AMI INTERNATIONAL
  S. DE R.L. DE C.V. 292
AMIAD WATER SYSTEMS 293
AMRESIST INC. 293
AMTEC HYDRACLAMP INC. 293
ANDREW S. MCCREATH
  & SON INC. 294
ANDRITZ AG 294
ANDRONACO INDUSTRIES 299
ANGSTROM INC. 299
ANGUIL ENVIRONMENTAL
  SYSTEMS INC. 299
ANT AUTOMATION 300
APEX CONTROL
  SYSTEMS INC. 300
APM 200
AQ TRANSFORMER
  SOLUTIONS INC. 300
ARCELORMITTAL
  NORTH AMERICA 10, 145, 147,
                149, 150, 152, 153,
                175, 177, 191, 192,
                199, 200, 204, 205, 210
  (AM/NS CALVERT LLC) 10, 192
                200, 205

  (DOFASCO G.P.) 10, 145, 147,
                150, 152, 175,
                191, 199, 204
  (LONG PRODUCTS
  CANADA G.P.) 11, 149, 152,
                175, 199, 210
  (MEXICO) 12, 147, 149,
                150, 153, 177
  (MINING CANADA G.P.) 13
  (TEXAS HBI) 13, 149
  (TUBULAR PRODUCTS) . . . 113, 220,
                222, 225
ARCO METAL S.A. DE C.V. 114, 222
ARKANSAS STEEL
  ASSOCIATES 154, 179
ARKO BY PMP 300
ARMOR PROTECTIVE
  PACKAGING 301
ARVA AG TECHNOLOGICAL
  CONSULTING 301
ARVOS SCHMIDTSCHE
  SCHACK LLC. 301
AS METALS TECHNOLOGIES 301
ASCENT TUBULAR
  PRODUCTS 114, 226
ASHLAND FOUNDRY &
  MACHINE WORKS 165
ASM INTERNATIONAL 609
ASME INTERNATIONAL 609
ASSA ABLOY/
  MEGADOOR USA 301
ASSOCIAÇÃO BRASILEIRA DE
  METALURGIA, MATERIAIS E
  MINERAÇÃO (ABM) 609
ASSOCIATION FOR IRON &
  STEEL TECHNOLOGY (AIST) . . . 609
ASSOCIATION OF WOMEN
  IN THE METAL INDUSTRIES
  (AWMI) 609
ASSOCIAZIONE ITALIANA DI
  METALLURGICA (AIM) 610
ASTECH INC. 165
ASTM INTERNATIONAL 610
ATI INC. 13, 154, 165, 179, 192, 211
ATKORE INTERNATIONAL . . . 115, 226
ATLANTIC TRACK &
  TURNOUT CO. 302
ATLANTIC TUBE &
  STEEL INC. 116, 220
ATLAX S.A. 153
AUSTRALTEK LLC 302
AUTOMATION PRODUCTS INC. -
  DYNATROLL® DIV. 303

INDEX

AVIS INDUSTRIAL CORP. 226
AZZ TUBULAR PRODUCTS 226

B

B&H MACHINE INC. 303
B.E. SPERANZA INC. 303
B.S.A. S.R.L. 303
BADGER ALLOYS INC. 165
BAHR BROS MFG. 165
BALD EAGLE AIR
　　KINETICS LLC. 304
BALTIMORE AIRCOIL CO. 304
BAR STOCK SPECIALTIES 304
BAR1 TRANSPORTATION 304
BAY CAST INC. 165
BEARING MANUFACTURING
　　INDIA. 304
BEARING SERVICE CO. 305
BEAVER VALLEY ALLOY
　　FOUNDRY CO. 15, 165
BEDA OXYGENTECHNIC
　　USA INC. 305
BENETECH INC. 305
BERG PIPE 117, 226
BERKLEY MACHINE WORKS &
　　FOUNDRY CO. 165
BERRY METAL CO. 305
BETA LASERMIKE PRODUCTS ... 306
BIJUR DELIMON
　　INTERNATIONAL
　　FARVAL/BIJUR/LUBESITE 306
BIRMINGHAM RAIL &
　　LOCOMOTIVE. 306
BK-SERVICES 307
BLACKHAWK
　　"COMBUSTIONEERING" LTD. ... 307
BLAIR STRIP STEEL CO. 15
BLASCHAK ANTHRACITE 307
BLASTECH MOBILE. 307
BLOOM ENGINEERING
　　CO. INC. 308
BLUE CREEK FOUNDRY 165
BLUESTONE
　　RESOURCES INC. 145
BM GROUP POLYTEC S.P.A. 308
BMD COMPANY LLC 308
BOC WATER
　　HYDRAULICS INC. 308
BOGNAR AND CO. INC. 309
BOLDROCCHI SRL. 309
BOLLFILTER CORP. 309

BORUSAN MANNESMANN. 227
BOSSTEK 310
BOWEN TECHNICAL
　　PRODUCTS & SERVICES 310
BPI INC. 310
BRADBURY CO. INC., THE 310
BRADKEN. 154, 163, 165
BRADLEY LIFTING CORP. 310
BRANDENBURG. 310
BRANDT ENGINEERED
　　PRODUCTS 311
BRAUN MASCHINENFABRIK
　　GMBH. 311
BRAZIL STEEL INSTITUTE 610
BRICKING SOLUTIONS. 311
BRILEX INDUSTRIES INC. 312
BRISTOL
　　METALS LLC. .... see ASCENT
　　　　TUBULAR PRODUCTS
BROKK INC. 312
BROWN STRAUSS STEEL. 16
BROWN TRANSPORT INC. 312
BRUKER AXS INC. 314
BSE AMERICA. 314
BUEHLER 314
BUELTMANN GMBH. 314
BUFFALO TRANSFORMER
　　SERVICES 315
BULK EQUIPMENT CORP. 315
BULL MOOSE
　　TUBE CO. 117, 220, 227
BURNS INDUSTRIAL
　　EQUIPMENT INC. 315
BUSCH VACUUM SOLUTIONS. ... 315
BUSHMAN EQUIPMENT INC. 316
BUTECH BLISS 316
BYER STEEL CORP. 16, 211

C

C&E PLASTICS INC. 317
CALDERYS. 317
CALDWELL GROUP INC., THE ... 317
CALIFORNIA STEEL
　　INDUSTRIES INC. 17, 192,
　　　　　　　　　　　　　200, 205, 227
CÁMARA NACIONAL DE LA
　　INDUSTRIA DEL HIERRO Y DEL
　　ACERO (CANACERO). 610
CAMCORP INC. 317
CANADA ALLOY
　　CASTINGS CO. 163

2023 AIST Directory — Iron and Steel Plants　623

INDEX

CANADIAN INSTITUTE OF STEEL
  CONSTRUCTION 610
CANADIAN PHOENIX STEEL
  PRODUCTS LTD................. 220
CANADIAN STEEL PRODUCERS
  ASSOCIATION (CSPA)......... 610
CARB-RITE CO..........see BOGNAR
  AND CO. INC.
CARBIDE INDUSTRIES LLC 318
CARBINITE METAL COATINGS ... 318
CARL ZEISS
  MICROSCOPY LLC 318
CARMEUSE AMERICAS.......... 320
CARPENTER
  TECHNOLOGY CORP. 17, 154,
  166, 179, 211
CASCADE STEEL ROLLING
  MILLS INC................. 19, 155,
  179, 211
CASEY EQUIPMENT CORP. 320
CAST TOOLS INC................. 166
CASTALLOY CORP. 166
CASTECH METALLURGY 163
CASTER MAINTENANCE CO...... 320
CASTING CONSULTANTS INC. ... 322
CASTING INDUSTRY SUPPLIERS
  ASSOCIATION (CISA).......... 610
CATTRON NORTH
  AMERICA INC................. 322
CBMM NORTH AMERICA INC..... 322
CENTRAL MACHINE & TOOL..... 166
CENTRIFUGAL CASTINGS INC.... 166
CENTRO-METALCUT............ 322
CENTURY TUBE CORP....... 118, 227
CERCO INC..................... 322
CERVIS INC..................... 324
CG THERMAL LLC 324
CHARTER
  MANUFACTURING CO...... 19, 155,
  179, 212
CHEN INTERNATIONAL.......... 227
CHICAGO HEIGHTS STEEL 20
CHICAGO STEEL
  HOLDINGS LLC................. 20
CHINESE SOCIETY FOR
  METALS 610
CHIZ BROS. INC................. 324
CID ASSOCIATES INC............ 324
CIM-TECH INC. 324
CINCINNATI GASKET &
  INDUSTRIAL GLASS 326
CINCINNATI THERMAL
  SPRAY .... see CTS INC.
CIVIL & ENVIRONMENTAL
  CONSULTANTS INC. 326

CLARKE ROLLER AND
  RUBBER LTD.................. 327
CLAUDIUS PETERS
  PROJECTS GMBH............. 327
CLAYTON ENGINEERING CO..... 327
CLEVELAND-
  CLIFFS INC........ 21, 145, 147, 149,
  150, 155, 166, 179,
  193, 197, 200, 205, 212
  (CLEVELAND-
  CLIFFS TUBULAR
  COMPONENTS) 118, 227
CLEVELAND GEAR CO. INC. 328
CLINGAN STEEL INC. 26
CMI HEAVY INDUSTRIES 328
CNC DESIGN PTY. LTD........... 328
COLT AUTOMATION.............. 329
COLT INTERNATIONAL BV 329
COLUMBIA STEEL 166
COLUMBIA MACHINE
  WORKS INC................... 329
COLUMBIANA
  FOUNDRY CO. 27, 166
COMBUSTION DYNAMICS LLC ... 329
COMMERCIAL CASTING CO...... 166
COMMERCIAL METALS
  COMPANY 27, 155, 182, 212
CONCRETE REINFORCING
  STEEL INSTITUTE 610
CONDUCTIX-WAMPFLER 330
CONDUIT RYMCO........ see RYMCO
CONSERO INC................... 330
CONTINENTAL STEEL &
  TUBE CO....................... 30
CONTRACTORS &
  INDUSTRIAL
  SUPPLY INC........see MAZZELLA
  COMPANIES
CONTROL CHIEF CORP.......... 330
CONTROLES Y SISTEMAS
  (C&S) SRL 330
CORE METALS GROUP LLC...... 330
COREWIRE LTD.................. 332
CORONADO STEEL CO. 167
CORPORACION
  POK S.A. DE C.V. 164
CORPORATESEARCH LLC....... 332
CRANE 1 SERVICES 332
CROWN TECHNOLOGY INC. 333
CRUCIBLE
  INDUSTRIES LLC 31, 156,
  167, 213
CSD ENGINEERS 333
CTS INC........................ 333
CV ENGINEERING 333

INDEX

D

D&S HOIST AND
  CRANE . . . . see CRANE 1 SERVICES
DALFORSÅN AB 334
DALTON INDUSTRIES LLC 334
DANIELI & C. OFFICINE
  MECCANICHE SPA 335
DATA-LINC GROUP 338
DAUBERT CHEMICAL CO. INC. . . . 338
DAUBERT CROMWELL 338
DAVID J. JOSEPH CO., THE 340
DAVIS ALLOYS 167
DB PIPING
  GROUP, THE 119, 220, 227
DE NORA WATER
  TECHNOLOGIES. 340
DEACERO S.A. DE C.V. 31, 153, 177
DEC INDUSTRIES LTD. 341
DEEP SOUTH CRANE &
  RIGGING .341
DELLNER BUBENZER 341
DELTA CENTRIFUGAL CORP. 167
DELTA STEEL TECHNOLOGIES. . . .341
DELTA USA INC. 342
DESHAZO LLC. 342
DIBENEDETTO APPRAISAL
  SERVICES 342
DILLON INDUSTRIAL FAN CO. 342
DITH REFRACTORIES 344
DIXON VALVE
  & COUPLING CO. 344
DLZ INDUSTRIAL LLC 344
DIALIGHT 342
DOUBLE G COATINGS
  CO. L.P.. . . . . .33, 206
DOUGLAS BROS. 227
DOVER HYDRAULICS INC. 344
DRAFTO CORP. 346
DRESSEL
  TECHNOLOGIES LLC. 346
DREVER INTERNATIONAL . . . see SMS
                               GROUP
DROPSA USA INC. 346
DRUMMOND CO. INC. 146
DTE ENERGY SERVICES. 146
DUNDEE PRODUCTS 227
DURA-BOND INDUSTRIES . . . 120, 228
DURALOY
  TECHNOLOGIES. 167, 348
DURAMETAL CORP. 167
DURANT METAL
  SHREDDING LLC 348
DÜRR SYSTEMS INC. 348
DW CLARK INC. 167
DYNAINDUSTRIAL LP 348
DYNAMIC MILL
  SERVICES CORP. 349

E

EAFAB CORP. 349
EAGLE ALLOY INC. 167
EAGLE FOUNDRY CO. 167
EATON STEEL BAR CO. 33
EBNER FURNACES INC. 350
EDDISONS CJM 350
EDW. C. LEVY CO. 430
EDWARDS VACUUM. 350
EES COKE BATTERY LLC 350
EFFORT FOUNDRY INC. 167
ELCON TECHNOLOGIES. 350
ELECTRALLOY 33, 156, 167
ELLWOOD GROUP INC. 34, 156, 167
EM MOULDS SPA 351
EMG-USA INC.. 351
EMPCO 351
ENCORE MATERIALS INC. 351
ENERTIME .351
ENGINEERS' SOCIETY OF
  WESTERN PENNSYLVANIA 610
ENPROTECH INDUSTRIAL
  TECHNOLOGIES LLC. 352
ENVEA INC. 352
E.P.R. S.R.L. 352
ERIE COPPER WORKS. 352
ERIEZ 354
ESMARK STEEL GROUP 36
ESSCO INC. 354
ETA ENGINEERING INC. 354
ETS SCHAEFER LLC 354
EUROPEAN STEEL ASSOCIATION
  (EUROFER) 611
EVERTZ KG, EGON/ETS. 356
EVRAZ NORTH AMERICA. 36, 152,
                156, 175, 182, 197,
                198, 213, 221, 228
EXACTRATION 356
EXLTUBE 228
EZG MANUFACTURING. 356

2023 AIST Directory — Iron and Steel Plants 625

INDEX

F

FABREEKA INTERNATIONAL INC. 358
FABRICATORS & MANUFACTURERS ASSOCIATION INTERNATIONAL 611
FABRIS INC. 358
FALK PLI 358
FALKONRY INC. 360
FARRAND CONTROLS. 360
FARWEST STEEL CORP. 37
FASTWAY INC. 360
FAVOR STEEL & FABRICATING 121
FEDERAL-MOGUL DEVA GMBH 360
FELKER BROS. CORP. 228
FERRAGON CORP. 38
FERROSER LTD. 360
FIBRECAST 362
FILTERTECH INC. 362
FIMEX S.A. DE C.V. 164
FINKL STEEL 41, 152, 156, 167
FINZER ROLLER 362
FISCHER GROUP 121
FISHER CAST STEEL PRODUCTS INC. 167
FIVES GROUP 362
FLAME TECHNOLOGIES INC. 364
FLANDERS. 364
FLETCHER ENGINEERED SOLUTIONS. 364
FLEXOSPAN. 364
FLOLO CORP. 364
FLUIDTECHNIK USA INC. 366
FLUOR METALS 366
FOERSTER INSTRUMENTS INC. 366
FONDERIA 177
FOOTHILLS STEEL FOUNDRY LTD. 163
FORCE CONTROL INDUSTRIES INC. 366
FOREMOST ENVIRONMENTAL CONSULTING INC. 366
FORGING INDUSTRY ASSOCIATION. 611
FORGING INDUSTRY EDUCATIONAL AND RESEARCH FOUNDATION 611
FORZA STEEL 222
FOSBEL INC. 366
FRANKLIN INDUSTRIES 213
FRIEDMAN INDUSTRIES INC. 41
FRISA STEEL 164
FUCHS LUBRICANTS CO. 368
FUNDIDORA MORELIA S.A. DE C.V. 164

G

GALLETTA ENGINEERING CORP. 368
GALVANIZERS ASSOCIATION 611
GALVAPRIME S.A. DE C.V. 43
GALVASID S.A. DE C.V. 43, 204
GAMMA-TECH LLC 370
GANTREX INC. 370
GARLOCK FAMILY OF COMPANIES 370
GAUTIER STEEL LTD. 43
GENERAL KINEMATICS 372
GEORG NORTH AMERICA INC. . . . 372
GERDAU 44
 (GERDAU CORSA S.A.P.I. DE C.V.) 44, 153, 178
 (GERDAU LONG STEEL NORTH AMERICA) 44, 152, 156, 176, 183, 210, 213
 (GERDAU SPECIAL STEEL NORTH AMERICA) 46, 157, 184, 214
GERLINGER CARRIER CO. (GCC INC.) 372
GERMAN STEEL FEDERATION 611
GESCO INC. (GRINDING ENGINEERING SERVICES CO.). 372
GFG PEABODY INC. 374
GKN HOEGANAES CORP. 157, 167
GLASSPORT CYLINDER WORKS. 374
GLIDEWELL SPECIALTIES FOUNDRY CO. INC. 47
GLOBAL GAUGE CORP. 374
GLOBAL STRATEGIC SOLUTIONS INC. 374
GLUNT INDUSTRIES INC. 375
GMB HEAVY INDUSTRIES 375
GO2 PARTNERS INC. 375
GOAD CO. 375
GONTERMANN-PEIPERS GMBH. 376
GORMAN-RUPP CO. 376
GPM INC. 376

INDEX

GRAFTECH INTERNATIONAL LTD. 376
GRANITE CITY PICKLING AND WAREHOUSE. 47
GRAPHITE METALLIZING CORP. 378
GRASS VALLEY STEELCAST. 168
GRAYCOR INDUSTRIAL CONSTRUCTORS INC. 378
GREAT LAKES METALS CORP. 47
GREENFIELD TECH PROJECTS 378
GREGORY INDUSTRIES INC. 48, 206
GREGORY TUBE. 122
GROWTHHIVE. 378
GRUPO COLLADO S.A. DE C.V. 48
GRUPO SIMEC S.A.B. DE C.V. 48, 153, 178
GUILD INTERNATIONAL 378
GULF STATES ENGINEERING INC. 380
GUND CO. INC., THE 380
G.W. BECKER INC. 380

H

H&K EQUIPMENT 382
HALL INDUSTRIES INC. 382
HANDLING SPECIALTY MANUFACTURING LTD. 382
HANNA STEEL. 122, 228
HANNECARD ROLLER COATINGS INC. — ASB INDUSTRIES 382
HANSEN GROUP INTERNATIONAL LLC 384
HARBISONWALKER INTERNATIONAL 384
HARBOR CASTINGS 168
HAROLD BECK & SONS INC. 384
HARRISON STEEL CASTINGS CO. 50, 157, 168
HARSCO ENVIRONMENTAL. 386
HASTEC GROUP. 387
HATCH LTD. 387
HAUHINCO. 388
HAVER & BOECKER NIAGARA . . . 388
HAYNES INTERNATIONAL INC. 50, 157, 168
HEG LTD. 388

HEICO FASTENING SYSTEMS. . . . 389
HEIDENHAIN CORP. 389
HEIDTMAN STEEL PRODUCTS INC. . 51
(HEIDTMAN TUBULAR PRODUCTS LLC) 123
HELMKE — MOTORS AND DRIVES. 389
HELWIG CARBON PRODUCTS. . . . 389
HENDERSON MANUFACTURING CO. INC. . . . 168
HENKEL (LOCTITE). 390
HENSLEY INDUSTRIES 157, 168
HERAEUS ELECTRO-NITE CO. LLC 390
HERKULES NORTH AMERICA 390
HERMETIK HYDRAULIK AB 390
HICKMAN, WILLIAMS & CO. 392
HIGHLAND CARBIDE TOOL CO. INC. 394
HIGHLAND FOUNDRY LTD. 163
HILLIARD BRAKE SYSTEMS 394
HJK CONSULTING ENGINEERS GMBH 394
HOFMANN INDUSTRIES INC. 123
HOH ENGINEERS INC. 394
HOISTCAM BY NETARUS LLC 394
HOLLAND. 396
HOLLTECK CO. INC. 396
HONGJI ELECTRODE MANUFACTURER CO. LTD. 396
HORSBURGH & SCOTT. 396
HOSE MASTER 396
HOTWORK-USA 397
HOWDEN GROUP 397
HOWELL FOUNDRIES LLC 168
HUBBELL 397
HUNT VALVE CO. 397
HURON CASTING INC. 168
HY-DAC RUBBER MFG. 397
HY-PRO FILTRATION 398
HYDRO INC. 398
HYDROTHRIFT CORP. 398
HYSTER CO. 398

I

I²R POWER. 399
IBA AMERICA LLC 399
ICL-IP AMERICA INC. 399
IDOM INC. 399
IKEUCHI USA INC. 400
ILLINOIS ELECTRIC WORKS 400

INDEX

IMS SYSTEMS INC. 400
IN-PLACE MACHINING CO. 400
INDUCTOTHERM CORP. 402
INDUSTRIAL ACCESSORIES
   CO. (IAC). 402
INDUSTRIAL HEATING
   EQUIPMENT ASSOCIATION. 611
INDUSTRIAL MAINTENANCE
   WELDING & MACHINING
   CO. INC. 402
INDUSTRIAL RUBBER
   PRODUCTS CO. 404
INDUSTRIAL
   SCIENTIFIC CORP. 404
INDUSTRIAS
   CH S.A.B. DE C.V. . . . . see GRUPO
                   SIMEC S.A.B. DE C.V.
INFOSIGHT CORP. 404
INJECTION ALLOYS INC. 404
INNERSPEC
   TECHNOLOGIES INC. 406
INNOVATING STEEL. 406
INOXIHP S.R.L. 406
INSTITUTE FOR BRIQUETTING
   AND AGGLOMERATION 611
INSTITUTE OF ELECTRICAL
   AND ELECTRONICS
   ENGINEERS INC. 611
INSTITUTE OF SCRAP
   RECYCLING INDUSTRIES
   INC. (ISRI). 612
INSTITUTO ARGENTINO DE
   SIDERURGIA. 612
INSTRON 406
INTECO PTI 406
INTEGRATED MILL
   SYSTEMS INC. 408
INTEGRATED POWER
   SERVICES (IPS). 408
INTEREP INC. 408
INTERFLOW TECHSERV INC. 408
INTERNATIONAL
   CASTING CORP. 168
INTERNATIONAL IRON
   METALLICS ASSOCIATION
   LTD. (IIMA) 612
INTERNATIONAL KNIFE &
   SAW INC. 409
INTERNATIONAL STAINLESS
   STEEL FORUM 612
INTERNATIONAL TECHNICAL
   CERAMICS LLC (ITC). 409
INTERPOWER INDUCTION
   USA. 409
IOMES GROUP LTD. 409
IRON AND STEEL INSTITUTE OF
   JAPAN. 612
IRWIN CAR AND EQUIPMENT 409
ISB STEEL TECH. 410
ISRA VISION PARSYTEC AG 410
ITIPACK SYSTEMS 410
ITR 412
IVACO ROLLING MILLS LP 52, 152,
                                     176, 211
IVC TECHNOLOGIES 412

J

J & L FIBER SERVICES INC. 168
JACKSON TUBE SERVICE INC. . . . 228
JACOBSON & ASSOCIATES. 412
JAPAN IRON AND STEEL
   FEDERATION 612
JEDDO COAL CO. 414
JENDCO CORP. 414
JERNKONTORET 612
JERSEY SHORE STEEL CO. . . . 53, 214
JGB ENTERPRISES INC. 414
JINDAL STEEL & POWER LTD. . . . 109
   (JINDAL SAW LTD.). 109
   (JINDAL STAINLESS LTD.) 109
   (JINDAL TUBULAR
      USA LLC) 124, 228
J.M. LAHMAN MFG. INC. 221
JMP SOLUTIONS INC. 414
JNE GROUP OF COMPANIES. 415
JOHANNES HUEBNER CORP. 415
JOHN COCKERILL INDUSTRY 416
JOHNSON POWER LTD. 416
JOINT PLANT
   COMMITTEE (JPC). 110
J.R. MERRITT CONTROLS INC. . . . 416
JSW STEEL. 110
   (JSW STEEL
      USA INC.). 53, 157, 184,
                             194, 198, 229
JTEKT NORTH
   AMERICA CORP. 416, 423
JUKOKE & CARBON UG 418
JVCKENWOOD USA CORP. 418
JVI VIBRATORY EQUIPMENT. 418

628   2023 AIST Directory — Iron and Steel Plants

INDEX

K

KALENBORN ABRESIST CORP. ... 419
KALYANI STEELS LTD. 110
KARK GMBH 419
KASTALON INC. 419
KELLY PIPE CO. LLC 124
KENNAMETAL INC. 168, 420
KENNEDY INDUSTRIES. 420
KENOSHA STEEL CASTINGS. 168
KEOKUK STEEL
  CASTINGS 157, 168
KETTENWULF INC. 420
KIEWIT 420
KIMZEY SOFTWARE
  SOLUTIONS. 420
KINETIC CO. 421
KINTNER INC. 421
KIRK EASTERN INC. 229
KLOECKNER METALS 54, 229
KLUBER LUBRICATION 421
KOBELCO METAL
  POWDER 157, 168
KOCKS PITTSBURGH CO. 421
KOCSIS USA 422
KOLD ROLL DE
  MONTERREY S.A. DE C.V. 54
KONECRANES PLC 422
KONRAD CORP. 422
KOYO BEARINGS
  NORTH AMERICA ...... see JTEKT
          NORTH AMERICA CORP.
KPF STEEL FOUNDRY 169
KRESS CORP. 423
KRK ASSOCIATES INC. 423
KSB SUPREMESERV
  NORTH AMERICA 423
KT-GRANT 424
KTSDI LLC 424
KUBOTA MATERIALS
  CANADA CORP. 425
KUBOTA METAL CORP. 163
KUTTNER NORTH AMERICA 425
KVA STAINLESS INC. 126
KYTOLA INSTRUMENTS. 425

L

L&L SPECIAL FURNACE
  CO. INC. 426
LAKOS FILTRATION
  SOLUTIONS. 426

LAMIFLEX INC. 426
LAP OF AMERICA LASER
  APPLICATIONS LLC. 426
LATIN AMERICAN STEEL
  ASSOCIATION (ALACERO). 612
LAVISA 426
THE LAWTON STANDARD
  FAMILY OF COMPANIES. 169
LECHLER INC. 426
LECO CORP. 428
LEGGETT & PLATT
  (AEROSPACE). 229
  (STERLING STEEL
  CO. LLC). 157, 184, 215
LEHIGH ANTHRACITE COAL 428
LEHIGH SPECIALTY MELTING. .. 162
LENOX INSTRUMENT CO. INC. .. 428
LEVY MARKETERS
  FOR INDUSTRY +
  TECH .... see GROWTHHIVE
LEXICON INC. 430
LEYBOLD VACUUM 430
LHOIST NORTH AMERICA 430
LIBERTY STEEL
  PRODUCTS INC. 55
LIBERTY
  STEEL USA 55, 157, 184, 214
LIFE CYCLE ENGINEERING 432
LIMAB NORTH AMERICA INC. .. 432
LINCOLN ELECTRIC CO., THE. .. 432
LINDE 434
LINTORFER
  EISENGIESSEREI GMBH 434
LITTELL STEEL CO. 436
LJB INC. 436
LM PERFILES Y HERRAJES
  S.A. DE C.V. 223
LOCK JOINT TUBE 229
LOGIKA TECHNOLOGIES INC. .. 436
LOGISTICS ETC. 436
LONGHORN TUBE 126, 229
LOUISIANA STEEL INC. 229
LUDECA INC. 437
LUMAR METALURGICA LTDA. .. 437
LUTHER HOLTON
  ASSOCIATES INC. 437

M

M A STEEL FOUNDRY LTD. 163
M. BRASHEM INC./
  MBI ROLLS LLC 437

INDEX

M E GLOBAL INC. 169
MACA SUPPLY CO. 169
MACH INDUSTRIAL GROUP. 229
MACHINE CONCEPTS INC. 438
MACK MANUFACTURING INC. . . . 438
MACPHERSON & COMPANY 438
MAGALDI
   TECHNOLOGIES LLC. 439
MAGIC STEEL SALES 56
MAGNECO/METREL INC. 439
MAGNETECH INDUSTRIAL
   SERVICES INC. 439
MAGNETEK 439
MAGNETIC LIFTING
   TECHNOLOGIES US. . . see CRANE 1
   SERVICES
MAGOTTEAUX 164, 169
MAINA ORGANI DI
   TRASMISSIONE S.P.A. 440
MAINTOCARE 440
MAJESTIC STEEL USA 57
MAJOR 440
MAJOR METALS CO. 229
MALMEDIE INC. 442
MANAGEMENT SCIENCE
   ASSOCIATES INC. 442
MANNESMANN. 126
MAPOMEGA INC. 442
MARMACOR INC. 442
MARUICHI STEEL
   TUBE LTD. 127, 230
MATERIAL SCIENCES
   CORP. 57, 204, 206
MATRIX METAL CASTING. 59
MATRIX TECHNOLOGIES INC. 443
MATTHEWS MARKING
   SYSTEMS. 443
MAX AICHER NORTH AMERICA . . . 211
MAXCESS. 443
MAYNARD STEEL
   CASTING CO. 158, 169
MAYRAN CASTINGS 164
MAZZELLA COMPANIES. 443
MCC INTERNATIONAL. 169
MCCLUSKEY &
   ASSOCIATES INC. 444
MCCONWAY & TORLEY LLC 169
MCDONALD STEEL CORP. 59
MCKEES ROCKS FORGINGS 444
MCKEOWN
   INTERNATIONAL INC. 444
MCNEIL INDUSTRIES –
   MAXAM BEARINGS. 445
MECON LTD. 445
MELTEC 169

MELTER S.A. DE C.V. 446
MERIT PUMP & EQUIPMENT
   CO. INC. 446
META-FIND, INC 446
METAL-MATIC INC. 230
METAL POWDER INDUSTRIES
   FEDERATION 612
METAL PRODUCTS AND
   ENGINEERING – U.S. LLC 446
METAL TREATING INSTITUTE. 612
METALHEAP.COM 447
METALLON. 447
METALS SERVICE CENTER
   INSTITUTE. 613
METALTEK
   INTERNATIONAL 158, 169, 447
MHI 613
MI-JACK PRODUCTS INC. 447
MICHELS CONSTRUCTION INC. . . 448
MICRO-EPSILON AMERICA 448
MICROCRANES INC. 448
MICROPOLY/PHYMET INC. 448
MID AMERICAN STEEL
   AND WIRE 184
MID-CONTINENT COAL AND
   COKE CO. 448
MID-CONTINENT STEEL AND
   WIRE INC. 60
MID RIVER MINERALS INC. 449
MIDDOUGH INC. 449
MIDREX TECHNOLOGIES INC. . . . 449
MIDWEST INDUSTRIAL
   SUPPLY INC. 450
MIDWEST METAL
   PRODUCTS INC. 170
MILL STEEL CO. 60
MINNCAST INC. 170
M.N. DASTUR & CO. (P) LTD. 450
MODULOC CONTROL
   SYSTEMS LTD. 450
MOFFITT CORP. 450
MOLTEN METALLURGY INC. 163
MOLYNEUX INDUSTRIES INC. 451
MONARCH STEEL CO. INC. 61
MONETT METALS INC. 170
MOOG FLO-TORK. 451
MOON FABRICATING CORP. 451
MORE S.R.L. 451
MORGAN ADVANCED MATERIALS –
   THERMAL CERAMICS. 452
MORGAN ENGINEERING 452
MOTION 452
MOTOROLA SOLUTIONS 453
MOVARESA 453

630   2023 AIST Directory — Iron and Steel Plants

INDEX

MRSI —
MAINTENANCE - RELIABILITY
SOLUTIONS INC. 453
MTS SENSORS . . . see TEMPOSONICS LLC
MTUS TECHNOLOGY INC. 453
MUNROE INC. 454

N

NALCO WATER,
AN ECOLAB CO. 454
NANJING REFMIN CO. LTD. 454
NATIONAL ASSOCIATION OF
STEEL PIPE DISTRIBUTORS . . . 613
NATIONAL CORRUGATED STEEL
PIPE ASSOCIATION (NCSPA). . . 613
NATIONAL FILTER MEDIA. 456
NATIONAL FOUNDRY &
MANUFACTURING CO. INC. 170
NATIONAL GALVANIZING L.P. 206
NATIONAL MACHINERY
EXCHANGE INC. 456
NATIONAL MINING
ASSOCIATION. 613
NATIONAL OILWELL VARCO 230
NATIONAL SLAG
ASSOCIATION. 613
NATIONAL SOCIETY
OF PROFESSIONAL
ENGINEERS 613
NAYLOR PIPE CO. 128, 230
NCCM CO. 456
NDC TECHNOLOGIES 458
NELSEN STEEL AND WIRE
CO. INC. 61
NEW YORK BLOWER CO. 458
NEWARK BRUSH CO. LLC 458
NEW CASTLE STAINLESS
PLATE LLC. 61
NICHOLAS ENTERPRISES INC. . . . 460
NIDEC INDUSTRIAL
SOLUTIONS. 460
NIPPON SANSO
HOLDINGS CORP. 460
NIPPON STEEL
(NIPPON STEEL PIPE
AMERICA INC. 230
(NIPPON STEEL PIPE
MEXICO). 223

NLMK
(NOVOLIPETSK) USA. . .62, 158, 184, 194, 202, 206
NMDC LTD. 111
NORD-LOCK INC. 460
NORDFAB DUCTING 460
NORTEK S.A. 460
NORTH AMERICAN CRANE
BUREAU INC. (NACB) 461
NORTH AMERICAN
HÖGANÄS CO. 62, 158, 170
NORTH AMERICAN
STAINLESS 63, 158, 170, 184
NORTH STAR
BLUESCOPE STEEL 63, 158, 185, 194, 206
NORTH STAR CASTEEL
PRODUCTS INC. 170
NORTHERN STAINLESS CORP. 170
NORTHFIELD
MANUFACTURING INC. 170
NORTHWEST PIPE CO. 129, 231
NOVASPECT INC. 461
NOVA STEEL INC. 63, 221, 223
NSK AMERICAS 462
NTN BEARING CORP. OF
AMERICA 462
NU-TECH RESOURCES. 462
NUCOR CORP. 64, 149, 158, 170, 185, 194, 198, 202, 204, 206, 215
(NUCOR TUBULAR
PRODUCTS). 129, 231
(NUCOR-YAMATO
STEEL CO.) 160, 187, 218
NUFLUX 462
NUPRO CORP. 464
NUTTALL GEAR LLC 464

O

OCMET INC. 464
ODDA DIGITAL SYSTEM AS 465
OHIO COATINGS CO. 69
OHIO MAGNETICS INC. 465
OIL SKIMMERS INC. 465
OILCO LIQUID HANDLING
SYSTEMS. 466
OKAYA SHINNICHI CORP.
OF AMERICA 232
OLYMPIC STEEL INC. 69
OMAHA STEEL CASTINGS CO. 170

2023 AIST Directory — Iron and Steel Plants   631

INDEX

OMEGA CASTINGS INC. 170
ONPOINT 466
OPTA GROUP LLC 466
OPTIMUS STEEL 70, 160, 187, 218
ORIND SPECIAL
   REFRACTORIES PVT. LTD 468
ORIVAL WATER FILTERS 468
OTC SERVICES INC 468
OUTOKUMPU STAINLESS
   USA LLC 70, 160, 171, 187
OXY-ARC INTERNATIONAL LP . . . 468
OXYLANCE INC. 469

P

PACESETTER .71
PACIFIC ALLOY CASTINGS 171
PALING TRANSPORTER LTD. 469
PALMER WAHL
   INSTRUMENTS INC. 469
PANNIER CORP. 470
PARAGON
   INDUSTRIES INC 131, 232
PARTS SUPER CENTER 470
PAUL WURTH SA . . . see SMS GROUP
PCC ENERGY GROUP 232
PCE INSTRUMENTS UK LTD 470
PEARCE FOUNDRY &
   MACHINE WORKS 171
PENATEK INDUSTRIES INC 171
PENINSULA ALLOY INC 164
PENN RADIANT 471
PENNA FLAME INDUSTRIES 471
PENNSYLVANIA
   EQUIPMENT INC 472
PENSCO LLC 472
PERFILES COMERCIALES
   SIGOSA S.A. DE C.V 71
PERFORMANCE
   IMPROVEMENT INC 472
PEWAG CHAIN INC. 473
PFEIFFER VACUUM 473
PHILADELPHIA NAVAL
   SHIPYARD FOUNDRY 171
PHILIP DOYLE
   MANUFACTURING INC. 473
PHILIPPI-HAGENBUCH INC 473
PHILLIPS TUBE GROUP 131, 232
PHOENIX SERVICES LLC 474
PHOENIX TUBE CO. INC. 131, 233
PICO CHEMICAL CORP. 474
PIEDMONT HOIST AND
   CRANE INC 474

PITTEK DIV. OF
   SWINDELL DRESSLER
   INTERNATIONAL CO. 474
PITTSBURGH AIR SYSTEMS –
   AIR INDUSTRIAL INC. 476
PKG EQUIPMENT INC 476
PLYMOUTH TUBE CO 132, 233
POLYONICS 476
POLYTEC INC 478
POSCO 204
POWER ELECTRONICS®
   INTERNATIONAL INC 478
POWER RESOURCES LLC 478
PRCO AMERICA INC 478
PRECISIONED
   COMPONENTS LLC 480
PRECISION
   MACHINE INC. . . . . . . see XTEK INC.
PRECISION SURFACE
   TECHNOLOGIES INC. 480
PRECITUBO 133, 223
PRECOAT METALS 71, 207
PRIME METALS
   ACQUISITION LLC 73
PRIMETALS
   TECHNOLOGIES LTD. 480
PRO-CHEM-CO INC. 484
PRO-TEC COATING CO. 74, 207
PROCESSBARRON 485
PROCO PRODUCTS INC 485
PROLAMSA 223, 233
PROMECON 485
PROTON PRODUCTS INC. 485
PROXITRON INC. 485
PRUFTECHNIK INC 486
PSI METALS NORTH
   AMERICA INC 486
PSNERGY 486
PT TECH LLC® 486
PTC ALLIANCE 133, 233
PYROTEK INC 486
PYTCO S.A. DE C.V 223

Q

QUAD ENGINEERING INC. 487
QUAKER CITY CASTINGS INC. 171
QUAKER HOUGHTON 488
QUAL-FAB INC. 488
QUALICAST CORP 488
QUALI-T-GROUP INC. 221

632   2023 AIST Directory – Iron and Steel Plants

INDEX

R

R&G LABORATORIES INC. 489
RABCO ENERGY
    SOLUTIONS INC. 489
RACO INTERNATIONAL L.P. 489
RAD-CON INC. 489
RADCOMM SYSTEMS CORP. 490
RADIAN ROBOTICS 490
RADIOMETRIC SERVICES AND
    INSTRUMENTS LLC (RSI) 490
RAMM METALS 490
RAMSA S.A. DE C.V. 164
RANGER STEEL 74
RAPID GEAR 492
RASHTRIYA ISPAT NIGAM LTD. 111
RATHBONE PRECISION
    METALS INC. 75
RAW MATERIAL
    SERVICES LLC 492
RDSTOLZ ENGINEERING LLC 492
R.E. WARNER &
    ASSOCIATES INC. 492
READING ANTHRACITE CO. 494
RED BUD INDUSTRIES 494
REDECAM USA LLC 494
REDHAWK INDUSTRIES 494
REDSTONE MACHINERY LLC 496
REFRACTORIES INSTITUTE. 613
REGAL CAST INC. 171
REGAL REXNORD MOTION
    CONTROL SOLUTIONS. 496
REICHARD INDUSTRIES LLC 496
REINHAUSEN
    MANUFACTURING INC. 496
RELIANCE STEEL &
    ALUMINUM CO. 75
REMELT SERVICES 171
REMIOR INDUSTRIES INC. 497
RENOLD INC. 497
REPUBLIC STEEL 76, 160,
                        171, 188, 218
REXA INC. 497
RFTS LLC 497
RGS MILL PRODUCTS CORP. 498
RHI MAGNESITA 498
RIO TINTO IRON AND
    TITANIUM. 150, 176
RITTERTECH 498
RMI—RAW MATERIALS AND
    IRONMAKING GLOBAL
    CONSULTING 498
RNP INDUSTRIES INC. 499
ROCK ISLAND ARSENAL 171
ROEMER ELECTRIC STEEL
    FOUNDRY 171
ROSCOE MOSS CO. 234
ROSER TECHNOLOGIES INC. 499
ROSS CONTROLS 499
ROTATOR PRODUCTS LTD. 500
ROVISYS. 500
R.T. PATTERSON CO. INC. 500
RUBICON REFRACTORIES INC. . . .501
RUHLIN CO., THE 501
RUSSULA CORP. 501
RYMCO 134

S

SAE INTERNATIONAL 613
SAFETY LAMP OF
    HOUSTON INC. 502
SAINT-GOBAIN
    PERFORMANCE CERAMICS
    & REFRACTORIES 502
SALEM-REPUBLIC
    RUBBER CO. 502
SALZGITTER GROUP 223, 234
SAMUEL, SON & CO. 77
(SAMUEL ASSOCIATED
    TUBE GROUP). 135, 221, 223
SANGRAF
    INTERNATIONAL INC. 502
SANYO SEIKI CO. LTD. 502
SARCLAD NORTH
    AMERICA LP 504
SARCO (SOUTH AFRICAN ROLL
    CO. PTY. LTD.). 504
SARGENT ELECTRIC CO. 504
SARRALLE EQUIPOS
    SIDERURGICOS 506
SAWBROOK STEEL
    CASTING CO. 171
SCANTECH INTERNATIONAL
    PTY. LTD. 506
SCHAEFFER INDUSTRIES 83
SCHENCK PROCESS LLC. 506
SCHENK VISION 507
SCHNEIDER ELECTRIC. 507
SCHONSHECK INC. 507
SCHUST 507
SEABEE FOUNDRY 171
SEARING
    INDUSTRIES INC. 135, 234
SEAUD SRL 508
SEIRIS 508

2023 AIST Directory — Iron and Steel Plants   633

INDEX

SELAS HEAT TECHNOLOGY
  CO. LLC 508
SEMAC LLC 508
SEMPER EXETER PAPER CO. 509
SENNEBOGEN LLC 509
SENTEK CORP. 509
SES LLC (STEEL EQUIPMENT
  SPECIALISTS)................ 510
SGM MAGNETICS CORP. 510
SHENANGO INDUSTRIES INC. 171
SHIMADZU SCIENTIFIC
  INSTRUMENTS INC. 512
SHINAGAWA ADVANCED
  MATERIALS AMERICAS 512
SHOWA DENKO CARBON INC. 512
SHUB MACHINERY................512
SHUTTLELIFT 512
SICON AMERICA LP.............512
SIDOCK GROUP INC............. 513
SIGNAL METAL
  INDUSTRIES INC............... 513
SIL-BASE CO. INC................ 513
SIMMERS CRANE DESIGN
  & SERVICES CO. 513
SIMPSON TECHNICAL
  SALES INC. 514
SINTERMET LLC.................514
S.I.T. AMERICA INC...............514
SIVYER STEEL CORP. 172
SLIPNOT® 514
SME 614
SMITH CASTINGS INC. 172
SMS GROUP 514
SOCIETY OF TRIBOLOGISTS
  AND LUBRICATION
  ENGINEERS (STLE) 614
SOCIETY OF WOMEN
  ENGINEERS (SWE)..............614
SOFIS CO. INC. 518
SOFTWEB SOLUTIONS INC. 518
SONGER SERVICES.............. 518
SOUTHERN ALLOY CORP. 172, 518
SOUTHERN CAST
  PRODUCTS INC................172
SOUTHWEST STEEL
  CASTING CO. 172
S.P. KINNEY ENGINEERS INC......519
SPANISH FORK FOUNDRY 172
SPARTAN STEEL
  COATING LLC 207
SPECIAL METALS CORP. 83
SPECIALTY STEEL INDUSTRY
  OF NORTH AMERICA 614
SPECIALTY STEEL
  WORKS INC. 84, 234

SPIRALCO 222
SPOKANE INDUSTRIES INC. 172
SPRAYING SYSTEMS CO.........519
SPRINGER CO. 519
SPUNCAST INC. 172, 519
SSAB AMERICAS LLC 86, 160, 188, 198
SSS CLUTCH CO. INC........... 520
ST. LOUIS PRECISION
  CASTING CO. 172
STAHLINSTITUT
  VDEH......... see GERMAN STEEL FEDERATION
STAINLESS FOUNDRY &
  ENGINEERING INC.............172
STANDARD ALLOYS & MFG. 172
STANDARD ELECTRIC
  SUPPLY CO.................... 520
STANDARD MACHINE 520
STANDARD STEEL LLC 87, 161, 172
STAR FOUNDRY AND
  MACHINE....................172
STEEL
  DYNAMICS INC. 88, 161, 188, 195, 202, 207, 218
STEEL EQUIPMENT CORP.........521
STEEL FOUNDERS' SOCIETY
  OF AMERICA..................614
STEEL MANUFACTURERS
  ASSOCIATION (SMA)...........614
STEELTAGS.COM 521
STEELTECH LTD. 173
STEEL TUBE INSTITUTE..........614
STELCO INC. 92, 145, 147, 150, 176, 191, 199, 204
STERLING PIPE &
  TUBE INC. 136, 234
STERLING STEEL CO. LLC........ 92
STEULER-KCH GMBH 522
STEVENS ENGINEERS &
  CONSTRUCTORS..............521
STIMPLE & WARD CO............521
STRATEGIC
  MATERIALS CORP. 173
STUCCHI USA 522
STUPP CORP. 234
STURM INC......................173
SUEZ WATER
  TECHNOLOGIES
  & SOLUTIONS......... see VEOLIA WATER TECHNOLOGIES & SOLUTIONS
SUMITOMO DRIVE
  TECHNOLOGIES............... 522
SUNCOKE ENERGY 146, 522

INDEX

SUPERIOR
   ENGINEERING LLC 524
SUPERIOR MACHINE CO.
   OF S.C. INC. 524
SUPERIOR METALS & ALLOYS 93
SWECOMEX S.A. DE C.V.
   (GRUPO CARSO) 224
SWEPCO TUBE 234
SWERIM AB 526
THE SYSTEMS GROUP 526

T

T. BRUCE SALES INC. 528
T-T ELECTRIC USA 529
T&B TUBE CO. 136, 234
T&M EQUIPMENT CO. INC. 528
TALLADEGA CASTINGS &
   MACHINE CO. 173
TALLERES Y ACEROS
   S.A. DE C.V. 153, 178
TALLMAN
   TECHNOLOGIES INC. 529
TAMINI
   TRASFORMATORI S.R.L. 529
TARRANT HYDRAULIC
   SERVICE .... see MOTION
TASACO INC. 530
TATA STEEL LTD.. 111
   (TATA STEEL
   PLATING USA) 93, 208
TAYLOR-WINFIELD
   TECHNOLOGIES INC. 532
TAYLOR DEVICES INC.. 530
THE TAYLOR & FENN CO. 173
TAYLOR MACHINE
   WORKS INC. 530
TDI GROUP LLC. 532
TECHNI-CAST CORP. 173
TECHNICAL WEIGHING
   SERVICES INC. 532
TECHNOS INC.. 532
TECHNOVATIONS
   INTERNATIONAL INC. (TII) 534
TEJAS TUBULAR
   PRODUCTS INC. 234
TEMCO INDUSTRIES INC. 534
TEMPOSONICS LLC 534
TENARIS 136, 153, 161,
                 189, 222, 235
TENOVA S.P.A. 534
TENUTE SRL 536

TERNIUM 93, 149, 153, 178,
             192, 200, 204, 208, 224
THE MINERALS, METALS &
   MATERIALS SOCIETY. 613
THERMA-FAB INC. 536
THERMAL-FLEX
   SYSTEMS INC. 536
THERMO FISHER SCIENTIFIC 536
   (THERMO FISHER SCIENTIFIC
   (ECUBLENS) SARL) 537
THOMPSON INDUSTRIAL
   SERVICES LLC 537
TIDEWATER CASTINGS INC. 173
TIMKEN CO., THE 537
TIMKENSTEEL CORP. 94, 161, 173,
                 189, 219, 235
TITAN BEARINGS 538
TMEIC CORP. AMERICAS 538
TML TECHNIK GMBH 538
TMS INTERNATIONAL LLC 540
TOKAI CARBON GE LLC 540
TORCUP OF WESTERN
   PENNSYLVANIA AND
   NORTHERN OHIO 540
TORQUE TECHNOLOGIES INC.... 542
TOTAL EQUIPMENT CO. 542
TR ELECTRONIC 542
TRAMCO PUMP CO. 542
TRANS CANADA WIRE &
   CABLE CO. 544
TRANS-LUBE
   LUBRICANTS INC. 544
TRANSCONTINENTAL
   ENGINEERED SYSTEMS INC....544
TRANSFORMERS AND
   RECTIFIERS (INDIA) LTD. 544
TRANSTECH 544
TRE SERVICES INC. 545
TREBNICK SYSTEMS INC. 545
TRI-STATE HYDRAULICS 545
TRIBCO INC.. 545
TRICON WEAR SOLUTIONS 545
TRIDENT ALLOYS INC. 173
TRIPLE-S STEEL
   HOLDINGS INC. 95
TRUMBULL METAL
   SPECIALTIES 173
TUBAC S.A. DE C.V. 138, 224
TUBACERO. 224
TUBACEX GROUP. 235
TUBE-MAC® PIPING
   TECHNOLOGIES LTD. 545
TUBERIA LAGUNA 224
TUBERÍAS PROCARSA
   S.A. DE C.V. 138, 224

2023 AIST Directory — Iron and Steel Plants   635

INDEX

TUBESA S.A. DE C.V. 139, 224
TUBULAR INDUSTRIES 235
TUBULAR STEEL INC. 139
TULLOCH ENGINEERING 546
TWIN BROTHERS
    MARINE LLC 139, 235
TYK AMERICA INC. 546

U

UESCO CRANES. 546
UHT–UVÅN HAGFORS
    TEKNOLOGI AB 548
UKCG GROUP LTD. 548
ULBRICH STAINLESS STEELS &
    SPECIAL METALS INC. 98
ULTRA ELECTRONICS,
    ENERGY. 548
UMECC 550
UNIFRAX LLC . . . . see ALKEGEN
UNILUX INC.. 550
UNION DRAWN STEEL II LTD. 99
UNION ELECTRIC
    STEEL CORP. 99, 162, 173
UNITED ROTARY
    BRUSH CORP.. 550
UNITED STATES CONTROLS 550
UNITED STATES ROLLER
    WORKS INC. 552
UNITED STATES STEEL
    CORPORATION 99, 146, 148,
                                151, 162, 189,
                                195, 203, 208
    (U. S. STEEL
    TUBULAR PRODUCTS) 140, 236
UNITED TUBE CORP.. 140
UNIVERSAL INDUSTRIAL
    GASES LLC 552
UNIVERSAL STAINLESS &
    ALLOY PRODUCTS INC. 102,
                                      162, 173
UNIVERSAL URETHANE
    PRODUCTS INC.. 552
UPA TECHNOLOGY 552
U.S. BORAX | RIO TINTO. 553
US PREMIER TUBE MILLS . . . 141, 236
U.S. TSUBAKI POWER
    TRANSMISSION LLC 553
USA BORESCOPES 553

V

VAHLE INC. 553
VAIL RUBBER WORKS INC. 554
VALBRUNA ASW
    STEEL INC. 152, 164, 176
VALBRUNA SLATER
    STAINLESS INC. 103, 162, 173
VALLOUREC
    (VALLOUREC CANADA) 141
    (VALLOUREC STAR LP) 141, 162,
                                      190, 236
VALVES INC. 554
VELCO GMBH 554
VENETA USA LLC 554
VENTILATION SYSTEMS LLC. 554
VENTILATORENFABRIK
    OELDE GMBH. 556
VENTURE STEEL INC. 104
VEOLIA WATER
    TECHNOLOGIES. 556
VEOLIA WATER
    TECHNOLOGIES &
    SOLUTIONS. 556
VERDER SCIENTIFIC INC. 556
VERICHEK TECHNICAL
    SERVICES INC.. 557
VEST INC. 141, 236
VESUVIUS USA 557
VH ENTERPRISES INC. 558
VICTORIA PRECISION ALLOYS 174
VILLACERO 104, 205, 224, 236
VINTON STEEL LLC 104, 162, 219
VIPER IMAGING 558
VIRGINIA CRANE
    (FOLEY MATERIAL
    HANDLING) 558
VISHAY PRECISION GROUP
    CANADA ULC (KELK). 558
VISTA SYSTEM AND
    PRODUCT ENGINEERS
    (VISTA SPE LLC) 560
VM5 LIGHTING
    SOLUTIONS LLC 560
VOESTALPINE BÖHLER
    WELDING UTP
    MAINTENANCE GMBH 560
VOITH TURBO 560
VOLLMER AMERICA INC. 562
VOSS INDUSTRIES 105
VR MASTER CO. LTD.. 562

INDEX

W

W. L. GORE &
  ASSOCIATES INC. 562
W. SILVER INC. 106, 219
WALBRIDGE 562
WALCO 562
WALKER MAGNETICS 564
WAUKESHA FOUNDRY CO. INC. ...174
WEAR-TEK 174
WEBCO INDUSTRIES INC. 236
WEBER SENSORS LLC 564
WEIR ESCO 152, 162, 164, 174
WELDED TUBE OF
  CANADA CORP. 222, 237
WELLS ENGINEERING PSC 564
WELSPUN TUBULAR 142, 237
WEST COAST FOUNDRY 174
WHEELABRATOR CAST
  PRODUCTS GROUP 174
WHEELING-NIPPON
  STEEL INC. 106, 209
WHEMCO 162, 174, 564
WHITING CORP. 567
WHITING EQUIPMENT
  CANADA INC. 568
WIKA MOBILE CONTROL LP 568
WINKLE INDUSTRIES 568
WINSERT INC...................174
WIRCO FOUNDRY................174
WIRE ASSOCIATION
  INTERNATIONAL INC...........614
WKW INDUSTRIAL SERVICES 571
WOLLASTON ALLOYS INC. 174
WOODINGS
  INDUSTRIAL CORP............ 570
WORCESTER FLUIDS
  TECHNOLOGY LLC 570
WORLD WIDE METRIC INC. 571
WORLDBRIDGE PARTNERS OF
  TOLEDO INC..................571
WORLD STEEL ASSOCIATION
  (WORLDSTEEL) 614
WORLDWIDE MATERIAL
  HANDLING....................571
WORTHINGTON
  INDUSTRIES 106, 209
WPT POWER CORP...............571
W.S. HAMPSHIRE INC........... 572
WS THERMAL PROCESS
  TECHNOLOGY INC. 572

X

XTEK INC...................... 572

Y

YATES INDUSTRIES INC.......... 575
YOUNGSTOWN TUBE CO.......... 237
YS TECH CO. LTD................ 575

Z

ZANASI USA.................... 576
ZAPTECH 576
ZEKELMAN
  INDUSTRIES INC......142, 222, 237
ZERO GRAVITY FILTERS......... 576
ZOLO
  TECHNOLOGIES..... see ONPOINT

NOTES

NOTES

E-BOOK DOWNLOAD INSTRUCTIONS

This print edition of the 2023 AIST *Directory — Iron and Steel Plants* includes a free copy of the 2023 AIST *Directory* E-Book.

To Download the E-Book:

1. Go to **Dropcards.com/2023Directory**
2. Enter the code written on the download card (located to the right of this page inside the back cover), then click *Submit* to begin downloading the .zip file.
3. Once the .zip file has downloaded, open the file and select *Extract All*. Select *Browse* to navigate to a folder on your computer where you would like to save your E-Book files.

To Open the E-Book:

The 2023 AIST *Directory* E-Book is provided as an **.EPUB** file. You will need an E-Book reader application (such as Kindle, Apple Books or Google Play Books) to access the file.

AIST recommends Adobe Digital Editions, a free E-Book reader software with versions for Windows, Macs and tablets/smartphones.

To download Adobe Digital Editions, go to **https://www.adobe.com/solutions/ebook/digital-editions/download.html** and choose *Download Digital Editions*.

Once installed, open Adobe Digital Editions and go to *File > Add to Library*. Select the 2023 *Directory* .EPUB file from the folder where you have saved it to open the E-Book.